Western USA

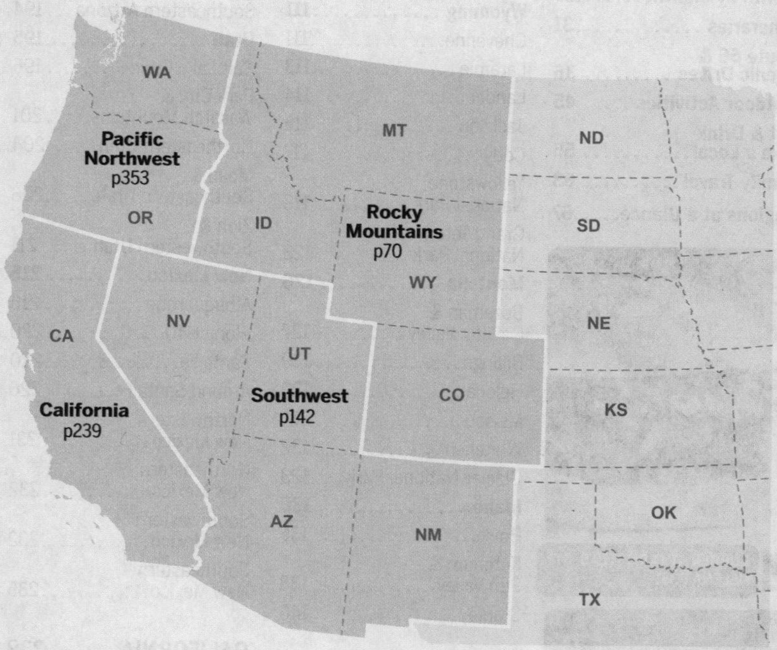

Anthony Ham, Amy C Balfour, Becky Ohlsen, Robert Balkovich, Greg Benchwick, Andrew Bender, Alison Bing, Celeste Brash, Stephanie d'Arc Taylor, Michael Grosberg, Ashley Harrell, John Hecht, Adam Karlin, MaSovaida Morgan, Christopher Pitts, Andrea Schulte-Peevers

PLAN YOUR TRIP

BURGER AT FARMSTEAD, ST HELENA P331

ANDREW MONTGOMERY/LONELY PLANET ©

MOTORCYCLISTS ON ROUTE 66 P36

SKY NOIR PHOTOGRAPHY BY BILL DICKINSON/ GETTY IMAGES ©

ON THE ROAD

Contents

UNDERSTAND

SURVIVAL GUIDE

SPECIAL FEATURES

Welcome to Western USA

Landscapes and legends draw adventurers to the West, where a good day includes locavore dining, vineyard wine-sipping, wildlife-watching, Native American history and outdoor adventure.

Great Outdoors

The landscapes here are stunners, from the high Rockies to the dramatic coastline, from the Great Plains' big-sky horizons to Glacier, Yellowstone and Grand Teton national parks. Some of America's most iconic animals animate the wild, including grizzlies, wolves, elk and bison. Elsewhere, surfers, kayakers and beachcombers flock to sunny San Diego and the rocky beaches of Oregon and Washington. Red rocks, plunging gorges and prickly-pear deserts lure hikers and cyclists to the Southwest and Grand Canyon. Over in the Rockies, snowcapped peaks offer some of the world's best skiing and snowboarding.

Regional Food & Wine

Fish tacos in San Diego, Sonoran dogs in Tucson, trout and bison in the Rockies, green and red chiles in New Mexico and wild salmon in the Pacific Northwest: regional specialties here are as diverse as the landscapes. One commonality? Chefs and consumers alike are focusing on fresh and locally grown food, a locavore trend that started in the West. Wine producers have embraced this eco-consciousness in an industry where Napa and Sonoma increasingly share the spotlight with Washington, Oregon and central California.

Urban Allure

Western cities have distinct personalities. In California there's the hey-bro friendliness of San Diego, the Hollywood flash of Los Angeles and silicon-meets-bohemian in San Francisco. Further north in Seattle, cutting-edge joins homegrown. Rootsy vibes and outdoor fun pair in Denver, while patio preening and spa pampering give Phoenix a compelling spoiled vibe. Artsy, historic Santa Fe is a world unto itself. And then there's Vegas, a glitzy neon playground where you can get hitched in the Elvis Chapel, spend your honeymoon in Paris and then bet the mortgage – all in the same weekend.

Hands-On History

Climb a wooden ladder into a cliff dwelling, poke around the ruins of a Pony Express station, contemplate where Native American tribes drove buffalo herds over cliffs, or simply join the congregation inside a 1700s Spanish mission. What else is there to explore? Crumbling forts and trading posts. Abandoned ghost towns. Adobe pueblos. Petroglyphs etched onto boulders and cliff faces. Wander historic sites like these for up-close and evocative links to the region's rich, multilayered past. And excellent museums? Western USA has them, many of them, in abundance.

Why I Love Western USA

By Anthony Ham, Writer

I love this place, and the love affair began out on the Great Plains. The combination of wildlife, Big Sky landscapes, and soulful Native American stories had me from the beginning. But the spirit of the American West is just as much about the new sophistications of the Pacific Northwest as it is the hardscrabble, red-rock canyons and old American stories of Utah, New Mexico and Arizona. And whichever side of the incomparable Rockies I find myself, from California to Colorado, I keep coming back to one thing: this is one beautiful, extraordinary place.

For more about our writers, see p480

Above: Mesa Verde National Park (p106)

Western USA

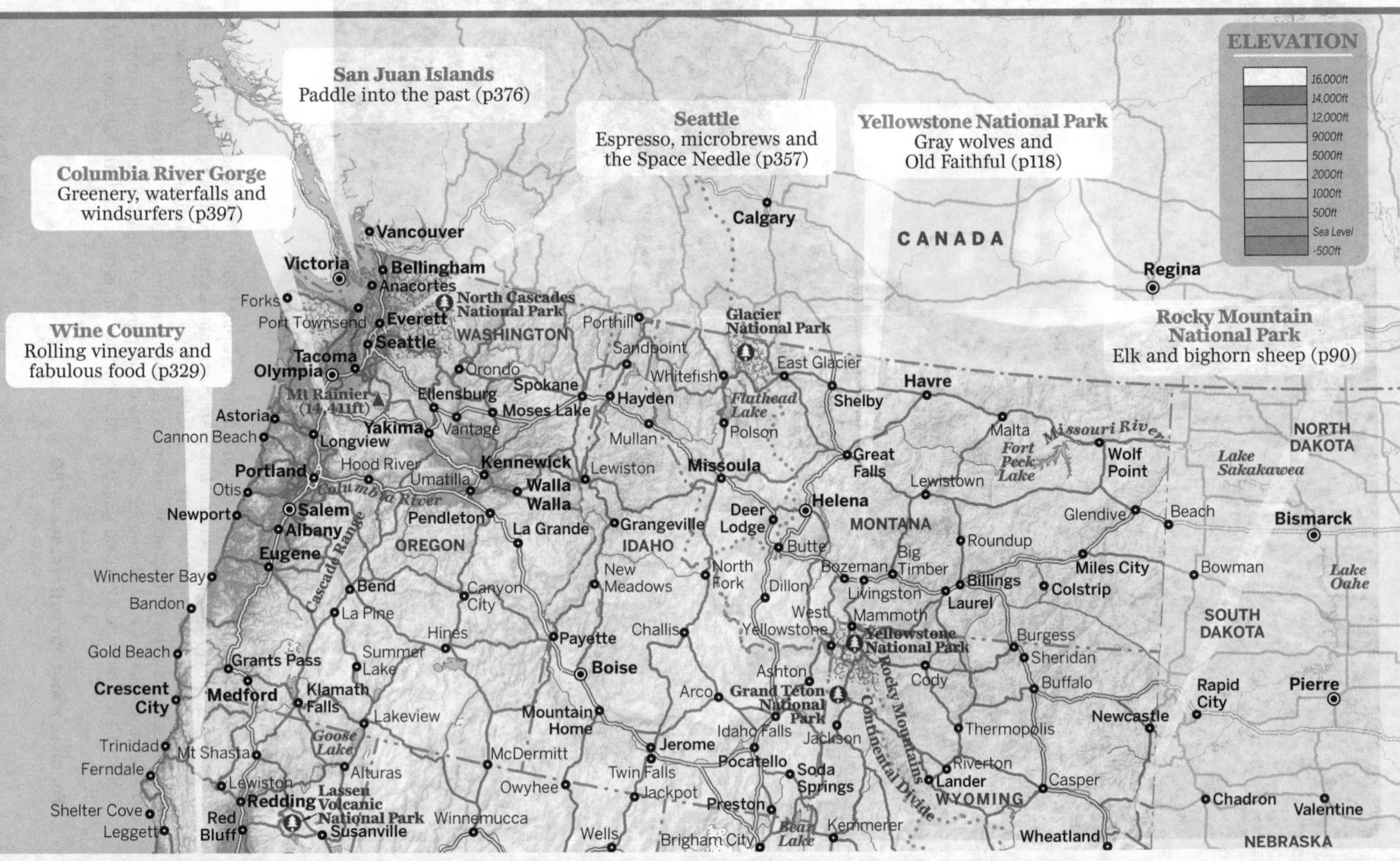
0 500 km
0 250 miles
ELEVATION
16,000ft
14,000ft
12,000ft
9000ft
5000ft
2000ft
1000ft
500ft
Sea Level
-500ft
San Juan Islands
Paddle into the past (p376)
Seattle
Espresso, microbrews and the Space Needle (p357)
Yellowstone National Park
Gray wolves and Old Faithful (p118)
Columbia River Gorge
Greenery, waterfalls and windsurfers (p397)
Wine Country
Rolling vineyards and fabulous food (p329)
Rocky Mountain National Park
Elk and bighorn sheep (p90)
CANADA
WASHINGTON
OREGON
IDAHO
MONTANA
WYOMING
NORTH DAKOTA
SOUTH DAKOTA
NEBRASKA
Vancouver
Victoria
Bellingham
Anacortes
Forks
Port Townsend
Everett
Seattle
Tacoma
Olympia
North Cascades National Park
Mt Rainier (14,411ft)
Astoria
Cannon Beach
Longview
Yakima
Vantage
Ellensburg
Orondo
Spokane
Moses Lake
Porthill
Sandpoint
Hayden
Mullan
Whitefish
Calgary
Glacier National Park
East Glacier
Flathead Lake
Polson
Shelby
Havre
Regina
Malta
Missouri River
Fort Peck Lake
Wolf Point
Lake Sakakawea
Bismarck
Lake Oahe
Portland
Hood River
Umatilla
Columbia River
Kennewick
Walla Walla
Lewiston
Missoula
Great Falls
Lewistown
Otis
Salem
Newport
Albany
Pendleton
La Grande
Grangeville
Deer Lodge
Helena
Glendive
Beach
Eugene
Cascade Range
Winchester Bay
Bandon
Bend
La Pine
Canyon City
New Meadows
North Fork
Butte
Dillon
Bozeman
Big Timber
Roundup
Billings
Laurel
Livingston
Colstrip
Miles City
Bowman
Hines
Payette
Challis
West Yellowstone
Mammoth
Yellowstone National Park
Burgess
Sheridan
Gold Beach
Grants Pass
Summer Lake
Boise
Ashton
Cody
Buffalo
Crescent City
Medford
Klamath Falls
Lakeview
Arco
Grand Teton National Park
Rocky Mountains
Continental Divide
Rapid City
Pierre
Mountain Home
Idaho Falls
Jackson
Thermopolis
Newcastle
Trinidad
Mt Shasta
Goose Lake
McDermitt
Jerome
Pocatello
Ferndale
Alturas
Twin Falls
Soda Springs
Riverton
Lander
Casper
Lewiston
Redding
Lassen Volcanic National Park
Owyhee
Jackpot
Preston
Chadron
Valentine
Shelter Cove
Red Bluff
Susanville
Winnemucca
Wells
Brigham City
Bear Lake
Kemmerer
Wheatland
Leggett

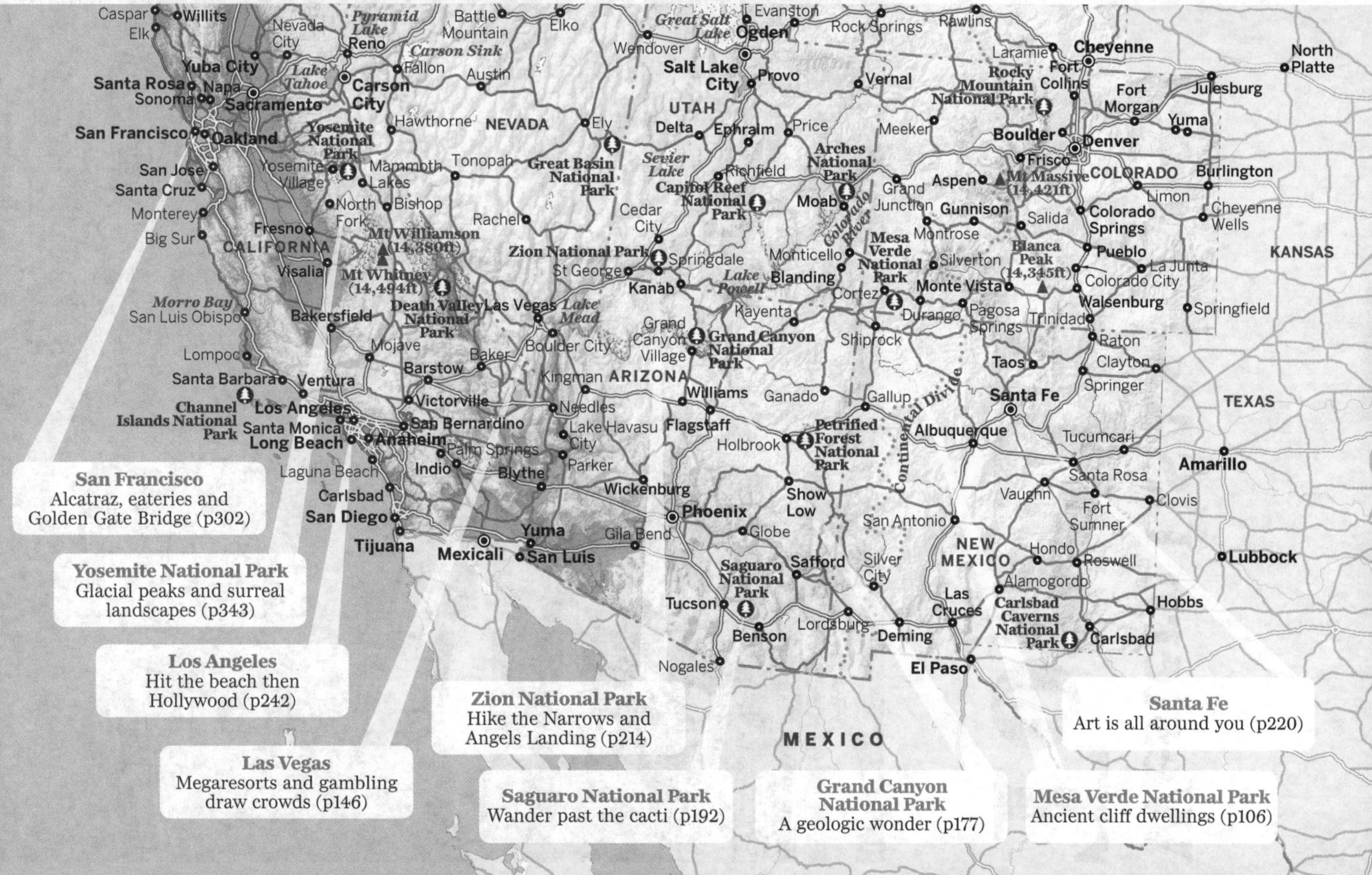

San Francisco
Alcatraz, eateries and Golden Gate Bridge (p302)
Yosemite National Park
Glacial peaks and surreal landscapes (p343)
Los Angeles
Hit the beach then Hollywood (p242)
Las Vegas
Megaresorts and gambling draw crowds (p146)
Zion National Park
Hike the Narrows and Angels Landing (p214)
Saguaro National Park
Wander past the cacti (p192)
Grand Canyon National Park
A geologic wonder (p177)
Mesa Verde National Park
Ancient cliff dwellings (p106)
Santa Fe
Art is all around you (p220)
CALIFORNIA
NEVADA
UTAH
ARIZONA
COLORADO
NEW MEXICO
KANSAS
TEXAS
MEXICO
Caspar
Elk
Willits
Santa Rosa
Sonoma
Napa
Yuba City
Nevada City
Sacramento
Lake Tahoe
Pyramid Lake
Reno
Carson City
Carson Sink
Fallon
Battle Mountain
Austin
Elko
San Francisco
Oakland
San Jose
Santa Cruz
Monterey
Big Sur
Morro Bay
San Luis Obispo
Lompoc
Santa Barbara
Ventura
Channel Islands National Park
Los Angeles
Santa Monica
Long Beach
Anaheim
Laguna Beach
Carlsbad
San Diego
Tijuana
Mexicali
Yuma
San Luis
Fresno
Visalia
Bakersfield
Mojave
Barstow
Victorville
San Bernardino
Palm Springs
Indio
Blythe
Yosemite National Park
Yosemite Village
Mammoth Lakes
North Fork
Bishop
Hawthorne
Tonopah
Rachel
Mt Williamson (14,380ft)
Mt Whitney (14,494ft)
Death Valley National Park
Baker
Las Vegas
Lake Mead
Boulder City
Kingman
Needles
Lake Havasu City
Parker
Ely
Great Basin National Park
Wendover
Great Salt Lake
Salt Lake City
Ogden
Evanston
Provo
Delta
Ephraim
Sevier Lake
Richfield
Capitol Reef National Park
Cedar City
Zion National Park
Springdale
St George
Kanab
Price
Vernal
Rock Springs
Rawlins
Arches National Park
Moab
Colorado River
Monticello
Blanding
Lake Powell
Kayenta
Grand Canyon Village
Grand Canyon National Park
Williams
Flagstaff
Ganado
Holbrook
Petrified Forest National Park
Wickenburg
Phoenix
Gila Bend
Show Low
Globe
Tucson
Saguaro National Park
Safford
Benson
Nogales
Lordsburg
Silver City
Deming
San Antonio
Gallup
Continental Divide
Albuquerque
Shiprock
Cortez
Mesa Verde National Park
Durango
Pagosa Springs
Silverton
Montrose
Grand Junction
Meeker
Aspen
Gunnison
Monte Vista
Blanca Peak (14,345ft)
Mt Massive (14,421ft)
Salida
Frisco
Boulder
Denver
Rocky Mountain National Park
Laramie
Fort Collins
Cheyenne
Fort Morgan
Julesburg
Yuma
North Platte
Burlington
Limon
Cheyenne Wells
Colorado Springs
Pueblo
La Junta
Colorado City
Walsenburg
Springfield
Trinidad
Raton
Clayton
Springer
Taos
Santa Fe
Tucumcari
Amarillo
Santa Rosa
Vaughn
Fort Sumner
Clovis
Hondo
Roswell
Lubbock
Alamogordo
Las Cruces
Carlsbad Caverns National Park
Carlsbad
Hobbs
El Paso

Western USA's Top 25

Yellowstone National Park

1 What makes the world's first national park (p118) so enduring? Geological wonders for one thing, from geysers and fluorescent hot springs to fumaroles and bubbling mud pots. Then there's the wildlife: grizzlies, black bears, wolf packs, elk, bison and moose, roaming across some 3500 sq miles of wilderness. Pitch a tent in Yellowstone's own Grand Canyon, watch wildlife in Lamar Valley, admire the Upper and Lower Falls, wait for Old Faithful to blow and hike through the primeval, fuming landscape for a real taste of what is truly the Wild West. Bottom left: Grand Prismatic Spring (p119)

San Francisco

2 Change is afoot in this boom-bust city, currently enjoying a very high-profile boom. Amid the growth, fog and clatter of old-fashioned trams, the diverse neighborhoods of San Francisco (p302) invite long days of wandering, with great indie shops, fabulous restaurants and bohemian nightlife. Highlights include peering into Alcatraz, strolling across the Golden Gate and dining inside the Ferry Building (pictured below). And you must take at least one ride on the trolley. How cool is San Francisco? Trust us – turn that first corner to a stunning waterfront view, and you'll be hooked.

LORCEL/SHUTTERSTOCK ©

2

ELIZA SNOW/GETTY IMAGES ©

Grand Canyon National Park

3 The sheer immensity of the canyon (p177) is what grabs you at first – a two-billion-year-old rip across the landscape that reveals the earth's geological secrets with commanding authority. But it's Mother Nature's artistic touches, from sun-dappled ridges and crimson buttes to lush oases and a ribbon-like river, that hold your attention and demand your return. To explore the canyon, take your pick of adventures: hiking, biking, rafting or mule riding. Or simply grab a seat along the Rim Trail and watch the earth change colors before you.

Los Angeles

4 A perpetual influx of dreamers, go-getters and hustlers gives this sprawling coastal city (p242) an energetic buzz. Learn the tricks of movie-making during a studio tour. Bliss out to acoustically perfect symphony sounds in the Walt Disney Concert Hall. Wander gardens and galleries at the hilltop Getty Museum (pictured below). And stargazing? Take in the big picture at the revamped Griffith Observatory or look for stylish, earthbound 'stars' at the Grove. Ready for your close-up, darling? You will be – an hour on the beach guarantees that sun-kissed LA glow.

MATT MUNRO/LONELY PLANET ©

HAYK_SHALUNTS/SHUTTERSTOCK ©; ARCHITECT: RICHARD MEIER

5

6

Coastal Highways

5 A drive along America's stunning western coastline is road tripping at its finest. In California, Hwy 1, also called the Pacific Coast Highway (p38; pictured above), Hwy 101 and I-5 pass dizzying sea cliffs, idiosyncratic beach towns and a few major cities: laid-back San Diego, rocker LA and beatnik San Francisco. North of the redwoods, Hwy 101 swoops into Oregon for windswept capes, rocky tide pools and, for *Twilight* fans, Ecola State Park, the stand-in for werewolf haven La Push, Washington. Cross the Columbia River into Washington for wet-and-wild Olympic National Park.

The Deserts

6 The saguaro cactus is one of the West's most enduring symbols. A denizen of the Sonoran Desert, it's a hardy survivor in a landscape both harsh and unforgiving, but also strangely beautiful. Five deserts – the Sonoran, Mojave, Chihuahuan, Great Basin and high Colorado Plateau – stretch across the Southwest and California, each with its own distinct climate. Each is also home to an amazing array of well-adapted reptiles, mammals and plants. This thriving diversity makes a stroll through the desert a wondrous, one-of-a-kind experience – try it at Saguaro National Park (p192; pictured above).

Santa Fe & Taos

7 Santa Fe (p220) is an old city with a young soul. Art lovers have flocked to Canyon Rd and the downtown galleries for years, but openings in the Railyard Arts District and Midtown – hello, Meow Wolf – have added a vibrant edge. Art and history partner up in style within the city's museums, and the food and shopping are first rate. With that turquoise sky as a backdrop, the experience is darn near sublime. Artists also converge in adobe Taos, where the vibe is quirkier, with ski bums and off-the-grid Earthships (pictured below).

California Wine Country

8 The Golden State is home to more than 100 wine regions. The rolling vineyards of Napa (p329), Sonoma and the Russian River Valley lure travelers north from San Francisco. Sample a world-class cab in chichi Napa, enjoy a picnic in laid-back Sonoma, or cap off an outdoor adventure with a complex pinot noir near the Russian River. Further south, day-trippers head to the lovely vineyards clustered east of Santa Barbara, a bucolic area made famous by the 2004 wine-centric movie *Sideways*.

7

SUE STOKES/SHUTTERSTOCK ©

8

HALBERGMAN/GETTY IMAGES ©

MIMI DITCHIE PHOTOGRAPHY/GETTY IMAGES ©

DANITA DELIMONT/ALAMY STOCK PHOTO ©

CRACKERCLIPS STOCK MEDIA/SHUTTERSTOCK ©

Yosemite National Park

9 Meander through wildflower-strewn meadows in valleys carved by rivers and glaciers, whose hard, endless work makes everything look simply colossal here (p343). Thunderous waterfalls tumble over sheer cliffs, ant-sized climbers scale the enormous granite domes of El Cap and Half Dome, while hikers walk beneath ancient groves of giant sequoias, the planet's biggest trees. Even the subalpine meadows of Tuolumne are magnificently vast. For the most sublime views, perch at Glacier Point on a full-moon night or drive the high country's dizzying Tioga Rd in summer.

Native American History & Culture

10 The Southwest is home to a fascinating array of Native American sites. To learn about America's earliest inhabitants, climb into the ancient clifftop homes of Ancestral Puebloans at Mesa Verde National Park (p106) in Colorado. For living cultures, visit the modern-day Pueblo of Taos, or Arizona's Navajo and Hopi Nations. As you'll discover here and in regional museums, many designs have religious significance. The baskets, rugs and jewelry crafted today often put a fresh spin on the ancient traditions – you may even see pottery emblazoned with a Harry Potter theme!

Seattle

11 A cutting-edge Pacific Rim city with an uncanny habit of turning locally hatched ideas into global brands, Seattle (p357) has earned its place in the pantheon of 'great' US metropolises with a world-renowned music scene, a mercurial coffee culture and a penchant for innovation and political progressiveness. But, while Seattle's trendsetters rush to unearth the next big thing, city traditionalists guard its soul with distinct urban neighborhoods, a homegrown food culture and what is arguably the nation's finest public market, Pike Place (pictured above).

Glacier National Park

12 Yep, the rumors are true. The namesake attractions at Glacier National Park (p133) are melting away. There were 150 glaciers in the area in 1850; today there are 26. But even without the giant ice cubes, Montana's sprawling national park is worthy of an in-depth visit. Road warriors can maneuver the thrilling 50-mile Going-to-the-Sun Road; wildlife-watchers can scan for elk, wolves and grizzlies (but hopefully not too close); and hikers have 700 miles of trails, trees and flora – including mosses, mushrooms and wildflowers – to explore.

Rocky Mountain National Park

13 From behind the line of RVs growling along Trail Ridge Rd, Rocky Mountain National Park (p90) can feel a bit overrun. But with boots laced and the trail unfurling beneath your feet, the park's majestic, untamed splendor becomes unforgettably personal. From epic ascents along the Longs Peak Trail and the Continental Divide to family-friendly romps to Calypso Falls, there's a vista for every ability and ambition. Don't be surprised if you find yourself humming the bars to *America the Beautiful* – Colorado is where it was written.

12

DENNIS_CASEY/GETTY IMAGES ©

13

TUPUNGATO/SHUTTERSTOCK ©

ROCLWYR/GETTY IMAGES ©

MARK SKERBINEK/EYEEM/GETTY IMAGES ©

San Juan Islands

14 Go back in time by hopping on a ferry to the San Juan Islands (p376), a low-key archipelago north of Puget Sound between Washington and Vancouver Island. Of the more than 450 'islands' (most are only rocky promontories), only about 60 are inhabited and just four are regularly served by ferries. Nature is the main influence here and each island has its own personality, both geographic and cultural. What can you do here? Start with cycling, kayaking and spotting orcas – then just sit back and relax.

Zion & Bryce Canyon National Parks

15 Towering cliffs hide waterfalls, slot canyons and hanging gardens in Zion National Park (p214). This lush wonderland lies in the shadow of Angels Landing, the terminus of one of the great North American day hikes. Upstream is the famous Narrows, where an overnight backpacking trip through the river takes you to the spectacle of Wall Street. Photographers should scoot to Bryce Canyon National Park (pictured above), where pastel-colored rock spires shimmer like trees in a magical forest of stone – a hypnotic, Tolkienesque place.

16
KRIS DAVIDSON/LONELY PLANET ©

17
SARO17/GETTY IMAGES ©

18
CHRISTOPHER GARDINER/SHUTTERSTOCK ©

Las Vegas

16 Just when you think you've got a handle on the West – majestic, sublime, soul-nourishing – here comes Vegas (p146) shaking its thing like a showgirl looking for trouble. Beneath the neon lights of the Strip, it puts on a dazzling show: dancing fountains, a spewing volcano, the Eiffel Tower. But Vegas saves its most dangerous charms for the gambling dens – seductive lairs where the fresh-pumped air and bright colors share one goal: separating you from your money. Step away for fine restaurants, Cirque du Soleil, Slotzilla and the Mob Museum.

Moab

17 Moab (p207) is the mountain-biking capital of the world, where the desert slickrock surrounding the town makes a perfect 'sticky' surface for knobbly tires. Challenging trails ascend steep bluffs, twist through forests and slam over 4WD roads into the wilds of canyon country. And you'll surely redefine adventure after ripping down 8000ft from Burro Pass through alpine streams, aspen groves, juniper scrub and desert slickrock along the Whole Enchilada. There's a reason why some Moab hotels have showers for bikes. One trip and you'll be hooked.

Columbia River Gorge

18 Can you ever have too many waterfalls? Carved by the mighty Columbia as the Cascade Range was uplifted, the Columbia River Gorge (p397) is a geological marvel. With Washington State on its north side and Oregon on its south, the gorge offers countless waterfalls and spectacular hikes, as well as a bounty of apples, pears and cherries. If you're into windsurfing or kiteboarding, head to Hood River, ground zero for these extreme sports. Whether you're a hiker, an apple lover or an adrenaline junkie, the gorge delivers. Above right: Multnomah Falls (p397)

Portland

19 It's easy to brag about PDX, and locals are sure to, but no one will think worse of you for it – after all, everyone loves this city (p385). It's as friendly as a big town, and home to a mix of students, artists, cyclists, hipsters, young families, old hippies, eco-freaks and everything in between. It has great food, music and culture aplenty, plus it's as sustainable as you can get. Come visit, but be careful – like everyone else, you might just want to move here. Below: Barista (p393)

Theme Parks

20 California is theme-park heaven, bringing Hollywood movie magic, Disney and roller coasters galore. Universal Studios Hollywood (p265; pictured) features movie-themed action rides and the Wizarding World of Harry Potter. Disneyland Park (p267) and neighboring Disney California Adventure are SoCal's most visited tourist attraction: beloved cartoon characters waltz arm in arm down Main Street, U.S.A., and fireworks explode over Sleeping Beauty Castle. Knott's Berry Farm (p269) was SoCal's original theme park.

JOSHUA RAINEY PHOTOGRAPHY/SHUTTERSTOCK ©

MAISLAM/GETTY IMAGES ©

Monument Valley & Canyon de Chelly

21 'May I walk in beauty' is the final line of a famous Navajo prayer. Beauty takes many forms on the Navajos' sprawling reservation, but makes its most famous appearance at Monument Valley (p188), an otherworldly cluster of buttes and towers. Beauty swoops in at Canyon de Chelly, where farmers till the land near age-old cliff dwellings. Elsewhere, beauty is in the connections, from the docent explaining Navajo clans, to the guide sharing photography tips in the light of Antelope Canyon. Below: Monument Valley

Microbreweries

22 Microbreweries are a specialty of the West, and you'll find at least one good one in outdoorsy towns all across the West, from Missoula to Moab. Though usually closely identified with their home towns, these popular watering holes share a few commonalities: boisterous beer sippers, deep-flavored brews with locally inspired names, and cavernous tap rooms that smell of hops, sweat and adventure. Hiking, biking or climbing near Boulder? Celebrate post-adventure with one of the 30 beers on tap at Avery (p86).

21

22

PATRICK ORTON/GETTY IMAGES ©

CASEYMARTIN/ GETTY IMAGES ©

LISSANDRA MELO/SHUTTERSTOCK

Snow Sports

23 The softest, lightest snow you'll ever ski combined with outrageous scenery and every type of terrain imaginable: Western resorts are among the world's best. Aspen (p97), Vail, Park City and Jackson Hole may sound like playgrounds for the rich and famous, but shredders and ski bums – and copious amounts of powder – have always found a way to keep it real. Launch off a cornice, slalom through trees, grind in a terrain park or face-plant repeatedly while learning to snowboard: one thing's certain, you'll end the day with a snow-encrusted smile. Above left: Vail (p95)

Route 66

24 As you step up to the counter at the Snow Cap Drive-In at Seligman, AZ, you know a prank is coming – a squirt of fake mustard, perhaps, or ridiculously incorrect change. Though it's all a bit hokey, you'd be disappointed if the owner forgot to 'get you.' It's these kitschy, down-home touches that make the Mother Road (p36) – which crosses California, Arizona and New Mexico – so memorable. Begging burros, the Wigwam Motel, the neon signs of Tucumcari – and a squirt of fake mustard beats a mass-consumption McBurger every time. Top right: Wigwam Motel (p189)

Flagstaff

25 Another thing the West does well? Mountain towns. Where outdoorsy types drop in from the trail and the slopes to swap stories and savor the microbrews. Many of the best double as gateways to the country's finest national parks. One favorite? Flagstaff (p173), which sits ruggedly on the Colorado Plateau in northern Arizona. Highlights include a thriving ale trail, innovative farm-to-table eateries, an observatory and Route 66's awesome Museum Club. And we almost forgot to mention the Grand Canyon, just 80 miles north. Above right: Lowell Observatory (p173)

Need to Know

For more information, see Survival Guide (p443)

Currency
US dollar ($)

Language
English, Spanish

Visas
Visitors from Canada, the UK, Australia, New Zealand, Japan and many EU countries do not require a visa for stays of less than 90 days. Other nations should see https://travel.state.gov.

Money
ATMs are widely available. Credit cards are normally required for hotel reservations and car rentals.

Cell Phones
GSM multiband models will work in the USA. If you have an unlocked phone, you can find prepaid SIM cards fairly easily.

Time
The 11 states follow either Mountain Standard Time (GMT/UTC minus seven hours) or Pacific Standard Time (GMT/UTC minus eight hours).

When to Go

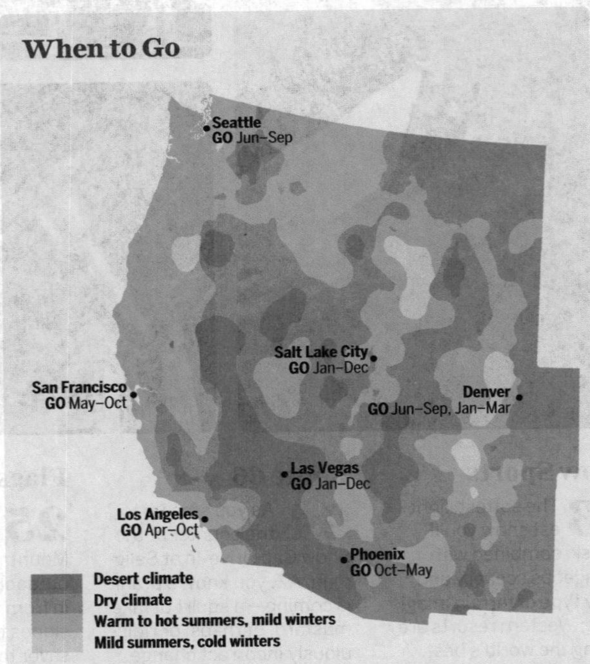

High Season (Jun–Aug)

- Summer temperatures (June to August) soar well above 100°F (38°C) and national parks are at maximum capacity.
- In winter (December to March), hit the slopes in the mountains; giddy-up at southern Arizona dude ranches.

Shoulder (Apr & May; Sep & Oct)

- Clouds may blanket the southern coast (May and June).
- Mountain towns shut down in spring.
- A good time to visit national parks, with milder temperatures, but some roads closed by snow.
- Blooming spring flowers; fiery autumn colors.

Low Season (Nov–Mar)

- Accommodation rates drop by the coast.
- Dark, wintery days, with snowfall in the mountains and heavier rains.

Useful Websites

Visit the USA (www.visittheusa.com) The USA's official tourism website.

National Park Service (www.nps.gov) Information on national parks and monuments.

Recreation.gov (www.recreation.gov) Camping reservations on federally managed lands.

Lonely Planet (www.lonelyplanet.com/usa) Destination info, bookings and forums.

Roadside America (www.roadsideamerica.com) Find offbeat tourist attractions.

Important Numbers

To call any regular number, dial the area code, followed by the seven-digit number.

USA country code	☎1
International access code	☎011
Emergency	☎911
National Sexual Assault Hotline	☎800-656-4673
Directory assistance	☎411
Statewide road conditions	☎511

Exchange Rates

Australia	A$1	$0.70
Canada	C$1	$0.74
China	Y10	$1.45
Europe	€1	$1.12
Japan	¥100	$0.92
Mexico	MXN10	$0.51
NZ	NZ$1	$0.66
UK	£1	$1.26

For current exchange rates, see www.xe.com.

Daily Costs

Budget: Less than $150

- Campgrounds and hostel dorms: $10–50
- Free activities (beach, park concerts): $0
- Food at farmers markets, taquerias: $6–15
- Bus, subway: $0–5

Midrange: $150–250

- Mom-and-pop motels, low-priced chains: $50–150
- Museums, national and state parks: $5–25
- Diners, local restaurants: $10–35
- Economy car rental per day: from $20

Top End: More than $250

- B&Bs, boutique hotels, resorts: from $175
- Meal in top restaurant, excluding drinks: $30–100
- Hiring guides; going to a show: from $100
- SUV or convertible rental per day: from $70

Opening Hours

Banks 8:30am–4:30pm Monday to Thursday, to 5:30pm Friday (and possibly 9am–noon Saturday)

Bars 5pm–midnight Sunday to Thursday, to 2am Friday and Saturday

Nightclubs 10pm–2am Thursday to Saturday

Post offices 9am–5pm Monday to Friday

Shopping malls 9am–9pm

Stores 10am–6pm Monday to Saturday, noon–5pm Sunday

Supermarkets 8am–8pm, some open 24 hours

Arriving in Western USA

Denver International Airport The easiest way to get from DIA to downtown is by train ($10.50, 35 minutes, every 15 minutes). The AB bus runs to Boulder ($10.50, 82 minutes, hourly). Shuttles run to all the major ski resorts.

Los Angeles International Airport Taxis cost about $47 to downtown, and door-to-door shuttles from $17 for shared rides. Free Shuttle G heads to Metro Green Line Aviation Station and free Shuttle C to the Metro Bus Center. FlyAway bus connects to downtown LA for $9.75.

Seattle-Tacoma International Airport Light-rail trains run regularly from the 4th floor of the parking garage to downtown ($3.25, 30 minutes, frequent); shuttle buses stop on the 3rd floor of the airport garage and cost from $20 one way; taxis cost from $55 to downtown (25 minutes).

Getting Around

Air Western USA has a decent regional air network, allowing you to save time by flying from one side to the other.

Car The best option for travelers who leave urban areas to explore national parks and more remote areas. Drive on the right.

Train Amtrak can be slow due to frequent delays, but trains are a convenient option for travel along the Pacific Coast. Cross-country routes to Chicago run from the San Francisco area and Los Angeles.

Bus Cheaper and slower than trains; can be a good option for travel to cities not serviced by Amtrak.

For much more on **getting around**, see p454

Accommodations

Find more accommodation reviews throughout the On the Road chapters (from p69).

Accommodation Types

Hotels Hotels range from the humble to the luxurious. Most have ample in-room amenities, cable TV and private bathrooms, and many have restaurants, bars, swimming pools and fitness centers.

Motels The mainstay of towns across America, motels are usually simpler than hotels and rooms have independent entrances opening onto the parking lot. Some have kitchenettes.

B&Bs Usually in the midrange, inviting homes offer a higher level of interaction and personal attention.

Camping From fee-paying campgrounds with tent and RV spots and basic amenities to primitive sites, America loves its outdoor living.

Dude ranches Converted farms and working ranches with accommodation and activities such as horseback riding, fly-fishing, mountain biking and the like. They range from rustic to luxurious.

Hostels Found in urban centers, especially in California, the Pacific Northwest and the Southwest. Some are connected to Hostelling International with segregated dorms.

Lodges Usually in national parks with a mix of rustic and comfortable accommodation.

Resorts Best for multiday stays, they're part of a wider complex that may include swimming pools, golf courses, tennis courts etc.

PRICE RANGES

The following price ranges do not include taxes, which average more than 10%, unless otherwise noted.

$ less than $150 (less than $200 in San Francisco)

$$ $150–$250 ($200–$350 in San Francisco)

$$$ more than $250 (more than $350 in San Francisco)

Best Places to Stay

Best on a Budget

From budget hotels to happening hostels, Western USA has a good smattering of high-quality budget accommodation. In addition to hostels and hotels, campground cabins, mountains huts and well-priced B&Bs sometimes fall into this category.

- Yotel San Francisco (p313), San Francisco, CA
- Hotel Mayflower (p315), San Francisco, CA
- Hostel Fish (p78), Denver, CO
- Shady Spruce Hostel (p131), Missoula, MT

Best for Families

Family-friendly accommodation is easy to find across the West, from resorts and dude ranches with a range of activities to places that go out of their way to make children feel welcome. Many standard rooms in US hotels have two double beds.

- Vista Verde Guest Ranch (p93), Steamboat Springs, CO
- Disney's Grand Californian Hotel & Spa (p268), Anaheim, CA
- Devil's Thumb Ranch (p94), Winter Park, CO
- Cody Cowboy Village (p118), Cody, WY

Best B&Bs

In Western USA, many B&Bs are high-end romantic retreats in restored historic homes that are run by personable, independent innkeepers who serve gourmet breakfasts. These B&Bs often take pains to evoke a theme – Victorian, rustic, Cape Cod – and amenities range from merely comfortable to indulgent. Rates normally top $120, and the best run $200 to $350. Some B&Bs have minimum-stay requirements, some exclude children and many exclude pets.

- C'est La Vie Inn (p396), Eugene, OR
- Valley of the Gods B&B (p211), Mexican Hat, UT
- Queen Anne Bed & Breakfast Inn (p78), Denver, CO
- Nagle Warren Mansion B&B (p112), Cheyenne, WY
- Briar Rose B&B (p85), Boulder, CO
- Inn at Halona (p220), Zuni Pueblo, NM

Best Lodges

Western USA has some fabulous lodges within national parks. Standard rooms start at around $120, but can easily be double that or more in high season. Since they represent the only option if you want to stay inside the park without camping, many are fully booked well in advance. Want a room today? Call anyway – you might be lucky and hit on a cancellation. In addition to on-site restaurants, they often offer touring services.

- Timberline Lodge (p399), Mt Hood, OR
- Vista Verde Guest Ranch (p93), Steamboat Springs, CO
- Sun Mountain Lodge (p380), Winthrop, WA
- El Tovar (p183), Grand Canyon, AZ

Booking

It's advisable to book well in advance during the summer months and school holiday weeks, and for ski-resort destinations. For popular national parks, it's not unusual to book a year out. Some local and state tourist offices offer hotel reservation services.

Timberline Lodge (p399), Oregon

Airbnb (www.airbnb.com) Search online for homes, apartments and other private accommodation with real-time availability.

Booking.com (www.booking.com) A vast range of hotels and other accommodation.

Hotwire (www.hotwire.com) This platform is one of the more popular online engines for booking hotels in the US.

Lonely Planet (lonelyplanet.com/hotels) Find independent reviews, as well as recommendations on the best places to stay – and then book them online.

National Park Service (www.nps.gov) Information on national parks and monuments, with camping reservations also possible.

Recreation.gov (www.recreation.gov) Camping reservations on federally managed lands.

If You Like...

National Parks

Yellowstone The nation's first park is a stunner: lakes, waterfalls, mountains, wildlife galore and a cauldron of geysers and springs. (p118)

Grand Canyon Two billion years of geological history? Yeah, yeah, that's cool, but have you seen that view? (p177)

Grand Teton Grazing bison, prowling grizzlies and snow-capped dagger peaks erupting from the valley floor. (p123)

Yosemite Flanked by El Capitan and Half Dome, Yosemite Valley is indeed cathedral-like, but the lush Sierra Nevada backcountry will have you singing hallelujah, too. (p343)

Southern Utah There's too much red-rock goodness in Utah to narrow it down to one fave. Arches, Canyonlands, Bryce, Zion, Capitol Reef – see 'em all! (p209)

Great Sand Dunes You can rub your eyes all you like, this massive sea of sand is no mirage. It's also one of the quietest places in the US. (p110)

Glacier Believed by many to be the most spectacular park in the US. (p133)

Rocky Mountain Wildlife-rich backcountry and wonderful landscapes await in northern Colorado. (p90)

Geology

Grand Canyon A 277-mile river cuts through two-billion-year-old rocks. (p177)

Yellowstone National Park Explosive geysers, rainbow-colored thermal pools and a supervolcano base create a dazzling show. (p118)

Arches National Park Drive, hike or bike past sandstone arches, windows, fins and a precariously balanced rock. (p209)

White Sands National Monument Ripples of chalk-white dunes mesmerize photographers and sand sledders alike. (p235)

Carlsbad Caverns National Park Descend to the 1800ft-long Big Room – a veritable underground cathedral concealed in a massive cave system. (p238)

Chiricahua National Monument A rugged wonderland of rock has been chiseled by rain and wind into pinnacles, bridges and balanced rocks. (p195)

Volcanoes The earth's shifting crust formed powerful volcanoes, like Mt Rainier or Mt St Helens, in Washington. (p383)

Dinosaur National Monument Touch a 150-million-year-old fossil at one of the largest dinosaur fossil beds in North America. (p205)

Yosemite National Park Granite mountains here have to be seen to be believed, and are loved by climbers. (p343)

Craters of the Moon This astonishing volcanic landscape is riven with caves and lava tubes, in Idaho. (p140)

Hiking

Grand Canyon Rim to Rim Earn bragging rights on this classic 17-mile trek. (p179)

Red Rock Country Hike to vortexes in Sedona, hoodoos in Bryce Canyon, and slender spans in Arches and Canyonlands National Parks. (p213)

Rocky Mountain National Park Longs Peak gets all the buzz, but there are summits, waterfalls, glacial lakes and trails galore. (p90)

Wonderland Trail Circumnavigate Mt Rainier's lofty peak – it's 93 miles of spectacular nature. (p382)

Maroon Bells There's a reason Aspen's breathtaking alpine backdrop has become the quintessential Colorado photograph. (p97)

Zion National Park Slot canyons, hanging gardens and lofty scrambles make this stunner an unmissable destination. (p214)

ANDRIY BLOKHIN/SHUTTERSTOCK ©

NICK FOX/SHUTTERSTOCK ©

Top: Bison, Antelope Island State Park (p207)

Bottom: Durango & Silverton Narrow Gauge Railroad (p107)

Highline Trail This natural high in Glacier National Park passes bighorn sheep, mountain wildflowers and snowcapped peaks, with a side-hike to glacier views. (p134)

Pacific Crest Trail It's 2650 spectacular miles from Canada to Mexico. (p51)

Half Dome Yosemite National Park's most spectacular trail offers incredible views. (p344)

Old West Sites

Lincoln Historic Site Billy the Kid's old stomping – and shooting – grounds during the Lincoln County War are well preserved. (p237)

Tombstone Famous for the gunfight at the OK Corral, this dusty town is also home to Boot Hill Graveyard and the Bird Cage Theater. (p194)

Whiskey Row A block of Victorian-era saloons in downtown Prescott has survived fires, filmmakers and tourists. (p169)

Pony Express Stations Rte 50 across Nevada, known as the Loneliest Road, traces the route of the Pony Express. (p160)

Durango & Silverton Narrow Gauge Railroad Channel the Old West on the steam-driven train that's chugged between Durango and Silverton for 125 years. (p107)

Wyoming Territorial Prison Laramie, WY, has the only prison ever to hold Butch Cassidy. (p113)

Garnet Ghost Town The poignant Montana outpost of a gold-rush boom town is now deserted. (p131)

Buffalo Bill Center of the West Cody's museum captures the spirit of an Old West icon. (p117)

Native American History & Culture

Mesa Verde National Park Climb to cliff dwellings that housed Ancestral Puebloans more than 700 years ago. (p106)

Indian Pueblo Cultural Center Offers an essential introduction to New Mexico's 19 Pueblos. (p216)

Acoma Pueblo Native guides lead guests on a history-filled tour through Sky City, a mesa-top village dating back to the 11th century. (p220)

Museum of Indian Arts & Culture Discover the origins and history of all the Native peoples living in the Southwest. (p225)

Little Bighorn Battlefield National Monument General George Custer made his famous 'Last Stand' against the Lakota Sioux on these Native American battlefields. (p130)

Chaco Canyon Some 100 years ago, these enigmatic remains were the cultural hub of the Four Corners. (p232)

Petroglyph National Monument Contemplate ancient petroglyphs, with some 23,000 examples. (p216)

First Peoples Buffalo Jump State Park Explore the old buffalo hunting grounds of northern Montana. (p416)

Cody Come for the mid-June powwow of the Shoshone and the Plains Indian Museum. (p117)

Wildlife

Yellowstone National Park A world wildlife highlight that is home to bears, grizzlies, bison and more. (p118)

Rocky Mountain National Park Come to see moose, bear and about a million elk. (p90)

Glacier National Park Bears roam in a remote and beautiful wilderness area. (p133)

Bosque del Apache National Wildlife Refuge More than 100,000 migratory birds roost here late October through March. (p233)

Antelope Island Some 600 bison roam Utah's Antelope Island alongside hundreds of thousands of migratory birds. (p207)

Southern Arizona Patagonia and Sierra Vista are hot spots for bird-watching, with plenty of mammals nearby. (p194)

Great Basin National Park See bighorn sheep, rattlesnakes, and even mountain lions if you're lucky. (p160)

Klamath Basin Watch the incredible bald eagle migration in February when the birds come to hunt wild geese. (p343)

Craft Beer

Ballard It's difficult to choose just one place up in the Pacific Northwest, so we'll go with this happening Seattle neighborhood. (p367)

Bend This Oregon town has the highest number of breweries per capita in the West. (p400)

Marble Brewery With a view of the Sandia Mountains, the rooftop deck is a fine place to sip a Red Ale. (p219)

Salt Lake City The city's exploding craft-beer scene offers a growing number of buzzy brewpubs. (p199)

Montana Has more than 70 craft breweries across the state from Billings and Bozeman to Helena. (p128)

Snake River Brewing Co Brilliant brewpub in beautiful Jackson, WY. (p117)

Fabulous Food

San Francisco Temptations await: real-deal taquerias and trattorias, top-notch Vietnamese, magnificent farmers markets and trailblazing chefs. (p302)

Chez Panisse Chef Alice Waters revolutionized California cuisine in the '70s with seasonal Bay Area locavorian cooking. (p329)

Santa Fe The best Southwestern flavors are found in the chile-laced New Mexican capital. (p220)

Las Vegas Great food is never a gamble in Sin City, with famous chefs and flavor-rich world cuisine. (p153)

Food Trucks LA sparked the mobile gourmet revolution, but the food-truck craze also thrives, well, everywhere. (p392)

Green Chiles Eat them roasted, stewed and slathered over enchiladas and cheeseburgers. Celebrate them at the Hatch Chile Festival. (p29)

Month by Month

TOP EVENTS

Sundance Film Festival, January

Telluride Bluegrass Festival, June

Burning Man, August

Great American Beer Festival, September

Halloween, October

January

Skiers and snowboarders descend on ski resorts across the region, but some mountain roads are impassable. Palm Springs and the southern deserts welcome travelers seeking warmer climes and saguaro-dotted landscapes.

Rose Parade

This famous New Year's Day parade of flower-festooned floats, marching bands and prancing equestrians draws about 700,000 spectators to Pasadena, CA, before the Rose Bowl college football game.

Sundance Film Festival

Park City, UT, unfurls the red carpet for indie filmmakers, actors and moviegoers who flock to the mountain town in late January for a week of cutting-edge films. (p203)

National Cowboy Poetry Gathering

Wranglers and ropers gather in Elko, NV, for a week of poetry readings and folklore performances. Started in 1985, this event has inspired cowboy poetry readings across the region.

Chinese New Year

In late January or early February, you'll find colorful celebrations and feasting anywhere there's a Chinatown. NYC throws a festive parade, to be sure, though San Francisco's is the best, with floats, firecrackers, bands and plenty of merriment.

February

It's the height of ski season, but there are plenty of distractions for those not racing down slopes: low-desert wildflowers bloom, whales migrate off the California coast, and dude ranches saddle up in southern Arizona.

Carnival in Colorado

Mardi Gras meets the mountains in Breckenridge, where folks celebrate with a street party, live jazz and, well, fire dancers.

Oregon Shakespeare Festival

In Ashland, tens of thousands of theater fans party with the Bard at this nine-month festival (that's right!), which kicks off in February and features world-class plays and Elizabethan drama. (p408)

March

Beer! Jet Skis! Parties! March is spring-break season, when hordes of college students converge on Arizona's lakes. Families ski or visit parks in warmer climes.

Spring Whale-Watching Week

Gray whales migrate along the Pacific Coast. Around Oregon's Depoe Bay, it's semi-organized, with docents and special viewpoints. The northward migration happens through June.

Frozen Dead Guy Days

Celebrate a cryogenically frozen town mascot, known as 'Grandpa Bredo,' in Nederland, CO, with festivities including coffin races, ice turkey bowling, a polar plunge and copious beer drinking.

M3F

This nonprofit Phoenix music fest pulls in big names – think Beck, the Avett Brothers and Trombone Shorty – and donates the proceeds to local charities. Also a good spot to check out up-and-coming local bands.

April

Wildflowers bloom in California's high deserts while migrating birds swoop into nature preserves in southern Arizona. For ski resorts, it's the end of the season, meaning slightly lower room prices.

Coachella Music & Arts Festival

Indie rock bands, cult DJs, superstar rappers and pop divas converge outside Palm Springs for this musical extravaganza, now held on two consecutive long weekends in mid-April.)

Gathering of Nations

More than 3000 Native American dancers and singers from the US and Canada compete in this powwow in late April in Albuquerque, NM. There's also a market with more than 800 artists and craftspeople. (p217)

May

A great time to visit most national parks. With children still in school, the masses don't show until Memorial Day weekend, the last weekend of the month.

Cinco de Mayo

Celebrate the victory of Mexican forces over the French army at the Battle of Puebla on May 5, 1862, with margaritas, music and merriment. Denver, Los Angeles and San Diego do it in style.)

Bay to Breakers

Tens of thousands run costumed, naked and/or clutching beer from Embarcadero to Ocean Beach in San Francisco on the third Sunday in May. The race dates from 1912.

Boulder Creek Festival

Start the summer in the Rockies on the Memorial Day weekend with food, drink, music, a rubber duck race and glorious sunshine. It closes with Bolder Boulder, a 10km race celebrated (and run) with all kinds of wacky merriment. (p84)

Sasquatch! Music Festival

Indie music fans converge on the outdoor Gorge Amphitheater in George, WA, near the Columbia River Gorge, for live music on Memorial Day weekend (www.sasquatchfestival.com).

June

High season begins for most of the West. Rugged passes are open, rivers are overflowing with snowmelt and mountain wildflowers are blooming. There may be gray fog (June gloom) over southern California beaches.

Pride Month

California's LGBTIQ+ pride celebrations occur throughout June, with costumed parades, coming-out parties, live music and more. The biggest, bawdiest celebrations are in Los Angeles (http://lapride.org) and San Francisco. (p323)

Telluride Bluegrass Festival

In mid-June, join 'Festivarians' for four days of camping and the high lonesome sounds of bluegrass in the mountain-flanked beauty of Telluride, CO. (p104)

Electric Daisy Carnival

The world's largest EDM (electronic dance music) fest, the Electric Daisy Carnival is a nonstop three-night party with DJs, carnival rides, art installations and performers at the Las Vegas Motor Speedway.

Custer's Last Stand

On the last weekend in June, there's a sometimes-fun, sometimes-poignant re-enactment of the Battle of Little Bighorn at Montana's Little Bighorn Battlefield National Monument, southeast of Billings. (p130)

Plains Indians Powwow

Around the middle of June, the Shoshone and other tribal nations of the Northern Plains gather in Cody, WY, for one of the most important gatherings of Native Americans in the American West.)

July

Vacationers head to beaches, theme parks, mountain resorts, and state and national parks – book well ahead and be prepared for crowds if visiting at this time. Broiling desert parks are best avoided.

Independence Day

Across the West, communities celebrate America's birth with rodeos, music festivals, barbecues, parades and fireworks on July 4.

Aspen Music Festival

From early July to mid-August, top-tier classical performers put on spectacular shows while students from orchestras led by sought-after conductors bring street corners to life with smaller groups.

Oregon Brewers Festival

During this fun beer festival in Portland, about 85,000 microbrew-lovers eat, drink and whoop it up on the banks of the Willamette River. Held the last full weekend in July. (p385)

Cheyenne Frontier Days

Celebrate the American cowboy and the legends of the Wild West with roping, riding and a parade at this 115-year-old Wyoming rodeo. (p112)

World Series of Poker

Everyone from Hollywood celebs and European soccer players to professional gamblers and maybe even your next-door neighbor vie for millions from June through mid-July, with the main championship event taking place in mid-July.

Grand Teton Music Festival

There are many reasons to visit Jackson, WY, in summer, and this fabulous classical music festival ranks high among them. It begins in July and continues in August. (p116)

August

Learn about Native American culture at art fairs, markets and ceremonial gatherings across the Southwest. Rodeos are popular in the West, while national parks remain crowded.

Santa Fe Indian Market

Santa Fe's most famous festival is held the third week of August on the historic plaza where more than 1100 artists from about 220 tribes and Pueblos exhibit. (p222)

Perseids

Peaking in mid-August, these annual meteor showers are the best time to catch shooting stars with your naked eye or a digital camera. Try darksky.org for info. For optimal viewing, head into the southern deserts.

Old Spanish Days Fiesta

A celebration of early rancho culture with parades, a rodeo, crafts exhibits and shows in Santa Barbara in early August.

Hatch Chile Festival

On Labor Day weekend, join green-chile lovers in Hatch, NM, for a parade, a mariachi competition and numerous chile-eating contests.

September

Summer's last hurrah is the Labor Day holiday weekend. It's a particularly nice time to visit the Pacific Northwest, where nights are cool and days are reliably sunny. Fall colors appear in the Rockies.

Burning Man

This outdoor celebration of self-expression is known for elaborate art displays, an easygoing barter system, blowing sand and the final burning of the man. The temporary city rises in the Nevada desert the week before Labor Day. (p160)

Great American Beer Festival

This three-day celebration of beer, held in Denver in late September or early October, is so popular it always sells out in advance, with 700 US breweries getting in on the sudsy action. More than 3500 beers available. (p78)

Bumbershoot

In early September, Seattle's biggest arts and cultural event hosts hundreds of musicians, artists, comedians, writers and theater troupes on various stages. (p363)

Santa Fe Fiesta & Burning of Zozobra

The original Burning Man (Old Man Gloom) – torched every September since 1924 – is the highlight of this 10-day fiesta in Santa Fe. (p222)

October

Shimmering aspens lure road-trippers to Colorado and northern New Mexico for the annual fall show. Watch for ghouls, ghosts and hard-partying maniacs as Halloween, on October 31, approaches.

Halloween

Hundreds of thousands of costumed revelers come out to play in LA's West Hollywood neighborhood and elsewhere for all-day partying, dancing, kids' activities and live entertainment.

Litquake

Author readings, discussions and literary events abound at this writer and arts festival, such as the legendary pub crawl in San Francisco, in mid-October.

Sedona Arts Festival

This fine-art show overflows with jewelry, ceramics, glass and sculptures in early October when 125 artists exhibit their works at Sedona's Red Rock High School.)

November

Temperatures drop across the West. Most coastal areas, deserts and parks are less busy, with the exception of the Thanksgiving holiday. The ski season begins.

Día de los Muertos

Mexican communities honor dead ancestors on November 1 and 2 with costumed parades, sugar skulls, graveyard picnics, candlelight processions and fabulous altars.

Thanksgiving

On the fourth Thursday of November, Americans gather with family and friends over daylong feasts – roast turkey, sweet potatoes, cranberry sauce, wine, pumpkin pie and loads of other dishes. NYC hosts a huge parade, and there's pro football on TV.

Wine Country Thanksgiving

More than 160 wineries in the Willamette Valley open their doors to the public for three days in late November.

Yellowstone Ski Festival

This Thanksgiving week celebration at West Yellowstone (www.skirunbikemt.com/yellowstone-ski-festival.html) is a great time for ski buffs and newcomers alike. Highlights include ski clinics and races. Nordic skiing kicks off around this time too.

December

'Tis the season for nativity scenes, holiday light shows and other celebrations of Christmas. The merriment continues through New Year's Eve. Expect crowds and higher prices at ski resorts.

Snow Daze

Vail, CO, marks the opening of the mountain with a weeklong festival featuring an expo village, parties and plenty of big-name live performances.

New Year's Eve

Americans are of two minds when it comes to ringing in the New Year. Some join festive crowds to celebrate, others plot a getaway to escape the mayhem. Whichever you choose, plan well in advance. Expect high prices.

Itineraries

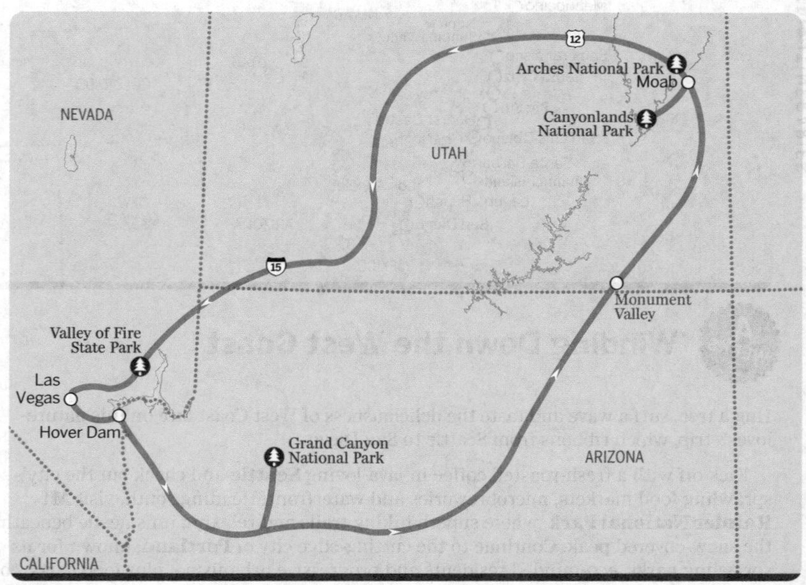

2 WEEKS Best of the Southwest

Cameras get a workout on this tour, which spotlights the most iconic sites in the Southwest. You'll loop past the region's most famous city, its biggest canyon and its most breathtaking red-rock scenery.

Start in **Las Vegas** and spend a few days traveling the world on the Strip. Partied out? Swoop east past **Hoover Dam**, then say hello to the **Grand Canyon**. Spend two days exploring America's most famous park. For a once-in-a-lifetime experience, descend from the South Rim into the chasm on a mule and spend the night at Phantom Ranch on the canyon floor. From the Grand Canyon head northeast to **Monument Valley**, with scenery straight out of a Hollywood Western, and then to the national parks in Utah's southeast corner – they're some of the most visually stunning in the country. Hike the shape-shifting canyons of **Canyonlands National Park**, mountain bike slickrock outside **Moab**, or take a photo of Balanced Rock in **Arches National Park**. Drive west along a spectacular stretch of pavement, Hwy 12, until it hooks up with I-15. Swing south for a sunset meditation at **Valley of Fire State Park**, before heading back to Las Vegas.

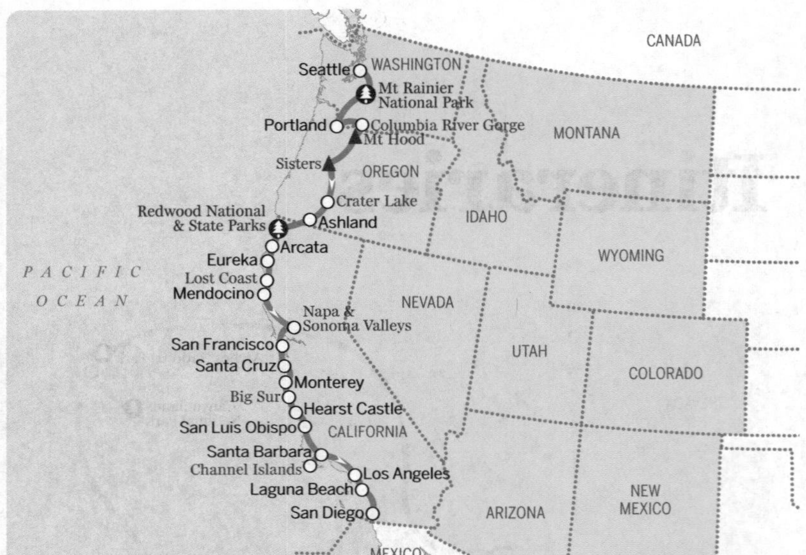

Winding Down the West Coast

Hug a tree, surf a wave and taste the deliciousness of West Coast fare on this nature-lover's trip, which ribbons from Seattle to San Diego.

Kick off with a fresh-roasted coffee in java-loving **Seattle** and check out the city's sprawling food markets, microbreweries and waterfront. Heading south, visit **Mt Rainier National Park**, where superb hiking trails and relaxing inns nestle beneath the snow-covered peak. Continue to the cutting-edge city of **Portland**, known for its sprawling parks, eco-minded residents and progressive urbanism – plus food carts, coffeehouse culture and great nightlife. Wonder at waterfalls and indulge in fresh roadside produce with a scenic drive east along the **Columbia River Gorge**, then turn south to get to **Mt Hood** for winter skiing or summer hiking. Further adventures await at the **Sisters**, a trio of 10,000ft peaks, and the striking blue waters of **Crater Lake**. Catch a Shakespearian play in sunny **Ashland**, then trade the mountains for the foggy coast. Enter California via Hwy 199 and stroll through the magnificent old-growth forests in **Redwood National and State Parks**.

Hug the coast as it meanders south through funky **Arcata** and seaside **Eureka**, lose yourself on the **Lost Coast**, and catch Hwy 1 through quaint **Mendocino**, where the scenic headlands and rugged shoreline make a wander mandatory. For wine tasting with a photogenic backdrop, travel inland to the rolling vineyards of the **Napa and Sonoma Valleys**, then, suitably provisioned, continue south to romantically hilly **San Francisco**. Return to scenic Hwy 1 through surf-loving **Santa Cruz**, stately bayfront **Monterey** and beatnik-flavored **Big Sur**. In no time, you'll reach the surreal **Hearst Castle** and laid-back, collegiate **San Luis Obispo**. Roll into Mediterranean-esque **Santa Barbara** for shopping and wine tasting then hop aboard a ferry in Ventura to the wildlife-rich **Channel Islands**. The pull from **Los Angeles** is strong. Go ahead – indulge your Hollywood fantasies then stroll the rugged hills of Griffith Park, followed by a cruise through LA's palm-lined neighborhoods. After racking up a few sins in the City of Angels, move south to wander the bluffs of **Laguna Beach** then cruise into picture-perfect **San Diego**.

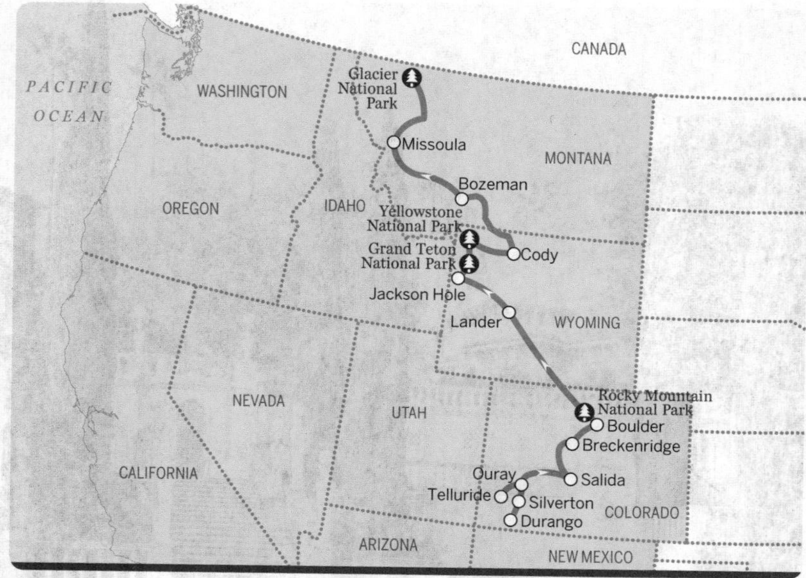

Rocky Mountain High

Pack your bathing suit, mountain bike and hiking boots for this high-altitude cruise atop the Continental Divide; it's big skies, big peaks and big wildlife the whole way.

Spend your first two days enjoying craft beers and singletrack mountain-biking trails in **Durango**, a fine mountain town. From here, take the Million Dollar Hwy (Hwy 550) north through the San Juan Mountains, sightseeing in **Silverton** and dipping into hot springs in **Ouray**. Take a side trip to **Telluride** for a festival – there's one almost every weekend in summer. From Montrose, drive east on Hwy 50 to the Arkansas River Valley and white-water rafting through Brown's Canyon National Monument in **Salida**. Hwy 24 continues past Colorado's tallest peaks; finish your first week in style with an overnight stay in historic **Breckenridge**.

Enjoy tubing, happy hour and people-watching in funky **Boulder**, then twist up to **Rocky Mountain National Park** to hike and horseback ride. While here, drive the thrilling Trail Ridge Rd up above the treeline. Continue north on I-25. In Wyoming, take I-80 west to Hwy 287; follow this highway to **Lander** for rock climbing.

Continue north to **Jackson Hole**, another fun gateway town. Anchored by a central park surrounded by chic stores and cowboy bars, it's a good place to relax, indulge in a gourmet meal or spend the night before rafting the Snake River. From here, it's an easy glide north into **Grand Teton National Park**, a scenic spot for a lazy lake day and bison photo ops. Next up is mighty **Yellowstone National Park**, where geysers, bears and hiking are highlights.

Start your last week with a drive to **Cody** in the west for a taste of Buffalo Bill and Wyoming cowboy life, then head north on the gorgeous Beartooth Hwy, following it into Montana then hooking onto I-90 west to **Bozeman** and **Missoula**; both are good places to stock up before the final push. **Glacier National Park** is a place to visit now – there are still some 26 glaciers hanging tight, but they may not be there for long. Scan for wildlife on a hike, then end with a drive on the stunning Going-to-the-Sun Road.

SERGEY DIDENKO/SHUTTERSTOCK ©; ARCHITECT: JULIA MORGAN

BLAZG/SHUTTERSTOCK ©

Top: Hearst Castle (p295), Central California

Bottom: Alcatraz (p316), San Francisco

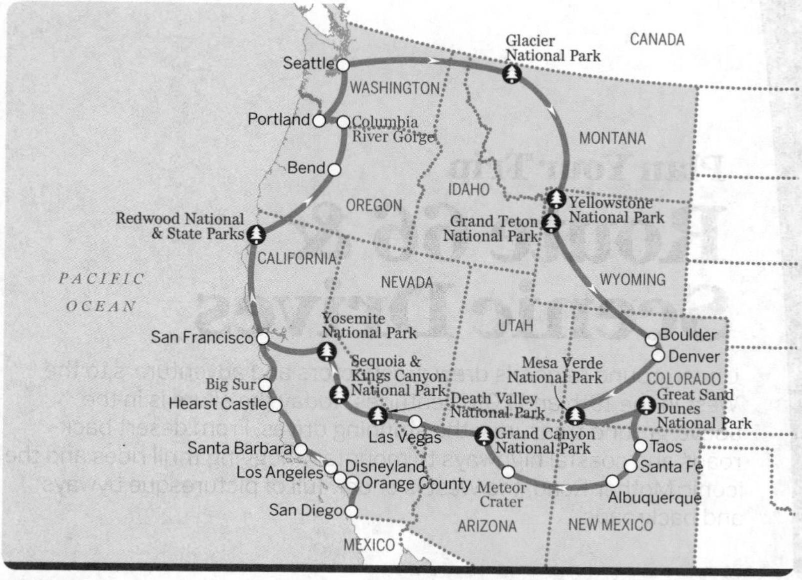

Western US Grand Tour

This lasso loop corrals the best of the West as it rolls north along the California coast, cruises through the lush landscapes of the Pacific Northwest, the alpine towns of the Rockies and the glowing red-rock beauty of the Southwest, with a final swing back into California for a hit-parade tour of the state's national parks.

From sunny **San Diego**, follow Hwy 1 north through the surf-loving coastal villages of **Orange County**, detouring to **Disneyland** before driving into shiny **Los Angeles**. Continue up the coast on scenic Hwy 1, stopping to shop and sample wine in glossy **Santa Barbara**. Gawk at gawdy **Hearst Castle** then continue north through woodsy **Big Sur**. Dine and shop then wander through Alcatraz in bohemian **San Francisco**. Return to Hwy 1 for the quirky towns dotting the northern California coast.

View the big trees in **Redwood National and State Parks** and continue into Oregon, taking time for outdoor fun in **Bend**. Soak in the greenery while traveling west along the **Columbia River Gorge**, then spend a few days savoring brews and views in **Portland**. Zip up the Space Needle in **Seattle** and drive east into wide-open Montana, heading for the outdoor wonders of **Glacier National Park**. Continue south into **Yellowstone National Park** where Old Faithful blasts regularly, and sightseers brake for buffalo, bison, bears and, if you're lucky, wolves. Swoosh below majestic peaks in **Grand Teton National Park** before swinging southeast through Wyoming's vast cowboy plains.

In Colorado, breathe deep in outdoorsy **Boulder** then uncover current hot spots in burgeoning **Denver**. The mining towns of central Colorado are next, followed by **Great Sand Dunes National Park** and **Mesa Verde National Park**. Just south in New Mexico, artist meccas **Taos** and **Santa Fe** are fab stops for one-of-a-kind gifts. Slurp green chile in **Albuquerque** and follow Route 66 west into Arizona, stopping at **Meteor Crater** before detouring north for **Grand Canyon National Park**. Continue west to **Las Vegas**, then drive into central California for **Death Valley National Park** and **Sequoia & Kings Canyon National Parks**, concluding with **Yosemite National Park**. Complete the loop with a glass of Californian wine in **San Francisco**.

Plan Your Trip

Route 66 & Scenic Drives

Underground minerals drew prospectors and adventurers to the West in the 19th and 20th centuries. Today the allure is in the above-ground treasures: the stunning drives. From desert backroads and coastal highways to mountain-hugging thrill rides and the iconic Mother Road, the West is chock-full of picturesque byways and backroads.

Road-Trip Necessities

Top Tips

- A prepared road-tripper is a happy road-tripper, especially out here, with lonely roads and unpredictable weather.
- Pack a spare tire and a tool kit (eg jack, jumper cables, ice scraper), as well as emergency equipment; if you're renting a car, consider buying a roadside safety kit.
- Bring good maps, especially if you're touring away from highways; don't depend on GPS units or phones as they may not work in remote areas.
- Carry extra water. You may need it if the car breaks down in the desert.
- Fill up the tank regularly; gas stations can be few and far between.
- Always carry your driver's license and proof of insurance.

Route 66

A wigwam motel. A meteor crater. Begging burros. And a solar-powered Ferris wheel overlooking the Pacific Ocean. Hmm, looks like 'Get your kitsch on Route 66' might be a better slogan for the stretch of Mother Road running through California, Arizona and New Mexico. It's a bit off-the-beaten path, but folks along the way will be very glad you're here.

Why Go

History, scenery and the open road. This alluring combination is what makes a Route 66 road trip so enjoyable. Navigators should note that I-40 and Route 66 overlap through much of New Mexico and Arizona.

In New Mexico, the neon signs of Tucumcari are a fun-loving welcome to the West. They also set the mood for adventure – the right mood to have before dropping into the scuba-ready **Blue Hole** (dive center 575-472-3370, visitor center 575-472-3763; http://santarosabluehole.com; 1085 Blue Hole Rd; parking $5; swimming 10am-7pm, diving 8am-8:30pm) in Santa Rosa. Fuel up on lip-smacking green-chile stew at Frontier (p218) in Albuquerque then grab a snooze at the 1937-built **El Rancho**

Scenic Drives

motel (☎505-863-9311; www.elranchohotel.com; 1000 E Hwy 66; r/ste from $102/174, motel r $88; P📶🐾) – John Wayne slept here! – in Gallup.

In Arizona, swoop off the highway for a grand drive through Petrified Forest National Park (p188). First up? Sweeping views of the Painted Desert. Trade panoramas for close-up views in the southern section of the park, where fossilized 225-million-year-old logs are clustered beside the main park road. You can snooze in a concrete tipi in Holbrook, west of the park. Next stop is the 'Take It Easy' town of Winslow where there's a girl, my Lord, in a flatbed Ford… Snap a photo of the famous corner then savor a spectacular dinner in the **Turquoise Room** (☎928-289-2888; www.theturquoiseroom.net; 305 E 2nd St, La Posada; breakfast & lunch $10-14, dinner $22-34; ⏰7am-4pm & 5-9pm) at La Posada Hotel. Meteor Crater (p189), east of Flagstaff, is a mighty big hole in the ground – and a good place to slow down and catch your breath. From here, Route 66 parallels the train tracks into energetic Flagstaff, passing the wonderful Museum Club (p176), a cabin-like roadhouse where everyone's having fun or is about to. Next up is Williams, a railroad town lined with courtyard motels and brimming with small-town charm.

Seligman is a quirky little village that greets travelers with retro motels, a roadkill cafe and a squirt of fake mustard at the Snow Cap Drive-In (p189). Burma Shave signs share funny advice on the way to Grand Canyon Caverns, where you'll be lured 21 stories underground for a tour or possibly an overnight stay. From here, highlights include an eclectic general store in Hackberry, the **Route 66 museum** (☎928-753-9889; www.gokingman.com; 120 W Andy Devine Ave; adult/senior/child $4/3/free; ⏰9am-5pm, last entry at 4pm) in Kingman and hay-loving burros in sun-baked Oatman.

Things stay sun-baked in California as the Mother Road swoops into the Mojave Desert and passes ghost towns heralded by lonesome railroad markers. In Victorville, the Brian Burger comes with a spicy kick at Emma Jean's Holland Burger Café (www.hollandburger.com). The vibe kicks up in stylish Pasadena before the road's final push to the Pacific. At the Santa Monica Pier (p251), hop on the solar-powered Ferris wheel and celebrate your journey with a panoramic sunset view.

When to Go

The best time to travel Route 66 is from May to September, when the weather is warm and you'll be able to take advantage of more outdoor activities.

The Route

This journey starts in Tucumcari, NM, then continues west through Arizona and California, roughly paralleling I-40 all the way to Barstow, CA. After Barstow, Route 66 south passes through San Bernardino on the I-15 before cutting west and heading into Pasadena. Follow I-110 to Santa Monica Blvd west to seaside Santa Monica.

Time & Mileage

Time: You might be able to do this trip in two or three days if you rush, but plan for six and enjoy the drive.

Mileage: About 1250 miles, depending on segments driven.

Pacific Coast Highway

Slip on your sunglasses, roll down the window and crank up your favorite song. The highways connecting Canada and Mexico on the West Coast were made for driving, and the ridiculously scenic Pacific Coast Hwy (PCH) is king of them all.

Why Go

This epic West Coast journey, which rolls through California, Oregon and Washington, takes in cosmopolitan cities, surf towns and charming coastal enclaves worthy of exploration. For many travelers, the biggest draw is the magnificent scenery: wild and remote beaches, cliff-top views overlooking crashing waves, rolling hills, and lush forests thick with redwoods and eucalyptus trees. But the route is not loved only for its looks. It's also got personality, offering beside-the-highway adventures for surfers, kayakers, scuba divers and hikers.

Highlights? Let's start with the cities. Coastal highways connect the dots between some of the West Coast's most striking municipalities, starting with surf-loving San Diego in Southern California and moving north through glitzy Los Angeles and techie San Francisco. Way up north, take a worthwhile detour to alternative-minded Seattle.

If you want to bypass urban areas, it's easy to stick to the places in between. In southern California, PCH rolls past the almost-too-perfect beaches of California's Orange County ('the OC') and Santa Barbara (the 'American Riviera'). Further north, Hwy 1 passes wacky Santa Cruz, a university town and surfers' paradise, then redwood forests along the Big Sur coast and north of Mendocino. Hwy 1 cruises past the sand dunes, seaside resorts and fishing villages of coastal Oregon; and finally, the wild lands of Washington's Olympic Peninsula, with its primeval rain forest and bucolic San Juan Islands, served by coastal ferries.

When to Go

There's no bad time of year to drive this route, although northern climes will be rainier and snowier during winter. Peak travel season is June through August, which isn't always the best time as many

THE HISTORY OF ROUTE 66

Launched in 1926, Route 66 would ultimately stretch from Chicago to Los Angeles, linking a ribbon of small towns and country byways as it rolled across eight states. The road gained notoriety during the Great Depression, when migrant farmers followed it west from the Dust Bowl across the Great Plains. Its nickname, 'The Mother Road,' first appeared in *The Grapes of Wrath*, John Steinbeck's novel about the era. Things got a little more fun after WWII, when newfound prosperity prompted Americans to get behind the wheel and explore. Nat King Cole recorded 'Get Your Kicks on Route 66' in 1946, which added to the road's allure. But just as things got going, the Feds rolled out the interstate system, which eventually caused the Mother Road's demise. The very last town on Route 66 to be bypassed by an interstate was Arizona's Williams, in 1984.

stretches of the coast are socked in by fog during early summer (locals call it 'June Gloom'). The shoulder seasons before Memorial Day (April and May) and after Labor Day (September and October) can be ideal, with sunny days, crisply cool nights and fewer crowds.

The Route

Highways stretch nearly 1500 miles from border to border, from Tijuana, Mexico, to British Columbia, Canada. In California, the coastal route jumps between I-5, Hwy 101 and Hwy 1 (when in doubt, just hug the coast) before committing to Hwy 101 in Oregon and Washington.

Time & Mileage

Time: No stopping? Give yourself four days because traffic and two-lane roads will slow you down; to fully enjoy the sights, allow 10 to 14 days.

Mileage: About 1500 miles.

LISAY/GETTY IMAGES ©

Palace Saloon (p170), Central Arizona

Highway 89/89A: Wickenburg to Oak Creek Canyon

Hwy 89 and its sidekick Hwy 89A cross some of Arizona's most scenic and distinct regions. The route described here travels north over the Weaver and Mingus mountains before rolling into Sedona and Oak Creek Canyon.

Why Go

This is our favorite drive in Arizona. It may not be the prettiest or wildest, but there's a palpable sense of the Old West infusing the trip, like you've slipped through the swinging doors of history. But the route's not stuck in the 19th century – far from it. Weekend art walks, a burgeoning wine trail, stylish indie-owned shops and restaurants all add some 21st-century sparkle.

For those interested in cowboy history, Wickenburg and its dude ranches are a good place to spend some time. Hwy 89 leaves town via Hwy 93 and soon tackles the Weaver Mountains, climbing 2500ft in 4 miles. The road levels out at mountain-topping Yarnell, site of a devastating fire in the summer of 2013, then passes grassy buttes and grazing cattle in the Peeples Valley. From here, one highlight is Prescott's infamous Whiskey Row, home of the historic Palace Saloon (p170). Thumb Butte is a hard-to-miss landmark west of downtown, and you'll pass the unusual boulders of Granite Dells on your way out of town.

Follow Hwy 89A to Jerome and hold on tight. This serpentine section of road brooks no distraction, clinging tight to the side of Mingus Mountain. If you dare, glance east for stunning views of the Verde Valley. The zigzagging reaches epic proportions in Jerome, a former mining town cleaved into the side of Cleopatra Hill. Pull over for art galleries, tasting rooms, quirky inns and an unusually high number of ghosts. Stand over a 1910ft-deep mining shaft at Audrey Headframe Park (p170) then visit the mining museum at Jerome State Historic Park (p170) next door.

Hwy 89A drops through another mining town, Clarkdale, on its way to Old Town Cottonwood. On the way to Sedona, detour to wineries on Page Springs Rd or loop into town via the Cathedral Rock (p170), passing Red Rock Loop Rd. Sedona is made for rejuvenation. It's a pretty place to commune with a vortex, dine on a fine meal or shop for art and Navajo rugs. This trip ends with a cannonball into Oak Creek Canyon where the namesake creek sparkles with riparian lushness in the shadows of a towering red-rock corridor.

When to Go

This route is best traveled in spring, summer and fall to avoid winter snow – although you might see a few flakes in the mountains in April or even May! In the dead of summer, you won't want to linger in low-lying, toasty Wickenburg.

The Route

From Wickenburg, follow Hwy 93 to Hwy 89 then track north to Prescott. North of town, pick up Hwy 89A, following it to Sedona.

Time & Mileage

Time: This route can be driven in a half-day, but we recommend two to three days for maximum enjoyment.

Mileage: 134 miles.

Million Dollar Highway

Stretching between Ouray and Silverton in southern Colorado is one of the most gorgeous alpine drives in the US. Part of the 236-mile San Juan Skyway, this section of US 550 is known as the Million Dollar Hwy because the road, they say, is filled with ore.

Why Go

Twenty-five miles of smooth, buttery pavement twists over three mountain passes, serving up views of Victorian homes, snowcapped peaks, mineshaft headframes and a gorge lined with rock. But the allure isn't just the beauty; part of the thrill is the driving. Hairpin turns and narrow, mountain-hugging pavement flips this route from a Sunday-afternoon drive to a NASCAR-worthy adventure.

Charming Ouray sits at nearly 7800ft, surrounded by lofty peaks. It also fronts the Uncompahgre Gorge, a steep, rocky canyon famous for its ice climbing. While here, take a hike or soak in the town's hot springs. From Ouray, the Million Dollar Hwy – completed in 1884 after three years of construction – hugs the side of the gorge, twisting past old mines that pock the mountainsides. Stay vigilant for the masochistic, spandex-clad cyclists pumping over the passes on the ribbon-thin road. In Silverton, step away from the car and enjoy the aspen-covered mountains or watch the steam-powered Durango & Silverton Narrow Gauge Railroad (p107) chug into town.

When to Go

Summer is the best time to visit. In winter, the highest pass sometimes closes and at other times you may need chains. You might even see snow on the ground in summer, though it likely won't be on the road.

The Route

From Ouray, follow Hwy 550 south to Silverton.

Time & Mileage

Time: The drive can be done in a few hours, but give yourself a day to see the sights.

Mileage: 25 miles.

Beartooth Highway

Depending on who's talking, the sky-high Beartooth Hwy is either the best way to get to Yellowstone, the most exciting motorcycle ride in the West or the most scenic highway in America. We reckon it's all of the above.

Why Go

Sometimes you just want to find a place so beautiful that it'll make you pull over, leave your car and yell 'Yeah!' In the West, that place is the Beartooth Hwy.

From Red Lodge, MT, this adventurous drive ascends Rock Creek Canyon's glaciated valley via a series of spaghetti-loop switchbacks, gaining an amazing 5000ft in elevation in just a few miles. Pull off at Rock Creek Vista Point Overlook for a short, wheelchair-accessible walk to superb views. The road continues up onto the high plateau, past 'Mae West Curve' and into Wyoming.

Twin Lakes has views of the cirque as well as the ski lift that carries the daring to an extreme spring ski run. After a series of switchbacks, look northwest for the Hellroaring Plateau and the jagged Bears Tooth (11,612ft). The route, flanked by alpine tundra, crests at the Beartooth Pass West Summit, the highest point at 10,947ft. Fifteen-foot snowbanks may linger here as late as June (sometimes even July).

After passing more lakes, the road descends past Beartooth Butte, a huge lump of the sedimentary rock that once covered the Beartooths. The highway drops to several excellent fishing areas on the Clark's Fork, then re-enters Montana, reaching Cooke City via Colter Pass (8066ft). The northeast entrance of Yellowstone is 4 miles from Cooke City.

When to Go

To add some hiking to your driving, visit in August. That's when the weather is typically the best for outdoor adventure. The road is usually only cleared of snow and open from around Memorial Day in late May to September.

The Route

From Red Lodge, follow Hwy 212 west – crossing into and out of Wyoming – to Cooke City, MT.

Time & Mileage

Time: It's hard to zip along the twisty Beartooth Hwy; allow at least an afternoon or morning to drive it.

Mileage: 68 miles.

Highway 12

Arguably Utah's most diverse and stunning route, Hwy 12 winds through remote and rugged canyons, linking several national and state parks – and several fantastic restaurants – in the state's red-rock center.

Why Go

With crimson canyons, sprawling deserts, thick forests and lofty peaks calling out for exploration, Hwy 12 in remote southern Utah works well for adventurous explorers. The trip kicks off at Bryce Canyon National Park where the eye-catching gold-and-crimson spires set the stage for the color-infused journey to come.

Traveling east, the first highlight is **Kodachrome Basin State Park** (☎435-679-8562; www.stateparks.utah.gov/parks/kodachrome-basin; 2905 S Kodachrome State Park Rd, off Cottonwood Canyon Rd, Cannonville; day use per vehicle/pedestrian $8/4; ⊙6am-10pm), home to petrified geysers and dozens of red, pink and white sandstone chimneys – some nearly 170ft tall. Pass through tiny Escalante and then, 8 miles down the road, pull over for the view at Head of the Rocks Overlook, atop the Aquarius Plateau. From here you'll lord it over giant mesas, towering domes, deep canyons and undulating slickrock, all unfurling in an explosion of color.

The adjacent Grand Staircase–Escalante National Monument (p212) is the largest park in the Southwest at nearly 1.9 million acres. The Lower Calf Creek Recreation Area, inside the park and beside Hwy 12, holds a picnic area and a pleasant campground. It's also the start of a popular 6-mile round-trip hike to the impressive 126ft Lower Calf Creek Falls. The razor-thin Hogback Ridge, between Escalante and Boulder, is pretty stunning, too.

The best section of the drive? Many consider it to be the switchbacks and petrified sand dunes between Boulder and Torrey. But it's not just the views. In Boulder, treat your taste buds to a locally sourced meal at Hell's Backbone Grill (p212), followed by homemade pie at the Burr Trail Outpost (p212), or enjoy a flavor-packed Southwestern dish at **Cafe Diablo** (☎435-425-3070; www.cafediablo.net; 599 W Main St; mains $20-36; ⊙3-9pm; 🌶) further north in Torrey.

MILLION DOLLAR HIGHWAY DETOUR

The drive between Ouray and Telluride is 50 miles – via the paved route. If you're feeling adventurous and have a 4WD (don't try it otherwise), consider the unpaved 16-mile road over Imogene Pass. On this old mining road you'll cross streams, alpine meadows and one of the state's highest passes. You'll also pass an old mine. We should mention one thing: this 'short cut' takes three hours. Still game?

Going-to-the-Sun Road (p134), Glacier National Park

When to Go

For the best weather and driving conditions – especially over 11,000ft Boulder Mountain – drive Hwy 12 between May and October.

The Route

From US Hwy 89 in Utah, follow Hwy 12 east to Bryce Canyon National Park. The road takes a northerly turn at Kodachrome Basin State Park then continues to Torrey.

Time & Mileage

Time: Although the route could be driven in a few hours, two to three days allows for a bit of exploration.

Mileage: 124 miles.

High Road to Taos

This picturesque byway in northern New Mexico links Santa Fe with Taos, rippling through a series of adobe villages and mountain-flanked vistas in and around the Truchas Peaks.

Why Go

Santa Fe and Taos are well-known artists' communities, lovely places brimming with galleries, studios and museums. Two cities this stunning should be linked by a beautiful byway, and the mountainous High Road to Taos obliges.

From Santa Fe follow Hwy 84/285 north. Exit onto Hwy 503 toward Nambe, where you can hike to waterfalls or simply meditate by the namesake lake. From here, the road leads north to picturesque Chimayo. Abandoned crutches line the wall in El Santuario de Chimayó (p229), also known as 'The Lourdes of America.' In 1816 this two-towered adobe chapel was built over a spot said to have miraculous healing powers. Take some time to wander through the community, and admire the fine weaving and woodcarving in family-run galleries.

Near Truchas, a village of galleries and century-old adobes, you'll find the **High Road Art Gallery** (☎505-689-2689; www.facebook.com/highroadartgallery; 1642 Hwy 76; ⊙10am-5pm, to 4pm winter). This cooperative on SR 676 sells a variety of artworks by local artists. Up Hwy 76, original paintings and carvings remain in good condition inside the **Church of San José de Gracia** (☎505-351-4360; Hwy 76, Las Trampas; ⊙by appointment, call ahead), considered one of the finest surviving 18th-century churches in the USA. Next is Picuris Pueblo, once one of the most powerful pueblos in the region. This ride ends at Penasco, a gateway to the Pecos Wilderness, and also home to the engagingly experimental **Peñasco Theatre** (☎575-770-7597; www.penascotheatre.org; 15046 Hwy 75). From here, follow Hwys 75 and 518 into Taos.

When to Go

The high season is summer, but spring can be a nice time to see blooming flowers. Fall presents a show of colorful leaves. With mountains on the route, winter is not the best time to visit.

The Route

From Santa Fe, take Hwy 84/285 west to Pojoaque and turn right on Hwy 503, toward Nambe. From Hwy 503, take Hwy 76 to Hwy 75, then drive into Taos on Hwy 518.

Time & Mileage

Time: Without stopping, this drive should take about half a day, but give yourself a full day if you want to shop and explore.

Mileage: 85 miles.

Going-to-the-Sun Road

A strong contender for the most spectacular drive in America, the 53-mile Going-to-the-Sun Road is the only paved road through Glacier National Park in Montana.

Why Go

Glaciers! Grizzlies! A mountain-hugging marvel of modern engineering! Yep, the Going-to-the-Sun Road inspires superlatives and exclamation points. But the accolades are deserved. The road, completed in 1933, crosses a ruggedly beautiful alpine landscape, twisting and turning over a lofty Continental Divide that's usually blanketed in snow. The views of the Great Plains beyond are also quite something.

From the park's west entrance, the road skirts the shimmering Lake McDonald. Ahead, the looming Garden Wall forms the 9000ft spine of the Continental Divide and separates the west side of the park from the east side. The road crosses the divide at Logan Pass (6880ft). From here, the 7.6-mile Highline Trail (one way) traces the park's mountainous backbone, with views of glaciated valleys, sawtooth peaks, wildflowers and wildlife. And the wildlife you might see? Mountain goats. Bighorn sheep. Moose. Maybe even a grizzly bear or an elusive wolverine. After Logan Pass, the road passes Jackson Glacier Overlook, where you can bear witness to one of the park's melting monoliths. Experts say that at current global temperatures, all of the park's glaciers will be gone by 2030, so now is the time to visit.

When to Go

This snow-attracting route opens late and closes early. It's typically drivable between mid-June and mid-September, but beware: in 2011, due to an unusually heavy snowpack, the road didn't completely open until July 13.

The Route

From the west entrance of Glacier National Park, follow the Going-to-the-Sun Road east to St Mary.

Time & Mileage

Time: It varies depending on conditions, but plan to spend at least a half-day on the drive.

Mileage: 53 miles.

GOING-TO-THE-SUN ROAD: A LEGEND & A LANDMARK

Going-to-the-Sun Road was named after Going-to-the-Sun Mountain. According to legend – or a story concocted in the 1880s – a deity of the Blackfeet Tribe once taught tribal members to hunt. After the lesson, he left an image of himself on the mountain as inspiration before he ascended to the sun. Today, the road is a National Historic Landmark and a National Civil Engineering Landmark, the only road in the country to hold both designations.

MORE SCENIC DRIVES

Hungry for more road trips? Here are a few good ones.

Turquoise Trail, NM This back route between Tijeras, near Albuquerque, and Santa Fe, was a major trade route for several thousand years. Today it rolls past art galleries, shops (with turquoise jewelry) and a mining museum. From I-40, follow Hwy 14 north to I-25. Also see www.turquoisetrail.org.

Apache Trail, AZ This isn't your grandmother's Sunday-afternoon drive – unless your grandmother likes 45 miles of rabid road. From Apache Junction east of Phoenix, follow Hwy 88 past a kid-friendly ghost town, the wildflowers of Lost Dutchman State Park and three Salt River lakes. In the middle of it all? A snarling dirt section that drops more than 1000ft in less than 3 miles. Hold tight!

The Loneliest Road Hwy 50 slices across Nevada, stretching east from Fallon to Great Basin National Park and the Utah state line. This remote highway unfurls past a singing sand dune, Pony Express stations, and mining towns. A burger at Middlegate Station is a tasty pit stop.

Eastern Sierra Scenic Byway, CA From Topaz Lake, follow Hwy 395 south along the eastern flank of the mighty Sierra Nevada, ending at Little Lake. The region holds 14,000ft peaks, ice-blue lakes, pine forests, desert basins and hot springs.

Historic Columbia River Highway

Lush foliage and trailblazing history are highlights on US 30, a carefully planned byway that ribbons alongside the Columbia River Gorge east of Portland, Oregon.

Why Go

Look, there's a waterfall. And another waterfall. And another... Just how many waterfalls can one scenic highway hold? Quite a few if that road is the Historic Columbia River Hwy. The original route – completed in 1922 – connected Portland to The Dalles. The first paved road in the Pacific Northwest, it was carefully planned and built with the pleasure of driving in mind rather than speed. Viewpoints were carefully selected, and stone walls and arching bridges stylishly complement the gorgeous scenery.

Also notable is the history. Lewis and Clark traveled this route as they pushed toward the Pacific Ocean in 1805. Fifty years later, Oregon Trail pioneers ended their cross-country trek with a harrowing final push through the gorge's treacherous waters. Today, although sections of the original byway have been closed, or replaced by US 84, much of US 30 is still open for driving and some closed portions can be traversed by hiking or cycling.

One roadside highlight is the Portland Women's Forum Park, which provides one of the best views of the gorge. Just east the 1916 Vista House, honoring the Oregon Trail pioneers, holds a visitor center. It's perched on Crown Point, a good viewpoint that also marks the western edge of the gorge. And did we mention those gushing cascades? For oohs and aahs, don't miss Multnomah Falls, Oregon's tallest waterfall at 642ft.

When to Go

Waterfalls are at their peak February to May, while summer is great for hiking.

The Route

To reach the historic highway, take exit 17, 28 or 35 off I-84 east of Portland. The western section of the original highway ends at Multnomah Falls. From here hop onto I-84 and continue east to exit 69 at Mosier where you can return to US 30.

Time & Mileage

Time: One day.

Mileage: 100 miles.

Plan Your Trip
Outdoor Activities

Whether you're a couch potato, a weekend warrior or an ironman (or maiden), the West has an outdoor activity for you. The best part? A stunning landscape as your backdrop. Scan for hummingbirds, paddle rapids, ride through epic powder, surf curling waves or hike into the world's most famous canyon.

Camping

Campers are absolutely spoiled for choice in the West. Pitch a tent beside alpine lakes and streams in Colorado, sleep under saguaro cacti in southern Arizona or snooze on gorgeous strands of California sand.

Campground Types & Amenities

Primitive or dispersed camping May have fire pits, but otherwise don't expect any amenities or even official sites; always free and possible in national forests (USFS) and on Bureau of Land Management (BLM) land.

Backcountry sites The most peaceful and only available to backpackers on public land. Permits and reservations may be required.

Developed campgrounds Typically found in state and national parks, with more amenities, including (sometimes) drinking water, toilets, picnic tables, barbecue grills and occasionally hot showers and a coin-op laundry.

RV (recreational vehicle) hookups and dump stations Available at many privately owned campgrounds, but only a few public-land campgrounds.

Private campgrounds Cater mainly to RVers and offer hot showers, swimming pools, wi-fi and family camping cabins; tent sites may be few and uninviting.

Best Outdoors

Ultimate Outdoor Experiences

Rafting the Colorado River through the Grand Canyon, AZ

Hiking to the summit of Half Dome, Yosemite National Park, CA

Cycling in Maroon Bells, Aspen, CO

Rock climbing in Joshua Tree National Park, CA

Scrambling to Angels Landing, Zion National Park, UT

Skiing in Vail, CO

Mountain biking in Moab, UT

Kayaking the San Juan Islands, WA

Soaking in hot springs in Ojo Caliente, NM

Glacier spotting in Glacier National Park, MT

Best Wildlife-Watching

Bears in Glacier National Park, MT

Bison, grizzlies and gray wolves in Yellowstone National Park, WY

Elk and bighorn sheep in Rocky Mountain National Park, CO

Birds in Patagonia-Sonoita Creek Preserve, AZ

Whales and dolphins in Monterey Bay, CA

Rates & Reservations

Many public and private campgrounds accept reservations for all or some of their sites, while a few are strictly first-come, first-served. Overnight rates range from free for the most primitive campsites to $50 or more for pull-through RV sites with full hookups.

These agencies let you search for campground locations and amenities; check availability and reserve campsites online:

Kampgrounds of America (http://koa.com) National chain of reliable but more expensive private campgrounds offering full facilities, particularly for RVs.

Recreation.gov (www.recreation.gov) Camping and cabin reservations for national parks, national forests, BLM land.

ReserveAmerica (www.reserveamerica.com) Reservations for state parks, regional parks and some private campgrounds across North America. See website for phone numbers by state.

Hiking & Trekking

Good hiking trails are abundant in the West. Fitness is a priority throughout the region, and most metropolitan areas have at least one large park with trails. National parks and monuments are ideal for both short and long hikes. If you're hankering for nights in the wilderness beneath star-filled skies, however, plan on securing a backcountry permit in advance, especially in places such as the Grand Canyon – spaces may be limited during summer. For longer-haul treks, consider the Pacific Crest Trail (p51) or the **Continental Divide Trail** (https://continentaldividetrail.org).

Hiking Resources

Wilderness Survival (1998), by Gregory Davenport, is easily the best book on surviving nearly every contingency. Useful websites:

American Hiking Society (https://americanhiking.org) Links to local hiking clubs and 'volunteer vacations' building trails.

Backpacker (www.backpacker.com) Premier national magazine for backpackers, from novices to experts.

SummitPost (www.summitpost.org) Routes, forums and trail descriptions for peaks and rock climbing.

Fees & Wilderness Permits

➡ State parks typically charge a daily entrance fee of $5 to $15; there's often a reduced fee, or no charge, if you walk or bike into these parks.

➡ National park entry averages $10 to $35 per vehicle for seven consecutive days; some national parks are free. Check the national park website for dates for Free Entrance Days (www.nps.gov/planyourvisit/fee-free-parks.htm).

➡ For unlimited admission to national parks, national forests and other federal recreation lands for one year, buy an 'America the Beautiful' pass ($80).

➡ Often required for overnight backpackers and extended day hikes, wilderness permits are issued at ranger stations and park visitor centers. Daily quotas may be in effect during peak periods (usually late spring through early fall).

➡ Some wilderness permits may be reserved ahead of time, and very popular trails (eg Half Dome, Mt Whitney) may sell out several months in advance.

➡ To hike in the forest surrounding Sedona, AZ, you'll need to buy a Red Rock Pass ($5 per day, $15 per week). National park interagency passes are accepted in lieu of the Red Rock Pass.

Cycling

The popularity of cycling is growing by the day in the US, with cities adding more cycle lanes and becoming more bike-friendly. An increasing number of greenways traverse urban areas and the countryside. You'll find die-hard enthusiasts in every town, and numerous outfitters offer guided trips for all levels and durations.

Many states offer social multiday rides, such as **Ride the Rockies** (www.ridetherockies.com) in Colorado. For a fee, you can join the peloton on a scenic, well-supported route; your gear is ferried ahead to that night's camping spot.

In Colorado, Aspen is a top cycling spot. Another standout ride is Arizona's **Mt Lemmon** (www.fs.usda.gov/main/coronado), a thigh-zinging, 28-mile climb from the Sonoran Desert floor to the 9157ft summit. You

WESTERN US NATIONAL PARKS

PARK	FEATURES	ACTIVITIES	BEST TIME
Arches (p209)	more than 2000 sandstone arches	scenic drives, day hikes	spring, fall
Bryce Canyon (p213)	brilliantly colored, eroded hoodoos	day & backcountry hikes, horseback riding	spring-fall
Canyonlands (p209)	epic Southwestern canyons, mesas & buttes	scenic viewpoints, back-country hikes, white-water rafting	spring, fall
Carlsbad Caverns (p238)	extensive cave system; free-tail bat colony	cave tours, backcountry hikes	spring-fall
Death Valley (p288)	hot, dramatic desert & unique ecology	scenic drives, day hikes	spring
Glacier (p133)	impressive glaciated land-scape; mountain goats	day & backcountry hikes, scenic drives	summer
Grand Canyon (p177)	spectacular 277-mile-long, 1-mile-deep river canyon	day & backcountry hikes, mule trips, river running	spring-fall
Grand Teton (p123)	towering granite peaks; moose, bison, wolves	day & backcountry hikes, rock climbing, fishing	summer-fall
Great Basin (p160)	desert mountains, caves and forests	day & backcountry hikes, scenic drives	summer-fall
Mesa Verde (p106)	preserved Ancestral Puebloan cliff dwellings, historic sites, mesas & canyons	short hikes	spring-fall
Olympic (p372)	temperate rainforests, alpine meadows, Mt Olympus	day & backcountry hikes	spring-fall
Petrified Forest (p188)	fossilized trees, petroglyphs, Painted Desert scenery	day hikes	year-round
Redwood (p338)	virgin redwood forest, world's tallest trees; elk	day & backcountry hikes	spring-fall
Rocky Mountain (p90)	stunning peaks, alpine tun-dra, the Continental Divide; elk, bighorn sheep, moose, beavers	day & backcountry hikes, cross-country skiing	summer-winter
Saguaro (p192)	giant saguaro cactus, desert scenery	day & backcountry hikes	fall-spring
Sequoia & Kings Canyon (p346)	sequoia redwood groves, granite canyon	day & backcountry hikes, cross-country skiing	summer-fall
Yellowstone (p118)	geysers & geothermal pools, impressive canyon; prolific wildlife	day & backcountry hikes, cycling, cross-country skiing	year-round
Yosemite (p343)	sheer granite-walled valley, waterfalls, alpine meadows	day & backcountry hikes, rock climbing, skiing	year-round
Zion (p214)	immense red-rock canyon, Virgin River	day & backcountry hikes, canyoneering	fall-spring

can also rent bikes on the South Rim of the Grand Canyon at Grand Canyon National Park (p179). Ride to Hermit's Rest on the park's Hermit Rd and the ever-lengthening **Greenway Trail** (www.nps.gov/grca/planyourvisit/bicycling.htm).

Top Cycling Towns

San Francisco, CA A pedal over the Golden Gate Bridge lands you in the stunningly beautiful, and stunningly hilly, Marin Headlands.

Boulder, CO Outdoors-loving town with loads of great biking paths, including the Boulder Creek Trail and Marshall Mesa mountain biking.

Portland, OR A trove of great cycling (on- and off-road) in the Pacific Northwest.

Surfing

The best surf in the continental USA breaks off the coast of California. There are loads of options – from the funky and low-key **Santa Cruz** to San Francisco's **Ocean Beach** – a tough spot to learn! – or bohemian **Bolinas**, 30 miles north. South, you'll find strong swells and Santa Ana winds in **San Diego**, **La Jolla**, **Malibu** and **Santa Barbara**, all of which sport warmer waters, fewer sharks of the great white variety and a saucy SoCal beach scene; the best conditions are from September to November. Along the coast of Oregon and Washington are miles of crowd-free beaches and pockets of surfing communities.

Top California Surfing Spots

Huntington Beach, Orange County (www.huntingtonbeachca.gov; ⏲5am-10pm; 🅿) The quintessential surf capital, with perpetual sun and a 'perfect' break, particularly during winter when the winds are calm.

Oceanside Beach, Oceanside One of SoCal's prettiest beaches boasts one of the world's most consistent surf breaks in summer. It's a family-friendly spot.

Rincon, Santa Barbara Arguably one of the planet's top surfing spots; nearly every major surf champion on the globe has taken Rincon for a ride.

MAD FOR MOUNTAIN BIKING

Mountain-biking enthusiasts will find trail nirvana in Crested Butte and Salida, CO; Moab, UT; Bend, OR; Ketchum, ID; Helena and Big Sky Resort, MT; and Marin, CA, the last being where Gary Fisher and Co bunny-hopped the sport forward by careening down the rocky flanks of Mt Tamalpais on home-rigged bikes. Montana alone has more than 60 mountain-biking trails covering nearly 1800 miles. For info about trails and trips, check out the MTB Project (www.mtbproject.com) and BikePacking (https://bikepacking.com/); the latter is especially good for long-distance hauls on epics such as the Colorado Trail and Arizona Trail. Great destinations include the following:

Kokopelli Trail, UT One of the premier bikepacking trails in the Southwest stretches 142 miles on a variety of terrain between Fruita, CO, and Moab, UT.

Monarch Crest, CO (p99) Extreme 20- to 35-mile adventure along the Continental Divide with fabulous high-altitude views. Near Salida.

Sun Top Loop, WA A 22-mile ride with challenging climbs and superb views of Mt Rainier and surrounding peaks on the western slopes of Washington's Cascade Mountains.

Downieville Downhill, CA (www.downievilleclassic.com) Not for the faint of heart, this piney trail, located near its namesake Sierra foothill town in Tahoe National Forest, skirts river-hugging cliffs, passes through old-growth forest and drops 4200ft in less than 14 miles.

McKenzie River Trail, Willamette National Forest, OR Twenty-five miles of blissful single-track winding through deep forests and volcanic formations. The town of McKenzie is about 50 miles east of Eugene.

Whole Enchilada, UT (☎435-259-2444; www.utah.com/mountain-biking/the-whole-enchilada; Sand Flats Rd, La Sal Mountains) Stitches together four incredible Moab trails, with more than 26 miles of riding and 7000ft of vertical drop from alpine forests all the way down onto the legendary slickrock.

Angel Fire Bike Park, NM (www.angelfireresort.com; 10 Miller Lane; all-day pass & lift ticket adult/child 7-12yr $49/39; ⏲mid-May–mid-Oct) More than 60 miles of bike trails in one of the Southwest's best mountain-biking parks.

Steamer Lane and Pleasure Point, Santa Cruz There are 11 world-class breaks, including the point breaks over rock bottoms, at these two sweet spots.

Swami's, Encinitas Located below Seacliff Roadside Park, this popular surfing beach has multiple breaks guaranteeing you some fantastic waves.

Surfing Resources

Surfer (www.surfer.com) Orange County–based magazine website with travel reports, gear reviews, newsy blogs and videos.

Surfline (www.surfline.com) Browse the comprehensive atlas, live webcams and surf reports for the lowdown from San Diego to Maverick's.

Surfrider (www.surfrider.org) Enlightened surfers can join up with this nonprofit organization, which aims to protect the coastal environment.

White-Water Rafting

There's no shortage of scenic and spectacular rafting in the West. In California, both the **Tuolumne** and **American Rivers** surge with moderate to extreme rapids, while in Idaho the Middle Fork of the Salmon River (p140) has it all: wildlife, thrilling rapids, a rich history, waterfalls and hot springs. The **North Fork of the Owyhee** – which snakes from the high plateau of southwest Oregon to the rangelands of Idaho – is rightfully popular and features towering hoodoos. In Salida, Colorado, **Brown's Canyon National Monument** stakes a claim as one of the most popular stretches of white water in the country. North of Moab, UT, look for wildlife on an easy float on the **Colorado River** or ramp it up several notches with a thrilling romp through class V rapids and the red rocks of Canyonlands National Park (p209). Also good are Snake River near Jackson, WY (p115), and Montana's Gallatin Valley (p127).

To book a spot on the Colorado River through the Grand Canyon, the quintessential river trip, make reservations at least a year in advance. And if you're not after white-knuckle rapids, fret not – many rivers have sections suitable for peaceful float trips or inner-tube drifts that you can enjoy with a cold beer in hand.

SPORTSTOCK/GETTY IMAGES ©

White-water rafting the Arkansas River (p100), Colorado

Kayaking & Canoeing

For exploring flatwater (no rapids or surf), opt for a kayak or canoe. For big lakes and the sea coast use a sea kayak. Be aware that kayaks are not always suitable for carrying bulky gear.

For scenic sea kayaking, you can push into the surf just about anywhere off the California coast. Popular spots include **La Jolla** as well as the coastal state parks just north of **Santa Barbara**. In the Pacific Northwest, you can enjoy world-class kayaking in and around the **San Juan Islands**, the **Olympic Peninsula** and **Puget Sound**. There's a full-moon paddle in Sausalito's **Richardson Bay**, CA. Sea-kayak rentals average $32 to $40 for two hours. Reputable outfitters will make sure you're aware of the tide schedule and wind conditions of your proposed route.

White-water kayaking is also popular wherever there's rafting. In the Pacific Northwest, where water tumbles down from the ice-capped volcanoes, look for bald eagles on the **Upper Sgakit River** o[r] slip through remote wilderness canyon[s] [on] the **Klickitat River**. Close to Portla[nd]

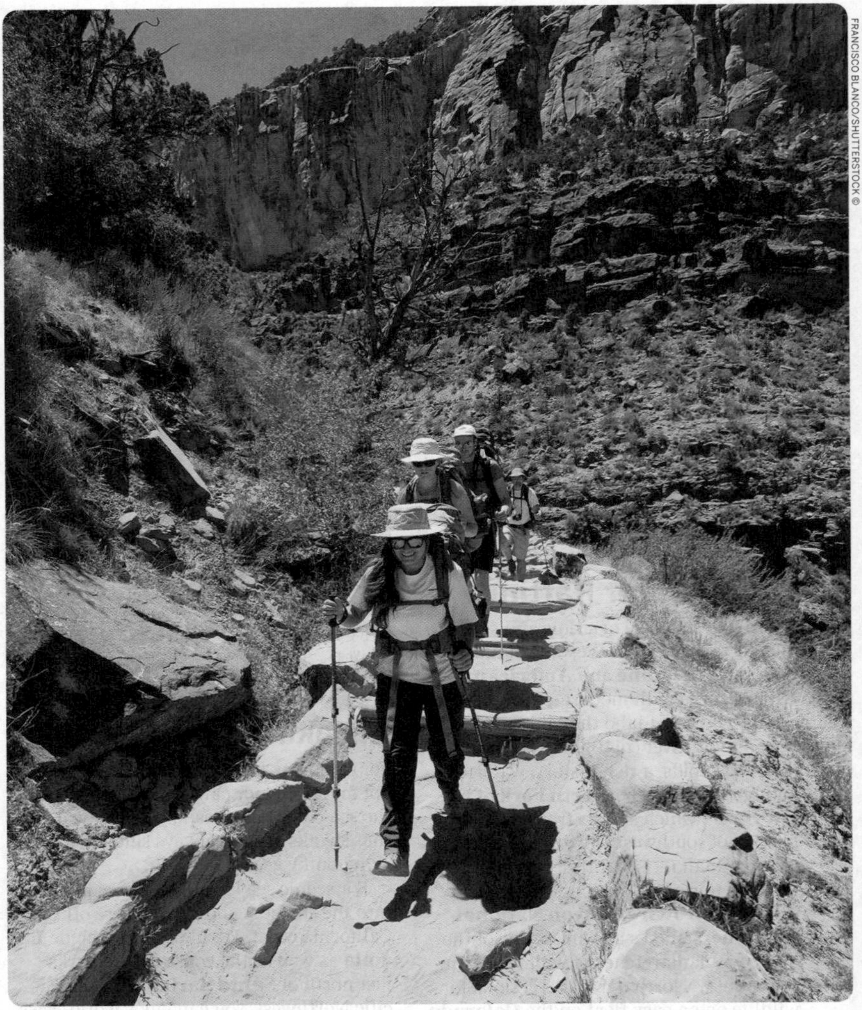

FRANCISCO BLANCO/SHUTTERSTOCK ©

GLADASSFANNY/GETTY IMAGES ©

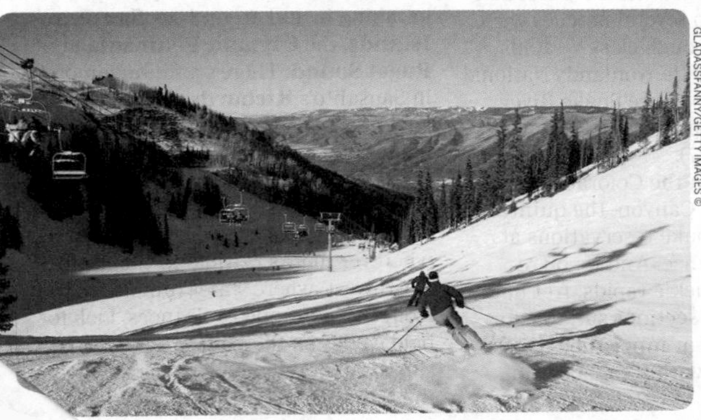

Top: Hikers on the Bright Angel Trail (p179), Grand Canyon National Park, Nevada

Bottom: Skiing at Aspen (p97)

the **Clackamas** and the **North Santiam**. For urban white-water kayaking, you can't beat Colorado. Look for white-water parks in **Salida** and **Boulder**.

Kayaking & Canoeing Resources

American Canoe Association (www.americancanoe.org) Organization supporting and providing information about canoeing and kayaking.

American Whitewater (www.americanwhitewater.org) Advocacy group for responsible recreation works to preserve America's wild rivers.

Canoe & Kayak (www.adventuresportsnetwork.com/sport/paddle-sports/canoe-kayak/) Special interest magazine for paddlers.

Kayak Online (www.kayakonline.com) Advice for buying gear and helpful links to kayaking manufacturers, schools and associations.

Skiing & Other Winter Sports

Skiing, snowboarding, snowshoeing, cross-country hut trips, backcountry snowcat tours, World Cup races, 22ft superpipes and ski mountaineering competitions: the West has some of the best snow – and most fun – in the world. The ski season typically runs from December to mid-April, though some resorts have longer seasons. In summer, many resorts offer mountain biking, hiking and adventure parks courtesy of

TOP TRAILS IN THE WEST

Ask 10 people for their top trail recommendations throughout the West and no two answers will be alike. The country is so varied and distances so enormous, there's little consensus. That said, you can't go wrong with the following all-star sampler.

South Kaibab/North Kaibab Trail, Grand Canyon, AZ (p179) A multiday cross-canyon tramp down to the Colorado River and back up to the rim.

Chasm Lake, Rocky Mountain National Park, CO (p90) The exposed climb to the summit of Longs Peak (14,259ft) is not recommended for casual hikers, but if you're in good shape, the 8.4-mile round-trip to Chasm Lake is equally amazing.

Angels Landing, Zion National Park, UT (p214) After a heart-pounding scramble over a narrow, precipice-flanked strip of rock, the reward is a sweeping view of Zion Canyon. It's a 5.4-mile round-trip hike.

Mt Washburn Trail, Yellowstone National Park, WY (p121) From Dunraven Pass, this wildflower-lined trail climbs 3 miles to expansive views from the summit of Mt Washburn (10,243ft). Look for bighorn sheep.

Pacific Crest Trail (PCT; ☎916-285-1846; www.pcta.org) Follows the spines of the Cascades and Sierra Nevada, traipsing 2650 miles from Canada to Mexico, passing through six of North America's seven ecozones.

Half Dome, Yosemite National Park, CA (p343) Scary and strenuous, but the Yosemite Valley views and sense of accomplishment are worth it. Park permit required.

Enchanted Valley Trail, Olympic National Park, WA (p372) Magnificent mountain views, roaming wildlife and lush rainforests – all on a 13-mile out-and-back trail.

Great Northern Traverse, Glacier National Park, MT (p133) A 58-mile haul that cuts through the heart of grizzly country and crosses the Continental Divide.

The Big Loop, Chiricahua National Monument, AZ (p195) A 9.5-mile hike along several trails that winds past an 'army' of wondrous rock pillars in southeastern Arizona once used as a hideout by Apache warriors.

Tahoe Rim Trail, Lake Tahoe, CA (p350) This 165-mile, all-purpose trail circumnavigates the lake from high above, affording glistening Sierra views.

Ruby Crest Trail, NV Extends for 36 uncrowded miles across the top of Nevada's Ruby Mountains.

chair lifts. Ski and snowboard packages (including airfares, hotels and lift tickets) are easy to find through resorts, travel agencies and online travel booking sites; these packages are often your best bet if your main goal is to ski.

Wherever you go, it won't come cheap. Find the best deals by purchasing multiday tickets – or better yet, a season pass – heading to lesser-known 'sibling' resorts, such **Alpine Meadows** (https://squawalpine.com) near Lake Tahoe, or checking out mountains that cater to locals, including Ski Santa Fe (p221) and Colorado's **Wolf Creek** (www.wolfcreekski.com).

Top 10 Ski Resorts

Vail, CO (p96) The largest (and most expensive) resort in Colorado, with legendary back bowls that have to be skied to be believed.

Aspen, CO (p97) It doesn't matter if you're a celebrity or a lifelong ski bum, Aspen's four mountains live up to the hype.

Sun Valley, ID (p139) Legendary Idaho resort popular with celebrities down through the years.

Jackson Hole, WY (p115) The expert's choice, with some of the steepest terrain in the US.

Salt Lake City, UT (p201) Does Utah have the best skiing? Brighton, Alta, Solitude, Snowbird and 500in of powder annually say yes.

Telluride, CO (p103) More than 4400ft of vertical, 2000 acres of terrain, 300in of snow and gulp-worthy views.

Lake Tahoe, CA (p351) Has a dozen resorts to play in, including Heavenly and Squaw Valley.

Taos, NM (p229) New ownership and expansions on- and off-mountain are keeping the Taos steeps in the mix.

Silverton, CO (p105) Top pick for the hard-core – there's no resort or fur-coat-wearing poseurs here, just a yurt and mind-blowing extreme terrain.

Big Sky, MT (p127) No attitude and no lift lines, just big-time skiing from the top of Lone Peak through 5800 acres of terrain.

Cross-Country Skiing & Snowshoeing

Most downhill ski resorts have cross-country (Nordic) ski trails. In winter, popular areas of national parks, national forests and city parks often have cross-country ski [illegible] snowshoe trails, and ice-skating rinks.

You'll find superb trail networks for Nordic skiers and snowshoers in California's **Royal Gorge**, North America's largest Nordic ski area, and Washington's sublime and crowd-free **Methow Valley**. Backcountry passionistas will be happily rewarded throughout the **Sierra Nevada**, with its many ski-in huts. There are 60 miles of trails around five ski-in huts in the **San Juan Mountains** (www.sanjuanhuts.com) in Colorado; the 10th Mountain Division Association (www.huts.org) manages more than 30 backcountry huts in the central Rockies. The **South Rim of the Grand Canyon** and the surrounding **Kaibab National Forest** are pretty spots for winter exploring.

The ranger stations at Nevada's Great Basin National Park (p160) lend out snowshoes for free for trekkers – there's snow here well into June.

Ski & Snowboard Resources

Cross-Country Ski Areas Association (https://xcski.org) Comprehensive information and gear guides for cross-country skiing and snowshoeing across North America.

Cross Country Skier (www.crosscountryskier.com) Magazine with Nordic-skiing news stories and destination articles.

Liftopia (www.liftopia.com) Shop for discount lift tickets.

Open Snow (https://opensnow.com) Get your daily powder report and forecast here.

Powder (www.powder.com) Online version of *Powder* magazine for skiers.

Ski (www.skimag.com) Online versions of *Ski* magazine.

SnoCountry Mountain Reports (www.snocountry.com) Snow reports for North America, plus events, news and resort links.

Rock Climbing & Canyoneering

In California, rock hounds test their mettle on the big walls, granite domes and boulders of world-class Yosemite National Park (p343), where the climbing season lasts from April to October. Climbers also flock to Joshua Tree National Park (p284), an otherworldly

AND LET'S NOT FORGET...

ACTIVITY	WHERE?	WHAT?	MORE INFORMATION
Horseback riding	Southern Arizona dude ranches, AZ	Old West country (most ranches close in summer due to the heat)	
	Grand Canyon South Rim, AZ	low-key trips through Kaibab National Forest; campfire rides	www.apachestables.com
	Yosemite National Park, CA	rides in Yosemite Valley, Tuolumne Meadows & near Wawona	www.travelyosemite.com
	Telluride, CO	all-season rides in the hills	www.ridewithroudy.com
	Durango, CO	day rides and overnight camping in Weminiuche Wilderness	www.vallecitolakeoutfitter.com
	Livingston, MT	rides in Yellowstone NP and Absaroka-Beartooth Wilderness	www.bearpawoutfittersmt.com
	Florence, OR	romantic beach rides	www.oregonhorsebackriding.com
	Jackson, WY	trail rides within sight of the Grand Tetons	www.millironranch.net
Diving	Blue Hole near Santa Rosa, NM	81ft-deep artesian well; blue water leads into a 131ft-long submerged cavern	https://visitsantarosanm.com
	La Jolla Underwater Park, CA	beginner-friendly; snorkelers enjoy nearby La Jolla Cove	www.sandiego.gov/lifeguards/beaches
	Channel Islands National Park, CA	kelp forests, sea caves off coastal islands	www.nps.gov/chis
	Point Lobos State Reserve, CA	fantastic shore diving; shallow reefs, caves; sea lions, seals, otters	www.pointlobos.org
	Puget Sound, WA	clear water, diverse marine life (including giant octopus!)	www.underwatersports.com
Hot-air ballooning	Sedona, AZ	float above red-rock country; picnic with bubbly	www.northernlightballoon.com
	Napa Wine Country, CA	colorful balloons float over vineyards	https://balloonrides.com; https://napavalleyballoons.com

shrine in southern California's sun-scorched desert. There, amid craggy monoliths and the country's oldest trees, they make their pilgrimage on 8000 routes, tackling sheer vertical, sharp edges and bountiful cracks. For beginners, outdoor outfitters at both parks offer guided climbs and instruction.

Outside Zion National Park (p214) in Utah, canyoneering classes teach the fine art of going down: rappelling off sheer sandstone cliffs into mysterious slot canyons. Some of the more intense routes are done in wetsuits, down the flanks of waterfalls and through ice-cold pools.

WHALE-WATCHING

Gray and humpback whales have the longest migrations of any mammal in the world – more than 5000 miles from the Arctic to Mexico, and back again. In the Pacific Northwest, most pass through from November to February (southbound) and March to June (northbound). Gray whales can be spotted off the California coast from December to April, while blue, humpback and sperm whales pass by in summer and fall. Bring binoculars! Top spots include the following:

Depoe Bay & Newport, OR (p405) Good whale-watching infrastructure; tour boats.

Puget Sound and San Juan Islands, WA (p376) Resident pods of orca.

Point Reyes Lighthouse, CA (p328) Gray whales pass by in December and January.

Monterey, CA (p298) Whales can be spotted year-round.

Channel Islands National Park, CA (p293) Take a cruise or peer through the telescope at the visitor center tower.

Cabrillo National Monument, CA (p276) The best place in San Diego to watch the gray-whale migration from January to March.

For ice climbing, try Ouray Ice Park (p103), off the Million Dollar Hwy in southwest Colorado. Inside a narrow slot canyon, 200ft walls and waterfalls are frozen in thick sheets.

Other great climbing spots include:

Grand Teton National Park, WY (p123) Good for climbers of all levels: beginners can take basic climbing courses and the more experienced can join two-day expeditions up to the top of Grand Teton itself; a 13,770ft peak with majestic views.

Sinks Canyon & Wild Iris, WY Some of the best climbing east of the Rockies, near the town of Lander.

Smith Rock, OR Sport-climbing mecca in central Oregon, with the country's first 5.14 route.

City of Rocks National Reserve, ID More than 500 routes up wind-scoured granite pinnacles 60 stories tall.

Bishop, CA This sleepy town in the Eastern Sierra is the gateway to excellent climbing in the nearby Owens River Gorge and Buttermilk Hills.

Red Rock Canyon, NV Ten miles west of Las Vegas is some of the world's finest sandstone climbing.

Indian Creek, UT Perfect multipitch sandstone cracks near Moab.

Devil's Tower, WY (www.nps.gov/deto; WY-110; 7-day vehicle pass $25; ⏲24hr, visitor center 8am-7pm) The 80-story butte of *Close Encounters of the Third Kind* fame is on every serious climber's bucket list.

Eldorado Canyon, CO More than 1000 superb granite multipitch climbs, right outside Boulder.

Flatirons, CO Not the best climbing in Boulder, but you can't miss the appeal of these 1000ft sandstone slabs.

Climbing & Canyoneering Resources

American Canyoneering Association (www.canyoneering.net) An online canyon database with links to courses, local climbing groups and more.

Climbing (www.climbing.com) Cutting-edge rock-climbing news and information since 1970.

CUSA (www.canyoneeringusa.com) Incredible online guide to Utah's canyoneering routes.

SuperTopo (www.supertopo.com) One-stop shop for rock-climbing guidebooks, downloadable topo maps and route descriptions.

Plan Your Trip

Eat & Drink Like a Local

Food served in the western part of the United States can't be slotted into one neat category because regional specialties abound – and they can vary widely. Half the fun of any trip is digging into a dish that has cultural and agricultural ties to a region, from green-chile enchiladas in New Mexico and grilled salmon in the Pacific Northwest to San Diego's delicious fish tacos and sizzling steaks in Arizona...

Staples & Specialties

Breakfast

Morning meals in the West, as in the rest of the country, are big business and taken very seriously. From a hearty serving of biscuits and gravy at a cowboy diner or a quick Egg McMuffin at the McDonald's drive-thru window to lavish Sunday brunches, Americans love their eggs and bacon, their waffles and hash browns, and their big glasses of orange juice. Most of all, they love that seemingly inalienable American right: a steaming cup of morning coffee with unlimited refills.

Lunch

After a mid-morning coffee break, an American worker's lunch hour (or half-hour these days) affords only a sandwich, quick burger or salad. The formal 'business lunch' is more common in big cities such as Los Angeles, where food is not necessarily as important as the conversation.

Dinner

Americans settle in to a more substantial weeknight dinner, usually early in the evening, which, given the workload of so many two-career families, might be

Eating Basics

Dos & Don'ts

Tip 10% to 15% of the total bill for standard service; tip 20% (or more) for excellent service.

It's customary to place your napkin on your lap.

Avoid putting your elbows on the table.

Wait until everyone is served to begin eating.

In formal situations, diners customarily wait to eat until the host has lifted a fork.

Must-Try Regional Specialties

Fish tacos (San Diego, CA)

Frito pie (NM)

Green-chile cheeseburgers (NM)

Navajo tacos (northeastern AZ)

Sonoran dogs (Tucson, AZ)

Rocky Mountain oysters (CO)

Bison burger (MT)

takeout (eg pizza or Chinese food) or prepackaged meals cooked in a microwave. Desserts tend toward ice cream, pies and cakes. Some families still cook a traditional Sunday night dinner, when relatives and friends gather for a big feast, or grill/barbecue outside and go picnicking on weekends.

Quick Eats

Eating a hot dog from a street cart or a taco from a roadside food truck is a convenient, and increasingly tasty, option in downtown business districts. Don't worry about health risks – these vendors are usually supervised by the local health department. Fast-food restaurants with drive-thru windows are ubiquitous, and you'll usually find at least one beside a major highway exit. At festivals and county fairs, pick from cotton candy, corn dogs, candy apples, funnel cakes, chocolate-covered frozen bananas and plenty of tasty regional specialties. Farmers markets and natural food markets often have more wholesome prepared foods.

California

Owing to its vastness and variety of microclimates, California is truly America's cornucopia for fruits and vegetables, and a gateway to myriad Asian markets. The state's natural resources are overwhelming, with wild salmon, Dungeness crab and oysters from the ocean; robust produce year-round; and artisanal products such as cheese, bread, olive oil, wine and chocolate.

Starting in the 1970s and '80s, star chefs such as Alice Waters and Wolfgang Puck pioneered 'California cuisine' by incorporating the best local ingredients into simple yet delectable preparations. The influx of Asian immigrants, especially after the Vietnam War, enriched the state's urban food cultures with Chinatowns, Koreatowns and Japantowns, along with huge enclaves of Mexican Americans who maintain their own culinary traditions across the state. Global fusion restaurants are another hallmark of California's cuisine scene.

North Coast & the Sierras

San Francisco hippies went back to the land in the 1970s for a more self-sufficient lifestyle, reviving traditions of making breads and cheeses from scratch and growing their own everything (note: farms from Mendocino to Humboldt are serious about No Trespassing signs). Hippie-homesteaders were early adopters of pesticide-free farming, and innovated hearty, organic cuisine that was health-minded yet satisfied the munchies.

On the North Coast, you can taste the influence of wild-crafted Ohlone and Miwok cuisine. In addition to fishing, hunting game and making bread from acorn flour, these Native Northern Californians also tended orchards and carefully cultivated foods along the coast. With such attentive stewardship, nature has been kind to this landscape, yielding bonanzas of wildflower honey and blackberries. Alongside traditional shellfish collection, sustainable caviar and oyster farms have sprung up along the coast. Fearless foragers have identified every edible plant, from Sierra's wood sorrel to Mendocino sea vegetables, though key spots for wild mushrooms remain closely guarded local secrets.

San Francisco Bay Area

In 2017, San Francisco had nearly 457 restaurants per 100,000 households – the highest number per household in the US. Hundreds of licensed food trucks crisscross the city.

Some city novelties have ended up with extraordinary staying power, including ever-

BREAKFAST BURRITOS

There's one Mexican-inspired meal that has been mastered in the West: the breakfast burrito. It's served in diners and delis in Colorado, in coffee shops in Arizona and beach-bum breakfast joints in California. In many ways, it's the perfect breakfast – cheap (usually under $6), packed with protein (eggs, cheese, beans), fresh veggies (or is avocado a fruit?), hot salsa, and rolled to go in paper and foil. Peel it open like a banana and inhale the savory steam.

FARMLAND, WILD FOODS & FISH

The diverse geography and climate – a mild, damp coastal region with sunny summers and arid farmland in the east – foster all types of farm-grown produce. Farmers grow plenty of fruit, from melons, grapes, apples and pears to strawberries, cherries and blueberries. Veggies thrive here too: potatoes, lentils, corn, asparagus and Walla Walla sweet onions, all of which feed local and overseas populations.

Many wild foods thrive, especially in the damper regions, such as the Coast Range. Foragers seek the same foods once gathered by local Native American tribes – year-round wild mushrooms, as well as summertime fruits and berries.

With hundreds of miles of coastline and an impressive system of rivers, Northwesterners have access to plenty of fresh seafood. Depending on the season, specialties include razor clams, mussels, prawns, albacore tuna, Dungeness crab and sturgeon. Salmon remains one of the region's most recognized foods, whether it's smoked or grilled, or in salads, quiches and sushi.

popular *cioppino* (Dungeness crab stew), chocolate bars invented by the Ghirardelli family, and sourdough bread, with original gold-rush-era mother dough still yielding local loaves with that distinctive tang. Dim sum is Cantonese for what's known in Mandarin as *xiao che* (small eats). It's served at *yum cha* (trolley-serviced meals), and there are dozens of places in San Francisco where you'll call it lunch.

Mexican, French and Italian food remain perennial local favorites, along with more recent SF ethnic food crazes: *izakaya* (Japanese bars serving small plates), Korean tacos, *banh mi* (Vietnamese sandwiches featuring marinated meats and pickled vegetables on baguettes) and *alfajores* (Arabic-Argentine crème-filled shortbread cookies).

SoCal

Los Angeles has long been known for its big-name chefs and celebrity restaurant owners. Robert H Cobb, owner of Hollywood's Brown Derby Restaurant, is remembered as the namesake of the Cobb salad (lettuce, tomato, egg, chicken, bacon and Roquefort). Wolfgang Puck launched the celebrity-chef trend with Sunset Strip's star-spangled Spago in 1982.

For authentic ethnic food in Los Angeles, head to Koreatown for flavor-bursting *kalbi* (marinated barbecued beef short ribs), East LA for tacos *al pastor* (marinated, fried pork), and Little Tokyo for ramen noodles made fresh daily.

Further south, surfers cruise Hwy 1 beach towns from Laguna Beach to La Jolla in search of the ultimate wave and quick-but-hearty eats such as breakfast burritos and fish tacos. And everybody stops for a date shake at Ruby's Crystal Cove Shake Shack south of Newport Beach.

Pacific Northwest

The late James Beard (1903–85), a chef, food writer and Oregon native, believed preparing food simply, without too many ingredients or complicated cooking techniques, allowed its natural flavors to shine. This philosophy has greatly influenced modern Northwest cuisine. Pacific Northwesterners don't like to think of their food as trendy or fussy, but at the same time, they love to be considered innovative, especially when it comes to 'green,' hyper-conscious eating.

The Southwest

Moderation is not a virtue when it comes to food in Arizona, New Mexico, Utah, southern Colorado and Las Vegas. These gastronomic wonderlands don't have time for the timid. Sonoran hot dogs, green-chili cheeseburgers, huevos rancheros, juicy slabs of steaks and endless buffets – take your Instagram photo then dig in and dine happy.

Two ethnic groups define Southwestern food culture: the Spanish and the Mexicans, who controlled territories from Texas to California until well into the 19th century. While there is little actual Spanish food

Sonoran hot dogs, a Southwestern classic

today, the Spanish brought cattle to Mexico, which the Mexicans adapted to their own corn-and-chili-based gastronomy to make tacos, tortillas, enchiladas, burritos, *chimichangas* (deep-fried burritos) and other dishes made of corn or flour pancakes filled with everything from chopped meat and poultry to beans. In Arizona and New Mexico, a few Native American dishes are served on reservations and during tribal festivals. Steaks and barbecue are always favorites on Southwestern menus, and beer is the drink of choice for dinner and a night out.

For a cosmopolitan foodie scene, visit Las Vegas, where top chefs from New York City, LA and even Paris sprout satellite restaurants.

Mexican & New Mexican Food

Mexican food is often hot and spicy. If you're sensitive, test the heat of your salsa before dousing your meal. In Arizona, Mexican food is of the Sonoran type, with specialties such as *carne seca* (dried beef). Meals are usually served with refried beans, rice and flour or corn tortillas; chiles are relatively mild. Tucsonans refer to their city as the 'Mexican food capital of the universe,' which, although hotly contested by a few other places, not least in Mexico itself, does carry a ring of truth. Colorado restaurants serve Mexican food, but they don't insist on any accolades for it.

New Mexico's food is distinct from, but reminiscent of, Mexican food. Pinto beans are served whole instead of refried; *posole* (a corn stew) may replace rice. Chiles aren't used so much as a condiment (like salsa) but more as an essential ingredient in almost every dish. *Carne adobada* (marinated pork chunks) is a specialty.

If a menu includes red or green chile dishes and sauces, it probably serves New Mexican–style dishes. The state is famous for its chile-enhanced Mexican standards. The town of Hatch, NM, is particularly known for its green chiles. For both red and green chile on your dish, order it Christmas-style

Native American Food

Modern Native American cuisine bears little resemblance to that eaten before the Spanish conquest, but it is distinct from

Southwestern cuisine. Navajo and Indian tacos – fried bread usually topped with beans, meat, tomatoes, chili and lettuce – are the most readily available. Chewy *horno* bread is baked in the beehive-shaped outdoor adobe ovens *(hornos)* using remnant heat from a fire built inside the oven, then cleared out before cooking.

Most other Native American cooking is game-based and usually involves squash and locally harvested ingredients such as berries and piñon nuts. Though becoming better known, it can be difficult to find. Your best bets are festival food stands, powwows, rodeos, Pueblo feast days and casino restaurants.

In the Southwest there's a new trend in upscale restaurants with a modern take on Native American food, using native ingredients like blue corn, wild mushrooms and venison in contemporary gourmet preparations.

The Rockies

Idaho, Montana and Wyoming have little new to add to the West's culinary mix, and what you're likely to find is a little bit of everything from elsewhere. With cattle such a big part of the local economies, especially in Wyoming and Montana, steaks, burgers and ribs are enduring menu highlights. In keeping with the recovering wildlife populations of the Great Plains, you'll often find elk or bison in amongst the beef. Boise, ID, and Jackson, WY, have particularly cosmopolitan eating scenes, with specialties from across the US as well as international cuisines. You'll find at least one Chinese restaurant with a buffet in most medium-sized towns, although freshness and quality vary greatly.

Vegetarians & Vegans

Most metro eateries offer at least one vegetarian dish, although very few are dedicated solely to meatless menus. These days, fortunately, almost every larger town has a natural-food grocer. You may go wanting in smaller towns in the hinterlands, and in those cases your best bet is pulling together a picnic from the local grocery store.

FAVORITE VEGETARIAN EATERIES

Green New American Vegetarian (p166), Phoenix, AZ

Lovin' Spoonfuls (☎520-325-7766; www.lovinspoonfuls.com; 2990 N Campbell Ave; breakfast & lunch $7-10, dinner $9-14.25; ⏰11am-9pm Mon-Fri, 9:30am-9pm Sat, 10am-3pm Sun; 🖉), Tucson, AZ

Macy's (p175), Flagstaff, AZ

Greens (p321), San Francisco, CA

City O' City (☎303-831-6443; www.cityocitydenver.com; 206 E 13th Ave; mains $9-14; ⏰7am-2am; 🖉; 🚌0, 6, 10, 16) 🍃, Denver, CO

Leaf (☎303-442-1485; www.leafvegetarianrestaurant.com; 2010 16th St; mains $13-18; ⏰11:30am-9pm Mon-Thu, 11:30am-10pm Fri, 10am-10pm Sat, 10am-9pm Sun; 🖉; 🚌204) 🍃, Boulder, CO

Sweet Melissa's (p114), Laramie, WY

One potential pitfall in the Southwest? Traditional Southwestern cuisine uses lard in beans, tamales *sopaipillas* (deep-fried puff pastry) and flour (but not corn) tortillas. Be sure to ask – even the most authentic places have a pot of pintos simmering for vegetarians.

Drinks

Work-hard, play-hard Americans are far from teetotalers. About 56% of Americans drink alcohol monthly.

Beer

Beer is about as American as Chevrolet, football and apple pie. According to a 2016 Gallup poll, about 43% of Americans who consume alcohol drink beer, while 32% of Americans regularly drink wine. Liquor trails the other two, with only 20% of Americans typically consuming spirits.

Craft & Local Beer

Microbrewery and craft-beer production has sky-rocketed in the US over the last 10 years. Craft-beer sales accounted for 13.2%

RICK POON/GETTY IMAGES ©

ANNAPOLISSTUDIOS/GETTY IMAGES ©

Top: Fresh California oysters

Bottom: Margarita cocktail

of the domestic beer market in 2018, and that figure rises with each passing year. The term 'microbrew' is used broadly, and tends to include beer produced by large, well-established brands such as Sam Adams and Sierra Nevada. According to the Brewers Association, however, a true craft brewery must produce no more than six million barrels annually. It must also be independently owned and the beer made with traditional ingredients.

In recent years it's become possible to 'drink local' all over the West as microbreweries pop up in urban centers, small towns and unexpected places. They're particularly popular in gateway communities outside national parks, including Moab, Flagstaff and Durango. Called brewpubs or taprooms, these breweries usually serve food and can have more than a dozen brews on tap at any one time.

Wine

There are nearly 9000 wineries in the US, and 2010 marked the first year that the US consumed more wine than France. To the raised eyebrows of European winemakers, who used to regard Californian wines as second class, many American wines are now even winning prestigious international awards. In fact, the nation is the world's fourth-largest producer of wine, behind Italy, France and Spain.

Wine isn't cheap in the US, but it's possible to procure a perfectly drinkable bottle of American wine at a liquor or wine shop for around $12.

Wine Regions

Today almost 90% of US wine comes from California, and Oregon and Washington wines have achieved international status.

BEER GOES LOCAL

In outdoorsy communities across the West, the neighborhood microbrewery is the unofficial community center – the place to unwind, swap trail stories, commune with friends and savor seasonal brews. Montana alone – hardly among the country's more populous states – has more than 70 microbreweries. Here are a few of our favorites from across the West:

Beaver Street Brewery (☎928-779-0079; www.beaverstreetbrewery.com; 11 S Beaver St; ⊙11am-10pm Sun-Thu, to midnight Fri & Sat) Flagstaff, AZ

OHSO Brewery & Distillery (☎602-955-0358; www.ohsobrewery.com; 4900 E Indian School Rd; ⊙11am-late Mon-Fri, from 9am Sat & Sun; 📶) Phoenix, AZ

Black Shirt Brewing Co (p80) Denver, CO

Mountain Sun (p86) Boulder, CO

Steamworks Brewing (☎970-259-9200; www.steamworksbrewing.com; 801 E 2nd Ave; ⊙11am-midnight Mon-Thu, to 2am Fri-Sun) Durango, CO

Squatters Pub Brewery (www.squatters.com; 147 W Broadway; dishes $10-24; ⊙11am-midnight Mon-Thu, to 1am Fri, 10am-1am Sat, 10am-midnight Sun), Salt Lake City, UT

Snake River Brewing Co (p117) Jackson, WY

North Coast Brewing Company (☎707-964-2739; www.northcoastbrewing.com; 455 N Main St; mains $17-25; ⊙restaurant 4-10pm Sun-Thu, to 11pm Fri & Sat, bar from 2pm daily; 📶) Fort Bragg, CA

Ecliptic Brewing (p393) Portland, OR

Fremont Brewing Company (p367) Seattle, WA

White Dog Brewing (☎208-906-0609; www.whitedogbrewing.com; 705 W Fulton St; ⊙11am-10pm Sun-Thu, to 11pm Fri & Sat), Boise, ID

Ten Mile Creek Brewery (☎406-502-1382; 48 N Last Chance Gulch; ⊙noon-8pm), Helena, MT

Katabatic Brewing (☎406-333-2855; www.katabaticbrewing.com; 117 W Park St; ⊙noon-8pm), Livingston, MT

Without a doubt, the country's hotbed of wine tourism is in Northern California, just outside of the Bay Area in the Napa and Sonoma Valleys. As other areas – Oregon's Willamette Valley, California's Central Coast and Arizona's Patagonia region – have evolved as wine destinations, they have spawned an entire industry of bed-and-breakfast tourism that goes hand in hand with the quest to find the perfect pinot noir.

There are many excellent 'New World' wines that have flourished in the rich American soil. The most popular white varietals made in the US are chardonnay and sauvignon blanc; best-selling reds include cabernet sauvignon, merlot, pinot noir and zinfandel.

Margaritas

In the Southwest it's all about the tequila. Margaritas are the alcoholic drink of choice, and synonymous with this region, especially in heavily Hispanic New Mexico, Arizona and southwestern Colorado. Margaritas vary in taste depending on the quality of the ingredients used, but all are made from tequila, a citrus liquor (Grand Marnier, Triple Sec or Cointreau) and either freshly squeezed lime or premixed Sweet & Sour.

Margaritas are either served frozen, on the rocks (over ice) or straight up. Most people order them with salt. Traditional margaritas are lime-flavored, but they come in a rainbow of other flavors – they're best ordered frozen.

Coffee

America runs on caffeine, and the coffee craze has only intensified in the last 25 years. Blame it on Starbucks. The world's biggest coffee chain was born amid the Northwest's progressive coffee culture in 1971, when Starbucks opened its first location across from Pike Place Market in Seattle.

The idea, to offer a variety of roasted beans from around the world in a comfortable cafe, helped fill the American coffee mug with more refined, complicated (and expensive) drinks compared to the ubiquitous Folgers and diner cups of joe. By the early 1990s, specialty coffeehouses were springing up across the country.

Independent coffee shops support a coffeehouse culture that encourages lingering; think free wi-fi and comfortable seating. That said, when using free cafe wi-fi, remember some basic etiquette: order something every hour, don't leave laptops unattended, and deal with interruptions graciously.

VINTAGE COCKTAILS

Across the US, it's become decidedly cool to party like it's 1929 by drinking retro cocktails from the days of Prohibition, when alcohol was illegal to consume. While Prohibition isn't likely to be reinstated, you'll find plenty of bars where the spirit of the Roaring Twenties and the illicit 1930s lives on, perhaps in the decor, sometimes even in the ingredients. Inspired by vintage recipes featuring spirits and elixirs, these cocktails, complete with ingredients such as small-batch liqueurs, whipped egg whites, hand-chipped ice and fresh fruit, are lovingly concocted by nattily dressed bartenders who regard their profession as something between an art and a craft.

Plan Your Trip

Family Travel

The West is a top choice for adventure-loving families. It offers superb attractions for all ages: amusement parks, zoos, science museums, unique campsites, hikes in wilderness reserves, body-boarding at beaches and bike rides through scenic forests. Most national and state parks offer kid-focused programs.

Children Will Love...

Outdoor Adventure

Yellowstone National Park, WY (p118) Watch powerful geysers, spy on wildlife and take magnificent hikes.

Grand Canyon National Park, AZ (p177) Gaze across one of the earth's great wonders, followed by a hike, a ranger talk and biking.

Olympic National Park, WA (p372) Explore the wild and pristine wilderness of one of the world's few temperate rainforests.

Zion National Park, UT (p214) Free shuttles, river access, rock scrambling and all levels of hikes mean there's something for all ages.

Oak Creek Canyon, AZ (p170) Swoosh over red rocks at Slide Rock State Park in Arizona.

Moab, UT (p207) Mountain biking, rafting, petroglyphs and rock climbing make this a great destination for teens.

San Diego, CA (p271) Bodyboard and explore tide pools on superb, laid-back beaches.

Great Sand Dunes National Park, CO (p110) An ankle-deep stream flows through giant sand dunes – younger kids will spend hours here.

Theme Parks

Disneyland, CA (p267) It's the attention to detail that amazes most at Mickey Mouse's enchantingly imagined Disneyland, in the middle of Orange County.

Keeping Costs Down

Eating

The US restaurant industry seems built on family-style service: children are not just accepted almost everywhere, they are usually encouraged by special children's menus with smaller portions and lower prices. In some restaurants children under a certain age even eat for free.

Sleeping

Motels and hotels typically have rooms with two beds, which are ideal for families. Many hotels have adjoining doors between rooms. Some offer 'kids stay free' programs, for children up to 12 or sometimes 18 years old.

Sightseeing

Child concessions often apply for tours, admission fees and transport, with some discounts as high as 50% off the adult rate. However, the definition of 'child' can vary from under 12 to under 16 years. Some sights also have discount rates for families. Most attractions give free admission to children under two years.

Transportation

Domestic airlines don't charge for children under two years. Very rarely, some resort areas (such as Disneyland) offer a 'kids fly free' promotion. Currently, children from two to 12 years enjoy 50% off the lowest Amtrak rail fare when they travel alongside a fare-paying adult.

Legoland, CA (☎760-918-5346; www.legoland.com/california; 1 Legoland Dr; adult/child 3-12yr from $95/89; ⌚hours vary, at least 10am-5pm year-round; P 👪) Younger kids will get a kick out of the Lego-built statues and low-key rides scattered across this amusement park in Carlsbad.

Universal Studios, CA (p265) Hollywood-movie-themed action rides, special-effects shows and a studio back-lot tram tour in Los Angeles.

Epic Discovery, CO (☎970-496-4910; www.epicdiscovery.com; day pass Ultimate/Little Explorer $94/54; ⌚10am-6pm Jun-Aug, Fri-Sun only Sep; 👪) Explore this eco-themed adventure park in Vail and Breckenridge.

Aquariums & Zoos

Arizona-Sonora Desert Museum, AZ (p189) Coyotes, cacti and docent demonstrations are highlights at this indoor-outdoor repository of flora and fauna in Tucson.

Monterey Bay Aquarium, CA (p298) Observe denizens of the deep next door to the California central coast's biggest marine sanctuary.

Aquarium of the Pacific, CA (p252) High-tech aquarium at Long Beach houses critters whose homes range from balmy Baja California to the chilly north Pacific; there's also a shark lagoon.

San Diego Zoo, CA (p274) This sprawling zoo is home to creatures great and small, with more than 3700 animals. It also supports some brilliant conservation programs.

Rainy-Day Activities

LA Museums, CA See stars (the real ones) at LA's Griffith Observatory (p248), dinosaur bones at the Natural History Museum of Los Angeles (p247) and the Page Museum at the La Brea Tar Pits (p249), then get hands-on at the amusing California Science Center (p247).

SF Museums, CA San Francisco's Bay Area is a mind-bending classroom for kids, especially at the interactive Exploratorium (p303) and ecofriendly California Academy of Sciences (p312).

Pacific Science Center, WA (p364) Fascinating, hands-on exhibits at this center in Seattle, plus an IMAX theater, planetarium and laser shows.

New Mexico Museum of Natural History & Science, NM (p219) Check out the Age of Supergiants in Albuquerque.

Denver Museum of Nature & Science, CO (p78) From space to local Ice Age fossils, with an IMAX and planetarium for good measure.

Mini Time Machine Museum of Miniatures, AZ (p193) You may not get many rainy days in Tucson, but when the monsoon season arrives this museum of tiny but intricate houses and scenes is a mesmerizing place to explore.

Museum of the Rockies, MT (p127) See the largest T. rex skeleton ever unearthed, with plenty of other dinosaur fossils and a planetarium, in Bozeman.

Region by Region

Rocky Mountains

The Rocky Mountain states (Colorado, Idaho, Montana and Wyoming) have plenty to offer families, although distances can be large so some careful planning will help you avoid going a long way.

The state of Colorado is like a giant playground: museums and water parks in Denver (p75), ziplines and horseback rides in the Rockies, rafting near Buena Vista (p100) and Salida (p99), cliff houses in Mesa Verde (p106) and ski resorts everywhere. Idaho has skiing at Sun Valley (p139) and rafting near Stanley (p140), and kids who love volcanoes will love Craters of the Moon National Monument & Preserve (p140).

Over in Wyoming, go looking for grizzlies, wolves, bison and elk in Yellowstone National Park (p118), with activities such as family white-water rafting also possible. Jackson (p115) has all sorts of family-friendly activities.

Southwest

The appeal of the Southwest for families may be less obvious, and the long distances will be a potential roadblock for some, especially those with younger children. But if your family is the kind that loves adventure, this is country seemingly designed for older kids who enjoy the outdoors: mountain biking, slot canyon adventures and a bevy of unbelievable fantasy-worthy landscapes.

Hike into Grand Canyon (p177), splash in Oak Creek (p170) and ponder the saguaro cacti (p192) outside Tucson. Water parks, dude ranches and ghost towns should also keep kids entertained. Utah's national parks have some weird and wonderful land formations, while Las Vegas (p146) has a surprising range of child-friendly activities and entertainment.

California

California seems custom-made for kids. See celebrity handprints in Hollywood (p247), ogle the La Brea tar pits (p249), and hit the beach in Santa Monica (p251) or San Diego (p271). Films hold a special place in children's hearts, and there are some fantastic studio tours to get them behind the scenes. Warner Bros Studio Tour (p253) will appeal to lovers of everything from Harry Potter to Batman, while Universal Studios Hollywood (p265) is like a stroll through every childhood movie they've ever watched. Beyond the movies, there are theme parks, including the grand-daddy of them all – Disneyland (p267).

Pacific Northwest

The Pacific Northwest – from the sun, sand and surf along the coast to the snow-covered slopes further inland – is a fun and exciting destination for families. Kids will love exploring the many child-oriented museums, amusement parks, zoos and animal safaris. National and state parks often organize family-friendly exhibitions or activities, and whale-watching can be a big hit. There are also plenty of kid-friendly hotels, restaurants, shops, playgrounds and even skateboard parks in the region. Finding things to do with your kids won't be a problem, but dragging them away from all that fun might be.

Portland, OR, is a wonderfully family-friendly city, with interactive, child-friendly museums, extensive parklands, Oregon Zoo (p388), Oaks Amusement Park (p389) and a host of other activities and attractions. Seattle is similar, with zoos and aquariums, terrific museums and the epic Seattle Center (p359). Throw in snow sports, whale-watching, and all manner of theme and water parks and it might just be one of the most family-friendly corners anywhere in the US.

Good to Know

- ➡ Look out for the icon for family-friendly suggestions throughout this guide.
- ➡ Playgrounds are easy to find in most cities – ask your hotel.
- ➡ Most resorts are child-friendly and many offer children's programs; some are adults-only.

Kids' Corner

Say What?

Stoked	Super excited
Danger dog	Popular LA street food
Pop	Soda; soft drink
Jojos	Potato wedges in the Pacific Northwest

Did You Know?

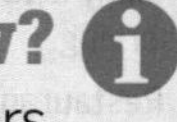

- Newborn grizzly bears weigh only 17oz (500g).
- Bozeman, MN, is home to the world's largest T. rex skull.

Have You Tried?

Fish taco
California meets Mexico

SONIA TAPIA/GETTY IMAGES ©

RAFALKRAKOW/GETTY IMAGES ©

Hiking in Yellowstone National Park (p118), Wyoming.

- Some hotels and motels offer rollaway beds or portable cribs for a small extra charge.
- Many B&Bs don't allow children; ask when reserving.
- Restaurants usually provide high chairs and booster seats. Some may also offer crayons and puzzles.
- In restaurants, you can ask if the kitchen will make a smaller order of a dish (check the price), or if they will split a normal-size main dish between two plates for the kids.
- Resort hotels may have on-call babysitting services; otherwise, ask the front-desk staff or concierge to help you make arrangements. Always check that babysitters are licensed and bonded, and ask what they charge per hour per child, whether there's a minimum fee, and if they charge extra for transportation or meals.
- Most tourist bureaus list local resources for childcare, plus recreation facilities, medical services and so on.
- Many public toilets have a baby-changing table (sometimes in men's toilets, too), and gender-neutral 'family' facilities appear in airports.
- Car-rental agencies should be able to provide an appropriate child seat, since these are required in every state, but you need to request it when booking and should expect to pay around $12 more per day.
- On domestic airlines, children aged two or over must have a seat, and discounts are unlikely.

Useful Resources

Lonely Planet Kids (www.lonelyplanetkids.com) Loads of activities and great family travel blog content.

My Family Travel Map: North America (shop.lonelyplanet.com) Unfolds into a colourful and detailed poster for kids to personalise with stickers to mark their family's travels. Ages five to eight.

Book: First Words Spanish (shop.lonelyplanet.com) A beautifully illustrated introduction to the Spanish language for ages five to eight.

Regions at a Glance

What image springs to mind when someone mentions the West? A saguaro cactus, or maybe the Grand Canyon? Either would be accurate – for Arizona. But the West holds so much more. Sun-kissed beaches in California. Lush forests in the Pacific Northwest. Epic singletrack trails in the Rockies. Yellowstone, the Grand Tetons and the Great Plains of Wyoming. Crimson buttes and crumbly hoodoos in Utah. There's a landscape for every mood and adventure.

Cultural travelers can explore Native American sites in Arizona and New Mexico. You'll find upscale shopping, fine dining and big-city bustle in Los Angeles, Phoenix, San Francisco, Denver and Seattle. For history buffs, there's Mesa Verde in Colorado, Spanish missions in California, and Old West towns just about everywhere. Ready to let loose? Two words: Las Vegas.

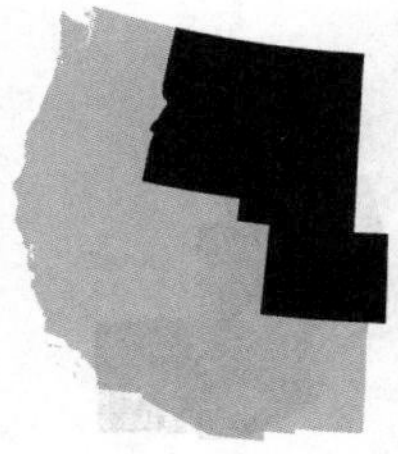

Rocky Mountains

Outdoor Adventure
Wild West Culture
Landscapes

Rugged Fun

Adrenaline junkie? Hit the Rockies, a world-class skiing, hiking, climbing and cycling destination. Everyone is welcome, with hundreds of races and group rides, and an incredible infrastructure of parks, trails and backcountry huts.

Modern Cowboys

Resonating with the echoes of the Wild West of the past, Montana and Wyoming are peopled by freedom-loving Rocky folk more often spotted in lycra, with a mountain bike hitched nearby, sipping a microbrew at a sunny outdoor cafe. Hard playing and slow living still rule.

Alpine Wonderland

The snow-covered Rocky Mountains are pure majesty. With chiseled peaks, clear rivers and mountain lions, bears and wolves in the backyard, the Rockies contain some of the world's most famous parks – Yellowstone, the Grand Tetons and Glacier – and endless clean mountain air.

p70

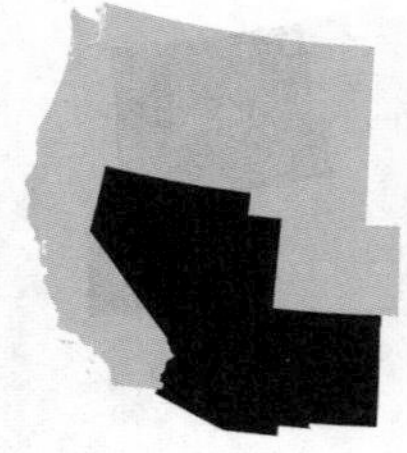

Southwest

Natural Scenery
Native Culture
Food

Red-Rock Country

The Southwest is famous for the jaw-dropping Grand Canyon, the dramatic red buttes of Monument Valley, the crimson arches of Moab and the fiery buttes of Sedona – just a few of the many geographic wonders in and around the spectacular national parks and forests.

Pueblos & Reservations

Visiting the Hopi and Navajo Nations or one of the 19 New Mexico Pueblos is a fine introduction to America's first inhabitants. This is your best bet for appreciating, and purchasing, crafts made by Native American people.

Good Eats

Try chile-smothered chicken enchiladas in New Mexico, a messy Sonoran hotdog in Tucson or grilled trout in Utah. In Vegas, stretch your fat pants and your budget at one of the extravagant buffets. For gourmands, the Strip restaurants offer the most intriguing epicurean experiences.

p142

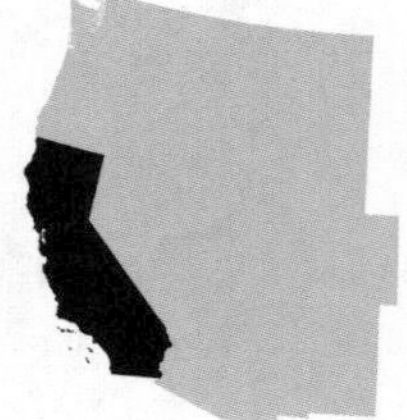

California

Beaches
Outdoors
Food & Wine

Gorgeous Shores

With more than 800 miles of coastline, California rules the sands: you'll find rugged, pristine beaches in the north and people-packed beauties in the south, with great surfing, sea kayaking and beach-walking all along the coast.

Romping Room

Ride the snow-covered slopes, raft on white-water rivers, kayak beside coastal islands, hike past waterfalls and climb boulders in the desert. The problem isn't choice in California, it's finding enough time to do it all.

King's Table

Fertile fields, talented chefs and an insatiable appetite for the new make California a major culinary destination. Browse the local food markets, sample Pinot and Chardonnay beside lush vineyards, and dine on farm-to-table fare.

p239

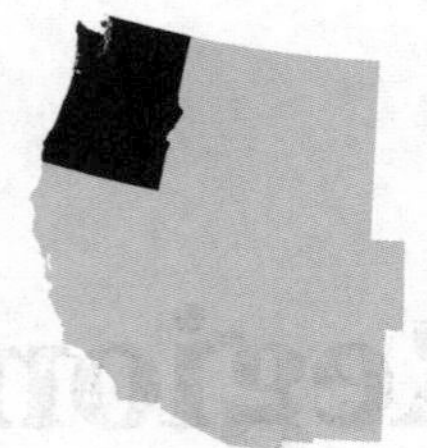

Pacific Northwest

Cycling
Food & Wine
National Parks

Pedal Power

Bicycle on paved, rolling roads in the tranquil San Juan Islands, cruise the bluff-dotted Oregon coast along Hwy 101 or pedal the streets of Portland, a city that embraces two-wheeled travel with loads of bike lanes, costumed theme rides and handcrafted bike shows.

Locavores & Oenophiles

No longer 'up and coming,' the food scene has arrived and smudged up its apron in the Pacific Northwest. In Portland and Seattle, chefs blend fish caught in local waters with vegetables harvested in the Eden-like valleys surrounding the Columbia River. Washington's wine is second only to California's.

Classic Playgrounds

The Northwest has four national parks, including three classics that date from the turn of the 20th century – Olympic, Mount Rainier and Crater Lake. The newest park is North Cascades, established in 1968.

p353

On the Road

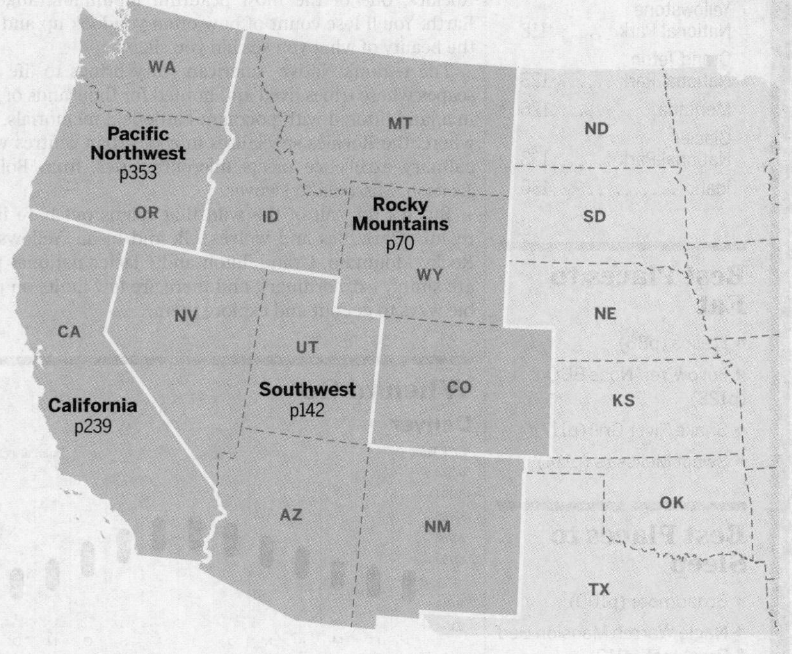
WA
MT
ND
Pacific Northwest
p353
OR
ID
Rocky Mountains
p70
SD
WY
NE
NV
CA
UT
CO
Southwest
p142
California
p239
KS
OK
AZ
NM
TX

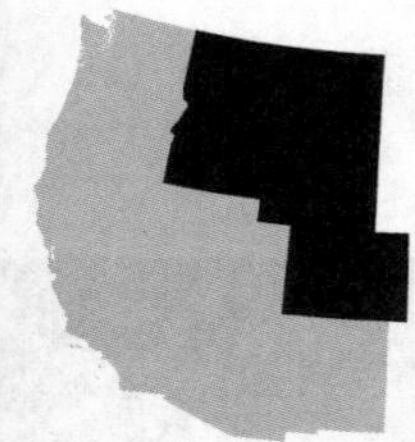

Rocky Mountains

Includes ➡

Best Places to Eat

- ➡ Frasca (p86)
- ➡ Follow Yer' Nose BBQ (p128)
- ➡ Snake River Grill (p117)
- ➡ Sweet Melissa's (p114)

Best Places to Sleep

- ➡ Broadmoor (p100)
- ➡ Nagle Warren Mansion Bed & Breakfast (p112)
- ➡ Mill House (p114)
- ➡ Wort Hotel (p116)

Why Go?

Welcome to where the US takes on truly epic proportions. Here in Colorado, Wyoming, Montana and Idaho, the Great Plains of the American West collide with the drama-filled Rockies, one of the most beautiful mountain ranges on Earth. You'll lose count of how often you look up and have the beauty of what you see bid you silent.

The region's Native American story brings to life landscapes where tribes lived and hunted for thousands of years in a land littered with poignant battlefield memorials. Elsewhere, the Rockies specialises in cool urban centres where culinary excellence meets microbreweries, from Boise to Jackson, Missoula to Denver.

But it's the call of the wild that reigns out here in the realm of grizzlies and wolves, elk and bison. Yellowstone, Rocky Mountain, Grand Teton and Glacier national parks are simply extraordinary, and there are few limits on possible ways to get out and explore them.

When to Go

Denver

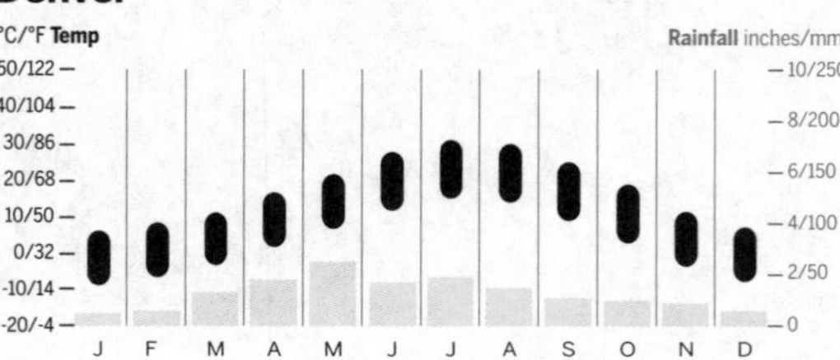

Jun–Aug Long days of sunshine for cycling, hiking, farmers markets and summer festivals.

Sep & Oct Fall foliage coincides with terrific lodging deals and far fewer crowds.

Jan–Mar Snow-dusted peaks, powdery slopes and deluxe après-ski parties.

History

When French trappers and Spaniards 'discovered' the Rocky Mountains in the late 18th century, they found the area was already home to several tribes of Native Americans, including the Nez Percé, the Shoshone, the Crow, the Lakota and the Ute. This fact merely slowed the European conquest, and countries began claiming, defending, buying and selling what they called 'unclaimed' territory.

A young US government purchased all lands east of the Continental Divide from France in the 1803 Louisiana Purchase. Shortly thereafter it dispatched Meriwether Lewis and William Clark to survey the area and see exactly what they had bought. Their epic survey covered nearly 8000 miles in two-and-a-half years, and tales of what they found urged on other adventurers, setting migration in motion.

Wagon trains voyaged to the Rockies and beyond right into the 20th century, and the process accelerated with the completion of the Transcontinental Railroad across southern Wyoming in the late 1860s.

To accommodate settlers, the US purged the western frontier of the Spanish, British and, in a truly shameful era, most of the Native American population. The government signed endless treaties to defuse Native American objections to increasing settlement, but always reneged and shunted tribes onto smaller reservations. Gold-miners' incursions into Native American territory in Montana and the building of US Army forts along the Bozeman Trail ignited a series of wars with the Lakota, Cheyenne, Arapaho and others.

ROCKY MOUNTAINS IN...

Two Weeks

Start your Rocky Mountain odyssey in the Denver area. Go tubing, vintage-clothes shopping or biking in outdoor-mad, boho Boulder (p84), then soak up the liberal rays while eavesdropping at a sidewalk cafe. Enjoy the vistas of Rocky Mountain National Park (p90) before heading west on I-70 to play in the mountains around Breckenridge (p94), which also has some of the best beginner slopes in Colorado. Go to ski and mountain-bike hot spot Steamboat Springs (p92) before crossing the border into Wyoming.

Get a taste of prairie-town life in Cheyenne (p111), then stop in Lander (p114) – rock-climbing destination extraordinaire. Continue northwest to chic Jackson (p115) and majestic Grand Teton National Park (p123) before hitting iconic Yellowstone National Park (p118). Save at least three days for exploring this geyser-packed natural wonderland.

Cross the state line into 'big sky country' and slowly make your way northwest through Montana, stopping in funky Bozeman (p127) and lively Missoula (p131) Wrap up your trip in Idaho, exploring Basque culture in up-and-coming Boise (p136).

One Month

With a month on your hands, you can really delve into the region's off-the-beaten-path treasures. Follow the two-week itinerary, but dip southwest into Colorado – a developing wine region – before visiting Wyoming. Ride the 4WD trails around Ouray (p102). Be sure to visit Mesa Verde National Park (p106) and its ancient cliff dwellings.

In Montana, you'll want to visit Glacier National Park (p133) before the glaciers disappear altogether. In Idaho, spend more time playing in Sun Valley (p138) and be sure to explore the shops, pubs and yummy organic restaurants in delightful little Ketchum (p138). You also have time to drive along a few of Idaho's fantastically remote scenic byways. Make sure you cruise Hwy 75 from Sun Valley north to Stanley (p140). Situated on the wide banks of the Salmon River, this stunning mountain hamlet is completely surrounded by national forestland and wilderness areas. Stanley is also blessed with world-class trout fishing and mild to wild rafting.

Take Hwy 21 (the Ponderosa Pine Scenic Byway) from Stanley to Boise. This scenic drive takes you through miles of dense ponderosa forests and past some excellent, solitary riverside camping spots – some of which come with their own natural hot-springs pools.

Rocky Mountain Highlights

1. **Yellowstone National Park** (p118) Spotting bears, wolves and bison between hot springs and geysers.
2. **Aspen** (p97) Reveling in Hollywood-gone-cowboy at Colorado's premier party resort.
3. **Grand Teton National Park** (p123) Hiking and climbing the craggiest of mountains.
4. **Boulder** (p84) Getting high on altitude in an urban outdoor paradise.
5. **Southern Colorado** (p101) Roaming the living Wild West towns of the San Juans.

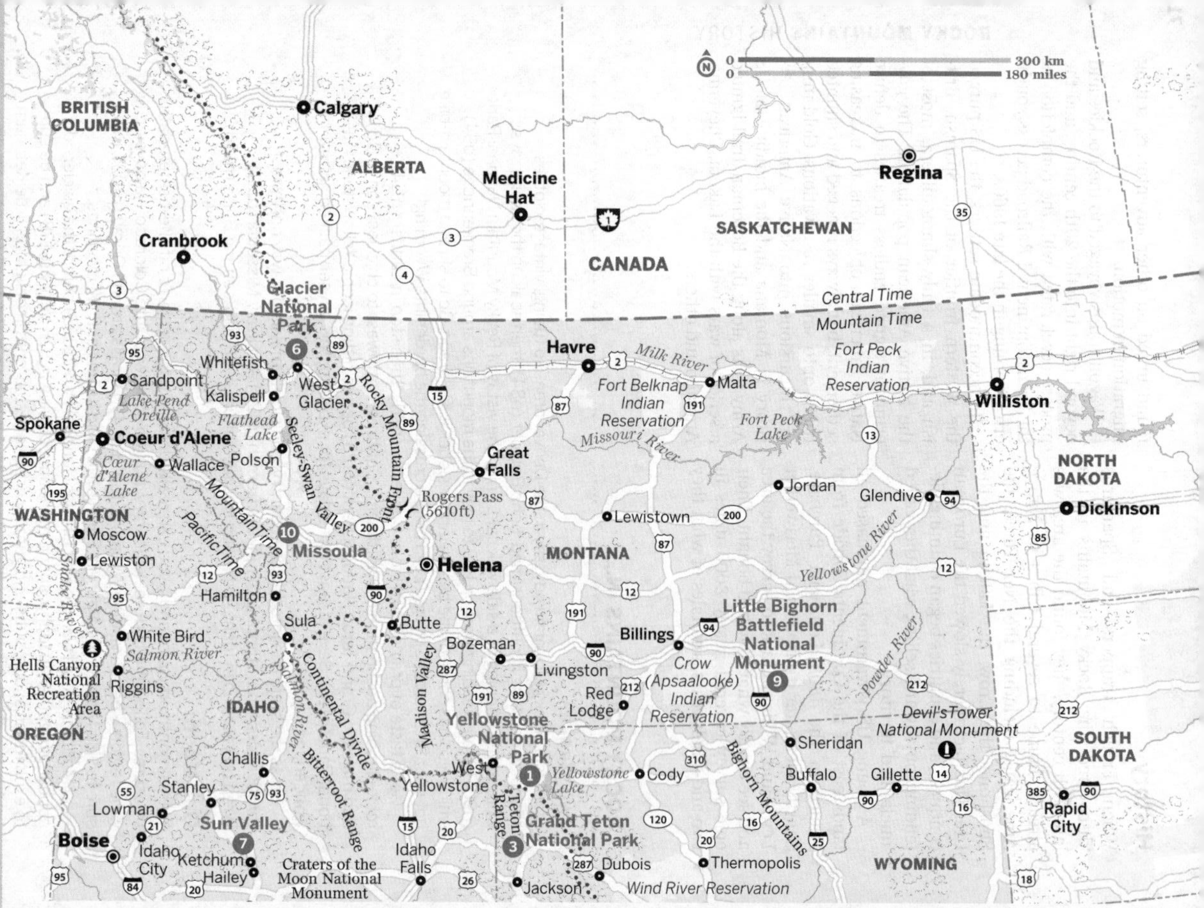

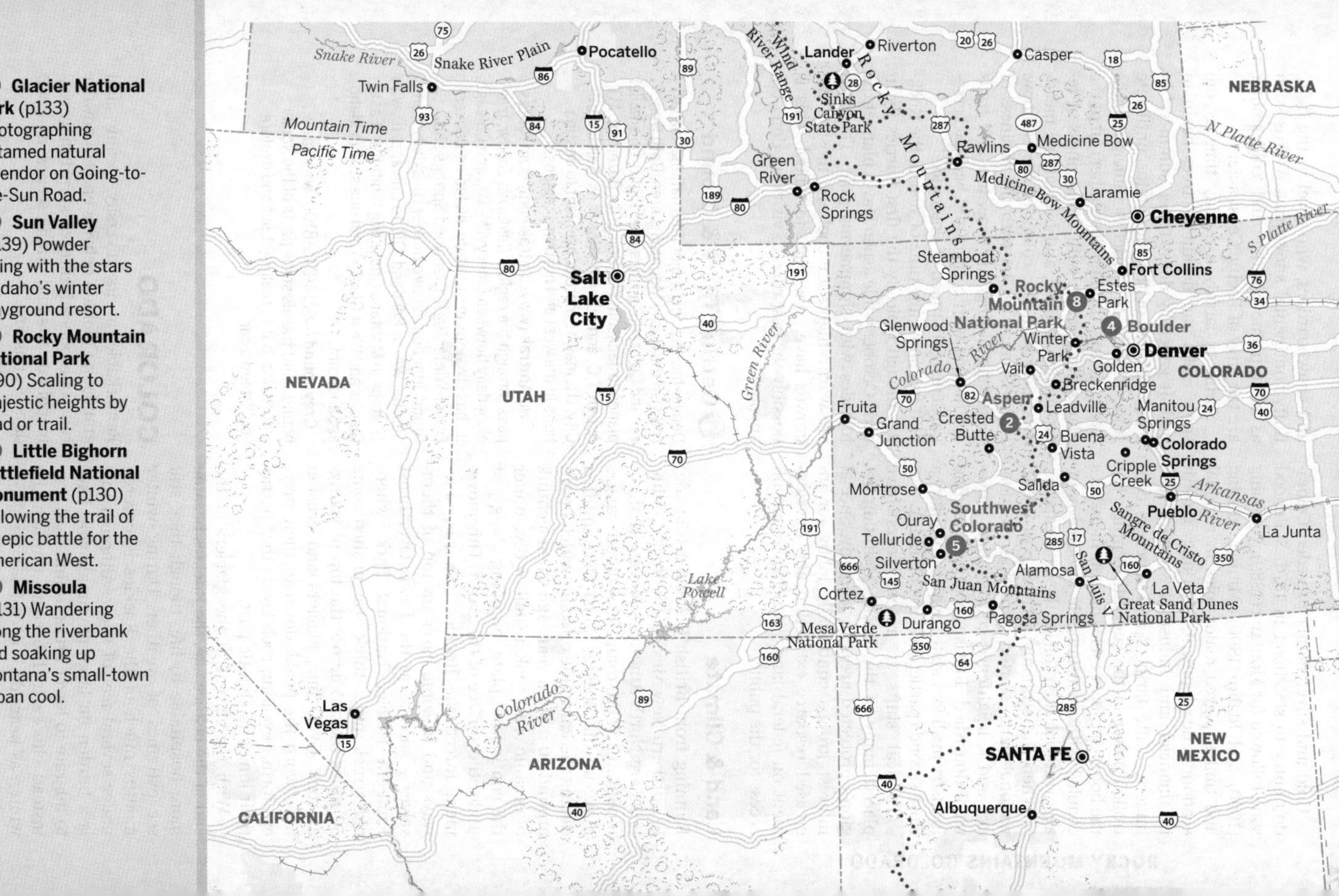

6 **Glacier National Park** (p133) Photographing untamed natural splendor on Going-to-the-Sun Road.

7 **Sun Valley** (p139) Powder skiing with the stars in Idaho's winter playground resort.

8 **Rocky Mountain National Park** (p90) Scaling to majestic heights by road or trail.

9 **Little Bighorn Battlefield National Monument** (p130) Following the trail of an epic battle for the American West.

10 **Missoula** (p131) Wandering along the riverbank and soaking up Montana's small-town urban cool.

Gold and silver mania preceded Colorado's entry to statehood in 1876. Statehood soon followed for Montana (1889), Wyoming (1890) and Idaho (1890). Mining, grazing and timber played major roles in regional economic development, sparking growth in financial and industrial support. The miners, white farmers and ranchers controlled power in the late 19th century, but the boom-and-bust cycles of their industries coupled with unsustainable resource management took their toll on the landscape.

When the economy thrived post-WWII, national parks started attracting vacationers, and a heightened conservation movement flourished. Tourism became a leading industry in all four states, with the military a close second (particularly in Colorado).

Political shifts in recent years have placed many of the Rocky Mountain region's protected areas in jeopardy. Special interest groups continually lobby for increased resource extraction and development on federal lands, which may cut off access for the public.

Land & Climate

Running from British Columbia (Canada) to northern New Mexico, the Rocky Mountains are North America's longest chain of mountains. More than 100 separate ranges make up the Rockies. Most were uplifted during the Laramide orogeny, which began around 80 million years ago when a chunk of oceanic crust took a shallow dive under the continental plate, bumping along just under the surface of the Earth. This movement forced the Rockies upwards, sideways and in some cases on top of themselves – such as at the Lewis Overthrust Fault in Glacier National Park, where older rock, miles thick, was pushed some 50 miles (80km) across the top of younger rock. Over time, glaciers and erosion have worn the peaks down to their present form, revealing rock layers that betray their long and chaotic past.

With the retreat of the glaciers at the end of the last ice age, the Rockies became more hospitable to life, though they still see extremes of weather. During winter months much of the Rockies is covered under several feet of snow. Although this is a burden on large mammals who have to migrate to lower areas to find food – or instead choose to hibernate through the winter, as bears do – it's a boon for skiers and snowboarders, who revel in the light, fluffy continental snow pack. Words such as 'champagne powder' and 'cold smoke' are the envy of Pacific Coast skiers.

Spring is largely a muddy time as the snow melts and deciduous trees begin to bud. It generally doesn't feel 'summery' in many regions of the mountains until late June. During the brief summer months (typically July through September) all of the plants must get on with the business of reproduction at once, and high alpine meadows glow with the colors of the rainbow. Humans must get on with the business of recreating during this time, too, and trails are flooded with cyclists and backpackers – particularly in much of Colorado.

It can snow any time of year in the Rockies, though typically the first flurries fly in early October while aspen leaves blanket the hillsides with shimmering gold. The days are warm, nights are cool and most of the crowds have gone back to school. This is possibly the best time to visit (but don't tell anyone).

Getting There & Around

Denver has the only major international airport (p83) in the Rocky Mountains area. Both Denver and Colorado Springs offer flights on smaller planes to Jackson, WY; Boise, ID; Bozeman, MT; Aspen, CO; and other destinations. Salt Lake City, UT, may be more convenient to destinations in the west and northern regions.

Two **Amtrak** (www.amtrak.com) train routes pass through the region. *California Zephyr*, traveling daily between Emeryville, CA, and Chicago, IL, has six stops in Colorado, including Denver, Fraser-Winter Park, Glenwood Springs and Grand Junction. *Empire Builder* runs daily from Seattle, WA, or Portland, OR, to Chicago, IL, with 12 stops in Montana (including Whitefish, East Glacier and West Glacier) and one stop in Idaho at Sandpoint.

Greyhound (☎214-849-8100; www.greyhound.com) travels some parts of the Rocky Mountains, but to really get out and explore you'll need a car.

COLORADO

Remarkable in its diversity, beauty and grandeur, Colorado delivers endless powder runs, outdoors adventures, surprisingly cosmopolitan arts and dining scenes, and 300 days of sunshine.

Information

Bureau of Land Management Colorado (BLM; ☎303-239-3600, 800-877-8339; www.co.blm.gov; 2850 Youngfield St, Lakewood; ⏲8:30am-4pm Mon-Fri; 🚌28) Provides information on historic sites, trails and more.

Camping USA (www.camping-usa.com) A great resource, with more than 12,000 campgrounds in its database.

Colorado Parks & Wildlife (CPW; Map p76; ☎303-297-1192; https://cpw.state.co.us; 1313 Sherman St, Denver; ⏲8am-5pm Mon-Fri) Manages more than 40 state parks and 300 wildlife areas; handles reservations for campgrounds.

Colorado Road & Traffic Conditions (☎511; www.codot.gov; ⏲24hr) Provides up-to-date information on Colorado highway and traffic conditions, including cycling maps.

Colorado Travel & Tourism Authority (☎800-265-6723; www.colorado.com) Offers detailed information on sights, activities and more throughout the state.

COLORADO FACTS

Nickname Centennial State

Population 5,700,000

Area 104,185 sq miles

Capital city Denver (population 693,100)

Other cities Boulder (population 97,385), Colorado Springs (population 445,830)

Sales tax 2.9% state tax, plus individual city taxes

Birthplace of Ute tribal leader Chief Ouray (1833–80); South Park creator Trey Parker (b 1969); actor Amy Adams (b 1974); climber Tommy Caldwell (b 1978)

Peaks higher than 14,000ft 53, 54 or 58 (depending on who's counting)

Politics Swing state

Famous for Sunny days (300 per year), the highest-altitude vineyards and longest ski run in the continental USA

Kitschiest souvenir Deer-hoof bottle-opener

Driving distances Denver to Vail 100 miles, Boulder to Rocky Mountain National Park 38 miles

Denver

Denver is rising. It's one of the fastest growing cities in the US. It's got beautiful weather and beautiful people. It's got good restaurants, even better bars, and a pretty lively arts and music scene.

Like other cities that are all grown up, each of Denver's neighborhoods has a flavor of its own.

For art, warehouses and street art, hit up River North (RiNo). Highlands and Lower Highlands (LoHi) have shopping and restaurant districts and a slightly less edgy attitude, while South Broadway is all leather and edge. At the core, you have the fun bars of Lower Downtown (LoDo), historic Five Points, the Santa Fe Arts District and the upscale Cherry Creek area. The entire city is connected through a beautiful series of bike paths and parks.

Best of all, within a couple hours' drive you have access to vast areas of wilderness, world-class skiing and hiking, and much, much more.

Sights & Activities

★Denver Art Museum MUSEUM

(DAM; Map p76; ☎ticket sales 720-865-5000; www.denverartmuseum.org; 100 W 14th Ave; adult/child $13/free, 1st Sat of month free; ⏲10am-5pm Tue-Thu, Sat & Sun, to 8pm Fri; P 👪; 🚌0, 52) The Denver Art Museum (DAM) is home to one of the largest Native American art collections in the USA, and puts on special multimedia exhibits that vary from treasures of British art to *Star Wars* costumes. The Western American Art section of the permanent collection is justifiably famous. This isn't an old, stodgy art museum, and the best part is diving into the interactive exhibits, which kids love.

★Confluence Park PARK

(Map p76; 2200 15th St; 👪; 🚌10, 28, 32, 44) Where Cherry Creek and South Platte River meet is the nexus and plexus of Denver's sunshine-loving culture. It's a good place for an afternoon picnic and there's a short white-water park for kayakers and tubers. Families also enjoy a small beach and shallow water areas for playing.

Children's Museum Denver Marisco Campus MUSEUM

(Map p76; ☎303-433-7444; www.mychildsmuseum.org; 2121 Children's Museum Dr; $14; ⏲9am-4pm Mon, Tue, Thu & Fri, to 7:30pm Wed, 10am-5pm Sat & Sun; 👪; 🚌10) This is one of the hottest tickets in town...well, at least

Denver

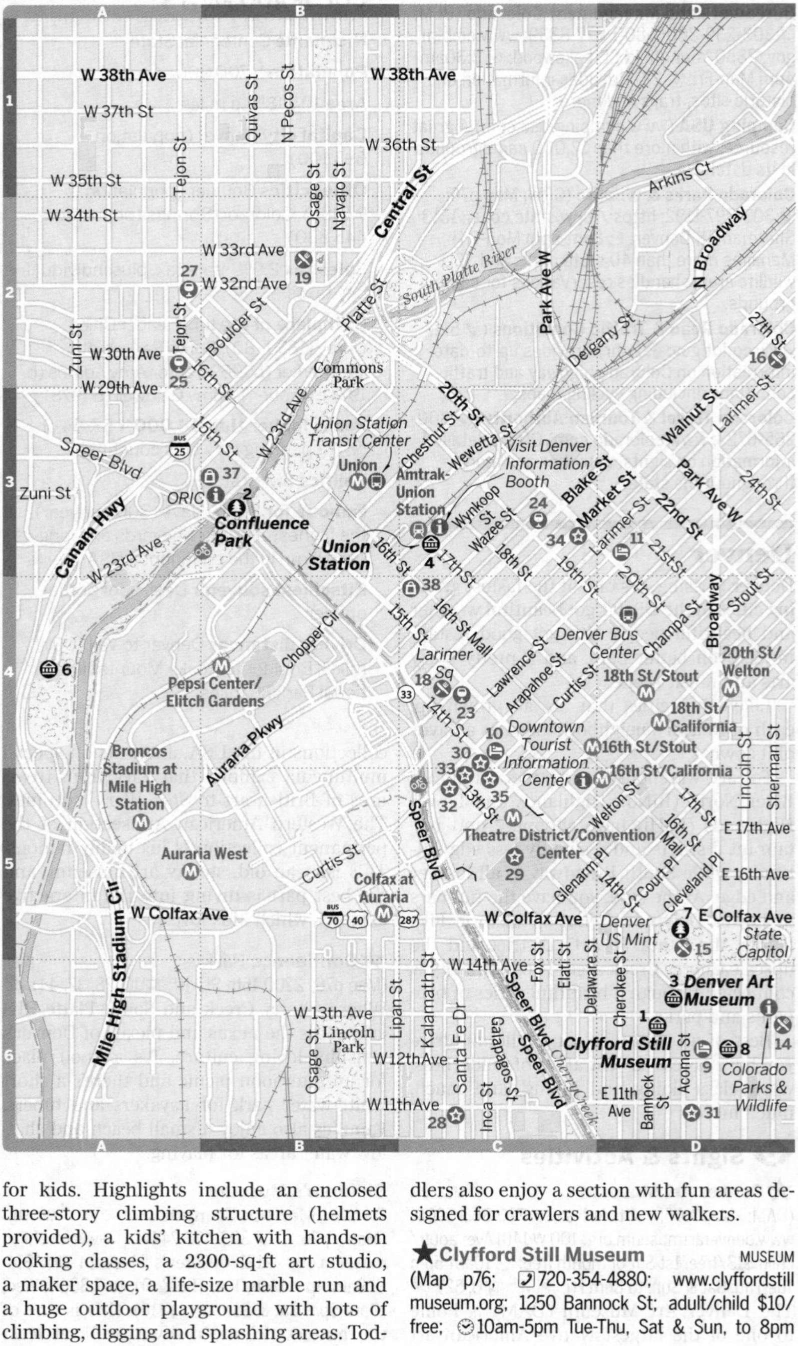

for kids. Highlights include an enclosed three-story climbing structure (helmets provided), a kids' kitchen with hands-on cooking classes, a 2300-sq-ft art studio, a maker space, a life-size marble run and a huge outdoor playground with lots of climbing, digging and splashing areas. Toddlers also enjoy a section with fun areas designed for crawlers and new walkers.

★Clyfford Still Museum MUSEUM

(Map p76; ☎720-354-4880; www.clyffordstillmuseum.org; 1250 Bannock St; adult/child $10/free; ⏲10am-5pm Tue-Thu, Sat & Sun, to 8pm

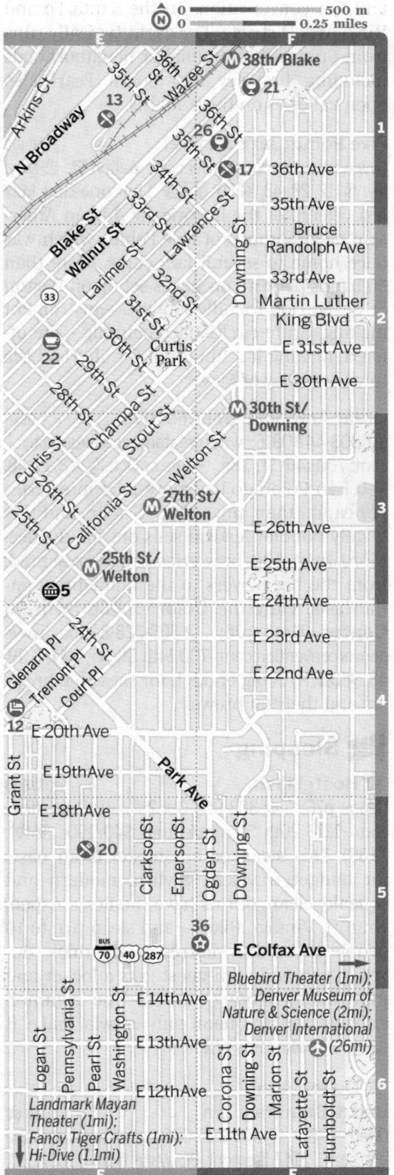

Fri; 👪; 🚌0, 52) Dedicated exclusively to the work and legacy of 20th-century American abstract expressionist Clyfford Still, this fascinating museum's collection includes more than 2400 pieces – 95% of his work – by the powerful and narcissistic master of bold. In his will, Still insisted that his body of work

Denver

Top Sights

1 Clyfford Still Museum D6
2 Confluence Park B3
3 Denver Art Museum D6
4 Union Station C3

Sights

5 Blair-Caldwell African American Museum E3
6 Children's Museum Denver Marisco Campus A4
7 Civic Center Park D5
8 History Colorado Center D6

Sleeping

9 Art – a Hotel D6
Crawford Hotel .... (see 4)
10 Curtis C4
11 Hostel Fish D3
12 Queen Anne Bed & Breakfast Inn E4

Eating

13 Acorn E1
14 City O' City D6
15 Civic Center Eats D5
16 Denver Central Market D2
17 Hop Alley F1
18 Rioja C4
19 Root Down B2
20 Steuben's Food Service E5

Drinking & Nightlife

21 Black Shirt Brewing Co F1
22 Crema Coffee House E2
23 Crú C4
24 Falling Rock Tap House C3
25 Linger A2
26 Tracks F1
27 Williams & Graham A2

Entertainment

28 Colorado Ballet C6
29 Colorado Convention Center C5
30 Colorado Symphony Orchestra C4
31 Curious Theatre D6
32 Denver Center for the Performing Arts C5
33 Denver Performing Arts Complex C5
34 El Chapultepec C3
35 Ellie Caulkins Opera House C5
36 Ogden Theatre F5
Opera Colorado .... (see 35)

Shopping

37 REI B3
38 Tattered Cover Bookstore C4

only be exhibited in a singular space, so Denver built him a museum. Free tours are offered throughout the week; check the website for dates and times.

History Colorado Center MUSEUM
(Map p76; ☎303-447-8679; www.historycoloradocenter.org; 1200 Broadway; adult/child $14/8; ⏱10am-5pm; P 🚸; 🚌0, 10) Discover Colorado's frontier roots and high-tech modern triumphs at this sharp, smart and charming museum. There are plenty of interactive exhibits, including a Jules Verne–esque 'Time Machine' that you push across a giant map of Colorado to explore seminal moments in the Centennial State's history. Periodically, story times for toddlers and low-sensory morning sessions are offered before the museum opens.

Blair-Caldwell African American Museum MUSEUM
(Map p76; ☎720-865-2401; https://history.denverlibrary.org/blair; 2401 Welton St, 3rd fl; ⏱noon-8pm Mon & Wed, 10am-6pm Tue, Thu & Fri, 9am-5pm Sat; P 🚸; 🚌43, 🚊D) FREE Tucked into the 3rd floor of a public library, this multimedia museum provides an excellent overview of the history of African Americans in the Rocky Mountain region – from migration and settlement to discrimination and achievements. Exhibits on Wellington Webb, Denver's first African American mayor, as well as Five Points, Denver's historically African American neighborhood, are particularly interesting.

Denver Museum of Nature & Science MUSEUM
(DMNS; ☎303-370-6000; www.dmns.org; 2001 Colorado Blvd; museum adult/child $19/14, IMAX $7/6, Planetarium $5/4; ⏱9am-5pm; P 🚸; 🚌20, 32, 40) A classic natural-science museum with excellent temporary exhibits on topics such as the biomechanics of bugs, Pompeii and mythical creatures. Permanent exhibits are equally engaging and include those cool panoramas we all loved as kids. The **IMAX Theatre** and **Gates Planetarium** are especially fun. The museum is located on the eastern edge of City Park, allowing for fun picnics or connected visits with the nearby zoo.

Festivals & Events

First Friday CULTURAL
(www.rivernorthart.com) FREE On the first Friday of every month, Denverites come out for an art stroll, cruising galleries for free wine and fun conversations in the Santa Fe and RiNo Arts Districts. The event typically runs from 6pm to 10pm. Smaller neighborhoods including Berkeley and South Pearl also open galleries on these nights.

Five Points Jazz Festival MUSIC
(www.artsandvenuesdenver.com; Welton St; ⏱May; 🚸; 🚌12, 28, 43, 🚊D) FREE This one-day jazz fest celebrates the historically African American neighborhood of Five Points, which was once home to several jazz clubs. More than 50 bands perform on stages set up on Welton St. Several kid-friendly activities – instrument making, drum circles, face painting – are offered, making it a fun event for all. Held the third Saturday of May.

Great American Beer Festival BEER
(☎303-447-0816; www.greatamericanbeerfestival.com; 700 14th St; $85; ⏱Sep or Oct; 🚌1, 8, 19, 48, 🚊D, F, H) Colorado has more microbreweries per capita than any other US state, and this hugely popular festival sells out in advance. More than 500 breweries are represented, from the big players to the home-brew enthusiasts. Only the **Colorado Convention Center** (Map p76; ☎303-228-8000; www.denverconvention.com; 700 14th St; 📶; 🚌1, 8, 19, 48, 🚊D, F, H) is big enough for these big brewers and their fat brews.

Sleeping

★Hostel Fish HOSTEL $
(Map p76; ☎303-954-0962; www.hostelfish.com; 1217 20th St; dm/r from $40/190; ❄📶; 🚌38) This swanked-out hostel is an oasis for budget travelers. Stylish, modern and squeaky clean, dorms have themes – Aspen, Graffiti, Vintage Biker – and sleep five to 10 people in bunks. Mattresses are thick, duvets plush and each guest gets a locker and individual charging station. The common kitchen and frequent pub crawls make it easy to make new friends.

★Queen Anne Bed & Breakfast Inn B&B $$
(Map p76; ☎303-296-6666; www.queenannebnb.com; 2147 Tremont Pl; r/ste from $165/230; P🚭❄📶; 🚌28, 32) 🍃 Soft chamber music wafting through public areas, fresh flowers, manicured gardens and evening wine tastings create a romantic ambience at this eco-conscious B&B in two late-1800s Victorian homes. Featuring period antiques, private hot tubs and exquisite hand-painted murals, each room has its own personality.

WORTH A TRIP

BEST DAY HIKES & RIDES FROM DENVER

There are literally hundreds of day hikes within an hour of Denver.

Golden Gate Canyon State Park (303-582-3707; www.cpw.state.co.us; 92 Crawford Gulch Rd; entrance $7, camping $20-26; 5am-10pm;) Located halfway between Golden and Nederland, this massive 12,000-acre state park has plenty of hiking trails and climbing opportunities.

Staunton State Park (303-816-0912; www.parks.state.co.us/parks; 12102 S Elk Creek Rd; individual pass/vehicle $4/8; 7am-9pm;) Colorado's newest state park sits on a historic ranch site 40 miles west of Denver. Ranging in elevation from 8100ft to 10,000ft, it has a rich variety of landscapes – from grassy meadows to dramatic granite cliffs.

Waterton Canyon (303-634-3745; www.denverwater.org/recreation/waterton-canyon-strontia-springs-resevoir; 11300 Waterton Rd; 30min before dawn-30min after dusk;) South of Denver, just west of Chatfield Reservoir, this pretty canyon has an easy 6.5-mile trail to the Strontia Springs Dam.

Buffalo Creek Mountain Bike Area (www.frmbp.org; 18268 S Buffalo Creek Rd, Pine; 7am-7pm;) If you're into singletrack mountain biking, this area has about 40 miles of bike trails, including the sections of the Colorado Trail that permit bikes.

★Crawford Hotel HOTEL $$$
(Map p76; 855-362-5098; www.thecrawfordhotel.com; 1701 Wynkoop St, Union Station; r from 290, ste from $529; ; 55L, 72L,120L, FF2, A, B, C, E, W) Set in the historic Union Station (p83), the Crawford Hotel is an example of Denver's amazing transformation. Rooms are luxurious and artful, with high ceilings and throwbacks such as the art-deco headboards and claw-foot tubs. Service is impeccable and the station's bar, the Terminal, is a fun hangout. Steps away, there's light-rail service to Denver International Airport (p83).

Curtis HOTEL $$$
(Map p76; 303-571-0300; www.thecurtis.com; 1405 Curtis St; r $309-449; ; 9, 10, 15, 20, 28, 32, 38, 43, 44) The Curtis is like stepping into a doo-bop Warhol wonderworld: 13 themed floors, each devoted to a different genre of American pop culture. Rooms are spacious and very mod. Attention to detail – either through the service or the decor – is paramount at the Curtis. While it's managed by the Doubletree, this is a one-of-a-kind hotel in the heart of downtown.

★Art – a Hotel BOUTIQUE HOTEL $$$
(Map p76; 303-572-8000; www.thearthotel.com; 1201 Broadway; r from $400; ; 0, 6, 10, 52) As the name suggests, this hotel has intriguing artwork in the guest rooms and common areas, befitting its location, just around the corner from the Denver Art Museum (p75). Rooms are sizable and modern, and the large patio (open to the general public) with firepits and great views is perfect for happy-hour cocktails.

Eating

Denver's food scene is booming, with new restaurants, cafes and food trucks seemingly opening every month. Downtown offers the greatest variety in Denver, though strollable neighborhoods like LoHi, RiNo, South Broadway, Uptown and Five Points hold some of Denver's best eateries. Out in the burbs, the city of Aurora has Denver's best ethnic food. Check out www.5280.com for new eats.

★Denver Central Market FOOD HALL $
(Map p76; www.denvercentralmarket.com; 2669 Larimer St; 8am-9pm Sun-Thu, to 10pm Fri & Sat; 44, 48) Set in a repurposed warehouse, this gourmet marketplace wows with its style and breadth of options. Eat a bowl of handmade pasta or an artisanal sandwich; consider a wood-fired pizza or street tacos. Or just grab a cocktail at the bar and wander between the fruit stand and chocolatier. Patrons eat at communal tables or on the street-side patio.

Civic Center Eats FOOD TRUCK $
(Map p76; 303-861-4633; www.civiccenterconservancy.org; cnr Broadway & Colfax Ave, Civic Center Park; mains $5-10; 11am-2pm Tue-Thu May-Oct; ; 0, 9, 10, 52) When the weather gets warm, head to **Civic Center Park** for lunch. There, a huge number of food

trucks – everything from BBQ and pizza to sushi and Indian – roll into the park and serve up hearty meals. Tables are set up, live bands play, office workers picnic on the grass. It's Denver at its best.

★ Hop Alley CHINESE $$

(Map p76; ☎720-379-8340; www.hopalleydenver.com; 3500 Larimer St; mains $10-25; ⊙5:30-10:30pm Mon-Sat; ; 12, 44) Hop Alley was a slur used for Denver's hardscrabble Chinatown in the 1880s, until a race riot and anti-Chinese legislation scattered the community. The moniker was reclaimed for this small bustling restaurant located in (what else?) a former soy-sauce plant. Come for authentic yet inventive Chinese dishes and equally creative cocktails, named after the signs of the Chinese zodiac.

★ Acorn AMERICAN $$$

(Map p76; ☎720-542-3721; www.denveracorn.com; 3350 Brighton Blvd, Source; dishes $14-30; ⊙11:30am-10pm Mon-Sat, from 5:30pm Sun; P; 12, 20, 48) The oak-fired oven and grill are the shining stars of this superb restaurant, where small plates of innovative and shareable eats make up meals. The menu changes seasonally but dishes like crispy fried pickles, oak-grilled broccolini and smoked-pork posole are hits. If dinner is too pricey, consider a midday meal (2:30pm to 5:30pm) – the menu is limited but more affordable.

Rioja MODERN AMERICAN $$$

(Map p76; ☎303-820-2282; www.riojadenver.com; 1431 Larimer St; mains $20-40; ⊙11:30am-2:30pm Wed-Fri, from 10am Sat & Sun, 5-10pm daily; ; 10, 28, 32, 38, 44) This is one of Denver's most innovative restaurants. Smart, busy and upscale, yet relaxed and casual – just like Colorado – Rioja features modern cuisine inspired by Italian and Spanish traditions and powered by modern culinary flavors.

Root Down MODERN AMERICAN $$$

(Map p76; ☎303-993-4200; www.rootdowndenver.com; 1600 W 33rd Ave; small plates $8-19, mains $14-35; ⊙5-10pm Sun-Thu, 5-11pm Fri & Sat, 11am-2pm Fri, 10am-2:30pm Sat & Sun; ; 19, 52) In a converted gas station, this is one of the city's most ambitious culinary concepts, marrying sustainable 'field-to-fork' practices, high-concept culinary fusions and a low-impact, energy-efficient ethos. The menu changes seasonally, but consider yourself lucky if it includes the sweet-potato falafel or Colorado lamb sliders. Vegetarian, vegan, raw and gluten-free diets very welcome.

Drinking & Nightlife

Denver's top nightlife districts include Uptown for gay bars and a young professional crowd, LoDo for loud sports bars and heavy drinking, RiNo for hipsters, LoHi for an eclectic mix, and South Broadway and Colfax for Old School wannabes.

★ Black Shirt Brewing Co BREWERY

(Map p76; ☎303-993-2799; www.blackshirtbrewingco.com; 3719 Walnut St; ⊙11am-10pm Sun-Thu, to midnight Fri & Sat; ; 12, 44, A) Artisanal brewers create the all-red-ale menu at the popular BSB; ales take anywhere from two months to three years to brew. So careful are they with the handcrafted beers, the brewers developed lopsided glasses to showcase the aromas. Live music is part of the culture here, as is good food. A kitchen offers brick-oven pizzas and gourmet salads.

★ Crema Coffee House CAFE

(Map p76; ☎720-284-9648; www.cremacoffeehouse.net; 2862 Larimer St; ⊙7am-5pm; ; 44) Noah Price, a clothing designer turned coffee impresario, takes his job seriously, selecting, brewing and pouring Denver's absolute-best coffee. The espresso and French-pressed are complete perfection, but it's the oatmeal latte, delicately infused iced teas and spectacularly eclectic menu – Moroccan meatballs to peanut-butter and jelly sandwiches with goat's cheese – that put this place over the top.

Williams & Graham COCKTAIL BAR

(Map p76; ☎303-997-8886; www.williamsandgraham.com; 3160 Tejon St; ⊙5pm-1am; 32, 44) Denver's top speakeasy looks like an old Western bookstore, but ask for a seat and the cashier pushes a wall of books and leads you deeper into the era. Polished wood, gleaming brass features, antique lamps, tin ceilings and mixologists in aprons await. Cocktails are creative and artfully prepared – almost too beautiful to drink. Almost.

Linger LOUNGE

(Map p76; ☎303-993-3120; www.lingerdenver.com; 2030 W 30th Ave; ⊙11:30am-2:30pm & 4-10pm Tue-Thu, to 11pm Fri, 10am-2:30pm & 4-11pm Sat, 10am-2:30pm Sun; 28, 32, 44) This rambling LoHi complex sits in the former Olinger mortuary. Come nighttime, they black out the 'O' and it just becomes Linger. There's an interesting international menu, but most people come for the tony feel and light-up-the-night rooftop bar, which even has a replica of the RV made famous by the Bill Murray smash *Stripes*.

Tracks GAY

(Map p76; ☎303-863-7326; www.tracksdenver.com; 3500 Walnut St; ⏰9pm-2am Fri & Sat, hours vary Sun-Thu; 🚌44, 🚊A) Denver's best gay dance club has an 18+ night on Thursday, and Friday drag shows. There's a definite pretty-boy focus, with good music and a scene to match. Saturday is the biggest dance night. No cover before 10pm, after 10pm it's $10.

Falling Rock Tap House BAR

(Map p76; ☎303-293-8338; www.fallingrocktaphouse.com; 1919 Blake St; ⏰11am-2am; 🚌0, 15, 20) High fives and hollers punctuate the scene when the Rockies triumph and beer drinkers file in to forget an afternoon of drinking Coors at the ball park. There are – count 'em – 80-plus beers on tap and the bottle list has almost 150. With all the local favorites, this is *the* place to drink beer downtown.

Crú WINE BAR

(Map p76; ☎303-893-9463; www.cruawinebar.com; 1442 Larimer St; ⏰2pm-midnight Mon-Thu, noon-2am Fri & Sat, 10:30am-3pm Sun; 🚌10, 28, 32, 38, 44) This classy Larimer Sq wine bar is decked out in wine labels and glassware, with dim lighting and gentle music. It looks so bespoke it's surprising to learn it's a chain (Dallas, Austin). Come for happy hour (4pm to 6:30pm Monday to Friday) when flights of wine are $3 off and light fare includes mussels and goat's cheese beignets.

☆ Entertainment

Denver is bursting with entertainment options. There's live music and theater practically everywhere, from intimate jazz clubs to the amazing Denver Center for the Performing Arts (p81). Denver is a four-sport town (one of few in the country) and also has professional soccer and lacrosse. Add to that comedy, movies, dance, up-and-coming all-ages shows, and yearly festivals and there's something for everyone.

★Denver Performing Arts Complex PERFORMING ARTS

(Map p76; ☎720-865-4220; www.artscomplex.com; cnr 14th & Champa Sts; 🚌9, 15, 28, 32, 38, 43, 44) This massive complex – one of the largest of its kind – occupies four city blocks and houses 10 major venues, including the historic **Ellie Caulkins Opera House** and the Boettcher Concert Hall. It's also home to the **Colorado Ballet** (Map p76; ☎303-837-8888; www.coloradoballet.org; 1075 Santa Fe Dr; ⏰box office 9am-5pm Mon-Fri; 👪; 🚌1, 9), **Denver Center for the Performing Arts** (Map p76; ☎303-893-4100; www.denvercenter.org; 1101 13th St; ⏰box office 10am-6pm Mon-Sat & 1hr before each show; 👪; 🚌9, 15, 28, 32, 38, 43, 44), **Opera Colorado** (Map p76; ☎303-468-2030; www.operacolorado.org; ⏰box office 10am-5pm Mon-Fri; 👪; 🚌9, 15, 28, 32, 38, 43, 44) and the Colorado Symphony Orchestra (p82). Not sure what you want to do tonight? Come here.

★Curious Theatre THEATER

(Map p76; ☎303-623-0524; www.curioustheatre.org; 1080 Acoma St; ⏰box office 2-6pm Tue-Sat; 🚌0, 6, 52) 'No guts, no story' is the tagline of this award-winning theater company, set in a converted church. Plays pack a punch with thought-provoking stories that take on social justice issues. Think race, immigration, sexuality. Stay for talks at the end of each show, when actors engage with the audience about everything from the plot to the set. Tickets from $18.

El Chapultepec JAZZ

(Map p76; ☎303-295-9126; www.thepeclodo.com; 1962 Market St; ⏰7am-1am, music from 9pm; 🚌38) This smoky, old-school jazz joint attracts a diverse mix of people. Since it opened in 1951, Frank Sinatra, Tony Bennett and Ella Fitzgerald have played here, as have Jagger and Richards. Local jazz bands take the tiny stage nightly, but you never know who might drop by.

Hi-Dive LIVE MUSIC

(☎303-733-0230; www.hi-dive.com; 7 S Broadway; 🚌0) Local rock heroes and touring indie bands light up the stage at the Hi-Dive, a venue at the heart of Denver's local live-music scene. During big shows it gets deafeningly loud, cheek-to-jowl with hipsters and humid as an armpit. In other words, perfection.

Ogden Theatre LIVE MUSIC

(Map p76; ☎303-832-1874; www.ogdentheatre.com; 935 E Colfax Ave; ⏰box office 10am-2pm Sat, 1hr before doors open show days; 🚌15) One of Denver's best live-music venues, the Ogden Theatre has a checkered past. Built in 1917, it was derelict for many years and might have been bulldozed in the early 1990s, but it's now listed on the National Register

OFF THE BEATEN TRACK

LIVE AT RED ROCKS!

Red Rocks Amphitheatre (☎720-865-2494; www.redrocksonline.com; 18300 W Alameda Pkwy, Morrison; ⏰5am-11pm; 👪) is set between 400ft-high red sandstone rocks 15 miles southwest of Denver. Acoustics are so good many artists record live albums here. The 9000-seat theater offers stunning views and draws big-name bands all summer. To see your favorite singer go to work on the stage is to witness a performance in one of the most exceptional music venues in the world. For many, it's reason enough for a trip to Colorado.

of Historic Places. Bands such as Edward Sharpe & the Magnetic Zeros and Lady Gaga have played here.

Colorado Symphony Orchestra CLASSICAL MUSIC
(CSO; Map p76; ☎303-623-7876; www.coloradosymphony.org; 1000 14th St, Boettcher Concert Hall; ⏰box office 10am-6pm Mon-Fri, from noon Sat; 👪; 🚌9, 15, 28, 32, 38, 43, 44) The Boettcher Concert Hall in the Denver Performing Arts Complex (p81) is home to this renowned symphony orchestra. The orchestra performs an annual 21-week Masterworks season, as well as concerts aimed at a broader audience – think live performances of movie scores during the screening of films such as *La La Land* or *Harry Potter and the Prisoner of Azkaban*.

Bluebird Theater LIVE MUSIC
(☎303-377-1666; www.bluebirdtheater.net; 3317 E Colfax Ave; 👪; 🚌15) This medium-sized theater is general admission standing room and has terrific sound and clear sight lines from the balcony. The venue often offers the last chance to catch bands – Denver faves the Lumineers and DeVotchKa both headlined here – on their way up to the big time.

Landmark Mayan Theatre CINEMA
(☎303-744-6799; www.landmarktheatres.com; 110 Broadway; 👪; 🚌0) Even without the fancy sound system and enormous screen, this is the best place in Denver to take in a film. The 1930s movie palace is a romantic, historic gem and – bonus! – it serves beer.

Shopping

★Tattered Cover Bookstore BOOKS
(Map p76; ☎303-436-1070; www.tatteredcover.com; 1628 16th St; ⏰6:30am-9pm Mon-Fri, 9am-9pm Sat, 10am-6pm Sun; 📶👪; 🚌10, 19, 28, 32, 44, MallRide) There are plenty of places to curl up with a book in Denver's beloved independent bookstore. Bursting with new and used books, it has a good stock of regional travel guides and nonfiction titles dedicated to the Western states and Western folklore. There's a second smaller location on Colfax near City Park.

REI SPORTS & OUTDOORS
(Recreational Equipment Incorporated; Map p76; ☎303-756-3100; www.rei.com; 1416 Platte St; ⏰9am-9pm Mon-Sat, to 7pm Sun; 👪; 🚌10, 28, 32, 44) The flagship store of this outdoor-equipment super-supplier is an essential stop if you are heading to the mountains or just cruising through Confluence. In addition to top gear for camping, cycling, climbing and skiing, it has a rental department, maps and the Pinnacle, a 47ft-high indoor structure of simulated red sandstone for climbing and rappelling.

Fancy Tiger Crafts ARTS & CRAFTS
(☎303-733-3855; www.fancytigercrafts.com; 59 Broadway; ⏰10am-7pm Mon & Wed-Sat, to 9pm Tue, 11am-6pm Sun; 👪; 🚌0) So you dig crochet and quilting? You knit a mean sweater and have a few too many tattoos? Welcome to Fancy Tiger Crafts, a sophisticated remodel of granny's yarn barn that's ground zero for Denver's crafty hipsters. There are classes in the back (including some by Jessica, 'mistress of patchwork') and a rad selection of fabric, yarn and books.

Information

The Tourist Information Center website (www.denver.org) has great information about events.

Downtown Tourist Information Center (Map p76; ☎303-892-1505; www.denver.org; 1575 California St; ⏰9am-6pm Mon-Fri, 9am-5pm Sat, 10am-2pm Sun May-Oct, 9am-5pm Mon-Fri, 9am-2pm Sat, 10am-2pm Sun Nov-Apr; 🚌9, 15, 20, MallRide, 🚊D, F, H) When you get to town, make for the largest and most central information center, located just off the 16th St Mall. You can load up on brochures, browse online travel pages and get solid information from knowledgeable staffers. A small gift shop sells high-quality souvenirs too.

ORIC (Outdoor Recreation Information Center; Map p76; ☎REI main line 303-756-3100;

www.oriconline.org; 1416 Platte St; hours vary; ; 10, 28, 32, 44) Inside REI, this information desk is a must for those looking to get out of town for outdoor adventure. It has maps and expert information on trip planning and safety. The desk is staffed by volunteers, so hours vary wildly, but arriving on a weekend afternoon is a good bet.

Visit Denver Information Booth (Map p76; 303-317-0629; www.visitdenver.com; Union Station; 9am-5:30pm Mon-Sat, 10am-2pm Sun; ; A) This Union Station desk is regularly staffed with knowledgeable folks who can help you curate an afternoon or a week.

Getting There & Away

AIR

Denver International Airport (DIA; 303-342-2000; www.flydenver.com; 8500 Peña Blvd; 24hr; ; A) is a major air hub and one of the country's busiest facilities. DIA has an automated subway that links the terminal to three concourses (Concourse C is almost 1 mile from the terminal).

DIA is 24 miles from downtown. Take the I-70 and exit 238 (Peña Blvd). From there, it's 12 miles to the main terminal. You'll see the Teflon-coated fiberglass roof that peaks out to mirror the mountains in the distance. A RTD Train (p83) will get you from the airport to Union Station as well.

BUS

Greyhound offers frequent buses on routes along the Front Range and on transcontinental routes. All buses stop at the **Denver Bus Center** (Map p76; 303-293-6555; 1055 19th St; 6am-midnight; ; 8, 48).

The **Epic Mountain Express** (800-525-6363; www.epicmountainexpress.com; 8500 Peña Blvd, Denver International Airport; ; A) has shuttle services from Denver International Airport (DIA), downtown Denver or Morrison to Summit County, including Breckenridge and Keystone (adult/child $66/35, 2½ hours) and Vail (adult/child $84/44, three hours).

The **Colorado Springs Shuttle** (877-587-3456; www.coloradoshuttle.com; 8500 Peña Blvd, Denver International Airport; ; A) offers trips from DIA to Colorado Springs (adult/child $50/25, two hours).

Regional Transportation District (RTD; Map p76; 303-299-6000; www.rtd-denver.com; 1600 Blake St; 10, 19, 28, 32, 44, MallRide) buses to Boulder (Rte FF1, $4.50) carry bicycles in the cargo compartment and offer frequent service from Union Station (p83). To reach Golden, take the 16L bus ($4.50) that stops at the corner of Colfax and Broadway.

TRAIN

Amtrak's (800-872-7245; www.amtrak.com) *California Zephyr* train runs daily between Chicago ($121 to $325, 19 hours) and San Francisco ($144 to $446, 33 hours) stopping in Denver's gorgeous **Union Station** (Map p76; 303-592-6712; www.unionstationindenver.com; 1701 Wynkoop St; P; 55L, 72L,120L, FF2, A, B, C, E, W).

Getting Around

TO/FROM THE AIRPORT

A complete Ground Transportation Center is centrally located on the 5th level of DIA's terminal, near the baggage claim. All transportation companies have their booths here and passengers can catch vans, shuttles and taxis outside the doors.

Complimentary hotel shuttles represent the cheapest means of getting to or from the airport. Courtesy phones for hotel shuttles are available in the Ground Transportation Center.

An RTD (p83) light-rail (Line A; $10.50, 45 minutes) transports people from DIA to downtown Denver, servicing Denver suburbs along the way.

Taxi service to downtown Denver costs around $60, excluding tip. Lyft and Uber are both popular.

There are a number of airport shuttle vans, such as **SuperShuttle** (800-258-3826; www.supershuttle.com; 24hr; A), and limousine services. Airport shuttles to the Front Range and mountain/ski areas are also not hard to come by.

BICYCLE

Denver has lots of bike lanes on the city streets and an excellent network of trails to get out of town. These include routes along the Platte River Pkwy, the Cherry Creek Bike Path and a network that heads all the way out to Golden (about a two-hour ride). You can get all the information you need from a pair of excellent websites: Bike Denver (www.bikedenver.org) and City of Denver (www.denvergov.org), both of which have downloadable bike maps for the city. Lyft and Jump both have bike shares here that are accessible with the app.

B-Cycle (303-825-3325; www.denverbcycle.com; 1-day membership $9; 5am-midnight;) is a bike-share company with more than 80 stations throughout Denver. The daily rate includes unlimited rides as long as they're under 30 minutes.

PUBLIC TRANSPORTATION

Regional Transportation District provides public transportation throughout the Denver and Boulder area (local/regional fares $3/5.25). The website has schedules, routes, fares and a trip planner.

TAXI

Two major taxi companies offer door-to-door service in Denver. Ridesharing services are huge.

Metro Taxi (☎303-333-3333; www.metrotaxidenver.com; ⏲24hr)

Yellow Cab (☎303-777-7777; www.denveryellowcab.com; ⏲24hr)

Boulder

Boulder comes with plenty of stereotypes. It's a hippie town. It's a yuppie town. It's pretentious. It's the most beautiful place on earth. Like many preconceived notions, many of these have at least a grain of truth. But the real Boulder, the one behind the layers of perception, is simply a wonderful place to be.

At the center of it all is the University of Colorado campus with its manicured quads and towering stone buildings. The college-town atmosphere also means Boulder has plenty of arts, culture, live music, hippie drum circles, and sharp-nosed intellectual debates.

Beyond the campus, the town is a lovely grouping of small retail enclaves, like the pedestrian Pearl Street Mall, walking paths, parks and Victorian houses dating back 100 years.

On the edge of town you have one of the best open-space park systems in the US, with amazing outdoor adventures right at your door.

Sights & Activities

★Chautauqua Park PARK

(☎303-442-3282; www.chautauqua.com; 900 Baseline Rd; 🚌HOP 2) This historic landmark park is the gateway to Boulder's most magnificent slab of open space adjoining the iconic Flatirons; its wide, lush lawn attracts picnicking families, sunbathers, Frisbee folk and students from nearby CU. It also gets lots of hikers, climbers and trail runners. It's a popular site so parking can be a hassle. During the summer the city of Boulder runs a free shuttle on the weekends from downtown and satellite parking lots (http://parktopark.org).

Dairy Arts Center ARTS CENTER

(☎303-440-7826; www.thedairy.org; 2590 Walnut St; prices vary; P 👪; 🚌HOP) A historic milk-processing factory turned arts center, the Dairy is one of Boulder's top cultural hubs. It's a state-of-the-art facility with three stages, four gallery spaces and a 60-seat cinema. There's always something going on – from lectures and plays to modern dance and art exhibits. There's a small cafe and bar on-site, too.

★Boulder Creek WATER SPORTS

(👪) An all-time favorite Boulder summer ritual is to tube down Boulder Creek. Most people put in at **Eben G Fine Park** (Boulder Canyon Dr; P 👪 🐾; 🚌205, N) and float as far as 30th St, or even 55th St. Be sure to check the water volume, especially early in the season; anything over 200 cu ft per second can be a real rodeo.

Eldorado Canyon State Park OUTDOORS

(☎303-494-3943; https://cpw.state.co.us/placestogo/parks/EldoradoCanyon; 9 Kneale Rd, Eldorado Springs; $9; ⏲dawn-dusk, visitor center 9am-5pm) Among the country's best rock-climbing areas, Eldorado has class 5.5 to 5.14 climbs focusing mostly on traditional crack climbing. Suitable for all visitors, a dozen miles of hiking trails also link up to Chautauqua Park. A public pool offers chilly swims in the canyon's famous spring water. Located 5 miles southwest of town.

Local Table Tours FOOD & DRINK

(☎303-909-5747; www.localtabletours.com; tours $49-79; ⏲hours vary; 🐾) 🍃 Go behind the scenes with one of these fun downtown walking tours presenting a smattering of great local cuisine and inside knowledge on food and wine. There are specialty tours for brews, cocktails, coffee and chocolate. The tours also highlight locally owned businesses with regional or sustainable food sources.

Festivals & Events

Bolder Boulder SPORTS

(☎303-444-7223; www.bolderboulder.com; adult/child from $73/58; ⏲Memorial Day; 👪; 🚌209, STAMPEDE) With more than 50,000 runners and pros mingling with costumed racers, live bands and sideline merrymakers, this may be the most fun 10km run in the US. To make it even better, it ends at Folsom Field, CU's football stadium.

Boulder Creek Festival MUSIC, FOOD

(☎303-777-6887; www.bouldercreekfest.com; Canyon Blvd, Central Park; ⏲May; 👪; 🚌203, 204, 225, AB, B, DASH, DD, DM, GS, SKIP) FREE Billed as the kick-off to summer and capped with the Bolder Boulder (p84), this summer festival is massive. At least 10 event areas feature more than 30 live entertainers and 500 vendors, plus a whole carnival ride zone. There's food and drink, entertainment and sunshine. What's not to love?

Sleeping

★Chautauqua Lodge & Cottages HISTORIC HOTEL $$
(☎303-952-1611; www.chautauqua.com; 900 Baseline Rd; r from $129, cottages from $200; ; HOP 2) Adjoining beautiful hiking trails to the Flatirons and in a leafy neighborhood inside Chautauqua Park, this is our top Boulder pick. It has contemporary rooms and one- to three-bedroom cottages with porches and patchwork-quilt beds. It's perfect for families and pets. All have full kitchens, though the wraparound porch of the Chautauqua Dining Hall is a local favorite for breakfast.

Boulder Adventure Lodge HOTEL $$
(A-Lodge; ☎303-444-0882; www.a-lodge.com; 91 Fourmile Canyon Dr; campsite/dm/r $45/65/189; ; N) You've come to Boulder to get outdoors, so why not stay nearer the action? Located a short distance from town, the A-Lodge has hiking, biking, climbing and fishing right from the property. Rooms are simple but well appointed, ranging from dorms to suites. There's a pool and firepit, generating a warm esprit de corps among guests and staff alike.

Briar Rose B&B B&B $$
(☎303-442-3007; www.briarrosebb.com; 2151 Arapahoe Ave; r from $184; ; JUMP) Gorgeous and comfy, this tranquil home is a stone's throw from Naropa University. A tall fence and landscaped garden insulate it from busy Arapahoe Ave. Inside there are cozy rooms with a Buddhist influence, reflecting the Zen monk practice of one of the owners. The organic vegetarian breakfast features a wide tea selection and there's one loaner bike.

★St Julien Hotel & Spa HOTEL $$$
(☎720-406-9696, reservations 877-303-0900; www.stjulien.com; 900 Walnut St; r/ste from $400/495; ; 205, HOP, SKIP) In the heart of downtown, Boulder's finest four-star option is modern and refined, with photographs of local scenery and cork walls that warm the ambience. With fabulous views of the Flatirons, the back patio hosts live world music, jazz concerts and popular Latin dance parties. Rooms are spacious and plush. The on-site spa is considered one of the best around.

Eating

★Rayback Collective FOOD TRUCK $
(☎303-214-2127; www.therayback.com; 2775 Valmont Rd; mains $6-12; 11am-10pm Mon-Fri, to 11pm Sat, to 9pm Sun; ; 205, BOLT) A plumbing-supplies warehouse turned urban oasis, Rayback is a snapshot of Boulder. A place to feel community. A huge outdoor space with firepit and lawn games. A lounge with cozy chairs and live music. A bar serving up Colorado brews and kombucha. A food-truck park with loads of good eats. Young, old and even furry friends are welcome here.

Rincón Argentino ARGENTINE $
(☎303-442-4133; www.rinconargentinoboulder.com; 2525 Arapahoe Ave; mains $4-13; 11am-8pm Mon-Thu, to 9pm Fri & Sat; ; JUMP) Don't be turned off by the shopping plaza setting: Rincón packs a wallop of authentic Argentinean flavors. It bakes fresh empanadas – savory, small turnovers filled with spiced meat, or mozzarella and basil – which are perfect with a glass of Malbec. It also offers *milanesas* (breaded-beef-cutlet sandwiches); and gourds of yerba maté, a high-octane coffee alternative.

Oak at Fourteenth MODERN AMERICAN $$
(☎303-444-3622; www.oakatfourteenth.com; 1400 Pearl St; mains $13-30; 11:30am-10pm Mon-Sat, from 5:30pm Sun; 205, 206) Zesty and innovative, locally owned Oak manufactures

BOULDER COUNTY FARMERS MARKET

Boulder County Farmers Market (☎303-910-2236; www.boulderfarmers.org; 13th St, btwn Canyon Blvd & Arapahoe Ave; 8am-2pm Sat Apr-Nov plus 4-8pm Wed May-Oct; ; 203, 204, 205, 206, 208, 225, DASH, JUMP, SKIP) is a massive spring and summer sprawl of colorful, mostly organic local food. Find flowers and herbs, as well as brain-sized mushrooms, delicate squash blossoms, crusty pretzels, vegan dips, grass-fed beef, raw granola and yogurt. Booths selling prepared food offer all sorts of international tasty treats. Live music is as standard as the family picnics in the park along Boulder Creek.

top-notch cocktails and tasty small plates for stylish diners. Standouts include the grilled bacon-wrapped pork tenderloin and cucumber sashimi drizzled with passion fruit. Portions at this farm-to-table eatery are minimal – when it's this scrumptious, you notice. Waiters advise well. The only downside: it tends to be noisy, so save your intimate confessions.

★Brasserie Ten Ten BISTRO **$$**
(☎303-998-1010; www.brasserietenten.com; 1011 Walnut St; mains $15-27; ⊙11am-10pm Mon-Thu, 11am-11pm Fri, 9am-11pm Sat, 9am-9pm Sun; 🚌203, 204, 225, AB, B) A go-to place for both students and professors, this sunny French bistro has a refined menu and an elegant atmosphere – think fresh flowers, marble high tops and polished brass. Sure, it's fancy, but not too uppity to offer killer happy-hour deals on crepes, sliders, mussels and beer. Don't miss the truffle fries.

Salt MODERN AMERICAN **$$**
(☎303-444-7258; www.saltthebistro.com; 1047 Pearl St; mains $15-30; ⊙11am-9pm Mon-Thu, 11am-11pm Fri & Sat, 10am-9pm Sun; 👪; 🚌208, HOP, SKIP) While farm-to-table is ubiquitous in Boulder, this is one spot that delivers and surpasses expectations. The handmade fettuccine with snap peas, radicchio and herb cream is a feverish delight. But Salt also knows meat: local and grass-fed, basted, braised and slow roasted to utter perfection. When in doubt, ask – the waiters really know their stuff.

★Frasca ITALIAN **$$$**
(☎303-442-6966; www.frascafoodandwine.com; 1738 Pearl St; mains $35, tasting menus $65-130; ⊙5:30-9:30pm Mon-Thu, to 10:30pm Fri, 5-10:30pm Sat; 🖉; 🚌HOP, 204) Deemed Boulder's finest by many (the wine service earned a James Beard award), Frasca has an impeccable kitchen and only the freshest farm-to-table ingredients. Rotating dishes range from earthy braised pork to housemade gnocchi and grilled quail served with leeks and wilted pea shoots. Reserve days, even weeks, in advance. Mondays offer 'bargain' $65 tasting menus with suggested wine pairings.

🍷 Drinking & Entertainment

★Mountain Sun BREWERY
(☎303-546-0886; www.mountainsunpub.com; 1535 Pearl St; ⊙11am-1am; 👪; 🚌HOP, 205, 206) As Boulder as it gets, this is the town's favorite brewery. It cheerfully serves a smorgasbord of fine brews and packs in everyone from yuppies to hippies. Best of all is its community atmosphere. The pub grub, especially the burgers and chili, is delicious and it's fully family-friendly, with board games and kids' meals.

Avery Brewing Company BREWERY
(☎303-440-4324; www.averybrewing.com; 4910 Nautilus Ct; ⊙11am-11pm Tue-Sun, from 3pm Mon; 🚌205) For craft breweries, how big is too big? Avery pushes the limit, with its imposing two-story building, complete with gift shop selling hats and tees. But the 1st-floor patio and tap room are lively and fun, while upstairs has a quieter restaurant feel. One thing's for sure: the beer's outstanding, from Apricot Sour to a devilish Mephistopheles Stout.

Bitter Bar COCKTAIL BAR
(☎303-442-3050; www.thebitterbar.com; 835 Walnut St; ⊙5pm-midnight Mon-Thu, to 2am Fri & Sat; 🚌HOP) A chic Boulder bar where killer cocktails – such as the lavender-infused Kiss the Sky or the elderflower tonic Guns n' Roses – make the evening slip happily out of focus. Happy hours that run till 8pm don't hurt either. The patio is great for conversation.

Boulder Dushanbe Teahouse TEAHOUSE
(☎303-442-4993; www.boulderteahouse.com; 1770 13th St; mains $8-24; ⊙8am-9pm; 👪; 🚌203, 204, 205, 206, 208, 225, DASH, JUMP, SKIP) It's impossible to find better ambience than at this incredible Tajik teahouse, a gift from Dushanbe, Boulder's sister city. The elaborate carvings and paintings were reassembled over an eight-year period on the edge of **Central Park** (Canyon Blvd; 🅿👪; 🚌206, JUMP).

eTown Hall LIVE MUSIC
(☎303-443-8696; www.etown.org; 1535 Spruce St; from $25; ⊙hours vary; 🚌HOP) Beautiful, brand-new and solar-powered, this repurposed church is the home of the eTown radio show (heard on National Public Radio). The show features rising and well-known artists and you can get in on it by attending a live taping in its 200-seat theater. Tapings run for two hours starting at 7pm, and are typically held on weeknights.

🛍 Shopping

★Pearl Street Mall AREA
(www.boulderdowntown.com; Pearl St, btwn 9th & 15th Sts; 👪🐾; 🚌205, 206, 208, HOP, SKIP) The highlight of downtown Boulder is the Pearl

Street Mall, a vibrant pedestrian zone filled with kids' climbing boulders and splash fountains, bars, galleries and restaurants. Street performers often come out in force on weekends, and there are featured concerts and events throughout the year (especially in the summer months).

★Boulder Book Store BOOKS
(☎303-447-2074; www.boulderbookstore.net; 1107 Pearl St; ⊙10am-10pm Mon-Sat, to 9pm Sun; 📶👪; 🚌208, HOP, SKIP) Boulder's favorite indie bookstore has a huge travel section downstairs, along with all the hottest new fiction and nonfiction. Check the visiting-authors lineup posted at the entry and on its website, or simply grab a corner to read for a while.

★Common Threads CLOTHING
(☎303-449-5431; www.shopcommonthreads.com; 2707 Spruce St; ⊙10am-6pm Mon, Tue & Thu-Sat, to 7pm Wed; 🚌205, BOLT, HOP) Vintage shopping at its most haute couture: this fun place is where to go for secondhand Choos and Prada purses. Prices are higher than at your run-of-the-mill vintage shop, but clothes, shoes and bags are always in good condition, and the designer clothing is guaranteed authentic. Offers fun classes on altering and creating clothes.

ℹ Information

Boulder Ranger District (☎303-541-2500; www.fs.usda.gov; 2140 Yarmouth Ave; ⊙8:30am-4:30pm Mon-Fri; 🚌204) This US Forest Service outpost provides information on the national forests that surround the Rocky Mountain National Park, including campgrounds and trails that cross between the two.

Boulder Visitor Center (☎303-442-2911; www.bouldercoloradousa.com; 2440 Pearl St; ⊙8:30am-5pm Mon-Fri; 🚌HOP) Set in the Boulder Chamber of Commerce, this visitor center offers basic information, maps and tips on nearby hiking trails and other activities. There's a more accessible **tourist information kiosk** (☎303-417-1365; cnr Pearl & 13th Sts; ⊙10am-8pm; 🚌208, HOP, SKIP) on the Pearl Street Mall in front of the courthouse.

Downtown Boulder (www.boulderdowntown.com) This alliance of downtown businesses offers comprehensive dining and event listings in the downtown area, including the Pearl Street Mall.

Get Boulder (www.getboulder.com) A local print and online magazine with helpful information on things to do in Boulder.

ℹ Getting There & Around

AIR

Denver International Airport (p83) Located just 45 miles from Boulder, this is the main entry point for travelers arriving by air.

Green Ride (☎303-997-0238; www.greenrideboulder.com; 4800 Baseline Rd, D110; one way $30-40) Serving Boulder and its satellite suburbs, this Denver International Airport shuttle is cheap and convenient, working on an hourly schedule (3:25am to 11:25pm). The cheapest service leaves from the depot. Additional travelers in groups are discounted.

SuperShuttle (☎303-444-0808; www.supershuttle.com; one way from $84) This shuttle provides a private van service to the airport. The base fare includes up to three people. Unless you have loads of luggage, parties of four or more are better served by a taxi.

BICYCLE

Owning a bicycle is almost a Boulder prerequisite. Most streets have dedicated bike lanes and the Boulder Creek Bike Path is a must-ride commuter corridor. There are plenty of places to get your hands on a rental.

Boulder B-Cycle (☎303-532-4412; https://boulder.bcycle.com; 24hr rental $8; ⊙office 9am-5pm Mon-Fri, 10am-3pm Sat) With rental cruisers stationed all over the city, this is a popular citywide program of hourly or daily bike rentals, but riders must sign up online first.

Full Cycle (☎303-440-7771; www.fullcyclebikes.com; 1211 13th St; daily rental $25-95; ⊙10am-7pm Mon-Fri, to 6pm Sat, to 5pm Sun; 👪; 🚌203, 204, 225, AB, B, DASH, DD, GS, SKIP) This terrific bike shop rents cruisers on the cheap, and higher-end road and full-suspension mountain bikes. Ask staff about the best cycling routes (from easy Boulder Creek Trail to the searing pain of the 4-mile ride up Flagstaff). There's another branch on E Pearl.

University Bicycles (☎303-444-4196; www.ubikes.com; 839 Pearl St; per day rental from $25; ⊙10am-7pm Mon-Fri, to 6pm Sat, to 5pm Sun; 👪; 🚌HOP) There are plenty of rental shops in this town, but this cavernous place has the widest range of rides and the most helpful staff.

CAR & MOTORCYCLE

RTD buses (p83) travel to Denver, Denver International Airport, Nederland and within Boulder. Dedicated bike lanes and paths make the city ideal for two-wheel traffic, and the downtown area is pleasantly walkable.

Western USA's National Parks

National parks are America's big backyards. No cross-country road trip would be complete without a visit to at least one of these remarkable natural treasures, rich in unspoiled wilderness, rare wildlife and history. The nation's five dozen national parks and over 350 other protected areas are managed by the National Park Service (NPS), which celebrated its centennial in 2016.

1

CHRISTOPHER KIMMEL/GETTY IMAGES ©

JEFF R CLOW/GETTY IMAGES ©

BJÖRN ALBERTS/GETTY IMAGES ©

1. Towering Redwoods
Experience the majesty of the world's tallest trees in Redwood National Park (p337).

2. Mesa Arch
Take in the surreal geology of Canyonlands National Park (p209).

3. Old Faithful Geyser
The world's oldest national park, Yellowstone National Park (p118) is still one of the most spectacular.

4. Vernal Falls
Yosemite National Park (p343) is one of the planet's busiest parks for good reason.

PETE SEAWARD/LONELY PLANET ©

Northern Mountains

With one foot on either side of the continental divide and behemoths of granite in every direction, Colorado's Northern Mountains offer out-of-this-world alpine adventures, laid-back skiing, kick-butt hiking and biking, and plenty of rivers to raft, fish and float.

Rocky Mountain National Park

The crown jewel of Colorado's national parks, **Rocky Mountain National Park** (www.nps.gov/romo; vehicle 1/7 days $25/35, motorcycle $25/30, foot & bicycle $15/20, annual passes $80) encompasses some 415 sq miles of granite mountain top, alpine lake, wildflower-filled meadow, hiking trails, star-filled nights and adventures large and small for everyone in your group.

Like many national parks, it can be a zoo in the height of the summer season. But leave the main trails behind and you will find beautiful quiet and solitude in the area that protects moose, elk, bighorn sheep, black bear and more. Climbers will be challenged on the area's high peaks, while families and sightseers will love driving over the rooftop of the Rockies on Trail Ridge Road, taking part in ranger-led activities and taking on short forays into the glorious wilderness.

Winter in the park is different. Expect stillness and a landscape blanketed in sweet snow.

Sights & Activities

With more than 300 miles of trails, traversing all aspects of its diverse terrain, the park is suited to every hiking ability. Those with kids in tow might consider the easy hikes in the **Wild Basin** to Calypso Falls, or to Gem Lake in the **Lumpy Ridge** area, while those with unlimited ambition, strong legs and enough trail mix will be lured by the challenge of summiting **Longs Peak**. Regardless, it's best to spend at least one night at 7000ft to 8000ft prior to setting out to allow your body to adjust to the elevation. Before July many trails are snowbound and high water runoff makes passage difficult. In winter avalanches are a hazard, and you should only enter if you know what you are doing and are well equipped. Dogs and other pets are not allowed on the trails. All overnight stays in the backcountry require **permits** (970-586-1242; www.nps.gov/romo; 1000 W Hwy 36, Estes Park, CO 80517).

The golden rule in Colorado mountaineering: if you haven't made the summit by noon, return (no matter how close you are). It's the best way to avoid getting hit by lightning.

★ **Moraine Park Discovery Center** MUSEUM
(970-586-1206; Bear Lake Rd; 9am-4:30pm Jun-Oct;) FREE Built by the Civilian Conservation Corps in 1923 and once the park's proud visitors lodge, this building has been renovated in recent years to host exhibits on geology, glaciers and wildlife. Kids will like the interactive exhibits and half-mile nature trail out the door.

Sleeping

Glacier Basin Campground CAMPGROUND $
(877-444-6777; www.recreation.gov; off Bear Lake Rd; RV & tent sites summer $26) This developed campground is surrounded by evergreens, offering plenty of sun and shade. It also sports a large area for group camping and accommodates RVs – though there are no electric hookups. It is served by the shuttle buses on Bear Lake Rd throughout the summer. Make reservations through the website.

Aspenglen Campground CAMPGROUND $
(877-444-6777; www.recreation.gov; State Hwy 34; tent & RV sites $26; summer only) With only 54 sites, this is the smallest of the park's reservable camping grounds. There are many tent-only sites, including some walk-ins; a limited number of trailers are allowed. This is the quietest campground in the park while still being highly accessible (5 miles west of Estes Park on US 34). Make reservations through the website.

Moraine Park Campground CAMPGROUND $
(877-444-6777; www.recreation.gov; off Bear Lake Rd; tent & RV sites summer $26, winter $18) In the middle of a stand of ponderosa pine forest off Bear Lake Rd, this is the biggest of the park's campgrounds, approximately 2.5 miles south of the Beaver Meadows Visitor Center (p91) and with 244 sites. The walk-in, tent-only sites in the D Loop are recommended if you want some quiet. Make reservations through the website.

Olive Ridge Campground CAMPGROUND $
(303-541-2500; www.recreation.gov; State Hwy 7; tent/RV site $15.75/31.50; mid-May–Nov) This well-kept USFS campground has access to four trailheads: St Vrain Mountain,

Wild Basin, Longs Peak and Twin Sisters. In the summer it can get full, though sites are mostly first-come, first-served.

Information

For private vehicles, the park entrance fee is $25 for one day and $35 for seven. Annual passes are $70. Individuals entering the park on foot, bicycle or bus pay $15 each for one day and $20 for seven. Motorcycles pay $25 for one day and $30 for seven.

Backcounty permits ($30 for a group of up to seven people for seven days) are required for overnight stays in the 260 designated backcountry camping sites in the park. A bear box to store your food in is required if you are staying overnight in the backcountry between May and October (established campsites already have them).

Alpine Visitor Center (www.nps.gov/romo; Fall River Pass; 10:30am-4:30pm late May–mid-Jun & early Sep–mid-Oct, 9am-5pm late Jun-early Sep;)

Beaver Meadows Visitor Center (970-586-1206; www.nps.gov/romo; US Hwy 36; 8am-9pm late Jun-late Aug, to 4:30pm or 5pm rest of the year;)

Kawuneeche Visitor Center (970-627-3471; 16018 US Hwy 34; 8am-6pm last week May–Labor Day, to 5pm Labor Day–Sep, to 4:30pm Oct-May;)

Getting There & Away

Trail Ridge Rd (US 34) is the only east–west route through the park; the US 34 eastern approach from I-25 and Loveland follows the Big Thompson River Canyon. The most direct route from Boulder follows US 36 through Lyons to the east entrances. Another approach from the south, mountainous Hwy 7, passes by **Enos Mills Cabin** (970-586-4706; www.enosmills.com; 6760 Hwy 7; adult/child $20/10; 11am-4pm Tue & Wed summer, by appointment only;) and provides access to campsites and trailheads on the east side of the divide. Winter closure of US 34 through the park makes access to the park's west side dependent on US 40 at Granby.

There are two entrance stations on the east side: **Fall River** (US 34) and **Beaver Meadows** (US 36). The **Grand Lake Entrance Station** (US 34) is the only entry on the west side. Year-round access is available through Kawuneeche Valley along the Colorado River headwaters to **Timber Creek Campground** (Trail Ridge Rd, US Hwy 34; tent & RV sites $26). The main centers of visitor activity on the park's east side are the Alpine Visitor Center (p91), high on Trail Ridge Rd, and Bear Lake Rd, which leads to campgrounds, trailheads and the Moraine Park Museum (p90).

North of Estes Park, Devils Gulch Rd leads to several hiking trails. Further out on Devils Gulch Rd, you pass through the village of Glen Haven to reach the trailhead entry to the park along the North Fork of the Big Thompson River.

Getting Around

The majority of visitors enter the park in their own cars, using the long and winding Trail Ridge Rd (US 34) to cross the Continental Divide. There are options for those without wheels, however. In summer a free shuttle bus operates from the **Estes Park Visitor Center** (970-577-9900; www.visitestespark.com; 500 Big Thompson Ave; 9am-8pm Jun-Aug, 8am-5pm Mon-Fri, 9am-5pm Sat, 10am-4pm Sun Sep-May) multiple times daily, bringing hikers to a park-and-ride location where you can pick up other shuttles. The year-round option leaves the Glacier Basin parking area and heads to Bear Lake, in the park's lower elevations. During the summer peak, a second shuttle operates between Moraine Park campground and the Glacier Basin parking area. The second shuttle runs on weekends only from mid-August through September.

Taking public transit or bikes is without a doubt the best way to get into the overcrowded park.

Estes Park

Estes Park is just seconds from one of the US's most popular national parks. The town itself is a hodgepodge of T-shirt shops and ice-cream parlors, sidewalks crowded with tourists and streets jammed with RVs. But when the sun reflects just right off Lake Estes, or you spend an afternoon with a lazy coffee on the riverwalk, you might just find a little piece of zen.

Activities

★**Colorado Mountain School** CLIMBING
(720-387-8944; https://coloradomountainschool.com; 341 Moraine Ave; half-day guided climbs per person from $300) Simply put, there's no better resource for climbers in Colorado – this outfit is the largest climbing operator in the region, has the most expert guides and is the only organization allowed to operate within Rocky Mountain National Park. It has a clutch of classes taught by world-class instructors.

Sleeping

Estes Park KOA CAMPGROUND $
(800-562-1887, 970-586-2888; www.estesparkkoa.com; 2051 Big Thompson Ave; tent sites $52-58, RV sites $52-85, cabins from $87;) With so

much excellent camping just up the road in Rocky Mountain National Park, it's hard to see the allure of this roadside RV-oriented camping spot. But for those in need of a staging day before a big adventure, the proximity to town is appealing.

★YMCA of the Rockies – Estes Park Center RESORT $$
(☎888-613-9622; www.ymcarockies.org; 2515 Tunnel Rd; r from $145, cabins from $160; P) Estes Park Center is not your typical YMCA boarding house. Instead it's a favorite vacation spot with families, boasting upmarket motel-style accommodations and cabins set on hundreds of acres of high alpine terrain. Choose from roomy cabins that sleep up to 10 or motel-style rooms for singles or doubles. Both are simple and practical.

Stanley Hotel HOTEL $$
(☎970-577-4000; www.stanleyhotel.com; 333 Wonderview Ave; r from $150; P) The white Georgian Colonial Revival hotel stands in brilliant contrast to the towering peaks of Rocky Mountain National Park that frame the skyline. A favorite local retreat, this best-in-class hotel served as the inspiration for Stephen King's cult novel *The Shining*. Rooms are decorated to retain some of the Old West feel while still ensuring all the creature comforts.

Black Canyon LODGE $$
(☎800-897-3730; www.blackcanyoninn.com; 800 MacGregor Ave; 1-/2-/3-bed r from $150/200/400; P) A fine place to splurge, this lovely, secluded 14-acre property offers luxury suites and a 'rustic' log cabin (which comes with a Jacuzzi). The rooms are dressed out with stone fireplaces, dark wood and woven tapestries in rich dark colors, just like you imagined.

Eating

Ed's Cantina & Grill MEXICAN $
(☎970-586-2919; www.edscantina.com; 390 E Elkhorn Ave; mains $9-12; ⊙11am-late Mon-Fri, 8am-10pm Sat & Sun;) With an outdoor patio right on the river, Ed's is a great place to kick back with a margarita. Serving Mexican and American staples, the restaurant is in a retro woodsy space with leather booth seating and bold primary colors.

Smokin' Dave's BBQ & Tap House BARBECUE $$
(☎866-674-2793; www.smokindavesbbq.com; 820 Moraine Ave; mains $8-20; ⊙11am-9pm Sun-Thu, to 10pm Fri & Sat;) Half-assed BBQ joints are all too common in Colorado's mountain towns, but Dave's fully delivers. The buffalo ribs and pulled pork come dressed in a slightly sweet, smoky, tangy sauce and the sweet-potato fries are crisply fried. Also excellent? The long, well-selected beer list. Check out its other location at the Golf Course.

Getting There & Away

The **Estes Park Shuttle** (☎970-586-5151; www.estesparkshuttle.com; one way/return $45/85) connects Denver's airport to Estes Park about four times a day. The trip takes two hours.

Steamboat Springs

Steamboat is Colorado magic. The area delivers big on adventures, family fun and some of the best champagne-powder skiing in the world, and yet the people here are delightfully direct and unassuming.

On the edge of Colorado's Western Slope, Steamboat got its roots a hundred years ago as a railway hub, and in the well-preserved Old Town area you'll have the chance to mix with real-life cowboys, dirt-bag ski bums and millionaires as you cruise past tony bistros and historic bars, and take summer walks along the Yampa River.

Activities

Steamboat Mountain Resort SNOW SPORTS
(☎ticket office 970-871-5252; www.steamboat.com; 2305 Mt Werner Circle; lift ticket adult/child $175/110; ⊙ticket office 8am-5pm) The stats of the Steamboat Ski Area speak volumes for the town's claim as 'Ski Town, USA' – 165 trails, 3668ft vertical and nearly 3000 acres. With excellent powder, super-fun tree runs and trails for all levels, this is the main draw for winter visitors and one of the best family skiing resorts in all of the US.

★Strawberry Park Hot Springs HOT SPRINGS
(☎970-879-0342; www.strawberryhotsprings.com; 44200 County Rd; per day adult/child $15/8; ⊙10am-10:30pm Sun-Thu, to midnight Fri & Sat;) Steamboat's favorite hot springs are actually outside the city limits. Offering great back-to-basics relaxation, the natural pools sit lovingly beside a river. After dark it is adults only and clothing optional (though most people wear swimsuits these days); you'll want a headlamp if you are visiting at this time. On weekends, expect a 15- to 45-minute wait to park.

Orange Peel Bikes CYCLING
(☎970-879-2957; www.orangepeelbikes.com; 1136 Yampa St; bike rental per day $45-75; ⏲10am-6pm Mon-Fri, to 5pm Sat; 👪) In a cone-shaped building at the end of Yampa (the building looks like a Martian outpost), this is perfectly situated for renting a bike to ride the trails crisscrossing Howelsen Hill. A staff of serious riders and mechanics can offer tons of information about local trails, including maps. This is the coolest bike shop in town, hands down.

Bucking Rainbow Outfitters RAFTING
(☎970-879-8747; www.buckingrainbow.com; 730 Lincoln Ave; inner tubes $20, rafting $50-100, fishing $150-500) This excellent outfitter has fly-fishing, rafting, outdoor apparel and the area's best fly shop, but it's most renowned for its rafting trips on the Yampa and beyond. Rafting trips run from half-day to full-day excursions. Two-hour in-town fly-fishing trips start at $155 per person. It has a tube shack that runs shuttles (included with rental) from Sunpies Bistro on Yampa St. It's a wonderful way to spend an afternoon.

Old Town Hot Springs HOT SPRINGS
(☎970-879-1828; www.oldtownhotsprings.org; 136 Lincoln Ave; adult/child $18/12, waterslide $2-7; ⏲5:30am-10pm Mon-Fri, 7am-9pm Sat, 8am-9pm Sun; 👪) Smack dab in the center of town, the water here is warmer than most other springs in the area. Known by the Utes as the 'medicine springs,' the mineral waters here are said to have special healing powers. Because there's a 230ft waterslide, a climbing wall and plenty of shallow areas, this is your best family-friendly hot springs in town.

Sleeping & Eating

★**Vista Verde Guest Ranch** RANCH $$$
(☎800-526-7433; www.vistaverde.com; 31100 Seedhouse Rd; per week per person summer/winter from $5125/3195; ❄📶) This is the most luxurious of Colorado's top-end guest ranches. Here you spend the day riding with expert staff, the evening around the fire in an elegantly appointed lodge, and the night in between high-thread-count sheets. If you have the means, this is it.

Rex's American Bar & Grill AMERICAN $
(☎970-870-0438; www.rexsgrill.com; 3190 S Lincoln Ave; mains $11-15; ⏲7am-11pm; P👪) Grass-fed steaks, elk sausage, bison burgers and other carnivorous delights are the ticket at this place, and they're so good that you'll have to forgive the restaurant's location – attached to the Holiday Inn. Rex's is also one of the most family-friendly spots in town and the latest dinner you'll find (serving until 11pm).

★**Laundry** AMERICAN $$
(☎970-870-0681; www.thelaundryrestaurant.com; 127 11th St; small plates $10-16, large plates $35-38; ⏲4:30pm-2am) This new-generation Steamboat eatery has some of the best food in town. You'll love creative takes on comfort food, charcuterie boards, big steaks, barbecue, creative presentations and pickled everything. Budget-busters will love sharing small plates – which all go a long way.

Information

Steamboat Springs Visitor Center (☎970-879-0880; www.steamboat-chamber.com; 125 Anglers Dr; ⏲8am-5pm Mon-Fri, 10am-3pm Sat) This visitor center, facing Sundance Plaza, has a wealth of local information. Its website is excellent for planning.

USFS Hahns Peak Ranger Office (☎970-879-1870; www.fs.usda.gov; 925 Weiss Dr; ⏲8am-5pm Mon-Sat) Rangers staff this office offering information about surrounding national forests, including Mount Zirkel Wilderness, plus hiking, mountain biking, fishing and other activities in the area. Permits are also available here.

Getting There & Away

Most people get into town by car from Denver via Rabbit Ears Pass on Hwy 40. Another options is **Yampa Valley Regional Airport** (YVRA; ☎970-276-5000; 11005 RCR 51A), with direct flights in winter from many US destinations. The airport is in Hayden, 22 miles west of Steamboat.

The **Go Alpine** (☎970-879-2800; www.goalpine.com; 1755 Lincoln Ave) taxi and shuttle service makes several daily runs between Steamboat and Denver International Airport (DIA; $93, four hours one way). It also makes trips to the Yampa Valley Regional Airport ($39 one way) and operates an in-town taxi.

Greyhound's US 40 service between Denver and Salt Lake City stops at the **Greyhound Terminal** (☎800-231-2222; www.greyhound.com; 1505 Lincoln Ave), about half a mile west of town. One-way tickets to Denver run from $35 to $43 (four hours).

The **Storm Mountain Express** (☎877-844-8787; www.stormmountainexpress.com) shuttle service runs to Yampa Valley Regional Airport ($39 one way) and beyond, though trips to DIA and Vail get very pricey.

Central Colorado

At the center of Colorado in the dizzying heights of the Rocky Mountains, you will find a million and one attractions. Much of the adventure centers in iconic ski resorts such as Aspen, Vail and Breckenridge. By summer, these are also great spots for hiking, mountain biking and other adventures into the vast alpine wilderness found here.

In the less-known areas around South Park and Leadville, you can still find world-class rafting, mountain climbing and vistas that go on for miles. There are alpine lakes to be visited, wildlife to be seen, backroads to mining ghost towns to be explored, steam trains to be ridden and much more.

It's also a place of fun-loving irreverence, wild parties and plenty of mountain-town high jinx. Part of the journey is connecting with the sun-kissed, broad-smiled locals.

Winter Park

Located less than two hours from Denver, unpretentious Winter Park Resort is a favorite with Front Rangers, who drive here to ski fresh tracks each weekend. Beginners can frolic on miles of heavily trafficked groomers while experts test their skills on Mary Jane's world-class bumps. For skiers with disabilities, the resort also offers one of the best adaptive skiing programs in the US.

The congenial oh-so-slightly '70s town is a wonderful base for year-round romping. Most services are found either in the ski village, which is actually south of Winter Park proper, or strung along US 40 (the main drag), which is where you'll also find the visitor center. Follow Hwy 40 and you'll get to Fraser – essentially the same town – then Tabernash and eventually the back of Rocky Mountain National Park.

Activities

In addition to downhill and cross-country skiing, Winter Park has some 600 miles of mountain-biking trails for all levels. The paved 5.5-mile **Fraser River Trail** runs through the valley from the ski resort to Fraser, connecting to different trail systems. Pick up trail maps at the **visitor center** (☎970-726-4118; www.winterpark-info.com; 78841 Hwy 40; ⏰9am-5pm). You can even bike in winter – it's known as fatbiking.

Sleeping & Eating

There are two first-come, first-served USFS campgrounds off Hwy 40 on the way into Winter Park: **Robber's Roost** (Hwy 40; tent & RV sites $20; ⏰mid-Jun–Aug; 🐾), which has no water, 5 miles from town, and **Idlewild** (Hwy 40; tent & RV sites $20; ⏰late May-Sep; 🐾), 1 mile from town. There's also plenty of free dispersed camping in the surrounding national forest; try heading up **Rollins Pass** (USFS Rd 149; ⏰mid-Jun–mid-Nov). In town, condos reign supreme, but there are also a few hotels and lodging worth checking out.

★ **Devil's Thumb Ranch** LODGE $$$

(☎970-726-7000; www.devilsthumbranch.com; 3530 County Rd 83; lodge from $350, cabins from $450; ❄📶🏊🐾) The classiest digs in the Winter Park area, this high-altitude ranch is a fantastic base for year-round **activities** (trail passes $10, horseback riding $85-175, zipline $55-110; 👪). Accommodations are plush, but not out of reach. The cowboy-chic lodge is a must for a romantic weekend escape. Cabins are a good bet for groups or for more privacy. Reserve well in advance.

★ **Pepe Osaka's Fish Taco** JAPANESE $

(☎970-726-7159; https://pepeosakasfishtaco.com; 78707 US Hwy 40; 2 tacos $13-15; ⏰4-9pm daily, plus noon-3pm Sat & Sun) You like sushi. You like fish tacos. And as it turns out, you love sushi tacos, because...why not? At this almost-but-not-quite Nikkei eatery (that's Japanese-Peruvian cuisine if you haven't been keeping up), dig in to some outstandingly spicy tuna tacos, *ahi poke* ceviche tacos and blackened mahi-mahi tacos *al pastor*. All served with delish fried plantains and margaritas.

Breckenridge & Around

Breckenridge is unique to Summit County in that the town wasn't built as a ski resort. Rather, it was built from the sweat and dreams of miners more than a hundred years ago. The quaint historic center now houses T-shirt shops, high-end restaurants and converted Victorian inns.

Sights & Activities

★ **Barney Ford Museum** MUSEUM

(www.breckheritage.com; 111 E Washington Ave; suggested donation $5; ⏰11am-3pm Tue-Sun, hours vary seasonally) FREE Barney Ford was an escaped slave who became a prominent entrepreneur and Colorado civil-rights pioneer, and made two stops in Breckenridge (where he ran a 24-hour chop stand serving delicacies such as oysters) over the course of his incredibly rich, tragic and triumphant life. He also owned a restaurant and hotel in Denver. The museum is set in his old home, where he lived from 1882 to 1890.

Breckenridge Ski Area SNOW SPORTS
(800-789-7669; www.breckenridge.com; lift ticket adult/child $189/123; 8:30am-4pm Nov–mid-Apr;) Breckenridge spans five mountains (Peaks 6 to 10), covering 2900 acres and featuring some of the best beginner and intermediate terrain in the state, as well as plenty of exhilarating high-alpine runs and hike-to bowls. There are also four terrain parks and a superpipe.

Sleeping

Bivvi Hostel HOSTEL $
(970-423-6553; www.thebivvi.com; 9511 Hwy 9; dm winter/summer from $85/29;) A modern hostel with a log-cabin vibe, the Bivvi wins points for style, friendliness and affordability. The four- to six-person dorm rooms come with private lockers, en suites and complimentary breakfast; chill out in the funky common room or out on the gorgeous deck, equipped with a gas grill and hot tub. Private rooms are also available.

Eating & Drinking

★**Breckenridge Distillery** AMERICAN $$
(970-547-9759; www.breckenridgedistillery.com; 1925 Airport Rd; small plates $10-18; 4-9pm Tue-Sat) Served in a big-city-cool dining space, the eclectic menu at this **distillery** (970-547-9759; www.breckenridgedistillery.com; 1925 Airport Rd; 11am-9pm Tue-Sat, to 6pm Sun & Mon) follows the delightful whims of its high-caliber chefs, jumping from the sublime *cacio e pepe* (Roman spaghetti and cheese) to chicken-liver profiteroles or dates and mascarpone without missing a beat. It's mostly small plates, perfect for sharing over the top-notch cocktails.

Crown CAFE
(970-453-6022; www.thecrownbreckenridge.com; 215 S Main St; 7:30am-8pm;) Breck's living room might as well be at the Crown, a buzzing cafe and social hub. Grab a mug of Silver Canyon coffee and a sandwich or salad, and catch up on all the latest town gossip.

CLIMBING YOUR FIRST FOURTEENER

Known as Colorado's easiest fourteener, **Quandary Peak** (www.14ers.com; County Rd 851) is the state's 15th-highest peak at 14,265ft. Though you'll see plenty of dogs and children, 'easiest' may be misleading – the summit remains 3 grueling miles from the trailhead. Go between June and September.

Broken Compass Brewing BREWERY
(970-368-2772; www.brokencompassbrewing.com; 68 Continental Ct; 11:30am-11pm) Set in an industrial complex at the north end of Airport Road, the Broken Compass is generally regarded as the best brewery in Breckenridge. Fill up with a pint of their Coconut Porter or Chili Pepper Pale and sink back with a couple of friends in the old chairlift. They run a shuttle every two hours between the brewery and town.

Information

Visitor Center (877-864-0868; www.gobreck.com; 203 S Main St; 9am-6pm;) Along with a host of maps and brochures, this center has a pleasant riverside museum that delves into Breck's gold-mining past.

Getting There & Away

Breckenridge is 80 miles west of Denver via I-70 exit 203, then Hwy 9 south.

Vail

Tucked beneath the Gore Range on I-70, Vail offers up just about everything you could ever ask for from a mountain resort. The village areas at the ski area base have cobblestone walkways and are designed to look and feel like a Tyrloean mountain town. The town has some of Colorado's best restaurants – and a gorgeous crowd of well-heeled spenders that light up the night when slopes close.

Sights & Activities

The draw to Vail is no secret. It's the endless outdoor activities in both winter and summer that make this resort so attractive. Remember, though, that the mud season (mid-April through May, plus November) holds little attraction for visitors – you can't ski, nor can you really get up into the mountains to hike around.

★Vail Mountain SNOW SPORTS
(☎970-754-8245; www.vail.com; lift ticket adult/child $189/130; ⏲9am-4pm Nov–mid-Apr; 👪) Vail Mountain is hands-down one of the best ski resorts in the world, with 5289 skiable acres, 195 trails, three terrain parks and, ahem, the highest lift-ticket prices on the continent. If you're a Colorado ski virgin, it's worth experiencing your first time here – especially on a bluebird fresh-powder day. Skiing more than three days? Consider the Epic Pass.

Vail to Breckenridge Bike Path CYCLING
(www.summitbiking.org) This paved, car-free bike path stretches 8.7 miles from East Vail to the top of Vail Pass (elevation gain 1831ft), before descending 14 miles into Frisco (it's 9 miles more if you go all the way to Breckenridge). If you're only interested in the downhill, hop on a shuttle from **Bike Valet** (☎970-476-7770; www.bikevalet.net; 616 W Lionshead Cir; bike rental per day from $51; ⏲9am-6pm; 👪) and enjoy the ride back to Vail.

Sleeping

Gore Creek Campground CAMPGROUND $
(☎877-444-6777; www.recreation.gov; Bighorn Rd; tent sites $22-24; ⏲mid-May–Sep; 🐾) This campground at the end of Bighorn Rd has 19 tent sites with picnic tables and fire grates nestled in the woods by Gore Creek. There is excellent fishing near here – try the Slate Creek or Deluge Lake trails; the latter leads to a fish-packed lake. The campground is 6 miles east of Vail Village via exit 180 (East Vail) off I-70.

★Sebastian Hotel HOTEL $$$
(☎800-354-6908; www.thesebastianvail.com; 16 Vail Rd; r winter/summer from $800/300; P ❄ 📶 🏊 🐾) Deluxe and modern, this sophisticated hotel showcases tasteful contemporary art and an impressive list of amenities, including a mountainside ski valet, luxury spa and 'adventure concierge.' Room rates dip in the summer, the perfect time to enjoy the tapas bar and spectacular pool area, with hot tubs frothing and spilling over like champagne.

Austria Haus HOTEL $$$
(☎866-921-4050; www.austriahaushotel.com; 242 E Meadow Dr; r winter/summer from $500/290; P ❄ 📶 🏊) One of Vail's longest-running properties, the Austria Haus offers both hotel rooms and condos (more information at www.austriahausclub.com), so make sure you're clear on what you're signing up for. In the hotel, charming details such as wood-framed doorways, Berber carpet and marble baths make for a pleasant stay. Fuel up at the generous breakfast spread in the morning.

Eating & Drinking

★Westside Cafe DINER $
(☎970-476-7890; www.westsidecafe.net; 2211 N Frontage Rd; mains $9-16; ⏲7am-3pm Mon-Wed, to 10pm Thu-Sun; 📶👪) Set in a West Vail strip mall, the Westside is a local institution. It does terrific all-day-breakfast skillets – like the 'My Big Fat Greek Skillet' with scrambled eggs, gyro, red onion, tomato and feta served with warm pita – along with all the usual high-cal offerings you need before or after a day on the slopes.

★Game Creek Restaurant AMERICAN $$$
(☎970-754-4275; www.gamecreekvail.com; Game Creek Bowl; 4-/5-course meal $115/135; ⏲5:30-9pm Tue-Sat Dec-Apr, 5:30-8:30pm Thu-Sat, 11am-2pm Sun late Jun-Aug; 🍷👪) This gourmet destination is nestled high in the spectacular Game Creek Bowl. Take the Eagle Bahn Gondola to Eagle's Nest and staff will shuttle you (via snowcat in winter) to their lodge-style restaurant, which serves an American-French menu starring wild boar, elk tenderloin and succulent leg of lamb. Reserve ahead.

Sweet Basil AMERICAN $$$
(☎970-476-0125; www.sweetbasilvail.com; 193 Gore Creek Dr; mains lunch $18-22, dinner $27-48; ⏲11:30am-2:30pm & 6pm-late) 🌿 In business since 1977, Sweet Basil remains one of Vail's top restaurants. The menu changes seasonally, but the eclectic American fare, which usually includes favorites such as Colorado lamb and seared Rocky Mountain trout, is consistently innovative and excellent. The ambience is also fantastic. Reservations are required – especially in high season.

Information

Vail Visitor Center (☎970-477-3522; www.vailgov.com; 241 S Frontage Rd; ⏲8:30am-5:30pm winter, to 8pm summer; 📶) Provides maps, last-minute lodging deals and information on the town and activities. It's located next to the Transportation Center. The larger Lionshead welcome center is located at the entrance to the parking garage.

Getting There & Around

The **Eagle County Regional Airport** (EGE; ☎970-328-2680; www.flyvail.com; 217 Eldon Wilson Dr, Gypsum) is 35 miles west of Vail and has services to destinations across the country (many of which fly through Denver) and rental-car counters.

Aspen

Live the dream. Aspen is one of the world's most famous mountain destinations.

The town's four ski slopes offer up some of Colorado's best champagne powder turns, and there are excellent restaurants at nearly every corner of the historic downtown area. Top it off with an understated chic that permeates nearly everything you do, eat, see and experience here, and you have the makings of the best mountain vacation ever.

Aspen takes on new shades and personalities with the seasons. In fall, the hills are set afire with the quaking of a million golden Aspen leaves; in winter, the slopes come to life and the party hits maximum velocity; come springtime, the flowers start to bud near the mirrored alpine lakes; and finally, in summer – ah, summer in Aspen! – everything unites with music festivals, arts, miles upon miles of trails to explore and perfect days under the bluebird Colorado sky.

Sights & Activities

Aspen Art Museum MUSEUM

(☎970-925-8050; www.aspenartmuseum.org; 637 E Hyman Ave; ⏰10am-6pm Tue-Sun) FREE This art museum's striking building features a warm, lattice-like exterior designed by Pritzker Prize–winner Shigeru Ban and contains three floors of gallery space. There's no permanent collection, just edgy, innovative contemporary exhibitions featuring paintings, mixed media, sculpture, video installations and photography by artists such as Mamma Andersson, Mark Manders and Susan Philipsz. Art lovers will not leave disappointed. Head up to the roof for views and a bite to eat at the cool cafe.

★ **Aspen Center for Environmental Studies** OUTDOORS

(ACES; ☎970-925-5756; www.aspennature.org; 100 Puppy Smith St, Hallam Lake; ⏰9am-5pm Mon-Fri; 👪) The Aspen Center for Environmental Studies manages the 25-acre Hallam Lake wildlife sanctuary that hugs the Roaring Fork River and miles of hiking trails in the Hunter Creek Valley. With a mission to advance environmental conservation, the center's naturalists provide free guided hikes and snowshoe tours, raptor demonstrations (eagles and owls are among the residents) and special programs for youngsters.

★ **Snowmass Ski Resort** SNOW SPORTS

(☎800-525-6200; www.aspensnowmass.com; 4-mountain lift ticket adult/child $174-116; ⏰9am-4pm Dec–mid-Apr; 👪) OK, the top winter activity here is pretty much a given: the pursuit of powder, and lots of it. Snowmass is undoubtedly built for families. There's some pretty steep terrain here if you want to get rad, but the overall draw is plenty of options for beginners, intermediates and advanced skiers. The Snowmass Village area has restaurants and hotels.

Maroon Bells HIKING

If you have but one day to enjoy a slice of pristine wilderness, spend it in the shadow of Colorado's most iconic mountains: the pyramid-shaped twins of **North Maroon Peak** (14,014ft) and **South Maroon Peak** (14,156ft). Eleven miles southwest of Aspen, it all starts on the shores of **Maroon Lake**, an absolutely stunning spot backed by the towering, striated summits.

Sleeping

★ **Difficult Campground** CAMPGROUND $

(☎877-444-6777; www.recreation.gov; Hwy 82; tent & RV sites $24-26; ⏰mid-May–Sep; 🐾) The largest campground in the Aspen area, Difficult is one of four sites at the foot of Independence Pass and the only one that takes reservations. Located 5 miles west of town, it also has the lowest altitude (8000ft). Higher up are three smaller campgrounds: Weller, Lincoln Gulch and Lost Man. Water is available, but no electrical hookups for RVs.

Annabelle Inn HOTEL $$

(☎877-266-2466; www.annabelleinn.com; 232 W Main St; r winter/summer from $250/200; P❄@📶) Personable and unpretentious, the cute and quirky Annabelle Inn resembles an old-school European-style ski lodge in a central location. Rooms are cozy without being too cute, and come with flat-screen TVs and warm duvets. After a long day of skiing or hiking, the hot tub and firepit await. The breakfast is fantastic.

Limelight Hotel HOTEL $$$

(☎855-925-3025; www.limelighthotel.com; 355 S Monarch St; r winter/summer from $500/250; P❄📶🏊🐾) Sleek and trendy, the Limelight's brick-and-glass modernism reflects Aspen's new school. Rooms are spacious, with stylish accoutrements: granite washbasins, leather headboards and mountain views from the balconies and rooftop terraces. Additional perks include shuttles that run to all the slopes and a fab breakfast. This is life on top! A sister Limelight is found in Snowmass (p97) near the Gondola.

Eating & Drinking

★Pyramid Bistro CAFE **$$**

(☎970-925-5338; www.pyramidbistro.com; 221 E Main St; mains lunch $12-18, dinner $19-29; ⏱11:30am-9:30pm;) Set on the top floor of **Explore Booksellers** (☎970-925-5336; www.explorebooksellers.com; 221 E Main St; ⏱10am-9pm;), this gourmet veggie cafe serves up some delightful creations, including sweet-potato gnocchi with goat's cheese, red-lentil sliders and quinoa salad with avocado, goji berries and sesame vinaigrette. Definitely Aspen's top choice for health-conscious fare.

Matsuhisa JAPANESE **$$$**

(☎970-544-6628; www.matsuhisarestaurants.com; 303 E Main St; mains $29-42, 2 pieces sushi $8-12; ⏱5:30pm-close) The original Colorado link in Matsuhisa Nobu's iconic global chain that now wraps around the world, this converted house is more intimate than its Vail sibling and still turns out spectacular dishes such as miso black cod, Chilean sea bass with truffle and flavorful uni (sea urchin) shooters.

Aspen Brewing Co BREWERY

(☎970-920-2739; www.aspenbrewingcompany.com; 304 E Hopkins Ave; ⏱noon-late;) With five signature flavors and a sun-soaked balcony facing the mountain, this is definitely the place to unwind after a hard day's play. Brews range from the flavorful This Year's Blonde and high-altitude Independence Pass Ale (its IPA) to the mellower Conundrum Red Ale and the chocolatey Pyramid Peak Porter.

Woody Creek Tavern PUB

(☎970-923-4585; www.woodycreektavern.com; 2 Woody Creek Plaza, 2858 Upper River Rd; ⏱11am-10pm) Enjoying a 100% agave tequila and fresh-lime margarita at the late, great gonzo journalist Hunter S Thompson's favorite watering hole is well worth the 8-mile drive – or **Rio Grande Trail** (www.riograndetrail.com; Puppy Smith St) bike ride – from Aspen. The walls at this rustic funky tavern, a local haunt since 1980, are plastered with newspaper clippings, photos of customers and paraphernalia.

Information

Aspen-Sopris Ranger District (☎970-925-3445; www.fs.usda.gov/whiteriver; 806 W Hallam St; ⏱8am-4:30pm Mon-Fri) The USFS Aspen-Sopris Ranger District operates around 20 campgrounds and covers Roaring Fork Valley and from Independence Pass to Glenwood Springs, including the Maroon Bells Wilderness. Come here for maps and hiking tips.

Aspen Visitor Center (☎970-925-1940; www.aspenchamber.org; 425 Rio Grande Pl; ⏱8:30am-5pm Mon-Fri) Located across from Rio Grande Park, this little visitor center can help you pick a hike, a restaurant or a far-out adventure.

Cooper Street Kiosk (cnr E Cooper Ave & S Galena St; ⏱10am-6pm) Maps, brochures and magazines.

Getting There & Around

Four miles northwest of Aspen on Hwy 82, the busy **Aspen-Pitkin County Airport** (ASE; ☎970-920-5380; www.aspenairport.com; 233 E Airport Rd;) has direct year-round flights from Denver, as well as seasonal flights direct to eight US cities, including Los Angeles and Chicago. Several car-rental agencies operate here. A free bus runs to/from the airport, departing every 10 to 15 minutes.

Roaring Fork Transportation Authority (RFTA; ☎970-925-8484; www.rfta.com; 430 E Durant Ave; ⏱6:15am-2:15am;) buses connect Aspen with the Highlands, Snowmass and Buttermilk via free shuttles, while the VelociRFTA serves the down-valley towns of Basalt ($4, 25 minutes), Carbondale ($6, 45 minutes) and Glenwood Springs ($7, one hour).

Salida

Under Colorado's sun, life just seems a little better here. You really can't beat the good-time mountain vibes, chart-topping wilderness access and historic charms of Salida. The sprawling, immaculately preserved historic downtown center has top-notch antiques and crafts shopping.

This is also raft-country USA. With the Arkansas running straight through town, you can access everything from class II family runs to big-time class V waters. Salida sits in a valley below a massive mountain range, meaning there is also excellent hiking, mountain biking and skiing to be had. It's really up to you. Adventure awaits on every corner.

When the sun sets, come back to town to cozy up at one of the many microbrews and hatch your plans for the next day's adventure. Most people come here in the summers.

Activities

Both bikers and hikers should note that some big-time trails – the **Continental Divide** (www.continentaldividetrail.org), the **Colorado Trail** (www.coloradotrail.org) and the **Rainbow Trail** – are within spitting distance of town. If you don't want to sweat it, a **gondola** (719-539-4091; www.monarchcrest.net; adult/child $10/5; 8:30am-5:30pm mid-May–mid-Sep) can haul you from Monarch Pass nearly 1000ft up to the top of the ridge. **Monarch ski area** (719-530-5000; www.skimonarch.com; 23715 Hwy 50; adult/child $84/40; Dec–mid-Apr) also has some surprisingly excellent terrain and affordable prices. The biggest draw around is of course the wicked rafting runs on the Arkansas (p100). You can do family-friendly floats, go fishing, or take on bigger challenges on runs such as Numbers, the Royal Gorge and Brown's Canyon from here.

★ Absolute Bikes CYCLING
(719-539-9295; www.absolutebikes.com; 330 W Sackett Ave; bike rental per day $25-105, tours from $175; 9am-6pm) The go-to place for bike enthusiasts, offering maps, gear, advice, rentals (cruisers and mountain bikes) and, most importantly, shuttles to the trailhead. Check out the great selection of guided rides, ranging from St Elmo ghost town to the Monarch Crest.

★ Monarch Crest Trail MOUNTAIN BIKING
One of the most famous rides in all of Colorado, the Monarch Crest is an extreme 20- to 35-mile adventure. It starts off at Monarch Pass (11,312ft), follows the exposed ridge 12 miles to Marshall Pass and then either cuts down to Poncha Springs on an old railroad grade or hooks onto the Rainbow Trail. A classic ride with fabulous high-altitude views.

Sleeping

Salida has a good hostel and hotel in town, along with a smattering of generic motels on the outskirts. The **Arkansas Headwaters Recreation Area** (719-539-7289; http://cpw.state.co.us; 307 W Sackett Ave; 8am-5pm, closed noon-1pm Sat & Sun) operates six campgrounds (bring your own water) along the river, including **Hecla Junction** (719-539-7289; http://coloradostateparks.reserveamerica.com; Hwy 285, Mile 135; tent & RV sites $18, plus daily pass $7). Another top campground is **Monarch Park** (877-444-6777; www.recreation.gov; off Hwy 50; tent & RV sites $18; Jun-Sep), up by the pass, near the hiking and biking along the Monarch Crest and Rainbow Trails.

★ Simple Lodge & Hostel HOSTEL $
(719-650-7381; www.simplelodge.com; 224 E 1st St; dm/d/q $24/65/84) If only Colorado had more spots like this. Run by the super-friendly Mel and Justin, this hostel is simple but stylish, with a fully stocked kitchen and a comfy communal area that feels just like home. It's a popular stopover for touring cyclists following the coast-to-coast Rte 50 – you're likely to meet some interesting folks here.

Eating

The Fritz TAPAS $
(719-539-0364; https://thefritzsalida.com; 113 E Sackett St; tapas $6-10, mains $11-16; 11am-9pm) This fun riverside watering hole serves up clever American-style tapas: think three-cheese mac with bacon, fries and truffle aioli, seared ahi wontons, and brie ciabatta with date jam. It also does a mean grass-fed-beef burger and other salads and sandwiches. Good selection of local beers on tap.

★ Amícas PIZZA $$
(719-539-5219; www.amicassalida.com; 127 F St; pizzas & paninis $6.90-13; 11am-9pm Mon-Wed, 7am-9pm Thu-Sun) Thin-crust wood-fired pizzas, panini, housemade lasagna and microbrews on tap? Amícas can do no wrong. This high-ceilinged, laid-back hangout is the perfect spot to replenish all those calories you burned off during the day. Savor a Michelangelo (pesto, sausage and goat cheese) or Vesuvio (artichoke hearts, sun-dried tomatoes, roasted peppers) alongside a cool glass of Headwaters IPA.

Information

Salida Chamber of Commerce (719-539-2068; www.nowthisiscolorado.com; 406 W Rainbow Blvd; 9am-5pm Mon-Fri) General tourist info.

USFS Ranger Office (719-539-3591; www.fs.usda.gov; 5575 Cleora Rd; 8am-4:30pm Mon-Fri) Located east of town off Hwy 50, with camping and trail info for the Sawatch and northern Sangre de Cristo Ranges.

WORTH A TRIP

RAFTING THE ARKANSAS RIVER

Running from Leadville down the eastern flank of Buena Vista, through Browns Canyon National Monument, and then rocketing through the spectacular Royal Gorge at class V speeds, the Arkansas River is the most diverse, the longest and arguably the wildest river in the state. Brace yourself for yet another icy splash as you plunge into a roaring set of big waves, or surrender to the power of the current as your hoot-hollering, thoroughly drenched crew unintentionally spins backwards around a monster boulder. Is this fun? You bet!

Getting There & Away

Located at the 'exit' of the Arkansas River Valley, Salida occupies a prime location at the crossroads of Hwys 285 and 50. Indeed, this used to be a railroad hub, and you'll likely spot an abandoned line or two while exploring the area. Gunnison, Colorado Springs, the Great Sand Dunes and Summit County are all within one to two hours' drive, provided you have your own car.

Colorado Springs

Colorado Springs is an interesting beast. The town has grown by leaps and bounds in recent years, but still retains some of its small-town charms. It's absolutely gorgeous, with Pikes Peak hanging over the city, the vertical sandstone towers of the Garden of the Gods, and cute little neighborhoods that make it feel like a cozy mountain town. It's also home to a big military presence and ultra-right-wing evangelicals. Beyond the politics, taking a day or two to explore everything the town and its environs have to offer should make it onto any Colorado Top Five list.

On the West Side of town, you'll find cute shops and bistros in Manitou Springs and Old Colorado City. As you head into the foothills, there is amazing hiking, mountain biking, outdoor adventures, cliff dwellings, cave tours, and a trip by car to the top of Pikes Peak.

Sights & Activities

★Pikes Peak MOUNTAIN
(☎719-385-7325; www.springsgov.com; highway per adult/child $15/5; ⊙7:30am-8pm Jun-Aug, to 5pm Sep, 9am-3pm Oct-May; P) Pikes Peak (14,110ft) may not be the tallest of Colorado's 54 fourteeners, but it's certainly the most famous. The Ute originally called it the Mountain of the Sun, an apt description for this majestic peak, which crowns the southern Front Range. Rising 7400ft straight up from the plains, more than half a million visitors climb it every year.

★Garden of the Gods PARK
(www.gardenofgods.com; 1805 N 30th St; ⊙5am-9pm; P) FREE This gorgeous vein of red sandstone (about 290 million years old) appears elsewhere along Colorado's Front Range, but the exquisitely thin cathedral spires and mountain backdrop of the Garden of the Gods are particularly striking. Explore the network of paved and unpaved trails, enjoy a picnic and watch climbers test their nerve on the sometimes flaky rock.

Sleeping

Mining Exchange HOTEL $$
(☎719-323-2000; www.wyndhamhotels.com; 8 S Nevada Ave; r from $225; P❄📶) Opened in 2012 and set in the former turn-of-the-century bank where Cripple Creek prospectors traded in their gold for cash (check out the vault door in the lobby), the Mining Exchange takes the prize for Colorado Springs' most stylish hotel. Twelve-foot-high ceilings, exposed brick walls and leather furnishings make for an inviting, contemporary feel.

★Broadmoor RESORT $$$
(☎866-620-7083; www.broadmoor.com; 1 Lake Ave; r from $335; P❄📶🏊🐾) One of the top five-star resorts in the US, the 784-room Broadmoor sits in a picture-perfect location against the blue-green slopes of Cheyenne Mountain. Everything here is exquisite: acres of lush grounds and a lake, a glimmering pool, world-class golf, myriad bars and restaurants, an incredible spa and ubercomfortable guest rooms. Check out the wilderness camps for closer proximity to nature.

★Garden of the Gods Resort RESORT $$$
(☎719-632-5541; www.gardenofthegodsclub.com; 3320 Mesa Rd; d/ste from $380/465; P❄📶🏊) The best views in town are had from this elegant resort that overlooks Garden of the Gods. Elegantly appointed with just the hint of southwest touches, the assortment of rooms, suites, cottages and casitas all have

easy access to the infinity pool and spa area. Stay and play deals are available for golfers.

Eating & Drinking

Shuga's CAFE $

(719-328-1412; www.facebook.com/shugasbar; 702 S Cascade Ave; dishes $8-9; 11am-midnight;) If you thought Colorado Springs couldn't be hip, stroll to Shuga's, a Southern-style cafe with a knack for knockout espresso drinks and hot cocktails. Cuter than a button, this little white house is decked out in paper cranes and red vinyl chairs; there's also patio seating. The food – Brie BLT on rosemary toast, Brazilian coconut shrimp soup – comforts and delights.

★**Uchenna** ETHIOPIAN $$

(719-634-5070; www.uchennaalive.com; 2501 W Colorado Ave, Suite 105; mains $12-22; noon-2pm & 5-8pm Tue-Sun;) Chef Maya learned her recipes from her mother before she moved to America, and you'll love the homey cooking and family-friendly vibe at this authentic Ethiopian restaurant. Go for well-spiced meat or veg options and mop everything up with the spongy *injera*.

★**Marigold** FRENCH $$

(719-599-4776; www.marigoldcafeandbakery.com; 4605 Centennial Blvd; mains lunch $8-13, dinner $11-24; bistro 11am-2:30pm & 5-9pm, bakery 8am-9pm Mon-Sat) Way out by the Garden of the Gods is this buzzy French bistro and bakery that's easy on both the palate and the wallet. Feast on delicacies such as snapper Marseillaise, garlic-and-rosemary rotisserie chicken, and gourmet salads and pizzas, but be sure to leave room for the double (and triple!) chocolate mousse cake or the lemon tarts.

Getting There & Away

A smart alternative to flying into Denver, **Colorado Springs Airport** (COS; 719-550-1900; www.flycos.com; 7770 Milton E Proby Pkwy;) is served principally by United and Delta, with flights to a number of major cities around the country. There is no public transportation into town, however, so you'll have to rent a car or take a cab.

Greyhound (800-231-2222; www.greyhound.com) buses ply the route between Colorado Springs and Denver (from $13, 1½ hours, up to six daily), departing from the **Colorado Springs Downtown Transit Terminal** (719-385-7433; 127 E Kiowa St; 8am-5pm Mon-Fri). Here you can find schedule information and route maps for all local buses.

Southern Colorado

Home to the dramatic San Juan and Sangre de Cristo mountain ranges, Colorado's bottom half is just as pretty as its top.

Crested Butte

Crested Butte is quite simply one of the best mountain towns in the whole world. There's an amazing ski area here, punctuated by some of the steepest lines in Colorado.

This was one of the birthplaces of mountain biking, and you can ride or hike for hundreds of miles on the wondrous trails found in the wilderness areas surrounding town. And the scenery is off-the-charts gorgeous, with Aspen-choked hillsides, scenic alpine lakes, towering snowcapped peaks and more.

Sights & Activities

★**Crested Butte Center for the Arts** ARTS CENTER

(970-349-7487; www.crestedbuttearts.org; 606 6th St; admission varies; 10am-6pm;) The arts center hosts shifting exhibitions of local artists and a stellar schedule of live music and performance pieces. There's always something lively and interesting happening here. The classes, workshops and lecture series are especially interesting.

★**Crested Butte Mountain Resort** SKIING

(970-349-2222; www.skicb.com; 12 Snowmass Rd; lift ticket adult/child $125/70;) One of Colorado's best, Crested Butte is known for its extreme lines, deep powder, ripping locals and down-home ski-town fun. This is one of America's last great ski areas, a place where skiing still stands for the renegade spirit, where locals occasionally take runs naked, and where freedom, irreverence and the simple joys of fresh powder on a bluebird day still stand true.

Alpineer MOUNTAIN BIKING

(970-349-5210; www.alpineer.com; 419 6th St; bike rental per day $29-75) This great local shop serves the mountain-biking mecca with maps, information and rentals, plus an excellent selection of men's and women's clothing. Skis and hiking and camping equipment can be rented here. Top tip: go ahead and splurge on a full-suspension bike (it feels like riding on a cloud).

Sleeping

Inn at Crested Butte BOUTIQUE HOTEL $$
(970-349-2111, toll-free 877-343-211; www.innatcrestedbutte.com; 510 Whiterock Ave; d $110-250;) This refurbished boutique hotel offers intimate lodgings in stylish and luxurious surrounds. With just a handful of rooms, some opening onto a balcony with views over Mt Crested Butte, and all decked out with antiques, flat-screen TVs, coffee makers and minibars, this is one of Crested Butte's nicest vacation addresses.

★ **Ruby of Crested Butte** B&B $$$
(800-390-1338; www.therubyofcrestedbutte.com; 624 Gothic Ave; d $300-350, ste from $400;) Thoughtfully outfitted, down to the bowls of jellybeans and nuts in the stylish communal lounge. Rooms are brilliant, with heated floors, flat-screen TVs with DVD players and DVD selections, iPod docks and deluxe linens. There's also a Jacuzzi, library, ski-gear drying room and use of retro townie bikes. Hosts help with dinner reservations and other services.

Eating & Drinking

★ **Secret Stash** PIZZA $$
(970-349-6245; www.secretstash.com; 303 Elk Ave; mains $12-18; 8am-late;) With phenomenal food, the funky-casual Stash is adored by locals, who also dig the original cocktails. The sprawling space was once a general store but is now outfitted with teahouse seating and tapestries. The house specialty is pizza; its Notorious Fig (with prosciutto, fresh figs and truffle oil) won the World Pizza Championship. Start with the salt-and-pepper fries.

Soupçon FRENCH $$$
(970-349-5448; www.soupconcb.com; 127 Elk Ave; mains $39-47; 6-10:30pm) Specializing in seduction, this petite French bistro occupies a characterful old mining cabin with just a few tables. The chefs keep it fresh with changing menus of local meat and organic produce. Reserve ahead.

★ **Montanya** BAR
(www.montanyarum.com; 212 Elk Ave; snacks $3-12; 11am-9pm;) The Montanya distillery receives wide acclaim for its high-quality rums. Its basiltini, made with basil-infused rum, fresh grapefruit and lime, will have you levitating. There are also tours, free tastings and worthy mocktails. The street-food inspired menu is pretty good as well. Expect this place to be packed and occasional live music. In the afternoon, it's a good family spot.

Information

Crested Butte Visitor Center (970-349-6438; www.crestedbuttechamber.com; 601 Elk Ave; 9am-5pm) Just past the entrance to town on the main road. Stocks loads of brochures and maps.

Getting There & Away

Crested Butte is about four hours' drive from Denver, and about 3½ hours from Colorado Springs. Head for Gunnison on US 50 and from there head north for about 30 minutes to Crested Butte on Hwy 135. In winter, there are regular flights to **Gunnison Airport** (GUC; 970-641-2304; www.gunnisoncounty.org/airport; 519 Rio Grande Ave).

Ouray

With gorgeous icefalls draping the box canyon and soothing hot springs dotting the valley floor, Ouray (you-ray) is privileged even for Colorado. For ice climbers it's a world-class destination, but hikers and 4WD fans can also appreciate its rugged and sometimes stunning charms. The town is a well-preserved quarter-mile mining village sandwiched between imposing peaks. The sun rarely shines here, and there is a bit of a Twin Peaks air about town.

Activities

★ **Million Dollar Highway** SCENIC DRIVE
The whole of US Hwy 550 has been called the Million Dollar Hwy, but more properly it's the amazing stretch south of Ouray through the Uncompahgre Gorge up to Red Mountain Pass at 11,018ft. The alpine scenery is truly awesome and driving south towards Silverton positions drivers on the outside edge of the skinny, winding road, a heartbeat away from free-fall.

Ouray Hot Springs HOT SPRINGS
(970-325-7073; www.ourayhotsprings.com; 1200 Main St; adult/child $18/12; 10am-10pm Jun-Aug, noon-9pm Mon-Fri, 11am-9pm Sat & Sun Sep-May;) For a healing soak or kiddish fun, try the historic Ouray Hot Springs. The natural spring water is crystal-clear and free of the sulfur smells plaguing other hot springs. There's a lap pool, waterslides, a climbing wall overhanging a splash pool and prime soaking areas (100°F to 106°F; 37.7°C to 41.1°C). The complex also offers a gym and massage service.

Ouray Ice Park CLIMBING
(☎970-325-4061; www.ourayicepark.com; County Rd 361; membership $40-150; ⏱7am-5pm mid-Dec–Mar; 👪) Enthusiasts from around the globe come to ice climb at the world's first public ice park, spanning a 2-mile stretch of the Uncompahgre Gorge. The sublime (if chilly) experience offers something for all skill levels. Get instruction through a local guide service.

Festivals & Events

Ouray Ice Festival CULTURAL
(☎970-325-4288; www.ourayicefestival.com; donation for evening events; ⏱Jan; 👪) The Ouray Ice Festival features four days of climbing competitions, dinners, slide shows and clinics. There's even a climbing wall set up for kids. You can watch the competitions for free, but various evening events require a donation to the ice park. Once inside, you'll get free brews from popular Colorado microbrewer New Belgium.

Sleeping & Eating

Amphitheater Forest Service Campground CAMPGROUND $
(☎877-444-6777; www.recreation.gov; US Hwy 550; tent sites $24; ⏱Jun-Aug) With great tent sites under the trees, this high-altitude campground is a score. Some of the gorgeous trees here are falling down, however, and the Forest Service has closed some of the campsites. On holiday weekends a three-night minimum applies. South of town on Hwy 550, take a signposted left-hand turn.

★**Wiesbaden** HOTEL $$
(☎970-325-4347; www.wiesbadenhotsprings.com; 625 5th St; r $133-350;) Quirky, quaint and new age, Wiesbaden even boasts a natural indoor vapor cave, which, in another era, was frequented by Chief Ouray. Rooms with quilted bedcovers are cozy and romantic, but the sunlit suite with a natural rock wall tops all. In the morning, guests roam in thick robes, drinking the free organic coffee or tea, post-soak or awaiting massages.

Box Canyon Lodge & Hot Springs LODGE $$
(☎970-325-4981, 800-327-5080; www.boxcanyonouray.com; 45 3rd Ave; r from $200;) It's not every hotel that offers geothermal heating, not to mention pineboard rooms that are spacious and fresh, and spring-fed barrel hot tubs – perfect for a romantic stargazing soak. With good hospitality that includes free apples and bottled water, it's popular, so book ahead.

Bon Ton Restaurant FRENCH, ITALIAN $$$
(☎970-325-4419; www.bontonrestaurant.com; 426 Main St; mains $16-40; ⏱5:30-11pm Thu-Mon, 9:30am-12:30pm Sat & Sun;) Bon Ton has been serving supper for a century in a beautiful room under the historic St Elmo Hotel. The French-Italian menu includes roast duck in cherry peppercorn sauce and tortellini with bacon and shallots. The wine list is extensive and the weekend Champagne brunch comes recommended.

Information

Ouray Visitor Center (☎970-325-4746, 800-228-1876; www.ouraycolorado.com; 1230 Main St; ⏱9am-6pm Mon-Sat, 10am-4pm Sun;) Located behind the Ouray hot-springs pool.

Getting There & Away

Ouray is on Hwy 550, 70 miles north of Durango, 24 miles north of Silverton and 37 miles south of Montrose. There are no bus services in the area and private transportation is necessary.

Telluride

Telluride is a unique destination cut off from much of the world by the towering peaks that surround the old mining town on three sides. No other town in Colorado feels this close to a Swiss mountain village.

Walking the downtown strip you have skyrocketing mountain ranges right in front of you. There's also a pretty darned good ski resort here, plenty of hiking and biking opportunities, and Colorado's best summer festivals. While there aren't that many restaurants and nightlife spots, what they do have is always high quality.

Activities

Telluride Ski Resort SNOW SPORTS
(☎970-728-7533, 888-288-7360; www.tellurideskiresort.com; 565 Mountain Village Blvd; adult/child full-day lift ticket $139/83) Known for its steep and deep terrain – with plunging runs and deep powder at the best times – Telluride is a real skier's mountain, but dilettantes love the gorgeous San Juan mountain views and the social town atmosphere. Covering three distinct areas, the resort is served by 16 lifts. Much of the terrain is for advanced and intermediate skiers, but there's still ample choice for beginners.

In summer, there is a **mountain bike park** (day lift ticket $36) here.

★Ashley Boling HISTORY
(970-728-6639; per person $20; by appointment) Local Ashley Boling has been giving engaging historical walking tours of Telluride for more than 20 years. They last over an hour and are offered year-round. Rates are for a minimum of three participants, but he'll cut a reasonable deal for two or more. By reservation.

Festivals & Events

Telluride Bluegrass Festival MUSIC
(800-624-2422; www.planetbluegrass.com; 1-/4-day pass $90/255; late Jun) This festival attracts thousands for a weekend of top-notch rollicking alfresco bluegrass. Stalls sell all sorts of food and local microbrews to keep you happy, and acts continue well into the night. Camping out for the four-day festival is very popular. Check out the website for info on sites, shuttle services and combo ticket-and-camping packages – it's all very organized!

Sleeping

★Telluride Town Park Campground CAMPGROUND $
(970-728-2173; www.telluride-co.gov/181/campground; 500 E Colorado Ave; campsite with/without vehicle space $33/19; mid-May–mid-Oct;) Right in the center of town, this convenient creekside campground has 43 campsites, along with showers, swimming and tennis. Sites are all on a first-come, first-served basis, unless it's festival time (consult ahead with festival organizers). Fancy some nightlife with your camping? Why not.

New Sheridan Hotel HOTEL $$
(970-728-4351, 800-200-1891; www.newsheridan.com; 231 W Colorado Ave; d from $220;) Elegant and understated, this historic brick hotel (erected in 1895) provides a lovely base camp for exploring Telluride. High-ceilinged rooms feature crisp linens and snug flannel throws. Check out the hot-tub deck with mountain views. In the bull's eye of downtown, the location is perfect, but some rooms are small for the price.

Inn at Lost Creek BOUTIQUE HOTEL $$$
(970-728-5678; www.innatlostcreek.com; 119 Lost Creek Lane, Mountain Village; r $275-500;) This lush boutique-style hotel in Mountain Village knows cozy. At the bottom of Telluride's main lift, it's also very convenient. Service is personalized, and impeccable rooms have alpine hardwoods, Southwestern designs and molded tin. There are also two rooftop spas. Check the website for packages.

Eating & Drinking

There's more good times to be had in Telluride than the rest of southern Colorado combined. But bring your wallet – those drinks aren't free or even close. Live bands spark it up.

Tacos del Gnar MEXICAN $
(970-728-7938; www.gnarlytacos.com; 123 S Oak St; mains $7-14; noon-9pm Tue-Sat;) The second outlet of a no-nonsense taco shop that puts flavor ahead of frills. Its fusion-style tacos, borrowing from Korean BBQ and Asian flavors, will make your taste buds sing. Do it.

Oak BARBECUE $$
(New Fat Alley; 970-728-3985; www.oakstelluride.com; 250 San Juan Ave, base of chair 8; mains $11-23; 11am-10pm;) You can pick something off the chalkboard or just take what the other guy has his face in – a cheap and messy delight. If in doubt, go for the pulled-pork sandwich with coleslaw on top. Do it right by siding it with a bowl of crispy sweet-potato fries. The beer specials are outrageous. And it's located right next to the free town Gondola.

★Chop House MODERN AMERICAN $$$
(970-728-4531; www.newsheridan.com; 231 W Colorado Ave, New Sheridan Hotel; mains $26-65; 5pm-2am) With superb service and a chic decor with embroidered velvet benches, this is an easy pick for an intimate dinner. Start with a cheese plate. From there the menu gets Western with exquisite elk short loin and ravioli with tomato relish and local sheep-milk ricotta. Top it off with a flourless dark chocolate cake in fresh caramel sauce.

New Sheridan Bar BAR
(970-728-3911; www.newsheridan.com; 231 W Colorado Ave, New Sheridan Hotel; 5pm-2am) It's rush hour for beautiful people, though in low season you'll find real local flavor and opinions. In summertime, beeline for the breezy rooftop. Old bullet holes in the wall testify to the plucky survival of the bar itself, even as the adjoining hotel sold off chandeliers and antiques to pay the heating bills when mining fortunes waned.

Entertainment

Fly Me to the Moon Saloon LIVE MUSIC
(970-728-6666; www.facebook.com/flymetothemoonsaloon; 132 E Colorado Ave; 3pm-2am) Let your hair down and kick up your heels to the tunes of live bands at this saloon, the best place in Telluride to party hard.

Sheridan Opera House THEATER
(970-728-4539; www.sheridanoperahouse.com; 110 N Oak St;) This historic venue has a burlesque charm and is always the center of Telluride's cultural life. It hosts the Telluride Repertory Theater, and frequently has special performances for children.

Information

Telluride Central Reservations (888-355-8743; 700 W Colorado Ave; 9am-5pm Mon-Sat, 10am-1pm Sun) Handles accommodations and sells festival tickets.

Telluride Visitor Center (888-353-5473, 970-728-3041; www.telluride.com; 230 W Colorado Ave; 10am-5pm winter, to 7pm summer) Well-stocked visitor center with good resources.

Wilkinson Public Library (970-728-4519; www.telluridelibrary.org; 100 W Pacific Ave; 10am-8pm Mon-Thu, to 6pm Fri & Sat, noon-5pm Sun;) Good resource for maps and local information, with some free public events.

Getting There & Around

In ski season **Montrose Regional Airport** (MTJ; 970-249-3203; www.montroseairport.com; 2100 Airport Rd), 65 miles north, has direct flights to/from Denver (on United), Houston, Phoenix and limited cities on the east coast. Commuter aircraft serve the mesa-top **Telluride Airport** (TEX; 970-778-5051; www.tellurideairport.com; 1500 Last Dollar Rd). At other times, planes fly into Montrose.

Telluride Express (970-728-6000; www.telluridexpress.com) provides low-cost shuttles to Telluride from the Montrose and Telluride Airports.

Silverton

Ringed by snowy peaks and steeped in the sooty tales of a tawdry mining town, Silverton would seem more at home in Alaska than the Lower 48. But here it is. And for those into snowmobiling, biking, fly-fishing or just basking in some very high-altitude sunshine, Silverton delivers. This is also home to one of America's unique ski mountains: the experts-only, one-chair wonder of Silverton Mountain.

It's a two-street town, but only one is paved. Greene St is where you'll find most businesses (think homemade jerky, fudge and feather art). Still unpaved, notorious Blair St – renamed Empire – runs parallel to Greene. During the silver rush, Blair St was home to thriving brothels and boozing establishments.

Activities

★**Silverton Railroad Depot** RAIL
(970-387-5416, toll-free 877-872-4607; www.durangotrain.com; 12th St; return adult/child 4-11yr from $114/80; departures 1:45pm, 2:30pm & 3pm;) You can buy one-way and round-trip tickets for the brilliant Durango & Silverton Narrow Gauge Railroad (p107) at the Silverton depot or via the website. The Silverton Freight Yard Museum is located at the Silverton depot; the train ticket provides admission two days prior to and following your ride on the train. The train service offers combination train-bus return trips (the bus route is much quicker).

★**Silverton Mountain Ski Area** SKIING
(970-387-5706; www.silvertonmountain.com; State Hwy 110; guided skiing $179, unguided skiing $79; guided skiing Thu-Sun Dec-Mar, unguided skiing late Mar-Apr) Silverton is an experts-only ski mountain that's perfect for advanced skiers looking to take it up a notch. The resort has just one lift to take you to the top. From there, you hike with your guide to any number of amazing lines with some of the best untracked powder in the state.

San Juan Backcountry DRIVING
(970-387-5565; www.sanjuanbackcountry.com; 1119 Greene St; tours $40-140; May-Oct;) Offering both 4WD tours and rentals, the folks at San Juan Backcountry can get you out and into the brilliant San Juan Mountain wilderness areas around Silverton. The tours are in modified open-top Chevy Suburbans and ATVs. Rafting trips down the Lower Animas by Durango are also possible.

Sleeping & Eating

Inn of the Rockies at the Historic Alma House B&B $$
(970-387-5336; www.innoftherockies.com; 220 E 10th St; r $125-200;) Opened by a local in 1898, this inn has 10 unique rooms furnished with Victorian antiques. The hospitality is first-rate and its breakfasts, served in a chandelier-lit dining room, merit special

mention. There's also a garden hot tub for soaking after a long day.

Wyman Hotel B&B $$
(☎877-504-5272; www.thewyman.com; 1371 Greene St; d from $250-375; ⊙closed Nov;) A handsome sandstone on the National Register of Historic Places, this revamped 1902 building offers sleek rooms with Scandinavian sensibilities and a fine-tuned minimalist touch. It's a stylish alternative to the usual bric-a-brac approach. Check out the historic caboose alongside a gravel patio out back.

Grand Restaurant & Saloon AMERICAN $$
(☎970-387-5527; www.grandimperialhotel.com; 1219 Greene St; mains $8-26; ⊙11am-3pm May-Oct, occasional dinners 5-9pm;) Stick with the burgers and club sandwiches at this atmospheric eatery, where the full bar is well patronised by locals and visitors. The player piano and historic decor are big draws.

Getting There & Away

Silverton is on Hwy 550 midway between Montrose, about 60 miles to the north, and Durango, some 48 miles to the south.

Other than private car, the only way to get to and from Silverton is by using the Durango & Silverton Narrow Gauge Railroad (p107), or the private buses that run its return journeys.

Mesa Verde National Park

More than 700 years after its inhabitants disappeared, Mesa Verde retains an air of mystery. No one knows for sure why the Ancestral Puebloans left their elaborate cliff dwellings in the 1300s. What remains is a wonderland for adventurers of all sizes, who can clamber up ladders to carved-out dwellings, see rock art and delve into the mysteries of ancient America.

Mesa Verde National Park (☎970-529-4465; www.nps.gov/meve; 7-day car/motorcycle pass May-Oct $25/20, Nov-Apr $15/10;) occupies 81 sq miles of the northernmost portion of the mesa. Ancestral Puebloan sites are found throughout the park's canyons and mesas, perched on a high plateau south of Cortez and Mancos.

Sights & Activities

If you only have time for a short visit, check out the Chapin Mesa Museum and try to get in on a ranger-guided tour of one of the dwellings (available only with in-person reservations up to two days in advance).

Mesa Verde rewards travelers who set aside a day or more to take ranger-led tours of Cliff Palace and Balcony House, explore Wetherill Mesa (the quieter side of the canyon), linger around the museum or participate in one of the campfire programs run at Morefield Campground.

Chapin Mesa Museum MUSEUM
(☎970-529-4475; www.nps.gov/meve; Chapin Mesa Rd; admission incl with park entry; ⊙8am-6:30pm Apr–mid-Oct, to 5pm mid-Oct–Apr;) The Chapin Mesa Museum has exhibits pertaining to the park and is a good first stop. Staff at the museum provide information on weekends when the park headquarters is closed.

Chapin Mesa ARCHAEOLOGICAL SITE
(ranger-led hikes $5; ⊙year-round, ranger-led hikes Apr-Oct) The largest concentration of Ancestral Puebloan sites is at Chapin Mesa, where you'll see the densely clustered **Far View Site** and the large **Spruce Tree House** (Chapin Mesa Rd; admission incl with park entry;) , the most accessible of sites, with a paved half-mile round-trip path. Spruce Tree House is currently closed to visitors, but you can see it easily from the museum overlook.

Wetherill Mesa ARCHAEOLOGICAL SITE
(guided tours per person $5) Wetherill Mesa is the second-largest concentration of sites. Visitors may enter stabilized surface sites and two cliff dwellings, including the Long House (ranger-led only), open from late May through August.

Aramark Mesa Verde HIKING
(☎970-529-4421; www.visitmesaverde.com; Mile 15, Far View Lodge; adult $70-75) The park concessionaire offers various guided private and group tours throughout the park daily from May to mid-October. Tours include bus transit and hikes. Book online or at the office at Far View Lodge.

Sleeping & Eating

Morefield Campground CAMPGROUND $
(☎970-529-4465; www.visitmesaverde.com; Mile 4; tent sites $33, RV sites with/without hookups $33/45; ⊙May-early Oct;) The park's camping option, located 4 miles from the entrance gate, has 445 regular tent sites on grassy grounds conveniently located near Morefield Village. The village has a general store, gas station, restaurant, showers and laundry. It's managed by Aramark.

Far View Lodge LODGE $$

(toll-free 800-449-2288; www.visitmesaverde.com; Mile 15; r $165-230; mid-Apr–Oct;) Perched on a mesa top 15 miles inside the park entrance, this tasteful Pueblo-style lodge has 150 Southwestern-style rooms, some with kiva fireplaces. Don't miss sunset over the mesa from your private balcony. Standard rooms don't have air-con (or TV) and summer daytimes can be hot. You can even bring your dog for an extra $10 per night.

Metate Room MODERN AMERICAN $$$

(800-449-2288; www.visitmesaverde.com; Mile 15, Far View Lodge; mains $20-36; 7-10am & 5:30-9:30pm Apr–mid-Oct, 5-7:30pm mid-Oct–Mar;) With an award in culinary excellence, this upscale restaurant in the Far View Lodge offers an innovative menu inspired by Native American food and flavors. Interesting dishes include stuffed poblano chilies, prickly-pear pork belly and cold smoked trout. Not your average national park dining, and the views are nothing short of spectacular.

Information

Mesa Verde Visitor & Research Center

(970-529-4465; www.nps.gov/meve; 7:30am-7pm Jun-early Sep, 8am-5pm early Sep–mid-Oct & mid-Apr–May, closed mid-Oct–mid-Apr;) This huge visitor center has water, wi-fi and bathrooms, in addition to information desks selling tickets for tours of Cliff Palace, Balcony House and Long House. It also displays museum-quality artifacts.

Durango

Durango is paradise unleashed. The historic mining town offers the perfect combination of easy access to adventures by river, by bike and by ski, super-cool locals, a fun nightlife scene powered by the local college kids, and plenty of great eateries, drinking holes, boutiques and more.

Activities

★Durango & Silverton Narrow Gauge Railroad RAIL

(970-247-2733; www.durangotrain.com; 479 Main Ave; return adult/child 4-11yr from $114/80;) Riding the Durango & Silverton Narrow Gauge Railroad is a Durango must. These vintage steam locomotives have been making the scenic 45-mile trip north to Silverton (3½ hours each way) for more than 125 years. The dazzling journey allows two hours for exploring Silverton. The Skyway Tour to Silverton operates only from May through October.

Mild to Wild Rafting RAFTING

(970-247-4789, toll-free 800-567-6745; www.mild2wildrafting.com; 50 Animas View Dr; trips from $55; 9am-5pm;) In spring and summer white-water rafting is one of the most popular sports in Durango. Mild to Wild Rafting is one of numerous companies around town offering rafting trips on the Animas River. Beginners should check out the one-hour introduction to rafting, while the more adventurous (and experienced) can run the upper Animas, which boasts class III to class V rapids.

Purgatory SKIING

(970-247-9000; www.purgatoryresort.com; 1 Skier Pl; lift ticket adult/child from $89/60; mid-Nov–Mar;) Durango's winter highlight is 25 miles north on Hwy 550. The resort offers 1200 skiable acres of varying difficulty, and boasts 260in of snow per year. Two terrain parks offer plenty of opportunities for snowboarders to catch big air. This is really a local's hill that offers up plenty of good groomers for families and a few steeper runs.

Sleeping

★Rochester House HOTEL $$

(970-385-1920, toll-free 800-664-1920; www.rochesterhotel.com; 721 E 2nd Ave; d $190-300;) Influenced by old Westerns (movie posters and marquee lights adorn the hallways), the Rochester is a little bit of old Hollywood in the new West. Rooms are spacious, with high ceilings. Two formal sitting rooms, where you're served cookies, and a breakfast room in an old train car are other perks at this pet-friendly establishment.

Antlers on the Creek B&B $$

(970-259-1565; www.antlersonthecreek.com; 999 Lightner Creek Rd; r from $180;) Tuck yourself into this peaceful creekside setting surrounded by sprawling lawns and cottonwoods and you may never want to leave. Between the spacious main house and the carriage house there are seven tasteful rooms with jetted tubs, plush bed linens and gas fireplaces. There's also a decadent three-course breakfast and hot tub in the outdoor gazebo. It's open year-round.

West Coast Beaches

From the wild, windswept beaches of Oregon to California's gorgeous sunkissed coast, the West Coast of the US holds some of the world's best loved and most iconic beaches. Whether you're sunning yourself on Huntington Beach, Orange County, with its perpetual sun, or surfing the amazing breaks of Rincon, Santa Barbara, you're sure to discover your perfect patch of coast.

1

MELPOMENE/SHUTTERSTOCK ©

2

COREY JENKINS/GETTY IMAGES ©

4

KRIS DAVIDSON/LONELY PLANET ©

1. Santa Monica beach
Santa Monica (p251) may be the epitome of Californian beach life.

2. La Jolla
Whether you're a surfer or a snorkeler, La Jolla is one of San Diego's (p271) most beloved beaches.

3. Huntington Beach
Southeast of Los Angeles, this city's beach (p270) epitomizes SoCal's surfing lifestyle.

4. Steamer Lane
Catch a wave on one of Santa Cruz's (p300) most famous surf breaks.

3

STEVE WHISTON - FALLEN LOG PHOTOGRAPHY/GETTY IMAGES ©

General Palmer Hotel HOTEL $$
(970-247-4747, toll-free 800-523-3358; www.generalpalmer.com; 567 Main Ave; r from $160;) With turn-of-the century elegance, this 1898 Victorian has a damsel's taste, with pewter four-poster beds, floral prints and teddies on every bed. Rooms are small but elegant, and if you tire of TV, there's a collection of board games at the front desk. Check out the cozy library and the relaxing solarium.

Eating & Drinking

★ **James Ranch** MARKET $
(970-385-9143; www.jamesranch.net; 33800 US Hwy 550; mains $5-18; 11am-7pm Mon-Sat) A must for those road-tripping the San Juan Skyway, the family-run James Ranch, 10 miles out of Durango, features a market and an outstanding farmstand grill featuring the farm's own organic grass-fed beef and fresh produce. Steak sandwiches and fresh cheese melts with caramelized onions rock. Kids dig the goats.

El Moro GASTROPUB $$
(970-259-5555; www.elmorotavern.com; 945 Main Ave; mains $12-30; 11am-midnight Mon-Fri, 9am-midnight Sat & Sun) There are two reasons to come here: drinking damned good custom cocktails at the bar and dining on some innovative small plates including Korean fried cauliflower, cheeses, housemade sausages and fresh salads. It's ground zero for Durango hipsters but really aims to please all.

★ **Bookcase & the Barber** COCKTAIL BAR
(970-764-4123; www.bookcaseandbarber.com; 601 E 2nd Ave, Suite B; 2pm-midnight) This modern speakeasy may be Durango's sexiest nightcap, hidden behind a heavy bookcase, with a dimly lit allure and exquisite cocktails worth the $12 price tag. Enter via the barbershop, but you'll need the password (found somewhere on their Facebook page). Try a spicy *paloma celosa* (jealous dove), a perfect tease of tequila, grapefruit and ancho chili.

Ska Brewing Company BREWERY
(970-247-5792; www.skabrewing.com; 225 Girard St; mains $9-15; 9am-9pm Mon-Fri, 11am-9pm Sat, to 7pm Sun) Big on flavor and variety, these are the best handcrafted beers in town. Although the small, friendly tasting-room bar was once mainly a production facility, over the years it's steadily climbed in popularity. Today it is usually jam-packed with friends meeting for an after-work beer.

Information

Durango Public Library (970-375-3380; www.durangopubliclibrary.org; 1900 E 3rd Ave; 9am-8pm Mon-Wed, 10am-5:30pm Thu, 9am-5:30pm Fri & Sat;) A handy resource for regional information.

Durango Welcome Center (970-247-3500, www.durango.org; 802 Main Ave; 9am-7pm Sun-Thu, to 9pm Fri & Sat;) An excellent information center located downtown. There is a second **visitor center** (111 S Camino del Rio) south of town, at the Santa Rita exit from US Hwy 550.

San Juan-Rio Grande National Forest HQ (970-247-4874; www.fs.fed.us/r2/sanjuan; 15 Burnett Ct; 9am-5pm Mon-Sat) Located a half-mile west of Durango off US Hwy 160. Offers camping and hiking information and maps.

Getting There & Around

Durango-La Plata County Airport (DRO; 970-247-8143; www.flydurango.com; 1000 Airport Rd) is 18 miles southwest of Durango via US Hwy 160 and Hwy 172. Both United and American Airlines have direct flights to Denver; United offers seasonal flights (summer only) to Chicago, Houston and LA; American flies to Dallas–Fort Worth and Phoenix.

Great Sand Dunes National Park

For all of Colorado's striking natural sights, the surreal **Great Sand Dunes National Park** (719-378-6399; www.nps.gov/grsa; 11999 Hwy 150; 8:30am-5pm Jun-Aug, 9am-4:30pm Sep-May;), a veritable sea of sand bounded by jagged peaks and scrubby plains, is a place of stirring optical illusions where nature's magic is on full display.

From the approach up Hwy 150, watch as the angles of sunlight make shifting shadows on the dunes; the most dramatic time is the day's end, when the hills come into high contrast as the sun drops low on the horizon. Hike past the edge of the dune field to see the shifting sand up close; the ceaseless wind works like a disconsolate sculptor, constantly rearranging the sandy landscape.

Most visitors limit their activities to the area where Medano Creek divides the main dune mass from the towering Sangre de Cristo Mountains. The remaining 85% of the park's area is designated wilderness: not for the unfit or fainthearted.

Hiking

There are no trails through this expansive field of sand, but it's the star attraction for hikers. Two informal hikes afford excellent panoramic views of the dunes. The first is a hike to High Dune (strangely, not the highest dune in the park), which departs from a parking area just beyond the visitor center. It's about 2.5 miles out to the peak and back, but be warned: it's not easy. As you trudge along up the hills of sand, it feels like you're taking a half-step back for every one forward. If you're up for it, try pushing on to the second worthy goal: just west of High Dune is Star Dune (750ft), the tallest in the park.

From the Great Sand Dunes National Park Visitor Center (p110), a short trail leads to the Mosca Picnic Area next to ankle-deep Medano Creek, which you must ford (when the creek is running) to reach the dunes. Across the road from the visitor center, the Mosca Pass Trail climbs up into the Sangre de Cristo Wilderness.

Sleeping & Eating

★Zapata Falls Campground CAMPGROUND $
(☎719-852-7074; www.fs.usda.gov; BLM Rd 5415; tent & RV sites $11; 🐾) Seven miles south of the national park, this campground offers glorious panoramas of the San Luis Valley from its 9000ft perch in the Sangre de Cristos. There are 23 first-come, first-served sites, but there is no water and the 3.6-mile access road is steep and fairly washed out, making for slow going. The payoff, however, is worth it, especially if you prefer a secluded location.

Zapata Ranch RANCH $$$
(☎719-378-2356; www.zranch.org; 5303 Hwy 150; 2-nights per person with full board $875) Ideal for horseback-riding enthusiasts, this exclusive preserve is a working cattle and bison ranch set amid groves of cottonwood trees. Owned and operated by the Nature Conservancy, the main inn is a refurbished 19th-century log structure, with distant views of the sand dunes. Stays include meals and horseback-riding excursions; other adventures such as rock climbing and rafting cost extra.

Getting There & Away

Great Sand Dunes National Park is 33 miles northeast of Alamosa. There is no public transit to get here.

WYOMING

Much of Wyoming is the essence of the Great Plains, a vast and empty land of windswept plains and sagebrush hills baking under brooding blue skies. What towns do exist are steeped in history and infused with pioneer grit. This is Oregon Trail and outlaw country, and the current inhabitants are content to keep this chunk of the West wild. Cody or Laramie offer a taste of the living past, while Jackson and Lander serve as the advanced outposts of the New West revolution.

But the country's least populated state is also home to some of its most dramatic mountains, most diverse wildlife and most unique geology. From the unspoiled Snowy Range near Laramie to the granite wilderness of the Wind River Range behind Lander, the peaks only become more impressive as you travel across Wyoming toward the archetypal – and truly grand – Teton Range, to say nothing of Yellowstone, one of the most beautiful places in America's Lower 48.

Information

Travel Wyoming (☎800-225-5996, 307-777-7777; www.travelwyoming.com) The state's excellent tourism portal.

Wapiti Ranger Station (☎307-587-3925) The oldest ranger station in the country.

Wyoming State Parks & Historic Sites (☎307-777-6323; http://wyoparks.state.wy.us) Information on Wyoming's 13 state parks and 26 historic sites. Campsite reservations are taken online or over the phone

Cheyenne

Once known as the 'Magic City' for its seemingly overnight growth on the edge of the plains, windy Cheyenne may not wow you with its looks, but like the rough-skinned cowboys you'll meet here, there's good-natured charm once you scratch the surface. Wander to the depot after hitting up the city's museums and you'll see this town is a solid step above a convenient pit stop on I-80.

Sights

Frontier Days Old West Museum MUSEUM
(☎307-778-7290; www.oldwestmuseum.org; 4610 Carey Ave; adult/child $10/free; ⏲9am-5pm; 👪) For a deep dive into Cheyenne's pioneer past and rodeo present, visit this museum year-

round on the Frontier Days rodeo grounds. It is chock-full of rodeo memorabilia, from saddles to trophies, displays cowboy art and photography, houses a fine collection of horse-drawn buggies, and dispenses nuggets of history – such as the story of Steamboat, the un-rideable bronco who likely isn't the one depicted on Wyoming's license plates (though many will tell you he is.)

Festivals & Events

Cheyenne Frontier Days RODEO
(307-778-7222; www.cfdrodeo.com; 4610 Carey Ave; rodeo per day $17-55, concerts $20-75; 2nd half of Jul;) During the last full week in July, the world's largest outdoor rodeo and celebration of all things Wyoming features 10 days of roping, bucking, riding, singing and dancing between air shows, parades, melodramas, carnivals and chili cook-offs. There's also a lively Frontier Town, Indian village and free morning 'slack' rodeos.

Sleeping & Eating

★ **Nagle Warren Mansion B&B** B&B $$
(307-637-3333; www.naglewarrenmansion.com; 222 E 17th St; r from $195;) This historic 1888 mansion is a rare find. The house still has the original carved leather ceiling, and is decked out with late-19th-century regional antiques in 12 spacious and elegant rooms. The property boasts a hot tub, a reading room tucked into a turret and classic 1954 Schwinn bikes for cruising. It's among Wyoming's most atmospheric places to stay.

★ **Historic Plains Hotel** HISTORIC HOTEL $
(307-638-3311; 1600 Central Ave; r from $140;) Around since 1911, this beautiful old belle drips with period atmosphere in the public areas; the antique lift is deliberately small so that cowboys wouldn't try to sneak their horses upstairs and into the rooms. Ask for a street-facing room; those facing onto the internal light well are a little dark.

★ **Bunkhouse Bar & Grill** STEAK $$
(307-632-6184; www.bunkhousebar.com; 1064 Happy Jack Rd; mains $10-28; 11am-9pm Sun-Thu, to 11:30pm Fri & Sat) West of Cheyenne on the W-210, this storied steakhouse is worth the trip. Around since 1898, they've learned a thing or two about local tastes – burgers, steaks and similar predilections rule. The house specialty is the remarkable Bunk-Nut Sandwich with fried Rocky Mountain oysters with American cheese on Texas toast... There's even live music on Friday and Saturday evening.

★ **Restaurant at the Plains** AMERICAN $$
(307-638-3311; www.theplainshotel.com; 1600 Central Ave; mains lunch $8-13, dinner $15-24; noon-3pm & 6-10pm Tue-Sun) Arguably Cheyenne's finest, the restaurant at the Historic Plains Hotel serves up some outstanding dinner dishes, such as crab-stuffed salmon or bourbon-glazed tenderloin, while lunch is a lighter affair with burgers, sandwiches and a soup-and-salad bar.

Drinking & Nightlife

Accomplice Brewing Company MICROBREWERY
(307-632-2337; www.accomplicebeer.com; 115 W 15th, Depot; 11am-10pm Sun-Thu, to midnight Fri & Sat;) Sample as many beers as you like as often as you like at the crowded pour-it-yourself taproom in Cheyenne's latest brewery to occupy the historic Depot building. The drafts are tasty – we particularly enjoyed the Nue Dogma Pale Ale and the Lincoln Squared IPA – and food options don't disappoint.

★ **Nagle Warren Mansion B&B** TEAHOUSE
(307-637-3333; www.naglewarrenmansion.com; 222 E 17th St; per person $12; 2-4pm Fri & Sat) For an old-world taste of the West, come for afternoon tea at this atmospheric mansion where you'll be served tea, scones, cookies, sandwiches and pastries – high tea as it used to be.

Information

Cheyenne Visitor Center (800-426-5009, 307-778-3133; www.cheyenne.org; 1 Depot Sq/121 W 15th St; 9am-5pm Mon-Fri, to 3pm Sat, 11am-3pm Sun;) Check the website for a comprehensive guide to Cheyenne. Downtown **trolley tours** (307-778-3133; www.cheyenne-trolley.com; 121 W 15th St, Depot Plaza; adult/child $12/6; 10am, 11:30am, 1pm, 2:30pm & 4pm May-Sep) leave from here.

Wyoming Travel & Tourism (800-225-5996; www.wyomingtourism.org; 5611 High Plains Rd; 9am-5pm Mon-Fri) At a rest area just south of Cheyenne on I-25, this info center has tons of information and kid-friendly displays about local wildlife, activities and the environment. Worth a stop.

Getting There & Around

For a capital city, Cheyenne is hard to reach. Black Hills Stage Lines/Express Arrow stops at the **bus terminal** (307-635-1327; www.grey

hound.com; 5401 Walker Rd, Rodeway Inn) at the northern end of town with direct service to Denver ($40, 2¼ hours) and Salt Lake City ($133, 8½ hours) as well as anywhere Greyhound travels. Sleepy **Cheyenne Airport** (CYS; 307-634-7071; www.cheyenneairport.com; 200 E 8th Ave) will get you to Denver every Thursday.

Laramie

Worth an overnight stop on your way across Wyoming, this prairie town has Wyoming's only four-year university (University of Wyoming), and has a constant flow of hip and lively students who re-energize an otherwise sleepy city. The small historic downtown, with its grid of brick buildings pressed up against the railroad tracks, can occupy an hour of window shopping, and a few museums on the pleasantly green university campus are informative ways to stretch your legs. The real reason to visit, however, is the Wyoming Territorial Prison): a well-preserved piece of frontier past with echoes of Butch Cassidy.

Sights

★Wyoming Territorial Prison MUSEUM
(307-745-3733; www.wyomingterritorialprison.com; 975 Snowy Range Rd; adult/child $7/3.50; 8am-7pm May-Sep, 10am-3pm Wed-Sat Oct-Apr;) See the only prison ever to hold Butch Cassidy, who was in for grand larceny in 1894–96, only to emerge a well-connected criminal who fast became one of history's greatest robbers. His story is told in thrilling detail in a back room, while the faces of other 'malicious and desperate outlaws' stare hauntingly at you as you explore the main cellblocks. Outside, tour the factory where convicts produced more than 700 brooms a day – one of the prison's short-lived revenue-generating schemes.

Geological Museum MUSEUM
(307-766-2646; www.uwyo.edu/geomuseum; SH Knight Geology Bldg, University of Wyoming; 10am-4pm Mon-Sat) FREE The Morrison Formation – a Jurassic sedimentary rock – stretches from New Mexico to Montana and is centered in Wyoming. This layer has produced many of the world's dinosaurs fossils, an impressive collection of which are on display in this tiny university museum, including a 75ft *Apatosaurus excelsus* (formerly known as the Brontosaurus) and a *Diatryma gigantea* (a 7ft-tall carnivorous bird discovered in Wyoming). Linger at the new 'Prep Lab' and watch researchers liberate brittle fossils from solid rock. Science!

Sleeping

Gas Lite Motel MOTEL $
(307-399-6176; 960 N 3rd St; s/d $55/65;) The Gas Lite Motel stands out – more due to the plastic horse and rooster on the roof and the tattered plywood cowboys lounging against the banisters than the modernity of the amenities. However, the rooms are clean if dated, the owners reasonably friendly, and the price is right if variable.

★Mad Carpenter Inn B&B $$
(307-742-0870; www.madcarpenterinn.net; 353 N 8th St; r $95-125;) With landscaped gardens, hot breakfast, and comfy, snug wood-trimmed rooms, the Mad Carpenter Inn has warmth and class to spare. A serious game room features billiards and ping-pong while the detached 'Doll House' with its kitchenette and Jacuzzi is an absolute steal for a couple looking for a quiet escape.

WYOMING FACTS

Nickname Equality State

Population 577,740

Area 97,914 sq miles

Capital city Cheyenne (population 63,600)

Other cities Laramie (population 32,300), Jackson (10,500), Cody (9890)

Sales tax 4%

Birthplace of Artist Jackson Pollock (1912–56)

Home of Women's suffrage, coal mining, geysers, wolves, Yellowstone

Politics Conservative to the core (except Teton County)

Famous for Rodeo, ranches, former vice-president Dick Cheney

Random fact Wyoming is the 10th-largest state by area but has the smallest population of any US state.

Tallest mountain Gannett Peak 13,809ft (4209m)

Driving distances Cheyenne to Jackson 432 miles

Eating & Drinking

★ Sweet Melissa's VEGETARIAN $

(☎ 307-742-9607; www.facebook.com/sweetmelissacafe; 213 S 1st St; mains $8.50-14; ⏲ 11am-9pm Mon-Thu, to 10pm Fri & Sat;) Sweet Melissa's makes delicious vegetarian and gluten-free dishes, no doubt the healthiest food for miles, such as gorgonzola-leek mac 'n' cheese. The cauliflower wings are bomber, as is the service.

Wyoming's Rib & Chop House AMERICAN $$

(☎ 307-460-9090; www.ribandchophouse.com; 2415 Grand Ave; mains $11-24; ⏲ 11am-10pm) For a real slice of modern Americana, wait in line at this wildly popular place, order from an extensive menu that ranges from slow-cooked ribs and Black Angus steaks to crab-stuffed mushrooms and lobster potpie, then watch from nearly a dozen TV screens streaming live sports.

Coal Creek Coffee Co COFFEE

(☎ 307-745-7737; www.coalcreekcoffee.com; 110 E Grand Ave; mains $5-11; ⏲ 6am-11pm;) With superlative brews, Coal Creek Coffee is everything you want in a coffeehouse: modern and stylish, even borderline hipster – but not in a bad way. When the fair-trade beans and expertly prepared lattes start to feel so 10am, roll over to Coal Creek Tap in the west wing where you'll find more than a dozen draft beers.

Getting There & Away

Five miles west of town on Hwy 130, **Laramie Regional Airport** (☎ 307-742-4164; www.laramieairport.com; 555 General Brees Rd) has twice-daily flights to Denver, as well as to a few smaller regional airstrips.

Greyhound (☎ 307-745-7394; www.greyhound.com; 1952 N Banner Rd) buses stop at the gas station everyone calls the 'Diamond Shamrock,' though it is unclear what brand it operates under these days. Destinations include Denver ($40, three hours).

Lander

Sprawled out near the foothills of the Wind River Range, Lander has always been a frontier town. Originally established as a fort on a spur of the Oregon Trail, it was later the end of the rail line and a frequent haunt of outlaws and horse thieves. It is also the gateway to the Wind River Indian Reservation, where indigenous Eastern Shoshone share 2.2 million acres of land with displaced Northern Arapaho at the base of the state's tallest peak.

Lander has a strong pedigree among climbers, hikers and other adventure seekers. But the town's remoteness means few stay for long, leaving Lander in relative peace, retaining its mellow blend of the Old and New West.

Sights & Activities

Sinks Canyon State Park PARK

(☎ 307-332-3077; www.sinkscanyonstatepark.org; 3079 Sinks Canyon Rd; tent & RV $11-16; ⏲ visitor center 9am-6pm Jun-Sep) Beautiful Sinks Canyon State Park, 6 miles southwest of Lander on Hwy 131, centers on a curious feature of the Middle Fork of the Popo Agie River, where the rushing water suddenly turns into a small cave and disappears into the soluble Madison limestone. Although the water bubbles up a quarter-mile downstream, scientists have learned it takes nearly two hours for it to make the subterranean journey before emerging warmer and with more volume.

Sleeping

Outlaw Cabins B&B $$

(☎ 307-332-9655; www.outlawcabins.com; 2411 Squaw Creek Rd; cabins $125) On a working ranch are a pair of real cabins done real nice. The Lawman was built by a county sheriff over 120 years ago, but has been maintained and restored for modern sensibilities. The Outlaw is our favorite, however, on account of its more Wild West vibe. Both are beautifully appointed with quiet porches made for sittin' on.

★ Mill House BOUTIQUE HOTEL $$

(☎ 307-349-9254; http://millhouselander.com/; 125 Main St; ste from $190;) Lander's most stylish address is an artful conversion of the town's old mill house, with exposed brick walls, hardwood floors and muted color schemes that carry a strong sense of contemporary style. You can book individual suites, each of which is different, or the whole house, but however you stay, this is one of Wyoming's best.

Eating

Middle Fork BREAKFAST $

(☎ 307-335-5035; www.themiddleforklander.com; 351 Main St; mains $6-11; ⏲ 7am-2pm Mon-Sat, 9am-2pm Sun;) A large hall with spartan ambience leaves you free to focus on the food – which is excellent. Homemade baked goods hold court with eggs Benedict and in-house corned-beef hash washed down with mimosas.

★Cowfish GRILL $$
(307-332-8227; www.cowfishlander.com; 148 Main St; brunch $9-16, dinner $17-35; 5-10pm Mon-Fri, 9am-2pm & 5-10pm Sat & Sun;) Spring for a candlelit dinner of brussels-sprout carbonara or coffee-rubbed rib eye at Lander's upscale restaurant suitable for date nights. The attached brewery serves the same food in a more casual atmosphere among the mash tuns (steel brewing vessels) that churn out a rotating menu of handcrafted beer experiments – many of which are excellent (sample a few before committing).

Information

Lander Visitor Center (307-332-3892; www.landerchamber.org; 160 N 1st St; 9am-5pm Mon-Fri)

Getting There & Away

Wind River Transportation Authority (307-856-7118; www.wrtabuslines.com; cnr West Main St & Baldwin Creek Rd, Shopko; one way $1) provides scheduled services Monday to Friday between Riverton and Lander, plus reserved service to Casper or Jackson (prices vary based on number of riders). You'll want a car, however, to access trailheads and climbing crags.

Jackson

Welcome to the other side of Wyoming, not to mention one of the state's most appealing towns. Hiding in a verdant valley between some of America's most rugged and wild mountains, Jackson looks similar to other towns in the state – false-front roof lines, covered wooden walkways, saloons on every block – but it ain't quite the same.

Here, hard-core climbers, cyclists and skiers (recognizable as sunburned baristas) outnumber cowboys by a wide margin, and you're just as likely to see a celebrity as a moose wandering the urban trails.

Although Jackson, being posh and popular, does have its downsides for the traveler, it does mean you'll find a lively urban buzz, a refreshing variety of foods and no shortage of things to do – both in and out of town.

Sights & Activities

★National Museum of Wildlife Art MUSEUM
(Map p124; 307-733-5771; www.wildlifeart.org; 2820 Rungius Rd; adult/child $15/6; 9am-5pm May-Oct, 9am-5pm Tue-Sat, 11am-5pm Sun Nov-Apr;) Major works by Bierstadt, Rungius, Remington and Russell breathe life into their subjects in impressive and inspiring ways. The outdoor sculptures and building itself (inspired, oddly, by a ruined Scottish castle) are worth stopping by to see even if the museum is closed.

National Elk Refuge WILDLIFE RESERVE
(Map p124; 307-733-9212; www.fws.gov/refuge/national_elk_refuge; Hwy 89; sleigh ride adult/child $25/15; 10am-4pm mid-Dec–mid-Apr) This refuge protects Jackson's herd of several thousand elk, offering them a winter habitat from November to May. During summer, ask at the Jackson visitor center (p117) for the best places to see elk. An hour-long horse-drawn sleigh ride is the highlight of a winter visit; buy tickets at the visitor center.

★Jackson Hole Mountain Resort SNOW SPORTS
(Map p124; 307-733-2292; www.jacksonhole.com; adult/child ski pass $155/94, Grand Adventure pass $75; Nov-Apr & Jun-Sep) This mountain is larger than life. Whether tackling Jackson Hole with skis, board, boots or mountain bike, you will be humbled. With more than 4000ft of vertical rise and some of the world's most infamous slopes, Jackson Hole's 2500 acres and average 400in of snow sit at the top of every serious shredder's bucket list.

★Continental Divide Dogsled Adventures TOUR
(Map p124; 307-455-3052; www.dogsledadventures.com; half-day tour incl transportation & lunch $305; Dec-Apr) Experience Wyoming's wintry backcountry from a dog's point of view with five-time Iditarod veteran Billy Snodgrass. Half-day trips include transportation from your Jackson hotel to Togwotee Pass, where you'll learn dogsled lore and the sport's history while teams of eight to 14 Alaskan huskies whisk you (and a guide) silently through the wilderness.

Jackson Hole Paragliding PARAGLIDING
(Map p124; 307-739-2626; www.jhparagliding.com; tandem flight $345; May-Oct) The only thing better than being in the Tetons is to be soaring above the Tetons. Tandem rides

with experienced pilots take off from Jackson Hole Mountain Resort (p115) in the mornings or **Snow King** (Map p124; ☎307-201-5464; https://snowkingmountain.com; 400 E Snow King Ave; lift ticket adult/child $58/48) in the afternoons. No experience necessary, but age and weight limits apply.

Festivals & Events

Grand Teton Music Festival MUSIC
(GTMF; ☎307-733-1128; www.gtmf.org; Walk Festival Hall, Teton Village; ⏲Jul & Aug) A near-continuous celebration of classical music in a fantastic summer venue. The Festival Orchestra plays every Friday at 8pm and Saturday at 6pm showcasing worldwide musicians and directors. The GTMF Presents program highlights and noted talent on most Wednesdays. Free family concerts provide a more informal way to experience things.

Sleeping

In Jackson, the quality of accommodations is high, but so are the prices. Jackson has plenty of lodging, both in town and at Jackson Hole Mountain Resort (p115), but reservations are still essential in summer and winter high season. There are a few camping options scattered in the forest nearby, but most require a long drive, often down poor roads.

The Hostel HOSTEL $
(Map p124; ☎307-733-3415; www.thehostel.us; 3315 Village Dr, Teton Village; dm $32-55, r $50-170; @📶🐾) This skier's favorite has been here so long it doesn't need a name – everybody knows the Hostel. Budget privates and cramped four-person bunk rooms are smack in the middle of everything (meaning you'll only be in them when you're sleeping). The spacious lounge, with fireplace and pool table, foosball and ski waxing station, are all chill places to socialize.

Antler Inn HOTEL $$
(Map p124; ☎307-733-2535; www.townsquareinns.com/antler-inn; 43 W Pearl Ave; r $85-220, cabin $115-290; ❄📶🐾) Right in the middle of the Jackson action, this sprawling complex provides clean and comfortable rooms, some with fireplaces and bathtubs. Stepping into the cheaper 'cedar log' rooms feels like you're coming home to a cozy Wyoming cabin, mostly because you are: they were hauled here and attached to the back of the hotel.

Modern Mountain Motel MOTEL $$$
(Map p124; ☎307-733-4340; https://mountainmodernmotel.com; 380 W Broadway; r $125-330; P📶🏊) Marrying functionality (there's room to store your snow gear) with style (wall-sized B&W photographs and wall maps), Modern Mountain Motel takes the old motel idea and updates it for the modern age. Despite having 135 rooms, they're often full, and deservedly so.

★ **Wort Hotel** HISTORIC HOTEL $$$
(Map p124; ☎307-733-2190; www.worthotel.com; 50 N Glenwood St; r from $450; ❄@📶) A distinctly Wyoming feel permeates this luxury historic hotel that has only gotten better with age. Knotty pine furniture and handcrafted bedspreads complement full-size baths and Jacuzzis while the best concierge service in Jackson helps you fill out your itinerary with outdoor adventures. Even if staying here is out of your reach, swing by the antique **Silver Dollar Bar** downstairs.

★ **Rusty Parrot Lodge & Spa** LODGE $$$
(Map p124; ☎888-739-1749; www.rustyparrot.com; 175 N Jackson St; r from $475; ❄📶) With a collection of Remington sculptures and amazing Western art, this elegant lodge oozes luxury. Service is top-notch and rooms pamper with well-tended bedroom fireplaces and a plush teddy bear posed on the bed. Those who don't ski will get distracted at the spa, where the arnica sports massages and herbal lavender wraps are pure hedonism.

The gourmet restaurant prepares innovative international cuisine.

Eating

Persephone BAKERY $
(Map p124; ☎307-200-6708; www.persephonebakery.com; 145 E Broadway; mains $8-13; ⏲7am-6pm Mon-Sat, to 5pm Sun; 📶) With rustic breads, oversized pastries and breakfast masterpieces, this tiny white-washed French bakery is worth waiting in line for (and you will). In summer the spacious patio provides more room for lingering with your coffee – or go for a pitcher of Bloody Mary.

★ **Gun Barrel** STEAK $$
(Map p124; ☎307-733-3287; http://jackson.gunbarrel.com; 852 W Broadway; mains $16-56; ⏲5:30pm-late) The line stretches out the door for Jackson's best steakhouse, where the buffalo prime rib and elk chop rival the grilled bone-in rib eye for the title of 'king cut.' For a fun game, try to match the meat

with the animal watching you eat it: this place was once the wildlife and taxidermy museum, and many original tenants remain.

Mangy Moose Saloon PUB FOOD **$$**
(Map p124; ☎307-733-4913; www.mangymoose.com; 3295 Village Dr, Teton Village; mains lunch $8-23, dinner $18-48; ⏲7am-9pm, saloon 11am-2am; 📶) For more than half a century Mangy Moose has been the rowdy epicenter for après-ski, big-name bands, slopeside dining and general mountain mischief at Jackson Hole Mountain Resort (p115). The cavernous pub offers a decent salad bar and cranks out bowls of chili, buffalo burgers and steaks from local farms, while the Rocky Mountain Oyster Cafe has your breakfast needs covered.

Snake River Grill AMERICAN **$$$**
(Map p124; ☎307-733-0557; www.snakerivergrill.com; 84 E Broadway; mains $22-62; ⏲5:30-9pm) With a roaring stone fireplace, an extensive wine list and snappy white linens, this grill creates notable American haute cuisine. Try the pan-roasted Alaskan halibut or the Wagyu short ribs. Or munch on a cast-iron bucket of truffle fries. Splurge on desserts such as roasted strawberry sorbet.

Drinking & Nightlife

From breweries to bars to concerts to theaters, there's no lack of things to fill your evenings in Jackson, especially during the summer and winter high seasons. Consult the *Jackson Hole News & Guide* (www.jhnewsandguide.com) for the latest happenings, or just head downtown and follow the sound of happy crowds.

★**Snake River Brewing Co** MICROBREWERY
(Map p124; ☎307-739-2337; www.snakeriverbrewing.com; 265 S Millward St; ⏲food 11am-11pm, drinks till late; 📶) With an arsenal of microbrews crafted on the spot (some award-winning), it's no wonder this is a favorite among the younger, outdoor-sports-positive crowd. Food (mains $13 to $21) includes wood-fired pizzas, bison burgers and pasta served in a modern-industrial warehouse with two floors and plenty of (but not too many) TVs broadcasting the game.

The Rose COCKTAIL BAR
(Map p124; ☎307-733-1500; www.therosejh.com; 50 W Broadway; ⏲5:30pm-2am Thu-Sat, 8pm-1:30am Sun, Tue & Wed) Slide into a red-leather booth at this swanky little lounge upstairs at the Pink Garter theater and enjoy the best craft cocktails in Jackson.

Information

The excellent *Jackson Hole Traveler Visitor Guide*, available from the visitor center, is an excellent resource.

Jackson Hole & Greater Yellowstone Visitor Center (Map p124; ☎307-733-3316; www.jacksonholechamber.com; 532 N Cache St; ⏲8am-7pm Jun-Sep; 📶) Everything you need to know about Jackson, the nearby national parks, wildlife and more. Enjoy a handful of exhibits, pick up hunting or fishing licenses, buy park passes and otherwise plan your visit with expert guidance.

Getting There & Around

Jackson Hole Airport (JAC; Map p124; ☎307-733-7682; www.jacksonholeairport.com; 1250 E Airport Rd) is inside Grand Teton National Park 7 miles north of Jackson. Daily direct flights go to Chicago, Dallas, Denver, Los Angeles, Minneapolis, Phoenix, Salt Lake City, and San Francisco, plus many more seasonal flights.

Alltrans (Mountain States Express; ☎800-652-9510, 307-733-1719; www.jacksonholealltrans.com) runs a shuttle to Salt Lake ($82, 5¼ hours) and Grand Targhee ski area (adult/child including lift pass $128/97) in winter.

Greyhound (www.greyhound.com) has long-haul buses to Denver (from $90, 23½ hours).

Cody

You have a few choices when it comes to getting into Yellowstone National Park, and approaching from the Cody side of life should be top on your list. Not just for the mesmerizing drive along the North Fork of the Shoshone – which Theodore Roosevelt once called the '50 most beautiful miles in America' – but also for the town.

Cody revels in its frontier image, a legacy that started with its founder, William 'Buffalo Bill' Cody: Chief of Scouts for the army, notorious buffalo hunter, and showman who spent years touring the world with his Wild West extravaganza. The town rallies around nightly rodeos in summer, rowdy saloons and a world-class museum that was started by Buffalo Bill's estate and is a worthy destination all by itself.

Sights

★**Buffalo Bill Center of the West** MUSEUM
(☎307-587-4771; www.centerofthewest.org; 720 Sheridan Ave; adult/child $19.50/13; ⏲8am-6pm May–mid-Sep, 8am-5pm mid-Sep–Oct, 10am-5pm Nov, Mar & Apr, 10am-5pm Thu-Sun Dec-Feb)

Do not miss Wyoming's most impressive human-made attraction. This sprawling complex of six museums showcases everything Western: from the spectacle of Buffalo Bill's world-famous Wild West shows and galleries featuring powerful frontier-oriented artwork, to the visually absorbing **Plains Indian Museum**. Meanwhile, the **Draper Museum of Natural History** brilliantly explores the Yellowstone region's ecosystem. Look for Teddy Roosevelt's saddle, the busy beaver ball and one of the world's last buffalo tepees. Entry is valid for two consecutive days – and you'll need 'em. Save a couple of bucks by booking online.

Sleeping

Irma Hotel HISTORIC HOTEL **$$**
(307-587-4221; www.irmahotel.com; 1192 Sheridan Ave; r $155-175, ste $230;) Built in 1902 by Buffalo Bill as the cornerstone of his planned city, this creaky hotel has old-fashioned charm with a few modern touches. The original high-ceiling historical suites are named after past guests (Annie Oakley, Calamity Jane), while the slightly more modern annex rooms are very similar but cheaper (and still have classic pull-chain toilets).

The Cody HOTEL **$$$**
(307-587-5915; www.thecody.com; 232 W Yellowstone Ave; d $260-290;) One of Cody's most luxurious hotels, the Cody combines New Western chic with green credentials, incorporating paneling made with recycled wood from park facilities and offering free bicycles to guests. Pay $10 extra for a balcony room away from the road, or $30 more for a king Jacuzzi suite. Breakfast included.

Cody Cowboy Village CABIN **$$**
(307-587-7555; www.thecodycowboyvillage.com; 203 W Yellowstone Ave; r & cabins $100-230; May–mid-Oct;) Popular and well-run, the modern and stylish duplex cabins or stand-alone suites come with small porch. There's a large outdoor plunge pool. Breakfast is included.

Eating

★**The Local** MODERN AMERICAN **$$**
(307-586-4262; www.thelocalcody.com; 1134 13th St; lunch $11-14, dinner $9-38; 9am-2pm & 5-8pm Tue-Sat;) When Cody's cowboy cuisine starts to weigh on your arteries, find the antidote in the Local's fresh, organic and locally sourced dishes. Think a falafel sandwich or grilled trout.

Cassie's Western Saloon STEAK **$$**
(307-527-5500; https://cassies.com; 214 Yellowstone Ave; lunch $12-29, steaks $22-50; food 11am-10pm, drinks to 2am) This classic roadhouse and former house of ill repute hosts heavy swilling, swingin' country-and-western music and the occasional bar fight. Strap on the feedbag at the attached supper club and tackle tender steaks ranging in size from 8oz to 36oz.

Entertainment

Cody Nite Rodeo SPECTATOR SPORT
(307-587-5155; www.codystampederodeo.com; 519 W Yellowstone Ave; adult/child $21/10.50; 8pm Jun-Aug) Experience a quintessential small-town rodeo at this summer-night Cody tradition. Note that animal welfare groups often criticize rodeo events as being harmful to animals.

Getting There & Away

Yellowstone Regional Airport (COD; 307-587-5096; www.flyyra.com; 2101 Roger Sedam Dr), Cody's small airport on the eastern edge of town, connects this otherwise isolated town with Salt Lake City and Denver in summer, and you can thank Buffalo Bill Cody for the scenic byway that bears his name and connects Cody to Yellowstone – a spectacular approach to the park.

Yellowstone National Park

Teeming with moose, elk, bison, grizzly bears and wolves, America's first **national park** (Map p120; 307-344-7381; www.nps.gov/yell; Grand Loop Rd, Mammoth; vehicle $35; North Entrance year-round, South Entrance May-Oct) also contains some of the country's wildest lands, just begging to be explored.

Yellowstone is home to more than 60% of the world's geysers – natural hot springs with unique plumbing that causes them to periodically erupt in towering explosions of boiling water and steam. And while these astounding phenomena and their neighboring Technicolor hot springs and bubbling mud pots draw in the crowds (more than 4 million people each year), the surrounding canyons, mountains and forests are no less impressive.

Sights

Geyser Country

Yellowstone's Geyser Country holds the park's most spectacular geothermal features (more than half the world's total), within the world's densest concentration of geysers (more than 200 spouters in 1.5 sq miles). It is Geyser Country that makes the Yellowstone plateau utterly and globally unique.

Highlights include **Old Faithful** (Map p120) and the **Upper Geyser Basin** (Map p120) and Grand Prismatic Spring (p119). The majority of the geysers line the Firehole River, the aquatic backbone of the basin, whose tributaries feed 21 of the park's 110 waterfalls. Both the Firehole and Madison Rivers offer superb fly-fishing, and the meadows along them support large wildlife populations.

Old Faithful Visitor Education Center VISITOR CENTER
(Map p120; ☎307-545-2751; Old Faithful; ⊙8am-8pm Jun-Sep, 9am-5pm Dec-Mar, hours vary spring & fall; 👪) This environmentally friendly center is all about the thermal features at Yellowstone, exploring the differences between geysers, hot springs, fumaroles and mud pots, and explaining why there are no geysers in Mammoth. Kids will enjoy the hands-on Young Scientist displays, which include a working laboratory geyser. Predicted eruption times are posted for a handful of the park's most famous gushers.

★**Grand Prismatic Spring** HOT SPRINGS
(Map p120; Midway Geyser Basin) At 370ft wide and 121ft deep, Grand Prismatic Spring is the park's largest and deepest hot spring. It's also considered by many to be the most beautiful thermal feature in the park. Boardwalks lead around the multicolored mist of the gorgeous pool and its spectacularly colored rainbow rings of algae. From above, the spring looks like a giant blue eye weeping exquisite multicolored tears.

Mammoth Country

Mammoth Country is renowned for its graceful geothermal terraces and the towering Gallatin Range to the northwest.

For visitors (and most elk) the focal point of the Mammoth region is Mammoth Junction (6239ft), 5 miles south of the North Entrance, on a plateau above Mammoth Campground. Just south of the junction is Mammoth Hot Springs, the area's main thermal attraction. From here roads go south to Norris (21 miles) and east to Tower-Roosevelt Junction (18 miles).

> WORTH A TRIP
>
> **SCENIC DRIVE: THE ROOF OF THE ROCKIES**
>
> Depending on who's talking, the **Beartooth Hwy** (www.beartoothhighway.com; Hwy 212; ⊙late May–mid-Oct) is either the best way to get to Yellowstone, the most exciting motorbike ride in the West or the most scenic highway in the USA. We'd say it is all three. The head-spinning tarmac snakes up the mountainside to deposit you in a different world, high above the tree line, onto a rolling plateau of mountain tundra, alpine lakes and Rocky Mountain goats. The views are superb, the fishing awesome and the hiking literally breathtaking.

Tower-Roosevelt Country

Fossil forests, the wildlife-rich **Lamar Valley** (Map p120), its tributary trout streams of Slough and Pebble Creeks and the dramatic and craggy peaks of the Absaroka Range are the highlights in this remote, scenic and undeveloped region.

Canyon Country

A series of scenic overlooks linked by hiking trails punctuate the cliffs, precipices and waterfalls of the Grand Canyon of the Yellowstone. Here the river continues to gouge out a fault line through an ancient golden geyser basin, most impressively at **Lower Falls**. South Rim Drive leads to the canyon's most spectacular overlook, at **Artist Point** (Map p120; South Rim Dr, Canyon), while **North Rim Drive** accesses the daring precipices of the Upper and Lower Falls.

Grand Canyon of the Yellowstone CANYON
(Map p120) Near Canyon Village, this is one of the park's true blockbuster sights. After its placid meanderings north from Yellowstone Lake, the Yellowstone River suddenly plummets over Upper Falls and then the much larger Lower Falls before raging through the 1000ft-deep canyon. Scenic overlooks and a network of trails along the canyon's

Yellowstone National Park

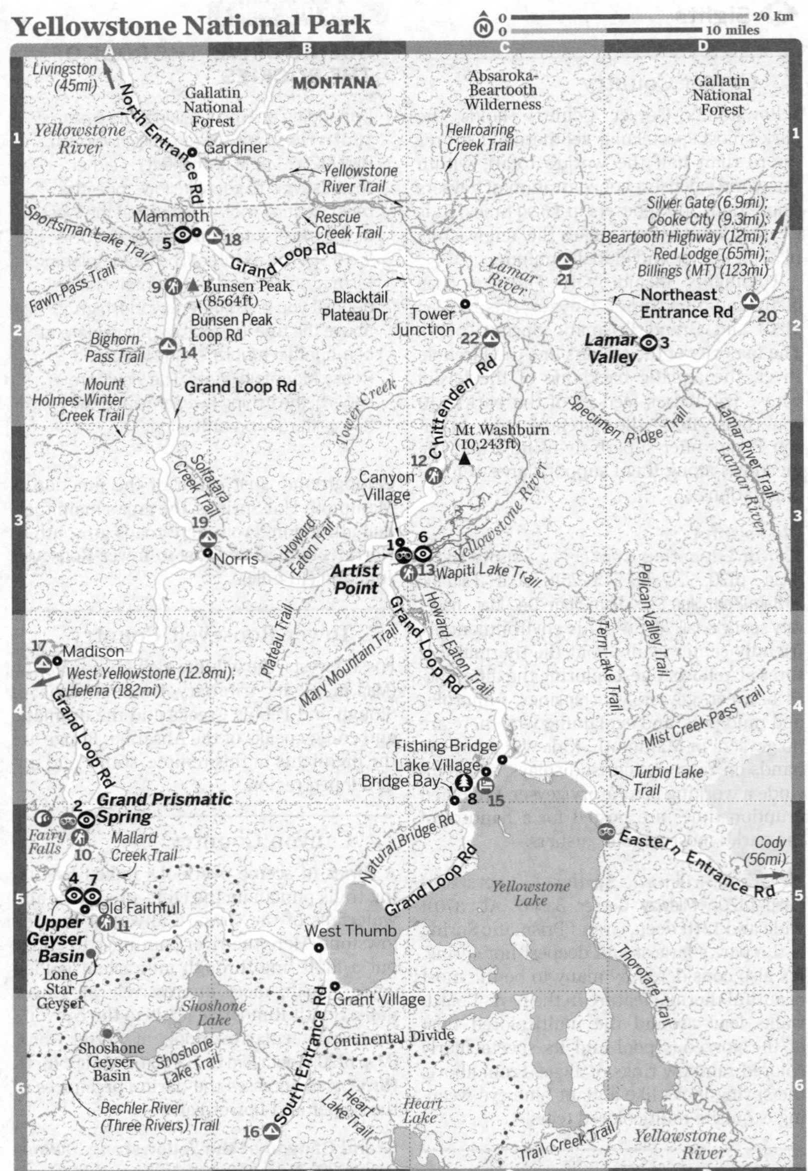

rims highlight its multicolored beauty from a dozen angles.

Lake Country

Yellowstone Lake (7733ft) is Lake Country's shimmering centerpiece – one of the world's largest alpine lakes, with the biggest inland population of cutthroat trout in the US. Yellowstone River emerges from the north end of the lake and flows through Hayden Valley into the Grand Canyon of the Yellowstone. The lake's southern and eastern borders flank the steep Absaroka Range

Yellowstone National Park

Top Sights
1 Artist Point ... B3
2 Grand Prismatic Spring ... A5
3 Lamar Valley ... D2
4 Upper Geyser Basin ... A5

Sights
5 Albright Visitor Center ... A2
6 Grand Canyon of the Yellowstone ... C3
7 Old Faithful ... A5
Old Faithful Visitor Education Center ... (see 7)
8 Yellowstone National Park ... C4

Activities, Courses & Tours
9 Bunsen Peak & Osprey Falls ... A2
10 Fairy Falls Trail & Twin Buttes ... A5
11 Lone Star Geyser Trail ... A5
12 Mt Washburn ... C3
13 South Rim Trail & Ribbon Lake ... C3

Sleeping
14 Indian Creek Campground ... A2
15 Lake Yellowstone Hotel ... C4
16 Lewis Lake Campground ... B6
17 Madison Campground ... A4
18 Mammoth Campground ... B2
19 Norris Campground ... A3
Old Faithful Inn ... (see 7)
20 Pebble Creek Campground ... D2
21 Slough Creek Campground ... C2
22 Tower Fall Campground ... C2

Eating
Lake Yellowstone Hotel Dining Room ... (see 15)
Mammoth Hot Springs Dining Room ... (see 5)

and the pristine Thorofare region, some of the wildest and remotest lands in the lower 48. This watery wilderness lined with volcanic beaches is best explored by **boat** (Map p124; ☎307-734-9227; www.jennylakeboating.com; round-trip shuttle adult/child 2-11yrs $15/8, scenic cruise US$19/11; 7am-7pm Jun-late Sep) or sea kayak.

Activities

★Bunsen Peak & Osprey Falls
HIKING, MOUNTAIN BIKING

(Map p120) Bunsen Peak (8564ft) is a popular early-season half-day hike that offers superb views in all directions. You can extend it to a more demanding day hike by continuing down the mountain's gentler eastern slope to the Bunsen Peak Rd and then *waaay* down (800ft) to the base of seldom-visited Osprey Falls.

Lone Star Geyser Trail
HIKING, CYCLING

(Map p120) This paved and pine-lined hike is an easy stroll (or family bike ride) along a former service road to one of the park's largest backcountry geysers. Isolated Lone Star erupts every three hours for two to 30 minutes and reaches 30ft to 45ft in height. It is definitely worth hanging around for an eruption if possible.

Mt Washburn
HIKING, MOUNTAIN BIKING

(Map p120; Tower-Roosevelt) This fairly strenuous two-hour uphill hike from Dunraven Pass trailhead to a mountaintop fire tower with 360-degree views over the park and nearby bighorn sheep is Yellowstone's most popular hike (6.4 miles round-trip, four hours). Alternatively, tackle the climb on a bicycle via the dirt Chittenden Rd from the north. The route's often blocked by snow until the end of June.

Fairy Falls Trail & Twin Buttes
HIKING

(Map p120) Tucked away in the northwestern corner of the Midway Geyser Basin, Fairy Falls (197ft) is a popular hike. Beyond Fairy Falls the trail continues to a hidden thermal area at the base of the Twin Buttes. The geysers are undeveloped, and you're likely to have them to yourself – a stark contrast to the throngs surrounding Grand Prismatic Spring (p119) below.

Sleeping

NPS and private campgrounds, along with cabins, lodges and hotels are all available in the park. Reservations, where possible, are essential in summer. Plentiful accommodations can also be found in the gateway towns of Cody, Gardiner and West Yellowstone.

The best budget options are the seven NPS-run campgrounds in **Mammoth** (Map p120; Mammoth; campsites $20; year-round), **Tower Fall** (Map p120; Tower-Roosevelt; campsites $15; mid-May–late Sep), **Indian Creek** (Map p120; Mammoth; campsites $15; early Jun–mid-Sep), **Pebble Creek** (Map p120; campsites $15; mid-Jun–late Sep), **Slough Creek** (Map p120; Tower-Roosevelt; campsites $15; mid-Jun–early Oct), Norris Campground (p122) and **Lewis Lake** (Map p120; South Entrance; campsites

$15; mid-Jun–Oct), which are first come, first served.

Xanterra (307-344-7311; www.yellowstonenationalparklodges.com) runs five more reservable campgrounds, all with cold-water bathrooms, flush toilets and drinking water. RV sites with full hookups are available at Fishing Bridge.

Norris Campground CAMPGROUND $

(Map p120; Norris; campsites $20; mid-May–Sep) Nestled in a scenic, open, lodgepole-pine forest on a sunny hill overlooking the Gibbon River and meadows, this is one of the park's nicest campgrounds. Sites are given on a first-come basis and the few loop-A riverside spots get snapped up quickly. Campfire talks are at 7:30pm and firewood is sold between 7pm and 8:30pm. Generators allowed 8am to 8pm.

Madison Campground CAMPGROUND $

(Map p120; 307-344-7311; www.yellowstonenationalparklodges.com; W Entrance Rd, Madison; campsites $26; May-Oct) The nearest campground to Old Faithful and the West Entrance occupies a sunny, open forest in a broad meadow above the Madison River. Bison and the park's largest elk herd frequent the meadows to its west, making for great wildlife-watching, and it's a fine base for fly-fishing the Madison. You can (and should) reserve your site in advance.

★ **Old Faithful Inn** HOTEL $$

(Map p120; 307-344-7311; www.yellowstonenationalparklodges.com; Old Faithful; d with shared/private bath from $167/288, r $368-437; early May-early Oct) A stay at this historic log masterpiece is a quintessential Yellowstone experience. The lobby alone is worth a visit, just to sit in front of the impossibly large rhyolite fireplace and listen to the pianist upstairs. The cheapest 'Old House' rooms provide the most atmosphere, with log walls and original washbasins, but bathrooms are down the hall.

Lake Yellowstone Hotel HOTEL $$$

(Map p120; 866-439-7375; www.yellowstonenationalparklodges.com; cottages $209, Sandpiper $305-341, hotel r $277-632; mid-May–early Oct; @) Commanding the northern lakeshore, this buttercup-yellow colonial behemoth sets romantics aflutter. It harks back to a bygone era, though the rooms that cost $4 in 1895 have appreciated somewhat. Lakeside rooms cost extra, sell out first and don't guarantee lake views. Small cottages have rooms with two double beds. Internet access is wired only, and available in main hotel rooms.

Eating

★ **Mammoth Hot Springs Dining Room** AMERICAN $$

(Map p120; Mammoth; dinner mains $12-26; 6:30-10am, 11:30am-2:30pm & 5-10pm May–mid-Sep;) There are a few surprises in this elegant place, including a delicious dinner starter of Thai-curry mussels. Dinner is a serious affair, with Montana meatloaf, and pistachio-and-parmesan-crusted trout. For dessert, try the 'Yellowstone caldera': a warm chocolate-truffle torte with a suitably molten center. Reservations only necessary in winter. From mid-September through October hours remain the same, except dinner is served until 9pm.

Lake Yellowstone Hotel Dining Room AMERICAN $$$

(Map p120; 307-344-7311; www.yellowstonenationalparklodges.com; Lake Village; dinner mains $16-37; 6:30-10am, 11:30am-2:30pm & 5-10pm mid-May–early Oct;) Save your one unwrinkled outfit to feast in style in Lake Yellowstone Hotel's dining room. Lunch options include trout, poached-pear salad and sandwiches. Dinner ups the ante with starters of lobster ravioli and mains of beef tenderloin, elk chops, quail and rack of Montana lamb. Dinner reservations are required.

Information

The park is open year-round, but most roads close in winter. Park entrance permits (hiker/vehicle $15/30) are valid for seven days. For entry into both Yellowstone and Grand Teton the fee is $50.

SOUTH RIM TRAIL

Southeast of the Yellowstone canyon's South Rimx, a network of **trails** Map p120) meanders through meadows and forests and past some small lakes, including **Ribbon Lake**. Linking several of these trails, the South Rim Trail loop hike (6 miles, four hours) combines awesome views of the Grand Canyon of the Yellowstone (p119) with a couple of lakes and even a backcountry thermal area.

BEAT THE CROWDS

Yellowstone's wonderland attracts up to 30,000 visitors daily in July and August and tops four million gatecrashers annually. Avoid the worst of the crowds with the following advice:

Visit in May or October Services may be limited, but there will be far fewer people.

Hit the trail Most (95%) of visitors never set foot on a backcountry trail; only 1% camp at a backcountry site (permit required).

Bike the park Most campgrounds have underutilized hiker/biker sites, and your skinny tires can slip through any traffic jam.

Mimic the wildlife Be active during the golden hours after dawn and before dusk.

Pack a lunch Eat at one of the park's many overlooked and often lovely scenic picnic areas.

Bundle up Enjoy a private Old Faithful eruption during the winter months.

Cell service is limited in the park, and wi-fi can only be found at Mammoth's **Albright Visitor Center** (Map p120; 307-344-2263; www.nps.gov/yell/planyourvisit/mammothvc.htm; Mammoth; 8am-6pm mid-Jun–Aug, 9am-5pm Sep–mid-Jun).

Getting There & Away

Most visitors to Yellowstone fly into Jackson, WY, or Bozeman, MT, but it's often more affordable to choose Billings, MT. You will need a car; there is no public transportation to or within Yellowstone National Park.

Grand Teton National Park

Awesome in their grandeur, the Tetons have captivated the imagination from the moment humans laid eyes on them. This **wilderness** (Map p124; 307-739-3300; www.nps.gov/grte; entrance per vehicle/motorcyclist $35/30, hiker or cyclist $20) is home to bear, moose and elk in number, and played a fundamental role in the history of American alpine climbing.

Some 12 imposing glacier-carved summits frame the singular Grand Teton (13,775ft). And while the view is breathtaking from the valley floor, it only gets more impressive on the trail. It's well worth hiking the dramatic canyons of fragrant forest to sublime alpine lakes surrounded by wildflowers in summer.

Sights & Activities

With almost 250 miles of **hiking trails**, options are plentiful. Backcountry-use permits are required for overnight trips. **Rock climbing** and **fishing** are also possible.

Cross-country skiing and **snowshoeing** are the best ways to take advantage of park winters. Pick up a brochure detailing routes at Craig Thomas Discovery & Visitor Center.

Craig Thomas Discovery & Visitor Center TOURIST INFORMATION
(Map p124; 307-739-3399; www.nps.gov/grte/planyourvisit/ctdvc.htm; Teton Park Rd, Moose; 8am-7pm Jun-Aug, hours vary Mar-May, Sep & Oct;) Your first stop should be this incredibly well-done visitor center. The raised-relief map helps you focus on where to go, while informative kid-friendly interactive displays show what you'll see. Rangers are on hand to help plan your visit, and you can get backcountry permits here, too.

Mormon Row GHOST TOWN
(Map p124; Antelope Flats Rd; P) This is possibly the most photographed spot in the park – and for good reason. The aged wooden barns and fence rails make a quintessential pastoral scene, perfectly framed by the imposing bulk of the Tetons. The barns and houses were built in the 1890s by Mormon settlers, who farmed the fertile alluvial soil irrigated by miles of hand-dug ditches.

Oxbow Bend RIVER
(Map p124; N Park Rd; P) One of the most famous scenic spots in Grand Teton National Park for wildlife-watching is Oxbow Bend, with the reflection of Mt Moran as a stunning backdrop. Dawn and dusk are the best times to spot moose, elk, sandhill cranes, ospreys, bald eagles, trumpeter swans, Canada geese, blue herons and white pelicans. The oxbow was created as the river's faster

Grand Teton National Park

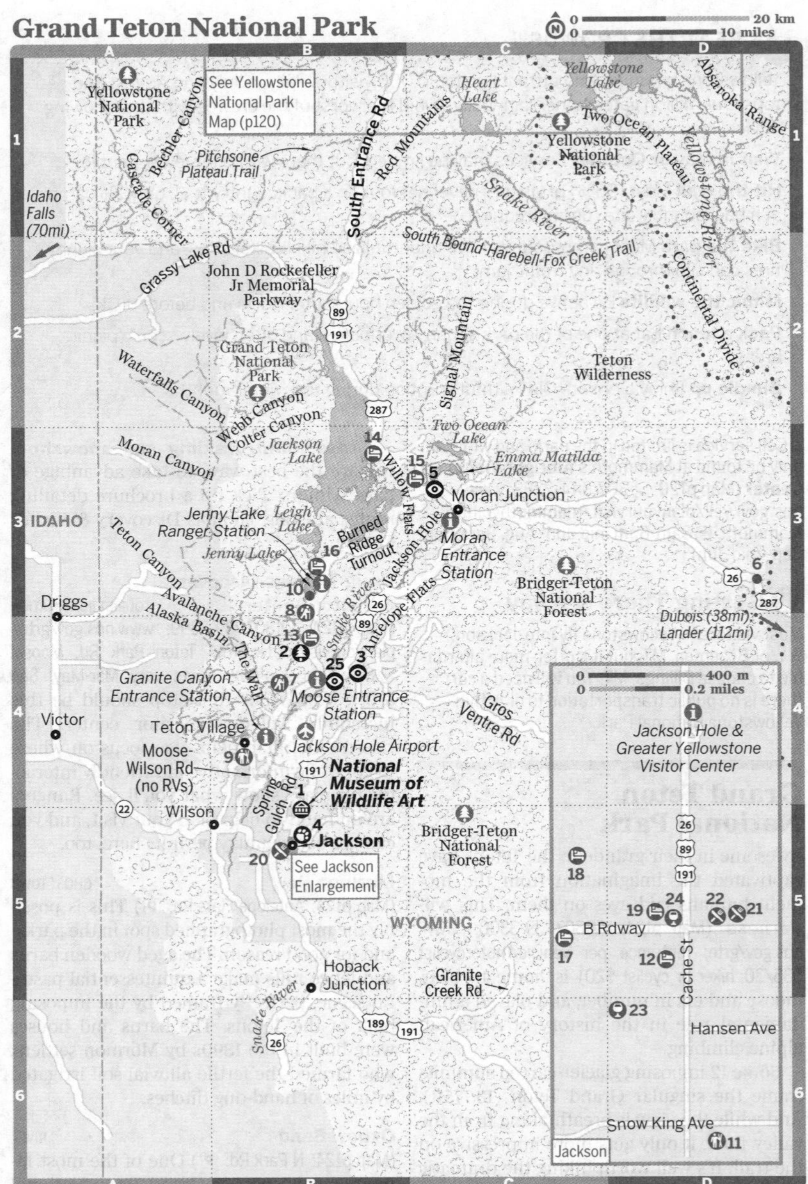

water eroded the outer bank while the slower inner flow deposited sediment.

Death Canyon Trail HIKING

(Map p124) Death Canyon is one of our favorite hikes – both for the challenge and the astounding scenery. The trail ascends a mile to the Phelps Lake overlook before dropping down into the valley bottom and following Death Canyon.

Garnet Canyon HIKING, CLIMBING

(Map p124) Garnet Canyon is the hard-won gateway to scrambles to Middle and South

Grand Teton National Park

Top Sights
1 National Museum of Wildlife Art B5

Sights
2 Grand Teton National Park B4
3 Mormon Row B4
4 National Elk Refuge B5
5 Oxbow Bend C3

Activities, Courses & Tours
Adventure Sports .... (see 25)
6 Continental Divide Dogsled Adventures D3
7 Death Canyon Trail B4
8 Garnet Canyon B3
9 Jackson Hole Mountain Resort B4
Jackson Hole Paragliding .... (see 9)
10 Jenny Lake Boating B3
11 Snow King Resort D6

Sleeping
12 Antler Inn D5
13 Climbers' Ranch B4
14 Colter Bay Village B3
15 Jackson Lake Lodge C3
16 Jenny Lake Lodge B3
17 Modern Mountain Motel C5
18 Rusty Parrot Lodge & Spa C5
The Hostel .... (see 9)
19 Wort Hotel D5

Eating
Blue Heron Lounge .... (see 15)
Dornan's Chuckwagon .... (see 25)
Dornan's Trading Post .... (see 25)
20 Gun Barrel B5
Jenny Lake Lodge Dining Room .... (see 16)
Mangy Moose Saloon .... (see 9)
21 Persephone D5
Pizza & Pasta Company .... (see 25)
22 Snake River Grill D5

Drinking & Nightlife
23 Snake River Brewing Co D6
24 The Rose D5

Information
25 Craig Thomas Discovery & Visitor Center B4

Teton and the technical ascent of Grand Teton – but you need technical climbing skills and an existing familiarity with the routes. However, even non-climbers will find the 4-mile hike to the starting point of the Grand Teton climb a memorable one.

Grand Teton Multiuse Bike Path CYCLING
(www.nps.gov/grte/planyourvisit/bike.htm; ⌚dawn-dusk May-Oct) Starting in the town of Jackson from Jackson Visitor Center (p117) and continuing 20 miles to the **Jenny Lake Ranger Station** (Map p124; ☎307-739-3343; 407 Jenny Lake Campground Road, Moose, WY; ⌚8am-5pm Jun-Aug), this multiuse path is an excellent way to see the park at a slow, intimate pace. For a shorter ride, rent bikes at **Dornan's** (Map p124; ☎307-733-3307; www.dornans.com; ⌚9am-6pm) in Moose for the 8-mile ride to Jenny Lake.

Sleeping

★Climbers' Ranch CABIN $
(Map p124; ☎307-733-7271; www.americanalpineclub.org/grand-teton-climbers-ranch; End Highlands Rd; dm $27; ⌚Jun-Sep; P) Started as a refuge for serious climbers, these rustic log cabins run by the American Alpine Club are now available to hikers, who can take advantage of the spectacular in-park location. There is a bathhouse with showers and a sheltered cook station with locking bins for coolers. Bring your own sleeping bag and pad (bunks are bare, but still a steal).

Colter Bay Village CABIN $$
(Map p124; ☎307-543-3100; www.gtlc.com/lodges/colter-bay-village; Colter Bay; tent cabins $76, cabins with bath $189-267; ⌚late May-Sep; P) In this busy village, comfortable log cabins, some original, are your best bet, available late May through September. Tent cabins (available June to early September) are very basic log-and-canvas structures sporting Siberian gulag charm. Expect bare bunks, a wood-burning stove, a picnic table and an outdoor grill. Bathrooms are separate and sleeping bags can be rented.

★Jackson Lake Lodge LODGE $$$
(Map p124; ☎307-543-3100; www.gtlc.com/lodges/jackson-lake-lodge; Jackson Lake Lodge Rd; r & cottages $339-459, ste $850; ⌚mid-May–early Oct; P) With soft sheets, meandering trails for long walks and enormous picture windows framing the peaks, the Teton's premier lodge is the perfect place to romance. Nearby, you may find the 348 cinder-block cottages overpriced for their viewless, barracks-like arrangement, though renovations have made them pleasant inside. The secluded Moose Pond View cottages feature amazing porch-side panoramas.

★ Jenny Lake Lodge LODGE **$$$**
(Map p124; ☎307-543-3100; www.gtlc.com/lodges/jenny-lake-lodge; Jenny Lake Scenic Dr; all-inclusive cabins from $542; ⏰Jun-early Oct; P) Worn timbers, down comforters and colorful quilts imbue these elegant cabins with a cozy atmosphere. It doesn't come cheap, but the Signature Stay package includes breakfast, five-course dinner, bicycle use and guided horseback riding. Rainy days are for hunkering down at the fireplace in the main lodge with a game or book from the stacks.

Eating

Pizza & Pasta Company PIZZA **$**
(Map p124; ☎307-733-2415; www.dornans.com; Moose; mains $10-13, pizzas $9-17; ⏰11:30am-9:30pm; 📶) If there is a more compelling place for pizza and beers than **Dornan's** (Map p124; ☎307-733-2415; www.dornans.com; Moose; ⏰8am-8pm) rooftop deck, looking across the Snake River and Menor's Ferry at the towering Tetons, we've yet to find it. Unfortunately service can be slow and the food comes second to the view. One of the only independently owned restaurants in the park, it's open year-round.

Blue Heron Lounge BARBECUE **$$**
(Map p124; ☎307-543-2811; www.gtlc.com/dining/blue-heron-lounge-jackson-lake-lodge; Jackson Lake Lodge; mains $11-23; ⏰11am-midnight mid-May–Sep) A must for sunset cocktails, this attractive wraparound bar features knee-to-ceiling windows. Alcohol and tasty small plates consisting of charcuterie and salads are locally sourced. If the weather is good, the outdoor grill offers great barbecue. Occasionally you'll hit on live music.

Dornan's Chuckwagon BARBECUE **$$**
(Map p124; ☎307-733-2415; www.dornans.com; Moose; breakfast & lunch mains $8-20, dinner $9-35; ⏰7-11am, noon-3pm & 5-9pm Jun-Aug) At this outdoor family favorite, breakfast means sourdough pancakes and eggs off the griddle, while lunchtime offers light fare and sandwiches. Come dinner, Dutch ovens are steaming. There's beef, ribs or trout, along with a bottomless salad bar. Picnic tables have unparalleled views of the Grand. Kids get special rates. There's live music from 5:30pm to 8:30pm, Tuesday to Thursday.

★ Jenny Lake Lodge Dining Room AMERICAN **$$$**
(Map p124; ☎307-543-3351; www.gtlc.com/dining/the-dining-room-at-jenny-lake-lodge; Jenny Lake Lodge; lunch $12-18, 5-course prix-fixe dinner $98; ⏰7:30-10am, 11:30am-1:30pm & 6-9pm) 🍃 A real splurge, this may be the only five-course wilderness meal of your life, and it's well worth it. For breakfast, crab-cake eggs Benedict is prepared to perfection. Elk tenderloin and daikon watermelon salad satisfy hungry hikers, and you can't beat the warm atmosphere snuggled in the Tetons. Dress up in the evening, when reservations are a must.

Information

Park permits (hiker/bicycle/vehicle $20/30/35) are valid for seven days.

Getting There & Away

Jackson Hole Airport (p117) lies inside the park's boundaries and sees a steady stream of traffic. Currently there is no regular shuttle service through the park, though several companies in Jackson provide guided tours.

The park begins 4.5 miles north of Jackson. There are three entrance stations. The closest to Jackson is the **South Entrance** (Map p124; Teton Park Rd, Moose Village; ⏰hours vary), west of Moose Junction. From Teton Village, the **Southwest Entrance** (Map p124; Moose-Wilson Rd; ⏰hours vary) is a mile or so north via the Moose–Wilson Rd. If driving south from Yellowstone, take the **North Entrance** (Map p124; Hwy 287; ⏰hours vary), 3 miles inside the park on US 89/191/287 just north of Moran Junction.

MONTANA

Welcome to Big Sky Country, where the Great Plains hit the Rockies and just about anything seems possible. Wilderness areas rule out here, whether it's the pre-Yellowstone valleys of Montana's south to Absaroka Beartooth, Bob Marshall or the American Prairie Reserve and the horizons-without-end in Montana's rural heartland. Not far away, Missoula and Bozeman are hip urban centers rich in brewpubs, great restaurants and scenes of emerging culinary excellence. Montana is also home to Little Bighorn Battlefield and, the state's major drawcard, the sculpted peaks of Glacier National Park, one of the most dramatically beautiful corners of the continent.

Information

There are tourist offices in towns across the state. The better ones are in **Bozeman** (☎406-586-5421; www.bozemancvb.com; 2000

Commerce Way; ⌚8am-5pm Mon-Fri), **Billings** (☎800-735-2635, 406-252-4016; www.visitbillings.com; 815 S 27th St; ⌚8:30am-5pm Mon-Fri), Helena (p130), **West Yellowstone** (☎406-646-7701; www.destinationyellowstone.com; 30 Yellowstone Ave; ⌚8am-8pm mid-May–Aug, 8am-4pm Mon-Fri Sep–mid-May; 📶) and Missoula (p132).

Visit Montana (☎800-847-4868; www.visitmt.com), the state's informative tourism website, has maps, guides and trip suggestions.

Bozeman & Gallatin Valley

Bozeman is what all those formerly hip, now-overrun Colorado mountain towns used to be like. The laid-back, old-school rancher legacy still dominates over the New West pioneers with their mountain bikes, skis and climbing racks. But that's changing rapidly. It is now one of the fastest-growing towns in America.

The brick buildings downtown, overflowing with brewpubs and boutiques, still retain their dusty historic appeal and you can spend days in the surrounding Bridger and Gallatin Mountains without seeing another human.

And, while Big Sky up the forested Gallatin Valley is besieged with condos and townhomes, Bridger Bowl is so underdeveloped you might question whether the place is still open. In short, get here quick so you can tell your kids about the time you were in Bozeman while it was still one of the coolest unknown towns in the Rockies.

Sights & Activities

★Museum of the Rockies MUSEUM

(☎406-994-2251; www.museumoftherockies.org; 600 W Kagy Blvd; adult/child $14.50/9.50; ⌚8am-6pm Jun-Aug, 9am-5pm Sep-May) The most entertaining museum in Montana should not be missed. It has stellar displays on the geological history of the Rockies, and dinosaur exhibits including an Edmontosaurus jaw with its incredible battery of teeth, the largest T. rex skull in the world, and a full T. rex (with only a slightly smaller skull). Laser planetarium shows are interesting, as is the living-history outdoors section (closed in winter).

★Bridger Bowl Ski Area SNOW SPORTS

(☎406-587-2111; www.bridgerbowl.com; 15795 Bridger Canyon Rd; lift ticket adult/child $64/25; ⌚mid-Dec–Apr) As the nation's leading nonprofit ski resort, it's all about the 'cold smoke,' not cold, hard cash, at Bridger Bowl. All you'll find at this small (2000 acres) community-owned hill 16 miles north of Bozeman is passionate skiers, reasonable prices and surprisingly great skiing.

Big Sky Resort SNOW SPORTS

(☎800-548-4486; www.bigskyresort.com; 50 Big Sky Resort Rd; ski/bike lift $142/46) The fourth-largest ski hill in North America is actually four mountains covering 5800 acres of skiable terrain (60% advanced/expert) that get more than 400in of powder a year. In short, Big Sky is big skiing. And when the snow melts, you get more than 40 miles of lift-served mountain-bike and hiking trails making it a worthy summer destination as well.

Explore Rentals OUTDOORS

(Phasmid; ☎406-922-0179; www.explore-rentals.com; 32 Dollar Dr; ⌚9am-5pm Mon-Sat, 10am-4pm Sun) Imagine stepping off the plane and there waiting for you is a car complete with luggage box, camping trailer, cook set, sleeping bags, backpacks, tent, bear spray and full fly-fishing setup – all ready to go for your ultimate outdoor adventure. Or maybe you just forgot your stove. Explore has that and (just about) everything else for rent. Reservations highly recommended.

Sleeping

Most big-box chain motels are north of downtown Bozeman on 7th Ave, near I-90, with a handful of budget options east of downtown. Camping is plentiful in the Gallatin Valley toward Big Sky.

★Howlers Inn B&B $$

(☎406-587-2050; www.howlersinn.com; 3185 Jackson Creek Rd; r $135-180, cabin $225; 📶) Wolf-watchers will love this beautiful sanctuary 15 minutes outside of Bozeman. Rescued captive-born wolves live in enclosed natural areas on 4 acres, supported by the profits of the B&B. There are three spacious Western-style rooms in the main lodge and a two-bedroom carriage house. Minimum two-night stay from May to mid-October.

The Lark MOTEL $$

(☎406-624-3070; www.larkbozeman.com; 122 W Main St; r $130-270; ❄📶) With a lively yellow palette and modern graphic design, this hip place is a big step up from its former life as a grungy motel. Rooms are fresh and the fine location puts it in walking distance of downtown's bars and restaurants.

MONTANA FACTS

Nickname Treasure State, Big Sky Country

Population 1,062,000

Area 147,040 sq miles

Capital city Helena (population 31,400)

Other cities Billings (population 109,600), Missoula (73,300), Bozeman (46,600)

Sales tax No state sales tax

Birthplace of Movie star Gary Cooper (1901–61); motorcycle daredevil Evel Knievel (1938–2007); actress Michelle Williams (b 1980)

Home of Crow, Blackfeet, Chippewa, Gros Ventre and Salish Native Americans

Politics Republican ranchers and oil barons generally edge out the Democratic students and progressives of left-leaning Bozeman and Missoula.

Famous for Fly-fishing, cowboys and grizzly bears

Random fact Some Montana highways didn't have a speed limit until the 1990s.

Driving distances Bozeman to Denver 695 miles, Missoula to Whitefish 133 miles

★ **Rainbow Ranch Lodge** RESORT $$
(406-995-4132; www.rainbowranchbigsky.com; Hwy 191; r $180-420;) Rustic but ultra-chic, Rainbow Ranch offers a select group of pondside or riverside rooms, most with roaring stone fireplaces, balconies and access to the romantic outdoor hot tub. The Pondside Luxury rooms are easily the most stylish. The lodge is 5 miles south of the Big Sky turnoff and 12 miles north of Yellowstone National Park.

Eating & Drinking

With plenty of breweries and an active live music scene, if you're not having fun in Bozeman, you're doing it wrong. Check the Bozone (www.bozone.com) for a good music calendar.

★ **Nova Cafe** CAFE $
(406-587-3973; www.thenovacafe.com; 312 E Main St; breakfast $7.50-13, mains $10-14; 7am-2pm;) A helpful map at the entrance shows you where the food you'll be eating comes from at this retro-contemporary locals' favorite. The hollandaise is a bit on the sweet side, but still excessively delicious – as is everything else. The forbidden rice salad with ginger and lemongrass is another highlight. There's a special menu for vegans, too.

★ **Follow Yer' Nose BBQ** BARBECUE $
(406-599 -7302; www.followyernosebbq.com; 504 N Broadway; mains $10-20; 2-8pm Sun-Tue, noon-8pm Wed-Sat) Lovers of some of Montana's best grills have for years been forced out into the backblocks of Paradise Valley for their fix. No longer. This city outpost does all the usual heavily smoked meats to perfection, alongside the **Bozeman Brewing Company** (406-585-9142; www.bozemanbrewing.com; 504 N Broadway; 2-8pm Mon-Thu, Sat & Sun, noon-8pm Fri), and better still, they do so year-round.

★ **Montana Ale Works** PUB
(406-587-7700; www.montanaaleworks.com; 611 E Main St; 4pm-close) Bozeman's former Northern Pacific freight warehouse brings industrial chic to this ever-reliable bar-restaurant, with excellent food (mains $11 to $26), pool tables and people-watching. Staff are happy to let you taste any of the 30 microbrews on tap, including the local Bozones.

★ **Rockford Coffee Roasters** CAFE
(406-556-1053; www.rockfordcoffee.com; 18 E Main St; 6:30am-7pm Mon-Fri, 7:30am-7pm Sat & Sun) Bozeman's best and coolest coffee cafe, Rockford's is where local artists and creative types hang out. The coffee is outstanding, and the high ceilings and exposed brick walls make for a classy but casual affair.

Bozeman Taproom & Fill Station BEER GARDEN
(406-577-2337; www.bozemantaproom.com; 101 N Rouse Ave; 11am-midnight Sun-Thu, to 1am Fri & Sat) One of Bozeman's coolest places to grab a pint and fill a growler has an open-air rooftop beer garden. Its 44 draft brews served from 75 taps can be combined in as many ways as you like with the 'build your own flight' program. Hot dogs and sandwiches keep your belly full while you sample them all.

Getting There & Away

Bozeman Yellowstone International Airport (BZN; 406-388-8321; www.bozemanairport.com; 850 Gallatin Field Rd), 8 miles northwest of downtown, serves most major hubs including

Atlanta, New York, Chicago, Denver, Seattle, Dallas, Salt Lake City, San Francisco and Minneapolis.

Jefferson Lines connects to Greyhound from a nondescript **bus depot** (Jefferson Lines; 612-499-3468; www.jeffersonlines.com; 1500 North 7th Ave; noon-5pm) on the southern side of the Super Walmart near the garden center. Between noon and 5pm, a well-marked Jefferson Lines car parked nearby can sell you tickets and check your luggage. Destinations include Missoula (from $55, 3½ hours), Billings (from $42, 2¼ hours) and Denver (from $149, 14¾ hours).

Billings

It's hard to believe laid-back Billings is Montana's largest city. The friendly oil-and-ranching center is not a must-see but makes for a decent overnight pit stop, or a point of departure for Yellowstone National Park via the breathtaking Beartooth Hwy.

Pompey's Pillar and the further away Little Bighorn Battlefield National Monuments are worthwhile stops for history buffs, and downtown has a certain unpolished charm for those who prefer the modern West.

Sleeping

The main knot of chain motels is outside Billings on I-90, exit 446, but there are a few standout independent options downtown – as well as a few mediocre ones.

Dude Rancher Lodge MOTEL $

(406-545-6331; www.duderancherlodge.com; 415 N 29th St; d from $75;) This historic motor lodge looks a little out of place in the downtown area, but has been well maintained, with about half the rooms renovated to good effect. Western touches like tongue-and-groove walls and cattle-brand carpet give it a welcoming rustic feel. The attached diner is a local breakfast favorite.

Northern Hotel HOTEL $$

(406-867-6767; www.northernhotel.com; 19 N Broadway; r/ste $165/215;) The historic Northern combines its previous elegance with fresh and modern facilities that are a solid step above generic business hotel. Breakfast and lunch are served in the attached 1950s diner.

Eating & Drinking

McCormick Cafe BREAKFAST $

(406-255-9555; www.mccormickcafe.com; 2419 Montana Ave; breakfast $6-10, meals $9-12; 7am-2pm Mon-Fri, 8am-2pm Sat & Sun;) For espresso, granola breakfasts, French-style crepes, good sandwiches and a lively atmosphere, stop by this downtown favorite that started life as an internet cafe.

★ **Walkers Grill** AMERICAN $$

(406-245-9291; www.walkersgrill.com; 2700 1st Ave N; tapas $8-14, mains $16-34; 4-10pm Mon-Thu, to 10:30pm Fri, 5-10:30pm Sat, 5-10pm Sun) Upscale Walkers offers good grill items and fine tapas at the bar accompanied by cocktails crafted by expert mixologists. It's an elegant, large-windowed space that would be right at home in Manhattan, though maybe without the barbed-wire light fixtures – or with. The menu changes with the seasons but is always filled with flavor. Check the website for live jazz.

Überbrew MICROBREWERY

(406-534-6960; www.facebook.com/uberbrew; 2305 Montana Ave; 11am-9pm, beer until 8pm) The most polished of Billings' half-dozen downtown brewpubs also happens to create award-winning beers that are a noticeable step above the rest. The food isn't half bad either: wash down a beer-marinated bockwurst with a glass of the White Noise Hefeweizen, which outsells the other drafts three to one.

Getting There & Away

Downtown Billings is just off I-90 occupying a wide valley of the Yellowstone River.

Helena

It's pretty easy to overlook diminutive Helena as you zip by on the interstate, but you'd be doing yourself a grave disservice. Penetrate the drab, utilitarian commerce sprawl toward Last Chance Gulch and old Helena where imposing brick and stone buildings – all arches and angles – portray a resolute commitment to permanence. It's in this historic core, rather than the uninspiring urban sprawl, that Helena's charm resides.

Activities

★ **Trail Rider** OUTDOORS

(406-449-2107; www.bikehelena.com/trail-rider; cnr Broadway & Last Chance Gulch; Wed-Sun late May-Sep) During the summer months a dedicated city bus pulling a bike trailer runs mountain bikers and hikers to one of three

WORTH A TRIP

CUSTER'S LAST STAND

The best detour from Billings is to the **Little Bighorn Battlefield National Monument** (☎406-638-2621; www.nps.gov/libi; 756 Battlefield Tour Rd; per car $25; ⏲8am-8pm Jun-Sep, to 4:30pm Oct-May), 65 miles outside town in the arid plains of the Crow (Apsaalooke) Indian Reservation. Home to one of the USA's best-known Native American battlefields, this is where General George Custer made his famous 'last stand.' Another way to look at it is that the victory by the Cheyenne and Lakota Sioux was something of a last victory for Native American peoples. Swift retaliation followed and, within a decade, these lands were under the control of government forces.

At Little Bighorn on 25 and 26 June 1876, Custer, and 272 soldiers, messed one too many times with Native Americans (including Crazy Horse and Sitting Bull of the Lakota Sioux), who overwhelmed the force in a frequently painted massacre. A visitor center tells the tale, including in the form of an excellent video.

A 5-mile road runs through the site, with frequent turnouts with information panels (including quotes from both government and Native American sources) that bring the battle alive. All across the fields and valleys, and within sight of the road, white tombstones mark the sites where soldiers fell. Crowning the battlefield is Last Stand Hill, while nearby the Indian Memorial is a fascinating tribute to the Sioux and Cheyenne stories. In summer, you can take one of the five daily tours with a Crow guide through **Apsaalooke Tours** (☎406-679-2790; www.crow-nsn.gov/apsaalooke-tours.html; adult/child $10/5; ⏲10am, 11am, noon, 2pm & 3pm Memorial Day-Labor Day).

The entrance to the site is a mile east of I-90 on US 212. If you're here for the last weekend of June, the **Custer's Last Stand Re-enactment** (www.littlebighornreenactment.com; Little Bighorn National Monument; adult/child $20/10; ⏲Jun) is an annual hoot, 6 miles west of Hardin.

trailheads for epic singletrack journeys back to town. Destinations include the Mt Helena Ridge Trail, the Mt Ascension trails, and the Continental Divide Trail at MacDonald pass.

Sleeping

Sanders B&B $$
(☎406-442-3309; www.sandersbb.com; 328 N Ewing St; r $150-175; ❄📶) Located in the old mansion district, this historic B&B once belonged to Wilbur Sanders, a frontier lawyer and Montana's first senator. It now has seven elegant guest rooms, a wonderful old parlor and a breezy front porch. Each bedroom is unique and thoughtfully decorated, and it's run by a relative of the Ringling Brothers Circus family, with appropriate memorabilia.

Eating & Drinking

Murry's CAFE $
(☎406-431-2886; www.murryscafe.com; 438 N Last Chance Gulch; breakfast & brunch $4-8.50, lunch mains $5-16; ⏲8am-3pm Mon-Fri, 9am-2pm Sat & Sun; 📶🖊) From spanakopita to soufflés, this little cafe on the southern end of downtown offers something a little different from the regular breakfast fare. Things really go off the hook during their Saturday and Sunday brunch when the name of the game is waffles – regular, stuffed, topped or drenched.

★**General Mercantile** COFFEE
(☎406-442-6028; www.generalmerc.com; 413 N Last Chance Gulch; ⏲8am-5:30pm Mon-Fri, 9am-5pm Sat, 11am-4pm Sun; 📶) You'll have to weave through all sorts of Montana eclectica for sale – hummingbird feeders, postcards and homemade jam – to get what is widely regarded as the best coffee in the universe. Take your espresso to a private nook where you can contemplate what you'd look like with a mermaid fin and an octopus mustache – both also available.

Information

Helena Visitor Center (☎406-442-4120; www.helenamt.com; 225 Cruse Ave; ⏲8am-5pm Mon-Fri) Local information.

Montana Fish, Wildlife & Parks (☎406-444-2535; http://fwp.mt.gov; 1420 E 6th Ave)

Montana Outfitters & Guides Association (☎406-449-3578; www.montanaoutfitters.org; 5 Microwave Hill Rd, Montana City) Clearinghouse for everything from fishing and dude ranches to hunting.

Getting There & Away

Helena Regional Airport (HNL; ☎406-442-2821; www.helenaairport.com; 2850 Mercer Loop), 2 miles north of downtown Helena, connects to regional hubs including Salt Lake City, Seattle, Denver and Minneapolis. A planned expansion is due to be completed in 2020. The **Salt Lake Express** (www.saltlakeexpress.com; 1415 N Montana Ave) bus heads south to join up with the Greyhound network at Butte ($29.25, 1¼ hours).

Missoula

Missoula regularly turns up near the top of the list for travelers' favorite small cities in America. With a walkable, low-rise city center, plenty of riverside walking trails, the in-town University of Montana and a palpable sense of civic pride, it's not difficult to see why. Missoulians love to get outside, and summer means an almost endless stream of farmers markets, concerts in the park, outdoor cinema and similar celebrations of community life, while students from the University of Montana ensure a real sense of energy coursing through its streets. Patio seating is the rule not the exception, and an afternoon outing will surely involve some human-powered activity on the miles of urban and foothills trails. The wandering Clark Fork River is popular with stand up paddleboarders where it cuts through town, and is a fly-fishing magnet downstream. Put simply, it's one of the most agreeable urban spaces in the West.

Sights & Activities

★Garnet Ghost Town GHOST TOWN

(☎406-329-3914; www.garnetghosttown.org; Bear Gulch Rd; adult/child $3/free; ⊙9:30am-4:30pm Jun-Sep; 🐾) More than a dozen buildings preserved in a state of 'arrested decay' transport you back to gold-rush days, when cities were built overnight and vanished almost as quickly. It's an evocative place, having been founded in the late 19th century, but deserted since the 1930s. Located 40 miles east of Missoula on dirt forest roads, accessible (and signposted) off the Missoula–Butte road (90) – check the website for detailed directions. Call in advance to arrange a guided tour.

Smokejumper Visitor Center MUSEUM

(☎406-329-4934; www.fs.fed.us/science-technology/fire/smokejumpers/missoula/center; 5765 West Broadway; ⊙8:30am-5pm Jun-Aug, guided tours 10am, 11am, 1pm, 2pm, 3pm & 4pm) FREE The visitor center on this active base for the heroic men and women who parachute into forests to combat raging wildfires has thought-provoking displays about an increasingly hazardous job. The real treat is touring the facility where the crew lives, trains and sews their own parachutes; tours last 45 minutes to an hour. For more on the perilous possibilities of the job, pick up a copy of Norman MacLean's *Young Men and Fire* (1992).

A Carousel for Missoula PLAYGROUND

(☎406-549-8382; www.carouselformissoula.com; 101 Carousel Dr, Caras Park; adult/child $2.25/0.75; ⊙11am-5:30pm Sep-May, 11am-7pm Jun-Aug; 👪) Hand-carved and individually painted by local artists, every horse that gallops around the classic carousel at Caras Park has a story to tell. But the bigger story is how a community rallied around one man's dream to restore a bit of whimsy to downtown. The carousel shares space with Dragon Hollow, a playground that excites the imagination.

Mount Sentinel HIKING

(Campus Dr) A steep switchback trail from behind the University of Montana football stadium leads up to a concrete whitewashed 'M' (visible for miles around) on 5158ft Mt Sentinel. Tackle it on a warm summer's evening for glistening views of this much-loved city and its spectacular environs. The trailhead is at Phyllis Washington Park on the eastern edge of campus.

Sleeping & Eating

★Shady Spruce Hostel HOSTEL $

(☎406-285-1197; www.shadysprucehostel.com; 204 E Spruce St; dm $35-40, s/ste $55/85; ❄📶) We're super-excited to see the resurgence of the hostel in the US, and this clean, bright and spacious new addition to the family nails it in all the right places. Although it's presence here is no longer news, they've maintained standards. Downtown is literally a block away from the converted house, but they have bikes for the walking-averse.

Goldsmith's B&B B&B $$

(☎406-728-1585; www.missoulabedandbreakfast.com; 809 E Front St; r $160-210; ❄📶🐾) Before being moved here in two massive pieces, this inviting riverside B&B was a frat house, and before that, home to the University of

Montana president. The modern-Victorian rooms are all comfortable, but we're partial to the Greenough Suite with its writing table and private river-view deck.

★ **Market on Front** CAFE $
(☎406-541-0246; www.marketonfront.com; 201 E Front St; mains $5-10; ⏲8am-7pm Mon-Fri, to 8pm Sat, to 7pm Sun; 📶) 🍃 Order a fresh-made sandwich or overflowing breakfast bowl, or take advantage of the gourmet grab-and-go picnic items such as local teas, organic chocolate and local beer. Or dine in – with all those windows it feels like you're outside anyway. Casual but cool atmosphere, free wi-fi, friendly staff, seriously good sandwiches – what's not to like.

★ **Pearl Cafe** FRENCH $$$
(☎406-541-0231; http://pearlcafe.us; 231 E Front St; mains $23-38; ⏲5-9pm Mon-Sat) Our pick as Missoula's culinary superstar, Pearl Cafe does French country cooking with a western-US twist – try the walnut and herb prawns, the grilled salmon with mustard butter or, for traditionalists, the classic filet mignon. Service is assured and the atmosphere is refined but not too stuffy; dress nice nonetheless.

Drinking & Nightlife

Missoula has a surprisingly high-profile music scene for a smaller town. Bars downtown provide choices between laid-back brewpubs and distilleries, or more traditional professional drinking establishments.

★ **Top Hat Lounge** LOUNGE
(☎406-830-4640; www.tophatlounge.com; 134 W Front St; ⏲11am-10pm Mon-Thu, to 2am Fri & Sat) Where Missoula goes to get its groove on. This dark venue features live music most weekends in a space large enough to cut a rug, but small enough to feel like the band is playing just for you. It's one of Montana's best live-music venues.

★ **Liquid Planet** COFFEE
(☎406-541-4541; www.liquidplanet.com; 223 N Higgins; ⏲7:30am-9pm; 📶) 🍃 Considering how much Missoula loves its beverages, it's no surprise Liquid Planet was born here. Opened by a university professor in 2003, it's a sustainable coffeehouse, cafe and bottle shop selling carefully curated wines and craft beers, loose-leaf tea, coffee beans (with handwritten pedigrees) and sports drinks.

Information

Missoula Visitor Center (☎800-526-3465; www.destinationmissoula.org; 101 E Main St; ⏲8am-5pm Mon-Fri) Destination Missoula has a useful website as well as a small walk-in space downtown.

Getting There & Away

Missoula International Airport (MSO; ☎406-728-4381; www.flymissoula.com; 5225 Hwy 10 W), 5 miles west of Missoula, serves Salt Lake City, Denver, Phoenix, LA, San Francisco, Portland, Seattle and Minneapolis, among others. Seasonal service to Atlanta and Chicago.

Greyhound (☎406-549-2339; www.greyhound.com; 1660 W Broadway) buses serve most of the state and stop at the depot, 1 mile west of town. Destinations include Bozeman (from $52, 3½ hours), Denver (from $164, 17¼ hours), Portland (from $78, 9½ hours) and Seattle (from $83, around 10 hours).

Whitefish

Tiny Whitefish blends an easygoing outdoorsy mountain town with a fur-lined playground for the glitterati. It's not quite there yet, thankfully, but there's something suspiciously refined about this charismatic and caffeinated New West town. It is home to an attractive stash of restaurants, a historic railway station and an underrated ski resort, as well as excellent biking and hiking on a rapidly growing network of trails. Whitefish is well worth a visit – just get here while it's still affordable. Locals, however, are decidedly unpretentious and measure their wealth not in terms of money, but how many days they get out on the slopes and how many outdoor adventures they have.

Activities

Whitefish Legacy Partners HIKING
(☎406-862-3880; www.whitefishlegacy.org; 525 Railway St; ⏲hours vary) Whitefish is surrounded by a growing network of trails ideal for hiking and mountain biking. The driving force behind the development, Whitefish Legacy Partners rallies support for the system with offerings such as guided walks focusing on wildflowers, bears and noxious weeds. Its focus is more on residents than tourists, but everyone's welcome.

Whitefish Mountain Resort SKIING
(☎406-862-2900; www.skiwhitefish.com; Big Mountain Rd; ski/bike lift $81/41) Big mountain skiiing

at Whitefish Mountain Resort (formerly Big Mountain), is a laid-back old-school affair, great for families, as well as expert skiers and snowboarders willing to hike up in order to rip up off-piste double black diamond glades. The mountain is known for its foggy days, but views from the summit are unsurpassed (when clear). On fresh powder days, locals ditch work and other responsibilities to make fresh tracks.

Sleeping

★Whitefish Bike Retreat HOSTEL $
(☎406-260-0274; www.whitefishbikeretreat.com; 855 Beaver Lake Rd; tent sites/dm/r $40/50/110; ❄📶) Celebrating all things bicycle, this forested compound run by passionate outdoorsperson Cricket Butler is a must-stay for two-wheel enthusiasts. The spacious polished-wood house with bunks, private rooms and a communal living area is a great place to hang when you're not hot-lapping the property trails or exploring the excellent Whitefish Trail that runs nearby. Hard-core cyclists can bike all the way here from town.

Firebrand BOUTIQUE HOTEL $$
(☎406-863-1900; www.firebrandhotel.com; 650 E 3rd St; r from $140; ❄@📶) Easily downtown Whitefish's nicest hotel, this handsome brick structure shelters large and supremely comfortable rooms, a spa and fitness center, a rooftop hot tub, a bar-restaurant and a genuine touch of class.

Lodge at Whitefish Lake RESORT $$$
(☎406-863-4000; www.lodgeatwhitefishlake.com; 1380 Wisconsin Ave; r from $285; ❄📶≋) Consistently ranked among Montana's top luxury hotels, the Lodge exudes refinement and sophistication. It offers a range of rooms, from standards to fully stocked condos, on the sprawling complex. The unifying theme is a classic, patrician decor and high levels of comfort. The lakefront restaurant and poolside tiki bar are both great places to catch the sunset.

Eating & Drinking

Loula's CAFE $
(☎406-862-5614; www.whitefishrestaurant.com; 300 E 2nd St; breakfast $7-12, lunch mains $8-13, dinner mains $10-20; ⏲7am-2pm Mon-Sun, 5-9:30pm Thu-Sun; 📶) Downstairs in the century-old Masonic temple building, this bustling cafe has local art on the wall and culinary artists in the kitchen. The highly recommended lemon crème–filled French toast dripping with raspberry sauce is a sinfully delicious breakfast, or try the truffle eggs Benedict. At other times, it's burgers, salads and dishes such as blackened wild salmon or chicken potpie.

★Spotted Bear Spirits DISTILLERY
(☎406-730-2436; www.spottedbearspirits.com; 503 Railway St, Suite A; ⏲noon-8pm; 📶) Award-winning spirits (vodka, gin, and agave) are paired with secret blends of herbs and spices to create unique, award-winning cocktails you won't find anywhere else. Grab a drink and head to the sofa upstairs for a relaxing break from your day. A Spotted Bear whisky is in the works and will be available in the next year or two.

Montana Coffee Traders COFFEE
(☎406-862-7667; www.coffeetraders.com; 110 Central Ave; ⏲7am-6pm Mon-Sat, 8am-4pm Sun; 📶) Whitefish's homegrown microroaster runs this always-busy cafe and gift shop in the old Skyles building in the center of town. The organic, fair-trade beans are roasted in an old farmhouse on Hwy 93 that you can tour (10am Friday by reservation).

Information

Whitefish Visitor Center (☎877-862-3548; www.explorewhitefish.com; 307 Spokane Ave; ⏲9am-5pm Mon-Fri) Professional and helpful office; the excellent website has loads of information on news, events, activities, and places to stay and eat.

Getting There & Away

Glacier Park International Airport (p136), located 11 miles south of Whitefish, has daily service to Denver, Minneapolis, Salt Lake and Seattle. Additional summer-only destinations include Chicago, Dallas and Los Angeles.

The most scenic way to get here is via **Amtrak** (☎406-862-2268; www.amtrak.com/empire-builder-train; 500 Depot St; ⏲6am-1:30pm, 4:30pm-midnight) on the *Empire Builder* line, which also connects to Glacier National Park via West Glacier ($7.50, 30 minutes) and East Glacier ($16, two hours).

Glacier National Park

Few places on earth are as magnificent and pristine as **Glacier** (www.nps.gov/glac; 7-day pass by car/foot & bicycle/motorcycle $35/20/30). Protected in 1910 during the first flowering of the American

WORTH A TRIP

NATIONAL BISON RANGE

National Bison Range (☎406-644-2211; www.fws.gov/refuge/national_bison_range; 58355 Bison Range Rd, Moiese; ⊙sunrise-sunset, visitor center 9am-5pm) is home to bison, black bear, a range of deer and antelope species, a handful of predators and more than 200 bird varieties. Located in Montana's northwest, the Range is a fabulous place to tick off wildlife species that you might not see elsewhere.

conservationist movement, Glacier ranks with Yellowstone, Yosemite and the Grand Canyon among the United States' most astounding natural wonders.

The glacially carved remnants of an ancient thrust fault have left us a brilliant landscape of towering snowcapped pinnacles laced with plunging waterfalls and glassy turquoise lakes. The mountains are surrounded by dense forests, which host a virtually intact pre-Columbian ecosystem. Grizzly bears still roam in abundance and smart park management has kept the place accessible and authentically wild.

Glacier is renowned for its historic 'parkitecture' lodges, the spectacular Going-to-the-Sun Rd and 740 miles of hiking trails. These all put visitors within easy reach of some 1489 sq miles of the wild and astonishing landscapes found at the crown of the continent.

Sights & Activities

Visitor centers and ranger stations in Glacier National Park sell field guides and hand out hiking maps. Those at Apgar and St Mary are open daily May to October, and Logan Pass Visitor Center is open when Going-to-the-Sun Rd is open. Many Glacier, Two Medicine and Polebridge Ranger Stations close at the end of September.

Logan Pass Visitor Center VISITOR CENTER
(☎406-888-7800; Going-to-the-Sun Rd; ⊙9am-7pm late Jun-late Aug, 9:30am-4pm Sep) Certainly in the most magnificent setting of all the park's visitor centers, the building has park information, interactive exhibits, and a good gift shop. Both the **Hidden Lake Overlook Trail** and the Highline Trail begin here.

Bird Woman Falls WATERFALL
(Going-to-the-Sun Rd) Standing at the artificially created Weeping Wall, look across the valley to this distant natural watery spectacle; the spectacular Bird Woman Falls drops 500ft from one of Glacier's many hanging valleys. There are several pull-outs along the western side of Going-to-the Sun Rd to view the falls.

Sunrift Gorge CANYON
(Going-to-the-Sun Rd) Just off Going-to-the-Sun Rd and adjacent to a shuttle stop lies this narrow canyon carved over millennia by the gushing glacial meltwaters of Baring Creek. Look out for picturesque **Baring Bridge**, a classic example of rustic Going-to-the-Sun Rd architecture, and follow a short trail down to misty **Baring Falls**. Most of the tree cover in this area was thinned out by the 2015 Reynolds Creek fire.

Jackson Glacier Overlook VIEWPOINT
This popular pull-over, located a short walk from the Gunsight Pass trailhead, offers telescopic views of the park's fifth-largest glacier, which sits close to its eponymous 10,052ft peak – one of the park's highest.

★**Going-to-the-Sun Road** SCENIC DRIVE
(www.nps.gov/glac/planyourvisit/goingtothesunroad.htm; ⊙late Jun-late Sep) A strong contender for the most spectacular road in America, the 50-mile Going-to-the-Sun Rd was built for the express purpose of giving visitors a way to explore the park's interior without having to hike. This marvel of engineering is a national historic landmark that crosses Logan Pass (6,646ft) and is flanked by hiking trails, waterfalls and endless views. The opening of the road marks the official start of the park's crowded summer season.

★**Highline Trail** HIKING
(Logan Pass) A Glacier classic, the Highline Trail contours across the face of the famous Garden Wall to Granite Park Chalet – one of two historic lodges only accessible by trail. The summer slopes are covered with alpine plants and wildflowers while the views are nothing short of stupendous. With only 800ft elevation gain over 7.6 miles, the treats come with minimal sweat.

Avalanche Lake Trail HIKING
(north of Lake McDonald) This low-commitment introduction to Glacier hiking pays big dividends in the form of a pristine alpine lake,

waterfalls and cascades. The 2.3-mile hike is relatively gentle and easily accessed by the shuttle. It's, therefore, invariably mobbed in peak season with everyone from flip-flop-wearing families to stick-wielding seniors making boldly for the tree line.

Glacier Park Boat Co BOATING
(☎406-257-2426; www.glacierparkboats.com; adult/child $18.25/9.25) Six historic boats – some dating back to the 1920s – ply five of Glacier's attractive mountain lakes, and some of them combine the float with a short **guided hike** led by interpretive, often witty, ranger guides. For those looking for a bit of a workout, it also rents rowboats ($18 per hour), kayaks ($18 per hour) and paddleboards ($10 per hour) at Lake McDonald, Mary, Many Glacier and Two Medicine.

Sleeping

There are 13 NPS campgrounds. For comprehensive information about camping in the park, see www.nps.gov.

★Izaak Walton Inn HISTORIC HOTEL $$
(☎406-888-5700; www.izaakwaltoninn.com; 290 Izaak Walton Inn Rd, Essex; r $109-179, cabins & cabooses $199-249; ⏲year-round; 📶) Perched on a hill within snowball-throwing distance of Glacier National Park's southern boundary, this historic mock-Tudor inn was originally built in 1939 to accommodate local railway personnel. It remains a daily flag-stop (request stop) on Amtrak's *Empire Builder* route – a romantic way to arrive. Caboose cottages with kitchenettes are available, along with a historic GN441 locomotive refurbished as a luxury four-person suite ($329).

★Many Glacier Hotel HISTORIC HOTEL $$
(☎303-265-7010; www.glaciernationalparklodges.com; 1 Many Glacier Rd; r $207-322, ste $476; ⏲mid-Jun–mid-Sep; 📶) Enjoying the most wondrous setting in the park, this massive, Swiss chalet–inspired lodge (some of the male staff even wear lederhosen) commands the northeastern shore of Swiftcurrent Lake. It was first built by the Great Northern Railway in 1915, and the comfortable, if rustic, rooms have been updated (restoration work continues) over the last 15 years. The deluxe rooms feature boutique-style elements, including high-end, contemporary tiled bathrooms.

Eating

In summer in Glacier National Park, there are grocery stores with camping supplies in Apgar, Lake McDonald Lodge, Rising Sun and at the Swiftcurrent Motor Inn. Most lodges have on-site restaurants. Dining options in West Glacier and St Mary offer mainly hearty hiking fare.

If cooking at a campground or picnic area, be sure to take appropriate bear safety precautions and do not leave food unattended.

★Serrano's Mexican Restaurant MEXICAN $$
(☎406-226-9392; www.serranosmexican.com; 29 Dawson Ave, East Glacier; mains $14-21; ⏲5-10pm May-Sep; 📶) East Glacier Park's most buzzed-about restaurant serves a mean chile relleno. Renowned for its excellent iced margaritas, Serrano's also has economical burritos, enchiladas and quesadillas in the vintage Dawson house log cabin, originally built in 1909. Expect a wait.

Belton Chalet Grill & Taproom AMERICAN $$$
(☎406-888-5000; www.beltonchalet.com; 12575 Hwy 2, West Yellowstone; mains $24-35; ⏲5-9pm, tap room from 3pm) 🍃 West Glacier's finest dining option, housed in one of its most historic buildings, has evolved with the times, the faux Swiss milkmaid waitress uniforms aside. The head chef, a Whitefish native now in his second season at the helm, has created a sophisticated menu featuring locally sourced ingredients and mains such as bison meatloaf with broccolini and bacon lardons (strips of fatty bacon).

FREE PARK SHUTTLE

See more with less stress by ditching the car and taking the park's free hop-on, hop-off **shuttle service** (www.nps.gov/glac; ⏲7am-7pm Jul & Aug) that hits all major points along Going-to-the-Sun Rd between Apgar and St Mary visitor centers. Buses run every 15 to 30 minutes depending on traffic from Apgar (every 40 minutes from St Mary on the east side), with the last trips down from Logan Pass leaving at 7pm.

Information

Glacier National Park Headquarters (406-888-7800; www.nps.gov/glac; West Glacier; 8am-4:30pm Mon-Fri)

Getting There & Around

Glacier Park International Airport (FCA; 406-257-5994; www.iflyglacier.com; 4170 Hwy 2 East, Kalispell;) in Kalispell has year-round service to Salt Lake, Minneapolis, Denver, Seattle and Las Vegas, and seasonal service to Atlanta, Oakland, LA, Chicago and Portland. Alaska, Allegiant, American Airlines, Delta and United have flights to FCA.

The **Great Falls International Airport** (GTF; www.flygtf.com) is 140 miles south of East Glacier.

Amtrak's *Empire Builder* (www.amtrak.com) stops daily at **West Glacier** (year-round) and **East Glacier Park** (Apr-Oct), with a whistle stop in Browning. Xanterra provides a shuttle (adult $6 to $10, child $3 to $5, 10 to 20 minutes) from West Glacier to their lodges on the west end, and Glacier Park Collection by Pursuit offers shuttles (from $15, one hour) connecting East Glacier Park to St Mary and Whitefish.

Glacier National Park runs a free hop-on, hop-off shuttle bus (p135) from **Apgar Transit Center** to St Mary over Going-to-the-Sun Rd during summer months; it stops at all major trailheads. Xanterra concession operates the classic guided **Red Bus Tours** (855-733-4522; www.glaciernationalparklodges.com/red-bus-tours; adult $46-100, child $23-50; mid-May–end Oct).

If driving a personal vehicle, be prepared for narrow, winding roads, traffic jams, and limited parking at most stops along Going-to-the-Sun Rd.

IDAHO

Wedged between Montana and Oregon, and often overlooked as a result, Idaho is truly one of Western USA's most underrated destinations. This rather large chunk of land has 114 mountain ranges and some of the most rugged mountains in the Lower 48. More than 60% of the state is public land, and with 3.9 million acres of wilderness, it's the third-wildest state in the union.

Boise, the state capital, is a pleasant place to linger, Sun Valley is a classic US ski resort, and the wild treasures range from Craters of the Moon National Park and the National Bison Range to Teton Valley and the dramatic Sawtooth National Recreation Area, one of the West's premier adventure areas.

Boise

One of the US's least-known state capitals, Boise can catch you unawares. Refreshingly modern, urban and trendy, Idaho's largest city has a lively downtown scene – complete with walking streets, bistros and sophisticated wine bars – that wouldn't look out of place on the East Coast. The network of trails that shoots up from town to the forested hills above rivals some of Colorado's best hiking destinations. Floating through the Greenbelt is as good as anything you'll find along Austin, Texas' beloved tubing circuit. Sample a steaming pan of paella in the Basque Block and you might as well be in Bilbao. With so much going on, it can be difficult for newbies to know what to make of Boise. But Boise is well worth the detour if you're anywhere nearby.

Sights & Activities

★Basque Block AREA

(www.thebasqueblock.com; Grove St, 6th St & Capitol Blvd) Boise is home to one of the largest Basque populations outside Spain, with up to 15,000 members of that community residing here. The original émigrés arrived in the 1910s to work as shepherds when sheep outnumbered people seven to one. Few continue that work today, but many extended families have remained, and the rich elements of their distinct culture are still very much alive – glimpses of which can be seen along Grove St between 6th St and Capitol Blvd.

Boise River Greenbelt PARK

(http://parks.cityofboise.org) The glowing emerald of Treasure Valley began as an ambitious plan in the 1960s to prevent development in the Boise River's floodplain and provide open space in a rapidly growing city. Today the growing collection of parks and museums along the tree-lined riverway is connected by more than 30 miles of multiuse paths, and hosts an insanely popular summer floating scene. A white-water park, complete with hydraulically controlled waves, is one of the largest in the country.

World Center for Birds of Prey BIRD SANCTUARY
(Peregrine Fund; 208-362-8687; www.peregrinefund.org/visit; 5668 W Flying Hawk Lane; adult/child $10/5; 10am-5pm Tue-Sun Mar-Nov, 10am-4pm Dec-Feb) The Peregrine Fund's worldwide raptor conservation programs have brought many species back from the brink of extinction – including the iconic California Condor, successfully bred in captivity here for release in California and the Grand Canyon. A pair of condors reside at the center, along with a dozen other impressive birds including the northern aplomado falcon, whose mating pairs work in tandem to hunt grassland sparrows. The live raptor presentations are excellent.

Idaho State Museum MUSEUM
(208-334-2120; https://history.idaho.gov/location/museum; 610 N Julia Davis Dr; adult/child $10/5; 10am-5pm Mon-Sat, noon-5pm Sun) After a multi-year renovation, which brought this museum back to life, traditional exhibits now share space with multimedia installations for a fascinating journey through the state's history. The Origins Gallery, with its Native American voices, is especially rewarding.

Ridge to Rivers Trail System HIKING
(208-493-2531; www.ridgetorivers.org;) Some 190 miles of hiking and mountain-biking trails meander the foothills northeast of town, crossing grasslands, scrub slopes and tree-lined creeks on their way to the Boise National Forest. The options are literally endless. The most convenient access is via Cottonwood Creek Trailhead east of the capitol building, or **Camel's Back Park** to the north.

Boise River Float PARK
(www.boiseriverraftandtube.com; 4049 S Eckert Rd, Barber Park; tube/kayak rental $12/35, 4-person raft $45; noon-5pm Mon-Thu, to 6pm Fri, 10am-6pm Sat & Sun;) There is no better way to spend a sunny summer day in Boise than floating down the river. Rent watercraft – from tubes to six-person rafts – at Barber Park (parking $5 Monday to Thursday, $6 Friday to Sunday) where you'll put in for a self-guided 6-mile, 1½- to three-hour float downstream to Ann Morrison Park. Open June through August depending on river flows.

Sleeping

★**Boise Guest House** GUESTHOUSE $$
(208-761-6798; www.boiseguesthouse.com; 614 N 5th St; ste $180-230;) A veritable home away from home, this appealing old house has a handful of contemporary-styled suites with kitchenettes and living areas comfortably arranged and tastefully decorated. All rooms have access to the large grill in the relaxing backyard, red-and-white cruiser bikes and laundry.

Inn at 500 HOTEL $$
(208-227-0500; www.innat500.com; 500 S Capitol Blvd; r $215-280, ste $290-325;) Finally, a luxury boutique hotel that doesn't give up at the lobby. Fine art, unique dioramas and blown glass – all from local artists – adorn the hallways and rooms, creating warm and inviting spaces a step above your standard high-quality-bed-in-a-box affair. All within walking distance of Boise's buzzing downtown.

Eating

Boise's vibrant downtown hosts numerous dining options from casual to formal. The concentration of Basque specialties downtown is a particular highlight, while options abound along 8th St. The hip Hyde Park region on 13th St is even more laid-back, and a great place to grab a snack after hiking.

★**Goldy's Breakfast Bistro** BREAKFAST $
(208-345-4100; www.goldysbreakfastbistro.com; 108 S Capitol Blvd; mains $6-20; 6:30am-2pm Mon-Fri, 7:30am-2pm Sat & Sun) Assuming an egg is just an egg, Goldy's offers 866,320 'Create Your Own Breakfast Combos.' Check our math – we were already drunk on hollandaise sauce when we put pen to napkin. Or go for the frittatas, bennies or massive breakfast burrito. Pass through the velvet curtain and go for a table on the internal balcony.

Fork MODERN AMERICAN $$
(207-287-1700; https://boisefork.com; 199 N 8th St; mains $10-34; 11:30am-10pm Mon-Thu, to 11pm Fri, 9:30am-11pm Sat, 9:30am-9pm Sun;) This cavernous corner restaurant occupying the old bank building downtown is good anytime, but excels during weekend brunch when things like the Dungeness crab scramble pair unbelievably well with the local favorite: asparagus fries. Try the Fork Lemonade for a refreshing pickup on a sunny summer day.

Drinking & Nightlife

★Bodovino WINE BAR

(208-336-8466; www.bodovino.com; 404 S 8th St; 11am-11pm Mon-Thu, to 1am Fri & Sat, 11am-9pm Sun;) Whether you're a sommelier or a swiller, the variety of vintages on tap here is nothing short of hazardous – especially considering the fact that you're on your own with walls of vending machines that decant tastes or pours from 144 different wines.

Bardenay DISTILLERY

(208-426-0538; www.bardenay.com; 610 Grove St; cocktails from $8; 11am-late Mon-Fri, from 10am Sat & Sun) Bardenay was the USA's very first 'distillery-pub,' and remains a one-of-a-kind watering hole. Located on Basque Block, it makes rum in-house and has whiskey aging for imminent release. A dizzying array of cocktails are created from spirits crafted in all three of Bardenay's Idaho locations, including the dizzying Sunday Morning Paper – a lemon-vodka-Bloody Mary experience.

IDAHO FACTS

Nickname Gem State

Population 1,754,000

Area 83,570 sq miles

Capital city Boise (population 226,600)

Other cities Idaho Falls (population 61,100)

Sales tax 6%

Birthplace of Lewis and Clark guide Sacagawea (1788–1812); politician Sarah Palin (b 1964); poet Ezra Pound (1885–1972)

Home of Star garnet, Sun Valley ski resort

Politics Reliably Republican with small pockets of Democrats, eg Sun Valley

Famous for Potatoes, wilderness, the world's first chairlift

North America's deepest river gorge Idaho's Hells Canyon (7900ft deep)

Driving distances Boise to Idaho Falls 280 miles, Lewiston to Coeur d'Alene 116 miles

Information

Visitor Center (208-810-7324; www.boise.org; 8th & Grove Sts, Grove Plaza; 9am-6pm Mon-Sat) This office has plenty of printed material on Boise and the wider area, while the website has a useful events calendar.

Getting There & Around

Small but busy **Boise Municipal Airport** (BOI; 208-383-3110; www.iflyboise.com; 3201 Airport Way, I-84 exit 53) is well connected, with nonstop flights to a range of locations including Denver, Las Vegas, Phoenix, Portland, Salt Lake City, Seattle, San Francisco, Los Angeles, Dallas and Chicago.

Greyhound services depart from the **bus station** (www.greyhound.com; 1212 W Bannock St; 6-11am & 4pm-midnight) with routes fanning out to Spokane (from $45, 8½ to 10 hours), Missoula (from $78, 15 hours), Pendleton (from $37, five hours), Portland (from $74, 9½ hours), Twin Falls (from $32, 2¼ hours) and Salt Lake City (from $64, seven hours).

The coolest way to get around downtown is by far the **Green Bike** (208-345-7433; https://boise.greenbike.com; per hr/month $5/15) system. Book online or download the app to unlock one of more than 100 bicycles locked at over 20 downtown stations, and feel the wind in your hair as you cruise the city in emissions-free style. The program has expanded to include the Boise River Greenbelt (p136) and area parks.

Ketchum & Sun Valley

Occupying one of Idaho's more stunning natural locations, Sun Valley is a living piece of ski history. It was the first purpose-built ski resort in the US (a venture by the Union Pacific Railroad to boost ridership) and opened in 1936 to much fanfare, thanks to both its luxury showcase lodge and the world's first chairlift.

The ski area and town of Ketchum were popularized early on by celebrities including Ernest Hemingway, Clark Gable and Gary Cooper (who received free trips as a marketing ploy by Averell Harriman – politician, railroad heir and Sun Valley's founder). It has maintained its love affair with swanky Hollywood clientele ever since.

For all that, Sun Valley remains a pretty and accessible place flush with hot springs, hiking trails, fishing, hunting and mountain biking, extending from Galena Pass down to the foothills of Hailey.

Activities

★Galena Lodge OUTDOORS
(☎208-726-4010; www.galenalodge.com; 15187 Hwy 75; XC ski pass adult/child $17/free; ⊙lodge 9am-4pm, kitchen 11am-3:30pm) Miles of mountain bike and groomed XC ski trails spiderweb out from this cool lodge that rents equipment and serves up lunch to keep you fueled for the day. It's 23 miles north of Ketchum.

Sun Valley Resort SNOW SPORTS
(☎888-490-5950; www.sunvalley.com; Ketchum; winter ski ticket $90-145) Sun Valley has been synonymous with luxury skiing ever since they invented the chairlift in 1936. But while you can now sit-to-ski elsewhere, people still flock here for the fluffy powder and celebrity spotting. Two mountains – mellow **Dollar Mountain** with its extensive terrain parks to the east of town and black-and-blue **Bald Mountain** to the west – provide plenty of variety.

Wood River Trail System OUTDOORS
(www.bcrd.org/wood-river-trail-summer.php) Good things happen when a community rallies behind outdoor activities. This paved urban trail system extends over 32 miles, connecting the major hubs of Sun Valley with the towns of Ketchum, Hailey and Bellevue (20 miles to the south) following the old Union Pacific Railroad line. Several shops rent bikes in the valley.

Sleeping

Ketchum has a small sprinkling of hotels, with at least one decent option in all categories. Rates vary with the seasons, winter being most expensive. For budget travelers, there's an in-town hostel and free camping on Bureau of Land Management (BLM) and Forest Service lands near town.

Tamarack Lodge HOTEL $$
(☎208-726-3344; www.tamaracksunvalley.com; 291 Walnut Ave; r/ste from $165/215;) Rooms are tasteful at this aging but clean downtown lodge that exudes a charming '1970s ski condo' vibe. Some rooms are a bit dark, but many have fireplaces and all have a balcony and use of the Jacuzzi and indoor pool.

★Limelight Hotel HOTEL $$$
(☎208-726-0888; www.limelighthotels.com/ketchum; 151 Main St; r $260-545;) Downtown Ketchum's coolest hotel, the Limelight has an appealing stone facade, muted earthy tones in the semi-luxurious rooms and some fine views from the floor-to-ceiling windows in rooms on the upper floors. With a bar, restaurants, equipment rental and other services, they have most bases covered.

Sun Valley Lodge HOTEL $$$
(☎208-622-2001; www.sunvalley.com; 1 Sun Valley Rd; inn/lodge from $355/445;) The celebrities already came in droves before the 2015 renovation that spruced up this swank 1930s-era lodge – Sun Valley's first and finest. Standard rooms have the exact same amenities as the higher end picks – including the spacious bathrooms with tub – just less floor space around the bed. Cheaper accommodation is available beyond the main lodge.

Eating & Drinking

You'll want to après-ski at **Apple's** (☎208-726-7067; www.facebook.com/applesbarandgrill; 205 Picabo St; ⊙11am-6pm) before checking out the valley's regular live-music scene. The more swanky bars are not averse to turning out the riffraff. If you unexpectedly find yourself in that category, the **Casino Club** (The Casbah; ☎208-726-9901; www.facebook.com/thecasbah36; 220 N Main St; ⊙11am-2am) has a stool for you.

The Kneadery BREAKFAST $
(☎208-726-9462; www.kneadery.com; 260 N Leadville Ave; mains $10-15; ⊙8am-2pm) A solid bet for breakfast or lunch, the Kneadery is off the main drag in an old split-log cabin outfitted with large fireplace, western art and a birchbark canoe hanging from the ceiling. The ambience is almost as fine as their pancakes.

★Enoteca INTERNATIONAL $$
(☎208-928-6280; www.ketchum-enoteca.com; 300 N Main St; mains $8-16; ⊙5-9pm) By the people who once presided over Ketchum Grill, Enoteca combines a classy, softly lit space with an enticing selection of large and small tapas-style plates. From wood-fired pizzas and mac and cheese to Idaho trout, from cured meats and cheeses to duck confit, it's all good. It offers a terrific wine list, too.

★Pioneer Saloon STEAK $$$
(☎208-726-3139; www.pioneersaloon.com; 320 N Main St; mains $15-36; ⊙5-10pm, bar 4pm-late)

WORTH A TRIP

CRATERS OF THE MOON

In Idaho's far south, between Sun Valley and Idaho Falls, **Craters of the Moon National Monument & Preserve** (208-527-1300; www.nps.gov/crmo; 1266 Craters Loop Rd; visitor center 8am-6pm late May–mid-Sep, to 4:30pm mid-Sep–late May) is one of Western USA's most unusual landscapes. Described by President Calvin Coolidge at the time of its recognition in 1924 as 'a weird and scenic landscape, peculiar to itself,' Craters of the Moon does indeed resemble a lunar land.

Beginning some 15,000 years ago, a series of volcanic eruptions laid waste to the Snake River Plain, leaving a blistered land of lunar-like craters, lava tubes caves and fissures. The last eruption took place a mere 2000 years ago. The results now cover 750,000 acres.

There's a **visitor center** at the entrance to the national monument, which is accessible along the US 93/26/20 between Arco and Carey. Beyond the center, a series of drives and hiking trails crisscross the reserve. The **North Crater Trail** and the summer-only **Tree Molds Trail** are the hiking highlights, while the **Loop Road**, accessible only from May to September, passes some of the most dramatic formations. These include **Devil's Orchard** (island-like lava fragments surrounded by cinders), **Inferno Cone** (with fabulous views from the summit) and the **Cave Area**.

For the best steak in Ketchum (and, some argue, Idaho) step into the former illicit gambling hall, now an unashamed Western den decorated with deer heads, antique guns (one being Hemingway's) and bullet boards. If red meat isn't your thing, they also have a range of fish options and a tasty mango-chutney and grilled-vegetable chicken kabob.

Information

Sun Valley/Ketchum Visitor Center (208-726-3423; www.visitsunvalley.com; 491 Sun Valley Rd; 6am-7pm;) Volunteers are a wealth of information when the station is staffed from 9am to 6pm. Maps and brochures available at all hours.

Getting There & Around

Friedman Memorial Airport (SUN; 208-788-4956; www.iflysun.com; 1616 Airport Circle, Hailey) is located 12 miles south of Ketchum in Hailey. It has daily service to most western-states hubs (LA, San Francisco, Seattle, Salt Lake City and Denver, as well as twice-weekly flights to Portland), though it can sometimes be more economical to fly into Boise and take the three-hour **Sun Valley Express** (Caldwell Transportation; 208-576-7381; www.sunvalleyexpress.com; adult/child $90/80) from there.

Mountain Rides (208-788-7433; www.mountainrides.org) offers free transportation throughout Ketchum; trips between Hailey and Ketchum cost $3/2 per adult/child.

Stanley

Barely more than a cluster of rustic log cabins just across from the jagged Sawtooth mountains, Stanley might be the most scenic small town in Idaho. For much of the year, the town is snowed in and very quiet, but it comes to life during the brief summer months as adventurers come to boat the world-class white water of the Middle Fork, fish the blue-ribbon rivers teeming with salmon and trout, or stock up on last-minute supplies before exploring the foreboding peaks and hidden valleys of the Sawtooth range.

Activities

★ Sawtooth National Recreation Area OUTDOORS
(208-423-7500; www.fs.usda.gov/sawtooth) You'll find rivers to boat, mountains to climb, more than 300 lakes to fish, and in excess of 700 miles of trails to hike or mountain bike in the dramatic Sawtooth National Recreation Area. It protects 1170 sq miles of America's public lands stretching between Stanley and Ketchum, offering unparalleled opportunities for exploration and recreation.

Solitude River Trips RAFTING
(208-806-1218, 800-396-1776; www.rivertrips.com; 6-day trip per person $2690; Jun-Aug) Offers top-notch, multiday trips on the famed Middle Fork of the Salmon. Camping is riverside and guides cook excellent food.

White Otter RAFTING

(☎208-788-5005; www.whiteotter.com; 100 Yankee Fork Rd & Hwy 75, Sunbeam; full-day float trips per person $160, half-day river rafting adult/child $80/65) One of few rafting outfits to be locally run, White Otter is recommended for fun class III day trips. It also arranges float trips in inflatable kayaks.

Sleeping & Eating

Sawtooth Hotel HOTEL $

(☎208-721-2459; www.sawtoothhotel.com; 755 Ace of Diamonds St; d with/without bath $115/80; ⏰mid-May–mid-Oct; 📶) Set in a nostalgic 1931 log motel, the Sawtooth updates the slim comforts of yesteryear, but keeps the hospitality effusively Stanley-esque. Six rooms are furnished old-country style, two with private bathrooms. Don't expect TVs or speedy wi-fi, but count on excellent dining (mains $14 to $23) with vegetarian and gluten-free options and a tiny selection of drinkable wines.

★ **Stanley Baking Company** BAKERY $

(www.stanleybakingco.com; 250 Wall St; mains $9-13; ⏰7am-2pm mid-May–Oct) Something of a legend, this middle-of-nowhere bakery and brunch spot is a must stop. Operating for five months of the year out of a small log cabin, Stanley Baking Co is the only place in town where you're likely to see a queue. The reason: off-the-ratings-scale homemade baked goods, oatmeal pancakes and a fabulous meatloaf sandwich.

Bridge Street Grill GRILL $$

(☎208-774-2208; www.bridgestgrill.com; Hwy 75, Lower Stanley; mains $11-23; ⏰11am-10pm) Although the town is literally surrounded by postcard-perfect scenery, somehow it's all the sweeter when viewed from the busy deck of Bridge Street Grill on the banks of the river – especially with a cold beer in hand and the remains of a green-chile-cheese Border Burger or house-smoked brisket on your plate.

Southwest

Includes ➡

Why Go?

Rugged. Beautiful. And fun. The Southwest is America's wild backyard, luring adventurous travelers with red-rock canyons, Wild West legends and the kicky delights of green-chile stew. Reminders of the region's Native American heritage and hardscrabble Wild West heyday dot the landscape, from enigmatic pictographs and abandoned cliff dwellings to crumbling Hispanic missions and rusty mining towns. Today, history making continues, with astronomers and rocket builders peering into starry skies, while artists and entrepreneurs flock to urban centers and quirky mountain towns. It's an ideal destination for road-trippers, with a splendid network of scenic drives linking the most beautiful and iconic sites. But remember: it's not just larger-than-life landscapes that make a trip through the Southwest memorable. Study that saguaro up close; ask a Hopi artist about their craft; savor that green-chile stew. You may cherish those smaller moments the most.

Best Places to Eat

- ➡ Kai Restaurant (p167)
- ➡ Cafe Pasqual's (p224)
- ➡ Red Iguana (p199)
- ➡ Kerouac's (p160)

Best Places to Sleep

- ➡ Washington School House (p203)
- ➡ NoMad (p152)
- ➡ La Fonda (p223)
- ➡ Arizona Biltmore Resort & Spa (p165)
- ➡ Hotel Luna Mystica (p229)

When to Go

Las Vegas

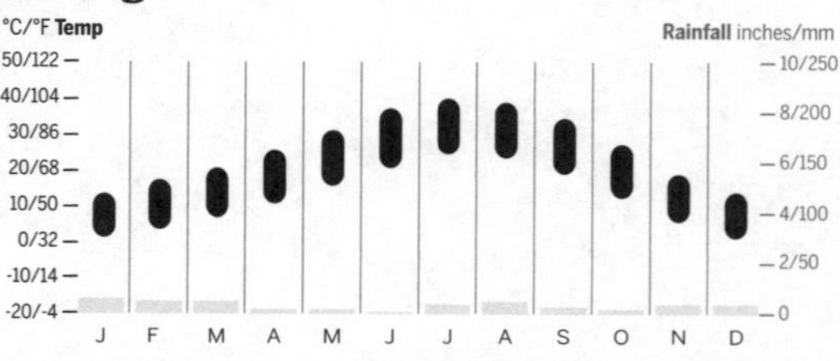

Jan Ski near Taos and Flagstaff. In Park City, hit the slopes and the Sundance Film Festival.

Jun–Aug High season for exploring national parks in New Mexico, Utah and northern Arizona.

Sep–Nov Hike to the bottom of the Grand Canyon or gaze at bright leaves in northern New Mexico.

History

By about AD 100, three dominant cultures were emerging in the Southwest: the Hohokam of the desert, the Mogollon of the central mountains and valleys, and the Ancestral Puebloans. Archaeologists originally called the Ancestral Puebloans the Anasazi, which comes from a Navajo term meaning 'ancient enemy' and has fallen out of favor.

Francisco Vásquez de Coronado led the first major expedition into North America in 1540. It included 300 soldiers, hundreds of Native American guides and herds of livestock. It also marked the first major violence between Spanish explorers and the native people.

In addition to armed conflict, Europeans introduced smallpox, measles and typhus, to which the Native Americans had no resistance. Pueblo populations were decimated by these diseases, shattering cultures and trade routes and proving a destructive force that far outstripped combat.

Development in the Southwest expanded rapidly during the 19th century, mainly due to railroad and geological surveys. As the US pushed west, the army forcibly removed entire tribes of Native Americans in horrifyingly brutal Indian Wars. Gold and silver mines drew fortune seekers, and the lawless mining towns of the Wild West mushroomed practically overnight. Soon the Santa Fe Railroad was luring a flood of tourists to the West.

Modern settlement is closely linked to water use. Following the Reclamation Act of 1902, huge federally funded dams were built to control rivers and irrigate the desert. Rancorous disagreements over water rights are ongoing, especially with the phenomenal boom in residential development and the extensive recent drought. The other major issue in recent years, especially in southern Arizona, has been illegal immigration across the border from Mexico.

Local Culture

Rugged individuality is the cultural idiom of the Southwest. But the reality? It's a bit more complex. The major identities of the region, centered on a trio of tribes – Anglo, Hispanic and Native American – are as vast and varied as the land that has shaped them. Whether their personal religion involves aliens, art, nuclear fission, slot machines, peyote or Joseph Smith, there's plenty of room for you in this beautiful, barely tamed chunk of America.

ℹ Getting There & Around

Las Vegas' McCarran International Airport (p157) and Phoenix's Sky Harbor International Airport (p169) are the region's busiest airports, with plenty of domestic and international connections.

Greyhound stops at major cities, but barely serves national parks or off-the-beaten-path towns such as Moab. Amtrak train service is even more limited, although it too links several southwestern cities and offers bus connections to others (including Santa Fe and Phoenix). The *California Zephyr* crosses Utah and Nevada; the *Southwest Chief* stops in Arizona and New Mexico;

SOUTHWEST IN...

One Week

Museums and a burgeoning arts scene set an inspirational tone in **Phoenix**. In the morning, follow Camelback Rd into **Scottsdale** for top-notch shopping and gallery-hopping in Old Town. Drive north to **Sedona** for spiritual recharging before pondering the immensity of the **Grand Canyon**. From here, choose either bling or buttes. For bling, detour onto **Route 66**, cross the bridge beside **Hoover Dam** then indulge your fantasies in **Las Vegas**. For buttes, drive east from the Grand Canyon into Navajo country, cruising beneath the giant rock formations in **Monument Valley Navajo Tribal Park** then stepping back in time at stunning **Canyon de Chelly National Monument**.

Two Weeks

Start in glitzy **Las Vegas** before kicking back in funky **Flagstaff** and peering into the abyss at **Grand Canyon National Park**. Check out collegiate **Tucson** and hike amid cacti at **Saguaro National Park**. Watch the gunslingers in **Tombstone** before settling into offbeat Victorian **Bisbee**. Secure your sunglasses for the blinding dunes of **White Sands National Monument** in New Mexico then sink into **Santa Fe**, a magnet for art-lovers. Explore the pueblo in **Taos** and watch the sunrise at awesome **Monument Valley Navajo Tribal Park**. Head into Utah for the red-rock national parks, **Canyonlands** and **Arches**. Do the hoodoos at **Bryce Canyon** then pay your respects at glorious **Zion**.

Southwest Highlights

1 Grand Canyon National Park (p177) Catching the sunset from a South Rim viewpoint

2 Santa Fe (p220) Exploring the cultural diversions, from Meow Wolf to international folk art.

3 Angels Landing (Zion) (p214) Staying brave while hiking this stunning slice of Utah canyonland.

4 Las Vegas (p146) Finding out it's even more brash, synthetic and irresponsible than you'd hoped!

5 Sedona (p170) Rejoicing that even monetised hippy culture can't tarnish this unique red-rock city.

6 Route 66 (p189) Winding along the Mother Road through remote landscapes and time-capsule townships.

7 Moab (p207) Celebrating the great outdoors while mountain biking, hiking, rafting or camping.

8 Monument Valley (p188) Snapping impossibly photogenic brick-red buttes and mesas, the stars of countless Westerns.

9 Acoma Pueblo (p220) Learning about one of the nation's oldest communities on a sky-high mesa.

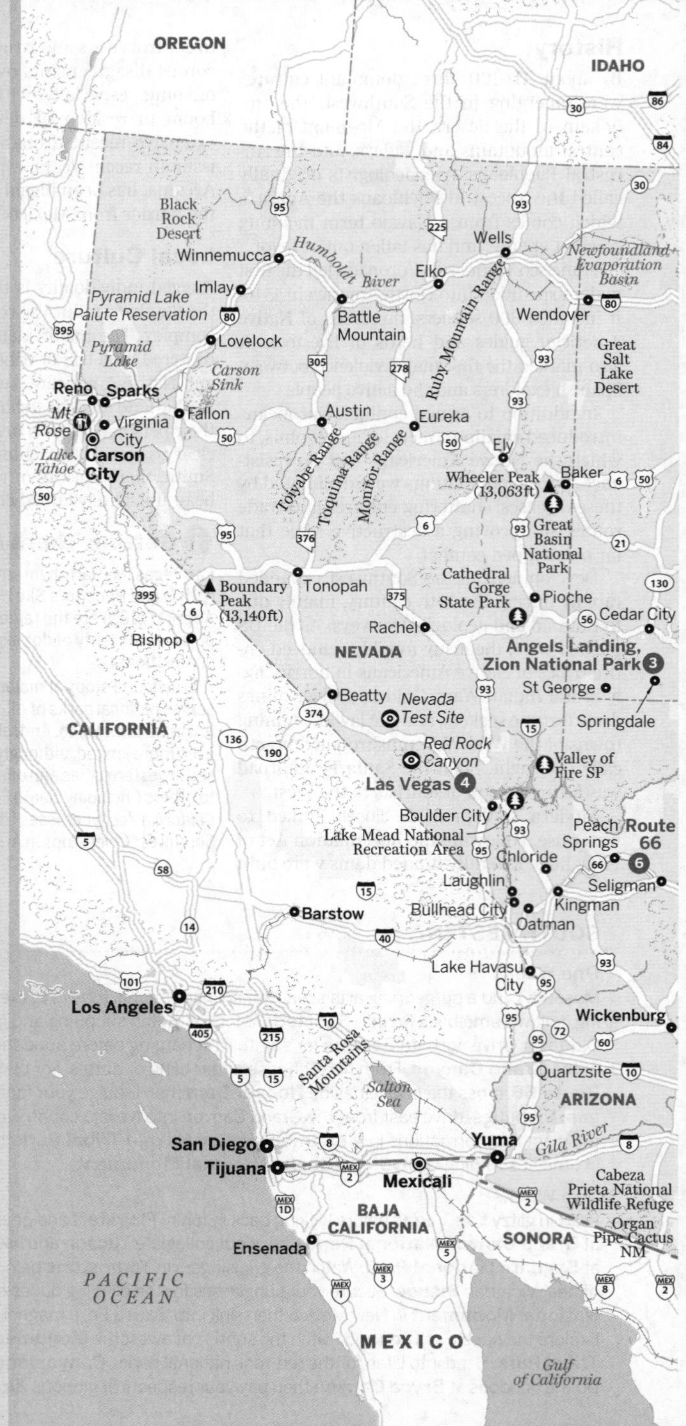

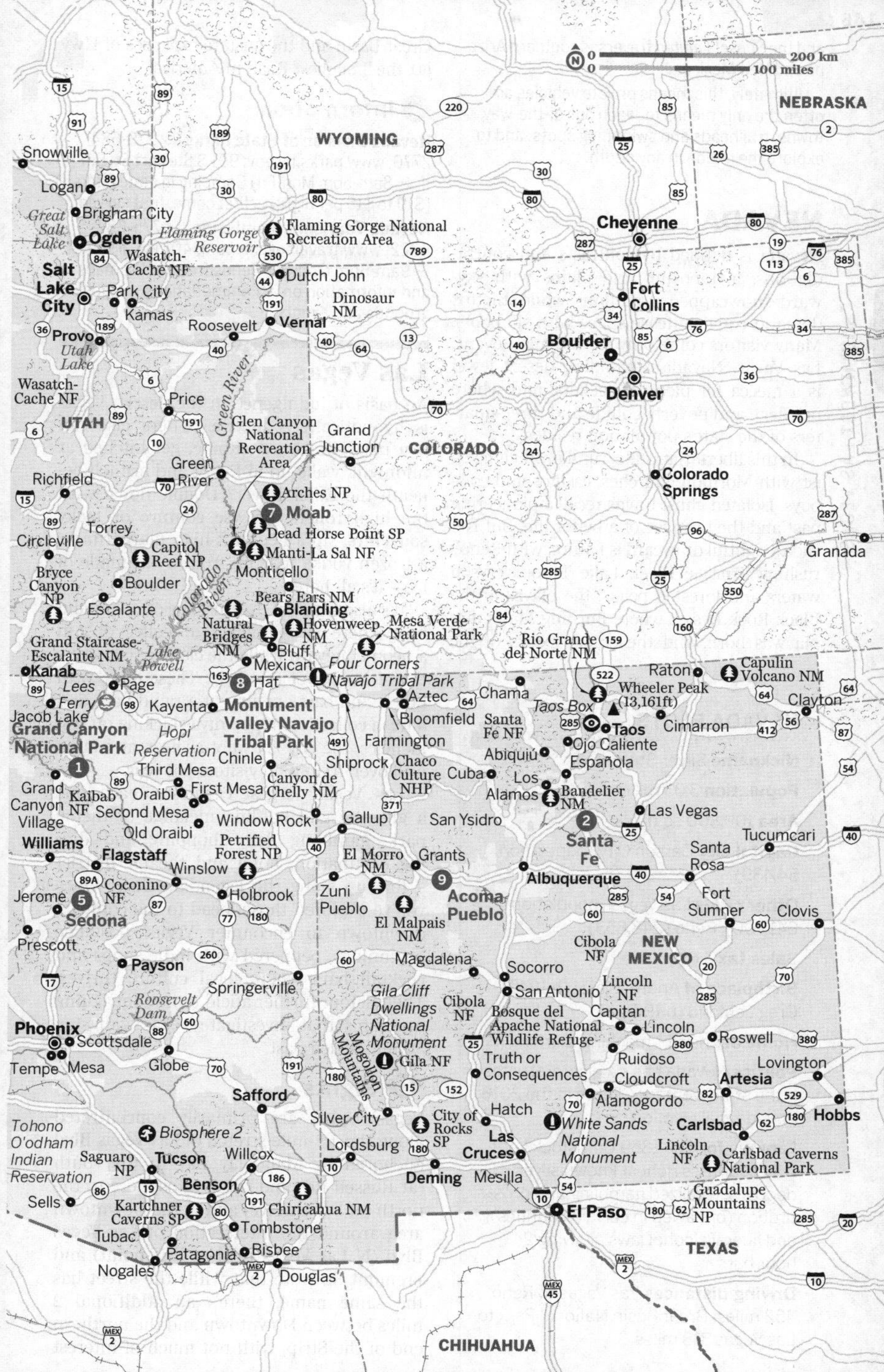
200 km
100 miles
WYOMING
NEBRASKA
Snowville
Logan
Brigham City
Great Salt Lake
Ogden
Flaming Gorge Reservoir
Flaming Gorge National Recreation Area
Wasatch-Cache NF
Salt Lake City
Park City
Kamas
Dutch John
Dinosaur NM
Roosevelt
Vernal
Provo
Utah Lake
Wasatch-Cache NF
Price
UTAH
Green River
Glen Canyon National Recreation Area
Grand Junction
COLORADO
Cheyenne
Fort Collins
Boulder
Denver
Colorado Springs
Granada
Richfield
Green River
Arches NP
Moab
Dead Horse Point SP
Manti-La Sal NF
Torrey
Circleville
Capitol Reef NP
Bryce Canyon NP
Boulder
Escalante
Colorado River
Monticello
Bears Ears NM
Blanding
Natural Bridges NM
Hovenweep NM
Mesa Verde National Park
Grand Staircase-Escalante NM
Lake Powell
Bluff
Mexican Hat
Four Corners Navajo Tribal Park
Kanab
Lees Ferry
Page
Jacob Lake
Kayenta
Monument Valley Navajo Tribal Park
Rio Grande del Norte NM
Raton
Capulin Volcano NM
Wheeler Peak (13,161ft)
Chama
Taos Box
Taos
Cimarron
Clayton
Aztec
Bloomfield
Farmington
Shiprock
Grand Canyon National Park
Hopi Reservation
Chinle
Canyon de Chelly NM
Third Mesa
First Mesa
Second Mesa
Oraibi
Old Oraibi
Grand Canyon Village
Kaibab NF
Window Rock
Chaco Culture NHP
Cuba
Santa Fe NF
Abiquiú
Ojo Caliente
Española
Los Alamos
Bandelier NM
Las Vegas
Santa Fe
Tucumcari
San Ysidro
Gallup
Williams
Flagstaff
Petrified Forest NP
Winslow
El Morro NM
Grants
Acoma Pueblo
Albuquerque
Santa Rosa
Jerome
Sedona
Coconino NF
Holbrook
Zuni Pueblo
El Malpais NM
Fort Sumner
Clovis
Prescott
Payson
Magdalena
Socorro
Cibola NF
NEW MEXICO
Roosevelt Dam
Springerville
Gila Cliff Dwellings National Monument
Cibola NF
San Antonio
Lincoln NF
Phoenix
Scottsdale
Tempe
Mesa
Globe
Mogollon Mountains
Bosque del Apache National Wildlife Refuge
Capitan
Lincoln
Roswell
Gila NF
Truth or Consequences
Ruidoso
Lovington
Cloudcroft
Artesia
Safford
Silver City
Alamogordo
Hobbs
Tohono O'odham Indian Reservation
Biosphere 2
City of Rocks SP
Hatch
White Sands National Monument
Carlsbad
Las Cruces
Lordsburg
Saguaro NP
Tucson
Willcox
Deming
Mesilla
Lincoln NF
Carlsbad Caverns National Park
Sells
Benson
Chiricahua NM
Kartchner Caverns SP
Tombstone
El Paso
Guadalupe Mountains NP
Tubac
Patagonia
Bisbee
Nogales
Douglas
TEXAS
CHIHUAHUA

and the *Sunset Limited* traverses southern Arizona and New Mexico.

Ultimately, this means private vehicles are often the only means to reach out-of-the-way towns, trailheads and swimming spots, and to explore the region in any depth.

NEVADA

Nevada is defined by contrasts and contradictions, juxtaposing arid plains with skyward, snowcapped mountains, while stilettos demand equal suitcase space with ski boots. Many visitors come only for the main event: Las Vegas. Nevada's twinkling desert jewel is a mecca for pleasure-seekers, and where privilege and poverty collide and three-quarters of the state's population resides.

In this libertarian state, rural brothels coexist with Mormon churches, casinos and cowboys. Isolated ghost towns recall a pioneering past and the promise of a better life. But Nevada's rightful drawcard is nature, with Reno's rushing Truckee River, Lake Tahoe's crystal waters and forested peaks, the playas of the Black Rock Desert where Burning Man's utopia was born, and the craggy peaks of the Great Basin and the austere expanses of Hwy 50, the 'Loneliest Road in America.'

NEVADA FACTS

Nickname Silver State

Population 3.03 million

Area 109,800 sq miles

Capital city Carson City (population 54,439)

Other cities Las Vegas (population 641,700), Reno (248,853)

Sales tax 4.6%

Birthplace of Andre Agassi (b 1970), Greg LeMond (b 1961)

Home of The slot machine, Burning Man

Politics Nevada has six electoral votes – the state went for Clinton in the 2016 presidential election

Famous for The 1859 Comstock Lode (the country's richest known silver deposit), legalized gambling and prostitution (outlawed in certain counties), and liberal alcohol laws allowing 24-hour bars

Driving distances Las Vegas to Reno 452 miles, Great Basin National Park to Las Vegas 313 miles

Information

Nevada Division of State Parks (☎775-684-2770; www.parks.nv.gov; 901 S Stewart St, 5th fl; ⏲8am-5pm Mon-Fri) Camping in state parks ($10 to $15 per night) is first come, first served.

Nevada Tourism Commission (☎775-687-4322; www.travelnevada.com; 401 N Carson St; ⏲9am-5pm Mon-Fri) Sends free books, maps and information on accommodations, campgrounds and events.

Las Vegas

An oasis of indulgence in the desert, Vegas is hypnotically seductive. Where else can you party in ancient Rome, get hitched at midnight, wake up in Egypt and brunch beneath the Eiffel Tower? Double down with the high rollers, browse couture or tacky souvenirs, sip a neon 3ft-high margarita or a frozen vodka martini from a bar made of ice – it's all here.

It's also a desert dreamscape of boom and bust, where once-famous signs collect dust in a neon boneyard while the clang of construction echoes over the Strip. These days, with hotels and bars opening at a rapid pace and a fresh collection of pop divas kicking off residencies, the city is as hot as ever, attracting well over 40 million visitors per year.

Las Vegas' largest casinos – each one a gigantic and baffling mélange of theme park, gambling den, shopping and dining destination, hotel and theater district – line up along the legendary Strip. Once you've explored those, head to the compact downtown to encounter Vegas' nostalgic beginnings, peppered with indie shops and cocktail bars where local culture thrives. Then detour further afield to find intriguing museums that investigate Vegas' gangster, atomic-fueled past.

Sights

Vegas' sights are primarily concentrated along the 4.2-mile stretch of Las Vegas Blvd anchored by Mandalay Bay to the south (at Russell Rd) and the Stratosphere to the north (at Sahara Ave) and in the Downtown area around the intersection of Las Vegas Blvd (N Las Vegas Blvd at this point) and Fremont St. Note that while the street has the same name, there's an additional 2 miles between Downtown and the northern end of the Strip, with not much of interest in between. It's not a great idea to walk between the two; this neighborhood can be a little dicey. Rideshares, the Monorail and Deuce bus services are by far the easiest ways to get around this spaced-out (in more ways than one) city.

The Strip

★Aria LANDMARK

(CityCenter; Map p148; www.aria.com; 3780 S Las Vegas Blvd; P) We've seen this symbiotic relationship before (think giant hotel anchored by a mall 'concept'), but the way that this futuristic-feeling complex places a small galaxy of hypermodern, chichi hotels in orbit around the glitzy **Shops at Crystals** (Map p148; www.simon.com/mall/the-shops-at-crystals; 10am-11pm Mon-Thu, to midnight Fri-Sun) is a first. The upscale spread includes the subdued, stylish **Vdara** (Map p148; 702-590-2111; www.vdara.com; 2600 W Harmon Ave, Aria; weekday/weekend ste from $103/189; P) , the hush-hush opulent **Waldorf Astoria** (Map p148; www.waldorfastorialasvegas.com; 3752 S Las Vegas Blvd; r from $200; P) and the dramatic architectural showpiece **Aria**, whose sophisticated casino provides a fitting backdrop to its many drop-dead-gorgeous restaurants. CityCenter's hotels have in excess of 6700 rooms!

★Bellagio CASINO

(Map p148; 702-693-7111; www.bellagio.com; 3600 S Las Vegas Blvd; 24hr; P) The Bellagio experience transcends its decadent casino floor of high-limit gaming tables and in excess of 2300 slot machines; locals say odds here are less than favorable. A stop on the World Poker Tour, Bellagio's tournament-worthy poker room offers kitchen-to-gaming-table delivery around the clock. Most, however, come for the property's stunning architecture, interiors and amenities, including the **Conservatory & Botanical Gardens** (Map p148; 24hr; P) FREE, **Gallery of Fine Art** (Map p148; 702-693-7871; adult/child under 12yr $18/free; 10am-8pm, last entry 7:30pm; P), unmissable **Fountains of Bellagio** (Map p148; shows every 30min 3-8pm Mon-Fri, noon-8pm Sat, 11am-7pm Sun, every 15min 8pm-midnight Mon-Sat, from 7pm Sun; P) FREE and the 2000-plus hand-blown glass flowers embellishing the hotel (p152) lobby.

★Caesars Palace CASINO

(Map p148; 866-227-5938; www.caesars.com/caesars-palace; 3570 S Las Vegas Blvd; 24hr; P) Caesars Palace claims that its smartly renovated casino floor has more million-dollar slots than anywhere in the world, but its claims to fame are far more numerous than that. Entertainment heavyweights Celine Dion and Elton John 'own' its custom-built **Colosseum** (Map p148; 866-227-5938; www.thecolosseum.com; tickets $55-500) theater, fashionistas saunter around **The Forum Shops** (Map p148; 702-893-4800; www.simon.com/mall/the-forum-shops-at-caesars-palace; 10am-11pm Sun-Thu, to midnight Fri & Sat), while Caesars' hotel guests quaff cocktails in the Garden of the Gods Pool Oasis. By night, megaclub **Omnia** (Map p148; 702-785-6200; www.omniaclubs.com/las-vegas; cover female/male from $20/40; 10:30pm-4am Tue & Thu-Sun) is one of the best places to get off your face this side of Ibiza.

NoMad CASINO

(Map p148; 702-730-7000; www.thenomadhotel.com; 3772 S Las Vegas Blvd; 24hr) If a Las Vegas casino can be classy, the NoMad comes in pretty close to the mark. High-limit roulette, blackjack and baccarat are available under a Tiffany-glass ceiling. The NoMad's pool is modeled on the Majorelle Gardens in Morocco, and is quietly relaxing on weekdays (weekend Jemaa parties are another story).

LINQ Casino CASINO

(Map p148; 800-634-6441; www.caesars.com/linq; 3535 S Las Vegas Blvd; 24hr; P) With a fresh, young and funky vibe, one of Vegas' newest casinos benefits from also being one of its smallest with just over 60 tables and around 750 slot machines. There's an airy, spacious feel to the place, tables feature high-backed, ruby-red, patent-vinyl chairs, and when you need to escape, the fun and frivolity of **LINQ Promenade** (Map p148; 800-634-6441; www.caesars.com/linq; 24hr; P) are just outside the door.

Venetian CASINO

(Map p148; 702-414-1000; www.venetian.com; 3355 S Las Vegas Blvd; 24hr; P) The Venetian's regal 120,000-sq-ft casino has marble floors, hand-painted ceiling frescoes and 120 table games, including a high-limit lounge and an elegant nonsmoking poker room, where women are especially welcome (unlike at many other poker rooms in town). When combined with its younger, neighboring sibling **Palazzo** (Map p148; 702-607-7777; www.palazzo.com; 3325 S Las Vegas Blvd; 24hr; P), the properties claim the largest

Las Vegas

Downtown Las Vegas
DOWNTOWN
Carson Ave
Promenade Pl
City Pkwy
Grand Central Pkwy
Bridger Ave
S 1st St
Casino Center Blvd
Bonneville Transit Center
Clark Ave
E Bonneville Ave
Garces Ave
California St
Main St
S 3rd St
S Las Vegas Blvd (The Strip)
E Charleston Blvd
Huntridge Circle Park
Franklin Ave
Colorado Ave
S 5th St
S 7th St
E Oakey Blvd
Retro Vegas (0.4mi); Arts Factory (0.5mi); Downtown Las Vegas (1mi; see inset)
Bell Trans Airport Shuttle
Presidential Limo
Western Ave
Fairfield Ave
W Sahara Ave
E Sahara Ave
SLS
Karen Ave
Las Vegas Country Club
Paradise Rd
Westgate
Circus Circus Dr
Circus Circus
Riviera Blvd
Meade Ave
S Highland Dr
S Industrial Rd
Las Vegas Convention Center
Sirius Ave
Convention Center Dr
Desert Inn Rd Super-Arterial
Las Vegas Convention & Visitors Authority
E Desert Inn Rd
Sammy Davis Jr Dr
Polaris Ave
Procyon Ave
Sierra Vista Dr
Spring Mountain Rd
Raku (1.25mi)
Treasure Island
Palazzo
Swenson St
THE STRIP
Sands Ave
E Twain Ave
Cassella Dr
LINQ Promenade
Harrah's/The LINQ
Ida Ave
Rio
Caesars Palace
Flamingo Wash
Flamingo/Caesars Palace
Bellagio Conservatory & Botanical Gardens
E Flamingo Rd
Bally's
Palms (0.4mi)
Bellagio
Bally's/Paris Las Vegas
University of Nevada, Las Vegas (UNLV)
Cosmopolitan
Planet Hollywood
Tropicana Wash
CityCenter
W Harmon Ave
E Harmon Ave
Aria
Monte Carlo
Koval La
Thomas & Mack Stadium
Tompkins Ave
MGM Grand
E Tropicana Ave
W Tropicana Ave
Excalibur
Tropicana
Gun Store (1.9mi)
E Reno Ave
Ali Baba La
Giles St
Mandalay Bay Rd
E Mandalay Bay Rd
McCarran International Airport
W Hacienda Ave
Mandalay Bay
Welcome to Las Vegas Sign (0.55mi)

Las Vegas

Top Sights

1 Aria ... B6
2 Bellagio ... B5
3 Bellagio Conservatory & Botanical Gardens ... B5
4 Caesars Palace ... B5
5 Cosmopolitan ... B5
6 LINQ Promenade ... B4
7 Mandalay Bay ... B7
8 MGM Grand ... B6
9 Palazzo ... B4

Sights

10 Aria ... B6
11 Arts Factory ... A2
Bellagio Gallery of Fine Art ... (see 2)
12 Fountains of Bellagio ... B5
13 High Roller ... B4
14 LINQ Casino ... B4
15 Mandalay Bay Beach ... B7
16 Mirage ... B4
17 Mirage Volcano ... B4
18 National Atomic Testing Museum ... D5
19 NoMad ... B6
20 Paris Las Vegas ... B5
21 Shark Reef Aquarium ... B7
22 Venetian ... B4

Activities, Courses & Tours

23 Gondola Ride ... B4
24 Qua Baths & Spa ... B5
25 Stratosphere Thrill Rides ... C1
26 VooDoo ZipLine ... A5

Sleeping

Aria Las Vegas Resort ... (see 10)
Aria Sky Suites & Villas ... (see 10)
Bellagio ... (see 2)
27 Cosmopolitan ... B5
28 Cromwell Las Vegas ... B5
29 Delano ... B7
30 Encore ... C3
Four Seasons Hotel ... (see 7)
LINQ Hotel ... (see 14)
Mandalay Bay ... (see 7)
NoMad ... (see 19)
31 SLS ... C2
32 Thunderbird Hotel ... A2
33 Vdara ... A5
34 Waldorf Astoria ... B6
35 Wynn ... B3

Eating

36 Carson Kitchen ... B1
Catch ... (see 10)
37 Esther's Kitchen ... A2
Giada ... (see 28)
38 Hugo's Cellar ... B1
39 Jaburrito ... B4
Joël Robuchon ... (see 8)
40 Lotus of Siam ... D2
Milk Bar ... (see 27)
Morimoto ... (see 8)
Peppermill ... (see 44)
41 Tacos El Gordo ... C3
42 Umami Burger ... C2
43 VegeNation ... B1

Drinking & Nightlife

Drai's Beachclub & Nightclub ... (see 28)
44 Fireside Lounge ... C3
Hakkasan ... (see 8)
45 NoMad Bar ... B6
46 Omnia ... B4
47 ReBAR ... A2
Skyfall Lounge ... (see 29)
XS ... (see 30)

Entertainment

48 Aces of Comedy ... B4
49 Colosseum ... B4
House of Blues Gospel Brunch ... (see 7)
50 Le Rêve the Dream ... B3
51 Legends in Concert ... B5
O ... (see 3)
52 Tix 4 Tonight ... B3

Shopping

53 Grand Canal Shoppes at the Venetian ... B4
54 Las Vegas Premium Outlets North ... A1
55 Planet 13 ... B3
Retro Vegas ... (see 37)
56 Shops at Crystals ... B5
57 The Forum Shops ... B4

Information

58 Clark County Marriage License Bureau ... B1
59 Office of Civil Marriages ... B1

casino space in Las Vegas. Unmissable on the Strip, a highlight of this miniature replica of Venice is a gondola ride (p151) down its Grand Canal.

★ Cosmopolitan CASINO

(Map p148; 702-698-7000; www.cosmopolitanlasvegas.com; 3708 S Las Vegas Blvd; 24hr; P)

Hipsters who thought they were too cool for Vegas finally have a place to go where they don't need irony to endure – or enjoy – the aesthetics of the Strip. Like the new Hollywood 'It' girl, the Cosmopolitan casino looks absolutely fabulous at all times. A steady stream of ingenues and entourages parade through the lobby (with some of the coolest design elements we've seen) along with anyone else who adores contemporary art and design.

★Mandalay Bay CASINO

(Map p148; 702-632-7700; www.mandalaybay.com; 3950 S Las Vegas Blvd; 24hr; P) Since opening in 1999, in place of the former '50s-era Hacienda, Mandalay Bay has anchored the southern Strip. Its theme may be tropical, but it sure ain't tacky, nor is its 135,000-sq-ft casino. Well-dressed sports fans find their way to the upscale race and sports book near the high-stakes poker room. Refusing to be pigeonholed, the Bay's standout attractions include the multilevel **Shark Reef Aquarium** (Map p148; 702-632-4555; www.sharkreef.com; adult/child $25/19; 10am-8pm Sun-Thu, to 10pm Fri & Sat; P), decadent day spas, oodles of signature dining and the unrivaled **Mandalay Bay Beach** (Map p148; 702-632-4760; www.mandalaybay.com/en/amenities/beach.html; pool 8am-7pm, Moorea Beach Club from 10am;).

Paris Las Vegas CASINO

(Map p148; 877-796-2096; www.caesars.com/paris-las-vegas; 3655 S Las Vegas Blvd; 24hr; P) This mini version of the French capital might lack the charm of the City of Light, but its efforts to emulate Paris' landmarks, including a 34-story Hotel de Ville and facades from the Opera House and Louvre, make it a fun stop for families and anyone yet to see the real thing. Its vaulted casino ceilings simulate sunny skies above myriad tables and slots, while its high-limit, authentic French roulette wheels, sans 0 and 00, slightly improve your odds.

High Roller FERRIS WHEEL

(Map p148; 702-777-2782; www.caesars.com/linq/high-roller; LINQ Promenade; adult/child from $22/9, after 5pm $32/19; 11:30am-1:30am; P; Flamingo or Harrah's/Linq) The world's largest observation wheel towers 550ft above LINQ Promenade (p147). Each of the 28 air-conditioned passenger cabins is enclosed by handcrafted Italian glass. Outside, 2000 colorful LED lights glow from dusk until dawn. One revolution takes about 30 minutes and each pod can hold 40 guests. From 4pm to 7pm, select pods host the adults-only (21-plus) 'happy half-hour' ($35, or $47 after 5pm) with an open bar (read all-you-can-drink) shared between your fellow riders. Things can get messy, fast.

Mirage Volcano LANDMARK

(Map p148; 702-791-7111; www.mirage.com; Mirage; shows 8pm, 9pm & 10pm daily) FREE When the Mirage's trademark artificial volcano erupts with a roar out of a 3-acre lagoon, it inevitably brings traffic on the Strip to a screeching halt. Be on the lookout for wisps of smoke escaping from the top, signaling that the fiery Polynesian-style inferno, with a soundtrack by a Grateful Dead drummer and an Indian tabla musician, is about to begin.

Downtown & Off the Strip

For tourists, the five-block **Fremont Street Experience** (702-678-5600; www.vegasexperience.com; Fremont St Mall; shows hourly dusk-midnight or 1am; Deuce, SDX) FREE is the focal point of Downtown, with its wealth of vintage casinos, where today's Vegas was born – and fear not, they're still going strong. Further south, the **Arts District** (www.18b.org) revolves around the **Arts Factory** (Map p148; 702-383-9907; www.theartsfactory.com; 107 E Charleston Blvd; 9am-6pm; Deuce, SDX), while heading east on Fremont St will take you to an adorable little hodgepodge of hip bars and happening restaurants.

★Mob Museum MUSEUM

(702-229-2734; www.themobmuseum.org; 300 Stewart Ave; adult/child $27/17; 9am-9pm; P; Deuce) It's hard to say what's more impressive: the museum's physical location in a historic federal courthouse where mobsters sat for federal hearings in 1950–51, the fact that the board of directors is headed up by a former FBI special agent, or the thoughtfully curated exhibits telling the story of organized crime in America. The museum features hands-on FBI equipment and mob-related artifacts, as well as interviews with real-life Tony Sopranos.

★Neon Museum – Neon Boneyard MUSEUM

(702-387-6366; www.neonmuseum.org; 770 N Las Vegas Blvd; 1hr tour adult/child $28/24; tours daily, schedules vary; 113) This nonprofit project is doing what almost no one else does: saving Las Vegas' history. Book ahead for a fascinating guided walking tour of the 'Neon Boneyard,' where irreplaceable vintage neon signs – Las Vegas' original art form – spend their retirement. Start exploring at the visitor center inside the salvaged

La Concha Motel lobby, a mid-century modern icon designed by African American architect Paul Revere Williams. Tours are usually given throughout the day, but are most spectacular at night.

National Atomic Testing Museum MUSEUM
(Map p148; ☎702-794-5151; www.nationalatomictestingmuseum.org; 755 Flamingo Rd E, Desert Research Institute; adult/child $22/16; ⏰10am-5pm Mon-Sat, noon-5pm Sun; 🚌202) Fascinating multimedia exhibits focus on science, technology and the social history of the 'Atomic Age,' which lasted from WWII until a worldwide ban on nuclear testing was declared in 1992. Experience a (legitimately scary) simulation of witnessing an atomic test, and examine southern Nevada's nuclear past, present and future, from Native American ways of life to the environmental legacy of atomic testing. Don't miss the ticket booth: it's a Nevada Test Site guard-station replica.

Activities

★Qua Baths & Spa SPA
(Map p148; ☎866-782-0655; www.caesars.com/caesars-palace; Caesars Palace; fitness center day pass $25, incl spa facilities $50; ⏰6am-8pm) Qua evokes the ancient Roman rituals of indulgent bathing. Try a signature 'bath liqueur,' a personalized potion of herbs and oils poured into your own private tub. The women's side includes a tea lounge, a herbal steam room and an Arctic ice room where artificial snow falls. On the men's side, there's a barber spa and big-screen sports TVs.

★Desert Adventures KAYAKING
(☎702-293-5026; www.kayaklasvegas.com; 1647 Nevada Hwy; full-day Colorado River kayak $195; ⏰9am-6pm Apr-Oct, 10am-4pm Nov-Mar) Would-be river rats should check in here for guided kayaking and SUP tours on Lake Mead and the Colorado River. Experienced paddlers can rent canoes and kayaks for DIY trips. Also offers fishing, hiking and boating guided tours – including smooth water floats on the Colorado River through Black Canyon ($199).

Gondola Ride BOATING
(Map p148; ☎877-691-1997; www.venetian.com/resort/attractions/gondola-rides.html; Venetian; shared ride per person $29, child under 3yr free, private 2-passenger ride $116; ⏰indoor rides 10am-11pm Sun-Thu, to midnight Fri & Sat, outdoor rides 11am-10pm, weather permitting; 👪) As in Venice itself, a gondola ride in Vegas is a touristy activity that nonetheless holds allure for visitors from all over the world. Choose between a moonlit outdoor cruise in the resort's miniature lake facing the Strip or float through winding indoor canals past shoppers and diners. Buy tickets inside the **Grand Canal Shoppes at the Venetian** (Map p148; ☎702-414-4525; www.grandcanalshoppes.com; 3377 S Las Vegas Blvd, Venetian; ⏰10am-11pm Sun-Thu, to midnight Fri & Sat).

THRILLS & SPILLS IN LAS VEGAS

Stratosphere (Map p148; ☎702-380-7777; www.stratospherehotel.com/ThrillRides; Stratosphere; elevator adult $20, incl 3 thrill rides $35, all-day pass $40; ⏰10am-1am Sun-Thu, to 2am Fri & Sat; 🚝Sahara) The world's highest thrill rides await, a whopping 110 stories above the Strip.

Sky Combat Ace (☎888-494-5850; www.skycombatace.com; 1420 Jet Stream Dr #100; from $299) A bona-fide fighter pilot takes you through the paces of air-to-air dogfights and extreme acrobatics!

VooDoo ZipLine (Map p148; ☎702-388-0477; www.voodoozipline.com; Rio; from $25; ⏰11am-midnight) At last, your chance to zipline between two skyscrapers.

Gravady (☎702-843-0395; www.gravady.com; 7350 Prairie Falcon Rd #120; 1hr flight adult/child $15/12; ⏰9am-9pm Mon-Wed, from 3:30pm Thu, 9am-11pm Fri & Sat, 11am-7pm Sun; 👪) Get bouncy with the kids at this high-energy trampoline park in Summerlin.

Speedvegas (☎702-874-8888; www.speedvegas.com; 14200 S Las Vegas Blvd; laps $39-99, experiences $395-1800; ⏰10am-4:30pm) Burn serious rubber at the wheel of a sports car on Vegas' only custom-built track.

Richard Petty Driving Experience (☎800-237-3889; www.drivepetty.com; 7000 N Las Vegas Blvd, Las Vegas Motor Speedway; ride-alongs from $136, drives from $199; ⏰hours vary) This is your chance to ride shotgun during a Nascar-style qualifying run.

Sleeping

Room rates in Las Vegas rise and fall every day; visiting on weekdays is almost always cheaper than weekends. Note that almost every Strip hotel also charges an additional 'resort fee' of $30 to $45 per day.

The Strip

★Cosmopolitan CASINO HOTEL **$**
(Map p148; ☎702-698-7000; www.cosmopolitanlasvegas.com; 3708 S Las Vegas Blvd; r from $140; P ❄ @ 📶 ≋ 🐾; 🚌Deuce) With at least eight distinctively different and equally stylish room types to choose from, Cosmo's digs are the hippest on the Strip. Ranging from oversized to decadent, about 2200 of its 2900 or so rooms have balconies (all but the entry-level category), many sport sunken Japanese tubs and all feature plush furnishings and design quirks you'll delight in uncovering.

★Mandalay Bay CASINO HOTEL **$$**
(Map p148; ☎702-632-7700; www.mandalaybay.com; 3950 S Las Vegas Blvd; r weekday/weekend from $79/388; P ❄ @ 📶 ≋) Anchoring the south Strip, upscale Mandalay Bay's (p150) same-named hotel has a cache of classy rooms worthy of your attention in their own right, not to mention the exclusive **Four Seasons Hotel** (Map p148; ☎702-632-5000; www.fourseasons.com/lasvegas; r weekday/weekend from $305/440; P ❄ @ 📶 ≋) and boutique **Delano** (Map p148; ☎702-632-7888; www.delanolasvegas.com; r weekday/weekend from $143/369; P ❄ @ 📶 ≋ 🐾) within its bounds. Plus there's a diverse range of noteworthy attractions and amenities, not least of which is Mandalay Bay Beach (p150).

★Bellagio CASINO HOTEL **$$**
(Map p148; ☎702-693-7111; www.bellagio.com; 3600 S Las Vegas Blvd; r weekday/weekend from $169/399; P ❄ @ 📶 ≋ 🐾) When it opened in 1998, Bellagio was the world's most expensive hotel. Aging gracefully, it remains one of America's finest. Its sumptuous oversized guest rooms fuse classic style with modern amenities and feature palettes of platinum, indigo and muted white-gold, or rusty autumnal oranges with subtle splashes of matcha green. Cashmere throws, mood lighting and automatic drapes complete the picture.

Aria Las Vegas Resort CASINO HOTEL **$$**
(Map p148; ☎702-590-7111; www.aria.com; 3730 S Las Vegas Blvd, CityCenter; r weekday/weekend from $119/169; P ❄ @ 📶 ≋) Aria's (p147) sleek resort hotel has no theme, unlike some of the Strip's other megaproperties. Instead, its 4000-plus deluxe rooms (520 sq ft) and 560 tower suites (920-plus sq ft) are all about soothing design, spaciousness and luxury, and every room has a corner view. If you've cash to burn, **Aria Sky Suites & Villas** (Map p148; ☎702-590-7111; www.aria.com; 3730 S Las Vegas Blvd, Aria; ste $400), a hotel-within-a-hotel, might be for you.

LINQ Hotel CASINO HOTEL **$$**
(Map p148; ☎800-634-6441; www.caesars.com/linq; 3535 S Las Vegas Blvd; r from $99; P ❄ 📶 ≋ 🐾) Launching onto the Las Vegas Strip in late 2014, LINQ, formerly the Quad, has cemented its position as a solid all-rounder. Its fresh, white rooms have fun splashes of color and sleek furniture, there's a wealth of available amenities (this being part of the Caesars group) and it has an enviable location at the center of its eponymous promenade (p147).

SLS HOTEL **$$**
(Map p148; ☎702-761-7000; www.slslasvegas.com; 2535 S Las Vegas Blvd; d from $102; P ❄ 📶 ≋) The SLS replaced the Sahara in 2011, and now the Sahara is replacing the SLS (the $100 million renovation is due to finish in 2020). In the meantime, you can nab a room here on the north Strip at very good rates compared to same-branded properties in other cities. The hotel's quirky style is infectious.

★Cromwell Las Vegas BOUTIQUE HOTEL **$$$**
(Map p148; ☎702-777-3777; www.caesars.com/cromwell; 3595 S Las Vegas Blvd; r from $288; P ❄ 📶 ≋ 🐾) If you're 20- to 30-something, can hold your own with the cool kids, or you're just effortlessly stylish whatever your demographic, there are a few good reasons to choose Cromwell, the best being its location and frequently excellent rates on sassy, entry-level rooms. The others? You've got your sights set on partying at **Drai's** (Map p148; ☎702-777-3800; www.draisgroup.com/las-vegas/; nightclub cover $20-50; ⊙nightclub 10:30pm-4am Thu-Sun, beach club 11am-6pm Fri-Sun) or dining downstairs at **Giada** (Map p148; ☎855-442-3271; www.caesars.com/cromwell; mains $24-60; ⊙5pm-10:30pm, brunch 9am-3pm Fri-Sun).

NoMad CASINO HOTEL **$$$**
(Map p148; www.thenomadhotel.com/las-vegas; 3772 S Las Vegas Blvd, Park MGM; r from $249; P ❄ 📶 ≋) The NoMad has taken things to truly a ridiculous level: it's a hotel within

a hotel within a hotel. It's a good thing the rooms are exquisite, most with freestanding bath tubs and custom-made furniture. There's a fun party vibe in the restaurant and bar, which spills out onto the classier-than-most casino floor.

Downtown & Off the Strip

★Thunderbird Hotel BOUTIQUE HOTEL **$**

(Map p148; ☎702-489-7500; www.thunderbirdhotellasvegas.com; 1215 S Las Vegas Blvd; d from $39; P ❄ 📶 🏊) Nestled between the north Strip and Fremont St, this retro renovated job is an instant winner with its great rates, funky fresh rooms with chunky, reclaimed-wood furniture, and fun, youthful vibe. It's not a hostel or a boutique hotel, but lies somewhere in between.

The neighborhood is dicey, especially after dark. Plan to drive or rideshare.

Golden Nugget CASINO HOTEL **$**

(☎702-385-7111; www.goldennugget.com; 129 Fremont St E; d from $49; P ❄ @ 📶 🏊) Pretend to relive the fabulous heyday of Vegas in the 1950s at this swank Fremont St address. Rooms in the Rush Tower are the best in the house.

Eating

The Strip has been studded with celebrity chefs for years. All-you-can-eat buffets and $10 steaks still exist, but today's high-rolling visitors demand ever more sophisticated dining experiences, with meals designed – although not personally prepared – by famous taste-makers.

The Strip

★Umami Burger BURGERS **$**

(Map p148; ☎702-761-7614; www.umamiburger.com; 2535 S Las Vegas Blvd, SLS; burgers $12-15; ⊙11am-10pm; P) This SLS (p152) burger offering is one of the best on the Strip, with its outdoor beer garden, extensive craft-beer selection and juicy boutique burgers made by the chain that won *GQ* magazine's 'burger of the year' crown. This is a great place to try the new, vegan 'Impossible' burger everyone keeps banging on about.

★Tacos El Gordo MEXICAN **$**

(Map p148; ☎702-982-5420; www.tacoselgordobc.com; 3049 S Las Vegas Blvd; small plates $3-12; ⊙10am-2am, to 4am Fri & Sat; P 🌶 👪; 🚌Deuce, SDX) This Tijuana-style taco shop from SoCal is just the ticket when it's way late, you've got almost no money left and you're desperately craving *carne asada* (beef) or *adobada* (chili-marinated pork) tacos in hot, handmade tortillas. Adventurous eaters will be lured by the authentic *sesos* (beef brains), *cabeza* (roasted cow's head) or tripe (intestines) variations.

★Milk Bar DESSERTS **$**

(Map p148; ☎7020-698-7000; www.cosmopolitanlasvegas.com; Cosmopolitan; soft serve from $6; ⊙9am-1am, to 2am Fri & Sat) Momofuku dessert program wünderkind Christina Tosi has brought her Milk Bar concept to Las Vegas, inspiring rapture and adoration. Try her cereal-milk soft serve, corn cookies or (and?) cake truffles and feel smug.

Jaburrito SUSHI **$**

(Map p148; ☎702-901-7375; www.jaburritos.com; LINQ Promenade; items $10-13; ⊙11am-11pm Sun-Thu, to midnight Fri & Sat) It's simple: hybridize a nori (seaweed) sushi roll with a burrito. What could go wrong? Nothing actually…they're awesome! Mochi ice-cream pops for dessert are extremely fun to eat.

Peppermill DINER **$$**

(Map p148; ☎702-735-4177; www.peppermilllasvegas.com; 2985 S Las Vegas Blvd; mains $13-31; ⊙24hr) Slide into a crescent-shaped booth at this retro casino coffee shop and revel in the old-school Vegas atmosphere. You can eavesdrop on Nevada cowboys and downtown politicos digging into a gigantic late-night bite or early breakfast. For tropical tiki drinks, step into a sexy booth at Peppermill's **Fireside Lounge** (Map p148; ☎702-735-7635).

★Joël Robuchon FRENCH **$$$**

(Map p148; ☎702-891-7925; www.mgmgrand.com; MGM Grand; tasting menus $120-425; ⊙5:30-10pm) The acclaimed 'Chef of the Century' leads the pack in the French culinary invasion of the Strip. Adjacent to the **MGM Grand's** (Map p148; ☎877-880-0880; www.mgmgrand.com; 3799 S Las Vegas Blvd; ⊙24hr; P 👪) high-rollers' gaming area, Robuchon's plush dining rooms, done up in leather and velvet, feel like a dinner party at a 1930s Paris mansion. Complex seasonal tasting menus promise the meal of a lifetime – and they often deliver.

★Morimoto FUSION **$$$**

(Map p148; ☎702-891-3001; www.mgmgrand.com; MGM Grand; mains $24-75; ⊙5-10pm, to 10:30pm Fri & Sat) Iron Chef Masaharu Morimoto's latest Vegas incarnation is in his

BUFFET ALL THE WAY

Extravagant all-you-can-eat buffets are a Sin City tradition. Here are three of the best:

Bacchanal Buffet (3570 Las Vegas Blvd S, Caesars Palace; $40-65 per adult, 7:30am-10pm Mon-Fri, from 8am Sat & Sun)

Wicked Spoon Buffet (3708 Las Vegas Blvd S, Cosmopolitan; $28-49 per adult, 8am-9pm Sun-Thu, to 10pm Fri & Sat)

Buffet at Wynn (3131 Las Vegas Blvd S; Wynn; $32-60 per person, 7:30am-9:30pm)

eponymous showcase restaurant, which pays homage to his Japanese roots and the cuisine of this city that has propelled him to legend status around the world. Dining here is an experience in every possible way and, we think, worth every penny.

★Catch SEAFOOD $$$

(Map p148; ☎702-590-5757; https://aria.mgmresorts.com; Aria; mains from $40; ⏰5:30-11:30pm; P ❄) Fresh from a $7 million renovation, this space had better be beautiful – and it does not disappoint. The seafood-centric menu is massive, focusing on Asian preparations including truffled sashimi and whole fish and crustaceans (the whole lobster, steamed in sake, is the thing to order if you're looking to impress your dining companion or someone across the room).

Downtown & off the Strip

★VegeNation VEGAN $

(Map p148; ☎702-366-8515; https://vegenationlv.com; 616 E Carson Ave; mains $13; ⏰8am-9pm Sun-Thu, to 10pm Fri & Sat; 📶 ✍) Faced with a health crisis, veteran chef Donald Lemperle adopted a plant-based diet, and used his learnings to open Downtown's most exciting new cafe. His kitchen sends out insanely delicious plant-based tacos, sandwiches, pizzas and desserts made from local products and community gardens to an adoring local fan base. You can even get CBD kombucha. Welcome to the new Vegas.

★Esther's Kitchen ITALIAN $$

(Map p148; ☎702-570-7864; www.estherslv.com; 1130 S Casino Center Blvd; pasta from $15; ⏰11am-3pm & 5-10pm Mon-Fri, from 10am Sat & Sun; ❄ 📶) Locals are justifiably mad for the housemade seasonal pasta and heritage sourdough at this little Arts District bistro. Everything is extremely delicious, but we're partial to the anchovy-garlic butter you can order with the sourdough, and a kale-cauliflower salad that has no right to be as delectable as it is.

★Carson Kitchen AMERICAN $$

(Map p148; ☎702-473-9523; www.carsonkitchen.com; 124 S 6th St; tapas & mains $8-22; ⏰11:30am-11pm Thu-Sat, to 10pm Sun-Wed; 🚌Deuce) This tiny eatery with an industrial theme of exposed beams, bare bulbs and chunky share tables hops with downtowners looking to escape the mayhem of Fremont St or the Strip's high prices. Excellent shared plates include rainbow cauliflower, watermelon and feta salad, and decadent mac 'n' cheese. There's also a creative drinks menu.

★Lotus of Siam THAI $$

(Map p148; ☎702-735-3033; www.lotusofsiamlv.com; 953 E Sahara Ave; mains $9-30; ⏰11am-2:30pm Mon-Fri, 5:30-10pm daily; ✍; 🚌SDX) Saipin Chutima's authentic northern Thai cooking has won almost as many awards as her distinguished, geographically diverse wine cellar. Critics have suggested this might be America's best Thai restaurant and we're sure it's at least very close. Although the strip-mall hole-in-the-wall may not look like much, those in the know flock here. Reservations essential.

Hugo's Cellar AMERICAN $$$

(Map p148; ☎702-385-4011; www.hugoscellar.com; Fremont St Mall, Fremont Street Experience, Four Queens Casino; mains $34-62; ⏰5-10pm) This is old-school Vegas, in the best way. In a dark and clubby space beneath Four Queens casino, Hugo's Cellar is a return to the days when service was king. Ladies are given a rose, salads are tossed table-side and service is attentive but not intrusive. Party like it's 1959 with veal Oscar, beef Wellington and cherries jubilee. Reservations essential.

Drinking & Nightlife

The Strip

★Hakkasan CLUB

(Map p148; ☎702-891-3838; http://hakkasannightclub.com; MGM Grand; cover $20-75; ⏰10:30pm-4am Thu-Sun) At this lavish Asian-inspired nightclub, international jet-set DJs such as Tiësto and Steve Aoki rule the jam-packed main dance floor bordered by VIP booths and floor-to-ceiling LED screens. More offbeat sounds spin in the intimate Ling Ling Club, revealing leather sofas and backlit amber glass.

Bouncers enforce the dress code: upscale nightlife attire (no athletic wear, collared shirts required for men).

NoMad Bar COCKTAIL BAR
(Map p148; ☎702-730-6785; www.mgmresorts.com; NoMad Hotel; cocktails $17; ⏲5-11pm Mon-Thu, to 1am Fri & Sat, 11am-5pm Sun) You have to walk across the restaurant to check in with the hostess at this bar – all the better for checking out the gorgeous decor (and people) at this sumptuous new addition to Vegas' craft cocktail scene. This place isn't just beautiful though – the drinks are truly out of this world, and well worth the hefty price tag.

Skyfall Lounge BAR
(Map p148; ☎702-632-7575; www.delanolasvegas.com; Delano; ⏲5pm-midnight Sun-Thu, to 1am Fri & Sat) Enjoy unparalleled views of the southern Strip from this rooftop bar atop Mandalay Bay's Delano (p152) hotel. Sit and sip cocktails as the sun sets over the Spring Mountains to the west, then dance the night away to mellow DJ beats, spun from 9pm.

XS CLUB
(Map p148; ☎702-770-0097; www.xslasvegas.com; Encore; cover $20-30; ⏲10:30pm-4am Fri-Sun) A few years in, XS is hitting its stride. Its extravagantly gold-drenched decor and over-the-top design mean you'll be waiting in line for cocktails at a bar towered over by ultra-curvaceous, larger-than-life golden statues of female torsos. Famous electronica DJs make the dance floor writhe, while high rollers opt for VIP bottle service at private poolside cabanas.

Downtown & off the Strip

Locals and in-the-know tourists make a beeline for the **Fremont East Entertainment District** (www.fremonteast.com) for the city's best grassroots nightlife. The precinct runs east of Las Vegas Blvd along Fremont St for about four blocks.

★ReBAR BAR
(Map p148; ☎702-349-2283; www.rebarlv.com; 1225 S Main St; ⏲1pm-midnight Sun-Wed, to 1am Thu, to 2am Fri & Sat) Las Vegas definitely revels in kitsch, and it absolutely loves drinking spots. ReBAR unites both. Located in the Arts District, it's a temple of nutty craft items, vintage bar signs, outrageous beer steins and one-of-a-kind doohickeys. Peruse the walls for that perfect retro souvenir, then sit down for a respectable selection of beers and spirits. Bask in the vintage glow.

☆ Entertainment

There's always plenty going on in Las Vegas, and Ticketmaster (www.ticketmaster.com) sells tickets for pretty much everything. **Tix 4 Tonight** (Map p148; ☎877-849-4868; www.tix4tonight.com; 3200 S Las Vegas Blvd, Fashion Show Mall; ⏲10am-8pm) offers half-price tickets for a limited lineup of same-day shows, plus smaller discounts on 'always sold-out' shows.

☆ Nightclubs & Live Music

Nightclubs are serious businesses in Las Vegas. Admission prices vary wildly, according to the mood of door staff, male-to-female ratio, the acts that night and how crowded the club may be. Avoid waiting in line by booking ahead with the club VIP host. Most bigger clubs have someone working the door in the late afternoon and early evening. Hotel concierges often have free passes for clubs, or can at least make reservations. Bottle service usually waives cover charges and waiting in line, but is hugely expensive.

★House of Blues Gospel Brunch LIVE PERFORMANCE
(Map p148; ☎702-632-7600; www.houseofblues.com/lasvegas; Mandalay Bay; adult/child under 11yr $54/27; ⏲seatings 10am & 1pm Sun; 👪) Saturday night sinners can find redemption at HOB's Sunday gospel brunch, where your ticket includes unlimited Bloody Marys and Southern and soul-food favorites such as jambalaya, chicken and waffles, jalapeño cornbread and warm banana-bread pudding. Buy tickets in advance, as they often sell out.

Legends in Concert LIVE MUSIC
(Map p148; ☎702-777-2782; www.legendsinconcert.com; Tropicana; tickets from $50; ⏲shows 4pm, 7:30pm & 9:30pm) Vegas' top pop-star impersonator show features real singing and dancing talent mimicking famous performers such as the Beatles, Elvis, Madonna, James Brown, Britney Spears, Shania Twain and many more.

☆ Production Shows

There are hundreds of shows to choose from in Vegas. Any Cirque du Soleil offering tends to be an unforgettable experience.

★ **Le Rêve the Dream** THEATER
(Map p148; ☎702-770-9966; http://boxoffice.wynnlasvegas.com; Wynn; tickets $115-175; ⊙shows 7pm & 9:30pm Fri-Tue) Underwater acrobatic feats by scuba-certified performers are the centerpiece of this intimate 'aqua-in-the-round' theater, which holds a million-gallon swimming pool. Critics call it a less-inspiring version of Cirque's *O*, while devoted fans find the romantic underwater tango, thrilling high dives and visually spectacular adventures to be superior. Beware: the cheapest seats are in the 'splash zone.'

O THEATER
(Map p148; ☎702-693-8866; www.cirquedusoleil.com/o; Bellagio; tickets $99-212; ⊙7pm & 9:30pm Wed-Sun) Phonetically speaking, it's the French word for water *(eau)*. With a lithe international cast performing in, on and above water, Cirque du Soleil's *O* tells the tale of theater through the ages. It's a spectacular feat of imagination and engineering, and you'll pay dearly to see it – it's one of the Strip's few shows that rarely sells discounted tickets.

★ **Aces of Comedy** COMEDY
(Map p148; ☎702-792-7777; www.mirage.com; 3400 S Las Vegas Blvd, Mirage; tickets $40-100; ⊙schedules vary, box office 10am-10pm Thu-Mon, to 8pm Tue & Wed) You'd be hard pressed to find a better A-list collection of famous stand-up comedians than this year-round series of appearances at the **Mirage** (Map p148; ☎702-791-7111; www.mirage.com; ⊙24hr; P), which delivers the likes of Jay Leno, Joe Rogan and George Lopez to the Strip. Buy tickets in advance online or by phone, or go in person to the Mirage's **Cirque du Soleil** (☎877-924-7783; www.cirquedusoleil.com/las-vegas; discount tickets from $49, full price from $69) box office.

VALLEY OF FIRE STATE PARK

Valley of Fire State Park (Map p180; ☎702-397-2088; www.parks.nv.gov/parks/valley-of-fire; Valley of Fire Hwy, Overton; per vehicle $10; ⊙7am-7pm) It's about 50 miles from Downtown Las Vegas to the Valley of Fire State Park **visitor center** (⊙8:30am-4:30pm). Make the center your first port of call to find out how best to tackle this masterpiece of Southwest desert scenery containing 40,000 acres of red Aztec sandstone, petrified trees and ancient Native American petroglyphs (at Atlatl Rock). Dedicated in 1935, the park was Nevada's first designated state park. Its psychedelic landscape has been carved by wind and water over thousands of years.

Shopping

★ **Las Vegas Premium Outlets North** MALL
(Map p148; ☎702-474-7500; www.premiumoutlets.com/vegasnorth; 875 S Grand Central Pkwy; ⊙9am-9pm Mon-Sat, to 8pm Sun; 🚻; 🚉SDX) Vegas' biggest-ticket outlet mall features 120 brands including high-end names such as Armani, Brooks Brothers, Diane von Furstenberg, Kate Spade, Michael Kors and Theory, alongside casual favorites such as Banana Republic, Diesel, Nike and Adidas.

Planet 13 DISPENSARY
(Map p148; ☎702-815-1313; www.planet13lasvegas.com; 2548 W Desert Inn Rd; ⊙24hr; 📶) File this under only-in-Vegas: this self-described 'cannabis superstore and entertainment complex' is an emporium the size of several city blocks devoted to all things weed. Your personal concierge walks you through the myriad products, from flower, seeds, edibles, CBD products and accessories. Even if you're not partial to a toke, this totally unprecedented shopping experience is worth a visit.

Retro Vegas VINTAGE
(Map p148; ☎702-384-2700; www.retro-vegas.com; 1131 S Main St; ⊙11am-6pm Mon-Sat, noon-5pm Sun; 🚉108, Deuce) Near Downtown's Arts District, this flamingo-pink-painted antiques shop is a primo place for picking up mid-20th-century modern and swingin' 1960s and '70s gems, from artwork to home decor, as well as vintage Vegas souvenirs such as casino-hotel ashtrays. Red Kat's secondhand clothing, handbags and accessories are also found here.

Information

EMERGENCY & MEDICAL SERVICES

Police ☎911 (emergencies) or ☎702-828-3111

Sunrise Hospital & Medical Center (☎702-731-8000; www.sunrisehospital.com; 3186 S Maryland Pkwy; ⊙24hr) Specialized children's trauma services available at a 24-hour emergency room.

University Medical Center (UMC; ☎702-383-2000; www.umcsn.com; 1800 W Charleston Blvd; ⊙24hr) Southern Nevada's most advanced trauma center has a 24-hour ER.

TOURIST INFORMATION

Las Vegas Convention & Visitors Authority (LVCVA; Map p148; ☎702-892-7575; www.

lasvegas.com; 3150 Paradise Rd; ⏰ 8am-5pm Mon-Fri; 🚇 Las Vegas Convention Center)

ℹ Getting There & Around

Vegas is served by **McCarran International Airport** (LAS; Map p148; ☎ 702-261-5211; www.mccarran.com; 5757 Wayne Newton Blvd; 📶), near the south end of the Strip. A free, wheelchair-accessible tram links outlying gates, while free shuttle buses link Terminals 1 and 3 and serve the **McCarran Rent-a-Car Center** (☎ 702-261-6001; www.mccarran.com/Transportation/RentalCars; 7135 Gillespie St; ⏰ 24hr).

Shuttle buses run to Strip hotels from $6 one way, and from $8 to Downtown and off-Strip hotels. You'll pay at least $15 plus tip for a taxi to the Strip – tell your driver to use surface streets, not the I-15 Fwy airport connector tunnel ('long-hauling'). Rideshare service runs from $13.

Greyhound runs long-distance buses connecting Las Vegas with Reno ($81, 9½ hours) and Salt Lake City (from $40, eight hours), as well as regular discounted services to/from Los Angeles (from $20, five to eight hours). You'll disembark at a downtown station just off the Fremont Street Experience. To reach the Strip, catch a south-bound **SDX** bus (two-hour pass $6). **Megabus** (www.megabus.com) runs daily direct routes from the **South Strip Transfer Terminal** (SSTT; ☎ 702-228-7433; www.rtcsnv.com; 6675 Gillespie St; ⏰ 24hr) to three destinations in southern California: Los Angeles (from $19, six hours), Anaheim (from $15, 6½ hours) and Riverside (from $10, 4¼ hours). Book in advance for best rates.

Day passes on the 24-hour Deuce and faster (though not 24-hour and not servicing all casinos) SDX buses are an excellent way to get around.

Around Las Vegas

Lake Mead and **Hoover Dam** are the most visited sites within the **Lake Mead National Recreation Area** (☎ info desk 702-293-8906, visitor center 702-293-8990; www.nps.gov/lake; Lakeshore Scenic Dr; 7-day entry per vehicle $10; ⏰ 24hr; 👪), which encompasses 110-mile-long Lake Mead, 67-mile-long Lake Mohave and many miles of desert around the lakes. The excellent **Visitor Center** (Alan Bible Visitor Center; ☎ 702-293-8990; www.nps.gov/lake; Lakeshore Scenic Dr, off US Hwy 93; per vehicle $25; ⏰ 9am-4:30pm), on Hwy 93 halfway between Boulder City and Hoover Dam, has information on recreation and desert life. From there, North Shore Rd winds around the lake and makes a great scenic drive.

Straddling the Arizona–Nevada border, the graceful curve and art-deco style of the 726ft **Hoover Dam** (☎ 866-730-9097, 702-494-2517; www.usbr.gov/lc/hooverdam; off Hwy 93; incl parking $10; ⏰ 9am-5pm; 👪) contrasts superbly with the stark landscape. Don't miss a stroll over the **Mike O'Callaghan-Pat Tillman Memorial Bridge** (Hwy 93), which features a pedestrian walkway with perfect views upstream of Hoover Dam.

For a relaxing lunch or dinner break, head to nearby downtown Boulder City, where **Milo's** (☎ 702-293-9540; www.milosbouldercity.com; 534 Nevada Hwy; mains $9-14; ⏰ 11am-9pm) serves fresh sandwiches, salads and gourmet cheese plates at sidewalk tables outside the wine bar.

Red Rock Canyon National Conservation Area NATURE RESERVE
(☎ 702-515-5350; www.redrockcanyonlv.org; 1000 Scenic Loop Dr; car/bicycle $15/5; ⏰ scenic loop 6am-8pm Apr-Sep, to 7pm Mar & Oct, to 5pm Nov-Feb; 👪) Red Rock's dramatic vistas are revered by Las Vegas locals and adored by visitors from around the world. Formed by extreme tectonic forces, it's thought the canyon, whose 3000ft red rock escarpment rises sharply from the valley floor, was formed around 65 million years ago. A 13-mile, one-way scenic loop drive offers mesmerizing vistas of the canyon's most striking features. Hiking trails and rock-climbing routes radiate from roadside parking areas.

The canyon is situated about 13 miles from the central Strip and just three miles from Summerlin.

Western Nevada

The state's western corner, carved by the conifer-clad Sierra Nevada, drops off near Genoa. It's a vast treeless steppe of sagebrush, unfurling itself like a plush green-gray carpet across the undulating plains of the Great Basin. From Lake Tahoe's sandy shores to the historic hamlet of Virginia City, to little Reno, Burning Man, Black Rock and beyond, Western Nevada has plenty to entice you.

Reno

In downtown Reno you can gamble at one of two-dozen casinos in the morning then walk down the street and shoot rapids at the Truckee River Whitewater Park. That's what makes 'The Biggest Little City in the World' so interesting – it's holding tight to its gambling roots but also earning kudos as a top-notch basecamp for outdoor adventure. Stealing a piece of California's tech-pie, the gargantuan

Tesla Gigafactory opened here in 2016, bringing plenty of cashed-up youngsters to town. The Sierra Nevada Mountains and Lake Tahoe are less than an hour's drive away, and the region teems with lakes, trails and ski resorts. Wedged between I-80 and the Truckee River, downtown's N Virginia St is casino central; south of the river it continues as S Virginia St.

Sights

★National Automobile Museum MUSEUM
(☎775-333-9300; www.automuseum.org; 10 S Lake St; adult/child $12/6; ⏲9:30am-5:30pm Mon-Sat, 10am-4pm Sun) Stylized street scenes illustrate a century's worth of automobile history at this engaging car museum. The collection is enormous and impressive, with one-of-a-kind vehicles – including James Dean's 1949 Mercury from *Rebel Without a Cause,* a 1938 Phantom Corsair and a 24-karat gold-plated DeLorean – and rotating exhibits with all kinds of souped-up and fabulously retro rides.

Discovery MUSEUM
(Terry Lee Wells Nevada Discovery Museum; ☎775-786-1000; www.nvdm.org; 490 S Center St; $10; ⏲10am-5pm Tue, Thu-Sat, to 8pm Wed, from noon Sun; P 👪) Since opening its doors in 2011 as a children's museum, the Discovery rapidly grew in popularity and expanded its focus to become a world-class, hands-on center for 'science, technology, engineering, art and math' (STEAM) learning, with 11 permanent, participatory exhibitions designed to inspire kids and young adults to have fun and develop an interest in these disciplines.

Nevada Museum of Art MUSEUM
(☎775-329-3333; www.nevadaart.org; 160 W Liberty St; adult/child $10/1; ⏲10am-5pm Wed & Fr-Sun, to 8pm Thu) In a sparkling building inspired by the geological formations of the Black Rock Desert north of town, a floating staircase leads to galleries showcasing temporary exhibits and eclectic collections on the American West, labor and contemporary landscape photography. In 2016 the museum opened its $6.2-million Sky Room function area. Visitors are free to explore and enjoy the space – essentially a fabulous rooftop penthouse and patio with killer views – providing it's not in use.

Galena Creek Recreation Area NATURE RESERVE
(☎775-849-4948; www.galenacreekvisitorcenter.org/trail-map.html; 18250 Mt Rose Hwy; ⏲24hr) FREE Nineteen miles from downtown Reno, a complex network of scenic hiking trails beginning at this recreation area within the Humboldt-Toiyabe National Forest gets you right into the heart of the wilderness. Check in with the **Galena Creek Visitor Center** (⏲9am-6pm Tue-Sun) when you arrive for the latest conditions and friendly advice.

> **RENO AREA TRAIL INFORMATION**
>
> For information about regional hiking and mountain-biking trails, including the Mt Rose summit trail and Tahoe-Pyramid Bikeway, download the *Truckee Meadows Trails Guide* (https://www.washoecounty.us/parks/files/TrailsGuideFinal.pdf).

Activities

Reno is a 30- to 60-minute drive from Tahoe ski resorts. Many hotels and casinos offer special stay-and-ski packages.

Mere steps from the casinos, the class II and III rapids at the city-run Truckee River Whitewater Park (www.reno.gov) are gentle enough for kids riding inner tubes, yet sufficiently challenging for professional freestyle kayakers. Two courses wrap around Wingfield Park, a small river island that hosts free concerts in summertime. **Tahoe Whitewater Tours** (☎775-787-5000; www.gowhitewater.com; 400 Island Ave; kayak rental from $48) and **Sierra Adventures** (☎775-323-8928, 866-323-8928; www.wildsierra.com; Truckee River Lane; kayak rental from $22) offer kayak trips and lessons.

Sleeping

Lodging rates vary widely, day by day. Sunday through Thursday are generally the best; Friday is more expensive and Saturday can be as much as triple the midweek rate.

In summer there's gorgeous high-altitude camping at **Mt Rose** (☎877-444-6777; www.recreation.gov; Mt Rose Hwy/Hwy 431; RV & tent sites $20-50; ⏲mid-Jun–Sep; P 🐕).

Sands Regency HOTEL $
(☎775-348-2200; www.sandsregency.com; 345 N Arlington Ave; r from $35; P ❄ 📶 🏊 🐾) The Sands Regency has some of the largest standard digs in town, decked out in a cheerful tropical palette of upbeat color. Empress Tower rooms are best. Rates triple on Friday and Saturday nights, but are great

value during the week (especially given the 17th-floor gym and outdoor pool).

★ Whitney Peak DESIGN HOTEL $$
(☎775-398-5400; www.whitneypeakhotel.com; 255 N Virginia St; d from $129; P ❄ 📶) What's not to love about this independent, inventive, funky, friendly, nonsmoking, non-gambling downtown hotel? Spacious guest rooms have a youthful, fun vibe celebrating the great outdoors and don't skimp on designer creature comforts. With an executive-level concierge lounge, an external climbing wall (if you're game), a decent on-site restaurant and friendly, professional staff, Whitney Peak is unbeatable in Reno.

Renaissance Reno Downtown HOTEL $$
(☎775-682-3900; www.marriott.com/hotels/travel/rnobr-renaissance-reno-downtown-hotel; 1 Lake St; r from $135; P 📶) It's part of a hotel group, but you could be forgiven for thinking it's a boutique hotel (in fact, it used to be). Renovated, oversized guest rooms follow a contemporary theme that's reminiscent of a stylish friend's cozy living room. With the best rooftop pool in town, this is a smart alternative to casino hotels.

Eating

★ Great Full Gardens HEALTH FOOD $
(☎775-324-2013; 555 S Virginia St; bowls from $10; ⊙8am-9pm, to 2pm Sun; P) Extensive menu chock-full of salads, smoothies and sandwiches that will make you feel healthy enough to justify another cocktail later on. Delicious grain bowls are categorized by lifestyle choice (vegan, paleo, macrobiotic). Chili fiends should not miss the housemade hot sauce.

Gold 'n Silver Inn DINER $
(☎775-323-2696; www.goldnsilverreno.com; 790 W 4th St; mains $6-20; ⊙24hr) A Reno institution for more than 50 years, this slightly divey but super-friendly 24-hour diner has a huge menu of home-style American favorites such as meatloaf, plated dinners, all-day breakfasts and burgers, not to mention seriously incredible caramel milkshakes.

Louis' Basque Corner BASQUE $$
(☎775-323-7203; www.louisbasquecorner.com; 301 E 4th St; dinner menu $12-29; ⊙11am-9:30pm Tue-Sat, from 4pm Sun & Mon) Get ready to dine on lamb, rabbit, sweetbreads and more lamb at a big table full of people you've never met before. After a picon punch you'll be getting along like *vieux amis*.

Wild River Grille GRILL $$
(☎775-847-455; www.wildrivergrille.com; 17 S Virginia St; mains $21-37; ⊙11am-9pm;) At the Wild River Grille you'll love the smart-casual dining and the varied menu of creative cuisine, from the Gruyère croquettes to the lobster ravioli, but most of all the wonderful patio overlooking the lovely Truckee River: it's also the best spot in town for a drink on a balmy summer's evening.

Drinking & Nightlife

★ Imperial Bar & Lounge BAR
(☎775-324-6399; www.imperialbarandlounge.com; 150 N Arlington Ave; ⊙11am-10pm, to 2am Fri & Sat) A classy bar inhabiting a relic of the past – this building was once an old bank, and in the middle of the wood floor you can see cement where the vault once stood. Sandwiches and pizzas go with 16 beers on tap and a buzzing happy-hour scene (3pm to 6pm).

Entertainment

The free weekly *Reno News & Review* (www.newsreview.com) is your best source for listings.

Information

Reno-Sparks Convention & Visitors Authority Visitor Center (☎775-682-3800; www.visitrenotahoe.com; 135 N Sierra St; ⊙9am-6pm)

Getting There & Around

About 5 miles southeast of downtown, **Reno-Tahoe International Airport** (RNO; www.renoairport.com; 📶) is served by most major airlines, with connections throughout the US to international routes.

The **North Lake Tahoe Express** (☎866-216-5222; www.northlaketahoeexpress.com; one way $49) operates a shuttle (six to eight daily, 3:30am to midnight) to and from the airport to multiple North Shore Lake Tahoe locations. The **South Tahoe Airporter** (☎866-898-2463; www.southtahoeairporter.com; adult/child one way $33/20) operates several daily shuttle buses from the airport to Stateline casinos.

Greyhound (☎800-231-2222; www.greyhound.com) offers several direct buses a day to Reno from San Francisco (from $18, from five hours): book in advance for lowest fares.

The **Amtrak** (☎800-872-7245; www.amtrak.com) *California Zephyr* train makes one daily departure from Emeryville/San Francisco ($55, 7½) to Reno.

The local **RTC Washoe** (☎775-348-0400; www.rtcwashoe.com) operates six wi-fi-equipped RTC Intercity buses each weekday to Carson City ($5, one hour), which loosely

WORTH A TRIP

BURNING MAN

Burning Man (https://burningman.org; $425; ⏲ Aug) For a week in August, 'Burners' from around the world descend on the Black Rock Desert to build the temporary Black Rock City, only to tear it all down again and set fire to an effigy of man. In between, there's peace, love, music, art, nakedness, drugs, sex and frivolity in a safe space where attendees uphold the principles of the festival.

connect with BlueGo buses – operated by **Tahoe Transportation District** (☎775-589-5500; www.tahoetransportation.org) – to the Stateline Transit Center in South Lake Tahoe (adult/child $4/2 with RTC Intercity transfer, one hour).

The Great Basin

A trip across Nevada's Great Basin is a serene, almost haunting experience. Anyone seeking the 'Great American Road Trip' will relish the fascinating historic towns and quirky diversions tucked away along lonely desert highways.

Along Highway 50

The transcontinental Hwy 50 cuts across the heart of Nevada, connecting Carson City in the west to Great Basin National Park in the east. Better known here by its nickname, 'The Loneliest Road in America,' it once formed part of the Lincoln Hwy, and follows the route of the Overland Stagecoach, the Pony Express and the first transcontinental telegraph line. Towns are few, and the only sounds are the hum of the engine or the whisper of wind.

About 25 miles southeast of Fallon, the **Sand Mountain Recreation Area** (☎775-885-6000; www.blm.gov/nv; 7-day permit $40, Tue & Wed free; ⏲24hr; P) is worth a stop for a look at its 600ft sand dune and the ruins of a Pony Express station. Just east, enjoy a juicy burger at an old stagecoach stop, **Middlegate Station** (☎775-423-7134; www.facebook.com/middlegate.station; 42500 Austin Hwy, cnr Hwys 50 & 361; mains $6-17; ⏲6am-2am) then toss your sneakers onto the **Shoe Tree** on the north side of Hwy 50 just ahead.

A fitting reward for surviving Hwy 50 is the awesome, uncrowded **Great Basin National Park** (☎775-234-7331; www.nps.gov/grba; 100 Great Basin; ⏲24hr) FREE. Near the Nevada–Utah border, it's home to 13,063ft Wheeler Peak, which rises abruptly from the desert. Hiking trails near the summit take in superb country with glacial lakes, ancient bristlecone pines and even a permanent ice field. Admission is free; in summer, you can get oriented at the **Lehman Caves Visitor Center** (www.nps.gov/grba; 5500 W Hwy 488, Baker; ⏲8am-4:30pm), just north of Baker. Stargazing is fantastic from the park's campgrounds.

If you want a roof over your head, try the **Stargazer Inn** (☎775-234-7323; stay@stargazernevada.com; 115 S Baker Ave, Baker, Hwy 50; r from $78; P ⊖ ❄ ᯤ 🐾) 🌿, a revamped roadside motel in Baker. The inn is also home to **Kerouac's** (☎775-234-7323; 115 S Baker Rd, Baker; pizzas from $12; ⏲7-10am & 5-8:30pm Apr-Oct; P ❄), known for its wood-fired pizzas and inventive cocktails.

Along Highways 375 & 93

Hwy 375 is dubbed the 'Extraterrestrial Hwy', both for its huge number of UFO sightings and because it intersects Hwy 93 near top secret **Area 51**, part of Nellis Air Force Base, supposedly a holding area for captured UFOs. Some people may find Hwy 375 more unnerving than the Loneliest Road; it's a desolate stretch of pavement where cars are few and far between. In the tiny town of Rachel, on Hwy 375, **Little A'Le' Inn** (☎775-729-2515; www.littlealeinn.com; 9631 Old Mill St, Rachel; RV sites $20, r $45-190; ⏲restaurant 8am-10pm; ❄ ᯤ 🐾) accommodates earthlings and aliens alike, and sells extraterrestrial souvenirs. Probings not included.

ARIZONA

Arizona is made for road trips. Yes, the state has its showstoppers – Monument Valley, the Grand Canyon, Cathedral Rock – but you'll remember the long, romantic miles under endless skies for as long as you do the icons in between. Each drive reveals more of the state's soul: for a dose of mom-and-pop friendliness, follow Route 66 into Flagstaff; to understand the sheer will of Arizona's mining barons, take a twisting drive through rugged Jerome; and Native American history becomes contemporary as you drive past mesa-top Hopi villages dating back 1000 years.

History

American Indian tribes and their ancestors inhabited Arizona for millennia before

Francisco Vásquez de Coronado set out from Mexico City in 1540, leading an expedition whose members were the first Europeans to clap eyes on the Grand Canyon and Colorado River. Settlers and missionaries followed in his wake, before the US annexed Arizona following the Mexican–American War in the mid-19th century. The Indian Wars, in which the US Army battled American Indians to protect settlers and claim land for the government, officially ended in 1886 with the surrender of Apache warrior Geronimo.

Railroad and mining expansion followed and people started arriving in ever larger numbers. After President Theodore Roosevelt visited Arizona in 1903 he supported the damming of its rivers to provide year-round water for irrigation and drinking, thus paving the way to statehood: in 1912 Arizona became the last of the 48 contiguous US states to be admitted to the Union.

The state shares a 250-mile border with Mexico and has found itself at the forefront of the immigration debate on repeated occasions. Most recently, some of the state's border facilities, notably at Yuma, have become overburdened as the number of Central American migrants seeking asylum has spiked. Detention centers have run out of space, resulting in the creation of temporary tent camps to house migrants who are waiting for their cases to be heard.

Information

Although Arizona is on Mountain Standard Time, it's the only western state that does not observe daylight saving time from spring to early fall – except for on the Navajo Reservation. Generally speaking, lodging rates in southern Arizona (including Phoenix, Tucson and Yuma) are much higher in winter and spring, considered to be the 'high season', so great deals can be found in the hotter areas in summer.

Arizona Office of Tourism (602-364-3700; www.tourism.az.gov) Free state information.

Arizona State Parks (877-697-2757; www.azstateparks.com) Sixteen of the state's parks have campgrounds, open to online reservations.

Public Lands Interpretative Association Information about USFS, NPS, Bureau of Land Management (BLM) and state lands and parks.

Phoenix

Phoenix is Arizona's indubitable cultural and economic powerhouse, a thriving desert metropolis boasting some of the best Southwestern and Mexican food you'll find anywhere. And with more than 300 days of sunshine a year, exploring the 'Valley of the Sun' is an agreeable proposition (except in the sapping heat from June to August).

Culturally, it offers an opera, a symphony, several theaters and three of the state's finest museums – the Heard, Phoenix Art and Musical Instrument Museums – while the Desert Botanical Garden is a stunning introduction to the region's flora and fauna. For sports fans, there are professional baseball, football, basketball and ice-hockey teams, and more than 200 golf courses.

Sights

Greater Phoenix consists of several distinct cities. Phoenix, the largest, combines a business-like demeanor with top-notch museums, a burgeoning cultural scene and great sports facilities. Southeast of here, lively, student-flavored Tempe (*tem*-pee), hugs 2-mile-long Tempe Town Lake, while suburban Mesa, further east, holds a couple of interesting museums. Two ritzy enclaves lie northeast of Phoenix – Scottsdale, known for its cutesy old town, galleries and lavish resorts, and the largely residential Paradise Valley.

ARIZONA FACTS

Nickname Grand Canyon State

Population 7.17 million

Area 113,998 sq miles

Capital city Phoenix (population 1,660,272)

Other cities Tucson (population 535,677), Flagstaff (71,975), Sedona (10,336)

Sales tax 5.6%

Birthplace of Cesar Chavez (1927–93), singer Linda Ronstadt (b 1946)

Home of The OK Corral, mining towns turned art colonies

Politics Majority vote Republican

Famous for Grand Canyon, saguaro cacti

Best souvenir Pink cactus-shaped neon lamp from roadside stall

Driving distances Phoenix to Grand Canyon Village 235 miles, Tucson to Sedona 230 miles

Phoenix

★Heard Museum MUSEUM

(Map p164; ☎602-252-8848; https://heard.org; 2301 N Central Ave; adult/senior/child $18/13.50/7.50; ⏲9:30am-5pm Mon-Sat, from 11am Sun; P) This extraordinary museum spotlights the history, life, arts and culture of American Indian tribes in the Southwest. Visitors will find art galleries, ethnographic displays, films, a get-creative kids' exhibit and an unrivaled collection of Hopi kachinas (elaborate spirit dolls, many gifted by Presidential nominee Barry Goldwater). The Heard emphasizes quality over quantity and is one of the best museums of its kind in America.

★Musical Instrument Museum MUSEUM

(☎480-478-6000; www.themim.org; 4725 E Mayo Blvd; adult/teen/child $20/15/10; ⏲9am-5pm; P) From Uganda thumb pianos to Hawaiian ukuleles to Indonesian boat lutes, the ears have it at this lively museum that celebrates the world's musical instruments. More than 200 countries and territories are represented within five regional galleries, with wireless recordings bringing many to life as you get within 'earshot' (headsets are provided). You can also bang a drum in the Experiences Gallery and listen to Taylor Swift or Elvis Presley rock out in the Artist Gallery.

★Desert Botanical Garden GARDENS

(Map p164; ☎480-941-1225; www.dbg.org; 1201 N Galvin Pkwy; adult/child $25/13; ⏲8am-8pm Oct-Apr, 7am-8pm May-Sep) Blue bells and Mexican gold poppies are just two of the colorful showstoppers blooming from March to May along the Desert Wildflower Loop Trail at this well-nurtured botanical garden, a lovely place to reconnect with nature while learning about desert plant life. Looping trails lead past a profusion of desert denizens, arranged by theme (including a Sonoran Desert nature loop and an edible desert garden). It's pretty dazzling year-round, but the flowering spring season is the busiest and most colorful.

Phoenix Art Museum MUSEUM

(Map p164; ☎602-257-1880; www.phxart.org; 1625 N Central Ave; adult/senior/child $23/20/14; ⏲10am-5pm Tue & Thu-Sat, 10am-9pm Wed, noon-5pm Sun; P 👪) Arizona's premier repository of fine art includes works by Claude Monet, Diego Rivera and Georgia O'Keeffe. Make a beeline for the Western Gallery, to see how the astonishing Arizona landscape has inspired everyone from the early pioneers to modernists. Got kids? Pick up a Kidpack at Visitor Services, examine the ingeniously crafted miniature period Thorne Rooms or visit the PhxArtKids Gallery.

Scottsdale

For a list of permanent and temporary public art displays, visit www.scottsdalepublicart.org.

Old Town Scottsdale AREA

(Map p164; www.oldtownscottsdaleaz.com) Tucked among Scottsdale's malls and bistros is its Old Town, a Wild West–themed enclave filled with cutesy buildings, covered sidewalks and stores hawking mass-produced 'Indian' artifacts. There's also a museum, sculptures, saloons, a few galleries with genuine American Indian art, and horse-drawn buggies and singing cowboys in the cooler months.

Taliesin West ARCHITECTURE

(☎888-516-0811; www.franklloydwright.org; 12621 N Frank Lloyd Wright Blvd; tours $35-75; ⏲8:30am-6pm Oct-May, shorter hours Jun-Sep, closed Tue & Wed Jun-Aug) Taliesin West was the desert home and studio of Frank Lloyd Wright, one of America's greatest 20th-century architects. A prime example of organic architecture, with buildings incorporating elements and structures found in surrounding nature, it was built between 1938 and 1940, and is still home to an architecture school. It's now a National Historical Monument, open to the public for informative guided tours – reservations are essential.

Tempe

Founded in 1885 and home to around 50,000 students, **Arizona State University** (ASU; Map p164; ☎480-965-2100; www.asu.edu) is the heart and soul of Tempe. The **Gammage Auditorium** (Map p164; ☎box office 480-965-3434, tours 480-965-6912; www.asugammage.com; 1200 S Forest Ave, cnr Mill Ave & Apache Blvd; entry free, performances from $50; ⏲box office 10am-5pm Mon-Thu summer, 10am-6pm Mon-Fri rest of year) was Frank Lloyd Wright's last major building. Easily accessible by light-rail from downtown Phoenix, **Mill Avenue**, Tempe's main drag, is packed with restaurants, themed bars and other collegiate hangouts. You could also check out **Tempe Town Lake** (Map p164; www.tempe.gov/lake), an artificial lake with boat rides and hiking paths.

Mesa

★Arizona Museum of Natural History MUSEUM

(☎480-644-2230; www.arizonamuseumofnaturalhistory.org; 53 N MacDonald St, Mesa; adult/senior/child $12/10/7; ⏲10am-5pm Tue-Fri, from 11am Sat, from 1pm Sun) Even if you're not staying in Mesa, this museum is worth a trip, especially if your kids are into dinosaurs (and aren't they all?). In addition to the multilevel Dinosaur Mountain, there are loads of life-sized casts of the giant beasts plus a touchable apatosaurus thighbone. Other exhibits highlight the Southwest's pre-conquest past, and that of the Americas more broadly, from a prehistoric Hohokam village to an entire hall on ancient Mesoamerican cultures.

Activities

★Camelback Mountain HIKING

(Map p164; ☎602-261-8318; www.phoenix.gov; ⏲sunrise-sunset) This 2704ft twin-humped mountain sits smack in the center of the Phoenix action. The two trails, the Cholla Trail (6131 E Cholla Lane) and the Echo Canyon Trail (4925 E McDonald Dr), are short but steep, with 1264ft of elevation gain over a mere 1.2 miles and lots of hands-on scrambling over boulders. A great workout followed by stellar views.Get here early – the Echo Canyon Trail in particular is extremely popular.

Salt River Recreation WATER SPORTS

(☎480-984-3305; www.saltrivertubing.com; 9200 N Bush Hwy; tubes & shuttle $17; ⏲9am-6:30pm May-late Sep) With Salt River Recreation you can float in an inner tube on the Lower Salt River through the stark Tonto National Forest. The launch is in northeast Mesa, about 15 miles north of Hwy 60 on Power Rd. Floats are two, three or five hours long, including the shuttle-bus ride back. Cash only.

Cactus Adventures MOUNTAIN BIKING

(☎480-688-4743; www.cactusadventures.com; half-day rental from $45; ⏲8am-8pm) Cactus Adventures rents hardtails and full-suspension bikes for use at South Mountain and offers guided hiking and biking tours at various parks (from $250). For rentals, staff will meet you at the trailhead. There is no shop; reserve ahead.

Ponderosa Stables HORSEBACK RIDING

(☎602-268-1261; www.arizona-horses.com; 10215 S Central Ave; 1/2/3hr rides $40/60/80; ⏲9am-8pm) This outfitter leads breakfast, lunch, dinner and sunset rides through the lovely and vast South Mountain Park. Reservations are required. The stables are around 7 miles south of downtown Phoenix, directly down Central Ave. Minimum of two riders for three-hour rides.

Festivals & Events

First Fridays ART

(www.artlinkphoenix.com; ⏲6-10pm 1st & 3rd Fri of month) Up to 20,000 people hit the streets of downtown Phoenix on the first and third Fridays of every month for this self-guided art walk, incorporating more than 70 galleries and performance spaces. Three trolleys ferry the cognoscenti from venue to venue.

Arizona State Fair FAIR

(☎602-252-6771; www.azstatefair.com; 1826 W McDowell Rd, Phoenix; ⏲Oct) This fair lures more than a million folks to the Arizona State Fairgrounds every October, with a rodeo, rides and amusements, livestock displays, a pie-eating contest and plenty of live performances.

PHOENIX FOR KIDS

Wet 'n' Wild Phoenix (☎623-201-2000; www.wetnwildphoenix.com; 4243 W Pinnacle Peak Rd, Glendale; over/under 42in tall $44/34, senior $34; ⏲10:30am-8pm Sun-Thu, to 10pm Fri & Sat Jun & Jul, reduced hours Mar-May & Aug-Oct) This water park has pools, tube slides, wave pools, waterfalls and floating rivers. It's in Glendale, 2 miles west of I-17 at exit 217.

Children's Museum of Phoenix (Map p164; ☎602-253-0501; www.childrensmuseumofphoenix.org; 215 N 7th St; $15; ⏲9am-4pm Tue-Sun; 👪) A tactile, climbable, paintable wonderland of interactive (and surreptitiously educational) exhibits.

Arizona Science Center (Map p164; ☎602-716-2000; www.azscience.org; 600 E Washington St; adult/child $18/13; ⏲10am-5pm) A high-tech temple of discovery; there are more than 300 hands-on exhibits and a planetarium.

Phoenix

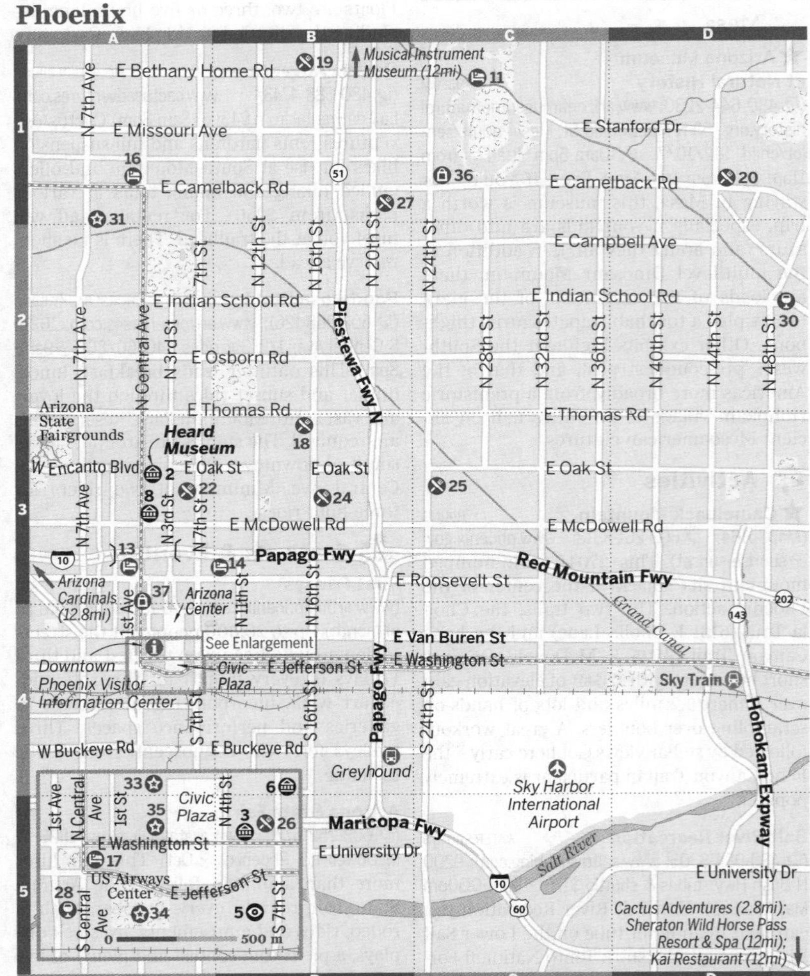

Sleeping

Phoenix

HI Phoenix Hostel HOSTEL **$**
(Map p164; ☎602-254-9803; www.phxhostel.org; 1026 N 9th St; dm/s/d $30/45/65;) Fall in love with backpacking all over again at this small hostel with fun owners who know Phoenix and want to enjoy it with you. The 22-bed hostel is located in a residential area and has relaxing garden nooks. The 'talking table' – at which laptops and other devices are banned from 8am to 10am and 5pm to 10pm each day – is a very sociable innovation.

Maricopa Manor B&B **$$**
(Map p164; ☎800-292-6403, 602-264-9200; www.maricopamanor.com; 15 W Pasadena Ave; ste $190-240;) This small, Spanish ranch-style place right near busy Central Ave has six individually appointed suites, many with French doors onto a deck overlooking the pool, garden and fountain areas. Although Maricopa Manor is central, it's well supplied with shady garden nooks, and privacy is easily achieved.

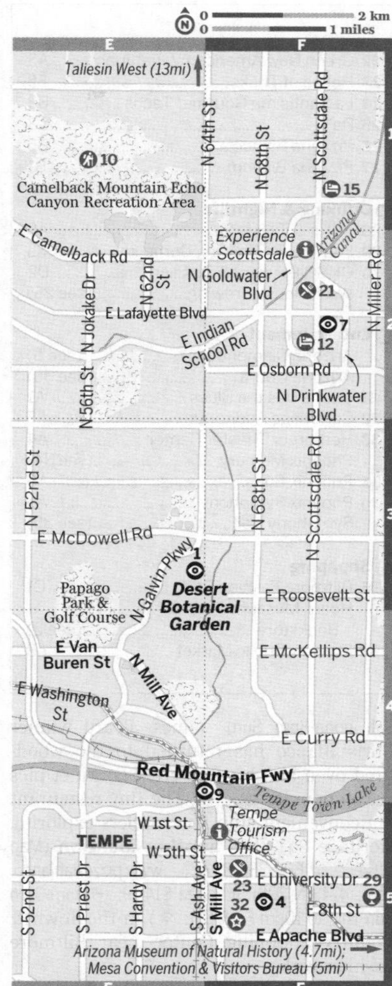

★Arizona Biltmore Resort & Spa RESORT $$$

(Map p164; ☎800-950-0086, 602-955-6600; www.arizonabiltmore.com; 2400 E Missouri Ave; d from $400; P ❄ @ 📶 ≋ 🐾) With architecture inspired by Frank Lloyd Wright and past guests including Irving Berlin, Marilyn Monroe and every president from Hoover to Bush the younger, the Biltmore is perfect for connecting to the magic of yesterday. A landmark, lending its name to much in the surrounding area, it boasts more than 700 beautifully appointed units, two golf courses, several pools and endless luxe touches.

Palomar Phoenix HOTEL $$$

(Map p164; ☎602-253-6633, reservations 877-488-1908; www.hotelpalomar-phoenix.com; 2 E Jefferson St; r/ste from $350/360; P ❄ 📶 ≋ 🐾) Shaggy pillows, antler-shaped lamps and portraits of blue cows. Yep, the 242 rooms of the Palomar are whimsical, and we like it. Larger than average and popping with fresh, modern style, the rooms come with yoga mats, animal-print robes and Italian Frette linens. There's a nightly wine reception, and Phoenix's major baseball and basketball stadiums are just around the corner.

Found:Re DESIGN HOTEL $$$

(Map p164; ☎602-875-8000; www.foundrehotels.com; 1100 N Central Ave; r $280-360; P ❄ 📶 ≋ 🐾) An art-driven hotel that exudes urban cool and a certain amount of cheekiness (you may want to avert your eyes from the Burt Reynolds nude upon entering), Found:Re's 104 rooms are plenty comfortable, with walk-in showers, quality linens, floor-to-ceiling windows and polished concrete floors. Pets stay free.

Scottsdale

Hotel Adeline MOTEL $$

(Map p164; ☎480-284-7700; www.hoteladeline.com; 5101 N Scottsdale Rd; d from $213; ❄ 📶 ≋ 🐾) Mid-century modern furnishings grace this renovated motel, a trendy alternative to Scottsdale's more sober upscale retreats. The palm-fringed pool is the center of the action for the younger crowd.

★Bespoke Inn, Cafe & Bicycles BOUTIQUE HOTEL $$$

(Map p164; ☎844-861-6715; www.bespokeinn.com; 3701 N Marshall Way; d from $450; P ❄ 📶 ≋ 🐾) A small slice of 'European' hospitality in downtown Scottsdale, this breezy eight-room hotel has chocolate scones to nibble in the chic cafe, an infinity pool to loll in and Pashley city bikes to roam the neighborhood on. Rooms are plush, with handsome touches such as handcrafted furniture and nickel bath fixtures. Gourmet meals are served at the on-site restaurant Virtu. Book early.

Tempe

Sheraton Wild Horse Pass Resort & Spa RESORT $$$

(☎602-225-0100; www.marriott.com; 5594 W Wild Horse Pass Blvd, Chandler; r from $360; P ❄ 📶 ≋) At sunset, scan the lonely horizon for the eponymous wild horses silhouetted against the South Mountains. Owned by the Gila Riv-

Phoenix

Top Sights
1 Desert Botanical Garden....E3
2 Heard Museum....A3

Sights
3 Arizona Science Center....B5
4 Arizona State University....F5
5 Chase Field....B5
6 Children's Museum of Phoenix....B4
7 Old Town Scottsdale....F2
8 Phoenix Art Museum....A3
9 Tempe Town Lake....F4

Activities, Courses & Tours
10 Camelback Mountain....E1

Sleeping
11 Arizona Biltmore Resort & Spa....C1
12 Bespoke Inn, Cafe & Bicycles....F2
13 Found:Re....A3
14 HI Phoenix Hostel....B3
15 Hotel Adeline....F1
16 Maricopa Manor....A1
17 Palomar Phoenix....A5

Eating
18 Barrio Café....B3
19 Dick's Hideaway....B1
20 Flower Child....D1
21 FnB....F2
22 Green New American Vegetarian....A3
23 House of Tricks....F5
24 La Santisima Gourmet Tacos....B3
25 Pa'la....C3
26 Pizzeria Bianco....B5
27 Pizzeria Bianco....B1

Drinking & Nightlife
28 Bitter & Twisted....A5
29 Four Peaks Brewing Company....F5
30 OHSO Brewery & Distillery....D2
Wren House Brewing....(see 25)

Entertainment
Arizona Diamondbacks....(see 5)
Arizona Opera....(see 35)
31 Char's Has the Blues....A1
32 Gammage Auditorium....F5
33 Herberger Theater Center....A4
Phoenix Mercury....(see 34)
34 Phoenix Suns....A5
35 Phoenix Symphony....A5
Symphony Hall....(see 35)

Shopping
36 Biltmore Fashion Park....C1
Heard Museum Shop & Bookstore....(see 2)
37 Phoenix Public Market....A3

er tribe and nestled on their sweeping reservation south of Tempe, this 500-room resort is a stunning alchemy of modern luxury and American Indian tradition. The domed lobby is a mural-festooned roundhouse, and rooms reflect the traditions of local tribes.

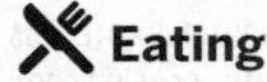

Eating

Phoenix

La Santisima Gourmet Tacos MEXICAN $
(Map p164; ☎602-254-6330; www.lasantisimagourmet.com; 1919 N 16th St; tacos $2.50-10; ⏰11am-10pm Mon-Sat, to 9pm Sun) Despite having 'gourmet' in the name, La Santisima keeps it real with plastic cutlery and rock music blaring in the background. Mexico City–style tacos are the headliners, but the real star may be the salsa bar, where you can choose from an array of fantastic creations ranging from pecan and peanut to jicama and Aztec chipotle. Great horchata too.

★**Pizzeria Bianco** PIZZA $$
(Map p164; ☎602-258-8300; www.pizzeriabianco.com; 623 E Adams St, Heritage Sq; pizza $14-19; ⏰11am-9pm Mon-Wed, 11am-10pm Thu-Sat, noon-8pm Sun) James Beard–winner Chris Bianco has returned to the wood-fired oven and his thin-crust gourmet pies are as popular as ever. The tiny restaurant – a convenient stop for travelers exploring Heritage Sq – has **another location** (Map p164; ☎602-368-3273; www.pizzeriabianco.com; 4743 N 20th St; pizza $14-19; ⏰11am-9pm Sun-Thu, to 10pm Fri & Sat; 📶) in the Town & Country Shopping Center, near Biltmore Fashion Park.

Flower Child AMERICAN $
(Map p164; ☎602-429-6222; www.iamaflowerchild.com; 5013 N 44th St; mains $8.25-12; ⏰11am-9pm) It may be a chain, but it's healthy, inexpensive and so, so good – veg out on salads, ancient grain bowls, pho and delectable small plates, plus kombucha and cold brew on tap. This location is just around the corner from Camelback Mountain.

Green New American Vegetarian VEGAN $
(Map p164; ☎602-258-1870; www.greenvegetarian.com; 2022 N 7th St; mains $7.25-9.75; ⏰11am-9pm Mon-Sat; 🌱) Your expectations of vegan food will be forever raised after dining at this hip cafe, where chef Damon

Brasch stirs up savory vegan and vegetarian dishes. Made with mock meats, the burgers, po'boys and Asian-style bowls taste as good, if not better, than their carnivorous counterparts. Order at the counter then take a seat in the garage-style digs.

★Barrio Café MEXICAN **$$**

(Map p164; ☎602-636-0240; www.barriocafe.com; 2814 N 16th St; mains $14-34; ⏲11am-10pm Tue-Sat, to 9pm Sun;) Barrio's staff wear T-shirts emblazoned with *comida chingona*, which translates as 'fucking good food,' and they don't lie. This is Mexican food at its most creative: how many menus have you seen featuring guacamole spiked with pomegranate seeds, buttered corn with chipotle, aged cheese, cilantro and lime, or goat's-milk-caramel-filled churros? Drinks are half-price from 2pm to 5pm daily. No reservations.

★Pa'la MEDITERRANEAN **$$**

(Map p164; ☎602-795-9500; www.palakitchen.com; 2107 N 24th St; mains $12-22; ⏲11am-9pm Wed-Sat, to 3pm Tue) It's small, simple and you order at the counter, but don't let the casual, eco-minded ambience fool you into thinking Pa'La is anything but extraordinary. Chef Claudio Urciuoli focuses on seasonal vegetables and sustainably sourced seafood hot off the grill to deliver culinary thrills at a reasonable price.

★Dick's Hideaway NEW MEXICAN **$$**

(Map p164; ☎602-241-1881; www.richardsonsnm.com; 6008 N 16th St; brunch $14-21, mains $16-32; ⏲8am-11pm Sun-Wed, to midnight Thu-Sat) At this pocket-sized ode to New Mexican cuisine, grab a small table beside the bar or settle in at the communal table in the side room and prepare for hearty servings of savory, chile-slathered New Mexican fare, from enchiladas to tamales to rellenos. We especially like the Hideaway for breakfast, when the Bloody Marys arrive with a shot of beer.

House of Tricks AMERICAN **$$$**

(Map p164; ☎480-968-1114; www.houseoftricks.com; 114 E 7th St; lunch $13-15, dinner $25-33; ⏲11am-10pm Mon-Sat) No, they don't do magic, but Robin and Robert Trick will still wow you with their eclectic, contemporary American menu with influences from the Southwest, the Med and Asia. The trellised garden patio usually buzzes with regulars and drop-ins, but the tables inside the vintage cottages are equally charming.

Scottsdale

Andreoli ITALIAN **$$**

(☎480-614-1980; www.andreoli-grocer.com; 8880 E Vía Linda; sandwiches from $9.25, mains $20-34; ⏲10am-9pm Mon-Sat) Opened by Calabria-born Giovanni Scorzo, this Italian deli has a perpetual line out the door, and for good reason. Whether you grab a panino to go or one of the daily housemade pasta specials to enjoy in the bric-a-brac interior, the ingredients are always top-of-the-line. No reservations.

★FnB GASTRONOMY **$$$**

(Map p164; ☎480-284-4777; www.fnbrestaurant.com; 7125 E 5th Ave; mains $26-36; ⏲5-10pm Tue-Sat, to 9pm Sun) Romantic ambience and culinary wizardry join forces to provide a dinner to remember in Scottsdale. Charleen Badman, named the Southwest's best chef in 2019, highlights local produce and wine in her modern creations – sample small veggie-driven plates such as grilled asparagus with polenta, egg and chiltepin, or roasted broccoli with yogurt, grapefruit and dakka. It's all quite divine. Reserve.

Tempe

★Kai Restaurant AMERICAN INDIAN **$$$**

(☎602-225-0100; 5594 W Wild Horse Pass Blvd, Chandler; mains $46-62, tasting menus $145-$245; ⏲5:30-9pm Tue-Sat) American Indian cuisine – based on traditional crops grown along the Gila River – soars to new heights at Kai ('seed'). Expect creations such as grilled buffalo tenderloin with smoked corn puree and cholla buds, or wild scallops with mesquite-smoked caviar and tepary-bean crackling. The unobtrusive service is flawless, the wine list expertly curated and the room decorated with American Indian art.

Kai is at the Sheraton Wild Horse Pass Resort & Spa on the Gila River Indian Reservation. Book ahead and dress nicely (no shorts or hats).

Drinking & Nightlife

★Wren House Brewing BREWERY

(Map p164; ☎602-244-9184; www.wrenhousebrewing.com; 2125 N 24th St; hnoon-10pm Sun-Thu, 11am-midnight Fri & Sat; W) Snag a stool in this reconverted house for some of Phoenix's best small-batch beer. The sin cuidados – a sour farmhouse ale with hints of apricot – is heavenly; for something that packs more punch, there are two triple IPAs to choose from.

vBitter & Twisted COCKTAIL BAR
(Map p164; ☎602-340-1924; www.bitterandtwistedaz.com; 1 W Jefferson St; ⏰4pm-2am Tue-Sat) Housed in the former Arizona Prohibition Headquarters, this stylish seating-only cocktail bar shakes up some serious mixes and slings some delicious food to keep drinkers upright. Particularly lip-smacking is the dragon dumpling burger – pork and beef with Sichuan pickle and dumpling sauce.

Four Peaks Brewing Company BREWERY
(Map p164; ☎480-303-9967; www.fourpeaks.com; 1340 E 8th St; ⏰11am-midnight Mon-Wed, 11am-2am Fri & Sat, 9am-midnight Sun; 📶) Hipsters, families, craft-beer obsessives and the plain thirsty congregate happily in this 1890s brick brewhouse, filling growlers of Kilt Lifter or Pitchfork Pale from the tap, or just chatting over a pint or two. There's also toothsome pub grub, tasting tours (Saturday, reserve online), a gift shop, and further locations in Tempe, Scottsdale and Phoenix Sky Harbor.

☆ Entertainment

Check *Arizona Republic Calendar* (www.azcentral.com/thingstodo/events) and *Phoenix New Times* (www.phoenixnewtimes.com) for listings.

Symphony Hall (Map p164; ☎602-262-6225; www.phoenixconventioncenter.com; 75 N 2nd St) hosts the **Arizona Opera** (Map p164; ☎602-266-7464; www.azopera.com) and the **Phoenix Symphony** (Map p164; ☎box office 602-495-1999; www.phoenixsymphony.org). The latter also performs at other regional venues. The **Arizona Diamondbacks** (Map p164; ☎602-462-6500; http://arizona.diamondbacks.mlb.com) play baseball at downtown's air-conditioned **Chase Field** (Map p164; ☎tours 602-462-6799; www.mlb.com/dbacks; 401 E Jefferson St; adult/senior/child $7/5/3; ⏰tours 9:30am, 11am, 12:30pm Mon-Sat, additional tours on game days), while the men's basketball team, the **Phoenix Suns** (Map p164; ☎602-379-7867; www.nba.com/suns), and the women's team, the **Phoenix Mercury** (Map p164; ☎602-252-9622; www.wnba.com/mercury), are also downtown, at **Talking Stick Resort Arena** (201 E Jefferson St). The **Arizona Cardinals** (☎623-433-7101; www.azcardinals.com; 1 Cardinals Dr, Glendale) play football in Glendale at **State Farm Stadium**, formerly the University of Phoenix Stadium, which hosted the Super Bowl in 2015.

Herberger Theater Center THEATER
(Map p164; ☎602-252-8497; www.herbergertheater.org; 222 E Monroe St; ⏰box office 10am-5pm Mon-Fri, from noon Sat & Sun & 1hr before performances) Housing several theater companies and three stages, the Herberger also plays host to visiting troupes and productions. The predominant fare is drama and musicals, but you can also catch dance, opera and exhibitions of local art here.

Char's Has the Blues BLUES
(Map p164; ☎602-230-0205; www.charshastheblues.com; 4631 N 7th Ave; ⏰8pm-1am) Dark, intimate and very welcoming, this shabby-fronted blues and R&B shack packs 'em in with solid acts most nights of the week, but somehow still manages to feel like a well-kept secret. The cover ranges from free to $7.

Shopping

Phoenix Public Market MARKET
(Map p164; ☎602-625-6736; www.phxpublicmarket.com; 721 N Central Ave; ⏰8am-1pm Sat Oct-Apr, 8am-noon Sat May-Sep) The largest farmers market in Arizona brings the state's best produce to one open-air jamboree of good tastes. Alongside fresh fruit and vegetables, you can find indigenous foods, wonderful bread, spices, pastes and salsas, organic meat, BBQ trucks and plenty more to eat on the spot. Jewelry, textiles and body products also make appearances.

Heard Museum Shop & Bookstore ARTS & CRAFTS
(Map p164; ☎602-346-8190; www.heardmuseumshop.com; 2301 N Central Ave; ⏰9:30am-5pm Mon-Sat, from 11am Sun; 📶) This museum store has a top-notch collection of American Indian original arts and crafts; the variety and quality of kachina dolls alone is impressive. Jewelry, pottery, American Indian books and a broad selection of fine arts can also be found, while the bookstore sells a wide array of books about the American Indian cultures of the Southwest.

Biltmore Fashion Park MALL
(Map p164; ☎602-955-8400; www.shopbiltmore.com; 2502 E Camelback Rd; ⏰10am-8pm Mon-Sat, noon-6pm Sun) Packed with high-end fashion retailers, this exclusive mall preens from its perch on Camelback just south of the Arizona Biltmore Resort.

Information

EMERGENCY & MEDICAL SERVICES

Police (emergency 911, non-emergency 602-262-6151; www.phoenix.gov/police; 620 W Washington St)

Both **Banner – University Medical Center Phoenix** (602-839-2000; www.bannerhealth.com; 1111 E McDowell Rd) and **St Joseph's Hospital & Medical Center** (602-406-3000; www.dignityhealth.org; 350 W Thomas Rd) have 24-hour emergency rooms.

TOURIST INFORMATION

Downtown Phoenix Visitor Information Center (Map p164; 877-225-5749; www.visitphoenix.com; 125 N 2nd St, Suite 120; 8am-5pm Mon-Fri) The Valley's most complete source of tourist information. Located across from the Hyatt Regency.

Experience Scottsdale (Map p164; 800-782-1117, 480-421-1004; www.experiencescottsdale.com; 7014 E Camelback Rd; 9am-6pm Mon-Sat, 10am-5pm Sun) In the Food Court of Scottsdale Fashion Square.

Mesa Convention & Visitors Bureau (800-283-6372, 480-827-4700; www.visitmesa.com; 120 N Center St; 8am-5pm Mon-Fri)

Tempe Tourism Office (Map p164; 866-914-1052; www.tempetourism.com; 222 S Mill Ave, Suite 120; 8:30am-5pm Mon-Fri)

Getting There & Away

Sky Harbor International Airport (PHX; Map p164; 602-273-3300; www.skyharbor.com; 3400 E Sky Harbor Blvd;) is 3 miles southeast of downtown Phoenix and served by airlines including United, American, Delta and British Airways. Its three terminals (Terminals 2, 3 and 4; Terminal 1 was demolished in 1990) and the parking lots are linked by free shuttles and the **Phoenix Sky Train** (www.skyharbor.com/phxskytrain; 24hr).

Greyhound (Map p164; 602-389-4200; www.greyhound.com; 2115 E Buckeye Rd) runs buses to Tucson ($14, two hours, nine daily), Flagstaff ($25, three hours, six daily), Albuquerque (from $68, 9½ hours, three daily) and Los Angeles (from $31, 7½ hours, 10 daily). Valley Metro's No 13 bus links the airport and the Greyhound station; tell the driver your destination is the Greyhound station.

For shared rides from the airport, the citywide door-to-door shuttle service provided by **Super Shuttle** (800-258-3826; www.supershuttle.com) costs about $14 to downtown Phoenix and Tempe, $19 to Old Town Scottsdale and Mesa. Alternatively, expect to pay $16 to $20 to downtown for a cab or rideshare.

The Phoenix Sky Train (p169) runs through Terminals 3 and 4 to the Metro light-rail station at 44th St and E Washington St, via the airport's east economy parking area. Bus 13 also connects the airport to town ($2 per ride).

Valley Metro (602-253-5000; www.valleymetro.org) operates buses all over the Valley and a 20-mile light-rail line linking north Phoenix with downtown Phoenix, Tempe/ASU and downtown Mesa. Fares for both light-rail and bus are $2 per ride (no transfers) or $4 for a day pass. Buses run daily at intermittent times.

Central Arizona

North of Phoenix, the wooded, mountainous and much cooler Colorado Plateau is draped with scenic sites and attractions. You can channel your inner goddess at a vortex, hike through ponderosa-perfumed canyons, admire ancient Native American dwellings and delve into Old West history.

The main hub, Flagstaff, is a lively and delightful college town that's the gateway to the Grand Canyon South Rim. Summer, spring and fall are the best times to visit. On I-17, you can drive the 145 miles between Phoenix and Flagstaff in just over two hours. Opt for the more leisurely Hwy 89 and you'll be rewarded with beautiful landscapes and intriguing diversions.

Prescott

With its historic Victorian-era downtown and colorful Wild West heritage, Prescott feels like the Midwest-meets-cowboy country. Boasting more than 500 buildings on the National Register of Historic Places, it's the home of the world's oldest rodeo, while the infamous strip of old saloons known as Whiskey Row still plies its patrons with booze. For an engaging roundup of local history, spend an hour at the **Sharlot Hall Museum** (928-445-3122; www.sharlot.org; 415 W Gurley St; adult/senior/child $9/8/5; 10am-5pm Mon-Sat, noon-4pm Sun May-Sep, to 4pm Oct-Apr) downtown.

Just south of downtown, the winningly retro **Motor Lodge** (928-717-0157; www.themotorlodge.com; 503 S Montezuma St; r/ste from $140/160;) welcomes guests with 12 snazzy bungalows arranged around a central driveway – it's indie lodging at its best. For breakfast, mosey into the friendly **Local** (928-237-4724; 520 W Sheldon St; mains $9.50-16; 7am-2:30pm;), where home baking and a classic Southwestern breakfast can be counted on. Cajun and Southwest specialties spice up the menu at delightful **Iron Springs Cafe** (928-443-8848; www.ironspringscafe.com; 1501 Iron Springs Rd; brunch & lunch $9-12.50,

ARIZONA'S BEST SCENIC DRIVES

Oak Creek Canyon A thrilling plunge past swimming holes, rockslides and crimson canyon walls on Hwy 89A between Flagstaff and Sedona.

Hwy 89/89A Wickenburg to Sedona The Old West meets the New Weston on this lazy drive past dude ranches, mining towns, art galleries and stylish wineries.

Patagonia–Sonoita Scenic Road This one's for the birds, and those who like to track them, in Arizona's southern wine country on Hwys 82 and 83.

Kayenta–Monument Valley Star in your own Western on an iconic loop past cinematic red rocks in Navajo country.

Vermilion Cliffs Scenic Road A solitary drive on Hwy 89A through the Arizona Strip linking condor country, the North Rim and Mormon hideaways.

dinner $9-25.50; ⏲11am-8pm Wed-Sat, 9am-2pm Sun), which sits inside an old train station 3 miles northwest of downtown.

On Whiskey Row, the **Palace** (☎928-541-1996; www.historicpalace.com; 120 S Montezuma St; ⏲11am-10pm Sun-Thu, to 11pm Fri & Sat) is an atmospheric place to drink; you enter through swinging saloon doors into a big room anchored by a Brunswick bar. The **visitor center** (☎928-445-2000; www.prescott.org; 117 W Goodwin St; ⏲9am-5pm Mon-Fri, 10am-2pm Sat & Sun) has tourist information.

Jerome

This resurrected ghost town was known as the 'Wickedest Town in the West' during its late-1800s mining heyday, but its buildings have now been restored to hold galleries, restaurants, B&Bs and wine-tasting rooms.

Feeling brave? Stand on the glass platform covering the 1910ft mining shaft at **Audrey Headframe Park** (Map p174; www.jeromehistoricalsociety.com; 55 Douglas Rd; ⏲8am-5pm) FREE – it's deeper than the Empire State Building by 650ft! Just ahead, the excellent **Jerome State Historic Park** (Map p174; ☎928-634-5381; www.azstateparks.com/jerome; 100 Douglas Rd; adult/child $7/4; ⏲8:30am-5pm) preserves the 1916 mansion of mining mogul Jimmy 'Rawhide' Douglas.

A hospital in the mining era, the **Jerome Grand Hotel** (Map p174; ☎928-634-8200; www.jeromegrandhotel.com; 200 Hill St; r$165-300, ste $400-525; ❄📶) plays up its past with medical relics in the hallways and an entertaining ghost tour kids will enjoy. The adjoining **Asylum Restaurant** (Map p174; ☎928-639-3197; www.asylumrestaurant.com; 200 Hill St; lunch $14-23.50, dinner $23.50-40; ⏲11am-3:30pm & 5-9pm; 📶), with its sweeping views, is a breathtaking spot for a fine meal and glass of wine.

Downtown, the **Spirit Room Bar** (Map p174; ☎928-634-8809; www.spiritroom.com; 166 Main St; ⏲11am-midnight) is a lively watering hole. Step into the **Flatiron Café** (Map p174; ☎928-634-2733; www.theflatironjerome.com; 416 Main St; mains $8-13.50; ⏲8:30am-3:30pm Thu-Mon) at the Y intersection for a gourmet breakfast or lunch; the specialty coffees are delicious. For information, call in at the **chamber of commerce** (Map p174; ☎928-634-2900; www.jeromechamber.com; 310 Hull Ave; ⏲11am-3pm most days).

Sedona

Nestled amid striking red sandstone formations at the south end of the 16-mile Oak Creek Canyon, Sedona attracts spiritual seekers, artists and healers, as well as day-trippers from Phoenix trying to escape the oppressive heat. Many New Age types believe that this area is the center of vortexes (not 'vortices' here in Sedona) that radiate the earth's power, and you'll find all sorts of alternative medicines and practices on display. More tangibly, the surrounding canyons offer outstanding hiking, biking, swimming and camping.

Sights & Activities

New Agers believe Sedona's rocks, cliffs and rivers radiate Mother Earth's mojo. The four best-known vortexes are **Bell Rock** (Map p174; Hwy 179) near the Village of Oak Creek east of Hwy 179; **Cathedral Rock** (Map p174; Back O Beyond Rd) near Red Rock Crossing; **Airport Mesa** (Map p174; Airport Rd); and **Boynton Canyon** (Map p174; Dry Creek Rd, Coconino NF). Airport Rd is also a great location for watching the Technicolor sunsets.

Red Rock State Park PARK

(Map p174; ☎928-282-6907; www.azstateparks.com/red-rock; 4050 Red Rock Loop Rd; adult/child $7/4; ⏲8am-5pm) Not to be confused with Slide Rock State Park (p171), this 286-acre park includes an environmental education center, picnic areas and 5 miles of well-marked, interconnecting trails in gorgeous red-rock country. Trails range from flat creekside saunters to moderate climbs to scenic ridges. Ranger-led activities include nature and bird walks. Swimming in the creek is prohibited. It's 9 miles west of downtown Sedona off Hwy 89A, on the eastern edge of the 15-mile Lime Kiln Trail.

Slide Rock State Park SWIMMING

(Map p174; ☎928-282-3034; www.azstateparks.com/slide-rock; 6871 N Hwy 89A; per car Mon-Thu $20, Fri-Sun $30 Mar-Sep, $10 Oct-Feb; ⏰8am-7pm May-Aug, shorter hours rest of year) One of Sedona's most popular and most crowded destinations, this state park 7 miles north of town features an 80ft sandstone chute that whisks swimmers through Oak Creek. Short trails ramble past an old homestead, farming equipment and an apple orchard, but the park's biggest draw is the set of wonderful natural rock slides.

West Fork Trail HIKING

(Map p174; Hwy 89A; day use per vehicle/bicycle $10/2; ⏰8am-7pm) This deservedly popular trail crosses Oak Creek a dozen times as it winds through the canyon, where walls soar more than 200ft in some places. The trail is marked for the first 3 miles, but you can scramble along the stream bed as far as 14 miles upstream. Parking is limited: arrive before 8:30am.

Pink Jeep Tours DRIVING

(Map p174; ☎800-873-3662; www.pinkadventuretours.com; 204 N Hwy 89A; ⏰6am-10pm) This veteran of Sedona's tour industry seems to have 4WDs everywhere. Once you join a tour, laughing and bumping around, you'll see why they're so popular. Pink runs 15 thrilling, bone-rattling off-road and adventure tours, most lasting from two hours (adult from $65, child from $60) to four hours (adult from $155, child from $140).

Sleeping

Sedona and nearby Oak Creek Canyon host many beautiful B&Bs, creekside cabins, motels and full-service resorts. Dispersed camping is not permitted in Red Rock Canyon. The Forest Service runs three campgrounds, without hookups, in the woods of Oak Creek Canyon, just off Hwy Alt 89. It costs $22 to camp, and you don't need a Red Rock Pass. Reservations are accepted for some sites at all three. Six miles north of town, Manzanita has 18 sites, showers and is open year-round; 11.5 miles north, Cave Springs has 84 sites, and showers; Pine Flat, 12.5 miles north, has 56 sites.

Cozy Cactus B&B $$$

(Map p174; ☎928-284-0082; www.cozycactus.com; 80 Canyon Circle Dr, Village of Oak Creek; d

VERDE VALLEY WINE TRAIL

Vineyards, wineries and tasting rooms are increasingly thick on the ground in the well-watered valley of the Verde River. Bringing star power is Maynard James Keenan, lead singer of the band Tool and owner of Caduceus Cellars and Merkin Vineyards. His 2010 documentary *Blood into Vine* takes a no-holds-barred look at the wine industry.

In Cottonwood, drive or float to **Alcantara Vineyards** (Map p174; ☎928-649-8463; www.alcantaravineyard.com; 3445 S Grapevine Way; wine tasting $10-15; ⏰11am-5pm) on the Verde River, then stroll through Old Town where **Arizona Stronghold** (Map p174; ☎928-639-2789; www.azstronghold.com; 1023 N Main St; wine tasting $9; ⏰noon-7pm Sun-Thu, to 9pm Fri & Sat), **Merkin Vineyards Osteria** (Map p174; ☎928-639-1001; www.merkinvineyardsosteria.com; 1001 N Main St; ⏰11am-9pm; 📶) and **Pillsbury Wine Company** (Map p174; ☎928-639-0646; www.pillsburywine.com; 1012 N Main St; wine tasting $8-12; ⏰11am-6pm Sun-Thu, to 9pm Fri & Sat) are three of the best wine-tasting rooms on oenophile-friendly Main St.

In Jerome, start at **Cellar 433** (Map p174; ☎928-634-7033; www.cellar433.com; 240 Hull Ave; wine tastings $10-12; ⏰11am-6pm Mon-Wed, to 7pm Thu-Sun) near the visitor center. From there, stroll up to Keenan's **Caduceus Cellars** (Map p174; ☎928-639-9463; www.caduceus.org; 158 Main St; wine tastings $15; ⏰11am-6pm Sun-Thu, to 8pm Fri & Sat), near the Connor Hotel.

Three wineries with tasting rooms hug a stretch of Page Springs Rd east of Cornville: bistro-housing **Page Springs Cellars** (Map p174; ☎928-639-3004; www.pagespringscellars.com; 1500 Page Springs Rd, Cornville; wine tasting $11; ⏰11am-7pm Sun-Wed, to 9pm Thu-Sat), the welcoming **Oak Creek Vineyards** (Map p174; ☎928-649-0290; www.oakcreekvineyards.net; 1555 N Page Springs Rd, Cornville; wine tasting $10; ⏰10am-6pm Sun-Thu, to 8pm Fri & Sat) and the mellow-rock-playing **Javelina Leap Vineyard** (Map p174; ☎928-649-2681; www.javelinaleapwinery.com; 1565 Page Springs Rd, Cornville; wine tasting $12; ⏰11am-6pm).

> **RED ROCK PASS**
>
> To park on National Forest land around Sedona and Oak Creek Canyon, you'll need to buy a Red Rock Pass, which is available at ranger stations, visitor centers and vending machines at most trailheads and picnic areas. Passes cost $5 per day or $15 per week and must be displayed under the windshield of your car. You don't need a pass if you're just stopping briefly for a photograph or to enjoy a viewpoint, or if you have one of the Federal Interagency Passes.

$275-345; ❄📶) This seven-room B&B, run by Carrie and Mark, works well for outdoorsy types – the Southwest-style house bumps up against Agave Trail, and is just around the bend from cyclist-friendly Bell Rock Pathway. Post-adventuring, get comfy beside the firepit on the back patio, perfect for wildlife-watching and stargazing, and enjoy the three-course breakfast that awaits you the next morning.

★El Portal INN $$$

(Map p174; ☎928-203-9405; www.elportalsedona.com; 95 Portal Lane; r $300-500; ❄📶🐾) 🍃 This discreet little inn is a beautiful blend of Southwestern and Craftsman style. It's a pocket of relaxed luxury tucked away in a corner across from the galleries and restaurants of Tlaquepaque, and marvelously removed from the chaos of Sedona's tourist-heavy downtown. The look is rustic but sophisticated, incorporating reclaimed wood, Navajo rugs, river rock and thick adobe walls.

Eating & Drinking

Sedona Memories DELI $

(Map p174; ☎928-282-0032; 321 Jordan Rd; sandwiches $8.50; ⏲10am-2pm Mon-Fri) This tiny local spot assembles gigantic sandwiches on slabs of homemade bread. A great choice for a picnic, as they pack 'em tight to-go, so there's less mess. You can also nosh on their quiet porch. If you call in your order, they'll toss in a free cookie.

Black Cow Café ICE CREAM $

(Map p174; ☎928-203-9868; 229 N Hwy 89A; medium ice cream $5; ⏲10:30am-9pm) Many claim the Black Cow's homemade ice cream is the best in town. Try the prickly pear.

★Elote Cafe MEXICAN $$$

(Map p174; ☎928-203-0105; www.elotecafe.com; Arabella Hotel, 771 Hwy 179; mains $23-29; ⏲5-10pm Tue-Sat) Come here for some of the best, most authentic Mexican food in the region. Elote Cafe serves unusual traditional dishes you won't find elsewhere, like the namesake *elote* (fire-roasted corn with spicy mayo, lime and cotija cheese) or smoked chicken in guajillo chilies. Reservations are not accepted: come early, order a margarita and get ready to make some new friends.

Hudson AMERICAN $$$

(Map p174; ☎928-862-4099; www.thehudsonsedona.com; Hillside Shopping Center, 671 Hwy 179; mains $15-43; ⏲11:30am-9pm) Prickly-pear ribs, butternut-squash ravioli, fireball chicken wings and a variety of salads bring an element of urban cool to Sedona. But it's not just the food that makes you want to linger past happy hour – those great big views from the half-moon banquettes and outdoor patio are equally enticing. Great bar too.

Information

Many places signed 'Tourist Information' really just want to sell you a timeshare. Stick to the following, which sell the Red Rock Pass and provide free hiking guides and maps.

Red Rock Country Visitor Center (Map p174; ☎928-203-2900; www.fs.usda.gov/coconino; 8375 Hwy 179; ⏲9am-4:30pm) Just south of the Village of Oak Creek.

Sedona Chamber of Commerce Visitor Center (Map p174; ☎928-282-7722; www.visitsedona.com; 331 Forest Rd; ⏲8:30am-5pm) Located in the pedestrian center of Uptown Sedona.

Getting There & Around

Ace Xpress (☎928-649-2720; www.acexshuttle.com; one way/round trip adult $68/109, child $35/55) and **Groome Transportation** (☎928-350-8466; www.groometransportation.com; one way adult/child $55/28) run shuttle services between Sedona and Phoenix's Sky Harbor International Airport.

Amtrak and Greyhound both stop in nearby Flagstaff.

Barlow Jeep Rentals (☎928-282-8700; www.barlows.us; 3009 W Hwy 89A; half-/1-/3-day Jeep rental $295/395/585; ⏲8am-6pm) is great for exploring 4WD roads. Free maps and trail information are provided. **Bob's Taxi** (☎982-282-1234) is a good local operator, while rental cars are available at **Enterprise** (☎928-282-2052; www.enterprise.com; 2090 W Hwy 89A; per day from $50; ⏲8am-5:30pm Mon-Fri, 9am-2pm Sat).

Flagstaff

Flagstaff's laid-back charms are many, from a pedestrian-friendly historic downtown crammed with eclectic vernacular architecture to hiking and skiing in the country's largest ponderosa pine forest. And the locals are a happy, athletic bunch, skewing more toward granola than gunslinger: buskers play bluegrass on street corners, while cycling culture flourishes. Northern Arizona University (NAU) gives Flag its college-town flavor, while its railroad history still figures firmly in the town's identity. Throw in a healthy appreciation for craft beer, freshly roasted coffee beans and an all-around good time, and you have the makings of the perfect northern Arizonan escape.

Sights

★ Lowell Observatory OBSERVATORY

(Map p174; ☎928-774-3358; www.lowell.edu; 1400 W Mars Hill Rd; adult/senior/child $17/16/10; ⏲10am-10pm Mon-Sat, to 5pm Sun) Astronomers, get ready to geek out! Sitting atop a hill just west of downtown, this national historic landmark – famous for the first sighting of Pluto in 1930 – was built by Percival Lowell in 1894. Check out the solar telescope or go on a tour during the day. Once evening falls, visitors can stargaze through on-site telescopes (weather permitting). A new exhibit, the Giovale Open Deck Observatory (GODO), which houses six telescopes alongside interactive displays, opened in October 2019.

★ Museum of Northern Arizona MUSEUM

(Map p174; ☎928-774-5213; www.musnaz.org; 3101 N Fort Valley Rd; adult/senior/child $12/10/8; ⏲10am-5pm Mon-Sat, noon-5pm Sun) Housed in an attractive Craftsman-style stone building amid a pine grove, this small but excellent museum spotlights local American Indian archaeology, history and culture, as well as geology, biology and the arts. Intriguing permanent collections are augmented by exhibitions on subjects such as John James Audubon's paintings of North American mammals. On the way to the Grand Canyon, it makes a wonderful introduction to the human and natural history of the region.

Riordan Mansion State Historic Park HISTORIC SITE

(Map p174; ☎928-779-4395; www.azstateparks.com/riordan-mansion; 409 W Riordan Rd; tour adult/child $10/5; ⏲9:30am-5pm May-Oct, 10:30am-5pm Thu-Mon Nov-Apr) Having made a fortune from their Arizona Lumber Company, brothers Michael and Timothy Riordan built this sprawling duplex in 1904. The Craftsman-style design was the brainchild of architect Charles Whittlesey, who also designed El Tovar in Grand Canyon Village. The exterior features hand-split wooden shingles, log-slab siding and rustic stone. Filled with Edison, Stickley, Tiffany and Steinway furniture, the interior is a shrine to arts and crafts.

Activities

Flagstaff Bicycle Revolution MOUNTAIN BIKING

(Map p174; ☎928-774-3042; www.flagbikerev.com; 3 S Mikes Pike; per 24hr hardtail/full suspension $45/70; ⏲8am-6pm Mon-Fri, 9am-5pm Sat & Sun) Flagstaff's best mountain-biking shop, with both hardtail (no rear suspension) and full-suspension bikes available to rent. You can ride directly to the trails from the shop, and it's sandwiched between great pizza and beer for postride celebrations.

Arizona Snowbowl SKIING

(Map p180; ☎928-779-1951; www.snowbowl.ski; 9300 N Snowbowl Rd; ski pass adult/child $89/59; ⏲9am-4pm Nov-Apr) About 14 miles north of downtown Flagstaff, Arizona Snowbowl is small but lofty, with eight lifts that service 55 ski runs between 9200ft and 11,500ft.

From June through mid-October, ride the chairlift to 11,500ft, where you can hike, hear ranger talks, go on a mini ropes course and take in the desert and mountain views.

Sleeping

Unlike in southern Arizona, summer is high season here.

★ Motel DuBeau MOTEL $

(Map p174; ☎928-774-6731; www.modubeau.com; 19 W Phoenix Ave; dm/r from $29/87; P@⊜) Built in 1929 as Flagstaff's first motel, the DuBeau has clean, well-run accommodations. In addition to private rooms, which all have refrigerators and cable TV, there is one seven-bed dorm room. There is also a kitchen and laundry facilities. Note there is no air-con in summer.

On-site Nomads serves beer, wine and meals.

★ Inn at 410 B&B $$

(Map p174; ☎928-774-0088; www.inn410.com; 410 N Leroux St; r $210-325; P❄⊜) This fully renovated 1894 house offers 10 spacious, beautifully decorated and themed

Flagstaff to Sedona

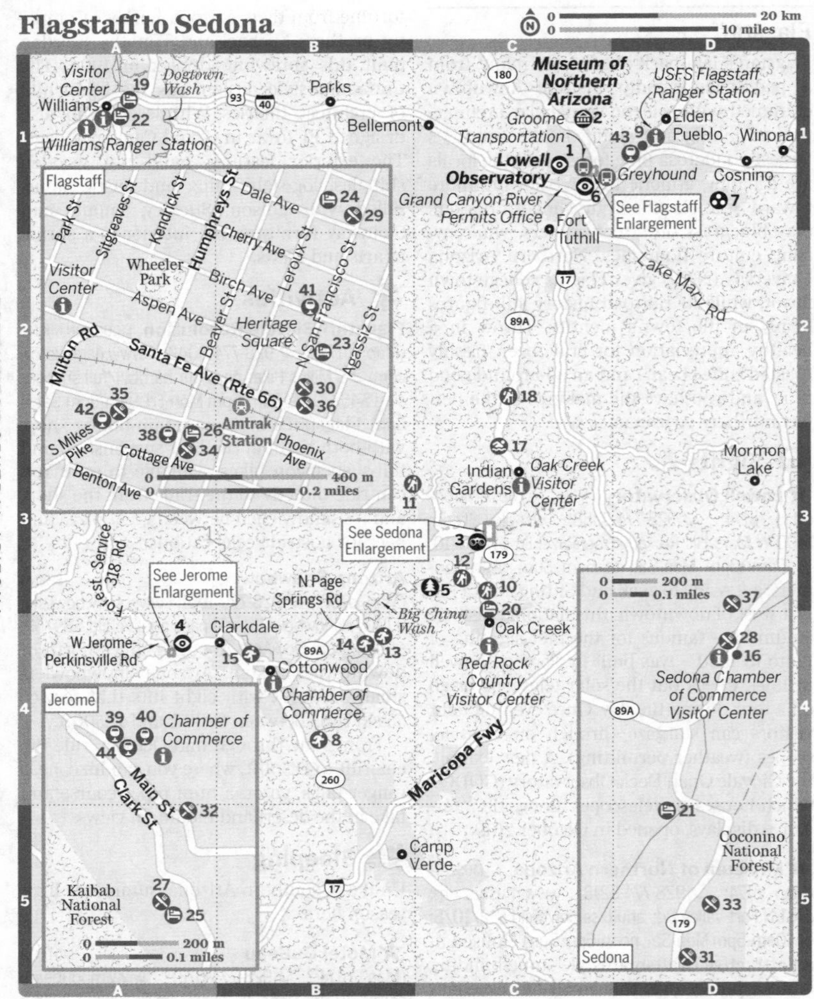

bedrooms, each with a fridge and bathroom, and many with four-poster beds and delightful views. A short stroll from downtown, the inn has a shady orchard garden and a cozy dining room, where a full gourmet breakfast and afternoon snacks are served.

Hotel Monte Vista HISTORIC HOTEL **$$**
(Map p174; ☎928-779-6971; www.hotelmontevista.com; 100 N San Francisco St; r $130-190; ❄📶) A huge, old-fashioned neon sign towers over this 1926 landmark hotel, hinting at what's inside: an array of feather lampshades, vintage furniture, bold colors and eclectic decor. Rooms are named for the movie stars who stayed here, and resident ghosts supposedly make regular appearances. Now for the downsides: it's noisy, wi-fi doesn't work in many rooms and street parking can be a headache.

✕ Eating

Flagstaff's college population and general dedication to living well translates into one of the best dining scenes in northern Arizona. There are a number of grocery stores in town – this is the best place to stock up before heading to the Grand Canyon.

Flagstaff to Sedona

★ Macy's CAFE $
(Map p174; ☎928-774-2243; www.macyscoffee.net; 14 S Beaver St; mains $6-9.50; ⏰6am-6pm;) The delicious coffee – house-roasted in the original, handsome, fire-engine-red roaster in the corner – at this Flagstaff institution has kept local students and caffeine devotees buzzing and sated since the 1980s. The all-vegetarian menu includes many vegan choices, along with traditional cafe grub including pastries, steamed eggs, waffles, yogurt and granola, salads and sandwiches.

Pizzicletta PIZZA $
(Map p174; ☎928-774-3242; www.pizzicletta.com; 203 W Phoenix Ave; pizzas $12-16; ⏰5-9pm Sun-Thu, to 10pm Fri & Sat) Tiny Pizzicletta, where the excellent thin-crusted wood-fired pizzas are loaded with gourmet toppings such as arugula and aged prosciutto, is housed in a sliver of a white-brick building. Inside there's an open kitchen, one long table with iron chairs, Edison bulbs and industrial surrounds. You can order in while you enjoy some suds at **Mother Road Brewing Company** (Map p174; ☎928-774-9139; www.motherroadbeer.com; 7 S Mikes Pike; ⏰2-9pm Tue & Wed, 2-10pm Thu, noon-10pm Fri & Sat, noon-9pm Sun;) next door.

★ Criollo Latin Kitchen FUSION $$
(Map p174; ☎928-774-0541; www.criollolatinkitchen.com; 16 N San Francisco St; lunch $12-16, dinner $19-23; ⏰11am-9pm Mon-Fri, from 9am Sat & Sun) Sister to Brix Restaurant & Wine Bar (p176) and **Proper Meats + Provisions** (Map p174; ☎928-774-9001; www.propermeats.com; 110 E Rte 66; sandwiches $12-14; ⏰10am-9pm), this on-trend Latin-fusion restaurant gives similar encouragement to local producers, sourcing ingredients from Arizona wherever possible. Set up your day with the Haitian brunch of slow-roasted pork with over-easy eggs, pinto beans and Ti-Malice hot sauce, or come back at happy hour (3pm to 6pm Monday to Friday) for fish tacos and $3.50 margaritas.

★**Coppa Cafe** CAFE $$$
(Map p174; ☎928-637-6813; www.facebook.com/coppacafeaz; 1300 S Milton Rd; lunch $11-15, mains $15-32; ⏰3-9pm Wed-Fri, 11am-3pm & 5-9pm Sat, 10am-3pm Sun; 📶) Brian Konefal and Paola Fioravanti, who met at an Italian culinary school, are the husband-and-wife team behind this friendly, art-strewn bistro with egg-yolk-yellow walls. Expect ingredients foraged from nearby woods (and further afield in Arizona) in dishes such as slow-roasted top loin with wildflower butter, or clay-baked duck's egg with a 'risotto' of Sonoran wheat and wild herbs.

Brix Restaurant & Wine Bar INTERNATIONAL $$$
(Map p174; ☎928-213-1021; www.brixflagstaff.com; 413 N San Francisco St; mains $23-40; ⏰5-9pm Tue-Sun) Brix offers seasonal, locally sourced and generally top-notch fare in a handsome room with exposed brick walls and an intimate copper bar. Sister business Proper Meats + Provisions (p175) supplies charcuterie, free-range pork and other fundamentals of delectable dishes, such as cavatelli with Calabrese sausage, kale and preserved lemon. The wine list is well curated, and reservations are recommended.

Drinking & Entertainment

For details about festivals and music programs, call the **Visitor Center** (Map p174; ☎928-213-2951; www.flagstaffarizona.org; 1 E Rte 66; ⏰8am-5pm Mon-Sat, 9am-4pm Sun) or check www.flagstaff365.com. On Friday and Saturday nights in summer, people gather on blankets for free music and family movies at Heritage Sq. The fun starts at 5pm.

On Thursday pick up a free copy of *Flagstaff Live!* (www.azdailysun.com/flaglive_new) for current shows and happenings around town.

★**Hops on Birch** PUB
(Map p174; ☎928-440-5380; www.hopsonbirch.com; 22 E Birch Ave; ⏰noon-1:30am; 🐾) Simple and handsome, Hops on Birch has 34 rotating beers on tap, live music five nights a week and a friendly local-crowd vibe. In classic Flagstaff style, dogs are as welcome as humans.

Museum Club BAR
(Map p174; ☎928-440-5214; www.museumclub.net; 3404 E Rte 66; ⏰11am-2am) This country-music roadhouse on Route 66 has been kicking up its heels since 1936. Inside what looks like a huge log cabin you'll find a large wooden dance floor, animal mounts and a sumptuous elixir-filled mahogany bar. The origins of the name? In 1931 it housed a taxidermy museum.

> **CAMPING AROUND FLAGSTAFF**
>
> Free dispersed camping is permitted in the Coconino National Forest surrounding Flagstaff. There are also campgrounds in Oak Creek Canyon to the south of town and Sunset Crater to the north.

Information

USFS Flagstaff Ranger Station (Map p174; ☎928-526-0866; www.fs.usda.gov/coconino; 5075 N Hwy 89; ⏰8am-4pm Mon-Fri) Provides camping and hiking information on the Mt Elden, Humphreys Peak and O'Leary Peak areas north of Flagstaff.

Visitor Center (p176) Located inside the Amtrak station, the visitor center has a great Flagstaff Discovery map and tons of information on things to do.

Getting There & Away

Greyhound (Map p174; ☎928-774-4573; www.greyhound.com; 880 E Butler Ave; ⏰10am-5:30am) stops in Flagstaff en route to/from Albuquerque, Las Vegas, Los Angeles and Phoenix. **Groome Transportation** (Map p174; ☎928-350-8466; www.groometransportation.com) has shuttles that run between Flagstaff, Grand Canyon National Park, Williams, Sedona and Phoenix's Sky Harbor International Airport.

Operated by **Amtrak** (☎928-774-8679; www.amtrak.com; 1 E Rte 66; ⏰24hr), the *Southwest Chief* stops at Flagstaff on its daily run between Chicago and Los Angeles.

Mountain Line Transit (☎928-779-6624; www.mountainline.az.gov; one way adult/child $1.25/0.60) has several fixed bus routes daily; pick up a user-friendly map at the visitor center. Buses are equipped with ramps for passengers in wheelchairs.

If you need a taxi, call **Action Cab** (☎928-774-4427; www.facebook.com/actioncabtaxiandtours). Several major car-rental agencies operate from the airport and downtown.

Williams

Affable Williams, 60 miles south of Grand Canyon Village and 35 miles west of Flagstaff, is a gateway town with character. Classic motels and diners line Route 66, and the old-school homes and train station give a nod to simpler times.

Most tourists visit to ride the turn-of-the-20th-century **Grand Canyon Railway** (Map p174; ☎800-843-8724; www.thetrain.com; 233 N Grand Canyon Bvd, Railway Depot; return adult/child from $67/32; ⊙departs 9:30am) to the Canyon's South Rim, which departs Williams 9:30am and returns at 5:45pm. Even if you're not a train buff, a trip is a scenic stress-free way to visit the Grand Canyon. Characters in period costumes provide historical and regional narration, and banjo folk music sets the tone.

The **Red Garter Inn** (Map p174; ☎800-328-1484; www.redgarter.com; 137 W Railroad Ave; d $175-200; ❄📶) is an 1897 bordello turned B&B where the ladies used to hang out the windows to flag down customers. The four rooms have nice period touches and the downstairs bakery has good coffee. The funky little **Grand Canyon Hotel** (Map p174; ☎928-635-1419; www.thegrandcanyonhotel.com; 145 W Route 66; dm $37, r $80-150; ⊙Apr-Nov; P❄@📶) has small themed rooms, a hostel-style dorm, a separate carriage house and no TVs. You can also sleep inside a 1929 Santa Fe caboose or a Pullman railcar at the **Canyon Motel & RV Park** (Map p174; ☎928-635-9371; www.thecanyonmotel.com; 1900 E Rodeo Rd; tent/RV sites from $30/42, railway car/cabooses from $110/205; ❄📶🏊), just east of downtown.

DON'T MISS

WALNUT CANYON

The Sinagua cliff dwellings at **Walnut Canyon** (Map p174; ☎928-526-3367; www.nps.gov/waca; I-40 exit 204; adult/child $15/free; ⊙8am-5pm Jun-Oct, from 9am Nov-May, trails close 1hr earlier) are set in the nearly vertical walls of a small limestone butte amid this stunning forested canyon. The mile-long Island Trail steeply descends 185ft (more than 200 stairs), passing 25 rooms built under the natural overhangs of the curvaceous butte. The shorter, wheelchair-accessible Rim Trail affords several views of the cliff dwellings from across the canyon.

Grand Canyon National Park

No matter how much you read about the **Grand Canyon** (Map p180; ☎928-638-7888; www.nps.gov/grca; 20 South Entrance Rd; ⊙7-day entry per car/person $35/20), or how many photographs you've seen, nothing really prepares you for the sight of it. The sheer immensity of the canyon grabs you first, followed by the dramatic layers of rock, which pull you in for a closer look. Next up are the artistic details – rugged plateaus, crumbly spires, maroon ridges – that flirt and catch your eye as shadows flicker across the rock.

Snaking along its floor are 277 miles of the Colorado River, which has carved the canyon over the past six million years and exposed rocks up to two billion years old – half the age of the earth. The two rims of the Grand Canyon offer quite different experiences; they lie more than 200 miles apart by road and are rarely visited on the same trip. Most visitors choose the South Rim with its easy access, wealth of services and vistas that don't disappoint. The quieter North Rim has its own charms; at 8200ft elevation (1000ft higher than the South Rim), its cooler temperatures support wildflower meadows and tall, thick stands of aspen and spruce.

June is the driest month, July and August the wettest. January has average overnight lows of 13°F (-11°C) to 20°F (-7°C) and daytime highs around 40°F (4°C). Summer temperatures inside the canyon regularly soar above 100°F (38°C). While the South Rim is open year-round, most visitors come between late May and early September. The North Rim is open from mid-May to mid-October.

ℹ Information

The most developed area in the Grand Canyon National Park is **Grand Canyon Village**, 6 miles north of the South Rim Entrance Station. The North Rim has one entrance, which is 30 miles south of Jacob Lake on Hwy 67; continue another 14 miles south to the actual rim. The North and South Rims are 215 miles apart by car, 21 miles on foot through the canyon, or 10 miles as the condor flies.

The park entrance ticket is valid for seven days and can be used at both rims. All overnight hikes and backcountry camping in the park require a permit. The **Backcountry Information Center** (Map p180; ☎928-638-7875; www.nps.gov/grca/planyourvisit/backcountry-permit.htm; Grand Canyon Village; ⊙8am-noon & 1-5pm, phone staffed 8am-5pm Mon-Fri; 🚌Village) accepts applications for backpacking permits ($10, plus $8 per person per night) starting four months before the proposed month. Your chances are decent if you apply early and provide alternative hiking itineraries.

WORTH A TRIP

SUNSET CRATER VOLCANO NATIONAL MONUMENT

Around AD 1064 a cinder cone erupted on this **spot** (Map p180; ☎928-526-0502; www.nps.gov/sucr; Park Loop Rd 545; car/motorcycle/bicycle & pedestrian $25/20/15; ⏲visitor center 9am-5pm, park 24hr), spewing ash across 800 sq miles, spawning the Kana-A lava flow. Now the 8029ft Sunset Crater is quiet, and short trails wind through the Bonito lava flow (formed c 1180) and up Lenox Crater (7024ft). More ambitious hikers and bikers can ascend O'Leary Peak (8965ft; 8-mile round trip), or there's a gentle, 0.3-mile, wheelchair-accessible loop overlooking the petrified flow.

Sunset Crater is 19 miles northeast of Flagstaff. Access fees include entry to nearby **Wupatki National Monument** (Map p180; ☎928-679-2365; www.nps.gov/wupa; Park Loop Rd 545; car/motorcycle/bicycle/pedestrian $25/20/15/15; ⏲visitor center 9am-5pm, trails sunrise-sunset), and are valid for seven days.

Reservations are accepted in person or by mail or fax, not by phone or email. For more information see www.nps.gov/grca/planyourvisit/backcountry-permit.htm.

If you arrive at the South Rim without a permit, head to the backcountry office, by **Maswik Lodge** (Map p180; ☎928-638-2631, advanced reservations 888-297-2757; www.grandcanyonlodges.com; 202 South Village Loop Dr, Grand Canyon Village; r South/North $215/304; P ❄ @ 📶; 🚌Village), to join the waiting list. As a conservation measure, the park no longer sells bottled water. Fill your flask at water filling stations along the rim or at **Canyon Village Market** (Map p180; ☎928-638-2262; www.visitgrandcanyon.com; Market Plaza, Grand Canyon Village; sandwiches & pizzas $6-11; ⏲6:30am-9pm late May-Sep, deli to 8pm, shorter hours rest of year; 🚌Village).

SOUTH RIM VISITOR CENTERS

Grand Canyon Visitor Center (Map p180; ☎park headquarters 928-638-7888; www.nps.gov/grca/planyourvisit/visitorcenters.htm; Grand Canyon Visitor Center Plaza, Grand Canyon Village; ⏲9am-5pm; 🚌Village, 🚌Kaibab/Rim, 🚌Tusayan (Mar 1-Sep 30)) Three hundred yards behind Mather Point, a large plaza holds the visitor center and the **Visitor Center Plaza Park Store** (Map p180; ☎Grand Canyon Association 800-858-2808; www.grandcanyon.org; ⏲8am-8pm Jun-Aug, shorter hours rest of year). Outdoor bulletin boards display information about trails, tours, ranger programs and the weather.

National Geographic Visitor Center (Map p180; ☎928-638-2468; www.explorethecanyon.com; 450 Hwy 64; IMAX adult/child $14/10; ⏲visitor center 8am-10pm Mar-Oct, 9am-8pm Nov-Feb, theater 8:30am-8:30pm Mar-Oct, 9:30am-6:30pm Nov-Feb; 🚌Tusayan) In Tusayan, 7 miles south of Grand Canyon Village; pay your $30 vehicle entrance fee here to spare yourself a potentially long wait at the park entrance. The IMAX theater screens the terrific film *Grand Canyon – The Hidden Secrets*.

In addition to the visitor centers already mentioned, information is available inside the park:

Desert View Watchtower (Map p180; ☎928-638-8960; www.nps.gov/grca/learn/photos-multimedia/mary-colter---indian-watchtower.htm; Desert View, Desert View Dr; ⏲8am-7pm Apr-Sep, to 6pm Oct-Mar; stairs close 30min before closing; P 🚻)

Kolb Studio (Map p180; ☎928-638-2771; www.nps.gov/grca/planyourvisit/art-exhibits.htm; Rim Trail, Grand Canyon Village Historic District; ⏲8am-7pm Mar-May & Sep-Nov, to 6pm Dec-Feb, to 8pm Jun-Aug; 🚌Village (Hermits Rest Route Transfer stop), 🚌Hermits Rest (Mar 1-Nov 30; Village Route Transfer))

Tusayan Museum & Ruins (Map p180; ☎928-638-7888; www.nps.gov/grca; Desert View Dr; ⏲9am-5pm; P 🚻)

Verkamp's Visitor Center (Map p180; ☎928-638-7888; www.nps.gov/grca/planyourvisit/verkamps.htm; Rim Trail, Grand Canyon Village Historic District; ⏲8am-7pm Mar-late May & Sep-Nov, to 6pm Dec-Feb, to 8pm late May-Aug; 🚌Village (Train Depot or Village East stop))

Yavapai Geology Museum (Map p180; ☎928-638-7888; www.nps.gov/grca/planyourvisit/yavapai-geo.htm; Rim Trail, Grand Canyon Village Historic District; ⏲8am-7pm Mar-late May & Sep-Nov, to 6pm Dec-Feb, to 8pm late May-Aug; P 🚻; 🚌Kaibab/Rim)

South Rim

If you don't mind bumping elbows with other travelers, you'll be fine on the South Rim, where you'll find an entire village worth of lodging, restaurants, bookstores, libraries, a supermarket and a deli. Museums and historic stone buildings illuminate the park's human history, and rangers lead daily programs on subjects from geology to resurgent condors. In summer, when day-trippers converge en masse, escaping the crowds can be as easy as taking a day hike below the rim or merely tramping a hundred yards away from a scenic overlook.

Activities

Driving & Hiking

A **scenic route** follows the rim on the west side of Grand Canyon Village along Hermit Rd. Closed to private vehicles March through November, the 7-mile road is serviced by free park shuttle buses; cycling is encouraged because of the relatively light traffic. Stops along the route offer spectacular views, and interpretive signs explain canyon features.

Desert View Drive starts east of Grand Canyon Village and follows the canyon rim for 26 miles to Desert View, the east entrance of the park. Pullouts offer tremendous views.

Hiking trails along the South Rim include options for every skill level. The **Rim Trail** is the most popular, and easiest, walk in the park. It dips in and out of the scrubby pines of Kaibab National Forest to connect scenic points and historical sights over 13 miles. Portions are paved, and every viewpoint is accessed by one of the three shuttle routes. Along the **Trail of Time**, bordering the Rim Trail just west of Yavapai Geology Museum, every meter represents one million years of geologic history.

Hiking down into the canyon itself is a serious undertaking; most visitors are content with short day hikes. Bear in mind that the climb back out of the canyon is much harder than the descent into it, and do not attempt to hike all the way to the Colorado River and back in a single day. On the most popular route, the beautiful **Bright Angel Trail**, the scenic 8-mile drop to the river is punctuated with four logical turnaround spots. Summer heat can be crippling; day hikers should either turn around at one of the two resthouses (a 3- or 6-mile round trip) or hit the trail at dawn to safely make the longer hikes to **Indian Garden** and **Plateau Point** (9.2- and 12.2-mile round trips, respectively).

The steeper and much more exposed **South Kaibab Trail** is one of the park's prettiest routes, combining stunning scenery and unobstructed 360-degree views with every step. Hikers overnighting at **Phantom Ranch** generally descend this way, and return the next day via the Bright Angel. Summer ascents can be dangerous, and during this season rangers advise day hikers to turn around at **Cedar Ridge** (about 3 miles round trip) for the park's finest short day hike.

Cycling

Bright Angel Bicycles & Cafe at Mather Point CYCLING

(Map p180; bike shop 928-638-3055, reservations 928-679-0992; www.bikegrandcanyon.com; Grand Canyon Visitor Center Complex; 24hr rental adult/child 16yr & under $47/31.50, 5hr rental $31.50/20, wheelchair $10.50, single/double stroller up to 8hr $18/31; 8am-6pm May–mid-Sep, 9am-5pm mid-Sep–Oct, 8am-5pm Mar & Apr; ; Village, Kaibab/Rim) Bicycle rental and tours. Reserve in advance online or by phone; with the exception of the peak stretch from June through mid-August, however, walk-ins can usually be accommodated. Helmets included; add-on pull-along trailer options available. The recommended seasonal two-hour **Hermit Shuttle Package** (adult/child $36/26) shuttles riders from the shop to **Hopi Point** (Map p180; www.nps.gov/grca; Rim Trail, Hermit Rd; P; Hermits Rest westbound (Mar 1-Nov 30)), and picks them up at **Hermits Rest** (Map p180; 928-638-2351; www.nps.gov/grca/learn/photosmultimedia/colter_hermits_photos.htm; Hermit Rd; 8am-8pm May-Sep, 9am-5pm Oct-Mar, 9am-6:30pm Apr; ; Hermits Rest (Mar 1-Nov 30)).

Tours

★**Grand Canyon Mule Rides** TOURS

(Map p180; 888-297-2757, next-day reservations 928-638-2631; www.grandcanyonlodges.com/plan/mule-rides; Bright Angel Lodge, Grand Canyon Village Historic District; 2hr mule ride $143, 1-/2-night mule ride incl meals & accommodations $606/875; per 2 people $1057/1440; rides available year-round, hours vary;) If you want to descend into the canyon, the only option is an overnight to Phantom Ranch (p181). These 10-mule trains follow the **Bright Angel Trail** (Map p180; www.nps.gov/grca; Rim Trail, Grand Canyon Village Historic District; ; Village, Hermits Rest (Mar 1-Nov 30)) 10.5 miles (5½ hours) down, spend one or two nights at Phantom Ranch, and return 7.8 miles (five hours) along the **South Kaibab Trail** (Map p180; www.nps.gov/grca; South Kaibab Trailhead, off Desert View Dr; Kaibab/Rim). Alternatively, the 4-mile Canyon Vistas ride stays on the rim.

Sleeping

The South Rim's six lodges are operated by **Xanterra** (Grand Canyon Lodges; advanced reservations 888-297-2757, international 303-297-2757, reservations within 48hrs 928-638-2631; www.xanterra.com; 10 Albright St, Grand Canyon).

Grand Canyon National Park

0 50 km
0 25 miles
N

A B C D E F G
1 2 3 4

St George Area Chamber of Commerce
St George
Utah Welcome Center
St George Regional Airport
UTAH
NEVADA
Hildale
Colorado City
Mesquite
15
Hurricane Cliffs
Kane County Office of Tourism 32
Kanab
1 Best Friends Animal Sanctuary
GSENM Visitor Center
Kaibab-Paiute Reservation
Fredonia
North Kaibab Ranger District Office
389
Paria Plateau
Arizona Strip
21
Paria Contact Station
Big Water
Big Water Visitor Center
Carl Hayden Visitor Center
Lake Powell
13
Navajo Mountain (10,388ft)
Horseshoe Bend
10
Page
Lees Ferry
Marble Canyon
5
29
28
Antelope Canyon
39
Jacob Lake
Kaibab Plateau Visitor Center
89 Alt
89
89T
Bitter Springs
Snake Gulch
Kaibab Plateau
67
Backcountry Information Center – North Rim
Colorado River
Bulrush Canyon
The Sunshine Route
Kanab Canyon
Kanab Creek
Valley of Fire State Park
8
Valley of Fire Visitor Center
Grand Wash River
ARIZONA
Hack Canyon
Robinson Wash
Tuweep
Lake Mead
Supai
Falls Area
34
35
Tourist Office
Havasu Canyon
See North Rim Enlargement
Point Imperial (8803ft)
12
27
Cape Royal (7876ft)
38
17
16
31
2
Desert View Watchtower
22
Heather Wash
19
See Grand Canyon Village Enlargement
Tusayan Ranger Station
Tusayan
Pearce Ferry
15
Colorado River
Hualapai Reservation
Rd
Diamond Bar Rd
Pierce Ferry
18
Coconino Plateau
Grand Canyon National Park Airport
Havasu Creek
Hualapai Hilltop Hwy
Hualapai Reservation
Dolan Springs
Stockton Hill Rd
Red Lake (dry)
Music Mountains
Peach Springs
Truxton
Visitor Center
14
Grand Canyon Caverns
66
64
Valle
Grand Canyon Railway
Cataract Creek
180
Cedar Wash
89
Wupatki National Monument
9
Tuba City
Moenkopi
160
Hopi Reservation
264
44
Cameron
Gray Mountain

North Rim
Uncle Jim Trailhead
North Kaibab Trail
Transept Trail
30
37
Bridle Trail
North Rim Visitor Center
Bright Angel Point Trailhead
Grand Canyon Lodge
3
Transept Trail Trailhead
0 1 km
0 0.5 miles

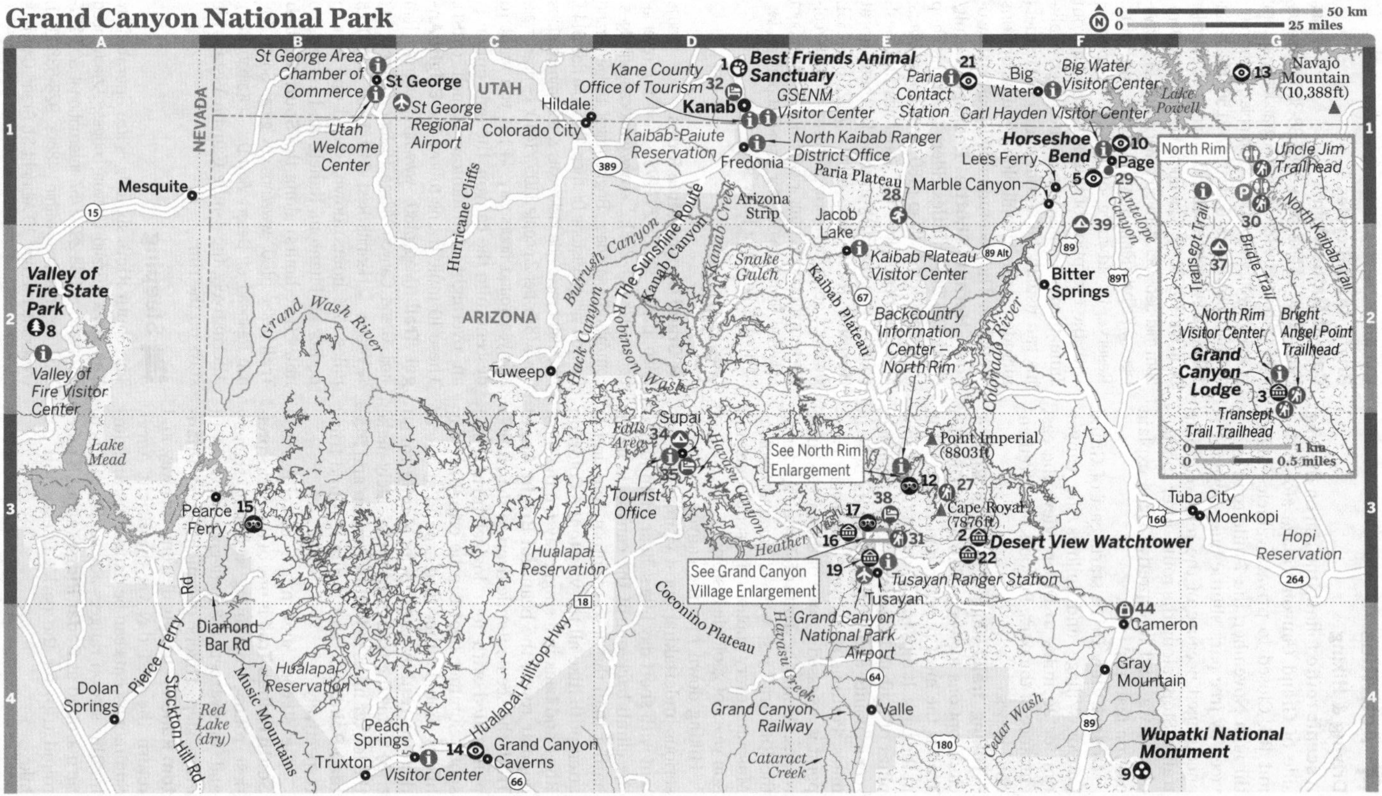

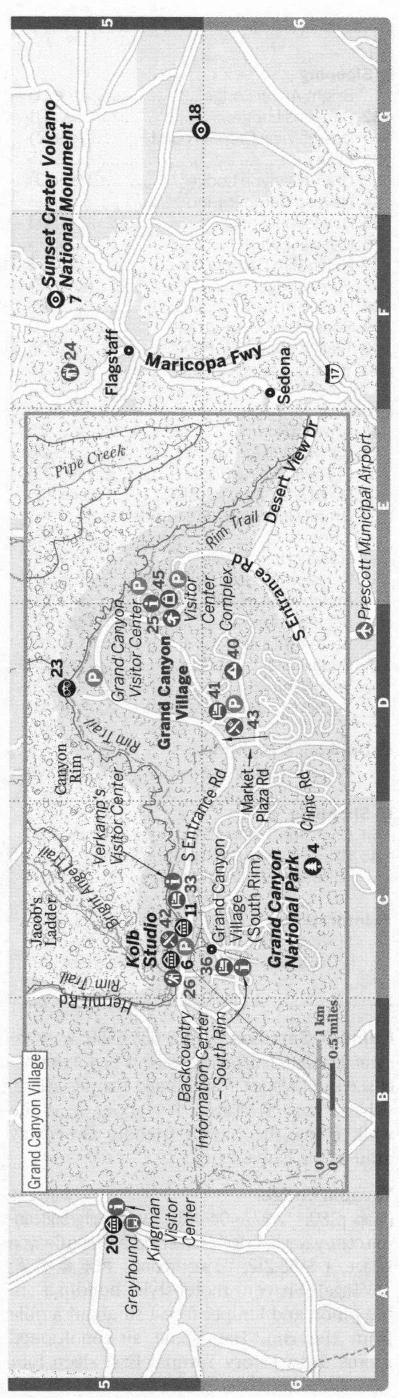

Contact them to make advance reservations (essential in summer), although it's best to call Phantom Ranch, down beside the Colorado River, directly. For same-day reservations or to reach a guest, call the South Rim **switchboard** (☎928-638-2631). If you can't find accommodations in the national park, try Tusayan (at South Rim Entrance Station), Valle (31 miles south), Cameron (53 miles east), Williams (about 60 miles south) or Flagstaff (80 miles southeast). All campgrounds and lodges are open year-round except Desert View.

★Desert View Campground CAMPGROUND $
(Map p180; www.nps.gov/grca/planyourvisit/cg-sr.htm; Desert View, Desert View Dr; campsites $12; ⊙mid-Apr–mid-Oct; P 🐾) In the piñon-juniper 25 miles from the tourist hub of Grand Canyon Village and close to the rim, this first-come, first-served 50-site NPS campground is relatively quiet, with a spread-out design that ensures a bit of privacy. The best time to secure a spot is mid-morning, when people are breaking camp, and it usually fills by noon.

Facilities include toilets and drinking water, but no showers or hookups; there's a general store with basic supplies next door.

★Bright Angel Lodge LODGE $
(Map p180; ☎advanced reservations 888-297-2757, reservations within 48hr 928-638-2631; www.grandcanyonlodges.com; Rim Trail, Grand Canyon Village Historic District; r/cabins from $140/243; P 📶; 🚌Village) This 1935 log-and-stone **historic lodge** (Map p180; ☎928-638-2631; www.nps.gov/grca/learn/photosmultimedia/colter_ba_photos.htm; Rim Trail, Grand Canyon Village Historic District; P 👪; 🚌Village) on the canyon ledge delivers simple charm and the small public spaces bustle with activity. Buckey and Powell Lodge rooms, an excellent choice for budget accommodations, offer bright, handsome and simple rooms (refrigerator, but no TV) only steps from the rim, while rustic Rim Cabins and suites are some of the South Rim's best accommodations.

Phantom Ranch CABIN, DORMITORY $
(Map p180; ☎888-297-2757; www.grandcanyonlodges.com; bottom of canyon, 9.9 miles below South Rim on Bright Angel, 7.4 miles below South Rim on South Kaibab, 13.6 miles below North Rim on North Kaibab; dm $65, cabin d $169, available by lottery; ❄) Bunks at this camp-like complex on the canyon floor are in private cabins sleeping two to 10 people and four hiker-only single-sex dorms, each with five bunks. Rates include bedding, soap and towels, but

Grand Canyon National Park

Top Sights

1	Best Friends Animal Sanctuary	D1
2	Desert View Watchtower	E3
3	Grand Canyon Lodge	G2
4	Grand Canyon National Park	C6
5	Horseshoe Bend	F1
6	Kolb Studio	C5
7	Sunset Crater Volcano National Monument	F5
8	Valley of Fire State Park	A2
9	Wupatki National Monument	F4

Sights

10	Antelope Point	F1
11	Bright Angel Lodge	C5
12	Bright Angel Point	E3
13	Dangling Rope	G1
14	Grand Canyon Caverns & Inn	C4
15	Grand Canyon West	B3
16	Hermits Rest	E3
17	Hopi Point	E3
18	Meteor Crater	G5
19	National Geographic Visitor Center & IMAX Theater	E3
20	Route 66 Museum	A5
21	The Toadstools	E1
22	Tusayan Museum & Ruin	E3
23	Yavapai Point and Geology Museum	D5

Activities, Courses & Tours

24	Arizona Snowbowl	F5
25	Bright Angel Bicycles & Cafe at Mather Point	D5
26	Bright Angel Trail	C5
	Canyon Trail Rides	(see 3)
27	Cape Final Trail	E3
28	Condor Release Site at Vermilion Cliffs	E1
29	Ekis' Antelope Canyon Tours	F1
	Grand Canyon Mule Rides	(see 6)
	Lake Powell Paddleboards	(see 29)
30	North Kaibab Trail	G1
31	South Kaibab Trail	E3

Sleeping

	Bright Angel Lodge	(see 11)
32	Canyons Lodge	D1
	Desert View Campground	(see 2)
33	El Tovar	C5
	Grand Canyon Lodge	(see 3)
34	Havasu Campground	D3
35	Havasupai Lodge	D3
36	Maswik Lodge	C6
37	North Rim Campground	G2
	Parry Lodge	(see 32)
38	Phantom Ranch	E3
39	Shash Diné EcoRetreat	F2
40	Trailer Village RV Park	D6
41	Yavapai Lodge	D6

Eating

42	Arizona Room	C5
43	Canyon Village Market	D6
	El Tovar Dining Room	(see 33)
	Floyd & Co Real Pit BBQ	(see 20)
	Grand Canyon Lodge Dining Room	(see 3)
	Harvey House Cafe	(see 11)
	Phantom Ranch Canteen	(see 38)
	Ranch House Grille	(see 29)
	Sego Restaurant	(see 32)
	State 48 Tavern	(see 29)
	Supai Cafe	(see 35)
	Vermillion 45	(see 32)
	Yavapai Lodge Restaurant	(see 41)

Drinking & Nightlife

	Beale Street Brews	(see 20)

Shopping

44	Cameron Trading Post	F4
45	Grand Canyon Association Park Store at the Visitor Center	E5

Information

	Navajo Parks & Recreation Department	(see 29)

meals are extra and must be reserved when booking your accommodations. Phantom is accessible by mule trip, on foot or via raft on the Colorado River.

Trailer Village RV Park CARAVAN PARK $
(Map p180; ☎877-404-4611; www.visitgrandcanyon.com; Market Plaza, Grand Canyon Village; RV sites with full hookups $49-59; ⏰year-round; P 📶 🐾; 🚌Village east-bound) A trailer park with RVs lined up tightly at paved pull-through sites on a rather barren patch of ground. You'll find picnic tables, barbecue grills and full hookups, but coin-operated showers and laundry are a half-mile walk to

Camper Services (☎928-638-6350; www.visitgrandcanyon.com/trailer-village-rv-park/rv-camper-services; Market Plaza, Grand Canyon Village; ⏰hours vary; 🚌Village). It's about a 1-mile walk along the bicycle-friendly Greenway Trail to the canyon rim.

Yavapai Lodge MOTEL $$
(Map p180; ☎877-404-4611; www.visitgrandcanyon.com/yavapai-lodge; Market Plaza, Grand Canyon Village; r $168-212; ⏰year-round; P ❄ @ 📶 🐾; 🚌Village) Sixteen motel-style buildings in the piñon and juniper forest sit about a mile from the rim. Handsome air-conditioned rooms at two-story Yavapai East sleep four

to six; family rooms include bunk beds. Pet-friendly drive-up rooms in single-story Yavapai West sleep up to four, but do not have air-conditioning and are more dated.

★El Tovar LODGE $$$
(Map p180; ☎advanced reservations 888-297-2757, reservations within 48hr 928-638-2631; www.grandcanyonlodges.com; Rim Trail, Grand Canyon Village Historic District; r $263-354; ⏲year-round; P ❄ 📶; 🚌Village west-bound (Train Depot stop)) Perched on the Rim Trail at the canyon edge, the public spaces of this 1905 wooden lodge ooze old-world national-park glamour and charm. Unfortunately, the 78 rooms and suites do not consistently share the historic aesthetic; some are lovely, with four-poster beds or a spectacular balcony, but standard rooms rival roadside motels. Stay here for the service and location.

Eating & Drinking

Grand Canyon Village has all the eating options you need, but nobody comes to Grand Canyon for the food! Arizona Room, El Tovar and **Harvey House Cafe** (Map p180; ☎928-638-2631; www.grandcanyonlodges.com/dine/harvey-house-cafe; Bright Angel Lodge, Grand Canyon Village Historic District; mains $13-21; ⏲6:30am-10pm; 👪; 🚌Village west-bound) are the only table-service restaurants on the South Rim, though several bars serve small plates and snacks. The other restaurants are cafeteria-style or fast food. You can make advanced reservations (dinner only) at Arizona Room and El Tovar.

Phantom Ranch Canteen (Map p180; ☎US 888-297-2757, outside US 303-297-2757; www.grandcanyonlodges.com/dine/phantom-ranch-cafe; Phantom Ranch, (bottom of the canyon); breakfast $23.65, dinner vegetarian stew/steak $24/48; ⏲breakfast 5am & 6:30am, Apr-Oct, 5:30am & 7am Nov-Mar, dinner 5pm & 6:30pm, canteen 8am-4pm & 8-10pm, from 8:30am Nov-Mar), below the rim near the Colorado River, offers family-style breakfasts and dinners by advanced reservation only.

Yavapai Lodge Restaurant CAFETERIA $
(Map p180; www.visitgrandcanyon.com; Yavapai Lodge, Grand Canyon Village; breakfast $7-9, lunch & dinner $10-16; ⏲7am-9pm; P 👪; 🚌Village) Breakfast buffet ($15) or à la carte; lunch and dinner are barbecue, hot and cold sandwiches and pizza, as well as beer and wine. Place your order on a touchscreen, pick up your drinks, and your number will be called when the food is ready. Efficient and convenient, but not much better than what you'd expect at a school cafeteria.

★El Tovar Dining Room AMERICAN $$$
(Map p180; ☎928-638-2631; www.grandcanyonlodges.com/dine/el-tovar-dining-room-and-lounge; El Tovar, Grand Canyon Village Historic District; mains $20-30; ⏲restaurant 6:30-10:30am, 11:15am-2pm & 4:30-9:30pm, lounge 11:30am-11pm; P 👪; 🚌Village) Classic national park dining at its best. Dark-wood tables are set with china and white linen, eye-catching murals spotlight American Indian tribes and huge windows frame views of the Rim Trail and canyon beyond. Breakfast options include El Tovar's pancake trio (buttermilk, blue cornmeal and buckwheat pancakes with pine-nut butter and prickly-pear syrup), and blackened trout with two eggs.

Arizona Room AMERICAN $$$
(Map p180; ☎ex 6432 928-638-2631; www.grandcanyonlodges.com/dine/arizona-room; Bright Angel Lodge, Grand Canyon Village Historic District; lunch $13-26, dinner $27-40; ⏲11:30am-3pm & 4:30-9:30pm Feb-Oct, dinner only Nov-Jan; 👪; 🚌Village) Antler chandeliers hang from the ceiling, picture windows overlook the Rim Trail and canyon beyond, and the seasonal menu gives a Western vibe. Reservations (dinner only) are accepted online or by phone 30 days in advance, but are usually available within the week.

Getting There & Around

Most people arrive at the canyon in private vehicles or on a tour. Parking can be a chore in Grand Canyon Village. Once inside the park, free park shuttles operate along three routes: around Grand Canyon Village, west along Hermits Rest Route and east along Kaibab Trail Route. Buses typically run every 15 minutes, from one hour before sunset to one hour afterward. In summer a free shuttle from Bright Angel Lodge, the Hiker's Express, has early-morning pickups at the Backcountry Information Center and Grand Canyon Visitor Center, and then heads to the South Kaibab trailhead.

North Rim

Solitude reigns supreme on the North Rim. There are no shuttles or bus tours, no museums, shopping centers, schools or garages. In fact, there isn't much of anything here beyond a classic rimside national park lodge, a campground, a motel, a general store and miles of trails carving through sunny meadows thick with wildflowers, willowy aspen and towering ponderosa pines

The entrance to the North Rim is 24 miles south of **Jacob Lake** on Hwy 67; Grand Canyon Lodge (p184) lies another 20 miles beyond. At 8000ft, it's about 10°F (6°C) cooler here than the South Rim – even on summer evenings you'll need a sweater. All facilities on the North Rim are closed from mid-October to mid-May, although you can drive into the park and stay at the campground until snow closes the road from Jacob Lake.

Activities

The short and easy, half-mile paved trail to **Bright Angel Point** (Map p180; www.nps.gov/grca) is a canyon must. Beginning from the back porch of Grand Canyon Lodge, it goes to a narrow finger of an overlook with fabulous views.

The **North Kaibab Trail** (Map p180; www.nps.gov/grca; Inner Canyon), the North Rim's only maintained rim-to-river trail, connects with trails to the South Rim in the Phantom Ranch (p181) area. The first 4.7 miles are the steepest, dropping 3050ft to **Roaring Springs** – a popular all-day hike. If you prefer a shorter day hike below the rim, walk just 0.75 miles down to **Coconino Overlook**, or 2 miles to the **Supai Tunnel** to get a taste of steep inner-canyon hiking. The 28-mile round trip to the Colorado River is a multiday affair.

For a short hike up on the rim, which works well for families, try the 4-mile round-trip **Cape Final Trail** (Map p180; www.nps.gov/grca; Cape Royal Rd), on the **Walhalla Plateau** east of Grand Canyon Lodge, which leads through ponderosa pines to sweeping views of the eastern Grand Canyon area.

Canyon Trail Rides TOURS

(Map p180; 435-679-8665; www.canyonrides.com; North Rim; 1/3hr mule ride $45/90; 7:30am, 8:30am, 12:30pm, 1:30pm, 2:30pm mid-May–mid-Oct) You can make reservations anytime for the upcoming year, but, unlike mule trips on the South Rim, you can usually book a trip upon your arrival at the park; just duck inside the Grand Canyon Lodge to the Mule Desk. Rides don't reach the Colorado River, but the North Kaibab Trail trip gives a taste of life below the rim.

Each of the three rides has specific age and weight restrictions, but if you're under 7 years old or weigh over 220lbs, you're out of luck.

Book in advance online or by calling 928-638-9875 within a week of your ride.

Sleeping & Eating

North Rim Campground CAMPGROUND $

(Map p180; 877-444-6777; www.recreation.gov; tent sites $18, RV sites $18-25; by reservation May 15-Oct 15, first-come, first-served Oct 16-31;) Operated by the NPS, this campground, 1.5 miles north of the Grand Canyon Lodge, offers shaded sites on level ground among the ponderosas. Sites 11, 14, 15, 16 and 18 have canyon views...and cost $25 – but site 10 is pretty sweet too. You can – and should – make reservations online up to six months in advance.

Walk-up sites are available for hikers and bikers only. There's water, a store, a snack bar, coin-operated showers and laundry facilities, but no hookups.

Grand Canyon Lodge HISTORIC HOTEL $$

(Map p180; advance reservations 877-386-4383, same-day reservations 928-638-2611; www.grandcanyonforever.com; r/cabins from $146/161; May 15-Oct 15) Guest rooms are not in the **lodge** (Map p180) itself; most are in log cabins nearby. Four of the Western Cabins have the only canyon views to speak of, and that's where you want to be if you can justify the $22 surcharge. Book them at least a year in advance.

Grand Canyon Lodge Dining Room AMERICAN $$

(Map p180; May-Oct 928-638-8560; www.grandcanyonforever.com/dining; breakfast $8-11, lunch $10-15, dinner $18-35; 6:30-10am, 11:30am-2:30pm & 4:30-9:30pm May 15-Oct 15;) While the solid dinner menu includes buffalo steak, western trout and several vegetarian options, don't expect great culinary memories – the view is the thing. Lunch is just OK, and the breakfast buffet is entirely forgettable; order something prepared. Although seats beside the window are wonderful, views from the dining room are so huge it really doesn't matter where you sit.

If you didn't make reservations in advance for dinner, you can still take advantage of the buffet across the lobby ($33; 4:30pm to 6:15pm) which has disappointing cafeteria sides to go with the delicious hand-cut steaks.

Information

Backcountry Information Center – North Rim (Map p180; 928-638-7875; www.nps.gov/grca; Administrative Bldg; 8am-5pm May 15-Oct 15) Backcountry permits for overnight camping on and below the rim, at Tuweep Campground, or camping anytime between November 1 and May 14.

RAFTING THE COLORADO

A boat trip down the Colorado is an epic, adrenaline-pumping adventure, which will take you beyond contact with civilization for several nights. The biggest single drop at Lava Falls plummets 37ft in just 300yd. But the true highlight is experiencing the Grand Canyon by looking up, not down from the rim. Its human history comes alive in ruins, wrecks and rock art. Commercial trips run from three days to three weeks and vary in the type of watercraft used.

Arizona Raft Adventures (Map p174; ☎800-786-7238, 928-526-8200; www.azraft.com; 4050 East Huntington Dr, Flagstaff, AZ 86004; 6-16-day raft trips $2305-4675, 8-/10-day motor trips $2945/3455) This multi-generational family-run outfit offers motor, oar and paddle (with opportunities for both paddling and floating) trips. Look online for details on photography, music, yoga and kayak 'specialty adventure' trips.

Arizona River Runners (☎800-477-7238, 602-867-4866; www.raftarizona.com; 15211 North Cave Creek Rd, Suite A, Phoenix AZ, 85032; 3-day combined ranch visit & motor trips from $1475, 13-day full-canyon oar trips from $4145) At its game since 1970, this outfit offers oar-powered and motorized trips. In addition to regular trips it has 'Hiker's Special' trips that take place over five to 15 days in the cooler temperatures of April. The company also caters to travelers with special needs, offering departures for people with disabilities.

Kaibab National Forest Visitor Center (Jacob Lake) Go here for the skinny on dispersed camping and viewpoints outside the park.

North Rim Visitor Center (Map p180; ☎928-638-7888; www.nps.gov/grca; ⊙8am-6pm May 15-Oct 15) Beside Grand Canyon Lodge, this is the place to get information on the park, and the starting point for ranger-led nature walks.

Getting There & Away

The only access road to the Grand Canyon North Rim is Hwy 67, which closes with the first snowfall and reopens in spring after the snowmelt (exact dates vary).

Although only 11 miles from the South Rim as the crow flies, it's a grueling 215-mile, four- to five-hour drive on winding desert roads between here and Grand Canyon Village. You can drive yourself or take the **Trans-Canyon Shuttle** (☎928-638-2820; www.trans-canyonshuttle.com; one way $90). Reserve at least two weeks in advance.

Although trails do connect the two rims, the three-day route should not be attempted by anyone except experienced canyon hikers in excellent physical condition.

Around the Grand Canyon

Havasupai Canyon

In a hidden side canyon off the Colorado River, complete with stunning, spring-fed waterfalls and azure swimming holes, this beautiful spot is hard to reach, but the hike down and back up makes the trip unique – and an amazing adventure.

Located on the Havasupai Indian Reservation, Havasu Canyon is just 35 miles directly west of the South Rim, but it's more like 195 miles by road. The four falls lie 10 miles below the rim, accessed via a moderately challenging hiking trail that starts from Hualapai Hilltop, and is reached by following a 62-mile road that leaves Route 66 7 miles east of Peach Springs.

All trips require an overnight stay, which must be reserved in advance.

The village of Supai, 8 miles along the trail, is home to **Supai Lodge** (Map p180; ☎928-448-2111, 928-448-2201; www.theofficialhavasupaitribe.com; Supai; r for up to 4 people $440, plus entrance fee per person $110; ⊙Feb-Nov; ❄), where basic motel-style rooms have nothing to recommend them bar the location. Reservations must be made a year in advance. The **Supai Cafe** (Map p180; Supai; mains $5.50-13; ⊙hours vary) serves hamburgers, bean burritos and a frybread taco.

The **Havasu Campground** (Map p180; ☎928-448-2180; www.havasupaireservations.com; Havasu Canyon; per person 3 nights $300-375; ⊙Feb-Nov), 2 miles beyond, has primitive campsites along a creek. There are several composting toilets, and drinking water is available. Although the campground accommodates 350 people per night, not all campsites are designated – expect a somewhat crowded experience. Getting a permit to camp is a maddeningly near-impossible thing – begin planning more than a year before your trip.

Continue deeper into Havasu Canyon to reach the waterfalls and blue-green swimming holes.

For detailed information about traveling into Havasu Canyon, see www.theofficialhavasupaitribe.com.

Hualapai Reservation

Run by the Hualapai Nation, around 215 driving miles west of the South Rim or 70 miles northeast of Kingman, the remote site known as Grand Canyon West is NOT part of Grand Canyon National Park.

If you're coming from Peach Springs, note that it's a two-hour drive, even though it looks closer. Check the directions on the website before you head out as there's no cell service here. Don't miss the Joshua Tree Forest on the way in.

Grand Canyon West VIEWPOINT
(Map p180; ☎928-769-2636, 888-868-9378; www.grandcanyonwest.com; Hualapai Reservation; per person $47-77; ⏲7am-7pm Apr-Sep, 8am-5pm Oct-Mar) The only way to visit Grand Canyon West, the section of the Grand Canyon overseen by the Hualapai Nation, is to purchase a package tour. These are based on a hop-on, hop-off shuttle ride, which loops to three stops along the rim. Tours include two viewpoints, cowboy activities at an ersatz Western town and informal American Indian performances. The **Skywalk**, a glass platform perched 4000ft above the canyon floor, is the primary draw, vertigo permitting.

Northern & Eastern Arizona

Between the brooding buttes of Monument Valley, the blue waters of Lake Powell and the fossilized logs of the Petrified Forest National Park are photogenic lands locked in ancient history. Inhabited by Native Americans for centuries, this region is dominated by the Navajo reservation – widely known as the Navajo Nation – which spills into surrounding states. The Hopi reservation is here as well, completely surrounded by Navajo land.

Lake Powell

The country's second-largest artificial reservoir, Lake Powell, stretches north from Arizona into Utah. Set amid striking red-rock formations, sharply cut canyons and dramatic desert scenery, and part of the **Glen Canyon National Recreation Area** (☎928-608-6200; www.nps.gov/glca; 7-day pass per vehicle $30, per pedestrian or cyclist $15), it's water-sports heaven. For stand-up paddleboard and kayak rentals, try **Lake Powell Paddleboards** (Map p180; ☎928-645-4017; www.lakepowellpaddleboards.com; 836 Vista Ave; per day SUP/kayak/bike $40/30/35; ⏲8am-6pm Apr-Sep, 9am-5pm Oct-Mar).

The lake was created by the construction of Glen Canyon Dam, 2.5 miles north of what's now the region's central town, Page. The Carl Hayden Visitor Center is located beside the dam.

To visit otherworldly **Antelope Canyon**, a stunning sandstone slot canyon, you must join a Navajo-led tour. Several tour companies offer trips into **Upper Antelope Canyon**, which is easier to navigate. Expect a bumpy ride and a bit of a cattle call; try **Roger Ekis' Antelope Canyon Tours** (Map p180; ☎928-645-9102; www.antelopecanyon.com; 22 S Lake Powell Blvd; adult/child from $60/50; ⏲tours 7am-4:30pm). The more strenuous **Lower Antelope Canyon** sees much smaller crowds.

A deservedly popular hike is the 1.2 mile round trip to **Horseshoe Bend** (Map p180; Hwy 89; parking $10; ⏲sunrise-sunset), where the Colorado wraps around a dramatic stone outcropping to form a perfect U on a jaw-dropping scale. The trailhead is south of Page off Hwy 89, across from mile marker 541.

Chain hotels line Page's main strip, Hwy 89, but there are independent alternatives along 8th Ave. Experience the beauty of the Navajo land from up close at **Shash Diné EcoRetreat** (Map p180; ☎928-640-3701; www.shashdine.com; off Hwy 89; r $150-200), a family ranch where visitors can stay in a traditional hogan, covered sheepherder wagon, canvas tent or cabin. Breakfast is included; at night bring your own food to enjoy around the campfire.

For breakfast in Page, the **Ranch House Grille** (Map p180; ☎928-645-1420; www.ranchhousegrille.com/page; 819 N Navajo Dr; mains $9-15; ⏲6am-3pm) has good food, huge portions and fast service. Later in the day, settle in at **State 48 Tavern** (Map p180; ☎928-645-1912; www.state48tavern.com; 614 N Navajo Dr; sandwiches $12-14, mains $18-27; ⏲5-10pm Wed-Fri & Mon, from 11am Sat & Sun), where dishes include pear-and-gorgonzola burgers and coconut shrimp tacos, and the beer selection is good.

Navajo Nation

The Navajo Nation is vast: at 27,000 sq miles it's bigger than some US states, and spreads across the junction of Arizona, New Mexico,

Colorado and Utah. It also contains natural beauty of staggering richness, and, of course, the living culture, language, institutions, farms and homes of the Diné (Navajo), the country's largest American Indian nation.

Unlike the rest of Arizona, the Navajo Nation observes mountain daylight saving time. During summer, the reservation is one hour ahead of Arizona. For details about hiking and camping, and required permits, visit www.navajonationparks.org.

During summer months, the park observes daylight saving time.

CAMERON

This historic settlement serves as the gateway to the east entrance of the Grand Canyon's South Rim, which is 32 miles away. The tiny, windswept community is one of the few worthwhile stops on Hwy 89 between Flagstaff and Page. The **Cameron Trading Post** (Map p180; ☎928-679-2231; www.camerontradingpost.com; Hwy 89; ⏲6am-10pm Mar-Oct, shorter hours Nov-Feb), just north of the Hwy 64 turnoff to the Grand Canyon, offers food, lodging, a gift shop and a post office.

NAVAJO NATIONAL MONUMENT

The sublimely well-preserved Ancestral Puebloan cliff dwellings of Betatakin and Keet Seel are protected within the **Navajo National Monument** (☎928-672-2700; www.nps.gov/nava; Hwy 564; ⏲visitor center 8am-5:30pm Jun-early Sep, 9am-5pm rest of year) FREE and can only be reached on foot. This walk in the park is no walk in the park, but there's truly something magical about approaching these ancient stone villages in relative solitude, among the piñon and juniper. The National Park Service controls access to the site and maintains the visitor center, which is informative and has excellent staff.

CANYON DE CHELLY NATIONAL MONUMENT

The many-fingered Canyon De Chelly (duh-*shay*) contains several beautiful Ancestral Puebloan sites, including ancient cliff dwellings. For centuries, though, it has been home to Navajo farmers, who winter on the rims then move to hogans (traditional roundhouses) on the canyon floor in spring and summer. The canyon is private Navajo property administered by the NPS. Enter hogans only with a guide and don't photograph people without their permission.

The only lodging in the park is **Thunderbird Lodge** (☎928-674-5842, 800-679-2473; www.thunderbirdlodge.com; Rural Rte 7; r $100-130; ❄📶🐾), just outside the canyon itself. It has comfortable rooms and an inexpensive cafeteria serving Navajo and American meals. The nearby Navajo-run campground has about 90 sites on a first-come, first-served basis ($14), with water but no showers. Cash only. The peaceful, Navajo-run **Spider Rock Campground** (☎928-781-2016, 928-781-2014; www.spiderrockcampground.com; Navajo Hwy 7; tent/RV sites $11/16, hogans $31-47; 📶🐾) on the South Rim Drive is surrounded by piñon and juniper trees

The Canyon de Chelly **visitor center** (☎928-674-5500; www.nps.gov/cach; Rte 7; ⏲8am-5pm) is 3 miles off Rte 191, beyond the small village of Chinle, near the mouth of the canyon. Two scenic drives follow the canyon's rim, but you can only explore the canyon floor on a guided tour. Stop by the visitor center, or check the park website, for a list of tour companies. The only unguided hiking trail you can follow in the park is a short but very

HOPI RESERVATION

Direct descendants of the Ancestral Puebloans, the Hopi have arguably changed less in the last five centuries than any other Native American group. Their village of Old Oraibi may be the oldest continuously inhabited settlement in North America. Hopi land is surrounded on all sides by the Navajo Nation. Hwy 264 runs past the three mesas (First, Second and Third Mesa) that form the heart of the reservation.

On Second Mesa, 8 miles west of First Mesa, the **Hopi Cultural Center Restaurant & Inn** (☎928-734-2401; www.hopiculturalcenter.com; Mile 379, Hwy 264; r from $100; ⏲restaurant 7am-9pm; ❄📶🐾) is as visitor-oriented as things get on the Hopi reservation. It provides food and lodging, and holds the small **Hopi Museum** (☎928-734-6650; Mile 379, Hwy 264; adult/child $3/1; ⏲8:30am-5pm Mon-Fri, 9am-3pm Sat), filled with historic photographs and cultural exhibits.

Photographs, sketching and recording are not allowed anywhere on the reservation. Alcohol and drug use are also prohibited.

spectacular round-trip route that descends to the amazing **White House Ruin**.

MONUMENT VALLEY NAVAJO TRIBAL PARK

When Monument Valley rises into sight from the desert floor, it is surprisingly familiar. Its brick-red spindles, sheer-walled mesas and grand buttes, stars of countless films, TV commercials and magazine ads, are part of the modern consciousness. And Monument Valley's epic beauty is only heightened by the barren landscape surrounding it.

For up-close views of the towering formations, visit the **Monument Valley Navajo Tribal Park** (435-727-5870; www.navajonationparks.org; per 4-person vehicle $20; drive 6am-7pm Apr-Sep, 8am-4:30pm Oct-Mar, visitor center 6am-8pm Apr-Sep, 8am-5pm Oct-Mar), where a rough and unpaved scenic driving loop covers 15 miles of stunning valley views. You can drive it yourself, or arrange a tour through one of the kiosks in the parking lot, which will take you to areas where private vehicles can't go (1½ hours $65; two-hour trail ride $150).

Inside the tribal park, the sandstone-colored **View Hotel** (435-727-5555; www.monumentvalleyview.com; Indian Rte 42, Monument Valley Navajo Tribal Park; r/ste from $210/349;) blends naturally with its surroundings, and most of the 95 rooms have private balconies facing the monuments. The Navajo-accented food at the adjoining restaurant (mains $11 to $15, no alcohol) aren't life-changing, but the vista makes up for all.

The peerlessly-situated **View Campground** (435-727-5802; www.monumentvalleyview.com/campground; Indian Rte 42, Monument Valley Navajo Tribal Park; tent & RV sites $30; Mar-Oct) is a cheaper option, while historic **Goulding's Lodge** (435-727-3231; www.gouldings.com; Monument Valley, Utah; d from $245, apt $310-330;), just over the road in Utah, offers basic rooms, camping and small cabins. Book early for summer. Kayenta, 20 miles south, has a handful of acceptable motels and borderline-acceptable restaurants; try the **Wetherill Inn** (928-697-3231; www.wetherill-inn.com; 1000 Main St/Hwy 163; r $155;) if everything in Monument Valley is booked.

Petrified Forest National Park

Home not only to an extraordinary array of fossilized logs that predate the dinosaurs but also the multicolored sandscape of the Painted Desert, this **national park** (928-524-6228; www.nps.gov/pefo; vehicle/cyclist $20/10; 7am-7pm mid-Apr–Aug, shorter hours rest of year) is a compulsory spectacle. The park straddles I-40 at exit 311, 25 miles east of **Holbrook**. Its **visitor center** (928-524-6228; 1 Park Rd, Petrified Forest National Park; 8am-6pm mid-Apr–mid-Oct, to 5pm rest of year), just half a mile north of I-40, holds maps and information on guided tours, while the 28-mile paved park road beyond offers a splendid scenic drive. There are no campsites, but a number of short trails, ranging from less than a mile to 2 miles, pass through the stands of petrified trees and ancient Native American dwellings. Those prepared for rugged backcountry camping need to pick up a free permit at the visitor center.

Western Arizona

Sun worshippers flock to the Colorado River in and around Lake Havasu City, while road-trippers cruise Route 66, which offers well-preserved stretches of classic highway near Kingman. Much further south, beyond I-10 towards Mexico, the wild, empty landscape is among the most barren in the West. If you're already here, there are some worthwhile sites, but there's nothing worth planning an itinerary around unless you're a Route 66 or boating fanatic.

Kingman & Around

Among Route 66 aficionados, Kingman is known as the main hub of the longest uninterrupted stretch of the historic highway, running from Topock to Seligman. Among its early-20th-century buildings is the former Methodist church at 5th and Spring Sts where Clark Gable and Carole Lombard eloped in 1939. Hometown hero Andy Devine had his Hollywood breakthrough as the perpetually befuddled driver of the eponymous *Stagecoach* in John Ford's Oscar-winning 1939 movie.

Pick up maps and brochures at the historic **Kingman Visitor Center** (Map p180; 928-753-6106, 866-427-7866; www.gokingman.com; 120 W Andy Devine Ave; 8am-5pm), housed in an old powerhouse and entailing a small but engaging Route 66 museum and a display of electric cars.

Wednesday through Sunday, drive up to the **Hualapai Mountain Resort** (928-757-3545; www.hmresort.net; 4525 Hualapai Mountain Rd; r/ste from $79/159; Wed-Sun;) and its restaurant, set amid towering pines. There's tasty pit-smoked meats at **Floyd & Co Real Pit BBQ** (Map p180; 928-757-8227; www.floydandcompany.com; 420 E Beale St; mains $8.50-13; 11am-8pm Tue-Thu, to 9pm Fri & Sat) and commendable coffee at **Beale Street Brews** (Map p180; 928-753-1404; www.bealestreetbrews.net; 510 E Beale St; 6am-6pm;).

Southern Arizona

This is a land of Stetsons and spurs, where cowboy ballads are sung around the campfire under starry, black-velvet skies and thick steaks sizzle on the grill. Anchored by the bustling college town of Tucson, it's a vast region, where long, dusty highways slide past rolling vistas and steep, pointy mountain ranges. Majestic saguaro cacti, the symbol of the region, stretch out as far as the eye can see.

Tucson

Fun-loving, outdoorsy and one of the most culturally invigorating places in the Southwest, Tucson (*too*-sawn) is an unexpected treasure. Set in a flat valley hemmed in by snaggletoothed mountains and swathes of saguaro, Arizona's second-largest city smoothly blends Native American, Spanish, Mexican and Anglo traditions. Distinct neighborhoods and 19th-century buildings give a rich sense of community and history not found in the more modern, sprawling Phoenix. The eclectic shops toting vintage garb, scores of funky restaurants and dive bars don't let you forget Tucson is a college town at heart, home turf to the 45,000-strong University of Arizona (UA).

Sights & Activities

Downtown Tucson and the historic district lie east of I-10 exit 258. The University of Arizona campus is a mile northeast of downtown; 4th Ave, the main drag here, is packed with cafes, bars and interesting shops. Many of Tucson's most fabulous treasures lie on the periphery, or even beyond town.

★**Arizona-Sonora Desert Museum** MUSEUM
(520-883-2702; www.desertmuseum.org; 2021 N Kinney Rd; adult/senior/child $22/20/9; 8:30am-5pm Oct-Feb, 7:30am-5pm Mar-Sep, to 10pm Sat Jun-Aug) Home to cacti, coyotes and palm-sized hummingbirds, this 98-acre ode to the Sonoran Desert is part zoo, part botanical garden and part museum – a trifecta that'll entertain young and old for half a day easily. Desert denizens, from precocious coatis to playful prairie dogs, inhabit natural enclosures, the grounds are thick with desert plants, and docents give demonstrations. Strollers and wheelchairs are available, and there's a gift shop, an art gallery, a restaurant and a cafe.

Arizona State Museum MUSEUM
(520-621-6302; www.statemuseum.arizona.edu; 1013 E University Blvd; adult/senior/child $8/6/

ROADSIDE ATTRACTIONS ON ROUTE 66

Four hundred miles of America's Highway stretches across Arizona, with plenty of kitschy sights, listed here from west to east, along the way.

Wild burros of Oatman Feral mules, the progeny of mining days, beg for treats in the middle of the road.

Grand Canyon Caverns & Inn (Map p180; 928-422-3223; www.gccaverns.com; Mile 115, Rte 66; tour adult/child from $16/11; 9am-5pm May-Sep, 9:30am-4pm Oct-Apr) A guided tour 21 stories underground loops past mummified bobcats, civil-defense supplies and a $900 motel room (or cave).

Burma Shave signs Red-and-white ads from a bygone era between Grand Canyon Caverns and Seligman.

Snow Cap Drive-In (928-422-3291; www.delgadillossnowcap.t2-food.com; 301 East Chino; mains $5-6.50; 10am-6pm Mar-Nov) Prankish burger and ice-cream joint open in Seligman since 1953.

Meteor Crater (Map p180; 800-289-5898; www.meteorcrater.com; Meteor Crater Rd; adult/senior/child $18/16/9; 7am-7pm Jun–mid-Sep, 8am-5pm mid-Sep–May) A 550ft-deep pockmark that's nearly 1 mile across, 38 miles east of Flagstaff.

Wigwam Motel (928-524-3048; www.galerie-kokopelli.com/wigwam; 811 W Hopi Dr; r $70-76;) Concrete wigwams with hickory logpole furniture in Holbrook.

free; 10am-5pm Mon-Sat) To learn more about the history and culture of the region's American Indian tribes, visit the Arizona State Museum, the oldest and largest anthropology museum in the Southwest. The exhibit covering the tribes' cultural histories is extensive but easy to navigate, and should appeal to newbies and history buffs alike. These galleries are complemented by much-envied collections of minerals and Navajo textiles.

Old Tucson Studios FILM LOCATION
(520-883-0100; www.oldtucson.com; 201 S Kinney Rd; adult/senior/child $20/18/11; generally 10am-5pm Fri-Sun, closed Sep;) Nicknamed 'Hollywood in the Desert,' this old movie set of Tucson in the 1860s was built in 1939 for the filming of *Arizona*. Hundreds of flicks followed, bringing in movie stars from Clint Eastwood to Leonardo DiCaprio. Now a Wild West theme park, it's all about shoot-outs, stagecoach rides, stunt shows and dancing saloon girls. Hours vary by month – check online before you go.

Tucson Museum of Art MUSEUM
(520-624-2333; www.tucsonmuseumofart.org; 140 N Main Ave; adult/senior/child $12/10/7; 10am-5pm Tue-Sun) For a small city, Tucson boasts an impressive art museum. There's a respectable collection of American, Latin American and modern art, and the permanent exhibition of pre-Columbian artifacts will awaken your inner Indiana Jones. The special exhibits are varied and interesting, there's a superb gift shop, and the block surrounding the building holds a number of notable historic homes. The museum stays open to 8pm on the first Thursday of the month, when admission is free from 5pm.

Pima Air & Space Museum MUSEUM
(520-574-0462; www.pimaair.org; 6000 E Valencia Rd; adult/senior/child $16.50/13.75/10; 9am-5pm, last entry 3pm) An SR-71 Blackbird spy plane and a massive B-52 bomber are among the stars of this extraordinary private aircraft museum. Allow at least two hours to wander through hangars and around the airfield where more than 300 'birds' trace the evolution of civilian and military aviation. Take a self-guided tour using the museum's GPS-guided app, or pay an extra $6 for the one-hour tram tour departing at 10am, 11:30am, 1:30pm and 3pm from November to May.

★ **Pedego** BIKE RENTALS
(520-441-9782; www.pedegoelectricbikes.com; 4340 N Campbell Ave, Suite 107B; half-/full-day cruisers from $45/65, mountain bikes $80/125; 7am-3pm Wed-Sun) If you've never had the pleasure of riding an electric bike – which use pedal-assist technology, so you still get some exercise – this is your chance. Conveniently located steps from the Loop, you'll have plenty to explore. Even better, rent a mountain bike. You'll never feel the same about those grueling uphills again.

Festivals & Events

Tucson Gem & Mineral Show CULTURAL
(520-332-5773; www.tgms.org; Feb) The most famous event on the city's calendar, held on the second full weekend in February, this is the largest gem and mineral show in the world. An estimated 250 retail dealers who trade in minerals, crafts and fossils take over the Tucson Convention Center and other venues around town.

Sleeping

Lodging prices vary considerably, with lower rates in summer and fall. To sleep under the stars and saguaros, try **Gilbert Ray Campground** (520-883-4200; www.webcms.pima.gov; 8451 W McCain Loop Rd; tent/RV sites $10/20;) near the western district of Saguaro National Park.

★ **Hotel Congress** HISTORIC HOTEL $
(520-622-8848; www.hotelcongress.com; 311 E Congress St; d from $120;) Perhaps Tucson's most famous hotel, this is where infamous bank robber John Dillinger and his gang were captured during their 1934 stay, when a fire broke out. Built in 1919 and beautifully restored, this charismatic place feels very modern, despite period furnishings such as rotary phones and wooden radios (no TVs). There are a popular cafe, bar and club on-site.

★ **Catalina Park Inn** B&B $$
(520-792-4541; www.catalinaparkinn.com; 309 E 1st St; r $125-195; late Sep–May; @) Style, hospitality and comfort merge seamlessly at this inviting B&B just west of the University of Arizona. Hosts Mark and Paul have poured their hearts into restoring this 1927 Mediterranean-style villa, and their efforts are on display in the six rooms, which vary in style. Don't miss the delicious breakfast – burritos, croissant French toast and more await in the mornings.

Under Canvas GLAMPING $$
(☎ 520-303-9412; www.undercanvas.com; 14301 E Speedway; tents from $149; ⊙ Sep-May; 📶🏊) Dreaming of spending the night in the Sonoran Desert but unsure about mixing sleeping bags with snakes? This high-end camp, just a 10-minute drive from the Saguaro National Park, could be for you. Unwind in one of three tent styles (Deluxe, Stargazer and Safari), all of which come with king-sized beds, bathrooms and showers.

★**Hacienda del Sol** RANCH $$$
(☎ 520-299-1501; www.haciendadelsol.com; 5501 N Hacienda del Sol Rd; r from $300; ❄@📶🏊) An elite hilltop girls' school built in the 1920s, this relaxing refuge has artist-designed Southwest-style rooms and teems with unique touches such carved ceiling beams and louvered exterior doors to catch the courtyard breeze. The Hacienda del Sol has sheltered Spencer Tracy, Katharine Hepburn, John Wayne and other legends, so you'll be sleeping with history. Its restaurant, the Grill, is fabulous too.

Eating

★**Tumerico** VEGETARIAN $
(☎ 520-240-6947; www.tumerico.com; 2526 E 6th St; meals $14; ⊙ 8am-8pm Wed-Sat, 10am-7pm Sun, 10am-3pm Tue; 🌿) How do we love thee? Let us count the ways: ranchero tacos stuffed with veggies and jackfruit, Frida Kahlo tostadas and cilantro pesto *sopes* (topped tortillas), coconut curry bowls, kombucha on tap and CBD lattes. The mysterious 'all powers' that accompanies each order includes soup, salsa, rice, beans, veggies and coffee. The bright orange turmeric shots, however, are extra.

Prep & Pastry BREAKFAST $
(☎ 520-326-7737; www.prepandpastry.com; 3073 N Campbell Ave; mains $9.50-14; ⊙ 7am-3pm) Tucson's to-die-for breakfast spot takes no reservations, so you'll have to join Yelp's waitlist to get in line. Indulgences range from duck confit to croissant sammies and French toast (stuffed with nutella, or with green chilies), plus more health-oriented options like the quinoa bowl and chickpea scramble. Mimosas, Bloody Marys and champagne turn breakfast into brunch.

★**Cafe Poca Cosa** MEXICAN $$
(☎ 520-622-6400; www.cafepocacosatucson.com; 110 E Pennington St; lunch $16-20, dinner $22-30; ⊙ 11am-9pm Tue-Thu, to 10pm Fri & Sat) Chef Suzana Davila's award-winning nuevo-Mexican bistro is a must for fans of Mexican food in Tucson. A Spanish-English blackboard menu circulates between tables because dishes change twice daily – it's all freshly prepared, innovative and beautifully presented. The undecided can't go wrong by ordering the 'Plato Poca Cosa' and letting Suzana decide what's best. Great margaritas too.

El Charro Café MEXICAN $$
(☎ 520-622-1922; www.elcharrocafe.com; 311 N Court Ave; lunch $10-15, dinner $13-20; ⊙ 10am-9pm; 🌿) This rambling, buzzing hacienda has been making great Mexican food on this site since 1922. It's particularly famous for the *carne seca,* sundried lean beef that's been reconstituted, shredded and grilled with green chile and onions. The fabulous margaritas pack a burro-stunning punch, and help while away the time as you wait for your table. Vegan options too.

Drinking & Entertainment

Congress St in downtown and 4th Ave near the University of Arizona are both busy party strips.

★**Che's Lounge** BAR
(☎ 520-623-2088; www.cheslounge.com; 350 N 4th Ave; ⊙ noon-2am) This slightly grungy but hugely popular watering hole does cheap beer and features a huge wraparound bar and the Geronimo's Revenge food truck (Thursday to Sunday). A popular college hangout, Che's rocks with live music most Saturday nights and on the patio on Sunday afternoons (4pm to 7pm) in summer.

Tap & Bottle BAR
(☎ 520-344-8999; www.thetapandbottle.com; 403 N 6th Ave; ⊙ noon-11pm Sun-Wed, to midnight Thu-Sat) Come to this brick-walled hangout for a fantabulous selection of draft beers, plus Belgians and sours in the back store, as well as wines by the glass.

Monsoon Chocolate CAFE
(☎ 520-396-3189; www.monsoonchocolate.com; 234 E 22nd St; ⊙ 10am-6pm Mon-Fri, 8am-6pm Sat, 10am-4pm Sun; 📶) Delightful single-origin chocolatier in southern Tucson, where, depending on the weather, you can sample a tongue-tingling Mexican hot chocolate or, more likely, a Frocho (chocloate granita with coconut cream), along with decadent mezcal chocolates, choco tacos and even s'mores. Simple cafe fare and excellent coffee is also served. Vegan and gluten-free options too.

Club Congress LIVE MUSIC (☎520-622-8848; www.hotelcongress.com; 311 E Congress St; ⏱live music from 7pm, club nights from 10pm) Skinny jeansters, tousled hipsters, aging folkies, dressed-up hotties – the crowd at Tucson's most happening club inside the grandly aging Hotel Congress defines the word eclectic. And so does the musical line-up, which usually features the finest local and regional talent, and DJs some nights. And for a no-fuss drink, there's the Lobby Bar for cocktails, or the Tap Room, open since 1919.

ℹ Information

General information on Tucson is available from the **Arizona University Visitor Center** (☎520-624-1817; www.visittucson.org; 811 N Euclid Ave; ⏱9am-5pm Mon-Fri, to 4pm Sat & Sun), while specific information on access and camping in the Coronado National Forest can be found at the downtown **Coronado National Forest Supervisor's Office** (☎520-388-8300; www.fs.usda.gov/coronado; 300 W Congress St, Federal Bldg; ⏱8am-4:30pm Mon-Fri).

ℹ Getting There & Around

Tucson International Airport (☎520-573-8100; www.flytucson.com; 7250 S Tucson Blvd; 📶) is 8 miles south of downtown and served by six airlines, with nonstop flights to Chicago, Houston, Los Angeles and Seattle.

Greyhound (☎520-792-3475; www.greyhound.com; 801 E 12th St) runs 10 buses daily to Phoenix (from $12, two hours), among other destinations. **Flixbus** (www.flixbus.com; 1119 E 6th St, University of Arizona, 6th St Garage) gets slightly better reviews for the Phoenix trip ($10).

The *Sunset Limited*, operated by **Amtrak** (☎520-623-4442; www.amtrak.com; 400 N Toole Ave), comes through on its way west to Los Angeles (10 hours, three weekly) and east to New Orleans (36 hours, three weekly).

The **Ronstadt Transit Center** (215 E Congress St, at 6th Ave) is the main hub for the public buses with **Sun Tran** (☎520-792-9222; www.suntran.com) that serve the entire metro area. Single/day fares are $1.75/4 if paying cash or using a ticket machine. The same fares apply on the **SunLink** (⏱7am-10pm Mon-Wed, 7am-2am Thu & Fri, 8am-2am Sat, 8am-8pm Sun) streetcar line.

Around Tucson

All the places listed here are less than 1½ hours' drive from Tucson, and make great day trips.

Saguaro National Park

Saguaros (sah-*wah*-ros) are icons of the American Southwest, and an entire cactus army of these majestic, ribbed sentinels is protected in this desert **playground** (☎Rincon 520-733-5153, Tucson 520-733-5158, park information 520-733-5100; www.nps.gov/sagu; 7-day pass per vehicle/motorcycle/bicycle $20/15/10; ⏱sunrise-sunset). Or, more precisely, playgrounds: the park is divided into east and west units, separated by 30 miles and Tucson itself. Both sections – the Rincon Mountain District in the east and Tucson Mountain District in the west – are filled with trails and desert flora; if you only visit one, make it the spectacular western half.

The larger section is the **Rincon Mountain District**, about 15 miles east of downtown. The **Red Hills Visitor Center** (☎520-733-5158; www.nps.gov/sagu; 2700 N Kinney Rd; ⏱9am-5pm) has information about day hikes, horseback riding and backcountry camping. The camping requires a permit ($8 per site per day) and must be obtained by noon on the day of your hike. The meandering 8-mile **Cactus Forest Scenic Loop Drive**, a paved road open to cars and bicycles, provides access to picnic areas, trailheads and viewpoints.

Hikers pressed for time should follow the 1-mile round-trip **Freeman Homestead Trail** to a grove of massive saguaro. For a full-fledged desert adventure, head out on the steep and rocky Tanque Verde Ridge Trail, which climbs to the summit of Mica Mountain (8666ft) and back in 20 miles (backcountry camping permit required for overnight use). If you'd rather someone (or something) else did the hard work, family-run **Houston's Horseback Riding** (☎520-298-7450; www.tucsonhorsebackriding.com; 12801 E Speedway Bvd; per person 2hr tour $80) offers trail rides in the eastern section of the Park.

West of town, the **Tucson Mountain District** has its own branch of the Red Hills Visitor Center. The **Scenic Bajada Loop Drive** is a 6-mile graded dirt road through cactus forest that begins 1.5 miles north of the visitor center. Two quick, easy and rewarding hikes are the 0.8-mile **Valley View Overlook** (awesome at sunset) and the half-mile **Signal Hill Trail** to scores of ancient petroglyphs. For a more strenuous trek we recommend the 7-mile **King Canyon Trail**, which starts 2 miles south of the visitor center, near the Arizona-Sonora Desert Museum. The half-mile informative **Desert Discovery Trail**, which is one mile northwest of the visitor center, is wheelchair accessible. Distances for all four hikes are round-trip.

As for the park's namesake cactus, don't refer to the limbs of the saguaro as branches. As park docents will quickly tell you, the mighty saguaro grows arms, not lowly branches – a distinction that makes sense when you consider their human-like features.

Saguaros grow slowly, taking about 15 years to reach a foot in height, 50 years to reach 7ft and almost a century before they begin to take on their typical many-armed appearance. The best time to visit is April, when the cacti begin blossoming with lovely white blooms – Arizona's state flower. By June and July, the flowers give way to ripe red fruit that local Native Americans eat. Their foot soldiers are the spidery ocotillo, the fluffy teddy bear cactus, the green-bean-like pencil cholla and hundreds of other plant species. It is illegal to damage or remove saguaros.

Trailers longer than 35ft and vehicles wider than 8ft are not permitted on the park's narrow scenic loop drives.

West of Tuscon

You want wide solitude? Follow Hwy 86 west from Tuscon into some of the emptiest parts of the Sonoran Desert – except for the ubiquitous green-and-white border-patrol trucks. The lofty **Kitt Peak National Observatory** (520-318-8726; www.noao.edu/kpno; Hwy 86; tours adult/child $11/7; 9am-3:45pm), about a 75-minute drive from Tucson, features the largest collection of optical telescopes in the world. Guided tours last about an hour. Book two to four weeks in advance for the worthwhile nightly observing program (adult $50; no programs from mid-July through August).

Clear, dry skies equal an awe-inspiring glimpse of the cosmos. Dress warmly, buy gas in Tucson (the nearest gas station is 30 miles from the observatory) and note that children under eight years of age are not allowed at the evening program. The picnic area draws amateur astronomers at night

To truly want to get away from it all, you can't get much further off the grid than the huge and exotic **Organ Pipe Cactus National Monument** (520-387-6849; www.nps.gov/orpi; Hwy 85; per vehicle $25) along the Mexican border. It's a gorgeous, forbidding land that supports an astonishing number of animals and plants, including 28 species of cacti, first and foremost its namesake organ-pipe. A giant columnar cactus, it differs from the more prevalent saguaro in that its branches radiate from the base.

The 21-mile **Ajo Mountain Drive** takes you through a spectacular landscape of steep-sided, jagged cliffs and rock tinged a faintly hellish red. There are 208 first-come, first-served sites at **Twin Peaks Campground** (877-444-6777; www.recreation.gov; 10 Organ Pipe Dr; tent & RV sites $20) by the visitor center.

DON'T MISS

MINI TIME MACHINE OF MUSEUM OF MINIATURES

Divided into the Enchanted Realm, Exploring the World and the History Gallery, this delightful **museum of miniatures** (520-881-0606; www.theminitimemachine.org; 4455 E Camp Lowell Dr, Tucson; adult/senior/child $10.50/8.50/7; 9am-4pm Tue-Sat, from 10am Sun) presents dioramas that are fantastical, historical and plain intriguing. You can also walk over a snow-globey Christmas village, peer into tiny homes constructed in the 1700s and 1800s, and search for the little inhabitants of a magical tree. The museum grew from a personal collection in the 1930s. Parents may find themselves having more fun than the kids.

South of Tuscon

The magnificent **Mission San Xavier del Bac** (520-294-2624; www.patronatosanxavier.org; 1950 W San Xavier Rd; donations appreciated; museum 8:30am-4:30pm, church 7am-5pm), on the San Xavier reservation 8 miles south of Tucson, is Arizona's oldest Hispanic-era building still in use. Completed in 1797, it's a graceful blend of Moorish, Byzantine and late-Mexican Renaissance architecture, with an unexpectedly ornate interior.

At exit 69, 16 miles south of the mission, the **Titan Missile Museum** (520-625-7736; www.titanmissilemuseum.org; 1580 Duval Mine Rd, Sahuarita; adult/senior/child $10.50/9.50/7; 9:45am-5pm Sun-Fri, from 8:45am Sat, last tour 3:45pm Nov-Apr, shorter hrs May-Oct) features an underground launch site for Cold War–era intercontinental ballistic missiles. Tours are chilling, informative and should be booked ahead.

HOT DIGGITY DOG

El Guero Canelo (☎520-295-9005; www.elguerocanelo.com; 5201 S 12th Ave; hot dogs $3.50-4, mains $7.75-10.50; ⏲10am-10pm Sun-Thu, 8:30am-midnight Fri & Sat) serves Tucson's signature dish, the Sonoran hot dog, a tasty example of what happens when Mexico's cuisine meets America's penchant for excess. It's a bacon-wrapped hot dog layered with tomatillo salsa, pinto beans, shredded cheese, mayo, ketchup, mustard, chopped tomatoes and onions. A specialty so popular it's spawned three more locations in Tucson; El Guero Canelo is the place to try them.

If history or shopping for crafts interest you, head 48 miles south of Tucson to the small village of Tubac (www.tubacaz.com), with more than 100 galleries, studios and shops clustered around a Spanish Colonial-era Presidio.

Patagonia & the Mountain Empire

This lovely riparian region, sandwiched between the Mexican border and the Santa Rita and Patagonia Mountains, is one of the shiniest gems in Arizona's jewel box. It's a tranquil destination for bird-watching and wine tasting. Bird-watchers and nature-lovers wander the gentle trails at the **Patagonia-Sonoita Creek Preserve** (☎520-394-2400; www.nature.org/arizona; 150 Blue Heaven Rd, Patagonia; $8; ⏲6:30am-4pm Wed-Sun Apr-Sep, 7:30am-4pm Wed-Sun Oct-Mar), an enchanting creekside willow and cottonwood forest managed by the Nature Conservancy. The peak migratory seasons are April through May, and late August through September.

For a leisurely afternoon of wine tasting, head to the villages and surrounding wineries of **Sonoita** and **Elgin**, north of Patagonia. If you're in Patagonia for dinner, try the satisfying gourmet pizzas at **Velvet Elvis** (☎520-394-0069; www.facebook.com/velvetelvispizza; 292 Naugle Ave, Patagonia; pizzas $12-26; ⏲11:30am-8:30pm Thu-Sun; 📶). Then get comfortable in the spacious rooms and inviting gardens at the **Duquesne House** (☎520-394-2732; www.theduquesnehouse.com; 357 Duquesne Ave, Patagonia; r $140; ❄@📶), a former boarding house for miners.

A small **visitor center** (☎520-394-7750; www.patagoniaaz.com; 299 McKeown Ave, Patagonia; ⏲10am-4pm daily Oct-May, Fri-Sun Jun-Sep) provides information.

Southeastern Arizona

Chockablock with places that loom large in Wild West folklore, southeastern Arizona is home to the wonderfully preserved mining town of Bisbee, the OK Corral in Tombstone, and a wonderland of stone spires at Chiricahua National Monument.

Kartchner Caverns State Park

This wonderland of spires, shields, pipes, columns, soda straws and other ethereal formations has been five million years in the making, but miraculously wasn't discovered until 1974. In fact, its very location was kept secret for another 25 years in order to prepare for its opening as **Kartchner Caverns State Park** (☎information 520-586-4100, reservations 877-697-2757; www.azstateparks.com/kartchner; 2980 Hwy 90; per vehicle $7, tours adult/child $23/13; ⏲park 7am-6pm, visitor center 8am-6pm late Dec–mid-May, shorter hrs rest of year). Two tours are available, both about 90 minutes long and equally impressive.

The Big Room tour closes to the public around mid-April, when a colony of migrating female cave myotis bats starts arriving from Mexico to roost and give birth to pups in late June. Mom and baby bats hang out until mid-September before flying off to their wintering spot. While a bat nursery, the cave is closed to the public.

There's a campground (with cabins) and the entrance is 9 miles south of I-10, off Hwy 90, exit 302.

Tombstone

Dubbing itself 'The Town too Tough to Die,' Tombstone was a booming mining town during its 19th-century heyday, when the whiskey flowed and six-shooters blazed over disputes large and small, most famously at the OK Corral. Now a National Historic Landmark, it attracts hordes of tourists to its old Western buildings, stagecoach rides and gunfight reenactments.

And yes, you must visit the **OK Corral** (☎520-457-3456; www.ok-corral.com; Allen St, btwn 3rd & 4th Sts; with/without gunfight $10/6; ⏲10am-4pm), site of the legendary gunfight where the Earps and Doc Holliday took on the McLaurys and Billy Clanton on October

26, 1881. The McClaurys, Clanton and many other casualties of those violent days now rest at the **Boothill Graveyard** (520-457-3300; www.tombstoneboothillgiftshop.com; 408 Hwy 80; adult/child $3/free; 8am-6pm) on Hwy 80 north of town.

Also make time for the dusty **Bird Cage Theater** (520-457-3421; www.tombstonebirdcage.com; 517 E Allen St; adult $14, senior & child $12; 9am-6pm), a one-time dance hall, saloon and bordello crammed with historic odds and ends. And a merman. The **Visitor Center** (888-457-3929; www.tombstonechamber.com; 395 E Allen St, at 4th St; 9am-4pm Mon-Thu, to 5pm Fri-Sun) has walking maps.

Bisbee

Oozing untidy, unforced old-world charm, Bisbee is a former copper-mining town that's now a delightful mix of aging bohemians, elegant buildings, sumptuous restaurants and charming hotels. Most businesses are in the Historic District (Old Bisbee), along Subway and Main Sts.

To burrow under the earth in a tour led by the retirees who once mined here, take the **Queen Mine Tour** (520-432-2071; www.queenminetour.com; 478 Dart Rd, off Hwy 80; adult/child $13/5.50; 9am-5pm). The Queen Mine Building, just south of downtown, also holds the local **visitor center** (520-432-3554; www.discoverbisbee.com; 478 Dart Rd; 8am-5pm Mon-Fri, 10am-4pm Sat & Sun), and is the obvious place to start exploring. Right outside of town, check out the **Lavender Pit**, an ugly yet impressive testament to strip mining.

Rest your head at **Shady Dell RV Park** (520-432-3567; www.theshadydell.com; 1 Douglas Rd, Lowell; trailers $105-145; closed summer & winter;), a retro trailer park where meticulously restored Airstream trailers are neatly fenced off and kitted out with fun furnishings. Swamp coolers provide cold air. You can sleep in a covered wagon at the quirky but fun **Bisbee Grand Hotel** (520-432-5900; www.bisbeegrandhotel.com; 61 Main St; d/ste from $94/135;), which brings the Old West to life with Victorian-era decor and a kick-up-your spurs saloon.

For good food, stroll up Main St and pick a restaurant – you can't go wrong. For fine American food, try stylish **Cafe Roka** (520-432-5153; www.caferoka.com; 35 Main St; mains $18.50-31.50; 5-9pm Wed-Sat, 4-8pm Sun), where four-course dinners include salad, soup, sorbet and a rotating choice of crowd-pleasing mains. Continue up Main St for wood-fired pizzas and punk-rock style at **Screaming Banshee** (520-432-1300; www.screamingbansheepizza.net; 200 Tombstone Canyon Rd; pizzas $14-19; 4-9pm Wed, 11am-10pm Thu-Sun). Bars cluster in the aptly named Brewery Gulch, at the south end of Main St.

Chiricahua National Monument

The towering rock spires at remote but mesmerizing **Chiricahua National Monument** (520-824-3560; www.nps.gov/chir; 12856 E Rhyolite Creek Rd; visitor center 8:30am-4:30pm;) FREE in the Chiricahua Mountains sometimes rise hundreds of feet high and often look like they're on the verge of tipping over. The **Bonita Canyon Scenic Drive** takes you 8 miles to Massai Point (6870ft) where you'll see thousands of spires positioned on the slopes like some petrified army. There are numerous hiking trails, but if you're short on time, hike the **Echo Canyon Trail** at least half a mile to the Grottoes, an amazing 'cathedral' of giant boulders where you can lie still and enjoy the wind-caressed silence. The monument is 36 miles southeast of Willcox off Hwy 186/181.

UTAH

Welcome to nature's perfect playground. From red-rock mesas to skinny slot canyons, powder-bound slopes and slickrock trails, Utah's diverse terrain will stun you. The biking, hiking and skiing are world-class. And with more than 65% of the state lands public, including 14 national parks and monuments, the access is simply superb.

Southern Utah is defined by red-rock cliffs, sorbet-colored spindles and seemingly endless sandstone desert. The pine-forested and snow-covered peaks of the Wasatch Mountains dominate northern Utah. Interspersed are old pioneer remnants, ancient rock art and ruins, and traces of dinosaurs.

Mormon-influenced rural towns can be quiet and conservative, but the rugged beauty has attracted outdoorsy progressives as well. Salt Lake City (SLC) and Park City, especially, have vibrant nightlife and progressive dining scenes. So pull on your boots and stock up on water: Utah's wild and scenic hinterlands await.

History

Traces of the Ancestral Puebloan and Fremont peoples, this land's earliest human inhabitants, remain in the rock art and ruins they left behind. But the modern Ute, Paiute and Navajo tribes were living here when settlers of European heritage arrived in large numbers. Led by Brigham Young (second president of the Mormon church), Mormons fled to this territory to escape religious persecution starting in the late 1840s. They set out to settle every inch of their new land, no matter how inhospitable, which resulted in skirmishes with Native Americans – and more than one abandoned ghost town.

For nearly 50 years after the United States acquired the Utah Territory from Mexico, petitions for statehood were rejected due to the Mormon practice of polygamy (taking multiple wives). Tension and prosecutions grew until 1890, when Mormon leader Wilford Woodruff had a divine revelation and the church officially discontinued the practice. Utah became the 45th state in 1896. The modern Mormon church, now called the Church of Jesus Christ of Latter-Day Saints (LDS), continues to exert a strong influence.

Information

Utah Office of Tourism (☎800-200-1160; www.utah.com) Publishes the free *Utah Travel Guide* and runs several visitor centers statewide. The website has links in six languages.

Utah State Parks & Recreation Department (☎801-538-7220; www.stateparks.utah.gov) Produces a guide to the 40-plus state parks; available online and at visitor centers.

UTAH FACTS

Nickname Beehive State

Population 3.16 million

Area 84,900 sq miles

Capital city Salt Lake City (population 200,591), metro area (1,152,633)

Other cities St George (population 84,400

Sales tax 4.85%

Birthplace of Entertainers Donny (b 1957) and Marie (b 1959) Osmond, beloved bandit Butch Cassidy (1866–1908)

Home of 2002 Winter Olympic Games

Politics Mostly conservative

Famous for Mormons, red-rock canyons, polygamy

Best souvenir Wasatch Brew Pub T-shirt: 'Polygamy Porter – Why Have Just One?'

Getting There & Around

International flights from Mexico, Canada, England, France and Holland land in Salt Lake City's airport (p201), as do domestic flights. Larger cities and tourist hubs have car-rental offices. An Amtrak train (www.amtrak.com) stops daily in Salt Lake City en route between Oakland, CA (19 hours) and Chicago (34 hours). Greyhound (www.greyound.com) runs long-distance service from Salt Lake City to Las Vegas, NV (eight hours), and Denver, CO (10½ hours).

Utah is not a large state, but it is largely rural – so unless you're staying in Salt Lake City or Park City, you'll need a car. If you're headed to the parks in southern Utah, your cheapest bet may be to fly into Las Vegas, and rent a ride there.

Salt Lake City

Sparkling Salt Lake City (SLC), with its bluebird skies and powder-dusted mountains, is Utah's capital city. The only Utah city with an international airport, it still manages to emanate a small-town feel. Downtown is easy to get around and fairly quiet come evening. It's hard to grasp that some 1.2 million people live in the metro area. While it's the Mormon equivalent of Vatican City, and the Church of Jesus Christ of Latter-Day Saints (LDS) owns a lot of land, less than half the population are church members. The university and excellent outdoor access have attracted a wide range of residents. A liberal spirit permeates the coffeehouses and yoga classes, where elaborate tattoos are the norm. Foodies find much to love among the multitude of international and organic dining options. And when the trail beckons, it's a scant 45 minutes from the Wasatch Mountains' brilliant hiking and skiing. Friendly people, great food and outdoor adventure – what could be better?

Sights & Activities

Mormon Church–related sights cluster mostly near the town center point for SLC addresses: the intersection of Main and South Temple Sts. (Streets are so wide – 132ft – because they were originally built so that four oxen pulling a wagon could turn around.) The downtown hub underwent a renaissance with the development of City Creek. To the east, the University-Foothills District has most of the museums and kid-friendly attractions.

Temple Square Area

Temple Square PLAZA

(www.visittemplesquare.com; cnr S Temple & N State Sts; grounds 24hr, visitor center 9am-9pm) FREE The city's most famous sight occupies a 10-acre block surrounded by 15ft-high walls. LDS docents give free, 30-minute tours continually, leaving from the visitor center at the entrance on North Temple St. Sisters, brothers and elders are stationed every 20ft or so to answer questions. (Don't worry, no one is going to try to convert you – unless you express interest.) The temple is closed for renovation from 2020 to 2024 but Temple Square's other sights remain open.

Church History Museum MUSEUM

(801-240-3310; https://history.lds.org/section/museum; 45 N West Temple St; 9am-9pm Mon-Fri, 10am-6pm Sat) FREE Adjoining Temple Sq (p197), this interactive museum has impressive exhibits of pioneer history and fine art.

Salt Lake Temple RELIGIOUS SITE

(801-240-2640; https://churchofjesuschristtemples.org/salt-lake-temple; 50 W North Temple St, Temple Sq) Lording over Temple Sq (p197) is the impressive 210ft-tall Salt Lake Temple. Atop the tallest spire stands a statue of the angel Moroni, who appeared to LDS founder Joseph Smith. Rumor has it that when the place was renovated, cleaners found old bullet marks in one of the gold-plated surfaces. The temple and ceremonies are private, open only to LDS members in good standing. The temple is closed for renovation from 2020 to 2024 to make it more earthquake-resistant.

Tabernacle CHRISTIAN SITE

(www.mormontabernaclechoir.org; Temple Sq; 9am-9pm) FREE The domed, 1867 auditorium – with a massive 11,000-pipe organ – has incredible acoustics. A pin dropped in the front can be heard in the back, almost 200ft away. Free daily organ recitals are held at noon Monday through Saturday, and at 2pm Sunday.

Beehive House HISTORIC SITE

(801-240-2681; www.lds.org/visitbeehivehouse; 67 E South Temple St; 10am-6pm Mon-Sat) FREE Brigham Young lived with one of his wives and families in the Beehive House during much of his tenure as governor and church president in Utah. The required tours vary; some offer historic house details over religious education, depending on the LDS docent.

Greater Downtown

Utah State Capitol HISTORIC BUILDING

(801-538-1800; www.utahstatecapitol.utah.gov; 350 N State St; 7am-8pm Mon-Thu, to 6pm Fri, 8am-6pm Sat & Sun, visitor center 9am-5pm Mon-Fri) FREE The grand, 1916 State Capitol is set among 500 cherry trees on a hill north of Temple Sq. Inside, colorful Works Progress Administration (WPA) murals of pioneers, trappers and missionaries adorn part of the building's dome. Free guided tours (hourly, 9am to 4pm, Monday to Friday) start at the 1st-floor visitor center; self-guided tours are available from the visitor center.

Clark Planetarium MUSEUM

(385-468-7827; www.clarkplanetarium.org; 110 S 400 W; adult/child $9/7; 10:30am-7pm Sun-Wed, to 11pm Thu-Sat) You'll be seeing stars at Clark Planetarium, home to the latest and greatest 3-D sky shows. There are free science exhibits and an IMAX theater, too. The planetarium is on the edge of the **Gateway** (801-456-0000; www.shopthegateway.com; 400 W 100 S; 10am-9pm Mon-Sat, noon-6pm Sun), a combination indoor-outdoor shopping complex anchored by the old railway depot.

University-Foothill District & Beyond

★Natural History Museum of Utah MUSEUM

(801-581-6927; www.nhmu.utah.edu; 301 Wakara Way, Rio Tinto Center; adult/child 3-12yr $15/10; 10am-5pm Thu-Tue, to 9pm Wed; P) Rio Tinto Center's stunning architecture forms a multistory indoor 'canyon' that showcases exhibits to great effect. Walk up through the layers as you explore both indigenous peoples' cultures and natural history. Past Worlds paleontological displays are the most impressive – an incredible perspective from beneath, next to and above a vast collection of dinosaur fossils offers the full breadth of prehistory.

This is the Place Heritage Park HISTORIC SITE

(801-582-1847; www.thisistheplace.org; 2601 E Sunnyside Ave; adult/child $14/10; 10am-5pm; P) Dedicated to the 1847 arrival of the Mormons, this heritage park covers 450 acres. The centerpiece is a living-history village where, June through August, costumed docents depict mid-19th-century life. Admission includes a tourist-train ride and activities. The rest of the year, access is limited to varying degrees at varyingly reduced prices; you'll at least be able to wander around the exterior of some 50 historic homes. Some are replicas, but some are originals, such as Brigham Young's farmhouse.

Red Butte Garden GARDENS
(www.redbuttegarden.org; 300 Wakara Way; adult/child $14/7; 9am-5pm Oct-Mar, to 7:30pm Apr & Sep, to 9pm May-Aug; P) Both landscaped and natural gardens cover a lovely 100 acres, with access to 5 miles of trails in the Wasatch foothills. Check online to see who's playing at the popular, outdoor summer concert series also held here. Daylight hours in low season and on concert days.

Sleeping

Downtown chain properties cluster around S 200 W near 500 S and 600 S; there are more in Mid-Valley (off I-215) and near the airport. At high-end hotels, rates are lowest on weekends. Parking downtown is often not included. Look for camping and alternative lodging in the Wasatch Mountains.

Kimball Condominiums CONDO $
(801-363-4000; www.thekimball.com; 150 N Main St; apt from $95; P) Just a half block from Temple Sq, these fully furnished condos range from older studio suites with wall beds to larger remodeled two-bedroom units that sleep up to six guests. All have kitchens and the location couldn't be better. Rates vary.

★ **Engen Hus** B&B $$
(801-450-6703; www.engenhusutah.com; 2275 E 6200 S; r $139-179;) Ideally positioned for mountain jaunts, this lovely home features four rooms with handmade quilts on log beds and flat-screen TVs. Hosts are knowledgeable about local hiking. The cozy quotient is high, with board games, a hot-tub deck and DIY laundry. Dig the buffet breakfast with the likes of caramel French toast. Has a room that's accessible to travelers in wheelchairs.

★ **Inn on the Hill** INN $$
(801-328-1466; www.inn-on-the-hill.com; 225 N State St; r $150-260; P@) Exquisite woodwork and Maxfield Parrish Tiffany glass adorn this sprawling, 1906 Renaissance Revival mansion-turned-inn. Guest rooms are classically comfortable, not stuffy, with jetted tubs and some fireplaces and balconies. Great shared spaces include patios, a billiard room, a library and a dining room where chef-cooked breakfasts are served.

DeSoto Tudor HOMESTAY $$
(801-503-9810, 801-835-4009; www.desototudoroncapitolhill.com; 545 DeSoto St E; ste $159;) Your on-site hosts Vince and Ken don't miss a beat during your stay in this homey one-bedroom suite on Capitol Hill. Expect an excellent breakfast, a generous supply of drinks and snacks stocked in the kitchen, a private outdoor hot tub overlooking the city and highly amusing conversation.

Hotel RL HOTEL $$
(801-521-7373; www.redlion.com/salt-lake; 161 W 600 S; r from $135; P@) Sleek comfort

SALT LAKE CITY FOR KIDS

Salt Lake is very child-friendly city. The wonderful hands-on exhibits at the **Discovery Gateway** (801-456-5437; www.discoverygateway.org; 444 W 100 S; $12.50; 10am-6pm Mon-Thu, to 7pm Fri & Sat, noon-6pm Sun;) stimulate imaginations and senses.

Kids can help farmhands milk cows at **Wheeler Historic Farm** (385-468-1755; www.wheelerfarm.com; 6351 S 900 E; wagon ride $3, house tour adult/child $4/2; dawn-dusk;) FREE, which dates from 1898. There's also tractor-drawn wagon rides in summer.

More than 800 animals inhabit zones such as the Asian Highlands on the landscaped 42-acre grounds at **Hogle Zoo** (801-584-1700; www.hoglezoo.org; 2600 Sunnyside Ave; adult/child $17/13; 9am-6pm Mar-Oct, 10am-5pm Nov-Feb; P). Daily animal encounter programs help kids learn more about their favorite species.

Tracy Aviary (801-596-8500; www.tracyaviary.org; 589 E 1300 S; adult/child $12/8; 9am-5pm;) lets little ones toss fish to the pelicans as one of its interactive programs and performances. Winged creatures from around the world call this bird park home.

With 55 acres of gardens, a full-scale working and petting farm, golf course, giant movie theater, museum, dining, shopping and a **Butterfly Biosphere** (801-768-2300; adult/child $20/15; 10am-8pm Mon-Sat; P), what doesn't Thanksgiving Point, located in Lehi, have? The on-site Museum of Ancient Life (p199) is one of the highest-tech and most hands-on dinosaur museums in the state. Lehi is 28 miles south of downtown SLC; to get there take exit 287 off I-15.

in a remodeled Red Lion hotel with almost 400 rooms, which feature black-and-white wall murals and flat-screen TVs. There's a classic diner attached, a modern-woodsy design lounge, 24-hour gym and outdoor pool and Jacuzzi. As big box hotels go, this one delivers.

Eating

Tosh's Ramen RAMEN $
(801-466-7000; www.toshsramen.com; 1465 S State St; mains $9-15; 11:30am-3pm & 5-9pm Mon-Sat; P) Ecstasy by the steaming oversized bowl, Tosh's ramen comes with silken broth and crunchy sprouts, topped with a poached egg if you like it that way. It couldn't get more authentic. Try to carve out some room for an order of sweet and spicy wings. Everyone is drawn to this happy place in a nondescript strip mall, so go early.

Oh Mai VIETNAMESE $
(801-467-6882; www.ohmaisandwich.com; 3425 State St; sandwiches $5-7; 10am-9pm Mon-Sat; P) This Vietnamese sandwich kitchen prepares crunchy banh mi baguettes with sweet and spicy fillings such as braised pork belly and jalapeño (that would be 'the sinner' sandwich), or opt for one of their vegan or vegetarian sammies. Oh Mai has other branches in town but many prefer the authenticity of the original South Salt Lake location.

Over the Counter Cafe BREAKFAST $
(801-487-8725; www.overthecountercafe.weebly.com; 2343 E 3300 S; mains $5-10; 6:30am-2pm; P) Hugely popular greasy spoon with booth seating and a convivial counter around an open grill. Regulars love the ancient-grains pancakes, blueberry-lemon French toast with fresh berries and the Flintstones-size ham steaks.

★**Red Iguana** MEXICAN $$
(801-322-1489; www.rediguana.com; 736 W North Temple St; mains $10-18; 11am-10pm Mon-Thu, to 11pm Fri & Sat, 9am-9pm Sun) Mexico at its most authentic, aromatic and delicious – no wonder the line is usually snaking out the door at this family-run restaurant. Ask for samples of the mole to decide on one of six chili- and chocolate-based sauces. The incredibly tender *cochinita pibil* (shredded roast pork) tastes like it's been roasting for days.

Del Mar al Lago PERUVIAN $$
(801-467-2890; www.facebook.com/delmar.al.lago; 310 W Bugatti Dr; mains $16-25; 11am-4pm & 6-9pm Mon-Thu, 11am-10pm Fri & Sat; P) Get ready for a treat. Chef Wilmer from Trujillo cooks up Peru's best dishes, including ceviche (fish marinated in lime), yucca fries and *causas* (seasoned mashed potatoes) with jalapeño aioli, and the Peruvian patrons say it's authentic.

White Horse AMERICAN $$
(801-363-0137; www.whitehorseslc.com; 325 Main St; mains $10-28; 11am-1am;) Shelves stacked high with top-notch spirits invite you to belly up to the counter and try one of the innovative cocktails mixed here. The trendy downtown spot serves excellent food as well, such as the Wagyu cheeseburger with smoked pork-belly bacon.

DON'T MISS

MUSEUM OF ANCIENT LIFE

This family-friendly **museum** (801-768-2300; www.thanksgivingpoint.org; 3003 N Thanksgiving Way, Lehi; museum only adult/child $20/15; 10am-8pm Mon-Sat; P) houses one of the world's largest displays of mounted dinosaurs. The exhibits, many of which are hands-on, are arranged chronologically and teach about fossils found all over the world. Little ones can dig for their own bones, search for hidden gnomes within the exhibits and practice paleontology in a Saturday lab (for an additional cost).

Drinking & Nightlife

Brewpubs and bars that also serve food are mainstays of SLC's nightlife, and no one minds if you mainly drink and nibble. A complete schedule of local bar music is available in the *City Weekly* (www.cityweekly.net).

★**Fisher Brewing Company** BREWERY
(801-487-2337; www.fisherbeer.com; 320 W 800 S; 11am-10pm Sun-Thu, to 1am Fri & Sat) A former auto shop in the Granary District has been converted into an employee-owned, small-batch brewery that produces the freshest beer around. Following in the footsteps of his great-great-grandfather Albert Fisher, a German immigrant who ran A. Fisher Brewing Company from 1884 to 1967, Tony Fisher and partners have revived a family tradition but on a smaller, more intimate scale.

Beer Bar PUB

(☎801-355-2287; www.beerbarslc.com; 161 E 200 S; ⏰11am-1am) With shared wooden tables and more than 140 beers and 13 sausage styles, Beer Bar is a hip little slice of Bavaria in Salt Lake City. The crowd is diverse and far more casual than at Bar X (p200) next door (a linked venue). A great place to meet friends and make friends, but it gets pretty loud.

Bar X COCKTAIL BAR

(☎801-355-2287; www.beerbarslc.com; 155 E 200 S; ⏰4pm-1am Mon-Sat, 7pm-1am Sun) So low-lit and funky, it's hard to believe you're down the street from Temple Sq (p197). Cozy up to the crowded bar with a Moscow Mule and listen to Motown or funk (or the guy at the next table saying to his date, 'Your voice is pretty').

Jack Mormon Coffee Co COFFEE

(☎801-359-2979; www.jackmormoncoffee.com; 82 E St; ⏰8am-6pm Mon-Sat; 📶) Utah's finest roaster also serves mean espresso drinks. When the temps rise, locals binge on a Jack Frost.

☆ Entertainment

Salt Lake City is as good as it gets in Utah when it comes to dance-club and live-music offerings. See the *City Weekly* (www.cityweekly.net) for listings. You'll also find a fair share of sporting events throughout the year. Classical entertainment options, especially around Temple Sq (p197), are plentiful.

> **THE BOOK OF MORMON, THE MUSICAL**
>
> Singing and dancing Mormon missionaries? You betcha…at least on Broadway. In the spring of 2011, *The Book of Mormon* musical opened to critical acclaim at the Eugene O'Neill Theatre in New York. The light-hearted satire about LDS missionaries in Uganda came out of the comic minds that also created the musical *Avenue Q* and the animated TV series *South Park*. No wonder people laughed them all the way to nine Tony Awards.
>
> The LDS church's official response? Actually quite measured, avoiding any direct criticism – though it was made clear that their belief is that while 'the Book, the musical' can entertain you, the scriptures of the actual Book of Mormon can change your life.

Music

★Mormon Tabernacle Choir LIVE MUSIC

(☎801-570-0080, 801-240-4150; www.tabernaclechoir.org) Hearing the world-renowned Mormon Tabernacle Choir is a must-do on any SLC bucket list. A live choir broadcast goes out every Sunday at 9:30am. September through November, and January through May, attend in person at the Tabernacle (p197). Free public rehearsals are held here from 7:30pm to 8:30pm Thursday.

Garage on Beck LIVE MUSIC

(☎801-521-3904; www.garageonbeck.com; 1199 Beck St; ⏰11am-1am) A former auto repair garage where you can catch live music performances on weekends in the rear patio. Note that this roadhouse bar and grill has limited parking.

Theater

There are concerts on Temple Sq (p197), at the **Library** (☎891-524-8200; www.slcpl.org; 210 E 400 S; ⏰9am-9pm Mon-Thu, 9am-6pm Fri & Sat, 1-5pm Sun; 👪) and in Red Butte Garden (p198) in the summertime. The Salt Lake City Arts Council provides a complete cultural events calendar on its website (www.slcgov.com/calendars). Most tickets can be reserved through **ArtTix** (☎801-355-2787, 385-468-1010; www.artsaltlake.org).

Eccles Theatre THEATER

(☎385-468-1010; www.artsaltlake.org; 131 S Main St) Opened in 2016, this gorgeous building has two theaters (one seating 2500 people), showing Broadway shows, concerts and other entertainment.

Sports

Utah Jazz BASKETBALL

(☎801-325-2500; www.nba.com/jazz; 301 S Temple St) Utah Jazz, the men's professional basketball team, plays at the **Vivint Smart Home Arena** (☎801-325-2000; www.vivintarena.com; 301 S Temple St), where concerts are also held.

Real Salt Lake SOCCER

(☎844-732-5849; www.rsl.com; 9256 State St, Rio Tinto Stadium; ⏰Mar-Oct) Salt Lake's winning Major League Soccer team (*ree*-al) has a loyal local following and matches are fun to take in at the **Rio Tinto Stadium** (☎801-727-2700; www.riotintostadium.com; 9256 State St, Sandy).

🔒 Shopping

An interesting array of boutiques, antiques and cafes line up along Broadway Ave (300

South), between 100 and 300 East. Drawing on Utah pioneer heritage, SLC has quite a few crafty shops and galleries scattered around; a few can be found on the 300 block of W Pierpont Ave. Many participate in the one-day **Craft Lake City Festival** (www.craftlakecity.com) in August.

Information

EMERGENCY & MEDICAL SERVICES

Local Police (801-799-3000; www.slcpd.com; 475 S 300 E; office 8am-5pm Mon-Fri)

Salt Lake Regional Medical Center (801-350-4111; www.saltlakeregional.org; 1050 E South Temple St; 24hr emergency)

University of Utah Hospital (801-581-2121; www.healthcare.utah.edu; 50 N Medical Dr)

TOURIST INFORMATION

Public Lands Information Center Recreation information for nearby public lands (state parks, BLM, USFS), including the Wasatch-Cache National Forest.

Visit Salt Lake (801-534-4900; www.visitsaltlake.com; 90 S West Temple St, Salt Palace Convention Center; 9am-5pm) Publishes a free visitor-guide booklet; large gift shop on-site at the visitor center.

Getting There & Around

Five miles northwest of downtown, **Salt Lake City International Airport** (SLC; 801-575-2400; www.slcairport.com; 776 N Terminal Dr;) has mostly domestic flights, though you can fly direct to Canada, Mexico, England, France and Holland. **Express Shuttle** (801-596-1600; www.expressshuttleutah.com; shared van to downtown $13-20) runs shared van services to the airport.

Greyhound (800-231-2222; www.greyhound.com; 300 S 600 W;) has buses to nationwide destinations. The **Union Pacific Rail Depot** (www.amtrak.com; 340 S 600 W) is serviced daily by **Amtrak** (800-231-2222; www.amtrak.com; 340 S 600 W) trains heading to Denver and California.

Utah Transit Authority (UTA; 801-743-3882; www.rideuta.com;) runs light-rail services to the international airport and downtown area. Bus 550 travels downtown from the parking structure between Terminals 1 and 2.

Park City & Wasatch Mountains

Utah offers some of North America's most awesome skiing, with fabulous low-density, low-moisture snow – between 300in and 500in annually – and thousands of acres of high-altitude terrain. The Wasatch Mountain Range, which towers over SLC, holds numerous ski resorts, abundant hiking, camping and mountain biking – not to mention chichi Park City, with its upscale amenities and famous film festival.

Salt Lake City Resorts

Because of Great Salt Lake–affected snow patterns, these resorts receive almost twice as much snow as Park City. The four resorts east of Salt Lake City sit 30 to 45 miles from the downtown core at the end of two canyons. In summer, access the numerous hiking and biking trails that lead off from both canyons.

Activities

★Alta SNOW SPORTS

(801-359-1078; www.alta.com; Little Cottonwood Canyon; day lift ticket adult/child $116/60) Dyed-in-the-wool skiers make a pilgrimage to Alta, at the top of the valley. No snowboarders are allowed here, which keeps the snow cover from deteriorating, especially on groomers. Wide-open powder fields, gullies, chutes and glades, such as **East Greeley**, **Devil's Castle** and **High Rustler**, have helped make Alta famous. Warning: you may never want to ski anywhere else.

★Snowbird SNOW SPORTS

(800-232-9542; www.snowbird.com; Hwy 210, Little Cottonwood Canyon; day lift ticket adult/child $125/60) The biggest and busiest of all the Salt Lake City resorts, with all-round great snow riding – think steep and deep. Numerous lift-assist summer hiking trails; aerial tramway runs year-round.

Solitude SNOW SPORTS

(801-534-1400; www.skisolitude.com; 12000 Big Cottonwood Canyon Rd; day lift ticket adult/child $109/75) Exclusive, European-style village surrounded by excellent terrain. The **Nordic Center** (801-536-5774; www.solitudemountain.com/winter-activities/nordic-skiing-nordic-center; day pass adult/child $20/15; 8:30am-4:30pm Dec–mid-Apr) has cross-country skiing in winter and nature trails in summer.

Brighton SNOW SPORTS

(801-532-4731; www.brightonresort.com; 8302 S Brighton Loop Rd; day lift-ticket adult $94, child under 11yr free;) Slackers, truants and boarders rule at Brighton. But don't be intimidated: the low-key resort where many Salt Lake residents first learned to ski remains a good first-timers' spot, especially if you want to snowboard. Thick stands of pines line sweeping groomed trails and wide boulevards, and from the top, the views are gorgeous.

Park City

With a dusting of snow, the century-old buildings on main street create a snow-globe scene come to life. A one-time silver boom-and-bust town, pretty Park City is now lined with condos and mansions in the valleys. Utah's premier ski village boasts fabulous restaurants and cultural offerings. It recently annexed the adjacent Canyons Resort to become the largest ski resort in North America.

Park City first shot to international fame when it hosted the downhill, jumping and sledding events at the 2002 Winter Olympics. Today it's the permanent home base for the US Ski Team. There's usually snow through mid-April.

Come summer, more residents than visitors gear up for hiking and mountain biking among the nearby peaks. June to August, temperatures average in the 70s (Fahrenheit; 20s Celsius); nights are chilly. Spring and fall can be wet and boring; resort services, limited in summer compared with winter, shut down entirely between seasons.

Sights

★Utah Olympic Park AMUSEMENT PARK

(☎435-658-4200; www.utaholympiclegacy.org; 3419 Olympic Pkwy; museum free, activity day-pass adult/child $80/55; ⏰9am-6pm, tours 11am-4pm) Visit the site of the 2002 Olympic ski jumping, bobsledding, skeleton, Nordic combined and luge events, which continues to host national competitions. There are 10m, 20m, 40m, 64m, 90m and 120m Nordic ski-jumping hills as well as a bobsled-luge run. The US Ski Team practices here year-round – in summer, the freestyle jumpers land in a bubble-filled jetted pool, and the Nordic jumpers on a hillside covered in plastic. Call for a schedule; it's free to observe.

★Park City Museum MUSEUM

(☎435-649-7457; www.parkcityhistory.org; 528 Main St; adult/child $12/5; ⏰10am-7pm Mon-Sat, noon-6pm Sun) A well-staged interactive museum touches on the highlights of the town's history as a mining boomtown, hippie hangout and premier ski resort. There are fascinating exhibits on the world's first underground ski lift, a real dungeon in the basement and a 3-D map of mining tunnels under the mountain.

Activities

Skiing is the big area attraction, but there are enough activities to keep you more than busy in both summer and winter. Most are based out of the three resort areas: Canyons (p203), Park City Mountain (p203) and Deer Valley.

Deer Valley SNOW SPORTS, ADVENTURE SPORTS

(☎435-649-1000, snowmobiling 435-645-7669; www.deervalley.com; 2250 Deer Valley Dr; day lift ticket adult/child $169/105, round-trip chairlift ride $22; ⏰snowmobiling 9am-5pm) Want to be pampered? Deer Valley, a resort of superlatives, has thought of everything – from tissue boxes at the base of slopes to ski valets.

CAN I GET A DRINK IN UTAH?

Yes, you can absolutely get a drink in Utah. Although a few unusual liquor laws remain, in recent years they've been relaxed and private-club membership bars are no more. Some rules to remember:

➡ Few restaurants have full liquor licenses: most serve beer and wine only. You have to order food to drink.

➡ Minors aren't allowed in bars.

➡ Mixed drinks and wine are available only after midday; 4% alcohol beer can be served from 10am. Full-strength bottled beer is sold in some bars and restaurants, and in most breweries.

➡ Mixed drinks cannot contain more than 1.5oz of a primary liquor, or 2.5oz total including secondary alcohol. Sorry, no Long Island iced teas or double shots.

➡ Packaged liquor can only be sold at state-run liquor stores; grocery and convenience stores can sell 4% alcohol beer and malt beverages. Sales in state-run stores are made from Monday through Saturday only.

Slalom, mogul and freestyle-aerial competitions in the 2002 Olympics were held here, but the resort is also famous for its superb dining, white-glove service and uncrowded slopes, as meticulously groomed as the gardens of Versailles.

Park City Mountain Resort SNOW SPORTS, ADVENTURE SPORTS
(435-649-8111; www.parkcitymountain.com; 1345 Lowell Ave; lift ticket adult/child $156/100;) From boarder dudes to parents with tots, everyone skis Park City Mountain Resort, host of the Olympic snowboarding and giant slalom events. The awesome terrain couldn't be more family-friendly – or more accessible, rising as it does right over downtown.

Canyons Village at Park City SNOW SPORTS, ADVENTURE SPORTS
(435-649-5400; www.parkcitymountain.com; 4000 Canyons Resort Dr; lift ticket adult/child $156/100) Bolstered by tens of millions of dollars in improvements, and now merged with Park City Mountain Resort (p203), Canyons seeks novelty with the first North American 'bubble' lift (an enclosed, climate-controlled lift), expanded services, 300 new acres of advanced trails and an increased snowmaking capability. The resort currently sprawls across nine aspen-covered peaks 4 miles outside of town, near the freeway.

Festivals & Events

Sundance Film Festival FILM
(888-285-7790; www.sundance.org/festival; late Jan) Independent films and their makers, and movie stars and their fans, fill the town to bursting for 10 days in late January. Passes, ticket packages and the few individual tickets sell out well in advance – plan ahead.

Sleeping

Mid-December through mid-April is winter high season, with minimum stays required; rates rise during Christmas, New Year's and the Sundance Film Festival. Off-season rates drop 50% or more. For better nightlife, stay in the old town. A complete list of condos, hotels and resorts in Park City is at www.visitparkcity.com.

Park City Hostel HOSTEL $
(435-731-8811; www.parkcityhostel.com; 1781 Sidewinder Dr; dm/r with shared bath from $45/90;) A welcome addition to a city seriously lacking in budget accommodations. Guests hang in a paneled lounge area downstairs and gather on the rooftop for weekly cookouts. Stay in a six-bed dorm (mixed or female-only) or private rooms with shared bathrooms. Organized outings include group bike rides and bar crawls.

Newpark Resort HOTEL $$
(435-649-3600; www.newparkresort.com; 1476 Newpark Blvd; r from $175;) A stylish hotel tucked into the shopping plaza. Extra points for heated floors and elevated beds with down duvets. Rooms have wood detail, flat-screen TV and coffeemaker; some include kitchen. There's a pool and hot tub, but breakfast isn't part of the package.

Peaks Hotel HOTEL $$
(435-649-5000; www.parkcitypeaks.com; 2346 Park Ave; d/ste $219/319;) Comfortable, contemporary rooms include access to a heated outdoor pool, hot tub, restaurant and bar. Great deals off-season. December through April, breakfast is included.

★Washington School House BOUTIQUE HOTEL $$$
(435-649-3800; www.washingtonschoolhouse.com; 543 Park Ave; r $1000;) Architect Trip Bennett oversaw the restoration that turned an 1898 limestone schoolhouse on a hill into a luxurious boutique hotel with 12 suites. How did the children ever concentrate when they could gaze out at the mountains through 9ft-tall windows instead? Rates drop to $405 from May to November.

Eating

Park City is well known for exceptional upscale eating – a reasonably priced meal is harder to find. The ski resorts have numerous eating options in season. Dinner reservations are required at all top-tier places in winter. From April through November restaurants reduce opening hours variably, and may take extended breaks, especially in May.

Five5eeds BREAKFAST $
(435-901-8242; www.five5eeds.com; 1600 Snow Creek Dr; mains $10-16; 7:30am-3pm;) An Australian-owned cafe that whips out some of the finest breakfast fare in town, such as eggs Benedict topped with spicy pulled pork, Moroccan-style baked eggs and many great vegetarian options. It also pours a nice strong cuppa.

Vessel Kitchen CAFE $
(435-200-8864; www.vesselkitchen.com; 1784 Uinta Way; mains $9-15; 11am-9pm;) Folks in the know head to this gourmet cafeteria in the shopping plaza for fast-value

eats. With kombucha on tap, avocado toast and lovely winter salads and stews, there's something for everyone, even kids. Other menu standouts include braised beef with sweet-potato hash and miso steelhead trout with spaghetti squash.

Cortona Italian Cafe ITALIAN $$
(435-608-1373; www.cortonaparkcity.com; 1612 Ute Blvd; mains $19-32; 5-8:30pm Tue-Sat) The fresh Tuscan-inspired pasta dishes you get at this small atmospheric Italian restaurant put the Main St competition to shame. Cortona's signature lasagna, which must be reserved ahead, is a menu highlight, as is the signature meatball-and-fettuccini dish. Everything is made to order and can take up to 30 minutes, but it's worth the wait. Reservations required.

Good Karma INDIAN, FUSION $$
(www.goodkarmarestaurants.com; 1782 Prospector Ave; breakfast $8-13, mains $15-25; 8am-9pm;) Whenever possible, local and organic ingredients are used in the Indo-Persian meals at Good Karma. Start the day with Punjabi eggs and dine on curries and grilled meats. You'll recognize the place by the Tibetan prayer flags flapping out front.

★**Riverhorse on Main** AMERICAN $$$
(435-649-3536; www.riverhorseparkcity.com; 540 Main St; mains $42-92; 5-9pm;) A fine mix of the earthy and exotic, with crab cake, stuffed acorn squash and macadamia-crusted halibut. There's a separate menu for vegetarians. A wall-sized window and the sleek modern design create a stylish atmosphere. Reserve ahead: this is a longtime, award-winning restaurant.

Drinking & Nightlife

Main St is where it's at. In winter there's action nightly; weekends are most lively off-season. Several restaurants, such as **Squatters** (435-649-9868; www.squatters.com; 1900 Park Ave; burgers $10-16, mains $11-24; 8am-10pm Sun-Thu, to 11pm Fri & Sat;) and **Wasatch Brew Pub** (435-649-0900; www.wasatchbeers.com; 250 Main St; mains $10-25; 11am-10pm Mon-Fri, from 10am Sat & Sun;), also have good bars. For better nightlife, stay in the old town.

★**High West Distillery** BAR
(435-649-8300; www.highwest.com; 703 Park Ave; 11am-9pm, tours 1pm & 2:30pm Mon-Thu & 11:30am, 1pm & 2:30pm Fri-Sun) This former livery and Model A–era garage is now home to Park City's most happenin' nightspot. The ski-in distillery was founded by a biochemist, and his bourbon and rye whiskeys have become legendary. Book a free tour to learn more about the process.

Spur BAR
(435-615-1618; www.thespurbarandgrill.com; 352 Main St; 10am-1am) Hosts live music every night with an eclectic offering of rock, folk, blues and electronica. Grab a drink and chill upstairs on a terrace overlooking the main drag, then head back downstairs and catch a band playing in the bar's back room.

Information

Visitor Information Center (435-658-9616; www.visitparkcity.com; 1794 Olympic Pkwy; 9am-6pm;) Vast visitor center with a coffee bar, a terrace and incredible views of the mountains at Olympic Park (p202). Visitor guides available online.

Getting There & Around

Downtown Park City is 5 miles south of I-80 exit 145, 32 miles east of Salt Lake City and 40 miles from Salt Lake City International Airport (p201). Hwy 190 (closed October through March) crosses over Guardsman Pass between Big Cottonwood Canyon and Park City.

Bus 902 (801-743-3882; www.rideuta.com; one way $4.50) goes between Salt Lake City and Park City several times daily in the ski season. There's also private shared van service **Canyon Transportation** (801-255-1841; www.canyon-transport.com; shared van to Park City adult/child $41/28) which offers shared vans from mountain locations to the airport and also has point-to-point transfers and jeep rentals delivered to your location.

The excellent free **public transit system** (435-615-5350; www.parkcity.org/departments/transit-bus; 558 Swede Alley; 7am-midnight) covers most of Park City, including the three ski resorts, and makes it easy not to need a car.

Northeastern Utah

Northeastern Utah is high-wilderness terrain, much of which is more than a mile above sea level. Most travelers come to see Dinosaur National Monument, but you'll also find other dino dig sites and museums, as well as Fremont Indian rock art and ruins in the area. Up near the Wyoming border, the Uinta Mountains and Flaming Gorge attract trout fishers and wildlife-lovers alike.

Vernal

As the closest town to Dinosaur National Monument, it's not surprising that Vernal welcomes you with a large pink allosaurus. The informative film, interactive exhibits, video clips and giant fossils at the **Utah Field House of Natural History State Park Museum** (☎435-789-3799; www.stateparks.utah.gov/parks/utah-field-house; 496 E Main St; adult/child $7/3.50; ⌚9am-7pm Jun-Aug, to 5pm Sep-May; 👪) make a great all-round introduction to Utah's dinosaurs.

Now partnered with OARS, **Don Hatch River Expeditions** (☎435-789-4316, 800-342-8243; www.donhatchrivertrips.com; 221 N 400 E; 1-day tour adult/child $119/99; ⌚May-Sep) runs a variety of one- to five-day trips locally and regionally.

The locally owned **Dinosaur Inn** (☎435-315-0123; www.dinoinn.com; 251 E Main St; r from $80; P❄📶🏊) provides the kind of down-home hospitality you'll rarely get at chain motels, which are numerous along Main St. **Holiday Inn Express & Suites** (☎435-789-4654; www.ihg.com; 1515 W Hwy 40; r $121-162; ❄📶🏊) offers a few upscale touches. For dinner, try the excellent pub food at **Vernal Brewing Company** (☎435-781-2337; www.vernalbrewingcompany.com; 55 S 500 E; mains $12-28; ⌚11:30am-8pm Mon-Thu, to 9pm Fri & Sat; P📶), or go Mexican at **Don Pedro's** (☎435-789-3402; www.facebook.com/donpedrosofvernal; 3340 N Vernal Ave; mains $11-20; ⌚11am-8:30pm Mon-Thu, to 9:30pm Fri & Sat, to 8pm Sun; P📶).

Dinosaur National Monument

Straddling the Utah-Colorado state line, **Dinosaur National Monument** (☎435-781-7700; www.nps.gov/dino; 11625 E 1500 S, Jensen; 7-day pass per vehicle/motorcycle/person only $25/20/15; ⌚24hr) protects a huge dinosaur fossil bed, discovered in 1909. Both states' sections are beautiful, but Utah has the bones. Don't miss the **Quarry Exhibit** (www.nps.gov/dino; per vehicle $20; ⌚8am-7pm Memorial Day–Labor Day, to 4:30pm rest of year), an enclosed, partially excavated wall of rock

BEARS EARS NATIONAL MONUMENT

When President Barack Obama designated **Bears Ears** (www.fs.fed.us/visit/bears-ears-national-monument) as a national monument in December 2016, his proclamation provided protection for 1.35 million acres of land filled with ancient cliff dwellings, ponderosa forests, 4000-year-old petroglyphs, mesas, canyons and glorious red-rock formations. But it didn't last long.

In December 2017, President Donald Trump countered Obama with a proclamation of his own, reducing the monument's size by a whopping 85% to 201,876 acres. He also issued a declaration that shrank Grand Staircase-Escalante National Monument (p212) nearly in half, cutting it from 1,880,461 acres to 1,003,863 acres.

Conservationists fear Trump's action could do serious ecological harm as his administration rallies to increase jobs in the fossil-fuel sector and it eases environmental protections on public lands to facilitate mining and development projects. Federal lawsuits have been filed to challenge the latest proclamation and both sides have dug in for a highly contentious years-long court battle.

Bears Ears was created as a national monument at the request of five Native American tribes. The Navajo, Hopi, Zuni, Ute Mountain and Ute Indian tribes unified in hopes that its protected status would safeguard archaeological sites dating back 8500 years; sadly, some of these ancient grounds continue to get vandalized and destroyed.

Some notable landmarks within the monument include the **Bears Ears Buttes**, **Cedar Mesa**, **White Canyon**, **San Juan River**, **Indian Creek**, **Comb Ridge**, **Goosenecks State Park** (☎435-678-2238; www.stateparks.utah.gov; Rd 316; vehicles $5, camp sites $10; ⌚24hr) and **Valley of the Gods** (www.blm.gov). Their treasures, described by David Roberts' *In Search of the Old Ones*, are nothing short of exquisite.

In Bluff, the **Bears Ears Education Center** (☎435-672-2402; www.friendsofcedarmesa.org/bears-ears-center; 567 W Main St; ⌚9am-5pm Thu-Mon Mar-Nov) 🍃, an initiative of the conservation nonprofit Friends of Cedar Mesa, was created as a grassroots effort to teach visitors about the importance of visiting Bears Ears with respect for nature and Native American culture. For more info visit www.friendsofcedarmesa.org and www.bearsearscoalition.org.

with more than 1600 bones protruding. In summer, shuttles run to the Quarry itself, 15 miles northeast of Vernal's **Quarry Visitor Center** (☎435-781-7700; www.nps.gov/dino/planyourvisit/quarry-exhibit-hall.htm; 11625 E 1500 S, Jensen; per vehicle $25; ⌚8am-5:30pm late May–mid-Sep, 9am-5pm mid-Sep–mid-May) on Hwy 149; out of season you drive there in a ranger-led caravan. Follow the Fossil Discovery Trail from below the parking lot (2.2 miles round trip) to see a few more giant femurs sticking out of the rock. The rangers' interpretive hikes are highly recommended.

In Colorado, the **Canyon Area** – 30 miles further east, outside Dinosaur, CO, and home to the monument's main **visitor center** (☎970-374-3000; 4545 E Hwy 40; ⌚8am-5pm May-Sep, 9am-5pm Sep-May) – holds some stunning overlooks, but thanks to its higher elevation is closed by snow until late spring. Both sections have numerous hiking trails, interpretive driving tours, Green or Yampa river access and campgrounds ($8 to 15 per campsite).

Flaming Gorge National Recreation Area

Named for its fiery red sandstone formations, this gorge-ous park has 375 miles of reservoir shoreline, part of the Green River system. Resort activities at **Red Canyon Lodge** (☎435-889-3759; www.redcanyonlodge.com; 2450 W Red Canyon Lodge, Dutch John; 2-/4-person cabin from $169/179; 📶🐾) include fly-fishing, rowing, rafting and horseback riding; its pleasantly rustic cabins have no TVs but there's wi-fi in the restaurant. **Nine Mile Bunk & Breakfast** (☎435-637-2572; www.9mileranch.com; 9 Mile Canyon Rd; r without/with bath from $80/90, cabins with shared bath $60-95, campsites $15; ⌚Apr-Nov) offers themed rooms, a log cabin and campgrounds, and can organise canyon tours.

Contact the **USFS Flaming Gorge Headquarters** (☎435-784-3445; www.fs.usda.gov/ashley; 25 W Hwy 43, Manila; park day use $5; ⌚8am-5pm Mon-Fri) for the public camping lowdown. The area's 6040ft elevation ensures pleasant summers.

Moab & Southeastern Utah

Experience the earth's beauty at its most elemental in this rocky-and-rugged desert corner of the Colorado Plateau. Beyond the few pine-clad mountains, there's little vegetation to hide the impressive handiwork of time, water and wind: the thousands of red-rock spans in Arches National Park, the sheer-walled river gorges from Canyonlands to Lake Powell, and the stunning buttes and mesas of Monument Valley. The town of Moab is the best base for adventure, with as much four-wheeling, white-knuckle rafting, outfitter-guided fun as you can handle. Or you can lose the crowd while looking for Ancestral Puebloan rock art and dwellings in miles of isolated and undeveloped lands.

Green River

The 'World's Watermelon Capital,' the town of Green River offers a good base for river running on the Green and Colorado Rivers. The legendary one-armed Civil War veteran, geologist and ethnologist John Wesley Powell first explored these rivers in 1869 and 1871. Learn about his amazing travels at the **John Wesley Powell River History Museum** (☎435-564-3427; www.johnwesleypowell.com; 1765 E Main St; adult/child $6/2; ⌚9am-7pm Mon-Sat, noon-5pm Sun Apr-Oct, 9am-5pm Nov-Mar), which doubles as the local visitor center.

Holiday River Expeditions (☎435-564-3273, 800-624-6323; www.bikeraft.com; 10 Holiday River St; day trip $210; ⌚8am-5pm May-Sep) runs one-day rafting trips in Westwater Canyon, as well as multiday excursions. Hikers should try the beginner-friendly and serpentine **Little Wild Horse canyon** (www.utah.com/little-wild-horse-canyon). At the Skyfall Guestrooms you'll find three colorful riverfront rooms, each themed after a unique geological formation in the area. Family-owned **Robbers Roost Motel** (☎435-564-3452; www.rrmotel.com; 325 W Main St; r from $53; P❄📶🐾) is a motorcourt budget-motel gem. Otherwise, there's the **Green River State Park campground** (☎800-322-3770; www.reserveamerica.com; Green River Blvd; tent & RV sites $35, cabins $75), or numerous chain motels where W Main St (Business 70) connects with I-70.

Residents and rafters alike flock to **Ray's Tavern** (☎435-564-3511; www.facebook.com/raystavern; 25 S Broadway; dishes $9-28; ⌚11am-9:30pm; 📶), the local beer joint, for hamburgers and fresh-cut french fries. Green River is 182 miles southeast of Salt Lake City and 52 miles northwest of Moab, and is a stop on the daily *California Zephyr* train, run by **Amtrak** (☎800-872-7245; www.amtrak.com; 250 S Broadway) to Denver, CO (from $62, 10¾ hours).

Moab

Doling out hot tubs and pub grub after a dusty day on the trail, Moab is southern Utah's adventure base camp. Mobs arrive to play in Utah's recreation capital. From the hiker to the four-wheeler, the cult of recreation borders on fetishism.

The town becomes overrun from March through October. The impact of all those feet, bikes and 4WDs on the fragile desert is a serious concern. People here love the land, even if they don't always agree about how to protect it. If the traffic irritates you, just remember – you can disappear into the vast desert in no time.

Activities

★**Canyonlands Field Institute** TOURS
(☎435-259-7750; www.cfimoab.org; 1320 S Hwy 191; 8:30am-4:30pm Mon-Fri) This nonprofit operation uses proceeds from guided tours to create youth outdoor-education programs and train local guides. It offers occasional workshops and seminars throughout the summer. Top tours include Colorado River trips and a geology- and archaeology-focused three-day outing.

Corona Arch Trail HIKING
(www.utah.com/hiking/arches-national-park/bowtie-corona-arches) To take in petroglyphs and two spectacular, rarely visited rock arches, hike the moderately easy Corona Arch Trail, the trailhead for which lies 10 miles up Potash Rd (Hwy 279). Follow cairns along the slickrock to **Bowtie** and **Corona Arches**. You may recognize Corona from a well-known photograph in which an airplane is flying through it – this is one big arch! The 3-mile walk takes two hours.

Sheri Griffith River Expeditions RAFTING
(☎435-259-8229; www.griffithexp.com; 2231 S Hwy 191; river trips from $95; 8am-6pm) Operating since 1971, this rafting specialist has a great selection of river trips on the Colorado, Green and Yampa Rivers – from family floats to Cataract Canyon rapids, and from a full day to a couple of weeks.

★**Rim Cyclery** MOUNTAIN BIKING
(☎435-259-5333; www.rimcyclery.com; 94 W 100 N; bike rentals per day from $40; 8am-6pm) Moab's longest-running family-owned bike shop not only does rentals and repairs, it also has a museum of mountain-bike technology, and rents cross-country skis in the winter.

WORTH A TRIP

ANTELOPE ISLAND STATE PARK

Antelope Island State Park (☎801-725-9263; https://stateparks.utah.gov/parks/antelope-island; Antelope Dr; day use per vehicle $10, tent & RV sites without hookups $20; 6am-10pm, visitor center 9am-6pm) White-sand beaches, birds and buffalo are what attract people to the pretty, 15-mile-long Antelope Island State Park. That's right, the largest island in the Great Salt Lake is home to a 600-strong herd of American bison (buffalo). The October roundup, for veterinary examination, is a thrilling wildlife spectacle. Hundreds of thousands of migratory birds stop to feast on tiny brine shrimp along the Great Salt Lake's shore en route to distant lands during fall and spring migrations.

Sleeping

Prices drop by as much as 50% outside March to October; some smaller places close November through March. Most lodgings have hot tubs and mini-refrigerators, and motels have laundries. Cyclists should ask whether a property provides *secure* bike storage, not just an unlocked closet.

Though there's a huge number of motels, they are often booked out. Reserve as far ahead as possible. For an extensive lodging list, see www.discovermoab.com.

Individual **BLM campsites** (☎435-259-2100; www.discovermoab.com/blm-campgrounds; Hwy 128; tent sites $20; year-round) along the Colorado River on Hwy 128 are first-come, first-served. In peak season, check with the Moab Information Center (p208) to see which sites are full.

Kokopelli Lodge MOTEL $
(☎435-259-7615; www.kokopellilodge.com; 72 S 100 E; r from $98;) Retro styling meets desert chic at this great-value budget motel. Amenities include a hot tub, BBQ grill and secure bike storage.

Moab Rustic Inn MOTEL $
(☎435-259-6177; www.moabrusticinn.com; 120 E 100 S; r from $119; P) Spacious rooms with full-size fridges, a heated swimming pool, friendly staff, central location and on-site laundry make this one of the best budget values in town.

DON'T MISS

ROBERT REDFORD'S SUNDANCE RESORT

Robert Redford's **ski resort** (801-223-4849; 8841 N Alpine Loop Rd; day lift ticket adult/child $85/58, ski & snowboard rentals from $35) could not be more idyllic. There are four chairlifts and a beginner area. Most terrain is intermediate and advanced, climbing 2150ft up the northeast slope of Mt Timpanogos. It hosts the Sundance Film Festival (p203) and the nonprofit Sundance Institute.

Pack Creek Ranch RANCH $$
(435-259-5091, 888-879-6622; www.packcreekranch.com; Abbey Rd, off La Sal Mountain Loop; cabins $175-265; P) This hidden Shangri-la's log cabins are tucked beneath mature cottonwoods and willow trees in the La Sal Mountains, 2000ft above Moab. Most feature fireplaces; all have kitchens and gas grills (bring groceries). No TV or phones. Edward Abbey is among the artists and writers who came here for inspiration. Amenities include an indoor hot tub and sauna.

★**Sunflower Hill Inn** INN $$$
(435-259-2974; www.sunflowerhill.com; 185 N 300 E; r $246-328; P) Wow! This is one of the best bets in town. A top-shelf B&B, Sunflower Hill offers 12 rooms in a quaint country setting. Grab a room in the cozier cedar-sided, early-20th-century home over the annex rooms. All rooms come with quilt-piled beds and antiques – some even have jetted tubs. Children under 10 not allowed.

Sorrel River Ranch LUXURY HOTEL $$$
(435-259-4642; www.sorrelriver.com; Mile 17, Hwy 128; r from $629; P@) Southeast Utah's only full-service luxury resort and gourmet restaurant was originally a 1903 homestead. The lodge and log cabins sit on 240 lush acres, with riding areas and alfalfa fields along the Colorado River. Details strive for rustic perfection, with bedroom fireplaces, handmade log beds, copper-top tables and Jacuzzi tubs. There is a two-night minimum stay during busy periods.

Eating

There's no shortage of places to fuel up in Moab, from backpacker coffeehouses to gourmet dining rooms. Pick up the *Moab Menu Guide* (www.moabmenuguide.com) at area lodgings. Some restaurants close or reduce their days from December through March.

Milt's Stop & Eat BURGERS $
(435-259-7424; www.miltsstopandeat.com; 356 Mill Creek Dr; mains $4-10; 11am-8pm Tue-Sun) Meet greasy goodness. A triathlete couple bought this classic 1954 burger stand and smartly changed nothing. Milt's is known for it's grass-fed beef-burgers, buffalo burgers, fresh-cut fries and brain freeze-inducing shakes. Be patient: the wait can be painfully long. It's a popular gathering spot after visiting the **Slickrock Trail** (435-259-2444; www.utah.com/mountain-biking/slickrock; Sand Flats Recreation Area, Sand Flats Rd; car/cyclist $5/2).

Thai Bella THAI $$
(435-355-0555; www.facebook.com/thaibella2019; 218 N 110 W; mains $15-30; 1-9:30pm Mon-Fri, from 3pm Sat & Sun;) Of the growing number of Thai restaurants in Moab this place reigns supreme. Popular menu items include spicy stir-fried drunken noodles, New Zealand sweet basil mussels, tom yum soup and an ample selection of vegetarian dishes. Meals are served in a two-story 1896 historic building with a shady garden area.

Sabaku Sushi SUSHI $$
(435-259-4455; www.sabakusushi.com; 90 E Center St; rolls $8-16, mains $17-19; 5-9pm Tue-Sun;) The ocean is about a million miles away, but with overnight delivery from Hawaii, you still get a creative selection of fresh rolls, catches of the day and a few Utah originals at this small hole-in-the-wall sushi joint. Go for happy hour (5pm to 6pm Tuesday through Thursday) for discounts on rolls.

★**Desert Bistro** SOUTHERN US $$$
(435-259-0756; www.desertbistro.com; 36 S 100 W; mains $28-45; 5-9pm) Stylized preparations of game and fresh, flown-in seafood are the specialty at this welcoming white-tablecloth restaurant inside an old house. Think bison filet mignon, seared scallops with lemon adobo and wedge salad with house-cured duck-breast bacon. Everything is made on-site, from freshly baked bread to delicious pastries. Great wine list, too. Reserve ahead.

Information

Moab Information Center (435-259-8825; www.discovermoab.com/visitor-center; 38 E Center St; 8am-7pm Mon-Sat, 9am-6pm Sun;) Excellent source of information on area parks, trails, activities, camping and weather. Extensive bookstore and helpful staff.

Getting There & Around

Moab is 235 miles southeast of Salt Lake City, 150 miles northeast of Capitol Reef National Park, and 115 miles southwest of Grand Junction, CO.

Canyonlands Field Airport (CNY; 435-259-0408; www.moabairport.com; 110 W Aviation Way, off Hwy 191), 16 miles north of town, receives flights from Denver. Major car-rental agencies, such as **Enterprise** (435-259-8505; www.enterprise.com; 1197 S Hwy 191; 8am-5pm Mon-Fri), have representatives at the airport.

SkyWest operates daily **United Airlines** (800-864-8331; www.united.com) flights to Denver.

There are also on-demand bus and shuttle van services, including **Porcupine Shuttle** (435-260-0896; www.porcupineshuttle.com), **Roadrunner Shuttle** (435-259-9402; www.roadrunnershuttle.com) and **Canyonlands Shuttle** (435-210-4757; www.canyonlandsshuttle.com), to get you to Grand Junction, CO, the airport and Salt Lake City.

A private vehicle is pretty much a requirement to get around Moab and the parks. Hwy 191 becomes Main St as it passes through town.

Vehicle traffic is heavy in high season. There are a number of bike paths in and around town; the Moab Information Center (p208) can offer a map guide.

Coyote Shuttle (435-260-2097; www.coyoteshuttle.com) and Porcupine Shuttle travel on request to Canyonlands Field Airport and do hiker-biker and river shuttles.

Arches National Park

Giant sweeping arcs of sandstone frame snowy peaks and desert landscapes at **Arches National Park** (435-719-2299; www.nps.gov/arch; Hwy 191; 7-day pass per vehicle/motorcycle/person only $30/25/15; 24hr, visitor center 7:30am-5pm Apr-Sep, 9am-4pm Oct-Mar). Explore the highest density of rock arches anywhere on earth: more than 2000 in a 119-sq-mile area. Nearly 1.5 million visitors make the pilgrimage here each year; it's just 5 miles north of Moab, and small enough for you to see most of it within a day. Many noteworthy arches are easily reached by paved roads and relatively short hiking trails. To avoid crowds, consider a moonlight exploration, when it's cooler and the rocks feel ghostly.

Highlights along the park's main scenic drive include **Balanced Rock**, perched beside the main park road, and, for hikers, the moderate-to-strenuous, 3-mile round-trip trail that ascends the slickrock to reach the unofficial state symbol, **Delicate Arch** (best photographed in the late afternoon).

Further along the road, the spectacularly narrow canyons and maze-like fins of the **Fiery Furnace** must be visited on three-hour, ranger-led hikes, for which advance reservation is usually necessary. It's not easy: be prepared to scramble up and over boulders, shimmy down between rocks and navigate narrow ledges.

The scenic drive ends 19 miles from the visitor center at **Devils Garden**. The trailhead marks the start of a 2- to 7.7-mile round-trip hike that passes at least eight arches, though most hikers only go the relatively easy 1.3 miles to Landscape Arch, a gravity-defying, 290ft-long behemoth. For stays between March and October, advance reservations are a must for the **Devils Garden Campground** (877-444-6777; www.recreation.gov; tent & RV sites $25). No showers, no hookups.

Because of water scarcity and heat, few visitors backpack, though it is allowed with free permits (available from the visitor center).

Canyonlands National Park

Red-rock fins, bridges, needles, spires, craters, mesas, buttes – **Canyonlands National Park** (435-719-2313; www.nps.gov/cany/index.htm; 7-day pass per vehicle/motorcycle/person $30/25/15, tent & RV sites without hookups $15-20; 24hr) is a crumbling beauty, a vision of ancient earth. Roads and rivers make inroads into this high-desert wilderness stretching 527 sq miles, but much of it is still untamed. You can hike, raft and 4WD here but be sure that you have plenty of gas, food and water.

The canyons of the Colorado and Green Rivers divide the park into four entirely separate areas. The appropriately named **Island in the Sky** district, just over 30 miles northwest of Moab, consists of a 6000ft-high flat-topped mesa that provides astonishing long-range vistas. Starting from the **visitor center** (435-259-4712; www.nps.gov/cany; Hwy 313; 8am-6pm Mar-Dec, 8am-5pm Fri-Tue Jan & Feb), a scenic drive leads past numerous overlooks and trailheads, ending after 12 miles at **Grand View Point**, where a sinuous trail runs for a mile along the very lip of the mesa. Our favorite short hike en route is the half-mile loop to oft-photographed **Mesa Arch**, a slender, cliff-hugging span that frames a magnficent view of Washer Woman Arch. Seven miles from the visitor center, the first-come, first served, 12-site **Island in**

the Sky Campground (Willow Flat; ☎435-719-2313; www.nps.gov/cany/planyourvisit/camping.htm; tent & RV sites $15; ⏰year-round) has vault toilets but no water, and no hookups. Determined mountain bikers can tackle primitive **White Rim Road** (Island in the Sky), a 70-mile route encircling the Island in the Sky.

Named for the spires of orange-and-white sandstone jutting skyward from the desert floor, the wild and remote **Needles** district is ideal for backpacking and off-roading. To reach the **visitor center** (☎435-259-4711; www.nps.gov/cany; Hwy 211; ⏰8am-4:30pm), follow Hwy 191 south for 40 miles from Moab, then take Hwy 211 west. This area is much more about long, challenging hikes than roadside overlooks. The awesome **Chesler Park/Joint Trail Loop** is an 11-mile route across desert grasslands, past towering red-and-white-striped pinnacles, and through deep, narrow slot canyons, at times just 2ft across. Elevation changes are moderate, but the distance makes it an advanced day hike. The first-come, first-served, 27-site **Needles Campground** (Squaw Flat; ☎435-719-2313; www.nps.gov/cany/planyourvisit/camping.htm; tent & RV sites $20; ⏰year-round), 3 miles west of the visitor center, fills up every day, spring to fall. It has flush toilets and running water, but no showers or hookups.

In addition to normal entrance fees, advance-reservation permits are required for overnight backpacking, mountain biking, 4WD trips and river trips. Permits are valid for 14 days and are issued at the **Island in the Sky Visitor Center** (☎435-259-4712; www.nps.gov/cany; Hwy 313; ⏰8am-6pm Mar-Dec, 8am-5pm Fri-Tue Jan & Feb), **Needles Visitor Center** (☎435-259-4711; www.nps.gov/cany; Hwy 211; ⏰8am-4:30pm) and **Hans Flat Ranger Station** (☎435-259-2652; www.nps.gov/cany; Recreation Rd 777, Hans Flat; ⏰8am-4:30pm). Reservations are available online (https://canypermits.nps.gov/index.cfm) and through the **Arches & Canyonlands National Park Headquarters** (☎435-719-2100; www.nps.gov/cany; 2282 SW Resource Blvd; ⏰8am-4:30pm Mon-Fri) in Moab. Remoter areas west of the rivers, only accessible southwest of the town of Green River, include **Horseshoe Canyon**, where determined hikers are rewarded with extraordinary ancient rock art, and the **Maze**, the park's remotest frontier.

> **LOCAL PASSPORTS**
>
> **Southeast Utah Parks Pass** Southeastern Utah national parks sell a Southeast Utah Parks Pass (per vehicle $55) that's good for a year's entry to Arches (p209) and Canyonlands (p209) National Parks (where a seven-day vehicle pass is $30) and Natural Bridges National Monument (p211).
>
> **National Park Service Passes** (www.nps.gov/findapark/passes.htm, per vehicle adult/senior $80/20) Available online and at parks, allow year-long access to all federal recreation lands in Utah and beyond – and are a great way to support the Southwest's amazing parks.

Dead Horse Point State Park

Tiny but stunning **Dead Horse Point State Park** (☎435-259-2614; www.stateparks.utah.gov/parks/dead-horse; Hwy 313; park day-use per vehicle $20, tent/RV sites $35/40, yurts $140; ⏰park 6am-10pm, visitor center 9am-5pm) has been the setting for numerous movies, including the climactic scenes of *Thelma & Louise*. It's not a hiking destination, but mesmerizing views merit the short detour off Hwy 313 en route to the Island in the Sky in Canyonlands National Park: look out at red-rock canyons rimmed with white cliffs, the Colorado River, Canyonlands and the distant La Sal Mountains. The excellent **visitor center** (☎435-259-2614; www.stateparks.utah.gov/parks/dead-horse; ⏰9am-5pm) has exhibits, on-demand videos, books and maps, along with ranger-led walks and talks in summer. To the south, the 21-site **campground** (☎800-322-3770; www.reserveamerica.com; campsites/yurts $40/140) has water; no showers, no hookups. Reserve ahead.

Bluff

One hundred miles south of Moab, this little community (population 320) makes a comfortable, laid-back base for exploring Utah's desolately beautiful southeastern corner. Founded by Mormon pioneers in 1880, Bluff sits surrounded by red rock and public lands near the junction of Hwys 191 and 162, along the San Juan River. Other than a trading post and a couple of places to eat or sleep, there's not much town.

For backcountry tours that access rock art and ruins, join **Far Out Expeditions** (☎435-672-2294; www.faroutexpeditions.com; 690 E Mulberry Ave; half-/full-day tours $200/325) on a day or multiday hike into the remote region. A rafting trip along the San Juan with **Wild**

Rivers Expeditions (435-672-2244; www.riversandruins.com; 2625 S Hwy 191, Bluff; half-day trip adult/child $200/140), a history and geology-minded outfitter, also includes ancient site visits. The hospitable **Recapture Lodge** (435-672-2281; www.recapturelodge.com; 250 Main St; d $98;) is a rustic, cozy place to stay. Owners know the region inside and out and can help with trip planning. You might also get off-grid at **Valley of the Gods B&B** (970-749-1164; www.valleyofthegodsbandb.com; off Hwy 261; s $145, d $175-195;) , one of the original ranches in the area.

Artsy **Comb Ridge Eat & Drink** (435-485-5555; www.combridgeeatanddrink.com; 680 Main St; breakfast mains $5-7, dinner mains $10-17; 11:30am-3pm & 5-9pm Wed-Sat, 9:30am-2pm & 5-9pm Sun;) serves standout single-pour coffee and blue-corn pancakes inside a timber and adobe cafe, while the Western-themed **Cottonwood Steakhouse** (435-672-2282; www.cottonwoodsteakhouse.com; 409 W Main St; mains $17-29; 5:30-9:30pm Mar-Nov;) serves substantial portions of barbecued steak and beans.

Hovenweep National Monument

Beautiful, little-visited **Hovenweep** (970-562-4282; www.nps.gov/hove; McElmo Rte, off Hwy 262; tent & RV sites $15; park dusk-dawn, visitor center 8am-6pm Jun-Sep, 9am-5pm Oct-May) FREE, meaning 'deserted valley' in the Ute language, showcases several neighboring Ancestral Puebloan sites, where impressive towers and granaries stand in shallow desert canyons. The Square Tower Group is accessed near the ranger station; other sites require long hikes. The **campground** (970-562-4282; www.nps.gov/hove; McElmo Rte, Hovenweep National Monument; tent & RV sites $10-15) has 31 basic, first-come, first-served sites (no showers, no hookups). The main access is east of Hwy 191 on Hwy 262 via Hatch Trading Post, more than 40 miles northeast of Bluff.

Natural Bridges National Monument

Fifty-five miles northwest of Bluff, the ultra-remote **Natural Bridges National Monument** (www.nps.gov/nabr; Hwy 275; 7-day pass per vehicle $20, camp sites $15; 24hr, visitor center 9am-5pm Apr–mid-Oct, 9am-5pm Thu-Mon mid-Oct–Mar) protects a white sandstone canyon (it's not red!) containing three impressive and easily accessible natural bridges. The oldest, **Owachomo Bridge**, spans 180ft but is only 9ft thick. The flat 9-mile Scenic Drive loop is ideal for overlooking. The campground offers 12 basic sites on a first-come, first served basis; no showers, no hookups. There is some primitive overflow camping space, but be aware that the nearest services are in Blanding, 40 miles east.

Zion & Southwestern Utah

Wonder at the deep-crimson canyons of Zion National Park; hike among the delicate pink-and-orange minarets at Bryce Canyon; drive past the swirling grey-white-and-purple mounds of Capitol Reef. Southwestern Utah is so spectacular that the vast majority of the territory has been preserved as national park or forest, state park or BLM wilderness. The whole area is ripe for outdoor exploration, with narrow slot canyons to shoulder through, pink sand dunes to scale and wavelike sandstone formations to seek out.

Capitol Reef National Park

Not as crowded as its fellow parks but equally scenic, **Capitol Reef** (435-425-3791; www.nps.gov/care/index.htm; cnr Hwy 24 & Scenic Dr; scenic drive per vehicle/pedestrian $20/10, tent & RV sites $20; 24hr, visitor center 8am-4:30pm) contains much of the 100-mile Waterpocket Fold, created 65 million years ago when the earth's surface buckled up and folded, exposing a cross-section of geologic history that is painterly in its colorful intensity.

Hwy 24 cuts grandly through the park, but make sure you head south on the **Capitol Reef Scenic Drive** (www.nps.gov/care/planyourvisit/scenicdrive.htm; 7-day pass per vehicle/person $20/10), a paved, dead-end 7.9-mile road that passes through orchards – a legacy of Mormon settlement. In season you can freely pick cherries, peaches and apples, and stop by the historic **Gifford Homestead** (435-425-3791; www.nps.gov/care/learn/historyculture/giffordhomestead.htm; Scenic Dr; 8am-5pm Mar-Oct) to see an old homestead museum and buy fruit-filled mini-pies. Great walks en route include the **Grand Wash** and **Capitol Gorge** trails, each following the level floor of a separate slender canyon. This terrific shady and green **campground** (435-425-3791; www.recreation.gov; Campground Rd, Fruita; sites $20) has no showers, no hookups and is first-come, first served; it fills early spring through fall.

Torrey

Just 15 miles west of Capitol Reef, the small pioneer town of Torrey serves as the base for most national-park visitors. In addition to a few Old West–era buildings, there are a dozen or so restaurants and motels.

Flirting with cowboy style, **Capitol Reef Resort** (☎435-425-3761; www.capitolreefresort.com; 2600 E Hwy 24; r $169-209, cabins & tipis from $269; P❄📶🏊) is one of the closest to the national park of the same name. Dressed with country elegance, each airy room at the 1914 **Torrey Schoolhouse B&B** (☎435-491-0230; www.torreyschoolhouse.com; 150 N Center St; r $125-165; ⊙Apr-Oct; ❄📶) has a story to tell. (Butch Cassidy may have attended a town dance here.) After consuming the gourmet breakfast, laze in the garden or the huge 1st-floor lounge.

Located behind an RV park, **Torrey Grill & BBQ** (☎435-609-6997; www.torreygrillandbbq.com; 1110 W Hwy 24; mains $18-24; ⊙5-9pm Mon-Sat Apr-Oct; P) serves praiseworthy dry-rubbed spare ribs, smoked beef tri-tip and home-style apple cobbler and ice cream in a rustic setting.

Boulder

Though the tiny outpost of **Boulder** (www.boulderutah.com; population 240) is just 32 miles south of Torrey on Hwy 12, you have to cross Boulder Mountain to reach it. From here, the attractive **Burr Trail Rd** heads east across the northeastern corner of the Grand Staircase–Escalante National Monument, eventually winding up on a gravel road that leads either up to Capitol Reef or down to Bullfrog Marina on Lake Powell.

The small **Anasazi State Park Museum** (☎435-335-7308; www.stateparks.utah.gov/parks/anasazi; 460 N Hwy 12; $5; ⊙8am-6pm Apr-Oct, to 4pm Nov-Mar) curates artifacts and a Native American site inhabited from AD 1130 to 1175. Rooms at **Boulder Mountain Lodge** (☎435-335-7460; www.boulder-utah.com; 20 N Hwy 12; r/apt/ste from $140/230/325; P❄@📶🐾) are plush, but it's the 15-acre wildlife sanctuary setting that's unsurpassed. An outdoor hot tub with mountain views is a soothing spot to bird-watch. The lodge's destination restaurant, **Hell's Backbone Grill** (☎435-335-7464; www.hellsbackbonegrill.com; 20 N Hwy 12, Boulder Mountain Lodge; breakfast $9-14, lunch $12-18, dinner $23-37; ⊙7am-2pm & 5-9pm Mar-Nov; 🖉) 🍃 serves soulful, earthy preparations of regionally inspired and sourced cuisine – book ahead – while the nearby **Burr Trail Outpost** (☎435-335-7565; www.burrtrailoutpost.com; 14 N Hwy 12; ⊙7:30am-7pm Apr-Sep, 8am-5pm Oct-Mar; 📶) offers organic coffee and scrumptious homemade desserts.

Grand Staircase–Escalante National Monument

The 2656-sq-mile **Grand Staircase–Escalante National Monument** (GSENM; ☎435-644-1300; www.blm.gov/visit/kanab-visitor-center; 745 Hwy 89, Kanab; ⊙24hr) FREE, a waterless region so inhospitable that it was the last to be mapped in the continental US, covers more territory than Delaware and Rhode Island combined. The nearest services, and GSENM visitor centers, are in Boulder and Escalante on Hwy 12 in the north, and Kanab on US 89 in the south. Otherwise, infrastructure is minimal, leaving a vast, uninhabited canyonland full of 4WD roads that call to adventurous travelers who have the time, equipment and knowledge to explore.

The most accessible and most used trail in the monument is the 6-mile round-trip hike to the magnificent multicolored waterfall on **Lower Calf Creek** (Hwy 12, Mile 75; day use $5; ⊙dawn-dusk), between Boulder and Escalante. The 14 sought-after creekside sites at **Calf Creek Campground** (☎435-826-5499; www.blm.gov/visit/calf-creek-recreation-area-campground; Hwy 12; tent & RV sites $15), just off Hwy 12, fill fast; no showers, no hookups, and no reservations taken.

Escalante

This national-monument gateway town of 800 souls is the closest thing to a metropolis for many a lonely desert mile. Thirty slow and winding miles from Boulder, and 65 from Torrey, it's a good place to base yourself before venturing into the adjacent Grand Staircase–Escalante National Monument. The **Escalante Interagency Visitor Center** (☎435-826-5499; www.blm.gov/visit/escalante-interacgency-visitor-center; 775 W Main St; ⊙8am-4:30pm) is a superb resource center with complete information on nearby monument and forest-service lands.

Escalante Outfitters (☎435-826-4266; www.escalanteoutfitters.com; 310 W Main St; natural history tours $45, fly-fishing from $225; ⊙7am-9pm) is a traveler's oasis: the bookstore sells maps, guides, camping supplies – and liquor(!) – while the pleasant cafe serves homemade breakfast, pizzas and salads. It also rents out tiny, rustic cabins (from $55). Longtime area outfitter **Excursions of Escalante** (☎800-839-7567; www.excursionsofescalante.com; 125 E Main St; all-day canyoneering $185; ⊙8am-5pm Mon-Fri, to noon Sat mid-Mar–Oct) leads canyoneering, climbing and photo hikes.

Other fine lodgings in town include **Canyons B&B** (☎435-826-4747; www.canyonsbnb.com; 120 E Main St; d $160; ⊙Mar-Nov; ❄📶) with upscale cabin rooms that surround a shady courtyard. Sleep in an upscale yurt on a tranquil 20-acre property with **Escalante Yurts** (☎435-826-4222; www.escalanteyurts.com; 1605 N Pine Creek Rd; yurts $235-345; P⊖❄📶). Savor exquisite pastries and great sandwiches at French-inspired **Mimi's Bakery & Deli** (☎435-826-4036; www.facebook.com/mimisbakeryescalante; 190 W Main St; pastries & sandwiches $3-7; ⊙7am-4pm Tue-Sat; 🖉).

Bryce Canyon National Park

The Grand Staircase, a series of uplifted rock layers that climb in clearly defined 'steps' north from the Grand Canyon, culminates in the Pink Cliffs formation at this deservedly popular **national park** (☎435-834-5322; www.nps.gov/brca; Hwy 63, Bryce; 7-day pass per vehicle/motorcycle/person only $35/30/20; ⊙24hr, visitor center 8am-8pm May-Sep, to 6pm Oct, to 4:30pm Nov-Mar, to 6pm Apr). Not actually a 'canyon', but an amphitheater eroded from the cliffs, it's filled with wondrous sorbet-colored pinnacles and points, steeples and spires, and totem-pole-shaped 'hoodoos'. The park is 50 miles southwest of Escalante; from Hwy 12, turn south on Hwy 63.

Rim Road Scenic Drive (8000ft) travels 18 miles, roughly following the canyon rim past the **visitor center** (☎435-834-5322; www.nps.gov/brca; Hwy 63; ⊙8am-8pm May-Sep, to 6pm Oct & Apr, to 4:30pm Nov-Mar; 📶), the lodge, incredible overlooks – don't miss **Inspiration Point** – and trailheads, ending at **Rainbow Point** (9115ft). From early May through early October, a free shuttle bus runs (8am until at least 5:30pm) from a staging area just north of the park to as far south as **Bryce Amphitheater**.

The park has two camping areas, both of which accept reservations through the park website. **Sunset Campground** (☎877-444-6777; www.recreation.gov; Bryce Canyon Rd; tent/RV site $20/30; ⊙Apr-Sep) is bit more wooded, but is not open year-round. Coin-op laundry and showers are available at the general store near **North Campground** (☎877-444-6777; www.recreation.gov; Bryce Canyon Rd; tent/RV sites $20/30). During summer, remaining first-come, first-served sites fill before noon.

DON'T MISS

NEWSPAPER ROCK STATE HISTORIC MONUMENT

This tiny recreation area showcases a single large sandstone rock **panel** (Hwy 211, Monticello) packed with more than 300 petroglyphs attributed to Ute and Ancestral Puebloan groups during a 2000-year period. The many red-rock figures etched out of a black 'desert varnish' surface make for great photos. It's located 50 miles south of Moab, east of Canyonlands National Park on Hwy 211.

The 1920s **Bryce Canyon Lodge** (☎435-834-8700, 877-386-4383; www.brycecanyonforever.com; Hwy 63; r & cabins $223-270; ⊙Apr-Oct; @📶) exudes rustic mountain charm. Rooms are in modern hotel-style units, with up-to-date furnishings, and thin-walled duplex cabins with gasfire places and front porches. No TVs. The lodge **restaurant** (☎435-834-5361; www.brycecanyonforever.com/dining; Bryce Canyon Rd; breakfast & lunch $10-20, dinner $10-35; ⊙7am-10pm Apr-Oct) 🍃 is excellent, if expensive, while **Bryce Canyon Pines Restaurant** (☎435-834-5441; www.brycecanyonrestaurant.com; Hwy 12; breakfast & lunch $9.50-14, dinner mains $12-24; ⊙7am-8pm) is a diner classic.

Just north of the park boundaries, **Ruby's Inn** (www.rubysinn.com; 1000 S Hwy 63) is a resort complex with multiple motel lodging options, plus a campground. You can also dine at several restaurants, admire Western art, wash laundry, shop for groceries, fill up with gas, and take a helicopter ride.

Eleven miles east on Hwy 12, the small-town of **Tropic** (www.brycecanyoncountry.com) has additional food and lodging.

Kanab

At the southern edge of Grand Staircase–Escalante National Monument, vast expanses of rugged desert surround remote Kanab (population 4687). Western filmmakers made dozens of movies here from the 1920s to the 1970s, and the town retains an Old West feel.

Animal-lovers can tour **Best Friends Animal Sanctuary** (Map p180; ☎435-644-2001; www.bestfriends.org; 5001 Angel Canyon Rd, Hwy 89; ⊙8am-5pm; 👪) FREE, the largest no-kill animal rescue center in the country.

John Wayne and Gregory Peck are among Hollywood notables who slumbered at the somewhat dated **Parry Lodge** (Map p180; ☎435-644-2601; www.parrylodge.com; 89 E Center St; r from $139-159; ⊙Mar-Nov; ❄📶≋🐾). The renovated **Canyons Lodge** (Map p180; ☎435-644-3069; www.canyonslodge.com; 236 N 300 W; r from $109-199; ❄@📶≋🐾) 🍃 motel has an art-house Western feel; rooms feature original artwork. Stay there, then eat downtown at French- and Italian-inspired **Vermillion 45** (Map p180; ☎435-644-3300; www.vermillion45.com; 210 S 110 E; mains $14-25; ⊙11am-11pm Wed-Sun) bistro or the classy **Sego** (Map p180; ☎435-644-5680; www.segokanab.com; 190 N 300 W; mains $13-30; ⊙6-10pm Mon-Sat Apr-Oct, 5-9pm Mon-Sat Nov-Mar; 📶), where you can expect gorgeous eats such as foraged mushrooms with goat's cheese and noodles with red-crab curry.

The **GSENM Visitor Center** (Map p180; ☎435-644-1300; www.blm.gov/visit/kanab-visitor-center; 745 E Hwy 89; ⊙8am-4:30pm) provides monument information; **Kane County Office of Tourism** (Map p180; ☎435-644-5033; www.visitsouthernutah.com; 78 S 100 E; ⊙8am-7pm) focuses on town and movie sites.

Zion National Park

Get ready for an overdose of awesome. **Zion National Park** (☎435-772-3256; www.nps.gov/zion; Hwy 9; 7-day pass per vehicle/motorcycle/person only $35/30/20; ⊙24hr, visitor center 8am-5pm Sep-May, to 7pm Jun-Aug) abounds in amazing experiences: gazing up at the red-and-white cliffs of **Zion Canyon**, soaring high over the **Virgin River**; peering beyond **Angels Landing** after a 1400ft ascent; or hiking downriver through the notorious **Narrows**. But it also holds more delicate beauties: weeping rocks, tiny grottoes, hanging gardens and meadows of mesa-top wildflowers. Lush vegetation and low elevation give the magnificent rock formations a far lusher feel than the barren parks in the east.

Most visitors enter the park along Zion Canyon floor; even the most challenging hikes become congested May through September (shuttle required). If you've time for only one activity, the 6-mile **Scenic Drive**, which pierces the heart of Zion Canyon, is the one. From mid-March through early-November, you have to take a free shuttle from the **visitor center** (☎435-772-3256; www.nps.gov/zion; Kolob Canyons Rd; ⊙8am-5pm late May-Sep, to 4:30pm rest of year), but you can hop off and on at any of the scenic stops and trailheads along the way.

Of the easy to moderate trails, the paved, mile-long **Riverside Walk** at the end of the road is a good place to start. The **Angels Landing Trail** is a much more strenuous, 5.4-mile vertigo-inducer (1400ft elevation gain, with sheer drop-offs), but the canyon views are phenomenal. Allow four hours round trip.

The most famous backcountry route is the unforgettable **Narrows**, a 16-mile journey into skinny canyons along the Virgin River's north fork (June through October). Plan on getting wet: at least 50% of the 12-hour hike is in the river. Split the hike into two days, reserving an overnight camping spot in advance, or finish it in time to catch the last park shuttle. A trailhead shuttle is necessary for this one-way trip.

Heading eastwards, Hwy 9 climbs out of Zion Canyon in a series of six tight switchbacks to reach the 1.1-mile Zion–Mt Carmel Tunnel, a 1920s engineering marvel. It then leads quickly into dramatically different terrain – a landscape of etched multicolor slickrock, culminating at the mountainous **Checkerboard Mesa**.

Reserve far ahead and request a riverside site in the canyon's cottonwood-shaded **Watchman Campground** (☎877-444-6777; www.recreation.gov; Hwy 9; tent sites $20, RV sites with hookups $30; 🐾); adjacent **South Campground** (☎877-444-6777; www.recreation.gov; Hwy 9; tent & RV sites $20; 🐾) is first-come, first-served only. Smack in the middle of the scenic drive, rustic **Zion Lodge** (☎888-297-2757, same day reservations 435-772-7700; www.zionlodge.com; Zion Canyon Scenic Dr; r/cabins $227/260; ❄@📶) has basic motel rooms and cabins with gas fireplaces. All have wooden porches with stellar red-rock cliff views, but no TVs. The lodge's full-service dining room, **Red Rock Grill** (☎435-772-7760; Zion Canyon

SCENIC DRIVE: HIGHWAY 12

Arguably Utah's most diverse and stunning route, **Hwy 12 Scenic Byway** (www.scenicbyway12.com; Hwy 12) winds through rugged canyonland on a 124-mile journey west of Bryce Canyon to near Capitol Reef. The section between Escalante and Torrey traverses a moonscape of sculpted slickrock, crosses narrow ridge backs and climbs over 11,000ft Boulder Mountain. Pretty much everything between Torrey and Panguitch is on or near Hwy 12.

Scenic Dr, Zion Lodge; breakfast & sandwiches $6-17, dinner $16.50-30; ⊙6:30-10am & 11:30am-10pm Mar-Oct, hours vary Nov-Feb), has similarly amazing views. Just outside the park, the town of Springdale offers many more services.

Note that you must pay the park entrance fee to drive on public Hwy 9 in the park, even if you are just passing through.

Springdale

Positioned at the main, south entrance to Zion National Park, Springdale is a perfect little park town – though its main drag can get bottlenecked with traffic. Stunning red cliffs form the backdrop to eclectic cafes, restaurants are big on organic ingredients, and galleries are interspersed with indie motels and B&Bs.

In addition to hiking trails in the national park, you can take outfitter-led climbing, canyoneering, mountain biking and 4WD trips on adjacent BLM lands. **Zion Adventure Company** (☎435-772-1001; www.zionadventures.com; 36 Lion Blvd; canyoneering day from $189; ⊙7am-8pm late May-late Sep, shorter hours rest of the year) offers excellent excursions, Narrows outfitting and hiker-biker shuttles, while **Zion Cycles** (☎435-772-0400; www.zioncycles.com; 868 Zion Park Blvd; half-/full-day rentals from $30/40, car racks from $15; ⊙9am-6pm Feb-Nov) is the most helpful bike shop in town.

Desert Pearl Inn (☎888-828-0898, 435-772-8888; www.desertpearl.com; 707 Zion Park Blvd; r $269-299; ❄@📶≋) offers the most stylish digs in town, while **Red Rock Inn** (☎435-772-3139; www.redrockinn.com; 998 Zion Park Blvd; r $105-309; ❄📶) has eight romantic country-contemporary cottages

Zion Canyon B&B (☎435-772-9466; www.zioncanyonbnb.com; 101 Kokopelli Circle; r $149-215; ❄📶) is the most traditional local B&B, with full gourmet breakfasts and mini-spa. The owners' creative collections of art and artifacts enliven the 1930s bungalow that is **Under the Eaves Inn** (☎435-772-9466; www.undertheeaves.com; 980 Zion Park Blvd; r $99-189; P❄📶); the morning meal is a coupon for a local restaurant.

For a coffee and *trés bonnes crepes* – both sweet and savory – make **MeMe's Cafe** (☎435-772-0114; www.memescafezion.com; 975 Zion Park Blvd; mains $11-18; ⊙7am-9pm) your first stop of the day. It also serves paninis and waffles, and for dinner, beef brisket and pulled pork. In the evening, the Mexican-tiled patio with twinkly lights at **Oscar's Cafe** (☎435-772-3232; www.cafeoscars.com; 948 Zion Park Blvd; mains $12-20, breakfast $6-13; ⊙7am-9pm) and the rustic **Bit & Spur Restaurant & Saloon** (☎435-772-3498; www.bitandspur.com; 1212 Zion Park Blvd; mains $14-30; ⊙5-11pm Mar-Oct, 5-11pm Fri-Sun Nov-Feb; 📶) are local-favored places to hang out, eat and drink. Reserve ahead for the excellent hotel-restaurant **King's Landing** (☎435-772-7422; www.klbzion.com; 1515 Zion Park Blvd, Driftwood Lodge; mains $18-38; ⊙5-9pm; 🖉).

NEW MEXICO

The Land of Enchantment casts a bewitching spell. Whether it's sunlight and shadow playing out across juniper-speckled hills, the electric glow of gypsum dunes at sunset or the Rio Grande Gorge cracking across the Taos Plateau, the landscape is undeniably mesmerizing. And it's all easily explored by hiking, cycling or paddling. The history is fascinating too, evidenced in the ancient pueblos, the homes and holding cells of trappers and outlaws, and the mud-brick churches filled with sacred art. And we haven't even mentioned the chile-smothered enchiladas, the thriving microbreweries or *Better Call Saul*. As for Meow Wolf, you'll want get in line right now.

Perhaps New Mexico's charm is best expressed in the simple but iconic paintings of Georgia O'Keeffe. The artist herself exclaimed, on her very first visit: 'Well! Well! Well!… This is wonderful! No one told me it was like this.'

But seriously, how could they?

History

Ancestral Puebloan civilization first began to flourish in the 8th century AD, and the impressive structures at Chaco Canyon were begun not long after. By the time Francisco Vasquez de Coronado got here in the 16th century, many Pueblo Indians had migrated to the Rio Grande Valley and were the dominant presence. After Santa Fe was established as the Spanish colonial capital in around 1610, Spanish colonists fanned out across northern New Mexico and Catholic missionaries began their often violent efforts to convert the Puebloans. Following the Pueblo Revolt of 1680, Native Americans occupied Santa Fe until 1692, when Don Diego de Vargas recaptured the city.

The US took control of New Mexico in 1846 during the Mexican-American War, and it became a US Territory in 1850. Native American wars with the Navajo, Apache and

Comanche further transformed the region, and the arrival of the railroad in the 1870s prompted an economic boom.

Painters and writers set up art colonies in Santa Fe and Taos in the early 20th century, and New Mexico became the 47th state in 1912. A top-secret scientific community descended on Los Alamos in 1943 and developed the atomic bomb. Some say that four years later, aliens crashed outside of Roswell...

Information

For information on the New Mexico stretch of Route 66, visit www.rt66nm.org.

New Mexico State Parks (www.emnrd.state.nm.us) Info about state parks, with a link to campsite reservations.

New Mexico Tourism (www.newmexico.org) Information about destination planning, activities and events.

Recreation.gov (www.recreation.gov) Reservations for national park and forest campsites and tours.

Albuquerque

A bustling desert crossroads, Albuquerque is just the right mix of urban and wild: the pink hues of the Sandia Mountains at sunset, the Rio Grande's cottonwood bosque, Route 66 diners and the hometown of Walter White and Saul Goodman. It's the largest city in the state, yet you can still hear the howls of coyotes when the sun goes down.

Good hiking and mountain-biking trails abound just outside of town, while the city's modern museums explore Pueblo culture, New Mexican art and space. Take the time to let your engine cool as you take a walk among the desert petroglyphs or order up a plate of red-chile enchiladas and a local beer – and with so many great breweries here it could take awhile.

Sights

Old Town

From its foundation in 1706 until the arrival of the railroad in 1880, the plaza, centering on the diminutive 1793 **San Felipe de Neri Church** (www.sanfelipedeneri.org; 2005 N Plaza NW, Old Town Plaza; 7am-5:30pm daily, museum 9:30am-4:30pm Mon-Fri, to 5pm Sat), was the hub of Albuquerque. Today Old Town is the city's most popular tourist area.

★Albuquerque Museum MUSEUM

(505-243-7255; www.cabq.gov/museum; 2000 Mountain Rd NW; adult/teen 13-18yr/child 4-12yr $6/6/3; 9am-5pm Tue-Sun; P) Formerly known as the Albuquerque Museum of Art & History, this showpiece museum shouldn't be missed. With an engaging Albuquerque history gallery that's imaginative, interactive and easy to digest and a permanent New Mexico art collection that extends to 20th-century masterpieces from Taos, it's a great place to explore as part of any visit to Old Town. There's free admission on Sunday mornings, and free guided walking tours of Old Town on Sunday, Tuesday, Thursday and Friday at 11am (April through November).

★American International Rattlesnake Museum MUSEUM

(505-242-6569; www.rattlesnakes.com; 202 San Felipe St NW; adult/child $6/4; 10am-6pm Mon-Sat, 1-5pm Sun Jun-Aug, 11:30am-5:30pm Mon-Fri, 10am-6pm Sat, 1-5pm Sun Sep-May) Anyone charmed by snakes and all things slithery will find this museum fascinating; for ophidiophobes, it's a complete nightmare, filled with the world's largest collection of different rattlesnake species. You'll also find snake-themed beer bottles and postmarks from every town named 'Rattlesnake' in the US.

Around Town

★Indian Pueblo Cultural Center MUSEUM

(IPCC; 505-843-7270; www.indianpueblo.org; 2401 12th St NW; adult/child 5-17yr $8.40/5.40; 9am-5pm; P) Collectively run by New Mexico's 19 Pueblos, this cultural center is an essential stop-off during even the shortest Albuquerque visit. Revamped in 2016, the museum today holds fascinating displays sharing the stories of the Pueblos' collective history and individual artistic traditions, while the galleries offer changing temporary exhibitions. They're arrayed in a crescent around a plaza that's regularly used for dances and crafts demonstrations. **Pueblo Harvest Cafe** (505-724-3510; www.puebloharvestcafe.com; 2401 12th St NW; lunch $13-20, dinner $12-40; 7am-9pm Mon-Sat, to 4pm Sun;) is recommended and there's also a large gift shop and retail gallery.

Petroglyph National Monument ARCHAEOLOGICAL SITE

(505-899-0205; www.nps.gov/petr; 6001 Unser Blvd NW; visitor center 8am-4:30pm; P) FREE The lava fields preserved in this large desert park, west of the Rio Grande, are adorned with more than 23,000 ancient petroglyphs (1000 BC–AD 1700). Several trails are scattered far and wide: **Boca Negra Canyon** is the busiest and most accessible (open 8:30am to 4:30pm; parking $1/2 weekday/weekend); **Piedras Marcadas** holds around 300 petroglyphs (sunrise to sunset); while **Rinconada Canyon** is a lovely desert walk (sunrise to sunset; 2.2 miles round trip), but with fewer visible petroglyphs.

Sandia Peak Tramway CABLE CAR
(505-856-7325; www.sandiapeak.com; 30 Tramway Rd NE; adult/youth 13-20yr/child $25/20/15, parking $2; 9am-9pm Jun-Aug, 9am-8pm Wed-Mon, from 5pm Tue Sep-May; P) The United States' longest aerial tram climbs 2.7 miles from the desert floor in the northeast corner of the city to the summit of 10,378ft Sandia Crest. Views are spectacular at any time, though sunsets are particularly brilliant. The summit complex holds gift shops, and a new fine dining restaurant and sky bar were adding the final touches during our research period. Hiking trails lead through the woods. If you plan on hiking down (or up), a one-way ticket costs $15.

Activities

The omnipresent Sandia Mountains and the less-crowded Manzano Mountains offer outdoor activities, including hiking, skiing (downhill and cross-country), mountain biking, rock climbing and camping.

Cycling is the ideal way to explore Albuquerque under your own steam. In addition to cycling lanes throughout the city, mountain bikers will dig the foothills trails east of town and the scenic **Paseo del Bosque** (www.cabq.gov; dawn-dusk), alongside the Rio Grande. For details of the excellent network of cycling lanes, see www.bikeabq.org.

The setting for the hit AMC dramas *Breaking Bad* and *Better Call Saul,* Albuquerque is a fun destination for fans, who can check out locations seen in both shows. Cyclists can tour with **Routes Rentals** (505-933-5667; www.routesrentals.com; 404 San Felipe St NW; 4/24hr rental from $20/35; 8am-6pm Mar-Nov, to 5:30pm Dec-Feb) or hop on an RV with **Breaking Bad RV Tours** (1919 Old Town Rd; 3hr tour per person $75).

Elena Gallegos Open Space HIKING, MOUNTAIN BIKING
(505-452-5200; www.cabq.gov; Simms Park Rd; weekday/weekend parking $1/2; 7am-9pm Apr-Oct, closes 7pm Nov-Mar) The western foothills of the Sandias are Albuquerque's outdoor playground, and the high desert landscape here is sublime. As well as several picnic areas, this section holds trailheads for hiking, running and mountain biking; some routes are wheelchair-accessible. Come early, before the sun gets too hot, or late, to enjoy the panoramic views at sunset amid the lonesome howls of coyotes. Basic trail maps are available on your way in.

Festivals & Events

Friday's *Albuquerque Journal* (www.abqjournal.com) includes exhaustive listings of festivals and activities.

Gathering of Nations Powwow CULTURAL
(www.gatheringofnations.com; late Apr) Dance competitions, displays of Native American arts and crafts, and the 'Miss Indian World' contest. Held in late April.

★**International Balloon Fiesta** BALLOON
(www.balloonfiesta.com; $10; early Oct) The largest balloon festival in the world. You simply haven't lived until you've seen a three-story-tall Tony the Tiger land in your

NEW MEXICO FACTS

Nickname Land of Enchantment

Population 2.1 million

Area 121,298 sq miles

Capital city Santa Fe (population 80,880)

Other cities Albuquerque (population 560,200), Las Cruces (102,296)

Sales tax 5.1% to 9.25%

Birthplace of John Denver (1943–97), Smokey Bear (1950–76)

Home of International UFO Museum & Research Center (Roswell)

Politics A 'purple' state, with a more liberal north and conservative south

Famous for Ancient pueblos, the first atomic bomb (1945), where Bugs Bunny should have turned left

State question 'Red or green?' (chili sauce, that is)

Highest/Lowest points Wheeler Peak (13,161ft) / Red Bluff Reservoir (2842ft)

Driving distances Albuquerque to Santa Fe 50 miles, Santa Fe to Taos 70 miles

hotel courtyard, and that's exactly the sort of thing that happens during the festival, which features mass dawn take-offs on each of its nine days, overlapping the first and second weekends in October.

Sleeping

★ El Vado MOTEL $

(☎510-361-1667; www.elvadoabq.com; 2500 Central Ave SW; r $137-150, ste $150-180) The white adobe walls of this revamped Route 66 motor court darn near glow as the sun rises, when you might just catch hot-air balloons rising almost overhead. Anchored by a central pool and flanked by a taproom and a handful of small eateries, this place – built in 1937 – exudes a hip-but-welcoming vibe. Mid-century modern decor.

Andaluz BOUTIQUE HOTEL $$

(☎505-388-0088; www.hotelandaluz.com; 125 2nd St NW; r/ste from $191/206; P❄@📶🐾) Albuquerque's finest historic hotel, built in the heart of downtown in 1939, has been modernized while retaining period details such as its stunning central atrium, where cozy arched nooks hold tables and couches. Rooms feature hypoallergenic bedding and carpets, the **Más Tapas Y Vino** (☎505-923-9080; tapas $8-22, mains $26-38; ⏰7am-2pm & 5-9:30pm) restaurant is notable, and there's a rooftop bar **Ibiza Bar & Patio**.

Böttger Mansion B&B $$

(☎505-243-3639; www.bottger.com; 110 San Felipe St NW; r $120-169; P❄@📶) The friendly proprietor gives this well-appointed B&B, built in 1912 and one minute's walk from the plaza, an edge over tough competition. Three of its seven themed, antique-furnished rooms have pressed-tin ceilings, one has a Jacuzzi, and sumptuous breakfasts are served in a honeysuckle-lined courtyard loved by bird-watchers. Past guests include Elvis, Janis Joplin and Machine Gun Kelly.

★ Los Poblanos B&B $$$

(☎505-344-9297; www.lospoblanos.com; 4803 Rio Grande Blvd NW; r/ste from $255/340; P❄@📶🏊) This amazing 20-room inn, on a 1930s rural ranch that's a National Historic Place, is five minutes' drive north of Old Town. Near the Rio Grande, it's set amid 25 acres of gardens, lavender fields and an organic farm. Gorgeous rooms feature kiva fireplaces, while produce from the farm is served at **Campo**, the on-site restaurant earning national acclaim for its wood-fired fare.

Breakfast is not included in the room price, but you can dine at Campo or pick up something quick at the **Farm Store**. For cocktails, it's hard to beat the rustically chic **Bar Campo**. The lavender blooms mid-June through July.

Eating

★ Pop Fizz MEXICAN $

(☎505-508-1082; www.pop-fizz.net; 1701 4th St SW, National Hispanic Cultural Center; popsicles from $2.50, snacks $6-9; ⏰11am-6pm Mon, to 7pm Tue-Thu & Sun, to 8pm Fri & Sat; 📶👪) These all-natural *paletas* (popsicles) straight-up rock: cool off with flavors such as cucumber chile lime, mango or pineapple habanero – or perhaps you'd rather splurge on a cinnamon-churro ice-cream taco? The kitchen also whips up all sorts of messy goodness, including carne asada fries, Sonoran dogs and Frito pies. The mango red chile is deliciously kicky.

★ Golden Crown Panaderia BAKERY $

(☎505-243-2424; www.goldencrown.biz; 1103 Mountain Rd NW; pastries $1-3, mains $10-25; ⏰7am-8pm Tue-Sat, from 10am Sun) Who doesn't love a friendly neighborhood cafe-bakery? Especially one in a cozy old adobe, with gracious staff, oven-fresh bread and pizza (with green chile or blue-corn crusts), fruity empanadas, smooth espresso coffees and cookies all round? Call ahead to reserve a loaf of quick-selling green-chile bread – then eat it hot, out on the patio.

Frontier NEW MEXICAN $

(☎505-266-0550; www.frontierrestaurant.com; 2400 Central Ave SE; mains $4-14; ⏰5am-1am; 👪) This giant cantina that sprawls across several rooms has to be seen to be believed: get in line for enormous buttery cinnamon rolls, smothered enchiladas and some of the best huevos rancheros in town. It may be fast-foody, but the atmosphere and prices are unbeatable.

Level 5 AMERICAN $$

(☎505-246-9989; www.hotelchaco.com; 2000 Bellemah Ave; $14-54; ⏰7am-2pm daily, 4:30-10pm Sun-Wed, to 11pm Thu-Sat) Whoa, that view. A breathtaking panorama of Albuquerque, flanked by the Sandia Mountains, accompanies your meal, whether dining inside or out at this sleek spot atop the Hotel Chaco. Service is upbeat but a little flighty, but the fancy fare on the short and seasonal menu delivers. Much of the produce is sourced from the hotel garden below.

★Artichoke Cafe MODERN AMERICAN **$$$**
(☎505-243-0200; www.artichokecafe.com; 424 Central Ave SE; lunch mains $12-19, dinner mains $24-39; ⏲11am-2:30pm & 5-9pm Mon-Fri, 5-10pm Sat, 5-9pm Sun) Elegant and unpretentious, this popular bistro prepares creative gourmet cuisine with panache and is always high on foodies' lists of Albuquerque's best. The Scottish Salmon at dinner is good. It's on the eastern edge of downtown, between the bus station and I-40.

Drinking & Entertainment

Popejoy Hall (☎505-277-3824; www.popejoypresents.com; 203 Cornell Dr NE) is the primary venue for big-name national acts, local opera, symphony and theater. **Launch Pad** (☎505-764-8887; www.launchpadrocks.com; 618 Central Ave SW) is best for local acts. To find out what's happening in town, pick up the free weekly *Alibi* (www.alibi.com).

★Marble Brewery MICROBREWERY
(☎505-243-2739; www.marblebrewery.com; 111 Marble Ave NW; ⏲noon-midnight Mon-Sat, to 10:30pm Sun) Convivial downtown brewpub, attached to its namesake brewery, with a snug interior for winter nights and a beer garden where local bands play early-evening gigs in summer. If it's nice out, snag a spot on the rooftop deck. Be sure to try its Red Ale. There's usually a food truck or two parked outside.

Java Joe's CAFE
(☎505-765-1514; www.downtownjavajoes.com; 906 Park Ave SW; ⏲6:30am-3:30pm; 🚻🐾) Best known these days for its explosive cameo role in *Breaking Bad*, this comfy coffee shop still makes a great stop-off for a java jolt or a bowl of the hottest chile in town.

Anodyne BAR
(☎505-244-1820; 409 Central Ave NW; ⏲4pm-2am Mon-Sat, 7pm-midnight Sun) An excellent spot for a game of pool, Anodyne is a huge space with book-lined walls, wood ceilings, plenty of overstuffed chairs, more than 100 bottled beers and great people-watching on Central Ave.

Information

EMERGENCY & MEDICAL SERVICES

Police (☎505-768-2200; www.cabq.gov/police; 400 Roma Ave NW)

Presbyterian Hospital (☎505-841-1234; www.phs.org; 1100 Central Ave SE; ⏲emergency 24hr)

UNM Hospital (☎505-272-2111; 2211 Lomas Blvd NE; ⏲emergency 24hr) Holds a level 1 trauma center.

TOURIST INFORMATION

Old Town Information Center (☎505-243-3215; www.visitalbuquerque.org; 303 Romero Ave NW; ⏲10am-5pm Nov-Apr, to 6pm May-Oct) Come here to get the scoop. In Plaza Don Luis.

Getting There & Around

AIR

New Mexico's largest airport, **Albuquerque International Sunport** (ABQ; ☎505-244-7700; www.abqsunport.com; 2200 Sunport Blvd SE; 📶), is 5 miles southeast of downtown and served by multiple airlines. Free shuttles connect the terminal building with the Sunport Car Rental Center at 3400 University Blvd SE, home to all the airport's car-rental facilities.

The **Sandia Shuttle** (☎888-775-5696; www.sandiashuttle.com; Santa Fe one way $33; ⏲8:45am-11:45pm) runs from the airport to Santa Fe 19 times per day.

BUS

The **Alvarado Transportation Center** (☎505-423-7433; www.cabq.gov/transit; 100 1st St SW,

ALBUQUERQUE FOR KIDS

Albuquerque has lots on offer for kids, from hands-on museums to cool hikes.

¡Explora! (☎505-224-8300; www.explora.us; 1701 Mountain Rd NW; adult/child 1-11yr $10/6; ⏲10am-6pm Mon-Sat, from noon Sun; 🅿🚻) From the lofty high-wire bike to the mind-boggling Light, Shadow, Color area, this gung-ho museum offers a hands-on exhibit for every type of child (don't miss the elevator).

New Mexico Museum of Natural History & Science (☎505-841-2800; www.nmnaturalhistory.org; 1801 Mountain Rd NW; adult/child 3-12yr $8/5; ⏲9am-5pm; 🅿🚻) Dinosaur-mad kids are certain to love this huge modern museum, on the northeastern fringes of Old Town. From the T. rex in the main atrium onwards, it's crammed with ferocious ancient beasts.

cnr Central Ave) is home to **Greyhound** (☎505-243-4435, 800-231-2222; www.greyhound.com; 320 1st St SW), which serves destinations throughout the state and beyond, though not Santa Fe or Taos.

ABQ Ride (☎505-243-7433; www.cabq.gov/transit; 100 1st St SW; adult/child $1/35¢, day pass $2) is a public bus system covering most of Albuquerque on weekdays and major tourist spots daily.

TRAIN

Amtrak's *Southwest Chief* stops at Albuquerque's **Amtrak Station** (☎800-872-7245; www.amtrak.com; 320 1st St SW), which is part of the Alvarado Transportation Center. Trains head east to Chicago (from $149, 26 hours) or west to Los Angeles (from $67, 16¾ hours), once daily in each direction.

A commuter light-rail line, the **New Mexico Rail Runner Express** (www.riometro.org; adult/child $10/5), shares the station. It makes several stops in the Albuquerque metropolitan area, but more importantly for visitors it runs all the way north to Santa Fe (one way $10, 1¾ hours), with eight departures on weekdays, four on Saturdays and three on Sundays.

Along I-40

Although you can zip between Albuquerque and Flagstaff, AZ, in less than five hours, the national monuments and pueblos along the way are well worth a visit. For a scenic loop, take Hwy 53 southwest from Grants, which leads to all the following sights except Acoma. Hwy 602 brings you north to Gallup.

Acoma Pueblo

The dramatic mesa-top 'Sky City' sits 7000ft above sea level and 367ft above the surrounding plateau. One of the oldest continuously inhabited settlements in North America, this place has been home to pottery-making Pueblo peoples since the 11th century. Guided tours leave from the **cultural center** (☎800-747-0181; www.acomaskycity.org; Rte 38; tours adult/child $25/17; ⏲tours 9-30am-3:30pm mid-Mar–Oct, to 2:30pm Nov–mid-Mar; Ⓟ) at the foot of the mesa and take 90 minutes. For the most dramatic drive to Sky City, take exit 102 from I-40, which is about 60 miles west of Albuquerque. Check the cultural center website before your visit for detailed directions. Also confirm it's not closed for ceremonial or other reasons.

El Morro National Monument

The 200ft sandstone outcropping at **El Morro National Monument** (☎505-783-4226; www.nps.gov/elmo; Hwy 53; ⏲visitor center 9am-6pm Jun-Aug, to 5pm Sep-May, trails close 1hr earlier; Ⓟ) FREE, also known as 'Inscription Rock,' has been a travelers' oasis for millennia. Thousands of carvings – from petroglyphs in the pueblo at the top (c 1275) to elaborate inscriptions by Spanish conquistadors and Anglo pioneers – offer a unique historical record. Make time for the **Mesa Top Trail** and its sweeping views in addition to the shorter **Inscription Rock Trail**. It's about 38 miles southwest of Grants via Hwy 53.

Zuni Pueblo

The Zuni are known for their delicately inlaid silverwork, which is sold in stores lining Hwy 53. Check in at the **Zuni Tourism Visitor Center** (☎505-782-7238; www.zunitourism.com; 1239 Hwy 53; 1hr tour $20; ⏲9am-5:30pm Mon-Fri, plus 9am-4pm Sat Jul-Sep) for information, photo permits and tours of the pueblo, which lead you among stone houses and beehive-shaped adobe ovens to the massive **Our Lady of Guadalupe Mission**, featuring impressive kachina (spirit) murals. The **A:shiwi A:wan Museum & Heritage Center** (☎505-782-4403; www.ashiwi-museum.org; Ojo Caliente Rd; ⏲8am-5pm Mon-Fri) FREE displays early photos and other tribal artifacts.

The friendly, eight-room **Inn at Halona** (☎505-782-4547; www.halona.com; 23b Pia Mesa Rd; r from $85; Ⓟ📶), decorated with local Zuni arts and crafts, is the only place to stay on the pueblo.

Santa Fe

Missions, museums and Meow Wolf. All are players in the story of 'the city different,' a place that makes its own rules without forgetting its long and storied past. Walking through its adobe neighborhoods, or around the busy plaza that remains its core, there's no denying that Santa Fe has a timeless, earthy soul. Indeed, its artistic inclinations are a principal attraction – there are more quality museums and galleries here than you could see in just one visit.

At more than 7000ft above sea level, Santa Fe is also the nation's highest state capital. Sitting at the foot of the Sangre de Cristo range, it makes a fantastic base for hiking, mountain biking and skiing. Après adventure, you can indulge in chile-smothered local cuisine, buy turquoise and silver directly from Native American jewelers in the Plaza, visit remarkable churches, or simply wander centuries-old, cottonwood-shaded lanes, daydreaming about one day moving here.

Sights

★The Plaza PLAZA

(Map p222) For more than 400 years, the Plaza has stood at the heart of Santa Fe. Originally it marked the far northern end of the Camino Real from Mexico; later, it was the goal for wagons heading west along the Santa Fe Trail. Today, this grassy square is peopled by tourists wandering from museum to margarita, food vendors, skateboarding kids and street musicians. Beneath the portico of the Palace of the Governors, along its northern side, Native Americans sell jewelry and pottery.

★Georgia O'Keeffe Museum MUSEUM

(Map p222; ☎505-946-1000; www.okeeffemuseum.org; 217 Johnson St; adult/child $13/free; ⏲10am-5pm Sat-Thu, to 7pm Fri) With 10 beautifully lit galleries in a rambling 20th-century adobe, this museum boasts the world's largest collection of O'Keeffe's work. She's best known for her luminous New Mexican landscapes, but the changing exhibitions here range through her entire career, from her early years through to her time at Ghost Ranch. Major museums worldwide own her most famous canvases, so you may not see familiar paintings, but you're sure to be bowled over by the thick brushwork and transcendent colors on show.

Meow Wolf MUSEUM

(☎505-395-6369; www.meowwolf.com; 1352 Rufina Circle; adult/child $29/21; ⏲10am-8pm Sun, Mon, Wed & Thu, to 10pm Fri & Sat, from 9am mid-Jun–mid-Aug; P 👪) If you've been hankering for a trip to another dimension but have yet to find a portal, the House of Eternal Return by Meow Wolf could be the place for you. The premise here is quite ingenious: visitors get to explore a recreated Victorian house for clues related to the disappearance of a Californian family, following a narrative that leads deeper into fragmented bits of a multiverse (often via secret passages), all of which are unique, interactive art installations.

Activities

The **Pecos Wilderness** and **Santa Fe National Forest**, east of town, have more than 1000 miles of hiking and biking trails, several of which lead to 12,000ft peaks. Contact the Public Lands Information Center for maps and details, and check weather reports for advance warnings of frequent summer storms.

Mellow Velo (Map p222; ☎505-995-8356; www.mellowvelo.com; 132 E Marcy St; mountain bikes per day from $40; ⏲9:30am-6pm Mon-Fri, to 5pm Sat & Sun mid-May–Oct, shorter hours Nov–mid-May) rents mountain bikes and provides trail information. Operators including **New Wave Rafting Co** (☎800-984-1444; www.newwaverafting.com; adult/child 6-11yr from $60/49; ⏲mid-Apr–Aug) offer white-water rafting adventures through the Rio Grande Gorge, the wild Taos Box and the Rio Chama Wilderness.

Dale Ball Trails MOUNTAIN BIKING, HIKING

(www.santafenm.gov/trails_1; Cerro Gordo Rd, off Upper Canyon Rd) More than 20 miles of mountain-biking and hiking trails, with fabulous desert and mountain views a quick drive from downtown. The 9.7-mile Outer Limits trail is a classic ride, combining fast singletrack in the north with the more technical central section. Hikers should check out the 4-mile round-trip trail to Picacho Peak, with a steep but accessible 1250ft elevation gain.

Ski Santa Fe SKIING

(☎505-982-4429; www.skisantafe.com; Hwy 475; lift ticket adult/13-23yr/child $80/62/54; ⏲9am-4pm Dec-Mar) Often overlooked for its more famous cousin outside Taos, the smaller Santa Fe ski area boasts the same dry powder (though not quite as much), with a higher base elevation (10,350ft). It caters to families and expert skiers, who come for the glades, steep bump runs and long groomers a mere 16 miles from town.

Santa Fe School of Cooking COOKING

(Map p222; ☎505-983-4511; www.santafeschoolofcooking.com; 125 N Guadalupe St; 2hr classes $80, 3hr classes from $82; ⏲9:30am-5:30pm Mon-Fri, to 5pm Sat, 10:30am-3:30pm Sun) Sign up for green- or red-chile workshops to master the basics of Southwestern cuisine, or try your hand at *chile rellenos* (stuffed chile peppers), tamales or more sophisticated flavors such as mustard mango habanero sauce. It also offers several popular restaurant walking tours.

Festivals & Events

★International Folk Art Market CULTURAL

(☎505-992-7600; www.folkartalliance.org; ⏲mid-Jul) The world's largest folk-art market

Santa Fe

draws around 150 artists from 50 countries to the Museum of International Folk Art for a festive weekend of craft shopping and cultural events in July.

Santa Fe Indian Market CULTURAL

(☎ 505-983-5220; www.swaia.org; ⏲ Aug) Around a thousand artists from about 220 tribes and pueblos show work at this world-famous juried show, held the weekend after the third Thursday in August. More than 100,000 visitors converge on the Plaza, at open studios, gallery shows and the Native Cinema Showcase. Come Friday or Saturday to see pieces competing for the top prizes; wait until Sunday before trying to bargain.

★ **Santa Fe Fiesta & Burning of Zozobra** CULTURAL

(☎ 505-913-1517; www.santafefiesta.org; ⏲ early Sep) This 10-day celebration of the 1692 resettlement of Santa Fe following the 1680 Pueblo Revolt includes concerts, a candlelit procession and the much-loved Pet Parade. Everything kicks off with the Friday-night torching of **Zozobra** (www.burnzozobra.com) – a 50ft-tall effigy of 'Old Man Gloom' – before some 60,000 people in Fort Marcy Park.

Sleeping

Silver Saddle Motel MOTEL $

(☎ 505-471-7663; www.santafesilversaddlemotel.com; 2810 Cerrillos Rd; r $68-85; P ❄ @ 📶 🐾) This old-fashioned, slightly kitschy Route 66 motel compound offers the best budget value in town. Some rooms have pleasant tiled kitchenettes, while all have shady wooden arcades outside and cowboy-inspired decor inside – get the Kenny Rogers or Wyatt Earp rooms if you can. It's located 3 miles southwest of the Plaza on busy Cerrillos Rd. Pet fee is $10 per night.

Black Canyon Campground CAMPGROUND $

(☎ 877-444-6777; www.recreation.gov; Hwy 475; tent & RV sites $10; ⏲ May–mid-Oct) A mere 8

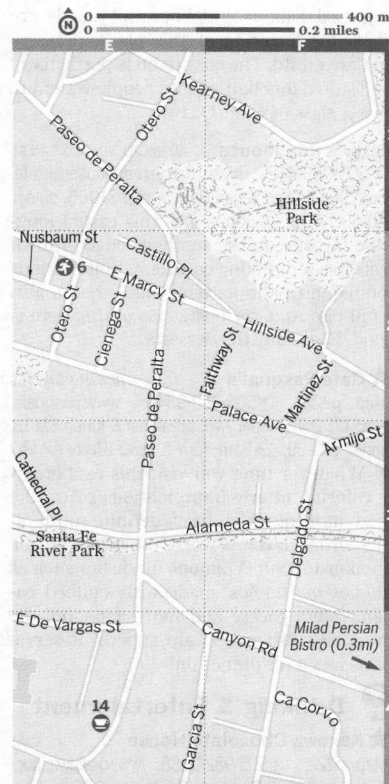

Santa Fe

Top Sights
1 Georgia O'Keeffe Museum C1
2 Palace of the Governors & New Mexico History Museum D2
3 The Plaza D2

Sights
4 New Mexico Museum of Art D2
5 State Capitol D4

Activities, Courses & Tours
6 Mellow Velo E2
7 Santa Fe School of Cooking C1

Sleeping
8 La Fonda D2
9 Las Palomas B2
10 Santa Fe Motel & Inn B4

Eating
11 Cafe Pasqual's D2
12 Tia Sophia's C2

Drinking & Nightlife
13 Bell Tower Bar D2
14 Kakawa Chocolate House E4
15 Santa Fe Spirits B4

Entertainment
16 Jean Cocteau Cinema B3
17 Lensic Performing Arts Center C2

Shopping
18 Blue Rain A4
19 Kowboyz B4
20 Santa Fe Farmers Market A4

miles from the Plaza is this gorgeous and secluded national forest service spot, complete with 36 sites and hiking and biking trails nearby. Water is available, but there are no hookups. If it's full, Hyde Memorial State Park is up the road, while the Big Tesuque and Aspen Basin campgrounds (free, but no potable water) are closer to the ski area.

★Santa Fe Motel & Inn HOTEL **$$**
(Map p222; ☎505-982-1039; www.santafemotel.com; 510 Cerrillos Rd; r from $159, casitas from $239; P ❄ @ 📶 🐾) Even the motel rooms in this downtown option, close to the Railyard and a real bargain in low season, have the flavor of a Southwestern B&B, with colorful tiles, clay sunbursts and tin mirrors. The courtyard casitas cost a little more and come with kiva fireplaces and little patios. Rates include a full hot breakfast, served outdoors in summer.

Las Palomas BOUTIQUE HOTEL **$$**
(Map p222; ☎505-982-5560; www.laspalomas.com; 460 W San Francisco St; r from $169; P ❄ 📶 🐾) Rustically modern rooms fill several low-slung buildings clustered near the intersection of W San Francisco St and Park Ave a half-mile from the plaza. A few quirks here and there – do these window shades shut all the way? – keep the pretension at bay at this glossy self-described compound. Rooms have gas or wood-fired fireplaces.

★La Fonda HISTORIC HOTEL **$$$**
(Map p222; ☎505-982-5511; www.lafondasantafe.com; 100 E San Francisco St; r from $419; P ❄ @ 📶 🏊 🐾) Long renowned as the 'Inn at the end of the Santa Fe Trail,' Santa Fe's loveliest historic hotel sprawls through an old adobe just off the Plaza. Retaining its beautiful folk-art windows and murals, it's both classy and cozy, with some wonderful top-floor luxury suites, and superb sunset views from the

rooftop **Bell Tower Bar** (Map p222; 100 E San Francisco St; ⌚3pm-sunset Mon-Fri, noon-sunset Sat & Sun May-Nov, closed Dec-Apr).

Eating

★La Choza NEW MEXICAN $

(☎505-982-0909; www.lachozasf.com; 905 Alarid St; lunch $10-18 dinner $12-25; ⌚11:30am-2:30pm & 5-9pm Mon-Sat; P ♿) Blue-corn burritos, a festive interior and an extensive margarita list make La Choza a perennial (and colorful) favorite among Santa Fe's discerning diners. Of the many New Mexican restaurants in Santa Fe, this one always seems to be reliably excellent. As with the Shed, its sister restaurant, arrive early or reserve.

Tia Sophia's NEW MEXICAN $

(Map p222; ☎505-983-9880; www.tiasophias.com; 210 W San Francisco St; breakfast $8-11, lunch $9-12; ⌚7am-2pm Mon-Sat, 8am-1pm Sun; ✎ ♿) Local artists and visiting celebrities outnumber tourists at this long-standing and always packed Santa Fe favorite. Breakfast is the meal of choice, with fantastic burritos and other Southwestern dishes, but lunch is pretty damn tasty too; try the perfectly prepared *chile rellenos* (stuffed chile peppers), or the rota of daily specials. The shelf of books helps entertain the little ones.

Clafoutis FRENCH $

(☎505-988-1809; 333 Cordova Rd; pastries $2-6, mains $5-13; ⌚7am-4pm Mon-Sat) As Oscar Wilde once quipped, the only way to get rid of temptation is to give in, and that sums up the approach you should take at this *super bon* French patisserie. Drop by for delectable pastries (*beignets* on Saturday!) or sit down for breakfast or lunch, with a tantalizing selection of crepes, omelets, quiches and brie sandwiches.

★Jambo Cafe AFRICAN $$

(☎505-473-1269; www.jambocafe.net; 2010 Cerrillos Rd; mains $10-17; ⌚11am-9pm Mon-Sat) Hidden within a shopping center, this African-flavored cafe is hard to spot from the road; once inside, though, it's a lovely spot, always busy with locals who love its distinctive goat, chicken and lentil curries, veggie sandwiches and roti flatbreads, not to mention the reggae soundtrack.

Milad Persian Bistro MIDDLE EASTERN $$

(☎505-303-3581; www.miladbistro.com; 802 Canyon Rd; small plates $3-16, mains $14-22; ⌚5-10pm Tue-Thu, from 11am Fri-Sun) The delicately seasoned kabobs and bountiful salads are made for lingering at this pleasant bistro on Canyon Rd. The cozy patio is particularly well suited for chatting and people-watching over a glass of wine. Or two.

Harry's Roadhouse AMERICAN, NEW MEXICAN $$

(☎505-989-4629; www.harrysroadhousesantafe.com; 96 Old Las Vegas Hwy; lunch $10-16, dinner $10-30; ⌚7am-9:30pm; ♿) This casual long-time favorite on the southern edge of town feels like a rambling cottage with its various rooms and patio garden – and there's also a full bar. And, seriously, *everything* here is good. Especially the desserts.

★Cafe Pasqual's NEW MEXICAN $$$

(Map p222; ☎505-983-9340; www.pasquals.com; 121 Don Gaspar Ave; breakfast & lunch $11-18, dinner $18-39; ⌚8am-3pm & 5:30-10pm; ✎ ♿) 🍃 Whatever time you visit this exuberantly colorful, utterly unpretentious place, the food, most of which has a definite south-of-the-border flavor, is worth every penny. The breakfast menu is famous for dishes such as *huevos motuleños,* made with sautéed bananas, feta cheese and more; later on, the meat and fish mains are superb. Reservations taken for dinner only.

Drinking & Entertainment

★Kakawa Chocolate House CAFE

(Map p222; ☎505-982-0388; www.kakawachocolates.com; 1050 Paseo de Peralta; ⌚9:30am-6pm Mon-Sat, from noon Sun) Chocolate addicts simply can't miss this ode to the sacred bean. This isn't your mom's marshmallow-laden hot chocolate, though – these rich elixirs are based on historic recipes and divided into two categories: European (eg 17th-century France) and Meso-American (Mayan and Aztec). Bonus: it also sells sublime chocolates (prickly-pear mescal) and spicy chile caramels.

★Santa Fe Spirits DISTILLERY

(Map p222; ☎505-780-5906; www.santafespirits.com; 308 Read St; ⌚3-8pm Sun, to 9pm Mon, to 9:30pm Tue-Thu, to 10pm Fri & Sat) The local distillery's tasting flight includes an impressive amount of liquor, including shots of Colkegan single malt, Wheeler's gin and Expedition vodka. Leather chairs and exposed rafters make the in-town tasting room an intimate spot for an aperitif; fans can reserve a spot on the hourly tours of the distillery.

★Santa Fe Opera OPERA

(☎505-986-5900; www.santafeopera.org; Hwy 84/285, Tesuque; tours adult/child $10/free; ⌚Jul

DON'T MISS

THE MUSEUM OF NEW MEXICO

The Museum of New Mexico administers four excellent museums in Santa Fe. Two are at the Plaza; two are on Museum Hill, 2 miles southwest.

Palace of the Governors & New Mexico History Museum (Map p222; 505-476-5100; www.palaceofthegovernors.org; 105 W Palace Ave; adult/child $12/free; 10am-5pm, closed Mon Nov-Apr) The oldest public building in the US, this low-slung adobe complex began as home to New Mexico's first Spanish governor in 1610. It was occupied by Pueblo Indians following their revolt in 1680, and after 1846 became the seat of the US Territory's earliest governors. During research the Palace was undergoing renovations; expect a new look after its scheduled 2020 reopening. The adjoining New Mexico History Museum engagingly tells the story of the state, beginning with the Spanish arrival in the 1500s. The Palace entrance is located in the History Museum.

New Mexico Museum of Art (Map p222; 505-476-5072; www.nmartmuseum.org; 107 W Palace Ave; adult/child $12/free; 10am-5pm Tue-Sun) Built in 1917 and a prime early example of Santa Fe's Pueblo Revival architecture, the New Mexico Museum of Art has spent a century collecting and displaying works by regional artists. A treasure trove of works by the great names who put New Mexico on the cultural map, from the Taos Society of Artists to Georgia O'Keeffe, it's also a lovely building in which to stroll around, with a cool garden courtyard. Constantly changing temporary exhibitions ensure its continuing relevance.

Museum of International Folk Art (505-476-1200; www.internationalfolkart.org; 706 Camino Lejo; adult/child $12/free; 10am-5pm, closed Mon Nov-Apr; P) Santa Fe's most unusual and exhilarating museum centers on the world's largest collection of folk art. Its huge main gallery displays whimsical and mind-blowing objects from more than 100 different countries. Tiny human figures go about their business in fully realized village and city scenes, while dolls, masks, toys and garments spill across the walls. Changing exhibitions in other wings explore vernacular art and culture worldwide.

Museum of Indian Arts & Culture (505-476-1269; www.indianartsandculture.org; 710 Camino Lejo; adult/child $12/free; 10am-5pm, closed Mon Sep-May; P) This top-quality museum sets out to trace the origins and history of the various Native American peoples of the entire Southwest, and explain and illuminate their widely differing cultural traditions. Pueblo, Navajo and Apache interviewees describe the contemporary realities each group now faces, while a truly superb collection of ceramics, modern and ancient, is complemented by stimulating temporary displays.

& Aug, tours 9am Mon-Fri Jun-Aug) Many visitors flock to Santa Fe for the opera alone: the theater is a marvel, with 360-degree views of sandstone wilderness crowned with sunsets and moonrises, while at center stage the world's finest talent performs magnificent masterworks. It's still the Wild West, though; you can even wear jeans. Shuttles run to and from Santa Fe ($25) and Albuquerque ($40); reserve online.

Lensic Performing Arts Center PERFORMING ARTS

(Map p222; 505-988-7050; www.lensic.org; 211 W San Francisco St) A beautifully renovated 1930 movie house, the theater hosts touring productions and classic films as well as seven different performance groups, including the Aspen Santa Fe Ballet and the Santa Fe Symphony Orchestra & Chorus.

Jean Cocteau Cinema CINEMA

(Map p222; 505-466-5528; www.jeancocteaucinema.com; 418 Montezuma Ave) Revived by George RR Martin in 2013, this is the top cinema in town for indie flicks; also has book signings, occasional live concerts and an in-theater bar.

Shopping

★Santa Fe Farmers Market MARKET

(Map p222; 505-983-4098; www.santafefarmersmarket.com; 1607 Paseo de Peralta, at Guadalupe St; 7am-1pm Sat Jun-Sep, 8am-1pm Sat Oct-May, also open Tue & Wed seasonally;) Local produce, much of it heirloom and organic, is on sale at this spacious indoor-outdoor market, alongside homemade goodies, inexpensive food, natural body products and arts and crafts.

Blue Rain ART
(Map p222; ☎505-954-9902; www.blueraingallery.com; 544 S Guadalupe St; ⏲10am-6pm Mon-Fri, to 5pm Sat) This large space in the Railyard district is the top gallery in town representing contemporary Native American and regional artists. There are generally several shows on at once, encompassing everything from modern pottery and sculpture to powerful landscapes and portraits.

Kowboyz CLOTHING
(Map p222; ☎505-984-1256; www.kowboyz.com; 345 W Manhattan Ave; ⏲10am-5:30pm) Secondhand shop selling everything you need to cowboy up. Shirts are a great deal; the amazing selection of boots, however, demands top dollar. Movie costumers in search of authentic Western wear often come here.

ℹ Information

EMERGENCY & MEDICAL SERVICES

Christus St Vincent Hospital (☎505-983-3361; www.stvin.org; 455 St Michaels Dr; ⏲24hr emergency)

Police (☎505-428-3710; 2515 Camino Entrada)

TOURIST INFORMATION

New Mexico Visitor Information Center (Map p222; ☎505-827-7336; www.newmexico.org; 491 Old Santa Fe Trail; ⏲10am-5pm Mon-Fri) Housed in the 1878 Lamy Building, this friendly place offers helpful advice and free coffee.

Public Lands Information Center (☎505-954-2002; www.publiclands.org; 301 Dinosaur Trail; ⏲8am-4:30pm Mon-Fri) Staff at this hugely helpful office have maps and information on public lands throughout New Mexico, and can talk you through all the hiking options.

Santa Fe Plaza Visitor Center (Map p222; ☎800-777-2489; www.santafe.org; 66 E San Francisco St, Suite 3, Plaza Galeria; ⏲10am-6pm) Pop into the Plaza Galeria center for maps and brochures. There is another visitor center at the Railyard (410 S Guadalupe St).

ℹ Getting There & Around

Daily flights to/from Denver, Dallas and Phoenix serve the small **Santa Fe Municipal Airport** (SAF; ☎505-955-2900; www.santafenm.gov/airport; 121 Aviation Dr), 10 miles southwest of downtown.

The **Sandia Shuttle Express** (☎888-775-5696; www.sandiashuttle.com; $33) connects Santa Fe with the Albuquerque Sunport.

North Central Regional Transit (Map p222; ☎505-629-4725; www.ncrtd.org) provides free shuttle bus service from downtown Santa Fe to Española on weekdays, where you can transfer to shuttles to Taos, Los Alamos, Ojo Caliente and other northern destinations. Pickup/drop-off is by the Santa Fe Trails bus stop at the Sheridan Transit Center on Sheridan St, a block northwest of the Plaza.

On weekends, the **Taos Express** (☎866-206-0754; www.taosexpress.com; $5; ⏲Sat & Sun) runs north to Taos from the corner of Guadalupe and Montezuma Sts, by the Railyard.

The Rail Runner (p220) commuter train offers eight daily connections (seven on weekends) with Albuquerque from its terminus in the Railyard and the South Capitol Station, a mile southwest. The trip takes about 1¾ hours. Arriving passengers can make use of the free Santa Fe Trails bus network.

Amtrak (800-872-7245; www.amtrak.com) serves Lamy station, 17 miles southeast, with 30-minute bus connections to Santa Fe.

If driving between Santa Fe and Albuquerque, try to take Hwy 14 (the Turquoise Trail), which passes through the old mining town (now arts colony) of Madrid, 28 miles south of Santa Fe.

The free **Santa Fe Pick-Up** meets arriving Rail Runner trains and loops around downtown until 5:30pm; it also heads out to Museum Hill. Runs past stops about every 15 minutes.

Santa Fe Trails (Map p222; ☎505-955-2001; www.santafenm.gov/transit; adult/child $1/free, day pass $2) operates buses from the Downtown Transit Center, with routes M, to Museum Hill, and 2, along Cerrillos Rd, being the most useful for visitors.

Around Santa Fe

Las Vegas

Not to be confused with Nevada's glittery gambling megalopolis, this Las Vegas is one of the loveliest towns in New Mexico, and the largest and oldest community east of the Sangre de Cristo Mountains. Its eminently strollable downtown has a pretty Old Town Plaza and holds some 900 Southwestern and Victorian buildings listed in the National Register of Historic Places.

Built in 1882 and carefully remodeled a century later, the elegant **Plaza Hotel** (☎505-425-3591; http://plazahotellvnm.com; 230 Plaza St; r $89-149; ❄@📶🐾) is Las Vegas' most celebrated lodging, as seen in the movie *No Country For Old Men*. Its sister property, the restored **Castañeda Hotel** (☎505-425-3591; www.castanedahotel.org; 524 Railroad Ave; r $89-149, ste $169; P❄📶🐾), was the first in a chain of trackside hotels from legendary hotelier Fred Harvey. It reopened its doors in 2019.

You can get sandwiches and coffee at **Traveler's Cafe** (☎505-426-8638; www.facebook.com/travelerscafenm; 1814 Plaza St; pastries

$1-4, salads & sandwiches $6-9; 7am-7pm Mon-Sat;), right on the plaza.

Los Alamos

When the top-secret Manhattan Project sprang to life in 1943, it turned the sleepy mesa-top village of Los Alamos into a busy laboratory of secluded brainiacs. Here, in the 'town that didn't exist,' the first atomic bomb was developed in almost total secrecy. Today you'll encounter a dynamic in which souvenir T-shirts emblazoned with atomic explosions and 'La Bomba' wine are sold next to books on pueblo history and wilderness hiking.

While you can't visit the **Los Alamos National Laboratory**, where classified cutting-edge research still takes place, the interactive **Bradbury Science Museum** (505-667-4444; www.lanl.gov/museum; 1350 Central Ave; 10am-5pm Tue-Sat, from 1pm Sun & Mon; P) FREE covers atomic history in fascinating detail. At the visitor center at the Manhattan Project National Historic Park you can learn more about the secret city and pick up a map pinpointing key sites downtown and across the mesa. The small but interesting **Los Alamos Historical Museum** (505-662-6272; www.losalamoshistory.org; 1050 Bathtub Row; $5; 9am-5pm Mon-Fri, 10am-4pm Sat & Sun) is on the nearby grounds of the former Los Alamos Ranch School – an outdoorsy school for boys that closed when the scientists arrived.

Grab a burger or enchiladas at the **Blue Window Bistro** (505-662-6305; www.labluewindowbistro.com; 1789 Central Ave; lunch $9-13, dinner $9-32; 11am-2:30pm Mon-Fri, 5-8:30pm Mon-Sat) followed by a beer at community-owned **Bathtub Row Brewing** (505-500-8381; www.bathtubrowbrewing.coop; 163 Central Park Sq; 2-10pm Sun-Thu, to 11pm Fri & Sat;).

Bandelier National Monument

Ancestral Puebloans dwelt in the cliffsides of beautiful Frijoles Canyon, now preserved within **Bandelier** (505-672-3861; www.nps.gov/band; Hwy 4; 1 week entry per vehicle $25; dawn-dusk; P). The adventurous can climb ladders to reach ancient caves and kivas (chambers) used until the mid-1500s. Backcountry camping (restricted to mesa tops from July to mid-September because of flood danger) requires a free permit, or there are around 100 sites at Juniper Campground, set among the pines near the monument entrance.

Note that from 9am to 3pm from mid-May 14 to mid-October, you have to take a shuttle bus to Bandelier from the **White Rock Visitor Center** (505-672-3193; www.nps.gov/band; 115 Hwy 4, White Rock; 8am-6pm mid-May–mid-Oct, 10am-2pm rest of year) 8.5 miles north on Hwy 4.

Abiquiu

The Hispanic village of Abiquiu (sounds like 'barbecue'), on Hwy 84 about 45 minutes' drive northwest of Santa Fe, is famous because artist Georgia O'Keeffe lived and painted here from 1949 until her death in 1986. With the Chama River flowing through farmland and spectacular rock landscape, this ethereal setting continues to attract artists.

Your first stop should be the new **Georgia O'Keeffe Welcome Center** (505-946-1000; www.okeeffemuseum.org; 21220 Hwy 84; 8:30am-5pm; P), which provides an overview of the O'Keeffe sights in the area. It's also the place to check-in for one-hour **tours** (505-685-4539; www.okeeffemuseum.org; standard tour $40; Tue-Sat early Mar–mid-Nov) of O'Keeffe's adobe house. Tours are often booked months in advance.

Set amid 21,000 Technicolor acres 15 miles northwest, **Ghost Ranch** (505-685-1000; www.ghostranch.org; Hwy 84; day pass adult/child $5/3; welcome center 8am-9pm; P) is a retreat center where O'Keeffe stayed many times. Besides fabulous hiking trails, it holds a **dinosaur museum** and offers basic **lodging** (505-685-1000; www.ghostranch.org; tent & RV sites $35-45, dm $99, r with/without bath from $169/159; @) plus horseback rides ($95) and various tours. To maximize your time here, review the website before your visit.

The lovely **Abiquiú Inn** (505-685-4378; www.abiquiuinn.com; 21120 Hwy 84; r from $170, casitas $250; P) is a sprawling collection of shaded fau -adobes. Its spacious casitas have kitchenettes, and the menu at the on-site restaurant, **Cafe Abiquiú** (505-685-4378; www.abiquiuinn.com; Abiquiú Inn; breakfast $6-12, lunch & dinner $10-29; 7am-9pm;), includes the usual array of New Mexican specialties.

Ojo Caliente

More than 150 years old, **Ojo Caliente Mineral Springs Resort & Spa** (505-583-2233; www.ojospa.com; 50 Los Baños Dr; r $209, cottages $249, ste from $319, tent & RV sites $40;

CANYON ROAD GALLERIES

Originally a Pueblo Indian footpath and later the main street through a Spanish farming community, Santa Fe's most famous art avenue embarked on its current incarnation in the 1920s, when artists led by Los Cinco Pintores (five painters who fell in love with New Mexico's landscape) moved in to take advantage of the cheap rent.

Today Canyon Rd is a top attraction, holding more than a hundred of Santa Fe's 300-plus galleries. The epicenter of the city's vibrant art scene, it offers everything from rare Native American antiquities to Santa Fe School masterpieces and in-your-face modern work. If gallery-hopping seems a bit overwhelming, don't worry, just wander.

Friday nights from May through October are particularly fun: that's when the galleries put on glittering openings, starting around 5pm and lasting until 7pm. Not only are these great social events, but you can also browse while nibbling on cheese, sipping Chardonnay or sparkling cider, and chatting with the artists.

P ❄ 📶) is one of the country's oldest health resorts – and Pueblo Indians have used the springs for centuries! Fifty miles north of Santa Fe on Hwy 285, it offers 11 soaking pools with several combinations of minerals. In addition to the pleasant, if nothing special, historic hotel rooms, the resort has several plush, boldly colored suites with kiva fireplaces and private soaking tubs, and New Mexican–style cottages. Its **Artesian Restaurant** (www.ojospa.com; 50 Los Baños Dr; lunch $11-16, dinner $16-38; ⏲7:30-11am, 11:30am-2:30pm & 5-9pm daily, to 9:30pm Fri & Sat summer; 📶 🖉) 🍃 prepares organic and local ingredients with aplomb.

Taos

A magical spot even by the standards of this Land of Enchantment, Taos remains forever under the spell of the powerful landscape that surrounds it: 12,300ft snowcapped peaks rise behind town, while a sage-speckled plateau unrolls to the west before plunging 800ft straight down into the Rio Grande Gorge. The sky can be a searing sapphire blue or an ominous parade of rumbling thunderheads so big they dwarf the mountains. And then there are the sunsets…

Taos Pueblo, a marvel of adobe architecture, ranks among the oldest continuously inhabited communities in the US, and stands at the root of a long history that also extends from conquistadors to mountain men to artists. The town itself is a relaxed and eccentric place, with classic mud-brick buildings, fabulous museums, quirky cafes and excellent restaurants. Its 5000 residents include bohemians and hippies, alternative-energy aficionados and old-time Hispanic families. It's both rural and worldly, and a bit otherworldly.

Sights

★Millicent Rogers Museum MUSEUM
(☎575-758-2462; www.millicentrogers.org; 1504 Millicent Rogers Rd; adult/child 6-16yr $10/2; ⏲10am-5pm; P) Rooted in the private collection of model and oil heiress Millicent Rogers, who moved to Taos in 1947, this superb museum, 4 miles northwest of the Plaza, ranges from Hispanic folk art to Navajo weaving, and even modernist jewelry designed by Rogers herself. The principal focus, however, is on Native American ceramics, and especially the beautiful black-on-black pottery created during the 20th century by Maria Martínez from San Ildefonso Pueblo.

Rio Grande Gorge Bridge BRIDGE, CANYON
(P) Constructed in 1965, this vertigo-inducing steel bridge carries Hwy 64 across the Rio Grande about 12 miles northwest of Taos. It's the seventh-highest bridge in the US (depending on your source), rising 565ft above the river and measuring 600ft long. The views from the pedestrian walkway, west over the empty Taos Plateau and down the jagged walls of the gorge, will surely make you gulp. Vendors selling jewelry, sage sticks and other souvenirs congregate on the eastern side.

The **West Rim Trail** rolls south for 9 miles from the rest area on the western side, with views of the plateau and the Sangre de Cristo Mountains.

Martínez Hacienda MUSEUM
(☎575-758-1000; www.taoshistoricmuseums.org; 708 Hacienda Way, off Lower Ranchitos Rd; adult/child $8/4; ⏲11am-4pm Mon, Tue, Fri & Sat, from noon Sun; P) Set amid the fields 2 miles southwest of the Plaza, this fortified adobe homestead was built in 1804. It served as a trading post, first for merchants venturing

north from Mexico City along the Camino Real, and then west along the Santa Fe Trail. Its 21 rooms, arranged around a double courtyard, are furnished with the few possessions that even a wealthy family of the era would have been able to afford. Cultural events are held here regularly.

Harwood Museum of Art MUSEUM

(☎575-758-9826; www.harwoodmuseum.org; 238 Ledoux St; adult/child $10/free; ⏲10am-5pm Tue-Fri, from noon Sat & Sun; Ⓟ) Attractively displayed in a gorgeous and very spacious mid-19th-century adobe compound, the paintings, drawings, prints, sculpture and photographs here are predominantly the work of northern New Mexican artists, both historical and contemporary. Founded in 1923, the Harwood is the second-oldest museum in New Mexico, and is as strong on local Hispanic traditions as it is on Taos' 20th-century school.

San Francisco de Asís Church CHURCH

(☎575-751-0518; St Francis Plaza, Ranchos de Taos; ⏲9am-4pm, hours vary in winter; Ⓟ) Just off Hwy 68 in Ranchos de Taos, 4 miles south of Taos Plaza, this iconic church was completed in 1815. Famed for the rounded curves and stark angles of its sturdy adobe walls, it was repeatedly memorialized by Georgia O'Keeffe in paint, and Ansel Adams with his camera. On weekends, Mass is celebrated at 5pm on Saturday and 8am (in Spanish) and 10am Sunday.

Earthships ARCHITECTURE

(☎575-613-4409; www.earthship.com; Hwy 64; self-guided tours $8; ⏲9am-5pm Jun-Aug, 10am-4pm Sep-May; Ⓟ) 🍃 Numbering 70 Earthships, with capacity for 60 more, Taos' pioneering community was the brainchild of architect Michael Reynolds. Built with recycled materials such as used automobile tires and cans, and buried on three sides, Earthships heat and cool themselves, make their own electricity and catch their own water; dwellers grow their own food. Stay **overnight** (☎575-751-0462; www.earthship.com; Hwy 64; earthships $169-410; Ⓟ📶🐾) 🍃 if possible; the self-guided 'tour' is disappointing. The visitor center is 1.5 miles west of the Rio Grande Gorge Bridge on Hwy 64.

Activities

During summer, white-water rafting is popular in the Taos Box, the steep-sided cliffs that frame the Rio Grande. There are also plenty of excellent hiking and mountain-biking trails. With a peak elevation of 11,819ft and a 3274ft vertical drop, **Taos Ski Valley** (☎866-968-7386; www.skitaos.org; lift ticket adult/teen/child $98/81/61; ⏲9am-4pm) offers some of the most challenging skiing and boarding in the US and yet remains low-key and relaxed.

Los Rios River Runners RAFTING

(☎575-776-8854; www.losriosriverrunners.com; adult/child half-day $54/44; ⏲late Apr-Sep) Half-day trips on the Racecourse – in one- and two-person kayaks, as you prefer – full-day trips on the Box (minimum age 12), and multinight expeditions on the scenic Chama. On its 'Native Cultures Feast and Float' you're accompanied by a Native American guide and have lunch homemade by a local Pueblo family. Its open season fluctuates based on water levels.

Sleeping

Hotel Luna Mystica CARAVAN PARK $

(☎505-977-2424; www.hotellunamystica.com; 25 ABC Mesa Rd; RVs $95-195, bunkhouse $25; Ⓟ📶🐾) Vintage Airstreams and RVs come with a view – a really big view – at this new trailer park that's perched between the Sangre de Cristos mountains and the Rio Grand Gorge on the Taos mesa about 8 miles northwest of downtown. Each snazzy trailer has its own

CHIMAYÓ

The so-called 'Lourdes of America' – the extraordinarily beautiful two-towered adobe chapel of **El Santuario de Chimayó** (☎505-351-4360; www.elsantuariodechimayo.us; 15 Santuario Dr; ⏲9am-6pm May-Sep, to 5pm Oct-Apr; Ⓟ) FREE – nestles amid the hills of the 'High Road' east of Hwy 84, 28 miles north of Santa Fe. It was built in 1826, on a site where the earth was said to have miraculous healing properties. Even today, the faithful come to rub the *tierra bendita* (holy dirt) from a small pit inside the church on whatever hurts. During Holy Week, about 30,000 pilgrims walk to Chimayó from Santa Fe, Albuquerque and beyond, in the largest Catholic pilgrimage in the USA. The artwork in the santuario is worth a trip on its own. Stop at **Rancho de Chimayó** (☎505-351-4444; www.ranchodechimayo.com; County Rd 98; lunch $9-11, dinner $12-27; ⏲11:30am-8:30pm Tue-Fri, from 8:30am Sat & Sun) afterward for lunch or dinner.

bathroom and kitchen, plus a firepit. All but the hostel-style bunkhouse include showers.

★ **Doña Luz Inn** B&B $$
(☎575-758-9000; www.stayintaos.com; 114 Kit Carson Rd; r $119-209; P❄@🛜🐾) Vibrant and fun, this central B&B is a labor of love by owner Paul Castillo. Rooms are decorated in colorful themes from Spanish colonial to Native American, with abundant art, murals and artifacts plus adobe fireplaces, and kitchenettes. If you don't mind stairs, the sumptuous Rainbow Room has a private rooftop deck and hot tub, offering fantastic views over the city.

★ **Historic Taos Inn** HISTORIC HOTEL $$
(☎575-758-2233; www.taosinn.com; 125 Paseo del Pueblo Norte; r from $179; P❄🛜) Lovely and lively old inn, where the 45 characterful rooms have Southwest trimmings such as heavy-duty wooden furnishings and adobe fireplaces (some functioning, some for show). The famed Adobe Bar spills into the cozy central atrium, and features live music every night – for a quieter stay, opt for one of the detached separate wings – and there's also a good **restaurant** (☎575-758-1977; www.taosinn.com; 125 Paseo del Pueblo Norte, Historic Taos Inn; breakfast & lunch $9-17, dinner $17-28; ⏰11am-3pm & 5-9pm Mon-Fri, 7:30am-2:30pm & 5-9pm Sat & Sun).

Eating

Taos Diner DINER $
(☎575-758-2374; 908 Paseo del Pueblo Norte; mains $4-14; ⏰7am-3pm; 👪) Diner grub at its finest, prepared with a Southwestern, organic spin. Mountain men, scruffy jocks, solo diners and happy tourists – everyone's welcome here. The breakfast burritos rock. There's another branch south of the plaza (216B Paseo del Pueblo Sur).

Love Apple NEW MEXICAN $$
(☎575-751-0050; www.theloveapple.net; 803 Paseo del Pueblo Norte; mains $16-18; ⏰5-9pm Tue-Sun) A real 'only in New Mexico' find, from the rustic setting in the converted 19th-century adobe Placitas Chapel, to the delicious, locally sourced and largely organic food. Everything – the local beefburger with red chile and blue cheese, the tamales with mole sauce, the wild boar tenderloin – is imbued with regional flavor. Cash only, with no ATM on-site.

★ **Lambert's** MODERN AMERICAN $$$
(☎575-758-1009; www.lambertsoftaos.com; 123 Bent St; lunch $10-15, dinner $23-38; ⏰11:30am-9pm; 🖋👪) Consistently hailed as the 'Best of Taos,' this charming old adobe north of the Plaza remains what it's always been: a cozy, romantic local hangout where patrons relax over sumptuous contemporary cuisine, with mains ranging from lunchtime's barbecue pork sliders to dinner dishes such as chicken mango enchiladas or Colorado rack of lamb.

The famed fresh-squeezed margaritas are $6 during happy hour (2:30pm to 6:30pm).

Drinking & Entertainment

Adobe Bar BAR
(☎575-758-2233; 125 Paseo del Pueblo Norte, Historic Taos Inn; ⏰11am-10pm, music from 6:30pm) There's something about the Adobe Bar. Everyone in Taos seems to turn up at some point each evening, to kick back in the comfy covered atrium, enjoying no-cover live music from bluegrass to jazz, and drinking the famed Cowboy Buddha margaritas. If you decide to stick around, you can always order food from the well-priced bar menu.

Taos Mesa Brewery BREWERY
(☎575-753-1900; www.taosmesabrewing.com; 20 ABC Mesa Rd; ⏰noon-11pm) This hangar-like space out by the airport has great beers, live music and à la carte tacos, making it a can't-miss après-ski/hike hangout. Indoor seating is limited – but that's to ensure there's space for the funk on Fridays, bluegrass on Saturdays and two-step on Sundays – or however it decides to mix it up. There's a **taproom** (☎575-758-1900; www.taosmesabrewing.com; 201 Paseo del Pueblo Sur; ⏰noon-11pm) in town.

Shopping

Taos has historically been a mecca for artists, demonstrated by the huge number of galleries and studios in and around town. Indie stores and galleries line the **John Dunn Shops** (www.johndunnshops.com) pedestrian walkway linking Bent St to Taos Plaza.

Just east of the Plaza, pop into **El Rincón Trading Post** (☎575-758-9188; 114 Kit Carson Rd; ⏰9am-5pm Mon-Fri, from 10am Sat, from 11am Sun) for classic Western memorabilia.

Information

Taos Visitor Center (☎575-758-3873; http://taos.org; 1139 Paseo del Pueblo Sur; ⏰9am-5pm; 🛜) This excellent visitor center stocks information of all kinds on northern New Mexico and doles out free coffee; everything, including the comprehensive *Taos Vacation Guide*, is also available online.

DON'T MISS

TAOS PUEBLO

Taos Pueblo (575-758-1028; www.taospueblo.com; Taos Pueblo Rd; adult/child under 11yr $16/free; 8am-4:30pm Mon-Sat, from 8:30am Sun, closed mid-Feb–mid-Apr) is centered on twin five-story adobe complexes, set either side of the Río Pueblo de Taos, against the stunning backdrop of the Sangre de Cristos mountains. The quintessential example of ancient Pueblo architecture, they're thought to have been completed by around 1450 AD. Modern visitors are thus confronted by the same staggering spectacle as New Mexico's earliest Spanish explorers, though a small and very picturesque Catholic mission church now stands nearby.

Residents lead short guided walking tours of the pueblo (by donation), which are recommended for a better understanding of the history and surroundings. You'll also have the chance to buy fine jewelry, pottery and other arts and crafts, and possibly sample flatbread baked in traditional beehive-shaped adobe ovens. Note that the pueblo closes for 10 weeks around February through April, and at other times for ceremonies and events; call ahead or check the website for dates.

Getting There & Away

From Santa Fe, take either the scenic 'High Road' along Hwys 76 and 518, with galleries, villages and sites worth exploring, or follow the lovely unfolding Rio Grande landscape on Hwy 68.

North Central Regional Transit (www.www.ncrtd.org) operates bus services through northern central New Mexico, including to Santa Fe; pickup/drop-off is at the Taos County offices off Paseo del Pueblo Sur, a mile south of the Plaza.

Taos Express (p226) has shuttle service to Santa Fe on Saturday and Sunday (one way adult/child $5/free), connecting with Rail Runner trains to and from Albuquerque.

Northwestern New Mexico

New Mexico's wild northwest is home to wide-open, empty spaces. It's still dubbed Indian country, and for good reason: huge swaths of land fall under the aegis of the Navajo, Zuni, Acoma, Apache and Laguna. This portion of New Mexico showcases remarkable ancient sites alongside modern, solitary Native American settlements. And when you've had your fill of culture, you can ride a historic narrow-gauge railroad through the mountains, hike around some trippy badlands or cast for huge trout.

Farmington & Around

The largest town in northwest New Mexico, Farmington makes a convenient base from which to explore the Four Corners area. The **visitors bureau** (505-326-7602; www.farmingtonnm.org; 3041 E Main St; 8am-5pm Mon-Sat) has more information. **Shiprock**, a 1700ft-high volcanic plug that rises over the landscape to the west, was a landmark for the Anglo pioneers and is a sacred site to the Navajo.

Fourteen miles northeast of Farmington, the 27-acre **Aztec Ruins National Monument** (505-334-6174; www.nps.gov/azru; 725 Ruins Rd; 8am-6pm mid-May–Aug, to 4pm Sep & Oct, 9am-4pm Nov–mid-May; P) FREE features the largest reconstructed kiva in the country, with an internal diameter of almost 50ft. A few steps away, let your imagination wander as you stoop through low doorways and dark rooms inside the West Ruin.

About 35 miles south of Farmington along Hwy 371, the undeveloped **Bisti/De-Na-Zin Wilderness Area** (www.blm.gov/visit/bisti-de-na-zin-wilderness) is a trippy, surreal landscape of strange, colorful rock formations, especially spectacular in the hours before sunset; desert enthusiasts shouldn't miss it. The Farmington **BLM office** (505-564-7600; www.blm.gov/new-mexico; 6251 College Blvd; 7:45am-4:30pm Mon-Fri) has information.

The lovely, three-room **Silver River Adobe Inn B&B** (505-325-8219; www.silveradobe.com; 3151 W Main St; r $115-205;) offers a peaceful respite among the trees along the San Juan River. Managing to be both trendy and kid-friendly, the hipish **Three Rivers Eatery & Brewhouse** (505-324-2187; www.threeriversbrewery.com; 101 E Main St; mains $10-27, pizza $8-22; 11am-10pm;) has good steaks, pub grub and its own microbrews. It's the best restaurant in town by a mile.

Chaco Culture National Historical Park

Featuring massive Ancestral Puebloan buildings set in an isolated high-desert environment, intriguing **Chaco** (☎505-786-7014; www.nps.gov/chcu; 7-day pass per vehicle $25; ⊙7am-sunset; P) contains evidence of 5000 years of human occupation.

In its prime, the community at Chaco Canyon was a major trading and ceremonial hub for the region – and the city the Puebloan people created here was masterly in its layout and design. **Pueblo Bonito** is four stories tall and may have had 600 to 800 rooms and kivas. As well as driving the self-guided loop tour, you can hike various backcountry trails. The 2-mile round-trip **hike** (Canyon Loop Rd) to the Pueblo Bonito Overlook ends with a bird's-eye view of its namesake pueblo and the canyon. For stargazers, there are evening astronomy presentations in summer. The park is in a remote area approximately 80 miles south of Farmington, far beyond the reach of any public transport. And the drive, much of it on an unpaved road, is extremely bumpy. **Gallo Campground** (☎877-444-6777; www.recreation.gov; tent & RV sites $15) is 1 mile east of the visitor center. No RV hookups.

Northeastern New Mexico

East of Santa Fe, the lush Sangre de Cristo Mountains give way to high and vast rolling plains. Dusty grasslands stretch to infinity and beyond – or at least to Texas. Cattle and dinosaur prints dot a landscape punctuated by volcanic cones. Ranching is an economic mainstay, and on many stretches of road you'll see more cattle than cars – and quite possibly herds of bison too. Boy Scouts congregate at Philmont Ranch in Cimarron in summer, but the opening of the new National Scouting Museum threatens to keep the town lively, or near lively, year-round.

The Santa Fe Trail, along which early traders rolled in wagon trains, ran from Missouri to New Mexico. You can still see the wagon ruts in some places off I-25 between Santa Fe and Raton. For a bit of the Old West without a patina of consumer hype, this is the place.

Cimarron

Cimarron once ranked among the rowdiest of Wild West towns; its name even means 'wild' in Spanish. According to local lore, murder was such an everyday occurrence in the 1870s that peace and quiet was newsworthy, one paper going so far as to report: 'Everything is quiet in Cimarron. Nobody has been killed in three days.'

Today, the town is more low-key, luring nature-minded travelers who want to enjoy the great outdoors. Driving to or from Taos, you'll pass through gorgeous **Cimarron Canyon State Park**, a steep-walled canyon with hiking trails, excellent trout fishing and camping. Also here is **Philmont Scout Ranch** (☎575-376-1136; www.philmontscoutranch.org; 17 Deer Run Rd; ⊙8am-5:30pm Jun-Aug, shorter hours rest of year; P) FREE, a 214-sq-mile adventure camp for the Boy Scouts of America. The ranch is the new home of the small-but-engaging **National Scouting Museum** (☎575-376-1136; www.philmontscoutranch.org; Hwy 21; ⊙8am-5pm; P) FREE, plus a few other themed museums.

You can stay or dine at what's reputed to be one of the most haunted hotels in the USA, the 1872 **St James** (☎575-376-2664; www.exstjames.com; 617 Collison St; r $85-135; ❄📶) – one room is so spook-filled that it's never been rented out! Many legends of the West stayed here, including Buffalo Bill, Annie Oakley, Wyatt Earp and Jesse James, and the front desk has a long list of who shot whom in the hotel bar. Another option is **Blu Dragonfly Brewing** (☎575-376-1110; www.bludragonflybrewing.com; 301 E 9th St; ⊙11am-9pm Mon-Thu, to 10pm Fri & Sat) down the road, which serves beer and barbecue.

Capulin Volcano National Monument

Rising 1300ft above the surrounding plains, **Capulin** (☎575-278-2201; www.nps.gov/cavo; 7-day pass per vehicle $20; ⊙8am-4:30pm; P) is the most accessible of several volcanoes in the area. A 2-mile road spirals up the mountain to a parking lot at the rim (8182ft), where trails lead around and into the crater. The entrance is 3 miles north of Capulin village, 30 miles east of Raton on Hwy 87.

Southwestern New Mexico

The Rio Grande Valley unfurls from Albuquerque down to the bubbling hot springs of funky Truth or Consequences and on toward Mexico and Texas. En route, it feeds one of New Mexico's agricultural treasures: Hatch, the so-called chile capital of the world. East of the river, the desert is so dry it's been known since Spanish times as the Jornada del Muerto. Loosely translated as the 'journey of the dead man,' it was a much-feared section of the El Camino Real de Tierra Adentro, a Spanish trade route established in 1598. Pretty appropriate that the area was chosen for the detonation of the first atomic bomb, at what's now the Trinity Site.

Away from Las Cruces, the state's second-largest city, residents in these parts are few and scattered. To the west, the rugged Gila National Forest is wild with backcountry adventure, while the Mimbres Valley is rich with archaeological treasures.

Truth or Consequences & Around

An offbeat joie de vivre permeates the funky little town of Truth or Consequences ('T or C'), which was built on the site of natural hot springs in the 1880s. Originally, called, sensibly enough, Hot Springs, it changed its name in 1950, after a then-popular radio game show called, you guessed it, Truth or Consequences. Publicity these days comes courtesy of Virgin Galactic CEO Richard Branson and other space-travel visionaries driving the development of nearby **Spaceport America** (844-727-7223; www.spaceportamerica.com; County Rd A021; adult/child $45/30), where wealthy tourists are expected to launch into orbit sometime soon. Less wealthy tourists can take a fascinating guided trip through the facility, hopping into a wild G-force machine along the way.

About 60 miles north, sandhill cranes and Arctic geese winter in the 90 sq miles of fields and marshes at **Bosque del Apache National Wildlife Refuge** (575-835-1828; www.fws.gov/refuge/bosque_del_apache; Hwy 1; per vehicle $5; dawn-dusk; P).

Sleeping

★Riverbend Hot Springs BOUTIQUE HOTEL **$$**
(575-894-7625; www.riverbendhotsprings.com; 100 Austin St; r $99-259, RV sites $75; P) This delightful place, occupying a fantastic perch beside the Rio Grande, is the only T or C hotel to feature outdoor, riverside hot tubs – tiled, decked and totally irresistible. Accommodation, colorfully decorated by local artists, ranges from motel-style rooms to a three-bedroom suite. Guests can use the public pools for free, and private tubs for $10. No children under 12 years.

Blackstone Hotsprings BOUTIQUE HOTEL **$$**
(575-894-0894; www.blackstonehotsprings.com; 410 Austin St; r $90-175; P) Blackstone embraces the T or C spirit with an upscale wink, decorating each of its 12 rooms in the style of a classic TV show, from *The Jetsons* to *The Golden Girls* to *I Love Lucy*. Best part? Each of the 10 rooms on the main property comes with its own oversized tub or waterfall fed from the hot springs.

Drinking & Nightlife

Passion Pie Cafe CAFE **$**
(575-894-0008; www.facebook.com/passionpiecafe; 406 Main St; breakfast & lunch mains $6-10; 7am-3pm;) Watch T or C get its morning groove on through the windows of this espresso cafe, and set yourself up with a breakfast waffle; the Elvis (with peanut butter) or the Fat Elvis (with bacon too) should do the job. Later on there are plenty of healthy salads and sandwiches.

Truth or Consequences Brewing Co MICROBREWERY
(575-297-0289; www.torcbeer.com; 410 N Broadway; 3-9:30pm Mon-Wed, noon-10pm Thu, to 11pm Fri & Sat, to 9:30pm Sun) Opening its doors in 2017, this spacious and welcoming watering hole already feels like a longtime neighborhood bar. The festive patio is the place to be while sipping the smooth ales and lagers – the specialties here. We liked the Cosmic Blonde. Solo travelers will feel welcome.

Las Cruces & Around

Las Cruces and its older and smaller sister city, Mesilla, sit at the edge of a broad basin beneath the fluted Organ Mountains, at the crossroads of two major highways, I-10 and I-25. An eclectic mix of old and young, Las Cruces is home to New Mexico State University (NMSU), whose 14,000 students infuse it with a healthy dose of youthful liveliness, while at the same time its 350 days of sunshine and numerous golf courses are turning it into a popular retirement destination.

Sights

For many, a visit to neighboring **Mesilla** (aka Old Mesilla) is the highlight of their time in Las Cruces. Wander a few blocks off Old Mesilla's plaza to gather the essence of a mid-19th-century Southwestern town of Hispanic heritage.

★New Mexico Farm & Ranch Heritage Museum MUSEUM
(575-522-4100; www.nmfarmandranchmuseum.org; 4100 Dripping Springs Rd; adult/child 4-17yr $5/3; 9am-5pm Mon-Sat, from noon Sun; P)

WORTH A TRIP

PEERING INTO THE COSMIC UNKNOWN

Beyond the town of Magdalena on Hwy 60, 130 miles southwest of Albuquerque, the amazing **Very Large Array** (VLA; 505-835-7410; https://public.nrao.edu/visit/very-large-array; junction US 60 & Hwy 52, Magdalena; adult/child under 17yr $6/free; 8:30am-sunset; P) radio telescope consists of 27 huge antenna dishes sprouting like giant mushrooms in the high plains. Watch a short film at the visitor center, then take a self-guided walking tour with a window peek into the control building.

This terrific museum doesn't just display engaging exhibits on the state's agricultural history – it's got livestock too. Enclosures on the working farm alongside hold assorted breeds of cattle, along with horses, donkeys, sheep and goats. The taciturn cowboys who tend the animals proffer little extra information, but they add color, and you can even buy a pony if you have $450 to spare. There are daily milking demonstrations, plus weekly displays of blacksmithing, spinning and weaving, and heritage cooking.

White Sands Missile Test Center Museum MUSEUM
(575-678-3358; www.wsmr.army.mil/PAO/Pages/RangeMuseum.aspx; off Hwy 70; museum 8am-4:30pm Mon-Fri, 10am-3pm Sat & Sun, missile park sunrise-sunset; P) FREE Explore New Mexico's military technology history with a visit to this museum, 25 miles east of Las Cruces along Hwy 70. It represents the heart of the White Sands Missile Range, a major testing site since 1945. There's a missile garden, a real V-2 rocket and a museum with lots of defense-related artifacts. Visitors have to park outside the Test Center gate and check-in with identification at the office before walking in.

Sleeping

Best Western Mission Inn MOTEL $
(575-524-8591; www.bwmissioninn.com; 1765 S Main St; r from $85; P) An optimal accommodation option: yes it's a roadside chain motel, but the rooms are beautifully kitted out with attractive tiling, stonework and colorful stenciled designs; they're sizable and comfortable; and the rates are great. Microwave and fridge in each room. Breakfast is included too.

Hotel Encanto de Las Cruces HOTEL $$
(505-522-4300; www.hotelencanto.com; 705 S Telshor Blvd; r/ste from $149/209; P @) The pick of the city's larger hotels, this Spanish Colonial resort property holds 200 spacious rooms, decorated in warm Southwestern tones, plus a palm-fringed outdoor pool, an exercise room, a restaurant and a lounge with patio. Pet fee is $25 per day.

Eating & Drinking

Chala's Wood-Fired Grill NEW MEXICAN $
(575-652-4143; 2790 Ave de Mesilla, Mesilla; mains $4-12; 8am-9pm Mon-Thu, to 10pm Fri & Sat, to 8pm Sun) With house-smoked carnitas and turkey, housemade bacon and chile-pork sausage, plus *calabacitas* (squash and corn), quinoa salad and organic greens, this place rises well above the standard New Mexican diner fare. Located at the southern end of Mesilla, it's kick-back casual and the price is right.

Double Eagle BAR
(575-523-6700; www.double-eagle-mesilla.com; 308 Calle de Guadalupe, Mesilla; 11am-10pm Mon-Sat, to 9pm Sun) A glorious melange of Wild West opulence, all dark wood and velvet hangings, this fabulous old bar on the Plaza is an atmospheric spot for a cocktail. The adjoining main dining room offers continental and Southwestern cuisine, especially steaks. The whole shebang is on the National Register of Historic Places and, of course, is haunted.

More than 40 specialty margaritas are on the menu.

Information

Las Cruces Visitors Center (575-541-2444; www.lascrucescvb.org; 336 S Main St; 8am-5pm Mon-Fri)

Mesilla Visitor Center (575-524-3262; www.oldmesilla.org; 2231 Ave de Mesilla, Mesilla; 8am-5pm Mon-Fri)

Getting There & Away

Greyhound (575-523-1824; www.greyhound.com; 800 E Thorpe Rd, Chucky's Convenience Store) Buses run to all major destinations in the area, including El Paso, Albuquerque and Tucson. The bus stop is about 7 miles north of town.

Las Cruces Shuttle Service (575-525-1784; www.lascrucesshuttle.com) Runs eight to 10 vans daily to the El Paso International Airport ($50 one way, $35 each additional person), and to Deming, Silver City and other destinations on request.

Silver City & Around

The spirit of the Wild West still hangs in the air in Silver City, 113 miles northwest of Las Cruces, as if Billy the Kid himself – who grew up here – might amble past at any moment. But things are changing, as the mountain-man/cowboy vibe succumbs to the charms of art galleries and coffeehouses.

Silver City is also the gateway to outdoor activities in the **Gila National Forest**, which is rugged country suitable for remote cross-country skiing, backpacking, camping and fishing. Two hours north of town, up a winding 42-mile road, is **Gila Cliff Dwellings National Monument** (575-536-9461; www.nps.gov/gicl; Hwy 15; adult/child under 16yr $10/free; trail 9am-4pm, visitor center 8am-4:30pm; P), occupied in the 13th century by the Mogollon people. Mysterious and relatively isolated, these remarkable cliff dwellings are easily accessed from a 1-mile loop trail and look very much as they would have at the turn of the first millennium. For pictographs, stop by the **Lower Scorpion Campground** and walk a short distance along the marked trail.

Weird rounded monoliths make the **City of Rocks State Park** an intriguing playground, with great **camping** (575-536-2800; www.emnrd.state.nm.us/SPD; 327 Hwy 61; tent/RV sites $10/14) among the formations; there are tables and firepits. For a rock-lined gem of a spot, check out campsite 43, the Lynx. Head 33 miles southeast of Silver City along Hwy 180 and Hwy 61.

For a smattering of Silver City's architectural history, overnight in the 22-room **Palace Hotel** (575-388-1811; www.silvercitypalacehotel.com; 106 W Broadway; r/ste from $62/98;). Exuding a low-key, turn-of-the-19th-century charm (no elevator, older fixtures), the Palace is a great choice for those tired of cookie-cutter chains.

Downtown eating options range from the comfy, come-as-you-are **Javalina** (575-388-1350; www.javalinacoffeehouse.com; 117 W Market St; 6am-6pm;) coffee shop to the gastronomically adventurous – and highly recommended – **Revel** (575-388-4920; www.eatdrinkrevel.com; 304 N Bullard St; mains lunch $10-23, dinner $17-40; 11am-9pm Mon & Tue, Thu & Fri, from 9am Sat & Sun). For a taste of local culture, head 7 miles north to Pinos Altos and the atmospheric **Buckhorn Saloon** (575-538-9911; www.buckhornsaloonandoperahouse.com; 32 Main St, Pinos Altos; mains $11-56; 4-10pm Mon-Sat), where the specialty is steak and there's live music most nights. Call for reservations.

Information

Gila National Forest Ranger Station (575-388-8201; www.fs.fed.us/r3/gila; 3005 E Camino del Bosque; 8am-4:30pm Mon-Fri)

Visitor Center (575-538-5555; www.silvercitytourism.org; 201 N Hudson St; 9am-5pm Mon-Sat, 10am-2pm Sun) This super-helpful office can provide everything you need to make the most of Silver City.

Southeastern New Mexico

Two extraordinary natural wonders are tucked away in New Mexico's arid southeast: the mesmerizing White Sands National Monument and the magnificent Carlsbad Caverns National Park. Also impressive, if less well known, are the thousands of petroglyphs at the Three Rivers Petroglyph Site and the sprawling lava flow at Valley of Fires Recreation Area. This region also swirls with some of the state's most enduring legends: aliens in Roswell, Billy the Kid in Lincoln, and Smokey Bear in Capitan. Most of the lowlands are covered by hot, rugged Chihuahuan Desert – once submerged under the ocean – but you can always escape to the cooler climes around the popular forest resorts of Cloudcroft or Ruidoso.

White Sands National Monument

Slide, roll and slither through brilliant towerings and hills. Sixteen miles southwest of Alamogordo (15 miles southwest of Hwy82/70), gypsum covers 275 sq miles to create a dazzling white landscape at this stark **monument** (575-479-6124; www.nps.gov/whsa; per vehicle/motorcycle $20/10 or adult/child under 16yr $10/free, whichever is less; 7am-9pm Jun-Aug, to sunset Sep-May; P). These captivating windswept dunes, which doubled as David Bowie's space-alien home planet in *The Man Who Fell to Earth*, are a highlight of any trip to New Mexico. Don't forget your sunglasses – the sand is as bright as snow!

Spring for a $19 plastic saucer at the visitor center gift store then sled one of the backdunes. It's fun, and you can sell the disc back for $5 at day's end. Check the park calendar for sunset strolls. Backcountry campsites, with no water or toilet facilities, are a mile from the scenic drive. Pick up a permit ($3, issued first-come, first-served) in person at the visitor center at least one hour before sunset.

Alamogordo & Around

In Alamogordo, a desert outpost famous for its space- and atomic-research programs, the four-story **New Mexico Museum of Space History** (575-437-2840; www.nmspacemuseum.org; 3198 Hwy 2001; adult/child 4-12yr $8/6; 10am-5pm Wed-Sat & Mon, from noon Sun;) has excellent exhibits on space research and flight, and shows outstanding science-themed films in its adjoining **New Horizons Dome Theater** (adult/child $8/6).

Motels stretch along White Sands Blvd, including a decent branch of **Super 8** (575-434-4205; www.wyndhamhotels.com; 3204 N White Sands Blvd; r from $73;). If you'd rather camp, hit **Oliver Lee State Park** (575-437-8284; www.nmparks.com; 409 Dog Canyon Rd; tent/RV sites $10/14), 12 miles south of Alamogordo. Grab good Mexican grub at the brisk **Rizo's** (575-434-2607; www.facebook.com/rizosmexican-restaurant; 1480 N White Sands Blvd; mains $6-17; 9am-9pm Tue-Sat, to 6pm Sun;).

Cloudcroft

Situated high in the mountains, little Cloudcroft provides welcome relief from the lowlands heat. With turn-of-the-19th-century buildings, it offers lots of outdoor recreation, is a good base for exploration and has a low-key feel. **High Altitude** (575-682-1229; www.highaltitudenm.com; 310 Burro Ave; rentals per day from $35; 10am-5:30pm Mon-Thu, to 6pm Fri & Sat, to 5pm Sun) rents mountain bikes and will point you in the right direction for a ride.

The **Lodge Resort & Spa** (800-395-6343; www.thelodgeresort.com; 601 Corona Pl; r/ste from $135/195;) is one of the Southwest's finest historic hotels. Rooms in the main Bavarian-style hotel are furnished with period and Victorian pieces, while the great-value **Cloudcroft Mountain Park Hostel** (575-682-0555; www.cloudcrofthostel.com; 1049 Hwy 82; dm $19, r without bathroom $37-64;) sits on 28 wooded acres west of town. **Rebecca's** (575-682-3131; www.thelodgeresort.com; Lodge Resort, 601 Corona Pl; mains lunch $9-20, dinner $24-40; 11:30am-3pm & 5:30-8pm Mon-Thu, 11:30am-3pm & 5:30-9pm Fri & Sat, 7-10:30am & 11am-2pm Sun) offers the best food in town. Grab a beer at **Cloudcroft Brewing Co** (575-682-2337; www.facebook.com/cloudcroft-brewingcompany; 1301 Burro Ave; 11am-9pm Sun & Mon, Wed & Thu, to 10pm Fri & Sat).

Ruidoso

Perched on the eastern slopes of Sierra Blanca Peak (11,981ft), Ruidoso is a year-round resort town that's downright bustling in summer, attracts skiers in winter, has a lively arts scene and is home to a renowned racetrack. The lovely Rio Ruidoso, a small creek with good fishing, runs through town.

Sights & Activities

Stretch your legs on the easily accessible forest trails on Cedar Creek Rd just west of Smokey Bear Ranger Station). Choose from the USFS Fitness Trail or the meandering paths at the Cedar Creek Picnic Area. Longer day hikes and backpacking routes abound in the White Mountain Wilderness, north of town. Always check fire restrictions around here – the forest closes during dry spells.

Hubbard Museum of the American West MUSEUM

(575-378-4142; www.hubbardmuseum.org; 26301 Hwy 70; adult/child 6-16yr $7/2; 9am-5pm Thu-Mon;) This town-run museum focuses on local history, with a wonderful gallery of old photos, and also displays Native American kachinas, war bonnets, weapons and pottery. Traces of its original incarnation as the Museum of the Horse linger in various horse-related exhibits – and be sure to check out the fascinating, if completely irrelevant, history of toilets in the restrooms.

Ski Apache SKIING

(575-464-3600; www.skiapache.com; 1286 Ski Run Rd, Alto; lift ticket adult/teen/child $74/65/54; 9am-4pm) Located 18 miles northwest of Ruidoso on the slopes of Sierra Blanca Peak, Ski Apache really is owned by the Apache. Potentially it's the finest ski area south of Albuquerque, a good choice for affordability and fun. Snowfall down here can be sporadic, though – check conditions ahead. In summer, ride the gondola (adult/child $35/25), hike, mountain bike and zipline (from $95).

Sleeping & Eating

Rental cabins are popular in Ruidoso. Most have kitchens and grills, and often fireplaces and decks. Some cabins in town are cramped, while newer ones are concentrated in the Upper Canyon. There's also free primitive camping along the forest roads on the way to the ski area; for campsite specifics, ask at the **ranger station** (575-257-

4095; www.fs.usda.gov/lincoln; 901 Mechem Dr; 8am-4pm Mon-Fri, plus Sat late May-early Sep).

Sitzmark Chalet HOTEL $
(575-257-4140; www.sitzmark-chalet.com; 627 Sudderth Dr; r from $83;) This ski-themed chalet offers 17 simple but nice rooms. Picnic tables, grills and an eight-person hot tub are welcome perks.

Upper Canyon Inn LODGE $$
(575-214-7170; www.uppercanyoninn.com; 215 Main Rd; r/cabin $149/169;) Rooms and cabins here range from simple good values to rustic-chic luxury. Bigger doesn't necessarily mean more expensive, so look at a few options. The pricier cabins have some fine interior woodwork and Jacuzzis. Check-in is at 2959 Sudderth Dr.

★ **Cornerstone Bakery** CAFE $
(575-257-1842; www.cornerstonebakerycafe.com; 1712 Sudderth Dr; mains $7-12; 7am-3pm Mon & Tue, Thu & Fri, to 4pm Sat & Sun;) Totally irresistible, hugely popular local bakery and cafe, where everything, from the breads, pastries and espresso to the omelets and croissant sandwiches, is just the way it should be. Stick around long enough and the Cornerstone may become your morning touchstone.

Entertainment

Ruidoso Downs Racetrack SPORTS GROUND
(575-378-4431; www.raceruidoso.com; 26225 Hwy 70; grandstand seats free; Fri-Mon mid-May–early Sep;) FREE National attention focuses on the Ruidoso Downs racetrack on Labor Day for the world's richest quarter-horse race, the All American Futurity, which has a purse of $3 million. The course is also home to the Racehorse Hall of Fame, and the small Billy the Kid Casino.

Flying J Ranch LIVE MUSIC
(575-336-4330; www.flyingjranch.com; 1028 Hwy 48N, Alto; adult/child $28/16; from 5:30pm Mon-Sat late May-early Sep, Sat only through mid-Sep;) Families with little ones will love this 'Western village,' 1.5 miles north of Alto, as it delivers a full night of entertainment, with gunfights, pony rides and Western music, to go with its cowboy-style chuckwagon dinner.

Information

Visitor Center (575-257-7395; www.ruidosonow.com; 720 Sudderth Dr; 8am-5pm Mon-Fri, 9am-3pm Sat) Stop by for information about things to do in the Ruidoso valley and Lincoln County.

WORTH A TRIP

ORGAN MOUNTAINS-DESERT PEAKS NATIONAL MONUMENT

New Mexico's newest **national monument** (575-522-1219; www.blm.gov/visit/omp; per vehicle $5; 8am-5pm;) consists of several components, totaling almost 500,000 acres and lying within a 50-mile radius of Las Cruces. While much of it is not developed for visitors, the Organ Mountains, which rise to 9000ft east of the city, are definitely worth exploring. Several trails leave from the **Dripping Springs Visitor Center**, including the lovely Dripping Springs trail itself, a 3-mile round trip that passes the century-old remains of a sanatorium and a hotel.

Lincoln & Capitan

Fans of Western history won't want to miss little Lincoln. Twelve miles east of Capitan along the **Billy the Kid National Scenic Byway** (www.billybyway.com), this is where the gun battles known as the Lincoln County War turned Billy the Kid into a legend. The whole town is beautifully preserved in close to original form, with its unspoiled main street designated as the **Lincoln Historic Site** (575-653-4082; www.nmmonuments.org/lincoln; US 380; adult/child $5/free; Visitor Center & Courthouse 9am-5pm, other Bldgs to 4:30pm;).

Buy tickets to the historic town buildings at the **Anderson-Freeman Visitors Center** (http://oldlincolntown.org; US 380; 9am-5pm), where you'll also find exhibits on Buffalo soldiers, Apaches and the Lincoln County War. Make the fascinating **Courthouse Museum**, the well-marked site of Billy's most daring – and violent – escape, your last stop. For overnighters, the **Wortley Hotel** (575-653-4300; www.wortleyhotel.com; 585 Calle La Placita/US 380; r from $125; Mar-Nov) has been a fixture since 1874. Enjoy a beer at **Bonito Valley Brewing Co** (575-653-4810; www.facebook.com/bonitovalleybrewing; 692 Calle La Placita; noon-9pm Thu-Mon), which recently opened right on the main drag.

Like Lincoln, cozy Capitan is surrounded by the beautiful mountains of Lincoln National Forest. The main reason to come is so the kids can visit **Smokey Bear Historical Park** (575-354-2748; www.emnrd.state.nm.us; 118 W Smokey Bear Blvd, Capitan; adult/child 7-12yr $2/1; 9am-4:30pm), where the original Smokey is buried.

DON'T MISS

CARLSBAD CAVERNS NATIONAL PARK

While a cave might not sound quite as sexy as redwoods, geysers or the Grand Canyon, there's no question that the one at **Carlsbad Caverns National Park** (575-785-2232, bat info 575-236-1374; www.nps.gov/cave; 727 Carlsbad Cavern Hwy; 3-day pass adult/child under 16yr $15/free; caves 8:30am-5pm late May-early Sep, to 3:30pm early Sep-late May; P) measures up on the national parks' jaw-droppingly ginormous scale: to simply reach the main chamber, you have to either take an elevator that drops the height of the Empire State Building or, more enjoyably, take a spooky 1.25-mile subterranean walk that goes down and down (and down) from the cave mouth into the yawning darkness.

Roswell

A mysterious object crashed at a ranch near Roswell in 1947. No one would have skipped any sleep over it, but the military made a big to-do of hushing it up, and for a lot of folks, that sealed it: the aliens had landed! International curiosity and local ingenuity have transformed the city into a quirky extraterrestrial-wannabe zone. Bulbous white heads glow atop the downtown streetlamps and busloads of tourists come to find souvenirs.

Believers and kitsch-seekers must check out the **International UFO Museum & Research Center** (575-625-9495; www.roswellufomuseum.com; 114 N Main St; adult/child 5-15yr $5/2; 9am-5pm), while the annual **Roswell UFO Festival** (www.roswellufofestival.com) beams down in early July.

Ho-hum chain motels line N Main St. About 36 miles south of Roswell, the **Heritage Inn** (575-748-2552; www.artesiaheritageinn.com; 209 W Main St, Artesia; r/ste $109/119; P) in Artesia is the nicest lodging in the area.

For simple, good Mexican fare, try **Los Cerritos** (575-622-4919; www.loscerritosmk.com; 2103 N main St; mains $7-15; 7am-9pm Mon-Sat, to 5pm Sun); for American eats, **Big D's Downtown Dive** (575-627-0776; www.facebook.com/bigdsdowntowndive; 505 N Main St; mains $7-13; 11am-9pm Mon-Sat) has the best salads, sandwiches and burgers in town. The tasty New Mexican dishes and fine margaritas at the **Adobe Rose** (575-476-6157; www.adoberoserestaurant.com; 1614 N 13th St, Artesia; mains lunch $10-23, dinner $12-32; 11am-9pm Mon & Wed, from 10:30am Thu, 11am-11pm Fri, 5-11pm Sat, 9am-3pm Sun) in Artesia earn their regional accolades.

Pick up local information at the **visitors bureau** (575-623-3442; http://roswell-nm.gov/749/Visitors-Center; 426 N Main St; 10am-3pm Sun & Mon, 9am-5pm Tue-Fri, 9am-4pm Sat;); **Greyhound** (575-622-2510; www.greyhound.com; 515 N Main St, Pecos Trails Transit) has buses to Las Cruces.

Carlsbad

Carlsbad is the closest town to Carlsbad Caverns National Park and the Guadalupe Mountains. To the northwest **Living Desert State Park** (575-887-5516; www.emnrd.state.nm.us; 1504 Miehls Dr N, off Hwy 285; adult/child 7-12yr $5/3; 8am-5pm Jun-Aug, from 9am Sep-May, last zoo entry 3:30pm) is a great place to see and learn about desert plants and wildlife. There's a good 1.3-mile trail that showcases different habitats of the Chihuahuan Desert, with live antelopes, wolves, roadrunners and more.

However, a recent boom in the oil industry means that even the most ordinary motel room in Carlsbad costs way more than it would elsewhere in the state – so it makes more sense to visit on a long day-trip from Roswell or Alamogordo. One unique, if perhaps overrated, boutique option is the **Trinity Hotel** (575-234-9891; www.thetrinityhotel.com; 201 S Canal St; r $239-269;), originally the First National Bank. The sitting room of one suite is inside the old vault, and the restaurant is Carlsbad's classiest.

The perky **Blue House Bakery & Cafe** (575-628-0555; www.facebook.com/BlueHouseBakeryAndCafe; 609 N Canyon St; pastries $3-6, mains $4-6; 6am-noon Mon-Sat) brews the best coffee in these parts. For a post-hike beer and pizza, try welcoming **Guadalupe Mountain Brewing Co** (575-887-8747; www.gmbrewingco.com; 3324 National Parks Hwy; 11am-2pm Tue-Fri, 5-9pm Tue-Thu, to 10pm Fri, 4-10pm Sat), between the national park and downtown Carlsbad.

Greyhound (575-628-3088; www.greyhound.com; 106 W Greene St/US 180) buses depart from Road Runner Express, 0.3 miles south of downtown. Destinations include El Paso, TX, and Las Cruces.

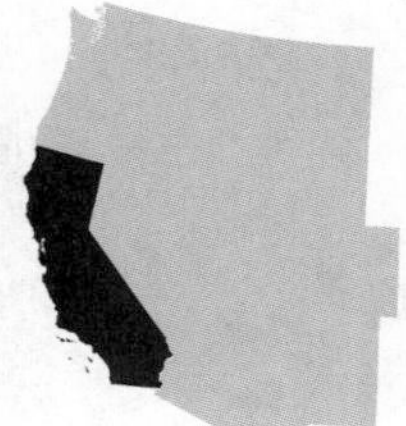

California

Includes ➡

Best Places to Eat

- Chez Panisse (p329)
- Grand Central Market (p258)
- June Bug Cafe (p345)
- Puesto at the Headquarters (p279)

Best Places to Sleep

- Arrive Hotel (p297)
- Auberge du Soleil (p297)
- Chateau Marmont (p256)
- McCloud River Mercantile Hote (p342)
- USA Hostels San Diego (p277)

Why Go?

From misty Northern California redwood forests to sun-kissed Southern California beaches, the enchanted Golden State makes Disneyland seem normal. Combining bohemian spirit and high-tech savvy, California embraces contrast and contradictions. It is home to both vibrant metropolises and rugged wilderness, snowy mountains and desert expanses, and miles and miles of spectacular coastline.

It was here that the hurly-burly gold rush kicked off in the mid-19th century, where poet-naturalist John Muir rhapsodized about the Sierra Nevada's 'range of light,' where Jack Kerouac and the Beat Generation defined what it meant to hit the road, and where the twin dream factories of tech and entertainment flourished.

Above all, this is a state that celebrates the good life – whether that means cracking open a bottle of old-vine zinfandel, climbing a 14,000ft peak or surfing the Pacific.

When to Go

Los Angeles

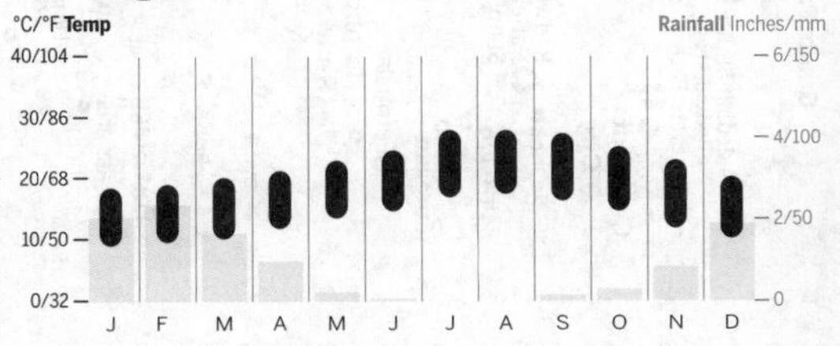

Jun–Aug Mostly sunny weather, occasional coastal fog; summer-vacation crowds.

Apr–May & Sep–Oct Cooler nights, many cloudless days; travel bargains galore.

Nov–Mar Peak tourism at ski resorts and in SoCal's warm deserts.

California Highlights

1. **Yosemite National Park** (p343) Chasing waterfalls and climbing granite domes in this Unesco World Heritage site.

2. **Los Angeles** (p242) Making the most of multicultural neighborhoods, Hollywood studios and red-carpet nightlife.

3. **Big Sur** (p296) Cruising Hwy 1 atop sculpted seacliffs on the bohemian Big Sur coast.

4. **San Francisco** (p302) Riding a cable car up dizzying hills in the often foggy, always fabulous city by the bay.

5. **Disneyland Resort** (p267) (Re) living your childhood dreams at the 'Happiest Place on Earth'.

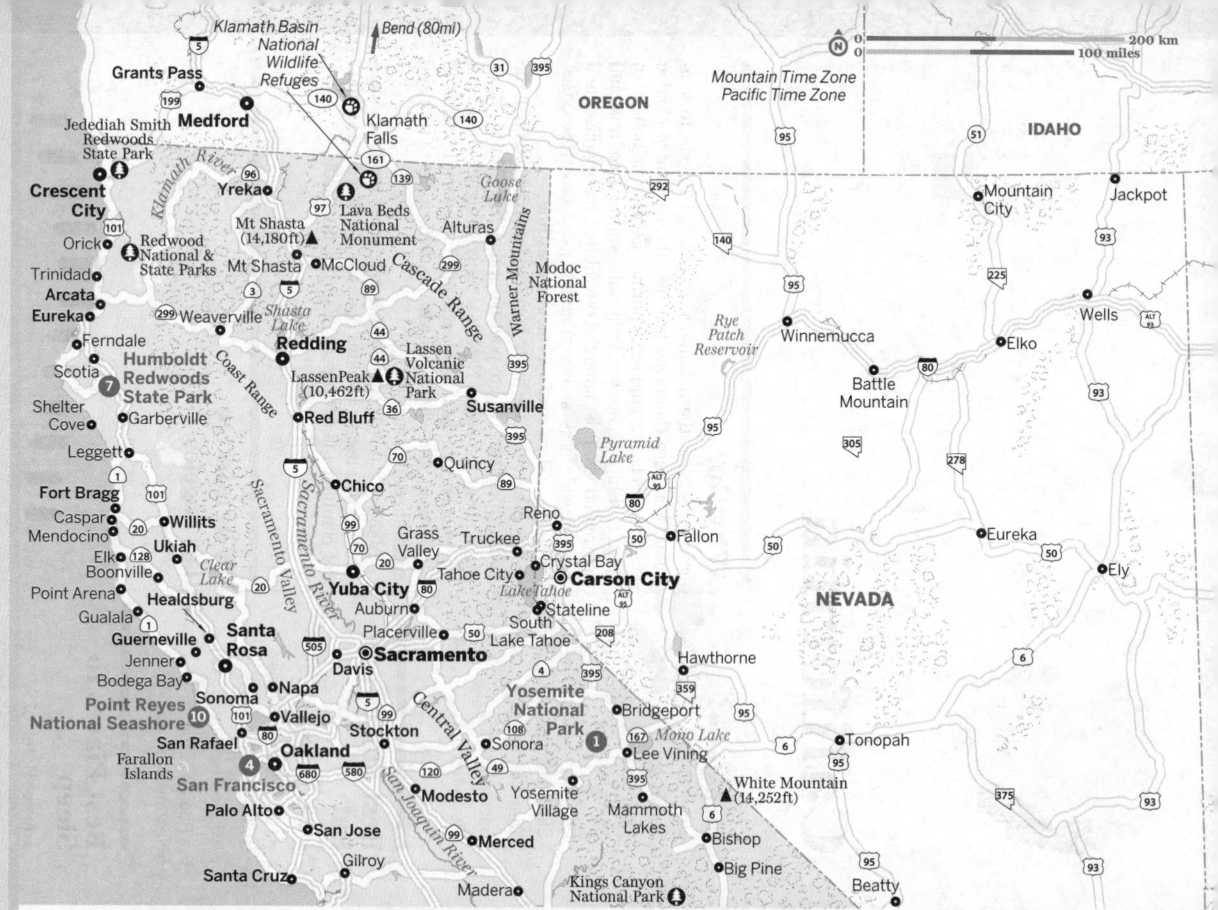

6 **San Diego** (p271) Surfing perfect waves off sunny beaches.

7 **Humboldt Redwoods State Park** (p336) Craning your neck at the world's tallest trees along the Avenue of the Giants.

8 **Palm Springs** (p282) Basking in the nonstop sun and mid-century-modern glam.

9 **Death Valley National Park** (p288) Trekking across sand dunes and uncovering Old West ghost towns.

10 **Point Reyes National Seashore** (p328) Spotting whales, elephant seals and tule elk on a wind-blown peninsula.

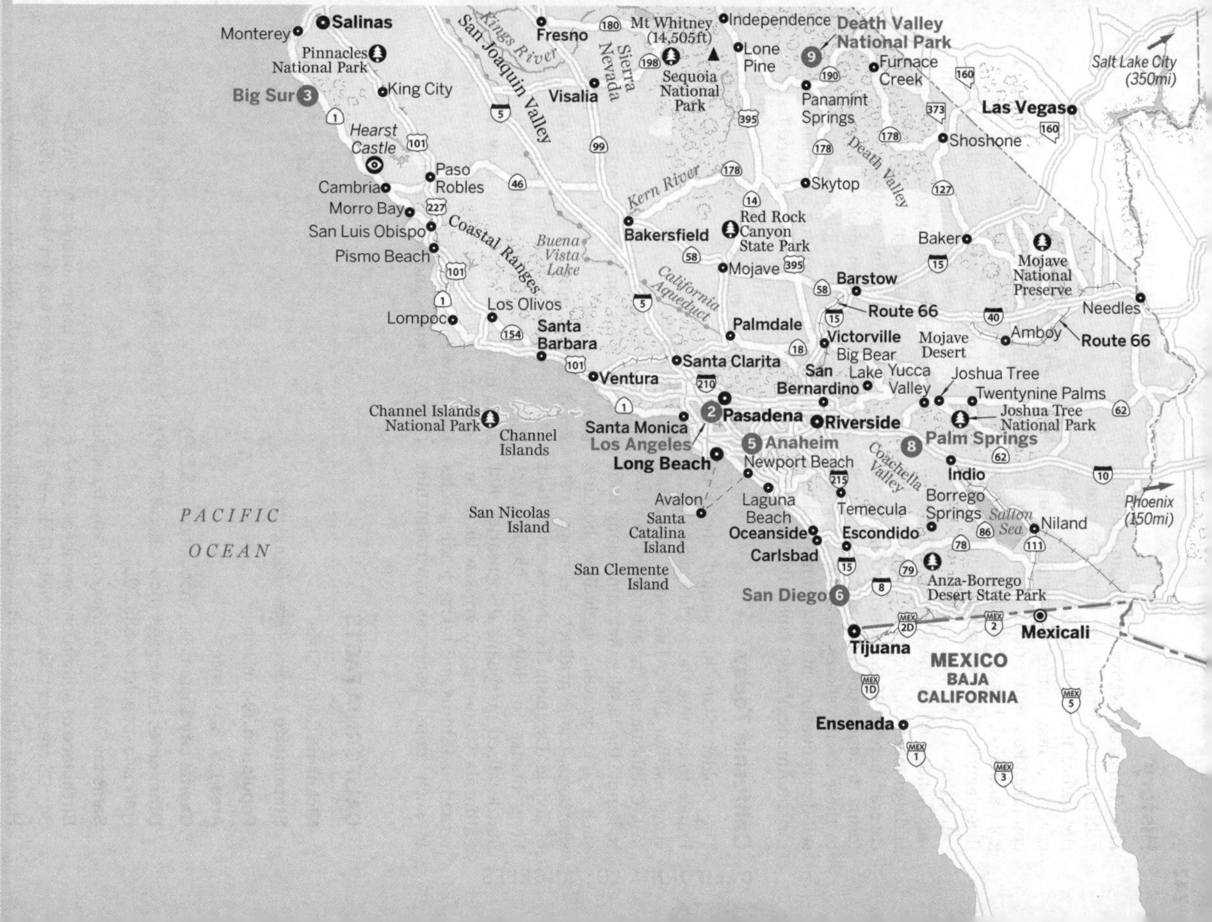

History

Five hundred Native American nations called this land home for some 150 centuries before 16th-century European arrivals gave it a new name: California. Spanish conquistadors and priests came here for gold and God, but soon relinquished their flea-plagued missions and ill-equipped presidios (forts) to Mexico. The unruly territory was handed off to the US in the Treaty of Hidalgo mere months before gold was discovered here in 1848. Generations of California dreamers continue to make the trek to these Pacific shores for gold, glory and self-determination, making homes and history on America's most fabled frontier.

California Today

The Golden State has surged ahead of France to become the world's sixth-largest economy. But like a kid that's grown too fast, California still hasn't figured out how to handle the hassles that come along with such rapid growth, including housing shortages, traffic gridlock and rising costs of living. Escapism is always an option here, thanks to Hollywood blockbusters and legalized marijuana dispensaries. But California is coming to grips with its international status and taking leading roles in such global issues as environmental standards, online privacy, marriage equality and immigrant rights.

LOS ANGELES

If you think you've already got LA figured out – celebutantes, smog, traffic, bikini babes and pop-star wannabes – think again. LA is best defined by simple life-affirming moments: a cracked-ice, jazz-age cocktail after midnight, a hike high into the sagebrush of Griffith Park, a pink-washed sunset over a Venice Beach drum circle, or a search for the perfect taco. With Hollywood and Downtown LA both undergoing an urban renaissance, the city's art, music, food and fashion scenes are all in high gear. Chances are, the more you explore, the more you'll love 'La-La Land.'

Sights

A dozen miles inland from the Pacific, Downtown LA combines history and highbrow arts and culture. Hip-again Hollywood awaits northwest of Downtown, while urban-designer chic and gay pride rule West Hollywood. South of WeHo, Museum Row is Mid-City's main draw. Further west are ritzy Beverly Hills, Westwood near the University of California, Los Angeles (UCLA) campus and West LA. Beach towns

CALIFORNIA FACTS

Nickname Golden State

State motto Eureka ('I Have Found It')

Population 39.5 million

Area 155,780 sq miles

Capital city Sacramento (population 508,529)

Other cities Los Angeles (population 3,990,456), San Diego (population 1,425,976), San Francisco (population 883,305)

Sales tax 7.25% to 10.25% (varies by municipality)

Birthplace of Author John Steinbeck (1902–68), photographer Ansel Adams (1902–84), US president Richard Nixon (1913–94), pop-culture icon Marilyn Monroe (1926–62)

Home of The highest and lowest points in the contiguous US (Mt Whitney, Death Valley), world's oldest, tallest and biggest living trees (ancient bristlecone pines, coast redwoods and giant sequoias, respectively)

Politics Majority Democrat, minority Republican, one in four Californians vote independent

Famous for Disneyland, earthquakes, Hollywood, hippies, Silicon Valley, surfing

Kitschiest souvenir 'Mystery Spot' bumper sticker

Driving distances Los Angeles to San Francisco 380 miles, San Francisco to Yosemite Valley 190 miles

CALIFORNIA IN...

One Week

California in a nutshell: start in beachy **Los Angeles**, detouring to **Disneyland**. Head up the breezy **Central Coast**, stopping in **Santa Barbara** and **Big Sur**, before getting a dose of big-city culture in **San Francisco**. Head inland to nature's temple, **Yosemite National Park**, then zip back to LA.

Two Weeks

Follow the one-week itinerary above, but at a saner pace. Add jaunts to NorCal's **Wine Country**; **Lake Tahoe**, perched high in the Sierra Nevada; the bodacious beaches of Orange County and laid-back **San Diego**; or **Joshua Tree National Park**, near the chic desert resort of **Palm Springs**.

One Month

Do everything described in the itineraries above, and more. From San Francisco, head up the foggy **North Coast**, starting in Marin County at **Point Reyes National Seashore**. Stroll Victorian-era **Mendocino** and **Eureka**, find yourself on the **Lost Coast** and ramble through fern-filled **Redwood National & State Parks**. Inland, snap a postcard-perfect photo of **Mt Shasta**, drive through **Lassen Volcanic National Park** and ramble in California's historic **Gold Country**. Trace the backbone of the **Eastern Sierra** before winding down into otherworldly **Death Valley National Park**.

include kid-friendly Santa Monica, boho Venice, star-powered Malibu and busy Long Beach. Leafy Pasadena lies northeast of Downtown.

Downtown

Though still sketchy in patches, Downtown (DTLA) continues the upward swing that began a decade or more ago. Within the large area that is Downtown, you'll find distinct neighbourhoods, each with their own unique identities and attractions.

Compact, colorful and car free, **El Pueblo de Los Angeles** historic district immerses you in LA's Spanish-Mexican roots. Its spine is festive **Olvera St** (Map p250; www.calleolvera.com; ; M Union Station, Union Station), where you can snap up handmade folkloric trinkets, then chomp on tacos and sugar-sprinkled churros.

Union Station (Map p250; www.amtrak.com; 800 N Alameda St; P), built on the site of LA's original Chinatown, opened in 1939 as America's last grand rail station. It's a glamorous exercise in Mission Revival style with art deco and American Indian accents. 'New' **Chinatown** (Map p250; www.chinatownla.com) is about a half mile north along Broadway and Hill St, crammed with dim-sum parlors, herbal apothecaries, curio shops, hipster-friendly restaurants and edgy art galleries.

Southwest of Union Station, **Little Tokyo** swirls with shopping arcades, Buddhist temples, traditional gardens, authentic sushi bars and noodle shops. Just east, a burgeoning **Arts District** is one of the city's creative centers, with restaurants and shops to match.

Despite the name, South Park isn't actually a park but an emerging neighborhood around the Convention Center and **LA Live** (Map p250; 213-763-5483; www.lalive.com; 800 W Olympic Blvd; P ; M Blue/Expo Lines to Pico Station), a dining and entertainment hub.

★Broad MUSEUM

(Map p250; 213-232-6200; www.thebroad.org; 221 S Grand Ave; 11am-5pm Tue & Wed, to 8pm Thu & Fri, 10am-8pm Sat, to 6pm Sun; P ; M Red/Purple Lines to Civic Center/Grand Park) FREE From the instant it opened in September 2015, the Broad (rhymes with 'road') became a must-visit for contemporary-art fans. It houses the world-class collection of local philanthropist and billionaire real-estate honcho Eli Broad and his wife Edythe, with more than 2000 postwar pieces by dozens of heavy hitters, including Cindy Sherman, Jeff Koons, Andy Warhol, Roy Lichtenstein, Robert Rauschenberg, Keith Haring and Kara Walker.

Greater Los Angeles

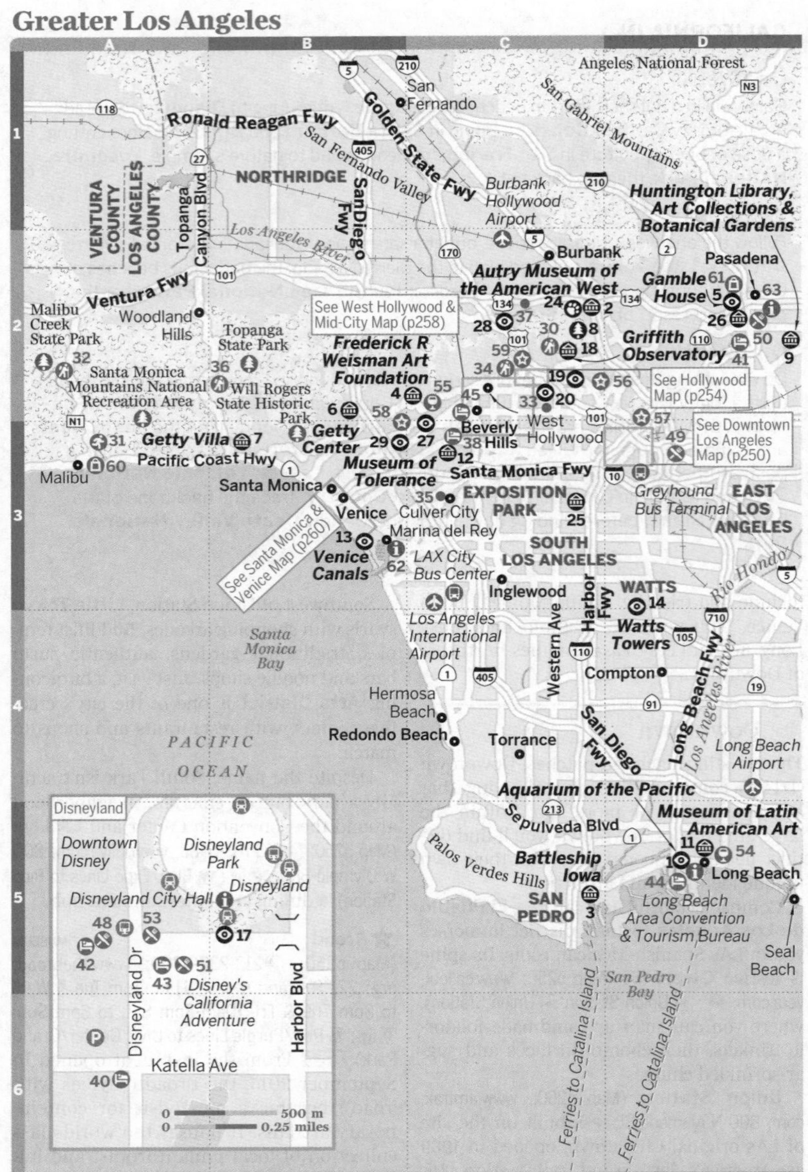

★ **Walt Disney Concert Hall** NOTABLE BUILDING (Map p250; ☎323-850-2000; www.laphil.org; 111 S Grand Ave; P; M Red/Purple Lines to Civic Center/Grand Park) FREE A molten blend of steel, music and psychedelic architecture, this iconic concert venue is the home base of the Los Angeles Philharmonic, but has also hosted contemporary bands such as Phoenix, and classic jazz musicians such as Sonny Rollins. The 2003 concert hall's visionary architect, Frank Gehry, pulled out all the stops for this building, a gravity-defying sculpture of heaving and billowing stainless steel.

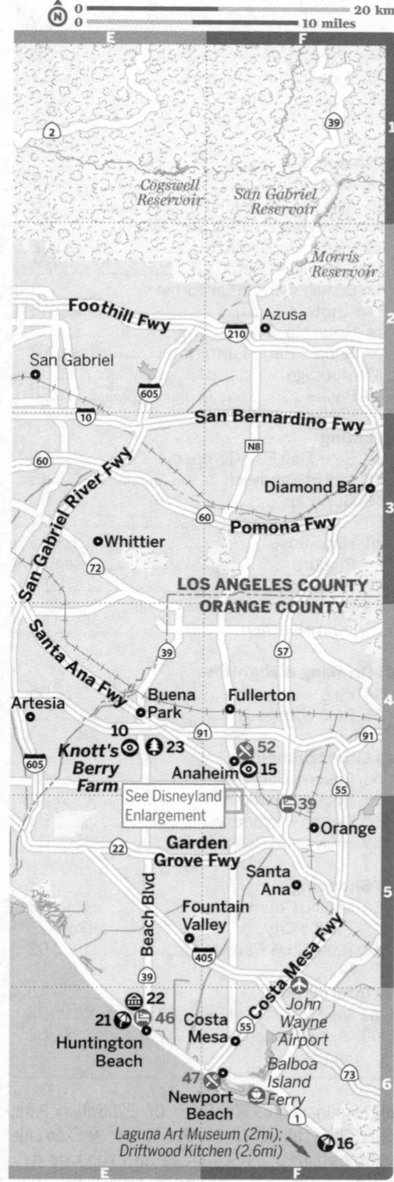

★MOCA Grand

MUSEUM

(Museum of Contemporary Art; Map p250; ☎213-626-6222; www.moca.org; 250 S Grand Ave; adult/child $15/free, 5-8pm Thu free; ⏲11am-6pm Mon, Wed & Fri, to 8pm Thu, to 5pm Sat & Sun; Ⓜ Red/Purple Lines to Civic Center/Grand Park) MOCA's superlative art collection focuses mainly on works created from the 1940s to the present. There's no shortage of luminaries, among them Mark Rothko, Dan Flavin, Willem de Kooning, Joseph Cornell and David Hockney, in regular and special exhibits. Their creations are housed in a 1986 building by 2019 Pritzker Prize–winning Japanese architect Arata Isozaki. Galleries are below ground, yet sky-lit bright.

Japanese American National Museum

MUSEUM

(Map p250; ☎213-625-0414; www.janm.org; 100 N Central Ave; adult/senior & child $12/6, 5-8pm Thu & all day 3rd Thu of month free; ⏲11am-5pm Tue, Wed & Fri-Sun, noon-8pm Thu; 👪; Ⓜ Gold Line to Little Tokyo/Arts District) A great first stop in Little Tokyo, this is the country's first museum dedicated to the Japanese immigrant experience. The 2nd floor is home to the permanent 'Common Ground' exhibition, which explores the evolution of Japanese-American culture since the late 19th century and offers moving insight into the painful chapter of America's WWII internment camps. Afterwards, relax in the tranquil garden and browse the well-stocked gift shop.

★Grammy Museum

MUSEUM

(Map p250; ☎213-765-6800; www.grammymuseum.org; 800 W Olympic Blvd; adult/child, senior & student $15/13; ⏲10:30am-6:30pm Sun, Mon, Wed & Thu, 10am-8pm Fri & Sat; P 👪; Ⓜ Blue/Expo Lines to Pico Station) The highlight of LA Live (p243), this museum's interactive exhibits define, differentiate and link musical genres. Spanning three levels, the rotating exhibitions might include threads worn by the likes of Michael Jackson, Whitney Houston and Beyoncé, scribbled words from the hands of Count Basie and Taylor Swift, and instruments once used by world-renowned rock deities. Inspired? Interactive sound chambers allow you to try your own hand at singing, mixing and remixing.

LA Plaza

MUSEUM

(La Plaza de Cultura y Artes; Map p250; ☎213-542-6259; www.lapca.org; 501 N Main St; ⏲noon-5pm Mon, Wed & Thu, to 6pm Fri-Sun; 👪; Ⓜ Union Station) FREE This museum offers snapshots of the Mexican-American experience in Los Angeles, from Spanish colonization in the late 18th century and the Mexican-American War (when the border crossed the original pueblo), to the Zoot Suit Riots, activist César Chávez and the Chicana movement. Exhibitions include a re-creation of 1920s

Greater Los Angeles

Top Sights

1 Aquarium of the Pacific........D5
2 Autry Museum of the American West........C2
3 Battleship Iowa........C5
4 Frederick R Weisman Art Foundation........C2
5 Gamble House........D2
6 Getty Center........B2
7 Getty Villa........B3
8 Griffith Observatory........C2
9 Huntington Library, Art Collections & Botanical Gardens........D2
10 Knott's Berry Farm........E4
11 Museum of Latin American Art........D5
12 Museum of Tolerance........C3
13 Venice Canals........B3
14 Watts Towers........D3

Sights

15 Anaheim Packing District........F4
California Science Center........(see 25)
Center Street Anaheim........(see 15)
16 Crystal Cove State Park........F6
17 Disneyland Resort........B5
18 Griffith Park........C2
19 Hollyhock House........C2
20 Hollywood Forever Cemetery........C2
21 Huntington City Beach........E6
22 International Surfing Museum........E6
23 Knott's Soak City........E4
24 Los Angeles Zoo & Botanical Gardens........C2
25 Natural History Museum of Los Angeles........C3
26 Norton Simon Museum........D2
27 Rodeo Drive........C3
Rose Garden........(see 25)
28 Universal Studios Hollywood........C2
29 Westwood Village Memorial Park Cemetery........B3

Activities, Courses & Tours

30 Bronson Cave........C2
31 Malibu Canyon........A3
32 Malibu Creek State Park........A2
33 Paramount Pictures........C2
34 Runyon Canyon........C2
35 Sony Pictures Studios........C3
36 Topanga State Park........B2
37 Warner Bros Studio Tour........C2

Sleeping

38 Avalon Hotel........C3
39 Ayres Hotel Anaheim........F5
40 Best Western Plus Stovall's Inn........A6
41 Bissell House B&B........D2
42 Disneyland Hotel........A5
43 Disney's Grand Californian Hotel & Spa........A5
44 Hotel Maya........D5
Knott's Berry Farm Hotel........(see 10)
45 Montage........C2
46 Paséa........E6

Eating

47 Bear Flag Fish Company........F6
48 Earl of Sandwich........A5
49 Guisados........D3
50 La Grande Orange........D2
51 Napa Rose........A5
Pigburd........(see 11)
52 Pour Vida........F4
53 Ralph Brennan's New Orleans Jazz Kitchen........A5

Drinking & Nightlife

54 Pike........D5
55 Polo Lounge........C2

Entertainment

56 Cavern Club Theater........C2
57 Dodger Stadium........D2
58 Geffen Playhouse........B3
59 Hollywood Bowl........C2

Shopping

60 Malibu Country Mart........A3
Pacific City........(see 46)
61 Rose Bowl Flea Market........D2

Information

62 Visit Marina Del Rey........B3
63 Visit Pasadena........D2

Main St as well as rotating showcases of modern and contemporary art by LA-based Latinx artists.

Exposition Park & Around

Just south of the University of Southern California (USC) campus, this park has a full day's worth of kid-friendly museums. Outdoor landmarks include the **Rose Garden** (Map p244; 213-763-0114; www.laparks.org/expo/garden; 701 State Dr, Exposition Park; 8:30am-sunset Mar 16–Dec 31; P; M Expo Line to Exposition Park/USC) FREE and the **Los Angeles Memorial Coliseum**, site of the 1932 and 1984 Summer Olympic Games. Parking costs around $10. From Downtown, take the Metro Expo Line or DASH minibus F.

★ Watts Towers LANDMARK
(Map p244; 213-847-4646; www.wattstowers.org; 1761-1765 E 107th St, Watts; tours 11am-3pm Thu & Fri, 10:30am-3pm Sat, noon-3pm Sun;

P; M Blue Line to 103rd St) The three 'Gothic' spires of the fabulous Watts Towers rank among the world's greatest monuments of folk art. In 1921 Italian immigrant Simon Rodia set out 'to make something big' and then spent 33 years cobbling together this whimsical free-form sculpture from concrete, steel and a motley assortment of found objects: green 7Up bottles to sea shells, tiles, rocks and pottery.

California Science Center MUSEUM
(Map p244; ☎film schedule 213-744-2019, info 323-724-3623; www.californiasciencecenter.org; 700 Exposition Park Dr, Exposition Park; IMAX movie adult/student & senior/child $8.95/7.95/6.75; ⏰10am-5pm; 👪) FREE Top billing at the Science Center goes to the Space Shuttle *Endeavour*, one of only four space shuttles nationwide, but there's plenty else to see at this large, multistory, multimedia museum filled with buttons to push, lights to switch on and knobs to pull. A simulated earthquake and a giant techno-doll named Tess bring out the kid in everyone. Admission is free, but special exhibits, experiences and IMAX movies cost extra.

Natural History Museum of Los Angeles MUSEUM
(Map p244; ☎213-763-3466; www.nhm.org; 900 Exposition Blvd, Exposition Park; adult/student & senior/child $15/12/7, LA County residents 3pm-5pm Mon-Fri free; ⏰9:30am-5pm; P 👪; M Expo Line to Expo/Vermont) Dinos to diamonds, bears to beetles, hissing roaches to African elephants – this museum will take you around the world and back, through millions of years in time. It's all housed in a beautiful 1913 Spanish Renaissance–style building that stood in for Columbia University in the first Toby McGuire *Spider-Man* movie – yup, this was where Peter Parker was bitten by the radioactive arachnid. There's enough to see here to fill several hours.

👁 Hollywood

Just as aging movie stars get the occasional face-lift, so has Hollywood. While it still hasn't recaptured its mid-20th-century 'Golden Age' glamour, its late 20th-century seediness is receding (albeit slowly). The **Hollywood Walk of Fame** (Map p254; www.walkoffame.com; Hollywood Blvd; M Red Line to Hollywood/Highland) honors more than 2600 celebrities with brass stars embedded in the sidewalk.

The Metro Red Line stops beneath **Hollywood & Highland** (Map p254; www.hollywoodandhighland.com; 6801 Hollywood Blvd; ⏰10am-10pm Mon-Sat, to 7pm Sun; 👪; M Red Line to Hollywood/Highland), a multistory mall with nicely framed views of the hillside **Hollywood sign** (erected in 1923 as an advertisement for a land development called Hollywoodland). Two-hour validated mall parking costs $3 (daily maximum $17).

★TCL Chinese Theatre LANDMARK
(Grauman's Chinese Theatre; Map p254; ☎323-461-3331; www.tclchinesetheatres.com; 6925

LOS ANGELES IN ...

Distances are ginormous in LA, so allow extra time for traffic and don't try to pack too much into a day.

One Day

Fuel up for the day at the **Original Farmers Market**, then go star-searching on the **Hollywood Walk of Fame** along Hollywood Blvd. Up your chances of spotting actual celebs by hitting the fashion-forward boutiques on paparazzi-infested **Robertson Boulevard**, or get a dose of nature at **Griffith Park**. Then drive west to the lofty **Getty Center** or head out to the **Venice Boardwalk** to see the seaside sideshow. Catch a Pacific sunset in **Santa Monica**.

Two Days

Explore rapidly evolving **Downtown LA**. Dig up the city's roots at **El Pueblo de Los Angeles**, then catapult to the future at dramatic **Walt Disney Concert Hall** and **Broad museum** topping Grand Ave's Cultural Corridor. Stop for a bite at **Grand Central Market,** then walk off lunch ambling between Downtown's historic buildings, **Arts District galleries** and **Little Tokyo**. At South Park's glitzy **LA Live** entertainment center, romp through the multimedia **Grammy Museum**. After dark, hit the dance floor at clubs in **Hollywood**.

Hollywood Blvd; ; Red Line to Hollywood/Highland) FREE Ever wondered what it's like to be in George Clooney's shoes? Find his foot- and handprints alongside dozens of other stars', forever set in the concrete forecourt of this world-famous movie palace, opened in 1927 and styled after an exotic pagoda complete with temple bells and stone heaven dogs from China. Join the throngs to find out how big Arnold's feet really are, or search for Betty Grable's legs, Whoopi Goldberg's braids, Daniel Radcliffe's wand or R2-D2's wheels.

★ **Hollywood Museum** MUSEUM
(Map p254; 323-464-7776; www.thehollywoodmuseum.com; 1660 N Highland Ave; adult/senior & student/child $15/12/5; 10am-5pm Wed-Sun; Red Line to Hollywood/Highland) For a taste of Old Hollywood, do not miss this musty temple to the stars, its four floors crammed with movie and TV costumes and props. The museum is housed inside the Max Factor Building, built in 1914 and relaunched as a glamorous beauty salon in 1935. At the helm was Polish-Jewish businessman Max Factor, Hollywood's leading authority on cosmetics. And it was right here that he worked his magic on Hollywood's most famous screen queens.

Hollywood Forever Cemetery CEMETERY
(Map p244; 323-469-1181; www.hollywoodforever.com; 6000 Santa Monica Blvd; guided tours $20; 8:30am-5pm, guided tours 10am most Saturdays; P) FREE Paradisiacal landscaping, vainglorious tombstones and epic mausoleums set an appropriate resting place for some of Hollywood's most iconic dearly departed. Residents include Cecil B DeMille, Mickey Rooney, Jayne Mansfield, punk rockers Johnny and Dee Dee Ramone and *Golden Girls* star Estelle Getty. Rudolph Valentino lies in the Cathedral Mausoleum (open 10am to 2pm), while Judy Garland rests in the Abbey of the Psalms.

Griffith Park

America's largest urban **park** (Map p244; 323-644-2050; www.laparks.org/griffithpark; 4730 Crystal Springs Dr; 5am-10:30pm, trails sunrise-sunset; P) FREE is five times the size of New York's Central Park, with an outdoor theater, **zoo** (Map p244; 323-644-4200; www.lazoo.org; 5333 Zoo Dr, Griffith Park; adult/senior/child $21/18/16; 10am-5pm, closed Christmas Day; P), observatory, museum, merry-go-round, antique and miniature trains, children's playgrounds, golf, tennis and over 50 miles of hiking paths, including to the original *Batman* TV series cave.

★ **Griffith Observatory** MUSEUM
(Map p244; 213-473-0890; www.griffithobservatory.org; 2800 E Observatory Rd; admission free, planetarium shows adult/student & senior/child $7/5/3; noon-10pm Tue-Fri, from 10am Sat & Sun; P ; DASH Observatory) FREE LA's landmark 1935 observatory opens a window onto the universe from its perch on the southern slopes of Mt Hollywood. Its planetarium claims the world's most advanced star projector, while its astronomical touch displays explore some mind-bending topics, from the evolution of the telescope and the ultraviolet x-rays used to map our solar system to the cosmos itself. Then, of course, there are the views, which (on clear days) take in the entire LA Basin, surrounding mountains and Pacific Ocean.

★ **Autry Museum of the American West** MUSEUM
(Map p244; 323-667-2000; http://theautry.org; 4700 Western Heritage Way, Griffith Park; adult/senior & student/child $14/10/6, 2nd Tue each month free; 10am-4pm Tue-Fri, to 5pm Sat & Sun; P) Established by singing cowboy Gene Autry, this expansive, underrated museum offers contemporary perspectives on the history and people of the American West, as well as their links to today's culture. Permanent exhibitions span Native American traditions to 19th-century cattle drives, daily frontier life (look for the beautifully carved vintage saloon bar) to costumes and artifacts from Hollywood westerns. Blockbuster temporary exhibits cover themes including Route 66, the 1960s and '70s Chicano newspaper *La Raza* and Native American artist Harry Fonseca.

West Hollywood & Mid-City

In WeHo, rainbow flags fly proudly over Santa Monica Boulevard, while celebs keep gossip rags happy by misbehaving at clubs on the fabled Sunset Strip. Boutiques along **Robertson Boulevard** and **Melrose Avenue** purvey sassy and ultrachic fashions for Hollywood royalty and celebutantes. WeHo's also a hotbed of cutting-edge interior design, fashion and art, particularly in the **West Hollywood Design District** (http://westhollywooddesigndistrict.com). Further south, some of LA's best museums line Mid-City's Museum Row along Wilshire Blvd east of Fairfax Ave.

★ **Los Angeles County Museum of Art** MUSEUM

(LACMA; Map p258; ☎323-857-6000; www.lacma.org; 5905 Wilshire Blvd, Mid-City; adult/senior & student/child $25/21/free, 2nd Tue each month free, some holidays free; ⏰11am-5pm Mon, Tue & Thu, to 8pm Fri, 10am-7pm Sat & Sun; P; 🚌Metro lines 20, 217, 720, 780 to Wilshire & Fairfax) The depth and wealth of the collection at the largest museum in the western US is stunning. LACMA holds all the major players – Rembrandt, Cézanne, Magritte, Mary Cassatt, Ansel Adams – plus millennia's worth of Chinese, Japanese, pre-Columbian and ancient Greek, Roman and Egyptian sculpture. Recent acquisitions include massive outdoor installations such as Chris Burden's *Urban Light* (a surreal selfie backdrop of hundreds of vintage LA streetlamps) and Michael Heizer's *Levitated Mass,* a surprisingly inspirational 340-ton boulder perched over a walkway.

La Brea Tar Pits & Museum MUSEUM

(Map p258; www.tarpits.org; 5801 Wilshire Blvd, Mid-City; adult/student & senior/child $15/12/7, 1st Tue of month Sep-Jun free; ⏰9:30am-5pm; P 👪) Mammoths, saber-toothed cats and dire wolves roamed LA's savanna in prehistoric times. We know this because of an archaeological trove of skulls and bones unearthed here at the La Brea Tar Pits, one of the world's most fecund and famous fossil sites. A museum has been built here, where generations of young dino hunters have come to seek out fossils and learn about paleontology from docents and demonstrations in on-site labs.

Beverly Hills & the Westside

Westwood is home to the well-tended UCLA campus, while Beverly Hills claims **Rodeo Drive** (Map p244), a prime people-watching spot – no trip to LA would be complete without a saunter along it. Guided tours of celebrity homes depart from Hollywood.

★ **Getty Center** MUSEUM

(Map p244; ☎310-440-7300; www.getty.edu; 1200 Getty Center Dr, off I-405 Fwy; ⏰10am-5:30pm Tue-Fri & Sun, to 9pm Sat; P 👪; 🚌734, 234) FREE In its billion-dollar, in-the-clouds perch, high above the city grit and grime, the Getty Center presents triple delights: a stellar art collection (everything from medieval triptychs to baroque sculpture and impressionist brushstrokes), Richard Meier's cutting-edge architecture, and the visual splendor of seasonally changing gardens. Admission is free, but parking is $20 ($15 after 3pm).

★ **Museum of Tolerance** MUSEUM

(Map p244; ☎reservations 310-772-2505; www.museumoftolerance.com; 9786 W Pico Blvd; adult/senior/student $15.50/12.50/11.50, Anne Frank Exhibit $15.50/13.50/12.50; ⏰10am-5pm Sun-Wed & Fri, to 9:30pm Thu, to 3:30pm Fri Nov-Mar; P) Run by the Simon Wiesenthal Center, this powerful, deeply moving museum uses interactive technology to engage visitors in discussion and contemplation around racism and bigotry. Particular focus is given to the Holocaust, with a major basement exhibition that examines the social, political and economic conditions that led to the Holocaust as well as the experience of the millions persecuted. On the museum's 2nd floor, another major exhibition offers an intimate look into the life and impact of Anne Frank.

★ **Frederick R Weisman Art Foundation** MUSEUM

(Map p244; ☎310-277-5321; www.weismanfoundation.org; 265 N Carolwood Dr; ⏰90min guided tours 10:30am & 2pm Mon-Fri, by appointment only) FREE The late entrepreneur and philanthropist Frederick R Weisman had an insatiable passion for art, a fact confirmed when touring his former Holmby Hills home. From floor to ceiling, the mansion (and its manicured grounds) bursts with extraordinary works from visionaries such as Picasso, Kandinsky, Miró, Magritte, Rothko, Warhol, Rauschenberg and Ruscha. There's even a motorcycle painted by Keith Haring. Tours should be reserved at least a few days ahead.

Westwood Village Memorial Park Cemetery CEMETERY

(Map p244; ☎310-474-1579; 1218 Glendon Ave, Westwood; ⏰8am-6pm; P) You'll be spending quiet time with entertainment heavyweights at this compact cemetery, hidden behind Wilshire Blvd's wall of high-rise towers. The northeast mausoleum houses Marilyn Monroe's simple crypt, while just south of it, the Sanctuary of Love harbors Dean Martin's crypt. Beneath the central lawn lie a number of iconic names, including actress Natalie Wood, pin-up Bettie Page, and crooner Roy Orbison (the latter lies in an unmarked grave to the left of a marker labeled 'Grandma Martha Monroe').

Downtown Los Angeles

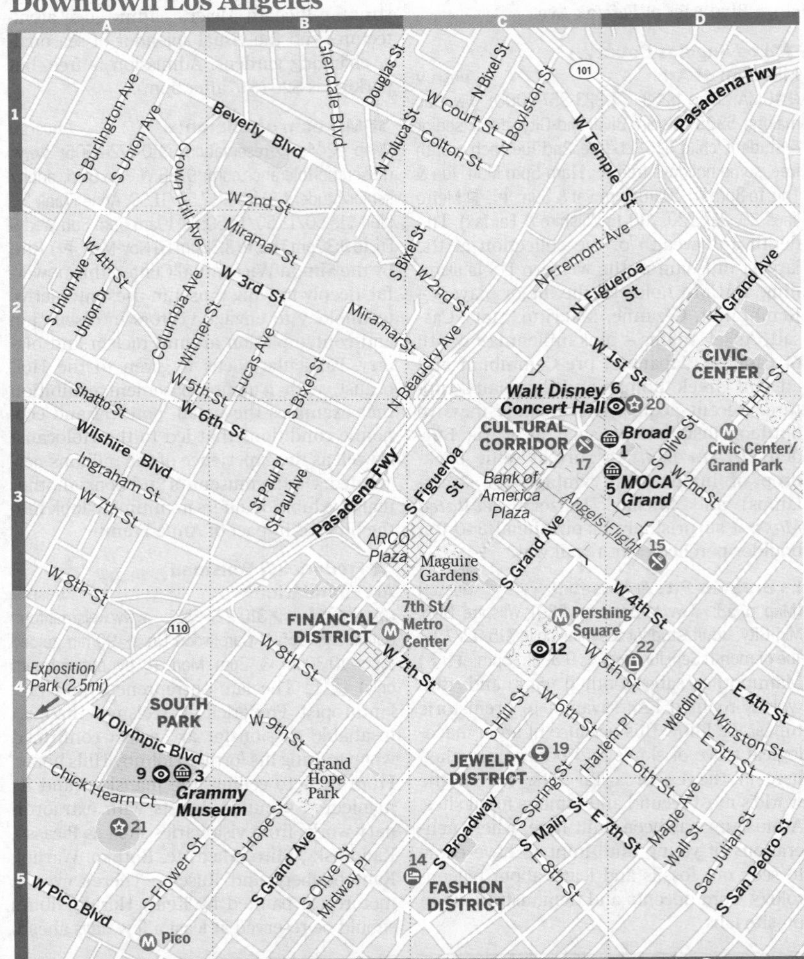

Malibu

The beach is king, of course, and whether you find a sliver of sand among the sandstone rock towers and topless sunbathers at **El Matador** (818-880-0363; 32215 Pacific Coast Hwy; P) or enjoy the wide loamy blonde beaches of Zuma and Westward, you'll have a special afternoon. Many A-listers have homes here and can sometimes be spotted shopping at the village-like **Malibu Country Mart** (Map p244; 310-456-7300; www.malibucountrymart.com; 3835 Cross Creek Rd; 10am-midnight Mon-Sat, to 10pm Sun; MTA line 534) shopping center.

One of Malibu's natural treasures is canyon-riddled **Malibu Creek State Park** (Map p244; 818-880-0367; www.malibucreekstatepark.org; 1925 Las Virgenes Rd, Cornell; parking $12; dawn-dusk), a popular movie and TV filming location with hiking trails galore (parking $12). A string of famous Malibu beaches include aptly named Surfrider near Malibu Pier, secretive El Matador, family fave Zuma Beach and wilder Point Dume (beach parking $3 to $12.50).

★Getty Villa MUSEUM

(Map p244; 310-430-7300; www.getty.edu; 17985 Pacific Coast Hwy, Pacific Palisades; 10am-

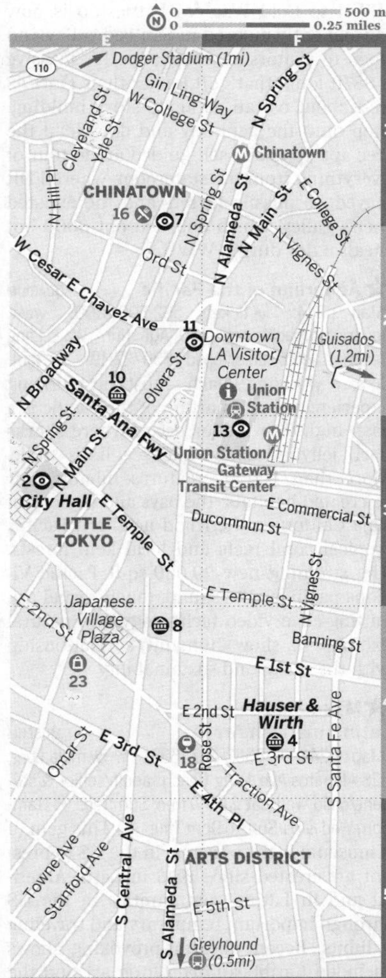

5pm Wed-Mon; P; line 534 to Coastline Dr) FREE Stunningly perched on an ocean-view hillside, this museum in a replica 1st-century Roman villa is an exquisite, 64-acre showcase for Greek, Roman and Etruscan antiquities. Dating back 7000 years, they were amassed by oil tycoon J Paul Getty. Galleries, peristiles, courtyards and lushly landscaped gardens ensconce all manner of friezes, busts and mosaics, along with millennia-old cut, blown and colored glass and brain-bending geometric configurations in the Hall of Colored Marbles. Other highlights include the Pompeii fountain and Temple of Herakles.

Downtown Los Angeles

Top Sights

1 Broad D3
2 City Hall E3
3 Grammy Museum A4
4 Hauser & Wirth F4
5 MOCA Grand D3
6 Walt Disney Concert Hall D3

Sights

7 Chinatown E1
8 Japanese American National Museum E4
9 LA Live A4
10 LA Plaza E2
11 Olvera Street E2
12 Pershing Square C4
13 Union Station F3

Sleeping

14 Ace Hotel C5

Eating

15 Grand Central Market D3
16 Howlin' Ray's E1
Manuela .... (see 4)
17 Otium C3

Drinking & Nightlife

18 Angel City Brewery E4
19 Clifton's Republic C4

Entertainment

LA Clippers .... (see 21)
LA Lakers .... (see 21)
20 Los Angeles Philharmonic D3
21 Staples Center A5

Shopping

22 Last Bookstore in Los Angeles D4
23 Raggedy Threads E4

Santa Monica

The belle by the beach mixes urban cool with a laid-back vibe. Tourists, teens and street performers throng car-free, chain-store-lined Third Street Promenade. For more local flavor, shop posh Montana Ave or eclectic Main St, backbone of the neighborhood once nicknamed 'Dogtown,' – the birthplace of skateboard culture. There's free 90-minute parking in most public garages downtown.

★ Santa Monica Pier LANDMARK

(Map p260; ☎310-458-8901; www.santamonicapier.org;) Once the very end of the legendary Route 66 and still the object of a tourist love affair, this much-photographed pier dates back to 1908 and is the city's most compelling landmark. It's dominated by **Pacific Park** (Map p260; 310-260-8744; www.pacpark.com; 380 Santa Monica Pier; per ride $5-10, all-day pass adult/child under 8yr $35/19; daily, seasonal hrs vary; ; Expo Line to Downtown Santa Monica) amusement park with arcades, carnival games, a Ferris wheel and roller coaster. Nearby is a vintage **carousel** (Map p260; 310-394-8042; adult/child $2/1; hrs vary;) and an **aquarium** (Map p260; 310-393-6149; www.healthebay.org; 1600 Ocean Front Walk; adult/child $5/free; 2-6pm Mon-Thu, 12:30-6pm Fri-Sun; ; Expo Line to Downtown Santa Monica). The pier is most photogenic when framed by California sunsets and when it comes alive with free concerts and outdoor movies in the summertime.

Venice

Prepare for sensory overload on Venice's **Boardwalk** (Ocean Front Walk; Map p260; Venice Pier to Rose Ave), a one-of-a-kind experience. Buff bodybuilders brush elbows with street performers and sellers of sunglasses, string bikinis, Mexican ponchos and cannabis, while cyclists and rollerbladers whiz by on the bike path, and skateboarders and graffiti artists get their own domains. A few blocks away, **Abbot Kinney Blvd** (Map p260; Big Blue Bus line 18) is the epicenter of 'new Venice', chockablock with trendy boutiques, restaurants and cafes. The **Venice Canals** (Map p244) offer a genteel escape among funky to modernist homes around the waterways that lent the neighborhood its name.

Long Beach

Stretching along LA County's southern flank, Long Beach forms half of America's busiest container-ship port along with the port of LA, across a channel. Yet there's little clue of the industrial edge in Long Beach's busy downtown – Pine Ave is crowded with restaurants and bars – and in the restyled waterfront. The Metro Blue Line connects Downtown LA with Long Beach in under an hour. Passport (www.lbtransit.com) minibuses shuttle around major tourist sights for free.

★ Battleship Iowa — MUSEUM, MEMORIAL

(Map p244; 877-446-9261; www.pacificbattleship.com; 250 S Harbor Blvd, San Pedro; adult/senior/child $20/17/12; 10am-5pm, last entry 4pm; ; Metro Silver Line) This WWII to Cold War–era battleship is now permanently moored in San Pedro Bay and open to visitors as a museum. It's massive – 887ft long (that's 5ft longer than *Titanic*) and about as tall as an 18-story building. Step onto the gangway and download the free app to take a self-guided audio tour of everything from the stateroom, where FDR stayed, to missile turrets and the enlisted men's galley, which churned out 8000 hot meals a day during WWII.

★ Aquarium of the Pacific — AQUARIUM

(Map p244; tickets 562-590-3100; www.aquariumofpacific.org; 100 Aquarium Way, Long Beach; adult/senior/child $30/27/19; 9am-6pm;) Long Beach's most mesmerizing experience, the Aquarium of the Pacific is a vast, high-tech indoor ocean where sharks dart, jellyfish dance and sea lions frolic. More than 11,000 creatures inhabit four re-created habitats: the bays and lagoons of Baja California, the frigid northern Pacific, tropical coral reefs and local kelp forests. The stunning new 29,000-sq-ft Pacific Visions pavilion uses sound, touch, visual art, cutting-edge video technology and natural exhibits to show humanity's relationship with the ocean and sustainability.

★ Museum of Latin American Art — MUSEUM

(Map p244; 562-437-1689; www.molaa.org; 628 Alamitos Ave, Long Beach; adult/senior & student/child Wed-Sat $10/7/free, Sun free; 11am-5pm Wed & Fri-Sun, to 9pm Thu;) This gem of a museum is the only one in the US to present art created since 1945 in Latin America and in Latino communities in the US through important temporary and traveling exhibits. Recent thought-provoking shows included Caribbean art, tattoo art and the works of LA's own Frank Romero.

Pasadena

Below the lofty San Gabriel Mountains, this city drips with wealth and gentility, feeling a world apart from urban LA. It's known for its early 20th-century arts-and-crafts architecture and the Tournament of Roses Parade on New Year's Day. Amble on foot around the shops, cafes, bars and restaurants of Old Town Pasadena, along Colorado Blvd east of Pasadena Ave. Metro Gold Line trains connect Pasadena and Downtown LA in 20 minutes.

★Huntington Library, Art Collections & Botanical Gardens — MUSEUM, GARDEN

(Map p244; ☎626-405-2100; www.huntington.org; 1151 Oxford Rd, San Marino; adult weekday/weekend & holidays $25/29, child $13, 1st Thu each month free; ⏲10am-5pm Wed-Mon; P) One of the most delightful, inspirational spots in LA, the Huntington is rightly a highlight of any trip to California thanks to a world-class mix of art, literary history and over 120 acres of themed gardens (any one of which would be worth a visit on its own), all set amid stately grounds. There's so much to see and do that it's hard to know where to begin; allow three to four hours for even a basic visit.

★Gamble House — ARCHITECTURE

(Map p244; ☎bookstore 626-449-4178, info 626-793-3334, tickets 844-325-0812; https://gamblehouse.org; 4 Westmoreland Pl, Pasadena; tours adult/student & senior/child $15/12.50/free; ⏲tours 10:30am, 11:30am & 1:30pm Tue, 11:30am-3pm Thu & Fri, noon-3pm Sat & Sun; P) This mansion in northwest central Pasadena has been called one of the 10 most architecturally significant homes in America. The 1908 masterpiece of California arts-and-crafts architecture was built by Charles and Henry Greene for Procter & Gamble heir David Gamble. Incorporating 17 woods, art glass and subdued light, the entire home is a work of art, with its foundation, furniture and fixtures all united by a common design and theme inspired by its Southern California environs and Japanese and Chinese architecture.

Norton Simon Museum — MUSEUM

(Map p244; ☎626-449-6840; www.nortonsimon.org; 411 W Colorado Blvd, Pasadena; adult/senior/student & child $15/12/free; ⏲noon-5pm Mon, Wed & Thu, 11am-8pm Fri & Sat, 11am-5pm Sun; P) Rodin's *The Burghers of Calais* standing guard by the entrance is only a mind-teasing overture to the full symphony of art in store at this exquisite museum. Norton Simon (1907–93) was an entrepreneur with a Midas touch and a passion for art who parlayed his millions into an admirable collection of Western art and Asian sculpture. Meaty captions really help tell each piece's story.

Activities

Despite spending a lot of time jammed on freeways, Angelenos love to get physical. Theirs is a city made for pace-quickening

STUDIO TOURS

Did you know it takes a week to shoot a half-hour sitcom? Or that you rarely see ceilings on shows because the space is filled with lights and lamps? You'll learn these and other nuggets of information about the make-believe world of film and TV while touring a working studio. Star-sighting potential is better than average, except during 'hiatus' (May to August) when studios are deserted. Reservations are required and so is photo ID.

Paramount (Map p244; ☎323-956-1777; www.paramountstudiotour.com; 5555 Melrose Ave; regular/VIP tours $60/189, After Dark tours $99; ⏲tours 9:30am-5pm, last tour 3pm) *Star Trek*, *Indiana Jones* and *Shrek* are among the blockbusters that originated at Paramount, the longest-operating movie studio and the only one still in Hollywood proper. Two-hour tours through the back lots and sound stages are available daily year-round and are led by passionate, knowledgeable guides.

Sony (Map p244; ☎310-244-8687; www.sonypicturesstudiostours.com; 10202 W Washington Blvd; tour $50; ⏲tours usually 9:30am, 10:30am, 1:30pm & 2:30pm Mon-Fri; M Expo Line to Culver City) Running on weekdays only, this two-hour tour includes visits to the sound stages where *Men in Black*, *Spider-Man*, and *Charlie's Angels* were filmed. Munchkins hopped along the Yellow Brick Road in *The Wizard of Oz*, filmed when this was still the venerable MGM studio.

Warner Bros (Map p244; ☎877-492-8687, 818-972-8687; www.wbstudiotour.com; 3400 Warner Blvd, Burbank; tours adult/child 8-12yr from $72/62; ⏲8:30am-3:30pm, extended hrs Jun-Aug; 🚌155, 222, 501 stop about 400yd from tour center) This tour offers the most fun and authentic look behind the scenes of a major movie studio. Consisting of a two-hour guided tour and a self-guided tour of Studio 48, the adventure kicks off with a video of WB's greatest film hits – among them *Rebel Without a Cause* and *La La Land* – before a tram whisks you to sound stages, back-lot sets and technical departments, including props, costumes and the paint shop. Tours run daily, usually every half-hour.

Hollywood

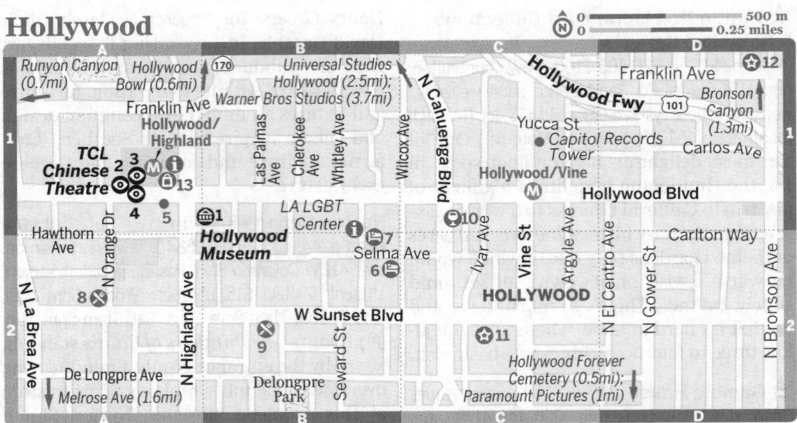

Hollywood

Top Sights
1 Hollywood Museum........B1
2 TCL Chinese Theatre........A1

Sights
3 Dolby Theatre........A1
4 Hollywood Walk of Fame........A1

Activities, Courses & Tours
5 TMZ Celebrity Tour........A1

Sleeping
6 Mama Shelter........B2
7 USA Hostels Hollywood........B2

Eating
8 In & Out Burger........A2
9 Luv2eat........B2

Drinking & Nightlife
Rooftop Bar at Mama Shelter........(see 6)
10 Tramp Stamp Granny's........C1

Entertainment
11 ArcLight Cinemas........C2
12 Upright Citizens Brigade Theatre........D1

Shopping
13 Hollywood & Highland........A1

thrills, with spectacular mountain hikes, one of the country's largest urban nature reserves and surf-pounded beach. Add to this almost 300 days of sunshine and you'll forgive the locals for looking so, so good.

Hiking

If hiking doesn't feel like an indigenous LA activity to you, you need to reassess. This town is hemmed in and defined by two mountain ranges and countless canyons. In the **San Gabriel Mountains**, trails wind from Mt Wilson into granite peak wilderness, once the domain of the Gabrielino people and the setting for California's last grizzly-bear sighting. The Chumash roamed the **Santa Monica Mountains** (www.nps.gov/samo/index.htm), which are smaller, but still offer spectacular views of chaparral-draped peaks with stark drops into the Pacific. The **Backbone Trail** spans the range, but our favorite hike is to Sandstone Peak. Day hikes in **Topanga Canyon State Park** (Map p244; 310-455-2465; www.parks.ca.gov; 20828 Entrada Rd, Topanga; per vehicle $10; 8am-dusk), **Malibu Canyon** (Map p244; Malibu Canyon Rd, Malibu), Point Mugu and **Leo Carrillo** (310-457-8143; www.parks.ca.gov; 35000 W Pacific Coast Hwy, Malibu; per car $12; 8am-10pm; P) state parks are also recommended. If you only have an hour or two, check out **Runyon** (Map p244; www.runyoncanyonhike.com; 2000 N Fuller Ave; dawn-dusk) or **Bronson** (Map p244; 818-243-1145; www.laparks.org; 3200 Canyon Dr; 5am-10:30pm) canyons in Hollywood. For more advice about trails in and around Southern California check out www.trails.com and www.modernhiker.com.

Yoga

The most popular style in town is Hatha yoga. Of course, it just wouldn't be LA without some unexpected offerings in the mix. Among the best are Vinyasa yoga classes to hip-hop and R&B beats at WeHo studio Y7 (www.y7-studio.com) and beer-and-yoga Sunday sessions at nearby Angel City Brewery (p262).

Cycling & In-line Skating

Get scenic exercise pedaling or skating along the paved **South Bay Bicycle Trail** (Map p260; sunrise-sunset;), which parallels the beach for most of the 22 miles between Santa Monica and Pacific Palisades. Rental shops are plentiful in busy beach towns. Warning: it's crowded on weekends.

Surfing & Swimming

Top beaches for swimming are Malibu's **Leo Carrillo State Park**, **Santa Monica State Beach** and the South Bay's **Hermosa Beach**. Malibu's **Surfrider Beach** is a legendary surfing spot. Parking rates vary seasonally, as does water quality – check the 'Beach Report Card' at http://brc.healthebay.org.

Tours

★Los Angeles Conservancy WALKING

(213-623-2489; www.laconservancy.org; adult/child $15/10) Downtown LA's intriguing historical and architectural gems – from an art deco penthouse to a beaux arts ballroom and a dazzling silent-movie theater – are revealed on this nonprofit group's 2½-hour walking tours. To see some of LA's grand historic movie theaters from the inside, the conservancy also offers the Last Remaining Seats film series, screening classic movies in gilded theaters.

★Esotouric BUS

(213-915-8687; www.esotouric.com; tours $64) Discover LA's lurid and fascinating underbelly on these offbeat, insightful and entertaining walking and bus tours themed around famous crime sites (Black Dahlia anyone?), literary lions (Chandler to Bukowski) and more.

TMZ Celebrity Tour BUS

(Map p254; 844-869-8687; www.tmz.com/tour; 6822 Hollywood Blvd; adult/child $52/32; tours depart 10am-5pm most days, check website for additional hours; Red Line to Hollywood/Highland) Cut the shame; we know you want to spot celebrities, glimpse their homes and laugh at their dirt. Super-fun tours by open-sided bus run for two hours, and you'll likely meet some of the TMZ stars...and perhaps even celebrity guests on the bus.

Dearly Departed BUS

(855-600-3323; www.dearlydepartedtours.com; tours $25-85) This long-running, occasionally creepy, frequently hilarious tour will clue you in on where celebs kicked the bucket, George Michael dropped his trousers, Hugh Grant received certain services and the Charles Manson gang murdered Sharon Tate. Some of the tours are not for kids, so choose carefully.

Festivals & Events

First Friday STREET CARNIVAL

(www.abbotkinneyfirstfridays.com; 5-11pm 1st Fri each month) Businesses along Abbot Kinney Blvd stay open late and the street is filled with food trucks at this monthly street fair.

Academy Awards FILM

(www.oscars.org; late Feb) On Tinseltown's biggest night, visitors can ogle their favorite film stars from the red-carpet-adjacent bleachers of the **Dolby Theatre** (Map p254; 323-308-6300; www.dolbytheatre.com; 6801 Hollywood Blvd; tours adult/child, senior & student $25/19; 10:30am-4pm; P; Red Line to Hollywood/Highland). Apply in November or December for one of around 700 lucky spots, or watch it on TV.

Día de los Muertos CULTURAL

(Day of the Dead; early Nov) LA's Mexican community honors its deceased relatives on and around November 2 with costumed parades, sugar skulls, graveyard picnics, candlelight processions and fabulous altars. Events are held across the city, including on Olvera St and at the Hollywood Forever Cemetery.

Sleeping

From rock-and-roll Downtown digs to fabled Hollywood hideaways and beachside escapes, LA serves up a dizzying array of slumber options. The key is to plan well ahead. Do your research and find out which neighborhood is most convenient for your plans and best appeals to your style and interests. Trawl the internet for deals, and consider visiting between January and April, when room rates and occupancy are usually at their lowest (Oscars week aside).

Downtown

Ace Hotel HOTEL $$$

(Map p250; 213-623-3233; www.acehotel.com/losangeles; 929 S Broadway; r/lofts from

LOCAL KNOWLEDGE

LA INSIDER MOVES

Classic Movies in Special Spaces It's always a scene (and surprisingly not creepy) when Cinespia (http://cinespia.org) screens films on the side of a giant mausoleum at Hollywood Forever Cemetery (p248), during summer. For a different experience, check the site for occasional screenings in historic Downtown theaters usually not open to the public.

Exploring Architecture Downtown LA's intriguing historical and architectural gems – from an art-deco penthouse to a beaux-arts ballroom and a dazzling silent-movie theater – are revealed on 2½-hour walking tours by the LA Conservancy (www.laconservancy.org). Each June, the conservancy also runs its own Last Remaining Seats film series in some of the same theaters as Cinespia.

Shop with the Chefs Farmers markets throughout the county serve up California's bounty with a heaping helping of local culture. Santa Monica's famous Wednesday and Saturday farmers markets (p261) tend to draw top chefs, and the Thursday market on the south lawn of **LA City Hall** (Map p250; ☎213-485-2121; www.lacity.org; 200 N Spring St; ⏰9am-5pm Mon-Fri) FREE donates 10% of its proceeds to Los Angeles River Artists and Business Association (LARABA).

Scenic Drives For awesome eyefuls, a couple of beautiful routes hide in plain sight. Twisty-turny Mulholland Dr forms the border between the LA Basin and San Fernando Valley, with breathtaking views on either side. Or head west from San Pedro along Palos Verdes Dr for 14 miles of stunning coastal views that may make you forget that you're in America's second-largest metropolis.

$300/450; P ❄ 📶 🏊) The ever-hip, buzzy, 182-room Ace is big on quirky details: Haas Brothers murals in the lobby and restaurant, whimsically themed cocktails at the rooftop bar and retro-inspired rooms with boxer-style robes, blank music sheets and, in many cases, record players or guitars. Small rooms can feel tight, so consider opting for a medium. Valet parking is $40 a night.

Hollywood

USA Hostels Hollywood HOSTEL $

(Map p254; ☎323-462-3777; www.usahostels.com; 1624 Schrader Blvd; dm $41-46, r with bath from $129; ❄ @ 📶; M Red Line to Hollywood/Vine) This sociable hostel puts you within steps of the Hollywood party circuit. Private rooms are a bit cramped, but making new friends is easy during staff-organized barbecues, comedy nights, hikes and various walking tours. Freebies include wi-fi, linens and continental breakfast with cook-your-own-pancakes. It has cushy lounge seating on the front porch and free beach shuttles.

★**Mama Shelter** BOUTIQUE HOTEL $$

(Map p254; ☎323-785-6666; www.mamashelter.com; 6500 Selma Ave; r from $189; ❄ @ 📶; M Red Line to Hollywood/Vine) Hip, affordable Mama Shelter keeps things playful with its lobby gumball machines, foosball table and live streaming of guests' selfies and videos. Standard rooms are small but cool, with quality beds and linen and subway-tiled bathrooms with decent-sized showers. Quirky in-room touches include movie scripts, masks and Apple TVs with free Netflix. The rooftop bar (p262) is one of LA's best.

West Hollywood & Mid-City

Palihotel BOUTIQUE HOTEL $$

(Map p258; ☎323-272-4588; www.pali-hotel.com; 7950 Melrose Ave, Mid-City; r from $175; P @ 📶) We love the rustic wood-paneled exterior, the polished-concrete floor in the lobby, the elemental Thai massage spa, and the 32 contemporary rooms with two-tone paint jobs, a wall-mounted flat-screen TV, and enough room for a sofa. Some have terraces. Terrific all-around value.

Chateau Marmont HOTEL $$$

(Map p258; ☎323-656-1010; www.chateaumarmont.com; 8221 W Sunset Blvd, Hollywood; r $465, ste from $845; P ⊖ ❄ 📶 🏊) The French-flavored indulgence may look dated, but this faux castle has long lured A-listers with its hilltop perch, five-star mystique and legendary discretion. Howard Hughes used to spy on bikini beauties from the same balcony suite that became the favorite of U2's Bono. If nothing else, it's worth stopping by for a cocktail at **Bar Marmont** (Map p258; ☎323-650-0575; www.chateaumarmont.com; 8171 Sunset Blvd, Hollywood; ⏲6pm-2am).

★Mondrian HOTEL **$$$**
(Map p258; ☎323-650-8999, reservations 800-606-6090; www.mondrianhotel.com; 8440 Sunset Blvd, West Hollywood; r/ste from $329/369; P@📶🏊) This chic, sleek tower has been an LA showplace since the 1990s. Giant doors facing the Sunset Strip frame the entrance, opening to a lobby of minimalist elegance: white walls, blond woods, billowy curtains and model-good-looking staff. Upstairs, mood-lit hallways with tiny light boxes (by famed light artist James Turrell) lead to recently renovated rooms with chandeliers, rain showers and down duvets.

Beverly Hills

Montage HOTEL **$$$**
(Map p244; ☎310-860-7800; www.montagebeverlyhills.com; 225 N Canon Dr, Beverly Hills; r/ste from $695/1175; P@📶🏊) Drawing on-point eye candy and serious wealth, the 201-room Montage balances elegance with warmth and affability. Models and moguls lunch by the gorgeous rooftop pool, while the property's sprawling five-star spa is a Moroccan-inspired marvel, with both single-sex and unisex plunge pools. Rooms are classically styled, with custom Sealy mattresses, dual marble basins, spacious showers and deep-soaking tubs.

Avalon Hotel HOTEL **$$$**
(Map p244; ☎310-277-5221; www.avalon-hotel.com/beverly-hills; 9400 W Olympic Blvd, Beverly Hills; r from $309; P⊖❄@📶🏊🐾) Mid-century modern gets a 21st-century spin at this fashion-crowd fave, which was Marilyn Monroe's old pad in its days as an apartment building. Funky retro rooms are all unique, but most have arched walls, marble slab desks and night stands, as well as playful art and sculpture. Perks include a sexy hourglass-shaped pool. Call it affordable glamour.

Santa Monica

HI Los Angeles – Santa Monica HOSTEL **$**
(Map p260; ☎310-393-9913; www.hilosangeles.org; 1436 2nd St; dm $38-70, r with shared bath $130-150, with private bath $180-220; ⊖❄@📶; Ⓜ Expo Line to Downtown Santa Monica) Near the beach and Promenade, this hostel has an enviable location and modernized facilities that rival properties charging much more. Its approximately 275 beds in single-sex dorms are clean and safe, private rooms are decorated with hipster chic and public spaces (courtyard, library, TV room, dining room, communal kitchen) let you lounge and surf.

Sea Shore Motel MOTEL **$$**
(Map p260; ☎310-392-2787; www.seashoremotel.com; 2637 Main St; r $140-195, ste $240-300; P❄📶) The friendly, family-run lodgings at this comfy 25-unit motel put you just a Frisbee toss from the beach on happening Main St (quadruple-pane windows help cut street noise). The tiled, rattan-decorated rooms are basic, but 2nd-floor rooms have high ceilings and, a few doors down, families can stretch out in suites (basically full apartments) with kitchen and balcony.

Palihouse BOUTIQUE HOTEL **$$$**
(Map p260; ☎310-394-1279; www.palihousesantamonica.com; 1001 3rd St; r from $295; P❄@📶🐾) LA's grooviest hotel brand (not named Ace) occupies the 38 rooms, studios and one-bedroom apartments of the 1927 Spanish Colonial Embassy Hotel, with antique-meets-hipster-chic style. Each comfy room is slightly different, but look for picnic-table-style desks and wallpaper with intricate sketches of animals. Most rooms have full kitchens (and we love the coffee mugs with lifelike drawings of fish).

Long Beach

Hotel Maya BOUTIQUE HOTEL **$$**
(Map p244; ☎562-435-7676; https://hotelmayalongbeach.com; 700 Queensway Dr, Long Beach; r from $179; P❄@📶🏊🐾) West of the *Queen Mary*, this boutique, waterside property hits you with hip immediately upon entering the rusted-steel, glass and magenta-paneled lobby. The feel continues in the 199 rooms (coral tile, river-rock headboards, Mayan-icon accents), set on 11 palmy acres in four 1970s-era hexagonal buildings with views of downtown Long Beach that are worth the upcharge.

Pasadena

Bissell House B&B B&B **$$**
(Map p244; ☎626-441-3535; www.bissellhouse.com; 201 S Orange Grove Ave, South Pasadena; r from $159; P📶🏊) Antiques, hardwood floors and a crackling fireplace make this secluded Victorian (1887) B&B on 'Millionaire's Row'

West Hollywood & Mid-City

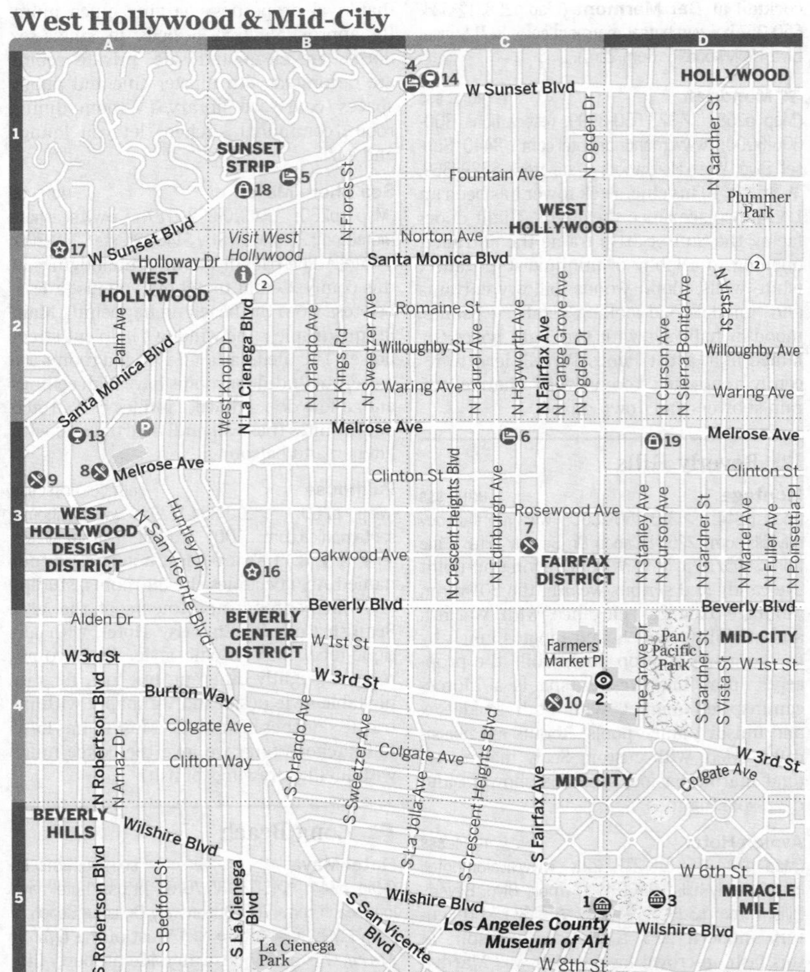

a bastion of warmth and romance. The hedge-framed garden feels like a sanctuary, and there's a pool for cooling off on hot summer days. The Prince Albert room has gorgeous wallpaper and a claw-foot tub. All seven rooms have private bathrooms.

Eating

Bring an appetite. A big one. LA's cross-cultural makeup is reflected at its table, which is an epic global feast. And while there's no shortage of just-like-the-motherland dishes – from Cantonese *xiao long bao* to Ligurian *farinata* – it's the takes on tradition that really thrill. Ever tried Korean-Mexican tacos? Or a vegan cream-cheese donut with jam, basil and balsamic reduction? LA may be many things, but a culinary bore isn't one of them.

Downtown

★Grand Central Market MARKET

(Map p250; www.grandcentralmarket.com; 317 S Broadway; 8am-10pm; ; Red/Purple Lines to Pershing Sq) Designed by prolific architect John Parkinson and once home to an office occupied by Frank Lloyd Wright, LA's beaux arts market hall has been satisfying

West Hollywood & Mid-City

Top Sights

1 Los Angeles County Museum of Art C5

Sights

2 Grove C4
3 La Brea Tar Pits & Museum D5

Sleeping

4 Chateau Marmont C1
5 Mondrian B1
6 Palihotel C3

Eating

7 Canter's C3
8 Catch LA A3
9 Gracias Madre A3
10 Original Farmers Market C4
11 Providence F3
12 Salt's Cure E2

Drinking & Nightlife

13 Abbey A3
14 Bar Marmont C1

Entertainment

15 Celebration Theatre F2
16 Largo at the Coronet B3
17 Whisky-a-Go-Go A2

Shopping

18 Fred Segal B1
19 Melrose Avenue D3

appetites since 1917 and today is DTLA's gourmet mecca. Lose yourself in its bustle of neon signs, stalls and counters, peddling everything from fresh produce and nuts, to sizzling Thai street food, hipster breakfasts, modern deli classics, artisanal pasta and specialty coffee.

Guisados TACOS $

(Map p244; ☎323-264-7201; www.guisados.co; 2100 E Cesar Chavez Ave, Boyle Heights; tacos from $2.95; ⌚9am-8pm Mon-Fri, to 9pm Sat, to 5pm Sun; Ⓜ Gold Line to Mariachi Plaza) Guisados' citywide fame is founded on its *tacos de guisados:* warm, thick, nixtamal tortillas made to order and topped with sultry, smoky, slow-cooked stews. Do yourself a favor and order the sampler plate ($7.25), a democratic mix of six mini tacos. The *chiles torreados* (blistered, charred chili) taco is a must for serious spice-lovers.

Howlin' Ray's CHICKEN, SOUTHERN $

(Map p250; ☎213-935-8399; www.howlinrays.com; 727 N Broadway, Suite 128, Far East Plaza, Chinatown; mains $9-16; ⌚11am-7pm Tue-Fri, 10am-7pm Sat & Sun; P; Ⓜ Gold Line to Chinatown) It's hard to overstate the phenomenon that is Howlin' Ray's. Customers gladly queue for two hours or more – check Twitter for current wait times – at this noisy takeout counter with a smattering of seats and many picnic tables. The reward: Nashville-style fried chicken, spiced from country (mild) to howlin' ('can't touch this!').

Manuela MODERN AMERICAN $$

(Map p250; ☎323-849-0480; www.manuela-la.com; 907 E 3rd St; mains lunch $16-21, dinner $22-48; ⌚11:30am-3:30pm & 5:30-10pm Wed &

Santa Monica & Venice

Thu, 11:30am-3:30pm & 5:30-11pm Fri, 10am-4pm & 5:30-11pm Sat, 10am-4pm & 5:30-10pm Sun;) This it-kid inside the **Hauser & Wirth** (Map p250; 213-943-1620; www.hauserwirthlosangeles.com; 901 E 3rd St; 11am-6pm Wed & Fri-Sun, to 8pm Thu) FREE arts complex boasts a woody warm, loftlike space and an oft-tweaked menu that beautifully fuses California meats, produce and seafood with smoky Southern accents. Pique the appetite with cream biscuits, barbecued oysters or yellow peach salad with whipped feta and honey vinegar, then lose yourself in mains with herbs from the onsite garden.

Santa Monica & Venice

Top Sights

1 Abbot Kinney Boulevard B5
2 Santa Monica Pier A2
3 Venice Boardwalk A5

Sights

4 Pacific Park A2
5 Santa Monica Pier Aquarium A2
6 Santa Monica Pier Carousel A2

Activities, Courses & Tours

7 South Bay Bicycle Trail A2

Sleeping

8 HI Los Angeles – Santa Monica A2
9 Palihouse A1
10 Sea Shore Motel A3

Eating

11 Cassia B1
12 Gjelina B5
13 Santa Monica Farmers Markets A1

Drinking & Nightlife

14 Basement Tavern A3

Otium MODERN AMERICAN **$$$**

(Map p250; 213-935-8500; http://otiumla.com; 222 S Hope St, Downtown; dishes $8-60; 11:30am-2:30pm & 5:30-10pm Tue-Thu, 11:30am-2:30pm & 5:30-11pm Fri, 11am-2:30pm & 5:30-11pm Sat, 11am-2:30pm & 5:30-10pm Sun; ; Red/Purple Lines to Civic Center/Grand Park) In a modernist pavilion beside the Broad (p243) is this fun, of-the-moment hot spot helmed by chef Timothy Hollingsworth. Prime ingredients conspire in unexpected ways, from the crunch of wild rice and amaranth in an eye-candy salad of avocado, beets and pomegranate, to octopus with green garlic, black trumpet mushroom and *tom kha* (Thai coconut broth) to 'large-format' steaks (to $185).

Hollywood

In & Out Burger BURGERS **$**

(Map p254; 800-786-1000; www.in-n-out.com; 7009 Sunset Blvd; burgers from $2.10; 10:30am-1am Sun-Thu, to 1:30am Fri & Sat; ; Red Line to Hollywood/Highland) This LA burger chain is a point of pilgrimage for locals and visitors alike. Yes, this is fast food, but In & Out has been hand-crafting burgers since 1948: fresh (not frozen) beef, hand-cut French fries etc. The basic burger comes piled with lettuce, tomato, secret spread (like Thousand Island dressing) and raw or sautéed onion.

Luv2eat THAI $

(Map p254; ☎323-498-5835; www.luv2eatthai.com; 6660 W Sunset Blvd, Hollywood; mains $9-16; ⏰11am-3:30pm & 4:30-11:30pm; Ⓟ) Don't let the odd name and strip-mall location put you off; Luv2eat is something of a temple for LA's Thai foodies. Cordon Bleu–trained, Polo Lounge (p263) alumna Chef Fern and Thailand-bred Chef Pla offer generous serves of authentic chefs' specials, dishes you don't normally see even in this town loaded with Thai restaurants. They nail the standards, too.

Salt's Cure MODERN AMERICAN $$

(Map p258; ☎323-465-7258; http://saltscure.com; 1155 N Highland Ave; mains lunch $12-24, dinner $18-36; ⏰11am-3pm Mon, to 10pm Tue-Fri, 10am-10pm Sat, 10am-3pm Sun) Wood-paneled, concrete-floored Salt's Cure is an out, proud locavore. From the in-season vegetables to the house-butchered and cured meats, the menu celebrates all things Californian. Expect sophisticated takes on rustic comfort grub, whether it's capocollo with chili paste or tender duck breast paired with impressively light oatmeal griddle cakes and blackberry compote.

★ **Providence** MODERN AMERICAN $$$

(Map p258; ☎323-460-4170; www.providencela.com; 5955 Melrose Ave; lunch mains $38-48, dinner tasting menus $120-240; ⏰noon-2pm & 6-10pm Mon-Fri, 5:30-10pm Sat, 5:30-9pm Sun; Ⓟ) Consistently near the top of every list of great LA restaurants, chef Michael Cimarusti's James Beard–winning, two-Michelin-starred darling turns superlative seafood into arresting, nuanced dishes that might see abalone paired with eggplant, turnip and nori, or spiny lobster conspire decadently with macadamia nut and earthy black truffle. À la carte options are available at lunch only.

West Hollywood & Mid-City

Original Farmers Market MARKET $

(Map p258; ☎323-933-9211; www.farmersmarketla.com; 6333 W 3rd St; ⏰9am-9pm Mon-Fri, to 8pm Sat, 10am-7pm Sun; Ⓟ👪) The Farmers Market is a great spot for a casual meal any time of day, especially if the rug rats are tagging along. Its narrow walkways are lined with choices: gumbo and diner classics to French bistro, Singapore-style noodles and tacos, sit-down or takeout. Before or afterwards, check out the **Grove** (Map p258; www.thegrovela.com; 189 The Grove Dr; Ⓟ👪; 🚌MTA lines 16, 17, 780 to Wilshire & Fairfax) mall, next door.

Gracias Madre VEGAN, MEXICAN $$

(Map p258; ☎323-978-2170; www.graciasmadreweho.com; 8905 Melrose Ave, West Hollywood; mains lunch $12-17, dinner $12-18; ⏰11am-11pm Mon-Fri, from 10am Sat & Sun; ✎) Gracias Madre shows just how tasty – and chichi – organic, plant-based Mexican cooking can be. Sit on the gracious patio or in the cozy interior and feel good as you eat healthily: sweet-potato flautas, coconut 'bacon,' plantain 'quesadillas,' plus salads and bowls. We're consistently surprised at innovations like cashew 'cheese,' mushroom 'chorizo' and heart-of-palm 'crab cakes.'

Canter's DELI $$

(Map p258; ☎323-651-2030; www.cantersdeli.com; 419 N Fairfax Ave, Mid-City; mains $8-29; ⏰24hr; Ⓟ) As old-school delis go, Canter's is hard to beat. A fixture in the traditionally Jewish Fairfax district since 1931, seen-it-all waitresses serve up the requisite pastrami, corned beef and matzo-ball soup, plus all-day breakfast, in a rangy room with deli and bakery counters up front.

Catch LA FUSION $$$

(Map p258; ☎323-347-6060; http://catchrestaurants.com/catchla; 8715 Melrose Ave, West Hollywood; shared dishes $8-39, dinner mains $34-79; ⏰11am-3pm Sat & Sun, 5pm-2am daily; Ⓟ) An LA-scene extraordinaire. You may well find sidewalk paparazzi stalking celebrity guests and a doorman to check your reservation, but all that's forgotten once you're in this 3rd-floor rooftop restaurant/bar above WeHo. The Pacific Rim–inspired menu features supercreative cocktails and shared dishes such as truffle sashimi, black-cod lettuce wraps, and scallop and cauliflower with tamarind brown butter.

Santa Monica

Santa Monica Farmers Markets MARKET $

(Map p260; www.smgov.net/portals/farmersmarket; Arizona Ave, btwn 2nd & 3rd Sts; ⏰Arizona Ave 8:30am-1:30pm Wed, 8am-1pm Sat; 👪) 🌿 You haven't really experienced Santa Monica until you've explored one of its outdoor farmers markets stocked with organic fruits, vegetables, flowers, baked goods and freshly shucked oysters. The mack daddy is the Wednesday market, around the intersection of 3rd and Arizona – it's the biggest and arguably the best for fresh produce, and is often patrolled by local chefs.

Cassia SOUTHEAST ASIAN $$$

(Map p260; ☎310-393-6699; www.cassiala.com; 1314 7th St; appetizers $12-18, mains $19-76; ⊙5-10pm Sun-Thu, to 11pm Fri & Sat; P) Ever since it opened in 2015, open, airy Cassia has made about every local and national 'best' list of LA restaurants. Chef Bryant Ng draws on his Chinese-Singaporean heritage in dishes such as *kaya* toast (with coconut jam, butter and a slow-cooked egg), 'sunbathing' prawns, and the encompassing Vietnamese pot-au-feu: short-rib stew, veggies, bone marrow and delectable accompaniments.

Venice

Gjelina AMERICAN $$$

(Map p260; ☎310-450-1429; www.gjelina.com; 1429 Abbot Kinney Blvd, Venice; veggies, salads & pizzas $10-18, large plates $15-45; ⊙8am-midnight; ; Big Blue Bus line 18) If one restaurant defines the new Venice, it's this. Carve out a spot on the communal table between the hipsters and yuppies, or get your own slab of wood on the elegant stone terrace, and dine on imaginative small plates (raw yellowtail spiced with chili and mint and drenched in olive oil and blood orange) and sensational thin-crust, wood-fired pizza.

Long Beach

Pigburd AMERICAN $$

(Map p244; ☎562-269-0731; http://pigburd.com; 743 E 4th St, East Village, Long Beach; mains $15-29; ⊙3-10pm Mon & Tue, 9am-10pm Wed, Thu & Sun, 9am-11pm Fri & Sat) There's much to love about this bistro near downtown Long Beach: small-family-farm–raised meats, eggs and produce, an evolving menu of comfort foods fashioned from the same, and low-key service, all under a high-rafter roof with generous windows to watch the world go by. *And* many of its staff are disabled veterans, so you're doing good while eating well.

Pasadena

La Grande Orange CALIFORNIAN $$

(Map p244; ☎626-356-4444; www.lgostationcafe.com; 260 S Raymond Ave, Pasadena; pizzas $15-17, mains $15-47; ⊙11am-10pm Mon-Thu, to 11pm Fri, 10am-11pm Sat, 9am-9pm Sun; P; M Gold Line to Del Mar) Pasadena's original train station (c 1911) has been handsomely renovated into this cheery, popular dining room beneath lovingly aged wooden beams. The kitchen in the former ticket booth serves a menu of New American cooking: mesquite-grilled burgers and seafood, salads and pricier Midwestern aged steaks. Watch today's Gold Line trains go by from the generous bar.

Drinking & Nightlife

Whether you're after an organic CBD espresso, a craft cocktail made with peanut-butter-washed Campari, or a saison brewed with Chinatown-sourced oolong tea, LA pours on cue. From postindustrial coffee roasters and breweries to mid-century lounges, classic Hollywood martini bars and cocktail-pouring bowling alleys, LA serves its drinks with a generous splash of wow. So do the right thing and raise your glass to America's finest town.

Downtown

Clifton's Republic COCKTAIL BAR

(Map p250; ☎213-627-1673; www.cliftonsla.com; 648 S Broadway; ⊙11am-midnight Tue-Thu, to 2am Fri, 10am-2:30am Sat, 10am-midnight Sun; ; M Red/Purple Lines to Pershing Sq) Opened in 1935 and back after a $10-million renovation, multilevel, mixed-crowd Clifton's defies description. Order drinks from a Gothic church altar amid taxidermied forest animals, watch burlesque performers shimmy in the shadow of a 40ft faux redwood, or slip through a glass-paneled door to a luxe tiki paradise where DJs spin in a repurposed speedboat.

Angel City Brewery MICROBREWERY

(Map p250; ☎213-622-1261; www.angelcitybrewery.com; 216 S Alameda St; ⊙4pm-1am Mon-Thu, to 2am Fri, noon-2am Sat, noon-1am Sun) Where suspension cables were once manufactured, craft brews are now made and poured. Located on the edge of the Arts District, this is a popular spot to knock back an India pale ale or chai-spiced Imperial stout, listen to some tunes and chow down some food-truck tacos.

Hollywood

Rooftop Bar at Mama Shelter BAR

(Map p254; ☎323-785-6600; www.mamashelter.com/en/los-angeles/restaurants/rooftop; 6500 Selma Ave; ⊙noon-1am Mon-Thu, 11am-2pm Fri & Sat, 11am-1am Sun; M Red Line to Hollywood/Vine) Less a hotel rooftop bar and more lush, tropical-like oasis with killer views of the

Hollywood sign and LA skyline, multicolored daybeds and tongue-in-cheek bar bites like 'boujee fries' and outré tacos. Pulling everyone from hotel guests to locals from the nearby Buzzfeed offices, it's a winner for languid cocktail sessions, landmark spotting and a game of giant Jenga.

Tramp Stamp Granny's BAR

(Map p254; ☎323-498-5626; www.trampstampgrannys.com; 1638 N Cahuenga Blvd; ⊙8pm-1am Tue & Wed, 6pm-1am Thu & Fri, 8pm-2am Sat; Ⓜ Red Line to Hollywood/Vine) In the heart of Hollywood, this piano bar owned by Darren Criss (star of *Glee* and *The Assassination of Gianni Versace*) is a little bit classy, a little bit trashy and a whole lot of fun. Talented pianists tickle the ivories as guests sing along to favorite tunes – look for theme nights (Disney, anyone?). Drinks are creative and strong.

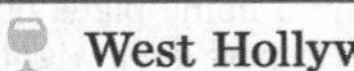

West Hollywood

Abbey GAY & LESBIAN

(Map p258; ☎310-289-8410; www.theabbeyweho.com; 692 N Robertson Blvd, West Hollywood; ⊙11am-2am Mon-Thu, from 10am Fri, from 9am Sat & Sun) It's been called the best gay bar in the world, and who are we to argue? Once a humble coffeehouse, the Abbey has expanded into the bar/club/restaurant of record in WeHo. It has so many different-flavored martinis and mojitos that you'd think they were invented here, plus a menu of upscale pub food (mains $14 to $21).

Beverly Hills

Polo Lounge COCKTAIL BAR

(Map p244; ☎310-887-2777; www.dorchestercollection.com/en/los-angeles/the-beverly-hills-hotel; Beverly Hills Hotel, 9641 Sunset Blvd, Beverly Hills; ⊙7am-1:30am) For a classic LA experience, dress up and swill martinis in the Beverly Hills Hotel's legendary bar. Charlie Chaplin had a standing lunch reservation at booth 1 and it was here that HR Haldeman and John Ehrlichman learned of the Watergate break-in in 1972. There's a popular Sunday jazz brunch (adult/child $95/20).

Santa Monica

Basement Tavern BAR

(Map p260; www.basementtavern.com; 2640 Main St; ⊙5pm-2am) A creative speakeasy, housed in the basement of the Victorian, and our favorite well in Santa Monica. We love it for its craft cocktails, cozy booths,

LGBTIQ LA

LA is one of the country's gayest cities and has made many contributions to gay culture. Your gaydar may well be pinging throughout the county, but the rainbow flag flies especially proudly in Boystown, along Santa Monica Blvd in West Hollywood, which is flanked by dozens of high-energy bars, cafes, restaurants, gyms and clubs. Most cater to gay men, although there's plenty for lesbians, trans and mixed audiences. Thursday through Sunday nights are prime time.

If nightlife isn't your bag, there are plenty of other ways to meet, greet and engage. Outdoor options include the **Frontrunners** (www.lafrontrunners.com) running club and the **Great Outdoors** (www.greatoutdoorsla.org) hiking club. The latter runs day and night hikes, as well as neighborhood walks. For insight into LA's fascinating queer history, book a walking tour with **Out & About Tours** (www.thelavendereffect.org/tours; tours from $30).

There's gay theater all over town, but the **Celebration Theatre** (Map p258; ☎323-957-1884; www.celebrationtheatre.com; 6760 Lexington Ave, Hollywood) ranks among the nation's leading stages for LGBT plays. The **Cavern Club Theater** (Map p244; www.cavernclubtheater.com; 1920 Hyperion Ave, Silver Lake) pushes the envelope, particularly with uproarious drag performers; it's downstairs from Casita del Campo restaurant. If you're lucky enough to be in town when the **Gay Men's Chorus of Los Angeles** (www.gmcla.org) is performing, don't miss out: this amazing group has been doing it since 1979.

The festival season kicks off in mid- to late May with the **Long Beach Pride Celebration** (☎562-987-9191; www.longbeachpride.com; 450 E Shoreline Dr, Long Beach; parade free, festival admission adult/child & senior $25/free; ⊙mid-May) and continues with the three-day **LA Pride** (www.lapride.org) in mid-June with a parade down Santa Monica Blvd. On Halloween (October 31), the same street brings out 500,000 outrageously costumed revelers of all persuasions.

island bar and nightly live-music calendar that features blues, jazz, bluegrass and rock bands. It gets way too busy on weekends for our taste, but weeknights can be special.

Long Beach

Pike BAR
(Map p244; ☎562-437-4453; www.pikelongbeach.com; 1836 E 4th St, Long Beach; ⊙11am-2am Mon-Fri, from 9am Sat & Sun; 🚌line 22) Adjacent to Retro Row, this nautical-themed dive bar, owned by Chris Reece of the band Social Distortion, brings in the cool kids for live-music acts every night – with no cover, thank you – and serves beer by the pitcher or bottle, and cocktails such as the Mezcarita and Greenchelada (a *michelada* with cucumber, jalapeño and lime).

☆ Entertainment

Hollywood Bowl CONCERT VENUE
(Map p244; ☎323-850-2000; www.hollywoodbowl.com; 2301 N Highland Ave; rehearsals free, performance costs vary; ⊙Jun-Sep) Summers in LA just wouldn't be the same without alfresco melodies under the stars at the Bowl, a huge natural amphitheater in the Hollywood Hills. Its annual season – which usually runs from June to September – includes symphonies, jazz bands and iconic acts such as Blondie, Bryan Ferry and Angélique Kidjo. Bring a sweater or blanket as it gets cool at night.

Upright Citizens Brigade Theatre COMEDY
(Map p254; ☎323-908-8702; http://franklin.ucbtheatre.com; 5919 Franklin Ave; tickets $5-12) Founded in New York by *Saturday Night Live* alums Amy Poehler and Ian Roberts along with Matt Besser and Matt Walsh, this sketch-comedy group cloned itself in Hollywood in 2005. With numerous nightly shows spanning anything from stand-up comedy to improv and sketch, it's arguably the best comedy hub in town. Valet parking costs $7.

There's a second location southeast at 5419 W Sunset Blvd, near Thai Town and off Western Ave.

Geffen Playhouse THEATER
(Map p244; ☎310-208-5454; www.geffenplayhouse.com; 10886 Le Conte Ave, Westwood) Entertainment megamogul David Geffen forked over $17 million to get his Mediterranean-style playhouse back into shape. The center's season includes both American classics and freshly minted works, and it's not unusual to see well-known film and TV actors treading the boards.

Los Angeles Philharmonic CLASSICAL MUSIC
(Map p250; ☎323-850-2000; www.laphil.org; 111 S Grand Ave) The world-class LA Phil performs classics and cutting-edge works at the Walt Disney Concert Hall (p244), under the baton of Venezuelan phenom Gustavo Dudamel.

Dodger Stadium BASEBALL
(Map p244; ☎866-363-4377; www.dodgers.com; 1000 Vin Scully Ave) Few clubs can match the Dodgers' history (Jackie Robinson, Sandy Koufax, Kirk Gibson and sportscaster Vin Scully), success and fan loyalty, and this 1950s-era stadium is still considered one of baseball's most beautiful, framed by views of palm trees and the San Gabriel Mountains. Best views are from behind home plate, or gorge in the all-you-can-eat pavilion in right field.

Largo at the Coronet LIVE MUSIC, PERFORMING ARTS
(Map p258; ☎310-855-0530; www.largo-la.com; 366 N La Cienega Blvd, Mid-City) Ever since its early days on Fairfax Ave, Largo has been progenitor of high-minded pop culture (it nurtured Zach Galifianakis to stardom). Now part of the Coronet Theatre complex, it features edgy comedy, such as Sarah Silverman and Nick Offerman, and nourishing night music such as the Preservation Hall Jazz Band.

ArcLight Cinemas CINEMA
(Map p254; ☎323-464-1478; www.arclightcinemas.com; 6360 W Sunset Blvd; Ⓜ Red Line to Hollywood/Vine) Assigned seats, exceptional celeb-sighting potential and a varied program that covers mainstream and art-house movies make this 14-screen multiplex the best around. If your taste dovetails with its schedule, the awesome 1963 geodesic Cinerama Dome is a must. Bonuses: age-21-plus screenings where you can booze it up, and Q&As with directors, writers and actors. Parking is $3 for four hours.

LA Lakers BASKETBALL
(Map p250; ☎888-929-7849; www.nba.com/lakers; tickets from $65) One of two NBA basketball teams in Los Angeles (the other is the **Clippers** (Map p250; ☎213-204-2900; www.nba.com/clippers; tickets from $20)), the Lakers are based at Downtown's **Staples Center**

LA FOR CHILDREN

Keeping kids happy is child's play in LA. The sprawling Los Angeles Zoo (p248) in family-friendly Griffith Park (p248) is a sure bet. Dino fans will dig the La Brea Tar Pits (p249) and the Natural History Museum (p247), while budding scientists crowd the Griffith Observatory (p248) and California Science Center (p247). For under-the-sea creatures, head to the Aquarium of the Pacific (p252) in Long Beach. The amusement park at Santa Monica Pier (p251) is fun for all ages. Activities for younger kids are more limited at tween/teen-oriented **Universal Studios Hollywood** (Map p244; ☎800-864-8377; www.universalstudioshollywood.com; 100 Universal City Plaza, Universal City; 1-/2-day regular admission from $109/149, child under 3yr free; ⏱daily, hours vary; P 👶; M Red Line to Universal City). In neighboring Orange County, Disneyland (p267) and Knott's Berry Farm (p269) are the first and last word in theme parks.

(Map p250; ☎213-742-7100; www.staplescenter.com; 1111 S Figueroa St). Although few teams can match the Lakers' legacy – many players are so legendary they go by one name: Kareem, Magic, Shaq, Kobe, LeBron – results on the court have been disappointing these last several seasons.

Shopping

Consider yourself a disciplined shopper? Get back to us after your trip. LA is a pro at luring cards out of wallets. After all, how can you *not* bag that supercute vintage-fabric frock? Or that tongue-in-cheek tote? And what about that mid-century-modern lamp, the one that perfectly illuminates that rare, signed Hollywood film script you scored? Creativity and whimsy drive this town, right down to its racks and shelves.

Downtown

Raggedy Threads VINTAGE

(Map p250; ☎213-620-1188; www.raggedythreads.com; 330 E 2nd St; ⏱noon-7pm Mon-Sat, to 6pm Sun; M Gold Line to Little Tokyo/Arts District) A tremendous vintage Americana store just off the main Little Tokyo strip. There's plenty of beautifully ragged denim, with a notable collection of pre-1950s workwear from the US, Japan and France. You'll also find a good number of Victorian dresses, soft T-shirts and a wonderful turquoise collection at decent prices.

Last Bookstore in Los Angeles BOOKS

(Map p250; ☎213-488-0599; www.lastbookstorela.com; 453 S Spring St; ⏱10am-10pm Mon-Thu, to 11pm Fri & Sat, to 9pm Sun) What started as a one-man storefront is now California's largest new-and-used bookstore, and a sight to behold spanning two levels of an old bank building. Eye up the cabinets of rare books before heading upstairs, home to a horror-and-crime book den, a book tunnel and a few art galleries to boot. The store also houses a terrific vinyl collection.

West Hollywood

Melrose Avenue FASHION & ACCESSORIES

(Map p258) This legendary, rock-and-roll shopping strip is as famous for its epic people-watching as for its consumer fruits. You'll see hair (and people) of all shades and styles, and everything from Gothic jewels to awesome vintage wear, custom sneakers to weed and stuffed porcupines, albeit sometimes for a price. The strip is located between Fairfax and La Brea Aves.

Fred Segal FASHION & ACCESSORIES

(Map p258; ☎323-432-0560; www.fredsegal.com; 8500 Sunset Blvd, West Hollywood; ⏱10am-9pm Mon-Sat, 11am-6pm Sun) No LA shopping trip is complete without a stop at Fred's. Recently relocated from its long-standing Melrose Ave location, this 13,000-sq-ft warren of high-end boutiques draws celebs and beautiful people for the very latest in Cal-casual couture under one impossibly chic, slightly snooty roof. The only time you'll see bargains (sort of) is during sales in summer and January.

Pasadena

Rose Bowl Flea Market MARKET

(Map p244; www.rgcshows.com; 1001 Rose Bowl Dr, Pasadena; admission from $9; ⏱9am-4:30pm 2nd Sun each month, last entry 3pm, early admission from 5am) Every month, rain or shine, since the 1960s, the Rose Bowl football field has hosted the 'Flea Market of the Stars,' with rummaging hordes seeking the next great treasure. Over 2500 vendors and some

NAVIGATING THE FASHION DISTRICT

Bargain hunters love the frantic, 100-block warren of fashion in southwestern Downtown that is the Fashion District. Deals can be amazing, but first-timers are often bewildered by the district's size and immense selection. For orientation, check out www.fashiondistrict.org.

20,000 buyers converge here. It's always a great time, and you can enjoy street-fair-style refreshments such as burgers, dogs, fries, sausages, sushi (this is LA), lemonade, cocktails etc.

Information

DANGERS & ANNOYANCES

Despite the apocalyptic panoply of dangers doled out by the entertainment industry – guns, violent crime, earthquakes – Los Angeles is generally a safe place to visit. Probably the greatest danger is posed by car accidents (buckle up and do not hold a phone while driving – it's the law), and the greatest everyday annoyance is traffic, which can mysteriously materialize – or inexplicably clear – when you least expect it.

MEDIA

Eater LA (http://la.eater.com) Up-to-the-minute news and reviews covering the city's ever-evolving food scene.

KCRW 89.9 FM (www.kcrw.com) LA's cultural pulse, the best radio station in the city beams National Public Radio (NPR), eclectic and indie music, intelligent talk, and hosts shows and events throughout Southern California.

LA Weekly (www.laweekly.com) Free alternative news, live music and entertainment listings.

LAist (http://laist.com) Arts, entertainment, food and pop-culture gossip.

Los Angeles Magazine (www.lamag.com) Monthly lifestyle magazine with a useful restaurant guide and some tremendous feature stories.

Los Angeles Times (www.latimes.com) Major, center-left daily newspaper.

MEDICAL SERVICES

Cedars-Sinai Medical Center (☎310-423-3277; http://cedars-sinai.edu; 8700 Beverly Blvd, West Hollywood; ⏲24hr) 24-hour emergency room skirting West Hollywood.

Keck Medicine of USC (☎323-226-2622; www.keckmedicine.org; 1500 San Pablo St, Downtown; ⏲24hr emergency room) 24-hour emergency department just east of Downtown.

Ronald Reagan UCLA Medical Center (☎310-825-9111; www.uclahealth.org; 757 Westwood Plaza, Westwood; ⏲24hr emergency room) 24-hour emergency room on the UCLA campus.

TOURIST INFORMATION

Downtown LA Visitor Center (Map p250; www.discoverlosangeles.com; Union Station, 800 N Alameda St; ⏲9am-5pm; Ⓜ Red/Purple/Gold Lines to Union Station) Maps and general tourist information in the lobby of Union Station.

Los Angeles Visitor Information Center (Map p254; ☎323-467-6412; www.discoverlosangeles.com; Hollywood & Highland, 6801 Hollywood Blvd; ⏲9am-10pm Mon-Sat, 10am-7pm Sun; Ⓜ Red Line to Hollywood/Highland) The main tourist office for Los Angeles, located in Hollywood. Maps, brochures and lodging information, plus tickets to theme parks and attractions.

Santa Monica Visitor Information Center (Map p260; ☎800-544-5319; www.santamonica.com; 2427 Main St) The main tourist information center in Santa Monica, with free guides, maps and helpful staff.

Getting There & Away

AIR

The main LA gateway is **Los Angeles International Airport** (LAX; Map p244; www.lawa.org/welcomeLAX.aspx; 1 World Way). Its nine terminals are linked by the free LAX Shuttle A, leaving from the lower (arrival) level of each terminal. Cabs and hotel and car-rental shuttles stop here as well. Ticketing and check-in are on the upper (departure) level.

The hub for most international airlines is the Tom Bradley International Terminal.

Some domestic flights also arrive at **Burbank Hollywood Airport** (BUR, Bob Hope Airport; Map p244; www.burbankairport.com; 2627 N Hollywood Way, Burbank), which is handy if you're headed for Hollywood, Downtown or Pasadena. To the south, on the border with Orange County, the small **Long Beach Airport** (Map p244; www.lgb.org; 4100 Donald Douglas Dr, Long Beach) is convenient for Disneyland and is served by Alaska, JetBlue and Southwest.

BUS

The main bus terminal for **Greyhound** (Map p244; ☎213-629-8401; www.greyhound.com; 1716 E 7th St) is in an industrial part of Downtown, so try not to arrive after dark. Some Greyhound buses go directly to the terminal in **North Hollywood** (11239 Magnolia Blvd) and a few also pass through **Long Beach** (1498 Long Beach Blvd).

CAR

From San Francisco and Northern California, the fastest route to LA is on I-5 through the San Joaquin Valley. Hwy 101 is slower but more picturesque, while the most scenic – and slowest – route is via Hwy 1 (Pacific Coast Hwy, or PCH).

From San Diego and other points south, I-5 is the obvious route. From Las Vegas or the Grand Canyon, take I-15 south to I-10 then head west into LA.

TRAIN

Amtrak (www.amtrak.com) trains roll into Downtown's historic **Union Station** (☎800-872-7245; www.amtrak.com; 800 N Alameda St). Interstate trains stopping in LA are the daily *Coast Starlight* to Seattle, the daily *Southwest Chief* to Chicago and the thrice-weekly *Sunset Limited* to New Orleans. The *Pacific Surfliner* travels numerous times daily between San Diego, Santa Barbara and San Luis Obispo via LA.

Getting Around

TO/FROM THE AIRPORT

LAX FlyAway (☎866-435-9529; www.lawa.org/FlyAway) buses travel nonstop for $9.75 to Downtown's Patsaouras Transit Plaza at Union Station (45 minutes), Hollywood ($8, one to 1½ hours), Van Nuys ($9, 50 minutes) and Long Beach ($9, 50 minutes).

For scheduled bus services, catch the free shuttle bus from the airport toward parking lot C. It stops by the LAX City Bus Center hub for buses serving all of LA County.

Taxis are readily available outside the terminals. The flat rate to Downtown LA is $46.50, plus $4 LAX airport surcharge and the customary 15% to 20% tip.

Fares for ride-hailing companies Uber and Lyft can cost 30% to 40% less than taxis. These companies both drop off and pick up passengers on the departure level (upstairs); board by the signs lettered A through G outside terminals.

CAR & MOTORCYCLE

The usual international car-rental agencies have branches near LAX and throughout LA. Offices and lots are outside the airport, but each company has free shuttles leaving from the lower level. LA's traffic is some of the worst traffic in the country. Avoid rush hour (7am to 9am and 3:30pm to 6:30pm).

PUBLIC TRANSPORTATION

Most public transportation is handled by **Metro** (☎323-466-3876; www.metro.net), which offers maps, schedules and trip-planning help through its website.

To ride Metro trains and buses, buy a reusable TAP card. Available from TAP vending machines at Metro stations with a $1 surcharge, the cards allow you to add a preset cash value or day passes. The regular base fare is $1.75 per boarding, or $7/25 for a day/week pass with unlimited rides.

TAP cards are accepted on DASH and municipal bus services and can be reloaded at vending machines or online on the TAP website (www.taptogo.net).

TAXI

With their (generally) cheaper fares and more convenient services, ride-hailing apps Uber and Lyft have drastically reduced demand for taxis in the region.

Beverly Hills Cab (☎800-273-6611; www.beverlyhillscabco.com) A solid, dependable company, with good rates to the airport and a wide service area.

Taxi Taxi (☎310-444-4444; www.santamonicataxi.com) Easily the best and most professional fleet available. It'll drive you anywhere, but can only pick up in Santa Monica.

SOUTHERN CALIFORNIAN COAST

Disneyland & Anaheim

Mickey is one lucky guy. Created by animator Walt Disney in 1928, this irrepressible mouse caught a ride on a multimedia juggernaut that rocketed him into a global stratosphere of recognition, money and influence. Plus, he lives in Disneyland, the 'Happiest Place on Earth,' an 'imagineered' hyper-reality where the streets are always clean, employees – called 'cast members' – are always upbeat and there are parades every day.

Today, **Disneyland Resort**® (Map p244; ☎714-781-4636; www.disneyland.com; 1313 Harbor Blvd; 1-day pass adult $104-149, child 3-9yr $96-141, 2-day pass adult/child 3-9yr $225/210; ⏲open daily, seasonal hr vary), which comprises the original Disneyland Park and newer Disney California Adventure theme park, remains a magical experience for the more than 14 million kids, grandparents, honeymooners and international tourists who visit every year.

Anaheim, the workaday city that grew up around the park, has itself developed some surprising pockets of cool that have nothing to do with the Mouse House.

Sights & Activities

Spotless, wholesome **Disneyland Park**® is still laid out according to Walt's original plans. It's here you'll find plenty of rides and some of the attractions most associated with the Disney name – Main Street USA, Sleeping Beauty Castle and Tomorrowland, plus the newest blockbuster, Star Wars: Galaxy's Edge.

Disneyland Resort's larger but less crowded park, **Disney California Adventure®**, celebrates the natural and cultural glories of the Golden State but lacks the original's density of attractions and depth of imagination. The best rides are on the old-fashioned California pleasure pier, Soarin' Around the World (a virtual hang glide), and Guardians of the Galaxy – Mission: BREAKOUT!, which drops you 183ft down an elevator chute.

Going on all the rides at both theme parks requires at least two days, as queues for top attractions can be an hour or more. To minimize wait times, arrive midweek (especially during summer) before the gates open, buy print-at-home tickets online and take advantage of the parks' Fastpass system, which pre-assigns boarding times at select rides and attractions. For seasonal park hours and schedules of parades, shows and fireworks, check the official website.

While of course Disneyland Resort dominates Anaheim tourism, it's worth visiting the redeveloped neighborhoods around city hall, the **Anaheim Packing District** (Map p244; www.anaheimpackingdistrict.com; S Anaheim Bl) and **Center Street** (Map p244; www.centerstreetanaheim.com; W Center St). By the latter is the Frank Gehry–designed **hockey rink** where the Anaheim Ducks practice; it's open to the public.

Sleeping

For the full-on Disney experience, there are three different hotels within Disneyland Resort, though there are less-expensive options just beyond the Disney gates in Anaheim. If you want a theme-park hotel for less money, try **Knott's Berry Farm** (Map p244; 714-995-1111; www.knotts.com/stay/knotts-berry-farm-hotel; 7675 Crescent Ave, Buena Park; r $79-169;).

Disneyland Resort

★Disney's Grand Californian Hotel & Spa RESORT **$$$**
(Map p244; info 714-635-2300, reservations 714-956-6425; https://disneyland.disney.go.com/grand-californian-hotel; 1600 S Disneyland Dr; r from $507;) Soaring timber beams rise above the cathedral-like lobby of the six-story Grand Californian, Disney's homage to the arts-and-crafts architectural movement. Cushy, recently renovated rooms have triple-sheeted beds, down pillows, bathrobes and all-custom furnishings. Outside there's a faux-redwood waterslide into the pool. At night, kids wind down with bedtime stories by the lobby's giant stone hearth.

Disneyland Hotel HOTEL **$$$**
(Map p244; 714-778-6600; www.disneyland.com; 1150 Magic Way, Anaheim; r from $409;) Though built in 1955, the year Disneyland opened, the park's original hotel has been rejuvenated with a dash of bibbidi-bobbidi-boo. There are three towers with themed lobbies (adventure, fantasy and frontier), and the 972 good-sized rooms now boast Mickey-hand wall sconces in bathrooms and headboards lit like the fireworks over Sleeping Beauty Castle.

Anaheim

Best Western Plus Stovall's Inn MOTEL **$$**
(Map p244; 714-778-1880; www.bestwestern.com; 1110 W Katella Ave; r $99-175;) Generations of guests have been coming to this 289-room motel about 15 minutes' walk to Disneyland. Around the side are two pools, two Jacuzzis, a fitness center, kiddie pool and a garden of topiaries (for real). The remodeled sleek and modern-design rooms sparkle; all have air-con, a microwave and minifridge. Rates include a hot breakfast and there's a guest laundry.

Ayres Hotel Anaheim HOTEL **$$**
(Map p244; 714-634-2106; www.ayreshotels.com/anaheim; 2550 E Katella Ave; r $139-259; ; ARTIC, Amtrak to ARTIC) This well-run minichain of business hotels delivers solid-gold value. The 133 recently renovated rooms have microwaves, minifridges, safes, wet bar, pillow-top mattresses and contemporary European-inspired design. Fourth-floor rooms have extra-high ceilings. Rates include a full breakfast buffet and evening social hours Monday to Thursday with craft beer, wine and snacks.

Eating & Drinking

From stroll-and-eat Mickey-shaped pretzels ($4) and jumbo turkey legs ($10) to deluxe, gourmet dinners (sky's the limit), there's no

WORTH A TRIP

KNOTT'S BERRY FARM

What, Disney's not enough for you? Find even more thrill rides and cotton candy at **Knott's Berry Farm** (Map p244; ☎714-220-5200; www.knotts.com; 8039 Beach Blvd, Buena Park; adult/child 3-11yr $84/54; ⊙from 10am, closing hours vary 5-11pm; P 🚸). This Old West–themed amusement park teems with packs of speed-crazed adolescents testing their mettle on a lineup of rides. Gut-wrenchers include the Boomerang 'scream machine,' wooden GhostRider and 1950s-themed Xcelerator. Younger kids will enjoy tamer action at Camp Snoopy. From late September through October, the park transforms at night into Halloween-themed 'Knott's Scary Farm.'

When summer heat waves hit, jump next door to **Knott's Soak City** (Map p244; ☎714-220-5200; www.knotts.com/play/soak-city; 8039 Beach Blvd, Buena Park; adult/child 3-11yr $53/43; ⊙10am-5pm, 6pm or 7pm mid-May–mid-Sep; P 🚸) water park. Save time and money by buying print-at-home tickets for either park online.

shortage of eating options, though most are pretty expensive and targeted to mainstream tastes. Phone **Disney Dining** (☎714-781-3463; http://disneyland.disney.go.com/dining) to make reservations up to 60 days in advance. Restaurant hours vary seasonally, sometimes daily. Check the Disneyland app or Disney Dining website for same-day hours.

If you want to steer clear of Mickey Mouse food, drive to the Anaheim Packing District (3 miles northeast), Old Towne Orange (7 miles southeast), Little Arabia (3 miles west) or Little Saigon (8 miles southwest).

Disneyland Resort

Earl of Sandwich SANDWICHES $

(Map p244; ☎714-817-7476; www.earlofsandwichusa.com; Downtown Disney; mains $6.50-9; ⊙8am-11pm Sun-Thu, to midnight Fri & Sat; 🚸) This counter-service chain near the Disneyland Hotel (p268) serves grilled sandwiches that are both kid- and adult-friendly. The 'original 1762' is roast beef, cheddar and horseradish, or look for chipotle chicken with avocado or holiday turkey. There are also pizza, salad and breakfast options.

Ralph Brennan's New Orleans Jazz Kitchen CAJUN $$

(Map p244; ☎714-776-5200; http://rbjazzkitchen.com; Downtown Disney; mains lunch $15.50-25, dinner $26.50-39.50; ⊙8am-10pm Sun-Thu, to 11pm Fri & Sat; 🚸) Hear live jazz combos on the weekends and piano on weeknights at this resto-bar with NOLA-style Cajun and Creole dishes: gumbo, po-boy sandwiches, jambalaya, plus a (less adventurous) kids menu and specialty cocktails. There's breakfast and lunch express service if you don't have time to linger.

★**Napa Rose** CALIFORNIAN $$$

(Map p244; ☎714-300-7170; https://disneyland.disney.go.com/dining; Grand Californian Hotel & Spa; mains $38-48; ⊙5:30-10pm; 🚸) High-back arts-and-crafts-style chairs, leaded-glass windows and towering ceilings befit Disneyland Resort's top-drawer restaurant. On the plate, seasonal 'California Wine Country' (read: NorCal) cuisine is as impeccably crafted as the Sleeping Beauty Castle. Kids menu available. Reservations essential. Enter the hotel from Disney California Adventure or Downtown Disney.

Anaheim

★**Pour Vida** MEXICAN $

(Map p244; ☎657-208-3889; www.pourvidalatinflavor.com; 185 W Center St Promenade; tacos $2-8; ⊙10am-7pm Mon, to 9pm Tue-Thu, to 10pm Fri, 9am-10pm Sat, 9am-8:30pm Sun) Chef Jimmy, who has worked in some of LA's top kitchens, returned to his Mexican roots to make some of the most gourmet tacos we've ever seen: pineapple skirt steak, tempura oyster, heirloom cauliflower...*caramba*! Even the tortillas are special, made with squid ink, spinach and a secret recipe. It's deliberately informal, all brick and concrete with chalkboard walls.

ℹ Information

For information or help inside the parks, just ask any cast member or visit Disneyland's **City Hall** (Map p244; ☎714-781-4565; Main Street USA) or Disney California Adventure's guest relations lobby.

Both can also help out with foreign-currency exchange. Multiple ATMs are found in both theme parks and at Downtown Disney.

WORTH A TRIP

MISSION SAN JUAN CAPISTRANO

Detour inland from the Orange County beaches to **Mission San Juan Capistrano** (☎949-234-1300; www.missionsjc.com; 26801 Ortega Hwy; adult/child $10/7; ⏰9am-5pm; 👪), one of California's most beautifully restored Spanish Colonial missions. Plan on spending at least an hour poking around the sprawling mission's tiled roofs, covered arches, lush gardens, fountains and courtyards – including the padre's quarters, soldiers' barracks and the cemetery.

The Serra Chapel – whitewashed outside with restored frescoes inside – is believed to be the oldest existing building in California (1782). It's certainly the only one still standing in which Junípero Serra (the founder of the mission) gave Mass. Serra founded the mission on November 1, 1776, and tended it personally for many years.

Admission includes a worthwhile free audio tour with interesting stories narrated by locals.

Travelex (☎714-687-7977; 100 West Lincoln Ave, inside US Bank, Anaheim; ⏰9am-5pm Mon-Fri, to 1pm Sat) Also exchanges foreign currency near Anaheim City Hall.

ℹ Getting There & Around

Disneyland and Anaheim can be reached by car (off the I-5 Fwy) or Amtrak or Metrolink trains at Anaheim's **ARTIC** (Anaheim Regional Transportation Intermodal Center; 2150 E Katella Ave, Anaheim) transit center. From here to Disneyland proper it's a short taxi, ride share or **Anaheim Resort Transportation** (ART; ☎888-364-2787; www.rideart.org; adult/child fare $3/1, day pass $6/2.50, multiple-day passes available) shuttle. The closest airport is Orange County's **John Wayne Airport** (SNA; Map p244; www.ocair.com; 18601 Airport Way, Santa Ana).

The miniature biodiesel Disneyland Railroad chugs in a clockwise circle around Disneyland, stopping at Main Street USA, New Orleans Square, Mickey's Toon Town and Tomorrowland, taking about 20 minutes to make a full loop. Between the Tomorrowland and Main Street USA stations, look out for dioramas of the Grand Canyon and a Jurassic-style 'Primeval World.' From Tomorrowland, you can catch the zero-emissions monorail directly to Downtown Disney.

Orange County Beaches

If you've seen *The OC* or *The Real Housewives*, you might imagine you already know what to expect from this giant quilt of suburbia connecting LA and San Diego, lolling beside 42 miles of glorious coastline. In reality, Hummer-driving hunks and Botoxed beauties mix it up with hang-loose surfers and beatnik artists to give each of Orange County's beach towns a distinct vibe of its own.

Seal Beach & Huntington Beach

Just across the LA-OC county line, old-fashioned **Seal Beach** is refreshingly noncommercial, with a quaint walkable downtown. Less than 10 miles further south along the Pacific Coast Hwy (Hwy 1), Huntington Beach – aka 'Surf City, USA' – epitomizes SoCal's surfing lifestyle. Fish tacos and happy-hour specials abound at bars and cafes along downtown HB's Main St, not far from a shortboard-sized **surfing museum** (Map p244; ☎714-960-3483; www.surfingmuseum.org; 411 Olive Ave; admission $3; ⏰noon-5pm Tue-Sun).

Here you'll find slick and serene **Paséa** (Map p244; ☎855-622-2472; http://meritagecollection.com/paseahotel; 21080 Pacific Coast Hwy; r May-Aug from $359, rest of year from $280; P ⊖ ❄ @ 🛜 ≋) hotel. Floors are themed for shades of blue, from denim to sky, and each of its 250 shimmery, minimalist, high-ceilinged rooms has an ocean-view balcony. As if the stunning pool, gym and Balinese-inspired spa weren't enough, it also connects to **Pacific City** (Map p244; www.gopacificcity.com; 21010 Pacific Coast Hwy; ⏰hours vary), with its unique and fun food court. Head here for pressed sandwiches (Burnt Crumbs – the spaghetti grilled cheese is so Instagrammable), Aussie meat pies (Pie Not), coffee (Portola) and ice cream (Han's). For the best views, take your meal to the deck.

Newport Beach & Balboa Peninsula

Next up is the ritziest of the OC's beach communities: yacht-filled Newport Beach. Families and teens steer toward Balboa Peninsula for its beaches, vintage wooden pier and quaint amusement center. From near the 1906 Balboa Pavilion, **Balboa Island**

Ferry (Map p244; www.balboaislandferry.com; 410 S Bay Front; adult/child $1/50¢, car incl driver $2; ⏲6:30am-midnight Sun-Thu, to 2am Fri & Sat) shuttles across the bay to Balboa Island for strolls past historic beach cottages and boutiques along Marine Ave.

Bear Flag Fish Company (Map p244; ☎949-673-3474; www.bearflagfishco.com; 3421 Via Lido; mains $10-16; ⏲11am-9pm Tue-Sat, to 8pm Sun & Mon;) is *the* place for generously sized, grilled and *panko*-breaded fish tacos, ahi burritos, spankin' fresh ceviche and oysters. Pick out what you want from the ice-cold display cases, then grab a picnic-table seat. About the only way this seafood could be any fresher is if you caught and hauled it off the boat yourself!

Laguna Beach

Continuing south, Hwy 1 zooms past the wild beaches of **Crystal Cove State Park** (Map p244; ☎949-494-3539; www.parks.ca.gov; 8471 N Coast Hwy; per car $15; ⏲6am-sunset; P) before winding downhill into Laguna Beach, the OC's most cultured seaside community. Secluded beaches, glassy waves and eucalyptus-covered hillsides create a Riviera-like feel. Art galleries dot the narrow streets of the 'village' and the coastal highway, where the **Laguna Art Museum** (☎949-494-8971; www.lagunaartmuseum.org; 307 Cliff Dr; adult/student & senior/child under 13yr $7/5/free, 5-9pm 1st Thu of month free; ⏲11am-5pm Fri-Tue, to 9pm Thu) exhibits modern and contemporary Californian works. Soak up the natural beauty right in the center of town at Main Beach.

Ocean views and ridiculous sunsets alone ought to be enough to bring folks in, but gourmet **Driftwood** (☎949-715-7700; www.driftwoodkitchen.com; 619 Sleepy Hollow Lane; mains lunch $15-37, dinner $25-44; ⏲9-10:30am & 11am-2:30pm Mon-Fri, 5-9:30pm Sun-Thu, to 10:30pm Fri & Sat, 9am-2:30pm Sat & Sun) steps up the food with seasonal menus centered around fresh, sustainable seafood, plus options for landlubbers.

If you're in town over summer, don't miss the **Festival of Arts** (www.foapom.com; 650 Laguna Canyon Rd; admission $7-10; ⏲noon-11:30pm Mon-Fri, 10am-11:30pm Sat & Sun Jul & Aug;), a two-month celebration of original artwork in almost all its forms. About 140 exhibitors display works ranging from paintings and hand-crafted furniture to scrimshaw. Plus there are kid-friendly art workshops and live music and entertainment daily.

San Diego

San Diego calls itself 'America's Finest City', and its breezy confidence and sunny countenance filter down to folks you encounter every day on the street. It feels like a collection of villages each with their own personality, but it's the nation's eighth-largest city and we're hard-pressed to think of a more laid-back place.

What's not to love? San Diego bursts with world-famous attractions for the entire family, including the zoo, the museums of Balboa Park, plus a bubbling Downtown, beautiful hikes for all, more than 60 beaches and America's most perfect weather.

Sights

Downtown & Embarcadero

San Diego's Downtown is the region's main business, financial and convention district. Whatever intense urban energy Downtown generally lacks, it makes up for in fun shopping, dining and nightlife in the historic **Gaslamp Quarter** (formerly a notorious strip of saloons, gambling joints and bordellos known as Stingaree), and the hipster havens of **East Village** and **North Park**. The waterfront **Embarcadero** is great for a stroll. In the northwestern corner of Downtown, vibrant **Little Italy** brims with progressive eats.

★ **Maritime Museum** MUSEUM
(Map p274; ☎619-234-9153; www.sdmaritime.org; 1492 N Harbor Dr; adult/child $18/8; ⏲9am-9pm late May-early Sep, to 8pm early Sep-late May;) Next to the new Waterfront Park, this collection of 11 historic sailing ships, steam boats and submarines is easy to spot: just look for the 100ft-high masts of the iron-hulled square-rigger *Star of India*, a tall ship launched in 1863 to ply the England–India trade route. Also moored here is a replica of the *San Salvador* that brought explorer Juan Rodriguez Cabrillo to San Diego's shore in 1542. It's easy to spend hours looking at the exhibits and clambering around the vessels.

USS Midway Museum MUSEUM
(Map p274; ☎619-544-9600; www.midway.org; 910 N Harbor Dr; adult/child $22/9; ⏲10am-5pm, last admission 4pm; P) The hulking aircraft carrier USS *Midway* was one of the navy's flagships from 1945 to 1991, last playing a

Greater San Diego

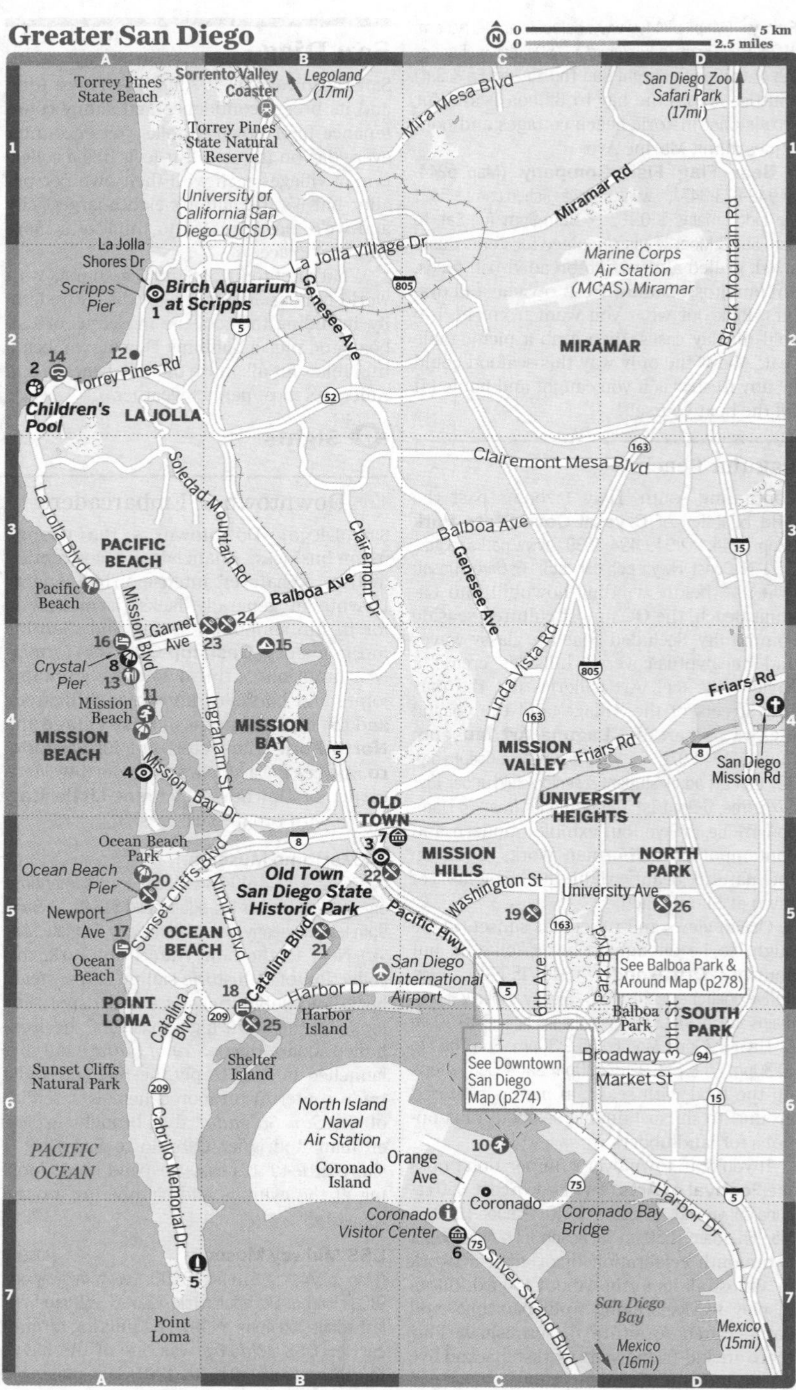

Greater San Diego

Top Sights
1 Birch Aquarium at Scripps ... A2
2 Children's Pool ... A2
3 Old Town San Diego State Historic Park ... B5

Sights
4 Belmont Park ... A4
5 Cabrillo National Monument ... A7
6 Hotel del Coronado ... C7
7 Junípero Serra Museum ... B5
8 Mission & Pacific Beaches Boardwalk ... A4
9 Mission Basilica San Diego de Alcalá ... D4

Activities, Courses & Tours
10 Bikes & Beyond ... C6
11 Cheap Rentals ... A4
12 Hike Bike Kayak ... A2
13 Pacific Beach Surf Shop ... A4
14 San Diego-La Jolla Underwater Park ... A2

Sleeping
15 Campland on the Bay ... B4
16 Crystal Pier Hotel & Cottages ... A4
Hotel del Coronado ... (see 6)
17 Inn at Sunset Cliffs ... A5
18 Pearl Hotel ... B5

Eating
19 Hash House a Go Go ... C5
20 Hodad's ... A5
21 Liberty Public Market ... B5
22 Old Town Mexican Café ... B5
23 Pacific Beach Fish Shop ... B4
24 Patio on Lamont ... B3
25 Point Loma Seafoods ... B6
26 Waypoint Public ... D5

combat role in the First Gulf War. On the flight deck, walk right up to some two dozen restored aircraft, including an F-14 Tomcat and F-4 Phantom jet fighter. Admission includes an audio tour along the narrow confines of the upper decks to the bridge, the admiral's war room, the brig and the 'pri-fly' (primary flight control; the carrier's equivalent of a control tower).

Museum of Contemporary Art MUSEUM
(MCASD Downtown; Map p274; ☎858-454-3541; www.mcasd.org; 1001 Kettner Blvd; adult/under 25yr $10/free; ⊙11am-5pm Thu-Tue) In an upcycled Santa Fe Depot baggage building, this well-respected museum presents changing exhibits drawn from a collection spanning the arc of artistic expression from the 1950s to the present. Genres where it's especially strong are minimalism, pop art, conceptual art and art from Southern California. The museum opens late and has free entry from 5pm to 8pm on the third Thursday of each month.

Coronado

Technically a peninsula, Coronado Island is joined to the mainland by a 2.2-mile-long bridge. The peninsula's main draw is the **Hotel del Coronado** (Map p272; ☎tours 619-522-8100, 619-435-6611; www.hoteldel.com; 1500 Orange Ave; tours $40; ⊙tours 10am daily, 2pm Sat & Sun; P) FREE, known for its seaside Victorian architecture and illustrious guestbook, which includes Thomas Edison, Babe Ruth and Marilyn Monroe.

At the entrance to the bay, **Point Loma** has sweeping views across sea and city from the Cabrillo National Monument (p276). **Mission Bay**, northwest of Downtown, has lagoons, parks and recreation, from water skiing to camping and SeaWorld. The nearby coastal neighborhoods – Ocean Beach, Mission Beach and Pacific Beach – epitomize the SoCal beach scene.

The hourly **Coronado Ferry** (Map p274; ☎800-442-7847; www.flagshipsd.com; 990 N Harbor Dr; one-way tickets $5; ⊙9am-9:30pm Sun-Thu, to 10:30pm Fri & Sat) departs from the Embarcadero's **Broadway Pier** (1050 N Harbor Dr) and from Downtown's convention center. All ferries arrive on Coronado at the foot of 1st St, where **Bikes & Beyond** (Map p272; ☎619-435-7180; www.bikes-and-beyond.com; 1201 1st St; per hr/day from $8/30; ⊙9am-sunset) rents cruisers and tandems, perfect for pedalling past Coronado's white-sand beaches that sprawl south along the Silver Strand.

Balboa Park

Balboa Park is an urban oasis brimming with more than a dozen museums, gorgeous gardens and architecture, performance spaces and a zoo. Early 20th-century beaux-arts and Spanish Colonial Revival–style buildings (the legacy of world's fairs) are grouped around plazas along east–west El Prado promenade.

The free Balboa Park Tram bus makes a continuous loop around the park; however, it's most enjoyable to walk, heading past the

Downtown San Diego

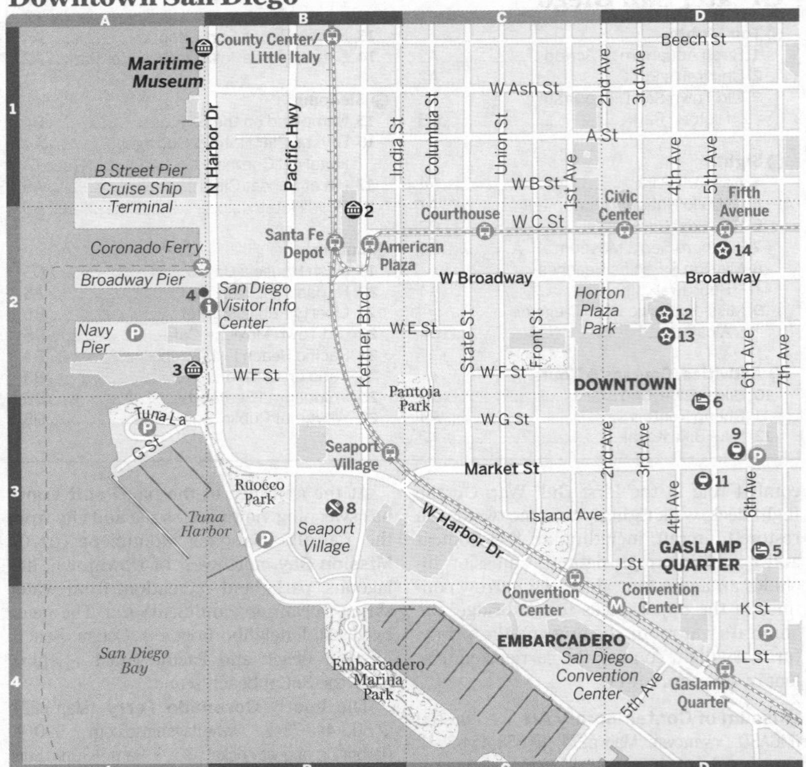

1915 **Spreckels Organ Pavilion** (Map p278; ☎619-702-8138; http://spreckelsorgan.org) FREE, the shops and galleries of the **Spanish Village Art Center** (Map p278; ☎619-233-9050; http://spanishvillageart.com; 1770 Village Pl; ⏲11am-4pm) FREE and the international-themed exhibition cottages by the **United Nations Building**.

San Diego Zoo ZOO

(Map p278; ☎619-231-1515; https://zoo.sandiegozoo.org; 2920 Zoo Dr; day pass adult/child from $56/46; 2-visit pass zoo &/or safari park adult/child $90/80; ⏲9am-9pm mid-Jun–early Sep, to 5pm or 6pm early Sep–mid-Jun; P 🚸) This justifiably famous zoo is one of SoCal's biggest attractions, showing more than 3000 animals representing more than 650 species in a beautifully landscaped setting, typically in enclosures that replicate their natural habitats. Its sister park is **San Diego Zoo Safari Park** (☎760-747-8702; www.sdzsafaripark.org; 15500 San Pasqual Valley Rd, Escondido; day pass adult/child from $56/46, 2-visit pass safari park &/or zoo adult/child $90/80; ⏲9am-6pm; P 🚸) in northern San Diego County.

Arrive early, as many of the animals are most active in the morning – though many perk up again in the afternoon. Pick up a map at the zoo entrance to find your favorite exhibits.

Fleet Science Center MUSEUM

(Map p278; ☎619-238-1233; www.rhfleet.org; 1875 El Prado; adult/child 3-12yr incl IMAX film $22/19; ⏲10am-5pm Mon-Thu, to 6pm Fri-Sun; 🚸) A top pick in Balboa Park, this hands-on science museum features interactive displays, including a room geared to the milk-tooth set. Look out for opportunities to build gigantic structures or to become a human battery, and ask about demonstrations of the mysterious Tesla Coil. The biggest draw, though, is the **Giant Dome Theater**, which presents several different films and planetarium shows daily.

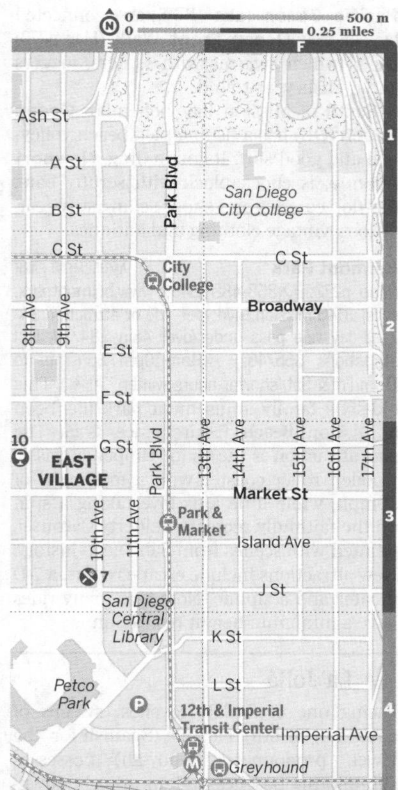

Downtown San Diego

Top Sights

1 Maritime Museum....................A1

Sights

2 Museum of Contemporary Art..........B2
3 USS Midway Museum...................A2

Activities, Courses & Tours

4 Flagship Cruises.....................A2

Sleeping

5 Kimpton Solamar......................D3
6 USA Hostels San Diego................D3

Eating

7 Basic................................E3
8 Puesto at the Headquarters...........B3

Drinking & Nightlife

9 Bang Bang............................D3
10 Noble Experiment....................E3
11 Prohibition Lounge..................D3

Entertainment

12 Arts Tix............................D2
13 Balboa Theatre......................D2
14 House of Blues......................D2

San Diego Natural History Museum MUSEUM
(The Nat; Map p278; ☎877-946-7797; www.sdnhm.org; 1788 El Prado; adult/child 3-17yr/under 2yr $29/12/free; ⊙10am-5pm; ⓗ) The 'Nat' houses 7.5 million specimens, including rocks, minerals, fossils and taxidermied animals, as well as an impressive dinosaur skeleton and an eye-opening exhibit on how climate change affects California's water supply, all in beautiful spaces. Kids love the 2-D and 3-D movies about the natural world in the giant-screen cinema and the fun and educational programs held most weekends.

San Diego Museum of Art MUSEUM
(SDMA; Map p278; ☎619-232-7931; www.sdmart.org; 1450 El Prado; adult/student/child under 17yr $15/8/free; ⊙10am-5pm Mon, Tue, Thu & Sat, to 8pm Fri, noon-5pm Sun) Pride of place in SDMA's permanent collection goes to its Spanish old masters (El Greco, Goya) and a respectable selection of works by other international heavy hitters from Matisse to Magritte, Cassat to Rivera. American landscape paintings are another focus, and the Asian galleries have some eye-catchers. On Fridays, admission is just $5 from 5pm to 8pm.

San Diego Air & Space Museum MUSEUM
(Map p278; ☎619-234-8291; www.sandiegoairandspace.org; 2001 Pan American Plaza; adult/youth/child under 2yr $20/$11/free; ⊙10am-4:30pm; ⓗ) An ode to flight, the circular museum houses an extensive display of historical aircraft and spacecraft (originals, replicas and models), including a hot-air balloon from 1783, an Apollo command module and a Vietnam-era Cobra helicopter. Also look for memorabilia from legendary aviators such as Charles Lindbergh and astronaut John Glenn or catch films in the 3-D/4-D theater.

Old Town & Mission Valley

★Old Town San Diego State Historic Park HISTORIC SITE
(Map p272; ☎619-220-5422; www.parks.ca.gov; 4002 Wallace St; ⊙visitor center & museums 10am-5pm May-Sep, 10am-4pm Mon-Thu, to 5pm Fri-Sun Oct-Apr; Ⓟⓗ) FREE On the site of San Diego's first European settlement, Old Town consists of a cluster of restored or rebuilt historic 19th-century buildings filled with

quaint exhibits, souvenir stores and cafes. A good place to start is at the visitor center in 1853 **Robinson-Rose House**; see the neat model of the pueblo in 1872 and pick up a self-guided tour pamphlet ($3). Staff also run free guided tours daily at 11am and 2pm.

Mission Basilica San Diego de Alcalá CHURCH

(Map p272; ☎619-281-8449; www.missionsandiego.org; 10818 San Diego Mission Rd; adult/child/under 5yr $5/2/free; ⏲9am-4:30pm; P) Padre Junípero Serra founded the first of California's 21 missions in 1769 on Presidio Hill near present-day Old Town but, five years later, it was moved about 6 miles upriver to be closer to water and more arable land. Destroyed, rebuilt and expanded multiple times, today's mission is the fifth on the site and an active parish. It's a lovely place to visit, not only for its historical significance but also to relax amid birdsong and bougainvillea in the serene garden.

Junípero Serra Museum MUSEUM

(Map p272; ☎619-232-6203; www.sandiegohistory.org/serra_museum; 2727 Presidio Dr; entry by donation; ⏲10am-4pm Fri-Sun early Jun-early Sep, to 5pm Sat & Sun early Sep-early Jun; P) This museum stands atop Presidio Hill, the original site of Mission San Diego de Alcalá. Inside the Spanish Revival building, a small collection of artifacts and pictures offers insight into the earliest days of European settlement.

Point Loma

On a map, Point Loma looks like an elephant's trunk guarding the entrance to San Diego Bay. Highlights are the **Cabrillo National Monument** (Map p272; ☎619-557-5450; www.nps.gov/cabr; 1800 Cabrillo Memorial Dr; per car/walk-ins $20/10; ⏲9am-5pm, tide pools to 4:30pm; P 👪) – at the end of the trunk; shopping and dining at **Liberty Public Market** (Map p272; ☎619-487-9346; http://libertypublicmarket.com; 2820 Historic Decatur Rd; dishes $5-20; ⏲11am-7pm; P 📶 🍷) – at its base; and seafood meals around **Shelter Island**.

Mission Bay & Beaches

San Diego's big three beach towns are ribbons of hedonism where armies of tanned, taut bodies frolic in the sand. West of amoeba-shaped Mission Bay, surf-friendly **Mission Beach** and its northern neighbor, **Pacific Beach** (aka 'PB'), are connected by car-free **Ocean Front Walk** (Map p272) FREE, which swarms with skaters, joggers and cyclists year-round.

South of Mission Bay, bohemian **Ocean Beach** (OB) has a fishing pier, beach volleyball and good surf. Its main drag, **Newport Avenue**, is chockablock with scruffy bars, flip-flop eateries and shops selling surf gear, tattoos, vintage clothing and antiques.

Belmont Park AMUSEMENT PARK

(Map p272; ☎858-488-1549; www.belmontpark.com; 3146 Mission Blvd; per ride or attraction $4-7, all-day ride pass under/over 48in $34/24, incl attractions $56/46; ⏲11am-10pm Sun-Thu, to 11pm Fri & Sat, shorter hours winter; P 👪) This old-style family amusement park has been a Mission Beach fixture since 1925. The star attraction is the Giant Dipper, a classic wooden roller coaster with a top speed of 50mph, while little kids love taking a spin on the faithfully recreated Liberty Carousel, painted with scenes from San Diego history. New attractions include escape rooms, a 7-D theater and a zipline. Note that many rides have a minimum height restriction.

La Jolla

Facing one of SoCal's loveliest sweeps of coastline, wealthy La Jolla (Spanish for 'the jewel,' pronounced la-hoy-ah) possesses shimmering beaches and an upscale downtown filled with boutiques and cafes. Oceanfront diversions include the **Children's Pool** (Map p272; 850 Coast Blvd; ⏲24hr; 👪) FREE – no longer for swimming, it's now home to barking sea lions; kayaking; exploring sea caves at **La Jolla Cove**; and snorkeling at **San Diego-La Jolla Underwater Park** (Map p272).

Torrey Pines State Natural Reserve STATE PARK

(☎858-755-2063; www.torreypine.org; 12600 N Torrey Pines Rd; ⏲7:15am-sunset, visitor center 9am-4pm Oct-Apr, to 6pm May-Sep; P 👪) FREE This reserve preserves the last mainland stands of the Torrey pine *(Pinus torreyana)*, a species adapted to sparse rainfall and sandy, stony soils. Steep sandstone gullies have eroded into wonderfully textured surfaces, and the views over the ocean and north, including whale-watching, are superb. Volunteers lead nature walks at 10am and 2pm on weekends and holidays. Several trails wind through the reserve and down to the beach.

SURFING IN SAN DIEGO

A good number of residents moved to San Diego just for the surfing, and gee, is it good. Even beginners will understand why surfing is so popular here.

Fall brings strong swells and offshore Santa Ana winds. In summer swells come from the south and southwest, and in winter from the west and northwest. Spring brings more frequent onshore winds, but the surfing can still be good. For the latest beach, weather and surf reports, call **San Diego County Lifeguard Services** (☎619-221-8824; www.sandiego.gov/lifeguards).

Beginners should head to Mission or Pacific Beach (p276) for beach breaks (soft-sand bottomed). About a mile north of Crystal Pier, **Tourmaline Surfing Park** is a crowded but good improvers' spot for those comfortable surfing reef.

Rental rates vary depending on the quality of the equipment, but figure on soft boards from around $7/20 per hour/day or $13/32 including wetsuit. Packages are available from **Cheap Rentals** (Map p272; ☎858-488-9070; https://cheap-rentals.com; 3689 Mission Blvd, Pacific Beach; bicycles per day from $15; ⏲10am-6pm) and **Pacific Beach Surf Shop** (Map p272; ☎858-373-1138; www.pbsurfshop.com; 4208 Oliver Ct; 90min private lessons $80-100; ⏲8am-6:30pm).

★**Birch Aquarium at Scripps** AQUARIUM
(Map p272; ☎858-534-3474; www.aquarium.ucsd.edu; 2300 Expedition Way; adult/child $19/15; ⏲9am-5pm; P) This state-of-the-art aquarium is a wonderous underwater world where you can watch sea horses dance, sharks dart, kelp forests sway, and even meet a rescued loggerhead turtle. The Hall of Fishes has more than 60 fish tanks, simulating marine habitats from the Pacific Northwest to tropical seas. The Tide Pool Plaza, with its fabulous ocean views, is the place to get touchy-feely with sea stars, hermit crabs, sea cucumbers, lobsters and tidal-zone critters.

Activities

There are plenty of hikes in and around San Diego, but most outdoor activities involve the ocean, which is a dream playground for surfers, paddleboarders, kayakers and boaters.

Flagship Cruises BOATING
(Map p274; ☎619-234-4111; www.flagshipsd.com; 990 N Harbor Dr; 2hr harbour tours adult/child $32/16) In business since 1915, this outfit runs harbor tours, dinner cruises and seasonal whale-watching cruises from its launchpad at the Embarcadero.

Hike Bike Kayak ADVENTURE SPORTS
(Map p272; ☎858-551-9510; www.hikebikekayak.com; 2222 Avenida de la Playa; kayak rentals from $35, tours $49-79; ⏲9am-sunset) HBK runs a variety of tours including the popular kayak exploration of La Jolla's cove and caves, and a bike tour down Mt Soledad and along the coast. Also rents kayaks, snorkeling gear and stand up paddleboards, bodyboards and surfboards.

Sleeping

The San Diego Tourism Authority runs a room **reservation line** (☎800-350-6205; www.sandiego.org).

For camping try **Campland on the Bay** (Map p272; ☎858-581-4260; www.campland.com; 2211 Pacific Beach Dr, Mission Bay; RV & tent sites $100-456 Jun-Aug, $55-364 Sep-May; P) in Mission Bay, or **KOA** (☎619-427-3601; www.sandiegokoa.com; 111 N 2nd Ave, Chula Vista; tent/RV with hookup sites from $60/90, std/deluxe cabins from $120/200; P@), about 8 miles south; both are full-service resorts geared toward families and groups.

Downtown & Around

★**USA Hostels San Diego** HOTEL $
(Map p274; ☎619-232-3100; www.usahostels.com; 726 5th Ave, Downtown; dm/r with shared bath from $32/80; @) There's lots of color, comforts and character at this convivial hostel in a former Victorian-era hotel. Dorms have upscale features such as air-conditioning, proper mattresses, reading lights and privacy screens. A full kitchen and a communal lounge invite chilling. Rates include linens, lockers and bagels for breakfast.

★**Kimpton Solamar** HOTEL $$
(Map p274; ☎619-819-9500; www.hotelsolamar.com; 435 6th Ave; r $150-300; P@) The 235-room Solamar delivers hip style without breaking the bank. Rooms sport hodge-podge decor with eccentric lamps,

Balboa Park & Around

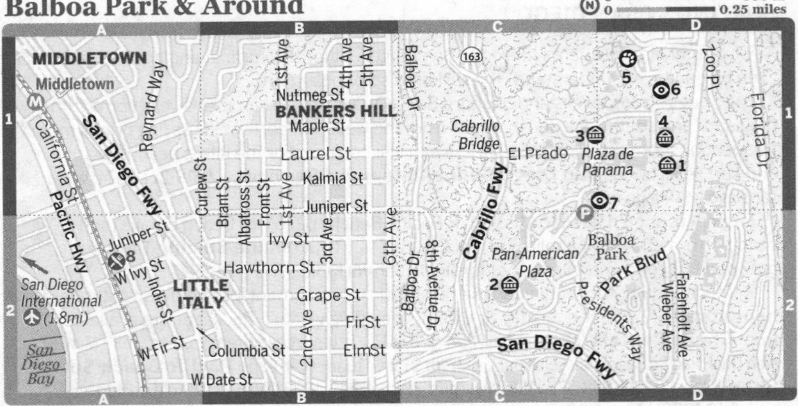

Balboa Park & Around

Sights

1 Fleet Science Center D1
2 San Diego Air & Space Museum C2
3 San Diego Museum of Art C1
4 San Diego Natural History Museum D1
5 San Diego Zoo D1
6 Spanish Village Art Center D1
7 Spreckels Organ Pavilion D1

Eating

8 Juniper & Ivy A2

patterned carpets, yoga mats and wallpapered bathrooms. Relax around the heated pool where there are cabanas and firepits or in the bar during the social hour with free drinks and snacks. Parking costs $47.

Beaches

Inn at Sunset Cliffs HOTEL $$

(Map p272; ☎619-222-7901; www.innatsunsetcliffs.com; 1370 Sunset Cliffs Blvd; r/ste from $200/315; P ⊖ ❄ @ ☎ ≋) Wake up to the sound of surf crashing onto the rocky shore at this privately owned 1950s charmer wrapped around a flower-bedecked courtyard with a heated pool. Spiffed up in 2018, the 24 rooms and suites (some with full kitchens) now sparkle in shiny white and blue hues and sport laminate flooring, blond furniture and attractive bathrooms.

Pearl Hotel BOUTIQUE HOTEL $$

(Map p272; ☎619-226-6100; www.thepearlsd.com; 1410 Rosecrans St, Point Loma; r $120-290; P ❄ ☎ ≋) This 1959 gem is showing its age, which is why new owners are giving it a big-bucks face-lift while preserving its mid-century-modern bone structure. The 23 rooms wrap around a peanut-sized swimming pool where guests and locals mingle during 'dive-in movies' on Wednesday nights.

Crystal Pier Hotel & Cottages COTTAGE $$$

(Map p272; ☎858-483-6983; www.crystalpier.com; 4500 Ocean Blvd, Pacific Beach; units Jun-Sep $225-450, Oct-Mar $185-350; P ⊖ ☎) Charming Crystal Pier consists of 29 breezy cottages from the 1930s built right on a wooden pier and flaunting dreamy ocean views from spacious decks. All but one have small kitchens, and newer, larger cottages sleep up to six. Book eight to 11 months in advance for summer reservations. Minimum-stay requirements vary by season. Rates include parking.

Hotel del Coronado LUXURY HOTEL $$$

(Map p272; ☎619-435-6611; www.hoteldel.com; 1500 Orange Ave; r from $319; P ⊖ ❄ @ ☎ ≋ 🐾) Now managed by Hilton, San Diego's iconic hotel provides the essential Coronado experience: over a century of history, a pool, full-service spa, well-equipped gym, shops, restaurants, manicured grounds and a white-sand beach. Even the basic rooms have luxurious marbled bathrooms. Make sure to book a room in the main Victorian-era hotel, not in the adjacent seven-story 1970s tower.

Eating

San Diego has a thriving dining culture, with an emphasis on Mexican and Californian cuisine and seafood. San Diegans eat dinner early, usually around 6pm or 7pm, and most restaurants are ready to close by 10pm. Breakfast is a big affair. There's a burgeoning farm-to-table and gourmet scene, especially in Little Italy and, to some extent, North Park.

Downtown & Around

★Old Town Mexican Café MEXICAN **$**
(Map p272; 619-297-4330; www.oldtownmexcafe.com; 2489 San Diego Ave; mains $5-17; 7-11pm Sun-Thu, to midnight Fri & Sat;) In business since the 1970s, this vibrant Mexican joint delivers authentic south-of-the-border fare despite the clichéd folkloric look. Marvel at staff churning out fresh tortillas at lightning speed while you sip a margarita and anticipate the arrival of menu stars such as crispy carnitas and succulent ribs.

★Puesto at the Headquarters MEXICAN **$$**
(Map p274; 610-233-8880; www.eatpuesto.com; 789 W Harbor Dr; 3 tacos $17; 11am-10pm) In the old San Diego Police Headquarters, this vibrant eatery serves modern Mexican street food that knocked our *zapatos* off. Start with some creamy guacamole before moving on to innovative tacos: chicken in hibiscus-chipotle sauce with avocado and pineapple-habanero salsa in a blue-corn tortilla. Sit on the spacious patio or inside amid murals and floating potted plants.

Basic PIZZA **$$**
(Map p274; 619-531-8869; www.barbasic.com; 410 10th Ave; small/large pizzas from $15/33; 11:30am-2am;) East Village hipsters feast on fragrant thin-crust brick-oven-baked pizzas under Basic's high ceiling (it's in a former warehouse). Toppings span the usual to the newfangled, such as the mashed pie with mozzarella, mashed potatoes and bacon. Wash them down with a craft beer or cocktail.

★Juniper & Ivy CALIFORNIAN **$$$**
(Map p278; 619-269-9036; www.juniperandivy.com; 2228 Kettner Blvd; small plates $13-28, mains $19-48; 5-10pm Sun-Thu, to 11pm Fri & Sat) Spearheading the new crop of Little Italy's fine-dining restaurants, J&I is the creation of star chef Richard Blais, who performs culinary sorcery with whatever is fresh, in season and locally available. While the menu is in constant flux, the sharing concept and the irresistible buttermilk biscuits are constant. It's all beautifully presented in the spacious setting of an open-beamed warehouse.

Balboa Park & Around

Waypoint Public GASTROPUB **$**
(Map p272; 619-255-8778; www.waypointpublic.com; 3794 30th St, North Park; mains $10-17; 11am-10pm Mon-Wed, to 11pm Thu, to 1am Fri, 8am-1am Sat, to 10pm Sun;) Waypoint's comfort-food menu is designed to pair with craft beer. The focus is squarely on burgers and sandwiches, including a wicked tri-tip with whiskey peppercorn sauce and blue cheese. For desert, beeramisu and lavender crème brûlée beckon. Walls are attractively done up in reclaimed wood, and glass garage doors roll up to the outside, all the better for hipster-watching in busy North Park.

★Hash House a Go Go AMERICAN **$$**
(Map p272; 619-298-4646; www.hashhouseagogo.com; 3628 5th Ave, Hillcrest; mains breakfast $12-22, dinner $15-29; 7:30am-2:30pm daily, 5:30-9pm Tue-Sun) This buzzing bungalow with its old-school dining room, busy bar and breezy patio dishes up rib-sticking 'twisted farm food' straight from the American Midwest. Towering Benedicts, large-as-your-head pancakes and – wait for it – hash seven different ways will keep you going for the better part of the day.

Beaches

★Pacific Beach Fish Shop SEAFOOD **$**
(Map p272; 858-483-1008; www.thefishshoppb.com; 1775 Garnet Ave; tacos/fish plates from $5/16; 11am-10pm) You can't miss this fishy-themed joint with its enormous swordfish hanging outside. Inside, it's a casual, communal bench affair. Choose from more than 10 types of fresh fish at the counter, from ahi to yellowtail, then pick your marinade (garlic butter to chipotle glaze) and your style – fish plate with rice and salad, taco or sandwich, perhaps?

★Hodad's BURGERS **$**
(Map p272; 619-224-4623; www.hodadies.com; 5010 Newport Ave, Ocean Beach; burgers $5-15; 11am-10pm) Since the flower-power days of 1969, OB's legendary burger joint has served great shakes, massive baskets of onion rings and succulent hamburgers wrapped in paper. The walls are covered in license plates; grunge/surf-rock plays (loud!); and your bearded, tattooed server might sidle into your booth to take your order. No shirt, no shoes, no problem, dude.

★**Point Loma Seafoods** SEAFOOD $
(Map p272; ☎619-223-1109; www.pointlomaseafoods.com; 2805 Emerson St, Point Loma; mains $8-17; ⊙9am-7pm Mon-Sat, 10am-7pm Sun) From California spiny lobster to harpoon-caught swordfish, the seafood at this been-there-forever fish market is off-the-boat-fresh and finds its destiny in sandwiches, salads, fried dishes and sushi. Order at the counter, then devour at a picnic table on the upstairs marina-view deck. Superb value for money.

Patio on Lamont AMERICAN $$
(Map p272; ☎858-412-4648; www.thepatioonlamont.com; 4445 Lamont St; mains lunch $8-17, dinner $16-38; ⊙11am-11pm Mon-Thu, to midnight Fri, 9am-midnight Sat, to 11pm Sun; 🐾) Although the wicker-chair look is getting a bit dated, this popular neighborhood restaurant is like a fine bottle of wine that gets better with age. Loyalists love the New American fare and the dog-friendly enclosed patio with wood-burning fireplace.

Drinking & Nightlife

As befits a cosmopolitan city, San Diego's bar scene is diverse, ranging from craft-beer bars, live-music pubs and classic American pool bars, to beach bars with tiki cocktails, gay clubs offering drag shows, and even a few speakeasies. You can also venture out to one of the 100-plus craft breweries or the vineyards in the Temecula area.

★**Bang Bang** CLUB
(Map p274; ☎619-677-2264; www.bangbangsd.com; 526 Market St; cover $20-30; ⊙5pm-midnight Wed, Thu & Sun, to 2am Fri & Sat) This Gaslamp hot spot serves sushi and Asian bites five nights a week and turns into a steamy dance club (EDM, minimal, deep house) on Fridays and Saturdays. Enter via a tiled Tokyo subway-style staircase to mingle with shiny happy people below a giant disco ball or share a giant punch bowl with your posse. Cocktails $15.

Noble Experiment BAR
(Map p274; ☎619-888-4713; http://nobleexperimentsd.com; 777 G St; ⊙6pm-2am Tue-Sun) A stack of kegs masquerading as a door inside the Neighborhood restaurant is your key to this 'speakeasy' that is so well known you need to make advance reservations. Once inside the 30-seat lair, order a Dealer's Choice and study the brass skulls and oil paintings while the bartender whips up a bespoke potion according to your tastes.

Prohibition Lounge COCKTAIL BAR
(Map p274; http://prohibitionsd.com; 548 5th Ave; ⊙8pm-1:30am Tue-Sun) Find the unassuming doorway on 5th Ave with 'Eddie O'Hare's Law Office' on it, then flip the light switch on to alert the door staff, who'll guide you into a sensuously lit basement exuding a 1920s Prohibition vibe. If your date doesn't make you swoon, the innovative craft cocktails will. Dress nicely and keep that cell phone off.

☆ Entertainment

Check out the San Diego *CityBeat* or *San Diego Union Tribune* for the latest movies, theater, galleries and music gigs around town. **Arts Tix** (Map p274; ☎858-437-9850; www.sdartstix.com; Horton Plaza Park, South Pavilion; ⊙10am-4pm Tue-Thu, to 6pm Fri & Sat, to 2pm Sun), in a kiosk on Horton Plaza, has discounted tickets (up to half-price) for same-day evening or next-day matinee performances; it also offers regular and discounted tickets to other events. Ticketmaster (www.ticketmaster.com) also sells tickets to gigs around the city.

Balboa Theatre PERFORMING ARTS
(Map p274; ☎619-570-1100; http://sandiegotheatres.org; 868 4th Ave) This elegant 1924 building began life as a vaudeville and movie theater, then presented Mexican films to a growing Latino audience in the 1930s before becoming a residence for US Navy bachelors during WWII. It now presents everything from Broadway shows to comedy and opera.

House of Blues LIVE MUSIC
(Map p274; ☎619-299-2583; www.houseofblues.com/sandiego; 1055 5th Ave; ⊙concerts usually 7pm) This Gaslamp venue presents an eclectic lineup of concerts (some free), a good-mood-inducing Sunday Gospel brunch, raucous party nights and other events. Come early for the daily happy hour (4pm to 6pm).

ℹ Information

MEDIA

Free listings magazines *San Diego Citybeat* (http://sdcitybeat.com) and *San Diego Reader* (www.sdreader.com) cover the active music, art and theater scenes. Find them in shops and cafes.

KPBS 89.5 FM (www.kpbs.org) National public radio station.

San Diego Magazine (www.sandiegomagazine.com) Glossy monthly.

San Diego Union Tribune (www.sandiegouniontribune.com) The city's major daily.

MEDICAL SERVICES

Scripps Mercy Hospital (☎619-294-8111; www.scripps.org; 4077 5th Ave; ⏰24hr) has a 24-hour emergency room. There are also 24-hour drugstores around the city, including CVS stores on Garnet Ave in Pacific Beach, on University Ave in North Park and on Market St in the Gaslamp Quarter.

TOURIST INFORMATION

Coronado Visitor Center (Map p272; ☎619-437-8788; www.coronadovisitorcenter.com; 1100 Orange Ave; ⏰9am-5pm Mon-Fri, 10am-5pm Sat & Sun)

San Diego Visitor Info Center (Map p274; ☎619-236-1242; www.sandiegovisit.org; 996 N Harbor Dr; ⏰9am-5pm) Across from the B St Cruise Ship Terminal; helpful staff offer very detailed neighborhood maps, sell discounted tickets to attractions and maintain a hotel-reservation hotline.

USEFUL WEBSITES

Gaslamp Quarter Association (http://gaslamp.org) Everything you need to know about the bustling Gaslamp Quarter, including parking secrets.

San Diego Tourism Authority (www.sandiego.org) Search hotels, sights, dining, rental cars and more, and make reservations.

ℹ Getting There & Away

AIR

Most flights arriving into **San Diego International Airport** (SAN; Map p272; ☎619-400-2400; www.san.org; 3325 N Harbor Dr; 📶), just 3 miles west of Downtown, are domestic. All major US airlines serve San Diego, as do Air Canada, British Airways, Lufthansa, Japan Airlines and WestJet.

BUS

Greyhound (Map p274; ☎619-515-1100; www.greyhound.com; 1313 National Ave; ⏰5am-11:45pm; 📶) buses depart frequently for Los Angeles (from $12, three to 3½ hours) and there are several daily departures to Anaheim (from $14, 2½ hours). Buses to San Francisco (from $49, 11 to 13 hours, about seven daily) require a transfer in LA.

Several Flixbus (www.flixbus.com) buses daily make the trip to LA, where you can transfer to destinations including Las Vegas, Palm Springs and San Francisco. Fares fluctuate with demand but are generally very competitive.

CAR & MOTORCYCLE

Allow at least two hours to drive the 125 miles between San Diego and LA Downtowns in off-peak traffic. With peak traffic, it's anybody's guess. If your car has two or more passengers, you can use the high-occupancy vehicle lanes, which shave off a fair amount of time in heavy traffic.

TRAIN

Amtrak runs the *Pacific Surfliner* several times daily to Anaheim (two hours), LA (three hours) and Santa Barbara (5¾ hours) from the historic **Santa Fe Depot** (Amtrak Station; ☎800-872-7245; www.amtrak.com; 1050 Kettner Blvd). Some trains continue north to San Luis Obispo (8½ hours). Within San Diego County, trains stop in Solana Beach, Oceanside, San Clemente and San Juan Capistrano. Fares start from around $35 and the coastal views are enjoyable.

ℹ Getting Around

While most people get around San Diego by car, it's possible to have an entire vacation here using your own two feet along with municipal buses and trolleys run by the Metropolitan Transit System (www.sdmts.com). Most buses/trolleys cost $2.25/2.50 per ride. Transfers are not available, so purchase a day pass (one-/two-/three-/four-day passes $5/9/12/15) if you're going to be taking more than two rides in a day. You will need a rechargeable Compass Card ($2 one-time purchase) available from ticket vending machines at trolley stations and the **MTS Transit Store** (☎619-234-1060; www.sdmts.com; 1255 Imperial Ave; ⏰8am-5pm Mon-Fri), which also has route maps. On buses, day passes may be purchased without a Compass Card ($7; exact fare required).

PALM SPRINGS & THE DESERTS

From swanky Palm Springs to desolate Death Valley, Southern California's desert region swallows up 25% of the entire state. What at first may seem harrowingly barren will eventually transform in your mind's eye to perfect beauty: weathered volcanic peaks, booming sand dunes, purple-tinged mountains, cactus gardens, tiny spring wildflowers pushing up from hard-baked soil, lizards scurrying beside colossal boulders and, in the night sky, uncountable stars. California's deserts are serenely spiritual, surprisingly chic and ultimately irresistible, whether you're a bohemian artist, movie star, rock climber or 4WD adventurer.

Palm Springs

The Rat Pack is back, baby, or at least its hangout is. In the 1950s and '60s, Palm Springs, some 100 miles east of LA, was the swinging getaway of Frank Sinatra, Elvis Presley and other Hollywood stars. Once the Rat Pack packed it in, Palm Springs surrendered to golfing retirees. However, in the mid-1990s, new generations discovered the city's retro-chic vibe and elegant mid-century-modern structures built by famous architects. Today, retirees and snowbirds mix comfortably with hipsters, hikers and a sizable LGBTQI+ community on getaways from LA and from across the globe.

Sights & Activities

Driving along the I-10, about 20 miles west of Palm Springs, keep an eye out for the **World's Biggest Dinosaurs** (951-922-8700; www.cabazondinosaurs.com; 50770 Seminole Dr, Cabazon; adult/child $13/11; 9am-6pm Mon-Fri, to 7pm Sat & Sun; P) on the north side of the freeway.

★Palm Springs Aerial Tramway — CABLE CAR

(760-325-1391; www.pstramway.com; 1 Tram Way, Palm Springs; adult/child $26/17, parking $8; 1st tram up 10am Mon-Fri, 8am Sat & Sun, last tram up 8pm, last tram down 9:45pm daily, varies seasonally; P) This rotating cable car climbs nearly 6000ft vertically and covers five different vegetation zones, from the Sonoran desert floor to pine-scented Mt San Jacinto State Park, in 10 minutes during its 2.5-mile journey. From the mountain station (8561ft), which is 30°F to 40°F (up to 22°C) cooler than the desert floor, you can enjoy stupendous views, dine in two restaurants (ask about ride 'n' dine passes), explore more than 50 miles of trails or visit the natural-history museum.

★Sunnylands — HISTORIC BUILDING, GARDENS

(760-202-2222; www.sunnylands.org; 37977 Bob Hope Dr, Rancho Mirage; visitor center & gardens free, house tours $48; house tours Wed-Sun, visitor center & gardens 8:30am-4pm Thu-Sun mid-Sep–early Jun; P) One of America's 'first families' of the 20th century, industrialist/diplomat/philanthropist couple Walter (1908–2002) and Leonore (1918–2009) Annenberg entertained seven US presidents, royalty, Hollywood celebrities and heads of state at their 200-acre winter retreat. The estate's art-filled main home, a 1966 mid-century-modern masterpiece by A Quincy Jones, is accessible only by 90-minute guided tour; book online far in advance. No reservations are required for the exhibits at the visitor center (built 2012) or magnificent desert gardens, inspired by impressionist paintings.

★Palm Springs Art Museum — MUSEUM

(760-322-4800; www.psmuseum.org; 101 Museum Dr, Palm Springs; adult/student $14/6; 10am-5pm Fri-Tue, noon-8pm Thu; P) Art fans should not miss this museum and its changing exhibitions drawn from a stellar collection of international modern and contemporary painting, sculpture, photography and glass art. The permanent collection includes works by Henry Moore, Ed Ruscha, Mark di Suvero, Frederic Remington and many more heavy hitters. Other highlights are glass art by Dale Chihuly and William Morris and a collection of pre-Colombian figurines. Free entry from 4pm to 8pm Thursdays.

Living Desert Zoo & Gardens — ZOO

(760-346-5694; www.livingdesert.org; 47900 Portola Ave, Palm Desert; adult/child $20/10; 9am-5pm Oct-May, 8am-1:30pm Jun-Sep; P) This amazing animal park showcases desert plants and animals alongside exhibits on regional geology and Native American culture. Highlights include a walk-through wildlife hospital and an African-themed village with a fair-trade market and storytelling grove. Camel rides, giraffe feeding, a spin on the endangered species carousel, and a hop-on, hop-off shuttle cost extra. It's educational, fun and worth the 15-mile drive down-valley. Allow for a visit of two to three hours.

Indian Canyons — HIKING

(760-323-6018; www.indian-canyons.com; 38520 S Palm Canyon Dr, Palm Springs; adult/child $9/5; 8am-5pm daily Oct-Jun, Fri-Sun Jul-Sep) Streams flowing from the San Jacinto Mountains sustain rich plant varieties in oases around Palm Springs. Home to Native American communities for centuries, these canyons are a hiker's delight. Follow the Palm Canyon trail to the world's largest oasis of fan-palm trees, the Murray Canyon trail to a seasonal waterfall, or the Andreas Canyon trail to rock formations along a year-round creek.

Sleeping

Palm Springs and the desert towns of the Coachella Valley offer an astonishing variety of lodging, including fine vintage-flair boutique hotels, full-on luxury resorts and chain motels. Some places don't allow children.

★ Arrive Hotel HOTEL $$
(760-227-7037; www.arrivehotels.com; 1551 N Palm Canyon Dr, Palm Springs; studios $190-390;) Rusted steel, wood and concrete are the main design ingredients of this stylish lair where the bar doubles as reception. The 32 spacious, phone-less rooms, some with enclosed patio, tick hipster boxes such as rain shower, Apple TV and fancy bath products. At weekends the pool, bar and restaurant turn into a lively party zone for both guests and locals.

★ El Morocco Inn & Spa BOUTIQUE HOTEL $$
(760-288-2527; http://elmoroccoinn.com; 66810 4th St, Desert Hot Springs; r $150-230; check-in 8:30am-7pm or by arrangement;) Heed the call of the casbah at this drop-dead gorgeous hideaway where the scene is set for romance. Twelve exotically furnished rooms wrap around a pool deck where your enthusiastic hosts serve free 'Morocco-tinis' during happy hour. The on-site spa offers tempting treatments; the Moroccan Mystical Ritual includes a 'Moroccan Rain' massage that uses seven detoxifying essential oils. Breakfast included.

Caliente Tropics MOTEL $$
(760-327-1391; www.calientetropics.com; 411 E Palm Canyon Dr, Palm Springs; r from $170;) Frank Sinatra and the Rat Pack once frolicked poolside at this newly spruced 1964 tiki-style motor lodge. Wrap up the day with a tropical potion in the dimly lit Reef Bar before drifting off to dreamland on quality mattresses in spacious rooms decorated with Polynesian posters.

★ L'Horizon BOUTIQUE HOTEL $$$
(760-323-1858; http://lhorizonpalmsprings.com; 1050 E Palm Canyon Dr, Palm Springs; r from $340;) The intimate William F Cody–designed retreat that saw celebs such as Marilyn Monroe and Ronald Reagan lounging poolside has been rebooted as a sleek and chic adults-only desert resort, with 25 bungalows scattered across generous grounds for maximum privacy. Treat yourself to alfresco showers, a chemical-free swimming pool and a private patio.

Eating

A lineup of zeitgeist-capturing restaurants has seriously elevated the level of dining in Palm Springs. The most exciting, including several with eye-catching design, flank N Palm Canyon Dr in the Uptown design district.

★ Cheeky's CALIFORNIAN $
(760-327-7595; www.cheekysps.com; 622 N Palm Canyon Dr; mains $9-15; 8am-2pm;) Waits can be long and service only so-so at this breakfast and lunch spot, but the farm-to-table menu dazzles with witty inventiveness. The kitchen tinkers with the offerings on a weekly basis but perennial faves such as custardy scrambled eggs and grass-fed burger with pesto fries never rotate off the list.

Trio CALIFORNIAN $$
(760-864-8746; www.triopalmsprings.com; 707 N Palm Canyon Dr; mains lunch $10-22, dinner $15-32; 11am-10pm Mon-Thu, to 11pm Fri, 10am-11pm Sat, 10am-10pm Sun;) The winning formula in this '60s modernist space: updated American comfort food (awesome Yankee pot roast) enjoyed surrounded by eye-catching artwork and picture windows. The $23 prix-fixe three-course dinner (served until 6pm) is a steal, and the all-day daily happy hour lures a rocking after-work crowd with bar bites and cheap drinks.

★ Workshop Kitchen + Bar AMERICAN $$$
(760-459-3451; www.workshoppalmsprings.com; 800 N Palm Canyon Dr; small plates $16-21, mains $28-38; 5-10pm Mon-Thu, to 11pm Fri & Sat, 10am-2pm Sun;) Hidden away in the back of the ornate 1920s El Paseo building, a large patio with olive trees leads to this starkly beautiful space. At its center is a long, communal table flanked by mood-lit booths. The kitchen crafts market-driven American classics reinterpreted for the 21st century and the bar is among the most happening in town.

Drinking & Nightlife

Drinking has always been in style in Palm Springs and many bars and restaurants have hugely popular happy hours that sometimes run all day. A handful of speakeasy bars spice up the cocktail scene and craft beer continues to be a draw. Friday is the big night out for the gay crowd.

Arenas Rd, east of Indian Canyon Dr, is nightlife central for the LGBTQI+ community.

★ Bootlegger Tiki COCKTAIL BAR
(760-318-4154; www.bootleggertiki.com; 1101 N Palm Canyon Dr; 4pm-2am) Crimson light bathes even pasty-faced hipsters with a healthy glow, as do the pretty crafted cocktails at this teensy tiki bar with blowfish lamps and rattan walls.

Birba BAR
(☎760-327-5678; www.birbaps.com; 622 N Palm Canyon Dr; ⏰5-11pm Tue-Sun Nov-May, 6-10pm Wed, Thu & Sun, to 11pm Fri & Sat Jun-Oct; 📶) On a balmy night, Birba's hedge-fringed patio with twinkle lights and a sunken firepit brings a dolce vita vibe to the desert. Unwind with a glass of frizzante or smooth cocktails such as the tequila-based Heated Snake, and stave off the blur with pizza or a plate of cheese and prosciutto.

Shopping

For art galleries, design and fashion boutiques – including the fabulous **Trina Turk** (☎760-416-2856; www.trinaturk.com; 891 N Palm Canyon Dr; ⏰10am-6pm Mon-Sat, 11am-5pm Sun) – head 'Uptown' to North Palm Canyon Dr. Thrift, vintage and consignment shops are scattered around downtown Palm Springs and down-valley along Hwy 111. For luxe labels, poke around Palm Desert's El Paseo, while bargain bunnies should steer 20 miles west on I-10 to the Desert Hills Premium Outlets mall.

Information

Palm Springs Historical Society (☎760-323-8297; www.pshistoricalsociety.org; 221 S Palm Canyon Dr; ⏰10am-4pm) Volunteer-staffed nonprofit organization. Maintains two museums and offers guided tours focusing on local history, architecture and celebrities.

Palm Springs Modern App Free app for iPhone and Android covering more than 80 iconic mid-century modern private homes and public buildings on three tours enhanced with videos, audio and photographs.

Palm Springs Visitors Center (☎760-778-8418; www.visitpalmsprings.com; 2901 N Palm Canyon Dr; ⏰9am-5pm) Well-stocked and well-staffed official visitor center in a 1965 Albert Frey–designed gas station at the Palm Springs Aerial Tram turnoff, 3 miles north of downtown.

Getting There & Around

Palm Springs International Airport (PSP; ☎760-318-3800; www.palmspringsairport.com; 3400 E Tahquitz Canyon Way) is a regional airport served year-round by 10 airlines, including United, American, Virgin, Delta and Alaska, and has flights throughout North America.

Palm Springs and the Coachella Valley are pancake-flat, and more bike lanes are being built all the time. Many hotels have loaner bicycles, or try **Bike Palm Springs** (☎760-832-8912; www.bikepsrentals.com; 194 S Indian Canyon Dr; std/kids/electric/tandem bikes half-day from $25/15/45/40, full day $35/20/60/50; ⏰8am-5pm Oct-May, to 10am Jun-Sep) or Palm Desert–based **Funseekers** (☎760-647-6042, 760-340-3861; www.palmdesertbikerentals.com; 73-865 Hwy 111, Palm Desert; bicycle per 24hr/3 days/week from $25/60/95; ⏰8:30am-5pm Mon-Fri, to 4pm Sat & Sun).

SunLine (☎760-343-3451; www.sunline.org; tickets $1) Alternative-fuel-powered public buses travel around the valley, albeit slowly. Bus 111 links Palm Springs with Palm Desert (one hour) and Indio (1½ hours) via Hwy 111. Buses have air-conditioning, wheelchair lifts and a bicycle rack. Cash only (bring exact change).

Buzz Trolley (www.sunline.org; ⏰noon-10pm Thu-Sat) This free shuttle operates from noon to 10pm Thursday through Sunday at more or less 20-minute intervals on a loop covering N Palm Canyon Dr from Via Escuela as far as Smoketree on E Palm Canyon and then back up Indian Canyon Dr.

Joshua Tree National Park

Looking like something from Dr Seuss, the whimsical Joshua trees (actually tree-sized yuccas) welcome visitors to this 794,000-acre **park** (☎760-367-5500; www.nps.gov/jotr; 7-day pass per car $30; 🅿🚻) at the transition zone of two deserts: the low and dry Colorado and the higher, moister and slightly cooler Mojave.

Rock climbers know 'JT' as the best place to climb in California; hikers seek out hidden, shady, desert-fan-palm oases fed by natural springs and small streams; and mountain bikers are hypnotized by the desert vistas.

In springtime the Joshua trees send up a huge single cream-colored flower. Mormon settlers named the trees for their branches stretching up toward heaven, which reminded them of the biblical prophet Joshua pointing the way to the promised land. The mystical quality of this stark, boulder-strewn landscape has inspired many artists, most famously the band U2, who titled their hit 1987 album *The Joshua Tree*.

Sights & Activities

If your time is limited, focus your exploration on the park's northern end where clumps of Joshua trees and otherworldly rock formations create a dramatic landscape. A drive from the west entrance in Joshua Tree to the Oasis Visitor Center in Twentynine Palms (or vice versa) takes about two hours and is a great introduction. Lots of roadside pullouts invite closer inspection as do numerous trails.

Barker Dam and **Hidden Valley** loop trails, both about 1 mile long, offer a quick

WORTH A TRIP

PIONEERTOWN

Looking like an 1870s frontier town, **Pioneertown** (Pioneertown Rd; 24hr;) FREE, about 5 miles north of 29 Palms Hwy/Hwy 62, was actually built in 1946 as a Hollywood Western movie set. Gene Autry and Roy Rogers were among the original investors, and more than 50 movies and several TV shows were filmed here in the 1940s and '50s. These days, it's fun to stroll around the old buildings and drop into the local honky-tonk for refreshments. Mock gunfights take place on 'Mane St' at 2:30pm every second and fourth Saturday, September to June.

Make a night of it and bed down at the **Pioneertown Motel** (760-365-7001; www.pioneertown-motel.com; 5040 Curtis Rd, Pioneertown; d from $185;), where yesteryear's silver-screen stars slept while filming. New owners have upgraded the elegant-rustic rooms with wooden A-frame ceilings, Native American rugs, decorative Western paraphernalia and the essential creature comforts.

immersion into JT's lunar landscape. For sunset-worthy views of the park and the entire Coachella Valley, drive up to **Keys View**.

If you're interested in pioneer history, book ahead for a tour of **Keys Ranch** (reservations 760-367-5522; www.nps.gov/jotr; tours adult/child 6-11yr $10/5, plus park admission; tours Oct-May;).

The southern end of the park is a stark and windy desert landscape. A highlight here is the **Cholla Cactus Garden** (0.25-mile loop). For a scenic 4WD route, tackle bumpy 18-mile **Geology Tour Road**, also open to mountain bikers.

Sleeping

Of the park's eight campgrounds, only **Cottonwood** (760-367-5500, reservations 877-444-6777; www.nps.gov/jotr; Pinto Basin Rd; tent & RV sites $20;) and **Black Rock** (760-367-5500, reservations 877-444-6777; www.nps.gov/jotr; Joshua Lane; tent & RV sites $20;) have potable water, flush toilets and dump stations. The two also accept reservations, as do **Indian Cove** (760-362-4367, reservations 877-444-6777; www.nps.gov/jotr; Indian Cove Rd, Twentynine Palms; tent & RV sites $20;) and Jumbo Rocks. The others are first-come, first-served and have pit toilets, picnic tables and fire grates. None have showers, but there are some at **Coyote Corner** (760-366-9683; www.jtcoyotecorner.com; 6535 Park Blvd, Joshua Tree; 9am-6pm) in Joshua Tree. Details are available at www.nps.gov/jotr or by calling 760-367-5500.

Between October and May, campsites fill by Thursday noon, especially during the springtime bloom. If you arrive too late, there's overflow camping on Bureau of Land Management (BLM) land north and south of the park as well as in private campgrounds. For details, see www.nps.gov/jotr/planyourvisit/camping-outside-of-the-park.htm.

Budget and midrange motels line Hwy 62. Twentynine Palms and Yucca Valley have mostly national chain motels, while pads in Joshua Tree as well as in Pioneertown and Landers north of Hwy 62 come with plenty of charm and character.

Harmony Motel MOTEL $
(760-401-1309, 760-367-3351; www.harmonymotel.com; 71161 29 Palms Hwy/Hwy 62, Twentynine Palms; r $90-95;) This immaculately kept 1950s motel, run by the charming Ash, was where U2 stayed while working on the *Joshua Tree* album. It has a small pool and seven large, cheerfully painted and handsomely decorated rooms (some with kitchenette) set around a tidy desert garden with serenely dramatic views. Free coffee and tea are available in the communal guest kitchen.

★ **Kate's Lazy Desert** CABIN $$
(845-688-7200; www.lazymeadow.com; 58380 Botkin Rd, Landers; Airstreams Mon-Thu $175, Fri & Sat $200;) Owned by Kate Pierson of the band B-52s, this desert camp has a coin-sized pool (May to October) and half-a-dozen artist-designed Airstream trailers to sleep inside. Sporting names such as 'Tinkerbell,' 'Planet Air' and ' Hot Lava,' each is kitted out with matching fantasia-pop design, a double bed and a kitchenette.

★ **Sacred Sands** GUESTHOUSE $$$
(760-974-2353, 760-424-6407; www.sacredsands.com; 63155 Quail Springs Rd, Joshua Tree; studios/ste $339/369;) In an isolated, pin-drop-quiet spot, these two desert-chic suites are the ultimate romantic retreat. Each has a kitchenette and a private patio with outdoor shower, hot tub and

hanging bed for sleeping under the stars. There are astounding views across the desert hills and into Joshua Tree National Park. Rates include a fridge stocked with breakfast supplies. Two-night minimum.

Eating

There's no food available inside the park, but there are supermarkets and convenience stores in the communities along Hwy 62 (especially Yucca Valley). Restaurants range from mom-and-pop-run greasy spoons to organic delis, funky diners and ethnic eats. On Saturday mornings, locals gather for gossip and groceries at the **farmers market** (www.joshuatreefarmersmarket.com; 61705 29 Palms Hwy/Hwy 62, Joshua Tree; 8am-1pm Sat) in Joshua Tree. Before hitting the trail, rocks or road, fuel up at **Crossroads Cafe** (760-366-5414; www.crossroadscafejtree.com; 61715 29 Palms Hwy/Hwy 62, Joshua Tree; mains $9-17; 7am-9pm;), a JT institution.

★La Copine INTERNATIONAL **$$**

(760-289-8537; www.lacopinekitchen.com; 848 Old Woman Springs Rd, Flamingo Heights; dishes $8-24; 2-7pm Thu-Sun;) It's a long road from Philadelphia to the high desert, but that's where Nikki and Claire decided to take their farm-to-table cuisine from pop-up to bricks and mortar. Their roadside bistro serves zeitgeist-capturing dishes such as the signature salad with smoked salmon and poached egg, rock shrimp ceviche or banh mi sandwich. No reservations.

Information

Entry permits ($30 per vehicle) are valid for seven days and are available at the three park entrances as well as National Park Service (NPS) visitor centers at **Joshua Tree** (www.nps.gov/jotr; 6554 Park Blvd, Joshua Tree; 8am-5pm;), **Oasis** (760-367-5522; www.nps.gov/jotr; 74485 National Park Dr, Twentynine Palms; 8:30am-5pm) and **Cottonwood** (www.nps.gov/jotr; Cottonwood Springs; 8:30am-4pm;). On weekends (Friday to Sunday) from November to February and daily in March and April, free shuttle buses loop around key stops in the northern park hourly from the Twentynine Palms Transit Center and the Oasis Visitor Center. No park pass is required.

There are no park facilities aside from restrooms, so bring all the drinking water and food you'll need. Get gas and stock up in the communities on 29 Palms Hwy (aka Hwy 62) along the park's northern boundary: Yucca Valley, Joshua Tree or Twentynine Palms. Coming from the south (via I-10), Indio is the nearest larger town.

Anza-Borrego Desert State Park

Shaped by an ancient sea and tectonic forces, enormous and little-developed **Anza-Borrego** (760-767-4205; www.parks.ca.gov; day use $10; P) covers 640,000 acres, making it the largest state park in California. Human history here goes back more than 10,000 years, as recorded by Native American pictographs and petroglyphs. The park is named for Spanish explorer Juan Bautista de Anza, who arrived in 1774 while pioneering a colonial trail from Mexico and no doubt running into countless *borregos*, the wild bighorn sheep that once ranged as far south as Baja California. (Today only a few hundred of these animals survive due to drought, disease, poaching and off-highway driving.) In the 1850s Anza-Borrego became a stop along the Butterfield Stagecoach line, which delivered mail between St Louis and San Francisco.

Sights & Activities

Two miles west of central Borrego Springs, the park **visitor center** (760-767-4205; www.parks.ca.gov; 200 Palm Canyon Dr, Borrego Springs; 9am-5pm daily Oct-May, Sat, Sun & holidays only Jun-Sep) has natural-history exhibits, information handouts and updates on road conditions. Driving through the park is free, but if you camp, hike or picnic, a day-use parking fee ($10 per car) applies. You'll need a 4WD to tackle most of the 500 miles of backcountry dirt roads. If you're hiking, always bring plenty of water.

Park highlights accessible without 4WD include the popular (and busy) 3-mile round-trip **Borrego Palm Canyon Nature Trail**, the easy 2-mile round-trip **Pictograph Trail** in Blair Valley, which has Native American pictographs and pioneer traces, and the fairly strenuous 6-mile round-trip **Maidenhair Falls Trail** into Hellhole Canyon. Check road and trail conditions at the visitor center before setting out.

Further south, you can soak in concreted hot-spring pools at **Agua Caliente Regional Park** (760-765-1188; www.sdparks.org; 39555 Great Southern Overland Stage Route of 1849/County Rte S2; per car $3, pools per person $3; 9:30am-sunset Sep-May).

More than 500 miles of the park's dirt and paved roads (but never hiking trails) are open to mountain bikes. Popular routes are Grapevine Canyon off Hwy 78 and Canyon

Sin Nombre in the Carrizo Badlands. Flatter areas include Blair Valley and Split Mountain. Get details at the visitor center.

Sleeping

A handful of motels and hotels cluster in and around Borrego Springs, but not all are open year-round. Otherwise, camping is the only way to spend the night in the park. In addition to developed campgrounds, free backcountry camping is permitted anywhere. Note that vehicles must be parked no more than one vehicle length off the road and that all campfires must be in metal containers. Gathering vegetation (dead or alive) is strictly prohibited.

Borrego Palm Canyon Campground CAMPGROUND **$**
(760-800-444-7275; www.reservecalifornia.com; 200 Palm Canyon Dr, Borrego Springs; tent/RV sites $25/35;) Near the Anza-Borrego Desert State Park Visitor Center (p286), this campground is a great base from which to explore the park. Despite its size, it fills up quickly on weekends, thanks in part to its modern amenities, including drinking water, flush toilets and hot, coin-operated showers.

★ **La Casa del Zorro** RESORT **$$$**
(760-767-0100; www.lacasadelzorro.com; 3845 Yaqui Pass Rd; r from $240 mid-Oct–Apr, $90-160 May–mid-Oct;) Completely updated, this venerable 1937 resort is again the region's grandest stay. The ambience exudes desert romance in 67 elegantly rustic poolside rooms and family-sized casitas sporting vaulted ceilings and marble bathtubs. A staggering 28 pools and Jacuzzis are scattered across the 42 landscaped acres, and there's a spa, five tennis courts, a fun bar and a gourmet restaurant.

Eating

Borrego Springs has a few restaurants, from spit-and-sawdust Mexican joints to fine dining. The best supermarket is **Center Market** (760-767-3311; www.centermarket-borrego.com; 590 Palm Canyon Dr, Borrego Springs; 8:30am-6:30pm Mon-Sat, to 5pm Sun;), also in Borrego Springs. In summer many places keep shorter hours or have closing days.

★ **Red Ocotillo** INTERNATIONAL **$$**
(760-767-7400; http://redocotillo.com; 721 Avenida Sureste, Borrego Springs; mains $11-20; 7am-8:30pm;) Empty tables are as rare as puddles in the desert at this artily painted charmer in a central Borrego Springs bungalow. Carb-load for a day on the trail with the breakfast burrito; tuck into bulging sandwiches at lunch; or wrap up the day with short ribs and serves of linguine with homemade pesto sauce. Lovely desert views from the patios.

Information

Borrego Springs has an ATM, two gas stations, a supermarket and a post office, all on Palm Canyon Dr. There's free public wi-fi around Christmas Circle.

Call the wildflower hotline (760-767-4684) for information on seasonal blooms.

Mojave National Preserve

If you're on a quest for the 'middle of nowhere,' you'll find it in the wilderness of the **Mojave National Preserve** (760-252-6100; www.nps.gov/moja; btwn I-15 & I-40;) FREE, a 1.6-million-acre jumble of sand dunes, Joshua trees, volcanic cinder cones and habitats for bighorn sheep, jackrabbit and desert tortoise. Warning: no gas is available here.

Southeast of Baker and the I-15 freeway, Kelbaker Rd crosses a ghostly landscape of cinder cones before arriving at **Kelso Depot**, a 1920s Mission-style railroad station. It now houses the park's main **visitor center** (760-252-6100; www.nps.gov/moja; Kelbaker Rd, Kelso; 9am-5pm), which has excellent natural and cultural history exhibits.

It's another 12 miles south on Kelbaker Rd to the **Kelso Dunes**. Under the right conditions they emanate low humming sounds caused by shifting sands – running downhill sometimes jump-starts the effect. From Kelso Depot, Kelso–Cima Rd takes off northeast.

Some 27 miles northeast of Kelso Depot, via Kelso–Cima Rd, **Cima Dome** is a 1500ft hunk of granite spiked with volcanic cinder cones and crusty lava outcrops. Its slopes are smothered in the world's largest **Joshua tree forest**. For close-ups, tackle the 3-mile round-trip **Teutonia Peak**; the trailhead is on Cima Rd, 5 miles northwest of Cima Junction.

There is no food inside the preserve, so stock up in Baker, on the northwestern edge along I-15, before heading out. Here, you'll also find plenty of cheap but charmless motels. Coming from the northeast, the casino hotels in Primm on the Nevada border offer slightly better options. If you're traveling on the I-40, Needles is the closest town to spend the night. Once you're in the preserve, camping is the only option.

OFF THE BEATEN TRACK

SALTON SEA & SALVATION MOUNTAIN

East of Anza-Borrego and south of Joshua Tree awaits a most unexpected sight: the **Salton Sea** (760-393-3810; www.parks.ca.gov; 100-225 State Park Rd, North Shore; day use per car $7; park 24hr, visitor center 10am-4pm; P), California's largest lake in the middle of its largest desert. It was created accidentally in 1905 after high spring flooding breached irrigation canals built to bring Colorado River water to farmland in the Imperial Valley. To this day, it provides habitat for around 400 species of migratory birds, but their survival is threatened by rising salinity from decades of phosphor and nitrogen in agricultural runoff that's yet to be cleaned up.

Perhaps even more bizarre is **Salvation Mountain** (760-624-8754; www.salvationmountaininc.org; 603 E Beal Rd, Niland; donations accepted; dawn-dusk; P), a 100ft-high hill of hand-mixed adobe and straw slathered in paint and decorated with flowers, found objects and Christian messages. It's the life's work of folk artist Leonard Knight (1931–2014).

Death Valley National Park

The very name evokes all that is harsh, hot and hellish – a punishing, barren and lifeless place of Old Testament severity. Yet closer inspection reveals that in **Death Valley** (760-786-3200; www.nps.gov/deva; 7-day-pass per car $30; P) nature is putting on a truly spectacular show: singing sand dunes, water-sculpted canyons, boulders moving across the desert floor, extinct volcanic craters, palm-shaded oases, stark mountains rising to 11,000ft and plenty of endemic wildlife. This is a land of superlatives, holding the US records for hottest temperature (134°F/57°C), lowest point (Badwater, 282ft below sea level) and largest national park outside Alaska (more than 5000 sq miles).

Furnace Creek is Death Valley's commercial hub, home to the park's main visitor center, a general store, gas station, post office, ATM, wi-fi, golf course, lodging and restaurants.

Park entry permits ($30 per vehicle) are valid for seven days and available from self-service pay stations at the park's access roads and at the visitor center.

Sights & Activities

In summer, stick to paved roads, limit your exertions outdoors to early morning hours and night, and visit higher-elevation areas of the park. From **Furnace Creek**, drive 5 miles southeast up to **Zabriskie Point** for spectacular views across the valley and golden badlands eroded into waves, pleats and gullies. Keep going for another 20 miles to **Dante's View** where, on clear days, you can simultaneously see the highest (Mt Whitney, 14,505ft) and lowest (Badwater) points in the contiguous USA.

Badwater is an eerily beautiful landscape of crinkly salt flats 15 miles south of Furnace Creek. Along the way, **Golden Canyon** is easily explored on a short hike. A 9-mile detour along **Artists Drive** through a narrow canyon is best in late afternoon when the exposed minerals and volcanic ash erupt in colorful fireworks.

Some 23 miles northwest of Furnace Creek, near Stovepipe Wells Village, you can trek across Sahara-like **Mesquite Flat** sand dunes – magical at sunrise and under a full moon – and scramble past the multihued rock walls of **Mosaic Canyon**.

About 55 miles northwest of Furnace Creek, whimsical **Scotty's Castle** (760-786-3200; www.nps.gov/deva; closed) was the desert home of Walter E Scott, alias 'Death Valley Scotty,' a quintessential teller of tall tales who captivated people with his stories of gold. The castle is closed due to flood damage until at least 2020.

Sleeping & Eating

Camping is plentiful but if you're looking for a place with a solid roof, in-park options are limited, pricey and often fully booked in springtime. Alternative bases are the gateway towns of Beatty (40 miles from Furnace Creek), Lone Pine (40 miles), Death Valley Junction (30 miles) and Tecopa (70 miles). Options a bit further afield include Ridgecrest (120 miles) and Las Vegas (140 miles).

If you're camping, bring in supplies from outside the park or else pay top dollar at stores in Stopepipe Wells, Furnace Creek and Panamint Springs. Generally speaking, restaurants here are expensive and mediocre.

Mesquite Spring Campground CAMPGROUND $
(☎760-786-3200; www.nps.gov/deva; Hwy 190; tent & RV sites $14) In the northern reaches of the park, this first-come, first-served campground has only 30 spaces and is a handy base for Ubehebe Crater and Racetrack Rd. At an elevation of 1800ft, it's also a lot cooler than the desert floor. Sites come with firepits and tables, and there's water and flush toilets. No RV hookups.

Ranch at Death Valley RESORT $$
(☎760-786-2345; www.oasisatdeathvalley.com; Hwy 190, Furnace Creek; d from $190; P ⊖ ❄ 🛜 ≋) Tailor-made for families, this rambling resort consists of 224 rooms with patios or balconies in one- and two-story buildings that flank lawns and lanes. Recent upgrades have resulted in a welcoming Spanish Colonial town square and an upgraded general store and saloon bar. The grounds also encompass a playground, a spring-fed swimming pool, tennis courts, a golf course and the **Borax Museum** (☎760-786-2345; www.furnacecreekresort.com; off Hwy 190, Furnace Creek; ⏲9am-9pm Oct-May, hours vary in summer; P 👪) FREE.

★**Inn at Death Valley** HOTEL $$$
(☎760-786-2345, reservations 800-236-7916; www.oasisatdeathvalley.com; Furnace Creek, Hwy 190; d from $390; P ⊖ ❄ @ 🛜 ≋) Roll out of bed, pull back the curtains and count the colors of the desert at this 1927 Spanish Mission–style hotel that emerged from a major rejuvenation in 2018. After a day of sweaty touring, languid valley views await as you relax by the spring-fed swimming pool with a spa and pool bar, in the warmly furnished lounge or in the library. A class act throughout.

Information

Furnace Creek Visitor Center (☎760-786-3200; www.nps.gov/deva; Furnace Creek; ⏲8am-5pm; 🛜) Modern visitor center with engaging exhibits on the park's ecosystem and indigenous tribes as well as a gift shop, clean toilets, (slow) wi-fi and friendly rangers to answer questions and help plan your day. First-time visitors should watch the gorgeously shot 20-minute movie. Check the schedule for ranger-led activities.

CENTRAL COAST

Too often forgotten or dismissed as 'flyover' country between San Francisco and LA, this fairy-tale stretch of California coast is packed with wild beaches, misty redwood forests where hot springs hide, and rolling golden hills of fertile vineyards and farm fields.

Coastal Hwy 1 pulls out all the stops, scenery-wise. Flower-power Santa Cruz and the historic port town of Monterey are gateways to the rugged wilderness of the bohemian Big Sur coast. It's an epic journey snaking down to vainglorious Hearst Castle, past lighthouses and edgy cliffs atop which endangered condors soar.

Get acquainted with California's agricultural heartland along inland Hwy 101, named El Camino Real (the King's Highway) by Spanish conquistadors and Franciscan friars. Colonial missions still line the route, which passes through Paso Robles' flourishing wine and craft-beer country. Then soothe your nature-loving soul in collegiate San Luis Obispo, ringed by sunny beach towns and volcanic peaks.

Santa Barbara

Perfect weather, beautiful buildings, excellent bars and restaurants, and activities for all tastes and budgets make Santa Barbara a great place to live (as the locals will proudly tell you) and a must-see place for visitors to Southern California. Check out the Spanish Mission church first, then just see where the day takes you.

Sights

Overlooking busy municipal beaches, 1872 **Stearns Wharf** (www.stearnswharf.org; ⏲daily; P 👪) FREE is the West's oldest continuously operating wooden pier; it's strung with touristy shops and restaurants. Outside town off Hwy 101, bigger palm-fringed **state beaches** await at Carpinteria, 12 miles east, and El Capitan and Refugio, more than 20 miles west.

★**Old Mission Santa Barbara** CHURCH
(☎805-682-4713; www.santabarbaramission.org; 2201 Laguna St; adult/child 5-17yr $12/7; ⏲9am-4:15pm Sep-Jun, to 5:15pm Jul & Aug; P) California's 'Queen of the Missions' reigns above the city on a hilltop perch more than a mile north of downtown. Its imposing Ionic facade, an architectural homage to an ancient Roman chapel, is topped by an unusual twin-bell tower. Inside the mission's 1820 stone church, notice the striking Chumash artwork. In the cemetery the elaborate mausoleums of early California settlers stand out, while the graves of thousands of Chumash lie largely forgotten.

WORTH A TRIP

RHYOLITE

Just outside the Death Valley eastern park boundary (about 35 miles from Furnace Creek), the ghost town of **Rhyolite** (off Hwy 374; 24hr; P) FREE epitomizes the hurly-burly, boom-and-bust story of Western gold-rush mining towns in the early 1900s; it had 8000 residents during its peak years between 1904 and 1916. Among the skeletal remains of houses, highlights are the Spanish Mission–style train station, a three-story bank building and a house made of 50,000 beer bottles.

Near Rhyolite, just east of Death Valley National Park, **Goldwell Open Air Museum** (702-870-9946; www.goldwellmuseum.org; off Hwy 374; park 24hr, visitor center 10am-4pm Mon-Sat, to 2pm summer; P) FREE was begun in 1984 by the late Belgian artist Albert Szukalski with his haunting version of Da Vinci's *Last Supper*. Other Belgian friends soon joined him and added further, often bizarre, sculptures. Today there are seven sculptures as well as a visitor center and a small store.

★MOXI MUSEUM
(Wolf Museum of Exploration & Innovation; 805-770-5000; www.moxi.org; 125 State St; adult/child $15/10; 10am-5pm;) This next-gen science museum is an interactive treasure trove of exhibits and experiences related to sound, technology, speed, light and color that are sure to delight and enlighten little ones. On three floors they can learn about music (by stepping inside a giant guitar), building a race car, or re-creating sound effects from famous movie scenes. Don't miss the views from the Sky Garden roof terrace and a nerve-challenging walk across a glass ceiling.

★Santa Barbara County Courthouse HISTORIC BUILDING
(805-962-6464; http://sbcourthouse.org; 1100 Anacapa St; 8am-5pm Mon-Fri, 10am-5pm Sat & Sun) FREE Built in Spanish-Moorish Revival style in 1929, the courthouse features hand-painted ceilings, wrought-iron chandeliers and tiles from Tunisia and Spain. On the 2nd floor, step inside the hushed mural room depicting Spanish-colonial history, then head up to El Mirador, the 85ft clock tower, for arch-framed panoramas of the city, ocean and mountains. Explore on your own or join a free hour-long tour offered at 2pm daily and 10:30am Monday to Friday, starting in the Mural Room on the 2nd floor.

Activities

Santa Barbara Sailing Center CRUISE
(805-962-2826; www.sbsail.com; Marina 4, off Harbor Way; 9am-6pm, to 5pm winter;) Climb aboard the *Double Dolphin*, a 50ft sailing catamaran, for a two-hour coastal or sunset cruise ($40); join a whale-watching trip ($50), offered from mid-February to mid-May; or hop on for a one-hour spin around the harbor to view marine life ($25). The outfit also offers kayak and SUP rentals and tours.

Condor Express CRUISE
(805-882-0088; https://condorexpress.com; 301 W Cabrillo Blvd; 150/270min cruises adult from $50/99, child 5-12yr from $30/50;) Take a whale-watching excursion aboard the high-speed catamaran *Condor Express*. Whale sightings are guaranteed, so if you miss out the first time, you'll get a free voucher for another cruise.

Sleeping

Prepare for sticker shock: even basic motel rooms by the beach command more than $200 in summer. Don't arrive without reservations and expect to find something reasonably priced, especially not on weekends. A good selection of renovated motels are tucked between the harbor and the 101 freeway, just about walking distance to everything. Cheaper motels cluster along upper State St and Hwy 101 northbound to Goleta and southbound to Carpinteria, Ventura and Camarillo.

★Santa Barbara Auto Camp CAMPGROUND $$
(888-405-7553; http://autocamp.com/sb; 2717 De La Vina St; d $180-390; P) Ramp up the retro chic and bed down with vintage style in one of six shiny silver Airstream trailers parked next to a historic RV park near upper State St, north of downtown. Sporting crisp mid-century-modern looks, all come with TV, fancy bedding and bath products, as well as a basic kitchen, patio with electric barbecue, and two cruiser bikes.

Harbor House Inn INN $$
(805-962-9745; www.harborhouseinn.com; 104 Bath St; r from $190; P) Two blocks

from the beach, this meticulously run inn offers bright sandy-hued studios with hardwood floors, small kitchens and mod cons such as SmartTVs with free Netflix and Hulu. If you're staying two nights or more, rates include a welcome basket of breakfast goodies. Make use of free loaner beach towels, chairs, umbrellas and three-speed bicycles.

★Hotel Californian BOUTIQUE HOTEL $$$
(www.thehotelcalifornian.com; 36 State St; r from $400; P ❄ 📶 ≋) Hotel Californian is the new kid on the once-run-down block that is the lower end of State St. Spearheading the area's rehabilitation, it would be worth staying here just for the prime location (next to the beach, Stearns Wharf and the Funk Zone) but its appeal goes way beyond geography. A winning architectural mix of Spanish Colonial and North African Moorish styles set a glamorous tone.

Eating

Restaurants abound along downtown's State St, and even the wharf and pier have a few gems among the touristy claptrap. More creative kitchens are found in the Funk Zone, while east of downtown, Milpas St has great taco shops. Book a week or two ahead for popular places or somewhere you're particularly keen to eat, especially on summer weekends..

La Super-Rica Taqueria MEXICAN $
(☎805-963-4940; 622 N Milpas St; tacos $2.50; ⏲11am-9pm Thu-Tue; 👪) Although there's plenty of good Mexican food in town, La Super-Rica is deluged daily by locals and visitors keen on tasting the dishes once so loved by the late culinary queen Julia Child. Join the line outside the airy casita to tuck into tacos, tamales and other Mexican staples, and see for yourself what the fuss is about.

★Mesa Verde VEGAN $$
(☎805-963-4474; http://mesaverderestaurant.com; 1919 Cliff Dr; shared plates $10-18; ⏲11am-9pm Mon-Fri, 11am-3:30pm & 5-9pm Sat & Sun; 🖉) 🍃 A top pick for plant-based dining, Mesa Verde has so many delicious, innovative all-vegan sharing plates on the menu that meat-avoiding procrastinators will be in torment. If in doubt, pick a selection and brace yourself for flavor-packed delights. Meat-eaters welcome (and possibly will be converted). Cash only.

★Lark CALIFORNIAN $$$
(☎805-284-0370; www.thelarksb.com; 131 Anacapa St; shared plates $12-32, mains $19-48; ⏲5-10pm Tue-Sun, bar to midnight; P) 🍃 A top spot to savor SoCal's bountiful farm and fishing goodness, chef-run Lark was named after an antique Pullman railway car and is based at a former fish market transformed into a buzzy casual restaurant in the Funk Zone. The menu morphs with the seasons, presenting inspiring flavor combinations such as crispy Brussels sprouts with dates or juniper-smoked duck breast. Make reservations.

Drinking & Nightlife

On lower State St, most of the boisterous watering holes have happy hours, tiny dance floors and rowdy college nights. The Funk Zone's eclectic mix of bars and wine-tasting rooms provides a trendier, more sophisticated alternative.

★Figueroa Mountain Brewing Co CRAFT BEER
(☎805-694-2252; www.figmtnbrew.com; 137 Anacapa St; ⏲11am-11pm) Father and son brewers have brought their gold-medal-winning hoppy IPA, Danish red lager and potent stout from Santa Barbara's Wine Country to the Funk Zone. Knowledgeable staff will help you choose. Clink glasses below vintage-style posters in the 'surf-meets-Old-West' taproom or on the open-air patio while acoustic acts play.

Information

Outdoors Santa Barbara Visitors Center (☎805-456-8752; http://outdoorsb.sbmm.org; 4th fl, 113 Harbor Way; ⏲11am-5pm Sun-Fri, to 3pm Sat) In the same building as the maritime museum, this volunteer-staffed visitor center offers info on Channel Islands National Park and has a harbor-view deck.

Santa Barbara Visitors Center (☎805-965-3021, 805-568-1811; www.santabarbaraca.com; 1 Garden St; ⏲9am-5pm Mon-Sat, 10am-5pm Sun Feb-Oct, to 4pm Nov-Jan) Drop by for maps and brochures and consult the helpful staff about how to get the most out of your stay. The website has handy downloadable DIY maps and itineraries, from food-and-drink routes to wine trails, art galleries and outdoors fun.

Getting There & Around

If you're driving on Hwy 101, take the Garden St or Carrillo St exits for downtown.

Greyhound (☎805-965-7551; www.greyhound.com; 224 Chapala St; 📶) operates a few direct buses daily to LA (from $14, three hours), Santa Cruz (from $42, six hours) and San Francisco (from $42, nine hours). **Amtrak** (800-872-7245; www.amtrak.com; 209 State St) trains run south to LA (from $31, 2¾ hours) via Carpinteria, Ventura and Burbank's airport, and north to San Luis Obispo (from $34, three hours) and Oakland (from $54, 8¾ hours), with stops in Paso Robles, Salinas and San Jose.

Local buses operated by the **Metropolitan Transit District** (MTD; 805-963-3366; www.sbmtd.gov) cost $1.75 per ride (exact change, cash only). Equipped with front-loading bike racks, these buses travel all over town and to adjacent communities; ask for a free transfer upon boarding. For bicycle rentals, **Wheel Fun Rentals** (805-966-2282; http://wheelfunrentalssb.com; 24 E Mason St; 8am-8pm Apr–mid-Oct, to 6pm mid-Oct–Mar;) has a handy location in the Funk Zone near Stearns Wharf.

Santa Barbara to San Luis Obispo

You can speed up to San Luis Obispo in less than two hours along Hwy 101, or take all day detouring to wineries, historical missions and hidden beaches.

Santa Ynez & Santa Maria Valleys

A scenic backcountry drive north of Santa Barbara follows Hwy 154, through the wine country (www.sbcountywines.com) of the Santa Ynez and Santa Maria Valleys. Ride along with **Sustainable Vine Wine Tours** (805-698-3911; www.sustainablevinewinetours.com; tours from $150), or follow the pastoral **Foxen Canyon Wine Trail** (www.foxencanyonwinetrail.com) north to discover cult winemakers' vineyards. In the town of **Los Olivos**, where two dozen more wine-tasting rooms await, **Los Olivos Wine Merchant & Café** (805-688-7265; www.winemerchantcafe.com; 2879 Grand Ave; mains $15-28; 11:30am-8pm Mon-Thu, to 8:30pm Fri, 11am-8:30pm Sat, 11am-8pm Sun) is a charming Cal-Mediterranean bistro with a wine bar.

Solvang

Point the compass south to the Danish-immigrant village of Solvang (www.solvangusa.com), which abounds with windmills and fairy-tale bakeries. Fuel up on bourbon vanilla French toast, charcuterie or bacon-wrapped tenderloin at **Succulent Café** (805-691-9444; www.succulentcafe.com; 1555 Mission Dr; mains breakfast & lunch $5-15, dinner $16-37; 10am-3pm Mon & Wed-Fri, 8:30am-3pm Sat & Sun, 5-9pm Sun & Mon;). For a picnic lunch or BBQ takeout, swing into **El Rancho Marketplace** (805-688-4300; http://elranchomarket.com; 2886 Mission Dr; 6am-11pm), east of Solvang's 19th-century Spanish Colonial **mission** (805-688-4815; www.missionsantaines.org; 1760 Mission Dr; adult/child under 12yr $5/free; 9am-5pm; P).

Lompoc & Around

From Solvang, follow Hwy 246 about 15 miles west of Hwy 101 to **La Purísima Mission State Historic Park** (805-733-3713; www.lapurisimamission.org; 2295 Purísima Rd, Lompoc; per car $6; park 9am-5pm, visitor center 10am-4pm Tue-Sun year-round, also 11am-3pm Mon Jul & Aug; P). Exquisitely restored, it's one of California's most evocative Spanish Colonial missions, with flowering gardens, livestock pens and adobe buildings. South of Lompoc off Hwy 1, Jalama Rd travels 20 twisting miles to windswept **Jalama Beach County Park** (805-568-2461; www.countyofsb.org/parks/jalama; Jalama Beach Rd, Lompoc; per car $10). Book ahead for its extremely popular **campground** (805-568-2460; www.countyofsb.org/parks/jalama.sbc; 9999 Jalama Rd, Lompoc; tent/RV sites/cabins from $35/50/190; P), which also has simple cabins with kitchenettes.

Pismo Beach & Around

Where Hwy 1 rejoins Hwy 101, **Pismo Beach** is a long, lazy stretch of sand with a **butterfly grove** (805-773-5301; www.monarchbutterfly.org; Hwy 1; 10am-4pm late Oct-Feb;) FREE, where migratory monarchs rest in eucalyptus trees from late October until February. Adjacent **North Beach Campground** (805-473-7220, reservations 800-444-7275; www.reservecalifornia.com; 399 S Dolliver St; tent & RV sites $35;) offers beach access and hot showers. Dozens of motels and hotels stand by the ocean and along Hwy 101, but rooms fill quickly, especially on weekends. **Pismo Lighthouse Suites** (805-773-2411; www.pismolighthousesuites.com; 2411 Price St; ste $190-500; P@) has everything vacationing families need, including a giant outdoor chessboard. In downtown Pismo, **Old West Cinnamon Rolls** (805-773-1428; www.oldwestcinnamonrolls.com; 861 Dolliver St; rolls $3-4; 6:30am-5:30pm;) offers gooey goodness. Uphill at the **Cracked Crab** (805-773-2722; www.crackedcrab.com; 751 Price St; mains $16-61; 11am-9pm Sun-Thu, to 10pm Fri & Sat;), make sure you don a plastic bib

OFF THE BEATEN TRACK

CHANNEL ISLANDS NATIONAL PARK

Channel Islands National Park (805-658-5730; www.nps.gov/chis; 1901 Spinnaker Dr, Ventura; visitor center 8:30am-5pm) FREE comprises five uninhabited islands off the coast of Ventura that are home to more than 150 endemic plant and animal species. It's a paradise for diving, hiking, kayaking, camping and other outdoor activities.

Boats leave from Ventura Harbor, 32 miles south of Santa Barbara on Hwy 101, where the park's **visitor center** (Robert J Lagomarsino Visitor Center; 805-658-5730; www.nps.gov/chis; 1901 Spinnaker Dr, Ventura; 8:30am-5pm;) has info and maps. The main tour-boat operator is **Island Packers Cruises** (805-642-1393; http://islandpackers.com; 1691 Spinnaker Dr, Ventura; Channel Island day trips from $59, wildlife cruises from $38); book ahead. If you want to camp, secure transportation first, then make a reservation on www.recreation.gov and bring food and water.

before a fresh bucket o' seafood gets dumped on your butcher-paper-covered table.

The nearby town of **Avila Beach** has a sunny waterfront promenade, an atmospherically creaky wooden fishing pier and a historical **lighthouse** (805-773-2411; www.pismolighthousesuites.com; 2411 Price St; ste $190-500;). Back toward Hwy 101, pick juicy fruit and feed the goats at **Avila Valley Barn** (805-595-2816; www.avilavalleybarn.com; 560 Avila Beach Dr; 9am-6pm May-Sep, 9am-5pm Apr, Oct & Nov, 9am-5pm Thu-Mon Dec-Mar;), then do some stargazing from a private redwood hot tub at **Sycamore Mineral Springs** (805-595-7302; www.sycamoresprings.com; 1215 Avila Beach Dr; 1hr per person $17.50-22.50; 8am-midnight, last reservation 10:30pm).

San Luis Obispo

Almost midway between LA and San Francisco, at the junction of Hwys 101 and 1, San Luis Obispo is a popular overnight stop for road-trippers. It also makes a handy base from which to explore coastal towns Pismo Beach, Avila Beach and Morro Bay, as well as Hearst Castle. SLO may not have any big-ticket sights, unless you count the Spanish-Colonial **mission** (805-543-6850; www.missionsanluisobispo.org; 751 Palm St; suggested donation $5; 9am-5pm late Mar-Oct, to 4pm Nov–mid-Mar;) and, perhaps, the kooky Madonna Inn. But this refreshingly low-key city does have an enviably high quality of life, helped along by CalPoly university students who inject a healthy dose of hubbub into the streets, bars and cafes. Thursdays are great time to be in SLO – the farmers market turns downtown's Higuera St into a party with live music and sidewalk BBQs.

Sleeping

Motels cluster off Hwy 101, especially off Monterey St northeast of downtown and around Santa Rosa St (Hwy 1). A slew of openings in recent times has increased the range of accommodations in town.

HI Hostel Obispo HOSTEL $
(805-544-4678; www.hostelobispo.com; 1617 Santa Rosa St; dm $33-45, r with shared bath from $65; closed 11am-4:30pm;) On a tree-lined street near SLO's train station, this avocado-colored hostel inhabits a converted Victorian, giving it a bit of a B&B feel. Meet fellow travelers in the communal kitchen, fireplace lounge or garden, or rent a bike (from $10 per day) to explore the town. Complimentary sourdough pancakes and coffee for breakfast. BYOT (bring your own towel). Check in from 4:30pm to 10pm.

Madonna Inn HOTEL $$
(805-543-3000; www.madonnainn.com; 100 Madonna Rd; r $209-329, plus resort fee per night $15;) The fantastically campy Madonna Inn is a garish confection visible from Hwy 101. Curious global tourists and irony-loving hipsters adore the 110 themed rooms – Yosemite Rock, Caveman and hot-pink Floral Fantasy (check out photos online) are sure to fulfil any fantasy. Even if you're not staying, it's worth a mind-bending spin around the main building. Wi-fi works in common areas only.

Eating & Drinking

Downtown SLO has several excellent restaurants, befitting the area's farm-to-fork focus and wine-country heritage.

Higuera St is littered with college-student-jammed bars. Craft-beer fans have plenty to look forward to, while grape-lovers will have no trouble finding places to sample regional wines.

Luna Red FUSION **$$**
(805-540-5243; www.lunaredslo.com; 1023 Chorro St; small plates $4-17, mains $23-27; 11:30am-10pm Mon-Thu, to 1am Fri, 10am-1am Sat, to 10pm Sun;) Local bounty from the land and sea pervades Luna's globally inspired small-plates menu meant for sharing, as is the big paella served straight from the pan. Cocktails and glowing lanterns create a sophisticated vibe indoors, although in fine weather the mission-view garden patio is the place to linger over weekend brunch or late-night drinks. Reservations recommended.

Guiseppe's Cucina Rustica ITALIAN **$$**
(805-541-9922; www.giuseppesrestaurant.com; 849 Monterey St; pizzas from $15, mains $15-39; 11:30am-3pm daily, 4:30-9:30pm Sun-Thu, to 10:30pm Fri & Sat;) Visit garlic-perfumed Guiseppe's for a leisurely lunch of toothsome salads, pizza and antipasti starring produce harvested on the owner's farm. Out the back, the facade of the heritage Sinsheimer Brothers building overlooks a shaded courtyard that's perfectly suited to languid dinners of chicken parmigiana and a glass of hearty SLO County red.

Luis Wine Bar WINE BAR
(805-762-4747; www.luiswinebar.com; 1021 Higuera St; 3-11pm Sun-Thu, to midnight Fri & Sat) This downtown wine bar is an urbane but unpretentious alternative to SLO's more raucous student-heavy drinking dens. About half of the roughly 60 wines on the list are available by the glass, and there's also a solid craft-beer selection, along with cheese and charcuterie platters.

Information

San Luis Obispo Visitor Center (805-781-2777; www.visitslo.com; 895 Monterey St; 9:30am-5pm Sun-Wed, to 6pm Thu-Sat)

Getting There & Away

Amtrak (800-872-7245; www.amtrak.com; 1011 Railroad Ave) runs daily Seattle–LA *Coast Starlight* and twice-daily SLO–San Diego *Pacific Surfliner* trains. Both routes head south to Santa Barbara (from $28, 2½ hours) and Los Angeles (from $43, 5½ hours). The *Coast Starlight* connects north via Paso Robles to Salinas (from $29, three hours) and Oakland (from $42, six hours). Several daily Thruway buses link to more regional trains.

Getting Around

SLO Transit (805-541-2877; www.slocity.org; single rides $1.50, day pass $3.25) provides daily bus service on eight fixed routes within city limits. It also runs the **Old SLO Trolley** (tickets 50¢; 5-9pm Thu year-round, 5-9pm Fri Jun-early Sep & 5-9pm Sat Apr-Oct), which loops between downtown and upper Monterey St every 20 minutes between 5pm and 9pm on Thursdays year-round, on Fridays from June to early September and on Saturdays from April through October.

SLO Regional Transit Authority (RTA; 805-541-2228; www.slorta.org; single-ride fares $1.75-3.25) operates countywide bus routes, including to the Hearst Castle Visitor Center (weekends only), Pismo Beach and Morro Bay. All routes converge on downtown's **transit center** (cnr Palm & Osos Sts).

Morro Bay to Hearst Castle

On this epic journey Hwy 1 snakes through wine country, along the coast and past lighthouses before arriving at the vainglorious Hearst Castle.

Morro Bay & Around

A dozen miles northwest of San Luis Obispo via Hwy 1, Morro Bay is a sea-sprayed fishing town where **Morro Rock**, a volcanic peak jutting up from the ocean floor, is your first hint of the coast's upcoming drama. (Never mind those distracting power-plant smokestacks.) Hop aboard boat cruises or rent kayaks along the Embarcadero, which is packed with touristy shops. Midrange motels cluster uphill off Harbor and Main Sts and along Hwy 1. A classic seafood shack, **Giovanni's Fish Market & Galley** (805-772-2123; www.giovannisfishmarket.com; 1001 Front St; mains $5-15; market 9am-6pm, restaurant 11am-6pm;) cooks killer fish and chips and garlic fries.

South of Morro Bay there are state parks for coastal hikes and **camping** (reservations 800-444-7275; www.reservecalifornia.com; campsites/RV sites $35/50;). First up is **Morro Bay State Park** (museum 805-772-2694, park 805-772-6101; www.parks.ca.gov; 60 State Park Rd; park entry free, museum adult/child under 17yr $3/free; park 6am-10pm, museum 10am-5pm;), which also has a child-oriented natural history museum. Further south, even wilder **Montaña de Oro State Park** (805-772-6101; www.parks.ca.gov; 3550 Pecho Valley Rd, Los Osos; 6am-10pm;) FREE features coastal bluffs, tide pools, sand dunes, peak hiking and mountain-biking trails. Its Spanish name (which means 'mountain of gold') comes from native California poppies that blanket the hillsides in spring.

Cayucos

Heading north of downtown Morro Bay along Hwy 1, giant platters of delicious Cal-Mexican grub await at unassuming **Taco Temple** (805-772-4965; www.tacotemple.com; 2680 Main St; mains $8-17; 11am-9pm;), a cash-only joint in a supermarket parking lot. Further north in laid-back Cayucos, **Ruddell's Smokehouse** (805-995–5028; www.smokerjim.com; 101 D St; dishes $5.50-13; 11am-6pm;) does a roaring trade in smoked-fish tacos by the beach. Vintage motels on Cayucos' Ocean Ave include the cute family-run **Seaside Motel** (805-995-3809; www.seasidemotel.com; 42 S Ocean Ave; d $110-180;). For more comfort, fall asleep to the sound of the surf at the **Shoreline Inn on the Beach** (805-995-3681; www.cayucosshorelineinn.com; 1 N Ocean Ave; r $200-250;).

Paso Robles Wine Country

North of Harmony (population: just 18 souls), Hwy 46 leads east into the vineyards of Paso Robles wine country (www.pasowine.com). For a hoppy antidote, swing by **Firestone Walker Brewing Company** (805-225-5913; www.firestonebeer.com; 1400 Ramada Dr; tours from $10; visitor center 10am-5pm Mon-Thu, to 6pm Fri-Sun;) off Hwy 101 in Paso Robles. It runs daily brewery tours (from $10; reservations recommended), or just stop by the visitor center for samples or into the restaurant for a meal.

Cambria & Hearst Castle

North of Harmony along Hwy 1, quaint Cambria has lodgings along unearthly pretty Moonstone Beach, where the **Blue Dolphin Inn** (805-927-3300; www.cambriainns.com; 6470 Moonstone Beach Dr; r $189-429;) has modern rooms with romantic fireplaces. Inland, **Bridge Street Inn** (805-215-0724; www.bsicambria.com; 4314 Bridge St; r $50-100, vans $30;) sleeps like a hostel but feels like a grandmotherly B&B, while the **Cambria Palms Motel** (805-927-4485; www.cambriapalmsmotel.com; 2662 Main St; r $100-125; check-in 3-9pm;) lulls guests to sleep with its 1950s retro vibe. An artisan cheese and wine shop turned breezy bistro, **Indigo Moon** (805-927-2911; www.indigomooncafe.com; 1980 Main St; mains lunch $10-22, dinner $18-38; 11am-3pm & 5-9pm;) dishes up market-fresh salads and sandwiches at lunch and more complex Cali fare at night. With a sunny patio and a takeout counter, **Linn's Easy as Pie Cafe** (805-924-3050; www.linnsfruitbin.com; 4251 Bridge St; dishes $8-12; 10am-7pm Mon-Thu, to 8pm Fri & Sat;) is famous for its olallieberry pie.

About 10 miles north of Cambria, hilltop **Hearst Castle** (reservations 800-444-4445; www.hearstcastle.org; 750 Hearst Castle Rd; tours adult/child 5-12yr from $25/12; from 9am;) is California's most famous monument to wealth and ambition. Newspaper magnate William Randolph Hearst entertained Hollywood stars and royalty at this fantasy estate that drips with European antiques, accented by shimmering pools and surrounded by flowering gardens. It can only be seen on tours – book ahead online or show up early in the day and hope for the best.

Across Hwy 1, overlooking a historic whaling pier, **Sebastian's** (805-927-3307; www.facebook.com/SebastiansSanSimeon; 442 SLO-San Simeon Rd; mains $9-14; 11am-4pm Tue-Sun) sells Hearst Ranch beef burgers and giant sandwiches for impromptu beach picnics. Five miles back south along Hwy 1, past a forgettable row of budget and midrange motels in San Simeon, **Hearst San Simeon State Park** (805-772-6101; www.reservecalifornia.com; Hwy 1; tent/RV sites $20/35) offers both primitive and developed creekside campsites.

Point Piedras Blancas is home to an **enormous elephant seal colony** that breeds, molts, sleeps, frolics and, occasionally, goes aggro on the beach. Keep your distance from these wild animals who move faster on the sand than you can. The signposted vista point, about 4.5 miles north of Hearst Castle, has interpretive panels. Seals haul out year-round, but the frenzied birthing and mating season runs from January through March. Nearby, the 1875 **Piedras Blancas Light Station** (805-927-7361; www.piedrasblancas.gov; Hwy 1, San Simeon; tours adult/child 6-17yr $10/5; tours 9:45am Mon, Tue & Thu-Sat mid-Jun–Aug, 9:45am Tue, Thu & Sat Sep–mid-Jun) is an outstandingly scenic spot; access is only via guided tours that can be booked online.

WORTH A TRIP

PINNACLES NATIONAL PARK

A study in geological drama, **Pinnacles National Park's** (831-389-4486; www.nps.gov/pinn; 5000 Hwy 146, Paicines; per car $15; park 24hr, east visitor center 9:30am-5pm, west visitor center 9am-4:30pm; P) craggy monoliths, sheer-walled canyons and twisting caves are the result of millions of years of erosion. In addition to hiking and rock climbing, the park's biggest attractions are its two talus caves. **Balconies Cave** is always open for exploration, while **Bear Gulch Cove** is generally closed from mid-May to mid-July when the resident colony of Townsend's big-eared bats raises their offspring. While in the park, keep an eye out for endangered California condors circling above.

Pinnacles is best visited during spring or fall; summer's heat is too extreme.

Big Sur

Much ink has been spilled extolling the raw beauty and energy of this 100-mile stretch of craggy coastline sprawling south of Monterey Bay. More a state of mind than a place you can pinpoint on a map, Big Sur has no traffic lights, banks or strip malls. When the sun goes down, the moon and stars are the only illumination – if summer fog hasn't extinguished them, that is.

Lodging, food and gas are pricey in Big Sur. Demand for rooms is high year-round, especially on weekends, so book ahead. The free *Big Sur Guide* (www.bigsurcalifornia.org), an info-packed newspaper, is available at roadside businesses. The day use parking fee (per car $10) charged at Big Sur's state parks is valid for same-day entry to all parks.

Gorda & Around

Coming from Hearst Castle, it's about 25 miles to blink-and-you-miss-it Gorda, home of **Treebones Resort** (805-927-2390; www.treebonesresort.com; 71895 Hwy 1; campsites $95, yurt with shared bath from $320; P), which offers back-to nature clifftop yurts. Basic United States Forest Service (USFS) campgrounds are just off Hwy 1 at shady **Plaskett Creek** (reservations 877-477-6777; www.recreation.gov; Hwy 1; tent & RV sites $35) and oceanside **Kirk Creek** (805-434-1996, reservations 877-444-6777; www.recreation.gov; Hwy 1; tent & RV sites $35).

Twenty miles north of Gorda is new-agey **Esalen Institute Hot Springs** (831-667-3000; www.esalen.org; 55000 Hwy 1; per person $35; 1am-3am), famous for its esoteric workshops and hot-tubbing from 1am to 3am. Same-day reservations can only be made online starting at 9am and usually sell out within minutes. It's surreal.

Another 3 miles north, partly closed **Julia Pfeiffer Burns State Park** (831-667-2315; www.parks.ca.gov; Hwy 1; day use per car $10; 30min before sunrise-30min after sunset; P) hides 80ft-high **McWay Falls**, one of California's only coastal waterfalls. From the viewpoint, you can photograph the water tumbling over granite cliffs into the ocean – or onto the beach, depending on the tide.

Henry Miller Memorial Library & Around

Head north from Julia Pfeiffer Burns State Park for another 8 miles to reach the beatnik **Henry Miller Memorial Library** (831-667-2574; www.henrymiller.org; 48603 Hwy 1; 11am-5pm Wed-Mon) FREE, the art and soul of Big Sur bohemia. It has a jam-packed bookstore, hosts concerts and other cultural events, and features eccentric outdoor sculptures. Just up the road, eating takes a backseat to dramatic panoramic views at clifftop **Nepenthe** (831-667-2345; www.nepenthebigsur.com; 48510 Hwy 1; mains lunch $18-24, dinner $18-52; 11:30am-10pm;), meaning 'island of no sorrow.'

Most of Big Sur's commercial activity is concentrated just north along Hwy 1, including private campgrounds with rustic cabins, motels, restaurants, gas stations and shops. Right by the post office, you can put together a picnic at the **Big Sur Deli & General Store** (831-667-2225; www.bigsurdeli.com; Big Sur Village; sandwiches $4-9; 7am-8pm;), attached to the laid-back **Big Sur Taphouse** (831-667-2197; www.bigsurtaphouse.com; Big Sur Village; noon-10pm;), with craft beer, Mexican pub grub and board games.

Just north, look left for the turnoff onto Sycamore Canyon Rd, which drops two narrow, twisting miles to crescent-shaped **Pfeiffer Beach** (805-434-1996; www.campone.com; Sycamore Canyon Rd; day use per car $10; 9am-8pm; P), where there's a towering offshore sea arch. Strong currents make it too dangerous for swimming. Dig down into the sand – it's purple!

Pfeiffer Big Sur State Park

Back on Hwy 1, drop by **Big Sur Station** (☎831-667-2315; 47555 Hwy 1; ⏰9am-4pm; 📶) for information on camping or hiking (or if you just need a bathroom and decent cell-phone coverage). Behind the station, **Pfeiffer Big Sur State Park** (☎831-667-2315; www.parks.ca.gov; 47225 Hwy 1; per car $10; ⏰30min before sunrise-30min after sunset; P 👪) 🍃 is crisscrossed by sun-dappled trails through redwood forests. Make reservations for the **campground** (☎reservations 800-444-7275; www.reservecalifornia.com; 47225 Hwy 1; tent & RV sites $35-50; P 🐾) or ramp up the luxury and watch the surf break far below from your private deck at the impossibly romantic **Post Ranch Inn** (☎831-667-2200; www.postranchinn.com; 47900 Hwy 1; d from $995; P 🚭 ❄ @ 📶 🏊).

Another gem is **Glen Oaks** (☎831-667-2105; www.glenoaksbigsur.com; 47080 Hwy 1; d $300-650; P 🚭 📶) 🍃, a 1950s redwood-and-adobe motor lodge turned luxe hideaway with woodsy cabins and cottages. Rooms at the nearby **Big Sur River Inn** (☎831-667-2700; www.bigsurriverinn.com; 46840 Hwy 1; mains breakfast & lunch $12-27, dinner $12-40; ⏰8am-9pm; P 📶) are a bit more ho-hum but the creekside restaurant serves solid American fare and a mean apple pie.

Andrew Molera State Park

Some 5 miles on from the Big Sur River Inn, don't skip **Andrew Molera State Park** (☎831-667-2315; www.parks.ca.gov; Hwy 1; day use per car $10; ⏰30min before sunrise-30min after sunset; P 👪) 🍃, a gorgeous trail-laced pastiche of grassy meadows, waterfalls, ocean bluffs and rugged beaches. Learn all about endangered California condors at the park's **Discovery Center** (☎831-620-0702; www.ventanaws.org/discovery_center; Andrew Molera State Park; ⏰10am-4pm Sat & Sun late May-early Sep; P 👪) 🍃 FREE. From the dirt parking lot, a 0.3-mile trail leads to a primitive no-reservations **campground** (Trail Camp; www.parks.ca.gov; Hwy 1; tent sites $25).

Point Sur State Historic Park

Six miles before the landmark **Bixby Creek Bridge**, you can take a tour (including a seasonal moonlight walk) of the 1889 lighthouse at **Point Sur State Historic Park** (☎831-625-4419; www.pointsur.org; off Hwy 1; adult/child 6-17yr from $15/5; ⏰tours 10am & 2pm Wed & Sat, 10am Sun Apr-Sep, 1pm Wed, 10am Sat & Sun Oct-Mar) FREE. Check online or call for tour schedules and directions to the meeting point. Arrive early since space is limited (no reservations).

Carmel-by-the-Sea

With borderline fanatical devotion to its canine citizens, quaint Carmel has the well-manicured feel of a country club. Watch behatted locals toting fancy-label shopping bags to lunch and dapper folk driving top-down convertibles along Ocean Ave, the village's slow-mo main drag.

Sights & Activities

Escape downtown Carmel's harried shopping streets and stroll tree-lined neighborhoods on the lookout for domiciles both charming and peculiar. The *Hansel and Gretel* houses on Torres St, between 5th and 6th Aves, are just how you'd imagine them. Another eye-catching house on Guadalupe St near 6th Ave is shaped like a ship and made from local river rocks and salvaged ship parts.

★Point Lobos State Natural Reserve STATE PARK
(☎831-624-4909; www.pointlobos.org; Hwy 1; per car $10; ⏰8am-7pm, last entry 6:30pm mid-Mar–early Nov, to 5pm early Nov–mid-Mar; P 👪) 🍃 They bark, they laze and bathe and they're fun to watch – sea lions are the stars in this state park some 4 miles south of Carmel, along with the dramatically rocky coastline and its excellent tide-pooling. Even a short hike through this spectacular scenery is rewarding. Note that parking inside the reserve is limited to 150 cars, and spaces fill quickly in summer. Arrive before 9:30am or after 3pm to avoid the crowds. Alternatively, park on Hwy 1 and walk in.

DRIVING HIGHWAY 1

Driving this narrow two-lane highway through Big Sur and beyond is very slow going. Allow at least three hours to cover the 140 miles between the Monterey Peninsula and San Luis Obispo, and much more if you want to stop and explore the coast. Don't travel Hwy 1 at night as it's too risky and, more to the point, it's futile, because you'll miss out on the terrific views. Watch out for cyclists and make use of signposted roadside pullouts to let faster-moving traffic pass.

★**Mission San Carlos Borromeo de Carmelo** CHURCH

(☎831-624-1271; www.carmelmission.org; 3080 Rio Rd; adult/child 7-17yr $9.50/5; ⏲9:30am-5pm) Carmel's strikingly beautiful mission is an oasis of solemnity with flowering gardens and a thick-walled basilica filled with Spanish Colonial art and artifacts. The mission was originally established by Franciscan friar Junípero Serra in 1770 in nearby Monterrey, but poor soil and the corrupting influence of Spanish soldiers forced the move to Carmel two years later. The mission became Serra's home base and he died here in 1784.

Sleeping

In summer and on weekends, shockingly overpriced boutique hotels, inns and B&Bs fill up quickly in Carmel-by-the-Sea. Ask the **Carmel Visitor Center** (☎831-624-2522; www.carmelcalifornia.org; Ocean Ave btwn Junipero & Mission, 2nd fl, Carmel Plaza; ⏲10am-5pm) about last-minute deals. For better-value lodgings, head north to Monterey.

Eating & Drinking

Low lighting and conversation-friendly sound levels characterize Carmel's old-world dining scene, although a few eateries are trying for a more modern, lively vibe. The best option for late-night drinks is the cool, energetic scene at **Barmel** (☎831-626-2095; www.facebook.com/BarmelByTheSea; San Carlos St btwn Ocean & 7th Aves; ⏲3pm-2am Mon-Sat, to midnight Sun).

★**Cultura Comida y Bebida** MEXICAN **$$**

(☎831-250-7005; www.culturacarmel.com; Dolores St btwn 5th & 6th Aves; mains $19-32; ⏲5:30pm-midnight daily, 10:30am-3:30pm Sat & Sun; 🍷) In a brick-lined courtyard, this vivaciously elegant restaurant pairs art and candlelight with food inspired by Oaxacan flavors and an entire library's worth of mezcal. The ambience is upscale but relaxed and suitable both for a date night or an outing with your posse. The Cultura mole with smoked pork and saffron tortillas is a signature dish.

La Bicyclette FRENCH **$$**

(☎831-622-9899; www.labicycletterestaurant.com; cnr Dolores St & 7th Ave; mains lunch $19-29, dinner $20-44; ⏲11am-3:30pm & 4:45-10pm) Rustic French comfort food using seasonal local ingredients and an open kitchen baking wood-fired-oven pizzas packs couples into this bistro. Excellent local wines by the glass. It's also a top spot for a leisurely lunch.

Monterey

Life in still delightfully rough-around-the-edges Monterey revolves around the sea. The city's biggest draw is a world-class aquarium overlooking Monterey Bay National Marine Sanctuary, which protects dense kelp forests and a sublime variety of marine life, including seals and sea lions, dolphins and whales.

Sights

The aquarium sits on the edge of **Cannery Row** (👪), which made Monterey the sardine capital of the world in the 1930s. Today it's an unabashedly touristic strip lined with souvenir shops and standard eateries in faux retro buildings. For more authenticity, take a stroll past downtown's cluster of restored buildings from the Spanish and Mexican periods.

★**Monterey Bay Aquarium** AQUARIUM

(☎info 831-648-4800, tickets 866-963-9645; www.montereybayaquarium.org; 886 Cannery Row; adult/child 3-12yr/13-17yr $50/30/40, tours $15; ⏲9:30am-6pm May-Aug, 10am-5pm Sep-Apr; 👪) 🍃 Monterey's most mesmerizing experience, this enormous aquarium occupies the site of a humongous sardine cannery. All kinds of aquatic creatures inhabit its halls and outside areas, from sea stars and slimy sea slugs to animated sea otters and surprisingly nimble 800lb tuna. The aquarium is much more than an impressive collection of glass tanks; thoughtful placards underscore the bay's cultural and historical contexts.

Monterey State Historic Park HISTORIC SITE

(☎831-649-2907, 831-649-7118; www.parks.ca.gov/mshp; 20 Custom House Plaza; ⏲Pacific House 10am-4pm Tue-Sun) FREE Old Monterey is home to an extraordinary assemblage of 19th-century brick and adobe buildings administered as a state park and linked by a 2-mile self-guided walking tour called the 'Path of History.' Pick up a copy at Pacific House Museum, which also doubles as the park HQ. Route highlights are the nearby Custom House and the Old Whaling Station. Note that buildings are open according to a capricious schedule dictated by state funding.

Activities

You can spot whales off the coast of Monterey Bay year-round. The season for blue and humpback whales runs from April to early December, while gray whales pass by from mid-December through March. **Sanctuary**

Cruises (☎info 831-917-1042, tickets 831-350-4090; www.sanctuarycruises.com; 7881 Sandholdt Rd; tours $45-55;) tour boats depart from Fisherman's Wharf and Moss Landing. Reserve trips at least a day in advance; be prepared for a bumpy, cold ride.

Monterey Bay Whale Watch BOATING
(☎831-375-4658; www.gowhales.com; Fisherman's Wharf; 3hr tours adult/child 4-12yr $49/39;) Right on Fisherman's Wharf, this is one of the oldest whale-watch tour operators in Monterey. Morning and afternoon boat rides are led by knowledgeable marine biologists for extra insight into the animals and their habitat. Sightings are guaranteed or you get another trip on them.

Adventures by the Sea CYCLING, KAYAKING
(☎831-372-1807; www.adventuresbythesea.com; 299 Cannery Row; per day bicycle $35, SUP set $50, 1-/2-seater kayak $35/60, kayak tours from $60; ⏲9am-sunset;) No matter if you fancy kayaking with sea otters, joining a kayak tour across the kelp-forest canopy, learning to paddleboard or exploring the area on a hybrid or e-bike, these folks can set you up. They have six locations in all, with Cannery Row being the largest and most central.

Aquarius Dive Shop DIVING
(☎831-375-1933; www.aquariusdivers.com; 2040 Del Monte Ave; snorkel-/scuba-gear rental $35/65, dive tours from $65; ⏲9am-6pm Mon-Thu, to 7pm Fri, 7am-7pm Sat, 7am-6pm Sun) Talk to this five-star PADI-certified operation for gear rentals, classes and guided dives into Monterey Bay.

Sleeping

Book ahead for special events, on weekends and in summer. To avoid the tourist congestion and jacked-up prices of Cannery Row, look to Pacific Grove. Cheaper motels line Munras Ave, south of downtown, and N Fremont St, east of Hwy 1.

HI Monterey Hostel HOSTEL $
(☎831-649-0375; www.montereyhostel.org; 778 Hawthorne St; dm $49-60, tr/q with shared bathroom $129/149;) Four blocks from Cannery Row and the aquarium, this simple, clean hostel houses single-sex and mixed dorms, as well as private rooms for three to five people. Days start with free make-your-own-pancake breakfasts and might conclude with barbecue parties or story-swapping in the lounge with piano. Check in from 2pm to 10pm

Monterey Hotel HOTEL $$
(☎831-375-3184; www.montereyhotel.com; 407 Calle Principal; r $210-450;) Steps from Fisherman's Wharf, this 1904 Victorian is honeycombed with 69 rooms that channel historic character, with antique furniture, ceiling fans, plantation shutters and fireplaces (in some). 'Historic' rooms are a tad twee; opt for the 'deluxe' categories if you need more elbow room. Breakfast included.

★**Jabberwock** B&B $$$
(☎831-372-4777; www.jabberwockinn.com; 598 Laine St; r $240-400;) Barely visible behind a shroud of foliage, this 1911 khaki-shingled Craftsman-style house hums a playful *Alice in Wonderland* tune through seven immaculate rooms, a few with fireplaces and Jacuzzis for two. Over afternoon wine and hors d'oeuvres, ask the genial hosts about the house's many salvaged architectural elements. Weekends have a two-night minimum. Breakfast included.

Eating

Away from the tourist zones, there's dining gold to be unearthed in Monterey. For casual indie eateries, head uphill from Cannery Row to Lighthouse Ave to feast on everything from Hawaiian barbecue and Thai flavors to sushi and kebabs. For more contemporary and upscale plates, head downtown around Alvarado St.

LouLou's Griddle in the Middle AMERICAN $
(☎831-372-0568; www.loulousgriddle.com; Municipal Wharf 2; mains $9-15; ⏲7:30am-3pm Wed-Mon;) Stroll down the municipal wharf to this zany diner, best for breakfasts of hubcap-sized pancakes and omelets served with fresh salsa and awesome fried potatoes. At lunchtime, you can fill the tummy with seafood and burgers.

Zab Zab NORTHERN THAI $
(☎831-747-2225; www.zabzabmonterey.com; 401 Lighthouse Ave; mains $11-19; ⏲11am-2:30pm & 5-9pm Tue-Fri, noon-9pm Sat & Sun;) Our pick of Lighthouse Avenue's lineup of low-key global eateries, Zab Zab channels the robust flavors of northeast Thailand. The bijou cottage is perfect in cooler weather, but during summer the best spot is on the deck surrounded by a pleasantly overgrown garden.

★**Montrio Bistro** CALIFORNIAN $$$
(☎831-648-8880; www.montrio.com; 414 Calle Principal; shared plates $6.50-20, mains $20-46; ⏲4:30-10pm Sun-Thu, to 11pm Fri & Sat;) With

'clouds' hanging from the ceiling and tube sculptures wriggling towards them, it's apparent that much thought has gone into the design of this dining-scene stalwart set inside a 1910 firehouse, Fortunately, the New American fare, prepared with ingredients hunted and gathered locally, measures up nicely. Drink and snack prices during happy hour (daily until 6:30pm) are practically a steal.

Information

Monterey Visitors Center (☎831-657-6400; www.seemonterey.com; 401 Camino el Estero; ⏲10am-6pm May-Aug, to 5pm Sep-Apr) Free tourist brochures and accommodations booking service for all of Monterey County.

Getting There & Away

Monterey-Salinas Transit (MST; ☎888-678-2871; www.mst.org; Jules Simoneau Plaza; single rides $1.50-3.50, day pass $10) operates local and countywide buses, including routes to Pacific Grove, Carmel, Big Sur (weekends only, daily in summer) and Salinas. Routes converge on downtown's **Transit Plaza** (cnr Pearl & Alvarado Sts).

From late May until early September, MST's free trolley loops around downtown, Fisherman's Wharf and Cannery Row between 10am and 7pm or 8pm daily (weekends only September to April).

Santa Cruz

Santa Cruz is counterculture central, a touchy-feely, new-agey city famous for its leftie-liberal politics and easygoing ideology – except when it comes to dogs (rarely allowed off-leash) and parking (meters run seven days a week).

Santa Cruz has a vibrant but chaotic downtown. On the waterfront is the famous beach boardwalk, and in the hills redwood groves embrace the University of California, Santa Cruz (UCSC) campus. Plan at least half a day here, but to appreciate the aesthetic of jangly skirts, crystal pendants and Rastafarian dreadlocks, stay longer and plunge headlong into the rich local brew of surfers, students, punks and eccentric characters.

Sights & Activities

One of the best things to do in Santa Cruz is simply stroll, shop and watch the sideshow along **Pacific Avenue** downtown. A 15-minute walk from there is the beach and the **Santa Cruz Wharf** (www.santacruzwharf.com), where seafood restaurants, gift shops and barking sea lions compete for attention.

Ocean-view **West Cliff Drive** follows the waterfront southwest of the wharf, paralleled by a paved recreational path. Great for sunsets, sandy **Natural Bridges State Beach** (☎831-423-4609; www.parks.ca.gov; 2531 W Cliff Dr; day use per car $10; ⏲beach 8am-sunset, visitor center 10am-4pm; P 👪), fronted by a natural sandstone bridge, is a family favorite and tops for wildlife-viewing.

Award-winning **Richard Schmidt Surf School** (☎831-423-0928; www.richardschmidt.com; 849 Almar Ave; lessons 2hr group/1hr private $100/130; 👪) offers small group lessons either at Cowell Beach or at Pleasure Point in Capitola. Experienced surfers can hire or buy boards and other gear at **O'Neill Surf Shop** (☎831-475-4151; www.oneill.com; 1115 41st Ave, Capitola; wetsuit/surfboard rental from $20/30; ⏲9am-8pm Mon-Fri, from 8am Sat & Sun).

★Santa Cruz Beach Boardwalk — AMUSEMENT PARK

(☎831-423-5590; www.beachboardwalk.com; 400 Beach St; boardwalk free, per ride $4-7, all-day pass $40; ⏲daily late May-Aug, most weekends Sep-Apr, weather permitting; P 👪) The West Coast's oldest beachfront amusement park, this 1907 boardwalk has a glorious old-school Americana vibe. The smell of cotton candy mixes with the salt air, which is punctuated by the squeals of kids hanging upside down on carnival rides. Famous thrills include the **Giant Dipper**, a 1924 wooden roller coaster, and the 1911 **Looff carousel**, both National Historic Landmarks. During summer, catch free movies on Wednesdays, and Friday-night concerts by rock veterans you may have thought already dead.

★Seymour Marine Discovery Center — MUSEUM

(☎831-459-3800; http://seymourcenter.ucsc.edu; 100 McAllister Way; adult/child 3-16yr $9/7; ⏲10am-5pm Tue-Sun Sep-Jun, daily Jul & Aug; P 👪) 🌿 This educational center is part of UCSC's Long Marine Laboratory. Interactive natural-science exhibits include tidal touch pools and aquariums, while outside you can gawk at the world's largest blue-whale skeleton.

Santa Cruz Surfing Museum — MUSEUM

(☎831-420-6289; 701 W Cliff Dr; entry by donation; ⏲10am-5pm Thu-Tue Jul 4-early Sep, noon-4pm Thu-Mon early Sep-Jul 3; 👪) A mile southwest of the wharf along the coast, this tiny museum inside an old lighthouse is packed with memorabilia, including vintage redwood surfboards. Fittingly, its location on Lighthouse Point overlooks two popular surf breaks.

★Santa Cruz Food Tour FOOD
(☎866-736-6343; www.santacruzfoodtour.com; per person $69; ⊙2:30-6pm Fri & Sun Apr-Oct) These congenial walking tours are the perfect way to plug into Santa Cruz's progressive, global and sophisticated food scene. Guides also deliver a healthy serving of local knowledge and interesting insights into Santa Cruz history, culture and architecture. You'll be walking for about 2 miles and will eat enough for most people not to need dinner afterwards.

Sleeping

Despite a couple of hotel openings, Santa Cruz does not have enough beds to satisfy demand: expect high prices at peak times for nothing-special rooms. Places near the beach boardwalk (p300) range from friendly to frightening. For a decent motel, cruise Ocean St inland or Mission St (Hwy 1). More hotels are in the pipeline, which should improve the city's accommodations options in the short- to mid-term.

Book well ahead to **camp** (☎800-444-7275; www.reservecalifornia.com; tent/RV sites $35/65) at state beaches off Hwy 1 south of Santa Cruz or up in the foggy Santa Cruz Mountains off Hwy 9. Family-friendly campgrounds include Henry Cowell Redwoods State Park in Felton and New Brighton State Beach in Capitola.

HI Santa Cruz Hostel HOSTEL $
(☎831-423-8304; www.hi-santacruz.org; 321 Main St; dm $28-42, r with shared bath $85-160; ⊙office 8-11am & 3-9pm; @ 📶) Budget overnighters dig this cute hostel set inside five rambling Victorian cottages and surrounded by flowering gardens, just two blocks from the beach. Whip up meals in the communal kitchen or watch a DVD (free rentals) in the funky furnished lounge with fireplace. Main con: the midnight curfew.

Dream Inn HOTEL $$$
(☎831-740-8069; www.dreaminnsantacruz.com; 175 W Cliff Dr; r $270-560; P ⊖ ❄ @ 📶 ≋) Proud of being Santa Cruz's only oceanfront hotel, the Dream Inn has good-sized rooms brimming with retro-chic charm and turquoise color accents. Catch hypnotic bay views from private balconies. The sleek swimming pool, fronted by sandy Cowell Beach, is just steps away.

Babbling Brook Inn B&B $$$
(☎831-427-2437; www.babblingbrookinn.com; 1025 Laurel St; r $280-370; ⊖ 📶) Built around a running creek amid meandering gardens and old pine and redwood trees, this wood-shingled inn has 13 cozy rooms named after impressionist painters and decorated in French-provincial style. Most have gas fireplaces, some have Jacuzzis and all have feather beds. There's afternoon wine and hors d'oeuvres, plus a full breakfast included.

Eating

There's some delicious dining to be done in Santa Cruz, which has seriously upped the kitchen ante in recent years. Seafood features prominently on menus, many of which are also driven by the regional-seasonal-organic trifecta. Pacific Ave in downtown has some excellent mid- to upscale options, while Mission St, near UCSC, and 41st Ave in Capitola offer cheaper eats.

★Soif CALIFORNIAN $$
(☎831-423-2020; www.soifwine.com; 105 Walnut Ave; mains $18-34; ⊙5-9pm Sun-Tue, noon-9pm Wed & Thu, noon-10pm Fri & Sat; 🖉) 🌿 A perennial local foodie fave, this chic and cosmopolitan lair harnesses mostly native products and turns them into triumphs of flavor pairings: Manila clams might cuddle with chorizo and fennel, or duck breast befriend roasted figs. There's a perfect wine match for each dish and, if you like it, you can pick up a bottle in the affiliated wine shop.

Akira Santa Cruz JAPANESE $$
(☎831-600-7093; www.akirasantacruz.com; 1222 Soquel Ave; nigiri $4-10, maki $7-17; ⊙11am-11pm; 🖉) Complemented by sake, craft brews and a buzzy surf-town ambience, Akira's menu harnesses briny-fresh tuna, salmon, eel and shellfish for a huge variety of sushi and new-gen spins on Japanese cuisine. Bento boxes for lunch ($11.50 to $16) are good value, and there's an entire page of classic and innovative vegetarian rolls.

Drinking & Nightlife

Santa Cruz's downtown overflows with bars, lounges and coffee shops. Heading west on Mission St (Hwy 1), craft breweries and wine-tasting rooms fill the raffish industrial ambience of the Swift and Ingalls St Courtyards.

★515 COCKTAIL BAR
(☎831-425-5051; www.515santacruz.com; 515 Cedar St; ⊙5pm-midnight Sun-Tue, to 1:30am Wed-Sat) This locally beloved cocktail parlor is the perfect place for a night of dapper drinking. Settle into a huge armchair amid the

vintage-chic decor to celebrate classic and masterfully concocted libations. Le Pamplemousse, a delicious blend of vodka, Aperol and citrus, is a perennial favorite.

Verve Coffee Roasters CAFE
(☎831-600-7784; www.vervecoffee.com; 1540 Pacific Ave; ⌚6:30am-9pm; 📶) To sip finely roasted artisan espresso or a cup of rich pour-over coffee, join the surfers and hipsters at this high-ceilinged industrial-zen cafe. Single-origin brews and house blends rule. The mod design is a study of how to get creative with wood.

Lupulo Craft Beer House CRAFT BEER
(☎831-454-8306; www.lupulosc.com; 233 Cathcart St; ⌚11:30am-10pm Mon-Thu, to 11:30pm Fri, 10am-11:30pm Sat, 11am-10pm Sun) Named with the Spanish word for hops, Lupulo Craft Beer House is an essential downtown destination for traveling beer fans. Modern decor combines with an ever-changing tap list – often including hard-to-get seasonal brews from local breweries – and good bar snacks ($4 to $15) such as empanadas, tacos and charcuterie plates. Almost 400 bottled and canned beers create delicious panic for the indecisive drinker.

ℹ Information

Santa Cruz Visitor Center (☎831-425-1234; www.santacruz.org; 303 Water St, Suite 100; ⌚9am-noon & 1-4pm Mon-Fri, 11am-3pm Sat & Sun)

ℹ Getting There & Around

Santa Cruz is 75 miles south of San Francisco via coastal Hwy 1 or Hwy 17, a nail-bitingly narrow, winding mountain road. Monterey is about 45 miles further south via Hwy 1.

Santa Cruz Shuttles (☎831-421-9883; www.santacruzshuttles.com) runs shared shuttles to/from airports at San Jose ($55), San Francisco ($85) and Oakland ($85).

Greyhound (☎831-423-4082; www.greyhound.com; 920 Pacific Ave; 📶) has a few daily buses to San Francisco (from $16, 3½ hours), Salinas (from $12, one hour), Santa Barbara (from $39, 5½ hours) and Los Angeles (from $22, nine hours).

Santa Cruz Metro (☎831-425-8600; www.scmtd.com; 920 Pacific Ave; single rides/day pass $2/6) operates local and countywide bus routes that converge on downtown's **Metro Center** (☎831-425-8600; www.scmtd.com; 920 Pacific Ave; single rides/day pass $2/6). The Highway 17 Express bus links Santa Cruz with San Jose's Amtrak/CalTrain station ($7, 50 minutes, once or twice hourly).

From late May through early September, the zero-emission **Santa Cruz Electric Shuttle** (www.santacruztrolley.com; per ride 25¢; ⌚noon-8pm late May-early Sep) connects downtown and the beach from noon to 8pm daily.

SAN FRANCISCO & THE BAY AREA

San Francisco

Grab your coat and a handful of glitter, and enter a wonderland of fog and fabulousness. So long, inhibitions; hello, San Francisco!

👁 Sights

Most major museums are downtown, though Golden Gate Park is home to the de Young Museum and the California Academy of Sciences. The city's most historic districts are the Mission, Chinatown, North Beach and the Haight. Galleries are clustered downtown and in North Beach, the Mission, Potrero Flats and Dogpatch. You'll find hilltop parks citywide, but Russian, Nob and Telegraph Hills are the highest and most panoramic.

👁 Downtown, Civic Center & SoMa

Downtown has all the amenities: art galleries, swanky hotels, first-run theaters, malls and entertainment megaplexes. High-end stores ring **Union Sq** (Map p308; btwn Geary, Powell, Post & Stockton Sts; 🚋Powell-Mason, Powell-Hyde, Ⓜ Powell, Ⓑ Powell) now, but this people-watching plaza has been a hotbed of protest, from pro-Union Civil War rallies to AIDS vigils.

Civic Center is a zoning conundrum, with great performances and Asian art treasures on one side of City Hall and dive bars and soup kitchens on the other. Some head to South of Market (SoMa) for high-tech deals, others for high art, but everyone gets down and dirty on the dance floor.

★San Francisco Museum of Modern Art MUSEUM
(SFMOMA; Map p308; ☎415-357-4000; www.sfmoma.org; 151 3rd St; adult/ages 19-24yr/under 18yr $25/19/free; ⌚10am-5pm Fri-Tue, to 9pm Thu, atrium 8am Mon-Fri; 👪; 🚌5, 6, 7, 14, 19, 21, 31, 38, Ⓜ Montgomery, Ⓑ Montgomery) The expanded San Francisco Museum of Modern Art is a mind-boggling feat, nearly tripling in size to accommodate a sprawling collection of

modern and contemporary masterworks over seven floors of galleries – but then, SFMOMA has defied limits ever since its 1935 founding. The museum was a visionary early investor in then-emerging art forms including photography, installations, video, performance art, digital art and industrial design. Even during the Depression, SFMOMA envisioned a world of vivid possibilities, starting in San Francisco.

Asian Art Museum MUSEUM

(Map p308; ☎415-581-3500; www.asianart.org; 200 Larkin St; adult/student/child $15/10/free, 1st Sun of month free; ⏰10am-5pm Tue, Wed & Fri-Sun, to 9pm Thu; 👪; Ⓜ Civic Center, Ⓑ Civic Center) Imaginations race from subtle Chinese ink paintings to seductive Hindu temple carvings and from elegant Islamic calligraphy to cutting-edge Japanese minimalism across three floors spanning 6000 years of Asian art. Besides the largest collection of Asian art outside Asia – 18,000 works – the museum offers excellent programs for all ages, from shadow-puppet shows and tea tastings with star chefs to mixers with cross-cultural DJ mash-ups.

Contemporary Jewish Museum MUSEUM

(Map p308; ☎415-655-7856; www.thecjm.org; 736 Mission St; adult/student/child $14/12/free, after 5pm Thu $8; ⏰11am-5pm Mon, Tue & Fri-Sun, to 8pm Thu; 👪; 🚌14, 30, 45, Ⓑ Montgomery, Ⓜ Montgomery) That upended blue-steel box miraculously balancing on one corner atop the Contemporary Jewish Museum is appropriate for an institution that upends conventional ideas about art and religion. Architect Daniel Libeskind designed this museum to be rational, mystical and powerful: building onto a 1907 brick power station, he added blue-steel elements to form the Hebrew word *l'chaim* (life). But it's the contemporary-art commissions that truly bring the building to life.

Museum of the African Diaspora MUSEUM

(MoAD; Map p308; ☎415-358-7200; www.moadsf.org; 685 Mission St; adult/student/child $10/5/free; ⏰11am-6pm Wed-Sat, noon-5pm Sun; Ⓟ 👪; 🚌14, 30, 45, Ⓜ Montgomery, Ⓑ Montgomery) MoAD assembles an international cast of characters to tell the epic story of diaspora, including a moving video of slave narratives told by Maya Angelou. Standouts among quarterly changing exhibits have included homages to '80s New Wave icon Grace Jones, architect David Adjaye's photographs of contemporary African landmarks and Alison Saar's sculptures of figures marked by history. Public events include poetry slams, Yoruba spiritual music celebrations and lectures examining the legacy of the Black Panthers' free-school-breakfast program.

Glide Memorial United Methodist Church CHURCH

(Map p308; ☎415-674-6090; www.glide.org; 330 Ellis St; ⏰celebrations 9am & 11am Sun; 👪; 🚌38, Ⓜ Powell, Ⓑ Powell) When the rainbow-robed Glide gospel choir enters singing their hearts out, the 2000-plus congregation erupts in cheers, hugs and dance moves. Raucous Sunday Glide celebrations capture San Francisco at its most welcoming and uplifting, embracing the rainbow spectrum of culture, gender, orientation, ability and socioeconomics. After the celebration ends, the congregation keeps the inspiration coming, serving 2000 meals a day and connecting homeless individuals and families with shelter and emotional support. Yes, Glide welcomes volunteers.

Powell St Cable Car Turnaround LANDMARK

(Map p308; www.sfmta.com; cnr Powell & Market Sts; 🚋Powell-Mason, Mason-Hyde, Ⓜ Powell, Ⓑ Powell) Peek through the passenger queue at Powell and Market Sts to spot cable-car operators leaping out, gripping the chassis of each trolley and slooowly turning the car atop a revolving wooden platform. Cable cars can't go in reverse, so they need to be turned around by hand here at the terminus of the Powell St lines. Riders queue up midmorning to early evening to secure a seat, with raucous street performers and doomsday preachers on the sidelines as entertainment.

Embarcadero

★Ferry Building LANDMARK

(Map p308; ☎415-983-8000; www.ferrybuildingmarketplace.com; cnr Market St & the Embarcadero; ⏰10am-7pm Mon-Fri, 8am-6pm Sat, 11am-5pm Sun; 👪; 🚌2, 6, 9, 14, 21, 31, Ⓜ Embarcadero, Ⓑ Embarcadero) Hedonism is alive and well at this transit hub turned gourmet emporium, where foodies happily miss their ferries over Sonoma oysters and bubbly, SF craft beer and Marin-raised beef burgers, and locally roasted coffee and just-baked cupcakes. Star chefs are frequently spotted at the farmers market (p319) that wraps around the building all year.

★Exploratorium MUSEUM

(Map p308; ☎415-528-4444; www.exploratorium.edu; Pier 15/17; adult/child $29.95/19.95,

6-10pm Thu $19.95; ⏲10am-5pm Tue-Sun, over 18yr only 6-10pm Thu; P 👪; M E, F) Is there a science to skateboarding? Do toilets really flush counterclockwise in Australia? At San Francisco's hands-on science museum, you'll find out things you wish you learned in school. Combining science with art and investigating human perception, the Exploratorium nudges you to question how you perceive the world around you. The setting is thrilling: a 9-acre, glass-walled pier jutting straight into San Francisco Bay, with large outdoor portions you can explore free of charge, 24 hours a day.

Transamerica Pyramid & Redwood Park NOTABLE BUILDING
(Map p308; www.thepyramidcenter.com; 600 Montgomery St; ⏲10am-3pm Mon-Fri; M Embarcadero, B Embarcadero) The defining feature of San Francisco's skyline is this 1972 pyramid, built atop a whaling ship abandoned in the gold rush. A half-acre redwood grove sprouted out front, on the site of Mark Twain's favorite saloon and the newspaper office where Sun Yat-sen drafted his Proclamation of the Republic of China. Although these transplanted redwoods have shallow roots, their intertwined structure helps them reach dizzying heights – Twain himself couldn't have penned a more perfect metaphor for San Francisco.

Chinatown & North Beach

Grant Ave is Chinatown's economic heart, but its soul is **Waverly Place** (Map p308; 🚌1, 30, 🚋California, Powell-Mason, M T), lined with historic clinker-brick buildings and flag-festooned temple balconies. Chinatown's 41 historic **alleyways** (Map p308; btwn Grant Ave, Stockton St, California St & Broadway; 🚌1, 30, 45, 🚋Powell-Hyde, Powell-Mason, California) have seen it all since 1849: gold rushes and revolution, incense and opium, fire and icy receptions. **Chinatown Alleyway Tours** (Map p308; ☎415-984-1478; www.chinatownalleywaytours.org; Portsmouth Sq; adult/student $26/16; ⏲tours 11am Sat; 👪; 🚌1, 8, 10, 12, 30, 41, 45, 🚋California, Powell-Mason, Powell-Hyde) and **Chinatown Heritage Walking Tours** (Map p308; ☎415-986-1822; https://tour.cccsf.us; Chinese Culture Center, Hilton Hotel, 3rd fl, 750 Kearny St; adult $30-40, student $20-30; 👪; 🚌1, 8, 10, 12, 30, 41, 45, 🚋California, Powell-Mason, Powell-Hyde) offer community-supporting, time-traveling strolls through defining moments in American history.

Wild parrots circle over the Italian cafes and bohemian bars of North Beach, serving enough espresso to fuel your own Beat poetry revival.

★Coit Tower PUBLIC ART
(Map p308; ☎415-249-0995; www.sfrecpark.org; Telegraph Hill Blvd; nonresident elevator fee adult/child $9/6, mural tour full/2nd fl only $9/6; ⏲10am-6pm Apr-Oct, to 5pm Nov-Mar; 🚌39) The exclamation mark on San Francisco's skyline is Coit Tower, with 360-degree views of downtown and wraparound 1930s Works Progress Administration (WPA) murals celebrating SF workers. Initially denounced as communist, the murals are now a national landmark. For a parrot's-eye panoramic view of San Francisco 210ft above the city, take the elevator to the tower's open-air platform. Book your docent-led, 30- to 40-minute mural tour online – tour all murals ($9), or just

SAN FRANCISCO IN...

One Day

Grab a leather strap on the Powell-Mason cable car and hold on: you're in for hills and thrills. Hop off at Washington Square Park, where parrots squawk encouragement for your hike up to **Coit Tower** for 1930s murals celebrating SF workers and 360-degree panoramas. Next, catch your prebooked ferry to **Alcatraz**, where D-Block solitary raises goose bumps. Hop the Powell-Mason cable car to North Beach, to take in free-speech landmark **City Lights Books**. Sample North Beach's best pasta at **Cotogna** then toast the wildest night in the west with potent Pisco sours at **Comstock Saloon**.

Two Days

Start your day in the Mission amid mural-covered garage doors lining **Balmy Alley**, then step inside meditative **Mission Dolores**. Break for burritos before hoofing it to the Haight for flashbacks at vintage boutiques and the Summer of Love site: **Golden Gate Park**. Glimpse bay views atop the **de Young Museum**, take a walk on the empirical side at the **California Academy of Sciences** and brave winds on the **Golden Gate Bridge**.

San Francisco & the Bay Area

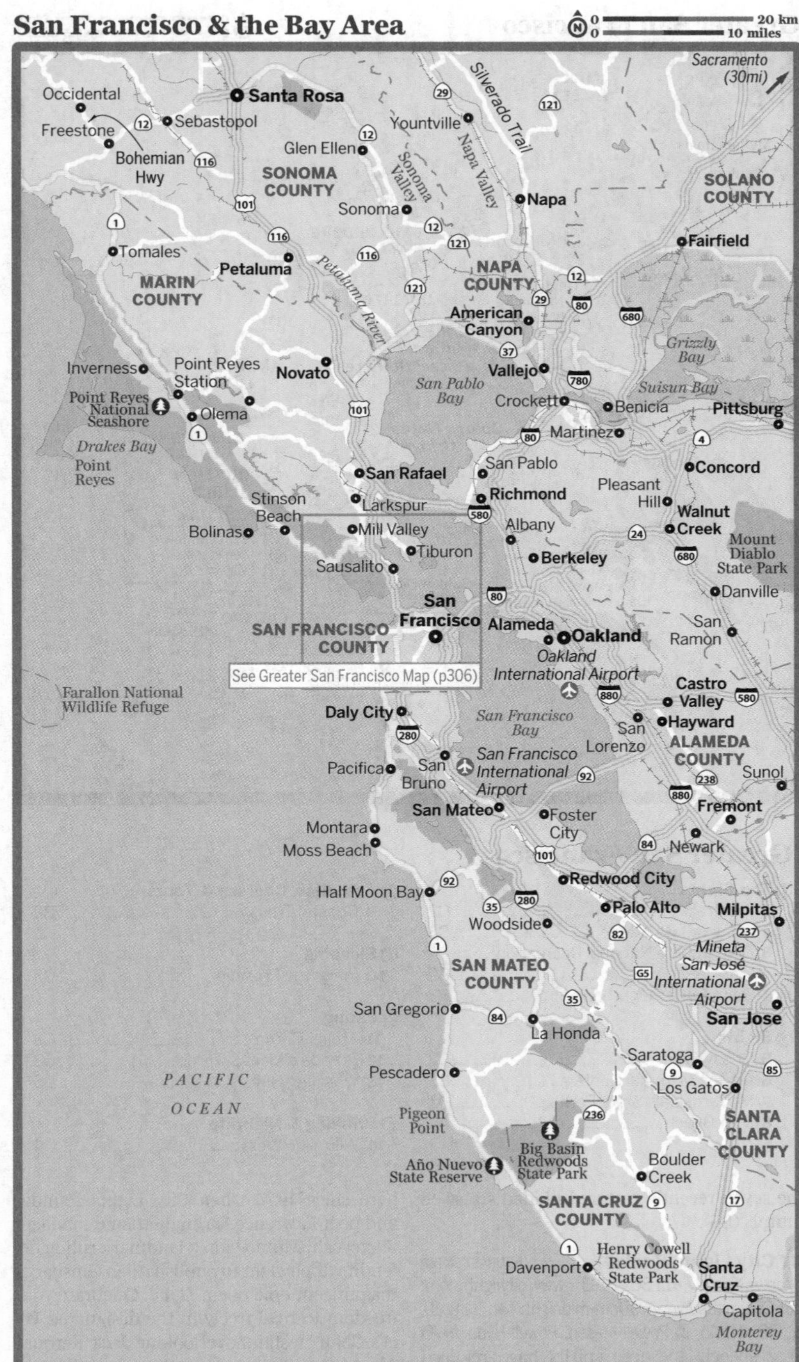

Greater San Francisco

Greater San Francisco

Top Sights
1 Alcatraz C2
2 Golden Gate Bridge C3
3 Golden Gate National Recreation Area B2
4 Point Bonita Lighthouse B3

Sights
5 Crissy Field C3
6 Marine Mammal Center B2
7 Mt Tamalpais State Park A1
8 Muir Beach A2

Activities, Courses & Tours
9 Coastal Trail B2

Sleeping
10 Inn at the Presidio C3

Eating
11 Atelier Crenn C3
12 Brenda's Meat & Three C3
13 Warming Hut C3

Drinking & Nightlife
14 Wild Side West C4

the seven recently restored hidden stairwell murals ($6).

★ **City Lights Books** CULTURAL CENTER
(Map p308; ☎415-362-8193; www.citylights.com; 261 Columbus Ave; ⊙10am-midnight; 🚻; 🚌8, 10, 12, 30, 41, 45, 🚋Powell-Mason, Powell-Hyde, Ⓜ T) Free speech and free spirits have rejoiced here since 1957, when City Lights founder and poet Lawrence Ferlinghetti and manager Shigeyoshi Murao won a landmark ruling defending their right to publish Allen Ginsberg's magnificent epic poem *Howl*. Celebrate your freedom to read freely in the designated Poet's Chair upstairs overlooking Jack Kerouac Alley, load up on zines on the mezzanine and

entertain radical ideas downstairs in the new Pedagogies of Resistance section.

Beat Museum MUSEUM
(Map p308; ☎800-537-6822; www.kerouac.com; 540 Broadway; adult/student $8/5, walking tours $30; ⏱museum 10am-7pm, walking tours 2-4pm Sat; 🚌8, 10, 12, 30, 41, 45, 🚋Powell-Mason, Ⓜ T) The closest you can get to the complete Beat experience without breaking a law. The 1000-plus artifacts in this museum's literary-ephemera collection include the sublime (the banned edition of Ginsberg's *Howl,* with the author's own annotations) and the ridiculous (those Kerouac bobblehead dolls are definite head-shakers). Downstairs, watch Beat-era films in ramshackle theater seats redolent with the odors of literary giants, pets and pot. Upstairs, pay your respects at shrines to individual Beat writers. A seismic retrofit may mean closures; call ahead.

Russian Hill & Nob Hill

You've seen the switchbacks of the 900 block of **Lombard Street** (Map p308; 🚋Powell-Hyde) in a thousand photographs. Incorrectly dubbed 'the world's crookedest street,' it is undeniably scenic, with its red-brick pavement and lovingly tended flowerbeds. While you're here, explore San Francisco's twin downtown hills – hop off a cable car, head to tiki-bar happy hour, hear a cathedral organ recital, or just watch the Bay Bridge lights twinkle.

★**Cable Car Museum** HISTORIC SITE
(Map p308; ☎415-474-1887; www.cablecarmuseum.org; 1201 Mason St; donations appreciated; ⏱10am-6pm Apr-Sep, to 5pm Oct-Mar; 👪; 🚋Powell-Mason, Powell-Hyde) FREE That clamor you hear riding cable cars is the sound of San Francisco's peak technology at work. Gears click and wire-hemp ropes whir as these vintage contraptions are hoisted up and over hills too steep for horses or buses – and you can inspect those cables close-up here, in the city's still-functioning cable-car barn. See three original 1870s cable cars stored here and browse a bonanza of SF memorabilia (actual cable-car bells!) in the museum shop.

★**Diego Rivera Gallery** GALLERY
(Map p308; ☎415-771-7020; www.sfai.edu; 800 Chestnut St; ⏱9am-7pm; 🚌30, 🚋Powell-Mason) FREE Diego Rivera's 1931 *The Making of a Fresco Showing the Building of a City* is a *trompe l'oeil* fresco within a fresco, showing the artist himself pausing to admire his own work and the efforts of workers around him, as they build the modern city of San Francisco. The fresco covers an entire wall of the Diego Rivera Gallery in the **San Francisco Art Institute** (SFAI; Map p308; ☎415-771-7020; www.sfai.edu; 800 Chestnut St; ⏱Walter & McBean Galleries 11am-7pm Tue, to 6pm Wed-Sat, Diego Rivera Gallery 9am-7pm; 🚌30, 🚋Powell-Mason) FREE. For sweeping views of the city Diego admired, head to the terrace cafe for espresso and panoramic bay vistas.

★**Grace Cathedral** CHURCH
(Map p308; ☎415-749-6300; www.gracecathedral.org; 1100 California St; suggested donation adult/child $3/2; ⏱8am-6pm Mon-Sat, to 7pm Sun, services 8:30am, 11am & 6pm Sun; 🚌1, 🚋California) San Francisco's Episcopal cathedral has been rebuilt three times since the gold rush and the current reinforced-concrete Gothic cathedral took 40 years to complete. Spectacular stained-glass windows include a 'Human Endeavor' series dedicated to science, depicting Albert Einstein uplifted in swirling nuclear particles. San Francisco history unfolds on murals covering the 1906 earthquake to the 1945 UN charter signing. People of all faiths wander indoor and outdoor inlaid-stone labyrinths, meant to guide restless souls through three spiritual stages: releasing, receiving and returning.

The Marina, Fisherman's Wharf & Presidio

Since the gold rush, this waterfront has been the point of entry for new arrivals – and it remains a major attraction for sea-lion antics and getaways to and from Alcatraz. To the west, the Marina has chic boutiques in a former cow pasture and organic dining along the waterfront. At the adjoining Presidio, you'll encounter Shakespeare on the loose and public nudity on a former army base.

★**Golden Gate Bridge** BRIDGE
(Map p306; ☎toll information 877-229-8655; www.goldengatebridge.org/visitors; Hwy 101; northbound free, southbound $7-8; 🚌28, all Golden Gate Transit buses) San Franciscans have passionate perspectives on every subject, especially their signature landmark, though everyone agrees that it's a good thing that the Navy didn't get its way over the bridge's design – naval officials preferred a hulking concrete span, painted with caution-yellow stripes, over the soaring art-deco design of architects Gertrude and Irving Murrow and engineer Joseph B Strauss, which, luckily, won the day.

Downtown San Francisco

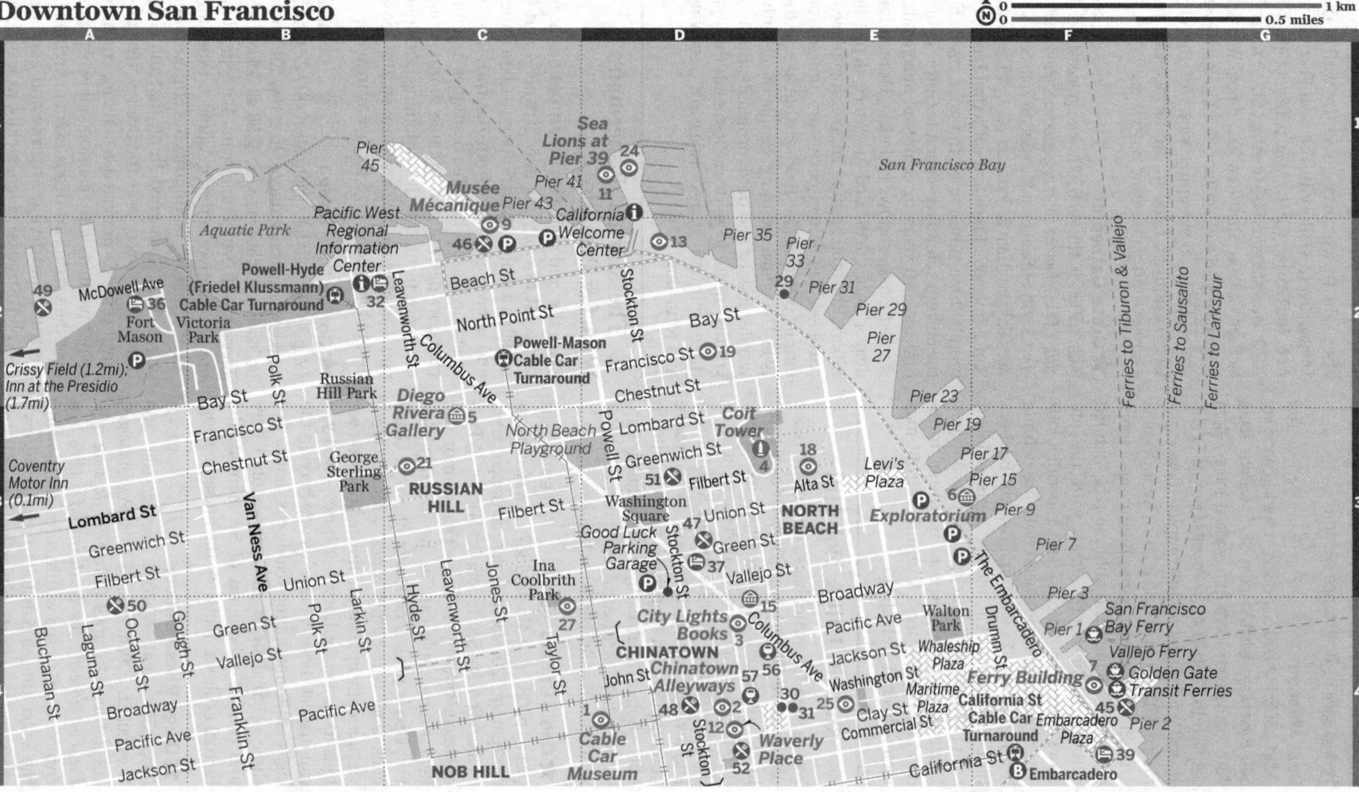

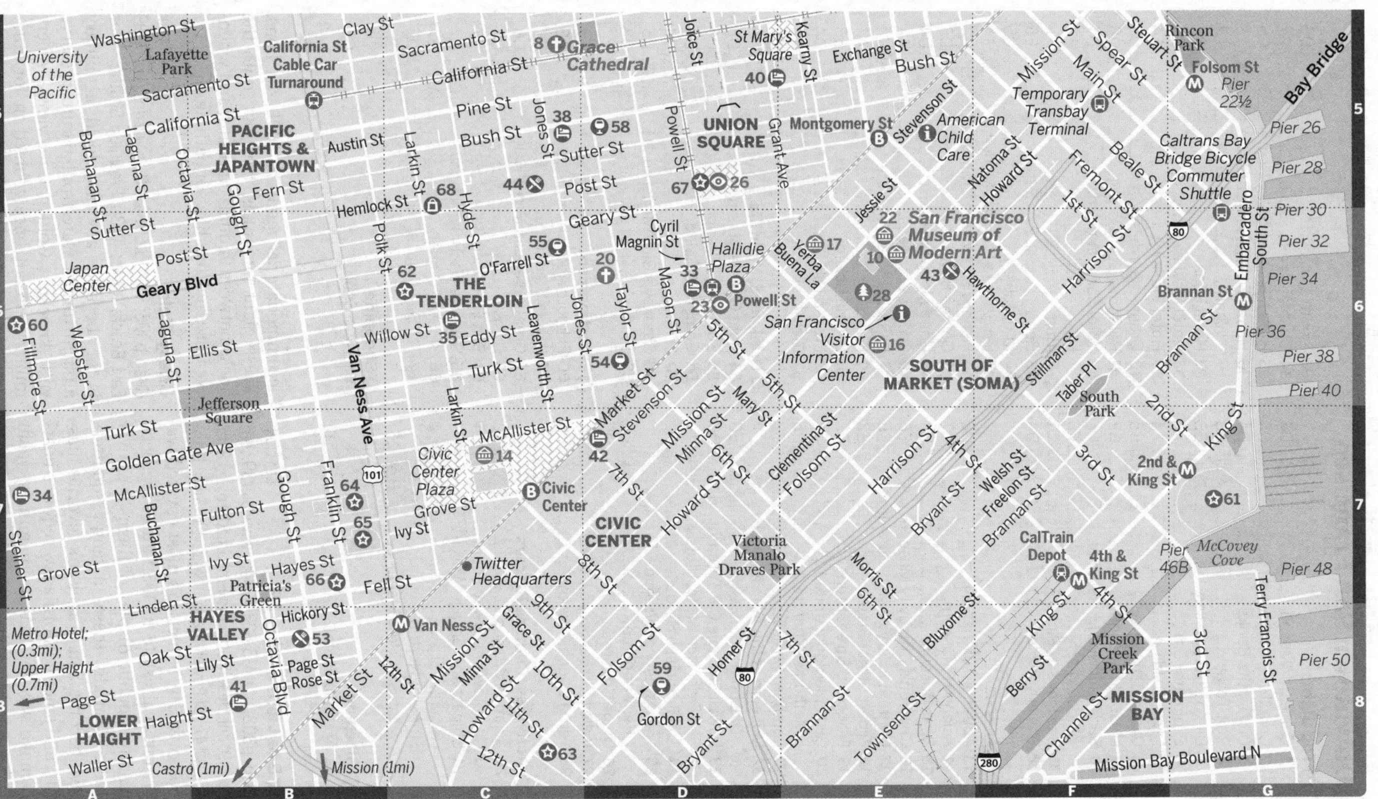

CALIFORNIA SAN FRANCISCO

Downtown San Francisco

Top Sights
1 Cable Car Museum ... D4
2 Chinatown Alleyways ... D4
3 City Lights Books ... D4
4 Coit Tower ... D3
5 Diego Rivera Gallery ... C3
6 Exploratorium ... E3
7 Ferry Building ... F4
8 Grace Cathedral ... C5
9 Musée Mécanique ... C2
10 San Francisco Museum of Modern Art ... E6
11 Sea Lions at Pier 39 ... D1
12 Waverly Place ... D4

Sights
13 Aquarium of the Bay ... D2
14 Asian Art Museum ... C7
15 Beat Museum ... D4
16 Children's Creativity Museum ... E6
17 Contemporary Jewish Museum ... E6
18 Filbert Street Steps ... E3
19 Francisco Street Steps ... D2
20 Glide Memorial United Methodist Church ... D6
21 Lombard Street ... C3
22 Museum of the African Diaspora ... E6
23 Powell St Cable Car Turnaround ... D6
San Francisco Art Institute ... (see 5)
24 San Francisco Carousel ... D1
25 Transamerica Pyramid & Redwood Park ... E4
26 Union Square ... D5
27 Vallejo Street Steps ... C4
28 Yerba Buena Gardens ... E6

Activities, Courses & Tours
29 Alcatraz Cruises ... E2
30 Chinatown Alleyway Tours ... E4
31 Chinatown Heritage Walking Tours ... E4
Emperor Norton's Fantastic Time Machine ... (see 26)

Sleeping
32 Argonaut Hotel ... B2
33 Axiom ... D6
34 Chateau Tivoli ... A7
35 HI San Francisco City Center ... C6
36 HI San Francisco Fisherman's Wharf ... A2
37 Hotel Bohème ... D3
38 Hotel Mayflower ... C5
39 Hotel Vitale ... F4
40 Orchard Garden Hotel ... D5
41 Parsonage ... B8
42 Yotel San Francisco ... D7

Eating
43 Benu ... E6
44 farm:table ... C5
45 Ferry Plaza Farmers Market ... F4
46 Fisherman's Wharf Crab Stands ... C2
47 Golden Boy ... D3
48 Good Mong Kok ... D4
49 Greens ... A2
In Situ ... (see 10)
50 Kaiyo ... A4
51 Liguria Bakery ... D3
52 Mister Jiu's ... D4
53 Rich Table ... B8

Drinking & Nightlife
54 Aunt Charlie's Lounge ... D6
55 Bourbon & Branch ... C6
56 Comstock Saloon ... D4
57 Li Po ... D4
58 Stookey's Club Moderne ... D5
59 Stud ... D8

Entertainment
60 Fillmore Auditorium ... A6
61 Giants Stadium ... G7
62 Great American Music Hall ... C6
63 Oasis ... C8
64 San Francisco Ballet ... B7
65 San Francisco Symphony ... B7
66 SFJAZZ Center ... B7
67 TIX Bay Area ... D5

Shopping
68 Hero Shop ... C5

★ Sea Lions at Pier 39 — SEA LIONS

(Map p308; 415-623-4734; www.pier39.com; Pier 39, cnr Beach St & the Embarcadero; 24hr; ; 47, Powell-Mason, E, F) Sea lions took over San Francisco's most coveted waterfront real estate in 1989 and have been making a public display of themselves ever since. Naturally these unkempt squatters have become San Francisco's favorite mascots, and since California law requires boats to make way for marine mammals, yacht owners have to relinquish valuable slips to accommodate as many as 1000 sea lions. These giant mammals 'haul out' onto the docks between January and July, and whenever else they feel like sunbathing.

Crissy Field — PARK

(Map p306; 415-561-4700; www.nps.gov; 1199 East Beach; P; 30, PresidiGo Shuttle) War is for the birds at Crissy Field, a military airstrip turned waterfront nature preserve with knockout Golden Gate views. Where military aircraft once zoomed in for landings, bird-watchers now huddle in the silent rushes of a reclaimed tidal marsh. Joggers pound beachside trails and the only security alerts are raised by puppies suspiciously sniffing surfers. On foggy days, stop by the certified-green **Warming Hut** (Map p306; ☎415-561-3042; www.parksconservancy.org/visit/eat/warming-hut.html; 983 Marine Dr; items $4-9; ⏲9am-5pm; P ♿; 🚌PresidiGo shuttle) to browse regional-nature books and warm up with fair-trade coffee.

The Mission & the Castro

The best way to enjoy the Mission is with a book in one hand and a burrito in the other, amid murals, sunshine and the usual crowd of filmmakers, techies, grocers, skaters and novelists. Calle 24 (24th St) is SF's designated Latino Cultural District, and the Mission is also a magnet for Southeast Asian Americans, lesbians and dandies. In the Castro, rainbow flags wave their welcome to all in the world's premier LGBTQ+ culture destination.

★Clarion Alley PUBLIC ART

(Map p312; https://clarionalleymuralproject.org; btwn 17th & 18th Sts; 🚌14, 22, 33, B16th St Mission, M16th St Mission) In this outstanding open-air street-art showcase, you'll spot artists touching up pieces and making new ones, with the full consent of neighbors and Clarion Alley Collective's curators. Only a few pieces survive for years, such as Megan Wilson's daisy-covered *Tax the Rich* or Jet Martinez' glimpse of Clarion Alley inside a forest spirit. Incontinent art critics often take over the alley's eastern end – pee-eew! – so topical murals usually go up on the western end.

★Women's Building NOTABLE BUILDING

(Map p312; ☎415-431-1180; www.womensbuilding.org; 3543 18th St; 🚌14, 22, 33, 49, B16th St Mission, MJ) A renowned and beloved Mission landmark since 1979, the nation's first women-owned-and-operated community center is festooned with one of the neighborhood's most awe-inspiring murals. The *Maestrapeace* mural was painted in 1994 and depicts hugely influential women, including Nobel Prize–winner Rigoberta Menchú, poet Audre Lorde, artist Georgia O'Keeffe and former US Surgeon General Dr Joycelyn Elders.

★Balmy Alley PUBLIC ART

(Map p312; ☎415-285-2287; www.precitaeyes.org; btwn 24th & 25th Sts; 🚌10, 12, 14, 27, 48, B24th St Mission) Inspired by Diego Rivera's 1930s San Francisco murals and provoked by US foreign policy in Latin America, 1970s Mission *muralistas* (muralists) led by Mia Gonzalez set out to transform the political landscape one mural at a time. The earliest works by Mujeres Muralistas ('Women Muralists') and Placa ('Mark-making') created a united artistic front. Today, murals span three decades, from a memorial for El Salvador activist Archbishop Óscar Romero to a homage to female artists, including Frida Kahlo and Georgia O'Keeffe.

Mission Dolores CHURCH

(Misión San Francisco de Asís; Map p312; ☎415-621-8203; www.missiondolores.org; 3321 16th St; adult/child $7/5; ⏲9am-4:30pm May-Oct, to 4pm Nov-Apr; 🚌22, 33, B16th St Mission, MJ) The city's oldest building and its namesake, whitewashed adobe Misión San Francisco de Asís was founded in 1776 and rebuilt from 1782. Today the modest adobe structure is overshadowed by the ornate adjoining 1913 **basilica**, built after the 1876 brick Gothic cathedral collapsed in the 1906 earthquake. It now features stained-glass windows depicting California's 21 missions and, true to Mission Dolores' name, seven panels depict the Seven Sorrows of Mary.

The Haight

Hippie idealism lives in the Haight, with street musicians, anarchist comic books and psychedelic murals galore. Browse local designs and go gourmet in Hayes Valley, where Zen monks and jazz legends drift down the sidewalks.

★Haight Street STREET

(Map p314; btwn Central & Stanyan Sts; 🚌7, 22, 33, 43, MN) Was it the fall of 1966 or the winter of '67? As the Haight saying goes, if you can remember the Summer of Love, you probably weren't here. The fog was laced with pot, sandalwood incense and burning military draft cards, entire days were spent contemplating trippy Grateful Dead posters, and the corner of **Haight and Ashbury Streets** (Map p314; 🚌6, 7, 33, 37, 43) became the turning point for an entire generation. The Haight's counterculture kids called themselves freaks and flower children; *San Francisco Chronicle* columnist Herb Caen dubbed them 'hippies.'

Golden Gate & Around

Hard-core surfers and gourmet adventurers meet in the foggy Avenues around Golden Gate Park. This is one totally chill global

village, featuring bluegrass and Korean BBQ, disc golf and tiki cocktails, French pastries and cult-movie matinees. Beyond the park, time seems to slow down, with the tranquil, mostly residential avenues stretching out toward Ocean Beach.

★ **Golden Gate Park** PARK

(Map p314; https://goldengatepark.com; btwn Stanyan St & Great Hwy; P 👪; 🚌5, 7, 18, 21, 28, 29, 33, 44, Ⓜ N) FREE From bonsai and buffalo to redwoods and protests, and from flowers, Frisbees and free music to free spirits, Golden Gate Park seems to contain just about everything San Franciscans love about their city. You could wander it for a week and still not see it all, with attractions including the **de Young Museum** (Map p314; ☎415-750-3600; http://deyoung.famsf.org; 50 Hagiwara Tea Garden Dr; adult/child $15/free, 1st Tue of month free; ⏲9:30am-5:15pm Tue-Sun; 🚌5, 7, 44, Ⓜ N), **California Academy of Sciences** (Map p314; ☎415-379-8000; www.calacademy.org; 55 Music Concourse Dr; adult/student/child $35.95/30.95/25.95; ⏲9:30am-5pm Mon-Sat, from 11am Sun; P 👪; 🚌5, 6, 7, 21, 31, 33, 44, Ⓜ N) , **San Francisco Botanical Garden** (Strybing Arboretum; Map p314; ☎415-661-1316; www.sfbg.org; 1199 9th Ave; adult/child $9/2, before 9am daily & 2nd Tue of month free; ⏲7:30am-5pm, extended hours in summer & spring, last entry 1hr before closing, bookstore 10am-4pm; 🚌6, 7, 44, Ⓜ N) , **Japanese Tea Garden** (Map p314; ☎415-752-1171; www.japaneseteagardensf.com; 75 Hagiwara Tea Garden Dr; adult/child $8/2, before 10am Mon, Wed & Fri free; ⏲9am-6pm Mar-Oct, to 4:45pm Nov-Feb; P; 🚌5, 7, 44, Ⓜ N), **Conservatory of Flowers** (Map p314; ☎415-831-2090; www.conservatoryofflowers.org; 100 John F Kennedy Dr; adult/student/child $9/6/3, 1st Tue of month free; ⏲10am-6pm Tue-Sun; 🚌5, 7, 21, 33, Ⓜ N) and **Stow Lake** (Map p314; www.sfrecpark.org; ⏲5am-midnight; 🚌7, 44, Ⓜ N).

The Mission & The Castro

Top Sights
1 Balmy Alley ... D3
2 Clarion Alley ... C1
3 Dolores Park ... B2
4 Rainbow Honor Walk ... A2
5 Women's Building ... C2

Sights
6 GLBT History Museum ... A2
7 Mission Dolores ... B1

Activities, Courses & Tours
8 Precita Eyes Mission Mural Tours ... D3

Sleeping
9 Parker Guest House ... B2

Eating
10 Al's Place ... C4
11 Californios ... C3
12 Frances ... A1
13 La Palma Mexicatessen ... D3

Drinking & Nightlife
14 20 Spot ... C2
15 El Rio ... C4
16 Jolene's ... D1
17 Trick Dog ... D2

Entertainment
18 Castro Theatre ... A2

Shopping
19 Adobe Books & Backroom Gallery ... D3
20 Community Thrift ... C2
21 Gravel & Gold ... C2

Tours

★Precita Eyes Mission Mural Tours WALKING
(Map p312; ☎415-285-2287; www.precitaeyes.org; 2981 24th St; adult/child $20/3; 12, 14, 48, 49, B 24th St Mission) Muralists lead weekend walking tours covering 60 to 70 Mission murals within a six- to 10-block radius of mural-bedecked Balmy Alley (p311). Tours last from one hour to two hours and 15 minutes (for the more in-depth, private Classic Mural Walk). Proceeds fund mural upkeep and overheads at this community arts nonprofit.

Public Library City Guides TOURS
(☎415-557-4266; www.sfcityguides.org) FREE Volunteer local historians lead nonprofit tours organized by neighborhood and theme: Victorian San Francisco, Castro Tales, Alfred Hitchcock's San Francisco, Gold Rush City, Deco Downtown, Secrets of Fisherman's Wharf, Russian Hill Stairways and more. Book ahead for the popular Diego Rivera Mural tour inside the Stock Exchange Luncheon Club. Tips are welcome.

Emperor Norton's Fantastic Time Machine WALKING
(Map p308; ☎415-548-1710; www.sftimemachine.com; $30; 11am Thu & Sat, waterfront tour 11am Sun; 30, 38, B Powell St, M Powell St, Powell-Mason, Powell-Hyde) Huzzah, San Francisco invented time-travel contraptions! They're called shoes, and you wear them to follow the self-appointed Emperor Norton (aka historian Joseph Amster) across 2 miles of the most dastardly, scheming, uplifting and urban-legendary terrain on Earth…or at least west of Berkeley. Sunday waterfront tours depart from the Ferry Building; all others depart from Union Sq's Dewey Monument.

Sleeping

San Francisco hotel rates are among the world's highest. Plan ahead – well ahead – and grab bargains when you see them. If you have the choice, San Francisco's boutique properties beat chains for a sense of place – but take what you can get at a price you can afford.

Downtown, Civic Center & SoMa

★HI San Francisco City Center HOSTEL $
(Map p308; ☎415-474-5721; www.sfhostels.org; 685 Ellis St; dm $33-70, r $90-165; @; 19, 38, 47, 49) The seven-story, 1920s Atherton Hotel was remodeled in 2001 into a much-better-than-average hostel, with private baths in all rooms, including dorms. And it scores bonus points for ecofriendliness: the place is powered mainly by solar panels, and shower heads change color based on the length of a shower.

★Yotel San Francisco HOTEL $
(Map p308; ☎415-829-0000; www.yotel.com/en/hotels/yotel-san-francisco; 1095 Market St; d $149-209; ; 6, 7, 9, 21, B Civic Center, M Civic Center) Newly situated within the long-standing Grant building, this chic downtown hotel is a West Coast first for parent company Yotel, a chain of compact, technology-forward luxury stays. Design choices conserve time and space at every turn, from

The Richmond, The Haight & Golden Gate Park

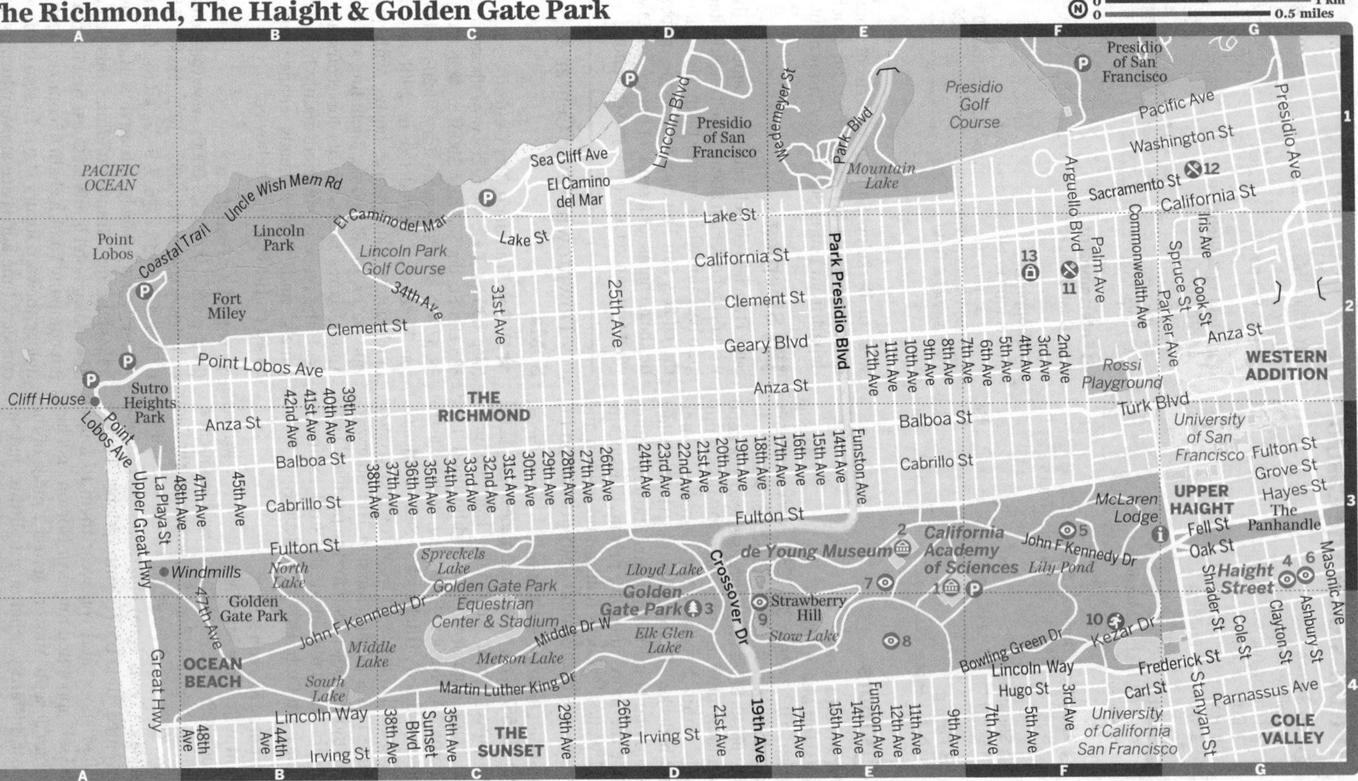

The Richmond, The Haight & Golden Gate Park

the self-check-in kiosks to the adjustable 'smartbeds' (which morph into couches) to the playful 'sky cabins,' cozy lofted sleeping quarters with extralong mattresses and large flat-screen TVs.

★Axiom BOUTIQUE HOTEL $$
(Map p308; ☎415-392-9466; www.axiomhotel.com; 28 Cyril Magnin St; d $189-342; @📶🐾; 🚋Powell-Mason, Powell-Hyde, B Powell, M Powell) Of all the downtown SF hotels aiming for high-tech appeal, this one gets it right. The lobby is razzle-dazzle LED, marble and riveted steel, but the games room looks like a start-up HQ, with arcade games and foosball tables. Guest rooms have low-slung, gray-flannel couches, king platform beds, dedicated routers for high-speed wireless streaming to Apple/Google/Samsung devices, and Bluetooth-enabled everything.

Hotel Vitale BOUTIQUE HOTEL $$$
(Map p308; ☎415-278-3700; www.hotelvitale.com; 8 Mission St; r $385-675; ❄@📶🐾; M Embarcadero, B Embarcadero) When your love interest or executive recruiter books you into the waterfront Vitale, you know it's serious. The office-tower exterior disguises a snazzy hotel with sleek, up-to-the-minute luxuries. Beds are dressed with silky-soft 450-thread-count sheets, and there's an excellent on-site spa with two rooftop hot tubs. Rooms facing the bay offer spectacular Bay Bridge views, and Ferry Building dining awaits across the street.

Hotel Mayflower HISTORIC HOTEL $
(Map p308; ☎415-673-7010; www.sfmayflowerhotel.com; 975 Bush St; d $130-190; P🚭❄📶; 🚌2, 3, 27) Location, comfort and character at half the cost of places down the block. Built in 1926, Hotel Mayflower has a Spanish Mission–style cloister lobby and vintage cage elevator straight out of a Hitchcock movie. Guest rooms are snug and simple but ship-shape, with sepia-toned San Francisco murals and wrought iron bed frames. Rates include muffin breakfasts; parking is a bargain at $20.

North Beach & Chinatown

★Hotel Bohème BOUTIQUE HOTEL $$
(Map p308; ☎415-433-9111; www.hotelboheme.com; 444 Columbus Ave; r $195-295; 🚭@📶; 🚌10, 12, 30, 41, 45, M T) Eclectic, historic and unabashedly romantic, this quintessential North Beach boutique hotel has jazz-era color schemes, wrought-iron beds, paper-umbrella lamps, Beat poetry and artwork on the walls. The vintage rooms are smallish, some face noisy Columbus Ave (quieter rooms are in back) and bathrooms are teensy, but novels beg to be written here – especially after bar crawls. No elevator or parking lot.

Orchard Garden Hotel BOUTIQUE HOTEL $$$
(Map p308; ☎415-393-9917; www.theorchardgardenhotel.com; 466 Bush St; r $278-332; P🚭❄@📶; 🚌2, 3, 30, 45, B Montgomery) 🍃 San Francisco's original LEED-certified, all-green-practices hotel uses sustainably grown wood, chemical-free cleaning products and recycled fabrics in its soothingly quiet rooms. Don't think you'll be trading comfort for conscience: rooms have unexpectedly luxe touches, like high-end down pillows, Egyptian-cotton sheets and organic bath products. Toast sunsets with a cocktail on the rooftop terrace. Book directly for deals, free breakfast and parking.

The Marina, Fisherman's Wharf & Presidio

★HI San Francisco Fisherman's Wharf HOSTEL $
(Map p308; ☎415-771-7277; www.hiusa.org; Fort Mason, Bldg 240; dm $40-64, r $116-160; P@📶; 🚌28, 30, 47, 49) Trading downtown convenience for a parklike setting with

Alcatraz

A HALF-DAY TOUR

Book a ferry from Pier 33 and ride 1.5 miles across the bay to explore America's most notorious former prison. The trip itself is worth the money, providing stunning views of the city skyline. Once you've landed at the ❶ **Ferry Dock & Pier**, you begin the 580yd walk to the top of the island and prison; if you need assistance to reach the top, there's a twice-hourly tram.

As you climb toward the ❷ **Guardhouse**, notice the island's steep slope; before it was a prison, Alcatraz was a fort. In the 1850s, the military quarried the rocky shores into near-vertical cliffs. Ships could then only dock at a single port, separated from the main buildings by a sally port (a drawbridge and moat in what became the guardhouse). Inside, peer through floor grates to see Alcatraz's original prison.

Volunteers tend the brilliant ❸ **Officers' Row Gardens**, an orderly counterpoint to the overgrown rose bushes surrounding the burned-out shell of the ❹ **Warden's House**. At the top of the hill, by the front door of the ❺ **Main Cellhouse**, beautiful shots unfurl all around, including a view of the ❻ **Golden Gate Bridge**. Above the main door of the administration building, notice the ❼ **historic signs & graffiti**, before you step inside the dank, cold prison to find the ❽ **Frank Morris cell**, former home to Alcatraz's most notorious jail-breaker.

TOP TIPS

➡ Book at least one month prior for self-guided daytime visits, longer for ranger-led night tours. For info on garden tours, see www.alcatrazgardens.org.

➡ Be prepared to hike; a steep path ascends from the ferry landing to the cell block. Most people spend two to three hours on the island. You need only reserve for the outbound ferry; take any ferry back.

➡ There's no food (just water) but you can bring your own; picnicking is allowed at the ferry dock only. Dress in layers as weather changes fast and it's usually windy.

Historic Signs & Graffiti
During their 1969–71 occupation, Native Americans graffitied the water tower: 'Home of the Free Indian Land.' Above the cellhouse door, examine the eagle-and-flag crest to see how the red-and-white stripes were changed to spell 'Free.'

Warden's House
Fires destroyed the warden's house and other structures during the Indian Occupation. The government blamed the Native Americans; the Native Americans blamed agents provocateurs acting on behalf of the Nixon administration to undermine public sympathy.

Officers' Row Gardens
In the 19th century soldiers imported topsoil to beautify the island with gardens. Well-trusted prisoners later gardened – Elliott Michener said it kept him sane. Historians, ornithologists and archaeologists choose today's plants.

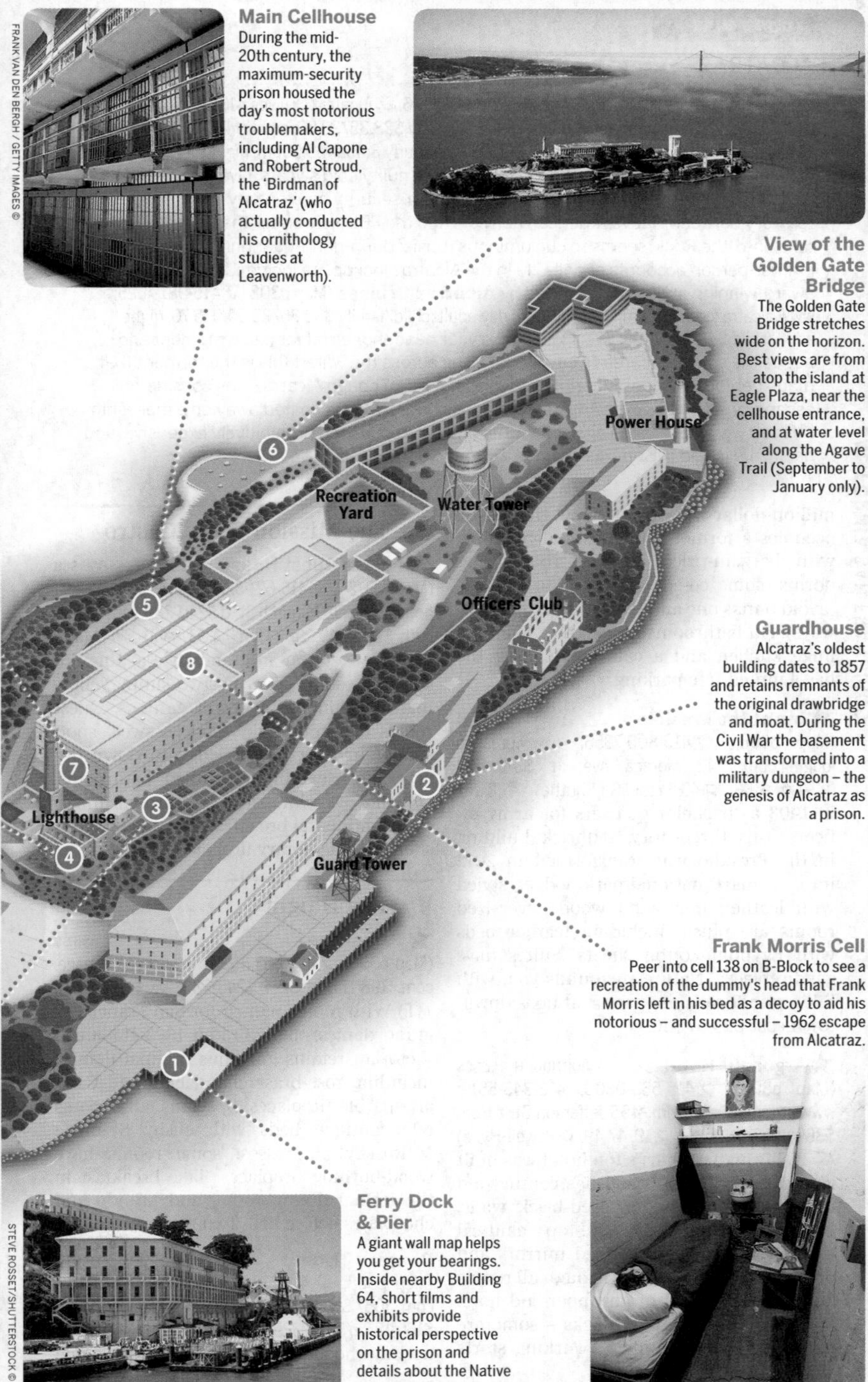

Main Cellhouse
During the mid-20th century, the maximum-security prison housed the day's most notorious troublemakers, including Al Capone and Robert Stroud, the 'Birdman of Alcatraz' (who actually conducted his ornithology studies at Leavenworth).
FRANK VAN DEN BERGH / GETTY IMAGES ©
FRANCKREPORTER/GETTY IMAGES ©
View of the Golden Gate Bridge
The Golden Gate Bridge stretches wide on the horizon. Best views are from atop the island at Eagle Plaza, near the cellhouse entrance, and at water level along the Agave Trail (September to January only).
Power House
6
Recreation Yard
Water Tower
5
Officers' Club
8
Guardhouse
Alcatraz's oldest building dates to 1857 and retains remnants of the original drawbridge and moat. During the Civil War the basement was transformed into a military dungeon – the genesis of Alcatraz as a prison.
7
2
3
Lighthouse
4
Guard Tower
Frank Morris Cell
Peer into cell 138 on B-Block to see a recreation of the dummy's head that Frank Morris left in his bed as a decoy to aid his notorious – and successful – 1962 escape from Alcatraz.
1
Ferry Dock & Pier
A giant wall map helps you get your bearings. Inside nearby Building 64, short films and exhibits provide historical perspective on the prison and details about the Native American Occupation.
STEVE ROSSET/SHUTTERSTOCK ©
OSCITY/SHUTTERSTOCK ©

DON'T MISS

ALCATRAZ

For over 150 years, the name **Alcatraz** (Map p306; Alcatraz Cruises 415-981-7625; www.alcatrazcruises.com; tours adult/child 5-11yr day $38.35/23.50, night $45.50/27.05; call center 8am-7pm, ferries depart Pier 33 half-hourly 8:45am-3:50pm, night tours 5:55pm & 6:30pm;) has given the innocent chills and the guilty cold sweats. Over the decades, it's been a military prison, a forbidding maximum-security penitentiary and disputed territory between Native American activists and the FBI. No wonder that first step you take onto 'the Rock' seems to cue ominous music: dunh-dunh-dunnnnh!

First-person accounts of daily life in the Alcatraz lockup are included on the award-winning audio tour provided by **Alcatraz Cruises** (Map p308; 415-981-7625; www.alcatrazcruises.com; Pier 33; tours day adult/child/family $38.35/23.50/115.70, night adult/child $45.50/27.05; M E, F). But take your headphones off for just a moment and notice the sound of carefree city life traveling across the water: this is the torment that made perilous escapes into riptides worth the risk. Though Alcatraz was considered escape-proof, in 1962 the Anglin brothers and Frank Morris floated away on a makeshift raft and were never seen again. Security and upkeep proved prohibitively expensive, and finally the island prison was abandoned to the birds in 1963.

million-dollar waterfront views, this hostel occupies a former army-hospital building, with bargain-priced private rooms and dorms (some co-ed) with four to 22 beds (avoid bunks one and two – they're by doorways). All bathrooms are shared. There's a huge kitchen and a cafe overlooking the bay. Limited free parking.

★ **Inn at the Presidio** HOTEL $$
(Map p306; 415-800-7356; www.presidiolodging.com; 42 Moraga Ave; r $310-495; P @ ; 43, PresidiGo Shuttle) Built in 1903 as bachelor quarters for army officers, this three-story, redbrick building in the Presidio was transformed in 2012 into a smart national-park lodge, styled with leather, linen and wood. Oversized rooms are plush, including feather beds with Egyptian-cotton sheets. Suites have gas fireplaces. Nature surrounds you, with hiking trailheads out back, but taxis downtown cost $25 to $30.

★ **Argonaut Hotel** BOUTIQUE HOTEL $$$
(Map p308; 415-563-0800, 415-345-5519; www.argonauthotel.com; 495 Jefferson St; r from $389; P ; 19, 47, 49, Powell-Hyde) Fisherman's Wharf's top hotel was built as a cannery in 1908 and has century-old wooden beams and exposed-brick walls. Rooms sport an over-the-top nautical theme, with porthole-shaped mirrors and plush, deep-blue carpets. Though all rooms have the amenities of an upper-end hotel – ultracomfy beds, iPod docks – some are tiny with limited sunlight. Parking starts at $65.

The Mission & the Castro

★ **Parker Guest House** B&B $$$
(Map p312; 415-621-3222; www.parkerguesthouse.com; 520 Church St; d $249-289, with shared bath $209-249; P @ ; 33, M J) Make your gay getaway in grand style at this Edwardian estate, covering two sunny yellow mansions linked by secret gardens. Guest rooms hit the swanky modern sweet spot: stately, inviting beds piled with down duvets and gleaming retro-tiled bathrooms. Unwind over wine in the sunroom, linger over continental breakfasts, or get cozy with sherry by the library fireplace.

The Haight

★ **Parsonage** B&B $$
(Map p308; 415-863-3699; www.theparsonage.com; 198 Haight St; r $240-280; @ ; 6, 71, M F) With rooms named for San Francisco's grand dames, this 23-room 1883 Italianate Victorian retains gorgeous original details, including rose-brass chandeliers and Carrara-marble fireplaces. Spacious, airy rooms offer antique beds with cushy SF-made McRoskey mattresses; some rooms have wood-burning fireplaces. Take breakfast in the formal dining room, and brandy and chocolates before bed. Two-night minimum.

Chateau Tivoli B&B $$
(Map p308; 415-776-5462; www.chateautivoli.com; 1057 Steiner St; d $205-215, with shared bath $160-185, q $220-325; ; 5, 22) The source of neighborhood gossip since 1892, this gilded

and turreted mansion graciously hosted Isadora Duncan, Mark Twain and (rumor has it) the ghost of a Victorian opera diva – and now you too can be Chateau Tivoli's guest. Nine antique-filled rooms and suites set the scene for romance; most have claw-foot bathtubs, though two share a bathroom. No elevator or TVs.

Eating

Downtown, Civic Center & SoMa

Ferry Plaza Farmers Market MARKET **$**

(Map p308; 415-291-3276; www.cuesa.org; cnr Market St & the Embarcadero; street food $3-12; 10am-2pm Tue & Thu, from 8am Sat; ; 2, 6, 9, 14, 21, 31, M Embarcadero, B Embarcadero) The pride and joy of SF foodies, the Ferry Building market showcases more than 100 prime purveyors of California-grown organic produce, pasture-raised meats and gourmet prepared foods at accessible prices. On Saturdays, join top chefs early for prime browsing, and stay for eclectic bayside picnics of Namu Korean tacos, RoliRoti porchetta, Dirty Girl tomatoes, Nicasio cheese samples and Frog Hollow fruit turnovers.

farm:table AMERICAN **$**

(Map p308; 415-300-5652; www.farmtablesf.com; 754 Post St; dishes $6-9; 7:15am-1pm Tue-Fri, 8am-2pm Sat & Sun; ; 2, 3, 27, 38) A ray of sunshine in the concrete heart of the city, this plucky little storefront showcases seasonal California organics in just-baked breakfasts and farmstead-fresh lunches. Daily specials include a rotation of homemade cereals, savory tarts and game-changing toast – mmmm, ginger peach and mascarpone on whole-wheat sourdough! Tiny space, but immaculate kitchen and great coffee.

★**In Situ** CALIFORNIAN, INTERNATIONAL **$$**

(Map p308; http://insitu.sfmoma.org; 151 3rd St, SFMOMA; mains $20-50; 11am-3:30pm Thu-Mon, 5-9pm Thu-Sat, 11am-3:30pm & 5-8pm Sun; 5, 6, 7, 14, 19, 21, 31, 38, B Montgomery, M Montgomery) The landmark gallery of modern cuisine attached to SFMOMA also showcases avant-garde masterpieces – but these ones you'll lick clean. Chef Corey Lee collaborates with more than 100 star chefs worldwide, scrupulously re-creating their signature dishes with California-grown ingredients so that you can enjoy Nathan Myhrvold's caramelized carrot soup, Tim Raue's wasabi lobster and Albert Adrià's Jasper Hill Farm cheesecake in one unforgettable sitting.

★**Benu** CALIFORNIAN, FUSION **$$$**

(Map p308; 415-685-4860; www.benusf.com; 22 Hawthorne St; tasting menu $310; 5:30-8:30pm Tue-Thu, to 9pm Fri & Sat; 10, 12, 14, 30, 45) SF has pioneered Asian fusion cuisine for 150 years, but the pan-Pacific innovation chef-owner Corey Lee brings to the plate is gasp-inducing: foie-gras soup dumplings – what?! Dungeness crab and truffle custard pack such outsize flavor into Lee's faux-shark's-fin soup, you'll swear Jaws is in there. A Benu dinner is an investment, but don't miss star sommelier Yoon Ha's ingenious pairings ($210). There's a 20% service charge.

North Beach & Chinatown

★**Liguria Bakery** BAKERY **$**

(Map p308; 415-421-3786; 1700 Stockton St; focaccia $4-6; 8am-2pm Tue-Fri, 7am-2pm Sat, 7am-noon Sun; ; 8, 30, 39, 41, 45, Powell-Mason, M T) Bleary-eyed art students and Italian grandmothers line up by 8am for cinnamon-raisin focaccia hot out of the 100-year-old oven, leaving 9am dawdlers a choice of tomato or classic rosemary and garlic. Latecomers, beware: when they run out, they close. Take yours in waxed paper or boxed for picnics – just don't kid yourself that you're going to save some for later. Cash only.

★**Golden Boy** PIZZA **$**

(Map p308; 415-982-9738; www.goldenboypizza.com; 542 Green St; slices $3.25-4.25; 11:30am-midnight Sun-Thu, to 2am Fri & Sat; 8, 30, 39, 41, 45, Powell-Mason) 'If you don't see it don't ask 4 it' reads the menu – Golden Boy has kept punks in line since 1978, serving Genovese focaccia-crust pizza that's chewy, crunchy and hot from the oven. You'll have whatever second-generation Sodini family *pizzaioli* (pizza-makers) are making and like it – especially pesto and clam-and-garlic. Grab square slices and draft beer at the bomb-shelter counter.

★**Mister Jiu's** CHINESE, CALIFORNIAN **$$**

(Map p308; 415-857-9688; http://misterjius.com; 28 Waverly Pl; mains $14-45; 5:30-10:30pm Tue-Sat; 30, California, M T) Success has been celebrated in this historic Chinatown banquet hall since the 1880s – but today, scoring a table at Mister Jiu's is reason enough for celebration. Build memorable banquets from chef Brandon Jew's ingenious Chinese/Californian signatures: quail

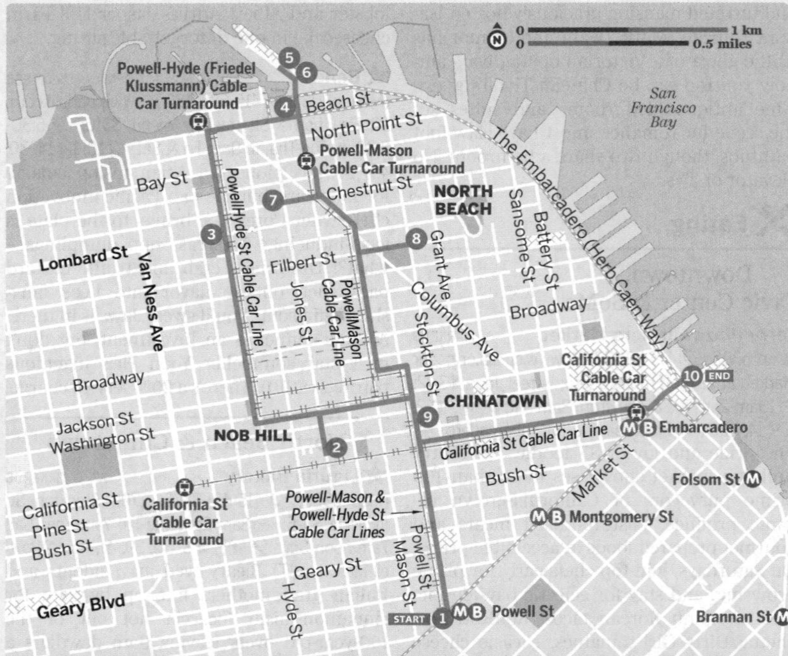

City Walk
SF by Cable Car

START POWELL ST CABLE CAR TURNAROUND
END FERRY BUILDING
LENGTH 2 MILES; TWO HOURS

The ultimate SF joyride is in a cable car. At the 1 **Powell St Cable Car Turnaround** (p303), you'll see operators turn the car atop a revolving wooden platform, and a vintage kiosk where you can buy an all-day Muni Passport for $23. Board the red-signed Powell-Hyde cable car and begin your 338ft ascent of Nob Hill.

Nineteenth-century city planners were sceptical of inventor Andrew Hallidie's 'wire-rope railway' – but after more than a century of near-continuous operation, his wire-and-hemp cables have seldom broken. Hallidie's cable cars even survived the 1906 earthquake and fire that destroyed 'Snob Hill' mansions, returning the faithful to the rebuilt 2 **Grace Cathedral** (p307) – hop off to say hello to SF's gentle patron St Francis.

Back on the Powell-Hyde car, enjoy Bay views as you careen past crooked, flower-lined 3 **Lombard Street** (p307) toward 4 **Fisherman's Wharf**. The waterfront terminus is named for 'Cable Car Lady' Friedel Klussmann, who saved cable cars from mayoral modernization plans in 1947.

At the wharf, emerge from the submarine 5 **USS Pampanito** to glimpse SF with the joyous relief of a WWII sailor on shore leave. Witness Western saloon brawls in vintage arcade games at the 6 **Musée Mécanique** (p325) before hitching the Powell-Mason cable car to North Beach.

Hop off to see Diego Rivera's 1934 cityscape at the 7 **San Francisco Art Institute** (p307), or follow your rumbling stomach directly to 8 **Liguria Bakery** (p319). Stroll through North Beach and Chinatown alleyways, or take the Powell-Mason line to time-travel through the 9 **Chinese Historical Society of America**. Nearby, catch a ride on the city's oldest line: the California St cable car. The terminus is near the 10 **Ferry Building** (p303), where champagne-and-oyster happy hour awaits.

and Mission-fig sticky rice, hot and sour Dungeness crab soup, Wagyu sirloin and tuna heart fried rice. Don't skip dessert – pastry chef Melissa Chou's salted plum sesame balls are flavor bombs.

★Good Mong Kok DIM SUM $

(Map p308; ☎415-397-2688; 1039 Stockton St; dumpling orders $2-5; ⏰7am-6pm; 🚌30, 45, 🚋Powell-Mason, California, Ⓜ T) Ask Chinatown neighbors about their go-to dim sum and the answer is either grandma's or Good Mong Kok. Lines snake out the door of this counter bakery for dumplings whisked from vast steamers into takeout containers to enjoy in Portsmouth Sq. The menu changes by the minute/hour, but expect classic pork *siu mai,* shrimp *har gow* and BBQ pork buns; BYO chili sauce and black vinegar.

The Marina, Fisherman's Wharf & Presidio

Fisherman's Wharf Crab Stands SEAFOOD $

(Map p308; Taylor St; mains $5-22; Ⓜ F) Men and women in rolled-up sleeves stir steaming cauldrons of Dungeness crab at several side-by-side takeout crab stands at the foot of Taylor St, the epicenter of Fisherman's Wharf. Crab season typically runs winter through spring, but you'll find shrimp and other seafood year-round.

★Kaiyo FUSION $$

(Map p308; ☎415-525-4804; https://kaiyosf.com; 1838 Union St; small plates $12-28, share plates $19-28; ⏰5-10pm Tue, Wed & Sun, to 11pm Thu & Sat, 10:30am-3pm Sat & Sun; 🚌41, 45) For a deliciously deep dive into the cuisine of the Japanese-Peruvian diaspora, head to Cow Hollow's most playful and inventive new restaurant, where the Pisco and whiskey cocktails are named for anime characters and a neon-green moss wall runs the length of the *izakaya*-style dining room. But the real adventure is the food.

Greens VEGETARIAN, CALIFORNIAN $$

(Map p308; ☎415-771-6222; www.greensrestaurant.com; 2 Marina Blvd, Bldg A, Fort Mason Center; mains $18-28; ⏰5:30-9pm Mon, 11:30am-2:30pm & 5:30-9pm Tue-Thu, 11:30am-2:30pm & 5-9pm Fri, 10:30am-2:30pm & 5-9pm Sat & Sun; 🌿👪; 🚌22, 28, 30, 43, 47, 49) 🍃 Career carnivores won't realize there's zero meat in the hearty black-bean chili, or in Greens' other flavor-packed vegetarian dishes, made using ingredients from a Zen farm in Marin. And, oh, what views! The Golden Gate rises just outside the window-lined dining room. The on-site cafe serves to-go lunches, but for sit-down meals, including Saturday and Sunday brunch, reservations are recommended.

★Atelier Crenn FRENCH $$$

(Map p306; ☎415-440-0460; www.ateliercrenn.com; 3127 Fillmore St; tasting menu $335; ⏰5-9pm Tue-Sat; 🚌22, 28, 30, 43) The menu arrives in the form of a poem and then come the signature white chocolate spheres filled with a burst of apple cider. If this seems an unlikely start to a meal, just wait for the geoduck rice tart in a glass dome frosted by liquid nitrogen, and about a dozen more plates inspired by the childhood of chef Dominique Crenn in Brittany, France.

The Mission & the Castro

★La Palma Mexicatessen MEXICAN $

(Map p312; ☎415-647-1500; www.lapalmasf.com; 2884 24th St; tamales, tacos & huaraches $3-10; ⏰8am-6pm Mon-Sat, to 5pm Sun; 🌿; 🚌12, 14, 27, 48, Ⓑ 24th St Mission) 🍃 Follow the applause: that's the sound of organic tortilla-making in progress. You've found the Mission mother lode of handmade tamales, and *pupusas* (tortilla pockets) with potato and *chicharones* (pork crackling), *carnitas* (slow-roasted pork), *cotija* (Oaxacan cheese) and La Palma's own tangy tomatillo sauce. Get takeout or bring a small army to finish the meal at sunny sidewalk tables.

★Al's Place CALIFORNIAN $$

(Map p312; ☎415-416-6136; www.alsplacesf.com; 1499 Valencia St; share plates $15-21; ⏰5:30-10pm Wed-Sun; 🌿; 🚌12, 14, 49, Ⓜ J, Ⓑ 24th St Mission) 🍃 The Golden State dazzles on Al's plates, featuring homegrown heirloom ingredients, pristine Pacific seafood and grass-fed meat. Painstaking preparation yields sun-drenched flavors and exquisite textures: crispy-skin cod with frothy preserved-lime dip, and grilled peach melting into velvety foie gras. Dishes are half the size but thrice the flavor of mains elsewhere – get two or three and you'll be California dreaming.

Frances CALIFORNIAN $$$

(Map p312; ☎415-621-3870; www.frances-sf.com; 3870 17th St; mains $26-34; ⏰5-10pm Sun & Tue-Thu, to 10:30pm Fri & Sat; 🚌24, 33, Ⓜ F, K, L, M) 🍃 Rebel chef-owner Melissa Perello earned a Michelin star for fine dining, then ditched downtown to start this market-inspired neighborhood bistro. Daily menus showcase rustic flavors and luxurious textures with impeccable technique – handmade ricotta *malfatti* pasta with buttery squash and crunchy pepitas, juicy pork chops with blood orange and earthy Japanese sweet potatoes – plus cult wine served by the ounce, directly from Wine Country.

The Haight

★Brenda's Meat & Three SOUTHERN US $$
(Map p306; ☎415-926-8657; http://brendasmeatandthree.com; 919 Divisadero St; mains $9-20; ⏰8am-10pm Wed-Mon; 🚌5, 21, 24, 38) The name means one meaty main course plus three sides – though only superheroes finish ham steak with Creole red-eye gravy and grits, let alone cream biscuits and eggs. Chef Brenda Buenviaje's portions are defiantly Southern, which explains brunch lines of marathoners and partiers who forgot to eat last night. Arrive early, share sweet-potato pancakes, and pray for crawfish specials.

Rich Table CALIFORNIAN $$
(Map p308; ☎415-355-9085; http://richtablesf.com; 199 Gough St; mains $17-37; ⏰5:30-10pm Sun-Thu, to 10:30pm Fri & Sat; 🚌5, 6, 7, 21, 47, 49, Ⓜ Van Ness) 🍃 Impossible cravings begin at Rich Table, where mind-bending dishes like porcini doughnuts, sardine chips, and *burrata* (mozzarella and cream) funnel cake blow up Instagram feeds nightly. Married co-chefs and owners Sarah and Evan Rich riff on seasonal San Francisco cuisine with the soul of SFJAZZ stars and the ingenuity of Silicon Valley regulars.

Golden Gate Park & Around

★Arsicault Bakery BAKERY $
(Map p314; ☎415-750-9460; 397 Arguello Blvd; pastries $3-7; ⏰7am-2:30pm Mon-Fri, to 3:30pm Sat & Sun; 🚌1, 2, 33, 38, 44) Armando Lacayo left his job in finance because he, like his Parisian grandparents before him, was obsessed with making croissants. After perfecting his technique, Lacayo opened a modest bakery in the Inner Richmond in 2015. Within a year, *Bon Appétit* magazine had declared it the best new bakery in America and the golden, flaky, buttery croissants regularly sell out.

★Spruce CALIFORNIAN $$$
(Map p314; ☎415-931-5100; www.sprucesf.com; 3640 Sacramento St; mains $19-44; ⏰11:30am-2pm & 5-10pm Mon-Thu, 11:30am-2pm & 5-11pm Fri, 10am-2pm & 5-11pm Sat, 10am-2pm & 5-9pm Sun; 🚌1, 2, 33, 43) 🍃 VIP all the way: Baccarat crystal chandeliers, tawny leather chairs, rotating art collections and 2500 wines. Ladies who lunch dispense with polite conversation, tearing into grass-fed burgers on house-baked English muffins loaded with pickled onions and heirloom tomatoes grown on the restaurant's own organic farm. Want fries with that? Oh, yes, you do: Spruce's are cooked in duck fat.

Drinking & Nightlife

San Francisco set the gold standard for Wild West saloons, until drinking was driven underground in the 1920s with Prohibition. Today San Francisco celebrates its historic saloons and speakeasies – and with Wine Country and local distillers providing a steady supply of America's finest hooch, the West still gets wild nightly.

★Bourbon & Branch BAR
(Map p308; ☎415-346-1735; www.bourbonandbranch.com; 501 Jones St; ⏰6pm-2am; 🚌27, 38) 'Don't even think of asking for a cosmo' reads the House Rules at this Prohibition-era speakeasy, recognizable by its deliciously misleading Anti-Saloon League sign. For award-winning cocktails in the liquored-up library, whisper the password ('books') at the O'Farrell entrance. Reservations required for front-room booths and Wilson & Wilson Detective Agency, the noir-themed speakeasy-within-a-speakeasy (password supplied with reservations).

★Comstock Saloon BAR
(Map p308; ☎415-617-0071; www.comstocksaloon.com; 155 Columbus Ave; ⏰4pm-midnight Mon, to 2am Tue-Thu, noon-2am Fri, 11:30am-2am Sat, 11:30am-4pm Sun; 🚌8, 10, 12, 30, 45, 🚋Powell-Mason, Ⓜ T) During this 1907 saloon's heyday, patrons relieved themselves in the marble trough below the bar – now you'll have to tear yourself away from Comstock's authentic pisco punch and martini-precursor Martinez (gin, vermouth, bitters, maraschino liqueur). Arrive to toast Emperor Norton's statue at happy hour (4pm to 6pm) and stay for the family meal (whatever kitchen staff's eating). Reserve booths to hear when ragtime-jazz bands play.

★Li Po BAR
(Map p308; ☎415-982-0072; www.lipolounge.com; 916 Grant Ave; ⏰2pm-2am; 🚌8, 30, 45, 🚋Powell-Mason, Powell-Hyde, Ⓜ T) Beat a hasty retreat to red-vinyl booths where Allen Ginsberg and Jack Kerouac debated the meaning of life under a golden Buddha. Enter the

LGBTIQ+ SF

It doesn't matter where you're from, who you love or who's your daddy: if you're here and queer, welcome home. The Castro is the heart of the gay cruising scene, but raging dance clubs and leather bars can be found in SoMa. Head to the Tenderloin for trans venues and queer cabaret, or the Mission for women's bars, arts venues and community spaces.

SF Pride (Jun) month is undoubtedly the biggest event on the calendar, with over 1.5 million people hitting parades and parties. While you're in town, check out America's first gay-history museum, **GLBT History Museum** (Map p312; 415-621-1107; www.glbthistory.org/museum; 4127 18th St; $5, 1st Wed of month free; 11am-6pm Mon-Sat, noon-5pm Sun, closed Tue fall-spring; Castro St), which showcases a century of San Francisco LGBTQ+ ephemera, or get to know LGBT icons as you walk through the Castro following the **Rainbow Honor Walk** (Map p312; http://rainbowhonorwalk.org; Castro St & Market St; Castro St).

The *Bay Area Reporter* (www.ebar.com) is released every Wednesday and has community news and events, or grab a copy of the *San Francisco Bay Times* (http://sfbaytimes.com). The free *Gloss Magazine* (www.glossmagazine.net) locks down nightlife and parties. Or head to the following:

Aunt Charlie's Lounge (Map p308; 415-441-2922; www.auntcharlieslounge.com; 133 Turk St; cover free-$5; noon-midnight Mon & Wed, to 2am Tue & Thu, to 12:30am Fri, 10am-12:30am Sat, 10am-midnight Sun; 27, 31, Powell, Powell) Knock-down, drag-out winner for gender-bending shows and dance-floor freakiness in a tiny space.

El Rio (Map p312; 415-282-3325; www.elriosf.com; 3158 Mission St; cover free-$10; 1pm-2am Mon-Sat, to midnight Sun; 12, 14, 27, 49, 24th St Mission) Mix it up with world music, salsa, house, live bands and SF's flirtiest patio.

Stud (Map p308; 415-863-6623; www.studsf.com; 399 9th St; cover $5-8; 5pm-2am Tue-Thu, to 4am Fri, 7pm-4am Sat, 7pm-2am Sun; 12, 19, 27, 47) Shows and DJs nightly, plus the tantalizing aroma of bourbon, cologne and testosterone.

Oasis (Map p308; 415-795-3180; www.sfoasis.com; 298 11th St; tickets $15-35; 9, 12, 14, 47, Van Ness) SF's dedicated drag venue, hostessed by SF drag icons Heklinka and D'Arcy Drollinger.

Jolene's (Map p312; 415-913-7948; http://jolenessf.com; 2700 16th St; 4pm-2am Thu-Fri, from 11am Sat & Sun; 12, 22, 55, 16th Mission St) Women on the dance floor, at the bar, all over the wallpaper, right at home.

Wild Side West (Map p306; 415-647-3099; www.wildsidewest.com; 424 Cortland Ave; 2pm-2am; 24) Cheers to queers and beers in the herstory-making sculpture garden.

1937 faux-grotto doorway and dodge red lanterns to place your order: Tsingtao beer or a sweet, sneaky-strong Chinese mai tai made with *baijiu* (rice liquor). Brusque bartenders, basement bathrooms, cash only – a world-class dive bar.

Stookey's Club Moderne LOUNGE

(Map p308; www.stookeysclubmoderne.com; 895 Bush St; 4:30pm-2am Mon-Sat, to midnight Sun; 1, Powell-Hyde, Powell-Mason, California) Dangerous dames lure unsuspecting sailors into late-night schemes over potent hooch at this art-deco bar straight out of a Dashiell Hammett thriller. Chrome-lined 1930s Streamline Moderne decor sets the scene for intrigue, and wisecracking white-jacketed bartenders shake the stiffest Corpse Reviver cocktails in town. Arrive early to find room on the hat rack for your fedora, especially on live jazz nights.

Trick Dog BAR

(Map p312; 415-471-2999; www.trickdogbar.com; 3010 20th St; 3pm-2am; 12, 14, 49) Drink adventurously with ingenious cocktails inspired by local obsessions: San Francisco muralists, Chinese diners or conspiracy theories. Every six months, Trick Dog adopts a new theme and the menu changes – proof you can teach an old dog new tricks and improve on classics like the Manhattan. Arrive early for bar stools or hit the mood-lit loft for high-concept bar bites.

20 Spot WINE BAR

(Map p312; 415-624-3140; www.20spot.com; 3565 20th St; 5-11pm Mon-Thu, to 12:30am Fri

& Sat; 14, 22, 33, B 16th St Mission) Find your California mellow at this neighborhood wine lounge in an 1885 Victorian building. After decades as Force of Habit punk-record shop – note the vintage sign – this corner joint has earned the right to unwind with a glass of Berkeley's Donkey and Goat sparkling wine and not get any guff. Caution: oysters with pickled persimmon could become a habit.

☆ Entertainment

Sign up at Gold Star Events (www.goldstarevents.com) for discounts on comedy, theater, concerts and opera, or stop by the **TIX Bay Area** (Map p308; 415-433-7827; http://tixbayarea.org; 350 Powell St; Powell-Mason, Powell-Hyde, B Powell, M Powell) Union Sq ticket booth for cheap tickets for same-day or next-day shows.

★San Francisco Symphony CLASSICAL MUSIC
(Map p308; box office 415-864-6000, rush-ticket hotline 415-503-5577; www.sfsymphony.org; Grove St, btwn Franklin St & Van Ness Ave; tickets $20-150; 21, 45, 47, M Van Ness, B Civic Center) From the moment conductor Michael Tilson Thomas bounces up on his toes and raises his baton, the audience is on the edge of their seats for another thunderous performance by the Grammy-winning SF Symphony. Don't miss signature concerts of Beethoven and Mahler, live symphony performances with such films as *Star Trek,* and creative collaborations with artists from Elvis Costello to Metallica.

★SFJAZZ Center JAZZ
(Map p308; 866-920-5299; www.sfjazz.org; 201 Franklin St; tickets $25-120; ; 5, 6, 7, 21, 47, 49, M Van Ness) Jazz legends and singular talents from Argentina to Yemen are showcased at North America's newest, largest jazz center. Hear fresh takes on classic jazz albums and poets riffing with jazz combos in the downstairs Joe Henderson Lab, and witness extraordinary main-stage collaborations by legendary Afro-Cuban All Stars, raucous all-women mariachis Flor de Toluache, and Balkan barnstormers Goran Bregović and his Wedding and Funeral Orchestra.

★Fillmore Auditorium LIVE MUSIC
(Map p308; 415-346-6000; http://thefillmore.com; 1805 Geary Blvd; tickets from $20; box office 10am-3pm Sun, plus 30min before doors open to 10pm show nights; 22, 38) Jimi Hendrix, Janis Joplin, the Grateful Dead – they all played the Fillmore and the upstairs bar is lined with vintage psychedelic posters to prove it. Bands that sell out stadiums keep rocking this historic, 1250-capacity dance hall, and for major shows, free posters are still handed out. To squeeze up to the stage, be polite and lead with the hip.

★Castro Theatre CINEMA
(Map p312; 415-621-6120; www.castrotheatre.com; 429 Castro St; adult/child, senior & matinee $13/10; M Castro St) Every night at the Castro, crowds roar as the mighty organ rises – and no, that's not a euphemism. Showtime at this 1922 art deco movie palace is heralded with Wurlitzer organ show tunes, culminating in sing-alongs to the Judy Garland anthem 'San Francisco.' Architect Timothy Pflueger's OTT Spanish-Moorish-Asian style inspired the *Wizard of Oz* sets, but earthquake-shy San Franciscans avoid sitting under his pointy metal chandelier.

★Giants Stadium BASEBALL
(AT&T Park; Map p308; 415-972-2000, tours 415-972-2400; http://sanfrancisco.giants.mlb.com; 24 Willie Mays Plaza; tickets $14-349, stadium tour adult/senior/child $22/17/12; tour times vary; ; M N, T) Baseball fans roar April to October at the Giants' 81 home games. As any orange-blooded San Franciscan will remind you, the Giants have won three World Series since 2010 – and you'll know the Giants are on another winning streak when superstitious locals wear team colors (orange and black) and bushy beards (the Giants' rallying cry is 'Fear the Beard!').

Great American Music Hall LIVE MUSIC
(Map p308; 415-885-0750; www.gamh.com; 859 O'Farrell St; shows $20-45; box office noon-6pm Mon-Fri, 5pm-close on show nights; ; 19, 38, 47, 49) Everyone busts out their best sets at this opulent 1907 bordello turned all-ages venue – indie rockers like the Band Perry throw down, international legends such as Salif Keita grace the stage, and John Waters hosts Christmas extravaganzas. Pay $25 extra for dinner with prime balcony seating to watch shows comfortably, or rock out with the standing-room scrum downstairs.

San Francisco Ballet DANCE
(Map p308; tickets 415-865-2000; www.sfballet.org; 301 Van Ness Ave, War Memorial Opera House; tickets $22-150; ticket sales over the phone 10am-4pm Mon-Fri; 5, 21, 47, 49, M Van Ness, B Civic Center) The USA's oldest ballet

SAN FRANCISCO FOR CHILDREN

San Francisco has the fewest kids per capita of any US city, yet many locals make a living entertaining kids – from Pixar animators to video-game designers – and this town is full of attractions for young people.

Hit the award-winning, hands-on exhibits at the Exploratorium (p303) to investigate the science of skateboarding and glow-in-the-dark animals, then free the world from Space Invaders at **Musée Mécanique** (Map p308; ☎415-346-2000; www.museemecanique.com; Pier 45, Shed A; ⏲10am-8pm; 👪; 🚌47, 🚋Powell-Mason, Powell-Hyde, Ⓜ E, F). Don't be shy: bark back at the sea lions at Pier 39 (p310), and ride a unicorn on the pier's vintage **San Francisco carousel** (Map p308; www.pier39.com; Pier 39; 1 ride $5, 3 rides $10; ⏲10am-9pm Sun-Thu, to 10pm Fri & Sat; 👪; 🚌47, 🚋Powell-Mason, Ⓜ E, F).

Chase butterflies through the rainforest dome, pet starfish in the petting zoo and squeal in the Eel Forest at the California Academy of Sciences (p312), or brave the shark tunnel at **Aquarium of the Bay** (Map p308; ☎415-623-5300; www.aquariumofthebay.org; Pier 39; adult/child/family $28/18/75; ⏲10am-8pm late May-early Sep, shorter hours rest of year; 👪; 🚌47, 🚋Powell-Mason, Ⓜ E, F). The **Children's Creativity Museum** (Map p308; ☎415-820-3320; http://creativity.org/; 221 4th St; $12.95; ⏲10am-4pm Tue-Sun summer, Wed-Sun rest of year; 👪; 🚌14, Ⓜ Powell, Ⓑ Powell) allows future tech moguls to design their own video games and animations, then let off some steam at the playgrounds in **Golden Gate Park** (Koret Children's Quarter; Map p314; ☎415-831-2700; www.golden-gate-park.com/childrens-playground.html; carousel per ride adult/child $2/1; ⏲sunrise-sunset, carousel 10am-4:15pm; 👪; 🚌7, 33, Ⓜ N), **Dolores Park** (Map p312; http://sfrecpark.org/destination/mission-dolores-park; Dolores St, btwn 18th & 20th Sts; ⏲6am-10pm; 👪🐾; 🚌14, 33, 49, Ⓑ 16th St Mission, Ⓜ J) or **Yerba Buena Gardens** (Map p308; ☎415-820-3550; www.yerbabuenagardens.com; cnr 3rd & Mission Sts; ⏲6am-10pm; 👪; Ⓜ Montgomery, Ⓑ Montgomery).

company is looking sharp in more than 100 shows annually, from *The Nutcracker* (the US premiere was here) to modern originals. Performances are at the War Memorial Opera House from January to May, and you can score $15 to $20 same-day standing-room tickets at the box office (open four hours before curtain on performance days only).

Shopping

★Park Life GIFTS & SOUVENIRS
(Map p314; ☎415-386-7275; www.parklifestore.com; 220 Clement St; ⏲10am-7pm Mon-Sat, to 6pm Sun; 🚌1, 2, 33, 38, 44) The Swiss Army knife of hip SF emporiums, Park Life is design store, indie publisher and art gallery rolled into one. Browse among presents too clever to give away, including toy soldiers in yoga poses, Park Life catalogs of Shaun O'Dell paintings of natural disorder, sinister Todd Hido photos of shaggy cats on shag rugs, and a Picasso bong.

★Community Thrift CLOTHING
(Map p312; ☎415-861-4910; www.communitythriftsf.org; 623 Valencia St; ⏲10am-6:30pm; 🚌14, 22, 33, 49, Ⓑ 16th St Mission) 🍃 When local collectors and retailers have too much of a good thing, they donate it to nonprofit Community Thrift, where proceeds go to 200-plus local charities – all the more reason to gloat over your $5 totem-pole teacup, $10 vintage windbreaker and $14 disco-era glitter romper. Donate your cast-offs (until 5pm daily) and show some love to the Community.

Adobe Books & Backroom Gallery BOOKS
(Map p312; ☎415-864-3936; www.adobebooks.com; 3130 24th St; ⏲noon-8pm Mon-Fri, from 11am Sat & Sun; 🚌12, 14, 48, 49, Ⓑ 24th St Mission) Wall-to-wall inspiration – including just-released fiction, limited-edition art books, rare cookbooks, well-thumbed poetry – plus zine-launch parties, comedy nights and art openings. Mingle with Mission characters debating all-time-greatest pulp-fiction covers and SF history (founder Andrew is a whiz) and see SF artists at the Backroom Gallery (well worth the walk to the back of the store) before they hit Whitney Biennials.

Gravel & Gold HOMEWARES
(Map p312; ☎415-552-0112; www.gravelandgold.com; 3266 21st St; ⏲noon-7pm Mon-Sat, to 5pm Sun; 🚌12, 14, 49, Ⓑ 24th St Mission) 🍃 Get back to the land and in touch with California's roots without leaving sight of a Mission sidewalk. Gravel & Gold celebrates

SAN FRANCISCO'S BEST SHOPPING AREAS

All those tricked-out dens, well-stocked spice racks and fabulous ensembles don't just pull themselves together – San Franciscans scour their city for them. Here's where to find what:

Polk Street Vintage looks, local art, indie designers and smart gifts.

Valencia Street Made-in-SF gifts, West Coast style and scents, pirate supplies.

Haight Street Vintage, drag glam, steampunk gear and hats galore, plus anarchist comics, vinyl LPs and skateboards for total SF makeovers.

Hayes Valley Local designers, gourmet treats, home decor.

Union Square Ringed by department stores and megabrands, including Neiman Marcus, Macy's, Saks and Apple.

California's hippie homesteader movement with hand-printed smock-dresses, signature boob-print totes and wiggly stoner-striped throw pillows. It's homestead California-style with hand-thrown stoneware mugs, Risograph posters and rare books on '70s beach-shack architecture – plus DIY maker workshops (see website).

Hero Shop FASHION & ACCESSORIES
(Map p308; ☎415-829-3129; http://heroshopsf.com; 982 Post St; ⏰11am-7pm Mon-Sat; 🚌2, 3, 19, 27, 38, 47, 49) On the cutting edge of the Tenderloin, Hero transforms casual browsers into SF fashionistas with statement pieces by rising-star local designers: Stevie Howell's boho silk tunics, Future Glory's handmade marbled-leather handbags, Culk's souvenir sweatshirts. It's no accident Hero's selection seems unusually well edited – owner Emily Holt left her job as *Vogue*'s fashion-trend editor to open this boutique.

ℹ Information

DANGERS & ANNOYANCES

Keep your city smarts and wits about you, especially at night in the Tenderloin, South of Market (SoMa), the Upper Haight and the Mission. If you're alone in these areas at night, consider ride-share or a taxi instead of waiting for a bus.

MEDICAL SERVICES

San Francisco City Clinic (☎415-487-5500; www.sfcityclinic.org; 356 7th St; ⏰8am-4pm Mon, Wed & Fri, 1-6pm Tue, 1-4pm Thu) Low-cost services.

San Francisco General Hospital (Zuckerberg San Francisco General Hospital and Trauma Center; ☎emergency 415-206-8111, main hospital 415-206-8000; https://zuckerbergsanfranciscogeneral.org; 1001 Potrero Ave; ⏰24hr; 🚌9, 10, 33, 48) Best ER for serious trauma.

University of California San Francisco Medical Center (☎415-476-1000; www.ucsfhealth.org; 505 Parnassus Ave; ⏰24hr; 🚌6, 7, 43, Ⓜ N) ER at leading university hospital.

TOURIST INFORMATION

SF Visitor Information Center (www.sanfrancisco.travel/visitor-information-center) Muni Passports, activities deals, and event calendars.

ℹ Getting There & Away

AIR

One of America's busiest, **San Francisco International Airport** (www.flysfo.com; S McDonnell Rd) is 14 miles south of downtown off Hwy 101 and accessible by BART (30 minutes). Travelers arriving at **Oakland International Airport** (OAK; ☎510-563-3300; www.oaklandairport.com; 1 Airport Dr; 📶; Ⓑ Oakland International Airport), 15 miles east of downtown, have a longer trip to reach San Francisco – but OAK has fewer weather-related flight delays than SFO.

BUS

From the **Temporary Transbay Terminal** (Map p308; cnr Howard & Main Sts; 🚌5, 38, 41, 71), you can catch the following buses:

AC Transit (☎510-891-4777; www.actransit.org; single ride East Bay/trans-Bay $2.35/5.50) Buses to the East Bay.

Greyhound (☎800-231-2222; www.greyhound.com) Buses leave daily for Los Angeles ($21 to $33, eight to 12 hours), Truckee ($32 to $40, 5½ hours) near Lake Tahoe and other major destinations.

Megabus (☎877-462-6342; https://us.megabus.com) Low-cost bus service to San Francisco from Los Angeles, Sacramento and Anaheim.

SamTrans (☎800-660-4287; www.samtrans.com) Southbound buses to Palo Alto and the Pacific coast.

TRAIN

Caltrain (www.caltrain.com; cnr 4th & King Sts) connects San Francisco with Silicon Valley hubs and San Jose.

Amtrak (☎800-872-7245; www.amtrak.com) serves San Francisco via stations in Oakland and Emeryville (near Oakland), with free shuttle-bus connections to San Francisco's Ferry Building and Caltrain station, and Oakland's Jack London Sq.

Getting Around

San Franciscans mostly walk, bike, ride Muni or ride-share instead of taking a car or cab. Traffic is notoriously bad and parking is next to impossible. Avoid driving until it's time to leave town. For Bay Area transit options, departures and arrivals, call 511 or check www.511.org. A *Muni Street & Transit Map* is available online.

Cable cars Frequent, slow and scenic, from 6am to 12:30am daily. Single rides cost $7; for frequent use, get a Muni Passport ($23 per day).

Muni streetcar and bus Reasonably fast, but schedules vary by line; infrequent after 9pm. Fares are $2.75 cash, or $2.50 with a reloadable Clipper card.

BART High-speed transit to East Bay, Mission St, SF airport and Millbrae, where it connects with Caltrain.

Taxi Fares are about $3 per mile; meters start at $3.50.

Marin County

Just across the Golden Gate Bridge from San Francisco, Marin County is a collection of wealthy, wooded hamlets that tenuously hang by haute hippie roots as a more conservative tech-era population moves in. Its southern peninsula nearly touches the north-pointing tip of the city, and is surrounded by ocean and bay. But Marin is wilder and more mountainous. Redwoods grow on the coastside hills, surf crashes against cliffs, and hiking and cycling trails crisscross blessedly scenic Point Reyes, Muir Woods and Mt Tamalpais. Nature is what makes Marin County such an excellent day trip or weekend escape from San Francisco.

Marin Headlands

The headland cliffs and hillsides rise majestically at the north end of the Golden Gate Bridge, their rugged beauty all the more striking given the fact that they're only a few miles from San Francisco's urban core. A few forts and bunkers are left over from a century of US military occupation – which is, ironically, the reason the headlands are today protected **parklands** (Map p306; 415-561-4700; www.nps.gov/goga; P) FREE, free of development. It's no mystery why this is one of the Bay Area's most popular hiking and cycling destinations: as the trails wind through the headlands, they afford stunning views of the sea, the Golden Gate Bridge and San Francisco and lead to isolated beaches and secluded picnic spots.

Historical **Point Bonita Lighthouse** (Map p306; 415-331-1540; www.nps.gov/goga/pobo.htm; 12:30-3:30pm Sat-Mon; P) FREE is a breathtaking half-mile walk from Field Rd parking area. From the tip of Point Bonita, you can see the Golden Gate Bridge and the San Francisco skyline. Harbor seals haul out seasonally on nearby rocks. For a longer walk, the **Coastal Trail** (Map p306; www.nps.gov/goga/planyourvisit/coastal-trail.htm) meanders 3.5 miles from **Rodeo Beach** (Map p306; www.parksconservancy.org/visit/park-sites/rodeo-beach.html; off Bunker Rd; P) inland, past abandoned military bunkers, to intersect the Tennessee Valley Trail. It then continues almost 3 miles along the headlands all the way to **Muir Beach** (Map p306; www.nps.gov/goga/planyourvisit/muirbeach.htm; off Pacific Way; P).

Above Rodeo Lagoon, the **Marine Mammal Center** (Map p306; 415-289-7325; www.marinemammalcenter.org; 2000 Bunker Rd; by donation, audio tour adult/child $9/5; 10am-4pm; P) rehabilitates injured, sick and orphaned sea mammals before returning them to the wild, and has educational exhibits about these animals and the dangers they face.

Mt Tamalpais State Park

Standing guard over Marin County, majestic Mt Tamalpais (Mt Tam) holds more than 200 miles of hiking and biking trails, lakes, streams, waterfalls and an impressive array of wildlife – from plentiful newts and hawks to rare foxes and mountain lions. Wind your way through meadows, oaks and madrone trees to breathtaking vistas over the San Francisco Bay, Pacific Ocean, towns, cities and forested hills rolling into the distance.

This serene 2572ft mountain, comprising **Mt Tamalpais State Park** (Map p306; 415-388-2070; www.parks.ca.gov/mttamalpais; per car $8; 7am-sunset; P), the Marin Municipal Water District, **Muir Woods National Monument**, several Marin County open-space areas and part of the Golden Gate Recreation Area, is a hiking paradise. You can download a map of the mountain's trails and get lots of hiking ideas at OneTam (www.onetam.org).

One of the best hikes on the mountain is the **Steep Ravine Trail**. From the park headquarters at **Pantoll Station** (Map p306; 415-388-2070; www.parks.ca.gov; 801 Panoramic Hwy; hours vary;), it follows a wooded creek to the coast (about 2.1 miles each way).

Point Reyes National Seashore

Windswept Point Reyes peninsula is a rough-hewn beauty that has always lured marine mammals and migratory birds; it's also home to scores of shipwrecks. **Point Reyes National Seashore** (☎415-654-5100; www.nps.gov/pore; P 👪) 🍃FREE protects 110 sq miles of pristine ocean beaches and coastal wilderness and has excellent hiking and camping opportunities. Be sure to bring warm clothing, as even the sunniest days can quickly turn cold and foggy.

Crowning the peninsula's westernmost tip, with wild terrain and ferocious winds, **Point Reyes Lighthouse** (☎415-669-1534; www.nps.gov/pore; end of Sir Francis Drake Blvd; ⏲10am-4:30pm Fri-Mon, lens room 2:30-4pm Fri-Mon; P) FREE feels like the end of the earth and offers the best whale-watching along the coast. The lighthouse sits below the headlands; to reach it you need to descend more than 300 stairs. Numerous beaches grace the peninsula, providing ample opportunities for swimming and animal-spotting: **Drakes** and **Heart's Desire** are both popular with families.

Pop into the **Bear Valley Visitor Center** (☎415-464-5100; www.nps.gov/pore; 1 Bear Valley Rd, Point Reyes Station; ⏲10am-5pm Mon-Fri, 9am-5pm Sat & Sun), a mile west of Olema, at Point Reyes National Seashore's headquarters, for maps, information and worthwhile exhibits.

Berkeley

Berkeley is synonymous with protest, activism and left-wing politics. Beyond those tropes is a busy, attractive city, a blend of yuppie and hippie and student, all existing side by side with great Asia-Pacific regional restaurants, twee toy stores, Latin American groceries, high-end organic food halls and the misty green campus of the University of California, Berkeley (aka 'Cal').

Sights

Telegraph Ave has traditionally been the throbbing heart of studentville in Berkeley, the sidewalks crowded with undergrads, postdocs and youthful shoppers squeezing their way past throngs of vendors, buskers and panhandlers.

★Tilden Regional Park PARK

(☎510-544-2747; www.ebparks.org/parks/tilden; ⏲5am-10pm; P 👪 🐾; 🚌AC Transit 67) 🍃FREE This 2079-acre park, in the hills east of town, is Berkeley's best. It has nearly 40 miles of hiking and multiuse trails of varying difficulty, from paved paths to hilly scrambles, including part of the magnificent Bay Area Ridge Trail. There's also a miniature steam train ($3), a children's farm and environmental education center, a wonderfully wild-looking botanical garden and an 18-hole golf course. Lake Anza is good for picnics and from spring through fall you can swim ($3.50).

University of California, Berkeley UNIVERSITY

(☎510-642-6000; www.berkeley.edu; ⏲hours vary; P; B Downtown Berkeley) 'Cal' is one of the country's top universities, California's oldest university (1866), and home to 40,000 diverse, politically conscious students. Next to **California Memorial Stadium** (☎510-642-2730; www.californiamemorialstadium.com; 2227 Piedmont Ave; ⏲hours vary; 👪; 🚌AC Transit 52), the **Koret Visitor Center** (☎510-642-5215; http://visit.berkeley.edu; 2227 Piedmont Ave; ⏲8:30am-4:30pm Mon-Fri, 9am-1pm Sat & Sun; 🚌AC Transit 36) has information and maps, and leads free campus walking tours (reservations required). Cal's landmark is the 1914 **Campanile** (Sather Tower; ☎510-642-6000; http://campanile.berkeley.edu; adult/child $4/3; ⏲10am-3:45pm Mon-Fri, 10am-4:45pm Sat, to 1:30pm & 3-4:45pm Sun; 👪; B Downtown Berkeley), with elevator rides ($4) to the top and carillon concerts. The **Bancroft Library** (☎510-642-3781; www.lib.berkeley.edu/libraries/bancroft-library; University Dr; ⏲archives 10am-4pm or 5pm Mon-Fri; B Downtown Berkeley) FREE displays the small gold nugget that started the California gold rush in 1848.

Sleeping

Graduate Berkeley BOUTIQUE HOTEL $$

(☎510-845-8981; www.graduatehotels.com/berkeley; 2600 Durant Ave; d $180-240; P 🚭 @ 📶 🐾; 🚌AC Transit 51B) Located a block from campus, this classic 1928 hotel has been cheekily renovated to highlight the connection to the university. The lobby is adorned with embarrassing yearbook photos and a ceiling mobile of exam books, and smallish rooms have dictionary-covered shower curtains and bongs repurposed into bedside lamps.

★Claremont Resort & Spa RESORT $$$

(☎510-843-3000; www.fairmont.com/claremont-berkeley; 41 Tunnel Rd; d from $300; P 🚭 @ 📶 🏊 🐾) The East Bay's classy crème de la crème, this Fairmont-owned historic hotel is a glamorous white 1915 building with elegant restaurants, a fitness center, swimming pools, tennis courts and a full-service spa. The bay-view rooms are superb. It's located at the foot of the Berkeley Hills, off Hwy 13 (Tunnel Rd) near the Oakland border. Parking is $30.

Eating & Drinking

★Cheese Board Collective PIZZA $

(☎510-549-3183; www.cheeseboardcollective.coop; 1504 & 1512 Shattuck Ave; slices/half-pizzas/whole pizzas $2.75/12/24; ⏰11:30am-3pm & 4:30-8pm Tue-Sat; ; AC Transit 7) Worker owned since 1971, this co-op boasts (surprise) a great collection of cheese, a bakery with a changing selection of fresh bread, and a new vegetarian pizza and salad every day; options may include asparagus and onion or crushed tomato and goat cheese. Live music is often playing at this delicious Berkeley institution. Expect lines!

★Great China Restaurant CHINESE $$

(☎510-843-7996; www.greatchinaberkeley.com; 2190 Bancroft Way; mains $13-21; ⏰11:30am-2:30pm Wed-Mon, 5:30-9pm Mon, Wed & Thu, to 9:30pm Fri, 5-9:30pm Sat & Sun; B Downtown Berkeley) Berkeley does not lack for good Chinese food, but this enormous, upscale restaurant elevates the genre with Northern Chinese specialties like duck-bone soup, cumin-braised lamb, steamed fish with ginger and scallions, and thrice-cooked pork belly. Come with friends and order as much as you can – your taste buds will not forget this.

Gather CALIFORNIAN $$

(☎510-809-0400; www.gatherrestaurant.com; 2200 Oxford St; dinner mains $18-30; ⏰11:30am-2pm & 5-9pm Mon-Thu, 11:30am-2pm & 5-10pm Fri, 10am-2pm & 5-10pm Sat, 10am-2pm & 5-9pm Sun; ; B Downtown Berkeley) When vegan foodies and passionate farm-to-table types dine out together, they often end up here. Inside a salvaged-wood interior punctuated by green vines streaking down over an open kitchen, dishes are created from locally sourced ingredients and sustainably raised meats. Reservations recommended.

★Chez Panisse CALIFORNIAN $$$

(☎cafe 510-548-5049, restaurant 510-548-5525; www.chezpanisse.com; 1517 Shattuck Ave; cafe dinner mains $21-35, restaurant prix-fixe dinner $75-125; ⏰cafe 11:30am-2:45pm & 5-10:30pm Mon-Thu, 11:30am-3pm & 5-11pm Fri & Sat, restaurant seatings 5:30pm & 8pm Mon-Sat; ; AC Transit 7) Foodies come to worship here at the church of Alice Waters, inventor of California cuisine. Panisse is located in a lovely arts-and-crafts house in Berkeley's 'Gourmet Ghetto,' and you can choose to pull out all the stops with a prix-fixe meal downstairs or go less expensive and a tad less formal in the upstairs cafe. Reservations accepted one month ahead.

Fieldwork Brewing Company BREWERY

(☎510-898-1203; www.fieldworkbrewing.com; 1160 6th St; ⏰11am-10pm Sun-Thu, to 11pm Fri & Sat; AC Transit 12) At this industrial brewery taproom you can sit down on the outdoor patio with a tasting flight of IPAs or a glass of rich Mexican hot-chocolate stout. It's dog-friendly, and there are racks for hanging up your bicycle inside the front door. There's a short menu of Mexican-Californian food too.

Getting There & Around

To get to Berkeley, catch a Richmond-bound train to one of three BART stations: Ashby, Downtown Berkeley or North Berkeley. Or drive over the Bay Bridge from San Francisico, then follow either I-80 (for University Ave, Berkeley Marina, downtown Berkeley and the university campus) or Hwy 24 (for College Ave and the Berkeley Hills).

Local buses, cycling and walking are the best ways to get around Berkeley.

NORTHERN CALIFORNIA

The Golden State goes wild in Northern California, with coast redwoods swirled in fog, Wine Country vineyards and hidden hot springs. Befitting this dramatic meeting of land and water is an unlikely mélange of local residents: timber barons and hippie tree huggers, dreadlocked Rastafarians and biodynamic ranchers, pot farmers and political radicals of every stripe. Come for the scenery, but stay for the top-notch wine and farm-to-fork restaurants, misty hikes among the world's tallest trees and rambling conversations that begin with 'Hey, dude!' and end hours later.

Wine Country

Surprising, lyrical, elegant and sophisticated, Northern California's Wine Country spans the diverse landscapes, people and flavors of Napa and Sonoma Counties.

With its rolling hills of grass, verdant valleys, evergreen-capped mountainsides and lulling rivers, the landscape here delivers surprises at every corner. But it's really the food and wine that draws people here. This is the epicurean capital of the United States, and the restaurants, wineries and tasting rooms rival anything Europe has to offer.

On the western side of the region, you have Sonoma County, where people still drive pickups and cold fingers of fog run all the way up the valleys from the sea to create amazing cold-weather wine varietals.

Head east of Eden for the world-class wineries of Napa County, which offers up truly out-of-this-world fine dining and plenty of open spaces for an afternoon picnic or hike.

Both valleys are a 90-minute drive from San Francisco and Oakland. Napa, further inland, has about 500 wineries and attracts the most visitors (expect heavy traffic on summer weekends). Sonoma County has more than 425 wineries and around 40 in Sonoma Valley, which is less commercial and less congested than Napa. If you have time to visit only one, for ease go with Sonoma.

Napa Valley

Napa Valley is exactly what you expect when you think of Wine Country: hillside chateau wineries, bold cabernets, vast expanses of perfectly ordered grape vines, grassy slopes speckled by the tungsten sun, restaurant dinners that go on for hours, and some of the finest and most luxurious small-scale boutique hotels anywhere in California.

Most journeys here start and end in the city of Napa proper. In the town center there are tasting rooms, live jazz and plenty of fine-dining options, plus the option to party late into the night at down-home pubs and eateries that draw a young local crowd.

Sights & Activities

★Hess Collection WINERY, GALLERY

(☎707-255-1144; www.hesscollection.com; 4411 Redwood Rd, Napa; museum & tours free, tasting $25-35; ⏰10am-5pm, last tasting 5pm) Art-lovers: don't miss Hess Collection, whose galleries display mixed-media and large-canvas works, including pieces by Francis Bacon and Robert Motherwell. In the elegant stone-walled tasting room, find well-known cabernet sauvignon and chardonnay, but also try the Viognier. There's garden service in the warmer months, which is lovely, as Hess overlooks the valley. Make reservations and be prepared to drive a winding road. Bottles are $30 to $100. A public tour runs at 10:30am.

★Robert Sinskey Vineyards WINERY

(☎707-944-9090; www.robertsinskey.com; 6320 Silverado Trail, Napa; bar tasting $40, seated food & wine pairings $70-175; ⏰10am-4:30pm; P) The fabulous hillside tasting room, constructed of stone, redwood and teak, resembles a small cathedral – fitting, given the sacred status here bestowed upon food and wine. It specializes in bright-acid organic pinot noir, plus exceptional aromatic white varietals, dry rosé and Bordeaux varietals such as merlot and cab franc, all crafted for the dinner table. Small bites accompany bar tastings, and seated food and wine experiences are curated by chef Maria Sinskey herself. Reserve ahead for sit-down tastings and culinary tours.

★Frog's Leap WINERY

(☎707-963-4704; www.frogsleap.com; 8815 Conn Creek Rd, Rutherford; tasting incl tour $25-35; ⏰10am-4pm by appointment only; P) Meandering paths wind through magical gardens and fruit-bearing orchards surrounding an 1884 barn and farmstead with cats and chickens. The vibe is casual and down-to-earth, with a major emphasis on *fun*. Sauvignon blanc is its best-known wine but the merlot merits attention. There's also a dry, restrained cabernet, atypical of Napa.

★Tres Sabores WINERY

(☎707-967-8027; www.tressabores.com; 1620 Sth Whitehall Lane, St Helena; tour & tasting $40; ⏰10:30am-3pm, by appointment;) At the valley's westernmost edge, where sloping vineyards meet wooded hillsides, Tres Sabores is a portal to old Napa – no fancy tasting room, no snobbery, just great wine in a spectacular setting. Bucking the cabernet custom, Tres Sabores crafts elegantly structured, Burgundian-style zinfandel and spritely sauvignon blanc, which the *New York Times* dubbed a top 10 of its kind in California. Reservations are essential.

Sleeping

Pricey and fabulous hotels are scattered throughout Napa Valley, with the most opulent stays perched in and around St Helena and Yountville. Calistoga is a bit more relaxed and affordable, and the best budget option, without question, is a yurt (or campsite) in **Bothe-Napa Valley State Park** (☎800-444-7275; www.parks.ca.gov; 3801 Hwy 128; camping & RV sites $35, yurts $55-70, cabins $150-225;).

Napa Winery Inn HOTEL $

(☎707-257-7220; www.napawineryinn.com; 1998 Trower Ave, Napa; r from $125; P@) Request a remodeled room at this good-value hotel, north of downtown, decorated with generic Colonial-style furniture. It has a hot tub and good service. There are complimentary wine receptions each night: weekdays 5:30pm to 6:30pm, to 7pm weekends.

★ Auberge du Soleil LUXURY HOTEL **$$$**
(☎707-963-1211; www.aubergedusoleil.com; 180 Rutherford Hill Rd, Rutherford; r $1325-4025;) The top splurge for a no-holds-barred romantic weekend, Auberge's hillside cottages are second to none. The view will very much define your lodging choice, but opting for a valley view room with panoramic windows is well worth the splurge. Most of the rooms come with a fireplace.

★ Carneros Resort & Spa RESORT **$$$**
(☎707-299-4900; www.carnerosresort.com; 4048 Sonoma Hwy, Napa; r from $500; P) Carneros Resort & Spa's contemporary aesthetic and retro small-town agricultural theme shatter the predictable Wine Country mold. The semidetached, corrugated-metal cottages look like itinerant housing, but inside they're snappy and chic, with cherry-wood floors, ultrasuede headboards, wood-burning fireplaces, heated-tile bathroom floors, giant tubs and indoor-outdoor showers.

Eating

★ Oxbow Public Market MARKET
(☎707-226-6529; www.oxbowpublicmarket.com; 610 & 644 1st St, Napa; ⊙7:30am-9:30pm; P) Showcasing all things culinary (produce stalls, kitchen shops and everywhere something to taste), Oxbow is foodie central with an emphasis on seasonal eating and sustainability. Some vendors and restaurants open early or close late. Come hungry.

Farmstead MODERN AMERICAN **$$**
(☎707-963-4555; www.longmeadowranch.com; 738 Main St, St Helena; mains $19-33; ⊙11:30am-9:30pm Mon-Thu, to 10pm Fri & Sat, 11am-9:30pm Sun;) An enormous open-truss barn with big leather booths and rocking-chair porch, Farmstead draws an all-ages crowd and farms many of its own ingredients – including grass-fed beef and lamb – for an earthy menu highlighting wood-fired cooking.

★ French Laundry CALIFORNIAN **$$$**
(☎707-944-2380; www.thomaskeller.com/tfl; 6640 Washington St, Yountville; prix-fixe dinner from $325; ⊙seatings 11am-12:30pm Fri-Sun, 5-9pm daily) The pinnacle of California dining, Thomas Keller's three-Michelin-star rated French Laundry is epic, a high-wattage culinary experience on par with the world's best. Book one month ahead on the online app Tock, where tickets are released in groupings. This is the meal you can brag about the rest of your life.

★ Restaurant at Meadowood CALIFORNIAN **$$$**
(☎707-967-1205; www.meadowood.com; 900 Meadowood Lane, St Helena; 12-course menu $275; ⊙5:30-9:30pm Tue-Sat) If you couldn't score reservations at French Laundry (p331), fear not: Meadowood – the valley's only other three-Michelin-star restaurant – has a slightly more sensibly priced menu, elegantly unfussy dining room and lavish haute cuisine that's not too esoteric. The restaurant at Auberge (p331) has better views, but Meadowood's food and service far surpass it.

Sonoma Valley

Here in the delightfully laid-back, unapologetic and fun-loving Sonoma Valley, winemakers ply their craft, foodies flock to amazing restaurants, and there are plenty of adventures to be had in the 13,000 acres of parkland.

Heading up valley, you pass through the tiny village of Glen Ellen, which has a handful of small eateries and access to the valley's best natural area at **Jack London State Historic Park** (☎707-938-5216; www.jacklondonpark.com; 2400 London Ranch Rd, Glen Ellen; per car $10, admission to cottage $3; ⊙9:30am-5pm; P) and then on to the gorgeous wineries and roadside attractions of the Kenwood area.

Sights & Activities

★ Gundlach-Bundschu Winery WINERY
(☎707-938-5277; www.gunbun.com; 2000 Denmark St, Sonoma; tasting $20-30, incl tour $30-60; ⊙11am-5:30pm Sun-Fri, to 7pm Sat Apr-Oct, to 4:30pm Nov-Mar; P) California's oldest family-run winery looks like a castle but has a down-to-earth vibe. Founded in 1858 by a Bavarian immigrant, its signatures are gewürztraminer and pinot noir, but 'Gun-Bun' was the first American winery to produce 100% merlot. Down a winding lane, it's a terrific bike-to winery with picnicking, hiking, a lake and frequent concerts, including a two-day folk-music festival in June. Tour the 1800-barrel cave by reservation only. Bottles are $20 to $50.

Benziger WINERY
(☎707-935-3000; www.benziger.com; 1883 London Ranch Rd, Glen Ellen; tasting $20-50, tours $25-50;

BOOKING TASTINGS

Because of strict county zoning laws, many Napa wineries cannot legally receive drop-in visitors; unless you've come strictly to buy, you'll have to call ahead. This is *not* the case with all wineries. We recommend booking one tasting, plus a lunch or dinner reservation, and planning your day around those appointments.

11am-5pm Mon-Fri, 10am-5pm Sat & Sun; P) If you're new to wine, make Benziger your first stop for Sonoma's best crash course in winemaking. The worthwhile tour (reservations recommended) includes an open-air tram ride (weather permitting) through biodynamic vineyards and a five-wine tasting. Great picnicking, excellent for families. The large-production wine is OK (head for the reserves); the tour's the thing. Bottles are $20 to $80.

Bartholomew Estate Winery WINERY
(707-509-0450; www.bartholomewestate.com; 1000 Vineyard Lane, Sonoma; tasting $15; 11am-4:30pm; P) Formerly Bartholomew Park Winery has transformed into Bartholomew Estate, ushering in a change of ownership and winemaker to the historic vineyards, which have been cultivated since 1857. You could easily while away an afternoon tasting the sauvignon blanc, rosé and zinfandel vintages, hiking the 3-mile trail through the grounds and admiring the plein-air artworks in the gallery adjacent to the tasting room.

Sleeping

The most sensible bases for exploring this valley are historic downtown Sonoma and lush, romantic Glen Ellen. To save some duckets, give Petaluma down south a second look or consider camping in the **Sugarloaf Ridge State Park** (707-833-6084; www.reservecalifornia.com/CaliforniaWebHome/; 2605 Adobe Canyon Rd, Kenwood; tent & RV sites $35, online reservation fee $7.99;).

Beltane Ranch B&B $$
(707-833-4233; www.beltaneranch.com; 11,775 Hwy 12, Glen Ellen; d $185-375; P) Surrounded by horse pastures and vineyards, Beltane is a throwback to 19th-century Sonoma. The cheerful 1890s ranch house has double porches lined with swinging chairs and white wicker. Though it's technically a B&B, each country-Americana-style room and the cottage has a private entrance – nobody will make you pet the cat. No phone or TV means zero distraction from pastoral bliss.

Olea Hotel BOUTIQUE HOTEL $$$
(707-996-5131; www.oleahotel.com; 5131 Warm Springs Rd, Glen Ellen; r from $340; P) This lovely property extends up a hillside off a Glen Ellen back road. Impeccably redeveloped following a brush with the 2017 fires, each room feels a little different, but comes with modern prints, and bright and shiny appointments. Some even have private balconies and fireplaces. Rooms 14, 15 and 16 have vaulted ceilings and the best views. There's a lovely pool and hot-tub area.

Eating

There are some very good restaurants in downtown Sonoma and Glen Ellen's Jack London Village. Also, don't miss the indulgent and fabulous food-and-wine pairing at **St Francis Winery** (707-538-9463; www.stfranciswinery.com; 100 Pythian Rd at Hwy 12, Santa Rosa; tasting $15, wine & cheese pairing $25, wine & food pairing $68; 10am-5pm).

★ **Cafe La Haye** CALIFORNIAN $$
(707-935-5994; www.cafelahaye.com; 140 E Napa St, Sonoma; mains $19-25; 5:30-9pm Tue-Sat) One of Sonoma's top tables for earthy New American cooking, La Haye only uses produce sourced from within 60 miles. Its dining room gets packed cheek-by-jowl and service can border on perfunctory, but the clean simplicity and flavor-packed cooking make it many foodies' first choice. Reserve well ahead.

Glen Ellen Star CALIFORNIAN, ITALIAN $$$
(707-343-1384; www.glenellenstar.com; 13648 Arnold Dr, Glen Ellen; pizzas $15-20, mains $24-50; 5:30-9pm Sun-Thu, to 9:30pm Fri & Sat;) Helmed by chef Ari Weiswasser, who once worked at Thomas Keller's French Laundry (p331), this petite Glen Ellen bistro shines a light on the best of Sonoma farms and ranches. Local, organic and seasonal ingredients star in dishes such as spring-lamb ragù, whole roasted fish with broccoli Di Cicco or golden beets with harissa crumble. Reservations recommended.

Healdsburg & Russian River Valley

'The River,' as locals call it, has long been a summer-weekend destination for Northern Californians who come to canoe, wander country lanes, taste wine, hike redwood forests and live at a lazy pace. In winter the river floods, and nobody's here.

The towns of this area are as diverse as the landscape. Without a doubt, the hippest and most sophisticated town, the once-sleepy farming village of Healdsburg has come to life with amazing restaurants, wonderful shops and tasting rooms, and plenty of glitz and glamour. Young, hip and growing, the county seat of Santa Rosa offers urban chic, while out-west towns like Sebastopol retain much of their downhome appeal.

Sights & Activities

★ Macrostie WINERY
(☎707-473-9303; www.macrostiewinery.com; 4605 Westside Rd, Healdsburg; tasting $25-35, with tour $55; ⊙11am-5pm Mon-Thu, 10am-5pm Fri-Sun) For its creamy and crisp chardonnays and earthy pinots, along with top-notch service and an elegant tasting room, Macrostie is the talk of Wine Country. The sit-down tastings are relaxed and highly personal, with gorgeous views of the vineyard. Visionary winemaker Heidi Bridenhagen holds the distinction of being the youngest female on the job in Sonoma Valley. Pair your tasting with a delicious charcuterie plate that includes three local cheeses, prosciutto, olives, almonds and dried fruit.

Francis Ford Coppola Winery WINERY, MUSEUM
(☎707-857-1471; www.francisfordcoppolawinery.com; 300 Via Archimedes, Geyserville; tasting $15-30; ⊙11am-6pm; P) The famous movie director's vineyard estate is a self-described 'wine wonderland.' Taking over historic Chateau Souverain, this hillside winery has a bit of everything: wine-tasting flights, a free museum of moviemaking memorabilia, a shameless gift shop and two modern Italian-American restaurants. The most satisfying tasting is the reserve flight ($25 to $30) upstairs. Bottles are $12 to $90. Outside you'll find boccie courts by two **swimming pools** (day pass adult/child $35/15; ⊙11am-6pm daily Jun-Sep, Fri-Sun Apr, May & Oct;).

Bella WINERY
(☎707-395-6136; www.bellawinery.com; 9711 W Dry Creek Rd, Healdsburg; tasting $20; ⊙11am-4:30pm; P) Atop the valley's north end, always-fun Bella has cool caves built into the hillside. The estate-grown grapes include 112-year-old vines from Alexander Valley. The focus is on big reds – zinfandel and syrah – but there's terrific rosé (good for barbecues) and late-harvest zinfandel (great with brownies). The wonderful vibe and dynamic staff make Bella special. Bottles are $25 to $55.

Sleeping

Russian River offers excellent resorts, inns and cottages, particularly in upscale Healdsburg and in and around Guerneville. Lodgings are harder to come by in small towns such as Duncan Mills, but wherever you find yourself, there's probably a campground nearby. Santa Rosa has plenty of options, and some cheaper spots for people on a budget.

★ Shanti Permaculture Farm FARMSTAY $
(☎707-874-2001; www.shantioccidental.com; 16,715 Coleman Valley Rd, Occidental; tent & RV sites $55-80, cottages & yurts $99-225;) Tucked back in the redwoods on scenic Coleman Valley Rd, this is the ultimate NorCal farmstay. The knowledgeable Oregonian owner educates guests about ecofriendly agricultural concepts such as biochar and *hugelkultur,* and shows off her chickens, ducks, goats and enormous llama. While the operation feels somewhat rustic, it is impressively MacGyvered and the one-bedroom cottage is surprisingly posh.

Astro BOUTIQUE HOTEL $$
(☎707-200-4655; www.theastro.com; 323 Santa Rosa Ave; r from $170;) A designer's dream, this throwback motel has wonderful and unique touches in each room. Most of the furnishings go back to the 1960s. Like what you see? No problem, all the furniture is for sale. Out back, a lounge and bar gives an easy central spot to gather, drink martinis or simply revel in the kitsch of 1960s Californiana.

★ Hotel Healdsburg HOTEL $$$
(☎707-431-2800; www.hotelhealdsburg.com; 25 Matheson St, Healdsburg; r from $314; @) Smack on the plaza, the fashion-forward HH has a coolly minimalist style of concrete and velvet, with requisite top-end amenities, including sumptuous beds and extradeep tubs. There's a full-service spa. The restaurant, **Dry Creek Kitchen** (☎707-431-0330; www.drycreekkitchen.com; 317 Healdsburg Ave; mains $32-44, tasting menu $29, wine pairing $48; ⊙5:30-9:30pm Sun-Thu, to 10pm Fri & Sat), is run by celeb-chef Charlie Palmer.

★ Applewood Inn INN $$$
(☎707-869-9093; www.applewoodinn.com; 13,555 Hwy 116, Guerneville; r $275-500; @) A hideaway estate on a wooded hilltop south of town, cushy Applewood has marvelous 1920s-era detail, with dark wood and heavy

furniture that echo the forest. Some rooms have Jacuzzi and couples' shower; some have fireplace. Amenities include a small spa and two heated pools, but the best perk is the coupon for complimentary tastings at more than 100 wineries.

Eating

Healdsburg is the area's culinary capital and its **Tuesday** (707-824-8717; www.healdsburgfarmersmarket.org; Plaza & Center Sts; 9am to 1pm May 29-Aug 28) and **Saturday** (www.healdsburgfarmersmarket.org; North & Vine Sts; 8:30am-noon Sat May-Nov) markets feature plenty of vendors and small tastings, but Santa Rosa, Sebastopol and Occidental are nothing to sneeze at, either. In general, this region is a foodie's dream, with prices far more reasonable than over in Napa Valley.

Chalkboard CALIFORNIAN **$$**
(707-473-8030; www.chalkboardhealdsburg.com; 29 North St, Healdsburg; mains $20-27; 4:30-9pm Mon-Fri, 11:30am-10pm Sat & Sun) With its tony grotto setting, sunny back patio and changing daily menu, this top restaurant focuses on pulling the freshest ingredients from local farms. The small-plate menu is ideal for sharing. Don't miss out on a housemade pasta or fresh melon soup to start, followed by locally caught scallops, crispy fried chicken and steak.

★ **Backyard** CALIFORNIAN **$$$**
(707-820-8445; www.backyardforestville.com; 6566 Front St, Forestville; mains lunch & brunch $14-30, dinner mains $22-30; 11:30am-9pm Mon & Fri, 9am-9pm Sat, to 8pm Sun) This relaxing, alfresco spot gets every fruit, vegetable and animal from local farmers or fishers and the chef knows just what to do with all of it. California-inspired dishes are simple and delicious; the steak, piquillo-pepper and duck-egg hash was perhaps the world's most perfect brunch. The coffee and artisanal doughnut holes are winners.

★ **SingleThread Farm-Restaurant-Inn** JAPANESE **$$$**
(707-723-4646; www.singlethreadfarms.com; 131 North St, Healdsburg; tasting menu per person $293; dinner daily from 5:30pm, lunch Sat & Sun from 11:30am) The most ambitious project in Northern California is SingleThread, a world-class restaurant and, secondarily, an inn, where *omotenashi* (warm hospitality in Japanese) reigns and dishes from an 11-course tasting menu are prepared in handmade Japanese *donabe* (earthenware pots). The cuisine is California-Japanese and guests book tickets in advance, offering up their preferences and dietary restrictions, and the chef abides.

North Coast

This is not the legendary California of the Beach Boys' song – there are no palm-flanked beaches and very few surfboards. The jagged edge of the continent is wild, scenic and even slightly foreboding, where spectral fog and an outsider spirit have fostered the world's tallest trees, most potent weed and a string of idiosyncratic two-stoplight towns. Explore hidden coves with a blanket and a bottle of local wine, scan the horizon for migrating whales and retreat at night to fire-warmed Victorians. As you travel further north, find valleys of redwood, wide rivers and mossy, overgrown forests. Expect cooler, damper weather too.

Coastal Highway 1 to Mendocino

Often winding precariously atop ocean cliffs, this serpentine slice of Hwy 1 passes salty fishing harbors and hidden beaches. Use roadside pullouts to scan the Pacific horizon for migrating whales or to amble coves bounded by startling rock formations and relentlessly pounded by the surf. The 110-mile stretch from Bodega Bay to Fort Bragg takes at least three hours of nonstop driving; at night or in the fog it takes steely nerves and much, much longer.

BODEGA BAY

Bodega Bay, the first pearl in a string of sleepy fishing villages, was the setting for Hitchcock's terrifying 1963 psycho-horror flick *The Birds*. Today the skies are free from bloodthirsty gulls, but you'd best keep an eye on that picnic basket as you explore the arched rocks, blustery coves and wildflower-covered bluffs of **Sonoma Coast State Park** (www.parks.ca.gov; per car $8), with beaches rolling beyond Jenner, 10 miles north. **Bodega Bay Sportfishing Center** (707-875-3495; www.bodegabaysportfishing.com; 1410b Bay Flat Rd; fishing trips from $130, whale-watching $60;) runs winter whale-watching trips. Landlubbers hike Bodega Head or saddle up at **Chanslor Ranch** (707-589-5040; https://chanslorstables.com; 2660 N Hwy 1; rides from $40; 9am-5pm).

Stop by classic dockside crab shack **Spud Point** (707-875-9472; www.spudpointcrab.com; 1910 Westshore Rd; mains $6.75-12; 9am-5pm;

(P 🍴) for salty-sweet crab sandwiches and real clam chowder (that consistently wins local culinary prizes).

JENNER & AROUND

Where the wide, lazy Russian River meets the Pacific, you'll find Jenner, a cluster of shops and restaurants dotting coastal hills. Informative volunteers protect the resident colony of harbor seals at the river's mouth during pupping season, between March and August. **Water Treks Ecotours** (☎707-865-2249; www.watertreks.com; 2hr kayak rental from $50, 4hr guided tours from $120; ⏲hours vary) rents kayaks on Hwy 1; reservations recommended.

Twelve miles north of Jenner, the salt-weathered structures of **Fort Ross State Historic Park** (☎707-847-3437; www.fortross.org; 19005 Hwy 1; per car $8; ⏲park sunrise-sunset, visitor center 10am-4:30pm) preserve an 1812 trading post and Russian Orthodox church. It's a quiet place, but the history is riveting: this was once the southernmost reach of Tsarist Russia's North American trading expeditions. The small, wood-scented museum offers historical exhibits and respite from the windswept cliffs.

SALT POINT STATE PARK

Several miles further north, **Salt Point State Park** (☎707-847-3221; www.saltpoint.org; 25050 Hwy 1; per car $8; ⏲park sunrise-sunset, visitor center 10am-3pm Sat & Sun Apr-Oct; P) abounds with hiking trails and tide pools and has two **campgrounds** (☎800-444-7275; www.reserveamerica.com; Salt Point State Park; tent & RV sites $35; P). At neighboring **Kruse Rhododendron State Natural Reserve**, pink blooms spot the misty greenwoods between April and June. Cows graze the fields on the bluffs heading north to **Sea Ranch** (www.tsra.org), where public-access hiking trails lead downhill from roadside parking lots (per car $7) to pocket beaches.

There are two good places to stay enroute to Point Arena: campers should head to **Gualala Point Regional Park** (☎707-785-2377; http://parks.sonomacounty.ca.gov; 42401 Hwy 1, Gualala; parking $7, tent & RV sites $35; ⏲6am-sunset summer, 8am-sunset winter; P) for the best drive-in camping on this stretch of the coast; in Anchor Bay, don't miss **Mar Vista Cottages** (☎707-884-3522; www.marvistamendocino.com; 35101 Hwy 1, Anchor Bay; cottages $195-310; P 🚭 📶 🐾). These elegantly renovated 1930s fishing cabins offer a simple, stylish seaside escape with a vanguard commitment to sustainability.

POINT ARENA & AROUND

Stop on Main St for the cutest patisserie on this stretch of coast, run by Franny and her mother, Barbara. The fresh berry tarts and creative housemade chocolates at **Franny's Cup & Saucer** (☎707-882-2500; www.frannyscupandsaucer.com; 213 Main St; cakes from $2; ⏲8am-4pm Wed-Sat) seem too beautiful to eat, until you take the first bite and immediately want to order another.

Two miles north of Point Arena town, detour to wind-battered **Point Arena Lighthouse** (☎707-882-2809; www.pointarenalighthouse.com; 45500 Lighthouse Rd; adult/child $8/1; ⏲10am-3:30pm mid-Sep–mid-May, to 4:30pm mid-May–mid-Sep; P), built in 1908. View the Fresnel lens in the museum then ascend 145 steps to get jaw-dropping coastal views. Eight miles north of the Little River crossing at Hwy 128 is **Van Damme State Park** (☎707-937-0851; www.parks.ca.gov; 8001 N Hwy 1, Little River; per car $8; ⏲hours vary; P), where the popular 5-mile round-trip Fern Canyon Trail passes through a lush river canyon with young redwoods, continuing another mile each way to a pygmy forest.

Mendocino

In Mendocino, a historical village perched on a gorgeous headland, baby boomers stroll around New England saltbox and water-tower B&Bs, quaint shops and art galleries. Wilder paths pass berry brambles, wildflowers and cypress trees standing guard over rocky cliffs and raging surf at Mendocino Headlands State Park (www.parks.ca.gov). The **Ford House Museum & Visitor Center** (☎707-937-5397; www.mendoparks.org; 45035 Main St; ⏲11am-4pm) is nearby.

Just south of town, paddle your way up the Big River with **Catch a Canoe & Bicycles, Too** (☎707-937-0273; www.catchacanoe.com; 10051 S Big River Rd, The Stanford Inn By The Sea; 3hr kayak, canoe or bicycle rental adult/child $35/15; ⏲9am-5pm). North of town, 1909 **Point Cabrillo Light Station** (☎707-937-6123; www.pointcabrillo.org; 45300 Lighthouse Rd; ⏲park sunrise-sunset, lighthouse 11am-4pm) FREE is a perfect winter whale-watching perch.

Accommodations standards are high in stylish Mendocino and so are prices; two-day minimums often crop up on weekends. For a range of cottages and B&Bs, contact **Mendocino Coast Reservations** (☎707-937-5033; www.mendocinovacations.com; 45084 Little Lake St; ⏲9am-4pm).

Alegria (707-937-5150; www.oceanfrontmagic.com; 44781 Main St; r $239-309;) is the perfect romantic hideaway: beds have views over the coast, decks have ocean views and all rooms have wood-burning fireplaces; outside, a gorgeous path leads to a big, amber-gray beach. The cluster of 1950s roadside cottages that is **Andiron Seaside Inn & Cabins** (707-937-1543; http://theandiron.com; 6051 N Hwy 1, Little River; d $134-284; P) is another good choice. With hip vintage decor, it's a refreshingly playful option amid the cabbage-rose and lace aesthetic of Mendocino.

For refined, inspired cooking, you can't do better than **Café Beaujolais** (707-937-5614; www.cafebeaujolais.com; 961 Ukiah St; lunch mains $11-20, dinner mains $24-42; 11:30am-2:30pm Wed & Thu, to 3pm Fri-Sun, 5:30-9pm daily; P), Mendocino's iconic, beloved country-Cal-French restaurant occupying an 1893 farmhouse. The locally sourced menu changes with the seasons, but the dry-aged duck breast is a gourmand's delight. Follow the boardwalk lit with fairy lights to cozy, casual **Luna Trattoria** (707-962-3093; www.lunatrattoria.com; 955 Ukiah St; mains $12-29; 5-9pm Tue-Thu & Sun, to 10pm Fri & Sat), serving up generous portions of Northern Italian fare. The bread and pastas are homemade, and there's a lovely garden out back.

Along Highway 101 to Avenue of the Giants

To get into the most remote and wild parts of the North Coast behind the 'Redwood Curtain' quickly, eschew winding Hwy 1 for inland Hwy 101, which occasionally pauses under the traffic lights of small towns. Diversions along the way include bountiful redwood forests past Leggett and the abandoned wilds of the Lost Coast.

A short detour off Hwy 101 just before Ukiah leads you to **Boonville**, home to Bavarian-style **Anderson Valley Brewing Company** (707-895-2337; www.avbc.com; 17700 Hwy 253, Boonville; tasting from $10, tours & disc-golf course free; 11am-6pm Sat-Thu, to 7pm Fri; P) and the impressive **Boonville Hotel** (707-895-2210; www.boonvillehotel.com; 14050 Hwy 128, Boonville; d $215-395; P); the in-house **restaurant** (lunch mains $10-15, dinner tasting menu from $48; 6-8pm Thu-Sat, from 5:30pm Sun Apr-Nov, 6-8pm Fri & Sat, 1-2:30pm Sun Dec-Mar; P), under the helm of renowned chef Perry Hoffman, features distinctive haute cuisine made up of seasonal produce, local seafood and meat, along with foraged greens and mushrooms.

UKIAH

Although Ukiah is mostly a place to gas up, it's worth stopping for an arty pizza at **Cultivo** (707-462-7007; www.cultivorestaurant.com; 108 W Standley St; pizzas $14-19, mains $19-24; 11:30am-9pm Mon-Thu, to 10pm Fri & Sat) or a vegetarian Asian-influenced meal at **Jyun Kang Vegetarian Restaurant** (707-468-7966; www.cttbusa.org; City of Ten Thousand Buddhas; mains $6-12; 11:30am-3pm Wed-Mon;).

LEGGETT

North of tiny Leggett on Hwy 101, take a dip in the Eel River at **Standish-Hickey State Recreation Area** (707-925-6482; www.parks.ca.gov; 69350 Hwy 101; day use per car $8, camping incl 1 car $35, extra car $8;), where hiking trails traipse through virgin and second-growth redwoods. South of Garberville on Hwy 101, **Richardson Grove State Park** (707-247-3318, 707-247-3378; www.parks.ca.gov; 1600 Hwy 101, Garberville; per car $8) also protects old-growth redwood forest beside the river. Both parks have developed **campgrounds** (reservations 800-444-7275; www.reservecalifornia.com; 1600 Hwy 101; tent & RV sites $35, cabins $80; P).

LOST COAST

The Lost Coast tempts hikers with the most rugged coastal backpacking in California. It became 'lost' when the state's highway bypassed the mountains of the King Range, which rises over 4000ft within a few miles of the ocean. From Garberville, it's 23 steep, twisting miles along a paved road to **Shelter Cove**, the main supply point but little more than a seaside subdivision with a general store, cafes and none-too-cheap ocean-view lodgings.

HUMBOLDT REDWOODS STATE PARK

Along Hwy 101, 82-sq-mile **Humboldt Redwoods State Park** (707-946-2409; www.parks.ca.gov; Hwy 101; P) FREE protects some of California's oldest redwoods, including more than half of the world's tallest 100 trees. Magnificent groves rival those in Redwood National Park, a long drive further north. If you don't have time to hike, at least drive the awe-inspiring **Avenue of the Giants**, a 32-mile, two-lane road parallel to Hwy 101. Book ahead for **campsites** (information 707-946-1811, reservations 800-444-7275; www.reservecalifornia.com; tent & RV sites $20-35; P).

Highway 101 from Eureka to Crescent City

There is a solid choice of accommodations throughout the southern redwood coast, including in Eureka, Arcata and Crescent City. Enthusiastic campers can choose between the wilderness options on the Lost Coast or more developed camping in the state parks.

You'll find a plethora of natural-food stores and markets along this stretch of the highway. Eureka and Arcata have a particularly fine choice of dining venues.

EUREKA

Past the strip malls sprawling around its edges, the heart of Eureka is Old Town, abounding with fine Victorian buildings, antique shops and restaurants. Cruise the harbor aboard the blue-and-white 1910 **Madaket** (Madaket Cruises; ☎707-445-1910; www.humboldtbaymaritimemuseum.com; 1st St; narrated cruises adult/child $22/18; ⏲1pm, 2:30pm & 4pm Tue-Sun, 1pm & 2:30pm Mon mid-May–mid-Oct) – 75-minute cruises cost adults $22 and depart from the foot of C St, while sunset cocktail cruises ($10) serve from the state's smallest licensed bar. The **visitor center** (☎707-733-5406; www.fws.gov/refuge/Humboldt_Bay/visit/VisitorCenter.html; Loleta; ⏲8am-5pm) is on Hwy 101, south of downtown.

Constructed in period style, the aesthetically remodeled rooms of the **Carter House Inns** (☎707-444-8062; www.carterhouse.com; 301 L St; r $184-395; P⊖☜🐾) have modern amenities and top-quality linens; suites have in-room Jacuzzis and marble fireplaces. It's also home to the sophisticated **Restaurant 301** (☎707-444-8062; www.carterhouse.com; 301 L St; mains $22-38; ⏲5-9pm) 🍃, serving up contemporary Californian fare using produce sourced from its organic gardens.

Exuding a cozy bistro-style ambience with red-and-white checkered tablecloths and jaunty murals, perennially popular **Cafe Nooner** (☎707-443-4663; www.cafenooner.com; 409 Opera Alley; mains $10-17; ⏲11am-4pm; 👪) serves organic and Med-inspired cuisine with choices that include a Greek-style meze platter, plus kebabs, salads and soups. For thin-crust pizza, head to perennially busy **Brick & Fire** (☎707-268-8959; www.brickandfirebistro.com; 1630 F St; dinner mains $17-24; ⏲11:30am-9pm Mon & Wed-Fri, 5-9pm Sat & Sun; ☜).

ARCATA

On the north side of Humboldt Bay, Arcata is a patchouli-dipped haven of radical politics. Biodiesel-fueled trucks drive in for the Saturday **farmers market** (www.humfarm.org; 9am to 2pm April to November, from 10am December to March) on the central plaza, surrounded by art galleries, shops, cafes and bars. Make reservations to soak at **Finnish Country Sauna & Tubs** (☎707-822-2228; http://cafemokkaarcata.com; 495 J St; per 30min adult/child $10.25/2; ⏲noon-11pm Sun-Thu, to midnight Fri & Sat; 👪). Northeast of downtown stands eco-conscious, socially responsible **Humboldt State University** (HSU; ☎707-826-3011; www.humboldt.edu; 1 Harpst St; P) 🍃.

Pop by Arcata's best grocery store, **Wildberries Marketplace** (☎707-822-0095; www.wildberries.com; 747 13th St, Arcata; sandwiches $5-8; ⏲6am-midnight; P🌶), to stock up on supplies, or linger over a 'brew with a view' at **Six Rivers Brewery** (☎707-839-7580; www.sixriversbrewery.com; 1300 Central Ave, McKinleyville; ⏲11:30am-11:30pm Sun-Wed, to 12:30am Thu-Sat), one of the first female-owned breweries in California.

TRINIDAD

Sixteen miles north of Arcata, Trinidad sits on a bluff overlooking a breathtakingly beautiful fishing harbor. Stroll sandy beaches or take short hikes around Trinidad Head after meeting tide-pool critters at the **HSU Telonicher Marine Laboratory** (☎707-826-3671; www.humboldt.edu/marinelab; 570 Ewing St; $1; ⏲9am-4:30pm Mon-Fri year-round, plus 10am-5pm Sat & Sun Aug-May; P👪) 🍃. Heading north of town, Patrick's Point Dr is dotted with forested campgrounds, cabins and lodges. **Patrick's Point State Park** (☎707-677-3570; www.parks.ca.gov; 4150 Patrick's Point Dr; per car $8; ⏲sunrise-sunset; P👪) 🍃 has stunning rocky headlands, beachcombing, an authentic reproduction of a Yurok village and a **campground** (☎information 707-677-3570, reservations 800-444-7275; www.reservecalifornia.com; 4150 Patrick's Point Dr; tent & RV sites $35 plus $8 for any additional vehicle; P🐾) with coin-operated hot showers.

REDWOOD NATIONAL PARK

Heading north, Hwy 101 passes Redwood National Park's **Thomas H Kuchel Visitor Center** (☎707-465-7765; www.nps.gov/redw; Hwy 101, Orick; ⏲9am-5pm Apr-Oct, to 4pm Nov-Mar; 👪). Together, the national park and three state parks – Prairie Creek, Del Norte and Jedediah Smith – are a World Heritage site containing more than 40% of the world's

WORTH A TRIP

ORR HOT SPRINGS

A soak in the thermal waters of the rustic **Orr Hot Springs** (707-462-6277; www.orrhotsprings.org; 13201 Orr Springs Rd; day use adult/child $30/25; by appointment 10am-10pm) is heavenly. While it's not for the bashful, the clothing-optional resort is beloved by locals, back-to-the-land hipsters, backpackers and liberal-minded tourists. Enjoy the private tubs, a sauna, a spring-fed, rock-bottomed swimming pool, steam room, massage and magical gardens. Make reservations.

There are also six yurts as well as **rooms** (707-462-6277; www.orrhotsprings.org; 13201 Orr Springs Rd; tent sites per adult/child $70/35, r & yurt $220, cottages $297.60;) on-site, should you wish to linger.

remaining old-growth redwood forests. The national park is free, while state parks have an $8 day-use parking fee and developed campgrounds (p336). This patchwork of state- and federally managed land stretches all the way north to the Oregon border, interspersed with several towns. Furthest south, you'll encounter **Redwood National Park** (707-464-6101, 707-465-7335; www.nps.gov/redw; Hwy 101, Orick;) FREE, where a 1½-mile nature trail winds through **Lady Bird Johnson Grove**.

PRAIRIE CREEK REDWOODS STATE PARK

Six miles north of Orick, the 10-mile Newton B Drury Scenic Parkway runs parallel to Hwy 101 through **Prairie Creek Redwoods State Park** (707-465-7335; www.parks.ca.gov; Newton B Drury Scenic Pkwy; day-use parking fee $8;). Roosevelt elk graze in the meadow outside the **visitor center** (707-488-2039; www.parks.ca.gov; Newton B Drury Scenic Pkwy; 9am-5pm May-Sep, to 4pm Oct-Apr), where sunlight-dappled hiking trails begin. Three miles back south, mostly unpaved Davison Rd heads northwest to Gold Bluffs Beach, dead-ending at the trailhead for unbelievably lush **Fern Canyon**.

North of tiny Klamath, Hwy 101 passes the **Trees of Mystery** (707-482-2251; www.treesofmystery.net; 15500 Hwy 101; museum free, gondola adult/child $18/9; 9am-4:30pm;), a kitschy roadside attraction.

DEL NORTE COAST REDWOODS STATE PARK

Next up, Del Norte Coast Redwoods State Park preserves virgin redwood groves and unspoiled coastline. The 4.5-mile round-trip **Damnation Creek Trail** careens over 1000ft downhill past redwoods to a hidden rocky beach, best visited at low tide. Find the trailhead at a parking turnout near mile marker 16 on Hwy 101.

CRESCENT CITY & AROUND

Backed by a fishing harbor and bay, Crescent City is drab because, after more than half the town was destroyed by a tidal wave in 1964, it was rebuilt with utilitarian architecture. When the tide's out, you can walk across to the 1856 **Battery Point Lighthouse** (707-464-3089; https://delnortehistory.org; South A St; adult/child $5/1; 10am-4pm Apr-Sep, 10am-4pm Sat & Sun Oct-Mar) from the south end of A St.

Beyond Crescent City, **Jedediah Smith Redwoods State Park** (707-465-7335; www.parks.ca.gov; Hwy 199, Hiouchi; day-use parking fee $8; sunrise-sunset;) is the northernmost park in the system. The redwood stands here are so dense that there are few trails, but a couple of easy hikes start near riverside swimming holes along Hwy 199 and rough, unpaved Howland Hill Rd, a 10-mile scenic drive. The Redwood National & State Parks' **Crescent City Information Center** (707-465-7306; www.nps.gov/redw; 1111 2nd St; 9am-5pm Apr-Oct, to 4pm Nov-Mar) has maps and info.

Sacramento

California's capital is a city of contrasts. Home to the **California State Capitol** (916-324-0333; http://capitolmuseum.ca.gov; 1315 10th St; 8am-5pm Mon-Fri, from 9am Sat & Sun;) FREE, here state legislators' SUVs go bumper-to-bumper with farmers' muddy, half-ton pickups at rush hour. The people of 'Sac' are a resourceful lot that have fostered small but thriving food, art and nightlife scenes. They rightfully crow about **Second Saturday**, the monthly Midtown gallery hop that is the symbol of the city's cultural awakening. Their ubiquitous farmers markets, farm-to-fork fare and craft beers are another point of pride.

Sights

★Golden 1 Center STADIUM

(box office 916-840-5700; www.golden1center.com; 500 David J Stern Walk) Welcome to the arena of the future. This gleaming home to the Sacramento Kings is one of the most advanced sports facilities in the country. Made with the highest sustainability standard, it's built from local materials, powered by solar and cooled by five-story airplane hangar doors that swing open to capture the pleasant Delta breeze.

★California Museum MUSEUM
(916-653-0650; www.californiamuseum.org; 1020 O St; adult/child $9/6.50; 10am-5pm Tue-Sat, from noon Sun;) This modern museum is home to the California Hall of Fame and so the only place to simultaneously encounter César Chávez, Mark Zuckerberg and Amelia Earhart. The California Indians exhibit is a highlight, with artifacts and oral histories of more than 10 tribes.

Sleeping

The capital is a magnet for business travelers, so Sacramento doesn't lack hotels. Many have good deals during legislative recesses. Unless you're in town for something at Cal Expo, stay Downtown or Midtown, where there's plenty to do within walking distance. If you're into kitschy motor lodges from the 1950s, cross the river into West Sac for the last-standing members of Motel Row on Rte 40.

Greens Hotel BOUTIQUE HOTEL $
(916-921-1736; www.thegreenshotel.com; 1700 Del Paso Blvd; r from $109;) This stylishly updated mid-century motel is one of Sacramento's hippest places to stay. The area is charming, with a cute coffee shop and an art gallery next door, and Greens' secure parking, pool and spacious grounds make this an ideal place for families to stop en route to or from Tahoe. The chic rooms are also classy enough for a romantic getaway.

★Citizen Hotel BOUTIQUE HOTEL $$
(916-442-2700; www.thecitizenhotel.com; 926 J St; r from $180;) After an elegant, ultrahip upgrade, this long-vacant 1927 beaux-arts tower became Downtown's coolest place to stay. The details are spot-on: luxe linens, wide-striped wallpaper and a rooftop patio with a great view of the city. There's an upscale farm-to-fork **restaurant** (916-492-4450; 926 J St; mains $29-55; 6:30-10:30am, 11:30am-2:30pm & 5:30-10pm Mon-Thu, to 11pm Fri, 8am-2pm & 5:30-11pm Sat, to 9pm Sun;) on the ground floor.

Eating & Drinking

Skip the overpriced fare in Old Sacramento or by the capitol and head Midtown or to the Tower District. A cruise up J St or Broadway passes a number of hip, affordable restaurants where tables spill onto the sidewalks in the summer. Many source farm-fresh ingredients.

La Bonne Soupe Cafe DELI $
(916-492-9506; 980 9th St; items $5-8; 11am-3pm Mon-Fri) In a new space as of 2018, this beloved French cafe continues to serve divine soup and sandwiches, assembled with such care that the line of downtowners snakes out the door. In a hurry? Skip it. This humble lunch counter is focused on quality that predates drive-through haste.

Be sure not to confuse it with the similarly named spot next door, La Bou Bakery & Cafe.

★Empress Tavern NEW AMERICAN $$$
(916-662-7694; www.empresstavern.com; 1013 K St; mains $24-41; 3-10pm Mon-Thu, to 11pm Fri, 5-11pm Sat) In the catacombs under the historic Crest Theater, this gorgeous restaurant hosts a menu of creative, meat-focused dishes (including family-style options like beef-cheek stroganoff and grilled-pork porterhouse). The space itself is just as impressive as the food; the arched brick ceilings and glittering bar feel like a speakeasy supper club from a bygone era.

★Fieldwork Brewing Company BREWERY
(916-329-8367; www.fieldworkbrewing.com; 1805 Capitol Ave; 11am-10pm Sun-Thu, to 11pm Fri & Sat) Bustling with activity, this ultrahip brewpub has 22 rotating taps of excellent draft beer. Playful variations of hoppy IPAs are the specialty (the Pulp IPA is a recurring favorite), but it does lighter seasonal brews like the Salted Watermelon Gose. It also has a small food menu and board games – making it an easy place to linger when the weather is sweltering.

Getting There & Around

Sacramento is at the intersection of major highways, and you'll likely pass through en route to other California destinations. The **Sacramento International Airport** (SMF; 916-929-5411; www.sacramento.aero/smf; 6900 Airport Blvd) is one of the nearest options for those traveling to Yosemite National Park.

The regional **Yolobus** (530-666-2877; www.yolobus.com) route 42B costs $2 and runs hourly between Sacramento International Airport and Downtown, and also goes to West Sacramento, Woodland and Davis. Local **Sacramento**

Regional Transit (RT; ☎916-321-2877; www.sacrt.com; fare $2.50) buses run around town and RT also runs a trolley between Old Sacramento and Downtown, as well as Sacramento's light-rail system, which is best for commuting from outlying communities.

Sacramento is also a fantastic city to cruise around by bike; rent them from **Trek Bicycles Sacramento** (☎916-447-2453; www.facebook.com/TrekBicycleSacramento; 2419 K St; per day $40-100; ⊙10am-7pm Mon-Fri, to 6pm Sat, 11am-5pm Sun).

Gold Country

Hollywood draws the dreamers and Silicon Valley lures fortune-hunters, but this isn't the first time droves of aspiring young folk have streamed into the Golden State. After a sparkle in the American River caught James Marshall's eye in 1848, more than 300,000 prospectors from America and abroad started digging for gold in the Sierra foothills. Soon California entered statehood with the official motto 'Eureka' solidifying its place as the land of opportunity.

The miner forty-niners are gone, but a ride along Hwy 49 through sleepy hill towns, past clapboard saloons and oak-lined byways is a journey back to the wild ride that was modern California's founding: umpteen historical markers tell tales of gold-rush violence and banditry.

Hwy 50 divides the Northern and Southern Mines. Winding Hwy 49, which connects everything, provides plenty of vistas of the famous hills. The Gold Country Visitors Association (https://visitgoldcountry.com) has many more touring ideas.

Getting There & Around

You can reach the region by train on the transcontinental line that links Sacramento and Truckee/Reno and has a stop in Auburn. Auburn is the main entry point of the area, a short hop on the I-80 from Sacramento. From Auburn pick up Hwy 49, the classic route through the Gold Country.

Northern Mines

Known as the 'Queen of the Northern Mines,' the narrow streets of Nevada City gleam with lovingly restored buildings, tiny theaters, art galleries, cafes and shops. The **visitor center** (☎530-265-2692; www.nevadacitychamber.com; 132 Main St; ⊙9am-5pm Mon-Fri, 11am-4pm Sat, noon-3pm Sun) dispenses information and self-guided walking-tour maps. On Hwy 49, the **Tahoe National Forest Headquarters** (☎530-265-4531; www.fs.usda.gov/tahoe; 631 Coyote St; ⊙8am-4:30pm Mon-Fri) provides camping and hiking information.

The six-room **Broad Street Inn** (☎530-265-2239; www.broadstreetinn.com; 517 W Broad St; r $119-134; ❄📶) in the heart of town is a favorite for its good-value modern rooms: brightly but soothingly furnished and elegant. Unusually friendly and fun, **Outside Inn** (☎530-265-2233; http://outsideinn.com; 575 E Broad St; d $94-230; P⊖❄📶🐾) is the best option for active explorers, while Peter Selaya's organic- and local-ingredient menu at elegant **New Moon Cafe** (☎530-265-6399; www.thenewmooncafe.com; 203 York St; dinner mains $25-44; ⊙11:30am-2pm Tue-Fri, 5-8pm Tue-Sun) changes with the seasons.

Moving on, just over a mile east of utilitarian **Grass Valley** and Hwy 49, **Empire Mine State Historic Park** (☎530-273-8522; www.empiremine.org; 10791 Empire St; adult/youth 6-16yr $7/3; ⊙10am-5pm; P) marks the site of one of the richest mines in California. From 1850 to 1956 it produced about 5.8 million troy ounces of gold – over $8 billion in today's market.

If it's hot, one of the best swimming holes in the area is at **Auburn State Recreation Area** (☎530-885-4527; www.parks.ca.gov; 501 El Dorado St; per car $10; ⊙7am-sunset). It's just east of Auburn, an I-80 pit stop about 25 miles south of Grass Valley.

Coloma is where California's gold rush started. Riverside **Marshall Gold Discovery State Historic Park** (☎530-622-3470; www.parks.ca.gov; Hwy 49, Coloma; per car $8; ⊙8am-8pm late May-early Sep, to 5pm early Sep-late May; P🐾) pays tribute to James Marshall's riot-inducing discovery, with restored buildings and gold-panning opportunities. The park is also home to **Argonaut Farm to Fork Cafe** (☎530-626-7345; www.argonautcafe.com; 331 Hwy 49, Coloma; items $8-12; ⊙8am-4pm; 📶), serving up truly delicious soups, sandwiches, baked goods and coffee.

Southern Mines

The towns of the Southern Mines – from Placerville to Sonora – receive less traffic and their dusty streets retain a whiff of Wild West, today evident in the motley crew of Harley riders and gold prospectors (still!) who populate them.

Some, like **Plymouth** (ol' Pokerville), **Volcano** and **Mokelumne Hill**, are virtual ghost towns, slowly crumbling into photogenic oblivion. Others, like **Sutter Creek**,

Murphys and **Angels Camp**, are gussied-up showpieces of Victorian Americana. Get off the beaten path at family-run vineyards and subterranean caverns, where geological wonders reward those who first navigate the touristy gift shops above ground.

Lacy B&Bs, cafes and ice-cream parlors are found in nearly every town. For something different, try the **Imperial Hotel** (209-267-9172; www.imperialamador.com; 14202 Old Hwy 49, Amador City; r $110-155, ste $125-195;) in Plymouth. Built in 1879, it's one of the area's most inventive updates, with sleek art-deco touches accenting the warm red brick, a genteel bar and a very good, seasonally minded restaurant (dinner mains $16 to $38).

A short detour off Hwy 49, **Columbia State Historic Park** (209-588-9128; www.parks.ca.gov; 11255 Jackson St; most businesses 10am-5pm; P) FREE preserves blocks of authentic 1850s buildings complete with shopkeepers and street musicians in period costumes. Near Sonora, **Railtown 1897 State Historic Park** (209-984-3953; www.railtown1897.org; 10501 Reservoir Rd, Jamestown; adult/child $5/3, incl train ride $15/10; 9:30am-4:30pm Apr-Oct, 10am-3pm Nov-Mar, train rides 10:30am-3pm Sat & Sun Apr-Oct; P) offers excursion trains through the surrounding hills where Hollywood Westerns including *High Noon* have been filmed.

California's Northern Mountains

Remote, empty and eerily beautiful, these are some of California's least visited wild lands, an endless show of geological wonders, clear lakes, rushing rivers and high desert. The major peaks – Lassen, Shasta and the Trinity Alps – have few geological features in common, but all offer backcountry camping under starry skies.

Redding to Mt Shasta

Much of the drive north of Redding is dominated by Mt Shasta, a 14,180ft snowcapped goliath at the southern end of the volcanic Cascades Range. It arises dramatically, fueling the anticipation felt by mountaineers who seek to climb its slopes.

Roadside motels are abundant, including in Mt Shasta city. Redding has the most chain lodgings, clustered near major highways. Campgrounds are abundant, especially on public lands.

Greyhound (www.greyhound.com) buses heading north and south on I-5 stop at the depot (628 S Weed Blvd) in Weed, 8 miles north of Mt Shasta city on I-5. Services include Redding (from $22, one hour and 20 minutes, four daily), Sacramento (from $40, 5½ hours, four daily) and San Francisco (from $55, 7½ hours, two or three times daily).

REDDING & AROUND

Don't believe the tourist brochures: Redding, the region's largest city, is a snooze. The best reason to detour off I-5 is the **Sundial Bridge**, a glass-bottomed pedestrian marvel designed by Spanish neofuturist architect Santiago Calatrava. It spans the Sacramento River at **Turtle Bay Exploration Park** (530-243-8850; www.turtlebay.org; 844 Sundial Bridge Dr; adult/child $16/12, after 2:30pm $11/7; 9am-5pm Mon-Sat, from 10am Sun late Mar-Oct, 9am-4:30pm Wed-Fri, from 10am Sat & Sun Nov–mid-Mar;), a kid-friendly science and nature center with botanical gardens.

Six miles west of Redding along Hwy 299, explore a genuine gold-rush town at **Shasta State Historic Park** (520-243-8194; www.parks.ca.gov; 15312 CA 299; museum entry adult/child $3/2; 10am-5pm Thu-Sun). Although the devastating Carr Fire ripped through this park in 2018, the main attractions were all salvaged. Three miles west, **Whiskeytown National Recreation Area** (530-246-1225; www.nps.gov/whis; 14412 Kennedy Memorial Dr, Whiskeytown; 10am-4pm) was the starting point of the fire, which burned 93% of the park's 42,000 acres before destroying 1604 nearby structures. The park's visitor center is back up and running, and people are again showing up at **Whiskeytown Lake** for its sandy beaches, water sports and camping opportunities. But the park's interior remains in rough shape, with several roads and all of the trails (including waterfall hikes and mountain-biking routes) still closed. In sleepy **Weaverville**, another 35 miles further west, **Joss House State Historic Park** (530-623-5284; www.parks.ca.gov; 630 Main St; tour adult/child $4/2; tours hourly 10am-4pm Thu-Sun; P) preserves an ornate 1874 Chinese immigrant temple.

SHASTA LAKE

North of Redding, I-5 crosses deep-blue Shasta Lake, California's biggest reservoir, formed by colossal **Shasta Dam** (530-247-8555; www.usbr.gov/mp/ncao/shasta-dam.html; 16349 Shasta Dam Blvd; visitor center 8am-5pm, tours 9am, 11am, 1pm & 3pm Sep-May, 9am, 10:15am, 11:30am, 1pm, 2:15pm, 3:30pm Jun-

Aug; P) FREE and ringed by houseboat marinas and RV campgrounds. High in the limestone megaliths on the lake's northern side are prehistoric **Lake Shasta Caverns** (530-238-2341; www.lakeshastacaverns.com; 20359 Shasta Caverns Rd, Lakehead; 2hr tour adult/child 3-15yr $30/18; tours every 30min 9am-4pm late May-early Sep, hourly 9am-3pm Apr-late May & early-late Sep, 10am, noon & 2pm Oct-Mar; P), where tours include a catamaran ride or a dinner cruise on the lake.

DUNSMUIR

Another 35 miles north on I-5, Dunsmuir is a teeny historic railroad town with vibrant art galleries inhabiting a quaint downtown district. Simple and elegant, **Café Maddalena** (530-235-2725; www.cafemaddalena.com; 5801 Sacramento Ave; mains $21-28; 5-9pm Thu-Sun Feb-Dec) put Dunsmuir on the foodie map. The menu was designed by chef Brett LaMott (of Trinity Cafe fame) and changes seasonally to feature dishes from southern Europe and northern Africa. Head over to **Dunsmuir Brewery Works** (530-235-1900; www.dunsmuirbreweryworks.com; 5701 Dunsmuir Ave; mains $8-14; 11am-8pm Sun, to 8:30pm Tue-Thu, to 9pm Fri & Sat Oct-Mar, extended hours Apr-Sep;) afterwards, for a crisp ale or perfectly balanced porter.

At the **Railroad Park Resort** (530-235-4440; www.rrpark.com; 100 Railroad Park Rd; tent/RV sites from $29/37, d $135-200;), 2 miles south of town, visitors can spend the night inside refitted vintage railroad cars and cabooses. The grounds are fun for kids, who can run around the engines and plunge in a centrally situated pool and hot tub.

Six miles south off I-5, **Castle Crags State Park** (530-235-2684; www.parks.ca.gov; 20022 Castle Creek Rd; per car $8; sunrise-sunset) shelters forested **campsites** (reservations 800-444-7275; www.reservecalifornia.com; tent & RV sites $25). Be awed by stunning views of Mt Shasta from the top of the park's hardy 5.6-mile round-trip **Crags Trail**.

Just north of Dunsmuir, a detour to the town of McCloud rewards with the **McCloud River Mercantile Hotel** (530-964-2330; www.mccloudmercantile.com; 241 Main St; r $139-275; P), built in 1897. This former lumber company store has been exquisitely restored, and features an old-fashioned candy counter and a 1930s-era soda fountain on the 1st floor. Oh, and the former butcher shop is now a delicious new restaurant, **McCloud Meat Market and Tavern**.

MT SHASTA CITY

Nine miles north of Dunsmuir, Mt Shasta City lures climbers, new-age hippies and back-to-nature types, all of whom revere the majestic mountain looming overhead. Usually open and snow-free beyond Bunny Flat from June until October, **Everitt Memorial Hwy** ascends the mountain to a perfect sunset-watching perch at almost 8000ft – simply head east from town on Lake St and keep going. For experienced mountaineers, climbing the peak above 10,000ft requires a Summit Pass ($25), available from **Mt Shasta Ranger Station** (530-926-4511; www.fs.usda.gov/stnf; 204 W Alma St; 8am-4:30pm Mon-Fri), which has weather reports and sells topographic maps. Stop by downtown's **Fifth Season** (530-926-3606; http://thefifthseason.com; 300 N Mt Shasta Blvd; 9am-6pm Mon-Fri, from 8am Sat, 10am-5pm Sun Apr-Nov, 8am-6pm Dec-Mar) outdoor-gear shop for equipment rentals. **Shasta Mountain Guides** (530-926-3117; http://shastaguides.com; 230 N Mt Shasta Blvd; 2-day climbs per person from $795) offers multiday mountaineering trips.

Only antique on the outside, bright Victorian 1904 **Shasta MountInn** (530-261-1926; www.shastamountinn.com; 203 Birch St; r $150-175; P) farmhouse is all relaxed minimalism, bold colors and graceful decor on the inside. Each airy room has a great bed and exquisite views of the luminous mountain. Pick up an organic, locally roasted coffee at **Seven Suns Coffee & Cafe** (530-926-9701; 1011 S Mt Shasta Blvd; 6am-4pm;) and stock up on groceries and organic produce at **Berryvale Grocery** (530-926-1576; www.berryvale.com; 305 S Mt Shasta Blvd; cafe items from $3; store 8am-8pm, cafe to 7pm;) .

Northeast Corner

LAVA BEDS NATIONAL MONUMENT

Lava Beds National Monument (530-667-8113; www.nps.gov/labe; 1 Indian Well HQ, Tulelake; 7-day entry per car $25; P) is a monument to centuries of turmoil. This park's got it all: lava flows, cinder and spatter cones, volcanic craters and amazing lava tubes. It was the site of the Modoc War, and ancient Native American petroglyphs are etched into rocks and pictographs painted on cave walls. Pick up info, flashlights and maps at the **visitor center** (530-667-8113; www.nps.gov/labe; Tulelake; 10am-4pm with extended but varying hours in summer, spring & fall), where hard hats and kneepads are available for purchase. Nearby is the park's basic **campground** (www.nps.gov/

labe/planyourvisit/campgrounds.htm; tent & RV sites $10; 🐾), where drinking water is available.

KLAMATH BASIN NATIONAL WILDLIFE REFUGE COMPLEX

Over 20 miles northeast of the park, the dusty town of **Tulelake** off Hwy 139 has basic motels, roadside diners and gas. Comprising six separate refuges in California and Oregon, **Klamath Basin National Wildlife Refuge Complex** is a prime stopover on the Pacific Flyway and an important wintering site for bald eagles. When the spring and fall migrations peak, more than a million birds can fill the sky. The **visitor center** (☎530-667-2231; www.klamathbasinrefuges.fws.gov; 4009 Hill Rd, Tulelake; ⏱9am-4pm) is off Hwy 161, about 4 miles south of the Oregon border. Self-guided 10-mile auto tours of the Lower Klamath and Tule Lake refuges provide excellent birding opportunities. Paddle the Upper Klamath refuge's 9.5-mile canoe trail by launching from **Rocky Point Resort** (☎541-356-2287; 28121 Rocky Point Rd, Klamath Falls, OR; canoe & kayak rental per hour/half-day/day $20/45/60; ⏱Apr-Oct; 👪🐾). For gas, food and lodging, drive into Klamath Falls, OR, off Hwy 97.

LASSEN VOLCANIC NATIONAL PARK

Quietly impressive **Lassen Volcanic National Park** (☎530-595-4480; www.nps.gov/lavo; 38050 Hwy 36 E, Mineral; 7-day entry per car mid-Apr–Nov $30, Dec–mid-Apr $10; P) 🍃 has hydrothermal sulfur pools, boiling mud pots and steaming pools, as glimpsed from the **Bumpass Hell** boardwalk. Tackle **Lassen Peak** (10,457ft), the world's largest known plug-dome volcano, on a strenuous, but nontechnical 5-mile round-trip trail. The park has two entrances: an hour's drive east of Redding off Hwy 44, near popular **Manzanita Lake Campground** (☎reservations 877-444-6777; www.recreation.gov; tent & RV sites $15-26; 🐾); and a 40-minute drive northwest of Lake Almanor off Hwy 89, by the **Kom Yah-mah-nee Visitor Facility** (☎530-595-4480; www.nps.gov/lavo; 21820 Lassen National Park Hwy, Mineral; ⏱9am-5pm, closed Mon & Tue Nov-Mar; 👪) 🍃. Hwy 89 through the park is typically snow-free and open to car from June though October.

Sierra Nevada

The mighty Sierra Nevada – baptized the 'Range of Light' by poet-naturalist John Muir – is California's backbone. This 400-mile phalanx of craggy peaks, chiseled and gouged by glaciers and erosion, both welcomes and challenges outdoor-sports enthusiasts. Cradling three national parks (Yosemite, Sequoia and Kings Canyon), the Sierra is a spellbinding wonderland of superlative wilderness, boasting the contiguous USA's highest peak (Mt Whitney), North America's tallest waterfall (Yosemite Falls) and the world's oldest and biggest trees (ancient bristlecone pines and giant sequoias, respectively).

Yosemite National Park

The jaw-dropping head-turner of America's national parks, and a Unesco World Heritage site, **Yosemite** (☎209-372-0200; www.nps.gov/yose/index.htm; per vehicle $35) (yo-*sem*-it-ee) garners the devotion of all who enter. From the waterfall-striped granite walls buttressing emerald-green Yosemite Valley to the sky-scraping giant sequoias catapulting into the air at Mariposa Grove, the place inspires a sense of awe and reverence – over four million visitors wend their way to the country's third-oldest national park annually. But lift your eyes above the crowds and you'll feel your heart instantly moved by unrivaled splendors: the haughty profile of Half Dome, the hulking presence of El Capitan, the drenching mists of Yosemite Falls, the gemstone lakes of the high country's subalpine wilderness and Hetch Hetchy's pristine pathways.

Sights

There are four main entrances to the park ($30 per vehicle): South Entrance (Hwy 41), Arch Rock (Hwy 140), Big Oak Flat (Hwy 120 W) and Tioga Pass (Hwy 120 E). Hwy 120 traverses the park as Tioga Rd, connecting Yosemite Valley with the Eastern Sierra.

Yosemite Valley

From the ground up, this dramatic valley cut by the meandering Merced River is so inspiring: rippling-green meadow grass, stately pines, cool, impassive pools reflecting looming granite monoliths, and cascading ribbons of glacially cold white water. Often overrun and traffic-choked, **Yosemite Village** is home to the park's main **visitor center** (☎209-372-0200; www.nps.gov/yose; 9035 Village Dr, Yosemite Village; ⏱9am-5pm), **museum** (www.nps.gov/yose; 9037 Village Dr, Yosemite Village; ⏱9am-5pm summer, 10am-4pm rest of year, often closed noon-1pm) 🍃 FREE, photography gallery, movie theater, general store and many more services. Half Dome Village (also known as Curry Village) is another valley hub, offering public showers and outdoor-equipment rental and sales, including camping gear.

Spring snowmelt turns the valley's famous waterfalls into thunderous cataracts; most are reduced to a mere trickle by late summer. **Yosemite Falls** is North America's tallest waterfall, dropping 2425ft in three tiers. A wheelchair-accessible trail leads to the bottom of this cascade or, for solitude and different perspectives, you can trek the grueling trail to the top (6.8 miles round trip). No less impressive are other waterfalls around the valley. A strenuous granite staircase beside **Vernal Fall** leads you, gasping, right to the waterfall's edge for a vertical view – look for rainbows in the clouds of mist.

You can't ignore the valley's monumental **El Capitan** (7569ft), an El Dorado for rock climbers. Toothed **Half Dome** (8842ft) soars above the valley as Yosemite's spiritual centerpiece. The classic photo op is at **Tunnel View** on Hwy 41 as you drive into the valley.

Glacier Point

Rising over 3000ft above the valley floor, dramatic Glacier Point (7214ft) practically puts you at eye level with Half Dome. It's at least an hour's drive from Yosemite Valley up Glacier Point Rd (usually open from May into November) off Hwy 41, or a strenuous hike along the **Four Mile Trail** (around 5 miles one way) or the less-crowded, waterfall-strewn **Panorama Trail** (8.5 miles one way). To hike one-way downhill from Glacier Point, reserve a seat on the **Glacier Point Hikers' Bus** (☎888-413-8869; one-way/return $26/52; ⏲mid-May–Oct).

Wawona

At Wawona, an hour's drive south of Yosemite Valley, drop by the **Pioneer Yosemite History Center** (www.nps.gov/yose/planyourvisit/upload/pyhc.pdf; Wawona; rides adult/child $5/4; ⏲24hr, rides 10am-2pm Wed-Sun May-Sep; P 👪) FREE, with its covered bridge, historic buildings and horse-drawn stagecoach rides. Further south stands towering **Mariposa Grove**, home to more than 500 giant sequoias including the Grizzly Giant. Free shuttle buses usually run to the grove from spring through fall.

Tuolumne Meadows

A 90-minute drive from Yosemite Valley, high-altitude Tuolumne Meadows (*twol*-uh-mee) draws hikers, backpackers and climbers to the park's northern wilderness. The Sierra Nevada's largest subalpine meadow (8600ft) is a vivid contrast to the valley, with wildflower fields, azure lakes, granite peaks, polished domes and cooler temperatures. Hikers and climbers have a paradise of options, and lake swimming and picnicking are also popular. Access is via scenic Tioga Rd (Hwy 120), which is only open seasonally. West of Tuolumne Meadows and **Tenaya Lake**, stop at **Olmsted Point** for epic vistas of Half Dome.

Hetch Hetchy

A 40-mile drive northwest of Yosemite Valley, Hetch Hetchy is the site of perhaps the most controversial dam in US history. Despite not existing in its natural state, Hetch Hetchy Valley remains pretty and mostly crowd-free. A 5.4-mile round-trip hike across the dam and through a tunnel to the base of **Wapama Falls** lets you get thrillingly close to an avalanche of water crashing down into the sparkling reservoir.

Activities

With more than 800 miles of hiking trails, you're spoiled for choice. Easy valley-floor routes can get jammed – escape the teeming masses by heading up. Other diversions include rock climbing, cycling, trail rides, swimming, rafting and cross-country skiing.

For overnight backpacking trips, wilderness permits (from $10) are required year-round. A quota system limits the number of hikers leaving daily from each trailhead. Make reservations up to 26 weeks in advance, or try your luck at the Yosemite Valley Wilderness Center (p345) or another permit-issuing station, starting at 11am on the day before you aim to hike.

Sleeping

Camping, even if it's car camping in a campground near busy Yosemite Village, enhances the being-out-in-nature feeling. Backcountry wilderness camping is for the prepared and adventurous. All lodging reservations within the park, including for facilities at Housekeeping Camp and Half Dome Village, are handled by **Aramark/Yosemite Hospitality** (☎888-413-8869; www.travelyosemite.com) and can be made up to 366 days in advance; reservations are critical from April to October. Rates – and demand – drop from December to March. Other park visitors overnight in nearby gateway towns like Fish Camp, Midpines, El Portal, Mariposa and Groveland; however, commute times into the park can be long.

★Majestic Yosemite Hotel HISTORIC HOTEL **$$$**
(☎reservations 888-413-8869; www.travelyosemite.com; 1 Ahwahnee Dr; r/ste from $580/1400; P ⊜ @ ≋ ≊) The crème de la crème of Yosemite's lodging, this sumptuous historic property (formerly called the Ahwahnee) dazzles with soaring ceilings and atmospheric lounges featuring mammoth stone fireplaces. Classic rooms have inspiring views of Glacier Point, Half Dome and Yosemite Falls. Cottages are scattered on the immaculately trimmed lawn next to the hotel. For high season and holidays, book a year in advance.

May Lake High Sierra Camp CABIN **$$$**
(www.travelyosemite.com/lodging/high-sierra-camps; tent & RV sites per person $155) Because it's the easiest of the High Sierra camps to access, May Lake is also the best for children – at least those who'll be untroubled by the mile-plus hike to get here. Views of Mt Hoffman are quite stunning. Breakfast and dinner included in rates, and showers available.

Yosemite Valley Lodge MOTEL **$$$**
(☎209-372-1001, reservations 888-413-8869; www.travelyosemite.com; 9006 Yosemite Lodge Dr; r from $260; P ⊜ @ ≋ ≊) A short walk from Yosemite Falls, this low-slung complex contains a wide range of eateries, a lively bar, a big pool and other amenities. The rooms, spread out over 15 buildings, feel like they're a cross between a motel and a lodge, with rustic wooden furniture and nature photography. Rooms have cable TV, a fridge and coffeemaker, and small patios or balcony panoramas.

Outside Yosemite

Gateway towns that have a mixed bag of motels, hotels, lodges and B&Bs include Fish Camp, Oakhurst, El Portal, Midpines, Mariposa, Groveland and, in the Eastern Sierra, Lee Vining.

★Yosemite Bug Rustic Mountain Resort HOSTEL **$**
(☎209-966-6666; www.yosemitebug.com; 6979 Hwy 140, Midpines; tent sites/dm/tent cabins from $25/38/65, r from $175, with shared bath from $139; P ⊜ @ ≋) This folksy place feels like a secret oasis tucked away on a forested hillside about 25 miles from Yosemite. A wide range of accommodations lines its narrow ridges (cabins, dorms, private rooms and permanent tents). The **June Bug Cafe** (☎206-966-6666; www.yosemitebug.com/cafe; Yosemite Bug Rustic Mountain Resort, 6979 Hwy 140, Midpines; mains $8-24; ⊙7-10am, 11am-2pm & 6-9pm; P ≋ ✎) is highly recommended and worth the trip alone, as are the massages and spa with hot tub and yoga studio ($12 per day).

★Evergreen Lodge CABIN **$$$**
(☎209-379-2606; www.evergreenlodge.com; 33160 Evergreen Rd, Groveland; tents $110-145, cabins $230-495; ⊙usually closed Jan–mid-Feb; P ⊜ ❄ @ ≋ ≊) Outside Yosemite National Park near the entrance to Hetch Hetchy, this classic, nearly century-old resort consists of lovingly decorated and comfy cabins (each with its own cache of board games) spread among the trees. Accommodations run from rustic to deluxe, and all cabins have private porches without a distracting phone or TV. Roughing-it guests can cheat with comfy, prefurnished tents.

Eating

You can find food options for all budgets and palates within the park, from greasy slabs of fast food to swanky cuts of top-notch steak. All places carry good vegetarian options. The **Village Store** (Yosemite Village; ⊙8am-8pm, to 10pm summer) has the best selection (including health-food items and some organic produce), while stores at Half Dome Village, Wawona, Tuolumne Meadows and the Yosemite Valley Lodge are more limited.

Information

Yosemite's entrance fee is $35 per vehicle, $30 per motorcycle or $20 for those on a bicycle or on foot and is valid for seven consecutive days. Passes are sold (you can use cash, checks, traveler's checks or credit/debit cards) at the various entrance stations. From late May to early October, passes are also sold at visitor centers in Oakhurst, Groveland, Mariposa and Lee Vining. You can also pay online (https://yourpassnow.com/ParkPass/park/yose).

Upon entering the park, you'll receive a National Park Service (NPS) map and a copy of the seasonal *Yosemite Guide* newspaper, which includes an activity schedule and current opening hours of all facilities. The official NPS website (www.nps.gov/yose) has the most comprehensive and current information.

For recorded park information, campground availability, and road and weather conditions, call 209-372-0200.

Yosemite Valley Visitor Center (p343)
Park's busiest information desk. Shares space with bookstore run by Yosemite Conservancy and part of the museum complex in the center of Yosemite Village.

Yosemite Valley Wilderness Center (☎209-372-0308; Yosemite Village; ⊙8am-5pm

May-Oct) Wilderness permits, maps and backcountry advice.

Yosemite Medical Clinic (☎209-372-4637, emergency 911; 9000 Ahwahnee Dr, Yosemite Village; ⏱9am-7pm Mon-Fri early Jun-early Jul, 9am-7pm Mon-Sat late Jul–mid-Sep, to 5pm Mon-Fri late Sep-late May) A 24-hour emergency service is available.

Getting There & Around

Yosemite is accessible by car year-round from the west (via Hwys 120 W and 140) and south (Hwy 41), and in summer also from the east (via Hwy 120 E). Roads are plowed in winter, but snow chains may be required. Gas up year-round at Wawona or Crane Flat inside the park (you'll pay dearly), at El Portal on Hwy 140 just outside its western boundary, or at Lee Vining at the junction of Hwys 120 and 395 outside the park in the east.

Roadside signs with red bears mark the many spots where bears have been hit by motorists (many hundreds have been injured and more than 100 killed since 1995), so think before you hit the accelerator, and follow the pokey posted speed limits – they are strictly enforced. Valley visitors are advised to park and take advantage of the **Yosemite Valley Shuttle Bus** (www.nps.gov/yose/planyourvisit/publictransportation.htm; ⏱7am-10pm). Even so, traffic in the valley can feel like rush hour in LA.

Yosemite is one of the few national parks that can easily be reached by public transportation. Greyhound buses and Amtrak trains serve Merced, west of the park, where they are met by buses operated by the **Yosemite Area Regional Transportation System** (YARTS; ☎877-989-2787; www.yarts.com), and you can buy Amtrak tickets that include the YARTS segment all the way into the park. Buses travel to Yosemite Valley along Hwy 140 several times daily year-round, with a variety of stops in Mariposa, Midpines and El Portal along the way. One-way tickets to Yosemite Valley are $16 ($9 child and senior, three hours) from Merced.

Cycling is an ideal way to take in Yosemite Valley. You can rent a wide-handled cruiser (per hour/day $12/34) or a bike with an attached child trailer (per hour/day $20.25/61) at the **Yosemite Valley Lodge** (per hour/day $12/34; ⏱8am-6pm summer only, weather dependent) or **Half Dome Village** (per hour/day $12/34; ⏱10am-4pm Mar-Oct). Strollers and wheelchairs are also rented here.

Sequoia & Kings Canyon National Parks

Joined by a high-altitude roadway bisecting a national forest and contiguous with a number of wilderness areas, these two parks combined offer vast stretches of alpine bliss. Groves of giant sequoias, wildflower-strewn meadows, gushing waterfalls, dramatic gorges and spectacular vistas reveal themselves at nearly every turn. General Grant Grove (p347) and the **Giant Forest** (off Generals Hwy), in Kings Canyon and Sequoia respectively, are obvious highlights.

Throw in opportunities for caving, rock climbing and backcountry hiking through granite-carved Sierra landscapes as well as backdoor access to 14,505ft Mt Whitney – the tallest peak in the lower 48 states – and you have all the ingredients for two of the best parks in the country.

The two **parks** (☎559-565-3341; www.nps.gov/seki; 7-day entry per car $35; 🅿🚻) though distinct, are operated as one unit with a single admission fee; for 24-hour recorded information, including road conditions, call the number listed or visit the parks' comprehensive website.

CAMPING IN YOSEMITE

Competition for sites at one of the park's 13 campgrounds is fierce from May to September, and there are no first-come, first-served campgrounds in Yosemite Valley. Those outside the valley tend to fill by noon, especially on weekends and around holidays.

All campgrounds have flush toilets, except for Tamarack Flat, Yosemite Creek and Porcupine Flat, which have vault toilets and no potable water. Those at higher elevations get chilly at night, even in summer, so pack accordingly. The **Yosemite Mountaineering School** (☎209-372-8344; www.travelyosemite.com; Half Dome Village; ⏱8:30am-5pm Apr-Oct) rents camping gear.

If you hold a wilderness permit, you may spend the nights before and after your trip in the backpacker campgrounds at Tuolumne Meadows, Hetch Hetchy, White Wolf and behind North Pines in Yosemite Valley.

Opening dates for seasonal campgrounds vary according to the weather. For the most accurate camping information, contact Yosemite National Park directly or visit www.nps.gov/yose/planyourvisit/campgrounds.htm.

Sights

Sequoia National Park

For a primer on the ecology and history of giant sequoias, the pint-sized **Giant Forest Museum** (559-565-3341; www.nps.gov/seki; 47050 Generals Hwy, cnr Crescent Meadow Rd; 9am-4:30pm winter, to 6pm summer; P) FREE will entertain both kids and adults. Hands-on exhibits teach about the life stages of these big trees, which can live for more than 3000 years, and the fire cycle that releases their seeds and allows them to sprout on bare soil.

Discovered in 1918 by two parks employees who were going fishing, unique **Crystal Cave** (www.recreation.gov; Crystal Cave Rd, off Generals Hwy; tours adult/child/youth from $16/5/8; late May-late Sep; P) was carved by an underground river and has marble formations estimated to be up to 100,000 years old. Tickets for the 50-minute introductory tour are only sold online in advance or at the Giant Forest Museum and Foothills Visitor Center, not at the cave. Bring a jacket.

Worth a detour is **Mineral King Valley** (Mineral King Rd), a late-19th-century mining and logging camp ringed by craggy peaks and alpine lakes. The 25-mile one-way scenic drive – navigating almost 700 white-knuckle hairpin turns – is usually open from late May until late October.

Kings Canyon National Park & Scenic Byway

Just north of Grant Grove Village, **General Grant Grove** (N Grove Trail, off Hwy 180; P) brims with majestic giants. Beyond, Hwy 180 begins its 30-mile drive down into Kings Canyon, serpentining past chiseled rock walls laced with waterfalls. The road meets the **Kings River**, its roar ricocheting off granite cliffs soaring over 8000ft high, making this one of North America's deepest canyons.

At the bottom of the canyon, **Cedar Grove** (off Hwy 180) is the last outpost before the rugged grandeur of the Sierra Nevada backcountry begins. A popular day hike climbs 8.2 miles round trip to gushing **Mist Falls** (Road's End, Hwy 180) from Roads End. A favorite of birders, an easy 1.5-mile nature trail loops around **Zumwalt Meadow** (off Hwy 108;), just west of Roads End. Watch for lumbering black bears and springy mule deer.

The scenic byway past Hume Lake to Cedar Grove Village is usually closed from mid-November to late April.

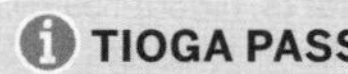

TIOGA PASS

Hwy 120 is the only road connecting Yosemite National Park with the Eastern Sierra, climbing through Tioga Pass (9945ft). Most maps mark this road 'closed in winter' which, while literally true, is also misleading. Tioga Rd is usually closed from the first heavy snowfall in October or November, not reopening until May or June. Call 209-372-0200 or check www.nps.gov/yose/planyourvisit/conditions.htm for current road conditions.

Activities

With more than 866 miles of marked trails, the parks are a backpacker's dream. Trails are officially open year-round to experienced hikers (you may need snow gear, snow shoes, navigation tools, crampons and ice picks in winter). Most come mid-May to October, when trails are far more accessible.

In Kings Canyon, Cedar Grove offers the best backcountry trail access, while in Sequoia head to Mineral King and Lodgepole. Jennie Lakes Wilderness in the Sequoia National Forest boasts pristine meadows and lakes at lower elevations.

Park-approved, bear-proof food canisters, which are always recommended, are mandatory in some places, especially for wilderness trips (eg Rae Lakes Loop). Rent bear canisters at park visitor centers and trailhead ranger stations or at the Lodgepole, Grant Grove and Cedar Grove Village markets (from around $5 per three-day trip). To prevent wildfires, campfires are usually only allowed in existing campfire rings in some backcountry areas.

Sleeping

Camping is the most affordable way to experience the parks, though sites fill up fast in high season (May to October). It's advisable to camp early, rather than wait until evening to secure your spot. Wilderness camping is free (permits required in quota season). Sequoia has one official in-park lodging option. The town of Three Rivers, just outside **Ash Mountain Entrance** (Generals Hwy, via Sierra Dr; car/walk-in/motorcycle $35/20/30), offers the most accommodations.

DNC Parks & Resorts (801-559-4930; www.visitsequoia.com) offers lodging in Sequoia and Kings Canyon National Parks.

NPS & USFS Campgrounds (877-444-6777; www.recreation.gov) provides a reservation service for many of the campgrounds in the parks, while some Sequoia National Forest lodgings can be organised through **Sequoia-Kings Canyon Park Services Company** (559-565-3388; www.sequoia-kingscanyon.com).

Cedar Grove Lodge LODGE $
(559-565-3096; www.visitsequoia.com; 108260 West Side Dr, Cedar Grove Village; r from $151; mid-May–mid-Oct;) The only indoor sleeping option in Kings Canyon, this riverside lodge offers 21 motel-style rooms. Three ground-floor rooms with shady furnished patios have spiffy river views and kitchenettes. All rooms have phones.

★ **Sequoia High Sierra Camp** CABIN $$$
(866-654-2877; www.sequoiahighsierracamp.com; off Forest Rte 13S12; tent cabins with shared bath incl all meals $500; early Jun–mid-Sep) A mile's hike deep into the Sequoia National Forest, this off-the-grid, all-inclusive resort is nirvana for those who don't think luxury camping is an oxymoron. Canvas bungalows are spiffed up with pillow-top mattresses, feather pillows and cozy wool rugs. Restrooms and a shower house are shared. Reservations are required and there's usually a two-night minimum stay. Prices are based on 2 people per tent.

Eating

Eating options are limited. Most visitors bring supplies, then enjoy campground cookouts and restock basic grocery items at the small markets in Lodgepole, Grant Grove and Cedar Grove villages (not open year-round). Simple eating options are at Wuksachi, John Muir and Cedar Grove, Lodgepole, Stoney Creek and Hume Lake, which have seasonal restaurants and snack bars. Three Rivers, just south of Sequoia, is the place to fill up.

The few park lodges – **Wuksachi** (information 866-807-3598, reservations 888-252-5757; www.visitsequoia.com; 64740 Wuksachi Way; r $123-340;), **John Muir** (877-436-9617; www.visitsequoiakingscanyon.com; 86728 Hwy 180, Grant Grove Village; r from $210;) and Cedar Grove (p348) – have restaurants, as do a couple of spots in the adjoining Sequoia National Forest. Three Rivers, just south of Sequoia, is a good place to fill up.

Information

Lodgepole Village and Grant Grove Village are the parks' main hubs. Both have visitor centers, post offices, markets and ATMs. Lodgepole has a coin-operated laundry and public showers (summer only). Expensive gas is available at Hume Lake (year-round) and Stony Creek (closed in winter) outside the parks on national-forest land.

Kings Canyon Visitor Center (559-565-4307; www.nps.gov/seki; Hwy 180, Grant Grove Village; 8am-5pm in summer, hours vary off-season) In the Grant Grove Village of Kings Canyon.

Lodgepole Visitor Center (559-565-4436; 63100 Lodgepole Rd, Lodgepole Village; 7am-5pm late May–mid-Oct) Located in the heart of Sequoia.

USFS Hume Lake District Office (559-338-2251; www.fs.fed.us/r5/sequoia; 35860 E Kings Canyon Rd/Hwy 180, Dunlap; 8am-4:30pm Mon-Fri) Stop here for recreation information, maps and campfire and wilderness permits for the Sequoia National Forest. The office is more than 20 miles west of the Big Stump Entrance.

Getting There & Around

Sequoia and Kings Canyon are both accessible by car only from the west, via Hwy 99 from Fresno or Visalia. It's 38 miles east on Hwy 198 from Visalia into Sequoia National Park – you pass through the gateway town of Three Rivers before entering the park. From Fresno, it's 47 miles east on Hwy 180 to Kings Canyon. The two roads are connected by the Generals Hwy, inside Sequoia. There is no access to either park from the east.

Car, motorcycle, shuttle bus, bike and foot are ways to get around the parks. The shuttles are only available in Sequoia National Park in the summer.

Eastern Sierra

Vast, empty and majestic, here jagged peaks plummet down into the desert, a dramatic juxtaposition that creates a potent scenery cocktail. Hwy 395 runs the entire length of the eastern side of the Sierra Nevada, with turnoffs leading to pine forests, wildflower-strewn meadows, placid lakes, hot springs and glacier-gouged canyons. Hikers, backpackers, mountain bikers, fishers and skiers all find escapes here.

Bishop, Lone Pine and Bridgeport have the most motels. Mammoth Lakes has a few motels and hotels and dozens of inns, B&Bs, condos and vacation rentals. Reservations are essential everywhere in summer.

Backcountry camping requires a wilderness permit, available at ranger stations.

BODIE STATE HISTORIC PARK

At **Bodie State Historic Park** (☎760-616-5040; www.parks.ca.gov/bodie; Hwy 270; adult/child $8/5; ⏲9am-6pm Apr-Oct, to 4pm Nov-Mar; road often closed in winter; P 🐾), the weathered buildings of a gold-rush boomtown sit frozen in time on a dusty, windswept plain. To get here, head east for 13 miles (the last three unpaved) on Hwy 270, about 7 miles south of Bridgeport. Snow usually closes the access road in winter and early spring.

MONO LAKE

Further south at **Mono Lake** (www.monolake.org; off Hwy 395), unearthly tufa towers rise from the alkaline water like drip sand castles. Off Hwy 395, **Mono Basin Scenic Area Visitor Center** (☎760-647-3044; www.fs.usda.gov/inyo; 1 Visitor Center Dr; ⏲8am-5pm May-Sep, hours vary Oct-Dec, closed Jan-Apr; 👪) has excellent views and educational exhibits, but the best photo ops are from the mile-long nature trail at the **South Tufa Area** (Test Station Rd, near Hwy 120; adult/child $3/free; P 👪). From the nearby town of Lee Vining, Hwy 120 heads west into Yosemite National Park via seasonal Tioga Pass.

A top regional draw, the open tasting room at **June Lake Brewing** (☎858-668-6340; www.junelakebrewing.com; 131 S Crawford Ave; ⏲noon-8pm Mon, Wed, Thu, Sun, to 9pm Fri & Sat) serves around 10 drafts, including Deer Beer Brown Ale and some awesome IPAs. Brewers swear the June Lake water makes all the difference. Flights are around $8.

MAMMOTH LAKES & AROUND

Continuing south on Hwy 395, detour along the scenic 16-mile **June Lake Loop** or push on to **Mammoth Lakes**, a popular four-seasons resort guarded by 11,053ft **Mammoth Mountain** (☎760-934-2571, 760-934-2571, 24hr snow report 888-766-9778; www.mammothmountain.com; access via Minaret Rd; adult/13-17yr/5-12yr/under 5yr from $79/65/32/free), a top-notch skiing area. The slopes morph into a mountain-bike park in summer, when scenic gondola rides run.

Warm and cozy, oozing traditional ski-lodge appeal, and only steps from the base of the Panorama Gondola, the location of **Mammoth Mountain Inn** (☎760-934-2581; www.themammothmountaininn.com; 10400 Minaret Rd; r from $129-239, condos from $259-1199; ❄ @ 📶 🏊) is spectacular no matter the time of year. In business since 1924, the charming year-round **Tamarack Lodge** (☎760-934-2442; www.tamaracklodge.com; 163 Twin Lakes Rd; r from $129, without bathroom from $99, cabins $255-425; P ⊖ @ 📶 🐾) 🍃 on Lower Twin Lake has a cozy fireplace lodge, a bar and an excellent restaurant, 11 rustic rooms and 35 cabins.

There's also camping and day hiking around Mammoth Lakes Basin and Reds Meadow, the latter near the 60ft-high basalt columns of **Devils Postpile National Monument** (☎760-934-2289; www.nps.gov/depo; access off Minaret Summit Rd/Reds Meadow Rd; shuttle day pass adult/child $8/4; ⏲Jun-Oct, weather depending), formed by volcanic activity.

The in-town **Mammoth Lakes Welcome Center & Ranger Station** (☎760-924-5500; www.visitmammoth.com; 2510 Hwy 203; ⏲8am-5pm, 8:30am-4:30pm winter) has helpful maps and information, and you can grab comfort food such as shepherd's pie, fondue and pork tenderloin at **Mammoth Tavern** (☎760-934-3902; www.mammothtavern.com; 587 Old Mammoth Rd; mains $14-35; ⏲4-9:30pm Tue-Thu & Sun, 5-10pm Fri & Sat). Alternatively, treat yourself to innovative, Norwegian-inspired creations, such as Canadian duck breast with arctic lingonberries and pan-seared day-boat scallops, at chef Ian Algerøen's **Skadi** (☎760-914-0962; www.skadirestaurant.com; 94 Berner St; mains $32-40; ⏲5pm-close Wed-Mon). Reservations required.

Hot-springs fans can soak in primitive pools off Benton Crossing Rd or view the geysering water at Hot Creek Geological Site, both off Hwy 395 southeast of town. Or detour to Benton to soak in your own hot-springs tub and snooze beneath the moonlight at **Benton Hot Springs** (☎760-933-2287; www.bentonhotsprings.

DON'T MISS

SUPERSIZED FORESTS

When it's time to pay your respects to the most massive trees on the planet, there's nowhere better to go than Sequoia National Park. Giant sequoias *(Sequoiadendron giganteum)* can live for almost 3000 years, and some of the ancient ones standing in the Giant Forest have been around since the fall of the Roman Empire. There the world's largest living specimen, the **General Sherman Tree**, is taller than a 27-story building and measures over 100ft around its massive trunk – crane your neck as you stare in awe at its leafy crown.

org; Hwy 120, Benton; tent & RV sites per 2 people $60-70, B&B r from $119;) , a small, historic resort in a 150-year-old former silver-mining town nestled in the White Mountains. Choose from 11 well-spaced campsites with private tubs or a room in the themed, antique-filled B&B, with semiprivate tubs.

BISHOP & AROUND

Further south, Hwy 395 descends into the Owens Valley. In frontier-flavored Bishop, the historical **Laws Railroad Museum** (760-873-5950; www.lawsmuseum.org; Silver Canyon Rd; suggested donation $10; 10am-4pm Sep-May, from 9.30am Jun-Aug;) is a kid-friendly attraction with rides on vintage trains. A gateway for packhorse trips, Bishop accesses the Eastern Sierra's best fishing and rock climbing. Budget a half-day for the thrilling drive up to the **Ancient Bristlecone Pine Forest**. These gnarled, otherworldly looking trees – the world's oldest – are found above 10,000ft on the slopes of the White Mountains. The road (closed by snow in winter and early spring) is paved to the **Schulman Grove Visitor Center** (760-873-2500; www.fs.usda.gov/inyo; White Mountain Rd; per person/car $3/6; 10am-5pm Jun-Aug, to 4pm Fri-Sun May-Jun), where hiking trails await. From Hwy 395 in Big Pine, take Hwy 168 east for 12 miles, then follow White Mountain Rd uphill for 10 miles.

LONE PINE & AROUND

Hwy 395 barrels south to **Manzanar National Historic Site** (760-878-2194; www.nps.gov/manz; 5001 Hwy 395; 9am-4:30pm;) FREE, which memorializes the camp where some 10,000 Japanese Americans were unjustly interned during WWII. Further south in Lone Pine, you'll finally glimpse Mt Whitney (14,505ft), the highest mountain in the lower 48 states. The heart-stopping, 12-mile scenic drive up **Whitney Portal Road** (closed in winter and early spring) is spectacular. Climbing the peak is hugely popular, but requires a permit (per person $21) that must be obtained on www.recreation.gov. Just south of town, the **Eastern Sierra Interagency Visitor Center** (760-876-6222; www.fs.fed.us/r5/inyo; cnr Hwys 395 & 136; 8am-5pm, 8:30am-4:30pm winter) issues wilderness permits, dispenses outdoor-recreation info and sells books and maps.

A popular launchpad for Mt Whitney trips and a locus of posthike washups (public showers are available), the **Whitney Portal Hostel & Hotel** (760-876-0030; www.whitneyportalstore.com; 238 S Main St; dm/d from $32/92;) has the cheapest beds in town – reserve dorms months ahead for July and August. Just off the main streets, at **Alabama Hills Cafe** (760-876-4675; www.alabamahillscafe.com; 111 W Post St; breakfast items $9.50-$14; 6am-3pm Fri-Sun, to 2pm Mon-Thu;), everyone's favorite breakfast joint, the portions are big, the bread is freshly baked and the soups hearty. Sandwiches and fruit pies make lunch an attractive option too.

West of Lone Pine, the bizarrely shaped boulders of the Alabama Hills have enchanted filmmakers of Hollywood Westerns. Peruse memorabilia and movie posters back in town at the **Museum of Western Film History** (760-876-9909; www.museumofwesternfilmhistory.org; 701 S Main St; adult/under 12yr $5/free; 10am-5pm Mon-Sat, to 4pm Sun;).

Lake Tahoe

Shimmering in myriad shades of blue and green, Lake Tahoe is the USA's second-deepest lake and, at 6245ft high, it is also one of the highest-elevation lakes in the country. Driving around the spellbinding 72-mile scenic shoreline will give you quite a workout behind the wheel. Generally, the north shore is quiet and upscale; the west shore, rugged and old-timey; the east shore, undeveloped; the south shore, busy and tacky, with aging motels and flashy casinos.

Information

Lake Tahoe Visitors Authority (775-588-5900; www.tahoesouth.com; 169 Hwy 50, Stateline, NV; 9am-5pm Mon-Fri) Tourist information, maps, brochures and money-saving coupons, with a second center in Stateline

Lake Tahoe Bicycle Coalition (www.tahoebike.org) publishes a bike map that's a great resource for pedaling around the area.

Desolation Wilderness Permits (877-444-6777; www.recreation.gov; per adult $5-10)

Getting There & Around

Greyhound buses from Reno, Sacramento and San Francisco run to Truckee, and you can also get the daily **Zephyr** (800-872-7245; www.amtrak.com) train here from the same destinations. From Truckee, take the **Truckee Transit** (530-550-1212; www.laketahoetransit.com) to Donner Lake, or **Tahoe Area Rapid Transit** (TART; 530-550-1212; https://tahoetruckeetransit.com; 10183 Truckee Airport Rd; single/day pass $1.75/3.50) buses to the north and west shores of the lake.

Tahoe Ski Trips (925-680-4386; www.tahoeskitrips.net; bus $89) offers shuttles connecting San Francisco and other Bay Area pickup locations with Tahoe's slopes.

From late fall through early spring, drivers should always pack snow chains in case a storm rolls in, and stash some emergency supplies (eg blankets, water, flashlights) in the trunk. Before hopping in the car, check road closures and conditions:

California Department of Transportation (Caltrans; 800-427-7623; www.dot.ca.gov)

Nevada Department of Transportation (NDOT; 877-687-6237, within Nevada 511; www.nevadadot.com)

With a saucy acronym and reliable service, bike-rack-equipped Tahoe Area Rapid Transit runs buses year-round along the north shore as far as Incline Village, down the western shore to **Ed Z'berg Sugar Pine Point State Park** (530-525-7982; www.parks.ca.gov; per car $10) and north to Squaw Valley and Truckee via Hwy 89. The main routes typically depart hourly from about 6am until 6pm daily.

SOUTH LAKE TAHOE & WEST SHORE

With retro motels and eateries lining busy Hwy 50, South Lake Tahoe gets crowded. Gambling at Stateline's casino hotels, just across the Nevada border, attracts thousands, as does the world-class ski resort **Heavenly** (775-586-7000; www.skiheavenly.com; 3860 Saddle Rd; adult/child 5-12yr/youth 13-18yr $154/85/126; 9am-4pm Mon-Fri, from 8:30am Sat, Sun & holidays;). In summer a trip up Heavenly's gondola guarantees fabulous views of the lake and the **Desolation Wilderness**, with its raw granite peaks, glacier-carved valleys and alpine lakes favored by hikers. Get maps, information and overnight wilderness permits (per adult or dog $5; day permits are free) from the **USFS Taylor Creek Visitor Center** (530-543-2674; www.fs.usda.gov/ltbmu; Visitor Center Rd, off Hwy 89; 8am-4:30pm late May-Oct). It's 3 miles north of the 'Y' intersection of Hwys 50/89, at **Tallac Historic Site** (530-544-7383; www.tahoeheritage.org; Tallac Rd; optional tour adult/child $10/5; 10am-4pm daily late May-Sep;) FREE, preserving swish early-20th-century vacation estates.

From sandy, swimmable **Zephyr Cove** (775-589-4901; www.zephyrcove.com; 760 Hwy 50; per car $10; sunrise-sunset) across the Nevada border or the in-town Ski Run Marina, **Lake Tahoe Cruises** (775-586-4906; www.zephyrcove.com; 760 Hwy 50; adult/child from $65/33) plies the 'Big Blue' year-round. Paddle under your own power with **Kayak Tahoe** (530-544-2011; www.kayaktahoe.com; 3411 Lake Tahoe Blvd; kayak single/double 1hr $25/35, 1 day $65/85, lessons & tours from $50; 9am-5pm Jun-Sep). Back on shore, boutique-chic motels include the **Alder Inn** (530-544-4485; www.alderinn.com; 1072 Ski Run Blvd; r $89-149;) and the hip **Basecamp Hotel** (530-208-0180; www.basecamphotels.com; 4143 Cedar Ave; d $109-229, 8-person bunk room $209-299, pet fee $40;), which has a rooftop hot tub, or pitch a tent at lakeside **Fallen Leaf Campground** (info 530-544-0426, reservations 877-444-6777; www.recreation.gov; 2165 Fallen Leaf Lake Rd; tent & RV sites $33-35, yurts $86; mid-May–mid-Oct;). Fuel up at vegetarian-friendly **Sprouts** (530-541-6969; www.sproutscafetahoe.com; 3123 Harrison Ave; mains $7-10; 8am-8pm;) natural-foods cafe, or with a peanut-butter-topped burger and garlic fries at the **Burger Lounge** (530-542-2010; 717 Emerald Bay Rd; dishes $6-10; 11am-8pm Jun-Sep, to 7pm Thu-Mon Oct-May;).

Hwy 89 threads northwest along the thickly forested west shore to **Emerald Bay State Park** (530-541-6498; www.parks.ca.gov; sunrise-sunset), where granite cliffs and pine trees frame a sparkling fjord-like inlet. A 1-mile trail leads steeply downhill to **Vikingsholm Castle** (530-525-7232; http://vikingsholm.com; tour adult/child 7-17yr $10/8; 10:30am-3:30pm or 4pm late May-Sep;), a 1920s Scandinavian-style mansion. From there, the **Rubicon Trail** ribbons 4.5 miles north along the lakeshore past petite coves to **DL Bliss State Park** (530-525-7277; www.parks.ca.gov; per car $10; late May-Sep;), offering sandy beaches. Further north, **Tahoma Meadows B&B Cottages** (530-525-1553; www.tahomameadows.com; 6821 W Lake Blvd; cottages $169-339, pet fee $20;) rents darling country cabins.

NORTH & EAST SHORES

A busy commercial hub, **Tahoe City** is great for grabbing food and supplies and renting outdoor-sports gear. It's not far from **Squaw Valley Alpine Meadows** (800-403-0206; www.squawalpine.com; 1960 Squaw Valley Rd, off Hwy 89, Olympic Valley; adult/child 5-12yr/youth 13-22yr $169/109/139; 9am-4pm Mon-Fri, from 8:30am Sat, Sun & holidays;), a mega-sized ski resort that hosted the 1960 Winter Olympics. Après-ski crowds gather at woodsy **Bridgetender Tavern & Grill** (530-583-3342; www.tahoebridgetender.com; 65 W Lake Blvd; 11am-11pm Mon-Thu, to midnight Fri, 9am-midnight Sat, to 11pm Sun) back in town. In the morning, gobble eggs Benedict with house-smoked salmon at down-home **Fire Sign Cafe** (www.firesigncafe.com; 1785 W Lake Blvd; mains $10-15; 7am-3pm;), 2 miles further south.

In summer, swim or kayak at **Tahoe Vista** or **Kings Beach**. Overnight at **Cedar Glen Lodge** (530-546-4281; www.tahoecedarglen.com; 6589 N Lake Blvd; r, ste & cottages $219-579, pet fee $30;), where rustic-themed cottages and rooms have kitchenettes, or well-kept, compact **Hostel Tahoe** (530-546-3266; www.hosteltahoe.com; 8931 N Lake Blvd; dm/d/q from $35/85/100;). East of Kings Beach's lakeside eateries, Hwy 28 barrels into Nevada. Catch a live-music show at a just-over-the-border casino, or for more happening bars and bistros, drive further to Incline Village.

With pristine beaches, lakes and miles of multiuse trails, **Lake Tahoe-Nevada State Park** (775-831-0494; www.parks.nv.gov; per car/bicycle $10/2; 8am-1hr after sunset; P) is the east shore's biggest draw. Summer crowds splash in the turquoise waters of **Sand Harbor**. The 13-mile **Flume Trail**, a mountain biker's holy grail, ends further south at **Spooner Lake**. Back in Incline Village, **Flume Trail Bikes** (775-298-2501; http://flumetrailtahoe.com; 1115 Tunnel Creek Rd; mountain-bike rental per day $35-67, shuttle $16, state park entrance $2; 8am-6pm, closed winter) offers bicycle rentals and shuttles.

TRUCKEE & AROUND

North of Lake Tahoe off I-80, Truckee is not in fact a truck stop but a thriving mountain town, with coffee shops, trendy boutiques and dining in downtown's historical district. Ski bums have several resorts to pick from, including glam **Northstar California** (530-562-1010; www.northstarcalifornia.com; 5001 Northstar Dr, off Hwy 267; adult/child 5-12yr/youth 13-18yr $160/94/131; 8am-5pm); kid-friendly **Sugar Bowl** (530-426-9000; www.sugarbowl.com; 629 Sugar Bowl Rd, off Donner Pass Rd, Norden; adult/child 6-12yr/youth 13-22yr $118/69/97; 9am-4pm); and **Royal Gorge** (530-426-3871; www.royalgorge.com; 9411 Pahatsi Rd, off I-80 exit Soda Springs/Norden, Soda Springs; adult/youth 13-22yr $35/20; 8:30am-4pm;), paradise for cross-country skiers.

West of Hwy 89, **Donner Summit** is where the infamous Donner Party became trapped during the fierce winter of 1846–47. About half survived – some by cannibalizing their dead friends. The grisly tale is chronicled at the museum inside **Donner Memorial State Park** (530-582-7892; www.parks.ca.gov; Donner Pass Rd; per car $5-10, varies seasonally; visitor center 10am-5pm; P), which offers **camping** (530-582-7894, reservations 800-444-7275; www.reservecalifornia.com; tent & RV sites $35; late May-late Sep). Nearby **Donner Lake** is popular with swimmers and paddlers.

On the outskirts of Truckee, green-certified **Cedar House Sport Hotel** (530-582-5655; www.cedarhousesporthotel.com; 10918 Brockway Rd; r $180-345, pet fee $50-100; P) offers stylish boutique rooms and an outstanding restaurant. Down pints of Donner Party Porter at **Fifty Fifty Brewing Co** (www.fiftyfiftybrewing.com; 11197 Brockway Rd; 11:30am-9pm Sun-Thu, to 9:30pm Fri & Sat).

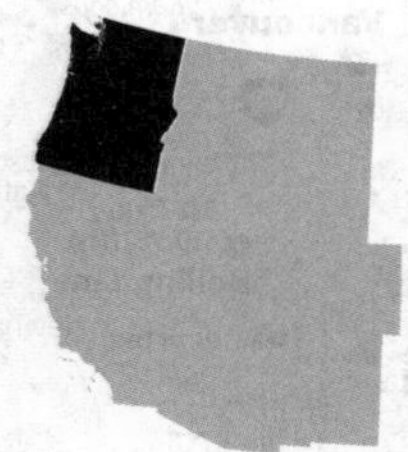

Pacific Northwest

Includes ➡

Best Places to Eat

- ➡ Ned Ludd (p392)
- ➡ Chow (p401)
- ➡ Ox (p392)
- ➡ Sitka & Spruce (p366)

Best Places to Sleep

- ➡ Timberline Lodge (p399)
- ➡ Crater Lake Lodge (p402)
- ➡ Hotel Monaco (p365)
- ➡ Olympic Lights B&B (p377)
- ➡ Historic Davenport Hotel (p381)

Why Go?

As much a state of mind as a geographical region, the northwest corner of the US is a land of subcultures and new trends, where evergreen trees frame snow-dusted volcanoes, and inspired ideas scribbled on the back of napkins become tomorrow's start-ups. You can't peel off the history in layers here, but you *can* gaze wistfully into the future in fast-moving, innovative cities such as Seattle and Portland, which are sprinkled with food carts, streetcars, microbreweries, green belts, coffee connoisseurs and weird urban sculpture.

Ever since the days of the Oregon Trail, the Northwest has had a hypnotic lure for risk-takers and dreamers; the metaphoric carrot still dangles. There's the air, so clean they ought to bottle it; the trees, older than many of Rome's Renaissance palaces; and the end-of-the-continent coastline, holding back the force of the world's largest ocean. Cowboys take note: it doesn't get much more 'wild' or 'west' than this.

When to Go

Seattle

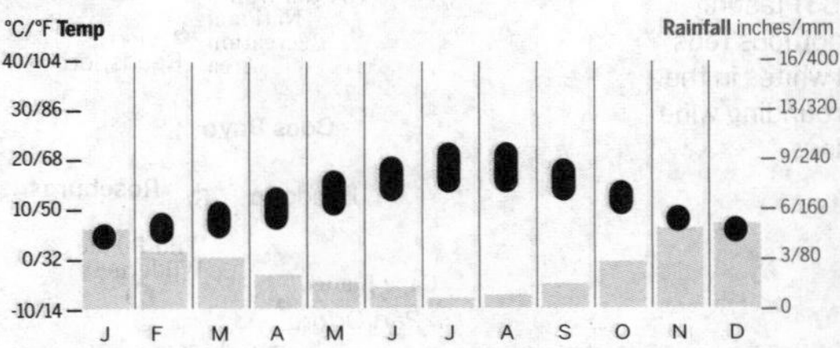

Jan–Mar Most reliable snow cover for skiing in the Cascades and beyond.

May Festival season: Portland Rose, International Film Festival and Oregon Shakespeare Festival.

Jul–Sep The best hiking months, between the spring snowmelt and the first fall flurries.

Pacific Northwest Highlights

1. **San Juan Islands** (p376) Cycling and kayaking around the quieter corners.
2. **Oregon Coast** (p402) Exploring this gorgeous region, from scenic Astoria to balmy Port Orford.
3. **Olympic National Park** (p372) Admiring trees older than Europe's Renaissance castles.
4. **Pike Place Market** (p358) Watching the greatest outdoor show in the Pacific Northwest.
5. **Portland** (p385) Walking the green and serene neighborhoods, energized by beer, coffee and food-cart treats.
6. **Crater Lake National Park** (p402) Witnessing the impossibly deep-blue waters and scenic panoramas.
7. **Bend** (p400) Mountain biking, rock climbing or skiing in this outdoor mecca.
8. **Walla Walla** (p383) Tasting sumptuous reds and whites in the surrounding wine regions.

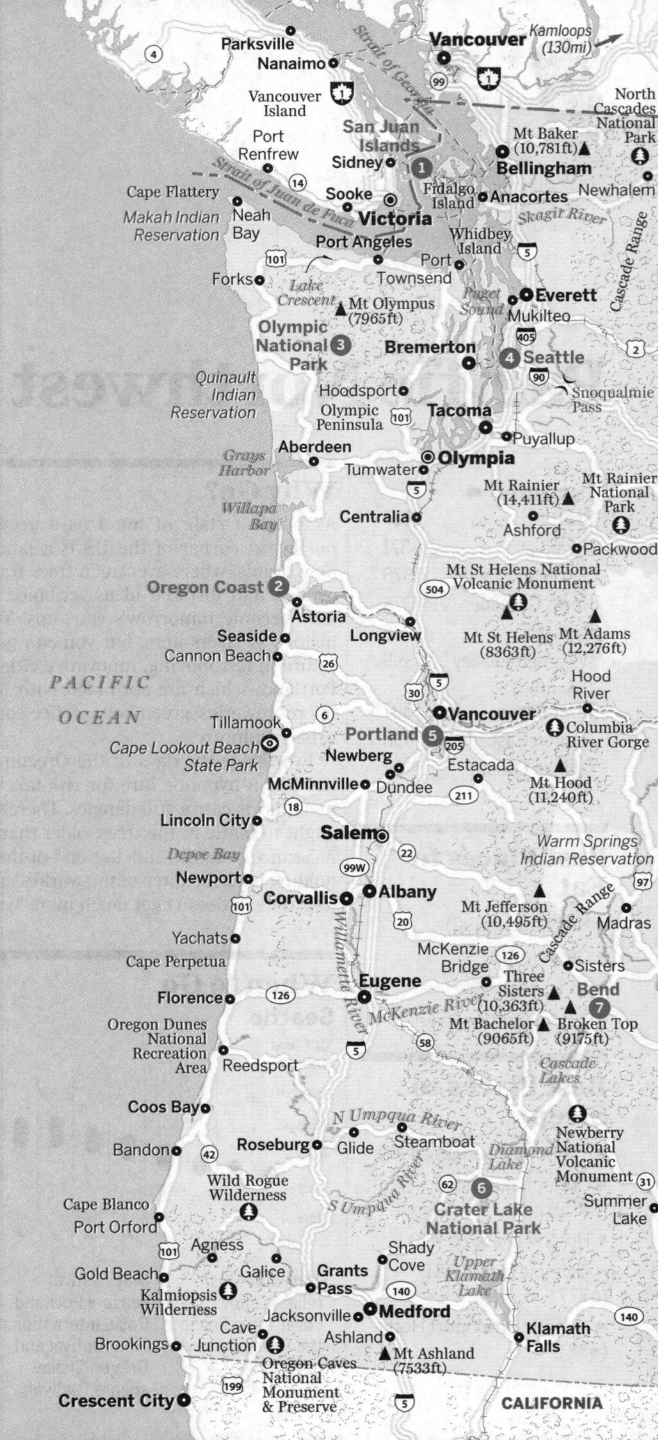

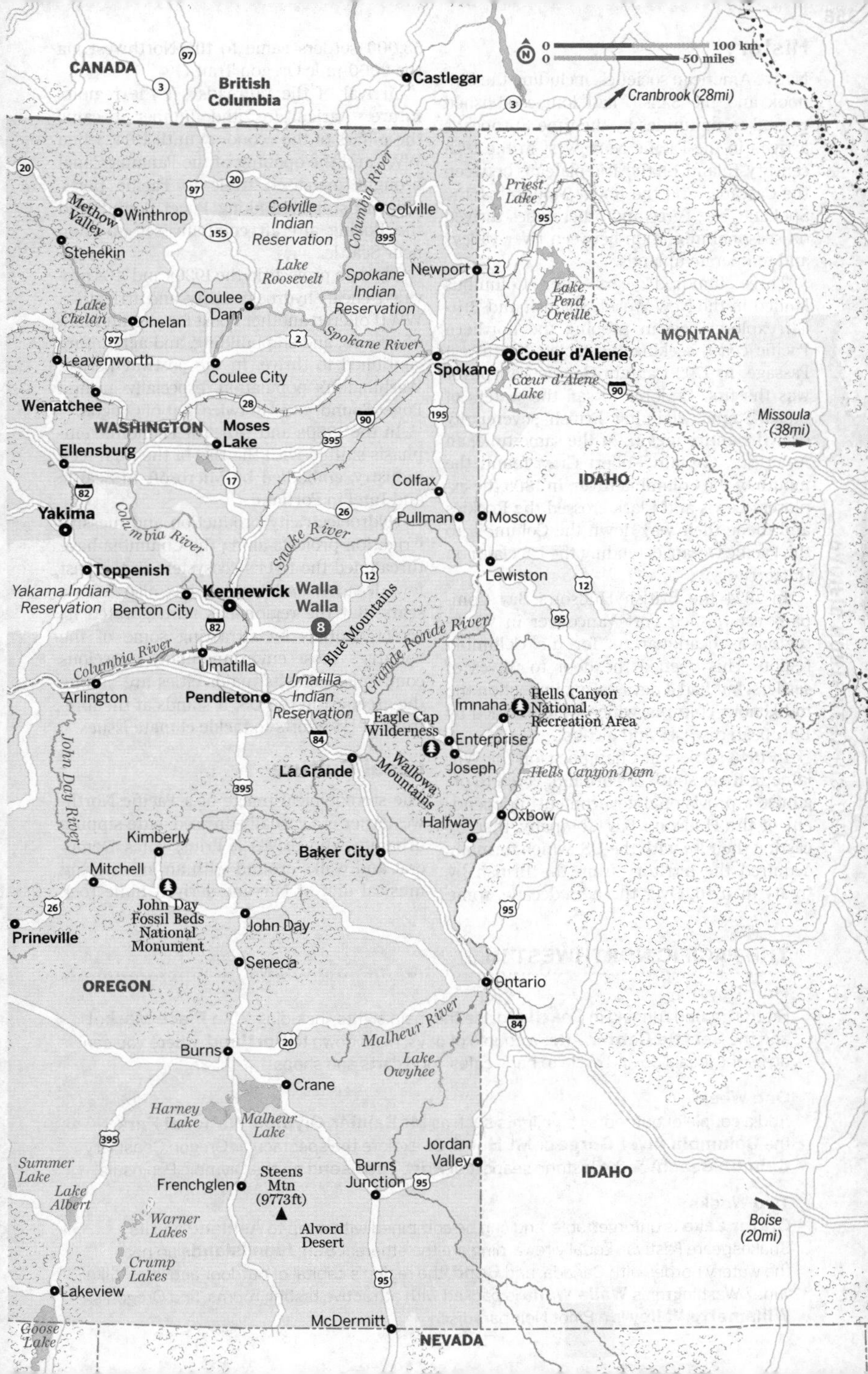

0 100 km
0 50 miles
CANADA
British Columbia
Castlegar
Cranbrook (28mi)
Methow Valley
Winthrop
Stehekin
Colville Indian Reservation
Columbia River
Colville
Lake Roosevelt
Spokane Indian Reservation
Newport
Priest Lake
Lake Pend Oreille
Coulee Dam
Lake Chelan
Chelan
Spokane River
Leavenworth
Coulee City
Spokane
Coeur d'Alene
Cœur d'Alene Lake
MONTANA
Missoula (38mi)
Wenatchee
WASHINGTON
Moses Lake
Ellensburg
Colfax
IDAHO
Yakima
Pullman
Moscow
Snake River
Toppenish
Lewiston
Yakama Indian Reservation
Benton City
Kennewick
Walla Walla
8
Blue Mountains
Grande Ronde River
Umatilla
Arlington
Pendleton
Umatilla Indian Reservation
Imnaha
Hells Canyon National Recreation Area
Eagle Cap Wilderness
Enterprise
Joseph
John Day River
La Grande
Wallowa Mountains
Hells Canyon Dam
Oxbow
Halfway
Kimberly
Baker City
Mitchell
John Day Fossil Beds National Monument
John Day
Prineville
Seneca
OREGON
Ontario
Malheur River
Burns
Lake Owyhee
Crane
Harney Lake
Malheur Lake
Jordan Valley
IDAHO
Summer Lake
Frenchglen
Steens Mtn (9773ft)
Burns Junction
Lake Albert
Warner Lakes
Alvord Desert
Boise (20mi)
Crump Lakes
Lakeview
Goose Lake
McDermitt
NEVADA

History

Native American societies, including the Chinook and the Salish, had long-established coastal communities by the time Europeans arrived in the Pacific Northwest in the 18th century. Inland, on the arid plateaus between the Cascades and the Rocky Mountains, the Spokane, Nez Percé and other tribes thrived on seasonal migration between river valleys and temperate uplands.

Three hundred years after Columbus landed in the New World, Spanish and British explorers began probing the northern Pacific coast, seeking the fabled Northwest Passage. In 1792 Captain George Vancouver was the first explorer to sail the waters of Puget Sound, claiming British sovereignty over the entire region. At the same time, an American, Captain Robert Gray, found the mouth of the Columbia River. In 1805 the explorers Lewis and Clark crossed the Rockies and made their way down the Columbia to the Pacific Ocean, extending the US claim on the territory.

In 1824 the British Hudson's Bay Company established Fort Vancouver in Washington as headquarters for the Columbia region. This opened the door to waves of settlers, but had a devastating impact on the indigenous cultures, which were assailed by European diseases and alcohol.

In 1843 settlers at Champoeg, on the Willamette River south of Portland, voted to organize a provisional government independent of the Hudson's Bay Company, thereby casting their lot with the US, which formally acquired the territory from the British by treaty in 1846. Over the next decade, some 53,000 settlers came to the Northwest via the 2000-mile Oregon Trail.

Arrival of the railroads set the region's future. Agriculture and lumber became the pillars of the economy until 1914, when WWI and the opening of the Panama Canal brought increased trade to Pacific ports. Shipyards opened along Puget Sound, and the Boeing aircraft company set up shop near Seattle.

Big dam projects in the 1930s and '40s provided cheap hydroelectricity and irrigation. WWII offered another boost for aircraft manufacturing and shipbuilding, and agriculture continued to thrive. In the postwar period, Washington's population, especially around Puget Sound, grew to twice that of Oregon.

In the 1980s and '90s, the economic emphasis shifted with the rise of the high-tech industry, embodied by Microsoft in Seattle and Intel in Portland.

Hydroelectricity production and massive irrigation projects along the Columbia have threatened the river's ecosystem in the past few decades, and logging has also left its scars. But the region has reinvigorated its eco-credentials by attracting some of the country's most environmentally conscious companies, and its major cities are among the greenest in the US. It stands at the forefront of US efforts to tackle climate issues.

Local Culture

The stereotypical image of a Pacific Northwesterner is a casually dressed, latte-sipping urbanite who drives a Prius, votes Democrat and walks around with an unwavering musical diet of Nirvana-derived indie rock

THE PACIFIC NORTHWEST IN...

Four Days

Hit the ground running in **Seattle** to see the main sights, including **Pike Place Market** and the **Seattle Center**. After a couple of days, head down to **Portland**, where you can do as the locals do and cycle to bars, cafes, food carts and shops.

One Week

Add a couple of outdoorsy highlights such as **Mt Rainier**, **Olympic National Park**, the **Columbia River Gorge** or **Mt Hood**. Or explore the spectacular Oregon Coast (try **Cannon Beach**) or the historic seaport of **Port Townsend** on the Olympic Peninsula.

Two Weeks

Crater Lake is unforgettable, and can be combined with a trip to **Ashland** and its Shakespeare Festival. Equally rewarding are the ethereal **San Juan Islands** up near the watery border with Canada, and **Bend**, the region's capital of outdoor activities. Like wine? Washington's **Walla Walla** is packed with attractive tasting rooms, and Oregon's **Willamette Valley** is a Pinot Noir paradise.

blaring from their headphones. But, as with most fleeting regional generalizations, the reality is far more complex.

Noted for their sophisticated cafe culture and copious microbrew pubs, the urban hubs of Seattle and Portland are the Northwest's most emblematic cities. But head east into the region's drier and less verdant interior, and the cultural affiliations become increasingly more traditional. Here, strung along the Columbia River Valley or nestled amid the arid steppes of southeastern Washington, small towns host raucous rodeos, tourist centers promote cowboy culture, and a cup of coffee is exactly that – no lattes, no matcha tea.

In contrast to the USA's hardworking eastern seaboard, life out west is more casual and less frenetic. Ideally, Westerners would rather work to live than live to work. Indeed, with so much winter rain, the citizens of the Pacific Northwest will dredge up any excuse to shun the nine-to-five treadmill and hit the great outdoors a couple of hours (or even days) early. Witness the scene in late May and early June, when the first bright days of summer prompt a mass exodus of hikers and cyclists to make enthusiastically for the national parks and wilderness areas for which the region is justly famous.

Getting There & Around

AIR

Seattle-Tacoma International Airport, aka 'Sea-Tac,' and Portland International Airport are the main airports for the region, serving many North American and several international destinations.

BOAT

Washington State Ferries (www.wsdot.wa.gov/ferries) links Seattle with Bainbridge and Vashon Islands. Other WSF routes cross from Whidbey Island to Port Townsend on the Olympic Peninsula, and from Anacortes through the San Juan Islands to Sidney, BC. Victoria Clipper (www.clippervacations.com) operates services from Seattle to Victoria, BC; ferries to Victoria also operate from Port Angeles. Alaska Marine Highway ferries (www.dot.state.ak.us/amhs) go from Bellingham, WA, to Alaska.

BUS

Greyhound (www.greyhound.com) provides service along the I-5 corridor from Bellingham in northern Washington down to Medford in southern Oregon, with connecting services across the US and Canada. East–west routes fan out toward Spokane, Yakima, the Tri-Cities (Kennewick, Pasco and Richland in Washington), Walla Walla and Pullman in Washington, and Hood River and Pendleton in Oregon. Private bus companies service most of the smaller towns and cities across the region, often connecting to Greyhound or Amtrak.

CAR

Driving your own vehicle is by far the most convenient way of touring the Pacific Northwest. Major and minor rental agencies are commonplace throughout the region. I-5 is the major north–south artery. In Washington I-90 heads east from Seattle to Spokane and into Idaho. In Oregon I-84 branches east from Portland along the Columbia River Gorge to link up with Boise in Idaho.

TRAIN

Amtrak (www.amtrak.com) runs train services north (to Vancouver, Canada) and south (to California), linking Seattle, Portland and other major urban centers with the *Cascades* and *Coast Starlight* routes. The famous *Empire Builder* heads east to Chicago from Seattle and Portland (joining up in Spokane).

WASHINGTON

Washington state is the heart of the Pacific Northwest. With that title comes everything you'd hope for, from the lush, green Olympic Peninsula to the wild white peaks of the Cascade Mountains and the relaxed, kayaker-friendly San Juan Islands. Head east and you'll see another side of the state: aridly beautiful, with upscale wineries and cowboy-style breakfasts in equal measure, plus orchards, wheat fields and pioneer history.

The biggest urban jolt is Seattle, but each of the state's main population centers – Spokane, Bellingham, Olympia – has its own charm. Still, to get the most out of visiting Washington, you'll want to leave the cities behind and lose yourself in the mountains and the woods, along the coast or on the islands. The best experiences here are mostly unmediated.

Seattle

Combine the brains of Portland, OR, with the beauty of Vancouver, Canada, and you'll get something approximating Seattle. It's hard to believe that the Pacific Northwest's largest metropolis was considered a 'secondary' US city until the 1980s, when a combination of bold innovation and unabashed individualism turned it into one of the dot-com era's biggest trendsetters, spearheaded by an unlikely alliance of coffee-sipping computer geeks and navel-gazing musicians.

WASHINGTON FACTS

Nickname Evergreen State

Population 7.3 million

Area 71,362 sq miles

Capital city Olympia (population 51,609)

Other cities Seattle (population 744,955), Spokane (population 217,108), Bellingham (population 89,045)

Sales tax 6.5%

Birthplace of Singer and actor Bing Crosby (1903–77), guitarist Jimi Hendrix (1942–70), computer geek Bill Gates (b 1955), political commentator Glen Beck (b 1964), musical icon Kurt Cobain (1967–94)

Home of Mt St Helens, Microsoft, Starbucks, Amazon.com, Evergreen State College

Politics Democrat governors since 1985

Famous for Grunge rock, coffee, Grey's Anatomy, *Twilight*, volcanoes, apples, wine, precipitation

State vegetable Walla Walla sweet onion

Driving distances Seattle to Portland174 miles, Spokane to Port Angeles 365 miles

Surprisingly elegant in places and coolly edgy in others, Seattle is notable for its strong neighborhoods, top-rated university, monstrous traffic jams and proactive city mayors who harbor green credentials. Although it has fermented its own pop culture in recent times, it has yet to create an urban mythology befitting Paris or New York, but it does have 'the Mountain.' Better known as Rainier, Seattle's unifying symbol is a 14,411ft mass of rock and ice, which acts as a perennial reminder to the city's huddled masses that raw wilderness, and potential volcanic catastrophe, are never far away.

Sights

Downtown

★Pike Place Market MARKET

(Map p360; 206-682-7453; www.pikeplacemarket.org; 85 Pike St, Pike Place; 9am-6pm Mon-Sat, to 5pm Sun; Westlake) A cavalcade of noise, smells, personalities, banter and urban theater sprinkled liberally around a spatially challenged waterside strip, Pike Place Market is Seattle in a bottle. In operation since 1907 and still as soulful today as it was on day one, this wonderfully local experience highlights the city for what it really is: all-embracing, eclectic and proudly unique. A 2017 expansion of the market infrastructure added vendor space, weather-protected common areas, extra parking, and housing for low-income seniors.

★Seattle Art Museum MUSEUM

(SAM; Map p360; 206-654-3210; www.seattleartmuseum.org; 1300 1st Ave, Downtown; adult/student $25/15; 10am-5pm Wed & Fri-Mon, to 9pm Thu; University St) While not comparable with the big guns in New York and Chicago, Seattle Art Museum is no slouch. Always re-curating its art collection with new acquisitions and imported temporary exhibitions, it's known for its extensive Native American artifacts and work from the local Northwest school, in particular by Mark Tobey (1890–1976). Modern American art is also well represented, and the museum gets some exciting traveling exhibitions (including Yayoi Kusama's infinity mirrors).

★Olympic Sculpture Park PARK

(Map p360; 206-654-3100; 2901 Western Ave, Belltown; sunrise-sunset; 33) FREE This ingenuous feat of urban planning is an official offshoot of the Seattle Art Museum and bears the same strong eye toward design and curation. There are more than 20 sculptures to stop at and admire in this green space that sprawls out over reclaimed urban decay. You can also enjoy them in passing while traversing the park's winding trails. Views of the Puget Sound and Olympic Peninsula in the background will delight anyone looking for some great pictures for social media.

Pioneer Square & the International District

Seattle's birthplace retains the grit of its 'Skid Row' roots with redbrick architecture and a rambunctious street life that's tempered by art galleries and locavore restaurants. The International District's legacy as home to many of the city's southeast Asian immigrant communities makes for unique shopping and exquisite dining, while SoDo (south of downtown) is an austere warehouse district that's steadily attracting new distilleries and dispensaries.

★ **Klondike Gold Rush National Historical Park** MUSEUM

(Map p360; ☎206-553-3000; www.nps.gov/klse; 319 2nd Ave S, Pioneer Sq; ⏲9am-5pm daily Jun-Aug, 10am-5pm Tue-Sun Sep-Feb, 10am-5pm daily Mar-May; 🚊First Hill Streetcar) FREE Eloquently run by the US National Park Service, this wonderful museum has exhibits, photos and news clippings from the 1897 Klondike gold rush, when a Seattle-on-steroids acted as a fueling depot for prospectors bound for the Yukon in Canada. Entry would cost $20 anywhere else; in Seattle it's free!

Wing Luke Museum of the Asian Pacific American Experience MUSEUM

(Map p360; ☎206-623-5124; www.wingluke.org; 719 S King St, International District; adult/child $17/12; ⏲10am-5pm Tue-Sun; 🚊First Hill Streetcar) The beautiful Wing Luke museum examines Asia Pacific American culture, focusing on prickly issues such as Chinese settlement in the 1880s and Japanese internment camps during WWII. Recent temporary exhibits include 'A Day in the Life of Bruce Lee.' There are also art exhibits and a preserved immigrant apartment. Guided tours are available; the first Thursday of the month is free (with extended hours until 8pm).

Seattle Center

★ **Space Needle** LANDMARK

(Map p360; ☎206-905-2100; www.spaceneedle.com; 400 Broad St, Seattle Center; adult/child $37.50/32.50, incl Chihuly Garden & Glass $49/39; ⏲9:30am-11pm Mon-Thu, 9:30am-11:30pm Fri & Sat, 9am-11pm Sun; 🚝Seattle Center) This streamlined, modern-before-its-time tower built for the 1962 World's Fair has been the city's defining symbol for more than 50 years. The needle anchors the complex now called the **Seattle Center** (Map p360; ☎206-684-8582; www.seattlecenter.com; 400 Broad St, Seattle Center; 🚝Seattle Center) and draws more than one million annual visitors to its flying saucer–like observation deck and pricey rotating restaurant.

★ **Museum of Pop Culture** MUSEUM

(Map p360; ☎206-770-2700; www.mopop.org; 325 5th Ave N, Seattle Center; adult/child $28/19; ⏲10am-5pm Jan-late May & Sep-Dec, 10am-7pm late May-Aug; 🚝Seattle Center) The Museum of Pop Culture (formerly EMP, the 'Experience Music Project') is an inspired marriage between super-modern architecture and legendary rock-and-roll history that sprang from the imagination (and pocket) of Microsoft co-creator Paul Allen (1953–2018). Inside its avant-garde frame, designed by Canadian architect Frank Gehry, you can tune into the famous sounds of Seattle (with an obvious bias toward Jimi Hendrix and grunge) or attempt to imitate the masters in the Interactive Sound Lab.

★ **Chihuly Garden & Glass** MUSEUM

(Map p360; ☎206-753-4940; www.chihulygardenandglass.com; 305 Harrison St, Seattle Center; adult/child $26/17, incl Space Needle $49/39; ⏲10am-8pm Sun-Thu, to 9pm Fri & Sat; 🚝Seattle Center) Opened in 2012 and reinforcing Seattle's position as a leading city of the arts, this exquisite exposition of the life and work of dynamic local sculptor Dale Chihuly is possibly the finest collection of curated glass art you'll ever see. It shows off Chihuly's creative designs in a suite of interconnected dark and light rooms before depositing you in an airy glass atrium and – finally – a landscaped garden in the shadow of the Space Needle. Glassblowing demonstrations are a highlight.

Capitol Hill

Capitol Hill is Seattle's most unashamedly hip neighborhood, where the exceptionally rich mix with the exceptionally eccentric. While gentrification has let some of the air out of its tires, this is still Seattle's best crash pad for dive-bar rock and roll, LGBTIQ+ mirth and on-trend dining. More straitlaced First Hill is home to an art museum and multiple hospitals.

Green Lake & Fremont

Fremont pitches young hipsters among old hippies in an unlikely urban alliance, and vies with Capitol Hill as Seattle's most irreverent neighborhood, with junk shops, urban sculpture and a healthy sense of its own ludicrousness. To the north, family-friendly Green Lake is a more affluent suburb centered on a park favored by fitness devotees.

Fremont Troll SCULPTURE

(N 36th St & Troll Ave, Fremont; 🚌62) The Fremont Troll is an outlandish sculpture that lurks beneath the north end of the Aurora Bridge at N 36th St. The troll's creators – artists Steve Badanes, Will Martin, Donna Walter and

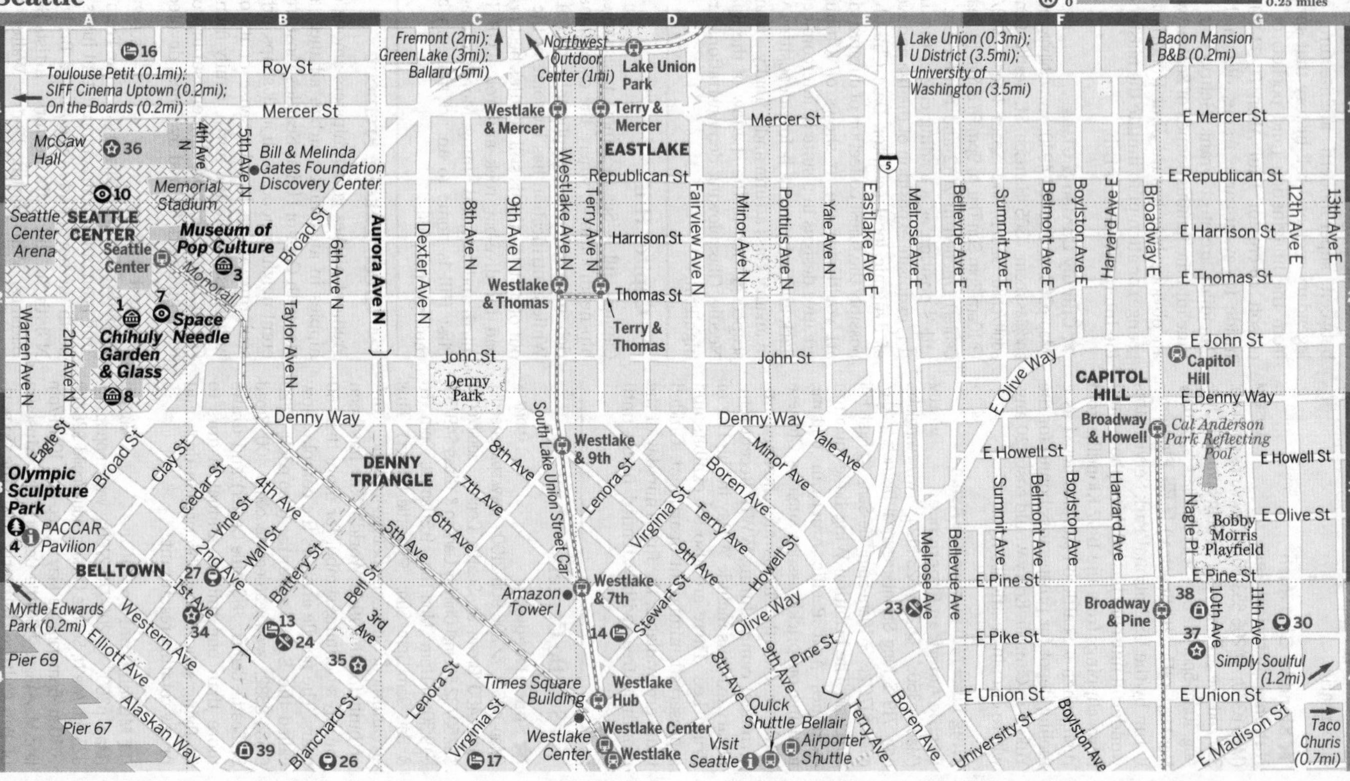
Seattle
500 m
0.25 miles
Toulouse Petit (0.1mi); SIFF Cinema Uptown (0.2mi); On the Boards (0.2mi)
Fremont (2mi); Green Lake (3mi); Ballard (5mi)
Northwest Outdoor Center (1mi)
Lake Union (0.3mi); U District (3.5mi); University of Washington (3.5mi)
Bacon Mansion B&B (0.2mi)
Myrtle Edwards Park (0.2mi)
Simply Soulful (1.2mi)
Taco Churis (0.7mi)
Roy St
Mercer St
E Mercer St
Lake Union Park
Westlake & Mercer
Terry & Mercer
EASTLAKE
Republican St
E Republican St
Harrison St
E Harrison St
Thomas St
E Thomas St
Westlake & Thomas
Terry & Thomas
John St
E John St
Capitol Hill
CAPITOL HILL
E Denny Way
Denny Way
Denny Park
McCaw Hall
Memorial Stadium
Bill & Melinda Gates Foundation Discovery Center
Seattle Center Arena
SEATTLE CENTER
Seattle Center
Museum of Pop Culture
Monorail
Space Needle
Chihuly Garden & Glass
4th Ave N
5th Ave N
Broad St
6th Ave N
Taylor Ave N
Aurora Ave N
Dexter Ave N
8th Ave N
9th Ave N
Westlake Ave N
Terry Ave N
Fairview Ave N
Minor Ave N
Pontius Ave N
Yale Ave N
Eastlake Ave E
Melrose Ave E
Bellevue Ave E
Summit Ave E
Belmont Ave E
Boylston Ave E
Harvard Ave E
Broadway E
12th Ave E
13th Ave E
Warren Ave N
2nd Ave N
E Olive Way
Broadway & Howell
Cal Anderson Park Reflecting Pool
E Howell St
E Olive St
Bobby Morris Playfield
Nagle Pl
E Pine St
E Pike St
E Union St
E Madison St
Broadway & Pine
10th Ave
11th Ave
Summit Ave
Belmont Ave
Boylston Ave
Harvard Ave
Melrose Ave
Bellevue Ave
University St
Eagle St
Clay St
Cedar St
Vine St
Wall St
Battery St
Bell St
Olympic Sculpture Park
PACCAR Pavilion
BELLTOWN
DENNY TRIANGLE
1st Ave
2nd Ave
3rd Ave
4th Ave
5th Ave
6th Ave
7th Ave
8th Ave
9th Ave
Western Ave
Elliott Ave
Alaskan Way
Pier 69
Pier 67
Blanchard St
Lenora St
Virginia St
Stewart St
Howell St
Olive Way
Pine St
Terry Ave
Boren Ave
Minor Ave
Yale Ave
South Lake Union Street Car
Westlake & 9th
Westlake & 7th
Amazon Tower I
Times Square Building
Westlake Hub
Westlake Center
Westlake
Visit Seattle
Quick Shuttle
Bellair Airporter Shuttle
1
2
3
4
7
8
10
13
14
16
17
23
24
26
27
30
34
35
36
37
38
39
A
B
C
D
E
F
G

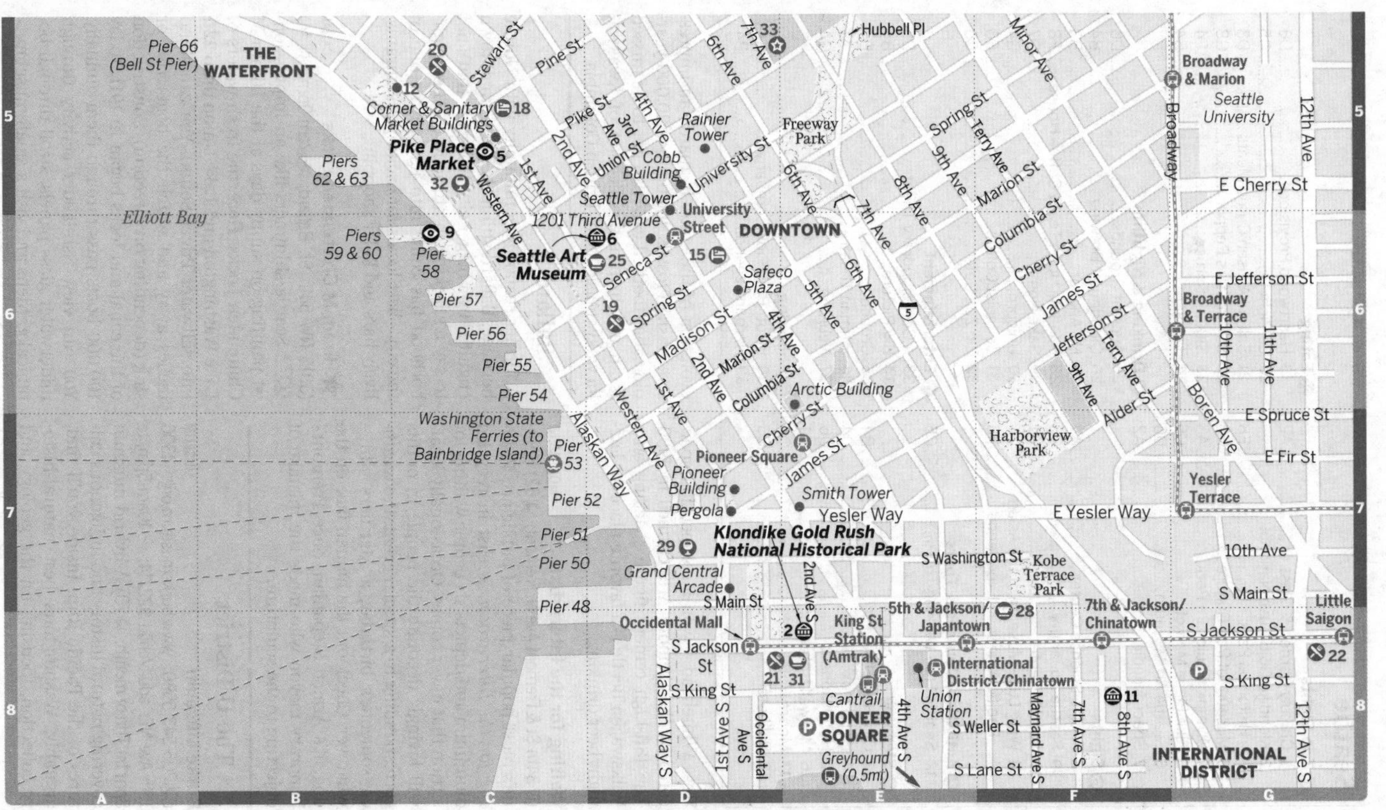
THE WATERFRONT
Pier 66 (Bell St Pier)
Elliott Bay
Piers 62 & 63
Piers 59 & 60
Pier 58
Pier 57
Pier 56
Pier 55
Pier 54
Washington State Ferries (to Bainbridge Island)
Pier 53
Pier 52
Pier 51
Pier 50
Pier 48
Pike Place Market
Corner & Sanitary Market Buildings
Stewart St
Pine St
Pike St
Union St
University St
Seneca St
Spring St
Madison St
Marion St
Columbia St
Cherry St
James St
Jefferson St
Terry Ave
Alder St
Yesler Way
E Yesler Way
S Washington St
S Main St
S Jackson St
S King St
S Weller St
S Lane St
1st Ave
2nd Ave
3rd Ave
4th Ave
5th Ave
6th Ave
7th Ave
8th Ave
9th Ave
Minor Ave
Hubbell Pl
Western Ave
Alaskan Way
Alaskan Way S
1st Ave S
Occidental Ave S
2nd Ave S
4th Ave S
7th Ave S
8th Ave S
Maynard Ave S
12th Ave S
Broadway
Boren Ave
10th Ave
11th Ave
12th Ave
E Cherry St
E Jefferson St
E Spruce St
E Fir St
Broadway & Marion
Seattle University
Broadway & Terrace
Yesler Terrace
Harborview Park
Freeway Park
DOWNTOWN
Rainier Tower
Cobb Building
Seattle Tower
University Street
1201 Third Avenue
Seattle Art Museum
Safeco Plaza
Arctic Building
Smith Tower
Pioneer Square
Pioneer Building
Pergola
Klondike Gold Rush National Historical Park
Grand Central Arcade
Occidental Mall
King St Station (Amtrak)
Cantrail
PIONEER SQUARE
Greyhound (0.5mi)
Union Station
International District/Chinatown
5th & Jackson/ Japantown
7th & Jackson/ Chinatown
Kobe Terrace Park
Little Saigon
INTERNATIONAL DISTRICT
2
5
6
9
11
12
15
18
19
20
21
22
25
28
29
31
32
33
53
A
B
C
D
E
F
G
5
6
7
8

Seattle

Top Sights
1 Chihuly Garden & Glass A2
2 Klondike Gold Rush National Historical Park E8
3 Museum of Pop Culture B2
4 Olympic Sculpture Park A3
5 Pike Place Market C5
6 Seattle Art Museum D6
7 Space Needle A2

Sights
8 Pacific Science Center A3
9 Seattle Aquarium C6
10 Seattle Center A1
11 Wing Luke Museum of the Asian Pacific American Experience F8

Activities, Courses & Tours
12 Seattle Free Walking Tours C5

Sleeping
13 City Hostel Seattle B4
14 Hotel Max D4
15 Hotel Monaco D6
16 Maxwell Hotel A1
17 Moore Hotel C4
18 Palihotel C5

Eating
19 Heartwood Provisions D6
20 Le Pichet C5
21 Salumi Artisan Cured Meats D8
22 Seven Stars Pepper G8
23 Sitka & Spruce E4
24 Tavolàta B4

Drinking & Nightlife
25 Ancient Grounds D6
26 Cloudburst Brewing B4
27 No Anchor B3
28 Panama Hotel Tea & Coffee House F8
29 Saké Nomi D7
30 Unicorn G4
31 Zeitgeist Coffee E8
32 Zig Zag Café C5

Entertainment
33 A Contemporary Theatre D5
34 Big Picture B4
35 Crocodile B4
36 Intiman Theatre A1
37 Neumos G4

Shopping
38 Elliott Bay Book Company G4
39 Herban Legends B4

Ross Whitehead – won a competition sponsored by the Fremont Arts Council in 1990. The 18ft-high cement figure snacking on a Volkswagen Beetle is a favorite place for late-night beer drinking.

Waiting for the Interurban MONUMENT
(N 34th St & Fremont Ave N, Fremont; 62) Seattle's most popular piece of public art, *Waiting for the Interurban,* is cast in recycled aluminum and depicts six people waiting for a train that never comes. Occasionally locals will lovingly decorate the people in outfits corresponding to a special event, the weather, someone's birthday, a Mariners win – whatever. Check out the human face on the dog; it's Armen Stepanian, once Fremont's honorary mayor, who made the mistake of objecting to the sculpture.

The U District

Burke Museum MUSEUM
(206-543-5590; www.burkemuseum.org; 4300 15th Ave NE; adult/child $22/14; 10am-5pm, to 8pm 1st Thu of month; 70) A hybrid museum covering natural history and indigenous cultures of the Pacific Rim. Inside you'll find, arguably, Washington's best natural-history collection, focusing on the geology and evolution of the state. It guards an impressive stash of fossils, including a 20,000-year-old saber-toothed cat. Also not to be missed is an awe-inspiring collection of Kwakwaka'wakw masks from British Columbia.

Ballard

A former seafaring community with Nordic heritage, Ballard still feels like a small town engulfed by a bigger city. However, that's not to say it's lacking in attractions. The neighborhood has come into its own as one of the city's best locals for exciting restaurants, lively bars and killer shopping.

★**Hiram M Chittenden Locks** CANAL
(3015 NW 54th St, Ballard; 7am-9pm; 44) FREE Seattle shimmers like an impressionist painting on sunny days at the Hiram M Chittenden Locks. Here, the fresh waters of Lake Washington and Lake Union drop 22ft into saltwater Puget Sound. You can stand inches away and watch the boats rise or sink (depending on direction). Construction of the canal and locks began in 1911; today 100,000 boats pass through them annually. You can view fish-ladder activity through underwater glass panels, stroll through botanical gardens and visit a small museum.

Activities

Cycling

Despite frequent rain and hilly terrain, cycling is still a major form of both transportation and recreation in the Seattle area. In 2014 the city finally inaugurated a public bike-sharing scheme, which closed in March 2017 due to lack of ridership. In 2018 several private companies, including Lyft and Lime, began the practice again.

In the city, commuter bike lanes are painted green on many streets, city trails are well maintained, and the friendly and enthusiastic cycling community is happy to share the road. The wildly popular 20-mile Burke-Gilman Trail winds from Ballard to Log Boom Park in Kenmore on Seattle's Eastside. There, it connects with the 11-mile long **Sammamish River Trail**, which winds past the Chateau Ste Michelle winery in Woodinville before terminating at Redmond's Marymoor Park.

Other good places to cycle are around **Green Lake** (206-684-4075; 7201 E Green Lake Dr N, Green Lake; 24hr; 62), which is congested but pretty, at sublime **Alki Beach** (206-684-4075; 1702 Alki Ave SW, West Seattle; 4am-11:30pm; 37) or, closer to downtown, through scenic **Myrtle Edwards Park** (206-684-4075; 3130 Alaskan Way, Belltown; 24hr; 33). The latter trail continues through Interbay to Ballard, where it links with the Burke-Gilman.

Anyone planning on cycling in Seattle should pick up a copy of the *Seattle Bicycling Guide Map,* published by the City of Seattle's Transportation Bicycle & Pedestrian Program and available online (www.cityofseattle.net/transportation/bikemaps.htm) and at bike shops.

Water Sports

Seattle is striated with kayak-friendly marine trails. The **Lakes to Locks Water Trail** links Lake Sammamish with Lake Washington, Lake Union and – via the Hiram M Chittenden Locks – Puget Sound. For launching sites and maps, check the website of the Washington Water Trails Association (www.wwta.org).

Northwest Outdoor Center KAYAKING
(206-281-9694; www.nwoc.com; 2100 Westlake Ave N, Lake Union; rental per hr kayak/SUP $18/20; 10am-8pm Mon-Fri, 9am-6pm Sat & Sun Apr-Sep, closed Mon & Tue Oct-Mar; 62) Located on the west side of Lake Union, this place rents kayaks and stand up paddleboards (SUPs) and offers tours and instruction in sea and white-water kayaking.

Tours

★ **Seattle Free Walking Tours** WALKING
(Map p360; www.seattlefreewalkingtours.org; 2001 Western Ave, Pike Place) FREE A nonprofit tour company that does an intimate two-hour walk taking in Pike Place, the waterfront and Pioneer Square, among other tours. Each tour is 'pay what you can,' and the company notes that comparable walking tours run around $20. Reserve online.

Festivals & Events

Seafair FAIR
(www.seafair.com; Jun-Aug) This waterfront festival is hugely popular and runs in one capacity or another from June through August. Come for music, pirate ships, food stalls and an excuse to be out in the nice weather.

Bumbershoot PERFORMING ARTS
(www.bumbershoot.com; Seattle Center; 3-day pass from $434; Sep) A fair few people – Seattleites or otherwise – would say that this is Seattle's finest festival, with major arts and cultural events at the Seattle Center on the Labor Day weekend in September. Bank on live music, comedy, theater, visual arts and dance, but also bank on crowds and hotels stuffed to capacity. Book well in advance!

Sleeping

Reserve ahead in summer, when hotels book up and prices tend to skyrocket.

SEATTLE CITYPASS

If you're going to be in Seattle for a while and plan on seeing its premier attractions, consider buying a Seattle **CityPASS** (www.citypass.com/seattle; per adult/child 5-12yr $99/79). Good for nine days, the pass gets you entry into five sights: the Space Needle, Seattle Aquarium, Argosy Cruises Seattle Harbor Tour, Museum of Pop Culture *or* Woodland Park Zoo and Pacific Science Center *or* Chihuly Garden & Glass. You wind up saving about 49% on admission costs and you never have to stand in line. You can buy one at any of the venues or online.

City Hostel Seattle HOSTEL $
(Map p360; 206-706-3255; www.hostelseattle.com; 2327 2nd Ave, Belltown; dm/d from $36/125; Westlake) This well-located, boutique 'art hostel' has colorful murals painted by local artists splashed on the walls of every room. There's also a common room, hot tub, in-house movie theater and all-you-can-eat breakfast. Dorms have four or six beds and some are women-only. There are also several private rooms, some with shared bathroom. Guests consistently praise the friendly staff.

Moore Hotel HOTEL $
(Map p360; 206-448-4851; www.moorehotel.com; 1926 2nd Ave, Belltown; d with/without bath from $165/117; 13) Old-world and allegedly haunted, the hip and whimsical Moore is undoubtedly central Seattle's most reliable bargain, offering fixed annual prices for its large stash of simple but cool rooms. Bonuses – aside from the dynamite location – are the cute ground-floor cafe, and zebra- and leopard-skin-patterned carpets.

Hotel Hotel Hostel HOTEL, HOSTEL $
(206-257-4543; www.hotelhotel.co; 3515 Fremont Ave N, Fremont; dm $34-36, d with/without bath $140/120; 5) Fremont's only real hotel is a good one, encased in a venerable old building replete with exposed brick and chunky radiators. In true Fremont fashion, Hotel Hotel is technically more of a hostel (with dorms), but it also passes itself off as an economical hotel on account of its private rooms with an assortment of shared and en-suite bathrooms.

The industrial-chic decor means it's comfortable without being fancy. A buffet breakfast is included in the price, and there is a common room and a kitchen.

★ **University Inn** BOUTIQUE HOTEL $$
(206-632-5055; www.universityinnseattle.com; 4140 Roosevelt Way NE; r from $226; 74) This spotless, modern, well-located place is good – especially when you factor in the waffles served with the complimentary breakfast. The hotel is four blocks from campus and just three from the bustle of 'the Ave.' The 102 rooms come in three levels of plushness. All of them offer such basics as a coffee maker, hair dryer and wi-fi; some have balconies, sofas and Bluetooth docking stations.

★ **Bacon Mansion B&B** B&B $$
(206-329-1864; www.baconmansion.com; 959 Broadway E, Capitol Hill; r with/without bath $244/189, ste from $269; 49) A 1909 Tudor-style mansion whose imposing exterior belies the quirky charm of its friendly hosts, this four-level B&B on a quiet residential street just past the Capitol Hill action is one of the best in the area. Among its charming amenities are a pleasant garden and a grand piano in the main room that guests are invited to play.

Graduate Seattle HOTEL $$
(206-634-2000; www.graduatehotels.com; 4507 Brooklyn Ave NE; r from $237;) This new kid on the block brings hip sophistication to the U District's hotel scene. Eclectic furniture and walls full of framed photographs almost make this place feel more like a passed-down vacation home than a new hotel, but then amenities such as the 24-hour gym and incredible rooftop bar bring it all back into focus.

★ **Palihotel** BOUTIQUE HOTEL $$$
(Map p360; 206-596-0600; www.palisociety.com; 107 Pine St, Downtown; r from $298;)

SEATTLE FOR CHILDREN

Make a beeline for the Seattle Center, preferably on the monorail, where food carts, street entertainers, fountains and green spaces will make the day fly by. One essential stop is the **Pacific Science Center** (Map p360; 206-443-2001; www.pacificsciencecenter.org; 200 2nd Ave N, Seattle Center; adult/child $26/18; 10am-5pm Mon-Fri, to 6pm Sat & Sun; ; Seattle Center), which entertains and educates with virtual-reality exhibits, laser shows, holograms, an IMAX theater and a planetarium. Parents won't be bored either.

Downtown on Pier 59, **Seattle Aquarium** (Map p360; 206-386-4300; www.seattleaquarium.org; 1483 Alaskan Way, Waterfront; adult/child $35/25; 9:30am-5pm; ; University St) is a fun way to learn about the natural world of the Pacific Northwest. Even better is **Woodland Park Zoo** (206-548-2500; www.zoo.org; 5500 Phinney Ave N, Green Lake; adult/child May-Sep $22.95/13.95, Oct-Apr $15.50/10.50; 9:30am-6pm May-Sep, to 4pm Oct-Apr; ; 5) in the Green Lake neighborhood, one of Seattle's greatest tourist attractions and consistently rated as one of the top 10 zoos in the country.

The rare new hotel that isn't a utilitarian business tower, Palihotel is an understated boutique (part of a small, but expanding, chain) whose early-20th-century 'forest green walls and overstuffed leather chairs' aesthetic is as chic as it is cozy. Although the theme is antique, the building's remodel ensures 21st-century luxuries like air-conditioning and rain showers.

★ **Hotel Monaco** BOUTIQUE HOTEL $$$

(Map p360; ☎206-621-1770; www.monaco-seattle.com; 1101 4th Ave, Downtown; d/ste $293/406; P @ ; University St) Whimsical and with dashes of European elegance, the downtown Monaco is a classic Kimpton hotel whose rooms live up to the hints given off in the illustrious lobby. Bed down amid the bold, graphic decor and reap the perks (complimentary bikes, fitness center, free wine tasting, in-room yoga mats).

Maxwell Hotel BOUTIQUE HOTEL $$$

(Map p360; ☎206-286-0629; 300 Roy St, Queen Anne; r/ste from $311/371; P @ ; RapidRide D Line) Located in Lower Queen Anne, the Maxwell has a huge designer-chic lobby with a floor mosaic and colorful furnishings that welcomes you with aplomb. Upstairs the slickness continues in 139 gorgeously modern rooms with hardwood floors and Scandinavian bedding. There's a small pool, a gym, free bike rentals and complimentary cupcakes.

Hotel Max BOUTIQUE HOTEL $$$

(Map p360; ☎206-441-4200; www.hotelmaxseattle.com; 620 Stewart St, Belltown; r from $263; P @ ; South Lake Union Streetcar) It's tough to get any hipper than a hotel that has a whole floor dedicated to Seattle's indie Sub Pop record label (that unleashed Nirvana on an unsuspecting world). The 5th floor pays homage to the music with giant grunge-era photos and record players with vinyls in every room. The art theme continues throughout the hotel (there's a Warhol in the lobby).

Eating

The best budget meals are to be found in Pike Place Market (p358). Take your pick from fresh produce, baked goods, deli items and takeout ethnic foods.

★ **Taco Chukis** TACOS $

(www.facebook.com/TacosChukis; 2215 E Union St, CD; tacos $2.20-2.75; 11am-9pm; 2) At the moment in Seattle there are few bites of food better than the signature taco at Taco Chukis. It's a simple design (juicy pork, guacamole, melted cheese and brilliantly tangy grilled pineapple) that's executed so well you're likely to get into line immediately after finishing to order a couple more.

★ **Salumi Artisan Cured Meats** SANDWICHES $

(Map p360; ☎206-621-8772; www.salumicuredmeats.com; 404 Occidental Ave S, Pioneer Sq; sandwiches $10.50-12.50; 11am-3pm Mon-Sat; International District/Chinatown) This well-loved deli used to be known for the long lines at its tiny storefront, and although it has moved to a bigger spot, you can still expect a wait for the legendary Italian-quality salami and cured-meat sandwiches (grilled lamb, pork shoulder, meatballs). You can expect a regular sandwich menu, as well as daily sandwich, soup and pasta specials.

Un Bien CUBAN $

(☎206-588-2040; www.unbienseattle.com; 7302 ½ 15th Ave NW, Ballard; mains $11-16; 11am-9pm Wed-Sat, to 8pm Sun; RapidRide D Line) Lines can get long at this Cuban take-out spot far from Ballard's commercial center, but the wait is worth it to finally sink your teeth into a perfectly juicy and tangy pork sandwich. The restaurant is owned by brothers working from family recipes and you can taste the affection in every bite.

★ **Bitterroot** BARBECUE $$

(☎206-588-1577; www.bitterrootbbq.com; 5239 Ballard Ave NW, Ballard; mains $11-19; 11am-2am; 40) People come to Bitterroot for two things: smoked meat and whiskey. Thankfully this restaurant with a pleasing modern roadhouse vibe does both exceptionally well. You can get your meat in sandwich form, or by itself with sides like cast-iron cornbread and roasted cauliflower. Likewise, the extensive whiskey menu comes neat or as an expertly mixed craft cocktail.

★ **Ma'Ono** HAWAIIAN $$

(☎206-935-1075; www.maonoseattle.com; 4437 California Ave SW, West Seattle; mains $12-17; 5-10pm Wed & Thu, 5-11pm Fri, 9am-3pm & 5-11pm Sat, 5-10pm Sun; 55) The fried chicken sandwich – served on a King's Hawaiian roll with cabbage and a perfectly spicy sauce – at this West Seattle spot is one of the best things between two slices of bread currently available in Seattle. Treat yourself to one during the always-packed brunch with a guava mimosa and side of roasted sweet potato with caramelized lime.

★Seven Stars Pepper SICHUAN $$

(Map p360; ☎206-568-6446; www.sevenstarspepper.com; 1207 S Jackson St, International District; mains $9-20; ⊙11am-3pm & 5-9:30pm Mon-Wed, 11am-9:30pm Thu, to 10pm Fri & Sat, to 9pm Sun; 🚇First Hill Streetcar) Don't be put off by Seven Stars Pepper's uninspiring location on the 2nd floor of a run-down strip mall: this Szechuan restaurant is one of the best in the city. Everything on the menu is exceptional, but the hand-cut *dan dan* noodles are a must-order. They are thick and flavorful with just the right amount of chewiness.

Le Pichet FRENCH $$

(Map p360; ☎206-256-1499; www.lepichetseattle.com; 1933 1st Ave, Pike Place; dinner mains $22-25; ⊙8am-midnight; 🚇Westlake) Say *bonjour* to Le Pichet, just up from Pike Place Market, a cute and very French bistro with pâtés, cheeses, wine, *chocolat* and a refined Parisian feel. Dinner features delicacies such as Niçoise chickpea crepes and Basque seafood stew. The specialty is a roast chicken (for two $45) – just know that there's an hour's wait when you order one.

★Sitka & Spruce MODERN AMERICAN $$$

(Map p360; ☎206-324-0662; www.sitkaandspruce.com; 1531 Melrose Ave, Capitol Hill; plates $16-35; ⊙11:30am-2pm & 5-10pm Tue-Thu, to 9pm Mon, to 11pm Fri, 10am-2pm & 5-11pm Sat, to 9pm Sun; 🌿; 🚌10) The king of all locavore restaurants, Sitka & Spruce was the pilot project of celebrated Seattle chef Matt Dillon. It has since become something of an institution and a trendsetter, with its country-kitchen decor and a constantly changing menu concocted with ingredients from Dillon's own Vashon Island farm. Sample items include housemade charcuterie and roasted-asparagus-and-liver parfait. Great choice for vegetarians too.

★Heartwood Provisions FUSION $$$

(Map p360; ☎206-582-3505; www.heartwoodsea.com; 1103 1st Ave, Downtown; mains $24-37; ⊙4:30-10pm Sun-Thu, to 11pm Fri & Sat, also 9:30am-2pm Sat & Sun; 🚇University St) Cocktails are having a moment as the alcoholic libation du jour in Seattle and nowhere is that more clear than at Heartwood, a handsome restaurant and bar with a menu of mixed drinks that is unmatched. Come for dinner, where each dish is infused with Southeast Asian flavors and has its own cocktail pairing (optional for an additional $7).

★Tavolàta ITALIAN $$$

(Map p360; ☎206-838-8008; 2323 2nd Ave, Belltown; mains $18-32; ⊙5-11pm; 🚌13) Owned by top Seattle chef Ethan Stowell, Tavolàta is a dinner-only, Italian-inspired eatery emphasizing homemade pasta dishes and hearty mains such as a rack of wild boar with fig *mostarda* (a sweet and spicy mustard and fruit sauce). Many consider it among the best Italian spots in the city.

Drinking & Nightlife

★Unicorn BAR

(Map p360; ☎206-325-6492; www.unicornseattle.com; 1118 E Pike St, Capitol Hill; ⊙2pm-1:45am Mon-Fri, from 11am Sat & Sun; 🚌11) Even if Unicorn's circus theme doesn't exactly tickle your fancy, its commitment to the spectacle makes it worth a visit. Cocktails like the Cereal Killer (made with Fruit Loop–flavored vodka) hark back to the joys of giant lollipops and cotton candy, while the colorful explosion of decoration and pinball machine collection are likely to make even hardened cynics smile.

★Ancient Grounds CAFE

(Map p360; ☎206-7749-0747; 1220 1st Ave, Downtown; ⊙7:30am-4:30pm Mon-Fri, noon-6pm Sat; 🚇University St) If it's not enough that this cozy coffee nook serves some of the best espresso shots in the city, Ancient Grounds also doubles as a showroom for a well-curated selection of antiques. While waiting for your latte you can pick through a rack of vintage kimonos or peruse a display of wooden masks from indigenous communities of the Pacific Northwest.

★Saké Nomi SAKE

(Map p360; ☎206-467-7253; www.sakenomi.us; 76 S Washington St, Pioneer Sq; flight of 3 $22; ⊙2-10pm Tue, Wed, Fri & Sat, from 5pm Thu, 2-6pm Sun; 🚇First Hill Streetcar) Regardless if you're a sake (Japanese rice wine) connoisseur or casual enjoyer, you're likely to expand your palate and your cultural horizons at this cozy retailer and tasting room in Pioneer Sq. The Japanese and American wife-husband duo who run the place have a clear love for what they do, which shows in their wonderfully educational tasting menu.

★Fremont Brewing Company BREWERY

(206-420-2407; www.fremontbrewing.com; 1050 N 34th St, Fremont; 11am-9pm; ; 62) This microbrewery, in keeping with current trends, sells its wares via an attached tasting room rather than a full-blown pub. Not only is the beer divine (try the seasonal bourbon barrel-aged Abominable), but the industrial-chic tasting room and 'urban beer garden' are highly inclusive spaces, where pretty much everyone in the 'hood comes to hang out at communal tables.

★Zeitgeist Coffee CAFE

(Map p360; 206-583-0497; www.zeitgeistcoffee.com; 171 S Jackson St, Pioneer Sq; 6am-7pm Mon-Fri, from 7am Sat, 8am-6pm Sun; ; First Hill Streetcar) Possibly Seattle's best (if also busiest) indie coffee bar, Zeitgeist brews smooth *doppio macchiatos* to go with its sweet almond croissants and other luscious baked goods. The atmosphere is trendy industrial, with brick walls and large windows for people-watching. Soups, salads and sandwiches are also on offer.

★Blue Moon BAR

(206-675-9116; www.bluemoonseattle.wordpress.com; 712 NE 45th St; 4pm-2am Mon-Fri, from 2pm Sat & Sun; 74) A legendary counter-culture dive that first opened in 1934 to celebrate the repeal of Prohibition, Blue Moon makes much of its former literary patrons – including Dylan Thomas and Allen Ginsberg. The place is agreeably gritty and unpredictable, with graffiti carved into the seats and punk poets likely to stand up and start pontificating at any moment. Frequent live music.

Zig Zag Café COCKTAIL BAR

(Map p360; 206-625-1146; www.zigzagseattle.com; 1501 Western Ave, Pike Place; 5pm-2am; University St) If you're writing a research project on Seattle's culinary history, you'll need to reserve a chapter for the Zig Zag Café. This is the bar that repopularized the gin-based Jazz Age cocktail 'The Last Word' in the early 2000s. The drink went viral and the Zig Zag's nattily attired mixers were rightly hailed as the city's finest alchemists.

Cloudburst Brewing MICROBREWERY

(Map p360; 206-602-6061; www.cloudburstbrew.com; 2116 Western Ave, Belltown; 2-10pm Wed-Fri, noon-10pm Sat & Sun; 13) The brainchild of former experimental brewer at Elysian Brewing, Steve Luke, Cloudburst Brewing became an instant Seattle favorite. Replicating the success of Luke's past brewing creations, Cloudburst Brewing features hoppy beers with sassy names, and the bare-bones tasting room is always packed to the gills with beer fans who want to support craft beer in Seattle.

BALLARD'S BARS & BEER CULTURE

Ballard's bars, breweries and pubs are almost a neighborhood in their own right. If you want the local gossip and unique libations of every stripe this is where you should gravitate. Look out for historic, century-old bars, modern cocktail lounges, inventive brewpubs – massive to nano – and gastropubs with carefully configured retro decor.

Panama Hotel Tea & Coffee House CAFE

(Map p360; 206-515-4000; www.panamahotel.net; 607 S Main St, International District; tea $3-6; 8am-9pm; ; First Hill Streetcar) The intensely atmospheric teahouse inside the Panama Hotel has such a thoroughly back-in-time feel that you'll be reluctant to pull out your laptop (although there is wi-fi). It's in a National Treasure–designated 1910 building containing the only remaining Japanese bathhouse in the US, and doubles as a memorial to the neighborhood's Japanese residents forced into internment camps during WWII.

No Anchor BAR

(Map p360; 206-448-2610; www.noanchorbar.com; 2505 2nd Ave, Belltown; noon-11pm Mon-Thu, noon-midnight Fri, 11am-midnight Sat, 11am-11pm Sun; 13) Most things on the menu at No Anchor feel like a big risk, and they often pay off. The cocktails feature ingredients such as maple syrup and toasted coconut, while the menu of bar bites has eccentric offerings such as pickled mussels. Beer novices will feel welcomed by the large draft menu featuring a 'what to pick' guide.

☆ Entertainment

Consult *The Stranger*, *Seattle Weekly* or the daily papers for listings. Tickets for big events are available at TicketMaster (www.ticketmaster.com).

★Crocodile LIVE MUSIC

(Map p360; 206-441-4618; www.thecrocodile.com; 2200 2nd Ave, Belltown; 13) Nearly old

GRUNGE: PUNK'S WEST COAST NIRVANA

Synthesizing Generation X angst with a questionable approach to personal hygiene, the music popularly categorized as 'grunge' first stage dived onto Seattle's scene in the early 1990s. The anger had been fermenting for years – not purely in Seattle but also in its sprawling satellite towns and suburbs. Some said it was inspired by the weather, others cited the Northwest's geographic isolation. It didn't matter which. Armed with dissonant chords and dark, sometimes ironic lyrics, a disparate collection of bands stepped sneeringly up to the microphone to preach a new message from a city that all of the touring big-name rock acts serially chose to ignore. There were Screaming Trees from collegiate Ellensburg, the Melvins from rainy Montesano and Nirvana from the timber town of Aberdeen, while Hole frontwoman Courtney Love had ties to Olympia and the converging members of Pearl Jam came from across the nation.

Historically, grunge's roots lay in West Coast punk, a musical subgenre that first found a voice in Portland, OR, in the late 1970s, led by the Wipers, whose leather-clad followers congregated in legendary dive bars such as Satyricon. Another musical blossoming occurred in Olympia, WA, in the early 1980s, where DIY musicians Beat Happening invented 'lo-fi' and coyly mocked the corporate establishment. Mixing in elements of heavy metal and scooping up the fallout of an itchy youth culture, Seattle quickly became alternative music's pulpit, spawning small, clamorous venues where boisterous young bands more interested in playing rock music than 'performing' could lose themselves in a melee of excitement and noise. It was a raucous, energetic scene characterized by stage diving, crowd-surfing and barely tuned guitars, but driven by raw talent and some surprisingly catchy tunes, the music filled a vacuum.

A crucial element in grunge's elevation to superstardom was Sub Pop Records, an independent Seattle label whose guerrilla marketing tactics created a flurry of hype to promote its ragged stable of cacophonous bands. In August 1988, Sub Pop released the seminal single 'Touch Me I'm Sick' by Mudhoney, a watershed moment. The noise got noticed, most importantly by the British music press, whose punk-savvy journalists quickly reported the birth of a 'Seattle sound,' later christened grunge by the brand-hungry media. Suitably inspired, the Seattle scene began to prosper, spawning literally hundreds of new bands, all cemented in the same DIY, anti-fashion, audience-embracing tradition. Of note were sludgy Soundgarden, who later went on to win two Grammys; metal-esque Alice in Chains; and the soon-to-be-mega Nirvana and Pearl Jam. By the dawn of the 1990s, every rebellious slacker with the gas money was coming to Seattle to hit the clubs. It was more than exciting.

What should have been grunge's high point came in October 1992, when Nirvana's second album, the hugely accomplished *Nevermind*, knocked Michael Jackson off the number-one spot, but the kudos ultimately killed it. After several years of railing against the mainstream, Nirvana and grunge had been incorporated into it. The media blitzed in, grunge fashion spreads appeared in *Vanity Fair* and half-baked singers from Seattle only had to cough to land a record contract. Many recoiled, most notably Nirvana vocalist and songwriter Kurt Cobain, whose drug abuse ended in suicide in his new Madison Park home in 1994. Other bands soldiered on, but the spark – which had burnt so brightly while it lasted – was gone. By the mid-1990s, grunge was officially dead.

enough to be called a Seattle institution, the Crocodile is a clamorous 560-capacity venue that first opened in 1991, just in time to grab the coattails of the grunge explosion. Everyone who's anyone in Seattle's alt-music scene has since played here, including a famous occasion in 1992 when Nirvana appeared unannounced, supporting Mudhoney.

★A Contemporary Theatre THEATER
(ACT; Map p360; ☎206-292-7676; www.acttheatre.org; 700 Union St, Downtown; University St) One of the three big theater companies in the city, the ACT fills its $30 million home at Kreielsheimer Pl with performances by Seattle's best thespians and occasional big-name actors. Terraced seating surrounds a central stage and the interior has gorgeous architectural embellishments.

Big Picture CINEMA
(Map p360; ☎206-256-0566; www.thebigpicture.net; 2505 1st Ave, Belltown; tickets $14.50) It's easy to miss Big Picture when exploring

Seattle's Belltown neighborhood. For those in the know, it's an 'underground' cinema experience with affordable tickets of first-run screenings in an intimate setting. Order a cocktail from the bar (where you can linger before your showtime), and then another to be delivered mid-screening.

Neumos LIVE MUSIC
(Map p360; ☎206-709-9442; www.neumos.com; 925 E Pike St, Capitol Hill; First Hill Streetcar) This punk, hip-hop and alternative-music joint is, along with the Crocodile (p367) in Belltown, one of Seattle's most revered small music venues. Its storied list of former performers is too long to include, but if they're cool and passing through Seattle, they've probably played here. The audience space can get hot and sweaty, and even smelly, but that's rock and roll.

Tractor Tavern LIVE MUSIC
(☎206-789-3599; www.tractortavern.com; 5213 Ballard Ave NW, Ballard; tickets $8-20; 8pm-2am; 40) One of Seattle's premier venues for folk and acoustic music, the Tractor books local songwriters and regional bands, plus quality touring acts. Music tends to run toward country, rockabilly, folk, bluegrass and old-time. It's an intimate place with a small stage and great sound; occasional square dancing is frosting on the cake.

Intiman Theatre THEATER
(Map p360; ☎206-441-7178; www.intiman.org; 201 Mercer St, Seattle Center; tickets from $25; ; Seattle Center) A beloved theater company based at the Cornish Playhouse in the Seattle Center. Artistic director Jennifer Zeyl curates magnificent stagings of Shakespeare and Ibsen as well as work by emerging artists.

Shopping

★Elliott Bay Book Company BOOKS
(Map p360; ☎206-624-6600; www.elliottbaybook.com; 1521 10th Ave, Capitol Hill; 10am-10pm Mon-Thu, to 11pm Fri & Sat, to 9pm Sun; First Hill Streetcar) Seattle's most beloved bookstore offers more than 150,000 titles in a large, airy, wood-beamed space with cozy nooks that can inspire hours of serendipitous browsing. In addition to the size, the staff recommendations and displays of books by local authors make this place extra special. Bibliophiles will be further satisfied with regular book readings and signings.

★Herban Legends DISPENSARY
(Map p360; ☎206-849-5596; www.herbanlegends.com; 55 Bell St, Belltown; 8am-11:45pm; 13) Herban Legends is both a brilliantly silly pun and one of Seattle's best dispensaries. It manages to feel very professionally run while maintaining a breezy vibe missing from other weed shops in town. The staff are always ready with a great recommendation and there is even a merch shop at the front should you want a coffee mug.

Lucca Great Finds GIFTS & SOUVENIRS
(☎206-782-7337; www.luccagreatfinds.com; 5332 Ballard Ave NW, Ballard; 11am-6pm Mon-Fri, to 7pm Sat, 10am-5pm Sun) One of the best things about this Ballard boutique is that it offers two shopping experiences: in the front is a chic PNW-themed homewares store that will have you redesigning your apartment in your head while you browse, and in the back is a stationery shop with reams of enviably stylish wrapping paper and rows of charming greeting cards.

Information

EMERGENCY & MEDICAL SERVICES

Harborview Medical Center (☎206-744-3000; www.uwmedicine.org/harborview; 325 9th Ave, First Hill; Broadway & Terrace) Full medical care, with emergency room.

Seattle Police (☎206-625-5011; www.seattle.gov/police)

MEDIA

KEXP 90.3 FM (stream at http://kexp.org) Legendary independent music and community station.

Seattle Magazine (www.seattlemag.com) A slick monthly lifestyle magazine.

Seattle Times (www.seattletimes.com) The state's largest daily paper.

TOURIST INFORMATION

Visit Seattle (Map p360; ☎206-461-5800; www.visitseattle.org; 701 Pike St, Downtown; 9am-5pm daily Jun-Sep, Mon-Fri Oct-May; Westlake) Information desk inside the Washington State Convention Center's 1st-floor lobby. You can pick up leaflets even when the desk is closed.

Getting There & Away

AIR

Sea-Tac International Airport (SEA; ☎206-787-5388; www.portseattle.org/Sea-Tac; 17801 International Blvd;) Located 13 miles south of downtown Seattle, Sea-Tac has flights all over the US and to some international destinations. Amenities include restaurants, money changers, baggage storage, car-rental agencies, a cell (mobile) phone waiting area (for drivers waiting to pick up arriving passengers) and free wi-fi.

BOAT

The **Victoria Clipper** (☎ 206-448-5000; www.clippervacations.com; 2701 Alaskan Way, Belltown) ferry from Victoria, BC, docks at Pier 69 just south of the Olympic Sculpture Park in Belltown. **Washington State Ferries** (Map p360; www.bainbridgeisland.com; 801 Alaskan Way, Pier 52, Waterfront; foot passenger/bike/car $8.50/9.50/19.15) services from Bremerton and Bainbridge Island use Pier 52.

BUS

Various intercity coaches serve Seattle and there is more than one drop-off point – it all depends on which company you are using.

Bellair Airporter Shuttle (Map p360; ☎ 866-235-5247; www.airporter.com; 705 Pike St, Downtown) Runs buses to Yakima, Bellingham and Anacortes, and stops at King Street Station (for Yakima) and the Washington State Convention Center (for Bellingham and Anacortes).

Cantrail (Map p360; www.cantrail.com; adult/child $45/23) Amtrak's bus connector runs four daily services to Vancouver (one way from $42) and picks up and drops off at King Street Station.

Greyhound (☎ 206-628-5526; www.greyhound.com; 503 S Royal Brougham Way, SoDo; Ⓡ Stadium) Connects Seattle with cities all over the country, including Chicago (from $157 one way, two days, three daily), San Francisco ($91, 20 hours, two daily) and Vancouver (Canada; $18, four hours, three daily). The company has its own terminal just south of King Street Station in SoDo, accessible on the Central Link light rail (Stadium Station).

Quick Shuttle (Map p360; ☎ 800-665-2122; www.quickcoach.com; tickets $29-59; 📶) Fast and efficient, with five to six daily buses to Vancouver ($43). Picks up at the Best Western Executive Inn in Taylor Ave N near the Seattle Center. Grab the monorail or walk to downtown.

TRAIN

King Street Station (☎ 206-296-0100; www.amtrak.com; 303 S Jackson St, International District) Amtrak serves Seattle's King Street Station. Three main routes run through town: the Amtrak Cascades (connecting to Vancouver, Canada; and Portland and Eugene, OR); the very scenic Coast Starlight (connecting Seattle to Oakland and Los Angeles, CA) and the Empire Builder (a cross-continental to Chicago, IL).

ℹ Getting Around

TO/FROM THE AIRPORT

There are a number of options for making the 13-mile trek from the airport to downtown Seattle. The most efficient is the light-rail service run by **Sound Transit** (www.soundtransit.org). It runs every 10 to 15 minutes between 5am and midnight; the ride between Sea-Tac Airport and downtown (Westlake Center) takes 36 minutes. There are additional stops in Pioneer Sq and the International District; the service was extended to Capitol Hill and the U District in 2016.

Shuttle Express (☎ 425-981-7000; www.shuttleexpress.com) has a help desk, and pickup and drop-off point on the 3rd floor of the airport garage. It offers rideshare services that are more comfortable than public transit, but less expensive than a cab.

Taxis are available at the parking garage on the 3rd floor. Fares to downtown start at around $55.

PUBLIC TRANSPORTATION

Buses are operated by **King County Metro Transit** (☎ 206-553-3000; http://kingcounty.gov/depts/transportation/metro.aspx), part of the King County Department of Transportation. The website has schedules, maps and a trip planner.

Pay as you enter the bus; there's a flat fee of $2.75/1.50 per adult/child; you'll receive a slip that entitles you to a transfer until the time noted.

Monorail (☎ 206-905-2620; www.seattlemonorail.com; adult/youth $2.25/1.25; ⏲ 7:30am-11pm Mon-Fri, 8:30am-11pm Sat & Sun) This cool futuristic train, built for the 1962 World's Fair, travels only between two stops: Seattle Center and Westlake Center. Fares are $2.25/1.25 per adult/child. Hours change slightly throughout the year, check the website for up-to-date info.

Seattle Streetcar (www.seattlestreetcar.org; $2.25) Two lines. One runs from downtown Seattle (Westlake) to South Lake Union; the other goes from Pioneer Sq via the International District, the Central District and First Hill to Capitol Hill. Stops allow connections with numerous bus routes. Trams run approximately every 15 minutes throughout the day.

TAXI

All Seattle taxi cabs operate at the same rate, set by King County: $2.60 at meter drop, then $2.50 per mile.

Seattle Orange Cab (☎ 206-522-8800; www.orangecab.net)

Seattle Yellow Cab (☎ 206-622-6500; www.seattleyellowcab.com)

STITA Taxi (☎ 206-246-9999; www.stitataxi.com)

Olympia

Small in size but big in clout, Washington state capital Olympia is a political, musical and outdoor powerhouse. Look no further than the street-side buskers on 4th Ave, the smartly attired bureaucrats marching across the lawns of the resplendent state legislature and the Gore-Tex-clad outdoor fiends overnighting before rugged sorties into the Olympic Mountains. Progressive Evergreen State College has long lent the place an artsy turn (creator of *The Simpsons* Matt Groening studied here), while the dive bars and pawn shops of downtown provided an original pulpit for riot-grrrl music and grunge.

Olympia's economy has struggled in the wake of the timber industry's collapse, with increasing homelessness among the knock-on effects. But while it may have a few rough edges, it's still a fun little city.

Sights

Washington State Capitol LANDMARK
(360-902-8880; www.olympiawa.gov/community/visiting-the-capitol.aspx; 416 Sid Snyder Ave SW; 7am-5:30pm Mon-Fri, 11am-4pm Sat & Sun) FREE Olympia's capitol complex is set in a 30-acre park overlooking Capitol Lake with the Olympic Mountains glistening in the background. The campus' crowning glory is the magnificent **Legislative Building**. Completed in 1927, it's a dazzling display of craning columns and polished marble, topped by a 287ft dome that is only slightly smaller than its namesake in Washington, DC. Free, 50-minute tours are available on the hour 10am to 3pm weekdays, 11am Saturday and Sunday, starting just inside the main doors.

Olympia Farmers Market MARKET
(360-352-9096; www.olympiafarmersmarket.com; 700 N Capitol Way; 10am-3pm Thu-Sun Apr-Oct, Sat & Sun Nov & Dec, Sat Jan-Mar) Second only to Seattle's Pike Place in size and character, Olympia's local market is a great place to shop for organic herbs, vegetables, flowers, baked goods and the famous specialty: oysters.

Sleeping & Eating

Most of Olympia's cool, budget-friendly options have been transformed into much-needed affordable housing, but there are a lot of private-room options (Airbnb etc), plus the usual chain hotels (not a great bargain here) and some nice B&Bs.

Swantown Inn B&B $$
(360-753-9123; www.swantowninn.com; 1431 11th Ave; r from $159;) In the tradition of Washington state B&Bs, the Swantown Inn features great personal service and meticulous attention to detail in an 1887 Queen Anne–style mansion that's listed on the state historical register. Within sight of the imposing capitol dome, there are four elegantly furnished rooms, and a formidable homemade breakfast.

★ **Traditions Cafe & World Folk Art** HEALTH FOOD $
(360-705-2819; www.traditionsfairtrade.com; 300 5th Ave SW; mains $6-12; 9am-6pm Mon-Sat, 11am-5pm Sun;) This comfortable hippie enclave at the edge of Heritage Park offers fresh salads and tasty, healthy sandwiches (smoked salmon with lemon-tahini dressing is a winner), coffee drinks, herbal teas, local ice cream, beer and wine. Posters advertise community-action events, and in the corner is a 'Peace and Social Justice Lending Library.' It's attached to an eclectic folk-art store.

Information

The **State Capitol Visitor Center** (360-902-8880; www.olympiawa.gov/community/visiting-the-capitol.aspx; 103 Sid Snyder Ave SW; 9am-5pm Mon-Fri), run by the Olympia-Lacey-Tumwater Visitor & Convention Bureau, offers information on the capitol campus, the Olympia area and Washington state. There's another visitor information office inside the main doors of the Legislative Building.

Olympic Peninsula

Surrounded on three sides by sea and exhibiting many of the characteristics of a full-blown island, the remote Olympic Peninsula is about as 'wild' and 'west' as America gets. What it lacks in cowboys it makes up for in rare, endangered wildlife and dense primeval forest. The peninsula's roadless interior is largely given over to the notoriously wet Olympic National Park, while the margins are the preserve of loggers, Native American reservations and a smattering of small but interesting settlements, most notably Port Townsend. Equally untamed is the western coastline, America's isolated end point, where tempestuous ocean and misty old-growth Pacific rainforest meet in aqueous harmony.

Olympic National Park

Declared a national monument in 1909 and a national park in 1938, the 1406-sq-mile **Olympic National Park** (www.nps.gov/olym; 7-day access per vehicle $30, pedestrian/cyclist $15, 1yr unlimited entry $55) shelters a unique rainforest, copious glaciated mountain peaks and a 57-mile strip of Pacific coastal wilderness that was added to the park in 1953. One of North America's great wilderness areas, most of it remains relatively untouched by human habitation. Opportunities for independent exploration in this huge backcountry region abound, be they for hiking, fishing, kayaking or skiing.

EASTERN ENTRANCES

The graveled Dosewallips River Rd follows the river from Hwy 101 (turnoff approximately 1km north of Dosewallips State Park); due to a washout, the gravel Dosewallips River Rd now ends just 8.5 miles in from Hwy 101, where hiking and bicycle trails begin. Even hiking smaller portions of the two long-distance paths, including the 14.9 mile Dosewallips River Trail, with views of glaciated **Mt Anderson**, is reason enough to visit the valley. Another eastern entry for hikers is the **Staircase Ranger Station** (360-877-5569; May-Oct), just inside the national-park boundary, 15 miles from Hoodsport on Hwy 101. Two campgrounds along the eastern edge of the national park are popular: **Dosewallips State Park** (888-226-7688; www.parks.state.wa.us/499/dosewallips; 306996 Hwy 101; primitive tent sites $12, standard tent sites $27-37, RV sites $30-45) and **Skokomish Park Lake Cushman** (360-877-5760; www.skokomishpark.com; 7211 N Lake Cushman Rd, Hoodsport; tent/RV sites from $33/52; late May-early Sep). Both have running water, flush toilets and some RV hookups. Reservations are accepted.

NORTHERN ENTRANCES

The park's easiest – and hence most popular – entry point is at **Hurricane Ridge**, 18 miles south of Port Angeles. At the road's end, an interpretive center gives a stupendous view of Mt Olympus (7965ft) and dozens of other peaks. The 5200ft altitude can mean you'll hit inclement weather, and the winds here (as the name suggests) can be ferocious. Aside from various summer trekking opportunities, the area maintains the small, family-friendly **Hurricane Ridge Ski & Snowboard Area** (www.hurricaneridge.com; all-lift day pass $30-40; 10am-4pm Sat & Sun mid-Dec–Mar).

Popular for boating and fishing is **Lake Crescent**, the site of the park's oldest and most reasonably priced **lodge** (888-896-3818; www.olympicnationalparks.com; 416 Lake Crescent Rd; lodge r from $139, cottage from $245; May-Nov, limited availability winter; P). Sumptuous Northwestern-style food is served in the lodge's ecofriendly restaurant. From **Storm King Ranger Station** (360-928-3380; 343 Barnes Point Rd; May-Sep) on the lake's south shore, a 1-mile hike climbs through old-growth forest to Marymere Falls.

Along the Sol Duc River, the **Sol Duc Hot Springs Resort** (360-327-3583; www.olympicnationalparks.com; 12076 Sol Duc Hot Springs Rd, Port Angeles; cabins from $200; Mar-Oct) has lodging, dining, massage and, of course, hot-spring pools, as well as great day hikes.

WESTERN ENTRANCES

Isolated by distance and home of one of the country's rainiest microclimates, the Pacific side of the Olympics remains the wildest. Only US 101 offers access to its noted temperate rainforests and untamed coastline. The **Hoh River Rainforest**, at the end of the 19-mile Hoh River Rd, is a Tolkienesque maze of dripping ferns and moss-draped trees. The **Hoh Rain Forest Visitor Center** (360-374-6925; 9am-4:30pm Sep-Jun, to 6pm Jul & Aug) has information on guided walks and longer backcountry hikes. The attached **campground** (360-374-6925; www.nps.gov/olym/planyourvisit/camping.htm; campsites $20; year-round) has no hookups or showers, and it's first-come, first-served.

A little to the south lies **Lake Quinault**, a beautiful glacial lake surrounded by forested peaks. It's popular for fishing, boating and swimming, and is surrounded by some of the nation's oldest trees. **Lake Quinault Lodge** (360-288-2900; www.olympicnationalparks.com; 345 S Shore Rd; r $250-450), a luxury classic of 1920s 'parkitecture,' has a massive fireplace, a manicured cricket-pitch-quality lawn and a dignified lakeview restaurant serving upscale American cuisine. For a cheaper sleep nearby, try the ultrafriendly **Quinault River Inn** (360-288-2237; www.quinaultriverinn.com; 8 River Dr; r $175, RV site $50) in Amanda Park, a favorite with anglers.

A number of short hikes begin just outside the Lake Quinault Lodge, or you cantry the longer **Enchanted Valley Trail**, a medium-grade 13-miler that begins from the Graves Creek Ranger Station at the end of South Shore Rd and climbs up to a large meadow resplendent with wildflowers and copses of alder trees.

Information

The park entry fee is $10/25 per person/vehicle, valid for one week and payable at park entrances. Many park visitor centers double as United States Forestry Service (USFS) ranger stations, where you can pick up permits for wilderness camping ($8).

Forks Chamber of Commerce (360-374-2531; www.forkswa.com; 1411 S Forks Ave; 10am-5pm Mon-Sat, 11am-4pm Sun, to 4pm Mon-Sat, 11am-4pm Sun winter;)

Olympic National Park Visitor Center (360-565-3130; www.nps.gov/olym; 3002 Mt Angeles Rd; 9am-6pm Jul & Aug, to 4pm Sep-Jun)

USFS Headquarters (360-956-2402; www.fs.fed.us/r6/olympic; 1835 Black Lake Blvd SW; 8am-4:30pm Mon-Fri)

Port Townsend

Inventive eateries, elegant *fin de siècle* hotels and an unusual stash of year-round festivals make Port Townsend an Olympic Peninsula rarity: a weekend vacation that doesn't require hiking boots. Cut off from the rest of the area by eight bucolic miles of two-lane highway, this is not the spot to base yourself for national-park exploration unless you don't mind driving a lot. Instead, settle in and enjoy one of the prettiest towns in the state.

Sights

Fort Worden State Park STATE PARK
(360-344-4412; www.parks.state.wa.us/511/fort-worden; 200 Battery Way; 6:30am-dusk Apr-Oct, 8am-dusk Nov-Mar) FREE This attractive park located within Port Townsend's city limits is the remains of a large fortification system constructed in the 1890s to protect the strategically important Puget Sound area from outside attack – supposedly from the Spanish during the 1898 war. Sharp-eyed film buffs might recognize the area as the backdrop for the movie *An Officer and a Gentleman*.

Visitors can arrange tours of the **Commanding Officer's Quarters** (360-385-1003; Fort Worden State Park, 200 Battery Way; adult/child $6/1; tours by appointment), a 12-bedroom mansion. You will also find the **Puget Sound Coast Artillery Museum** (www.coastartillerymuseum.org; adult/child $4/2; 11am-4pm), which tells the story of early Pacific coastal fortifications. And there are cultural and musical programs year-round at the **Centrum** (www.centrum.org; Fort Worden State Park).

Hikes lead along the headland to **Point Wilson Lighthouse Station** and some wonderful windswept beaches. On the park's fishing pier is the **Port Townsend Marine Science Center** (360-385-5582; www.ptmsc.org; 532 Battery Way; adult/child $5/3; noon-5pm Fri-Sun Apr-Oct;), featuring four touch tanks and kid-friendly interpretive programs. There are also several camping and lodging possibilities.

Sleeping & Eating

Manresa Castle HISTORIC HOTEL $
(360-385-5750; www.manresacastle.com; cnr 7th & Sheridan Sts; d from $75, ste $149-229;) One of Port Townsend's signature buildings has been turned into a historic hotel-restaurant that's light on fancy gimmicks but heavy on period authenticity. This 40-room mansion, built by the town's first mayor, sits high on a bluff above the port and is one of the first buildings to catch your eye as you arrive by ferry.

★ **Palace Hotel** HISTORIC HOTEL $$
(360-385-0773; www.palacehotelpt.com; 1004 Water St; r from $150;) Built in 1889, this beautiful Victorian building was once a brothel run by the locally notorious Madame Marie, who did business out of the 2nd-floor corner suite. It's been reincarnated as an attractive, character-filled period hotel with antique furnishings (plus all the modern amenities). Pleasant common spaces; kitchenettes available. The cheapest rooms share a bathroom. Rates are higher on festival weekends.

Doc's Marina Grill AMERICAN $$
(360-344-3627; www.docsgrill.com; 141 Hudson St; mains $13-28; 11am-11pm) With a great location by Port Townsend's marina, Doc's offers something for everyone. There are burgers, sandwiches, fish-and-chips, various salads, pastas, steaks, seafood and a few vegetarian options. It's housed in a historic building that was a nurses' barracks back in the 1940s.

★ **Finistere** FRENCH $$$
(360-344-8127; www.restaurantfinistere.com; 1025 Lawrence St; dinner mains $24-34, tasting menu $50; 3-9pm Wed-Fri, 10am-2pm & 3-9pm Sat & Sun) When Sweet Laurette (formerly in this location) closed, local foodies despaired, but Finistere is a worthy replacement. With

a staff whose experience includes Per Se, Canlis, Tilth and other swoon-inducing restaurant names, you expect (and get) a high level of food and service: think saffron risotto with seafood, rabbit lasagna, steak tartare, multiple cheese-plate options, and smoked-salmon tartine for brunch.

Information

Visitor Center (☎360-385-2722; www.ptchamber.org; 2409 Jefferson St; ⏰9am-5pm Mon-Fri, 10am-4pm Sat & Sun) Pick up a useful walking-tour map and guide to the downtown historic district here.

Getting There & Away

Washington State Ferries (☎206-464-6400; www.wsdot.wa.gov/ferries/; car & driver/passenger $11.90/3.45) operates daily trips about every 90 minutes (more in high season) to Coupeville on Whidbey Island from the downtown terminal (35 minutes).

Port Angeles

One might wonder if Port Angeles suffers from abandonment issues. People come here mainly to leave: whether by ferry to Victoria, Canada, or on excursions into the northern parts of Olympic National Park. Most of the town – propped up by the lumber industry and backed by the steep-sided Olympic Mountains – is strictly utilitarian, but the downtown core near the ferry dock has plenty of charm.

Activities

The **Olympic Discovery Trail** (www.olympicdiscoverytrail.com) is a 30-mile off-road hiking and cycling trail between Port Angeles and Sequim, starting at the end of Ediz Hook, the sand spit that loops around the bay. Bikes can be rented at **Sound Bikes & Kayaks** (☎360-457-1240; www.soundbikeskayaks.com; 120 E Front St; bike rental per hr/day $10/40; ⏰10am-6pm Mon-Sat, 11am-4pm Sun).

Sleeping & Eating

Downtown Hotel HOTEL $
(☎360-565-1125; www.portangelesdowntownhotel.com; 101 E Front St; d with/without bath $80/60;) Nothing special on the outside but surprisingly spacious and tidy within, this no-frills, family-run place down by the ferry launch is Port Angeles' secret bargain. The dated but comfy rooms are decked out in wicker and wood, and several have water views. The cheapest rooms share a bathroom in the hallway. The soundproofing isn't great, but the location is tops.

Olympic Lodge HOTEL $$
(☎360-452-2993; www.olympiclodge.com; 140 Del Guzzi Dr; d from $140;) This is the most comfortable place in town, offering gorgeous rooms, an on-site bistro, a swimming pool with hot tub, and complimentary cookies and soup in the afternoon. Prices vary widely depending on day and month.

★**Next Door Gastropub** AMERICAN $$
(☎360-504-2613; www.nextdoorgastropub.com; 113 W First St; burgers $13-16, mains $11-24; ⏰11am-midnight Mon-Thu, 11am-1am Fri & Sat, 10am-midnight Sun) Arguably the best place to eat on the peninsula and definitely serving the best burger (go for the Mrs Newton with bacon, fig jam and Brie), this small, lively pub is like a little slice of Portland someone dropped here. It's no secret, so expect to wait a *looong* time for a table. Great beer list and a Sunday brunch.

Information

Port Angeles Visitor Center (☎360-452-2363; www.portangeles.org; 121 E Railroad Ave; ⏰9:30am-5:30pm Mon-Fri, 10am-5:30pm Sat, noon-3pm Sun May-Sep, 10am-5pm Mon-Sat, noon-3pm Sun Oct-Apr) Adjacent to the ferry terminal, this small office is loaded with brochures and staffed by enthusiastic volunteers.

Getting There & Away

Clallam Transit (☎360-452-4511; www.clallamtransit.com; fares per person $1-10, day pass from $3) Buses go to Forks and Sequim, where they link up with other transit buses that circumnavigate the Olympic Peninsula.

Coho Vehicle Ferry (☎888-993-3779; www.cohoferry.com; car & driver one way $66, foot passenger $19) Runs to/from Victoria, Canada (1½ hours, twice daily, four times daily in summer).

Dungeness Line (☎360-417-0700; www.dungeness-line.com; Gateway Transit Center, 123 E Front St; one way to Seattle from $39) Runs buses twice a day between Port Angeles, Sequim, Port Townsend, downtown Seattle and Seattle-Tacoma International Airport.

Northwest Peninsula

Several Native American reservations cling to the extreme northwest corner of the continent and are welcoming to visitors. The small weather-beaten settlement of **Neah Bay** on Hwy 112 is home to the Makah Indian Reservation, whose **Makah Museum**

(☎360-645-2711; www.makahmuseum.com; 1880 Bayview Ave; adult/child 5yr & under $6/free; ⏲10am-5pm) displays artifacts from one of North America's most significant archaeological finds, the 500-year-old Makah village of Ozette. Several miles beyond the museum, a short boardwalk trail leads to stunning **Cape Flattery**, a 300ft promontory that marks the most northwesterly point in the lower 48 states.

Convenient to the Hoh River Rainforest and the Olympic coastline is **Forks**, a one-horse lumber town that's now more famous for its *Twilight* paraphernalia. It's a central town for exploring Olympic National Park; a good accommodation choice is the **Miller Tree Inn** (☎360-374-6806; www.millertreeinn.com; 654 E Division St; r from $175; 📶🐾).

Northwest Washington

Wedged between Seattle, the Cascades and Canada, northwest Washington draws influences from three sides. Its urban hub is collegiate Bellingham, while its outdoor highlight is the pastoral San Juan Islands, an extensive archipelago that glimmers like a sepia-toned snapshot from another era. Anacortes is the main hub for ferries to the San Juan Islands and Victoria, Canada.

Whidbey Island

While not as detached (there's a bridge connecting it to adjacent Fidalgo Island at its northernmost point) or nonconformist as the San Juans, Whidbey Island is almost as quiet and pastoral. Having six state parks is a bonus, along with a plethora of B&Bs, two historic fishing villages (Langley and Coupeville), famously good clams and a thriving artist's community.

Deception Pass State Park (☎360-675-2417; www.parks.state.wa.us/497/deception-pass; 41229 N State Hwy 20; day pass $10; ⏲dawn-dusk) straddles the eponymous steep-sided strait that flows between Whidbey and Fidalgo Islands, and incorporates lakes, islands, campsites and 38 miles of hiking trails.

Ebey's Landing National Historical Reserve (☎360-678-6084; www.nps.gov/ebla; 162 Cemetery Rd, Coupeville) FREE comprises 17,400 acres encompassing working farms, sheltered beaches, two state parks and the town of **Coupeville**. This small settlement is one of Washington's oldest towns and has an attractive seafront, antique stores and a number of old inns, including the **Captain Whidbey Inn** (☎360-678-4097; www.captainwhidbey.com; 2072 W Captain Whidbey Inn Rd; r/cabins from $205/420; 📶), a newly updated log-built inn dating to 1907. For the famous fresh local clams, head to **Christopher's** (☎360-678-5480; www.christophersonwhidbey.com; 103 NW Coveland St; lunch mains $12-16, dinner mains $16-26; ⏲11:30am-2pm & 5-8pm Sun, Mon, Wed & Thu, to 8:30pm Fri & Sat).

ℹ Getting There & Around

Regular **Washington State Ferries** (WSF; ☎888-808-7977; www.wsdot.wa.gov/ferries) link Clinton to Mukilteo and Coupeville to Port Townsend. Free **Island Transit** (☎360-678-7771; www.islandtransit.org) buses run the length of Whidbey every hour daily, except Sundays, from the Clinton ferry dock.

Bellingham

Welcome to a green, liberal and famously livable settlement with a distinctively libertine, nothing-is-too-weird ethos. Mild in both manners and weather, the city is an unlikely alliance of espresso-sipping students, venerable retirees and all-weather triathletes, with brewpubs on every corner. Bellingham's downtown has been revitalized in recent years with intra-urban trails, stylishly refurbished warehouses, independent food co-ops, tasty brunch spots and – in genteel Fairhaven – a rejuvenated historic district.

Sights & Activities

Bellingham offers outdoor sights and activities by the truckload. **Whatcom Falls Park** is a natural wild region that bisects Bellingham's eastern suburbs. The change in elevation is marked by four sets of waterfalls, including **Whirlpool Falls**, a popular summer swimming hole.

Fairhaven Bicycles CYCLING
(☎360-733-4433; www.fairhavenbicycles.com; 1108 11th St; bike rental per day from $50; ⏲10am-6pm Mon & Wed-Sat, 11am-5pm Sun) Bellingham is one of the most bike-friendly cities in the Northwest, with a well-maintained intra-urban trail going as far south as **Larrabee State Park** (www.parks.state.wa.us/536/larrabee; Chuckanut Dr; ⏲dawn-dusk). This outfit rents bikes and has maps on local routes.

Moondance Sea Kayak Adventures KAYAKING
(www.moondancekayak.com; 348 Cove Rd; half-day tours adult/child $70/60; ⏲Apr-Sep) If you're interested in getting out on the water, try

this outfit, which runs family-friendly guided trips in Chuckanut Bay, launching from Larrabee State Park (p375).

Sleeping & Eating

Larrabee State Park CAMPGROUND $
(888-226-7688, 360-676-2093; www.parks.state.wa.us/536/larrabee; Chuckanut Dr; primitive sites $12, tent/RV sites from $27/35) Seven miles south of Bellingham, along scenic Chuckanut Dr, these campsites sit among Douglas firs and cedars with access to Chuckanut Bay and its 20-plus miles of hiking and biking trails. Light sleepers should note that trains pass by the campground frequently throughout the night; bring earplugs.

Heliotrope Hotel MOTEL $
(360-201-2914; www.heliotropehotel.com; 2419 Elm St; r with shared bath $99, r/ste from $109/130;) A 1950s motor inn that's been given a stylish makeover, this fun motel has 17 ground-floor rooms in various configurations, plus a secluded grassy yard with a firepit and a central lobby area designed to encourage hanging out. There's no breakfast but staff have lots of suggestions for restaurants (and nightlife) within walking distance.

★ **Hotel Bellwether** BOUTIQUE HOTEL $$$
(360-392-3100; www.hotelbellwether.com; 1 Bellwether Way; r from $250;) Bellingham's finest and most charismatic hotel lies on the waterfront and offers views of Lummi Island. Standard rooms (some with water views) come with Italian furnishings and Hungarian-down duvets, but the finest pick is the 900-sq-ft lighthouse suite (from $599), a converted three-story lighthouse with a wonderful private lookout. There's a spa and a restaurant on the premises.

★ **Pepper Sisters** MODERN AMERICAN $$
(360-671-3414; www.peppersisters.com; 1055 N State St; mains $11-17; 4:30-9pm Tue-Thu & Sun, to 9:30pm Fri & Sat;) This cheerful, colorful restaurant serves innovative food that is hard to categorize – let's call it New Mexican cuisine with a Northwestern twist. Try the grilled eggplant tostada, chipotle-and-pink-peppercorn enchilada or Southwest pizza (with green chilies, jack cheese and tomatillo sauce); there's even a chicken-strip-free kids' menu.

Colophon Cafe CAFE $
(1208 11th St, Fairhaven; sandwiches $8-16, soups $8-10; 9am-8pm Mon-Thu, 9am-9pm Fri & Sat, 10am-7pm Sun) Linked with Fairhaven's famous literary haven, **Village Books** (www.villagebooks.com; 1210 11th St; 9am-9pm Mon-Sat, 10am-7pm Sun), the Colophon is a multiethnic eatery for people who like to follow their panini with Proust. Renowned for its African peanut soup and chocolate brandy cream pies, the cafe has indoor seating along with an outside wine garden and is ever popular with the local literati.

Information

Downtown Info Center (360-671-3990; www.bellingham.org; 1306 Commercial St; 11am-3pm Tue-Sat, to 5pm summer) A downtown location of Bellingham's visitor info center.

Getting There & Away

Bellingham is the terminal for **Alaska Marine Highway** (AMHS; 800-642-0066; www.dot.state.ak.us/amhs; 355 Harris Ave; per person one way from $460) ferries, which travel once a week up the Inside Passage to Juneau, Skagway and other southeast Alaskan ports.

The **Bellair Airporter Shuttle** (www.airporter.com) runs around the clock to Sea-Tac Airport (round trip $74) and Anacortes (round trip $35).

San Juan Islands

There are 172 landfalls in this expansive archipelago, but unless you're rich enough to charter your own yacht or seaplane, you'll be restricted to seeing the big four – San Juan, Orcas, Shaw and Lopez Islands – all served daily by Washington State Ferries. Communally, the islands are famous for their tranquility, whale-watching opportunities, sea kayaking and general nonconformity.

A great way to explore the San Juans is by sea kayak or bicycle. Cycling-wise, Lopez is flat and pastoral and San Juan is worthy of an easy day loop, while Orcas offers the challenge of undulating terrain and a steep 5-mile ride to the top of Mt Constitution.

Getting There & Around

Two airlines have scheduled flights from the mainland to the San Juans. **Kenmore Air** (866-435-9524; www.kenmoreair.com) flies from Lake Union and Lake Washington to Lopez, Orcas and San Juan Islands daily on three- to 10-person seaplanes. Fares start at around $150 one way. **San Juan Airlines** (800-874-4434; www.sanjuanairlines.com) flies from Anacortes and Bellingham to the three main islands.

Washington State Ferries (p375) leave Anacortes for the San Juans; some continue to Sidney, Canada, near Victoria. Ferries run to Lopez Island (45 minutes), Orcas Landing (60 minutes) and Friday Harbor on San Juan Island (75 minutes). Fares vary by season; the cost of the entire round trip is collected on westbound journeys only (except those returning from Sidney).

Shuttle buses ply Orcas and San Juan Island between May and October.

San Juan Island

San Juan Island is the archipelago's unofficial capital, a harmonious mix of low forested hills and small rural farms that resonates with a dramatic and unusual 19th-century history. The only real settlement is Friday Harbor, home to the visitor center and **Chamber of Commerce** (360-378-5240; www.sanjuanisland.org; 165 1st St S, Friday Harbor; 10am-5pm).

Sights

San Juan Island National Historical Park HISTORIC SITE
(360-378-2240; www.nps.gov/sajh; visitor center 8:30am-5pm Jun-Aug, to 4:30pm Sep-May) FREE Known more for their scenery than their history, the San Juans nonetheless hide one of the 19th century's oddest political confrontations, the so-called 'Pig War' between the USA and Britain. This curious standoff is showcased in two separate historical parks at either end of the island, which once housed opposing **American** (360-378-2240; www.nps.gov/sajh; 4668 Cattle Point Rd, Friday Harbor; grounds 8:30am-11pm) FREE and **English** (360-378-2240; www.nps.gov/sajh; 8:30am-11pm) FREE military encampments.

Lime Kiln Point State Park STATE PARK
(360-902-8844; www.parks.state.wa.us/540/lime-kiln-point; 1567 Westside Rd; 8am-dusk) Clinging to the island's rocky west coast, this beautiful park overlooks the deep Haro Strait and has a reputation as one of the best places in the world to view whales from the shoreline. The word is out, however, so the view areas are often packed with hopeful picnickers. There's a small **interpretive center** (360-378-2044; 11am-4pm Jun-mid-Sep) FREE in the park, along with trails, a restored lime kiln and the landmark **Lime Kiln Lighthouse**, built in 1919.

Sleeping & Eating

San Juan County Park Campground CAMPGROUND $
(360-378-1842; https://secure.itinio.com/sanjuan/island/campsites; 380 West Side Rd; hiker & cyclist sites per person $10, campsites from $35) San Juan's best campground is beautifully located in a county park on the scenic western shoreline. The site includes a beach and boat launch, along with 20 tent pitches, flush toilets and picnic tables. At night the lights of Victoria, Canada, flicker theatrically from across the Haro Strait. Reservations are mandatory during peak season.

★ **Olympic Lights B&B** B&B $$
(888-211-6195, 360-378-3186; www.olympiclights.com; 146 Starlight Way; r $165-185; Jun-Sep;) Once the centerpiece of a 320-acre estate, this splendidly restored 1895 farmhouse now hosts an equally formidable four-room B&B that stands on an open bluff facing the snow-coated Olympic Mountains. Sunflowers adorn the garden and the hearty breakfasts include homemade buttermilk biscuits. Two-night minimum.

Market Chef DELI $
(360-378-4546; 225 A St, Friday Harbor; sandwiches from $9; 10am-4pm Mon-Fri) Super-popular and famous for its delicious sandwiches, including its signature curried-egg salad with roasted peanuts and chutney, or roast beef and rocket. Salads are also available; local ingredients are used. If you're in town on a Saturday in summer, visit Market Chef at the San Juan Island Farmers Market (10am to 1pm).

★ **Duck Soup Inn** FUSION $$$
(360-378-4878; www.ducksoupsanjuans.com; 50 Duck Soup Lane; mains $21-39; 5-10pm Wed-Sun Apr-Oct) It ain't cheap, but it's really good. Situated 4 miles northwest of Friday Harbor amid woods and water, Duck Soup offers the best island fine dining using the fruits of its own herb garden to enhance menu items such as oysters, scallops and Ethiopian lentil stew. The extensive wine list includes island-produced chardonnay.

Orcas Island

More rugged than Lopez yet less crowded than San Juan, Orcas has struck a delicate balance between friendliness and frostiness, development and preservation, tourist dollars and priceless privacy – for the time being, at least. The ferry terminal is at Orcas Landing, 8 miles south of the main village, Eastsound.

On the island's eastern lobe is **Moran State Park** (☎360-376-6173; 3572 Olga Rd; Discover Pass required at some parking lots per day/year $10/35; ⏰6:30am-dusk Apr-Sep, 8am-dusk Oct-Mar), dominated by Mt Constitution (2409ft), with 40 miles of trails and an amazing 360-degree mountaintop view. **Camping** (☎360-376-2326; www.moranstatepark.com; campsites from $25) is a great option here.

Sleeping

★Golden Tree Hostel HOSTEL $

(☎360-317-8693; www.goldentreehostel.com; 1159 North Beach Rd, Eastsound; dm/d with shared bath $47/110; ⏰Apr-Oct; @📶🏊) Located in an 1890s-era heritage house, this hip hostel offers cozy rooms and pleasant common spaces, along with a hot tub and sauna in the grassy garden. Options include a tipi, a bus and a geodesic dome. There's even a separate recreation building with pool, Foosball, shuffleboard and darts. Bicycle rentals are $20. Friday pizza nights. Reserve in summer.

Doe Bay Village Resort & Retreat HOSTEL $

(☎360-376-2291; www.doebay.com; 107 Doe Bay Rd, Olga; campsites from $60, cabins from $100, yurts from $80; 📶🐾) One of the least expensive resorts in the San Juans, Doe Bay has the atmosphere of an artists' commune combined with a hippie retreat. Accommodations include sea-view campsites and various cabins and yurts, some with views of the water.

Outlook Inn HOTEL $$

(☎360-376-2200; www.outlookinn.com; 171 Main St, Eastsound; r/ste from $109/250; @📶🐾) Eastsound's oldest and most eye-catching building, the Outlook Inn (1888) is an island institution. Budget rooms are cozy and neat (try for room 30), while the luxurious suites have fireplaces, Jacuzzis and stunning water views from their balconies. Excellent attached cafe.

Eating & Drinking

★Brown Bear Baking BAKERY $

(cnr Main St & North Beach Rd, Eastsound; pastries $7; ⏰8am-4pm Thu-Mon) No one wants to pay $7 for a pastry, but the trouble is that once you start eating the baked goods here, nothing else will do. Options include croissants *aux amandes*, quiche using fresh Orcas Island eggs and roast veggies, caramel sticky buns and fruit pie. Balance the nutritional ledger with one of the hearty soups or sandwiches.

★Inn at Ship Bay SEAFOOD $$$

(☎877-276-7296; www.innatshipbay.com; 326 Olga Rd; mains $27-36; ⏰5-10pm Tue-Sat) Locals unanimously rate this place as the best fine-dining experience on the island. The chefs work overtime preparing everything from scratch using the freshest local ingredients. Seafood is the specialty and it's served in an attractive 1860s orchard house a couple of miles south of Eastsound. There's also an on-site 11-room hotel (doubles from $195). Reservations recommended.

Island Hoppin' Brewery BREWERY

(www.islandhoppinbrewery.com; 33 Hope Lane, Eastsound; ⏰11am-9pm) The location just off Mt Baker Rd near the airport makes this tiny brewery hard to find, but the locals sure know it's there – this is *the* place to go to enjoy local brews on tap. Don't come hungry – only snacks are served, but you're welcome to bring your own food. A ping-pong table adds some action.

Lopez Island

If you're going to Lopez – or 'Slow-pez,' as locals prefer to call it – take a bike. With its undulating terrain and salutation-offering residents (who are famous for their three-fingered 'Lopezian wave'), this is the ideal cycling isle. A leisurely pastoral spin can be tackled in a day, with good overnight digs available next to the marina in the **Lopez Islander Resort** (☎360-468-2233; www.lopezfun.com; 2864 Fisherman Bay Rd; r from $159; 📶🏊). For something more upscale, try the **Edenwild Inn** (☎360-468-3238; www.edenwildinn.com; Lopez Rd, Lopez Village; ste from $218; 📶), a Victorian mansion set in lovely formal gardens.

If you arrive cycleless, call up **Village Cycles** (☎360-468-4013; www.villagecycles.net; 214 Lopez Rd; rental per hr $7-13), which can deliver a bicycle to the ferry terminal for you.

North Cascades

Dominated by Mt Baker and – to a lesser extent – the more remote Glacier Peak, the North Cascades region is made up of a huge swath of protected forests, parks and wilderness areas that dwarf even the expansive Rainier and St Helens parks to the south. The crème de la crème is the North

Cascades National Park, a primeval stash of old-growth rainforest, groaning glaciers and untainted ecosystems whose savage beauty goes unexplored by all but 2500 or so annual visitors who penetrate its rainy interior. Dotting this rugged landscape are a tiny handful of small towns, many of which are not much more than a gas station, a cafe and a general store.

Mt Baker

Rising like a ghostly sentinel above the sparkling waters of upper Puget Sound, Mt Baker has been mesmerizing visitors to the Northwest for centuries. A dormant volcano that last belched smoke in the 1850s, this haunting 10,781ft peak shelters 12 glaciers, and in 1999 registered a record-breaking 95ft of snow in one season.

Well-paved Hwy 542, known as the Mt Baker Scenic Byway, climbs 5100ft to **Artist Point**, 56 miles from Bellingham. Near here you'll find the **Heather Meadows Visitor Center** (Mt Baker Hwy, Mile 56; ⌚10am-4pm mid-Jul–late Sep) and a plethora of varied hikes, including the 7.5-mile **Chain Lakes Loop** that leads you around a half-dozen lakes surrounded by huckleberry meadows.

Receiving more annual snow than any ski area in North America, the **Mt Baker Ski Area** (☎360-734-6771; www.mtbaker.us; lift tickets adult/child $61/38) has 38 runs, eight lifts and a vertical rise of 1500ft. The resort has gained something of a cult status among snowboarders, who have been coming here for the Legendary Baker Banked Slalom every January since 1985.

On your way up the mountain, stop for a bite at authentic honky-tonk bar and restaurant **Graham's** (☎360-599-9883; 9989 Mt Baker Hwy, Glacier; mains $9-14; ⌚noon-9pm Mon-Fri, 8am-9pm Sat & Sun) and grab munchies at **Wake & Bakery** (☎360-599-1658; www.getsconed.com; 6903 Bourne St, Glacier; snacks from $4; ⌚7:30am-5pm), both in the town of **Glacier**.

Leavenworth

Blink hard and rub your eyes. This isn't some strange Germanic hallucination. Leavenworth is a former lumber town that underwent a Bavarian makeover back in the 1960s after the re-routing of the cross-continental railway threatened to put it permanently out of business. Swapping wood for tourists, Leavenworth today has successfully reinvented itself as a traditional *Romantische Strasse* village, right down to the beer, sausages and lederhosen-loving locals (25% of whom are of German descent). The classic *Sound of Music* mountain setting helps, as does the fact that Leavenworth serves as the main activity center for sorties into the nearby Alpine Lakes Wilderness.

The **Leavenworth Chamber of Commerce** (☎509-548-5807; https://leavenworth.org; 940 US 2; ⌚8am-5pm Mon-Thu, 8am-6pm Fri & Sat, 10am-4pm Sun) can advise on the local outdoor activities. Highlights include the best climbing in the state at **Castle Rock** in Tumwater Canyon, about 3 miles northwest of town off US 2.

The **Devil's Gulch** is a popular off-road mountain-bike trail (25 miles, four to six hours). Local outfitters **Der Sportsmann** (☎509-548-5623; www.dersportsmann.com; 837 Front St; cross-country ski/snowshoe rental $18/16; ⌚10am-6pm Mon-Thu, to 7pm Fri, 9am-7pm Sat, 9am-6pm Sun) rents mountain bikes.

Sleeping & Eating

Hotel Pension Anna HOTEL $$
(☎509-548-6273; www.pensionanna.com; 926 Commercial St; r from $240; 📶) The most authentic Bavarian hotel in town is also spotless and incredibly friendly. Each room is kitted out in imported Austrian decor, and the European-inspired breakfasts (included) may induce joyful yodels. A recommended room is the double with hand-painted furniture, but the spacious suite in the adjacent St Joseph's chapel is perfect for families.

Enzian Inn HOTEL $$
(☎509-548-5269; www.enzianinn.com; 590 US 2; d from $240; 📶🏊) At this Leavenworth classic the day starts with a blast on an alpenhorn before breakfast. If that doesn't send you running for your lederhosen, consider the free putting green (with resident grass-trimming goats), the indoor and outdoor swimming pools, and the nightly pianist pounding out requests in the Bavarian lobby.

München Haus GERMAN $
(☎509-548-1158; www.munchenhaus.com; 709 Front St; brats $4-7; ⌚11am-8pm, to 10pm Fri & Sat) The Haus is 100% alfresco, meaning that the hot German sausages and pretzels are essential stomach warmers in winter, while the Bavarian brews will cool you down in summer. The casual beer-garden atmosphere is complemented by an aggressively jaunty accordion soundtrack, laid-back staff, a kettle of cider relish and an epic mustard bar. Hours vary outside summer.

Lake Chelan

Long, slender Lake Chelan is central Washington's watery playground. The town of Chelan, at the lake's southeastern tip, is the primary base for accommodations and services, and has a **USFS Ranger Station** (509-682-4900; www.fs.usda.gov/detail/okawen/about-forest/offices; 428 W Woodin Ave; 7:45am-4:30pm Mon-Fri).

Lake Chelan State Park (509-687-3710; https://parks.state.wa.us/531/Lake-Chelan; 7544 S Lakeshore Rd; primitive/standard sites from $12/27) has 144 campsites; a number of lakeshore campgrounds are accessible only by boat. If you'd rather sleep in a real bed, try the great-value **Midtowner Motel** (800-572-0943; www.midtowner.com; 721 E Woodin Ave; r from $125;) or the delightful **Riverwalk Inn** (509-682-2627; www.riverwalkinnchelan.com; 205 E Wapato Ave; d $69-199;), both in town.

Several wineries have also opened in the area and many have excellent restaurants. Try **Tsillan Cellars** (509-682-9463; www.tsillancellars.com; 3875 US 97A; noon-6pm) or the swanky Italian **Sorrento's Ristorante** (509-682-9463; https://tsillancellars.com/dining; 3875 US 97A; mains $20-38; 5pm-late daily, plus noon-3pm Sat, 11am-3pm Sun).

Link Transit (509-662-1155; www.linktransit.com) buses connect Chelan with Wenatchee and Leavenworth ($2.50 one way).

Beautiful **Stehekin**, on the northern tip of Lake Chelan, is accessible only by **boat** (509-682-4584; www.ladyofthelake.com; 1418 W Woodin Ave; one way $22-37, round trip to Stehekin $61), or a long hike across Cascade Pass, 28 miles from the lake. You'll find lots of information about hiking, campgrounds and cabin rentals at www.stehekin.com. Most facilities are open from mid-June to mid-September.

Methow Valley

The Methow's combination of powdery winter snow and abundant summer sunshine has transformed this valley into one of Washington's primary recreation areas. You can bike, hike and fish in summer, and cross-country ski on the second-biggest snow trail network in the US in winter.

The 200km of trails are maintained by the nonprofit **Methow Valley Sport Trails Association** (MVSTA; 509-996-3287; www.methowtrails.org; 309 Riverside Ave, Winthrop; 8:30am-3:30pm Mon-Fri), which in winter provides the most comprehensive network of hut-to-hut (and hotel-to-hotel) skiing in North America. An extra blessing is that few people seem to know about it. For classic accommodations and easy access to the skiing, hiking and cycling trails, decamp at the exquisite **Sun Mountain Lodge** (509-996-2211; www.sunmountainlodge.com; 604 Patterson Lake Rd; r from $285, cabins from $415;), 10 miles west of the town of Winthrop. Winthrop is also the locus of the area's best eating: try the fine-dining **Arrowleaf Bistro** (509-996-3920; www.arrowleafbistro.com; 253 Riverside Ave; mains $22-28; 4-10pm Wed-Sun).

North Cascades National Park

Even the names of the lightly trodden, dramatic mountains in **North Cascades National Park** (www.nps.gov/noca) sound wild and untamed: Desolation Peak, Jagged Ridge, Mt Despair and Mt Terror. Not surprisingly, the region offers some of the best backcountry adventures outside of Alaska.

The **North Cascades Visitor Center** (206-386-4495, ext 11; 502 Newhalem St, Newhalem; 9am-5pm mid-May–Sep), in the small settlement of Newhalem on Hwy 20, is the best orientation point for visitors and is staffed by expert rangers who can enlighten you on the park's highlights.

Built in the 1930s for loggers working in the valley (which was soon to be flooded by Ross Dam), the floating cabins at the **Ross Lake Resort** (206-486-3751; www.rosslakeresort.com; 503 Diablo St, Rockport; cabins $205-385; mid-Jun–late Oct;) on the eponymous lake's west side are the state's most unique accommodations. There's no road in – guests can either hike the 2-mile trail from Hwy 20 or take the resort's tugboat-taxi-and-truck shuttle from the parking area near Diablo Dam.

Northeastern Washington

Spokane

Washington's second-biggest population center is situated at the nexus of the Pacific Northwest's 'Inland Empire', on the banks of the Spokane River. It's home to the impressive Northwest Museum of Arts & Culture, Gonzaga University, the 1974 World's Fair site, and a dramatic waterfall right in the middle of a well-preserved historic downtown core. There are plenty of rough edges left, but a patient visitor can find a lot of surprising beauty and charm in this oft-maligned city.

Sights

★Northwest Museum of Arts & Culture MUSEUM
(MAC; ☎509-456-3931; www.northwestmuseum.org; 2316 W 1st Ave; adult/child $10/5; ⌚10am-5pm Tue-Sun, to 8pm 3rd Thu of month;) In a striking state-of-the-art building in the beautiful Browne's Addition neighborhood, this museum is well worth a visit. It has one of the finest collections of Native American artifacts in the Northwest, and stages ambitious temporary exhibits several times a year that illuminate key regional artists (such as glass master Dale Chihuly) and cultural phenomena (pioneer quilts, indigenous beadwork etc).

Riverfront Park PARK
(www.spokaneriverfrontpark.com;) The site of the 1974 World's Fair and Exposition, this downtown park has numerous highlights, including a 17-point **Sculpture Walk** and the scenic **Spokane Falls**. A short gondola ride, the **Spokane Falls SkyRide** (adult/child $7.75/5.75; ⌚11am-7pm) takes you directly across the falls, or get an equally spectacular view from the **Monroe Street Bridge**, built in 1911 and still one of the largest concrete arches in the USA. An ongoing renovation project means that a few areas of the park are closed due to construction.

Sleeping & Eating

Hotel Ruby MOTEL $
(☎509-747-1041; www.hotelrubyspokane.com; 901 W 1st Ave; r from $81;) An arty redesign of a formerly basic motel, the Ruby has a '70s feel, with cool original art on the walls and a sleek cocktail lounge adjoining the lobby. Rooms have mini fridge and microwave, and you can use the gym at the nearby sister hotel, Ruby 2, cool in its own right (rooms from $78). The downtown location rules.

★Historic Davenport Hotel HISTORIC HOTEL $$
(☎800-899-1482; www.thedavenporthotel.com; 10 S Post St; r from $200;) This historic landmark (opened in 1914) is considered one of the best hotels in the country. Even if you're not staying here, linger in the exquisite lobby or have a drink in the Peacock Lounge. The adjacent, modern Davenport Tower sports a safari-themed lobby and bar.

★Ruins AMERICAN, FUSION $$
(☎509-443-5606; 825 N Monroe St; small plates $6-17; ⌚11am-3pm & 5-10pm Tue-Fri, 9:30am-2pm & 5-11pm Sat, 9:30am-2pm & 5-9pm Sun, 5-10pm Mon) This stylish little place has a constantly changing menu of mostly small plates and snacks to pair with perfectly crafted cocktails. Expect fresh twists on anything from pad Thai to street tacos, banh mi to burgers, plus some heartier fare (recently a carne asada plate) for sharing – or not. Slip in late and grab a seat at the bar.

★Wild Sage American Bistro NORTHWESTERN US $$$
(www.wildsagebistro.com; 916 W 2nd Ave; mains $18-42; ⌚4-9pm Mon-Thu, to 10pm Fri-Sun) The intimate yet simple decor and fresh local ingredients, creatively and elegantly prepared, see Wild Sage consistently rated as one of Spokane's top dining spots. The Alaskan halibut, honey-Dijon chicken and coconut-cream layer cake come highly recommended, and there's a gluten-free menu and an excellent selection of wines and craft cocktails.

Drinking & Entertainment

Atticus Coffee COFFEE
(222 N Howard St; tea/espresso from $2/3; ⌚7:30am-6pm Mon-Sat, 9am-5pm Sun) As much a well-curated gift shop as a coffeehouse, this bookish, bright and convivial cafe serves an amazing selection of loose teas and perfect coffee. Good luck resisting the urge to pick up a handmade mug, artisan soap or kitty-faced pot holder while you're here. Wi-fi is available Monday to Friday.

No-Li Brewhouse BREWERY
(☎509-242-2739; www.nolibrewhouse.com; 1003 E Trent Ave; mains $12-18; ⌚11:30am-10pm Sun-Thu, 11am-11pm Fri & Sat) A massively popular hangout near Gonzaga University, Spokane's best microbrewery serves some weird and wonderful flavors, including a tart cherry ale and an imperial stout with coffee, chocolate and brown-sugar tones. Food-wise, check out the cod and chips cooked in batter made with the brewery's own pale ale.

Information

Visitor Information Center (☎888-776-5263, 509-744-3341; www.visitspokane.com; 620 W Spokane Falls Blvd; ⌚10am-7pm Jun-Sep, to 6pm rest of year) Near the riverfront, this office has plenty of information on the city and region.

Getting There & Away

Spokane International Airport (www.spokaneairports.net) Alaska, American, Delta, Frontier, Southwest and United airlines all offer nonstop services to 16 destinations including Seattle, Portland OR; San Francisco, CA; Denver, CO;

WORTH A TRIP

GRAND COULEE DAM

While the more famous Hoover Dam (conveniently located between Las Vegas and the Grand Canyon) gets around 1.6 million visitors per year, the four-times-larger and arguably more significant **Grand Coulee Dam** (inconveniently located far from everything) gets only a trickle of tourism. If you're in the area, don't miss it – it's one of the country's most spectacular displays of engineering and you'll get to enjoy it crowd-free.

The **Grand Coulee Dam Visitor Center** (☎509-633-9265; www.usbr.gov/pn/grandcoulee/visit; ⏲9am-11pm mid-May–Jul, to 10:30pm Aug, to 9:30pm Sep, to 5pm Oct–mid-May) details the history of the dam and surrounding area with movies, photos and interactive exhibits. Free guided tours of the facility run daily at 10am, noon, 2pm and 3:30pm and involve taking a glass-walled elevator 465ft down into the Third Power Plant, where you can view the generators from an observation deck.

Minneapolis, MN; Salt Lake City, UT; and Phoenix, AZ.

Spokane Intermodal Center (221 W 1st Ave) Buses and trains depart from this station.

South Cascades

More rounded and less hemmed in than their saw-toothed cousins to the north, the South Cascades are nonetheless higher. Their pinnacle in more ways than one is 14,411ft Mt Rainier, the fifth-highest mountain in the lower 48 states and arguably one of the most dramatic stand-alone mountains in the world. Further south, fiery Mt St Helens needs zero introduction, while unsung Adams glowers way off to the east like a sulking middle child.

Mt Rainier National Park

The USA's fifth-highest peak outside Alaska, majestic Mt Rainier is also one of its most beguiling. Encased in a 368-sq-mile national park, the mountain's snowcapped summit and forest-covered foothills boast numerous hiking trails, huge swaths of flower-carpeted meadows, and an alluring conical peak that presents a formidable challenge for aspiring climbers.

Mt Rainier National Park (www.nps.gov/mora; car $30, pedestrian & cyclist $15, 1yr pass $55) has four entrances. Call 800-695-7623 for road conditions. The National Park Service (NPS) website includes downloadable maps and descriptions of dozens of park trails. The most famous is the hard-core, 93-mile-long Wonderland Trail, which completely circumnavigates Mt Rainier and takes 10 to 12 days to tackle.

Campgrounds in the park have running water and toilets, but no showers or RV hookups. Reservations at park **campsites** (☎800-365-2267; www.nps.gov/mora; campsites $20) are strongly advised during summer and can be made up to two months in advance by phone or online. For overnight backcountry trips, you'll need a wilderness permit – check the NPS website for details.

NISQUALLY ENTRANCE

The busiest and most convenient gate to Mt Rainier National Park, Nisqually lies on Hwy 706 via Ashford, near the park's southwest corner. It's open year-round. Longmire, 7 miles inside the Nisqually entrance, has a **museum and information center** (☎360-569-6575; Hwy 706, Longmire; ⏲museum 9am-4:30pm year-round, info center May-Oct) FREE, a number of important trailheads, and the rustic **National Park Inn** (☎360-569-2275; Hwy 706, Longmire; r with/without bath from $203/138; ❄), complete with an excellent restaurant.

More hikes and interpretive walks can be found 12 miles further east at loftier **Paradise**, which is served by the informative **Henry M Jackson Visitor Center** (☎360-569-6571; Paradise; ⏲10am-5pm daily May-Oct, Sat & Sun Nov-Apr), and the vintage **Paradise Inn** (☎360-569-2275; Paradise; r with/without bath from $182/123; ⏲mid-May–Oct; 🚭), a historical 'parkitecture' inn constructed in 1916. Climbs to the top of Rainier leave from the inn; excellent four-day guided ascents are led by **Rainier Mountaineering Inc** (☎888-892-5462; www.rmiguides.com; 30027 Hwy 706 E, Ashford; 4-day climb $1163).

OTHER ENTRANCES

The three other entrances to Mt Rainier National Park are **Ohanapecosh**, accessed via Hwy 123 and the town of Packwood, where lodging is available; **White River**, off Hwy 410, literally the highroad (6400ft) to the beautiful viewpoint at the **Sunrise Lodge**

Cafeteria (Sunrise Park Rd, Sunrise; mains $6-12; 10am-7pm Jul & Aug, 11am-3pm Sat & Sun Sep); and remote Carbon River in the northwest corner, which gives access to the park's inland rainforest.

Mt St Helens National Volcanic Monument

What it lacks in height, Mt St Helens makes up for in fiery infamy – 57 people perished on the mountain when it erupted with a force of 1500 atomic bombs on May 18, 1980. The cataclysm began with an earthquake measuring 5.1 on the Richter scale, which sparked the biggest landslide in recorded history and buried 230 sq miles of forest under millions of tons of volcanic rock and ash. Today it's a fascinating landscape of recovering forests, new river valleys and ash-covered slopes. There's an $8 per adult fee to enter the National Monument.

NORTHEASTERN ENTRANCE

From the main northeast entrance on Hwy 504, your first stop should be the Silver Lake Visitor Center (360-274-0962; https://parks.state.wa.us/245/Mount-St-Helens; 3029 Spirit Lake Hwy; adult/child $5/free; 9am-4pm Mar–mid-May & mid-Sep–Oct, to 5pm mid-May–mid-Sep, 9am-4pm Thu-Mon Nov-Feb;), which has films, exhibits and free information about the mountain (including trail maps). For a closer view of the destructive power of nature, venture to the Johnston Ridge Observatory (360-274-2140; www.fs.usda.gov; 24000 Spirit Lake Hwy; day use $8; 10am-6pm mid-May–Oct), situated at the end of Hwy 504, which looks directly into the mouth of the crater. A welcome stop in an accommodations-light area, the Eco Park Resort (360-274-7007; www.ecoparkresort.com; 14000 Spirit Lake Hwy, Toutle; campsites $25, 6-person yurts $95, cabins $150;) offers campsites and RV hookups, and basic two- or four-person cabins.

SOUTHEASTERN & EASTSIDE ENTRANCES

The southeastern entrance via the town of Cougar on Hwy 503 holds some serious lava terrain, including the 2-mile-long Ape Cave lava tube, which you can explore year-round; be prepared for the chill as it remains a constant 41°F (5°C). Bring two light sources per adult or rent lanterns at Apes' Headquarters (360-449-7800; Forest Rd 8303; 10am-5pm mid-Jun–early Sep) for $5 each.

The eastside entrance is the most remote, but the harder-to-reach Windy Ridge viewpoint on this side gives you a palpable, if eerie, sense of the destruction from the blast. It's often closed until June. A few miles down the road you can descend 600ft on the mile-long Harmony Trail (hike 224) to Spirit Lake.

Central & Southeastern Washington

The sunny, dry, near-California-looking central and southeastern parts of Washington harbor one not-so-secret weapon: wine. The fertile land that borders the Nile-like Yakima and Columbia River Valleys is awash with enterprising new wineries producing quality grapes that now vie with the Napa and Sonoma Valleys for recognition. Yakima and its more attractive cousin Ellensburg once held the edge, but nowadays the real star is Walla Walla.

Yakima & Ellensburg

The main reason to stop in Yakima is to visit one of the numerous wineries that lie between here and Benton City; pick up a map at the visitor center (800-221-0751; www.visityakima.com; 101 N 8th St; 8:30am-5pm Mon-Fri).

A better layover is Ellensburg, a diminutive settlement 36 miles to the northwest that juxtaposes the state's largest rodeo (each Labor Day) with a town center that has some well-preserved historic buildings. Grab your latte at local roaster D&M Coffee (509-925-5313; www.dmcoffee.com; 323 N Pearl St; 7am-8pm;) and eat at the unconventional Yellow Church Cafe (509-933-2233; www.theyellowchurchcafe.com; 111 S Pearl St; lunch mains $12-17, dinner mains $14-27; 11am-9pm Mon-Thu, 8am-9pm Fri-Sun;) or fantastic upstart the Red Pickle (509-367-0003; 301 N Pine St; mains from $10, cocktails $8; 11am-9pm Wed-Sun, 4-9pm Tue).

Greyhound services both cities, with buses to Seattle, Spokane and points in between.

Walla Walla

Walla Walla has converted itself into the hottest wine-growing region outside of California. While venerable Marcus Whitman College is the town's most obvious cultural attribute, you'll also find zany coffee bars, cool wine-tasting rooms, fine Queen Anne architecture, and one of the state's freshest and most vibrant farmers markets.

Sights & Activities

You don't need to be sloshed on wine to appreciate Walla Walla's historical and cultural heritage. Its Main St has won countless historical awards, and to bring the settlement to life, the local **chamber of commerce** (509-525-0850; www.wwvchamber.com; 29 E Sumach St; 8:30am-5pm Mon-Fri) has concocted some interesting walking tours, complete with leaflets and maps. Main St and environs are also crammed with tasting rooms. Expect tasting fees of $5 to $10.

Fort Walla Walla Museum MUSEUM
(509-525-7703; www.fwwm.org; 755 Myra Rd; adult/child $9/4; 10am-5pm Mar-Oct, to 4pm Nov-Feb;) This museum occupies the fort's old cavalry stables, with a recreated pioneer village outside. The main exhibit hall contains displays on the Lewis and Clark expedition, local agriculture and military history, and the four large stable buildings hold collections of farm implements, a jail cell and a plastic replica of a 33-mule team used for harvesting wheat in the 1920s.

Waterbrook Wine WINE
(509-522-1262; www.waterbrook.com; 10518 W US 12; tasting $5-15; 11am-5pm Sun-Thu, to 6pm Fri & Sat) About 10 miles west of town, this large, extremely manicured modern winery feels a bit slick and commercial, but it has attentive staff and the pond-side patio is a great place to sample from the long selection of wines on a sunny day. Full menu served Thursday to Sunday.

Amavi Cellars WINE
(509-525-3541; www.amavicellars.com; 3796 Peppers Bridge Rd; tasting $10; 10am-4pm) South of Walla Walla, amid a scenic spread of grape and apple orchards, you can sample some of the most talked-about wines in the valley (try the syrah and cabernet sauvignon). The classy yet comfortable patio has views of the Blue Mountains.

Sleeping & Eating

Walla Walla Garden Motel MOTEL $
(509-529-1220; www.wallawallagardenmotel.com; 2279 Isaacs Ave; s/d from $72/94;) A simple family-run motel halfway to the airport, the Garden Motel is welcoming and bike-friendly, with safe bike storage and plenty of local maps.

Marcus Whitman Hotel HOTEL $$
(509-525-2200; www.marcuswhitmanhotel.com; 6 W Rose St; r from $159;) Walla Walla's best-known landmark is also the town's only tall building, impossible to miss with its distinctive rooftop turret. In keeping with the settlement's well-preserved image, the redbrick 1928 beauty has been elegantly renovated and decorated, with ample rooms and suites in rusts and browns, embellished with Italian-crafted furniture, huge beds and great views over the nearby Blue Mountains.

Graze CAFE $
(509-522-9991; www.grazeplaces.com; 5 S Colville St; sandwiches $8-12; 10am-7:30pm Mon-Sat, to 3:30pm Sun;) Amazing sandwiches are packed for your picnic or (if you can get a table) eaten in at this simple cafe. Try the turkey-and-pear panini with provolone and blue cheese or the flank-steak torta with pickled jalapeños, avocado, tomato, cilantro and chipotle dressing. There are plenty of vegetarian options.

★ **Saffron Mediterranean Kitchen** MEDITERRANEAN $$$
(509-525-2112; www.saffronmediterraneankitchen.com; 125 W Alder St; flatbreads $14-16, mains $25-45; 2-9pm Mon-Fri, noon-9pm Sat & Sun) This place isn't about cooking, it's about alchemy: Saffron takes seasonal, local ingredients and turns them into pure gold. The Med-inspired menu lists dishes such as asparagus-fontina flatbread, wood-grilled quail with dates and olives, and eggplant, lamb and pork-belly lasagna. Then there are the intelligently paired wines – and gorgeous atmosphere. Reserve.

Getting There & Away

Alaska Airlines has two daily flights to Seattle-Tacoma International Airport from **Walla Walla Regional Airport** (www.wallawallaairport.com; 45 Terminal Loop), northeast of town off US 12.

Greyhound buses run once daily to Seattle ($47, six hours) via Pasco, Yakima and Ellensburg; change buses in Pasco for Spokane.

OREGON

It's hard to slap a single characterization onto Oregon's geography and people. Its landscape ranges from rugged coastline and thick evergreen forests to barren, fossil-strewn deserts, volcanoes and glaciers. As for its denizens, you name it – Oregonians run the gamut from pro-logging conservatives to tree-hugging liberals. What they have in common is an independent spirit, a love of the outdoors and a fierce devotion to where they live.

It doesn't usually take long for visitors to feel a similar devotion. Who wouldn't fall in love with the spectacle of glittering Crater Lake, the breathtaking colors of the Painted Hills in John Day or the hiking trails through deep forests and over stunning mountain passes? And then there are the towns: you can eat like royalty in hip Portland, see top-notch dramatic productions in Ashland or sample an astounding number of brewpubs in Bend.

OREGON FACTS

Nickname Beaver State

Population 4.25 million

Area 98,466 sq miles

Capital city Salem (population 169,800)

Other cities Portland (population 647,800), Eugene (population 169,000), Bend (population 94,520)

Sales tax None

Birthplace of Former US president Herbert Hoover (1874–1964), actor and dancer Ginger Rogers (1911–95), writer and merry prankster Ken Kesey (1935–2001), filmmaker Gus Van Sant (b 1952), *The Simpsons* creator Matt Groening (b 1954)

Home of Oregon Shakespeare Festival, Nike, Crater Lake

Politics Democrat governors since 1987

Famous for Forests, rain, microbrews, coffee, anti-fascism demonstrators

State beverage Milk (dairy's big here)

Driving You can't pump your own gas in most of Oregon. Portland to Eugene 110 miles, Portland to Astoria 96 miles

Portland

Best coffee. Most food carts. Top craft breweries. Number-one hipster haven. Portland is a city of indie-spirited superlatives and humble, off-beat charms.

Sights

Downtown

★Tom McCall Waterfront Park PARK

(Map p386; Naito Pkwy) This popular riverside park, which lines the west bank of the Willamette River, was finished in 1978 after four years of construction. It replaced a freeway with 1.5 miles of paved sidewalks and grassy spaces, and now attracts joggers, in-line skaters, strollers and cyclists. During summer the park is perfect for hosting large outdoor events such as the **Oregon Brewers Festival** (www.oregonbrewfest.com; Tom McCall Waterfront Park; admission free, 10-token tasting package $20, additional tokens $1; late Jul). Walk over the Steel and Hawthorne bridges to the **Eastbank Esplanade**, making a 2.6-mile loop.

★Pioneer Courthouse Square LANDMARK

(Map p386; www.thesquarepdx.org; Red, Blue, Green) The heart of downtown Portland, this brick plaza is nicknamed Portland's 'living room' and is the most-visited public space in the city. When it isn't full of sunbathers or office workers lunching, the square hosts concerts, festivals, rallies, farmers markets, and even summer Friday-night movies – aka **Flicks on the Bricks** (Map p386; https://thesquarepdx.org/events; 7pm Fri Jul & Aug).

Oregon Historical Society MUSEUM

(Map p386; 503-222-1741; www.ohs.org; 1200 SW Park Ave; adult/child $10/5; 10am-5pm Mon-Sat, noon-5pm Sun; Red, Blue) Along the tree-shaded **South Park Blocks** (Map p386) sits the state's primary history museum, which in 2019 unveiled a permanent 7000-sq-ft interactive exhibit that delves into Oregon's history, peoples and landscape. Stations include a canoe-building exercise, a walk-through covered-wagon replica and historical role-playing games. There are interesting sections on various immigrant groups, Native American tribes and the travails of the Oregon Trail. Temporary exhibits furnish the downstairs space. Check the website for free admission days.

Portland Art Museum MUSEUM

(Map p386; 503-226-2811; www.portlandartmuseum.org; 1219 SW Park Ave; adult/child $20/free; 10am-5pm Tue, Wed, Sat & Sun, to 8pm Thu & Fri; 6, 38, 45, 55, 58, 68, 92, 96, NS Line, A-Loop) Alongside the South Park Blocks, Portland Art Museum's excellent exhibits include Native American carvings, Asian and American art, photography and English silver. The museum also houses the Whitsell Auditorium, a first-rate theater

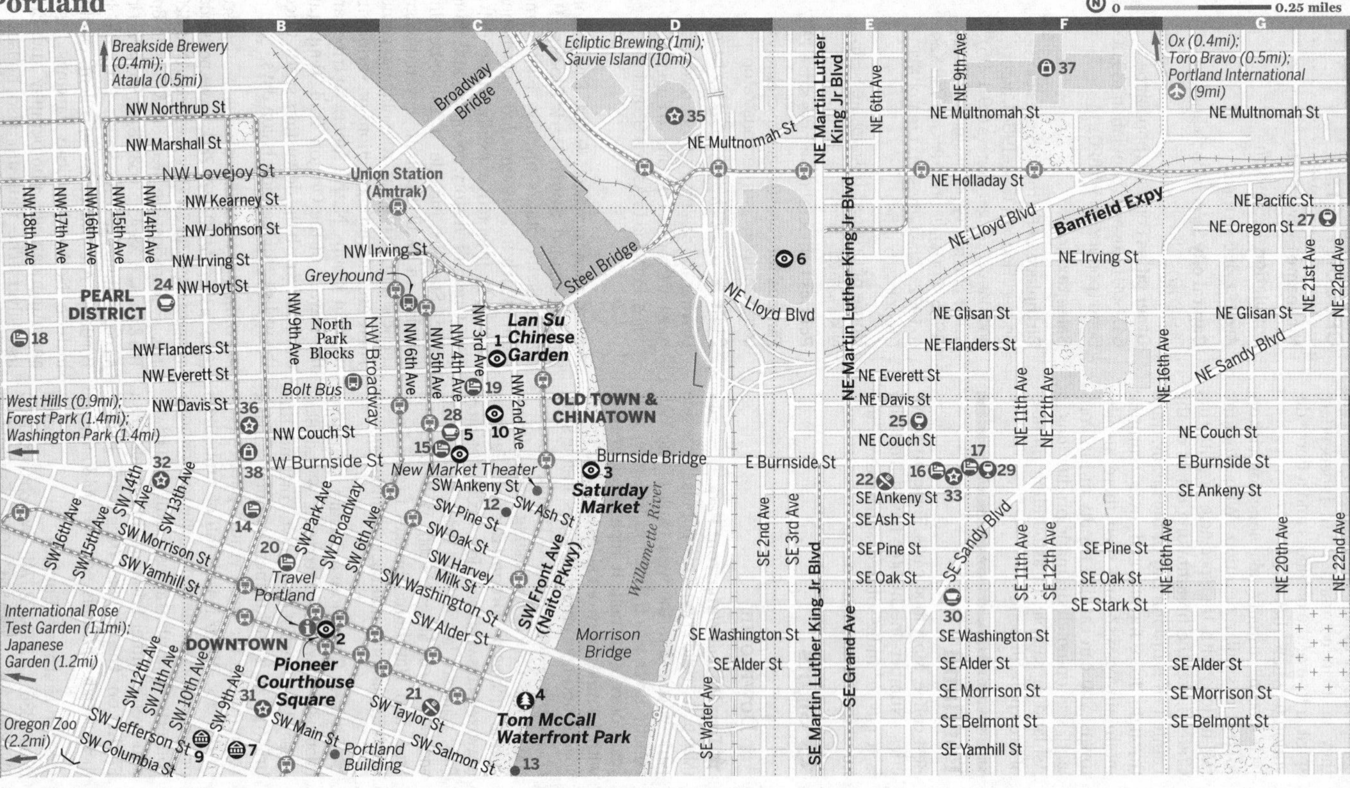

Portland
500 m
0.25 miles
Breakside Brewery (0.4mi); Ataula (0.5mi)
Ecliptic Brewing (1mi); Sauvie Island (10mi)
Ox (0.4mi); Toro Bravo (0.5mi); Portland International (9mi)
West Hills (0.9mi); Forest Park (1.4mi); Washington Park (1.4mi)
International Rose Test Garden (1.1mi); Japanese Garden (1.2mi)
Oregon Zoo (2.2mi)
PEARL DISTRICT
OLD TOWN & CHINATOWN
DOWNTOWN
Union Station (Amtrak)
Greyhound
Bolt Bus
North Park Blocks
Lan Su Chinese Garden
Saturday Market
Pioneer Courthouse Square
Tom McCall Waterfront Park
Travel Portland
Portland Building
New Market Theater
Willamette River
Broadway Bridge
Steel Bridge
Burnside Bridge
Morrison Bridge
Banfield Expy
NE Martin Luther King Jr Blvd
SE Martin Luther King Jr Blvd
SE Grand Ave
NE Sandy Blvd
SE Sandy Blvd
NE Lloyd Blvd
E Burnside St
W Burnside St
SW Front Ave (Naito Pkwy)
NW Broadway
SW Broadway

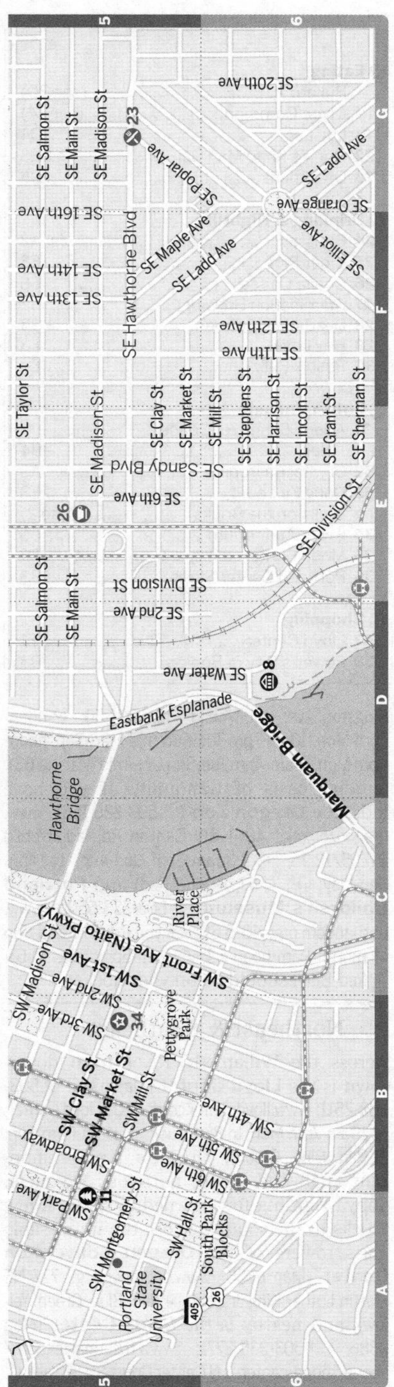

that frequently screens rare or international films and that is part of the Northwest Film Center and school.

Old Town & Chinatown

The core of rambunctious 1890s Portland, once-seedy **Old Town** had a well-earned reputation as the lurking ground of unsavory characters. Now it's home to some lovely historic buildings, plus Waterfront Park, Saturday Market and a few good pockets of nightlife.

Old Town is generally lumped together with the city's historic **Chinatown** – no longer the heart of the Chinese community (that's moved to outer Southeast) but still home to the ornate **Chinatown Gateway** (Map p386; cnr W Burnside St & NW 4th Ave; 20), tranquil **Lan Su Chinese Garden** (Map p386; 503-228-8131; www.lansugarden.org; 239 NW Everett St; adult/student $11/8; 10am-7pm mid-May–mid-Oct, to 5pm mid-Oct–mid-Mar, to 6pm mid-Mar–mid-May; 8, 77, Blue, Red) and the so-called **Shanghai Tunnels** (Map p386; 503-622-4798; 120 NW 3rd Ave; adult/child $13/8; 12, 19, 20, Blue, Red), some of which can be toured.

★ Saturday Market MARKET
(Map p386; 503-222-6072; www.portlandsaturdaymarket.com; 2 SW Naito Pkwy; 10am-5pm Sat, 11am-4:30pm Sun Mar-Dec; ; 12, 16, 19, 20, Red, Blue) The best time to walk along the Portland Waterfront is on a weekend, when you can catch this famous market showcasing arts and crafts, street entertainers and food carts.

The Pearl District & Northwest

Encompassing three distinctive districts, Northwest Portland is home to some of the city's top art galleries, trendy restaurants and plentiful shopping options – all connected by wonderfully walkable streets. Nob Hill's craftsman-style storefronts house neighborhood-feel restaurants and retail shops amid century-old Victorian homes. In the face of Portland's rapid development, industrial Slabtown is up and coming with new high-rise residences and more. Characterized by its cobblestone streets and old loading docks, the once-industrial Pearl District is now one of the state's chicest neighborhoods, boasting a wealth of galleries, eateries and boutiques.

Portland

Top Sights
1 Lan Su Chinese Garden C2
2 Pioneer Courthouse Square B4
3 Saturday Market D3
4 Tom McCall Waterfront Park C4

Sights
5 Chinatown Gateway C3
6 Oregon Convention Center E2
7 Oregon Historical Society B4
8 Oregon Museum of Science & Industry D6
9 Portland Art Museum B4
10 Shanghai Tunnels C3
11 South Park Blocks A5

Activities, Courses & Tours
12 Pedal Bike Tours C3
13 Portland Spirit C4

Sleeping
14 Ace Hotel B3
15 Hoxton C3
16 Jupiter Hotel E3
17 Jupiter Next F3
18 Northwest Portland Hostel A2
19 Society Hotel C2
20 Woodlark B3

Eating
Bullard .... (see 20)
Clyde Common .... (see 14)
21 Luc Lac C4
22 Nong's Khao Man Gai E3
23 OK Omens G5

Drinking & Nightlife
24 Barista A2
25 Cider Riot E3
26 Coava Coffee E5
27 Culmination Brewing G2
28 Deadstock Coffee C3
29 Hey Love F3
30 Push x Pull E4

Entertainment
31 Arlene Schnitzer Concert Hall B4
32 Crystal Ballroom A3
33 Doug Fir Lounge E3
Flicks on the Bricks .... (see 2)
34 Keller Auditorium B5
35 Moda Center D1
36 Portland Center Stage B3

Shopping
37 Lloyd Center F1
38 Powell's City of Books B3

West Hills

★Forest Park
PARK

(503-223-5449; www.forestparkconservancy.org) Abutting the more manicured Washington Park to the south (to which it is linked by various trails) is the far wilder 5100-acre Forest Park, an urban Northwest forest that harbors plants and animals and hosts an avid hiking fraternity. The **Portland Audubon Society** (503-292-6855; www.audubonportland.org; 5151 NW Cornell Rd; 9am-5pm, nature store 10am-6pm Mon-Sat, to 5pm Sun; 20) FREE maintains a bookstore, wildlife rehabilitation center and 4.5 miles of trails within its Forest Park sanctuary.

Washington Park
PARK

(www.washingtonparkpdx.org; ; 63, Blue, Red) Tame and well-tended Washington Park contains several key attractions within its 410 acres of greenery. The **International Rose Test Garden** (www.waparkrosefriends.org; 400 SW Kingston Ave; 7:30am-9pm; 63) FREE is the centerpiece of Portland's famous rose blooms; there are more than 700 varieties on show here, plus great city views. Further uphill is the **Japanese Garden** (503-223-1321; www.japanesegarden.org; 611 SW Kingston Ave; adult/child $16.95/11.50; noon-7pm Mon, 10am-7pm Tue-Sun mid-Mar–Sep, noon-4pm Mon, 10am-4pm Tue-Sun Oct–mid-Mar; 63), another oasis of tranquility. If you have kids, the **Oregon Zoo** (503-226-1561; www.oregonzoo.org; 4001 SW Canyon Rd; adult/child $17.95/12.95; 9:30am-6pm Jun-Aug, to 4pm Sep-May; ; 63, Blue, Red) and **Portland Children's Museum** (503-233-6500; www.portlandcm.org; 4015 SW Canyon Rd; $11, 2nd Sun of month 9am-noon $3; 9am-5pm; ; 63, Red, Blue) should be on your docket.

Northeast & Southeast

Across the Willamette River from downtown is the **Lloyd Center** (Map p386; 503-282-2511; www.lloydcenter.com; 2201 Lloyd Center; 10am-7pm Mon, to 8pm Tue-Sat, 11am-6pm Sun; Red, Blue, Green), Oregon's largest shopping mall and where notorious ice-queen Tonya Harding first learned to skate. A few blocks to the southwest are the unmissable glass towers of the **Oregon Convention Center** (Map p386; www.oregoncc.org; 777 NE Martin Luther King Jr Blvd; Red, Blue, Green, Yellow), and nearby is the **Moda Center** (Map p386; 503-235-8771; www.rosequarter.com/venue/moda-center; 1 N Center Court St; Yellow), home of professional basketball team the Trailblazers.

Further up the Willamette, **N Mississippi Ave** used to be full of run-down buildings, but is now a hot spot of trendy shops and eateries. Northeast is artsy **NE Alberta St**, a long ribbon of art galleries, boutiques and cafes (don't miss the **Last Thursday** (☎503-823-1052; www.lastthurspdx.org; ⏲6-9pm last Thu of month) street-art event here). **SE Hawthorne Blvd** (near SE 39th Ave) is affluent hippy territory, with gift stores, cafes, coffee shops and two branches of Powell's bookstores. One leafy mile to the south, **SE Division St** has become a foodie destination, with plenty of excellent restaurants, bars and pubs. The same is true of **E Burnside at NE 28th Ave**, though it has a more concentrated and upscale feel.

Activities

Hiking

Portland boasts the 5100-acre Forest Park (p388) within city limits, which will keep avid hikers busy for a while. There's also a network of trails in **Hoyt Arboretum** (☎503-865-8733; www.hoytarboretum.org; 4000 Fairview Blvd; ⏲trails 5am-10pm, visitor center 9am-4pm Mon-Fri, from 10am Sat & Sun; 🚊Washington Park) FREE, easily reached by light rail, and more to explore at **Tryon Creek State Natural Area** (☎503-636-9886; www.oregonstateparks.org; 11321 SW Terwilliger Blvd).

If that's not enough, the hiking wonderlands of Mt Hood (p398) and the Columbia River Gorge (p397) are each less than an hour's drive away.

Cycling

Portland often tops lists of the USA's most bike-friendly cities.

Look for pleasant paths along the **Willamette River** downtown, or try the 21-mile **Springwater Corridor**, which heads out to the suburb of Boring.

Mountain bikers can head to **Leif Erikson Dr**, or for singletrack and technical trails, **Hood River** and **Mt Hood** (both about an hour's drive away) have great options.

For scenic farm country, head to **Sauvie Island** (www.sauvieisland.org; Hwy 30; daily parking pass $10), 10 miles northwest of downtown Portland.

Everybody's Bike Rentals & Tours CYCLING
(☎503-358-0152; www.pdxbikerentals.com; 305 NE Wygant St; rentals per hr $8-25, tours per person from $39; ⏲10am-5pm; 🚌6) It's true that Portland is best seen by bicycle, and this company offers low-key, fun tours of the city and its surroundings – whether you're into food and farms or beer and parks. Try the 'Beyond Portlandia' tour for an off-the-beaten-path glimpse of the city. Bicycle rentals, from commuters to mountain bikes, are also available.

Kayaking

Situated close to the confluence of the Columbia and Willamette Rivers, Portland has miles of navigable waterways.

Portland Kayak Company KAYAKING
(☎503-459-4050; www.portlandkayak.com; 6600 SW Macadam Ave; rental per hr from $14; ⏲10am-6pm Mon-Fri, from 9am Sat, to 5pm Sun; 🚌43) Kayaking rentals (minimum two hours), instruction and tours – notably a three-hour circumnavigation of Ross Island on the Willamette River ($49), available at 10am and 2pm daily and at sunset (starts 6pm) May through September.

PORTLAND FOR CHILDREN

Washington Park has the most to offer families with young kids. Here you'll find the world-class Oregon Zoo (p388), which is set in a beautiful natural environment parents will also enjoy. Next door is the Portland Children's Museum (p388) and **World Forestry Center** (☎503-228-1367; www.worldforestry.org; 4033 SW Canyon Rd; adult/child $8/5; ⏲10am-5pm, closed Tue & Wed Labor Day-Memorial Day; 👪; 🚌63, 🚊Blue, Red), both offering fun learning activities and exhibits.

On the other side of the **Willamette River**, the **Oregon Museum of Science and Industry** (OMSI; Map p386; ☎503-797-4000; www.omsi.edu; 1945 SE Water Ave; adult/child $14.50/9.75; ⏲9:30am-7pm Jun-Aug, to 5:30pm Tue-Sun Sep-May; 👪; 🚌9, 17, 🚋A Loop, B Loop, 🚊Orange) is a top-notch destination with a theater, planetarium and even a submarine to explore. Further south is **Oaks Amusement Park** (☎503-233-5777; www.oakspark.com; 7805 SE Oaks Park Way; ride bracelets $19-41, individual rides $4.95, skating $7-7.50; ⏲hours vary; 👪; 🚌35, 99), home to pint-size roller coasters, miniature golf and carnival games.

Tours

Pedal Bike Tours CYCLING
(Map p386; 503-243-2453; www.pedalbiketours.com; 133 SW 2nd Ave; tours from $49; 10am-6pm; 15, 16, 51, Blue, Red) Offers all sorts of themes – history, doughnuts, beer – plus day trips to the Columbia Gorge. The three-hour 'bike and boat' package includes a historic bike tour of downtown and a sightseeing cruise with **Portland Spirit** (Map p386; 503-224-3900; www.portlandspirit.com; cnr SW Salmon St & Waterfront; sightseeing/dinner cruise from $32/78; 4, 10, 14, 15, 30).

Portland Walking Tours WALKING
(503-774-4522; www.portlandwalkingtours.com; per person $23-79) Food, chocolate, underground and even ghost-hunting tours are available daily. A tour of 'makers and their spaces' offers a glimpse behind the scenes of Portland's indie-creative side, from crafts and woodworking to leather goods and a brewery. Each tour meets at a different location; reservations recommended.

Festivals & Events

Pickathon MUSIC
(www.pickathon.com; 16581 SE Hagen Rd, Happy Valley; weekend pass $325; Aug) This family-friendly music festival has been going strong for more than 20 years, thanks to outstanding music lineups and a fun, stress-free atmosphere. Camping is free with a weekend pass, and kids under 12 get in free with a parent. Bicycling to the festival is strongly encouraged. It's in Happy Valley, 10 miles southeast of downtown.

Feast Portland FOOD & DRINK
(www.feastportland.com; tickets from $25; mid-Sep) Taste the food and drink that's at the forefront of Oregon cuisine at this festival, with more than 30 events of varying sizes and levels of involvement. Proceeds benefit an organization that fights hunger. Book early as some events sell out months ahead.

Sleeping

Tariffs listed are for the summer season, when reservations are a good idea. Prices at top-end hotels are highly variable depending on occupancy and day of the week.

Hawthorne Portland Hostel HOSTEL $
(503-236-3380; www.portlandhostel.org; 3031 SE Hawthorne Blvd; dm $35-39, d with shared bath $77; ; 14) This ecofriendly hostel with two private rooms and spacious dorms has a great Hawthorne location. There are summertime open-mike nights in the grassy backyard, and bicycle rentals (and a fix-it station) are available. The hostel composts and recycles, harvests rainwater for toilets, and has a nice eco-roof. Discounts are offered to those who are bicycle touring.

Northwest Portland Hostel HOSTEL $
(Map p386; 503-241-2783; www.nwportlandhostel.com; 425 NW 18th Ave; dm $36-42, d with shared bath from $100; ; 77) Perfectly located between the Pearl District and NW 21st and 23rd Aves, this friendly, clean hostel takes up four old buildings and features plenty of common areas, including a small deck and garden patio. Dorms are spacious and private rooms can be as nice as those in hotels, though all share outside bathrooms. Non-HI members pay $3 extra.

★**Kennedy School** HOTEL $$
(503-249-3983; www.mcmenamins.com/kennedyschool; 5736 NE 33rd Ave; r $135-235; ; 70) This former elementary school is now home to a hotel (sleep in old classrooms!), a restaurant with a great garden courtyard, several bars, a microbrewery and a movie theater. Guests can use the soaking pool for free. The whole school is decorated in the McMenamins' distinctive art style – mosaics, fantasy paintings and historical photographs.

★**Ace Hotel** BOUTIQUE HOTEL $$
(Map p386; 503-228-2277; www.acehotel.com; 1022 Harvey Milk St; s with shared bath from $200, d from $285; P) A well-established brand, the Ace fuses industrial, minimalist and retro styles to great effect. From the photo booth in its lobby to the recycled fabrics and salvaged-wood furniture in its rooms, the hotel feels very chic and very Portland. There's a Stumptown coffee shop and underground bar on-site, and **Clyde Common bistro** (Map p386; 503-228-3333; www.clydecommon.com; 1014 Harvey Milk St; mains $25-40; 6-11pm Sun-Wed, to midnight Thu-Sat, brunch 10am-3pm Sat & Sun) adjoins the lobby. The location can't be beat.

★**Society Hotel** HOTEL $$
(Map p386; 503-445-0444; www.thesocietyhotel.com; 203 NW 3rd Ave; dm $55, d from $130; ; 8, 77, Red, Blue, Green, Orange) This pretty hotel in the historic 1881 Mariners Building – originally a lodging house for sailors – has impeccable fashion sense. Options include dorms as well as private rooms. There's a lively bar and rooftop deck, plus

Wednesday wine tastings and drag bingo on Thursday. Some corner rooms have huge windows designed to catch sunlight.

Jupiter Next BOUTIQUE HOTEL **$$**
(Map p386; ☎503-230-9200; https://jupiterhotel.com; 900 E Burnside St; d from $180) Jupiter Next, the upmarket big sister of the adjacent '60s-retro **Jupiter Hotel** (Map p386; ☎503-230-9200; www.jupiterhotel.com; 800 E Burnside St; d from $149; ; 20), brings a modern boutique offering to Portland's central eastside district. The six-floor geometric structure is completely bedecked in roofing shingles and its 67 rooms have oversized windows that offer postcard-perfect views of the city. Extra touches include digital concierges and bedside CBD chocolates.

Hey Love (Map p386; ☎503-206-6223; www.heylovepdx.com; 920 E Burnside St, Jupiter Next; 7am-2am), the hotel's tropical tippling den, serves tasty international fare daily for lunch and dinner, in addition to weekend brunch.

★**Hoxton** BOUTIQUE HOTEL **$$$**
(Map p386; ☎503-770-0500; https://thehoxton.com/oregon/portland/hotels; 15 NW 4th Ave; d from $275;) From London-based Hoxton hoteliers comes this US outpost, right inside the Chinatown Gateway. An airy, Northwestern modernist aesthetic – clean lines, natural materials and mid-century accents – features throughout expansive communal areas and the 119 rooms, ranging in usual Hoxton sizes (Shoebox, Snug, Cozy and Roomy). Standards include breakfast bag delivery, books curated by locals and rip-off-free munchies for purchase at reception.

★**Woodlark** BOUTIQUE HOTEL **$$$**
(Map p386; ☎503-548-2559; https://woodlarkhotel.com; 813 SW Alder St; d from $275;) Stitching together two revived National Historic Register buildings, this new boutique hotel delivers sumptuous design with swanky amenities. Mid-century modern furnishings, tropical plants and elemental accents make up the opulent lobby, while forest-green-upholstered headboards and foliage-themed wallpaper feature throughout the 150 rooms. Luxury plant-based toiletries, in-room streaming fitness programs, and menus for pillows and spiritual texts come standard.

Eating

Portland has become nationally recognized for its food scene, with dozens of young, top-notch chefs pushing the boundaries of ethnic and regional cuisines and making the most of locally sourced, sustainably raised ingredients.

★**Luc Lac** VIETNAMESE **$**
(Map p386; ☎503-222-0047; www.luclackitchen.com; 835 SW 2nd Ave; mains $9-13; 11am-2:30pm & 4pm-midnight Sun-Thu, 11am-2:30pm & 4pm-4am Fri & Sat) This bustling Vietnamese kitchen draws downtown lunch crowds and late-night bar-hoppers with superbly executed classics such as *pho,* vermicelli bowls and banh mi. Count on queuing any time of day to score a seat in the swanky dining room, where pink paper parasols hang from the ceiling. Happy hour (4pm to 7pm) has a more relaxed vibe and small plates run just $3.

★**Yonder** SOUTHERN US **$**
(☎503-444-7947; www.yonderpdx.com; 4636 NE 42nd Ave; mains $8-17; 11am-9pm Wed-Sun) Yonder's excellent fried chicken is available 'dusted' (adorned with dry spice), 'dipped' (tossed in a zesty sauce) or 'hot' (just spicy enough to be memorable, without injury), served with cornbread or a biscuit with sweet sorghum butter. Add a side of pimento mac 'n' cheese or bacon-braised collard greens, then wash it down with a craft cocktail. Down-home good!

Nong's Khao Man Gai THAI **$**
(Map p386; ☎503-740-2907; www.khaomangai.com; 609 SE Ankeny St; mains $11-16; 10:50am-9pm; 20) The widely adored food cart where it all started has closed, but Nong's brick-and-mortar locations still dish out her signature menu item: tender poached chicken with rice in a magical sauce. A handful of other options (including vegetarian) and add-ons are available, as well as occasional specials.

There's another branch located at 417 SW 13th Ave.

★**Stammtisch** GERMAN **$$**
(☎503-206-7983; www.stammtischpdx.com; 401 NE 28th Ave; small plates $5-9, mains $14-24; 3pm-1:30am Mon-Fri, 11am-1:30am Sat & Sun; ; 19) Dig into serious German food – with a beer list to match – at this dark and cozy neighborhood pub. Don't miss the *Maultaschen* (a gorgeous pasta pocket filled with leek fondue in a bright, lemony wine sauce), the clams with *Landjäger* sausage in white wine broth, or the paprika-spiced roast chicken.

PORTLAND'S FOOD CARTS

Some of Portland's most amazing food comes from humble little kitchens-on-wheels. Found all over town clumped together in parking lots or otherwise unoccupied spaces, food carts offer hungry wanderers a chance to try unusual dishes at low prices, and they often have covered seating areas if you don't like to walk while you eat. Many of Portland's beloved eateries got their start as food carts, with specialties that were such hits that brick-and-mortar locations were established to serve increasing demands.

★Bullard SOUTHERN US **$$**
(Map p386; ☎503-222-1670; www.bullardpdx.com; 813 SW Alder St; dinner mains $16-32; ⏲11am-3pm & 5-10pm Mon-Thu, 11am-3pm & 5-11pm Fri, 10am-11pm Sat, 10am-10pm Sun) Inside the Woodlark hotel (p391) is this nod to chef Doug Adams' roots and chosen home, where the meat-centric menu is decidedly Texas-meets-Oregon. 'Supper' plates showcase the likes of 12-hour smoked Painted Hills beef ribs served with fresh flour tortillas, grilled rainbow trout with a black-eyed pea and celery salad, and a pork chop with heirloom hominy and local collard greens.

★Tasty n Daughters AMERICAN **$$**
(☎503-621-1400; www.tastyndaughters.com; 4537 SE Division St; small plates $3-14, mains $12-19; ⏲9am-2:30pm & 5-10pm) After a nine-year run, chef John Gorham, of **Toro Bravo** (☎503-281-4464; www.torobravopdx.com; 120 NE Russell St; tapas $3-17, mains $13-24; ⏲5-10pm Mon-Thu, to 11pm Fri & Sat) fame, took brunch favorite Tasty n Sons, formerly on N Williams, to southeast Portland. The reboot – renamed to accurately reflect his offspring – retained favorites like *shakshuka* and patatas bravas, but added fresh pasta and seafood to the menu. Most notable is a new Turkish influence – the pide breakfast pizza is a must.

OK Omens AMERICAN **$$**
(Map p386; ☎503-231-9959; www.okomens.com; 1758 SE Hawthorne Blvd; dishes $8-18; ⏲5pm-midnight; 🚌14) OK Omens is a hit, not least for its epic wine list and menu of adventurous shareable dishes. Crowd favorites include a spicy Caesar-style salad with buttermilk fried chicken, hoisin-roasted carrots, adorable cheddar-filled beignets, crab pasta topped with thinly sliced jalapeños, and burgers. On Sunday, happy hour lasts all day.

★Ava Gene's ITALIAN **$$$**
(☎971-229-0571; www.avagenes.com; 3377 SE Division St; mains $25-35; ⏲5-10pm Mon-Thu, to 11pm Fri, 4:30-11pm Sat, 4:30-10pm Sun; 🚌4) This renowned trattoria-inspired eatery – owned by Duane Sorenson, who founded Stumptown Coffee (p393) – serves rustic Italian cuisine, with exquisite pasta and vegetable dishes as highlights. Exceptional ingredients, a great wine list and cocktails, and outstanding service make it a swoon-worthy dining experience worth seeking out. Reserve ahead.

★Ox STEAK **$$$**
(☎503-284-3366; www.oxpdx.com; 2225 NE Martin Luther King Jr Blvd; mains $14-56; ⏲5-10pm Sun-Thu, to 11pm Fri & Sat; 🚌6) One of Portland's most popular restaurants is this upscale, Argentine-inspired steakhouse. Start with the smoked bone-marrow clam chowder, then go for the gusto: the grass-fed beef rib eye. If there's two of you, the *asado* (barbecue grill; $94) is a good choice, allowing you to try several different cuts. Reserve ahead.

★Ataula SPANISH **$$$**
(☎503-894-8904; www.ataulapdx.com; 1818 NW 23rd Pl; tapas $9-17, paella dishes $35-40; ⏲4:30-10pm Tue-Sat; 🚌15, 77) This critically acclaimed Spanish tapas restaurant offers outstanding cuisine. If these are on the menu, try the *nuestras bravas* (sliced, fried potatoes in milk aioli), *croquetas* (salt-cod fritters), *xupa xup* (chorizo 'lollipop') and *ataula montadito* (salmon with mascarpone yogurt and black-truffle honey). Great cocktails, too. Be sure to reserve.

Ned Ludd AMERICAN **$$$**
(☎503-288-6900; www.nedluddpdx.com; 3925 NE Martin Luther King Jr Blvd; small plates $3-18, mains $25-28; ⏲5-9pm Sun-Thu, to 10pm Fri & Sat; 🚌6) 🍃 Quintessentially Portland, this offbeat, upscale joint exudes thick artisan vibes, from its rustic-peasant decor to the prominent brick wood-fired oven where all dishes are cooked. The beautifully presented small plates are rotated daily. This is not a place to simply fill your tummy but one in which to sample eclectic 'American craft' delicacies.

🍷 Drinking & Nightlife

Drinking, whether it's coffee or a craft brew, cider or kombucha, is practically a sport in Portland. In winter it's a reason to hunker down and escape the rain; in summer, an excuse to sit on a patio or deck and soak up the long-awaited sunshine. Whatever your poison, there's bound to be a handcrafted, artisan version of it here.

★Push x Pull COFFEE

(Map p386; https://pushxpullcoffee.com; 821 SE Stark St; ⏲7am-5pm Mon-Fri, 8am-4pm Sat & Sun) A labor of love by a group of java-obsessed pals, this roastery and cafe specializes in natural-process coffees and offers a rotating selection of single-origins, plus local baked goods. Bright wood paneling and turquoise-painted walls that perfectly match the industrial schoolhouse furniture and espresso machines make for a cheery space – not to mention the delightfully friendly owners and staff.

★Barista COFFEE

(Map p386; ☎503-274-1211; www.baristapdx.com; 539 NW 13th Ave; ⏲6am-7pm Mon-Fri, from 7am Sat & Sun; 🚌77) One of Portland's best coffee shops, this tiny, stylish shop is owned by award-winning barista Billy Wilson. Beans are sourced from specialty roasters. Three other locations in town.

Coava Coffee COFFEE

(Map p386; ☎503-894-8134; www.coavacoffee.com; 1300 SE Grand Ave; ⏲6am-6pm Mon-Fri, 7am-6pm Sat & Sun; 📶; 🚌6, 15, 🚋B Loop) The decor takes the concept of 'neo-industrial' to extremes, but it works – Coava delivers where it matters. The pour-over makes for a fantastic cup of java, and the espressos are exceptional, too. Also at 2631 SE Hawthorne Blvd.

★Proud Mary CAFE

(☎503-208-3475; https://proudmarycoffee.com; 2012 NE Alberta St; ⏲7am-4pm Mon-Fri, from 8am Sat & Sun) From the land of flat whites and avocado toast comes Proud Mary, the notable Melbourne-based coffee roaster that aptly chose Portland for their first US outpost. In addition to superb coffee, they sling delicious, Insta-worthy breakfast, brunch and lunch plates such as vanilla and ricotta hotcakes, a smoked pork-belly satay sandwich and Aussie meat pies. Smoothies and fresh juices, too.

Deadstock Coffee COFFEE

(Map p386; ☎971-220-8727; www.deadstockcoffee.com; 408 NW Couch St; ⏲7:30am-5pm Mon-Fri, 9am-6pm Sat, 10am-4pm Sun) Deadstock's ethos that 'coffee should be dope' comes through in its signature concoctions and blends, such as the LeBronald Palmer (a mix of iced coffee, sweet tea and lemonade) and 'Fresh Prince' (Ethiopian light-roast beans). Owner Ian Williams once worked his way from janitor to shoe designer at Nike HQ, and it's the world's only coffee shop dedicated to sneaker culture.

Stumptown Coffee Roasters COFFEE

(☎503-230-7702; www.stumptowncoffee.com; 4525 SE Division St; ⏲6am-7pm Mon-Fri, from 7am Sat & Sun; 📶; 🚌4) Stumptown was the first micro roaster to put Portland on the coffee map, and this small, narrow space is where it all started.

★Breakside Brewery BREWERY

(☎503-444-7597; www.breakside.com; 1570 NW 22nd Ave; ⏲11am-10pm Sun-Thu, to 11pm Fri & Sat; 🚌8) Known for experimental brews laced with fruits, vegetables and spices, plus a nationally lauded IPA, Breakside expanded beyond its original location at 820 NE Dekum St in northeast Portland and opened a bigger venue in Slabtown in 2017. Sixteen taps, great grub and two levels of seating (plus a large patio) in a cheery industrial space make it one of Portland's finest brewpubs.

★Culmination Brewing MICROBREWERY

(Map p386; ☎971-254-9114; www.culminationbrewing.com; 2117 NE Oregon St; plates $5-16; ⏲noon-9pm Sun-Thu, to 10pm Fri & Sat; 🚌12) At this comfortable tasting room in a refurbished old warehouse, you'll find some of the city's best beers (including the top-notch Phaedrus IPA plus a whole array of limited-edition seasonals) and a brief but unusually ambitious food menu. If the *pêche* is available, try it – even if you don't normally like 'fruit' beers.

Ecliptic Brewing BREWERY

(☎503-265-8002; www.eclipticbrewing.com; 825 N Cook St; ⏲11am-10pm Sun-Thu, to 11pm Fri & Sat; 🚌4) It's in kind of a chilly industrial space, but the beer speaks for itself – Ecliptic was founded by John Harris, who previously brewed for McMenamins, Deschutes and Full Sail. The brewery's astronomically named creations (such as the Craft Beer medal–winning Spica Pilsner) are ambitious and wildly successful. Food includes lamb picatta, tempura asparagus and a goat's cheese and beet melt sandwich.

Cider Riot BREWERY

(Map p386; ☎503-662-8275; www.ciderriot.com; 807 NE Couch St; ⏲4-11pm Mon-Fri, noon-11pm Sat, noon-9pm Sun; 🚌12, 19, 20) Portland's best cider company now has its very own pub and tasting room, so you can sample Everybody

DON'T MISS

POWELL'S CITY OF BOOKS

Powell's City of Books (Map p386; 800-878-7323; www.powells.com; 1005 W Burnside St; 9am-11pm; 20) is one of the USA's largest independent bookstores, with a whole city block of new and used titles, and a well-attended series of readings.

There's another branch at 3723 SE Hawthorne Blvd (with a Home and Garden bookstore next door), and one at the airport.

Pogo, Never Give an Inch or Plastic Paddy at the source. Ciders here are dry and complex, made with regional apples and hyper-regional attitude.

Entertainment

Music, particularly of the indie rock persuasion, is one of Portland's primary exports – but jazz, punk, electronic, blues, metal, hip-hop and other genres also have a place in the scene, with acts playing both renowned local venues and unassuming neighborhood bars. Other entertainment runs the gamut from theater and ballet to burlesque and drag, and there's plenty of cinema and sports, too.

Live Music

Doug Fir Lounge LIVE MUSIC
(Map p386; 503-231-9663; www.dougfirlounge.com; 830 E Burnside St; 7am-2:30am; 20) Combining futuristic elements with a rustic log-cabin aesthetic, this venue has helped transform the LoBu (lower Burnside) neighborhood from seedy to slick. Doug Fir books great bands and the sound quality is usually tops. The attached restaurant offers a killer breakfast and weekend brunch, and a bar menu ($8 to $13) until close.

Crystal Ballroom LIVE MUSIC
(Map p386; 503-225-0047; www.crystalballroompdx.com; 1332 W Burnside St; 20) This large, historic ballroom has hosted some major acts, including James Brown and Marvin Gaye in the early '60s, and Devendra Banhart and Two Door Cinema Club today. The bouncy, 'floating' dance floor makes dancing almost effortless.

Mississippi Studios LIVE MUSIC
(503-288-3895; www.mississippistudios.com; 3939 N Mississippi Ave; 4) This intimate bar is good for checking out budding acoustic talent along with more-established musical acts. Excellent sound system, and good restaurant-bar with patio (and awesome burgers) next door.

Performing Arts

Portland Center Stage THEATER
(Map p386; 503-445-3700; www.pcs.org; 128 NW 11th Ave; tickets from $25; 4, 8, 44, 77) The city's main theater company performs in the Portland Armory – a renovated Pearl District landmark with state-of-the-art features.

Arlene Schnitzer Concert Hall CLASSICAL MUSIC
(Map p386; 503-248-4335; www.portland5.com; 1037 SW Broadway; 10, 14, 15, 35, 36, 44, 54, 56) This beautiful, if not acoustically brilliant, downtown venue, built in 1928, hosts a wide range of shows, lectures, concerts and other performances.

Keller Auditorium PERFORMING ARTS
(Map p386; 503-248-4335; www.portland5.com; 222 SW Clay St; 38, 45, 55, 92, 96) Built in 1917 and formerly known as the Civic Auditorium, Keller hosts a wide range of performers, from big-name musicians (Sturgill Simpson) to the Portland Opera (www.portlandopera.org) and the Oregon Ballet Theatre (www.obt.org), along with some Broadway productions.

Shopping

Portland's downtown shopping district extends in a two-block radius from Pioneer Courthouse Sq and hosts all of the usual suspects. The Pearl District is dotted with high-end galleries, boutiques and home-decor shops. On weekends, you can visit the quintessential Saturday Market by the Skidmore Fountain. For a pleasant, upscale shopping street, head to NW 23rd Ave.

Eastside has lots of trendy shopping streets that also host restaurants and cafes. SE Hawthorne Blvd is the biggest, N Mississippi Ave is the newest and NE Alberta St is the most artsy and funkiest.

Information

EMERGENCY & MEDICAL SERVICES

Legacy Good Samaritan Medical Center (503-413-7711; www.legacyhealth.org; 1015 NW 22nd Ave) Convenient to downtown.

Portland Police Bureau (503-823-0000; www.portlandoregon.gov/police; 1111 SW 2nd Ave) Police and emergency services.

MEDIA

KBOO 90.7 FM (www.kboo.fm) Progressive local station run by volunteers; alternative news and views.

Portland Mercury (www.portlandmercury.com) Free local sibling of Seattle's *The Stranger.*

Willamette Week (www.wweek.com) Free weekly covering local news and culture.

TOURIST INFORMATION

Travel Portland (Map p386; 503-275-8355; www.travelportland.com; 701 SW 6th Ave, Pioneer Courthouse Sq; 8:30am-5:30pm Mon-Fri, 10am-4pm Sat Nov-Apr, plus 10am-2pm Sun May-Oct; Red, Blue, Green, Yellow) Super-friendly volunteers staff this office in Pioneer Courthouse Sq. There's a small theater with a 12-minute film about the city, and TriMet bus and light-rail offices inside.

Getting There & Away

AIR

Portland International Airport (503-460-4234; www.flypdx.com; 7000 NE Airport Way; ; Red) Award-winning Portland International Airport has daily flights all over the US, as well as to several international destinations. It's situated just east of I-5 on the banks of the Columbia River (a 20-minute drive from downtown).

BUS

Bolt Bus (Map p386; 877-265-8287; www.boltbus.com) Connects Portland with Seattle (from $25), Bellingham ($40), Eugene ($15) and Vancouver ($50), among other cities. Buses leave from the corner of NW 8th Ave and NW Everett St.

Greyhound (Map p386; 503-243-2361; www.greyhound.com; 550 NW 6th Ave; Green, Orange, Yellow) Greyhound connects Portland with cities along I-5 and I-84. Destinations beyond Oregon include Chicago, Denver, San Francisco, Seattle and Vancouver.

TRAIN

Union Station (800-872-7245; www.amtrak.com; 800 NW 6th Ave; 17, Green, Yellow) Amtrak services depart from here for Chicago, Oakland, Seattle and Vancouver.

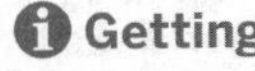

Getting Around

TO/FROM THE AIRPORT

Tri-Met's light-rail MAX red line takes about 40 minutes to get from downtown to the airport (adult/child $2.50/1.25). If you prefer a bus, **Blue Star** (503-249-1837; www.bluestarbus.com; per person one way from $14) offers shuttle services between PDX and several downtown stops.

Taxis charge around $35 to $40 (not including tip) from the airport to downtown.

BICYCLE

Clever Cycles (503-334-1560; www.clevercycles.com; 900 SE Hawthorne Blvd; rentals per day $30, cargo bikes $60; 11am-6pm Mon-Fri, to 5pm Sat & Sun; 10, 14) Rents folding, family and cargo bikes.

CAR

Parking on the east side of the city is generally easy to find; downtown, SmartPark garages, some with electric-vehicle charging stations, offer affordable parking (see www.portlandoregon.gov/transportation/35272). Downtown, Northwest and the Pearl District often have metered parking; finding a spot here can be harder. Carshare programs are also popular.

It only became legal to pump your own gasoline in Oregon in 2019. Most stations have free full-serve attendants on-site, who will do everything from start to finish.

CHARTER SERVICE

For custom bus or van charters and tours, try **EcoShuttle** (503-548-4480; www.ecoshuttle.net; per 3hr from $500). Its vehicles run on 100% biodiesel.

PUBLIC TRANSPORTATION

The MAX light rail connects to most of the major metro areas (and suburbs) and is easily navigable. Buses connect with many stops.

TAXI

Cabs are available 24 hours by phone. Downtown, you can sometimes flag them down, and some bartenders will call you a cab on request. **Broadway Cab** (503-333-3333; www.broadwaycab.com) and **Radio Cab** (503-227-1212; www.radiocab.net) are two reliable operators. Rideshare services are usually abundant in Portland.

Willamette Valley

The Willamette Valley, a fertile 60-mile-wide agricultural basin, was the Holy Grail for Oregon Trail pioneers who headed west more than 170 years ago. Today it's the state's breadbasket, producing more than 100 kinds of crops – including renowned pinot noir grapes. Salem, Oregon's capital, is about an hour's drive from Portland at the northern end of the valley, and most of the other attractions in the area make easy day trips as well. Toward the south is Eugene, a dynamic college town worth a day or two of exploration.

Salem

Oregon's legislative center is renowned for its cherry trees, art-deco capitol building and Willamette University.

The university's **Hallie Ford Museum of Art** (☎503-370-6855; www.willamette.edu/arts/hfma; 700 State St; adult/child $6/free, Tue free; ⊙10am-5pm Tue-Sat, 1-5pm Sun) showcases the state's best collection of Pacific Northwest art, including an impressive Native American gallery.

The **Oregon State Capitol** (☎503-986-1388; www.oregonlegislature.gov; 900 Court St NE; ⊙8am-5pm Mon-Fri) FREE, built in 1938, looks like a background from a lavish Cecil B De-Mille movie; free tours are offered. Rambling 19th-century **Bush House** (☎503-363-4714; www.salemart.org; 600 Mission St SE; adult/child $6/3; ⊙tours 1-4pm Thu-Sun Apr-Sep, Fri-Sun Oct-Mar) is an Italianate mansion now preserved as a museum with historical accents, including original wallpapers and marble fireplaces.

You can get oriented at the **Visitors Information Center** (☎503-581-4325; www.travelsalem.com; 388 State St; ⊙9am-5pm Mon-Fri, 10am-4pm Sat; 📶). Salem is served daily by **Greyhound** (www.greyhound.com; 500 13th St SE) buses and **Amtrak** (☎503-588-1551; www.amtrak.com; 500 13th St SE) trains.

Eugene

'Track Town' offers a great art scene, fine restaurants, boisterous festivals, miles of riverside paths and several lovely parks. Its location at the confluence of the Willamette and McKenzie Rivers, just west of the Cascades, means there's plenty of outdoor recreation on offer – especially around the McKenzie River region, the Three Sisters Wilderness and Willamette Pass.

Sights

Saturday Market MARKET

(☎541-686-8885; www.eugenesaturdaymarket.org; 8th Ave & Oak St; ⊙10am-5pm Sat Apr–mid-Nov) For great fun and a quintessential introduction to Eugene's peculiar vitality, don't miss the Saturday Market, held each Saturday from April through November. Local artisans sell handcrafted works, and there's live music throughout the day on the stage in the food court. Between Thanksgiving and Christmas it's renamed the **Holiday Market** (☎541-686-8885; www.holidaymarket.org; 796 W 13th Ave, Lane Events Center; ⊙10am-6pm mid-Nov–Dec) and moves indoors to the Lane Events Center.

Alton Baker Park PARK

(100 Day Island Rd) This popular 400-acre riverside park, which provides access to the **Ruth Bascom Riverbank Trail System**, a 12-mile bikeway that flanks both sides of the Willamette, is heaven for cyclists and joggers. There's good downtown access via the DeFazio Bike Bridge.

University of Oregon UNIVERSITY

(☎541-346-1000; www.uoregon.edu; 1585 E 13th Ave) Established in 1872, the University of Oregon is the state's foremost institution of higher learning, with a focus on the arts, sciences and law. The campus is filled with historic ivy-covered buildings and includes a **Pioneer Cemetery**, with tombstones that give a vivid insight into life and death in the early settlement. Campus tours are held in summer.

Sleeping

Eugene has a handful of budget chain motels and hotels, plus a couple of lovely inns and a hostel. Prices can rise sharply during key football games (September to November) and at graduation (mid-June).

Eugene Whiteaker International Hostel HOSTEL $

(☎541-343-3335; www.eugenehostel.org; 970 W 3rd Ave; dm/r from $35/50; ⊖@📶) This casual hostel in an old, rambling house has an artsy vibe, nice front and back patios to hang out on, and a free simple breakfast. Towels and bedding are included in the price.

★**C'est La Vie Inn** B&B $$

(☎541-302-3014; www.cestlavieinn.com; 1006 Taylor St; r from $180; ⊖❄@📶) This gorgeous Victorian house, run by a friendly French woman and her American husband, is a neighborhood showstopper. Beautiful antique furniture fills the living and dining areas, while the four tastefully appointed rooms (each named for a French artist) offer comfort and luxury. Hosts provide a full breakfast, as well as afternoon port and other nice touches.

Eating & Drinking

Krob Krua Thai Kitchen THAI $

(☎541-636-6267; www.krobkrua.com; 254 Lincoln St; mains $7-9; ⊙11am-9pm Tue-Sun) Superb Thai curries, noodles, salads, soups and wok-fired dishes are served at this joint in the same space as **WildCraft Cider Works** (☎541-735-3506; https://wildcraftciderworks.com; 232 Lincoln St; ⏲11:30am-9pm Tue-Thu, to 11pm Fri & Sat, to 8pm Sun), where you can enjoy your food in the tasting room and wash it down with a cider. Spring for the Dungeness crab and shrimp dumplings, the namesake *krob krua* noodles with beef, or the green-curry fried rice.

★Izakaya Meiji Company IZAKAYA **$$**
(☎541-505-8804; www.izakayameiji.com; 345 Van Buren St; small plates $3-13; ⏲5pm-1am) This hip *izakaya* (Japanese pub serving small plates) in the heart of the Whiteaker district draws nightly crowds with handcrafted libations, sake, shochu and over 100 different whiskeys, plus a seasonal menu of shareable dishes. Feeling adventurous? Try the *shiokara,* an acquired delicacy of salted, fermented squid viscera. Or just stick with the curry udon. You can't go wrong here.

Beppe & Gianni's Trattoria ITALIAN **$$**
(☎541-683-6661; www.beppeandgiannis.net; 1646 E 19th Ave; mains $15-26; ⏲5-9pm Sun-Thu, to 10pm Fri & Sat) One of Eugene's most beloved restaurants, Beppe & Gianni's serves up homemade pastas and excellent desserts. Expect a wait, especially on weekends.

★Ninkasi Brewing Company BREWERY
(☎541-344-2739; www.ninkasibrewing.com; 272 Van Buren St; ⏲noon-9pm Sun-Wed, to 10pm Thu-Sat) If you like hops, head to this tasting room to sample some of Oregon's most distinctive and innovative microbrews at the source. There's a sweet patio with occasional food trucks, or you can bring in your own food. Brewery tours are at 11am on Monday, Wednesday and Friday, and at 4pm Tuesday, Thursday and Saturday.

ℹ Information

Visitor Center (☎541-484-5307; www.eugenecascadescoast.org; 754 Olive St; ⏲8am-5pm Tue-Fri, from 9am Mon) This center is open weekdays. On weekends, stop by the visitor center (☎541-484-5307; www.eugenecascadescoast.org; 3312 Gateway St, Springfield; ⏲9am-6pm) in Springfield for information.

ℹ Getting There & Around

Located about 7 miles northwest of the center, **Eugene Airport** (☎541-682-5544; www.flyeug.com; 28801 Douglas Dr) offers domestic flight services.

Greyhound (☎541-344-6265; www.greyhound.com; 987 Pearl St) provides long-distance services to Salem, Corvallis, Portland, Medford, Grants Pass, Hood River, Newport and Bend.

Trains leave from the **Amtrak station** (☎541-687-1383; www.amtrak.com; 433 Willamette St) for Portland's Union Station ($28, three hours, nine daily); Seattle, WA; and Vancouver, Canada, among other places.

Local bus service is provided by **Lane Transit District** (☎541-687-5555; www.ltd.org). For bike rentals, head to **Paul's Bicycle Way of Life** (☎541-344-4105; www.bicycleway.com; 556 Charnelton St; rentals per day $24-48; ⏲10am-6pm Mon-Fri, to 5pm Sat & Sun).

Columbia River Gorge

The fourth-largest river in the US by volume, the mighty Columbia runs 1243 miles from Alberta, Canada, into the Pacific Ocean just west of Astoria. For the final 309 miles of its course, the heavily dammed waterway delineates the border between Washington and Oregon and cuts though the Cascade Mountains via the spectacular Columbia River Gorge. Sheltering numerous ecosystems, waterfalls and magnificent vistas, the land bordering the river is protected as a National Scenic Area and is a popular sporting nexus for windsurfers, cyclists, anglers and hikers.

Not far from Portland, **Multnomah Falls** is a huge tourist draw, while **Vista House** offers stupendous gorge views. And if you want to stretch your legs, the Gorge is riddled with hiking trails.

Hood River & Around

Famous for its surrounding fruit orchards and wineries, the town of Hood River – 63 miles east of Portland on I-84 – is also a huge mecca for windsurfing and kiteboarding. Premier wineries have taken hold in the region, providing good wine-tasting opportunities as well.

⊙ Sights & Activities

Mt Hood Railroad RAIL
(☎800-872-4661; www.mthoodrr.com; 110 Railroad Ave; adult/child from $35/30; 👪) Built in 1906, the railroad once transported fruit and lumber from the upper Hood River Valley to the main railhead in Hood River. The vintage trains now transport tourists beneath Mt Hood's snowy peak and past fragrant orchards. The line is about 21 miles long and ends in pretty Parkdale. See the website for schedules and fares. Reserve in advance.

Cathedral Ridge Winery WINE
(☎800-516-8710; www.cathedralridgewinery.com; 4200 Post Canyon Dr; tastings from $15; ⏲11am-5pm) This attractive winery in pretty farm country at the edge of town has signature red blends and a slew of awards on display. In nice weather, sit outdoors and take in the awesome view of Mt Hood. Various tours and tastings are available.

Hood River Waterplay WATER SPORTS
(☎541-386-9463; www.hoodriverwaterplay.com; I-84 exit 64; 2hr windsurfing course $99, SUP lessons per hr from $48; ⏲May-Oct) Interested in windsurfing, kayaking, SUP, catamaran sailing and so on? Contact this company, with rentals and classes at its waterfront location.

Discover Bicycles CYCLING
(☎541-386-4820; www.discoverbicycles.com; 210 State St; rentals per day $40-100; ⏲10am-6pm Mon-Sat, to 5pm Sun) This shop rents road bikes, hybrids, mountain bikes, e-bikes and mountain e-bikes and can give advice on area trails.

Sleeping & Eating

Hood River Hotel HISTORIC HOTEL $$
(☎541-386-1900; www.hoodriverhotel.com; 102 Oak St; d/ste from $110/152;) Located right in the heart of downtown, this lovingly restored 1913 hotel offers comfortable, hip yet vintage rooms. Beds are comfy but some bathrooms are minuscule. The suites have the best amenities and views. Kitchenettes are also available, and there's an excellent restaurant and a relaxing sauna on the premises. Heat in the winter is via ancient steam radiator plus space heaters.

Columbia Gorge Hotel HOTEL $$$
(☎800-345-1921; www.columbiagorgehotel.com; 4000 Westcliff Dr; r $149-439;) Hood River's most famous place to stay is this historic Spanish-style hotel, set high on a cliff above the Columbia. The atmosphere is classy and the grounds are lovely, and there's a fine restaurant on the premises. Rooms have antique beds and furnishings. River-view rooms cost more but are worth it.

★**pFriem Tasting Room** GASTROPUB $$
(☎541-321-0490; www.pfriembeer.com; 707 Portway Ave; mains $13-18; ⏲11:30am-9pm) The highly regarded beers at this brewery are matched by a hearty menu that is definitely not run-of-the-mill: think mussels and *frites*, beef tongue, pork terrine, and a stew made with braised lamb and duck confit. It's located near the waterfront along a stretch of industrial-chic development and tables are cozied up right up to the brewing vats.

Information

Chamber of Commerce (☎541-386-2000; www.hoodriver.org; 720 E Port Marina Dr; ⏲9am-5pm Mon-Fri, 10am-4pm Sat & Sun Apr-Oct, 9am-5pm Mon-Fri Nov-Mar) Visitor information for Hood River and the surrounding area.

Getting There & Away

Greyhound (☎541-386-1212; www.greyhound.com; 110 Railroad Ave) Hood River is connected to Portland by daily Greyhound buses (from $21, one hour, three daily).

Oregon Cascades

The Oregon Cascades offer plenty of dramatic volcanoes that dominate the skyline for miles around. Mt Hood, overlooking the Columbia River Gorge, is the state's highest peak, and has year-round skiing plus a relatively straightforward summit ascent. Tracking south you'll pass Mt Jefferson and the Three Sisters before reaching Crater Lake, the ghost of erstwhile Mt Mazama that collapsed in on itself after blowing its top approximately 7000 years ago.

Mt Hood

The state's highest peak, 11,240ft Mt Hood pops into view over much of northern Oregon whenever there's a sunny day, exerting an almost magnetic tug on skiers, hikers and sightseers. In summer, wildflowers bloom on the mountainsides and hidden ponds shimmer in blue, making for some unforgettable hikes; in winter, downhill and cross-country skiing dominates people's minds and bodies.

Mt Hood is accessible year-round on Hwy 26 from Portland (56 miles), and from Hood River (44 miles) on Hwy 35. Together with the Columbia River Hwy, these routes comprise the Mt Hood Loop, a popular scenic drive. **Government Camp**, the center of business on the mountain, is at the pass over Mt Hood.

Activities

Skiing

Hood is rightly revered for its skiing. There are six ski areas on the mountain, including **Timberline** (☎503-272-3158; www.timberlinelodge.com; Government Camp; lift tickets adult/child $73/63), which lures snow-lovers with the longest ski season in the US (nearly year-round). Closer to Portland, **Mt Hood**

SkiBowl (☎503-272-3206; www.skibowl.com; Hwy 26; lift tickets $59, night skiing $43) is no slacker either. It's the nation's largest night-ski area and popular with city slickers who ride up for an evening of powder play. The largest ski area on the mountain is **Mt Hood Meadows** (☎503-337-2222; www.skihood.com; lift tickets adult/child up to $89/44), where the best conditions usually prevail.

Hiking

The Mt Hood National Forest protects an astounding 1200 miles of trails. A Northwest Forest Pass ($5 per day) is required to park at most trailheads.

One popular trail loops 7 miles from near the village of Zigzag to beautiful **Ramona Falls**, which tumbles down mossy columnar basalt. Another heads 1.5 miles up from US 26 to **Mirror Lake**, continues half a mile around the lake, then tracks 2 miles beyond to a ridge.

The 41-mile **Timberline Trail** circumnavigates Mt Hood through scenic wilderness. Noteworthy portions include the hike to McNeil Point and the short climb to Bald Mountain. From Timberline Lodge, Zigzag Canyon Overlook is a 4.5-mile round trip.

Climbing Mt Hood should be taken seriously, as deaths do occur, though dogs have made it to the summit and the climb can be done in a long day. Contact **Timberline Mountain Guides** (☎541-312-9242; www.timberlinemtguides.com; 2-day summit per person $780) for guided climbs.

Sleeping & Eating

Most area **campsites** (☎877-444-6777; www.recreation.gov; tent & RV sites $16-39) have drinking water and vault toilets. Reserve on busy weekends, though some walk-in sites are usually set aside. For more information, contact a nearby ranger station.

★Timberline Lodge LODGE **$$**
(☎800-547-1406; www.timberlinelodge.com; 27500 Timberline Rd; bunk r $165-221, d from $180;) As much a community treasure as a hotel, this gorgeous historic lodge offers a variety of rooms, from dorms that sleep up to 10 to deluxe fireplace rooms. There's a year-round heated outdoor pool, and the ski lifts are close by. Enjoy awesome views of Mt Hood, nearby hiking trails, two bars and a good dining room. Rates vary widely.

Huckleberry Inn INN **$$**
(☎503-272-3325; www.huckleberry-inn.com; 88611 E Government Camp Loop; r $95-165, 10-bed dm $160;) Simple and comfortably rustic rooms are available here, along with bunk rooms that sleep up to 10. It's in a great central location in Government Camp. The casual restaurant (which doubles as the hotel's reception) serves good breakfasts. Peak holiday rates are higher.

Rendezvous Grill & Tap Room AMERICAN **$$**
(☎503-622-6837; www.thevousgrill.com; 67149 E Hwy 26, Welches; mains $12-29; ⏱11:30am-8pm Tue-Sun, to 9pm Fri & Sat) This excellent restaurant offers outstanding dishes such as wild salmon with caramelized shallots and artichoke hash or chargrilled pork chop with rhubarb chutney. Lunch means gourmet sandwiches, burgers and salads on the patio. Bonus: excellent cocktails.

Mt Hood Brewing Co PUB FOOD **$$**
(☎503-272-3172; www.mthoodbrewing.com; 87304 E Government Camp Loop, Government Camp; mains $12-24; ⏱11am-9pm) Government Camp's only brewery-restaurant offers a friendly, family-style atmosphere and pub fare including hand-tossed pizzas, sandwiches and short ribs.

Information

For maps, permits and information, contact regional ranger stations. If you're approaching from Hood River, visit the **Hood River Ranger Station** (☎541-352-6002; 6780 OR 35, Parkdale; ⏱8am-4:30pm Mon-Fri). The **Zigzag Ranger Station** (☎503-622-3191; 70220 E Hwy 26; ⏱7:45am-4:30pm Mon-Sat) is more handy for Portland arrivals. Mt Hood **Information Center** (☎503-272-3301; 88900 E Hwy 26; ⏱9am-5pm) is in Government Camp. The weather changes quickly here; carry chains in winter.

Getting There & Away

From Portland, Mt Hood is one hour (56 miles) by car along Hwy 26. Alternatively, you can take the prettier and longer approach via Hwy 84 to Hood River, then Hwy 35 south (1¾ hours, 95 miles).

The **Central Oregon Breeze** (☎800-847-0157; www.cobreeze.com; Government Camp Rest Area, Government Camp Loop) shuttle between Bend and Portland stops briefly at Government Camp, 6 miles from the Timberline Lodge. **Sea to Summit** (☎503-286-9333; www.seatosummit.net; round trip from $59) runs regular shuttles from Portland to the ski areas during the winter.

Sisters

Once a stagecoach stop and trade town for loggers and ranchers, today Sisters is a bustling tourist destination whose main street is lined with boutiques, art galleries and eateries housed in Western-facade buildings. Visitors come for the mountain scenery, spectacular hiking, fine cultural events and awesome climate – there's plenty of sun and little precipitation here.

At the southern end of Sisters, the **city park** (City Park Camping; ☎541-323-5220; www.ci.sisters.or.us/creekside-campground; S Locust St; tent/RV sites $20/40; ⊙Apr-Nov) has campsites, but no showers. For ultra comfort, bag a room in the luxurious **Five Pine Lodge** (☎866-974-5900; www.fivepinelodge.com; 1021 Desperado Trail; d from $242, cabins from $265;).

For refined French food you might not expect out here, head to **Cottonwood Cafe** (☎541-549-2699; www.cottonwoodinsisters.com; 403 E Hood Ave; breakfast $9-13, lunch mains $11-13; ⊙8am-3pm), while **Three Creeks Brewing** (☎541-549-1963; www.threecreeksbrewing.com; 721 Desperado Ct; mains $12-26, pizzas $10-14; ⊙11:30am-9pm Sun-Thu, to 10pm Fri & Sat) is the place for home brew and pub grub.

Information

Chamber of Commerce (☎541-549-0251; www.sisterscountry.com; 291 E Main Ave; ⊙10am-3pm Mon-Fri)

Getting There & Away

Cascades East Transit (☎541-385-8680; https://cascadeseasttransit.com; one-way fare $1.50) connects Sisters with Bend (30 minutes, three daily) and Redmond (25 minutes, three daily).

Bend

Bend is where all lovers of the outdoors should live – it's an absolute paradise. You can ski fine powder in the morning, paddle a kayak in the afternoon and play golf into the evening. Or would you rather go mountain biking, hiking, mountaineering, stand up paddleboarding, fly-fishing or rock climbing? It's all close by and top drawer. Plus, you'll probably be enjoying it all in great weather, as the area gets nearly 300 days of sunshine each year.

Sights

★High Desert Museum MUSEUM

(☎541-382-4754; www.highdesertmuseum.org; 59800 Hwy 97; adult/child $12/7; ⊙9am-5pm May-Oct, 10am-4pm Nov-Apr;) This excellent museum, about 3 miles south of Bend, charts the exploration and settlement of the West, using reenactments of a Native American camp, a hard-rock mine and an old Western town. The region's natural history is also explored; kids love the live snake, tortoise and trout exhibits, and watching the birds of prey and otters is always fun.

Guided walks and other programs are well worth attending – don't miss the raptor presentation.

Activities

Bend is a mountain-biking paradise, with hundreds of miles of awesome trails to explore. The good Bend Area Trail Map ($12.99; www.adventuremaps.net/shop/product/product/bend-area-trail-map) is available at the Visit Bend tourist office and elsewhere.

The king of Bend's mountain-biking trails is **Phil's Trail** (www.bendtrails.org/trail/phils-trail-complex) network, which offers a variety of excellent fast singletrack forest trails just minutes from town. If you want to catch air, don't miss the Whoops Trail. You can rent a bike from adventure-oriented **Cog Wild** (☎541-385-7002; www.cogwild.com; 255 SW Century Dr, Suite 201; half-day tours from $60, rentals $35-80; ⊙9am-6pm).

Bend is also the gateway to some of Oregon's best skiing, 22 miles southwest of town at **Mt Bachelor Ski Resort** (☎800-829-2442; www.mtbachelor.com; lift tickets adult/child $99/56, cross-country day pass $21/14; ⊙Nov-May;).

Sleeping

There's an endless supply of cheap motels, hotels and services on 3rd St (US 97). Because of festivals and events, Bend's lodging rates head north most weekends, and booking ahead is recommended.

Bunk + Brew Hostel HOSTEL $

(☎458-202-1090; www.bunkandbrew.com; 42 NW Hawthorne Ave; dm $45, d $109-139;) This super-cosy, central and social hostel lets you bunk in the oldest brick building in Bend. Everything is small but feels like home, plus a sauna and new bathhouse were under construction when we passed. Make friends in the kitchen or movie/video-game room or take off on a walking or biking beer tour of town literally right out the door.

★McMenamins Old St Francis School HOTEL $$

(☎541-382-5174; www.mcmenamins.com; 700 NW Bond St; r from $189;) Surely one of

DON'T MISS

SMITH ROCK STATE PARK

Smith Rock State Park (☎800-551-6949; www.oregonstateparks.org; 9241 NE Crooked River Dr; day use $5) Best known for its glorious rock climbing, Smith Rock State Park boasts rust-colored 800ft cliffs that tower over the pretty Crooked River. Nonclimbers have several miles of fine hiking trails, some of which involve a little simple rock scrambling. Nearby Terrebonne has a climbing store, along with some restaurants and grocery stores. The formations in the park are simply spectacular.

There's camping right next to the park, or at Skull Hollow (no water; campsites $5), 8 miles east. The nearest motels are a few miles south in Redmond.

Smith Rock Climbing Guides Inc (☎541-788-6225; www.smithrockclimbingguides.com; Smith Rock State Park, Terrebonne; half-day per person from $65) This company offers a variety of climbing instruction (basic, lead, trad, multipitch, aid and self-rescue), along with guided climbs to famous routes at Smith Rock State Park. Gear is included. Prices depend on the number in your group. Open by appointment.

McMenamins' best venues, this old schoolhouse has been remodeled into a hotel – two rooms even have side-by-side claw-foot tubs. The fabulous tiled saltwater Turkish bath alone is worth the stay; nonguests can soak for $5. A restaurant-pub, three bars, a movie theater and artwork complete the picture.

★Oxford Hotel BOUTIQUE HOTEL **$$$**
(☎541-382-8436; www.oxfordhotelbend.com; 10 NW Minnesota Ave; r from $319;) Bend's premier boutique hotel is deservedly popular. The smallest rooms are still huge (470 sq ft) and are decked out with ecofriendly features such as soy-foam mattresses and cork flooring. High-tech aficionados will love the iPod docks and smart-panel desks. Suites (with kitchen and steam shower) are available, and the basement restaurant is slick.

The modern design and chic, cool-tone muted color scheme would fit in fine in a major city, so it simply sparkles in the more town-sized Bend.

Eating

The Bite FOOD TRUCK **$**
(☎541-610-6457; www.thebitetumalo.com; 19860 7th St, Tumalo; mains $8-16; ⊙11am-9pm) Great setting in Tumalo, between Bend and Sisters. Get your beer on tap at the Bite bar then purchase food from one of the handful of food trucks to eat at outdoor picnic tables or indoors by the bar. People regularly drive out here just to order the delectable, sustainable and wild-caught sushi at the Ronin Sushi cart.

★El Sancho MEXICAN **$**
(☎458-206-5973; www.elsanchobend.com; 335 NE Dekalb Ave; tacos $2.75-3.25; ⊙11am-10pm) Fantastic, great-value Mexican served in a cool atrium-like setting that opens up in summer or is heated in winter. Every taco, from the chipotle chicken to Oaxacan cheese and green chile, is as good as you'll find anywhere. Extras include fried plantains, tamales, chicken tortilla soup and kick-ass margaritas and pisco sours.

★Chow AMERICAN **$**
(☎541-728-0256; www.chowbend.com; 1110 NW Newport Ave; mains $10-17; ⊙7am-2pm) The signature poached-egg dishes here are spectacular and involve layers of delicious things like polenta cakes, roasted vegetables, Mexican cheeses and cornmeal-crusted tomatoes (don't miss the housemade hot sauces). Gourmet sandwiches including crab patty or braised corned beef are served for lunch. Much of the produce is grown in the garden, and there are good cocktails, too.

★Sunriver Brewing Co GASTROPUB **$$**
(☎541-408-9377; www.sunriverbrewingcompany.com; 1005 NW Galveston Ave; mains $12-15; ⊙11am-10pm Sun-Thu, to 11pm Fri & Sat) In a town of many, many breweries, Sunriver stands out, not only for its delicious, award-winning beers (try the flagship Vicious Mosquito IPA), but also for its great food – from bratwurst sausages with fried brussels sprouts to a creamy mac 'n' cheese topped with sockeye salmon. The pub front opens up to let the outside in on sunny days.

★Bos Taurus STEAK **$$$**
(☎541-241-2735; www.bostaurussteak.com; 163 NW Minnesota Ave; mains $20-79; ⊙5-10pm) Like a museum of the finest beef, Bos Taurus is a must-splurge for meat lovers. The chefs here picked their cattle ranches via blind taste

test and everything beyond has also been refined to the smallest detail. There's always a fish dish and coq au vin on the menu for nonbeef eaters. Service is impeccable. Reserve ahead.

Zydeco AMERICAN **$$$**
(☎541-312-2899; www.zydecokitchen.com; 919 NW Bond St; dinner mains $17-38; ⏲11:30am-2:30pm & 5-9pm Mon-Fri, 5-9pm Sat & Sun) Zydeco is one of Bend's most acclaimed restaurants, and with good reason. Start with the duck fries (french fries fried in duck fat) or beet salad with goat cheese, then move on to your main course: seared ahi tuna, crawfish jambalaya or roasted duck with mushroom gravy. Reserve.

ℹ Information

Visit Bend (☎541-382-8048; www.visitbend.com; 750 NW Lava Rd; ⏲9am-5pm Mon-Fri, 10am-4pm Sat & Sun) Great information, plus maps, books and recreation passes available for purchase.

ℹ Getting There & Around

Central Oregon Breeze (☎541-389-7469; www.cobreeze.com; 3405 N Hwy 97, Circle K) offers transport to Portland two or more times daily ($52 one way, reserve ahead).

High Desert Point (☎541-382-4193; www.oregon-point.com/highdesert-point; Hawthorne Station) buses link Bend with Chemult, where the nearest train station is located (65 miles south). It also has bus services to Eugene, Ontario and Burns.

Cascades East Transit (☎541-385-8680; www.cascadeseasttransit.com) is the regional bus company in Bend, covering La Pine, Mt Bachelor, Sisters, Prineville and Madras. It also provides bus transport within Bend.

Newberry National Volcanic Monument

Newberry National Volcanic Monument (☎541-593-2421; www.fs.usda.gov/recarea/deschutes/recarea/?recid=66159; Hwy 97; day use $5; ⏲May-Sep) showcases 400,000 years of dramatic seismic activity. Start your visit at the **Lava Lands Visitor Center** (☎541-593-2421; www.fs.usda.gov; 58201 S Hwy 97; ⏲9am-5pm late May-Oct), 13 miles south of Bend. Nearby attractions include **Lava Butte**, a perfect cone rising 500ft, and **Lava River Cave**, Oregon's longest lava tube. Four miles west of the visitor center is **Benham Falls**, a good picnic spot on the Deschutes River.

Newberry Crater was once one of the most active volcanoes in North America, but after a large eruption a caldera was born. Close by are **Paulina Lake** and **East Lake**, deep bodies of water rich with trout, while looming above is 7985ft **Paulina Peak**.

Crater Lake National Park

It's no exaggeration: Crater Lake is so blue, you'll catch your breath. And if you get to see it on a calm day, the surrounding cliffs are reflected in those deep waters like a mirror. It's a stunningly beautiful sight. **Crater Lake** (☎541-594-3000; www.nps.gov/crla; 7-day vehicle pass winter/summer $15/25) is Oregon's only national park.

The classic tour is the 33-mile rim drive (open from approximately June to mid-October), but there are also exceptional hiking and cross-country-skiing opportunities. Note that because the area receives some of the highest snowfalls in North America, the rim drive and north entrance are sometimes closed up until early July.

You can stay at the **Cabins at Mazama Village** (☎888-774-2728; www.craterlakelodges.com; d $160; ⏲late May-Sep; 🚭) or the majestic **Crater Lake Lodge** (☎888-774-2728; www.craterlakelodges.com; r from $197; ⏲late May–mid-Oct; 🚭📶), opened in 1915. Campers head to **Mazama Campground** (☎888-774-2728; www.craterlakelodges.com; Mazama Village; tent/RV sites $22/32; ⏲Jun–mid-Oct; 📶🐾). For more information, head to **Steel Visitor Center** (☎541-594-3000; www.nps.gov/crla/planyourvisit/visitorcenters.htm; Park Headquarters; ⏲9am-5pm May-Oct, 10am-4pm Nov-Apr).

Oregon Coast

This magnificent littoral zone is paralleled by Hwy 101, a scenic highway that winds its way through towns, resorts, state parks (more than 70 of them) and wilderness areas. Everyone from campers to gourmets will find a plethora of ways to enjoy this exceptional region, which is especially popular in summer (reserve accommodations in advance).

Astoria

Named after America's first millionaire, John Jacob Astor, Astoria sits at the 5-mile-wide mouth of the Columbia River and was the first US settlement west of the Mississippi. The city has a long seafaring history and has seen its old harbor, once home to poor artists and writers, attract fancy hotels and restaurants in recent years. Inland are many historical houses, including lovingly restored Victorians – a few converted into romantic B&Bs. It's nonbeach-y vibe gives it a special ambience on the coast.

Sights

Adding to the city's scenery is the 4.1-mile **Astoria-Megler Bridge**, the longest continuous truss bridge in North America, which crosses the Columbia River into Washington state. See it from the **Astoria Riverwalk**, which follows the trolley route. **Pier 39** is an interesting covered wharf with an informal cannery museum and a couple of places to eat.

Columbia River Maritime Museum MUSEUM
(503-325-2323; www.crmm.org; 1792 Marine Dr; adult/child $14/5; 9:30am-5pm;) Astoria's seafaring heritage is well interpreted at this wave-shaped museum. It's hard to miss the retired Coast Guard boat, frozen mid-rescue, through a huge outside window. Other exhibits highlight the salmon-packing industry and the Chinese immigrants who made up the bulk of its workforce; the river's commercial history; and the crucial job of the bar pilot.

You get a keen sense of the treacherous conditions that define this area, known for good reason as the 'Graveyard of the Pacific.'

Fort Stevens State Park PARK
(ext 21 503-861-3170; www.oregonstateparks.org; 100 Peter Iredale Rd, Hammond; day use $5) Ten miles west of Astoria, this park holds the historic military installation that once guarded the mouth of the Columbia River. Near the **Military Museum** (503-861-2000; http://visitftstevens.com; day-use fee $5; 10am-6pm May-Sep, to 4pm Oct-Apr) are gun batteries dug into sand dunes – interesting remnants of the fort's mostly demolished military stations (truck and walking tours available).

There's a popular beach at the small *Peter Iredale* 1906 shipwreck, and good ocean views from parking lot C. There's also camping and 12 miles of paved bike trails.

Sleeping & Eating

Fort Stevens State Park CAMPGROUND $
(503-861-1671; https://oregonstateparks.org; 100 Peter Iredale Rd, Hammond; tent/RV sites $22/32, yurts/cabins $46/90) About 560 sites (most for RVs) are available at this popular campground 10 miles west of Astoria. Great for families; reserve in summer. Entry off Pacific Dr.

Commodore Hotel BOUTIQUE HOTEL $$
(503-325-4747; www.commodoreastoria.com; 258 14th St; d with/without bath from $164/89;) Hip travelers should make a beeline for this stylish hotel, which offers attractive but small, minimalist rooms. Choose a room with bathroom or go Euro style (sink in room, bathroom down the hall; 'deluxe' rooms have better views). There's a lounge-style lobby with cafe, free samples of local microbrews from 5pm to 7pm, an impressive movie library and record players to borrow.

Bowpicker SEAFOOD $
(503-791-2942; www.bowpicker.com; cnr 17th & Duane Sts; dishes $8-12; 11am-6pm Wed-Sun) On just about every list of great seafood shacks is this adorable place in a converted 1932 gillnet fishing boat, serving beer-battered chunks of albacore and steak fries and that's it. Some say it's the best fish-and-chips in the US.

Fort George Brewery PUB FOOD $
(503-325-7468; www.fortgeorgebrewery.com; 1483 Duane St; mains $7-17, pizzas $14-26; 11am-11pm, from noon Sun) Fort George has established itself as one of the state's best and

LEWIS & CLARK: JOURNEY'S END

In November 1805 William Clark and his fellow explorer Meriwether Lewis of the Corps of Discovery staggered, with three dozen others, into a sheltered cove on the Columbia River, 2 miles west of the present-day Astoria-Megler Bridge, completing what was indisputably the greatest overland trek in American history.

After the first truly democratic ballot in US history (in which a woman and a black slave both voted), the party elected to make their bivouac 5 miles south of Astoria at Fort Clatsop, where the Corps spent a miserable winter in 1805–06. Today this site is called the **Lewis and Clark National Historical Park** (503-861-2471; www.nps.gov/lewi; 92343 Fort Clatsop Rd; adult/child $5/free; 9am-6pm mid-Jun–Aug, to 5pm Sep–mid-Jun). Here you'll find a reconstructed Fort Clatsop, along with a visitor center and historical reenactments in summer.

most reliable craft brewers. Its atmospheric brewery-restaurant is in a historic building that was the original settlement site of Astoria. Apart from the excellent beer, you can get gourmet burgers, housemade sausages, salads and, upstairs, wood-fired pizza. Head to the Lovell Taproom for views over the production line.

Astoria Coffeehouse & Bistro AMERICAN $$
(503-325-1787; www.astoriacoffeehouse.com; 243 11th St; breakfast & lunch mains $6-18, dinner mains $15-32; 7am-9pm Sun, to 10pm Mon-Thu, to 11pm Fri & Sat) Small, popular cafe with attached bistro offering an eclectic menu – things like coconut chicken red curry, chili-relleno burger, fish tacos and build-your-own mac 'n' cheese. Everything is made in-house, even the ketchup. There's sidewalk seating and excellent cocktails. Expect a wait at dinner and Sunday brunch. Excellent and changing $5 breakfast and lunch specials available daily.

Getting There & Away

Northwest Point (503-484-4100; http://oregon-point.com/northwest-point) Daily buses head to Seaside, Cannon Beach and Portland; check the website for schedules.

Pacific Transit (360-642-9418; www.pacifictransit.org) Buses go over the border to Washington.

Cannon Beach

Charming Cannon Beach is one of the most popular beach towns on the Oregon coast. Several premier hotels here cater to a fancier clientele, as do the town's many boutiques and art galleries. In summer the streets are ablaze with flowers. Lodging is expensive, and the streets are jammed: on a warm, sunny Saturday, you'll spend a good chunk of time just finding a parking spot.

Sights & Activities

Photogenic **Haystack Rock**, a 295ft sea-stack, is the most spectacular landmark on the Oregon coast and is accessible from the beach at low tide. Birds cling to its ballast cliffs and tide pools ring its base.

The coast to the north, protected inside **Ecola State Park** (503-436-2844; https://oregonstateparks.org; day use $5), is the Oregon you may have already visited in your dreams: sea stacks, crashing surf, hidden beaches and gorgeous pristine forest. The park is 1.5 miles from town and is crisscrossed by paths, including part of the **Oregon Coast Trail**, which leads over Tillamook Head to the town of Seaside.

The Cannon Beach area is good for surfing, though not the beach itself. The best spots are **Indian Beach** in Ecola State Park, 3 miles to the north, and **Oswald West State Park**, 10 miles south. **Cleanline Surf Shop** (503-738-2061; www.cleanlinesurf.com; 171 Sunset Blvd; board/wetsuit rentals from $20/15; 10am-6pm Sun-Fri, 9am-6pm Sat) is a friendly local shop that rents out boards and wetsuits.

Sleeping

Cannon Beach is pretty exclusive; for budget choices head 7 miles north to Seaside.

★**Ocean Lodge** HOTEL $$$
(503-436-2241, 888-777-4047; www.theoceanlodge.com; 2864 S Pacific St; d $219-369;) This gorgeous place has some of Cannon Beach's most luxurious rooms, most with ocean view and all with fireplace and kitchenette. A complimentary continental breakfast, an 800-DVD library and pleasant sitting areas are available to guests. Located on the beach at the southern end of town.

Eating & Drinking

Here you'll find everything from coffee shops to one that doubles as a fine restaurant. If you're just after a warm cup of buttery clam chowder with a view, stop in at **Mo's** (503-436-1111; www.moschowder.com; 195 W Warren Way; chowder $4.25-10; 11am-9pm;).

★**Irish Table** IRISH $$$
(503-436-0708; www.theirishtable.com; 1235 S Hemlock St; mains $26-30; 5:30-9pm Fri-Tue) Excellent restaurant hidden at the back of Sleepy Monk Coffee, serving a fusion of Irish and Pacific Northwest cuisine made with local and seasonal ingredients. The menu is small and simple, but the choices are tasty; try the vegetarian shepherd's pie, lamb-loin chops or seared Piedmontese flat-iron steak. If the curried mussels are on the menu, don't hesitate.

Sleepy Monk Coffee COFFEE
(503-436-2796; www.sleepymonkcoffee.com; 1235 S Hemlock St; drinks & snacks $2-7; 8am-3pm Mon, Tue & Thu, to 4pm Fri-Sun) For organic, certified-fair-trade coffee, try this little coffee shop on the main street. Sit on an Adirondack chair in the tiny front yard and

enjoy the rich brews, all tasty and roasted on the premises. Good homemade pastries, too.

Information

Chamber of Commerce (503-436-2623; www.cannonbeach.org; 207 N Spruce St; 10am-5pm) Has good local information, including tide tables.

Getting There & Around

Northwest Point (541-484-4100; www.oregon-point.com/northwest-point) Buses run from Astoria to Portland (and vice versa) every morning (one way $18, three hours), stopping at Cannon Beach (two hours). Buy tickets online or at the Beach Store, next to Cannon Beach Surf.

Sunset Empire Transit (503-861-7433; www.ridethebus.org; 900 Marine Dr; one-way fare $3) Buses go to Seaside ($1, 13 minutes) or Astoria ($1, 30 minutes) plus other coastal stops. The Cannon Beach bus runs the length of Hemlock St to the end of Tolovana Beach; the schedule varies depending on day and season.

Tillamook County Transportation (The Wave; 503-815-8283; www.tillamookbus.com) Buses go south toward Manzanita ($3, 30 minutes) and Lincoln City ($9, two hours) several times daily.

Newport

Tied with Astoria as home to Oregon's largest commercial fishing fleet, Newport is a lively tourist city with several fine beaches and a world-class aquarium. In 2011 it became the Pacific Fleet Headquarters of NOAA (National Oceanic and Atmospheric Administration). Good restaurants – along with some tacky attractions, gift shops and barking sea lions – abound in the historic bayfront area, while bohemian Nye Beach offers art galleries and a friendly village atmosphere. The area was first explored in the 1860s by fishing crews who found oyster beds at the upper end of Yaquina Bay.

Sights

The world-class **Oregon Coast Aquarium** (541-867-3474; www.aquarium.org; 2820 SE Ferry Slip Rd; adult/3-12yr/13-17yr $25/15/20; 10am-6pm Jun-Aug, to 5pm Sep-May;) is an unmissable attraction, featuring a sea-otter pool, surreal jellyfish tanks and Plexiglas tunnels through a shark tank. Nearby, the **Hatfield Marine Science Center** (541-867-0100; www.hmsc.oregonstate.edu; 2030 SE Marine Science Dr; 10am-5pm Jun-Aug, to 4pm Thu-Mon Sep-May;) FREE is much smaller, but still worthwhile.

For awesome tide-pooling and views, don't miss the **Yaquina Head Outstanding Natural Area** (541-574-3100; www.blm.gov/learn/interpretive-centers/yaquina; 750 NW Lighthouse Dr; vehicle fee $7; 8am-sunset, interpretive center 10am-6pm) FREE, site of the coast's tallest lighthouse and an interesting interpretive center.

Sleeping & Eating

Campers can head to large and popular **South Beach State Park** (541-867-4715; https://oregonstateparks.org; tent/RV sites $21/31, yurts $47;), 2 miles south on Hwy 101. Book-lovers can stay at the **Sylvia Beach Hotel** (541-265-5428; www.sylviabeachhotel.com; 267 NW Cliff St; d $150-260;) and nautical and romantic types at the shipshape **Newport Belle** (541-867-6290; http://newportbelle.com; 2126 SE Marine Science Dr, South Beach Marina, H Dock; d $165-175; Feb-Oct;).

For crab po'boys, pan-fried oysters and other tasty seafood, head to **Local Ocean Seafoods** (541-574-7959; www.localocean.net; 213 SE Bay Blvd; mains $17-35; 11am-9pm, to 8pm winter) – it's especially great on warm days, when the glass walls open to the port area.

Information

Visitor Center (541-265-8801; www.newportchamber.org; 555 SW Coast Hwy; 8:30am-5pm Mon-Fri)

Yachats & Around

One of the Oregon coast's best-kept secrets is the neat and friendly little town of Yachats (ya-*hots*). Lying at the base of massive Cape Perpetua, Yachats offers the memorable scenery of a rugged and windswept land. People come here to get away from it all, which isn't hard to do along this relatively undeveloped stretch of coast.

Lining the town is the 804 Coast Trail, providing a lovely walk and access to tide pools and fabulous ocean vistas. It hooks up with the Amanda trail to the south, eventually arriving at Cape Perpetua Scenic Area.

Sights

★**Cape Perpetua Scenic Area** PARK
(www.fs.usda.gov; Hwy 101; day use $5) Located 3 miles south of Yachats, this volcanic remnant was sighted and named by England's

Captain James Cook in 1778. Famous for dramatic rock formations and crashing surf, the area contains numerous trails that explore ancient shell middens, tide pools and old-growth forests. Views from the cape are incredible, taking in coastal promontories from Cape Foulweather to Cape Arago.

For spectacular ocean views, head up Overlook Rd to the **Cape Perpetua** day-use area.

Deep fractures in the old volcano allow waves to erode narrow channels into the headland, creating effects such as **Devil's Churn**, about a half-mile north of the visitor center. Waves race up this chasm, shooting up the 30ft inlet to explode against the narrowing sides of the channel. For an easy hike, take the paved **Captain Cook Trail** (1.2 miles round trip) down to tide pools near **Cooks Chasm**, where at high tide the geyser-like spouting horn blasts water out of a sea cave. (There's also parking along Hwy 101 at Cooks Chasm.)

The **Giant Spruce Trail** (2 miles round trip) leads up Cape Creek to a 500-year-old Sitka spruce with a 15ft diameter. The **Cook's Ridge–Gwynn Creek Loop Trail** (6.5 miles round trip) heads into deep old-growth forests along Gwynn Creek; follow the Oregon Coast Trail south and turn up the Gwynn Creek Trail, which returns via Cook's Ridge.

The **visitor center** (541-547-3289; www.fs.usda.gov/siuslaw; 2400 Hwy 101; vehicle fee $5; 9:30am-4:30pm Jun-Aug, 10am-4pm Sep-May) details human and natural histories, and has displays on the Alsi tribe.

Heceta Head Lighthouse LIGHTHOUSE
(541-547-3416; www.hecetalighthouse.com; day use $5; 11am-3pm, to 2pm winter) Built in 1894 and towering precipitously above the churning ocean, this lighthouse, 13 miles south of Yachats on Hwy 101, is supremely photogenic and still functioning. Tours are available; hours may be erratic, especially in winter, so call ahead. Park at Heceta Head State Park for views.

Sea Lion Caves CAVE
(541-547-3111; www.sealioncaves.com; 91560 Hwy 101, Florence; adult/child $14/8; 9am-5pm;) Fifteen miles south of Yachats is an enormous sea grotto that's home to hundreds of Steller sea lions. An elevator descends 208ft to a dark interpretive center, and a caged-off observation area lets you watch (and smell) the sea lions jockeying for the best seat on the rocks. From late September to November there are no sea lions in the cave.

Kids in particular will love this stop. There are lots of interesting coastal birds to look for here as well.

Sleeping & Eating

Ya'Tel Motel MOTEL $
(541-547-3225; www.yatelmotel.com; cnr Hwy 101 & 6th St; d $69-119;) This eight-room motel has personality, along with large, clean rooms, some with kitchenette. A large room that sleeps six is also available ($119). Look for the (changeable) sign out front, which might say something like, 'Always clean, usually friendly.'

Green Salmon Coffee House CAFE $
(541-547-3077; www.thegreensalmon.com; 220 Hwy 101; coffee drinks $2-7; 7:30am-2:30pm;) Organic and fair trade are big words at this eclectic cafe, where locals meet for tasty breakfast items (pastries, lox bagels, homemade oatmeal). The inventive list of hot beverages ranges from regular drip coffee to lavender rosemary cocoa to CBD infused. Vegan menu available, plus a used-book exchange.

Oregon Dunes National Recreation Area

Stretching for 50 miles between Florence and Coos Bay, the Oregon Dunes form the largest expanse of coastal dunes in the USA. They tower up to 500ft and undulate inland as far as 3 miles to meet coastal forests, harboring curious ecosystems that sustain an abundance of wildlife, especially birds. The area inspired Frank Herbert to pen his epic sci-fi *Dune* novels. Hiking trails, bridle paths, and boating and swimming areas are available, but avoid the stretch south of Reedsport as noisy dune buggies dominate. Find out more at the **Oregon Dunes National Recreation Area Visitor Center** (541-271-6000; www.fs.usda.gov/siuslaw; 855 Hwy 101; 8am-4:30pm Mon-Sat Jun-Aug, Mon-Fri Sep-May) in Reedsport.

State parks with camping include popular **Jessie M Honeyman** (800-452-5687, 541-997-3641; https://oregonstateparks.org; 84505 Hwy 101 S; tent/RV sites $21/31, yurts $46;), 3 miles south of Florence, and pleasant, wooded **Umpqua Lighthouse** (541-271-4118; https://oregonstateparks.org; 460 Lighthouse Rd; tent/RV sites $19/29, yurts/deluxe yurts $43/92;

), 4 miles south of Reedsport. There's plenty of other camping in the area, too.

Port Orford

Occupying a rare natural harbor and guarding plenty of spectacular views, the scenic hamlet of Port Orford sits on a headland wedged between two magnificent state parks. **Cape Blanco State Park** (541-332-2973; https://oregonstateparks.org; Cape Blanco Rd) FREE, 9 miles to the north, is the second-most-westerly point in the continental US, and the promontory is often lashed by fierce 100mph winds. As well as hiking, visitors can tour the **Cape Blanco Lighthouse** (541-332-2207; https://oregonstateparks.org; 91814 Cape Blanco Rd; admission by donation; 10am-3:15pm Wed-Mon Apr-Oct) – built in 1870, it's the oldest and highest operational lighthouse in Oregon.

Six miles south of Port Orford, in **Humbug Mountain State Park** (541-332-6774; https://oregonstateparks.org; Hwy 101), mountains and sea meet in aqueous disharmony, generating plenty of angry surf. You can climb the 1750ft peak on a 3-mile trail through old-growth cedar groves.

For an affordable stay try **Castaway-by-the-Sea Motel** (541-332-4502; www.castawaybythesea.com; 545 W 5th St; d $110-140, ste $140-185;); for a more luxurious cabin, **Wildspring Guest Habitat** (866-333-9453; www.wildspring.com; 92978 Cemetery Loop Rd; d $298-328;). Eating well in this fishing village means a visit to slick **Redfish** (541-366-2200; www.redfishportorford.com; Hawthorne Gallery, 517 Jefferson St; mains $10-32; 11am-9pm Mon-Fri, 10am-9pm Sat & Sun) for the freshest seafood in town.

Southern Oregon

With a warm, sunny and dry climate that belongs in nearby California, Southern Oregon, the state's 'banana belt,' is an exciting place to visit. Rugged and remote landscapes are entwined with a number of designated 'wild and scenic' rivers, which are famous for their challenging white-water rafting, world-class fly-fishing and excellent hiking.

Ashland

This pretty city is the cultural center of Southern Oregon thanks to its internationally renowned Oregon Shakespeare Festival (OSF), which runs for nine months of the year and attracts hundreds of thousands of theatergoers from all over the world. The festival is so popular that it's Ashland's main attraction, packing it out in summer and bringing in steady cash flows for the town's many fancy hotels, upscale B&Bs and fine restaurants.

Even without the OSF, however, Ashland is still a pleasant place whose trendy downtown streets buzz with well-heeled shoppers and youthful bohemians. In late fall and early winter – those few months when the festival doesn't run – folks come to ski at nearby Mt Ashland. And wine-lovers, take note: the area has several good wineries worth seeking out.

Sights & Activities

Lithia Park PARK
(59 Winburn Way) Adjacent to Ashland's three splendid theaters lies what is arguably the loveliest city park in Oregon, the 93 acres of which wind along Ashland Creek above the center of town. Unusually, the park is in the National Register of Historic Places. It is embellished with fountains, flowers, gazebos and an ice-skating rink (winter only), plus a playground and woodsy trails.

Schneider Museum of Art MUSEUM
(541-552-6245; http://sma.sou.edu; 1250 Siskiyou Blvd; suggested donation $5; 10am-4pm Mon-Sat) If you like contemporary art, check out this Southern Oregon University museum, where new exhibitions go up every month or so. The university also puts on theater and opera performances, along with classical concerts.

Momentum River Expeditions RAFTING
(541-488-2525; www.momentumriverexpeditions.com; 3195 East Main St 2; 1-day rafting trips $185; Apr-Sep) This outfit runs one- to three-day rafting trips on the Upper Klamath River. Unlike many Oregon rivers that get low into summer, the Upper Klamath has strong flowing rapids deep into the season. It also offers multi-sport trips that combine rafting with mountain biking, running and backcountry camping.

Sleeping

From May to October, try to arrive with reservations. Rooms are cheaper in Medford, 12 miles north of Ashland.

Ashland Hostel HOSTEL $
(541-482-9217; www.theashlandhostel.com; 150 N Main St; dm $30, r $50-139;)

DON'T MISS

OREGON SHAKESPEARE FESTIVAL

As a young town, Ashland was included in the Methodist Church's cultural education program, called the Chautauqua Series. By the 1930s, one of the venues, Chautauqua Hall, had deteriorated to a dilapidated wooden shell. Angus Bowmer, a drama professor at the local college, noted the resemblance of the roofless structure to drawings of Shakespeare's Globe Theatre. He convinced the town to sponsor two performances of Shakespeare's plays and a boxing match (the Bard would have approved) as part of its 1935 July 4 celebration. The plays proved a great success, and the **OSF** (OSF; 541-482-4331; www.osfashland.org; cnr Main & Pioneer Sts; tickets $30-136; Tue-Sun Feb-Oct) was off and running.

Though it's rooted in Shakespearean and Elizabethan drama, the OSF does an equal amount of revivals and international contemporary theater. Eleven productions run in three theaters: the outdoor **Elizabethan Theatre** (June to October), the **Angus Bowmer Theatre** and the intimate **Thomas Theatre**. No children under six. Performances sell out quickly, but the box office sometimes has (usually discounted) rush tickets an hour before showtime.

Check with the **OSF Welcome Center** (541-482-2111; 76 N Main St; 11am-5pm Tue-Sun) for other events, including scholarly lectures, play readings, concerts and pre-show talks. There are backstage tours (adult/child $20/14), which should be booked a week or so in advance.

This is a central and somewhat upscale hostel (shoes off inside!) in a bungalow on the National Register. Most private rooms share bathrooms; some can be connected to dorms. Hangout spaces include the cozy basement living room and the shady front porch. No pets, and no alcohol or smoking on the premises; call ahead, as reception times are limited. All ages are welcome.

Palm BOUTIQUE HOTEL $$

(541-482-2636; www.palmcottages.com; 1065 Siskiyou Blvd; d $141-289;) Fabulous small motel remodeled into 16 charming garden-cottage rooms and suites (some with kitchens). It's an oasis of green on a busy avenue, complete with grassy lawns and a saltwater pool. A house nearby harbors three large suites (from $249). Lots of ecopractices from zero gasoline use to free charging stations for electric vehicles.

Eating & Drinking

Morning Glory CAFE $

(541-488-8636; 1149 Siskiyou Blvd; mains $10-17; 8am-1:15pm) This colorful, casual cafe is one of Ashland's best breakfast joints. Creative dishes include the Alaskan-crab omelet, vegetarian hash with roasted chilies, and shrimp cakes with poached eggs. For lunch there's gourmet salad and sandwiches. Go early or late to avoid a long wait.

Agave MEXICAN $

(541-488-1770; www.agavetaco.net; 5 Granite St; tacos $3.75-6; 11:30am-8pm Tue-Sun, later hours summer) Tasty and creative tacos are cooked up at this popular restaurant. There's the regular stuff such as *carnitas* (little meats) and grilled chicken, but for something more exotic go for the shredded duck or sautéed lobster. There's ceviche, salads and tamales, too.

Caldera Brewery & Restaurant BREWPUB $$

(541-482-4677; www.calderabrewing.com; 590 Clover Lane; mains $10-23; 11am-10pm;) This bright, airy brewery-restaurant just off I-5 has pleasant outdoor seating and views of the countryside. It's kid-friendly until 10pm and serves pizza, fancy pasta, burgers and good salads. Wash it all down with one of the 40 beers on tap. Also located at 31 Water St, on the river in downtown Ashland, with more of a cozy pub atmosphere.

Greenleaf DINER $$

(541-482-2808; www.greenleafrestaurant.com; 49 N Main St; mains $10-16; 8am-8pm;) This casual diner, with booths as well as counter seating, focuses on sustainable ingredients in innovative combinations. There are lots of vegetarian options, and the specials board is well worth checking out, although the regular menu is so massive that you might not ever need to venture that far. There's a whole gluten-free menu, too.

Ashland Chamber of Commerce (☎541-482-3486; www.ashlandchamber.com; 110 E Main St; ⏲9am-5pm Mon-Fri)

Jacksonville

This small but endearing former-gold-prospecting town is the oldest settlement in southern Oregon and a National Historic Landmark. The town's main drag is lined with well-preserved buildings dating from the 1880s, now converted into boutiques and galleries. Music-lovers shouldn't miss the September **Britt Festival** (☎541-773-6077; www.brittfest.org; cnr 1st & Fir Sts; tickets around $42; ⏲Jun-Sep), a world-class musical experience that brings in top-name performers. Seek more enlightenment at the **Chamber of Commerce** (☎541-899-8118; www.jacksonvilleoregon.org; 185 N Oregon St; ⏲10am-3pm daily May-Oct, to 2pm Mon-Sat Nov-Apr).

Jacksonville is full of fancy B&Bs; for budget motels head 6 miles east to Medford. The **Jacksonville Inn** (☎541-899-1900; www.jacksonvilleinn.com; 175 E California St; r $159-325;) is the most pleasant abode, shoehorned downtown in an 1863 building with regal antique-stuffed rooms. There's a fine restaurant on-site.

Oregon Caves National Monument & Preserve

This very popular cave (singular) lies 19 miles east of Cave Junction on Hwy 46. Three miles of passages are explored via 90-minute cave tours that include 520 rocky steps and dripping chambers running along the River Styx. Dress warmly, wear shoes with good traction and be prepared to get dripped on.

Cave Junction, 28 miles south of Grants Pass on US 199 (Redwood Hwy), provides the region's services – though one of the best accommodations in the area is **Out 'n' About Treesort** (☎541-592-2208; www.treehouses.com; 300 Page Creek Rd, Takilma; tree houses $150-330;) – super-fun tree houses in Katilma, 12 miles south. For fancy lodgings right at the cave there's the impressive **Oregon Caves Chateau** (☎541-592-3400; www.oregoncaveschateau.com; 20000 Caves Hwy; r $117-212; ⏲May-Oct;) – be sure to grab a milkshake at the old-fashioned soda fountain here.

Eastern Oregon

Oregon east of the Cascades bears little resemblance to its wetter western cohort, either physically or culturally. Few people live here – the biggest town, Pendleton, numbers only 17,000 – and the region holds high plateaus, painted hills, alkali lake-beds and the country's deepest river gorge.

John Day Fossil Beds National Monument

Within the soft rocks and crumbly soils of John Day country lies one of the world's greatest fossil collections, laid down between six and 50 million years ago. The national monument includes 22 sq miles at three different units: Sheep Rock Unit, Painted Hills Unit and Clarno Unit. Each has hiking trails and interpretive displays.

Visit the excellent **Thomas Condon Paleontology Center** (☎541-987-2333; www.nps.gov/joda; 32651 Hwy 19, Kimberly; ⏲10am-5pm daily Mar-May, Sep & Oct, 10am-5pm Tue-Sat Nov-Feb) FREE, 2 miles north of US 26 at the **Sheep Rock Unit**. Displays include a three-toed horse and petrified dung-beetle balls, along with many other fossils and geologic history exhibits. If you feel like walking, take the short hike up the Blue Basin Trail.

The **Painted Hills Unit**, near the town of Mitchell, consists of low-slung, colorfully banded hills formed about 30 million years ago. Ten million years older is the **Clarno Unit**, which exposes mud flows that washed over an Eocene-era forest and eroded into distinctive, sheer white cliffs topped with spires and turrets of stone.

Rafting is popular on the John Day River, the longest free-flowing river in the state. **Oregon River Experiences** (☎800-827-1358; www.oregonriver.com; 4-/5-/9-day trips per person $675/795/1365; ⏲May-Jun) offers trips of up to nine days. There's also good fishing for smallmouth bass and rainbow trout; find out more at the Oregon Department of Fish & Wildlife (www.dfw.state.or.us).

Most towns in the area have at least one hotel; these include the atmospheric **Historic Oregon Hotel** (☎541-462-3027; www.theoregonhotel.net; 104 E Main St, Mitchell; d with/without bath from $65/55;) in Mitchell. The town of John Day has most of the district's services and there are several public campgrounds in the area (sites $5), including Lone Pine and Big Bend, both on Hwy 402.

Wallowa Mountains Area

The Wallowa Mountains, with their glacier-hewn peaks and crystalline lakes, are among the most beautiful natural areas in Oregon. The only drawback is the large number of visitors who flock here in summer, especially to the pretty Wallowa Lake area.

Escape them all on one of several long hikes into the nearby **Eagle Cap Wilderness**, such as the 6-mile one-way jaunt to **Aneroid Lake** or the 8-mile trek on the **Ice Lake Trail**.

Just north of the mountains, in the Wallowa Valley, **Enterprise** is a homely backcountry town with several motels – try the **Ponderosa** (541-426-3186; www.theponderosamotel.com; 102 E Greenwood St; r from $90;). If you like beer and good food, don't miss the town's microbrewery, **Terminal Gravity Brewing** (541-426-3000; www.terminalgravitybrewing.com; 803 SE School St; mains $9-17; 11am-9pm, to 8pm Sun & Mon). Just 6 miles south is Enterprise's fancy cousin, the upscale town of **Joseph**. Expensive bronze galleries and artsy boutiques line the main strip, along with some good eateries.

Hells Canyon

The mighty Snake River has taken 13 million years to carve its path through the high plateaus of eastern Oregon to its present depth of 8000ft, creating America's deepest gorge.

For perspective, drive 30 miles northeast from Joseph to Imnaha, where a slow-going 24-mile gravel road leads up to **Hat Point**. From here you can see the Wallowa Mountains, Idaho's Seven Devils, the Imnaha River and the wilds of the canyon itself. This road is open from late May until snowfall; give yourself two hours each way for the drive.

For white-water action and spectacular scenery, head down to **Hells Canyon Dam**, 25 miles north of the small community of Oxbow. A few miles past the dam, the road ends at the **Hells Canyon Visitors Center** (www.fs.usda.gov; Hells Canyon Rd, Hells Canyon Dam; 8am-4pm May-Oct), which has good advice on the area's campgrounds and hiking trails. Beyond here, the Snake River drops 1300ft through wild rapids accessible only by jet boat or raft. **Hells Canyon Adventures** (800-422-3568; www.hellscanyonadventures.com; 4200 Hells Canyon Dam Rd; jet-boat tours adult/child from $100/70; May-Sep) is the main operator running raft trips and jet-boat tours (reservations required).

The area has many campgrounds and more solid lodgings. Just outside Imnaha is the beautiful **Imnaha River Inn** (541-577-6002; www.imnahariverinn.com; 73946 Rimrock Rd; s/d without bath from $75/135), a B&B replete with Hemingway-esque animal trophies. For more services, head to the towns of Enterprise, Joseph and Halfway.

Steens Mountain & Alvord Desert

The highest peak in southeastern Oregon, Steens Mountain (9773ft) is part of a massive, 30-mile-long fault-block range that was formed about 15 million years ago.

Beginning in Frenchglen, the gravel 59-mile **Steens Mountain Loop Rd** is Oregon's highest road, offers the range's best sights, and has access to camping and hiking trails. You'll see sagebrush, bands of juniper and aspen forests, and finally fragile rocky tundra at the top. **Kiger Gorge Viewpoint**, 25 miles up from Frenchglen, is especially stunning. It takes about three hours all the way around if you're just driving through, but you'll want to see the sights, so give yourself much more time. You can also see the eastern side of the Steens via the **Fields-Denio Rd**, which goes through the Alvord Desert between Hwys 205 and 78. Take a full tank of gas and plenty of water, and be prepared for weather changes at any time of year.

Frenchglen, with a population of roughly 12, nonetheless supports the historic **Frenchglen Hotel** (541-493-2825; www.frenchglenhotel.com; 39184 Hwy 205; d/tr without bath $79/87, Drovers' Inn d/q $125/145; mid-Mar–early Nov;), with eight small rooms, huge meals (reserve for dinners), a small store with a seasonal gas pump and not much else. There are camping options on the Steens Mountain Loop Rd, such as the BLM's pretty **Page Springs** ($8 per vehicle, open year-round). A few other campgrounds further into the loop are very pleasant, but accessible in summer only. Water is available at all of these campgrounds. Free backcountry camping is also allowed in the Steens.

Understand Western USA

Western USA Today

Western USA is a window on a nation in turmoil. Southwestern states like California, New Mexico and Arizona are America's ground zero when it comes to immigration, while the nation's political dividing lines seem to run through the heart of the West. The environment is also increasingly a talking point, whatever the political climate, from arguments over how (or whether) to combat human-induced climate change, to the extreme weather events that appear to grow in intensity with each passing year.

Best on Film

Stagecoach (1939) Monument Valley may be the true star of this John Ford Western.

Butch Cassidy & the Sundance Kid (1969) The adventures of two real-life outlaws hiding in Utah.

Thelma & Louise (1991) Two gal pals run from the law and into stunning Southwest scenery.

Fear and Loathing in Las Vegas (1998) A darkly comic adaptation of Hunter S Thompson's road-movie classic.

The Revenant (2015) A harrowing thriller set in the lawless 1820s frontier, with wilderness Montana as backdrop.

Best in Print

The Grapes of Wrath (John Steinbeck; 1939) Dust Bowl migrants travel west to California.

Desert Solitaire (Edward Abbey; 1968) Essays about the Southwest and industrial tourism by no-holds-barred eco-curmudgeon.

Ceremony (Leslie Marmon Silko; 1977) Novel based in the rich heritage of New Mexico's Pueblo people.

Wild (Cheryl Strayed; 2013) Author hikes the Pacific Crest Trail solo after the death of her mother.

The Earth is Weeping (Peter Cozzens; 2017) Landmark coverage of the 19th-century wars for the American West.

The Immigration Debate

Out here in the West, the national debate on immigration carries extra significance. The latest estimates suggest that California, Arizona and New Mexico, each sharing a border with Mexico, are collectively home to more than three million undocumented migrants (and rising). From the Trump administration's policy of separating children of undocumented immigrants from their parents in 2018 to the appearance of anti-immigration militias and the president's threat to close the border with Mexico in 2019, the heightened tensions surrounding immigration are taking their toll here more than anywhere else. The result is an intolerable strain upon local social services, government agencies, and the cross-border trade upon which these states depend. And then there's President Trump's promised border wall, with its capacity to divide opinion arguably greater than its ability to stem the tide of arrivals from the south. It should be hardly surprising, therefore, that the way this debate plays out over the coming years will be watched particularly closely in the Southwest.

Political Fault Lines

Today's America can seem more divided than at any time in its recent history. Whether or not that's true, poll numbers point to a deep schism and the West is no exception. In the 2016 presidential elections, Hillary Clinton won California by more than 29% and swept the West Coast, winning Oregon and Washington by double-digit margins; New Mexico wasn't far behind, with a victory margin of 8.3%. The reverse happened in Idaho, Montana and Wyoming, where President Trump took each state by more than 30%; his margin of victory in Wyoming was a remarkable 70.1% to 22.5%. In only three states was the margin close – Hillary Clinton carried Nevada by 2.4% and Colorado by 2.8%, while

Donald Trump won Arizona by 4.1%. When drawn on a map, it's a reminder that the increasingly entrenched dividing line between red and blue states, between liberal coast and conservative interior, runs through the very heart of the American West. In such a climate, the death of respected Arizona senator John McCain, much respected on both sides of the party divide, on 25 August 2018 felt very much like the end of an era.

Climate Change

If immigration is the most divisive issue in modern America, climate change is not far behind. Since winning the November 2016 presidential election, President Trump and his conservative allies have wound back numerous Obama-era regulations that were designed to reduce the impact of human-induced global warming. In June 2017 President Trump announced plans to withdraw from the Paris Agreement, an agreement between 195 nations to mitigate global warming. On the other side of the debate, California enacted the *Global Warming Solutions Act of 2006*, and has numerous policies encouraging clean and alternative sources of energy, with the aim of returning the levels of harmful gases in the air to 80% of 1990 levels by 2050. At the time of writing, Oregon's state legislature was moving forward with an attempt to become the second state to introduce a similar cap-and-trade emissions law. And in 2019, the governor of neighboring Washington, Jay Inslee, launched an ultimately unsuccessful bid to be the Democrat nominee for president, running a single-issue campaign on his plans to address climate change.

Extreme Weather

In the summer of 2018, with drought conditions and record temperatures fanning the flames, California experienced its worst wildfire season on record. The unusually long and intense wildfire season lasted from June to November, and culminated in the Camp Fire in Butte County in the state's north – 86 people were killed and the town of Paradise (pop 26,000) was destroyed. In the winter that followed, avalanches reached record levels across the Rockies, especially in Colorado; the hurricane season began early and swept with rare and often devastating force across the Great Plains region; and flooding from Western rivers wrought devastation upon Nebraska, Missouri, Iowa and other Midwestern states. According to the Environmental Protection Authority, temperatures have increased by almost 2°F (1°C) in the last century, and although the exact causes of extreme weather events are unclear, climate change, residential development and government policy may all be factors. In October–November 2019 communities were again forced to face the threat of widespread fires.

AREA: **1.2 MILLION SQ MILES**

CURRENCY: **US DOLLAR ($)**

GDP: **US$5.2 TRILLION**

POPULATION: **75.84 MILLION**

if Western USA were 100 people

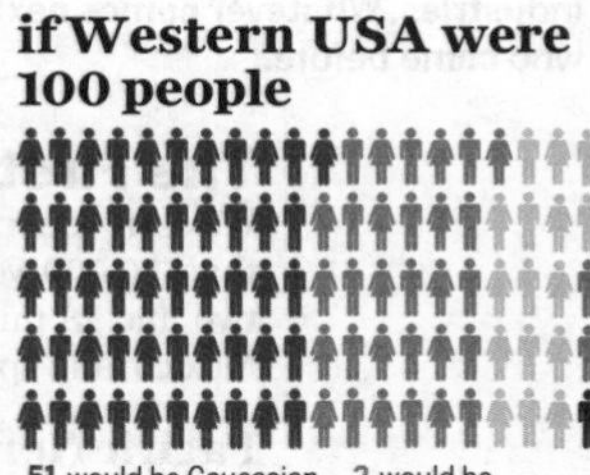

51 would be Caucasian
30 would be Latino
10 would be Asian
6 would be African American
2 would be Native American
1 would be other

belief systems

(% of population)

Protestant unaffiliated Catholic

5 Mormon
2 Jewish
other

population per sq mile

WESTERN USA

USA

CALIFORNIA

≈ 20 people

History

Throughout time, the West has been a place for seekers to reinvent fortunes. Its first inhabitants crossed the Bering Strait between modern-day Russia and Alaska and moved south to form diverse Native American communities that adapted to weather and landscape to build complex, sustainable societies. They were followed by the Spanish, explorers like Lewis and Clark, gold-rush enthusiasts and today's immigrants and tech industries. Whatever comes next will be highly influenced by the frontier spirit of those who came before.

The First Americans

Western America's earliest inhabitants crossed the Bering Strait more than 20,000 years ago. When Europeans arrived, somewhere between two and 18 million Native American people lived north of present-day Mexico, and spoke more than 300 languages.

The Apache Wars: The Hunt for Geronimo, the Apache Kid, and the Captive Boy Who Started the Longest War in American History (Paul Andrew Hutton; 2016) is a memorable history of the frontier wars in the southwest.

Pacific Northwest

In the Pacific Northwest, early coastal inhabitants went out to sea in pursuit of whales or sea lions, or depended on catching salmon and cod and collecting shellfish. On land they hunted deer and elk while gathering berries and roots. Food was stored for the long winters, when free time could be spent on artistic, religious and cultural pursuits. The construction of ornately carved cedar canoes led to extensive trading networks that stretched along the coast.

Inland, a regional culture based on seasonal migration developed among tribes. During salmon runs, tribes gathered at rapids and waterfalls to net or harpoon fish. In the harsh landscapes of Oregon's southern desert, tribes were nomadic peoples who hunted and scavenged in the northern reaches of the Great Basin desert.

California

By AD 1500, more than 300,000 Native Americans spoke some 100 distinct languages in the California region. Central-coast fishing communities built subterranean roundhouses and saunas, where they held

TIMELINE

20,000–40,000 BC

The first peoples to come to the Americas arrive from Central Asia by migrating over a wide land bridge between Siberia and Alaska (when sea levels were lower than today).

8000 BC

Widespread extinction of ice-age mammals, including the woolly mammoth, due to cooperative hunting by humans and a warming climate. People begin hunting smaller game and gathering native plants.

1300

The entire civilization of Ancestral Puebloans living in Mesa Verde, CO, abandons the area, possibly due to drought, leaving behind a sophisticated city of cliff dwellings.

ceremonies, told stories and gambled for fun. Northwest hunting communities constructed big houses and redwood dugout canoes, while the inhabitants of southwest California created sophisticated pottery and developed irrigation systems that made farming in the desert possible. Native Americans in California had no written language but observed oral contracts and zoning laws.

Within a century of the arrival of Spanish colonists in 1769, California's Native American population was decimated to 20,000 by European diseases, conscripted labor regimes and famine.

Cattle Kingdom: The Hidden History of the Cowboy West (Christopher Knowlton; 2017) is one of the best histories of the region, from cattle barons and cowboys to Teddy Roosevelt.

The Southwest & Southern Colorado

Archaeologists believe that the Southwest's first inhabitants were hunters. As the population grew, wild game became extinct, forcing hunters to augment their diets with berries, seeds, roots and fruits. After 3000 BC, contacts with farmers in what is now central Mexico led to the beginnings of agriculture in the Southwest.

By about 100 AD, three dominant cultures were emerging in the Southwest: the Hohokam of the desert, the Mogollon of the central mountains and valleys, and the Ancestral Puebloans – formerly known as the Anasazi.

The Hohokam lived in the deserts of Arizona, adapting to desert life by creating an incredible river-fed irrigation system. They also developed low earthen pyramids and sunken ball courts with earthen walls. By about 1400, the Hohokam abandoned their villages. There are many theories on this tribe's disappearance, but it most likely involved a combination of drought, overhunting, conflict among groups and disease.

The Mogollon culture settled near the Mexican border from 200 BC to 1400 AD. They lived in small communities, often elevated on isolated mesas or ridgetops, and built simple pit dwellings. Although they farmed, they depended more on hunting and foraging for food. By around the 13th or 14th century, the Mogollon had probably been peacefully incorporated into the Ancestral Puebloan groups from the north.

The Ancestral Puebloans inhabited the Colorado Plateau, also called the Four Corners area. This culture left the richest archaeological sites and ancient settlements that are still inhabited in the Southwest. Their descendants live in Pueblo Indian communities in New Mexico. The oldest links with the Ancestral Puebloans are found among the Hopi tribe of northern Arizona. The mesa-top village of Old Oraibi, now inhabited by the Hopi, has been inhabited since the 1100s, making it the oldest continuously inhabited settlement in North America.

Many modern Pueblo Indians object to the term 'Anasazi,' a Navajo word meaning 'enemy ancestors'; it's no longer used.

The Great Plains

The seemingly endless plains that begin east of the Rockies, sweeping east through Montana, Wyoming and beyond, play a significant role in

1492

Christopher Columbus 'discovers' America, eventually making three voyages to the Caribbean. He dubs the indigenous inhabitants 'Indians,' mistakenly thinking he'd reached the Indian subcontinent.

1598

A large force of Spanish explorers, led by Don Juan de Oñate, stops near present-day El Paso, TX, and declares the land to the north New Mexico for Spain.

c 1600

Santa Fe, America's oldest capital city, is founded. The Palace of Governors is the only 17th-century structure that survives into the 21st century; the rest of Santa Fe is destroyed by a 1914 fire.

1787–91

The Constitutional Convention in Philadelphia draws up the US Constitution. The Bill of Rights is later adopted as constitutional amendments articulating citizens' rights.

the story of the American West. Numerous Native American tribes called the plains home, among them the Lakota Sioux, Shoshone, Crow, Cheyenne and others. Prior to the European arrival and the push to colonize the West, the Great Plains were a vast realm of shifting alliances and territorial boundaries. All the tribal nations that lived in the region hunted vast herds of bison, including sophisticated strategies that drove entire herds off the cliffs. One place where the tradition took place and can still be imagined is the **First Peoples Buffalo Jump State Park** (☎406-866-2217; http://stateparks.mt.gov/first-peoples-buffalo-jump; 342 Ulm-Vaughn Rd; ⏰8am-6pm mid-Apr–mid-Sep, 10am-4pm Wed-Sat, noon-4pm Sun mid-Sep–mid-Apr) in northern Montana.

In 1680, during the Pueblo Revolt, the northern New Mexico Pueblo banded together to drive out the Spanish after the latter's bloody campaign to destroy Puebloan ceremonial objects. The Spanish were pushed south of the Rio Grande and the Pueblo people held Santa Fe until 1682.

The Europeans Arrive

The Spanish arrived in the Southwest in the 1540s, looking for the Seven Cities of Gold. Missions and missionaries followed in the 1700s as the Spanish staked their claim along the California coast.

Spain's Mission Impossible

Francisco Vázquez de Coronado led the first major expedition into North America from the south in 1540. In addition to 300 soldiers, the traveling party included hundreds of Native American guides and herds of livestock. It also marked the first major violence between the Spanish and the native people.

The expedition's goal was to reach the fabled, immensely rich Seven Cities of Cibola. For two years, the expedition traveled through what is now Arizona, New Mexico and as far east as Kansas. Instead of gold and precious gems, the expedition found adobe pueblos, which they violently commandeered. During the Spaniards' first few years in northern New Mexico, they tried to defeat the pueblos, with much bloodshed.

When 18th-century Russian and English trappers arrived trading valuable otter pelts from Alta California, Spain concocted a plan for colonization. For the glory of God and the tax coffers of Spain, missions would be built across the state and within 10 years these would be going concerns run by local converts.

The Spanish established Santa Fe as the capital of the province of New Spain around 1610. The city remains New Mexico's capital today and is the oldest state capital in what is now the USA.

Spain's missionizing plan was approved in 1769, and Franciscan Padre Junípero Serra secured support to set up *presidios* (military posts) alongside several missions in northern and central California in the 1770s and '80s. Clergy relied on soldiers to round up conscripts to build missions. In exchange for their labor, Native Americans were allowed one meal a day (when available) and a place in God's kingdom – which came much sooner than expected due to the smallpox the Spanish brought with them. In the Southwest, more than half of the pueblo populations were decimated by smallpox, measles and typhus.

1803

Napoleon sells the Louisiana Territory to the US for $15 million, thereby extending the boundaries of the new nation from the Mississippi River to the Rocky Mountains.

1803–06

President Jefferson sends Meriwether Lewis and William Clark west. Guided by Shoshone tribeswoman Sacagawea, they trailblaze from St Louis, MO, to the Pacific Ocean and back.

1811

Pacific Fur Company mogul John Jacob Astor establishes Fort Astoria, the first permanent US settlement on the Pacific Coast. He later becomes the country's first millionaire.

1841

Wagon trains follow the Oregon Trail, and by 1847 over 6500 emigrants a year are heading West, to Oregon, California and Mormon-dominated Utah.

Westward, Ho!

As the 19th century dawned on the young nation, optimism was the mood of the day. With the invention of the cotton gin in 1793 – followed by threshers, reapers, mowers and later combines – agriculture was industrialized, and US commerce surged. The 1803 Louisiana Purchase doubled US territory, and expansion west of the Appalachian Mountains began in earnest.

Exploiting the West's vast resources became a patriotic duty in the 1840s – a key aspect of America's belief in its Manifest Destiny. During the early territorial days, movement of goods and people from the East to the West was very slow. Horses, mule trains and stagecoaches represented state-of-the-art transportation at the time.

An estimated 400,000 people trekked west across America between 1840 and 1860, lured by tales of gold, promises of religious freedom and visions of fertile farmland. The 'Wild West' years soon followed with ranchers, cowboys, miners and entrepreneurs staking claims and raising hell. Law, order and civilization arrived, hastened by the telegraph, the transcontinental railroad and a continual flow of new arrivals who just wanted to settle down and enjoy their piece of the American pie.

You can follow the Lewis and Clark expedition on its extraordinary journey west to the Pacific and back again online at www.pbs.org/lewisandclark, featuring historical maps, photo albums and journal excerpts.

LEWIS & CLARK

After President Thomas Jefferson bought the Louisiana Territory from Napoleon in 1803 for $15 million, he sent his personal secretary, Meriwether Lewis, west to chart North America's western regions. The goal was to find a waterway to the Pacific while exploring the newly acquired Louisiana Purchase and establish a foothold for American interests. Lewis, who had no training for exploration, convinced his good friend William Clark, an experienced frontiersman and army veteran, to tag along. In 1804 the 40-member party, called the Corps of Discovery, left St Louis.

The expedition fared relatively well, in part because of the presence of Sacagawea, a young Shoshone woman who had been forcibly married to a French-Canadian trapper in the entourage. Sacagawea proved invaluable as guide, translator and ambassador to the area's Native Americans, and gave birth to a son while on the expedition. York, Clark's African American slave, also softened tensions between the group and the Native Americans they encountered en route.

The party traveled some 8000 miles in about two years, documenting everything they came across in their journals. Meticulous notes were made about 122 animals and 178 plants, with some new discoveries along the way. In 1805 the party finally reached the mouth of the Columbia River and the Pacific Ocean at Cape Disappointment, and bedded down for the winter nearby, thus establishing Fort Clatsop.

Lewis and Clark returned to a hero's welcome in St Louis in 1806.

1844

First telegraph line is inaugurated with the phrase 'What hath God wrought?'. In 1845 Congress approves a transcontinental railroad, completed in 1869. Together, telegraph and train open the frontier.

1846–48

The battle for the West is waged with the Mexican–American War. The war ends with the 1848 Treaty of Guadalupe Hidalgo that gives most of present-day Arizona and New Mexico to the USA.

1847

Mormons fleeing religious persecution in Illinois start arriving in Salt Lake City; over the next 20 years more than 70,000 Mormons head to Utah via the Mormon Pioneer Trail.

1849

After the 1848 discovery of gold near Sacramento, an epic cross-country gold rush sees 60,000 'forty-niners' flock to California's mother lode. San Francisco's population explodes to 25,000.

One of the major routes was the Oregon Trail. Spanning six states, it sorely tested the families who embarked on this perilous trip. Their belongings were squirreled away under canvas-topped wagons, which often trailed livestock. The journey could take up to eight months, and by the time the settlers reached eastern Oregon their food supplies were almost gone. Other major routes included the Santa Fe Trail and the Old Spanish Trail, which ran from Santa Fe into central Utah and across Nevada to Los Angeles in California. Regular stagecoach services along the Santa Fe Trail began in 1849; the Mormon Trail reached Salt Lake City in 1847.

Among the provisions recommended for those traveling the Oregon Trail were coffee (15lb per person), bacon (25lb per person), 1lb of castile soap, citric acid to prevent scurvy, and a live cow for milk and emergency meat.

The arrival of more people and resources via the railroad led to further land exploration and the frequent discovery of mineral deposits. Many Western mining towns were founded in the 1870s and 1880s; some, like Santa Rita, are now ghost towns, while others, like Tombstone and Silver City, remain active.

The Long Walk & Apache Conflicts

For decades, US forces pushed west across the continent, killing or forcibly moving whole tribes of Native Americans who were in their way. The most widely known incident is the forceful relocation of many Navajo in 1864. US forces, led by Kit Carson, destroyed Navajo fields, orchards and houses, and forced the people into surrendering or withdrawing into remote parts of Canyon de Chelly. Eventually, they were starved out. About 10,000 Navajo were rounded up and marched 400 miles east to a camp at Bosque Redondo, near Fort Sumner, NM. Hundreds of Native Americans died from sickness, starvation or gunshot wounds along the way. The Navajo call this 'The Long Walk,' and it remains an important part of Navajo history.

Further north on the Great Plains, massacres took place against the Shoshone at Bear River (Idaho) in 1863, and of the Cheyenne and Arapaho in Sand Creek (Colorado) a year later. The 1876 victory of a Native American coalition led by Crazy Horse, inspired by Sitting Bull, and comprised of the Sioux, Northern Cheyenne and Arapaho at the Battle of the Little Bighorn, also known as Custer's Last Stand, was the last victory for the Plains tribes. The retaliatory campaigns were devastating and decisive, and the massacre of the Lakota (Sioux) at Wounded Knee (in modern-day South Dakota) in 1890 effectively marked the end of Native American resistance across the Great Plains.

Junípero Serra was canonized as a Catholic saint by Pope Francis in 2015. The process was not without controversy, with historians and Native Americans pointing to the mistreatment of native peoples under his watch.

The last serious conflicts were between US troops and the Apache. This was partly because raiding was the essential path to manhood for the Apache. As US forces and settlers moved into Apache land, they became targets for the raids that were part of the Apache way of life. These continued under the leadership of Mangas Coloradas, Cochise, Victorio and, finally, Geronimo. The latter surrendered in 1886 and was for a time confined to a reservation in Arizona after being promised that he and the Apache would

1861–65

American Civil War erupts between North and South. The celebration of the war's end on April 9, 1865, is marred by President Lincoln's assassination five days later.

1864

Kit Carson forces around 10,000 Navajo to walk 400 miles to a camp near Fort Sumner. Hundreds of Native Americans die from sickness, starvation and gunshot wounds along 'The Long Walk.'

1876

At the Battle of the Little Bighorn, in what is now southeastern Montana, a Native American force of Sioux, Arapaho and Cheyenne, led by Crazy Horse, defeat the US Army led by General Custer.

1881

Wyatt Earp, his brothers Virgil and Morgan, and Doc Holliday, kill Billy Clanton and the McLaury brothers in the famous gunfight at the OK Corral in Tombstone, AZ.

be imprisoned for two years then allowed to return to their homeland. As with many promises made during these years, this one, too, was broken.

Even after the wars were over, Native Americans were treated like second-class citizens. Non–Native Americans used legal loopholes and technicalities to take over reservation land. Many children were removed from reservations and shipped off to boarding schools where they were taught in English and punished for speaking their own languages or behaving 'like Indians' – this practice continued into the 1930s.

The moving Boarding School Experience exhibit at the Heard Museum in Phoenix traces the forced relocation of Native American children to federally run boarding schools in the 1800s and 1900s for 'Americanization.'

Reforming the Wild West

When the great earthquake and fire hit San Francisco in 1906, it signaled change for California. With public funds for citywide water mains and fire hydrants siphoned off by corrupt bosses, there was only one functioning water source in San Francisco. When the smoke lifted, one thing was clear: it was time for the Wild West to change.

While San Francisco was rebuilt at a rate of 15 buildings per day, California's reformers set to work on city, state and national politics, one plank at a time. Californians concerned about public health and trafficking in women pushed for passage of the 1914 statewide Red Light Abatement Act. The Mexican Revolution (1910–20) brought a new wave of migrants and revolutionary ideas, including ethnic pride and worker solidarity. As California's ports grew, longshoremen's unions coordinated a historic 83-day strike in 1934 along the entire West Coast that forced concessions for safer working conditions and fair pay.

THE WILD WEST

Romanticized tales of gunslingers, cattle rustlers, outlaws and train robbers fuel Wild West legends. Good and bad guys were designations in flux – a tough outlaw in one state became a popular sheriff in another. Gunfights were more frequently the result of mundane political struggles in emerging towns than storied blood feuds. New mining towns mushroomed overnight, playing host to rowdy saloons and bordellos where miners would come to brawl, drink and gamble. Riders and swift horses were the backbone of the short-lived but legendary Pony Express (1860–61). They carried letters between Missouri and California in an astounding 10 days!

Legendary figures Billy the Kid and Sheriff Pat Garrett, both involved in the infamous Lincoln County War, were active in the late 1870s. Billy the Kid reputedly shot and killed more than 20 men in a brief career as a gunslinger – he himself was shot and killed by Garrett at the age of 21. In 1881 Wyatt Earp, along with his brothers Virgil and Morgan, and Doc Holliday, shot dead Billy Clanton and the McLaury brothers (Frank and Tom) in a blazing gunfight at the OK Corral in Tombstone – the showdown took less than a minute. Both sides accused the other of cattle rustling, but the real story will never be known.

1882

Racist sentiment, particularly in California (where over 50,000 Chinese immigrants had arrived since 1848) leads to the Chinese Exclusion Act, the only US immigration law to exclude a specific race.

1919

The Grand Canyon becomes the USA's 15th national park, and a dirt road to the North Rim is built from Kanab. By 2018, the park is visited by 6.38 million people annually.

1938

Route 66 becomes the first cross-country highway to be completely paved, including more than 750 miles across Arizona and New Mexico. The Mother Road is officially decommissioned in 1984.

1945

The first atomic bomb is detonated in the ironically named Jornada del Muerto (Journey of the Dead Man) Valley in southern New Mexico, which is now part of the White Sands Missile Range.

EUREKA!

Real-estate speculator, lapsed Mormon and tabloid publisher Sam Brannan was looking to unload some California swampland in 1848 when he heard rumors of gold flakes found near Sutter's Mill, 120 miles from San Francisco. Figuring this news should sell some newspapers and raise real-estate values, Brannan published the rumor as fact. Initially the story didn't generate excitement. So Brannan ran another story, this time verified by Mormon employees at Sutter's Mill who had sworn him to secrecy. Brannan reportedly kept his word by running through the San Francisco streets, brandishing gold entrusted to him as tithes for the Mormon church, shouting, 'Gold on the American River!'

Other newspapers hastily published stories of 'gold mountains' near San Francisco. By 1850, the year California was fast-tracked for admission as the 31st state, its non-Native population had ballooned from 15,000 to 93,000. Most arrivals weren't Americans, but Peruvians, Australians, Chileans and Mexicans, with some Chinese, Irish, Hawaiian and French prospectors.

At the height of the Depression in 1935, some 200,000 farming families fleeing the drought-stricken Dust Bowl in Texas and Oklahoma arrived in California, where they found scant pay and deplorable working conditions at major farming concerns. California's artists alerted middle America to the migrants' plight, and the nation rallied around Dorothea Lange's haunting documentary photos of famine-struck families and John Steinbeck's harrowing fictionalized account in his 1939 novel *The Grapes of Wrath*.

WWII & the Atomic Age

The West took on a more important economic and technological role during WWII. Scientists developed the atomic bomb in the secret city of Los Alamos. War-related industries, such as timber production and work at naval yards and airplane factories, thrived in the Pacific Northwest and California.

Los Alamos

In 1943 Los Alamos, NM, then home to a boys school perched on a 7400ft mesa, was chosen as the top-secret headquarters of the Manhattan Project, the code name for the research and development of the atomic bomb. The 772-acre site, accessed by two dirt roads, had no gas or oil lines and only one wire service, and it was surrounded by forest.

Isolation and security marked every aspect of life on 'the hill.' Not only was resident movement restricted and mail censored, there was also no outside contact by radio or telephone. Perhaps even more unsettling was the fact that most residents had no idea why they were living in Los

1947

An unidentified object falls in the desert near Roswell. The government first calls it a crashed disk, then a day later a weather balloon, and mysteriously closes off the area.

1964

Congress passes the Civil Rights Act, outlawing discrimination on the basis of race, color, religion, sex or national origin. First proposed by Kennedy, it is one of President Johnson's crowning achievements.

1973

The debut of the MGM Grand signals the dawn of the corporate-owned 'megaresort,' and sparks a building bonanza along Las Vegas' Strip that's still going strong.

1976

Designed by Steve Wozniak, the Apple Computer 1 is released. With 4KB of memory, it costs $666. Apple becomes integral to the identity of Silicon Valley.

Alamos. Knowledge was on a 'need to know' basis; everyone knew only as much as their job required.

In just under two years, Los Alamos scientists successfully detonated the first atomic bomb at the Trinity site, now White Sands Missile Range.

After the US detonated the atomic bomb in Japan, the secret city of Los Alamos was exposed to the public. The city continued to be cloaked in secrecy, however, until 1957, when restrictions on visiting were lifted.

Twenty-year-old artist and vagabond Everett Ruess explored the Four Corners region in the early 1930s. He disappeared under mysterious circumstances outside of Escalante, UT, in November 1934. Read his evocative letters in the book *Everett Ruess: A Vagabond for Beauty*, with an afterword by Edward Abbey.

Changing Workforce & New Industries

California's workforce permanently changed in WWII, when women and African Americans were recruited for wartime industries and Mexican workers were brought in to fill labor shortages. Contracts in military communications and aviation attracted an international elite of engineers, who would launch California's high-tech industry. Within a decade after the war, California's population had grown by 40%, reaching almost 13 million.

The war also brought economic fortune to the Pacific Northwest, when the area became the nation's largest lumber producer and both Oregon's and Washington's naval yards bustled, along with William Boeing's airplane factory. The region continued to prosper through the second half of the 20th century, attracting new migrations of educated, progressively minded settlers from the nation's east and south.

After the war, industry took on new forms, with Silicon Valley's dot-com industry drawing talented entrepreneurs to the Bay Area in the 1990s. The film industry still holds strong in Los Angeles, but tax incentives have drawn filmmakers to other western enclaves, particularly New Mexico.

California's Civil Rights Movement

When 117,000 Japanese Americans along the West Coast were ordered into internment camps by President Roosevelt in 1942, the San Francisco-based Japanese American Citizens League immediately filed suits that advanced all the way to the Supreme Court. These lawsuits established groundbreaking civil-rights legal precedents, and in 1992 internees received reparations and an official letter of apology for internment signed by President George HW Bush.

Adopting the nonviolent resistance practices of Mahatma Gandhi and Martin Luther King Jr, labor leaders César Chávez and Dolores Huerta formed United Farm Workers in 1962 to champion the rights of underrepresented immigrant laborers. While civil rights leaders marched on Washington, Chávez and Californian grape pickers marched on Sacramento, bringing the issue of fair wages and the health risks of pesticides to the nation's attention. When Bobby Kennedy was sent to investigate, he sided with Chávez, bringing Latinos into the US political fold.

On November 7, 1893, Colorado became the first US state – and one of the first places in the world – to grant women the right to vote.

1994

Amazon, one of the first major companies to sell products online, is launched in Seattle. Originally starting as a bookseller, it does not become annually profitable until 2003.

1999

From November 30 to December 1, 40,000 protesters in Seattle take on economic globalization at the World Trade Organization's international trade negotiations.

2002

Salt Lake City hosts the Winter Olympics, becoming the most populated place to ever hold the games. Women also compete in bobsled racing for the first time.

2008

Barack Obama is elected president of the United States, the first African American to hold the office.

Hollywood & Counterculture

In 1908 California became a convenient movie location for its consistent sunlight and versatile locations, although its role was limited to doubling for more exotic locales and providing backdrops for period-piece productions. But gradually, California began stealing the scene in movies and iconic TV shows with waving palms and sunny beaches.

For behind-the-scenes stories about Wild West legends, along with their photographs, pick up the monthly magazine *True West* (www.truewestmagazine.com), or visit the website to see who's in the spotlight.

Not all Californians saw themselves as extras in a movie, however. WWII sailors discharged for insubordination and homosexuality in San Francisco found themselves at home in North Beach's bebop jazz clubs, bohemian coffeehouses and, later, the City Lights bookstore. San Francisco became the home of free speech and free spirits, and soon everyone who was anyone was getting arrested: Beat poet Lawrence Ferlinghetti for publishing Allen Ginsberg's epic poem 'Howl', comedian Lenny Bruce for uttering the F-word onstage, and Carol Doda for going topless. When flower power faded, other Bay Area rebellions grew in its place: Black Power, gay pride and medical marijuana clubs.

But while Northern California had the more attention-grabbing counterculture from the 1940s to '60s, nonconformity in sunny Southern California shook America to the core. In 1947, when Senator Joseph McCarthy attempted to root out suspected communists in the movie industry, 10 writers and directors who refused to admit communist alliances or to name names were charged with contempt of Congress and barred from working in Hollywood. The Hollywood Ten's impassioned defenses of the Constitution were heard nationwide, and major Hollywood players boldly voiced dissent and hired blacklisted talent until California lawsuits put a legal end to McCarthyism in 1962.

On January 28, 1969, an oil rig dumped 200,000 gallons of oil into Santa Barbara Channel, killing dolphins, seals and some 3600 shore birds. The beach community organized a highly effective protest, spurring the establishment of the Environmental Protection Agency (1970).

In 2014 the series *Silicon Valley* premiered on HBO. Co-created by Mike Judge, the comedy follows the ups and downs of an internet start-up company and its quirky founders.

Geeking Out

When California's Silicon Valley introduced the first personal computer in 1968, Hewlett-Packard's 'light' (40lb) machine cost just $4900 (about $29,000 today). Hoping to bring computer power to the people, Steve Jobs (aged 22) and Steve Wozniak (aged 26) introduced the Apple II at the 1977 West Coast Computer Faire. It had unfathomable memory (4KB of RAM) and microprocessor speed (1MHz).

By the mid-1990s, an entire dot-com industry boomed in Silicon Valley with online start-ups, and suddenly people were getting their mail, news, politics, pet food and, yes, sex online. But when dot-com profits weren't forthcoming, venture funding dried up, and fortunes in stock

2010
Arizona passes controversial legislation requiring police officers to ask for identification from anyone they suspect of being in the US without authorization. Immigration-rights activists call for a boycott of the state.

2012
Colorado and Washington become the first states to legalize recreational marijuana for adults aged 21 and older.

2015
In a five-four decision, the US Supreme Court decides that same-sex marriage is a right guaranteed by the Constitution. Thirteen states banning such unions comply with the ruling and issue same-sex marriage licenses.

2016
A divided nation elects Donald Trump as the 45th president of the US through a majority in the electoral college, despite Hillary Clinton having won the popular vote.

options disappeared on one nasty Nasdaq-plummeting day: March 11, 2000. Overnight, 26-year-old VPs and Bay Area service-sector employees alike found themselves jobless. But as online users continued to look for useful information and one another in those billions of web pages, search engines and social-media websites boomed. Between 2011 and 2015, social-media giant Facebook jumped from 2000 employees to 6800.

Meanwhile, California biotech was making strides. In 1976 an upstart company called Genentech cloned human insulin and introduced the hepatitis B vaccine. California voters approved a $3 billion bond measure in 2004 for stem-cell research, and by 2008 California had become the biggest funder of stem-cell research and the focus of Nasdaq's Biotech Index.

America Turns Inward

After a highly contentious campaign season, Donald Trump defied the pollsters and became the 45th president of the US on November 8, 2016. His platform, 'America First,' has set the stage for the current phase of US politics. With precarious relations with NATO and new terms for many international alliances, a new era has begun. This is not to say that all of America waxes nostalgic for the 'good old days.' Shortly after Trump's inauguration, half a million people stood up against the administration at the Women's March on Washington on January 21, 2017, joined by five million marchers worldwide. This initial tour de force of dissent was followed by subsequent marches for science and climate change. And, on a topic that carries particular currency out West, immigration from Central America has become a defining issue of the Trump presidency.

The engaging *Cowgirls: Women of the American West* (Teresa Jordan; 1992) journeys in search of the cowgirls, past and present, who run ranches and ride rodeos across the West.

On January 27, 2017, President Trump issued an executive order suspending entry from seven countries in the Middle East and North Africa and cutting the US refugee program. While various courts have banned implementation of the ban, it has a huge psychological impact on immigrant communities and there's speculation that it could result in a brain drain from Silicon Valley and tech industries. Companies like Google, Expedia and Amazon have spoken out against the ban. His tirades against immigrants and frequent wars of words with Mexico over illegal immigration from Central America have also been felt across the Southwest. Numerous groups have sprung up to protest against the government's immigration policies and their impacts upon migrants. Among those located in the region is the El Paso–based Detained Migrant Solidarity Committee (www.facebook.com/DMSCElPaso).

2017

The US pulls out of the Paris Agreement, joining Nicaragua and Syria as the only countries not participating in the climate accord.

2018

Senator John McCain, Vietnam war hero, senator for Arizona from 1987 until his death, and one-time Republican presidential candidate, dies. Tributes pour in from both sides of politics.

2019

President Trump declares a national emergency to enable him to reallocate funds from other agencies, without congressional approval, in order to pay for a border wall between the US and Mexico.

2019

Oregon's Democrat-led Congress seeks to follow California's lead and introduce strong legislation designed to combat climate change; Republican state senators flee the state to deny the Democrat majority quorum.

Way of Life

If you believe the headlines, Westerners are a quirky bunch, with angry Arizonans up in arms about illegal immigration, hair-pulling housewives in Orange County, and pot-smoking deadbeats in Colorado. And, according to *Portlandia* comedy sketches, Portland brims with bike-riding, organic-obsessed hipsters who want to put a bird on everything. Are these accurate depictions? Yes and no. The headlines may reflect some regional attitudes, but most folks are just trying to go about their lives with as little drama as possible.

Regional Identity

The cowboy has long been a symbol of the West – brave, self-reliant, and a solitary seeker of truth, justice and a straight shot of whiskey. The truth behind the myth? For a start, many aspects of the cowboy culture had their origins not in the US, but in Mexico's cattle-ranching traditions. Those who settled the US West were indeed self-reliant and brave. They had to be. In that harsh and unforgiving landscape, danger was always a few steps behind opportunity. As the dangers dissipated, however, and settlers put down roots, the cowboy stereotype became less accurate. Like the red-rock mesas that have weathered into new and varying forms over the years, the character of the populace has also evolved. Stereotypes today, accurate or not, are regionally based, and the residents of Portland, San Diego, Santa Fe, Cheyenne and Phoenix are perceived very differently from one another.

California

Hey dude, don't stick a label on me, that's so uncool. And what's the label? According to the stereotype, Californians are laid-back, self-absorbed, health-conscious, open-minded and eco-aware. The stats behind the stereotype? According to the the National Oceanic and Atmospheric Administration (NOAA), more than 25.5 million Californians lived in a coastal shoreline county in 2010 – the highest number for any coastal state. The state's southern beaches are sunniest and most swimmable, thus Southern California's inescapable associations with surf, sun and classic prime-time TV soaps like *Baywatch* and *The O.C.*

California's adult prison and jail population was 202,700 in 2017. The state was second only to Texas, which housed 218,505 inmates.

Self-help, fitness and body modification are major industries throughout California, successfully marketed since the 1970s, while exercise and good food help keep Californians among the fittest in the nation. Politically, the scene is not rosy for Republicans. In 2018 only 25% of registered voters in the state were Republicans while 44% were registered Democrats and 27% were considered Independent.

Environmentally, Golden Staters have zoomed ahead of the national energy-use curve in their smog-checked cars; more hybrid cars are sold here than in any other state. Expect California to be the first place in the world to legalize fully self-driving vehicles in the not-too-distant future.

Pacific Northwest

And what about those folks living in Washington and Oregon? Tree-hugging hipsters with activist tendencies and a penchant for latte? That's pretty accurate, actually. Many locals are proud of their independent spirit, profess a love for nature and, yes, will separate their plastics when it's time to recycle. They're a friendly lot and, despite the common tendency to denigrate Californians, most are transplants themselves. Why did they all come here? Among other things, for the lush scenery, the good quality of life and less of of the pretension that often afflicts bigger, more popular places. Primping up and putting on airs is not a part of Northwestern everyday life, and wearing Gore-Tex outerwear to restaurants, concerts or social functions will rarely raise an eyebrow.

Rocky Mountain States

The iconic Western cowboy? You're likely to find the real deal here. Ranching is big business in these parts, and the solitary cowboy – seen riding a bucking bronco on the Wyoming license plate – is an appropriate symbol for the region. It takes a rugged individualist to scratch out a living on the lonely, windswept plains – plains that can leave big-city travelers feeling slightly unmoored.

Politically, the northern Rockies – Wyoming, Montana and Idaho – skew conservative, although you will find pockets of liberalism in the college and resort towns. Wyoming may have been the first territory to give women the right to vote, in 1869, but this nod to liberal thinking has been overshadowed by Wyoming's association with former vice-president Dick Cheney, the divisive Republican who was a six-term national congressman. In addition to ranching, the other big industry in Wyoming is energy; Wyoming coal powers nearly one-fifth of America's electricity, but the state is also emerging as one of the largest generators of wind-powered energy.

Colorado is the West's most recognizable swing state. For every bastion of liberalism like Boulder there's an equally entrenched conservative counterpart like Colorado Springs. Yet, a growing urban population has it leaning left: in the 2016 presidential election, Clinton garnered almost 3.5 million more votes than Trump. In 2018 Democrats won the race for the most US Congressional seats, taking four to the Republicans' three, while the Colorado governor's mansion has been in Democrat hands since 2006.

Southwest

The Southwest has long drawn stout-hearted settlers – Mormons, cattle barons, prospectors – pursuing different agendas than those of the average American. Scientists flocked to the empty spaces to develop and test atomic bombs and soaring rockets. Astronomers built observatories on lonely hills and mountains, making the most of the dark skies and unobstructed views. A new generation of idealistic entrepreneurs has transformed former mining towns into New Age art enclaves and Old West tourist attractions.

Every September, 70,000 euphoric souls descend upon the Nevada desert for Burning Man, an annual camping extravaganza, art festival and rave where freedom of expression, costume and libido are all encouraged. There are controversial plans to raise the number of tickets sold to 100,000.

Better known for her writing about Africa, Alexandra Fuller, now a resident of Wyoming, has written the memorable *The Legend of Colton H. Bryant* (2008), the true story of an ill-starred, modern Wyoming cowboy.

THE SPORTING LIFE

Westerners cherish their sports, whether they're players themselves or just watching their favorite teams. Here is a breakdown of the West's professional teams by sport.

National Football League AFC West: Denver Broncos, Oakland Raiders (due to move to Las Vegas at the time of writing), Los Angeles Chargers; NFC West: Arizona Cardinals, Los Angeles Rams, San Francisco 49ers, Seattle Seahawks

National Basketball Association Western Conference Pacific: Golden State Warriors, Los Angeles Clippers, Los Angeles Lakers, Phoenix Suns, Sacramento Kings; Northwest: Denver Nuggets, Portland Trail Blazers, Utah Jazz

Women's National Basketball Association Los Angeles Sparks, Las Vegas Aces, Phoenix Mercury, Seattle Storm

Major League Baseball American League West: Los Angeles Angels, Oakland Athletics, Seattle Mariners; National League West: Arizona Diamondbacks, Colorado Rockies, Los Angeles Dodgers, San Diego Padres, San Francisco Giants

EQUAL MARRIAGE RIGHTS FOR ALL

Forty thousand Californians were already registered as domestic partners when, in 2004, San Francisco Mayor Gavin Newsom issued marriage licenses to same-sex couples in defiance of a California same-sex marriage ban. Four thousand same-sex couples promptly got hitched. The state ban was nixed by California courts in June 2008, but then Proposition 8 passed in November 2008 to amend the state's constitution and prohibit same-sex marriage. Civil-rights activists challenged the constitutionality of the proposition, and federal courts eventually ruled that the law unconstitutionally violated the equal-protection and due-process clauses. In 2013 the US Supreme Court did not appeal and same-sex marriages resumed in the Golden State. In June 2015 the US Supreme Court settled the question across the country by ruling that the Constitution guarantees a right to same-sex marriage.

In recent years high-profile efforts to stop illegal immigration have impacted the 'let's coexist' vibe, most vocally in the southern reaches of Arizona, though the state remains politically split between conservatives and liberals. President Trump's proposal for a border wall – with costs estimated up to $70 billion – is at its most controversial in this region, where the public actually understands what the 1900-mile border looks like..

Population & Multiculturalism

California, with 39.5 million residents, is the most populous state in the USA. California has the country's highest Asian American population, 5.7 million, and the highest Latino population at 15.5 million, both numbers from the 2010 census. In 2014, Latinos became the state's largest racial or ethnic group. Latino culture is deeply enmeshed with that of California, and most residents see the state as an easygoing multicultural society that gives everyone a chance to live the American Dream.

Divisions over illegal immigration are no abstract concepts across the Southwest. California alone had an estimated 1.5 million to 2.2 million undocumented immigrants in 2017 – about 4% to 5% of the state population.

Colorado, Arizona and New Mexico all have large Native American and Latino populations. These residents take pride in maintaining their cultural identities through preserved traditions and oral history lessons.

Religion

Although Californians are less churchgoing than the American mainstream, and one in five Californians professes no religion at all, it remains one of the most religiously diverse states. About a third of Californians are Catholic, due in part to the state's large Latino population, while another third are Protestants. About 1% of California's population is Muslim. LA has the third-largest Jewish community in North America behind NYC and southern Florida. About 2% of California's population identifies as Buddhist and another 2% as Hindu.

The only US president to have been born west of the Rockies (or in any Western states) was Richard Nixon who was born in California and was president from 1969 to 1974.

About a third of Pacific Northwesterners have no religious affiliation. Those who are religious tend to adhere to Christianity and Judaism. Asian Americans have brought Buddhism and Hinduism, and New Age spirituality is no stranger here.

The Southwest has its own anomalies. In Utah, 67% of the state's population identifies as Mormon, with smaller populations in Idaho (21%), Nevada (9%) and Wyoming (9%). The church stresses traditional family values; drinking, smoking and premarital sex are frowned upon. Family and religion are also core values for Native Americans and Hispanics throughout the Southwest. For the Hopi, tribal dances are such sacred events that they are mostly closed to outsiders. And, although many Native Americans and Hispanics are living in urban areas, working as professionals, large family gatherings and traditional customs are still important facets of daily life.

Native Americans

According to the 2010 census, California has the largest Native American population in the country, with Arizona and New Mexico ranking in the top 10. The Navajo tribe is the largest western tribe, second only to the Cherokee nationwide.

Culturally, tribes today grapple with questions about how to prosper in contemporary America while protecting their traditions from erosion and their lands from further exploitation, and how to lift their people from poverty while maintaining their sense of identity and the sacred.

The Tribes

Apache

The Southwest has a number of major Apache reservations, including New Mexico's **Jicarilla Apache Indian Reservation** and **Mescalero Apache Indian Reservation** (http://mescaleroapachetribe.com), and Arizona's San Carlos Apache Reservation and White Mountain Apache Reservation, which includes Fort Apache. All the Apache tribes descend from Athabascans who migrated from Canada around 1400. They were nomadic hunter-gatherers who became warlike raiders, particularly of Pueblo tribes and European settlements, and they fiercely resisted relocation to reservations.

The most famous Apache is Geronimo, a Chiricahua Apache who resisted the American takeover of native lands. He was finally subdued by the US Army with the help of White Mountain Apache scouts.

For decades, traditional Navajo and Hopi have thwarted US industry efforts to strip-mine sacred Big Mountain. Black Mesa Indigenous Support (www.supportblackmesa.org) tells their story.

Havasupai

The Havasupai Indian Reservation (www.havasupaireservations.com) abuts Arizona's Grand Canyon National Park beneath the canyon's South Rim. The tribe's one village, Supai, can only be reached by an 8-mile hike or a mule or helicopter ride from road's end at Hualapai Hilltop.

Havasupai (hah-vah-*soo*-pie) means 'people of the blue-green water,' and tribal life has always been dominated by the Havasu Creek tributary of the Colorado River. Reliable water meant the ability to irrigate fields, which led to a season-based village lifestyle. The deep Havasu Canyon also protected the community from others; this extremely peaceful people basically avoided Western contact until the 1800s. Today, the tribe relies on tourism, and Havasu Canyon's gorgeous waterfalls draw a steady stream of visitors. The tribe is related to the Hualapai (p428).

The Hopi Arts Trail spotlights artists and galleries on the three mesas that are the heart of the Hopi reservation. For a map, as well as a list of artists and galleries, visit https://hopiartstrail.com.

Hopi

Surrounded by the Navajo Reservation in northeast Arizona, the Hopi Reservation (p187) covers more than 1.5 million acres. Most Hopi live in 12 villages at the base and on top of three mesas jutting from the main Black Mesa; Old Oraibi, on Third Mesa, is considered (along with Acoma Pueblo) the continent's oldest continuously inhabited settlement. Like all Pueblo peoples, the Hopi are descended from the Ancestral Puebloans (formerly known as Anasazi).

Hopi (*ho*-pee) translates as 'peaceful ones' or 'peaceful person,' and perhaps no tribe is more renowned for leading such a humble, traditional and

ETIQUETTE

When visiting a reservation, ask about and follow any specific rules. Almost all tribes ban alcohol, and some ban pets and restrict cameras. All require permits for camping, fishing and other activities. Tribal rules may be posted at the reservation entrance, or you can visit the tribal office or check the reservation's website.

When you visit a reservation, you are visiting a unique culture with customs that may be unfamiliar. Be courteous, respectful and open-minded, and don't expect locals to share every detail of their lives.

Ask first, document later Some tribes restrict cameras and sketching entirely; others may charge a fee, or restrict them at ceremonies or in certain areas. *Always ask before taking pictures or drawing.* If you want to photograph a person, ask permission first; a tip is polite and often expected.

Pueblos are not museums The incredible adobe structures are homes. Public buildings will be signed; if a building isn't signed, assume it's private. Don't climb around. *Kivas* (sacred buildings) are nearly always off limits.

Ceremonies are not performances Treat ceremonies like church services; watch silently and respectfully, without talking, clapping or taking pictures; wear modest clothing. Pow-wows are more informal, but unless they're billed as theater, they are for the tribe, not you.

Privacy and communication Many Native Americans are happy to describe their tribe's general religious beliefs, but not always, or to the same degree, and details about rituals and ceremonies are often considered private. Always ask before discussing religion and respect each person's boundaries. Also, Native Americans consider it polite to listen without comment; silent listening, given and received, is a sign of respect.

deeply spiritual lifestyle. The Hopi practice an unusual, near-miraculous technique of 'dry farming.' The soil isn't plowed; instead, seeds are planted in 'wind breaks' and natural water catchments. Their main crop has always been corn, which is central to their creation story.

Hopi ceremonial life is complex and intensely private, and extends into all aspects of daily living. Following the 'Hopi Way' is considered essential to bringing the life-giving rains, but the Hopi also believe it fosters the wellbeing of the entire human race. Each person's role is determined by their clan, which is matrilineal. Even among themselves, the Hopi keep certain traditions of their individual clans private.

The Hopi are skilled artisans; they are famous for their pottery, coiled baskets and silverwork, as well as for their ceremonial kachina (spirit) dolls.

California had the largest Native American population (648,172) of all US states in 2017. But New Mexico had the highest number of Native Americans as a proportion of the total population (10.7%) of all states in the lower 48. Montana was fourth at 5.67%.

Hualapai

The Hualapai Reservation (http://hualapai-nsn.gov) occupies around 1 million acres along 108 miles of the Grand Canyon's South Rim. Hualapai (*wah*-lah-pie) means 'people of the tall pines.' Because this section of the Grand Canyon was not readily arable, the Hualapai were originally seminomadic, gathering wild plants and hunting small game.

Today, forestry, cattle ranching, farming and tourism are the economic mainstays. The tribal headquarters are in Peach Springs, AZ, which was the inspiration for 'Radiator Springs' in the animated movie *Cars*. Hunting, fishing, rafting and the lofty Skywalk are prime draws.

Navajo

Nationwide, there are about 300,000 Navajo, making it the USA's second-largest tribe after the Cherokee. The Navajo Reservation (www.discovernavajo.com) is by far the largest and most populous in the US. Also called the Navajo Nation and Navajoland, it covers 17.5 million acres (over 27,000 sq miles) in Arizona and parts of New Mexico and Utah.

The Navajo were feared nomads and warriors who both traded with and raided the Pueblos and who fought settlers and the US military. They also borrowed generously from other traditions: they acquired sheep and horses from the Spanish, learned pottery and weaving from the Pueblos, and picked up silversmithing from Mexico. Today, the Navajo are renowned for their woven rugs, pottery and inlaid silver jewelry, as well as for their intricate sandpainting, which is used in healing ceremonies.

For a helpful introduction to Navajo culture, stop by the Explore Navajo Interactive Museum (www.explorenavajo.com) in Tuba City, AZ, on the way to Monument Valley from Grand Canyon National Park.

Pueblo

New Mexico contains 19 Pueblo reservations, with links and introductions provided by the Indian Pueblo Cultural Center (www.indianpueblo.org). Four reservations lead west from Albuquerque: Isleta, Laguna, Acoma and Zuni. Fifteen pueblos fill the Rio Grande Valley between Albuquerque and Taos: Sandia, San Felipe, Santa Ana, Zia, Jemez, Santo Domingo, Cochiti, San Ildefonso, Pojoaque, Nambé, Tesuque, Santa Clara, Ohkay Owingeh (or San Juan), Picuris and Taos.

These tribes are as different as they are alike. Nevertheless, the term 'pueblo' (Spanish for 'village') is a convenient shorthand for what these tribes share: all are believed to be descended from the Ancestral Puebloans and to have inherited their architectural style and their agrarian, village-based life – often atop mesas.

Pueblos are unique among Native Americans. These adobe structures can have up to five levels, connected by ladders, and are built with varying combinations of mud bricks, stones, logs and plaster. In the central plaza of each pueblo is a kiva, an underground ceremonial chamber that connects to the spirit world. Catholic churches are prominent in the pueblos, a legacy of missionaries, and many Pueblos hold both Christian and native religious beliefs.

Sioux

The Sioux is not one tribe, but a consortium of three major tribes – Eastern Dakota, Western Dakota and Lakota – speaking different dialects but sharing a common culture. Each tribe also has various sub-branches.

Prior to European arrival they lived in the southeast, but were first encountered by Europeans in modern-day Minnesota, Iowa and Wisconsin. The Sioux slowly expanded west to what is now the Dakotas, Nebraska and Montana by 1800.

The Sioux were fierce defenders of their lands, and fought many battles to preserve them. These included the Battle of the Little Bighorn in 1876 in modern-day Montana, also known as Custer's Last Stand, where a combined army of Lakota Sioux, Northern Cheyenne and Arapaho defeated the US Army; Crazy Horse and Sitting Bull were both Lakota Sioux. The Sioux also fought the Black Hills war and suffered the infamous Wounded Knee Massacre (both in neighboring South Dakota) in 1890, although the slaughter of the buffalo (on which they had survived) did as much to remove them from their lands as anything else. That spirit of protest endures today: the Sioux were among the founders of the American Indian Movement in 1968.

Most (78%) Native Americans live off reservations, and 72% live in urban environments. An estimated 140,000 Native Americans live in San Francisco's Bay Area.

Today, the Sioux live in Minnesota, Nebraska, Montana, North Dakota and South Dakota – the latter contains the two-million-acre Pine Ridge Reservation, the nation's second largest.

Shoshone

The Shoshone crossed the Rockies around 1500 AD and became one of the most significant Native American tribes on the Great Plains. Their traditional lands now range across Wyoming, southern Idaho, Nevada and Utah, with four major linguistic groupings.

Under pressure from their traditional enemies, the Cheyenne and Lakota Sioux, the Shoshone became widely dispersed in the 17th and 18th centuries; some even reached Texas where they became the Comanches. Those who remained stood in the path of the inexorable expansion of white settlers and their resistance was finally broken at the 1863 Bear River Massacre (in present-day Idaho), where more than 400 Shoshone men, women and children were killed by US soldiers. Although Shoshone raids forced the rerouting of the mail route through Wyoming in subsequent decades, the tribe were still confined to reservations and their numbers much reduced, like so many other peoples in the region.

Although only around 1000 people speak the Shoshone language, language classes are offered through Idaho State University, and the Shoshone community is actively working to build renewable-energy partnerships.

The Battle of the Little Bighorn on June 25–26, 1876, was known to Native Americans as the Battle of the Greasy Grass. It was an overwhelming victory for the Lakota Sioux, Northern Cheyenne and Arapaho, with 274 US casualties. Estimates of Native American casualties range from 36 to 300.

Arts

By purchasing arts from Native Americans themselves, visitors have a direct, positive impact on tribal economies, which depend in part on tourist dollars. Many tribes run craft outlets and galleries, usually in the main towns of reservations. The Indian Arts and Crafts Board (www.doi.gov/iacb) lists Native American–owned galleries and shops state-by-state online – click on 'Source Directory' then 'State and Country Listings.'

Pottery & Basketry

Pueblo pottery is perhaps most acclaimed of all Native American pottery. Initially, local clay determined color, so that Zia pottery was red, Acoma white, Hopi yellow, Cochiti black and so on. Santa Clara is famous for its carved relief designs, and San Ildefonso for its black-on-black style, which was revived by world-famous potter Maria Martinez. The Navajo and Ute Mountain Utes also produce well-regarded pottery.

Pottery is nearly always synonymous with village life, while more portable baskets were often preferred by nomadic peoples. Among the tribes who stand out for their exquisite basketry are the Jicarilla Apache (whose name means 'basket maker'), the Kaibab Paiute, the Hualapai and the Tohono O'odham. Hopi coiled baskets, with their vivid patterns and kachina iconography, are also notable.

Navajo Weaving

Navajo legend says that Spider Woman taught humans how to weave, and she seems embodied today in the iconic sight of Navajo women patiently shuttling handspun wool on weblike looms, creating the Navajo's legendary rugs (originally blankets), so tight they hold water. Preparation of the wool, and sometimes the dyes, is still done by hand. Finishing a rug takes months, and occasionally years.

Authentic Navajo rugs are expensive, ranging from hundreds to thousands of dollars. Not average souvenirs, they are artworks that will last a lifetime, whether displayed on the wall or the floor. Take time to research, even a little, so you recognize when quality matches price.

The Pulitzer Prize–winning *House Made of Dawn* (N Scott Momaday; 1968), about a Pueblo youth, launched a wave of Native American literature.

Silver & Turquoise Jewelry

Jewelry using stones and shells has always been a native tradition; silverwork did not arrive until the 1800s, along with Anglo and Mexican contact. In particular, Navajo, Hopi and Zuni became renowned for combining these materials with inlaid-turquoise silver jewelry. In addition to turquoise, jewelry often features lapis, onyx, coral, carnelian and shells.

Authentic jewelry is often stamped or marked by the artisan, and items may come with an Indian Arts and Crafts Board certificate; always ask. Price may also be an indicator: a high tab doesn't guarantee authenticity, but an absurdly low one probably signals trickery. A crash course can be had at the August Santa Fe Indian Market (p222).

Arts & Architecture

Art created in the American West is often marked by a striking collision of personality, attitude and landscape: the take-it-or-leave-it cow skulls in Georgia O'Keeffe paintings; the prominent shadows in an Ansel Adams' photograph of Yosemite's Half Dome; the gonzo journalism of Hunter S Thompson in the sun-baked Southwest; even Nirvana's grunge seems inseparable from its rainy Seattle roots. The landscape is a presence; beautiful yet unforgiving. The results, whether Hollywood mainstream or restless indie, are always worth exploring.

Literature

Social Realism

Arguably the most influential author ever to emerge from California was Nobel Prize–winner John Steinbeck, who was born in Salinas in 1902. His masterpiece of social realism, *The Grapes of Wrath* (1939), tells of the struggles of migrant farm workers. His California-centric *Of Mice and Men* (1937) is another literary masterpiece and window on America during the Great Depression, while *Travels with Charley* (1962) is a non-fiction work following the author's travels along the borders of the US (or at least the lower-48 part), including the West Coast, Montana and other Western US states.

Pulp Noir & Mysteries

In the 1930s San Francisco and Los Angeles became the capitals of the pulp detective novel. Dashiell Hammett (*The Maltese Falcon;* 1929–30) made San Francisco's fog a sinister character. The king of hard-boiled crime was Raymond Chandler, who thinly disguised his hometown of Santa Monica as Bay City.

Since the 1990s, a renaissance of California crime fiction has been masterminded by James Ellroy (*L.A. Confidential;* 1990); Elmore Leonard (*Rum Punch;* 1992); and Walter Mosley (*Devil in a Blue Dress;* 1990), whose Easy Rawlins detective novels are set in South Central LA's impoverished neighborhoods. *Heartsick* (2007), a thriller by Chelsea Cain, is set in Portland, OR.

But not all detectives work in the cities. Tony Hillerman, an enormously popular author from Albuquerque, NM, wrote *People of Darkness* (1980), *Skinwalkers* (1986), *The Sinister Pig* (2003) and *Skeleton Man* (2004). His award-winning mystery novels take place on Navajo, Hopi and Zuni reservations.

In Northern California, professional hell-raiser Jack London (1876–1916) grew up and cut his teeth in Oakland. He turned out a massive volume of influential fiction, including tales of the late-19th-century Klondike Gold Rush in the iconic *Call of the Wild* (1903).

Movers & Shakers

After the chaos of WWII, the Beat Generation brought about a provocative new style of writing: short, sharp, spontaneous and alive. Based in San Francisco, the scene revolved around Jack Kerouac (*On the Road,* 1957), Allen Ginsberg ('Howl,' 1956) and Lawrence Ferlinghetti, the Beats' patron and publisher.

Joan Didion nailed California culture in *Slouching Towards Bethlehem* (1968), a collection of essays that takes a caustic look at 1960s flower power and the Haight-Ashbury district. Tom Wolfe also put '60s San Francisco in perspective with *The Electric Kool-Aid Acid Test* (1968), which follows Ken Kesey's band of Merry Pranksters.

In the 1970s Charles Bukowski's autobiographical novel *Post Office* (1971) captured down-and-out downtown LA, while Richard Vasquez's *Chicano* (1970) took a dramatic look at LA's Latino communities.

Hunter S Thompson, who died by suicide in early 2005, wrote *Fear and Loathing in Las Vegas* (1971), set in the temple of American excess in the desert; it's a high-octane road-trip novel.

Eco Warriors, Social Commentators & New Voices

Edward Abbey, noted for his strong environmental and political views, created the thought-provoking and seminal works *Desert Solitaire* (1968) and *The Journey Home: Some Words in Defense of the American West* (1977). His classic *The Monkey Wrench Gang* (1975) is a comic fictional account of real people who planned to blow up Glen Canyon Dam before flooding could occur.

Rebecca Solnit snaps the reins of environmental advocacy, with fine-tuned lyric prose on politics and place, most notably her book of essays, *A Field Guide to Getting Lost* (2005). Conservationist and poet Terry Tempest Williams examines our relationship with wilderness, honing in on her native Utah. Her latest is *The Hour of Land: A Personal Topography of America's National Parks* (2016).

The bestselling novel *Where'd You Go, Bernadette* (Maria Semple; 2012) has fun with Seattle stereotypes while tracing the disappearance of the title character, a feisty but reclusive famous architect.

Wild, Cheryl Strayed's 2012 memoir about dealing with loss while hiking the Pacific Coast Trail, helped create a boom in thru-hiking. Wallace Stegner's western-set novel *Angle of Repose* won the Pulitzer Prize in 1972. His book of essays *Where the Bluebird Sings to the Lemonade Springs* (1992) discusses the harmful consequences of mythologizing the West.

Former Tucsonian Barbara Kingsolver published two novels with Southwestern settings, *The Bean Trees* (1988) and *Animal Dreams* (1990). She shares her thoughts about day-to-day life in the Southwest in a series of essays in *High Tide in Tucson* (1995). Set on the Oregon coast, *Mink River* (2010) by Brian Doyle is a work of fiction filled with myths and storytelling.

One of America's most popular modern writers, Annie Proulx is another adopted Westerner. Born in Connecticut, she lived for a time in Saratoga, WY, and now lives in Port Townsend, WA. Her collections of short stories include *Close Range: Wyoming Stories* (1999), *Bad Dirt: Wyoming Stories 2* (2004), and *Fine Just the Way It Is: Wyoming Stories 3* (2008). She also wrote *Bird Cloud: A Memoir* (2011) about the experience of setting up home in the West.

Louise Erdrich is another prolific and highly respected writer about the West. Her fiction is filled with Native American stories and characters – the outstanding *The Round House* (2012) won the National Book Award for fiction.

David Baron's *The Beast in the Garden* (2004) is a gripping story of what happens when people move into the domain of wild animals, in this case mountain lions around Boulder, CO. *The Solace of Open Spaces* (Gretel Ehrlich; 1985) is an ode in prose to the plains and big-sky country of Wyoming.

One of the most exciting new voices to emerge in recent years is Tara Westover, with her 2018 memoir *Educated*. Recounting her abusive and fundamentalist upbringing in rural Idaho, and Westover's remarkable subsequent journey through some of the most esteemed educational institutions on earth; it's a real tour de force.

Music

Rockin' Out

The first homegrown rock-and-roll talent to make it big in the 1950s was Ritchie Valens, whose 'La Bamba' was a rockified version of a Mexican folk song. When Joan Baez and Bob Dylan had their Northern California fling in the early 1960s, Dylan plugged in his guitar and played folk rock. When Janis Joplin and Big Brother and the Holding Company developed their shambling musical stylings in San Francisco, folk rock splintered into psychedelia. Meanwhile, both Jim Morrison and The Doors and The Byrds blew minds on LA's famous Sunset Strip. The epicenter of LA's psychedelic rock scene was the Laurel Canyon neighborhood, just uphill from the Sunset Strip and the legendary **Whisky-a-Go-Go nightclub** (Map p258; ☎310-652-4202; www.whiskyagogo.com; 8901 W Sunset Blvd, West Hollywood).

At the Museum of Pop Culture (www.mopop.org) in the Seattle Center, the 'Nirvana: Taking Punk to the Masses' exhibit traces the rise of grunge rockers Nirvana and singer/songwriter Kurt Cobain.

Rap & Hip-Hop

Since the 1980s, LA has been a hotbed for West Coast rap and hip-hop. Eazy-E, Ice Cube and Dr. Dre released the seminal N.W.A. (Niggaz Wit Attitudes) album, *Straight Outta Compton* (1989). Death Row Records, cofounded by Dr. Dre, has launched megawatt rap talents including Long Beach bad boy Snoop Dogg and the late Tupac Shakur, who started his rap career in Marin County and was fatally shot in 1996 in Las Vegas in a suspected East Coast/West Coast rap feud.

Throughout the 1980s and '90s, California maintained a grassroots hip-hop scene closer to the streets in LA and in the heart of the Black Power movement in Oakland. In the late 1990s the Bay Area birthed underground artists like E-40 and the 'hyphy movement,' a reaction against the increasing commercialization of hip-hop. Also from Oakland, Michael Franti & Spearhead blend hip-hop with funk, reggae, folk, jazz and rock stylings into messages for social justice and peace.

Meanwhile, during the late '90s and early 2000s, Korn from Bakersfield and Linkin Park from LA County combined hip-hop with rap and metal to popularize 'nu metal.' Today's darling is Compton-born Kendrick Lamar, with seven Grammys under his belt.

Grunge & Indie

Grunge started in the mid-1980s and was heavily influenced by cult group the Melvins. Distorted guitars, strong riffs, heavy drumming and gritty styles defined the unpolished musical style. Grunge didn't explode until the record label DGC Records released Nirvana's *Nevermind* in 1991, skyrocketing 'Seattle sound' into mainstream music. True purists, however, shunned Nirvana for what they considered selling out to commercialism while overshadowing equally worthy bands like Soundgarden and Alice in Chains. The general popularity of grunge continued through the early 1990s, but the very culture of the genre took part in its downfall. Bands lived hard and fast, never really taking themselves seriously. Many eventually succumbed to internal strife and drug abuse. The final blow was in 1994, when Kurt Cobain – the heart of Nirvana – committed suicide.

Cobain's wife, Courtney Love, was a talent in her own right, and she fronted alternative rock band Hole from 1989 until they disbanded in 2002. Their punk rock sound mellowed a little through the years – the debut *Pretty on the Inside* (1991) was followed by the hugely successful *Live Through This* (1994) and *Celebrity Skin* (1998); they briefly re-formed to release *Nobody's Daughter* (2010).

For an engaging introduction to a global array of musical instruments, don't miss the Musical Instrument Museum (www.mim.org) in Phoenix, AZ, home to more than 7000 instruments from about 200 countries and territories.

A few western cities are especially connected with indie music. Seattle was the original stomping grounds for Modest Mouse, Death Cab for Cutie and The Postal Service. Olympia, WA, has been a hotbed of indie rock and riot grrls. Portland, OR, has boasted such diverse groups as folktronic hip-hop band Talkdemonic, alt-band The Decemberists and multigenre Pink Martini, not to mention The Shins (originally from Albuquerque, NM), The Dandy Warhols, Blind Pilot and Elliott Smith. Washington-based Sleater-Kinney, with Carrie Brownstein, Corin Tucker and Janet Weiss, hit the road again in 2015 after a nearly 10-year hiatus, and released *The Center Won't Hold* in 2019.

Elsewhere, New Mexico band Beirut is where indie rock meets world music, in the able hands of Santa Fe native Zach Condon. For something entirely different, Meat Puppets are prolific Phoenix rockers known for their genre-bending psychedelic punk sound.

Top Music Festivals

Telluride Bluegrass Festival, CO

Grand Teton Music Festival, WY

Grand Targhee Bluegrass Music Festival, WY

M3F (McDowell Mountain Music Festival), AZ

Aspen Music Festival, CO

Film

The Industry

The moviemaking industry grew out of the humble orchards of Hollywoodland, a residential neighborhood of Los Angeles. Entrepreneurial moviemakers, many of whom were European immigrants, established studios in the early 1900s. German-born Carl Laemmle built Universal Studios in 1915, selling lunch to curious guests coming to watch the magic of moviemaking; Polish immigrant Samuel Goldwyn joined with Cecil B DeMille and others to form Paramount; and Jack Warner and his brothers, born to Polish parents, arrived a few years later from Canada.

LA's perpetually balmy weather meant that most outdoor scenes could be easily shot there. Fans loved early silent-film stars like Charlie Chaplin and Harold Lloyd, and the first big Hollywood wedding occurred in 1920 when Douglas Fairbanks wed Mary Pickford, becoming Hollywood's first 'royal' couple. The silent-movie era gave way to 'talkies' after 1927's *The Jazz Singer*, a Warner Bros musical starring Al Jolson, premiered in downtown LA, ushering in Hollywood's glamorous Golden Age.

Hollywood & Beyond

From the 1920s, Hollywood became the industry's social and financial hub, but only one major studio, Paramount Pictures, stood in Hollywood proper. Most movies have been shot elsewhere around LA, from Culver City (at MGM, now Sony Pictures), to Studio City (at Universal Studios) and Burbank (at Warner Bros and later at Disney).

It's one of modern cinema's most recognizable scenes: in *Forrest Gump* (1994), Forrest stopped his cross-country run in Monument Valley, which straddles the Utah–Arizona line.

Today's high cost of filming has sent location scouts outside the state. During his two terms as governor of New Mexico (2003–11), Bill Richardson wooed production teams to the state by offering a 25% tax rebate on expenditures. His efforts helped inject more than $3 billion into the economy.

Las Vegas, NV, had a starring role in 2009's blockbuster comedy *The Hangover*, an R-rated buddy film that grossed more than $467 million worldwide. The three-film *The Hangover* series, with further films in 2011 and 2013, grossed US$1.4 billion.

Westerns & Beyond

Though many Westerns have been shot in SoCal, a few places in Utah and Arizona have doubled as film and TV sets so often that they have come to define the American West. In addition to Utah's Monument Valley, first popularized by director John Ford in *Stagecoach*, movie-worthy destinations include Moab, UT, in *Thelma and Louise* (1991) and Dead Horse Point State Park for *Mission Impossible: 2* (2000); Lake Powell, UT/AZ, for *Planet of the Apes* (1968); and Tombstone, AZ, for the eponymous *Tombstone* (1993). Scenes in *127 Hours* (2010), the film version of Aron Ralston's harrowing time trapped in Bluejohn Canyon in Canyonlands National Park, UT, were shot in and around the canyon.

Joel and Ethan Coen shot the 2007 Oscar-winner *No Country for Old Men* around Las Vegas, NM (doubling for 1980s' West Texas). The Coen brothers returned to film their remake of *True Grit* (2010), basing their headquarters in Santa Fe and shooting on several New Mexico ranches. Reese Witherspoon earned an Academy Award nomination for best actress for *Wild* (2015) based on the Cheryl Strayed memoir and directed by Jean-Marc Vallée. It was mostly set on the Pacific Crest Trail (p51).

Arizona drug-war movie *Sicario* (2015) was directed by Denis Villeneuve and starred Emily Blunt, Benicio del Toro and Josh Brolin. In the same year, the sexually charged *Fifty Shades of Grey* (2011), directed by Sam Taylor-Johnson, was set in Seattle, WA.

In Albuquerque, NM, *Breaking Bad* fans can take a self-guided tour of locations that appeared in the series. Visit www.visitalbuquerque.org/albuquerque/film-tourism for an interactive map and details about locations.

Small Screen

The first TV station began broadcasting in Los Angeles in 1931. Through the following decades, iconic images of LA were beamed into living rooms across America in shows such as *Dragnet* (1950s), *The Beverly Hillbillies* (1960s), *The Brady Bunch* (1970s), *LA Law* (1980s–90s), *Baywatch*, *Melrose Place* and *The Fresh Prince of Bel-Air* (1990s), through to teen 'dramedies' *Beverly Hills, 90210* (1990s) and *The O.C.* (2000s), the latter set in Newport Beach, Orange County. Fans of reality TV will spot Southern California starring in everything from the first two seasons of *Top Chef* (2006 and 2007) to *The Real Housewives of Orange County* (2006 to 2019).

Southern California has also been a versatile backdrop for edgy cable-TV dramas, from Showtime's *Weeds* (2005–12), about a pot-growing SoCal widow, to TNT's cop show *The Closer* (2005–12), about homicide detectives in LA, and FX's *The Shield* (2002–8), which fictionalized police corruption in the City of Angels.

But SoCal isn't the only TV backdrop. Former *X-Files* writer Vince Gilligan brought more of his off-beat brilliance to the small screen with *Breaking Bad* (2008–13), set and shot in sun-baked Albuquerque. Its prequel, *Better Call Saul*, debuted in 2015. Portland will never be the same after *Portlandia*, a sketch comedy series (2011–18) on IFC that pokes fun at the cultural quirks of young urbanites.

Architecture

Westerners have adapted imported styles to the climate and available materials, building cool, adobe-inspired houses in Tucson, AZ, and fog-resistant redwood-shingle houses in Mendocino, CA.

Southwestern Styles

Regional influences rule the Southwest. First and foremost are the ruins of the Ancestral Puebloans – most majestically their cliff communities – and Taos Pueblo. These traditional designs and examples are echoed in the Pueblo Revival style of Santa Fe's New Mexico Museum of Art (p225) and are speckled across the city and the region today.

Adobe dominates many New Mexico cityscapes and landscapes, while the mission-style architecture of the 17th and 18th centuries is visible in religious and municipal buildings such as Santa Fe's **State Capitol** (Map p222; ☎505-986-4589; www.nmlegis.gov/visitors; cnr Paseo de Peralta & Old Santa Fe Trail; ⏰7am-6pm Mon-Fri, plus 9am-5pm Sat Jun-late Aug).

Master architect Frank Lloyd Wright was also a presence in the Southwest, most specifically at Taliesin West (p162) in Scottsdale, AZ. More recently, Route 66's kitschy motels and neon signs are icons of the American road trip.

Top Film Festivals

- *AFI Fest (www.afi.com/afifest)*
- *Outfest (www.outfest.org)*
- *San Francisco International Film Festival (https://sffilm.org/sf-film-festival)*
- *Sundance Film Festival (www.sundance.org/festivals/sundance-film-festival)*
- *Telluride Film Festival (www.telluridefilmfestival.org)*
- *Seattle International Film Festival (www.siff.net/festival)*

Spanish Missions & Victorian Queens

The first Spanish missions were built around courtyards, using materials that Native Americans and colonists found on hand: adobe, limestone and grass. Many missions crumbled into disrepair as the church's influence waned, but the style remained practical for the climate. Early

California settlers later adapted it into the rancho adobe style, as seen at El Pueblo de Los Angeles and in San Diego's Old Town (p275).

During the mid-19th-century gold rush, California's nouveau riche imported materials to construct mansions matching European fashions, and raised the stakes with ornamental excess. Many favored the gilded Queen Anne style. Outrageous examples of Victorian architecture, including 'Painted Ladies' and 'gingerbread' houses, can be found in such Northern California towns as San Francisco, **Ferndale** (707-786-4000; www.gingerbread-mansion.com; 400 Berding St; r $175-495; P) and Eureka (p337).

Founded in New Mexico by Michael Reynolds, the Earthship (www.earthship-global.com) is a brilliant architectural model based around sustainability, the use of recycled materials in construction and harmony with the local environment. The results are stunning, and expanding around the world.

Some architects rejected frilly Victorian styles in favor of the simple, classical lines of Spanish Colonial architecture. Mission-revival details are restrained and functional: arched doors and windows, long covered porches, fountains, courtyards, solid walls and red-tiled roofs.

Arts & Crafts & Art Deco

Simplicity was the hallmark of the arts-and-crafts style. Influenced by both Japanese design principles and England's arts-and-crafts movement, its woodwork and handmade touches marked a deliberate departure from the Industrial Revolution. SoCal architects Charles and Henry Greene (Greene and Greene) and Bernard Maybeck in Northern California popularized the versatile one-story bungalow, which became trendy at the turn of the 20th century. Today you'll spot them in Pasadena and Berkeley with their overhanging eaves, terraces and sleeping porches harmonizing indoors and outdoors.

In the 1920s the international art deco style took elements from the ancient world – Mayan glyphs, Egyptian pillars, Babylonian ziggurats – and flattened them into modern motifs to cap stark facades and outline streamlined skyscrapers, notably in LA and downtown Oakland. 'Streamline moderne' kept decoration to a minimum and mimicked the aerodynamic look of ocean liners and airplanes, as seen at LA's Union Station (p243).

A few years later master architect Frank Lloyd Wright was designing homes in the Romanza style, following the principle that for every indoor space there's an outdoor space, and this flowing design is best exhibited in LA's **Hollyhock House** (Map p244; 323-913-4031; www.barnsdall.org/hollyhock-house/about; Barnsdall Art Park, 4800 Hollywood Blvd, Los Feliz; adult/student/child $7/3/free; tours 11am-4pm Thu-Sun; P; M Red Line to Vermont/Sunset), constructed for heiress Alice Barnsdale. His part-time home and studio in Scottsdale, AZ, Taliesin West (p162), complements and showcases the surrounding desert landscape.

Postmodern Evolutions

Jim Heimann's *California Crazy and Beyond: Roadside Vernacular Architecture* (1980) is a romp through the zany, whimsical world of California, where lemonade stands look like giant lemons and motels are shaped like tipis.

Architectural styles have veered away from strict high modernism, and unlikely postmodern shapes have been added to the landscape. Richard Meier made his mark on West LA with the Getty Center (p249), a cresting wave of a building atop a sunburned hilltop. Canadian-born Frank Gehry relocated to Santa Monica. His billowing, sculptural style for LA's Walt Disney Concert Hall (p244) winks cheekily at shipshape Californian streamline moderne. Renzo Piano's signature inside-out industrial style can be glimpsed in the sawtooth roof and red-steel veins on the Broad Contemporary Art Museum extension of the Los Angeles County Museum of Art (p249).

San Francisco has lately championed a brand of postmodernism by Pritzker Prize–winning architects that magnifies and mimics California's great outdoors, especially in Golden Gate Park (p312). Swiss architects Herzog & de Meuron clad the de Young Museum (p312) in copper, which will eventually oxidize green to match its park setting. Nearby, Renzo Piano literally raised the roof on sustainable design at the LEED (Leadership in Energy and Environmental Design) platinum-certified California Academy of Sciences (p312), capped by a living garden.

Land & Wildlife

Crashing tectonic plates, mighty floods, spewing volcanoes, frigid ice fields: for millions and millions of years, the American West was an altogether unpleasant place. But from this fire and ice sprang a kaleidoscopic array of stunning, wildlife-rich landscapes bound by a common modern trait: an undeniable ability to attract explorers, naturalists, artists and outdoor adventurers. They're all drawn by the natural drama – of the Rockies, of an extraordinary coastline and of the epic Great Plains.

The Land

As Western novelist and essayist Wallace Stegner noted in his book *Where the Bluebird Sings to the Lemonade Springs* (1992), the West is home to a dozen or so distinct and unique subregions. Their one commonality? In Stegner's view it's the aridity. Aridity, he writes, sharpens the brilliance of the light and heightens the clarity of the air in most of the West. It also leads to fights over water rights, a historic and ongoing concern.

California

Geology & Earthquakes

California is a complex geologic landscape formed from fragments of rock and earth crust scraped together as the North American continent has drifted westward over hundreds of millions of years. Crumpled coast ranges, the downward-bowing Central Valley and the still-rising Sierra Nevada are evidence of gigantic forces that have been exerted as the continental and ocean plates continue to crush together.

About 25 million years ago, the ocean plates stopped colliding and instead started sliding against each other, creating the massive San Andreas Fault. Because this contact zone doesn't slide smoothly, but catches and slips irregularly, it rattles California with an ongoing succession of tremors and earthquakes.

The state's most famous earthquake in 1906 measured 7.9 on the Richter scale and demolished San Francisco, leaving more than 3000 people dead and 250,000 homeless. The Bay Area made headlines again in 1989 when the Loma Prieta earthquake (magnitude 7.1) caused a section of the Bay Bridge to collapse. Los Angeles' last 'big one' was in 1994, when the Northridge quake (magnitude 6.7) caused parts of the Santa Monica Fwy to fall down. With $44 billion in damages, it is the most costly quake in US history – so far.

California claims both the highest point in the contiguous US (Mt Whitney; 14,505ft) and the lowest elevation in North America (Badwater Basin, Death Valley; 282ft below sea level) – plus they're only 90 miles apart, as the condor flies.

The Coast to the Central Valley

Much of California's coast is fronted by rugged coastal mountains that capture winter's water-laden storms. San Francisco divides the Coast Ranges roughly in half, with the foggy North Coast remaining sparsely populated, while the Central and Southern California coasts have a balmier climate and many more people.

In the northernmost reaches of the Coast Ranges, nutrient-rich soils and abundant moisture foster forests of giant trees. On their eastern flanks, the Coast Ranges subside into gently rolling hills that give way to the 450-mile-long Central Valley, an agricultural powerhouse producing more than 230 different types of crops, from nuts to fruits and vegetables. The region produces one third of all produce grown in the United States.

On the evening of July 5, 2011, a mile-high dust storm with an estimated 100-mile width enveloped Phoenix after reaching speeds of more than 50mph. Visibility dropped to between zero and one-quarter of a mile. Phoenix International Airport temporarily closed. An eerily similar storm swept through Phoenix on July 9, 2018.

Mountain Highs

On the eastern side of the Central Valley looms the world-famous Sierra Nevada. At 400 miles long and 50–80 miles wide, it's one of the largest mountain ranges in the world and is home to 13 peaks over 14,000ft. The vast wilderness of the High Sierra (lying mostly above 9000ft) presents an astounding landscape of glaciers, sculpted granite peaks and remote canyons. The soaring Sierra Nevada captures storm systems and their water, with most of the precipitation over 3000ft falling as snow. These waters eventually flow into half a dozen major river systems that provide the vast majority of water for San Francisco and LA as well as farms in the Central Valley.

The Deserts & Beyond

With the west slope of the Sierra Nevada capturing the lion's share of water, all lands east of the Sierra crest are dry and desertlike, receiving less than 10in of rain a year. Surprisingly, some valleys at the eastern foot of the Sierra Nevada are well watered by creeks and support a vigorous economy of livestock and agriculture.

Areas in the northern half of California, especially on the elevated Modoc Plateau of northeastern California, are a cold desert at the western edge of the Great Basin, blanketed with hardy sagebrush shrubs and pockets of juniper trees. Temperatures increase as you head south, with a prominent transition as you descend from Mono Lake into the Owens Valley east of the Sierra Nevada. This southern hot desert (part of the Mojave Desert) includes Death Valley, one of the hottest places on earth.

The Southwest

Extremely ancient rocks (among the oldest on the planet) exposed in the deep heart of the Grand Canyon (p177) show that the region was under water two billion years ago. Younger layers of rocks in southern Utah reveal that this region was continuously or periodically under water. About 286 million years ago, near the end of the Paleozoic era, a collision of continents into a massive landmass known as Pangaea deformed the earth's crust and produced pressures that uplifted the ancestral Rocky Mountains. Though this early mountain range lay to the east, it formed rivers and sediment deposits that began to shape the Southwest.

Visit www.publiclands.org for a one-stop summary of recreational opportunities on government land in the West, regardless of managing agency. The site provides links to relevant books and maps for purchase and includes updates about current fire restrictions and closures.

Around 60 million years ago North America underwent a dramatic separation from Europe, sliding westward over a piece of the earth's crust known as the East Pacific Plate and leaving behind an ever-widening gulf that became the Atlantic Ocean. The East Pacific Plate collided with the North American Plate. This collision, named the Laramide orogeny, resulted in the birth of the modern Rocky Mountains and uplifted an old basin into a highland known today as the Colorado Plateau. Fragments of the East Pacific Plate also attached themselves to the leading edge of the North American Plate, transforming the Southwest from a coastal area to an interior region increasingly detached from the ocean.

In contrast to the compression and collision that characterized earlier events, the earth's crust began stretching in an east–west direction about 30 million years ago. The thinner, stretched crust of New Mexico and Texas cracked along zones of weakness called faults, resulting in a rift valley where New Mexico's Rio Grande now flows. These same forces created the stepped plateaus of northern Arizona and southern Utah.

UNIQUE LANDSCAPE FEATURES IN THE SOUTHWEST

Badlands Crumbling, mineral-filled soft rock; found in the Painted Desert at Petrified Forest National Park (p188), at Capitol Reef National Park (p211) and in the Bisti Badlands (p231).

Hoodoos Sculptured spires of rock weathered into towering pillars; showcased at Bryce Canyon National Park (p213) and Arches National Park (p209).

Natural Bridges Formed when streams cut through sandstone layers; three bridges can be seen at Natural Bridges National Monument (p211).

Goosenecks Early-stage natural bridges formed when a stream U-turns across a landscape; visible from Goosenecks Overlook at Capitol Reef National Park (p211).

Mesas Hulking formations of layered sandstone where the surrounding landscape has been stripped away; classic examples can be found at Monument Valley (p188) and elsewhere on the Arizona–Utah border.

During the Pleistocene glacial period, large bodies of water accumulated throughout the Southwest. Utah's **Great Salt Lake** is the most famous remnant of these mighty Ice Age lakes. Basins with now completely dry, salt-crusted lakebeds are especially conspicuous on a drive across Nevada.

For the past several million years the dominant force has probably been erosion. Not only do torrential rainstorms readily tear through soft sedimentary rocks, but the rise of the Rocky Mountains generates large, powerful rivers that wind throughout the Southwest, carving mighty canyons in their wake. Nearly all of the contemporary features in the Southwest, from arches (Arches National Park (p209) has more than 2000 sandstone arches) to hoodoos (natural rock columns), are the result of weathering and erosion.

Geology of the Grand Canyon

Arizona's Grand Canyon (p177) is the best-known geologic feature in the Southwest and for good reason: not only is it on a scale so massive it dwarfs the human imagination, but it also records two billion years of geologic history – a huge amount of time considering the earth is just 4.6 billion years old. The canyon itself, however, is young, a mere five to six million years old.

Carved by the powerful Colorado River as the land bulged upward, the 277-mile-long canyon reflects the differing hardness of the 10-plus layers of rocks in its walls. Shales, for instance, crumble easily and form slopes, while resistant limestones and sandstones form distinctive cliffs.

The layers making up the bulk of the canyon walls were laid during the Paleozoic era, 542 to 251 million years ago. These formations perch atop a group of one- to two-billion-year-old rocks lying at the bottom of the inner gorge of the canyon. Between these two distinct sets of rock is the Great Unconformity, a several-hundred-million-year gap in the geologic record where erosion erased 12,000ft of rock and left a huge mystery.

From desert plants and animals to gunslingers and Native Americans to hiking and cycling, www.desertusa.com deals the goods on the allure of the Southwestern desert.

Pacific Northwest

From 16 to 13 million years ago, eastern Oregon and Washington witnessed one of the premier episodes of volcanic activity in the planet's history. Due to shifting stresses in the earth's crust, much of interior western North America began cracking along thousands of lines and releasing enormous amounts of lava that flooded over the landscape. On multiple occasions, so much lava was produced that it filled the Columbia River

One of America's most respected narrative non-fiction writers, John McPhee travelled the 40th parallel to write about US geology for a project called *Annals of the Former World* (1998). The results include *Basin and Range* (1982; covering Utah and California), *Rising from the Plains* (1986; Wyoming), and *Assembling California* (1993).

channel and reached the Oregon coast, forming prominent headlands including Cape Lookout. Today, the hardened lava flows of eastern Oregon and Washington are easily seen in spectacular rimrock cliffs and flat-top mesas.

Not to be outdone, the ice ages of the past two million years created a massive ice field from Washington to British Columbia – and virtually every mountain range in the rest of the region was blanketed by glaciers.

The Rockies & the Great Plains

The Rockies

The Rocky Mountains run for 3000 miles from northern British Columbia in Canada to the Rio Grande in New Mexico. North America's longest range of mountains, the Rockies are actually the sum total of more than 100 distinct massifs. Important ranges that fall within the Rockies purview include the Sangre de Cristo Mountains), the Front Range (Colorado), the Wind River Range and Big Horn Mountains of Wyoming, and the Absaroka-Beartooth ranges in Montana.

The ranges formed between 80 and 55 millions years ago when a tectonic plate beneath the ocean forced its way beneath the continental shelf and pushed the earth upwards. Tectonic instability and glacial erosion, processes which continue to this day, shaped the mountains to those you see today. **Mt Elbert** (www.14ers.com; ⏲Jun-Sep) in Colorado (14,440 feet) is the highest peak in the Rockies.

Human beings first inhabited the Rockies when the last Ice Age ended, a mere 12,000 years ago. In the millennia since, the Rockies have been variously inhabited by many Native American tribes, among them the Apache, Arapaho, Cheyenne, Crow, Shoshone and Sioux. Their semi-nomadic lifestyles saw them inhabit the mountains in spring and summer, when they could fish, hunt deer and elk, and forage tubers and berries. In the cooler temperatures of fall and winter, they moved down to where vast herds of bison ranged across the plains.

The Great Plains

The Rockies' alter ego, the Great Plains dominate the interior of the continental United States. Reaching from west of the Mississippi River to the Rockies, stretching 500 miles east–west and more than 2000 miles north–south, the Great Plains is dominated by grasslands, often known as prairies.

Plains such as these are formed over millions of years, through the erosion of hills and mountains as ice and water push down the slopes and deposit sediments in layers. The Great Plains of Western USA are no exception. Their formation began around a billion years ago. Prior to the formation of the Rockies, which began to appear 80 million years ago, rising sea levels meant that the plains were for a time covered by shallow inland seas. After the Rockies appeared, the waters retreated (or seeped into the earth, creating vast underground aquifers) and the process of erosion and creation of sedimentary layers accelerated, extending the boundaries of the plains. The Plains' formation was largely completed, at least for now, when massive ice sheets or glaciers covered the Plains during the Ice Age, thereby smoothing and flattening the plains.

The plains consume North and South Dakota, Nebraska and Kansas in their entirety, and cover much of Wyoming, Montana, Colorado, New Mexico, Oklahoma and Texas.

To read more about two of Western USA's most iconic species, track down the recent *Path of the Puma: The Remarkable Resilience of the Mountain Lion* (Jim Williams; 2018) and *Down from the Mountain: The Life and Death of a Grizzly Bear* (Bryce Andrews; 2019).

Wildlife

Although the staggering numbers of animals that greeted the first European settlers are now a thing of the past, it is still possible to see wildlife thriving in the West in the right places and at the right times of year.

Bears

The black bear is among the most notorious animal in the Rockies. Adult males weigh from 275lb to 450lb; females weigh about 175lb to 250lb. They measure 3ft high on all fours and can be taller than 5ft when standing on their hind legs.

Black bears also roam the Pacific Northwest, the Southwest and California. They feed on berries, nuts, roots, grasses, insects, eggs, small mammals and fish, but can become a nuisance around campgrounds and mountain cabins where food is not stored properly.

According to the California Department of Fish and Wildlife, the state's mountain forests are home to an estimated 30,000 to 40,000 black bears, whose fur actually ranges in color from black to dark brown, cinnamon and even blond.

The grizzly bear, which can be seen on California's state flag, once roamed California's beaches and grasslands in large numbers, eating everything from whale carcasses to acorns. Grizzlies were particularly abundant in the Central Valley. The grizzly was extirpated in the early 1900s after relentless persecution. Grizzlies are classified as an endangered species in Colorado, but they are almost certainly gone from the state; the last documented grizzly in Colorado was killed in 1979. In 2016, scientists estimated there were between 674 and 839 grizzlies wandering the Yellowstone National Park area.

The best places to see bears are Yellowstone National Park (p118) and Glacier National Park (p133).

Wolves

The wolf is a potent symbol of America's wilderness. This smart, social predator is the largest species of canine – averaging more than 100lb and reaching nearly 3ft at the shoulder. An estimated 400,000 once roamed the continent from coast to coast, from Alaska to Mexico.

Wolves were not regarded warmly by European settlers. The first wildlife legislation in the British colonies was a wolf bounty. As 19th-century Americans tamed the West, they slaughtered the once-uncountable herds of bison, elk, deer and moose, replacing them with domestic cattle and sheep; wolves found the new creatures equally tasty.

To stop wolves from devouring the livestock, the wolf's extermination soon became official government policy. Up until 1965, for $20 to $50 an animal, wolves were shot, poisoned, trapped and dragged from dens; in the lower 48 states, only a few hundred gray wolves remained in northern Minnesota and Michigan.

In 1944 naturalist Aldo Leopold called for the return of the wolf. His argument was ecology, not nostalgia. His studies showed that wild ecosystems need their top predators to maintain a healthy biodiversity; in complex interdependence, all animals and plants suffered with the wolf gone.

An extremely adaptable creature, the coyote looks similar to a wolf but is about half the size, ranging from 15lb to 45lb. An icon of the Southwest, coyotes are found all over, even in cities.

Despite dire predictions from ranchers and hunters, gray wolves were reintroduced to the Greater Yellowstone region in 1995–96 and Mexican wolves to Arizona in 1998.

Protected and encouraged, wolf populations have made a remarkable recovery, with more than 6000 now counted in the continental US, and a further 8000 in Alaska. A recent study suggests that the introduction of wolves to Yellowstone may be helping the grizzly population there – wolves eat elk, leaving more berries for the grizzlies. In 2019, the US Fish and Wildlife Service proposed removing the gray wolf from the endangered species list; a decision is pending.

Bison

The American bison (or Great American buffalo) is the USA's national animal and the symbol of the devastation wrought upon the wildlife of the American West, but also its part renewal. Ten thousand years ago, vast herds of bison wandered from Alaska to New Mexico and all the way east to Florida. They play an important role in the mythology of many Native American tribes, who hunted the bison for meat and skins. The estimated population at the end of the 18th century was around 65 million – in herds so thick they 'darkened the whole plains,' as explorers Lewis and Clark wrote. By 1889, there were just 541 bison left in America. Overcoming near extinction, new herds arose from these last survivors, so that one of America's noblest animals can again be admired in its gruff majesty. These days, there are believed to be somewhere between 15,000 and 30,000 bison roaming free, with a total population of half a million on fenced and private lands. The easiest places to see them are Yellowstone National Park (p118), Grand Teton National Park (p123) and surrounds in Wyoming, as well as Montana's National Bison Range (p134).

In 2020, four hydroelectric dams on the Klamath River will be demolished to improve fish passage and water quality on the Oregon–California waterway. The hope is to one day reclaim the Klamath's status as one of the most productive salmon and steelhead (trout) rivers in the West.

In winter, the bison sports a long and shaggy brown winter coat, which turns lighter in winter; calves are a much lighter shade of brown. Up to 9.2ft long and weighing 2800lb, bisons are herbivores which graze on grasslands – the prairie is their natural habitat – usually in the same area for a couple of hours before moving on; they are known to move up to two miles in a day. They can be deceptively fast, running at up to 40mph; in the last two decades of the 20th century, bisons injured more people in Yellowstone National Park (79) than did bears (24).

Environmental Issues

Growth in the West comes with costs. In the Pacific Northwest, the production of cheap hydroelectricity and massive irrigation projects along the Columbia River have led to the near-irreversible destruction of the river's ecosystem. Dams have all but eliminated most runs of native salmon and have further disrupted the lives of remaining Native Americans who depend on the river. Logging of old-growth forests has left ugly scars. Washington's Puget Sound area and Portland's extensive suburbs are groaning under the weight of rapidly growing population centers.

Ongoing controversies include arguments about the locations of nuclear-power plants and the transport and disposal of nuclear waste in the Southwest, notably at Yucca Mountain, 90 miles from Las Vegas. Fracking, an aggressive practice of extracting oil and gas through hydraulic fracturing, has taken hold of much of the West, supplying economic mini-booms in formerly depressed areas but also setting off environmental problems ranging from compromised water tables to a fatality from an exploding home in Colorado.

Read Marc Reisner's *Cadillac Desert: The American West and Its Disappearing Water* (rev. 1993) for a thorough account of how exploding populations in the West have utilized every drop of available water.

Climate Change

A report published by the National Academy of Sciences in 2016 states that human-caused climate change is behind the exponential increase in wildfires in the Western US. The report finds the threat to be greatest in the Northwest, including Idaho, Wyoming, Montana, eastern Oregon and eastern Washington.

Records show that regional temperatures have increased while snowpack has decreased. Rising sea levels and drier forests bring layered consequences to human activity and whole ecosystems. With the United States' exit from the Paris Agreement on climate in 2017, many states (including Washington, California and Oregon) as well as cities (including LA, Seattle and Denver) are keeping the agreement's commitments for the sake of their own futures.

Survival Guide

Directory A–Z

Accessible Travel

➡ The USA can be an accommodating place for those with a physical disability. The *Americans with Disabilities Act* (ADA) requires that all public buildings, private buildings built after 1993 (including hotels, restaurants, theaters and museums) and public transit be wheelchair accessible. Nevertheless, do call ahead to confirm what is available. Some local tourist offices publish detailed accessibility guides.

➡ Download Lonely Planet's free Accessible Travel guides from http://lptravel.to/AccessibleTravel.

➡ Telephone companies offer relay operators, available via teletypewriter (TTY) numbers, for the hearing impaired. Most banks provide ATM instructions in Braille, and via earphone jacks for hearing-impaired customers. All major airlines, Greyhound buses and Amtrak trains will assist travelers with disabilities; just describe your needs when making reservations at least 48 hours in advance. Service animals (guide dogs) are allowed to accompany passengers, but bring documentation.

➡ Some car-rental agencies – such as Avis and Hertz – offer hand-controlled vehicles and vans with wheelchair lifts at no extra charge, but you must reserve them well in advance. Accessible Vans of America (www.accessiblevans.com) rents accessible vans throughout the USA. In many cities and towns, public buses are accessible to wheelchair riders; just let the driver know that you need the lift or ramp.

➡ Many national and some state parks and recreation areas have wheelchair-accessible paved, graded dirt or boardwalk trails. The website for the Rails-to-Trails Conservancy (www.traillink.com/activity/wheelchair-accessible-trails) lists wheelchair-accessible trails by state.

➡ US citizens and permanent residents with permanent disabilities are entitled to a free 'America the Beautiful' Access Pass, which gives free entry to all federal recreation lands (eg national parks).

Resources

Some helpful resources for travelers with disabilities:

Access Northern California (http://accessnca.org) Extensive links to accessible-travel resources, publications, tours and transportation, including outdoor recreation opportunities, plus a searchable lodgings database and an events calendar.

Arizona Raft Adventures (www.azraft.com) Can accommodate disabled travelers on rafting trips through the Grand Canyon.

Disabled Sports USA (☎301-217-0960; www.disabledsportsusa.org) Offers sports, adventure and recreation programs for those with disabilities. Also publishes *Challenge* magazine.

Mobility International USA (☎541-343-1284; www.miusa.org; 132 E Broadway, No 343, Eugene; ⏰9am-5pm Mon-Fri) Advises USA-bound disabled travelers on mobility issues.

Splore (https://discovernac.org/programs/splore-outdoor-adventures) Offers accessible outdoor adventure trips in Utah.

Customs Regulations

For a complete and current list of US customs regulations, visit the official portal for US Customs and Border Protection (www.cbp.gov).

Duty-free allowances per person are typically as follows:

➡ 1L of liquor (provided you are at least 21 years old)

➡ 100 cigars and 200 cigarettes (if you are at least 18)

➡ $200 worth of gifts and purchases ($800 if a returning US citizen)

If you arrive with $10,000 or more in US or foreign currency, it must be declared.

Heavy penalties apply for attempting to import illegal drugs. Other forbidden items include drug paraphernalia, firearms, lottery tickets, items with fake brand names, and most goods made in Cuba, Iran, Myanmar (Burma) and parts of Sudan. Any fruit, vegetables or other food or plant material must be declared (whereby you'll undergo a time-consuming search) or left in the bins in the arrival area.

Discount Cards

America the Beautiful Interagency Annual Pass (www.nps.gov/planyourvisit/passes.htm; $80) This pass admits the driver and all passengers in a single, noncommercial vehicle, or four adults aged 16 or older, to all national parks and federal recreational lands (eg USFS, BLM) for one year. Children aged 15 and younger are admitted free. Purchase the pass online or at any national park entrance station. US citizens and permanent residents 62 years and older are eligible for an annual/lifetime Senior Pass ($20/80), which grants free entry and 50% off some recreational-use fees such as camping, as does the lifetime Access Pass (free to US citizens or permanent residents with a permanent disability). These passes are available in person or by mail. A free annual US Military Pass for current members of the US armed forces and their dependents is available at recreation sites with Common Access card or Military ID (Form 1173).

American Association of Retired Persons (www.aarp.org) This advocacy group for Americans 50 years and older offers member discounts on hotels (usually 10%), car rentals and more. People over 65 years (sometimes 55, 60 or 62) often qualify for the same discounts as students; any ID showing your birth date should suffice as proof of age.

American Automobile Association (AAA; www.aaa.com) Members of AAA and its foreign affiliates (eg CAA, AA) qualify for small discounts on Amtrak trains, car rentals, motels and hotels (usually 5% to 15%), chain restaurants, shopping, tours and theme parks.

International Student Identity Card (www.isic.org; $20) Offers savings on airline fares, travel insurance and local attractions for full-time students. For nonstudents under 31 years, an International Youth Travel Card ($20) grants similar benefits. Cards are issued by student unions, hosteling organizations and travel agencies.

Student Advantage Card (www.shopandtravelusa.com/sa-mobile) Offers international and US students 10% savings on Amtrak and 20% on Greyhound, plus discounts at some chain shops and car rentals.

Electricity

Embassies & Consulates

International travelers needing to contact their home country's embassy while in the US should visit www.embassy.org for contact information of all foreign embassies in Washington, DC. Some countries have consulates in LA; look under 'Consulates' in the yellow pages, or call local directory assistance.

Health

Health Insurance

The USA offers excellent health care. The problem is that, unless you have good insurance, it is prohibitively expensive. It's *essential* to purchase travel health insurance if your regular policy doesn't cover you when you're abroad. Even with insurance, you will probably have to pay out of pocket for treatment and then chase up reimbursement afterwards.

- Overseas visitors with travel health-insurance policies may need to contact a call center for an assessment by phone before getting medical treatment.
- Keep all receipts and documentation for billing and insurance claims and reimbursement purposes.
- If you plan on doing any adventure sports (skiing, diving etc), check to make sure insurance covers this – some policies specifically exclude 'extreme' activities.

Availability & Cost of Health Care

- Medical treatment in the USA is of the highest caliber, but the expense could kill you. Many health-care professionals demand payment at the time of service, especially from out-of-towners and international visitors.
- For medical emergencies call 911 or go to the nearest 24-hour hospital emergency room, or ER); in other instances, phone around to find a doctor who will accept your insurance.
- Some health-insurance policies require you to get pre-authorization for medical treatment before seeking help.

➡ Carry any medications you may need in their original containers, clearly labeled. Bring a signed, dated letter from your doctor describing all medical conditions and medications (including generic names).

Environmental Hazards

ALTITUDE SICKNESS

➡ Visitors from lower elevations undergo rather dramatic physiological changes as they adapt to high altitudes.

➡ Symptoms, which tend to manifest during the first day after reaching altitude, may include headache, fatigue, loss of appetite, nausea, sleeplessness, increased urination and hyperventilation due to overexertion.

➡ Symptoms normally resolve within 24 to 48 hours.

➡ The rule of thumb: don't ascend until the symptoms descend.

➡ More severe cases may display extreme disorientation, ataxia (loss of coordination and balance), breathing problems (especially a persistent cough) and vomiting. These folks should descend immediately and get to a hospital.

➡ To avoid the discomfort characterizing the milder symptoms, drink plenty of water and take it easy – at 7000ft, a pleasant walk around Santa Fe can wear you out faster than a steep hike at sea level.

DEHYDRATION, HEAT EXHAUSTION & HEATSTROKE

➡ Take it easy as you acclimatize, especially on hot summer days and in the desert.

➡ Drink plenty of water. One gallon per person per day minimum is recommended when you're active outdoors.

➡ Dehydration (lack of water) or salt deficiency can cause heat exhaustion, often characterized by heavy sweating, pale skin, fatigue, lethargy, headaches, nausea, vomiting, dizziness, muscle cramps and rapid, shallow breathing.

➡ Long, continuous exposure to high temperatures can lead to possibly fatal heatstroke. Warning signs include altered mental state, hyperventilation and flushed, hot and dry skin (ie sweating stops). Hospitalization is essential. Meanwhile, get out of the sun, remove clothing that retains heat (cotton is OK), douse the body with water and fan continuously; ice packs can be applied to the neck, armpits and groin.

HYPOTHERMIA

➡ Skiers and hikers will find that temperatures in the mountains and desert can quickly drop below freezing, especially during winter or if you are canyoneering. Even a sudden spring shower or high winds can lower your body temperature dangerously fast.

➡ Instead of cotton, wear synthetic or woolen clothing that retains warmth even when wet. Carry waterproof layers (eg Gore-Tex jacket, plastic poncho, rain pants) and high-energy, easily digestible snacks such as chocolate, nuts and dried fruit.

➡ Symptoms of hypothermia include exhaustion, numbness, shivering, stumbling, slurred speech, dizzy spells, muscle cramps and irrational or even violent behavior.

➡ To treat hypothermia, get out of bad weather and change into dry, warm clothing. Drink hot liquids (no caffeine or alcohol) and snack on high-calorie food.

➡ In advanced stages, carefully put hypothermia sufferers in a warm sleeping bag cocooned inside a wind- and waterproof outer wrapping. Do not rub victims, who must be handled gently.

TAP WATER

You can drink tap water anywhere you find it in Western USA.

Insurance

Getting travel insurance to cover theft, loss and medical problems is highly recommended.

➡ Some policies do not cover 'risky' activities such as scuba diving, motorcycling and skiing, so read the fine print. Make sure the policy at least covers hospital stays and an emergency flight home.

➡ Paying for your airline ticket or rental car with a credit card may provide limited travel accident insurance.

➡ If you already have private health insurance or a homeowner's or renter's policy, it is critical to find out what those policies cover and get supplemental insurance. You do not want to have a medical emergency in the US and then find you are not covered – the costs for even minor treatments are often astronomical.

➡ If you have prepaid a large portion of your vacation, trip cancellation insurance may be a worthwhile expense.

➡ Worldwide travel insurance is available at www.lonelyplanet.com/travel-insurance. You can buy, extend and claim online anytime – even if you're already on the road.

Internet Access

➡ Travelers will have few problems staying connected in tech-savvy USA. Most hotels, guesthouses, hostels and motels have wi-fi (usually free); ask when reserving.

➡ Across the US, most cafes and some restaurants offer free wi-fi. Some cities have wi-fi-connected parks and plazas, and the public library is always a good standby. Most libraries have public internet terminals (albeit with time limits) in addition to wi-fi.

➡ Non-US laptops may need an AC adapter, plus a plug adapter for US sockets; both are available at larger electronics shops, such as Best Buy.

Legal Matters

In everyday matters, there is no system for paying traffic or other fines on the spot if you are stopped by police. Attempting to pay a fine to an officer is frowned upon at best and may result in a charge of bribery. For traffic offenses, the police officer or highway patroller will explain the options to you. There is usually a 30-day period to pay a fine. Most matters can be handled by mail.

If you are arrested, you have a legal right to an attorney and you are allowed to remain silent. There is no legal reason to speak to a police officer if you don't wish, but never walk away from an officer until given permission to do so.

Anyone who is arrested is legally allowed to make one phone call. If you can't afford a lawyer, a public defender will be appointed to you free of charge. Foreign visitors who don't have a lawyer, friend or family member to help should call their embassy; the police will provide the number upon request.

As a matter of principle, the US legal system presumes a person innocent until proven guilty. Each state has its own civil and criminal laws, and what is legal in one state may be illegal in others.

EATING PRICE RANGES

The following price ranges refer to an average main course at dinner, not including drinks, appetizers, desserts, taxes or tip. Note the same dishes at lunch will usually be cheaper, maybe even half-price.

$ less than $15

$$ $15–$25

$$$ more than $25

LGBTIQ+ Travelers

LGBTIQ+ travelers will find lots of places where they can be themselves without thinking twice. Beaches and big cities typically are the most gay-friendly destinations.

Attitudes

Most major US cities have a visible and open LGBTIQ+ community.

The level of acceptance varies across the West. In some places, there is absolutely no tolerance whatsoever, and in others acceptance is predicated on LGBTIQ+ people not 'flaunting' their sexual preference or identity. In rural areas and extremely conservative enclaves, it's unwise to be openly out, as violence and verbal abuse can sometimes occur. When in doubt, assume locals follow a 'don't ask, don't tell' policy.

After a 2015 US Supreme Court decision, same-sex marriage is now legal in all 50 states.

Hot Spots

San Francisco stakes a strong claim to being America's LGBTIQ+ capital, while Los Angeles, Seattle, Las Vegas, Palm Springs and Denver also have vibrant gay scenes and publicly active LGBTIQ+ communities.

Resources

Advocate (www.advocate.com) Gay-oriented news website reports on business, politics, arts, entertainment and travel.

Gay Travel (www.gaytravel.com) Online guides to US destinations.

GLBT National Help Center (www.glbthotline.org) A national hotline for counseling, information and referrals.

National LGBTQ Task Force (www.thetaskforce.org) National activist group's website covers news, politics and current issues.

OutTraveler (www.outtraveler.com) Has useful online city guides and travel articles to various US and foreign destinations.

Purple Roofs (www.purpleroofs.com) Lists gay-owned and gay-friendly B&Bs and hotels nationwide.

Money

ATMs are widely available. Credit cards are normally required for hotel reservations and car rentals.

ATMs

➡ ATMS are located at most banks, shopping malls, airports, and grocery and convenience stores.

➡ Expect a minimum surcharge of $2.50 per transaction, in addition to any fees charged by your home bank. Some ATMs in Las Vegas charge more.

➡ Most ATMs are connected to international networks and offer decent foreign-exchange rates.

➡ Withdrawing cash from an ATM using a credit card usually incurs a hefty fee and high interest rates; check with your credit-card company for a PIN.

Cash

Most people do not carry large amounts of cash for everyday use, relying instead on credit cards, debit cards and smartphones. It is good to have some cash on hand on road trips, as you may need it for campsites or the occasional cafe or restaurant.

Credit Cards

Major credit cards are almost universally accepted. In fact, it's almost impossible to rent a car, book a room or buy tickets over the phone without one. A credit card may also be vital in emergencies. Visa, MasterCard and American Express are the most widely accepted.

Money Changers

➡ Exchange money at major airports, some banks and all currency-exchange offices such as American Express or Travelex. Always inquire about rates and fees.

➡ Outside big cities, exchanging money may be a problem, so make sure you have a credit card and sufficient cash on hand.

Taxes

➡ Sales tax varies by state and county, with state sales taxes ranging from zero in Montana to 7.25% in California.

➡ Hotel taxes vary by city.

Tipping

Tipping is *not* optional. Only withhold tips in cases of outrageously bad service.

Airport skycaps and hotel bellhops $2 per bag, minimum $5 per cart

Bartenders 10% to 15% per round, minimum $1 per drink

Concierges Nothing for simple information, up to $20 for securing last-minute restaurant reservations, sold-out show tickets etc

Housekeeping staff $2 to $4 daily, left under the card provided; more if you're messy

Parking valets At least $2 when handed back your car keys

Restaurant staff and room service 10% to 20%, unless a gratuity is already charged

Taxi drivers 10% to 15% of metered fare, rounded up to the next dollar

Traveler's Checks

➡ Traveler's checks have pretty much fallen out of use.

➡ Larger restaurants, hotels and department stores will occasionally accept traveler's checks (in US dollars only), but small businesses, markets and fast-food chains may refuse them.

➡ Visa and American Express are the most widely accepted issuers of traveler's checks.

Opening Hours

Banks 8:30am–4:30pm Monday to Thursday, to 5:30pm Friday (and possibly 9am–noon Saturday)

Bars 5pm–midnight Sunday to Thursday, to 2am Friday and Saturday

Nightclubs 10pm–2am Thursday to Saturday

Post offices 9am–5pm Monday to Friday

Shopping malls 9am–9pm

Stores 10am–6pm Monday to Saturday, noon–5pm Sunday

Supermarkets 8am–8pm, some open 24 hours

Photography

➡ Digital-camera memory cards are widely available at chain retailers such as Best Buy and Target.

➡ Some Native American tribal lands prohibit photography and video completely; when it's allowed, you may be required to purchase a permit. Always ask permission if you want to photograph someone close up; anyone who then agrees to be photographed may expect a small tip.

➡ For more advice on picture-taking, consult Lonely Planet's *Guide to Travel Photography*.

Post

➡ For 24-hour postal information, including post office locations and hours, contact the US Postal Service (www.usps.com), which is reliable and inexpensive.

➡ For sending urgent or important letters and packages either domestically or overseas, Federal Express (www.fedex.com) and United Parcel Service (www.ups.com) offer more expensive door-to-door delivery services.

Public Holidays

On the following national public holidays, banks, schools and government offices (including post offices) are closed, and transportation, museums and other services operate on a Sunday schedule. Holidays falling on a weekend are usually observed the following Monday.

New Year's Day January 1

Martin Luther King Jr Day Third Monday in January

Presidents' Day Third Monday in February

Memorial Day Last Monday in May

Independence Day July 4

Labor Day First Monday in September

Columbus Day Second Monday in October

Veterans Day November 11

Thanksgiving Fourth Thursday in November

Christmas Day December 25

During spring break (March and April), grade school and college students get a week off from school. For students of all ages, summer vacation runs from June to August.

Safe Travel

Western USA is a reasonably safe place to visit.

➡ The greatest danger is posed by car accidents – the risks increase at night.

➡ LA has the most crime, though tourists are unlikely to run into trouble.

➡ Wildlife can pose problems in national parks if you don't heed proper precautions (eg proper food storage).

Telephone

Dialing Codes

➡ US phone numbers consist of a three-digit area code followed by a seven-digit local number.

➡ When dialing a number within the same area code, you generally have to dial the entire 10-digit number, but not always.

➡ If you are calling long distance, dial ☎1 plus the area code plus the phone number.

➡ Toll-free numbers begin with ☎800, 866, 877 or 888 and must be preceded by 1.

➡ For direct international calls, dial ☎011 plus the country code plus the area code (usually without the initial '0') plus the local phone number.

➡ For international call assistance, dial ☎00.

➡ If you're calling from abroad, the country code for the US is ☎1 (the same as Canada, but international rates apply between the two countries).

Cell Phones

➡ Expect little to no coverage in remote or mountainous areas.

➡ SIM cards are sold at telecommunications and electronics stores. These stores also sell inexpensive prepaid phones, including some airtime. Verizon and AT&T have the two largest networks in the US. Verizon tends to have better coverage in rural areas.

Payphones & Phonecards

➡ Where payphones still exist, they are usually coin-operated, although some may only accept credit cards (eg in national parks).

➡ Local calls usually cost 35¢ to 50¢ minimum.

➡ For long-distance calls, you're usually better off buying a prepaid phonecard, sold at convenience stores, supermarkets, newsstands and electronics stores.

Time

➡ Most of Colorado, Wyoming, Montana, Idaho, Utah, New Mexico and Arizona follow Mountain Standard Time (GMT/UTC minus seven hours). California, Nevada, Oregon and Washington generally follow Pacific Standard Time (GMT/UTC minus eight hours). There are some variations within a state, usually based on location or season.

➡ Daylight Saving Time (DST) pushes the clocks ahead one hour. It runs from the second Sunday in March to the first Sunday in November.

➡ Arizona does not observe DST; during that period the state is one hour behind other Southwestern states. The Navajo Reservation, which lies in Arizona, New Mexico and Utah, does use Daylight Saving Time. The Hopi Reservation, which is surrounded by the Navajo Reservation in Arizona, follows the rest of Arizona.

GOVERNMENT TRAVEL ADVICE

The following government websites offer travel advisories and information for travellers.

Australian Department of Foreign Affairs & Trade (www.smartraveller.gov.au)

Canadian Department of Foreign Affairs & International Trade (www.voyage.gc.ca)

French Ministère des Affaires Étrangères et Européennes (www.diplomatie.gouv.fr/fr/conseils-aux-voyageurs)

German Auswärtiges Amt (www.auswaertiges-amt.de/de/ReiseUndSicherheit)

Italian Ministero degli Affari Esteri (www.viaggiaresicuri.mae.aci.it)

Japanese Ministry of Foreign Affairs (www.anzen.mofa.go.jp)

Netherlands Buitenlandse Zaken (www.nederlandwereldwijd.nl/reizen/reisadviezen)

New Zealand Ministry of Foreign Affairs & Trade (www.safetravel.govt.nz)

UK Foreign & Commonwealth Office (www.gov.uk/foreign-travel-advice)

US Department of State (https://travel.state.gov/content/travel/en/traveladvisories/traveladvisories.html/)

PRACTICALITIES

Newspapers & Magazines Leading national newspapers include the *New York Times*, *Wall Street Journal* and *USA Today*; *Time* and *Newsweek* are mainstream news magazines.

Radio & TV National Public Radio (NPR) can be found at the lower end of the FM dial. The main TV broadcasting channels are ABC, CBS, NBC, FOX and PBS (public broadcasting); the major cable channels are CNN (news), ESPN (sports), HBO (movies) and Weather Channel.

Smoking Most Western states are entirely smoke-free in restaurants, bars and workplaces. The exception is Nevada – casinos in particular are still quite smoky. You may still encounter smoky lobbies in chain hotels and budget-minded inns, but for the most part accommodations are smoke-free.

Weights & Measures Weights are measured in ounces (oz), pounds (lb) and tons; liquids in fluid ounces (fl oz), pints (pt), quarts (qt) and gallons (gal); and distance in inches (in), feet (ft), yards (yd) and miles (mi).

➡ The US date system is written as month/day/year. Thus, the 8th of June, 2019, becomes 6/8/19.

Toilets

Public toilets are free. If you can't find a public toilet, head to a gas station, restaurant or cafe (you may need to purchase something).

Tourist Information

➡ Most tourist offices have a website, from which you can download free travel guides. Offices also field phone calls; some local offices maintain daily lists of hotel room availability, but few offer reservation services. All tourist offices have self-service racks of brochures and discount coupons; some also sell maps and books.

➡ State-run 'welcome centers,' usually placed along interstate highways, tend to have materials that cover wider territories, and offices are usually open longer hours, including weekends and holidays.

➡ Many cities have an official convention and visitor bureau (CVB); these sometimes double as tourist bureaus, but since their main focus is drawing the business trade, CVBs can be less useful for independent travelers.

➡ Keep in mind that, in smaller towns, where the local chamber of commerce runs the tourist bureau, their lists of hotels, restaurants and services usually mention only chamber members; the town's cheapest options may be missing.

➡ Similarly, in prime tourist destinations, some private 'tourist bureaus' are really agents who book hotel rooms and tours on commission. They may offer excellent service and deals, but you'll get what they're selling and nothing else.

Visas

Visitors from Canada, the UK, Australia, New Zealand, Japan and many EU countries do not require a visa for stays of less than 90 days. Other nations should see https://travel.state.gov.

Be warned that all visa information is highly subject to change. US entry requirements keep evolving as national security regulations change. All travelers should double-check current visa and passport regulations before coming to the USA.

The US State Department (https://travel.state.gov) maintains the most comprehensive visa information, providing downloadable forms, lists of US consulates abroad and even visa wait times calculated by country.

Visa Waiver Program

➡ Pursuant to the Visa Waiver Program, many travelers visiting the US for sightseeing or for short visits will not need a visa to enter the country.

➡ According to VWP requirements, citizens of certain countries may enter the US for stays of 90 days or fewer without a US visa. This list is subject to continual rejigging. Check https://travel.state.gov to see which countries are included under the waiver and for a summary of current VWP requirements.

➡ Citizens of a VWP country must have a passport that meets current US standards and receive approval from the Electronic System for Travel Authorization (ESTA) in advance. Register online with the Department of Homeland Security (https://esta.cbp.dhs.gov/esta) at least 72 hours before arrival. The fee is $14. Canadians are currently exempt from ESTA.

➡ Visitors from VWP countries arriving by air or sea must arrive on an approved air or sea carrier. They must also demonstrate that their trip is for 90 days or fewer and that they have a round-trip or onward ticket.

➡ All foreign visitors entering the US from abroad require a passport. In most cases, passports must be valid for at least six months after the end of your intended stay in the USA. If your passport doesn't meet current US standards, you'll be turned back at the border. If your passport was issued on or after October 26, 2006 it must be an e-passport with a digital photo and an integrated chip containing biometric data.

➡ For assistance, check out the Visa Wizard on the State Department (https://travel.state.gov) website.

Visa Applications

➡ With the exception of most Canadian citizens and those travelers entering under the Visa Waiver Program (VWP), all foreign visitors to the US need a visa. For more details about visa requirements, visit https://travel.state.gov.

➡ Most visa applicants must schedule a personal interview, to which you must bring all your documentation and proof of fee payment. Wait times for interviews vary, but afterward, barring problems, visa issuance takes from a few days to a few weeks.

➡ You'll need a recent color photo (2in by 2in), and you must pay a nonrefundable $160 processing fee, plus in a few cases an additional visa issuance reciprocity fee. You'll also need to fill out the online DS-160 nonimmigrant visa electronic application.

➡ Depending on the type of visa requested, applicants may have to provide documentation confirming the purpose of their trip, their intent to depart the US after their trip and an ability to cover all costs related to the trip. Visit the website for more details.

Short-Term Departures & Re-entry

It's temptingly easy to make trips across the border to Canada or Mexico, but upon return to the USA, non-Americans will be subject to the full immigration procedure.

➡ Always take your passport when you cross the border.

➡ If your immigration card still has plenty of time on it, you will probably be able to re-enter using the same one, but if it has nearly expired, you will have to apply for a new card, and border control may want to see your onward air ticket, sufficient funds and so on.

➡ Citizens of most Western countries will not need a visa to visit Canada, so shouldn't have a problem passing through on the way to Alaska.

➡ Travelers entering the USA by bus from Canada may be closely scrutinized. A round-trip ticket that takes you back to Canada will most likely make US immigration feel less suspicious.

➡ At the time of writing, most visitors did not need a visa for short-term travel in Mexico (under 90 to 180 days, depending on your nationality).

Women Travelers

Women traveling alone or in groups should not expect to encounter any particular problems in the USA. The community website www.journeywoman.com facilitates women exchanging travel tips, and has links to other helpful resources.

The booklet *Her Own Way*, published by the Canadian government, is filled with general travel advice; download the PDF or read it online at https://travel.gc.ca/travelling/publications/her-own-way.

Some women carry a whistle, mace or cayenne-pepper spray in case of assault. If you purchase a spray, contact a police station to find out about local regulations. Laws regarding sprays vary from state to state, and federal law prohibits them being carried on planes.

If you're assaulted, consider calling a rape-crisis hotline before calling the police, unless you are in immediate danger, in which case you should call ☎911. Be aware that not all police have as much sensitivity training or experience assisting sexual-assault survivors as staff at rape-crisis centers, who will tirelessly advocate on your behalf and act as a link to other community services, including hospitals and police. Telephone books have listings of local rape-crisis centers, or contact the 24-hour National Sexual Assault Hotline (☎800-656-4673). Alternatively, go straight to a hospital emergency room.

National advocacy groups that may be useful:

National Organization for Women (https://now.org/) A grassroots movement fighting for women's rights.

Planned Parenthood (www.plannedparenthood.org) Offers referrals to women's health clinics throughout the country.

Transportation

GETTING THERE & AWAY

Flights, cars and tours can be booked online at www.lonelyplanet.com/bookings.

Entering Western USA

If you are flying into the US, the first airport where you land is where you must go through immigration and customs, even if you are continuing on the flight to another destination. Fingerprints are taken and biometric information is checked upon entry.

Passport

- Under the Western Hemisphere Travel Initiative (WHTI), all travelers must have a valid machine-readable passport (MRP) when entering the USA by air, land or sea.
- Exceptions to the above are only for most US citizens and some Canadian and Mexican citizens traveling by land or sea who can present other WHTI-compliant documents (eg pre-approved 'trusted traveler' cards).
- All foreign passports must meet current US standards and be valid for the length of your stay. Certain nationalities need passports that are valid for a minimum of six months longer than the intended stay.

Air

Airports

Western USA's primary international airports:

Los Angeles International Airport (LAX; Map p244; www.lawa.org/welcomeLAX.aspx; 1 World Way) California's largest and busiest airport, 20 miles southwest of downtown LA, near the coast.

San Francisco International Airport (SFO; www.flysfo.com; S McDonnell Rd) Northern California's major hub, 14 miles south of downtown, on San Francisco Bay.

Seattle-Tacoma International (SEA; ☎206-787-5388; www.portseattle.org/Sea-Tac; 17801 International Blvd; 🛜) Known locally as 'Sea-Tac.'

Major regional airports with limited international service:

Albuquerque International Sunport (ABQ; ☎505-244-7700; www.abqsunport.com; 2200 Sunport Blvd SE; 🛜) Serving Albuquerque and all of New Mexico.

Denver International Airport (DEN; ☎303-342-2000; www.flydenver.com; 🛜) Serving southern Colorado.

LA/Ontario International Airport (ONT; ☎909-937-2700; www.flyontario.com; 2500 E Airport Dr; 🛜) In Riverside County, east of LA.

McCarran International Airport (LAS; Map p148; ☎702-261-5211; www.mccarran.com; 5757 Wayne Newton Blvd; 🛜) Serves Las Vegas, NV, and southern

CLIMATE CHANGE & TRAVEL

Every form of transport that relies on carbon-based fuel generates CO_2, the main cause of human-induced climate change. Modern travel is dependent on airplanes, which might use less fuel per mile per person than most cars but travel much greater distances. The altitude at which aircraft emit gases (including CO_2) and particles also contributes to their climate change impact. Many websites offer 'carbon calculators' that allow people to estimate the carbon emissions generated by their journey and, for those who wish to do so, to offset the impact of the greenhouse gases emitted with contributions to portfolios of climate-friendly initiatives throughout the world. Lonely Planet offsets the carbon footprint of all staff and author travel.

Utah. Las Vegas is 290 miles from the South Rim of Grand Canyon National Park and 277 miles from the North Rim.

Mineta San Jose International Airport (SJC; 408-392-3600; www.flysanjose.com; 1701 Airport Blvd) In San Francisco's South Bay.

Oakland International Airport (OAK; 510-563-3300; www.oaklandairport.com; 1 Airport Dr; ; Oakland International Airport) In San Francisco's East Bay.

Palm Springs International Airport (PSP; 760-318-3800; www.palmspringsairport.com; 3400 E Tahquitz Canyon Way, Palm Springs) In the desert, east of LA.

Portland International Airport (PDX; 503-460-4234; www.flypdx.com; 7000 NE Airport Way; ; Red) About 12 miles from downtown Portland, OR.

Salt Lake City International Airport (SLC; 801-575-2400; www.slcairport.com; 776 N Terminal Dr;) Serving Salt Lake City and northern Utah; a good choice if you're headed to the North Rim of Grand Canyon National Park and the Arizona Strip.

San Diego International Airport (SAN; Map p272; 619-400-2400; www.san.org; 3325 N Harbor Dr;) Four miles northwest of downtown.

Sky Harbor International Airport (PHX; Map p164; 602-273-3300; www.skyharbor.com; 3400 E Sky Harbor Blvd;) Serving Phoenix and the Grand Canyon; one of the 10 busiest airports in the country. Phoenix is 220 miles from the South Rim of Grand Canyon National Park and 335 miles from the North Rim.

Tucson International Airport (TUS; 520-573-8100; www.flytucson.com; 7250 S Tucson Blvd;) Serving Tucson and southern Arizona.

Vancouver International Airport (YVR; 604-207-7077; www.yvr.ca; 3211 Grant McConachie Way, Richmond;) Located 6 miles south of Vancouver, Canada, on Sea Island; between Vancouver and the municipality of Richmond.

Security

➡ To get through airport security checkpoints, you'll need a boarding pass and photo ID. Thirty-minute wait times are standard.

➡ Some travelers may be required to undergo a secondary screening, involving hand pat-downs and carry-on luggage searches.

➡ Airport security measures restrict many common items (eg pocket knives) from being carried on planes. Check current restrictions with the Transportation Security Administration (TSA; www.tsa.gov).

➡ Currently, TSA requires that all carry-on liquids and gels be stored in 3.4oz or smaller bottles placed inside a quart-sized clear plastic ziplock bag. Exceptions, which must be declared to checkpoint security officers, include medications.

➡ All checked luggage is screened for explosives. TSA may open your suitcase for visual confirmation, breaking the lock if necessary. Leave your bags unlocked or use a TSA-approved lock like Travel Sentry (www.travelsentry.org).

Land

Border Crossings

➡ It is relatively easy crossing from the USA into Canada or Mexico; it's crossing back into the USA that can pose problems if you haven't brought your required documents. Check the ever-changing passport and visa (p450) requirements with the US Department of State (www.state.gov/travel) beforehand. US Customs and Border Protection (https://bwt.cbp.gov) tracks current wait times at every land border crossing.

DEPARTURE TAX

Departure tax is included in the price of a ticket.

➡ Some borders are open 24 hours, but most are not.

➡ Have your papers in order, be polite and don't make jokes or casual conversation with US border officials.

➡ Drug cartel violence and crime are serious dangers along the US–Mexico border.

Bus

➡ Greyhound (www.greyhound.com) has direct connections between Canada and the Northern US, but you may have to transfer to a different bus at the border. You can also book through Greyhound Canada (www.greyhound.ca).

➡ Northbound buses from Mexico into the USA can take some time to cross the US border; US immigration may insist on checking every person on board.

Car & Motorcycle

➡ If driving into the USA from Canada or Mexico, bring your vehicle's registration papers, liability insurance and driver's license; an international driving permit (IDP) is a good supplement, but not a requirement.

➡ If you're renting a car or motorcycle, ask if the agency allows its vehicles to be taken across the Mexican or Canadian borders; chances are it doesn't, and if it does you'll need prior permission.

TO & FROM CANADA

➡ Canadian auto insurance is typically valid in the USA, and vice versa.

➡ If your papers are in order, taking your own car across the US–Canada border is usually quick and easy.

➡ On weekends and holidays, especially in summer,

CROSSING THE MEXICAN BORDER

The issue of crime-related violence in Mexico has been front and center in the international press for a number of years now. Nogales, AZ, for example, is safe for travelers, but Nogales, Mexico, is a major locus for the drug trade and its associated violence. We cannot safely recommend crossing the border for an extended period until the security situation changes. You're fine for day trips, but anything past that may be risky.

The US Department of State (https://travel.state.gov) recommends travelers visit its website before traveling to Mexico. Here you can check for travel updates and warnings and confirm the latest border-crossing requirements. Before leaving, US citizens can sign up for the Smart Traveler Enrollment Program (https://step.state.gov/step) to receive email updates.

US and Canadian citizens entering the US from Mexico at airports must present a valid passport. To enter by land or sea, US and Canadian citizens are required to present a valid WHTI-compliant document, such as a passport, US passport card, enhanced driver's license or trusted traveler card (NEXUS, SENTRI, Global Entry or FAST). Check the latest requirements as this may change.

US and Canadian children under 16 years can also enter using a birth certificate, a consular report of birth abroad, naturalization certificate or Canadian citizenship card. All other nationals must carry a passport and, if needed, a visa for entering Mexico and re-entering the US. Regulations change frequently, so get the latest scoop at www.cbp.gov.

border-crossing traffic can be heavy and the waits long.

➡ Occasionally the authorities of either country will decide to search a car *extremely* thoroughly. Remain calm and be polite if faced with this situation.

TO & FROM MEXICO

➡ Very few car-rental companies will let you take a car from the US into Mexico.

➡ Unless you're planning an extended stay in Tijuana, taking a car across the Mexican border is more trouble than it's worth. Instead take the trolley from San Diego or leave your car on the US side and walk across.

➡ US auto insurance is not valid in Mexico, so even a short trip into Mexico's border region requires you to buy Mexican car insurance, available for around $25 per day at most border crossings, as well as from the American Automobile Association (www.aaa.com).

➡ For a longer driving trip into Mexico beyond the border zone or Baja California, you'll need a Mexican *permiso de importación temporal de vehículos* from Banjercito (temporary vehicle import permit; www.gob.mx/banjercito).

➡ Expect long border-crossing waits, as security has tightened and the number of those crossing rises with each passing year.

➡ See Lonely Planet's *Mexico* guide for further details.

Train

➡ Amtrak (www.amtrakcascades.com) operates the daily *Cascades* rail service between Eugene, OR, and Vancouver, Canada, with connecting bus services to destinations not served by train.

➡ **VIA Rail** (☎888-842-7245; www.viarail.ca) also serves Vancouver, BC, with routes running north and east across Canada.

➡ US/Canadian customs and immigration inspections happen at the border, not upon boarding.

➡ Currently, no train service connects Arizona or California with Mexico.

Sea

If you're interested in taking a cruise ship to America – as well as to other interesting ports of call – a good specialized travel agency is Cruise Web (https://cruiseweb.com).

You can also travel to and from the USA on a freighter, though it will be much slower and less cushy than a cruise. Nevertheless, freighters aren't spartan (some advertise cruise-ship-level amenities) and they are much cheaper (sometimes by half). Trips range from a week to two months; stops at interim ports are usually quick.

For more information, try Cruise & Freighter Travel Association (www.travltips.com), which has listings for freighter cruises and other boat travel.

GETTING AROUND

Air

The domestic air system is extensive and reliable, with

a number of competing airlines, hundreds of airports and thousands of flights daily. Flying is usually more expensive than traveling by bus, train or car, but it's the best option if you're in a hurry.

Airlines in the Western USA

Overall, air travel in the USA is very safe (much safer than driving on the nation's highways); for comprehensive details by carrier, check out www.airsafe.com.

The main domestic carriers in the West:

Alaska Airlines (800-252-7522; www.alaskaair.com) Serves Alaska and the Western US, with flights to the East Coast and Hawaii.

American Airlines (800-433-7300; www.aa.com) Nationwide service.

Delta (800-221-1212; www.delta.com) Nationwide service.

Frontier Airlines (801-401-9000; www.flyfrontier.com) Denver-based airline with service across the continental US.

JetBlue Airways (800-538-2583; www.jetblue.com) Nonstop connections between Eastern and Western US cities, plus Florida, New Orleans and Texas.

Southwest Airlines (800-435-9792; www.southwest.com) Service across the continental USA.

Spirit Airlines (801-401-2222; www.spirit.com) Florida-based airline serving many US gateway cities.

United Airlines (800-864-8331; www.united.com) Nationwide service.

Virgin America (877-359-8474; www.virginamerica.com) Flights between East and West Coast cities plus Las Vegas, Austin and Dallas.

Bicycle

Regional bicycle touring is popular. It means coasting over winding back roads (because bicycles are often not permitted on freeways) and calculating progress in miles per day, not miles per hour. Cyclists must follow the same rules of the road as automobiles, but don't expect drivers to respect your right of way. Wearing a helmet is mandatory for riders under 18 years of age in California and many Western cities.

Some helpful resources for cyclists:

Adventure Cycling Association (www.adventurecycling.org) Excellent online resource for purchasing bicycle-friendly maps and long-distance route guides.

Better World Club (www.betterworldclub.com) Annual membership ($40, plus $15 enrollment fee) entitles you to two 24-hour emergency roadside pickups with transportation to the nearest bike-repair shop within a 30-mile radius.

Bikepacking (www.bikepacking.com) Info on multiday mountain-biking trips through the backcountry.

Renting & Purchase

- You can rent bikes by the hour, the day or the week in most cities and major towns.
- Rentals start from around $20 per day for beach cruisers, and from $40 or more for basic mountain bikes; ask about multiday and weekly discounts.
- Most rental companies require a credit-card security deposit of several hundred dollars.
- Buy new models from specialty bike shops, sporting-goods stores and discount-warehouse stores, or used bicycles via noticeboards at hostels, cafes and universities.
- To buy or sell used bikes, check online bulletin boards such as Craigslist (www.craigslist.com).

Transporting Bicycles

- Some local buses and trains are equipped with bicycle racks.
- Greyhound transports bicycles as luggage (surcharge $30 to $40), which must be packed in wood, canvas or a substantial container, and properly secured.
- Most of Amtrak's *Cascades*, *Pacific Surfliner*, *Capital Corridor* and *San Joaquin* trains feature onboard racks where you can secure your bike unboxed; try to reserve a spot when making your ticket reservation (surcharge up to $10).
- On Amtrak trains without racks, bikes must be put in a box ($15) and checked as luggage (fee $10). Not all stations or trains offer checked-baggage service.
- Before flying, you'll need to disassemble your bike and box it as checked baggage; contact the airline directly for details, including applicable surcharges (typically $150 to $200). There may be no surcharge for lighter and smaller bikes (under 50lb and 62 linear inches).

Boat

There is no river or canal public transportation system in the West, but there are many smaller, often state-run, coastal ferry services. Most larger ferries will transport private cars, motorcycles and bicycles.

Off the coast of Washington, ferries reach the scenic San Juan Islands. Several of California's Channel Islands are accessible by boat, as is Catalina Island, offshore from Los Angeles. On San Francisco Bay, regular ferries operate between San Francisco and Sausalito, Larkspur, Tiburon, Angel Island, Oakland, Alameda and Vallejo.

Bus

- Greyhound (www.greyhound.com) is the major

long-distance bus company, with routes throughout the USA and Canada. Greyhound has stopped service to many small towns; routes generally trace major highways and stop at larger population centers. To reach country towns on rural roads, you may need to transfer to local or county bus systems; Greyhound can usually provide contact information.

➡ Most baggage has to be checked in; label it loudly and clearly to avoid it getting lost. Larger items, including skis, surfboards and bicycles, can be transported, but there may be an extra charge. Call to check.

➡ Greyhound often has excellent online fares – web-only deals will net you substantial discounts over buying at a ticket counter.

➡ The frequency of bus services varies widely. Despite the elimination of many tiny destinations, nonexpress Greyhound buses still stop every 50 to 100 miles to pick up passengers. Long-distance buses stop for meal breaks and driver changes.

➡ Greyhound buses are usually clean, comfortable and reliable. The best seats are typically near the front away from the bathroom. Limited onboard amenities include freezing air-con (bring a sweater) and slightly reclining seats; select buses have electrical outlets and wi-fi. Smoking on board is prohibited.

➡ Many bus stations are clean and safe, but some are in dodgy or potentially unsafe areas; in such places, jump in a cab or head for your connecting bus as soon as you arrive.

Costs

➡ Fares vary depending on when you're traveling and how much flexibility you need; online rates are the best and often very competitive.

➡ Discounts (on unrestricted fares only) are available for veterans (10%), students (10%), seniors (5%) and children (varies).

➡ Special promotional discounts are often available on www.greyhound.com, though may come with restrictions or blackout periods.

Reservations

➡ Greyhound bus tickets can be bought over the phone or online. You can print tickets at home or pick them up at the terminal using 'Will Call' service (bring photo ID).

➡ Seating is normally first-come, first-served. Greyhound recommends arriving an hour before departure to get a seat.

➡ Travelers with disabilities who need special assistance should call ☎800-752-4841 (TDD/TTY ☎800-345-3109) at least 48 hours before traveling; there are limited spaces for those in wheelchairs, although wheelchairs are also accepted as checked baggage. Service animals, such as guide dogs, are allowed on board.

Useful Bus Routes

SERVICE	PRICE ($)	TIME (HR)
Las Vegas–Los Angeles	from 28	5¼–7
Los Angeles–San Francisco	from 32	7½–11½
Phoenix–Tucson	from 12	2
Seattle–Portland	from 17	4
Denver–Salt Lake City	from 92	10½–12¼

Car & Motorcycle

A car allows maximum flexibility and convenience, and is essentially the only way to explore the Western interior and its wide-open spaces.

Automobile Associations

For 24-hour emergency roadside assistance, free maps and discounts on lodging, attractions, entertainment, car rentals and more:

American Automobile Association (AAA; www.aaa.com)

Better World Club (www.betterworldclub.com)

Car Rental

➡ To rent your own wheels, you'll typically need to be at least 25 years old, hold a valid driver's license and have a major credit card, not a check or debit card. Companies may rent to drivers under 25 but over 21 for a surcharge (around $25 to $30 per day). A credit card is usually needed for a deposit.

➡ With advance reservations, you can often get an economy-sized vehicle with unlimited mileage from around $20 per day, plus insurance, taxes and fees. Airport locations may have cheaper rates but higher fees; if you get a fly-drive package, local taxes may be extra when you pick up the car. City-center branches may offer free pickups and drop-offs.

➡ Rates generally include unlimited mileage (check the mileage cap), but expect surcharges for additional drivers and one-way rentals. Some rental companies let you pay for your last tank of gas upfront; this is rarely a good deal.

➡ You may get a better deal by booking through discount-travel websites such as Priceline (www.priceline.com) or Hotwire (www.hotwire.com), or by using online travel-booking sites, such as Expedia (www.expedia.com), Orbitz (www.orbitz.com) or Travelocity (www.travelocity.com). You can also compare rates across travel sites at Kayak (www.kayak.com).

- A few major car-rental companies (including Avis, Budget, Enterprise, and Hertz) offer 'green' fleets of hybrid, clean diesel or electric rental cars, but they're in short supply. Reserve well in advance. Also try **Simply Rent-a-Car** (☎323-653-0022; www.simplyrac.com) in Los Angeles, which offers free delivery and pickup from some locations; or **Zipcar** (☎866-494-7227; www.zipcar.com), which is available in California (Los Angeles, San Diego and the San Francisco Bay area) and Denver, Portland and Seattle. This car-sharing club charges usage fees (per hour or daily), and includes free gas, insurance (damage fee of up to $1000 may apply) and limited mileage. Apply online. Monthly memberships run from $8 to $55 and higher, and the application fee is $30. Drivers from outside the US will need to present passport, driver's license and accident history prior to rental.
- To compare independent car-rental companies, try Car Rental Express (www.carrentalexpress.com), which is especially useful for finding cheaper long-term rentals, or Auto Europe (www.autoeurope.com).
- If you are under 25 years old and in LA, San Francisco or Orange County, check out Super Cheap Car Rental (www.supercheapcar.com), which has no surcharge for drivers aged 21 to 24; daily fee applies for drivers aged 18 to 21.

Driver's Licences

- Foreign visitors can legally drive a car in some states using their home driver's license, but other states may require an additional international driving permit (IDP); for info see www.usa.gov/visitors-driving.
- An IDP will also have more credibility with US traffic police, especially if your home license doesn't have a photo or isn't in English. Your automobile association at home can issue an IDP, valid for one year, for a small fee. Always carry your home license together with the IDP.
- To drive a motorcycle in the USA, you will need a valid motorcycle license. International visitors need a driver's permit from their home country, or an IDP specially endorsed for motorcycles.

Fueling Up

Many gas stations in the West have fuel pumps with automated credit-card pay screens. Most machines ask for your zip code. For foreign travelers, or those with cards issued outside the US, you'll have to pay inside before pumping gas. Tell the clerk how much money you'd like to put on the card. If there's still credit left, go back inside and have the difference refunded to the card.

You cannot pump your own gas in Oregon except at rural gas stations.

Insurance

- Liability insurance covers you for people and property you might hit.
- For a rental vehicle, a collision damage waiver (CDW) is available for about $30 per day. Before renting a car, check your auto-insurance policy to see if you're already covered. Your policy probably includes liability protection but check anyway.
- Some credit cards offer reimbursement coverage for collision damages when you use the card to rent a car. There may be exceptions for rentals of more than 15 days or for exotic models, Jeeps, vans and 4WD vehicles. If there's an accident, you may have to pay the rental-car company first and then seek reimbursement from the credit-card company. Check your credit card's policies carefully before renting.
- Many rental agencies stipulate that damage a car suffers while being driven on unpaved roads is not covered by the insurance they offer. Check with the agent when you make your reservation.

Motorcycle & RV Rental

If you dream of cruising across America on a Harley, EagleRider (www.eaglerider.com) has offices in major cities nationwide and rents other kinds of adventure vehicles, too. Motorcycle rental and insurance are expensive.

Companies specializing in recreational vehicles (RVs) and pop-up camper rentals:

- **Adventures on Wheels** (www.adventuresonwheels.com)
- **Apollo RV** (☎800-777-779; www.apollorv.com)
- **Cruise America** (www.cruiseamerica.com)
- **Jucy Rentals** (☎800-650-4180; www.jucyusa.com)

Road Conditions & Hazards

- Road hazards include potholes, city commuter traffic, wandering wildlife, and distracted and enraged drivers.
- Where winter driving is an issue, some cars are fitted with snow tires; snow chains are sometimes required in mountain areas. Driving off-road, or on dirt roads, is often forbidden by rental-car companies, and it can be very dangerous in wet weather.
- In deserts and range country, livestock sometimes grazes next to unfenced roads. These areas are signed as 'Open Range' or with the silhouette of a steer. Where deer, elk and other wild animals frequently appear roadside, you'll see signs with the silhouette of a leaping deer. Take these signs seriously, particularly at night.

For nationwide traffic and road-closure information, visit www.fhwa.dot.gov/trafficinfo.

For current road conditions within a state, call 511. From outside a state, try the following:

Arizona (888-411-7623; www.az511.com)

California (800-427-7623; www.dot.ca.gov)

Colorado (303-639-1111; www.codot.gov/travel)

Idaho (888-432-7623; http://511.idaho.gov)

Montana (800-226-7623)

Nevada (877-687-6237; www.nvroads.com)

New Mexico (800-432-4269; https://nmroads.com)

Oregon (503-588-2941; www.tripcheck.com)

Utah (866-511-8824; www.udot.utah.gov)

Washington (800-695-7623; www.wsdot.wa.gov)

Wyoming (888-996-7623; www.wyoroad.info)

Road Rules

➡ Cars drive on the right-hand side of the road.

➡ The use of seat belts and child safety seats is required in every state. Most car-rental agencies rent child safety seats for around $13 per day, but you must reserve them when booking.

➡ In some states, motorcyclists are required to wear helmets.

➡ On interstate highways, the speed limit is sometimes raised to 80mph. Unless otherwise posted, the speed limit is generally 55mph or 65mph on highways, 25mph to 35mph in cities and towns and as low as 15mph in school zones (strictly enforced during school hours). It's forbidden to pass a school bus when its lights are flashing.

➡ When emergency vehicles (ie police, fire or ambulance) approach from either direction, pull over safely and get out of the way.

➡ It is almost always illegal to talk on a handheld cell (mobile) phone or send texts while driving; use a hands-free device or pull over for a call.

➡ The maximum legal blood-alcohol concentration for drivers is 0.08%. Penalties are very severe for 'DUI' – driving under the influence of alcohol and/or drugs. Police can give roadside sobriety checks to assess if you've been drinking or using drugs. If you fail, they'll require you to take a breath test, urine test or blood test to determine the level of alcohol or drugs in your body. Refusing to be tested is treated the same as if you'd taken the test and failed.

➡ In some states it is illegal to carry 'open containers' of alcohol in a vehicle, even if they are empty.

Local Transportation

Airport Shuttles

Shuttle buses provide inexpensive and convenient transport to/from airports in most cities. Most are 12-seat vans; some have regular routes and stops (which include the main hotels), and some pick up and deliver passengers 'door to door' in their service area. Average costs run from $15 to $25 per person.

Bicycle

Some cities are more amenable to bicycles than others, but most have at least a few dedicated bike lanes and paths. Bikes can usually be carried on public transportation.

Bus

Most cities and larger towns have dependable local bus systems, though they are often designed for commuters and provide limited service in the evening and on weekends. Costs average about $2 per ride. Limited routes in tourist areas may be free.

Subway & Train

The largest systems are in Los Angeles and the San Francisco Bay Area. Other cities may have small, one- or two-line rail systems that mainly serve downtown.

Taxi

➡ Taxis are metered, with average flagfall fees of $2.50 to $3.75, plus $2 to $3 per mile.

➡ Credit cards may be accepted.

➡ Taxis may charge extra for baggage and/or airport pickups.

➡ Drivers expect a 10% to 15% tip, rounded up to the next dollar.

➡ Ridexsharing companies are a very popular alternative to taxis.

Train

Amtrak (www.amtrak.com) operates a fairly extensive rail system throughout the USA. Fares vary according to the type of train and seating (eg reserved or unreserved coach seats, business class, sleeping compartments). Trains are comfortable, if a bit slow, and are equipped with dining and lounge cars on long-distance routes.

Amtrak routes in the West:

California Zephyr Daily service between Chicago and Emeryville (from $138, 52 hours), near San Francisco, via Denver, Salt Lake City, Reno and Sacramento.

Coast Starlight Travels the West Coast daily from Seattle to LA (from $98, 35½ hours) via Portland, Sacramento, Oakland and Santa Barbara; wi-fi may be available.

Southwest Chief Daily departures between Chicago and LA (from $143, 43¼ hours) via Kansas City, Albuquerque, Flagstaff and Barstow.

Sunset Limited Thrice-weekly service between New Orleans and LA (from $173, 46½ hours) via Houston, San Antonio, El Paso, Tucson and Palm Springs.

Useful Routes

SERVICE	PRICE ($)	TIME (HR)
Los Angeles–Flagstaff	from 59	11½
Los Angeles–Oakland/San Francisco	from 53	12
San Francisco/Emeryville–Salt Lake City	from 102	18½
Seattle–Oakland/San Francisco	from 89	22¼

SCENIC ROUTES

Historic locomotives chug through mountain ranges and other scenic landscapes across the West. Most trains run in the warmer months only, and they can be extremely popular, so book ahead.

Cumbres & Toltec Scenic Railway (☎888-286-2737; www.cumbrestoltec.com; adult/child 2-12yr from $100/50; ⊙late May–mid-Oct) A living, moving museum from Chama, NM, into Colorado's Rocky Mountains.

Durango & Silverton Narrow Gauge Railroad (p107) Ends at historic mining town Silverton in Colorado's Rocky Mountains.

Empire Builder (www.amtrak.com) This stunning journey connects Whitefish with Glacier National Park in northern Montana.

Grand Canyon Railway (p177) Vintage steam and diesel locomotives with family-oriented entertainment running between Williams, AZ, and Grand Canyon National Park.

Mount Hood Railroad (www.mthoodrr.com) Rolls south from the Columbia River Gorge toward Mt Hood.

Pikes Peak Cog Railway (www.cograilway.com) An 8.9-mile track outside Colorado Springs that climbs from the plains to the 14,115ft peak.

Skunk Train (www.skunktrain.com) Runs between Fort Bragg, CA, on the coast, and Willits, further inland, passing through redwoods.

Reservations

Reservations can be made from 11 months in advance up to the day of departure. Space on most trains is limited and certain routes can be crowded, especially during summer and holiday periods, so it's a good idea to book as far in advance as you can.

Tickets

➡ Purchase tickets at train stations, by phone or online.

➡ Fares depend on the day of travel, the route, the type of seating etc. Fares may be slightly higher during peak travel times such as summer.

➡ Usually seniors over 61 years and veterans with a Veterans Advantage Card receive 15% discount; students with an ISIC or Student Advantage Card receive 10% discount. AAA members and US military personnel and families also save 10%. Up to two children aged two to 12 years who are accompanied by an adult get 50% off. Special promotions can become available anytime, so check online or ask.

Train Passes

➡ Amtrak's USA Rail Pass (www.amtrak.com/rail-passes) is valid for coach-class travel for 15 ($459), 30 ($689) or 45 ($899) days; children aged two to 12 years pay half-price. Actual travel is limited to eight, 12 or 18 one-way 'segments,' respectively. A segment is *not* the same as a one-way trip; if reaching your destination requires riding more than one train, you'll use multiple pass segments.

➡ Purchase rail passes online; make advance reservations for each travel segment.

➡ For travel within California, consider the seven-day California Rail Pass (adult/child $159/$79.50), which must be used within 21 consecutive days.

Behind the Scenes

SEND US YOUR FEEDBACK

We love to hear from travelers – your comments keep us on our toes and help make our books better. Our well-traveled team reads every word on what you loved or loathed about this book. Although we cannot reply individually to your submissions, we always guarantee that your feedback goes straight to the appropriate authors, in time for the next edition. Each person who sends us information is thanked in the next edition – the most useful submissions are rewarded with a selection of digital PDF chapters.

Visit **lonelyplanet.com/contact** to submit your updates and suggestions or to ask for help. Our award-winning website also features inspirational travel stories, news and discussions.

Note: We may edit, reproduce and incorporate your comments in Lonely Planet products such as guidebooks, websites and digital products, so let us know if you don't want your comments reproduced or your name acknowledged. For a copy of our privacy policy visit lonelyplanet.com/privacy.

WRITER THANKS

Amy C Balfour

Thank you Brandon Dekema and Christy Germscheid for your Enchanted Circle tips and Angel Fire hospitality! Thanks also to Todd Norman, Matt Redington, John White, Marty Robertson, Elizabeth Edgren, Charise May and Ellen McBee. Much obliged for the meet-up and the Central New Mexico suggestions, Michael Benanav – all right on! Thank you to my talented co-writers – to Chris Pitts for the New Mexico background – and editors, and cheers to Ben Buckner for this awesome assignment.

Becky Ohlsen

I would like to thank editor Ben Buckner for the gig, Celeste Brash for her work on the previous edition, Paul Smith for being a great travel companion, and all the dedicated volunteers at the many wonderful tiny museums, state parks, national parks and campgrounds visited along the way.

Robert Balkovich

Thank you, as always, to my friends and family for your continued support while I run hither and thither and yon. Special thanks to Karin, for sharing your love of Seattle with me and setting me off on the right foot, and to Lynae for the wonderful home away from home where I made many great memories.

Greg Benchwick

This book wouldn't be possible without my family. Dad, Mom, Cara, Bry and little baby Violeta. Love you guys. Thanks to the beautiful editors, cartographers and whole team at Lonely Planet for making an amazing book. And to the on-the-ground people that helped along the way, like Chris at Pine Needles in Durango and the lovely Sara.

Celeste Brash

Thanks to my husband Josh and my kids who have come with me on so many Oregon trips over the years. And to many friends old and new that helped out this time around, including Ticari, Chris & Ashley, Nathan, Dana, Jon & Kara, Ron & Nisa, Elizabeth, Pattye, Rachel Cabakoff, Amanda Castleman, Dave Nevins, Amy Hunter, all my LP co-authors and Ben Buckner for seeing this through.

Stephanie d'Arc Taylor

As always, I don't do anything without support and inspiration from Queen Xtine. My home team: Maya G, A&E, Daniel and Danielle. Carlo, grazie. The friendly park rangers at Great Basin and staff at Kerouac's (I'm not stalking you, promise). That guy at Napa Auto Parts in Lone Pine. At LP: Ben Buckner, Lauren Keith, Alicia Johnson, Martine Power and Sasha Drew for your attention. Thanks to my late father for showing me the calm beauty of the Basin & Range.

Michael Grosberg

Many thanks to all those who shared their experiences, knowledge and deep passion for Glacier, Whitefish and Waterton including Brian Schott, Greg Fortin, Riley Polumbus, Rhonda Fitzgerald, Chris Schustrom, Cricket Butler, BJ Elzinga, Marc Ducharme, Michelle Gaudet, Kimmy Walt, Angel Esperanueva and Monica Jungster. And to Carly, Rosie, Willa and Boone for keeping in touch while in the wilderness.

Ashley Harrell

Thanks to: editors Sarah Stocking and Martine Power, along with my co-authors, for their hard work on this book; Freda Moon for the advice on Mendocino; Amy Benziger for putting up with my research detours in Tahoe (and in general); the nice Norwegian couple who stopped in Sequoia to pick up two dirty hitchhikers, and Steven Sparapani and Osa Peligrosa, for joining me on an epic road trip across 3,000 awe-inspiring miles of Northern California.

John Hecht

Many thanks to all the kind folks in Utah who offered their help, be that in the brewpubs, on the trails or wherever else our paths may have crossed. I also want to thank destination editor Ben Buckner, the book's co-writers and my lovely wife Lau for all their support.

Adam Karlin

Thanks to Ben Buckner for adding me to the team, and to Rachel, Sanda and Isaac for your ceaseless love and support.

Christopher Pitts

Thanks to the inordinately kind people of Arizona, in particular my Mom, Michael and Maddie in Scottsdale, and Ellen and Norman for their great tips. In Cochise Stronghold, thanks to Tolin for leading the way on the Sheepshead. At home, bises as always to my dearest partners in crime, Perrine, Elliot and Celeste.

ACKNOWLEDGEMENTS

Climate map data adapted from Peel MC, Finlayson BL & McMahon TA (2007) 'Updated World Map of the Köppen-Geiger Climate Classification', Hydrology and Earth System Sciences, 11, 163344.

Illustration pp316-17 by Michael Weldon.

Cover photograph: Sunset at McDowell Sonoran Preserve, Scottsdale, Arizona; Tom Mackie/AWL Images ©

THIS BOOK

This 5th edition of Lonely Planet's *Western USA* guidebook was curated by Anthony Ham, Amy C Balfour, Becky Ohlsen and Lauren O'Connell, and researched and written by Anthony, Amy, Becky, Robert Balkovich, Greg Benchwick, Andrew Bender, Alison Bing, Celeste Brash, Stephanie d'Arc Taylor, Michael Grosberg, Ashley Harrell, John Hecht, Adam Karlin, MaSovaida Morgan, Christopher Pitts and Andrea Schulte-Peevers. The previous edition was written by Hugh McNaughtan, Brett Atkinson, Loren Bell, Greg Benchwick, Andrew Bender, Sara Benson, Alison Bing, Cristian Bonetto, Celeste Brash, Jade Bremner, Nate Cavalieri, Michael Grosberg, Ashley Harrell, Carolyn McCarthy, Becky Ohlsen, Christopher Pitts, Liza Prado, Josephine Quintero, Andrea Schulte-Peevers, Helena Smith, John A Vlahides, Benedict Walker and Clifton Wilkinson. This guidebook was produced by the following:

Destination Editors Ben Buckner, Sarah Stocking

Senior Product Editors Martine Power, Vicky Smith

Regional Senior Cartographer Alison Lyall

Product Editor Joel Cotterell

Book Designer Gwen Cotter

Cartographer Valentina Kremenchutskaya

Assisting Editors Judith Bamber, Katie Connolly, Sam Cook, Melanie Dankel, Barbara Delissen, Andrea Dobbin, Carly Hall, Gabrielle Innes, Kellie Langdon, Jodie Martire, Lou McGregor, Rosie Nicholson, Lauren O'Connell, Kristin Odijk, Susan Paterson, Monique Perrin, Mani Ramaswamy, Sarah Reid, Monica Woods

Assisting Cartographer Rachel Imeson

Assisting Book Designer Fergal Condon

Cover Researcher Meri Blazevski

Thanks to Megan Bell, Hannah Cartmel, Linda de Vos, Sasha Drew, Bailey Freeman, Andi Jones, Kate Kiely, Trisha Ping, Angela Tinson

Index

A

B

C

Map Pages **000**
Photo Pages **000**

Map Pages **000**
Photo Pages **000**

Map Pages **000**
Photo Pages **000**

Map Pages **000**
Photo Pages **000**

Map Legend

Sights

- Beach
- Bird Sanctuary
- Buddhist
- Castle/Palace
- Christian
- Confucian
- Hindu
- Islamic
- Jain
- Jewish
- Monument
- Museum/Gallery/Historic Building
- Ruin
- Shinto
- Sikh
- Taoist
- Winery/Vineyard
- Zoo/Wildlife Sanctuary
- Other Sight

Activities, Courses & Tours

- Bodysurfing
- Diving
- Canoeing/Kayaking
- Course/Tour
- Sento Hot Baths/Onsen
- Skiing
- Snorkeling
- Surfing
- Swimming/Pool
- Walking
- Windsurfing
- Other Activity

Sleeping

- Sleeping
- Camping
- Hut/Shelter

Eating

- Eating

Drinking & Nightlife

- Drinking & Nightlife
- Cafe

Entertainment

- Entertainment

Shopping

- Shopping

Information

- Bank
- Embassy/Consulate
- Hospital/Medical
- Internet
- Police
- Post Office
- Telephone
- Toilet
- Tourist Information
- Other Information

Geographic

- Beach
- Gate
- Hut/Shelter
- Lighthouse
- Lookout
- Mountain/Volcano
- Oasis
- Park
- Pass
- Picnic Area
- Waterfall

Population

- Capital (National)
- Capital (State/Province)
- City/Large Town
- Town/Village

Transport

- Airport
- BART station
- Border crossing
- Boston T station
- Bus
- Cable car/Funicular
- Cycling
- Ferry
- Metro/Muni station
- Monorail
- Parking
- Petrol station
- Subway/SkyTrain station
- Taxi
- Train station/Railway
- Tram
- Underground station
- Other Transport

Routes

- Tollway
- Freeway
- Primary
- Secondary
- Tertiary
- Lane
- Unsealed road
- Road under construction
- Plaza/Mall
- Steps
- Tunnel
- Pedestrian overpass
- Walking Tour
- Walking Tour detour
- Path/Walking Trail

Boundaries

- International
- State/Province
- Disputed
- Regional/Suburb
- Marine Park
- Cliff
- Wall

Hydrography

- River, Creek
- Intermittent River
- Canal
- Water
- Dry/Salt/Intermittent Lake
- Reef

Areas

- Airport/Runway
- Beach/Desert
- Cemetery (Christian)
- Cemetery (Other)
- Glacier
- Mudflat
- Park/Forest
- Sight (Building)
- Sportsground
- Swamp/Mangrove

Note: Not all symbols displayed above appear on the maps in this book

Adam Karlin

Yellowstone, Grand Teton, Zion, Bryce Canyon and Grand Canyon National Parks Adam has contributed to dozens of Lonely Planet guidebooks, covering an alphabetical spread that ranges from the Andaman Islands to the Zimbabwe Border. As a journalist, he has sent dispatches from every continent barring Antarctica (one day!).

MaSovaida Morgan

Oregon MaSovaida is a travel journalist whose wayfaring tendencies have taken her to more than 50 countries across all seven continents. As a Lonely Planet author, she contributes to guidebooks on destinations throughout Southeast Asia, the Middle East, Europe and the Americas.

Christopher Pitts

Arizona Chris's first expedition in life ended in failure when he tried to dig from Pennsylvania to China at the age of six. He went on to study Chinese in university, living for several years in China. After more than a decade in Paris, the lure of Colorado's sunny skies and outdoor adventure proved too great to resist.

Andrea Schulte-Peevers

California Born and raised in Germany and educated in London and at UCLA, Andrea has traveled the distance to the moon and back in her visits to some 75 countries. She has earned her living as a professional travel writer for more than two decades and authored or contributed to nearly 100 Lonely Planet titles.